AMERICAN DECADES

1960 - 1969

AMERICAN DECADES
1960-1969

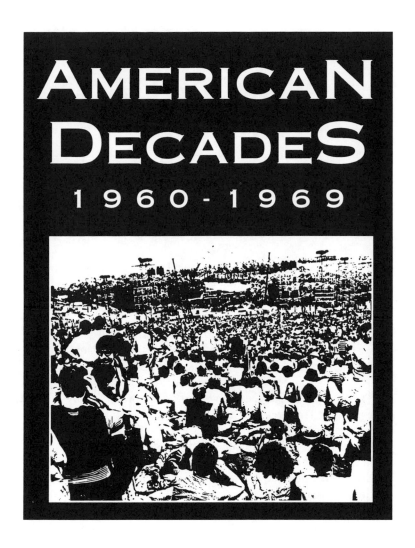

EDITED BY
RICHARD LAYMAN

ASSOCIATE EDITOR
JAMES W. HIPP

A MANLY, INC. BOOK

 Gale Research Inc.

An International Thomson Publishing Company

I(T)P

NEW YORK • LONDON • BONN • BOSTON • DETROIT • MADRID
MELBOURNE • MEXICO CITY • PARIS • SINGAPORE • TOKYO
TORONTO • WASHINGTON • ALBANY NY • BELMONT CA • CINCINNATI OH

AMERICAN
DECADES
1960-1969

Matthew J. Bruccoli and Richard Layman, *Editorial Directors*

Printed in the United States of America

Published simultaneously in the United Kingdom
by Gale Research International Limited
(An affiliated company of Gale Research Inc.)

Library of Congress Catalog Card Number   94-078811
ISBN 0-8103-8883-9

I(T)P™

The trademark **ITP** is used under license.
10 9 8 7 6 5 4 3

CONTENTS

INTRODUCTION

A New World to be Won. The early 1960s in America were a time of hope, energy, and prosperity, a time when the United States settled confidently into its role as a superpower possessed of military might and financial clout. "It is a time for a new generation of leadership, to cope with new problems and new opportunities," the new president John F. Kennedy told the nation in 1960. "For there is a new world to be won."

Prosperity. Unemployment was between five and six percent in the first half of the decade, and inflation hovered between 1 and 2 percent. The gross national product, the value of goods produced by the national workforce, increased almost 36 percent between 1960 and 1965, and salaries increased about 20 percent during the same period. Generally, people had more money than ever before and more goods available to spend it on.

The Global Village. The world seemed to have shrunk in the 1960s. Transcontinental and even intercontinental travel became easy and efficient for the first time. Delta Airlines ran eleven flights a day from Chicago to Miami in 1966 carrying passengers to vacationland for $74.40 each, and those who did not travel were able routinely to see and hear people from other parts of the country and the world on television. In 1969 fifty-eight million of the nation's sixty-two million households had television sets. Advances in transportation and in communication, the two pillars of commerce, had turned the world into what Marshall McLuhan called a global village.

New Awareness. People's universes expanded as they were exposed daily to television newscasts that informed them about the day's events and confronted them with current issues. A significant portion of the populace, newly empowered with information and the freedom that affluence brings, focused their attentions on matters that extended beyond their homes and neighborhoods. Civil rights, equal rights for women, and the war on poverty were the domestic issues that mobilized activists and stimulated debate during the 1960s. Interest in foreign affairs was dominated by the increasing tensions of the cold war and, in the last half of the decade, the war in Vietnam.

Activism. The 1960s were an activist decade. Frustrated by the delays in enforcing civil rights affirmed during the 1950s by Congress, blacks and supportive whites took to the streets first in peaceful, and then in violent, protest. When they gathered together to demand equitable treatment in school, in the workplace, and in the administration of public benefits, they were met with force by guardians of the old order. At public schoolhouse doors in Mississippi and Alabama black students were turned away by state officials, and federal authorities mobilized troops to enforce laws that promised equality and liberty. When federal power was unable to ensure the rights the government granted and the deliberate action of the legislature and the judiciary seemed unresponsive to the demands of the disenfranchised, radicals took matters into their own hands, rioting and terrorizing in the name of social justice.

Individual Rights. People in the 1960s paid careful attention to individual rights. Women began to discover parallels between racial and sexual discrimination. Feminists initiated their own assault on the old order, demanding that their dignity be recognized, that their achievements be given equal consideration with those of men, and that they be allowed to assume control over their own destinies without the interference of domineering males. The ethical implications of abortion and the question of who had authority to regulate it were issues of fundamental importance. The birth-control pill, first distributed for the purpose of contraception in the early 1960s, sparked what was called the sexual revolution, as the primary burden of risk for women was removed from sexual activity. Media commentators imagined a generation without morals, and feminist theorists imagined a generation of women freed from their sexual masters; neither prognostication was entirely accurate. The female workforce increased by about 50 percent during the 1960s, and as women began to forsake domestic labor for paying jobs, they came to have an increasing voice in the nation's affairs that grew more insistent with the passage of time.

The Youth Revolt. The most disturbing protest of the 1960s was that of youth against the values of their parents and what President Johnson called the Great Society of their political leaders. The focus of youth protest was civil rights and feminism early in the decade, but with the increasing U.S. involvement in the Vietnam War and the accompanying threat of military draft students lost tolerance of their elders' attempts to maintain order in the nation and in the world. Though it was encouraged and to some extent influenced by a highly organized, even authoritarian student protest movement, the youth revolution was basically anarchic; its purpose was to question and subvert authority, and it proceeded on moral or, some would say, pseudomoral grounds. The basic assumption of the youth protest movements of the decade was that society had become corrupted by materialism. Social inequities that had deprived blacks, women, and the poor of their rights and an imperialistic foreign policy that had led to the war in Vietnam and the escalation of the cold war were equally attributable to powerlust and greed. The best remedy was a return to basic values that would disarm the forces of perversity by robbing them of their purpose. The result would be a world of love and peace, beauty, and serenity. While the most radical acted on their beliefs, paradoxically, by employing terrorist tactics, the philosophy infused a generation with the energy of righteousness and the confusion of reform.

Fading Optimism. Much of the optimism had gone out of American life by the end of the 1960s; it was replaced by grief, cynicism, and fear. John F. Kennedy, the president who had for many symbolized the hope of America; Martin Luther King, Jr., the Nobel Prize–winning leader who had promoted nonviolence to redress social injustice; Malcolm X, the forceful advocate of black pride; and Robert Kennedy, the presidential candidate who promised peace and order, were all assassinated. American military power, or the threat of it, was frustrated by poorly armed guerrilla soldiers in third-world countries on at least three continents. The social programs of the progressive Democratic presidents combined with the war debt had set the stage for a volatile economy plagued by inflation and tax increases. The idealism of the early 1960s had hardened into hostility as nonviolent protest evolved into displays of black power and "turn on, tune in, and drop out" replaced "make love not war" as the slogan of disaffected youth. By the end of the decade women may have held nearly half the jobs in the United States, but they only made 60 percent as much as their male coworkers. The race to the moon that had provided so much nationalistic spirit during the decade was finally ended successfully, and then the manned space program was scaled back in acknowledgement of the criticism that unmanned flights were more productive and cheaper.

The Burdens. The United States suffered the burden of power during the 1960s, which included the commitment to react responsibly even when others do not. That burden included the struggle for dominance with the Soviet Union in a global war of tactics; challenges of other nations who did not wish to subordinate themselves to American interests; and rude scrutiny from its own citizens as they struggled to comprehend the obligations of wealth and the responsibilities of dominion.

The Benefits. The United States also enjoyed the benefits of power during the 1960s, which supplied the resources to accomplish grand achievements. Those benefits included the ability to penetrate outer space and to find practical application for the scientific knowledge gathered there; to understand physiological processes so precisely that medical researchers could transplant organs, eradicate diseases, and increase longevity; to develop commerce so that goods to enrich people's lives could be delivered throughout the world. It was a time when American maturity was tested and American capacity was demonstrated.

—R.L.

PLAN OF THIS VOLUME

This is one of nine volumes in the *American Decades* series. Each volume will chronicle a single twentieth-century decade from thirteen separate perspectives, broadly covering American life. The volumes begin with a chronology of world events outside of America, which provides a context for American experience. Following are chapters, arranged in alphabetical order, on thirteen categories of American endeavor ranging from business to medicine, from the arts to sports. Each of these chapters contains the following elements: first, a table of contents for the chapter; second, a chronology of significant events in the field; third, Topics in the News, a series, beginning with an overview, of short essays describing current events; fourth, anecdotal sidebars of interesting and entertaining, though not necessarily important, information; fifth, Headline Makers, short biographical accounts of key people during the decade; sixth, People in the News, brief notices of significant accomplishments by people who mattered; seventh, Awards of note in the field (where applicable); eighth, Deaths during the decade of people in the field; and ninth, a list of Publications during or specifically about the decade in the field. In addition, there is a general bibliography at the end of this volume, followed by an index of photographs and an index of subjects.

ACKNOWLEDGMENTS

This book was produced by Manly, Inc.

Production coordinator is George F. Dodge. Photography editors are Bruce Andrew Bowlin and Josephine A. Bruccoli. Photographic copy work was performed by Joseph M. Bruccoli. Layout and graphics supervisor is Penney L. Haughton. Copyediting supervisor is Bill Adams. Typesetting supervisor is Kathleen M. Flanagan. Julie E. Frick is editorial associate. The production staff includes Phyllis A. Avant, Ann M. Cheschi, Melody W. Clegg, Patricia Coate, Brigitte B. de Guzman, Denise W. Edwards, Sarah A. Estes, Joyce Fowler, Laurel M. Gladden, Mendy Gladden, Stephanie C. Hatchell, Leslie Haynsworth, Rebecca Mayo, Kathy Lawler Merlette, Jeff Miller, Pamela D. Norton, Delores I. Plastow, Patricia F. Salisbury, William L. Thomas, Jr., and Robert Trogden. Nicholas Charles Layman was intern assistant.

Walter W. Ross and Robert S. McConnell did library research. They were assisted by the following librarians at the Thomas Cooper Library of the University of South Carolina: Linda Holderfield and the interlibrary-loan staff; reference librarians Gwen Baxter, Daniel Boice, Faye Chadwell, Cathy Eckman, Gary Geer, Qun "Gerry" Jiao, Jean Rhyne, Carol Tobin, Carolyn Tyler, Virginia Weathers, Elizabeth Whiznant, and Connie Widney; circulation-department head Thomas Marcil; and acquisitions-searching supervisor David Haggard.

AMERICAN
DECADES
1960-1969

WORLD EVENTS: SELECTED OCCURRENCES OUTSIDE THE UNITED STATES

1960

- Federico Fellini's film *La Dolce Vita* premieres.
- Alan Sillitoe's *The Loneliness of the Long Distance Runner* is published.
- Harold Pinter's play *The Caretaker* premieres.
- Alain Resnais's film *Last Year at Marienbad* premieres.

1 Jan. Soviet premier Nikita Khrushchev indicates in a New Year's toast that the Soviet Union might disarm unilaterally if it fails to reach an arms agreement with the West.

3 Jan. The Moscow State Symphony becomes the first Soviet orchestra to play in the United States.

4 Jan. Albert Camus dies in an automobile accident near Paris.

8 Jan. West Berlin students hold mass demonstrations against recent outbreaks of neo-Nazism and anti-Semitism.

12 Jan. Soviet police expose a black-market rock 'n' roll ring that produces phonograph records on X-ray plates.

19 Jan. The United States and Japan sign a treaty of mutual cooperation and security.

24 Jan. Pope John XXIII presides over the first diocesan ecclesiastical council held in Rome.

1 Feb. In Algeria a revolt by European immigrants collapses.

5 Feb. The Soviet Exhibition in Havana is disrupted by anti-Communist demonstrators, who are fired upon by Cuban police.

7 Feb. Ancient biblical scrolls are discovered in a cave one thousand feet above the Dead Sea.

8 Feb. After successfully detonating an atomic bomb in the Sahara, France becomes the world's fourth nuclear power.

18 Feb. The Winter Olympics begin in Squaw Valley, California.

19 Feb. Despite appeals by anti-U.S. leftist Chileans, several hundred thousand turn out to welcome President Dwight Eisenhower to Santiago.

1 Mar. The Moroccan resort city of Agadir is leveled by earthquakes, a tidal wave, and fires, killing nearly twelve thousand and leaving almost all of the city's population homeless.

14 Mar. In New York, Israeli premier David Ben-Gurion and West German chancellor Konrad Adenauer meet for the first time and discuss German-Israeli relations.

18 Mar. Accused of leading Chinese priests in espionage against Communist China, Roman Catholic bishop James Edward Walsh, a U.S. citizen, is sentenced by the Shanghai People's Court to twenty years in prison.

21 Mar. Cuban soldiers shoot down an American private plane and capture its pilot and copilot, who are suspected of attempting to rescue Cuban political prisoners.

21 Mar. South African police open fire on twenty thousand antiapartheid demonstrators, killing fifty-six.

9 Apr. South African white supremacist prime minister Hendrik Verwoerd is shot and wounded by a white man in Johannesburg.

16 Apr. Major American publishing houses Alfred A. Knopf and Random House announce their merger.

26 Apr. Prompted by a student uprising against government election policies, South Korea's National Assembly demands the immediate resignation of President Syngman Rhee.

5 May Soviet premier Khrushchev presents evidence to the Supreme Soviet that an American U-2 plane had been shot down over the Soviet Union and that its pilot Gary Powers had been captured.

6 May Princess Margaret Rose of the British royal family marries Antony Armstrong-Jones, a commoner.

7 May Twenty-three-year-old Mikhail Tol of Soviet Latvia becomes the youngest world chess champion in the twentieth century after defeating Mikhail Botvinnick in a two-month series held in Moscow.

7 May The Paris summit meeting between Khrushchev and Eisenhower breaks down, with each side blaming the other for its collapse.

11 May The SS *France,* the world's longest passenger liner, is launched at Saint Nazaire, France.

20 May *La Dolce Vita,* by Italian director Federico Fellini, wins the award for best film at the Cannes Film Festival.

23 May The Israeli government announces that it is holding former Nazi SS colonel Adolf Eichmann, accused of war crimes, to stand trial.

27 May Turkish dictator Adnan Menderes is overthrown in a military coup.

30 May Boris Pasternak dies at age seventy in his villa outside Moscow.

1 June Benjamin Britten's opera *A Midsummer Night's Dream* premieres at Jubilee Hall in Aldeburgh, England.

9 June Typhoon Mary, packing 135-MPH winds, hits Hong Kong, leaving many dead and 120,000 homeless.

13 June A Rome court announces the annulment of Ingrid Bergman's marriage to Roberto Rossellini.

16 June At the request of Japanese officials President Eisenhower agrees to postpone his visit to Japan due to anti-American rioting.

20 June U.S. boxer Floyd Patterson defeats Ingemar Johansson of Sweden to reclaim the world heavyweight boxing title.

20 June	Algerian rebels agree to take part in Paris peace talks after nearly six years of war.
30 June	The Republic of Congo is born after Belgian king Baudouin I proclaims the country's independence.
1 July	The Republic of Somalia is formed after merging the former British Somaliland with the former UN trust territory of Somalia.
11 July	Kremlin officials announce that the Soviet Union has shot down an American RB-47 reconnaissance jet after it violated Soviet airspace. Of the six crewmen two survived and are held in the Soviet Union.
14 July	The UN Security Council authorizes Secretary-General Dag Hammarskjöld to send UN troops to the Republic of Congo to restore peace to the emerging nation plagued by civil war.
21 July	Fifty-nine-year-old Francis Chichester wins the transatlantic solo race aboard his sloop *Gypsy Moth* in a record time of forty days.
24 July	Marshal Andrei A. Grechko succeeds Ivan S. Konev as supreme commander of Warsaw Pact forces.
27 July	At the Geneva test-ban talks the United States, Great Britain, and the Soviet Union agree in principle to bar atmospheric tests as well as all underground detonations registering at more than 4.75 on the Richter scale.
29 July	Dr. Andre Danjon, director of the Paris Observatory, reports that the day has been lengthened one-tenth of a second because of three solar eruptions in July 1959 that slowed the earth's rotation.
3 Aug.	An English translation of *The Last Temptation of Christ,* by Nikos Kazantzakis, is published in New York.
6 Aug.	Bangu of Brazil defeats Kilmarnock of Scotland 2–0 in New York to win the American Challenge Cup in the International Soccer League's first title playoff.
11 Sept.	The Rome summer Olympics end, the Soviet athletes having won the most medals.
19 Sept.	Soviet premier Nikita Khrushchev and Cuban leader Fidel Castro arrive in New York under heavy police security for the convening of the UN General Assembly.
5 Oct.	Jean Anouilh's play *Becket* opens in New York.
10 Oct.	The coast of East Pakistan along the Bay of Bengal is struck by a cyclone and a tidal wave, killing five thousand people.
12 Oct.	At the United Nations, Soviet premier Khrushchev pounds his desk with his shoe in protest over a speech by a Philippine delegate condemning Soviet colonialism in Eastern Europe.
21 Oct.	Britain announces its first nuclear submarine, the *Dreadnought.*
28 Oct.	For the seventeenth time since 1901 the Nobel Peace Prize Committee announces that no prize will be given.
2 Nov.	In the first major test of Great Britain's new obscenity laws, a London court rules that D. H. Lawrence's *Lady Chatterley's Lover* is not obscene.
7 Nov.	The Soviet team wins the Olympic chess tournament in Leipzig, East Germany, with the United States placing second.

| 1 Dec. | Accused by his political enemies of inciting rebellion, Congolese premier Patrice Lumumba is arrested by Congolese troops. |
| 13 Dec. | A new Congolese government is proclaimed by Antoine Gizenga, former deputy premier in the Lumumba government. |

1961

- Iris Murdoch's *A Severed Head* is published.
- Shelagh Delaney's play *A Taste of Honey* premieres.
- Psychologist Carl Gustav Jung dies.
- Goya's portrait of the duke of Wellington is stolen from the National Gallery in London.
- François Truffaut's film *Jules et Jim* premieres.
- Muriel Spark's *The Prime of Miss Jean Brodie* is published.

Jan.	British physicist Sir John Cockcroft wins the 1961 Atoms for Peace Award.
Jan.	French voters endorse plan for Algerian self-determination.
2 Jan.	Soviets begin exchanging old rubles for new, revalued ones at a rate of ten to one.
3 Jan.	The United States announces it has severed diplomatic ties with Cuba.
17 Jan.	Deposed Congolese premier Patrice Lumumba is murdered.
31 Jan.	Israeli premier David Ben-Gurion resigns.
Mar.	The Soviet Union places a spacecraft carrying a dog in orbit around the earth.
12 Apr.	Soviet cosmonaut Yuri Gagarin becomes the first man to orbit the earth.
17–20 Apr.	At Cuba's Bay of Pigs, Castro's forces repulse an invasion of Cuban exiles backed by the United States.
26 Apr.	The French army puts down a dissidents' revolt in Algiers.
30 May	Dominican Republic dictator Rafael Trujillo is assassinated.
June	Arthur Ramsey becomes the one hundredth archbishop of Canterbury.
June	France breaks peace negotiations with Algerian nationalists.
June	Kuwait becomes independent.
30 June	The U.S. government abandons its efforts to exchange U.S. bulldozers for Cuban exiles captured during the failed Bay of Pigs invasion.
July	British troops are sent to Kuwait to counter an Iraqi threat of invasion.
July	His forces having curbed all political freedoms, Gen. Park Chung Hee becomes chairman of South Korea's military junta.
13 Aug.	The Soviet Union closes the border between East and West Berlin.
15–17 Aug.	East Germany constructs the Berlin Wall.
18 Sept.	UN secretary-general Dag Hammarskjöld dies in a plane crash in Africa.
23 Oct.	The Soviet Union detonates a bomb of between thirty and fifty megatons, creating the largest explosion in history to date.

26–28 Oct.	U.S. and Soviet tanks face off at the border between East and West Berlin.
3 Nov.	U Thant of Burma is elected secretary-general of the United Nations.
12 Nov.	West Germany announces that it will pay up to ten thousand dollars to each of the seventy-three Polish women used in Nazi experiments.
11 Dec.	Adolf Eichmann is convicted in Israel for his role in the deaths of six million Jews during World War II.

1962

- Aleksandr Solzhenitsyn's *One Day in the Life of Ivan Denisovich* is published.
- Anthony Burgess's *A Clockwork Orange* is published.
- Doris Lessing's *The Golden Notebook* is published.
- Akira Kurosawa's *Yojimbo* is released.
- *Shoot the Piano Player*, directed by François Truffaut, is released.
- Ingmar Bergman's *Through a Glass Darkly* is released.
- David Lean's *Lawrence of Arabia* is released.
- U.S. and Soviet tank forces back down from a confrontation at the border between East and West Berlin.

4 Jan.	The first International Gimbel Award is given to Begum Liaquat Ali Khan, Pakistani ambassador to Italy, for her role in the emancipation of Pakistani women.
7 Jan.	Indonesian president Bung Sukarno escapes an assassination attempt when a grenade explodes behind his car, killing three bystanders.
18 Jan.	North Vietnam announces that Communist-held territory in the south will be governed by the Vietnam People's Revolutionary party.
3 Feb.	The United States places an embargo on virtually all U.S.-Cuba trade.
10 Feb.	U-2 pilot Gary Powers and Soviet spy Rudolf Abel are secretly exchanged at the border between East and West Germany.
20 Feb.	The Israeli Knesset votes to maintain military rule over the Arabs in Israeli-occupied lands.
27 Feb.	The presidential palace in Saigon, South Vietnam, is bombed by dissident South Vietnamese air force officers flying U.S. planes; President Diem escapes injury.
7 Mar.	The British Royal College of Physicians concludes that cigarette smoking is a cause of lung cancer.
12 Mar.	The British Ministries of Health and Education launch an information program to warn the public about the dangers of smoking.
14 Mar.	The seventeen-nation Geneva disarmament talks begin; both superpowers — the United States and the Soviet Union — are represented.
18 Mar.	France and the Algerian provisional government announce the signing of a truce ending the nearly seven-year-long Muslim rebellion against French rule in Algeria.

22 Mar.	British anthropologist Louis Leakey announces his 1961 discovery of the remains of a humanlike creature estimated to have lived fourteen million years ago.
28 Mar.	Argentine president Arturo Frondizi is ousted by a bloodless military coup.
7 Apr.	A military court in Havana, Cuba, sentences to thirty years in prison 1,179 prisoners captured in the 1961 Bay of Pigs invasion; the Cuban government offers to suspend the sentences in exchange for $62 million.
8 Apr.	In a national referendum French voters overwhelmingly approve the Algerian peace agreement.
10 Apr.	A two-sided Pablo Picasso painting (*Death of a Harlequin* and *Woman Sitting in a Garden*) is purchased in London for $224,000, a record sum paid for a painting by a living artist.
17 May	Ingemar Johansson knocks out Wales fighter Dick Richardson in Göteburg, Sweden, in the eighth round to win the European heavyweight boxing championship.
31 May	Nazi war criminal Adolf Eichmann is executed by hanging in Israel.
3 June	A New York–bound Air France jet chartered by members of the Atlanta Art Association crashes shortly after takeoff from Orly International Air Field in Paris; 130 of the 132 passengers are killed in the worst single aviation disaster to date.
3 June	In Venezuela three thousand government troops crush an uprising by five hundred marines at Venezuelan naval headquarters in Puerto Cabello.
7 June	In Algeria the Secret Army Organization steps up its terrorist bombing campaign against the Muslim-led Algerian provisional government.
17 June	In Santiago, Chile, Brazil defeats Czechoslovakia 3–1 to defend its World Cup soccer title.
30 June	The Vatican censures Fr. Pierre Teilhard de Chardin's *The Phenomenon of Man*, a book in which the late French priest attempts to reconcile church teachings and evolution.
1 July	In Saskatchewan, Canada, nearly all of the doctors go on strike to protest the new health-care plan modeled after the British National Health Service.
4 July	British yachtsman Francis Chichester sets a transatlantic solo voyage record of thirty-three days aboard the *Gypsy Moth III*.
10 July	The first privately owned satellite, a *Telstar* built by American Telephone and Telegraph, successfully relays television images from the United States to Europe.
18 July	A military junta overthrows the Peruvian government in a bloodless coup.
30 July	Eastern and Western European countries continue their dispute over Berlin air rights; Western planes flying over East Berlin are harassed by Soviet fighter jets.
9 Aug.	German-born Swiss writer and 1946 Nobel Prize laureate Hermann Hesse dies at age eighty-five in Montagnola, Switzerland.
14 Aug.	Violence between East and West Berliners continues along the Berlin Wall as an East German patrolman is killed in an exchange of gunfire.
21 Aug.	Soviet cosmonauts contradict Western reports that their two spaceships docked when they tell reporters that the spaceships had not come within three miles of each other.

28 Sept.	A Canadian satellite, the first satellite designed and built by a country other than the United States or the Soviet Union, is launched into orbit from California.
8 Oct.	The U.S. Defense Department reports that forty-six American soldiers have died in Vietnam since U.S. large-scale intervention in the Vietnamese war began in 1961.
20 Oct.	India-Tibet border conflict erupts as Indian and Communist China army troops engage in full-scale fighting.
22 Oct.	U.S. president John F. Kennedy announces the imposition of a naval blockade against Cuba in response to evidence that the Soviets are constructing missile installations on the island and shipping military weapons there.
23 Oct.	Dick Tiger of Nigeria scores a fifteen-round decision over Gene Fullmer in San Francisco to win boxing's world middleweight championship.
24 Oct.	The U.S. quarantine on arms shipments to Cuba officially begins.
28 Oct.	Soviet premier Nikita Khrushchev announces that he has ordered the withdrawal of all Soviet missiles from Cuba in response to Kennedy's 27 October pledge not to invade Cuba.
20 Nov.	The United States ends its quarantine of Cuba after the Soviets agree to remove all their jet bombers from the island.
21 Nov.	The Soviet Union cancels its special military alert that had been ordered during the Cuban missile crisis.
25 Nov.	Candidates loyal to President Charles de Gaulle are victorious in National Assembly elections, marking the first time in modern French history that a single unified party has won control of Parliament.
30 Nov.	At the United Nations U Thant is elected to a four-year term as secretary-general of the organization.
Dec.	A team of English surgeons successfully transplants a dead man's kidney into a living patient at the Leeds General Infirmary.
20 Dec.	In the Dominican Republic's first free elections in thirty-eight years, Juan Bosch of the Dominican Revolutionary party is elected president.
24 Dec.	The Cuban government exchanges 1,113 prisoners captured in the Bay of Pigs invasion for $53 million worth of medicine and baby food offered by the U.S.-based Cuban Families Committee.
31 Dec.	North Vietnamese leader Ho Chi Minh vows to outlast American aid to South Vietnam and wage guerrilla war for ten years if necessary.

1963

- Federico Fellini's *8 1/2* is released.
- Tony Richardson's *Tom Jones* is released.
- Ingmar Bergman's *The Silence* is released.
- Aleksandr Solzhenitsyn's *One Day in the Life of Ivan Denisovich* is published in the West.

25 Jan.	North and South Korea announce that they have agreed to field a joint team for the 1964 Olympic Games in Tokyo.

29 Jan.	France blocks Great Britain's application to join the European Economic Community.
5 Feb.	The conservative Canadian government headed by John Diefenbaker is overthrown by a no-confidence vote concerning Canadian defense policies.
7 Feb.	Likely in response to Indonesia's refusal to allow Israeli and Nationalist Chinese participation in the 1962 Asian Games in Jakarta, the executive board of the International Olympic Committee bars Indonesia from the Olympics.
9 Feb.	Having been overthrown the previous day by anti-Communist air force officers, Iraqi premier Abdul Karim Dassim is executed by his captors.
22 Feb.	Norwegian explorer Helge Ingstad reports the discovery of Nordic artifacts in Newfoundland; dating about A.D. 1000, the artifacts, Ingstad argues, are proof of a Viking settlement in America five hundred years before the arrival of Christopher Columbus.
9 Mar.	Accused by Communist China of using poison chemicals to kill civilians and crops in Vietnam, U.S. officials explain that the chemicals are defoliants and are harmless to human and animal life.
21 Mar.	An eruption of the Agung volcano on the island of Bali kills an estimated fifteen hundred persons.
27 Mar.	Russian poet Yevgeny Yevtushenko is denounced by delegates to the Union of Writers Conference in Moscow for having allowed Western publication of his *Precocious Autobiography*.
2 Apr.	A Soviet fighter plane fires on a private twin-engine plane flying an air corridor to West Berlin.
15 Apr.	Tens of thousands protest nuclear weapons at a peace rally in Hyde Park, London.
17 Apr.	Canadian prime minister Diefenbaker resigns after the opposition Liberal party gains a majority in Parliament.
22 Apr.	Liberal party leader Lester Pearson becomes Canada's new prime minister.
1 May	Soviet premier Khrushchev salutes Cuban premier Castro at a May Day celebration in Moscow.
22 May	The North Atlantic Treaty Organization approves plans for a NATO nuclear alliance.
27 May	Jomo Kenyatta is elected the first African prime minister of Kenya.
31 May	Pope John XXIII receives last rites.
3 June	Pope John XXIII dies at age eighty-one.
5 June	British war secretary John Profumo resigns after admitting that he lied to Parliament about his relationship with Christine Keeler, who had ties to the Soviet Union.
16 June	Valentina V. Tereshkova, a Soviet cosmonaut, becomes the first woman in space.
16 June	Israeli prime minister David Ben-Gurion resigns.
21 June	Giovanni Battista Cardinal Montoni is elected as Pope Paul VI.

26 June	During a visit to West Germany in which he pledges U.S. support in resisting communism, President Kennedy proclaims, "Ich bin ein Berliner."
27 June	Henry Cabot Lodge is appointed U.S. ambassador to South Vietnam.
20 July	U.S., British, and Soviet negotiators draft a nuclear test-ban treaty.
24 July	Cuba takes over the U.S. embassy building in Havana after Cuban accounts in U.S. banks are frozen.
30 July	After disappearing in Beirut, British journalist H. A. R. Philby is given asylum by the Soviet Union.
8 Aug.	A masked gang escapes with more than $5 million taken from a mail train near London; after being caught, the twelve are sentenced to a total of 307 years in prison.
30 Aug.	An emergency hot line between Washington and Moscow is opened.
15 Sept.	Malaysia is officially created.
7 Oct.	A hurricane kills five thousand people in Haiti and leaves one hundred thousand homeless.
10 Oct.	British prime minister Harold Macmillan announces his retirement.
12–16 Nov.	Prof. Frederick C. Barghoorn, chair of the Soviet studies department at Yale University, is arrested in the Soviet Union and charged with espionage; at President Kennedy's request he is released four days later.
22 Nov.	President Kennedy is shot and killed in Dallas.
9 Dec.	Zanzibar and Pemba become independent of Britain.
11 Dec.	Kenya becomes independent of Britain.

1964

•	René Magritte's artwork *The Man in the Bowler Hat* is shown.
4 Jan.	Pope Paul VI tours the Holy Land and meets with Patriarch Benedictos of Jerusalem; it is the first meeting of the heads of the Roman Catholic and Eastern Orthodox churches in five hundred years.
26 Mar.	Defense Secretary Robert S. McNamara claims that U.S. forces will remain in Vietnam until the possibility of a Communist takeover is no longer a threat.
27 May	Jawaharlal Nehru, the prime minister of India since its independence in 1948, dies at age seventy-four.
29 May	Quebecois members of the Canadian Parliament accept Prime Minister Lester Pearson's proposal for a new flag with a maple-leaf design; they reject his recommendation to keep the Union Jack.
12 June	Eight South African antiapartheid leaders, including Nelson Mandela, are sentenced to life imprisonment.
7 Aug.	Congress's Tonkin Gulf Resolution authorizes President Lyndon B. Johnson to "take all necessary measures to repel any armed attack against forces of the United States and to prevent further aggression."

14 Sept.	Pope Paul VI opens the third session of the Ecumenical Council, Vatican II, in Saint Peter's Basilica in Rome.
5 Oct.	Fifty-seven East Germans escape to West Berlin by tunnel.
9 Oct.	The Summer Olympics begin in Tokyo.
12 Oct.	The Soviet Union launches the first successful space flight with more than one cosmonaut.
15 Oct.	Nikita Khrushchev is replaced as premier of the Soviet Union by Leonid Brezhnev.
15 Oct.	Harold Wilson, leader of the Labour party, becomes prime minister of Britain.
16 Oct.	China conducts its first nuclear test explosion.
23 Oct.	The republic of Zambia, formerly the British protectorate Northern Rhodesia, becomes an independent nation.
2 Nov.	Saudi Arabian religious and political authorities dethrone the sick King Saud and crown his half brother, Crown Prince Faisal.

1965

- Goya's portrait of the duke of Wellington, which was stolen in 1961, is returned to London's National Gallery.
- Architect Le Corbusier dies.
- David Lean's movie *Dr. Zhivago* is released.
- Federico Fellini's film *Juliet of the Spirits* premieres.

4 Jan.	In his State of the Union address President Lyndon Johnson invites an exchange of Soviet and U.S. television broadcasts.
4 Jan.	T. S. Eliot dies at seventy-six in London.
14 Jan.	The two Irish prime ministers meet for the first time since 1922, when Ireland was partitioned.
19 Jan.	The United States claims that a recent Soviet underground nuclear test is likely in violation of the test-ban treaty.
21 Jan.	Indonesia formally withdraws from the United Nations.
23 Jan.	Winston Churchill dies in London at age ninety.
24 Jan.	Fashion reports indicate that European designers have turned to plastics in creating new household items.
30 Jan.	The United States agrees to widen cultural ties with the Soviet Union.
1 Feb.	Troops loyal to the Laos government repel an attempted coup by army officers.
8 Feb.	The Soviet Union pledges air-defense aid to North Vietnam following U.S. air attacks.
12 Feb.	Twenty-one protesters die in language riots in southern India.
19 Feb.	UN secretary-general U Thant says that the severe financial crisis at the United Nations will force the organization to seek additional funds for 1965.

20 Feb.	It is announced that the UN will try to help India lower its birth rate.
23 Feb.	Syria hangs Farhan Attassi, a naturalized U.S. citizen, for alleged spying.
24 Feb.	U.S. officials admit that U.S. military advisers have taken a more active role in the Vietnam War.
24 Feb.	UN secretary-general U Thant calls for negotiations that would lead to the United States pulling out of Vietnam.
26 Feb.	Indonesia seizes rubber estates belonging to U.S. concerns.
27 Feb.	It is reported that Communist China has opened its borders to visits by Japanese private citizens.
1 Mar.	The Russian film *The Overcoat* opens in New York City.
3 Mar.	Great Britain announces massive cuts in defense spending.
4 Mar.	Two thousand students attack the U.S. embassy in Moscow.
14 Mar.	Israel and West Germany agree to talks aimed at establishing diplomatic relations between the two countries.
17 Mar.	Jean-Paul Sartre cancels a U.S. lecture tour in protest over American involvement in the Vietnam War.
18 Mar.	Cosmonaut Aleksei Leonev takes a ten-minute walk in space.
29 Mar.	A bomb explosion at the U.S. embassy in Saigon kills six.
3 Apr.	The United States launches a satellite powered by a nuclear reactor.
3 Apr.	The United States accuses the Soviet Union of harassing U.S. ships at sea.
4 Apr.	East German guards prohibit West Berlin mayor Willy Brandt from driving into Berlin from West Germany.
8 Apr.	The Vatican names Cardinal Konig as its envoy to atheists.
25 Apr.	For the first time U.S. officials confirm that North Vietnamese troops are fighting in the south of Vietnam.
25 Apr.	The U.S.-supported ruling junta in the Dominican Republic is overthrown.
28 Apr.	President Johnson announces that 405 U.S. Marines have landed in the Dominican Republic to protect and evacuate American citizens.
13 May	Israel and West Germany establish diplomatic relations.
22 May	A cease-fire begins in the Dominican Republic.
24 May	Art buyers in New York and London are linked by satellite television.
5 June	U.S. officials acknowledge that U.S. troops are engaged in active combat in Vietnam.
7 June	U.S. consul Allison Wanamaker is murdered by guerrillas in Argentina.
13 June	Israeli philosopher Martin Buber dies at age eighty-seven in Jerusalem.
18 June	Nguyen Cao Ky becomes South Vietnamese premier.

28 June	Six nations join in opening the Comsat telephone system.
6 July	France withdraws its delegate from the Common Market.
15 July	U.S. spacecraft *Mariner 4* sends back to Earth the first photos of Mars taken from space.
19 July	Former South Korean president Syngman Rhee dies in Honolulu at age ninety.
20 July	The British House of Lords approves a ban on the death penalty for murder.
5 Aug.	Greek premier George Athansiadas-Novas resigns as thousands of backers of former prime minister George Papandreou continue to protest.
1 Sept.	Fighting between India and Pakistan over Kashmir begins to escalate.
5 Sept.	Dr. Albert Schweitzer dies in Gabon at age ninety.
10 Sept.	In a draft declaration issued by the Vatican, the Catholic church exonerates the Jews of collective responsibility in the killing of Christ.
17 Sept.	Stephanos Stephanopoulos becomes Greek prime minister.
21–22 Sept.	India and Pakistan agree to a UN-sponsored cease-fire in Kashmir.
14 Oct.	Paul Cézanne's *Maisons a l'Estaque* sets a new world's auction record for impressionist art.
15 Oct.	Soviet writer Mikhail Sholokhov wins the Nobel Prize for literature.
25 Oct.	The United Nations Children's Fund wins the Nobel Peace Prize.
12 Nov.	Philippine senator Ferdinand Marcos wins his country's presidential election.
24 Nov.	Soviet officials sentence U.S. tourist Newcomb Mott to eighteen months in prison for crossing the Soviet border without authorization.
27 Nov.	The Vatican recovers stolen manuscripts by Italian poets Petrarch and Torquato Tasso.
30 Nov.	France calls on the United States to pull out of Vietnam.
10 Dec.	It is reported that the role of the South Vietnamese army in its war with the North has diminished greatly as the U.S. troop buildup continues.
15 Dec.	British author W. Somerset Maugham dies in Nice, France, at age ninety-one.
19 Dec.	Five international teams of scientists report having identified indications of the primordial flash that occurred when the universe was born.
19 Dec.	President Charles de Gaulle wins 54.7 percent of the vote in the French presidential elections.
20 Dec.	U.S. field commanders are given permission to pursue enemy troops into Cambodia.
21 Dec.	The Soviet Union pledges to increase aid to North Vietnam.
25 Dec.	Mexico begins a televised literacy program.
27 Dec.	A gas rig collapses in the North Sea, killing thirteen.
30 Dec.	Ferdinand Marcos begins his presidential term in the Philippines.

- Book of quotations of Chairman Mao is published.

- Michelangelo Antonioni's film *Blow-Up* is released.

19 Jan. Indira Gandhi, daughter of former prime minister Jawaharlal Nehru, is elected prime minister of India.

3 Feb. An unmanned Soviet craft, *Luna 9,* makes the first soft landing on the moon.

17 Feb. France launches its first satellite into orbit.

1 Mar. In the first physical contact with another planet, a Soviet spacecraft crashes onto the surface of Venus.

12 Mar. France announces that it plans to withdraw from the North Atlantic Treaty Organization.

23 Mar. The archbishop of Canterbury, the Most Reverend Arthur Michael Ramsey, meets in Rome with Pope Paul VI.

3 Apr. The Soviet Union's *Luna 10* becomes the first man-made object to orbit the moon.

10 Apr. British novelist Evelyn Waugh dies at age sixty-two in Taunton, Somerset, England.

21 Apr. The world's third heart-transplant operation is performed in Houston, Texas.

10 May In a runoff election the Guatemalan Congress elects Mendez Montenegro as president.

13 May China accuses the United States of violating its airspace and shooting down a Chinese military training plane.

30 May Two Buddhist monks burn themselves to death in protest over government policies in South Vietnam.

3 June It is reported that in May a widespread purge called the Great Proletarian Cultural Revolution took place in Communist China.

6 June For the first time in the history of Communist China an army official, Lo Jui-ching, is publicly criticized in the government press.

15 June The Syrians and Israelis engage in a three-hour sea and air battle in and over the Sea of Galilee.

19 June South Vietnamese troops end Buddhist resistance in Hue.

28 June Argentine president Arturo Illia is ousted by a three-man military junta led by Lt. Gen. Juan Carlos Ongania.

29 June British prime minister Harold Wilson publicly criticizes recent U.S. bombing missions in Vietnam.

30 June The United States begins to withdraw its military forces from France.

1 July The United States begins to withdraw troops from the Dominican Republic.

1 July Congolese president Joseph Mobutu orders that the European names of his country's cities be changed to African names.

4 July	In Belfast, Northern Ireland, a thirty-pound concrete block is dropped on the roof of a car containing Queen Elizabeth II and Prince Philip; no one is injured.
9 July	Egyptian president Gamal Nasser declares that the Arab countries will never accept Israel as their neighbor.
11 July	In protest over U.S. policy in Vietnam the Soviet Union announces that its athletes will not participate in the eighth annual U.S.-Soviet track meet.
14 July	Welsh nationalists for the first time win a seat in the British House of Commons.
16 July	Communist Chinese officials report that Chairman Mao recently swam fifteen kilometers in an hour and five minutes in the Yangtze River.
18 July	A lawsuit challenging South Africa's right to govern South-West Africa is dismissed by the International Court of Justice.
19 July	Argentina and Great Britain open talks on the future of the Falkland Islands.
12 Aug.	North Korea asserts its independence from both Communist Chinese and Soviet influence and declares that it will follow its own path.
13 Aug.	A parade of ten thousand East German soldiers marks the fifth anniversary of the construction of the Berlin Wall.
17 Aug.	North Korea aligns itself with the Soviet Union after accusing Communist China of "Trotskyism."
20 Aug.	It is reported that a majority of Roman Catholics use some form of artificial birth control.
24 Aug.	Pro-Mao Chinese youths called Red Guards continue to carry out the Cultural Revolution by breaking into private homes to destroy all items deemed Western.
30 Aug.	North Vietnam and Communist China sign an aid agreement.
1 Sept.	In a speech delivered in Cambodia, French president Charles de Gaulle urges the United States to withdraw from Vietnam.
6 Sept.	South African prime minister Hendrik Verwoerd is stabbed to death by an assassin during a session of Parliament.
6 Sept.	Syria announces that a coup attempt organized by Baath party founder Michel Aflak has been crushed.
14 Sept.	New South African prime minister B. J. Vorster pledges to continue his country's apartheid policy.
19 Sept.	The last American troops leave the Dominican Republic.
20 Oct.	Israeli writer Shmuel Agnon wins the Nobel Prize for literature.
22 Oct.	At the United Nations the U.S. delegation opposes sanctions against South Africa on the grounds that they would be counterproductive.
23 Oct.	The International Cancer Congress convenes in Tokyo.
1 Nov.	Eight U.S. soldiers are killed by North Koreans in the demilitarized zone.

24 Nov.	U.S. scientists ask Pope Paul VI to reconsider the church's anti–birth control policy.
29 Nov.	In a fifty-seven to forty-seven vote the United Nations refuses Communist China entry into the organization.
Dec.	Dr. Audouin Dollfus of France's Meudon Observatory discovers a tenth satellite of the planet Saturn.
1 Dec.	The West German Parliament elects Kurt-Georg Kiesinger as chancellor.
2 Dec.	An agreement on the first international treaty governing the exploration of space is reached at the United Nations.
21 Dec.	An American tourist is sentenced by a Soviet court to three years in a labor camp for having exchanged money on the black market.
26 Dec.	The European Economic Community rejects Spain's application for membership on the grounds that it is not a democracy.

1967

- Tom Stoppard's play *Rosenkrantz and Guildenstern Are Dead* premieres.
- Gabriel García Márquez's novel *Cien años de soledad* (One Hundred Years of Solitude) is published.
- French painter René Magritte dies.
- The Cultural Revolution in China leads to virtual civil war as anti-Mao peasants repeatedly clash with pro-Mao Red Guards.

4 Jan.	Pope Paul VI bans unorthodox liturgies such as jazz masses.
5 Jan.	Harold Pinter's play *The Homecoming* opens in New York.
16 Jan.	Lynden Oscar Pindling becomes the first black prime minister of the Bahama Islands.
20 Jan.	Cuba executes Enrique Gonzalez Rodriguez for allegedly acting as an agent for the Central Intelligence Agency.
20 Jan.	In the first meeting between a Roman Catholic pontiff and a Communist head of state, Pope Paul VI confers with Soviet president Nikolai Podgorny.
31 Jan.	Romania becomes the first Eastern Bloc country to recognize West Germany.
3 Feb.	Canadian prime minister Lester Pearson announces the creation of a government commission on the status of women in Canadian society.
13 Feb.	Canada denies entry to LSD proponent Timothy Leary.
21 Feb.	Mao Tse-tung orders Red Guards to cease political activity.
1 Mar.	Marshall McLuhan's *The Medium Is the Message* is published.
5 Mar.	Col. Fidel Sanchez Hernandez wins presidential elections in El Salvador.
5 Mar.	Mohammed Mossadegh, prime minister of Iran from 1951 to 1953, dies in Teheran at age eighty-six.
6 Mar.	Svetlana Stalina, only daughter of the late Joseph Stalin, asks for U.S. asylum at the U.S. embassy in New Delhi.

15 Mar.	Artur Da Costa e Silva becomes president of Brazil.
15 Apr.	The Soviets announce that they will introduce a profit system in 390 state farms.
19 Apr.	Konrad Adenauer, former chancellor of West Germany, dies in Rhondorf, West Germany, at age ninety-one.
20 Apr.	René Ribiere and Gaston Deferre, two French politicians, fight a duel after a heated argument in the French Assembly; neither man is hurt.
21 Apr.	The interim government of Premier Panayotis Kanellopoulos of Greece is overthrown in a military coup.
24 Apr.	Miniskirts for girls and long hair for boys are banned in Greece.
25 Apr.	Swaziland, a former British colony, becomes a self-governing British protectorate.
26 Apr.	Eugene Blake, general secretary of the World Council of Churches, calls on the United States to stop the bombing in North Vietnam.
19 May	U.S. planes bomb downtown Hanoi.
5 June	The Six Day War between Israel and Syria, Jordan, and the United Arab Republic begins; Israel expands its borders as a result.
17 June	China detonates its first hydrogen bomb.
23–25 June	President Johnson and Soviet premier Aleksey Kosygin meet in Glassboro, New Jersey, about arms control, Vietnam, and the Middle East.
26 June	U.S. and Panamanian officials meet to discuss passing U.S. control of the Panama Canal to Panama.
28 June	Jerusalem is reunited with Israel.
4 July	Britain's House of Commons passes a bill that eliminates criminal charges for private homosexual acts between consenting adults.
24 July	French president de Gaulle, during a visit to Canada, proclaims "Long live free Quebec" in Montreal; Canadian prime minister Lester B. Pearson condemns the statement.
25 July	During a visit to Turkey, Pope Paul VI becomes the first Roman Catholic pontiff to enter an Eastern Orthodox church.
3 Aug.	President Johnson announces that the United States will send forty-five thousand to fifty thousand more men to Vietnam.
6–7 Aug.	A Colombian plane is hijacked by five supporters of Fidel Castro and forced to land in Cuba.
27 Aug.	India sets up camps for nearly five hundred Tibetans who left their country due to persecution from China's Red Guards.
17 Sept.	In Kayseri, Turkey, forty-two people are killed and more than six hundred wounded during riots at a soccer game.
20 Sept.	The British luxury liner the *Queen Elizabeth II* is launched.
23 Sept.	North Vietnam and the Soviet Union agree that the Soviet Union will continue to provide North Vietnam with military and economic assistance.

24 Sept.	The Organization of American States agrees to fight Cuban-promoted revolutionary activities in the Western Hemisphere.
9 Oct.	Cuban revolutionary Che Guevara is executed by Bolivian troops.
18 Oct.	The Soviet Union lands a spacecraft on the surface of Venus, revealing that the atmosphere consists largely of carbon dioxide and that temperatures range from 104° to 536° Fahrenheit.
21 Oct.	The discovery of a new Dead Sea scroll is announced.
26 Oct.	The shah of Iran proclaims himself king of kings and makes his wife his country's first crowned queen.
31 Oct.	Queen Elizabeth II announces that membership in the House of Lords by heredity will be eliminated.
3 Dec.	Dr. Christiaan Barnard performs the world's first successful heart transplant on Louis Washkansky in Cape Town, South Africa.
11 Dec.	The first supersonic airliner, the Concorde, is unveiled by Britain and France.
17 Dec.	Australian prime minister Harold Holt disappears while swimming and is assumed dead.
21 Dec.	Heart-transplant recipient Louis Washkansky dies of pneumonia.

1968

- Britain's Theatres Act ends the lord chamberlain's censorship powers.
- The Aswan Dam in Egypt is completed.
- The gross national product of Japan climbs 12 percent, making the country second only to the United States economically.
- The West German Volkswagen accounts for 57 percent of automobiles imported into the United States and outsells many domestic models.

1 Jan.	C. Day Lewis becomes Great Britain's poet laureate.
5 Jan.	The Czechoslovak Communist party elects Alexander Dubcek as its first secretary, indicating a movement toward political liberalization in Czechoslovakia.
12 Jan.	Martin Buber's *A Believing Humanism* is published by Simon and Schuster.
21 Jan.	The North Vietnamese launch a massive attack against a U.S. marine base at Kesanh.
23 Jan.	The U.S. intelligence-gathering ship *Pueblo* is captured by North Korean patrol boats.
30 Jan.	A major Tet offensive is launched as North Vietnamese and Viet Cong forces attack numerous cities in South Vietnam.
31 Jan.	The U.S. embassy in Saigon is overrun and held for six hours by Viet Cong.
6 Feb.	Six American soldiers opposed to U.S. involvement in Vietnam are granted asylum by the Swedish government.
6 Feb.	The scheduled publication of Aleksandr Solzhenitsyn's *The Cancer Ward* in a Soviet literary magazine is canceled by Soviet officials.

8–11 Mar.	Thousands of students in Poland fight police in protests against Communist party involvement in cultural matters.
16 Mar.	Hundreds of men, women, and children in the South Vietnamese village of My Lai are massacred by U.S. soldiers under orders from Lt. William L. Calley, Jr.; the news is suppressed for more than a year.
27 Mar.	Yuri Gagarin, the first man in space, dies in a plane crash.
6 Apr.	Pierre Trudeau is elected leader of Canada's Liberal party; he becomes the new prime minister on 20 April.
21 Apr.	The International Olympic Committee recommends that South Africa be excluded from the 1968 games.
23 Apr.	In shifting to a decimal monetary system, Britain issues its first five- and ten-pence coins.
27 Apr.	Britain legalizes most abortions.
26 June	Iwo Jima is returned to Japan after more than twenty-three years of U.S. administration.
29 July	In an encyclical letter Pope Paul VI says that Roman Catholics should limit the sizes of their families only by abstinence or the rhythm method.
20–22 Aug.	Warsaw Pact troops invade Czechoslovakia.
22 Aug.	In a visit to Colombia, Pope Paul VI becomes the first Roman Catholic pontiff to visit South America.
24 Aug.	France becomes the fifth nation to possess nuclear weapons.
29 Sept.	Greek voters support a new constitution that limits their rights and strips the king of most of his power.
9 Oct.	Five Soviet citizens are arrested for protesting the invasion of Czechoslovakia.
16 Dec.	The Spanish government reverses a 1492 order expelling Jews from the country.
27 Dec.	The United States announces that it will sell fifty fighter jets to Israel.

1969

- Aleksandr Solzhenitsyn is removed from the Soviet Writers' Union.
- Samuel Beckett receives the Nobel Prize for literature.
- The Museum of Modern Art in New York purchases the art collection of the late expatriate writer Gertrude Stein for $6 million.
- Federico Fellini's film *Satyricon* is released.
- Ken Russell's movie *Women in Love* is released.
- Yasser Arafat is elected chair of the executive committee of the Palestine Liberation Organization.

12 Jan.	Approximately five thousand people march in London to protest discrimination against nonwhites; hundreds clash with police.
17 Mar.	Golda Meir is sworn in as premier of Israel.

28 Apr.	Charles de Gaulle resigns as president of France after voters reject his proposed constitutional reforms.
1 July	Queen Elizabeth II makes her son Charles Prince of Wales and Earl of Chester.
7 July	Canada's House of Commons approves a bill making French the second official language.
14 July	El Salvadoran troops invade Honduran territory.
20 July	U.S. astronauts make the first manned landing on the moon.
22 July	Generalissimo Francisco Franco of Spain names Prince Juan Carlos as his successor to lead the country.
31 July	Pope Paul VI is the first Roman Catholic pontiff to visit Africa.
3 Sept.	North Vietnamese president Ho Chi Minh dies at age seventy-nine.
17 Oct.	A subsidiary of the Gulf Oil Corporation, the Bolivia Gulf Company, is taken over by the Bolivian government.
31 Oct.	A U.S. Marine hijacks a jet from California to Rome in the first transatlantic hijacking.
3 Nov.	President Richard M. Nixon appeals to "the great silent majority of my fellow Americans" to support his policies on Vietnam and his social policies.

Civil-rights demonstrators arriving in Montgomery, Alabama, on 25 March 1965 after a fifty-four-mile march to protest denial of voting rights to blacks

THE ARTS

by DARREN HARRIS-FAIN

CONTENTS

Sidebars and tables are listed in italics.

1960

Movies *The Apartment*, directed by Billy Wilder and starring Jack Lemmon and Shirley MacLaine; *Elmer Gantry*, starring Burt Lancaster and Jean Simmons; *Little Shop of Horrors*, directed by Roger Corman; *Psycho*, directed by Alfred Hitchcock and starring Anthony Perkins; *Spartacus*, directed by Stanley Kubrick and starring Kirk Douglas, Tony Curtis, Peter Ustinov, and Jean Simmons.

Fiction John Barth, *The Sot-Weed Factor*; E. L. Doctorow, *Welcome to Hard Times*; John Hersey, *The Child Buyer*; Harper Lee, *To Kill a Mockingbird*; Flannery O'Connor, *The Violent Bear It Away*; John O'Hara, *Sermons and Soda-Water*; John Updike, *Rabbit, Run*.

Popular Songs Paul Anka, "Puppy Love"; Ray Charles, "Georgia on My Mind"; Chubby Checker, "The Twist"; Elvis Presley, "Are You Lonesome Tonight?" and "It's Now or Never"; Johnny Preston, "Running Bear."

- The second annual Photography in the Fine Arts Project is held at the IBM Gallery in New York; it is twice as big and occupies three times as much space as the original.

- Leslie Fiedler's controversial *Love and Death in the American Novel* quickly becomes one of the best-known books in the history of American literary criticism.

- *Astounding Science Fiction*, one of the most popular science-fiction magazines since the 1930s, changes its name to *Analog*.

3 Jan. The Moscow State Symphony begins a successful seven-week tour of the United States at Carnegie Hall in New York. It is the first Soviet orchestra to perform in the United States.

Mar. Seven of the eight major film studios are crippled by an actors' strike.

4 Mar. Baritone Leonard Warren collapses and dies during a performance of *La forza del destino* at the Metropolitan Opera House in New York.

16 Mar. The merger of Alfred A. Knopf, Inc., and Random House, Inc., is completed, with Random in control.

3 July The city council of Newport, Rhode Island, votes to cancel remaining performances at the annual Newport Jazz Festival due to riots led by drunken high-school and college students.

2 Nov. Dimitri Mitropoulos collapses and dies while conducting at La Scala Opera House in Milan, Italy.

1961

Movies *The Absent-Minded Professor*, starring Fred MacMurray; *Breakfast at Tiffany's*, starring Audrey Hepburn and George Peppard; *El Cid*, starring Charlton Heston; *The Hustler*, starring Paul Newman and Jackie Gleason; *Judgment at Nuremberg*, starring Montgomery Clift; *The Misfits*, directed by John Huston and starring Clark Gable and Marilyn Monroe; *101 Dalmatians*, Disney animation; *Splendor in the Grass*, directed by Elia Kazan and starring Natalie Wood and Warren Beatty; *West Side Story*, starring Richard Beymer and Natalie Wood.

Fiction John Hawkes, *The Lime Twig;* Joseph Heller, *Catch-22;* John O'Hara, *Assembly;* Robert A. Heinlein, *Stranger in a Strange Land;* Walker Percy, *The Moviegoer;* J. D. Salinger, *Franny and Zooey;* Isaac Bashevis Singer, *The Spinoza of Market Street;* John Steinbeck, *The Winter of Our Discontent.*

Popular Songs Ray Charles, "Hit the Road, Jack"; Jimmy Dean, "Big Bad John"; Dion, "Runaround Sue"; the Kingston Trio, "Where Have All the Flowers Gone?"; the Marvelettes, "Please, Mr. Postman"; Roy Orbison, "Cryin' "; the Shirelles, "Will You Still Love Me Tomorrow?"; the Tokens, "The Lion Sleeps Tonight."

- The Museum of Modern Art holds a retrospective exhibit of the work of Mark Rothko.

- Robert A. Heinlein's *Stranger in a Strange Land* becomes the first science-fiction novel to appear on *The New York Times* best-seller list.

27 Jan. Soprano Leontyne Price first performs at the New York Metropolitan Opera.

29 July Ten paintings worth $300,000 are stolen from the private collection of G. David Thompson of Pittsburgh; others (including a Picasso) are damaged.

28 Aug. A contract dispute concerning the musicians at the Metropolitan Opera in New York is settled when the musicians and the company agree to abide by binding arbitration by Secretary of Labor Arthur Goldberg.

13 Nov. Cellist Pablo Casals performs at a White House dinner honoring Puerto Rican governor Luis Muñoz Marín.

1962

Movies *The Birdman of Alcatraz,* starring Burt Lancaster; *Days of Wine and Roses,* starring Jack Lemmon and Lee Remick; *Dr. No,* starring Sean Connery; *Lawrence of Arabia,* directed by David Lean and starring Peter O'Toole; *Lolita,* directed by Stanley Kubrick and starring James Mason; *The Manchurian Candidate,* starring Laurence Harvey, Frank Sinatra, and Angela Lansbury; *The Music Man,* starring Robert Preston and Shirley Jones; *Mutiny on the Bounty,* starring Marlon Brando and Trevor Howard; *To Kill a Mockingbird,* starring Gregory Peck; *What Ever Happened to Baby Jane?,* starring Joan Crawford and Bette Davis.

Fiction James Baldwin, *Another Country;* William S. Burroughs, *The Ticket That Exploded;* Ken Kesey, *One Flew Over the Cuckoo's Nest;* Vladimir Nabokov, *Pale Fire;* Katherine Anne Porter, *Ship of Fools;* Isaac Bashevis Singer, *The Slave;* Kurt Vonnegut, Jr., *Mother Night.*

Popular Songs Tony Bennett, "I Left My Heart in San Francisco"; Gene Chandler, "Duke of Earl"; Ray Charles, "I Can't Stop Loving You"; the Four Seasons, "Big Girls Don't Cry" and "Sherry"; Little Eva, "The Loco-Motion"; Bobby "Boris" Pickett, "The Monster Mash"; Elvis Presley, "Return to Sender"; Neil Sedaka, "Breaking Up Is Hard to Do."

- William S. Burroughs's novel *Naked Lunch* (1959), initially published in Paris, is published in America for the first time.

- After the death of Clara Langhorne Clemens Samossoud, the last surviving child of Mark Twain, his antireligious *Letters from the Earth* is published for the first time, as a book edited by Bernard De Voto.

30 May Benny Goodman begins a six-week tour of Russia in Moscow arranged by the U.S. State Department. Some jazz aficionados feel a more respected all-around musician such as Duke Ellington should represent America, while others think a younger, more "modern" musician would be more appropriate.

25 Sept. Philharmonic Hall, the first completed building of the Lincoln Center for the Performing Arts in New York, is inaugurated by Leonard Bernstein and the New York Philharmonic. First Lady Jacqueline Kennedy is guest of honor.

25 Oct. John Steinbeck is announced as the 1962 recipient of the Nobel Prize in literature.

12 Dec. French minister of culture André Malraux announces that France will loan the United States Leonardo da Vinci's Mona Lisa for a short period for an American touring exhibit.

1963

Movies *The Birds*, directed by Alfred Hitchcock and starring Tippi Hedren; *Cleopatra*, starring Elizabeth Taylor and Richard Burton; *Hud*, starring Paul Newman; *It's a Mad Mad Mad Mad World*, directed by Stanley Kramer; *Lilies of the Field*, starring Sidney Poitier; *The Nutty Professor*, starring Jerry Lewis; *Tom Jones*, starring Albert Finney.

Fiction Mary McCarthy, *The Group;* Sylvia Plath, *The Bell Jar;* Thomas Pynchon, *V.;* J. D. Salinger, *Raise High the Roofbeam, Carpenters, and Seymour: An Introduction;* Kurt Vonnegut, Jr., *Cat's Cradle.*

Popular Songs The Angels, "My Boyfriend's Back"; the Beach Boys, "Surfin' U.S.A."; Johnny Cash, "Ring of Fire"; the Chiffons, "He's So Fine" and "One Fine Day"; the Crystals, "Then He Kissed Me"; the Four Seasons, "Walk Like a Man"; Leslie Gore, "It's My Party"; the Kingsmen, "Louie, Louie"; Steve Lawrence, "Go Away, Little Girl"; Peter, Paul and Mary, "Blowin' in the Wind" and "Puff, the Magic Dragon"; the Singing Nun, "Dominique"; Bobby Vinton, "Blue Velvet."

- John Cleland's erotic eighteenth-century-style novel *Memoirs of a Woman of Pleasure*, better known as *Fanny Hill*, is banned in several cities, but the courts declare it not to be obscene. Meanwhile, a bookseller in New Orleans is arrested for selling James Baldwin's novel *Another Country*.

- A member of the New York Public Library board of trustees borrows and burns the children's book *My Mother Is the Most Beautiful Woman in the World*, Rebecca Reyher's retelling of a Russian folktale, because the book contains passages "favorable to Russia." He is suspended from the board for six weeks or until he replaces the book.

- Andrew Wyeth becomes the first painter to receive the Presidential Medal of Freedom.

1964

8 Jan.   Leonardo da Vinci's Mona Lisa is shown at the National Gallery in Washington, D.C., the first time the painting has ever appeared outside the Louvre in Paris. During its three-and-a-half-week stay it attracts 500,000 visitors. When the painting moves to New York, 23,872 people show up on a rainy day to see it.

7 May   The Guthrie Theatre in Minneapolis, the first major regional theater in the Midwest, opens.

Movies   *Becket,* starring Richard Burton and Peter O'Toole; *Dr. Strangelove or: How I Learned to Stop Worrying and Love the Bomb,* directed by Stanley Kubrick and starring Peter Sellers, George C. Scott, and Slim Pickens; *Goldfinger,* starring Sean Connery; *Mary Poppins,* starring Julie Andrews and Dick Van Dyke; *My Fair Lady,* starring Rex Harrison and Audrey Hepburn; *Zorba the Greek,* starring Anthony Quinn.

Fiction   Saul Bellow, *Herzog;* Thomas Berger, *Little Big Man;* Richard Brautigan, *A Confederate General from Big Sur;* William S. Burroughs, *Nova Express;* James Gould Cozzens, *Children and Others;* John Hawkes, *Second Skin.*

Popular Songs   The Animals, "The House of the Rising Sun"; Louis Armstrong, "Hello, Dolly!"; the Beach Boys, "Fun, Fun, Fun" and "I Get Around"; the Beatles, "Can't Buy Me Love," "A Hard Day's Night," "I Feel Fine," "I Want to Hold Your Hand," "She Loves You," and "Twist and Shout"; Manfred Mann, "Do Wah Diddy Diddy"; Martha and the Vandellas, "Dancing in the Street"; Dean Martin, "Everybody Loves Somebody"; Roy Orbison, "Pretty Woman"; the Temptations, "The Way You Do the Things You Do"; Mary Wells, "My Guy."

- *A Moveable Feast,* Ernest Hemingway's memoirs of his early years in Paris, is published.

- After three years of court battles in various states, the U.S. Supreme Court rules that Henry Miller's novel *Tropic of Cancer* is not obscene.

- *The Deputy,* by German playwright Rolf Hochhuth, is picketed at its New York performance by Catholics outraged at its suggestion that Pope Pius XII had tacitly allowed the Nazis to commit genocide during World War II.

28 Feb.   Jazz pianist Thelonious Monk is featured in a cover story in *Time* magazine.

May   After remodeling, the Museum of Modern Art reopens with a new gallery, named the Steichen Photography Center after Edward Steichen, its photography department director from 1947 to 1962.

1965

Movies   *Cat Ballou,* starring Lee Marvin and Jane Fonda; *Doctor Zhivago,* directed by David Lean and starring Omar Sharif and Julie Christie; *The Greatest Story Ever Told,* starring Max Von Sydow, Charlton Heston, and Telly Savalas; *The Sound of Music,* starring Julie Andrews and Christopher Plummer; *Thunderball,* starring Sean Connery.

Fiction   Robert Coover, *The Origin of the Brunists;* Frank Herbert, *Dune;* Jerzy Kosinski, *The Painted Bird;* Norman Mailer, *An American Dream;* Flannery O'Connor, *Everything That Rises Must Converge.*

1965

Popular Songs

Fontella Bass, "Rescue Me"; the Beach Boys, "California Girls" and "Help Me, Rhonda"; the Beatles, "Eight Days a Week," "Ticket to Ride," and "Yesterday"; James Brown, "Papa's Got a Brand New Bag"; the Byrds, "Turn! Turn! Turn!"; Petula Clark, "Downtown"; Bob Dylan, "Like a Rolling Stone"; Four Tops, "I Can't Help Myself"; The McCoys, "Hang On, Sloopy"; Roger Miller, "King of the Road"; the Righteous Brothers, "Unchained Melody" and "You've Lost That Lovin' Feelin' "; the Rolling Stones, "Get Off of My Cloud" and "(I Can't Get No) Satisfaction"; Sonny and Cher, "I Got You Babe"; the Supremes, "Stop! In the Name of Love"; the Temptations, "My Girl"; Dionne Warwick, "What the World Needs Now."

- A three-person music jury suggests that the advisory board for the Pulitzer Prizes grant jazz musician, composer, and bandleader Duke Ellington a special citation for his lifework. The board rejects the recommendation, leading one jury member to voice his dissatisfaction with the decision publicly. Ellington, 66, shrugs it off: "Fate doesn't want me to be too famous too young," he says.

- The Metropolitan Museum in New York stages a successful exhibit, "Three Centuries of American Painting," of more than four hundred works from those of colonial times to those by Jasper Johns, Robert Rauschenberg, and Mark Rothko.

- More than seventy thousand listeners attend the first of the New York Philharmonic's free concerts in Central Park.

26 Apr. Charles Ives's Symphony No. 4 (1916) is performed in its entirety for the first time by the American Symphony Orchestra, conducted by Leopold Stokowski. A grant is required to finance the extra rehearsals needed for the extremely difficult piece.

1966

Movies

Batman, starring Adam West, Burt Ward, Burgess Meredith, Cesar Romero, Frank Gorshin, and Lee Meriwether; *The Chase,* starring Marlon Brando, Robert Redford, and Jane Fonda; *The Group,* starring Candice Bergen; *One Million Years B.C.,* starring Raquel Welch; *Who's Afraid of Virginia Woolf?,* starring Richard Burton, Elizabeth Taylor, George Segal, and Sandy Dennis.

Fiction

John Barth, *Giles Goat-Boy;* Truman Capote, *In Cold Blood;* William H. Gass, *Omensetter's Luck;* Bernard Malamud, *The Fixer;* Thomas Pynchon, *The Crying of Lot 49.*

Popular Songs

The Beach Boys, "Good Vibrations"; the Beatles, "Eleanor Rigby," "Paperback Writer," and "We Can Work It Out"; the Lovin' Spoonful, "Did You Ever Have to Make Up Your Mind?" and "Summer in the City"; Loretta Lynn, "Don't Come Home a-Drinkin' (with Lovin' on Your Mind)"; the Mamas and the Papas, "Monday, Monday"; the Monkees, "I'm a Believer" and "Last Train to Clarksville"; Napoleon XIV, "They're Coming to Take Me Away, Ha Ha"; Staff Sgt. Barry Sadler, "The Ballad of the Green Berets"; Simon and Garfunkel, "I Am a Rock" and "The Sounds of Silence"; Frank Sinatra, "Strangers in the Night"; Nancy Sinatra, "These Boots Are Made for Walkin'"; Percy Sledge, "When a Man Loves a Woman"; the Supremes, "You Can't Hurry Love"; the Troggs, "Wild Thing"; the Young Rascals, "Good Lovin'."

- Jazz pianist Earl Hines tours the Soviet Union, sponsored by the U.S. State Department. The tour is a tremendous success: in thirty-five concerts in eleven cities Hines plays for nearly one hundred thousand jazz fans.

- *The Sound of Music* (1965), having earned $70 million in one year, becomes the top-grossing movie in American motion-picture history.

- Berry Gordy, Jr., the founder of Motown, changes the name of the Supremes to Diana Ross and the Supremes.

11 May Joseph H. Hirschhorn donates his art collection, including fifty-six hundred paintings, drawings, and sculptures, to the United States. The collection's value is appraised at $50 million.

8 Dec. Paul Mellon donates his collection of British rare books, paintings, drawings, and prints to Yale University. The collection's value is appraised at more than $35 million.

1967

Movies *Bonnie and Clyde,* starring Warren Beatty and Faye Dunaway; *Cool Hand Luke,* starring Paul Newman; *The Graduate,* starring Dustin Hoffman and Anne Bancroft; *Guess Who's Coming to Dinner,* starring Sidney Poitier, Spencer Tracy, and Katharine Hepburn; *In the Heat of the Night,* starring Sidney Poitier and Rod Steiger; *The Jungle Book,* Disney animation.

Fiction Donald Barthelme, *Snow White;* Richard Brautigan, *Trout Fishing in America;* Norman Mailer, *Why Are We in Vietnam?;* William Styron, *The Confessions of Nat Turner;* Gore Vidal, *Washington, D.C.*

Popular Songs The Doors, "Light My Fire"; Aretha Franklin, "Respect" and "(You Make Me Feel Like) A Natural Woman"; Bobbie Gentry, "Ode to Billie Joe"; Arlo Guthrie, "Alice's Restaurant"; Engelbert Humperdinck, "Release Me"; Jefferson Airplane, "Somebody to Love" and "White Rabbit"; Procol Harum, "A Whiter Shade of Pale"; Smokey Robinson and the Miracles, "I Second That Emotion"; the Rolling Stones, "Let's Spend the Night Together" and "Ruby Tuesday"; Tommy James and the Shondells, "I Think We're Alone Now"; the Turtles, "Happy Together"; Frankie Valli, "Can't Take My Eyes Off of You."

- M-G-M Studios turns down a $10 million offer to broadcast *Gone with the Wind* on television.

18 Feb. The National Gallery of Art in Washington arranges to purchase Leonardo da Vinci's *Ginevra dei Benci* from Prince Franz Joseph of Liechtenstein for $5–6 million, the highest price to that time for a single painting.

8–10 Apr. The Academy Awards ceremony, slated for 8 April, is postponed two days due to the 9 April funeral of Martin Luther King, Jr., who was killed four days before, when five participants say they will not attend if the show goes on as planned. Academy president Gregory Peck also cancels the Governors' Ball.

26 Apr. Pablo Picasso's *Mother and Child* sells for $532,000, the highest price to that time for a single painting by a living artist.

Dec. Unable to compete with television news, the last of the movie newsreel companies, Universal News, closes.

1968

Movies

Barbarella, starring Jane Fonda; *Funny Girl,* starring Barbra Streisand; *The Green Berets,* directed by and starring John Wayne; *The Lion in Winter,* starring Katharine Hepburn and Peter O'Toole; *Night of the Living Dead,* directed by George Romero; *The Odd Couple,* starring Jack Lemmon and Walter Matthau; *Planet of the Apes,* starring Charlton Heston and Roddy McDowall; *The Producers,* directed by Mel Brooks and starring Zero Mostel and Gene Wilder; *Romeo and Juliet,* directed by Franco Zeffirelli and starring Leonard Whiting and Olivia Hussey; *Rosemary's Baby,* directed by Roman Polanski and starring Mia Farrow; *2001: A Space Odyssey,* directed by Stanley Kubrick and starring Keir Dullea.

Fiction

John Barth, *Lost in the Funhouse: Fiction for Print, Tape, Live Voice;* Richard Brautigan, *In Watermelon Sugar;* Robert Coover, *The Universal Baseball Association, Inc., J. Henry Waugh, Prop.;* James Gould Cozzens, *Morning Noon and Night;* Ronald Sukenick, *Up;* John Updike, *Couples;* Gore Vidal, *Myra Breckinridge.*

Popular Songs

The Beatles, "Hey Jude"; James Brown, "Say It Loud (I'm Black and I'm Proud)"; the Doors, "Hello, I Love You"; Marvin Gaye, "I Heard It through the Grapevine"; Bobby Goldsboro, "Honey"; Ohio Express, "Yummy Yummy Yummy"; the Rascals, "People Got to Be Free"; Otis Redding, "(Sittin' on) The Dock of the Bay"; Jeannie C. Riley, "Harper Valley P.T.A."; the Rolling Stones, "Jumpin' Jack Flash"; Simon and Garfunkel, "Mrs. Robinson"; Steppenwolf, "Born to Be Wild"; Dionne Warwick, "Do You Know the Way to San Jose?"

- The Academy of Motion Picture Arts and Sciences announces that it will no longer offer separate Oscars for films in color and in black and white because of the rapidly shrinking number of black-and-white films. Separate awards had been given in cinematography since 1939, art direction since 1940, and costume design since 1948.

- Bosley Crowther, the influential film critic of *The New York Times,* retires after disagreeing with most critics and moviegoers over *Bonnie and Clyde* (1967), which he disliked and the public loved.

- *Switched-On Bach,* an album of music by Johann Sebastian Bach performed on the Moog synthesizer by Walter (later, after a sex change, Wendy) Carlos, is popular with classical listeners as well as young people. A second album the following year, *The Well-Tempered Synthesizer,* is equally successful.

1969

Movies

Butch Cassidy and the Sundance Kid, starring Paul Newman and Robert Redford; *Easy Rider,* starring Peter Fonda, Dennis Hopper, and Jack Nicholson; *Goodbye, Mr. Chips,* starring Peter O'Toole; *The Love Bug,* starring Dean Jones and Buddy Hackett; *Midnight Cowboy,* starring Dustin Hoffman and Jon Voight; *The Prime of Miss Jean Brodie,* starring Maggie Smith; *True Grit,* starring John Wayne; *The Wild Bunch,* directed by Sam Peckinpah and starring William Holden and Ernest Borgnine.

Fiction

Robert Coover, *Pricksongs and Descants;* Ursula K. Le Guin, *The Left Hand of Darkness;* N. Scott Momaday, *The Way to Rainy Mountain;* Vladimir Nabokov, *Ada, or Ardor;* Joyce Carol Oates, *Them;* Mario Puzo, *The Godfather;* Ishmael Reed, *Yellow Back Radio Broke Down;* Philip Roth, *Portnoy's Complaint;* Ronald Sukenick, *The Death of the Novel and Other Stories;* Kurt Vonnegut, Jr., *Slaughterhouse-Five.*

Popular Songs

The Archies, "Sugar, Sugar"; the Beatles, "Get Back"; Johnny Cash, "A Boy Named Sue"; Creedence Clearwater Revival, "Proud Mary"; Bob Dylan, "Lay Lady Lay"; the Fifth Dimension, "Aquarius/Let the Sunshine In"; Merle Haggard, "Okie from Muskogee"; Peter, Paul and Mary, "Leaving on a Jet Plane"; Elvis Presley, "Suspicious Minds"; Frank Sinatra, "My Way"; B. J. Thomas, "Raindrops Keep Falling on My Head"; Stevie Wonder, "My Cherie Amour"; Tommy James and the Shondells, "Crimson and Clover."

- Ten-year retrospectives are held featuring the work of pop artists Claes Oldenburg (at the Museum of Modern Art) and Roy Lichtenstein (at the Guggenheim Museum).

- Twenty-five writers at *Newsday,* convinced that they could write a best-selling sex novel of the type popular at the time, create *Naked Came the Stranger* by "Penelope Ashe" — which indeed became a best-seller.

- In response to the new MPAA ratings system, many newspapers either refuse to advertise X-rated movies or list only the title, rating, and theater for such films.

OVERVIEW

Revolution. Compared with other upheavals of the 1960s, artistic activity seems almost tame. During the 1960s Americans were confronted with a broad range of pressing social issues, and creative artists of the decade responded by voicing their concerns. Writers spoke out against the Vietnam War, and scores of black artists and writers, guided by what they called the Black Aesthetic, forged a Black Arts Movement that urged promotion of black values and causes through art. Popular music of the era evolved from the dance music rock 'n' roll of the 1950s to socially conscious folk music and rock music with lyrics of protest and frustration. The 1960s were a decade of free expression. It was the message that mattered for many. Others, though, frustrated by the futility of encouraging social reform, adopted a nihilistic approach. Notable sculptors, artists, dancers, musicians, and writers, acting independently of one another, came at the same time to one of two conclusions: either that nothing mattered but form or that only absurd responses were possible to world problems. Both positions provided the ultimate creative refuge from seemingly insoluble issues.

Photography. Perhaps the quietest revolution in the arts during the 1960s occurred in photography, which gained greater acceptance as an art form during the decade. This increased respect was attested to by the 350-item Henri Cartier-Bresson exhibit at the IBM Gallery in New York in 1960; the exhibit of abstract photography, "The Sense of Abstraction," at the Museum of Modern Art the same year; and the 1962 "Ideas in Images" exhibit that toured the country. Some photographers worked at expanding the possibilities of the medium. The most noteworthy was Diane Arbus, who left fashion photography to focus on creating a disturbing series of photos of people at their worst.

Art. If some photographers seemed bent on capturing ugliness, certainly many observers felt the same about much modern art. Abstract expressionism, the wildly emotional painting style that scandalized the 1950s, was accepted by the critical establishment as the most respected approach to art in the 1960s. Abstract expressionist works sold for seven-figure sums, and critics alike

waited to see what the next innovative movement would be.

The New Art. There were several new movements — all with their supporters and detractors. The most popular, fittingly, was pop art, which employed commercial techniques and drew on artifacts from everyday culture such as comic strips, movies, and items available at local grocery stores. After pop art came op art, which used optical illusions. More serious in intent was minimalism: sculptors created massive geometric works of uniform color and material while painters placed simple geometric forms on canvas. Both efforts were a repudiation of abstract expressionism, which valued personality. In minimalism personality meant nothing, and the art referred to nothing; the sculpture or painting was intended to draw attention to its materials and form.

Modern Dance. This emphasis on form over content had been a central tenet of modern-dance choreographers such as Merce Cunningham for decades, but those critics and audiences who took modern dance seriously tended to prefer the psychological dramas of artists such as Martha Graham over the innovations of younger choreographers. By the 1960s, however, not only was modern dance sufficiently developed to embrace different approaches, but audiences and critics embraced them as well — from the mythic dances of Graham to the plotless dances of Cunningham to the equally abstract works of Alwin Nikolais, Paul Taylor, Twyla Tharp, and others.

Ballet. Ballet had a less successful decade in comparison, but the art was hardly moribund. Established choreographers, such as George Balanchine and Jerome Robbins, continued to create impressive new dances, and smaller companies rose up to supplement the offerings of powerhouses such as American Ballet Theatre and New York City Ballet. Classical dance in the West also added a superstar when Rudolf Nureyev defected from the Soviet Union and joined the Royal Ballet in England as partner to the equally glamorous Margot Fonteyn.

Classical Music. While no new style emerged in classical dance during the 1960s, in the world of classical music styles became increasingly challenging for listeners and composers alike. Though audiences tended to favor works from the baroque era to the romantics that featured traditional melodic and harmonic approaches, works by classic composers were performed side by side with those by contemporary composers whose music was calculated to subvert traditional approaches. However, a division between composers and audiences that became especially pronounced due to experiments in atonality and other harsh-sounding techniques earlier in the century continued to grow. Avant-garde composers such as John Cage and Milton Babbitt attracted critical adulation, but new works of theirs were often not performed again after their premieres. An increase in recordings of new music helped to broaden its audience, but not much. More accessible were the efforts of minimalist composers, who featured repeated melodies and rhythms in their works in response to the increasing complexity of much contemporary classical music.

Classical Musicians. The 1960s are notable in classical music for the dearth of musicians well known to the general public apart from those already established. Certainly the most famous remained Leonard Bernstein, who focused his considerable energies on conducting rather than composing during the decade. Several musicians made it into the news for one reason or another — pianist Arthur Rubinstein for a remarkable comeback tour, conductor Leopold Stokowski for his return to Boston, pianist Vladimir Horowitz for his return to live concerts after a twelve-year absence — but the really famous musicians of the decade were popular, not classical.

Jazz. Many of the popular musicians of the 1960s were jazzmen, including performers as diverse as Louis Armstrong, Dave Brubeck, John Coltrane, the influential and innovative Miles Davis, Duke Ellington, Dizzy Gillespie, and Thelonious Monk. New developments in jazz also brought attention to innovative performers such as Ornette Coleman for his "free jazz," a highly improvisational, atonal form, and Gunther Schuller with his notion of the "Third Stream," which combined jazz improvisation with written classical styles.

New Styles. As in art, jazz styles diversified during the 1960s. At the beginning of the decade bebop was king, but it was challenged by faddish forms. For instance, 1962 was the year of the bossa nova, which combined American jazz with the Brazilian samba; prominent jazz musicians such as Stan Getz and Gillespie had highly successful bossa nova records. The bossa nova craze was short-lived, and by the mid 1960s jazz was torn between the music of earlier innovators, now established, such as Gillespie, Davis, and Monk, and innovators such as Coleman. Even "easy-listening" jazz, such as that performed by Herb Alpert and the Tijuana Brass, had its audience, as did fusions between rock and jazz performed by groups such as Blood, Sweat and Tears and Frank Zappa's Mothers of Invention. Further, in the mid 1960s many saw the revival of big-band music as a major trend in jazz, and the folk-music revival helped to spur a renewed interest in Dixieland jazz.

Folk Music. Folk music was many things to many people, but it included a revival of older forms such as bluegrass as well as a more commercial style performed by musicians such as Joan Baez, Bob Dylan, and Peter, Paul and Mary that nevertheless had its roots in older songs by performers such as the Weavers and Woody Guthrie. Though this new style of folk music prospered in the early 1960s, it faded out toward the end of the decade as the new rock music gained a prominence distinct from its origins in rock 'n' roll.

Rock and Pop. Rock 'n' roll music underwent a remarkable transformation during the 1960s — from songs with fluffy lyrics set to a catchy beat to the more sophisticated and harder-hitting approach of rock. Compare anything by the Beach Boys with Jefferson Airplane's "Somebody to Love," or, for that matter, anything by the early Beatles with anything by the later Beatles, and one can hear the difference. In certain respects this development was less of a transformation and more of a branching, a splintering of rock 'n' roll into different camps. The more easygoing style of early rock 'n' roll was maintained, for instance, in what came to be known as pop, or light, rock. The decade also produced early soul music with the Motown phenomenon and the merging of folk music with rock by performers as distinct as Dylan and Simon and Garfunkel.

The Reign of Youth. Different as these styles were, they had one important distinction in common: they ruled popular music in America. The music of teenagers and college students was what sold best; and while songsters their parents appreciated, such as Frank Sinatra and Tony Bennett, were not excluded from the charts, they definitely were exceptions in a field of younger, faster, and louder performers.

Theater. Rock even invaded the Broadway stage on occasion, most notably with the hit musical *Hair* (1968), but for the most part musicals remained the province of older audiences with more conservative tastes. This was due in part to the fact that little changed for Broadway musicals during the 1960s; in fact, hit musicals such as *Hello, Dolly!* (1964) and *Fiddler on the Roof* (1964) tended to reflect nostalgia for older musical styles. Plays were not much different as far as Broadway offerings were concerned, although experimental contemporary playwrights, such as the Americans Edward Albee and Arthur Kopit and the Britishers Harold Pinter and Tom Stoppard, began to gain a following during the decade, very often Off Broadway.

Literature. American literature also began to recognize promising new writers during the 1960s, but often this was obscured by the fact that it lost so many great older ones. Two of the nation's most famous and respected writers died early in the decade: Ernest Hemingway committed suicide in 1961 and William Faulkner suffered a fatal heart attack in 1962. Well-known poets also died during the decade, among them William Carlos

Williams, E. E. Cummings, Robert Frost, and Carl Sandburg. In 1962 it was announced that a sixth American, John Steinbeck, was to be awarded the Nobel Prize in Literature, which Faulkner had received for 1949 and Hemingway for 1954; Steinbeck died as well before the decade was over. With these deaths and this sense that even middle-aged writers such as Norman Mailer were beyond their prime, American fiction entered a new phase, with younger writers such as John Updike and Thomas Pynchon coming to the fore, along with an even newer group of experimental writers, such as the metafictionists and the black humorists, whose attitudes toward fiction were simultaneously cynical and innovative. Younger readers were often taken with the black humorists, especially figures such as Joseph Heller, Ken Kesey, and Kurt Vonnegut, Jr., who made them laugh while supporting their antiwar views.

Movies. Catering to youth was not only a preoccupation of popular music and an indirect concern of some writers; it was also the driving force of Hollywood during the 1960s. Concerned that television would usurp its audiences and thereby its profits, the film industry strove to present movies that did things television could not. In part this meant big-budget epics, but more importantly it meant more sex and violence. The phenomenal success of the James Bond films during the 1960s is a case in point. Additionally, the Bond films subtly assuaged both British and American anxieties about the state of their declining empires.

The Decline of "Family Entertainment." As movies became racier and more violent, many Americans stayed away from the theaters in protest against the decrease in "family entertainment." The Bond films were fairly tame, but other movies began to depart from family-values standards as mainstream movies in America never had before, depicting nudity, detailed sexual themes, profanity from heroes, and realistic on-screen deaths. The Motion Picture Association of America (MPAA) regulated content with a self-imposed production code, but during the decade the code became increasingly ineffectual. While the federal government stepped out of the film-censorship business for the most part in the 1950s, state and local governments threatened to step in, until the fears of most concerned citizens were settled with the establishment of an MPAA ratings system that determined what films were appropriate for what ages. Significantly, sex was reserved for adult audiences, while violence was considered acceptable for teens and for children accompanied by an adult.

TOPICS IN THE NEWS

ART AND HUMANITIES FUNDING

Business and Art. The business of America may be business, as a U.S. president once remarked, but during the 1960s the business of America, both in the private and public sectors, became increasingly involved with art.

Philanthropy. One exhibition shows this trend: backed by $500,000 to purchase art, Chase Manhattan Bank showed its collection at the Whitney Museum of Art in New York in 1960. Similarly, in 1962 S. C. Johnson and Son (of Johnson Wax) paid $750,000 for 102 works by contemporary American painters, including Andrew Wyeth and Willem de Kooning. The works were shown for a month at the Milwaukee Art Center then sent on tour abroad. In 1963 the New York Metropolitan Opera received $135,000 from American Export and Isbrandtsen Lines to stage a new production of Giuseppi Verdi's opera *Aida.*

No Help from the Government. Grant organizations such as the Ford Foundation were already providing generous financial assistance to performers and artistic organizations in the 1950s, but they stepped up their efforts in the early 1960s, in part responding to a perceived lack of such support from the government, which had not directly aided artists or groups since the New Deal launched during the Depression in the 1930s. In 1963, for instance, the Ford Foundation announced that it would give $7,756,750 to support ballet in America over the next ten years, and the same year the Pittsburgh Symphony was saved with a $5 million endowment from a handful of organizations and individuals working together. Apart from funds given to artists and organizations through its cultural exchange programs, in the early 1960s the United States stood out as the only industrialized nation that did not provide some financial support for the arts.

The Government Steps In. On 15 November 1961 a

Congressional subcommittee began investigating the financial situations of musical organizations and musicians. In 1964 the National Collection of Fine Arts at the Smithsonian Institution received $7 million to renovate the former Patent Office Building in order to create a national museum; the same year it supported American entries in the Venice Biennale through the U.S. Information Agency, the first time the federal government had directly sponsored U.S. contributors to that prestigious international exhibit. The highlight of the decade came in 1965 with the passage of several acts for education funding — which had an indirect effect on the arts — and the signing of the Federal Aid to the Arts Bill by President Lyndon B. Johnson on 29 September — establishing what became known as the National Endowment for the Arts and the National Endowment for the Humanities. A portion of the $20 million allocated per year for the next three years, he announced, would go toward the foundation of the American Film Institute, which would be dedicated to preserving deteriorating old films and to promoting motion pictures as an art form. Less than a month later the Ford Foundation announced that it would give $85 million to fifty orchestras in America — the largest donation to the arts ever.

Windfalls. Such assistance was a breath of fresh air for the arts in America. For instance, in 1966 modern-dance choreographers Alvin Ailey, Merce Cunningham, Paul Taylor, and Alwin Nikolais each received $5,000 from the National Council on the Arts; the same year Martha Graham received $40,000 to produce two new works and $141,000 to mount a national tour of her company.

Controversies to Come. There was only one problem with government-subsidized art. Since they were footing the bill, lawmakers and taxpayers often felt that they ought to control grants and that certain recipients did not deserve federal support, especially if their art challenged conventional notions. Who controls creativity, how creative artists should be supported, and the role of art in American life are issues raised by the controversy that continue to be debated today.

Source:
Stephen Miller, *Excellence and Equity: The National Endowment for the Humanities* (Lexington: University Press of Kentucky, 1984).

ART EVERYWHERE: AN EXPLOSION OF ART MOVEMENTS

Growing Museums, Growing Audiences. Increased funding for the arts and humanities led to increased public exposure to art and ideas during the 1960s. In addition to regional theaters and public radio and television — the most obvious results of this funding — new museums and new programs in existing museums attracted a larger audience. For example, the new Munson-Williams-Proctor Institute in Utica, New York, which opened in 1960, included a baby-sitting service and an art room for children in an effort to attract families. Also popular were the

---

HAPPENINGS

Happenings were introduced in the art world in the late 1950s and were identified as a distinct form with Allan Kaprow's ninety-minute piece *18 Happenings in 6 Parts* (1959). Very much an avant-garde form, happenings attracted only small audiences during their height in the early 1960s.

Using ordinary objects and avant-garde theatrical techniques, the creators of happenings consciously posed several challenges to the conventional art world. First, in staging exhibits as events rather than as a collection of objects, they questioned the notion of art as static. By employing commonplace objects, they questioned the division between art and life. By occasionally encouraging audience participation, they broke down the division between artist and public. Sometimes described as "living sculptures," happenings were often staged in art galleries, though other locations were not uncommon. In 1962, for instance, Kenneth Koch and Jean Tinguely's *The Construction of Boston* was presented Off-Broadway. It included projections with captions and a Venus de Milo that bled different colors when shot with a replica of a Revolutionary War rifle.

Happenings had their roots in artistic movements from early in the century such as dada and surrealism as well as the more recent multimedia experiments of artists such as John Cage and others at Black Mountain College in North Carolina during the early 1950s. Some were carefully planned; others were spontaneous. All, however, gave the appearance of spontaneity, since they included discontinuous pieces employing music, drama, and art in unpredictable combinations. Though happenings became less popular with artists by the mid 1960s, they were an important predecessor to performance art.

Sources: Adrian Henri, *Environments and Happenings* (London: Thames & Hudson, 1974);
Allan Kaprow, *Assemblage, Environments and Happenings* (New York: Abrams, 1966).

---

increased number of museums on college campuses, successfully linking art history and appreciation with actual exhibits, including exhibits of photography, which gained increased acceptance as an artistic medium during the 1960s. Established museums also reported increased attendance throughout the 1960s — partially the result of highly publicized exhibits such as the 1963 loans of Leonardo da Vinci's *La Gioconda* (better known as Mona Lisa, 1503–1507) and James Whistler's *Arrangement in Grey and Black* (better known as Whistler's Mother, 1871–1872) by the Louvre in Paris.

Growing Prices. Art was also in the news as art prices continued to rise to unprecedented levels. In a 1961 New York auction the Metropolitan Museum of Art paid $2.3 million for Rembrandt's *Aristotle Contemplating the Bust of Homer* (1653), the highest amount ever paid for a single painting and just one of a series of records set and broken. In 1962, for instance, the Dallas Museum paid $58,000 for a painting by Andrew Wyeth, the highest then given for a work by a living American artist. In 1967 New York art dealer David Mann purchased Picasso's *Mother and Child* (1902) for $532,000, the record for a single work by a living artist, and in the same year the National Gallery in Washington, D.C., was said to have paid $5.8 million for *Ginevra dei Benci* (1474?), the first painting by Leonardo da Vinci to find a permanent American home, setting a record price for a single work.

Abstract Expressionism. The 1950s were dominated by abstract expressionism, the art movement linking wildly abstract painting with highly emotional expressiveness. It was controversial during the 1950s but emerged in the 1960s as the most important style — or so the influential magazine *Art News* claimed in a 1960 article. Other critics, however, believed that the movement had peaked and that something new was on the horizon. They were right. Fitting the popular image of the 1960s as a decade of experimentation and protest, painters and sculptors rebelled against the authority of abstract expressionism, which itself had been a rebellion against earlier orthodoxies.

Other Styles. Abstract expressionism did not grind to a halt during the 1960s, but its position as *the* American painting style was no longer secure. A hallmark of American art during the 1960s is its variety, with representational and various abstract styles existing almost comfortably together. Some abstract painters turned to geometric forms devoid of emotional content, while other painters returned to figurative works. In 1963, for example, the Jewish Museum in New York featured an exhibit called "Towards a New Abstraction," in which the "hard-edge" works of geometric abstract painters such as Ellsworth Kelly were displayed, while several exhibits of the work of Wyeth, the most respected representational painter in America at the time, drew large crowds.

Pop Art. One type of revolt against prevailing standards in painting and sculpture was at first labeled new realism, which included works by sculptors George Segal and Claes Oldenburg and painters Roy Lichtenstein and Andy Warhol. In the early 1960s, for instance, Oldenburg created fanciful versions of everyday consumer objects from papier-mâché, plaster, and cloth. The painters' use of popular culture — Lichtenstein used comic books and strips and Warhol used artifacts such as soup cans, soap boxes, and movie magazines — led to one of the most discussed movements during the 1960s, pop art.

A happening, staged by Park Commissioner Thomas Hoving, in New York's Central Park

Both a critique and celebration of popular culture, pop art, like many art movements of the 1960s, broke down the boundary between art and ordinary life. Some saw pop art as a challenge to artistic conventions, while more-skeptical observers saw it as blatantly commercial, since works were sold for high prices. Its popularity also spread to dance, as modern-dance and even some ballet companies adopted pop art settings for new works.

Op Art. On the heels of pop art came op art, a distant cousin of the geometric abstraction of hard-edge painting that relied on patterned effects creating the optical illusion of movement or depth within the work. Enthusiastically greeted by some art lovers bored with abstract expressionism or pop art, this international movement was featured in a 1964 exhibit called "The Responsive Eye" at the Museum of Modern Art in New York. Like pop art, op art was denounced as a gimmick by some critics.

Sculpture. In all this diversity was a hunger for art, even of avant-garde works, on the part of the public. By 1966, however, art sales were diminishing, with some speculating that buyers were waiting to see what the next new thing in art would be. The answer was sculpture: in the late-1960s kinetic sculptures, which employed moving parts similar to Alexander Calder's well-known mobiles, and minimalist works came to the fore. Both kinetic sculptures and process art — such as Hans Haacke's condensation cubes, clear plastic cubes with moisture that changed states according to climatic changes — introduced time as an element of the artwork, thus removing the focus from the work as a completed object. These and other artistic approaches also challenged what artists saw as the objectification and commercialization of art. Conceptual artists, for instance, responded to the success of minimalism by asserting the importance of the ideas behind the art rather than the completed object. Earth art was even more drastic, as artists such as Robert Smithson created enormous sculpural works from natural materials. Such pieces naturally could not be shown in galleries, nor were they finished products; instead, they were intended to be subjected to the processes of erosion over time.

Welcome to Postmodernism. By the end of the decade some critics and scholars were speculating that art had passed out of a modernist phase and had entered postmodernism. Two aspects of postmodernism that fit the arts during the 1960s are diversity of style and the use of previous styles in new works. These trends characterize subsequent art in America.

Sources:

Barbara Haskell, *Blam! The Explosion of Pop, Minimalism, and Performance, 1958–1964* (New York: Whitney Museum of American Art / Norton, 1984);

Bruce D. Kurtz, *Contemporary Art 1965–1990* (Englewood Cliffs, N. J.: Prentice Hall, 1992);

Frank Popper, *Origins and Development of Kinetic Art* (Greenwich, Conn.: New York Graphic Society, 1968);

Irving Sandler, *American Art of the 1960s* (New York: Harper & Row, 1988);

Daniel Wheeler, *Art Since Mid-Century. 1945 to the Present* (New York: Vendome, 1989).

THE ART OF LESS: MINIMALISM

Back to Basics. As the gulf between high and low culture widened in art, music, and literature during the 1960s, works in these arts often became increasingly difficult and complex. In response, some artists and composers went the opposite direction, creating works with a bare-bones, back-to-basics approach that drew attention to form and materials rather than content or meaning. The result was named minimalism by art critic Barbara Rose.

CARNEGIE HALL THREATENED

Since 1891 Carnegie Hall had been the most highly regarded concert hall in New York. However, in early 1960 it appeared that Carnegie Hall was slated for demolition by its owners after their contract with the New York Philharmonic expired in 1959 and the orchestra planned to move to Lincoln Center, then under construction. A committee, headed by violinist Isaac Stern, campaigned to save the auditorium, and in April 1960 the New York state legislature authorized the city to purchase the building. It did so, turning it over to a new corporation with Stern as president. Carnegie Hall reopened in September following renovations to the building.

Painting. Minimalism first appeared in paintings by artists, such as Frank Stella, who rejected the emotional content of abstract expressionism. Instead, such work — called post-painterly abstraction — removed subjects and personality entirely from the picture; the work was not a picture of anything save itself. The resulting works, similar to Ellsworth Kelly's hard-edge paintings, consisted of flat color in geometric shapes.

Sculpture. The trend was first identified as minimalism in sculpture when artists such as Carl Andre, Donald Judd, and Robert Morris began creating physically imposing works with simple geometric forms of untreated materials, often of a single color. The focus was on the materials, since the objects were not intended to represent anything.

Music. In the late 1960s the term also was applied to a new movement in music. While many serious composers were writing scores of increasing complexity, others scaled back to write pieces influenced by African and Asian music with simpler instrumentations — often relying on electronic keyboards and percussion instruments — and repeated phrases and rhythms that gradually changed in the course of the piece. The best-known minimalist composers were Philip Glass, Steve Reich, and Terry Riley.

The Influence of Minimalism. Minimal art requires minimal talent, according to some critics. However, minimalism introduced a new concern for the substance of art as opposed to content or technique, and it became a major trend in the arts of the 1960s.

Sources:

Kenneth Baker, *Minimalism: Art of Circumstance* (New York: Abbeville, 1988);

Barbara Haskell, *Blam! The Explosion of Pop, Minimalism, and Performance, 1958–1964* (New York: Whitney Museum of American Art / Norton, 1984);

Michael Nyman, *Experimental Music: Cage and Beyond* (London: Studio Vista, 1974).

FOLK MUSIC

Different Interpretations. In the early 1960s "folk music" was defined broadly. For some it included the "hillbilly music" that provided the roots of modern country-and-western music; for others it included rural and working-class tunes such as those performed by Woody Guthrie and Pete Seeger; and for others it included popularized, often sanitized versions, by performers such as Burl Ives and the Kingston Trio. Then something new happened.

The New Stars. In 1962 the first of a new generation of performers appeared, most prominently Joan Baez, Bob Dylan, and Peter, Paul and Mary, all unaffected musicians whose straightforward delivery of a repertoire that included traditional songs and new compositions after traditional models attracted a large, appreciative audience. In particular, folk musicians addressed contem-

American rock 'n' roll in the early 1960s was dominated by American performers. Then came the Beatles in 1964, launching a British Invasion that at times threatened to overwhelm the industry. Home-grown groups such as the Beach Boys earned a respectable number of hits, to be sure, but no one was as popular as the boys from Liverpool.

Screen Gems, realizing that imitation is the sincerest form of avarice, created their own American response to the Fab Four. The Monkees — Davy Jones, Mike Nesmith, Peter Tork, and Mickey Dolenz — were banded together for a prime-time series on ABC-TV in 1966 featuring music similar to that of the Beatles and using techniques related to those from the Beatles' films *A Hard Day's Night* (1964) and *Help!* (1965). Despite the fact that the four were selected by Screen Gems for their talent as actors, with less attention paid to their musical abilities, the Monkees' "Last Train to Clarksville" and "I'm a Believer" were both number-one hit singles. The group, created as a take-off, was surprisingly resilient. Their material was supplied by talented songwriters, including Neil Diamond and Nesmith.

At first the Monkees only sang; the instrumentals were provided by studio musicians. However, they tried to learn how to play the instruments they pretended to play on television so they could tour. At first they could not reproduce the studio sound, a circumstance masked by screaming fans in live audiences. Nonetheless, the group, and especially Nesmith, were bothered by the deception, and in a 1967 press conference he admitted that they did not play the instruments on their albums and that the record company would not permit them to do so. After a conflict with Screen Gems, the band was allowed to play as well as sing. They continued to score hit singles and albums. The television show was cancelled late in 1968, prompting Tork's departure, but the Monkees continued until Nesmith left the following year.

If the success of a rock band created for television was surprising, even more so was the popularity of the Archies, ostensibly composed of comic-book characters. The best of the "bubble-gum rock" phenomenon, the Archies was created by producer Don Kirshner for a Saturday-morning animated television show based on the long-standing comic book characters. Amazingly, the Archies had four Top 40 hits, all by Jeff Barry and performed by studio musicians: "Bang-Shang-a-Lang" (1968), "Sugar, Sugar" (1969), "Jingle Jangle" (1969), and "Who's Your Baby?" (1970). Not only was "Sugar, Sugar" a number-one hit, it sold more than six million copies, more than any other single during 1969. In 1971 Ron Dante, the voice of Archie, joined the editorial staff of the literary magazine the *Paris Review*.

Sources: Glenn A. Baker with Tom Czarnota and Peter Hogan, *Monkeemania: The True Story of The Monkees* (New York: St. Martin's, 1986);

Jon Pareles and Patricia Romanowski, eds., *The Rolling Stone Illustrated Encyclopedia of Rock and Roll* (New York: Rolling Stone Press / Summit Books, 1983);

Edward Reilly, Maggie McManus, and William Chadwick, *The Monkees: A Manufactured Image — The Ultimate Reference Guide to Monkee Memories and Memorabilia* (Ann Arbor, Mich.: Pierian, 1987).

porary issues facing college students, notably civil rights and, later, the Vietnam War.

The Folk-Music Revival. While performers such as Baez and Dylan — and later Judy Collins and Joni Mitchell — were popular, the folk-music phenomenon spurred a new interest in less-played indigenous forms such as bluegrass and Dixieland jazz. Soon songs such as Seeger's "If I Had a Hammer" and Dylan's "Blowin' in the Wind" were adopted by folk performers of all sorts. Folk festivals drew large crowds attracted by a musical display of back-to-basics values that were expressed in simple lyrics to hummable tunes performed by free spirits.

Folk and Rock. Always considered in its new incarnation a close relative to rock 'n' roll, folk music was gradually electrified. In 1965, for instance, Dylan introduced a "folk rock" group, with electric instruments, angering many who felt he had sold out. The following year the group the Lovin' Spoonful, which also combined elements of folk and rock, had a number-one hit with "Summer in the City" and came to national fame. Further blows came as Dylan continued to distance himself from protest songs, which were taken up by the new rock performers. The new rock was largely serious in intent, while softer music for entertainment was labeled as "pop," formerly the designation for all popular music.

Decline. By 1967, when rock music had invaded much of the territory of folk music in terms of social commentary, the folk-music phenomenon seemed to have faded into the background. Even performers such as Bobbie

Gentry with "Ode to Billie Joe" (1967) and Simon and Garfunkel, whose music owed distinct debts to the folk idiom, were said to be too sophisticated in their song-writing styles to be actual folk musicians. Folk and rock continued to blend into the 1970s, but folk music, as it was known in the early 1960s, became a part of history rather than remaining a popular form.

Sources:

Kristin Baggelaar and Donald Milton, *Folk Music: More Than a Song* (New York: Crowell, 1976);

Phil Hood, ed., *Artists of American Folk Music: The Legends of Traditional Folk, the Stars of the Sixties, the Virtuosi of New Acoustic Music* (New York: Quill, 1986);

Sarah Lifton, *The Listeners' Guide to Folk Music* (New York: Facts on File, 1983);

Irwin Stambler and Grelun Landon, *Encyclopedia of Folk, Country, and Western Music,* second edition (New York: St. Martin's Press, 1983).

FROM ROCK 'N' ROLL TO ROCK AND POP

Rock 'n' Roll Dead? By 1960 rock 'n' roll was the most popular music among young people — not only in America but internationally. However, it comprised only one segment of American popular music, which also included country music, rhythm and blues, folk music and crooners such as Frank Sinatra. In fact, the charts early in the 1960s reflected such a diversity of musical styles that some unfriendly to the new music in the late 1950s announced that rock 'n' roll was passé. In February 1962 New York radio station WINS, which had been among the first in the country to jump aboard the rock 'n' roll bandwagon, instituted a new policy by playing sixty-six straight hours of Frank Sinatra as a death knell to rock 'n' roll.

Revival. Reports of its demise were highly exaggerated. In April WINS began playing rock 'n' roll again, including Chubby Checker's "The Twist," which had set off a national dance craze in 1960. Rock 'n' roll flourished in the early 1960s, during which time sentimental songs, dance music, and doo-wop proliferated. Then, in 1964, the British Invasion arrived, led by a group that would prove to be a tremendous influence on American rock 'n' roll: the Beatles.

The Boys from Liverpool. The Beatles — singer-songwriter-guitarists John Lennon and Paul McCartney, guitarist George Harrison, and drummer Ringo Starr — began producing hit singles in 1963 in England, some of which found their way to American charts. With the band's February 1964 appearance on *The Ed Sullivan Show* and their subsequent U.S. tour, Beatlemania was born in America. Thousands of screaming fans lined up to see the Fab Four, as they were called, whose distinctive collarless jackets and long mop-top hairstyles set a fashion trend. The Beatles also appeared in a film in 1964, *A Hard Day's Night.* Their singles dominated the American charts in that year and appeared there regularly until their breakup in 1970.

The Beatles

The British Invasion. Following in their wake came other British bands with their own distinct sounds, including the Rolling Stones and the Animals. Both were influenced by American rock 'n' roll and rhythm and blues, yet both, in turn, influenced rock 'n' roll in the United States. The Beach Boys were often considered America's answer to the British Invasion, and the Monkees were created to cash in on the craze.

Rock Grows Up. Though many older listeners still disdained rock 'n' roll, it gradually gained greater acceptance as British groups such as the Beatles and the Rolling Stones earned new respect and as it seeped into the national consciousness. Moreover, listeners who appreciated rock 'n' roll in the 1950s as teens became adults in the 1960s. The music likewise matured, further contributing to its elevated status. Among the reasons for its evolution were more-sophisticated studio techniques and experimentation with recording methods and instrumentation. The Beach Boys with *Pet Sounds* (1966) and the Beatles with *Sgt. Pepper's Lonely Hearts Club Band* (1967) were in the forefront. In addition, this new "rock music" — as distinct from rock 'n' roll — became identified with the youth movements in sex, drugs, and protest, especially after the Summer of Love in 1967, and people actually began paying attention to the lyrics of songs. The first International Pop Festival in Monterey, California, also took place in 1967 and drew large crowds.

The Birth of Hard Rock. Rock groups and performers of the late 1960s definitely possessed a harder edge than their predecessors in rock 'n' roll. Especially influential was the "San Francisco sound," originating from the Haight-Ashbury district, with such bands as the Grateful

Dead, Jefferson Airplane, and Big Brother and the Holding Company with Janis Joplin. From them came the term *psychedelic rock,* since the music was sometimes performed as part of the background for taking psychedelic drugs. An extension of this, acid rock, was pioneered by Jimi Hendrix and others. The music became louder and faster, the lyrics more explicit.

Pop. On the other side of the coin was pop, which still had its roots in rock 'n' roll but wore a friendlier face. Pop could also include crooners such as Sinatra, but such performers were playing for an aging audience. The money was with youth, and the market became more and more fragmented in the following decades in order to cater to increasingly specialized audiences.

Sources:

Gene Anthony, *The Summer of Love: Haight-Ashbury at Its Highest* (Berkeley, Cal.: Celestial Arts, 1980);

R. J. Gleason, *The Jefferson Airplane and the San Francisco Sound* (New York: Ballantine, 1969);

Jim Miller, ed., *The Rolling Stone Illustrated History of Rock and Roll* (New York: Rolling Stone Press / Random House, 1976).

Diana Ross (center) and the Supremes, Cindy Birdsong and Mary Wilson

HIPPIES AND THEIR MUSIC: WOODSTOCK

The Making of a Legend. One of many popular-music festivals of the 1960s, the Woodstock Music and Arts Fair of 15–17 August 1969 began as an organized event, descended into chaos, and emerged as the most legendary rock festival in history, known simply as Woodstock. It has since come to symbolize an era of peaceful, free-loving, drug-taking hippie youth, carefree before harsher realities hit — such as the untimely drug-related deaths of rockers Jimi Hendrix and Janis Joplin and the shootings of student protesters and bystanders at Kent State University — all the following year. During and after the 1970s thousands of rock fans claimed to have been present at Woodstock, and it is quite possible they were: the festival attracted nearly half a million people, most in their teens and twenties.

A Surprising Turnout. The promoters of the event hardly expected such a turnout — they expected perhaps two hundred thousand at the most. Given the fact that Woodstock featured most of the top performers in rock and that it promised to be a gathering of like-minded hippies and fellow travelers, the surprise was that there were not more. Perhaps they were detained by the traffic jams into the small rural community near Bethel, New York; and after all, the six-hundred-acre farm owned by Max Yasgur, where the festival was held, could hold only so many.

A Peaceful Gathering. Those who did make it, however, formed a large enough crowd to cause the promoters to despair of charging admission beyond a certain point and certainly enough to overload the available facilities. While there were about eighty arrests for possession of hard drugs, police did not bother making arrests for marijuana possession because there were far too many cases.

The gathering was nonviolent: there were no arrests for fighting. This was hardly remarkable, though, since Woodstock represented the peak of "flower power," promoted by hippies who encouraged people to make love, not war.

The Stars of Woodstock. Although thunderstorms cut some performances short, those in attendance were not disappointed when they actually paid attention to what was happening on stage. The musicians present included Joan Baez; Blood, Sweat and Tears; Creedence Clearwater Revival; Crosby, Stills, Nash and Young; the Grateful Dead; Arlo Guthrie; Jimi Hendrix; Jefferson Airplane; Janis Joplin; Ravi Shankar; Sly and the Family Stone; and the Who.

Source:

Jack Curry, *Woodstock: The Summer of Our Lives* (New York: Weidenfeld & Nicolson, 1989).

MOTOWN

The Motown Sound. Black rhythm and blues provided the foundation for rock 'n' roll in the 1950s, and, as racial attitudes relaxed, black performers such as Chuck Berry, the Coasters, and Chubby Checker attracted large audiences. However, it was not until the 1960s that black performers in general received unrestricted radio play. The music that came from the Motor City of Detroit, Michigan, in the 1960s, was the Motown Sound.

Early Success. In creating Tamla Motown in 1959, Berry Gordy, Jr., established the first major label owned and operated by blacks. The music he produced had its roots in gospel, jazz, and rhythm and blues, but the Motown Sound, with its rock 'n' roll beat backed by orches-

Anne Bancroft in *The Graduate* (1967)

tral accompaniment, was definitely commercial pop music — and in terms of commercial and popular success, it took off in the early 1960s. This success was due in part to the songwriting efforts of Lamont Dozier and brothers Eddie and Brian Holland, who created such hits as "Please Mr. Postman" by the Marvelettes and "Baby Love," "Stop! In the Name of Love," "Where Did Our Love Go?," and "You Can't Hurry Love" by the Supremes. Another important songwriter for Motown was Smokey Robinson, who wrote "My Guy" (performed by Mary Wells) and "The Way You Do the Things You Do" (performed by The Temptations), as well as "The Tracks of My Tears" which he performed with the Miracles.

Popular Performers. Motown also could attribute its success to the talented performers it recorded, many of whom were discoveries of the company. In addition to the performers already named, Motown featured the Four Tops, Marvin Gaye, Gladys Knight and the Pips, Martha and the Vandellas, and Little Stevie Wonder, a blind child prodigy reminiscent of Ray Charles. In 1969 Gordy discovered more child wonders in the Jackson Five, featuring the eleven-year-old Michael Jackson. Most of all, however, Motown prospered because the Motown Sound was a welcome addition to popular music during the 1960s.

Motown at Its Height. In 1971 Gordy moved operations to Los Angeles, and Motown became a less distinctive form of popular music. However, during the 1960s it produced several excellent songs and singers, often intro-

ducing them to white audiences, and exerted an influence on what has since become known as soul music.

Sources:
David Morse, *Motown and the Arrival of Black Music* (London: Studio Vista, 1971);

Don Waller, *The Motown Story* (New York: Scribners, 1985).

MOVIES

The Death of the Studio System. During the summer of 1961 20th Century-Fox took its back lot apart, a poignant symbol of the dismantling of the Hollywood studio system that became final later in the 1960s. Rather than creating motion pictures, the studios gradually assumed the role of financing and distributing films made by producers, directors, and actors not on the studio bankroll.

Rising Costs, Shrinking Audiences. Motion pictures entered the 1960s in fairly bad shape in general: fewer movies were being made, and they were attracting smaller audiences. The most common scapegoat was television, but as expenses increased so did the number of admissions required to produce enough revenue to cover them. Such increases were justified by some; after all, *Ben-Hur* (1959) had cost fifteen million dollars to make yet grossed one hundred million dollars. Not every movie could be *Ben-Hur,* but to studios it seemed a safer bet to invest in stars and spectacle in hopes of large profits than in low-budget films with unknown actors or stories. *Cleopatra* (1963), starring Elizabeth Taylor and Richard Burton, was released after years of delays and a cost of

The Motion Picture Association of America (MPAA) had long opposed efforts at censorship and continued to do so in the early 1960s. As films became increasingly "adult," however, the demand for some sort of ratings system grew. One model was the recently enacted system in England, which labeled movies as appropriate for all audiences, for children in the company of adults, and for adults only. Some communities and individual theaters adopted their own systems, but studios were apprehensive that any ratings system would limit the potential audience for a film. Eventually, many came to see this as preferable to protests from censorship forces, at first labeling some of their own films as inappropriate for children.

The MPAA, however, countered efforts in the mid 1960s to impose mandatory labeling on motion pictures, such as that proposed by the state of New York that would limit the entrance of children to certain films identified by its licensing board. Instead, the MPAA endorsed the Green Sheet, a monthly publication that recommended — but did not enforce — suggested age ranges for particular films. The MPAA also had its own Production Code, established by Will H. Hays in 1934 as a means for film producers to monitor the contents of their products.

Throughout the 1960s, however, the effectiveness of the Code, which was entirely voluntary, gradually slipped further and further. In 1964 the Code approved Billy Wilder's *Kiss Me, Stupid*, but the Catholic Legion of Decency — which became the National Catholic Office of Motion Pictures the following year — slapped its C (condemned) rating on the film, criticizing the movie's "crude and suggestive dialogue, a leering treatment of marital and extra-marital sex, and a prurient preoccupation with lechery."

In 1965 the MPAA passed a film including nudity (*The Pawnbroker*) for the first time, announcing that it was revising the Production Code to bring it into line with current standards of acceptability. The new changes went into effect the following year, in which the film version of Edward Albee's *Who's Afraid of Virginia Woolf?*, which contained scenes and language that earlier would have been censored, was released with the caveat "Suggested for Mature Audiences." Ironically, the film was approved by the National Catholic Office for Motion Pictures.

Nonetheless, while filmmakers and many filmgoers no longer took either the Code's or the Legion's pronouncements as seriously as they once had, many observers felt by the mid 1960s that some form of ratings system, such as that contemplated by New York, was imminent. This was especially so in 1967, which pushed the envelope even further in terms of sex and violence with the seduction of a young man by his girlfriend's mother in *The Graduate* and the graphic death scenes in *Bonnie and Clyde*. More controversial still was the success in 1967 of the 1966 British film *Blow-Up*, directed by Italian Michelangelo Antonioni. Though its sex scenes precluded approval by the Code, the movie was released anyway to a large and appreciative audience.

The inevitable happened on 1 November 1968: the MPAA initiated a voluntary ratings system throughout the industry as a way to circumvent public outrage and government censorship. The four categories were: G, for general audiences; M, for mature audiences (later replaced by PG, parental guidance suggested); R, for restricted (with no one under seventeen admitted without a parent or adult guardian); and X, admission restricted to persons sixteen or older. The age boundary between R and X proved flexible at first and eventually rose. The ratings applied only to films produced by the MPAA or those by independent or foreign producers submitted for classification.

Application was somewhat erratic at first. For instance, any treatment of homosexuality or lesbianism, no matter how tasteful or discreet, seemed to warrant an automatic X rating, as in *The Killing of Sister George* (1968) and *Midnight Cowboy* (1969). On the other hand, it seemed as if no amount of violence on the screen could warrant a similar restriction.

Source: Robert Sklar, *Film: An International History of the Medium* (New York: Abrams, 1993).

---

thirty-seven million dollars. In addition, unions and guilds often insisted on better wages, driving their demands home with strikes that crippled the industry, and aggressive agents arranged increasingly sweeter deals for their clients, enabling actors such as Taylor and Marlon Brando to receive as much as one million dollars per

Poster for John Schlesinger's 1969 Academy Award–
winning movie

since the code had been adopted. Nor did many theaters limit their showings only to films that followed the production code or that met with the approval of the most energetic watchdog organization, the Catholic Legion of Decency. Such unapproved movies ranged from cheap exploitation flicks to quality foreign films and mainstream domestic offerings. Consequently, many lamented the dearth in "family entertainment." In particular, popu-

picture. To cut costs, studios resorted to filming outside the United States: in 1960 half of American studio films were made abroad, and more in 1961.

The Decline of the Production Code. Potential moviegoers who stayed away from the big screens were not necessarily watching the little screen at home: some were staying home in a silent protest against the nature of many of the films available, which became increasingly violent and sexual as the decade progressed. The movie industry had adhered to a self-imposed production code since 1934, but the code itself became less stringent through the 1960s. Consequently, subjects previously kept from the screen, including extramarital affairs, premarital sex, prostitution, homosexuality, and drug addiction, found their way into successful mainstream movies. Nudity also appeared for the first time in Hollywood pictures, most notably in *The Carpetbaggers* (1964). The code formerly maintained a "law of compensating values," in which characters who defied social conventions paid the price; but *Breakfast at Tiffany's* (1961), in which a call girl ends up happily with a man who has been kept by a married woman, demonstrated clearly that either social conventions or the price paid for defying them had changed dramatically

WEST SIDE STORY

It is common for a hit Broadway show to be adapted into a movie that, though possibly competent and generally entertaining, lacks the punch of the live show. Not so with the 1961 film version of *West Side Story*, which took a competent Broadway musical (1957) and turned it into a phenomenally popular movie. Set in contemporary New York City, the musical is a love story involving a Puerto Rican girl and an Anglo boy and the tensions their romance creates in their respective communities. Many consider it to be one of the greatest American film musicals of all time.

The same creative talents worked on both the musical and the movie. Leonard Bernstein composed the music, Stephen Sondheim wrote the lyrics, and Jerome Robbins provided the choreography. The movie's stars, Richard Beymer and Natalie Wood, while adequate in their parts, did not even sing their own songs. What then made the movie so popular?

The market, for one. Whereas the Broadway audience consisted mainly of adults in New York who could afford the price of admission, the movie audience could include adults across the country as well as young people drawn to the Romeo-and-Juliet story about adolescent love. The movie soundtrack, released on record, popularized the music. Moreover, the movie, filmed on location in New York, seemed more real than the stage show, despite the fact that it has young hoodlums periodically breaking into song and dance.

Winning ten Academy Awards, second only to *Ben-Hur* (1959) with eleven, did not hurt the movie's reputation. In addition to winning for Best Picture, *West Side Story* took the Oscars for supporting actor, supporting actress, director, color cinematography, color art direction, sound, musical score, editing, and color costume design.

Source: Mason Wiley and Damien Bona, *Inside Oscar: The Unofficial History of the Academy Awards* (New York: Ballentine, 1988).

lar European films, such as *I Am Curious (Yellow)* (1969), steamed the screens with treatments of sexuality far more open than even the raciest American movie.

Concern over Content. Though the current motion-picture rating system was not inaugurated until the end of the decade, audiences had plenty of guides as to what might or might not be appropriate viewing material for themselves or their children, most noticeably the Catholic Legion of Decency (changed to the National Catholic Office of Motion Pictures in 1965). Many Protestants and Catholics, for instance, agreed in their condemnations of films such as Billy Wilder's *The Apartment* (1960) and *Kiss Me, Stupid* (1964), to which the Legion of Decency gave its C (condemned) rating. While government censorship of films all but ended in the 1950s, cities and states often initiated attempts at regulation in response to morally outraged citizens.

Targeting Young Audiences. While some films often met with adult disapproval, their appeal to youth was obvious, and studios began to direct more of their efforts to this increasingly prosperous target audience. One such attempt included musicals released in 1965 such as *Beach Blanket Bingo, Girl Happy,* and *How to Stuff a Wild Bikini.* In addition, those who saw these movies were often attracted by stars and subjects they could not see on television. Especially popular were the James Bond films starring Sean Connery as Agent 007 of Her Majesty's Secret Service. Made in England, these films combined just enough sex and violence to titillate viewers but not enough to offend most. After the success of *Goldfinger* in 1964, the earlier Bond films *Dr. No* (1962) and *From Russia, with Love* (1963) were rereleased in 1965 and did better than many new films.

The Rebirth of the Industry. Another protest against American studio films was launched by independent filmmakers who advocated a "New American Cinema" as an alternative to what they viewed as the formulaic big-budget picture. However, their films never attracted near the number of moviegoers the studios did even at their lowest point, and by the mid 1960s movies appeared to be on the upswing again, drawing audiences lured by big-budget extravaganzas with exotic settings such as *Lawrence of Arabia* (1962) and *Cleopatra.* As domestic films again gained favor, foreign films were offered less frequently to American audiences. By 1965 the American motion-picture industry had rebounded fully, and American pictures filled screens across America. Part of this productivity was fueled, ironically, by the success of television, whose productions were often filmed on studio lots, and by sales of older movies to television networks.

Sources:

Richard S. Randall, *Censorship of the Movies: The Social and Political Control of a Mass Medium* (Madison & London: University of Wisconsin Press, 1968);

David Shipman and others, *The Chronicle of the Movies: A Year-by-Year History from "The Jazz Singer" to Today* (New York: Crescent, 1991);

Robert Sklar, *Film: An International History of the Medium* (New York: Abrams, 1993).

REGIONAL THEATER

Like opera, ballet has generally been considered an elite art in America. It seems surprising, therefore, that one of the major trends in dance during the 1960s was a proliferation of regional ballet companies featuring young performers; in 1960 there were an estimated 150 such companies in the United States, and by 1968 the number had risen to 200. This development is less surprising, however, given the fact that the country experienced a significant increase in regional theaters, galleries, and performances during the 1960s.

While some critics found the offerings of the New York theaters limited in the early 1960s, others praised the innovations and experiments that regional theaters such as Arena Stage in Washington, D.C., took on. Their sometimes precarious existence, already encouraged by the Ford Foundation and Rockefeller Foundation, was eased after 1965 by grants from the National Endowment for the Arts.

Along with major regional theaters and companies stood more provincial ones with more conservative tastes. Even these were welcome, however, seen by commentators as a necessary part of developing an appreciation for live drama and dance in the general public and as a training ground for young artists and directors.

All of this was part of a general trend in America during the decade to expose more people to the arts and to encourage young talent. Television was seen as an especially pernicious threat, so to counteract its influence regional theaters and companies sought to offer quality entertainment featuring local talent. In addition, much of the social and political activism of the 1960s was translated into community-improvement efforts such as those represented by regional theaters.

Sources: Tyrone Guthrie, *A New Theatre* (New York, Toronto & London: McGraw-Hill, 1964);

"Major Regional Theaters," in *Dictionary of Literary Biography, volume 7: Twentieth-Century American Dramatists, Part 2: K–Z,* edited by John MacNicholas (Detroit: Gale, 1981), pp. 405–453.

ON THE STAGE

The British Invasion. The best-known British Invasion of the 1960s occurred in rock 'n' roll, but American theaters also experienced an influx of talent from the United Kingdom, prompting one member of Actors Equity to claim that "New York is a British Festival." Irish playwright Brendan Behan's *The Hostage* was widely dis-

Uta Hagen, Ben Piazza, Avra Petrides, and Arthur Hill in the Broadway production of Edward Albee's *Who's Afraid of Virginia Woolf?* (1962)

cussed in 1960, as were Samuel Beckett's *Krapp's Last Tape* and Shelagh Delaney's *A Taste of Honey*. In the 1960s American theaters discovered British talents ranging from Harold Pinter and Tom Stoppard to the antic revue *Beyond the Fringe*.

Edward Albee and the Theater of the Absurd. One of the most respected dramatists, however, was an American: Edward Albee's one-act play *The Zoo Story* (1960) attracted the critics' attention and prepared the way for his biggest success, *Who's Afraid of Virginia Woolf?* (1962). Albee, perhaps incorrectly, was lumped in with other playwrights identified by critic Martin Esslin in 1961 as creators of the theater of the absurd. According to Esslin, these playwrights incorporated the existentialist ideas of French philosophers such as Jean-Paul Sartre and Albert Camus, particularly their notions that life is essentially meaningless, that former supports such as religion and society have collapsed, and that all efforts to make sense out of life are absurd. The resulting works were said to illustrate this human condition. Playwrights identified under this label whose works were performed during the 1960s in America include Albee and Arthur Kopit along with French writers Eugène Ionesco and Samuel Beckett and British playwright Pinter.

Few Outstanding Plays. American theater of the early 1960s, torn between depicting social realism and experi-

mentalism, did neither to the satisfaction of critics. Apart from Albee, who blended each strand skillfully in his dramas, no single figure or play stands out. No "serious" figure, that is — Neil Simon's light comedies such as *Barefoot in the Park* (1963) and *The Odd Couple* (1965) launched a commercially successful if critically maligned career. One exceptional play was Robert Bolt's *A Man for All Seasons* (1961), about the Renaissance man Sir Thomas More. Many of the most innovative productions, of course, occurred Off Broadway, such as Albee's early one-act plays; Kopit's comic *Oh Dad, Poor Dad, Mama's Hung You in the Closet and I'm Feelin' So Sad* (1962), directed by Jerome Robbins; Arthur Miller's autobiographical *After the Fall* (1964); and LeRoi Jones's powerful one-act play *Dutchman* (1964). Others premiered at regional theaters, including Terence McNally's *And Things That Go Bump in the Night* (1964) at the Guthrie Theatre in Minneapolis and Kopit's *Indians* (1968) at Arena Stage in Washington, D.C.

Musicals. Two musicals by the last of the great Broadway partnerships were running in 1960: Richard Rodgers and Oscar Hammerstein II's *The Sound of Music*, which premiered the year before, and Alan Jay Lerner and Frederick Loewe's *Camelot*. Beyond that, the Broadway musical seemed lost, and Hammerstein's death in 1960 appeared to signal the end of an era. Meredith Willson and Richard Morris's *The Unsinkable Molly Brown* (1960) and Charles Strouse, Lee Adams, and Michael Stewart's *Bye, Bye Birdie* (1960) were minor successes, but neither was very influential. The most successful musical of 1961, Abe Burrows and Frank Loesser's *How to Succeed in Business without Really Trying*, was praised for its innovative dance routines, while Stephen Sondheim, Burt Shevelove, and Larry Gelbart's *A Funny Thing Happened on the Way to the Forum* (1962) pleased audiences with its uninhibited humor. A better year came in 1964, which experienced three exuberant productions: Jerry Herman and Michael Stewart's *Hello, Dolly!* starring Carol Channing, Jule Styne, and Isobel Lennart; Bob Merrill's *Funny Girl* starring Barbra Streisand; and Jerry Boek, Joseph Stein, and Sheldon Harnick's *Fiddler on the Roof* starring Zero Mostel. An unconventional musical appeared on Broadway in 1968. A "tribal love-rock musical" by Gerome Ragni, James Rado, and Galt MacDermot, *Hair* was one of the most financially successful plays of the time — perhaps in part to its brief but controversial full-cast nude scene.

Ballet. The two powerhouses in the American ballet world continued to be American Ballet Theatre (ABT) and the New York City Ballet. Primarily a touring company, ABT spent almost half of 1960 in Europe and the Soviet Union on the President's Program for Cultural Exchange. To a large extent the New York City Ballet stayed in America, featuring new works by its artistic director George Balanchine. This pattern set the program for the two companies for the remainder of the decade.

Modern Dance. Just as Balanchine continued to dominate ballet, so Martha Graham continued to dominate modern dance during the 1960s. Other prominent figures include Alvin Ailey, Merce Cunningham, Alwin Nikolais, and Paul Taylor (particularly his comically disturbing *Insects and Heroes*, 1961). Younger dancers and choreographers, such as Twyla Tharp, began to push the barriers of modern dance even further in their avant-garde offerings.

Sources:

Doris Auerbach, *Sam Shepard, Arthur Kopit, and the Off Broadway Theater* (Boston: Twayne, 1982);

Martin Gottfried, *Broadway Musicals* (New York: Abrams, 1979);

Joseph H. Mazo, *Prime Movers: The Makers of Modern Dance in America* (New York: Morrow, 1977);

Don McDonagh, *The Rise and Fall and Rise of Modern Dance*, revised edition (Pennington, N. J.: A Cappella, 1990).

POETRY AND POLITICS: THE BLACK ARTS MOVEMENT AND THE BLACK AESTHETIC

From Negro to Black. After the death of Richard Wright in 1960, the two most respected Negro writers in America were Ralph Ellison and James Baldwin. As the civil rights movement progressed throughout the decade and some factions became increasingly militant, the term

Cover for an issue of a New York City political magazine that was an important vehicle for the Black Aesthetic–Black Power Coalition

---

WRITERS AND VIETNAM

Few Americans were impartial on the matter of the Vietnam War, and artists were no exception. In particular, many writers spoke out on the conflict in southeast Asia — most against it. In *Cannibals and Christians* (1966), for instance, Norman Mailer attacked the war, while John Steinbeck offered a more traditionally patriotic stance the same year in *America and Americans*. Renowned poet Robert Lowell joined Mailer in the October 1967 march on the Pentagon that Mailer chronicled in *The Armies of the Night* (1968), and other poets, such as Denise Levertov and Allen Ginsberg, spoke out against the war, both in their poetry and in speeches. In 1968 poet Robert Bly, given the National Book Award for his volume *The Light around the Body*, made the headlines by announcing that he would donate his one-thousand-dollar prize to a group that helped people evade the draft "as an appropriate use of an award for a book of poems mourning the war."

Negro was rejected by many in favor of *Black*, especially in phrases such as Black Power and names of groups, such as the Black Panthers. As "Negro" writers, Ellison and Baldwin were deemed by some to be insufficiently militant, despite their incisive critiques of race relations in America. Such writers, their critics said, relied too heavily on white literary models, when what was needed, they claimed, was a Black Aesthetic that wedded poetry and politics, art and social concerns. The Black Arts Movement was born.

A Separate Art. According to writers and critics such as Amiri Baraka (formerly LeRoi Jones), Larry Neal, and Addison Gayle, Jr., blacks and whites occupied separate cultures and so should have separate arts. In an essay in *The Black Aesthetic* (1971), edited by Gayle, Hoyt Fuller proclaims that whites and blacks exist in "two separate and naturally antagonistic worlds." Consequently, when white novelist William Styron wrote *The Confessions of Nat Turner* (1967) from the point of view of a runaway slave, ten black writers attacked him in *William Styron's Nat Turner* (1968) for his presumption. Black literary attacks on whites in general were not uncommon, as seen in the anger displayed by contributors to Baraka and Neal's 1968 anthology *Black Fire* and the works of poets such as Nikki Giovanni, Don L. Lee (later Haki R. Madhubuti), and Sonia Sanchez. More significantly, black writers and artists turned inward, viewing themselves as members of a close-knit black community. Even Gwendolyn Brooks, an established poet admired by both blacks and whites, changed the content and style of her work in response to the movement.

Art as Education and Inspiration. The rhetoric was revolutionary and intentionally shocking, but behind it stood the notion that art, rather than being an elitist activity, should speak directly to all blacks. As Ron Karenga writes in *The Black Aesthetic,* black art should "expose the enemy, praise the people and support the revolution." Therefore, according to the Black Aesthetic, black art should realistically represent black life. The plays, poems, and essays produced by the Black Arts Movement, then, were intended to be educational and inspirational while promoting race-centered attitudes. Also seen as role models were black performers, from Miles Davis and John Coltrane to Aretha Franklin, whose sound was thought to express the soul of black consciousness.

Critics. Some whites took offense at the language and ideas of the Black Arts Movement. Its advocates could counter that it was never intended for whites in the first place, but eventually some blacks began to criticize the movement as well, claiming that it was too restrictive in the roles and approaches it prescribed for black artists; others were troubled by its racism and sexism.

Impact. In addition to its artistic contributions at the time, the Black Aesthetic and the Black Arts Movement were significant in focusing more attention on the work of all black artists, not just those approved by white critics, and in questioning the aesthetic standards of certain critics by showing that their judgments were culturally based rather than universal.

Sources:

Jeffrey Louis Decker, ed., *Dictionary of Literary Biography Documentary Series, volume 8: The Black Aesthetic Movement* (Detroit, New York & London: Gale, 1991);

Addison Gayle, Jr., ed., *The Black Aesthetic* (Garden City, N.Y.: Doubleday, 1971);

LeRoi Jones and Larry Neal, eds., *Black Fire: An Anthology of Afro-American Writing* (New York: Morrow, 1968);

Larry Neal, "The Black Arts Movement," *Drama Review,* 12 (Summer 1968): 29–39.

REASONS NOT TO KILL YOURSELF EVEN THOUGH LIFE IS MEANINGLESS: THE RISE OF BLACK HUMOR

Origins. During the 1960s there were plenty of reasons to be depressed: leaders were assassinated, the military was involved in one questionable conflict after another, and French philosophers claimed that life was meaningless. The response of several writers of experimental fiction was to laugh in the face of death and despair, and the reaction was so widespread that it earned a name: black humor.

Comic Antiheroes. Writers of black humor portrayed antiheroes caught up in an absurd world in which traditional values seemed no longer to apply and in which the individual appeared lost in a maze of systems. As bleak as they were, the novels were still funny. Examples include John Barth's *The Sot-Weed Factor* (1960), Joseph Heller's

---

CATCH-22

If you were among the thousands who played Trivial Pursuit during the 1980s and had said that the phrase *catch-22* came before the book of the same title in response to one of the Literature questions, you would have been wrong: the book came first.

Have you ever been in a situation in which you want a job but are told you do not have experience, and you know you cannot get experience unless you get the job? That's catch-22. As Webster's defines it, the term can also refer to anything that is illogical or unreasonable; something that causes the opposite of the desired effect; a case with two alternatives, both bad; or simply as a catch. As used in the source of the phrase, however, catch-22 refers to a no-win problem whose solution is impossible because the situation presents a self-reversing paradox.

In Joseph Heller's 1961 novel *Catch-22* there are several examples of what the term means, but the best known involves its protagonist Yossarian, a bombardier in World War II who wants to stop fighting and go home. Only there's a catch — Catch-22, to be precise. A man "would be crazy to fly more missions and sane if he didn't, but if he was sane, he had to fly them. If he flew them he was crazy and didn't have to; but if he didn't, he was sane and had to." Used in the novel as an indictment of illogical bureaucratic policy, catch-22 has since become a commonly used term.

Source: Stephen W. Potts, *"Catch-22": Antiheroic Antinovel* (Boston: Twayne, 1989).

Catch-22 (1961), Thomas Pynchon's *V.* (1963), John Hawkes's *Second Skin* (1964), and Kurt Vonnegut, Jr.'s *Slaughterhouse-Five* (1969). Both *Catch-22* and *Slaughterhouse-Five,* for instance, include serious depictions of the horrors and stupidity of war, but both also include comic characters and situations. In *Slaughterhouse-Five,* the reader follows both Billy Pilgrim's horrific experiences during the war and his abduction by one-eyed aliens shaped like plungers. Pynchon's *The Crying of Lot 49* (1966) includes, in addition to its themes of conspiracy and paranoia, a strip-poker game for which the protagonist prepares by putting on every item of clothing in her suitcase and a hilarious description of a grisly Jacobean play.

Legacy. Certainly black humor existed before the 1960s, but it was at its height during the decade. Nor has it entirely disappeared: black humor has remained a fre-

John Barth

quent approach in modern fiction in the decades since the 1960s.

Sources:

Bruce Jay Friedman, ed., *Black Humor* (New York: Bantam, 1965);

Max F. Schulz, *Black Humor Fiction of the Sixties: A Pluralistic Definition of Man and His World* (Athens: Ohio University Press, 1973).

SELF-REFLEXIVE REFLECTIONS: METAFICTION

Vanity, Vanity. For many intellectuals in the late 1960s, God was dead and so was the novel. After the heyday of realism in the nineteenth century and the experiments of the modernists in the early part of the twentieth, it seemed as if there truly was nothing new to do in fiction. However, some writers proceeded to use this very situation as both subject and technique. The writers of metafiction, as it was called, wrote about the process of writing when there is nothing left to write about, and since all possible techniques had been used, they used all possible techniques to comment on the situation. This new metafiction, also called superfiction or surfiction by some, differed from self-reflexive fiction of the past — in which the author would comment on the story — in the postmodern assumption that reality is an artificial construction rather than something that can be captured by literature.

Barth. The prophet and chief practitioner of metafic-

tion was John Barth, who began employing its techniques in his 1960 novel *The Sot-Weed Factor*, polished them in his novel *Giles Goat-Boy* (1966), and spelled out its main points in an often-cited essay, "The Literature of Exhaustion," published in *Atlantic Monthly* in 1967. He proclaimed that fiction had reached a dead end, a point of exhaustion, but that a promising possibility lay in the use of multiple literary styles since no single approach presented itself. Barth did this himself in his collection *Lost in the Funhouse* (1968), which playfully parodies various literary techniques in stories either based on myth or deliberately reflecting the presence of a creator.

The Metafictionists. Other writers to use metafictional techniques and to address metafictional concerns in their work included Donald Barthelme, who in *Snow White* (1967) casts the fairy tale in a modern setting and interrupts the narrative process to comment on how he is creating the novel and even to quiz the reader on its progress; Robert Coover, especially in his experimental collection *Pricksongs and Descants* (1969); and Kurt Vonnegut, Jr., who includes himself as a character in his novel *Slaughterhouse-Five* (1969).

A New Approach. The metafiction trend peaked in the mid 1970s as readers and writers alike conceded that, even if the novel were dead, it could still be preferable to these experimental alternatives, and subsequent writers have been able to resuscitate the form. However, the metafictional approach has remained a viable option for writers.

Sources:

Robert E. Scholes, *Fabulation and Metafiction* (Urbana: University of Illinois Press, 1979);

Patricia Waugh, *Metafiction: The Theory and Practice of Self-Conscious Fiction* (London & New York: Methuen, 1984).

SLOUCHING TOWARD POPULARITY: FACTION AND THE NEW JOURNALISM

Faction. One of the most-discussed books of the 1960s was Truman Capote's *In Cold Blood* (1966). Variously promoted as a "nonfiction novel" and as "faction," the book was based on actual murders in Kansas on 15 November 1959, the trial in May 1960, and the hanging of the murderers in April 1965. Capote, already a well-known novelist, interviewed people in Kansas and wrote about the story in the form of a novel. Sales of the book skyrocketed, and Capote, no resister of publicity, basked in the limelight. Scores of imitations followed, with varying success. The most notable example, Norman Mailer's *The Armies of the Night: History as a Novel, the Novel as History* (1968), was about his participation in an October 1967 peace march on the Pentagon and includes Mailer as a character.

The New Journalism. Almost as popular were books with firmer roots in journalism — or the New Journalism, to be precise. The New Journalism was a controversial movement emerging in the mid 1960s that wedded fictional techniques with reporting. After a start in fictionlike stories in the *New York Herald Tribune* and in magazines such as *Esquire*, the *Village Voice*, and *Rolling Stone*, the New Journalism moved to books, thanks primarily to the popularity of its unofficial spokesman, Tom Wolfe. His first collection of magazine pieces, *The Kandy-Kolored Tangerine-Flake Streamline Baby* (1965), sold well, as did his book about the doings of writer Ken Kesey and his Merry Pranksters, *The Electric Kool-Aid Acid Test* (1968).

Unconventional Nonfiction. A whole series of nonfiction books told in the form of fiction soon appeared, including Hunter S. Thompson's *Hell's Angels: A Strange and Terrible Saga* (1966) and George Plimpton's *Paper Lion* (1966). Like Wolfe, neither writer pretended to reportorial objectivity; instead, each became a part of the story he told. In an era that prized personal involvement, both succeeded. Equally successful was Joan Didion's collection *Slouching towards Bethlehem* (1968), a series of ironic, well-crafted essays on topics ranging from celebrities to California living to Las Vegas weddings.

The Real Story. As it developed, the New Journalism became a form of writing all its own. No longer simply reporting in a fictional style, it became known for its odd subjects, interesting range of styles, and its insistence on showing the story behind the story.

Source:
Tom Wolfe and E. W. Johnson, eds., *The New Journalism* (New York: Harper & Row, 1973).

TO BEDLAM AND BACK: THE NEW AMERICAN POETRY

The New American Poetry. Donald M. Allen signaled the beginning of a new era in American poetry early in the decade with the publication of his anthology *The New American Poetry, 1945–1960* in 1960. In addition to publishing Beat poets from the 1950s such as Lawrence Ferlinghetti, Allen included many younger or little-known poets whose approaches sometimes differed radically from the carefully constructed and highly intellectual poetry then favored by most professors and critics.

Against Modernism. Like most of the new art movements and much of the experimental fiction of the late 1950s and the 1960s, this new poetry was an explicit rejection of modernism, which had dominated the arts in America and Europe since the early decades of the twentieth century. For instance, in his book *In Defense of Ignorance* (1960) poet Karl Shapiro attacks the influence of modernism on American poetry and criticism, particularly that generated by advocates of American-born British poet T. S. Eliot. Instead, many of the new poets adopted Walt Whitman or William Carlos Williams as models.

Confessional Poetry. In particular, confessional poetry rebelled against the impersonality advocated by modernist ideals. Poets such as John Berryman, Robert

A POET READS FOR THE PRESIDENT

On 20 January 1961 Robert Frost, the unofficial poet laureate of America, read his original poem "The Gift Outright" at the inauguration of President John F. Kennedy, the only poet to read at a presidential inauguration in the history of the country. The presence of the 86-year-old poet from New England, one of the most popular literary figures in the United States, indicated not only Kennedy's canny populist instincts but also the high esteem with which he and his wife Jacqueline held the arts. James Dickey read one of his poems at an inaugural gathering for President Jimmy Carter in 1977, but a poet did not read again at the actual ceremony until Maya Angelou at the inauguration of President Bill Clinton in 1993.

Source: Lawrence Thompson and R. H. Winnick with Edward Connery Lathem, *Robert Frost: A Biography* (New York: Holt, Rinehart & Winston, 1981).

Lowell, Sylvia Plath, Theodore Roethke, and Anne Sexton, all trained as modernist poets, as well as Allen Ginsberg from the Beat movement of the 1950s, broke new ground beginning in the late 1950s and through the 1960s in their intensely personal poems dealing with madness, guilt, and other emotional topics largely absent in earlier American poetry. Though the poets themselves were hardly ideal personal models — some had spent time in mental hospitals and some had committed suicide — their poetry was considered worthy of emulation.

New Directions Discouraged. Such success, however, was fairly limited in terms of audience. Many poets felt that the public as well as publishers and critics were unresponsive to new directions in poetry. For instance, at the National Book Awards Symposium in March 1968, poets such as John Ashbery, Robert Creeley, and Ginsberg complained that experiments in poetry were discouraged by critics and reviewers. In addition, many readers were put off by the use of personal revelation from the confessional poets on the one hand and the street language and rhythms from popular music in the work of poets allied with the Black Arts Movement on the other.

Diversity. Poets such as Ashbery, and, to a certain extent, Berryman, indicated another direction for American poetry: toward the abstruse and virtually nonsensical, a sharp contrast with the confessional poets and those who wrote about traditional subjects in traditional forms. Such divisions had always existed to a certain extent, but in the 1960s a split between poems using ordinary language about common experience and highly difficult works became especially pronounced, continuing for the

During the 1950s writer John Updike was widely considered one of the most promising new voices in American literature with his stories in *The New Yorker* and his first novel, *The Poorhouse Fair* (1959). He entered his maturity as a writer, ironically, with a novel about a man who resists the responsibilities that maturity entails in his 1960 novel *Rabbit, Run.*

Harry "Rabbit" Angstrom, the protagonist of *Rabbit, Run,* is a frustrated salesman nostalgic for the glory days of his youth. The novel captures not only the tension in Angstrom between the responsibilities of family life and the yearning for freedom but also the minutiae of American culture during the 1950s as experienced by a middle-class, suburban Everyman.

Rabbit, Run was a tremendous success both with the reading public and with academics. In its equally popular sequels — *Rabbit, Redux* (1971), *Rabbit Is Rich* (1981), and *Rabbit at Rest* (1990) — Updike portrays Angstrom's life over the next three decades.

Source: Donald J. Greiner, *John Updike's Novels* (Athens: Ohio University Press, 1984).

next decades. As in art, poetry during the 1960s went from adherence of a uniform code to extreme diversity.

Sources:

David Perkins, *A History of Modern Poetry: Modernism and After* (Cambridge, Mass. & London: Belknap Press–Harvard University Press, 1987);

Robert S. Phillips, *The Confessional Poets* (Carbondale & Edwardsville: Southern Illinois University Press, 1973).

WHAT'S EVERYONE READING? POPULAR FICTION AND NONFICTION

Unusual Best-Sellers. Histories of twelve hundred pages generally do not sell well, but William L. Shirer's *The Rise and Fall of the Third Reich* (1960), about Nazi Germany, proved an exception by selling more than half a million copies and remaining on the best-seller list through 1961. It was a good decade for nonfiction in general, though best-seller-list definitions of what constituted nonfiction in some cases seemed arbitrary, including Charles M. Schulz's "Peanuts" collections and Rod McKuen's books of poems, for example. Readers are always interested in sex, and Helen Gurley Brown's *Sex and the Single Girl* (1962) found a voracious readership.

Best-Selling Literature. Despite the concerns of critics, professors, and others that quality fiction was being smothered by a mass of popular fiction, it was also a good decade for literature: J. D. Salinger's *Franny and Zooey* (1961), Katherine Anne Porter's *Ship of Fools* (1962), William Faulkner's *The Reivers* (1962), Mary McCarthy's *The Group* (1963), Saul Bellow's *Herzog* (1964), Bernard Malamud's *The Fixer* (1966), Truman Capote's *In Cold Blood* (1966), Philip Roth's controversial *Portnoy's Complaint* (1969), and Kurt Vonnegut, Jr.'s *Slaughterhouse-Five* (1969) all reached the best-seller lists.

Beach Reading. In 1960 President John F. Kennedy mentioned that British author Ian Fleming's *From Russia, with Love* (1957) was one of his ten favorite novels. Soon Fleming's thrillers featuring secret agent James Bond were wildly successful, from bookstores to the big screen. Fleming's books had plenty of company on popular-fiction bookshelves. One of the most popular (though not critically acclaimed) novelists of the decade was Harold Robbins, and books such as Morris West's *The Shoes of the Fisherman* (1963), about the election of a

In July 1960 a previously unknown southern writer named Harper Lee (1926–) published a first novel that briefly made her a household name. *To Kill a Mockingbird* was an instant success, selling half a million copies in one year and winning the 1961 Pulitzer Prize for fiction.

The response was understandable, since Lee had a terrific story and told it well. Set in a rural Alabama town in the 1930s, *To Kill a Mockingbird* is the story of six-year-old Jean Louise ("Scout") as she experiences two sets of events: her widowed father's defense of a black man wrongly accused of raping a white woman, and her realization that the reclusive "Boo" Radley is neither strange nor evil, as the townspeople think. In both cases Lee demonstrates the follies of prejudice. Such a theme was particularly relevant in the early 1960s, when Americans were still adjusting to desegregation and when the civil rights movement was beginning to grow in strength. Without seeming to preach to her readers, Lee made a strong case for tolerance and understanding.

A successful film of *To Kill a Mockingbird* was released in 1962, with a screenplay by Horton Foote and starring Gregory Peck as attorney Atticus Finch, Scout's father. Each received an Academy Award for his work. The popularity of the book and the movie led to great expectations for Lee's next novel, which she was said to have begun in 1961, but she has not published anything since *To Kill a Mockingbird.*

new pope; Irving Wallace's *The Man* (1964), about a black vice-president who becomes the first black president; Arthur Hailey's *Hotel* (1965) and *Airport* (1968); Jacqueline Susann's *Valley of the Dolls* (1966); James Clavell's *Tai-Pan* (1966); and Gore Vidal's racy *Myra Breckinridge* (1968) all sold well.

Genre Fiction. In fiction categorized by traditionally popular subjects, romance novels and science fiction and fantasy were in, while the realms of detective novels and Westerns, losing major talents, sought to rediscover their purpose and audience. Certain science-fiction and fantasy writers, such as Robert A. Heinlein with his novel *Stranger in a Strange Land* (1961) and British author J. R. R. Tolkien with his *Lord of the Rings* trilogy (1954–1955), became cult favorites on college campuses. So did many of the writers of science fiction's New Wave, including Harlan Ellison, who edited the much-discussed New Wave anthology *Dangerous Visions* (1967). In addition, horror fiction had its first best-selling novel with Ira Levin's *Rosemary's Baby* (1967), which prefigured the horror-fiction boom of the 1970s.

YOUNG ADULT AND CHILDREN'S LITERATURE

More Books. Books for children and young adults continued their dramatic rise begun in the 1950s. There was a boom in demand for children's books and books for young adults due to increased library funding resulting from the education acts passed in 1965.

Concerned Parents and Librarians. Also on the rise was the concern of parents and others about the content of the books. A popular target was J. D. Salinger's *The Catcher in the Rye* (1951), an adult novel popular with adolescent readers that self-appointed censors found objectionable due to its language, certain sexual situations, and its criticism of the adult world. In general, books for children and young adults became controversial for presenting critical observations of adults, often couched in more-realistic settings, and for showing children in ways some parents and librarians preferred not to see them. The work of many new young-adult writers, influenced by Salinger, would have been labeled as adult fiction only a decade earlier; examples include Emily Neville's *It's Like This, Cat* (1963), S. E. Hinton's *The Outsiders* (1967), and Paul Zindel's *My Darling, My Hamburger* (1969). Books for younger children, though not nearly as graphic, nevertheless stirred controversy, especially Maurice Sendak's *Where the Wild Things Are* (1963), which featured ferocious monsters that some adults believed would frighten young children. Nonetheless, it became one of the best-selling children's books of the decade, challenging Dr. Seuss's popular *Green Eggs and Ham* (1960).

Picture Books. In picture books, the art became better and better, sometimes to the detriment of the stories it

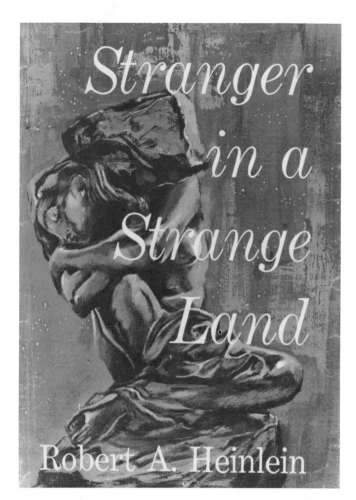

Dust jacket for the first science-fiction novel to appear on *The New York Times* best-seller list

illustrated. At times glorious art fleshed out stories or poems that earlier would have been found in collections, allowing individual stories or poems to be published as complete books.

Messages for Children. Not all books for children and young adults during the 1960s were controversial, of course, even though most carried implicit messages. In Leo Lionni's *Swimmy* (1963), for example, a small fish gets other small fish to group together to scare away the big fish, while Ezra Jack Keats's *The Snowy Day* (1962) broke new ground in making nothing of the fact that the protagonist was black, which after all was obvious from the illustrations. Another popular book, E. L. Konigsberg's *From the Mixed-Up Files of Mrs. Basil E. Frankweiler* (1967), for intermediate readers, showed children as independent persons rather than as accessories of their parents, reflecting new attitudes toward children espoused by psychologists and educators.

Sources:
Lee Burress, *Battle of the Books: Literary Censorship in the Public Schools, 1950–1985* (Metuchen, N. J.: Scarecrow, 1989);

Kenneth L. Donelson and Alleen Pace Nilsen, *Literature for Today's Young Adults,* third edition (Glenview, Ill. & London: Scott, Foresman, 1989).

HEADLINE MAKERS

EDWARD ALBEE

1928-

PLAYWRIGHT

Early Promise. Playwright Edward Albee stood out in the midst of what many critics saw as a dreary period for American theater in the 1960s. His one-act plays *The Zoo Story* (1960), *The Sandbox* (1960), *The Death of Bessie Smith* (1960), and *The American Dream* (1961) were critical and commercial Off-Broadway successes, and then he impressed everyone with his first full-length play, *Who's Afraid of Virginia Woolf?* (1962). Starring Uta Hagen and Arthur Hill as Martha and George, it ran for 644 performances on Broadway and was launched on an international tour.

Later Developments. His reputation was further enhanced by his 1962 stage adaptation of Carson McCullers's *The Ballad of the Sad Cafe,* which opened on Broadway the following year. After *Who's Afraid of Virginia Woolf?* Albee was the most sought-after playwright in America: he took part in an Off-Broadway production of Ugo Betti's *Corruption in the Palace of Justice* in 1963 and was said to be working on two plays, a novel, and an opera simultaneously. The experience was a heady one for a young playwright whose first work had appeared only five years earlier. Before that, he had attended various private schools and college (without graduating) and had worked at odd jobs. Indeed, it appeared as if his youthful promise had been exhausted in the early 1960s, a perception negated in part by the successful 167-performance run of his play *Tiny Alice* from 1964 to 1965 and by *A Delicate Balance* (1966), hailed by many as the outstanding American play in 1966 (it received the Pulitzer Prize for drama) but criticized by several observers. It fared better, however, than his dramatization of James Purdy's

novel *Malcolm,* which appeared early in 1966 and was withdrawn after seven performances.

Reputation. With plays such as *Box* (1968) and *Quotations from Chairman Mao Tse-Tung* (1968) Albee was identified with the theater of the absurd, whose vogue helped his reputation somewhat. Despite writing two Pulitzer Prize–winning plays since the 1960s, his popularity has never been as high as it was in the early 1960s.

Sources:

Richard E. Amacher, *Edward Albee,* revised edition (Boston: Twayne, 1982);

Matthew Charles Roudane, *Understanding Edward Albee* (Columbia: University of South Carolina Press, 1987).

DAVE BRUBECK

1920-

JAZZ PIANIST, COMPOSER

Intellectual Jazz. One of the most innovative and popular figures in jazz during a decade filled with innovative and popular performers was pianist and composer Dave Brubeck. At the same time, Brubeck was one of the most controversial figures in jazz: while he and his quartet, which included alto saxophonist Paul Desmond and drummer Joe Morello, were highly successful, especially on the college campuses where they often took their music, some criticized their work for being overly intellectual, claiming it lacked genuine feeling.

Popular Complexity. It was understandable that Brubeck's music was consciously complex, since he had trained under some of the most experimental classical composers of the twentieth century, including Darius Milhaud. Brubeck experimented with quotation from classical composers in his jazz compositions — thus anticipating Gunther Schuller's concept of a "Third

Stream" combining classical and jazz techniques — and incorporated atonality, counterpoint, and unusual time signatures. In stark contrast to the "free jazz" or "progressive jazz" of figures such as Ornette Coleman, which was admired only by a small coterie of jazz fans, the Brubeck Quartet's intelligent lyricism was widely appreciated. The quartet's single "Take Five" (1962), for instance, written in 5/4 time, reached the top ten on the pop music charts. Indeed, in polls conducted by *Playboy* and *Downbeat*, Brubeck and his quartet invariably did well through most of the 1960s.

Sources:

Brian Case and Stan Britt, *The Harmony Illustrated Encyclopedia of Jazz,* third edition, revised by Chrissie Murray (New York: Harmony, 1986);

Leonard Feather, *The Pleasures of Jazz* (New York: Horizon, 1976).

JOHNNY CASH

1932-

COUNTRY MUSICIAN

A Solid Reputation. Since the 1950s country music had gained an increasing amount of respect in American culture, in contrast to its earlier status as "hillbilly music." One of the singers and songwriters responsible for this improvement was Johnny Cash, who solidified his position during the 1960s as one of the greatest country musicians.

The Sun Records Days. Cash began his recording career in 1955 and was one of the pioneers of rockabilly, a combination of country music with rhythm and blues or rock 'n' roll, at Sun Records in Memphis. With his pared-down accompaniments, steady rhythms, and inimitable baritone on recordings such as "I Walk the Line" (1956), he quickly became a star, engaging in dozens of recordings and tour dates by the 1960s.

Ring of Fire. In 1961 June Carter, a descendant of the legendary Carter family, joined Cash's tour group, and she and Cash co-wrote his 1963 hit "Ring of Fire." In the mid 1960s Cash ruined his marriage and nearly killed himself through drug addiction. Aided by Carter, whom he married in 1968, and a return to the religion of his youth, Cash overcame his addiction and came back stronger than ever. In 1969 he enjoyed a Top 40 hit with "A Boy Named Sue" and became the star of his own television show, which ran until 1971. Cash has remained a popular performer ever since and has influenced several younger musicians.

Sources:

Johnny Cash, *Man in Black* (Grand Rapids, Mich.: Zondervan, 1975);

Christopher S. Wren, *Winners Got Scars Too: The Life and Legends of Johnny Cash* (New York: Dial, 1971).

JOHN COLTRANE

1926-1967

JAZZ SAXOPHONIST

A Link between Styles. The career of John Coltrane, one of the most influential jazz saxophonists of the 1960s and after, bridges the mature bebop of the 1950s and the experimental developments of the late 1960s.

Sheets of Sound. Coltrane played with bebop masters Dizzy Gillespie, Miles Davis, and Thelonious Monk during the 1950s before starting his own quartet in 1960. Composed of Coltrane, pianist McCoy Tyner, bassist Jimmy Garrison, and drummer Elvin Jones, the group allowed Coltrane to expand on the melodic and harmonic possibilities of jazz. Coltrane's music from this period, usually described as consisting of "sheets of sound," was both structurally complex and emotionally rich, including long improvisations, unorthodox chords, and elements of Eastern music. The effect was popular with many jazz fans, particularly on Coltrane's famous version of "My Favorite Things" (1961).

Innovations Cut Short. In 1966, impressed with Ornette Coleman's experiments in free jazz that evaded conventional harmonic structure altogether, Coltrane went in a new direction to explore the new sound. Although he died of cancer the following year, Coltrane has remained a major influence for many young musicians, who revere him as one of the great performers of jazz.

Sources:

William Shadrack Cole, *John Coltrane* (New York: Schirmer, 1976);

Cuthbert Ormond Simpkins, *Coltrane: A Biography* (New York: Herndon House, 1975);

J. C. Thomas, *Chasin' the Trane: The Music and Mystique of John Coltrane* (Garden City, N.Y.: Doubleday, 1975).

BOB DYLAN

1941-

FOLK AND ROCK PERFORMER, SONGWRITER

The Man from Minnesota. Soon after coming to national attention in 1962, Bob Dylan was recognized as one of the most promising songwriters and performers in the new folk-music revival. Born Robert Zimmerman in Duluth, Minnesota, he moved to New York in 1960 and soon established himself in the folk-music scene, playing in coffeehouses in Greenwich Village.

Protest Songs. In 1962 he recorded his first album,

a compilation of traditional folk songs in the manner of his hero Woody Guthrie, called *Bob Dylan*. The same year he wrote "Blowin' in the Wind," which rhetorically questioned establishment attitudes and claimed that "the answer . . . is blowin' in the wind." This stance of youthful challenge and expectation of imminent social change was popular with young listeners; the song was successfully recorded by Peter, Paul & Mary the following year, setting the stage for Dylan's own successful version of his 1963 album *The Freewheelin' Bob Dylan,* which also included the hits "A Hard Rain's a-Gonna Fall" and "Masters of War." Such songs established Dylan as a masterful writer of intelligent protest songs, as did his album *The Times They Are a-Changin'* (1964).

New Directions. Dylan refused to stay in one place as an artist. In a 1964 profile in *The New Yorker,* for instance, he said that he would continue to write protest songs, but that this would become less prominent in his work. Indeed, in 1965 he upset many folk-music fans by combining folk music with elements of rock; some were particularly bothered by his new use of electric instruments as opposed to the guitar and harmonica he had used before. However, his entry into rock was partly responsible for the increased maturity of the field. Dylan and others wrote rock songs and lyrics as sophisticated as those he had written as a folk musician.

Further Innovations. He experimented with psychedelic rock, which sought to emulate or enhance the effects of psychedelic drugs through deliberate distortion, on *Blonde on Blonde* (1966), then returned to acoustic instruments on his 1968 album *John Wesley Harding* and the country-influenced *Nashville Skyline* (1969). Such continuous exploration has characterized his work since.

Sources:
Clinton Heylin, *Bob Dylan: Behind the Shades — A Biography* (New York: Summit, 1991);
Robert Shelton, *No Direction Home: The Life and Music of Bob Dylan* (New York & London: Morrow, 1986).

JIMI HENDRIX

1942-1970

ROCK GUITARIST

A Great Rock Guitarist. Jimi Hendrix was born James Marshall Hendrix in Seattle. He taught himself to play by listening to blues recordings; left-handed, he used a restrung right-handed guitar. He became known in the late 1960s for doing even stranger things with the instrument, such as playing it behind his back, playing it with his teeth, and setting it on fire. At times his stage pyromania overshadowed his mu-

sical pyrotechnics, but he is now recognized as perhaps the most influential rock guitarist in history.

Play Fast, Die Young. Hendrix began his career as a studio musician in the early 1960s and formed his own band in 1965. The following year he created a new band, the Jimi Hendrix Experience, and started to form a new sound, called acid rock, that employed intentional feedback and other deliberate distortions. His stage antics rather than his music gained him notoriety at the 1967 Monterey Pop Festival (captured on film in the cinema verité documentary *Monterey Pop,* 1968), but the band did have a Top 40 hit with their version of Bob Dylan's "All Along the Watchtower" in 1968. That year Hendrix directed his efforts to studio recordings, but he appeared with his new group, Band of Gypsies, in 1969 at Woodstock, where he gave a memorable performance of "The Star-Spangled Banner." He died from asphixiation resulting from a drug overdose the following year.

Sources:
Curtis Knight, *Jimi: An Intimate Biography of Jimi Hendrix* (New York: Praeger, 1974);
Charles Shaar Murray, *Crosstown Traffic: Jimi Hendrix and the Post-War Rock 'n' Roll Revolution* (New York: St. Martin's Press, 1989).

JANIS JOPLIN

1943-1970

ROCK SINGER

A Symbol of the 1960s. Janis Joplin was more than just one of the most talented blues and rock vocalists of the twentieth century: she was also a personality, a symbol of rebellion adopted by youth anxious to "let it all hang out" in the late 1960s. Uninhibited both as a performer and in her personal life, Joplin personified what many saw as the spirit of rock in the late 1960s, and her untimely death was a sobering reminder of where the excesses of the rock spirit could lead.

Youthful Success. An outcast as an adolescent, Joplin ran away from her Port Arthur, Texas, home at age seventeen and worked as a singer in different cities before joining the rock group Big Brother and the Holding Company in San Francisco in 1966. Thanks to Joplin's versatile, roaring vocals and equally unrestrained performance style, the group stopped the show at the Monterey Pop Festival in 1967. The following year their album *Cheap Thrills* had exceptional sales, spurred in part by media stories about Joplin's lifestyle of sex, drugs, and alcohol abuse. Joplin left the band in 1968 and formed her own group, which recorded *Kosmic Blues* (1969). Her arrest in 1969 in a confrontation with police only increased her popularity with many young fans, but she was overwhelmed by her success.

Youthful Excess. Joplin's fierce vocal style led some to worry that she would ruin her remarkable voice. To this she responded, "Why should I hold back now and sound mediocre just so I can sound mediocre twenty years from now?" She never had the chance to find out: she died of a heroin overdose in 1970.

Source:

Jon Pareles and Patricia Romanowski, eds., *The Rolling Stone Illustrated Encyclopedia of Rock and Roll* (New York: Rolling Stone Press/Summit, 1983).

KEN KESEY

1935-

NOVELIST

Nonconformist Writer. During the 1960s writer Ken Kesey was as famous for his promotion of the hippie lifestyle as he was for anything he published. Stepping into the shoes vacated by the Beat Generation of the 1950s, Kesey and his circle of followers, called the Merry Pranksters, stood out even among nonconformists in an age of rebellion against conformity.

Novels. Kesey became famous at age twenty-seven with his first novel, *One Flew Over the Cuckoo's Nest* (1962). The protagonist, Randle J. McMurphy, is a patient in a mental hospital. Though the consequences of his actions are sometimes disastrous, to many readers he was a figure admirable for his dramatic challenges to convention and authority. This stance made the character, and Kesey by extension, popular with young readers in particular. Kesey's next novel, *Sometimes a Great Notion* (1964), was less successful, perhaps because its conservative Oregonians were a radical departure from what readers most admired in *One Flew Over the Cuckoo's Nest*.

On the Road. For the remainder of the 1960s Kesey stopped writing and became a character himself. To celebrate the publication of *Sometimes a Great Notion*, he and the Merry Pranksters left California in a bus painted with psychedelic designs in psychedelic colors to tour the country. Not only was the trip an echo of Jack Kerouac's Beat novel *On the Road* (1957), the driver was Kerouac's friend and inspiration, Neal Cassady. The trip came to an anticlimax in Millbrook, New York, where Kesey, who had used LSD (lysergic acid diethylamide) since participating in government-sanctioned experiments in 1959, hoped to join Timothy Leary as a fellow LSD researcher. Instead, Leary turned Kesey and his Pranksters away.

Acid Tests. Kesey and the Merry Pranksters returned to California and immersed themselves in the San Francisco youth culture. In 1965 and 1966 they sponsored Acid Tests, in which they distributed LSD to others (sometimes without their knowledge) and observed the effects, and involved themselves with rock bands, such as the Grateful Dead, in performances involving light shows and movies from their trip. In 1966 Kesey was arrested for marijuana possession and spent five months in jail. After he was released, he retreated to Oregon, devoting himself to literary projects and collaborations but writing few books of his own.

Sources:

Paul Perry, *On the Bus: The Complete Guide to the Legendary Trip of Ken Kesey and the Merry Pranksters and the Birth of the Counterculture*, edited by Ken Bobbs, Michael Schwartz, and Neil Ortenberg (New York: Thunder's Mouth Press, 1990);

Tom Wolfe, *The Electric Kool-Aid Acid Test* (New York: Farrar Straus & Giroux, 1968).

STANLEY KUBRICK

1928-

FILM WRITER, DIRECTOR, PRODUCER

Notable Director. Though producing a film only every few years, writer and director Stanley Kubrick stands out as one of the most notable and unconventional filmmakers of the 1960s. Kubrick is a perfect example of what critics in the 1960s called the auteur theory, the belief that, despite the collaborative nature of film, the director infuses the work with his or her personal artistry and vision.

Early Potential. He began writing, producing, and directing low-budget films in the 1950s, scoring a success with the World War I film *Paths of Glory* (1957). One of its stars, Kirk Douglas, was producing *Spartacus* (1960), and he hired Kubrick as its new director. Though this was his first experience with a larger budget, the 1960 film dissatisfied Kubrick, who preferred doing things his way. His adaptation of Vladimir Nabokov's 1955 novel *Lolita* (1962), though memorable for Peter Sellers's antic portrayal of Clare Quilty, was panned by critics, but audiences came in droves for his next two efforts.

Maturity. *Dr. Strangelove or: How I Learned to Stop Worrying and Love the Bomb* (1964), which Kubrick called a "nightmare comedy" about the threat of nuclear war, was both a critical and commercial success. Critical opinion was more divided on *2001: A Space Odyssey* (1968), based on a science-fiction story by Arthur C. Clarke, but the film was an enormous hit. Fans praised its philosophical bent and its special effects, which revolutionized science-fiction film. Though Kubrick has directed various pictures since, he is largely identified with *2001*, which also forever linked Richard Strauss's *Also Sprach Zarathustra*, the theme music of the movie, with space exploration and portentous discoveries in popular culture.

Sources:

Thomas Nelson, *Kubrick: Inside a Film Artist's Maze* (Bloomington: Indiana University Press, 1982);

Gene Phillips, *Stanley Kubrick: A Film Odyssey* (New York: Popular Library, 1975);

Alexander Walker, *Stanley Kubrick Directs,* expanded edition (New York: Harcourt Brace Jovanovich, 1972).

SIDNEY POITIER

1927-

ACTOR

The Noble Mr. Poitier. "You're like us, but you're not like us," says Lulu to the character played by Sidney Poitier in the 1967 British film *To Sir, with Love.* Such sentiments were shared by many filmgoers concerning the actor and the roles he played — especially white filmgoers, comforted during a decade of racial unrest by this handsome black man who played friendly, hard-working characters who, though allowed to reveal "ethnic" characteristics occasionally, spoke "standard" English flawlessly and almost always wore a tie. The first black leading man in Hollywood, he was also the only one to win an Academy Award for Best Actor.

A Responsible Model. Born in Miami to parents from the Bahamas, where he spent his youth, Poitier began his acting career on the New York stage in 1946. He made his first film in 1950 and had several roles during the decade. His portrayal in *The Blackboard Jungle* (1955) of a black urban youth with promise was indicative of things to come. After an acclaimed performance in the 1961 film version of Lorraine Hansberry's play *A Raisin in the Sun* (1959), Poitier was invariably cast as a responsible role model for blacks and whites alike. In his Oscar-winning performance in *The Lilies of the Field* (1963), for instance, he plays a laborer who gets swept into building a chapel for a convent in the Southwest.

Important Roles. Poitier's most active year was 1967, with two important roles: *In the Heat of the Night,* as an investigator looking into a murder in a bigoted southern town; and *Guess Who's Coming to Dinner?,* as the fiancé of a white woman whose parents have difficulty accepting their future son-in-law, no matter how smart he is or how respectable his family.

Lifetime Achievements. Though not militant like some blacks in the 1960s, Poitier contributed to promoting a positive image of blacks, both through his roles and his private life. In the 1970s he turned his attention to directing, with occasional roles. In 1990 he received a Lifetime Achievement Award from the American Film Institute.

Sources:

William Hoffman, *Sidney* (New York: Stuart, 1971);

Sidney Poitier, *This Life* (New York: Knopf, 1980).

THOMAS PYNCHON

1937-

NOVELIST

Mystery Writer. Paranoia and conspiracy theories abounded during the 1960s, proferring speculations about topics ranging from the assassination of President John F. Kennedy to the Vietnam War to whether or not the U.S. Air Force was storing aliens and UFOs in Dayton, Ohio. It was hardly surprising, then, that the works of an author for whom paranoia and conspiracies were major plot devices should appear during the decade — an author made all the more appealing by the fact that apparently no one knew where he was or what he looked like. His name was Thomas Pynchon, and only two published photographs of him are known: one from his high-school yearbook and one from his Navy years. In his efforts to avoid publicity, he became one of the most discussed writers of the 1960s.

A Cult Phenomenon. After studying at Cornell University, Pynchon burst on the literary scene with his first novel, *V.,* in 1963. A long, difficult book, it was not a best-seller, but it did gain Pynchon a cult following and respectful attention from critics. A similar response greeted his next novel, *The Crying of Lot 49* (1966), which was shorter and somewhat more accessible. Nonetheless, the reader has to struggle with Pynchon's writing in both books: he loads his books with detail ranging from science and history to trivia from popular culture.

The In Crowd. For many readers Pynchon's appeal was that, apart from using black humor along with other writers during the 1960s, he belonged in a category all his own. To read Pynchon — or at least to claim to have read Pynchon — likewise placed one in a special group. Moreover, there was an air of mystery about Pynchon. Since he never gave interviews, readers did not know when to expect his latest offering, nor were they distracted by a cult of personality. Fans had to wait eight years after *The Crying of Lot 49* for his next novel, *Gravity's Rainbow* (1974).

Sources:

Judith Chambers, *Thomas Pynchon* (New York: Twayne, 1992);

Robert D. Newman, *Understanding Thomas Pynchon* (Columbia: University of South Carolina Press, 1986).

ROBERT RAUSCHENBERG

1925-

ARTIST

Representative Artist. One of the most respected and representive artists of the 1960s, Robert Rauschenberg experimented with a variety of new styles during the decade. Like those of Jasper Johns, Rauschenberg's works bridge the transition from abstract expressionism to pop art and beyond. He was among a handful of contemporary artists to have work presented in a retrospective. At the Jewish Museum of New York in 1963 many of his "combine" paintings, which feature assorted materials such as photographs, newspapers, clocks, and stuffed animals, were displayed to an appreciative public. Similarly, an exhibition of his work at Whitechapel Gallery in London broke previous attendance records. The following year he won two million lire in the prestigious Venice Biennale. He was the first American to win the prize.

Pioneering New Styles. During the 1960s Rauschenberg also helped to design sets for experimental modern dances staged by Merce Cunningham to the equally experimental music of John Cage, and in the late 1960s he became identified as one of the artists involved in a new style called luminal art, which featured movement and light as integral aspects of the work. In 1968, when "environments" were all the rage in the art world, Rauschenberg was praised for his efforts, particularly one in which people walked through a thirty-six-foot-long room as the sounds they made triggered the projection of a series of images onto a wall.

Later Career. In the 1970s Rauschenberg became involved with performance art and other experimental styles, and he continued to influence many young artists.

Sources:
Mary Lynn Kotz, *Rauschenberg, Art and Life* (New York: Abrams, 1990);

Calvin Tomkins, *Off the Wall: Robert Rauschenberg and the Art World of Our Time* (Garden City, N.Y.: Doubleday, 1980).

BARBRA STREISAND

1942-

SINGER, ACTRESS

Funny Girl. Barbra Streisand first came to the attention of audiences and critics with a small role in *I Can Get It for You Wholesale* (1962), her first Broadway role, in which she stopped the show. In her second, as Fanny Brice in *Funny Girl* (1964), she *was* the show. The musical was critically acclaimed primarily for the presence of this young singer and comedian from Brooklyn, and it ran for a total of 1,348 performances.

If You Ain't Got Elegance. A star was born: Streisand recorded three albums in 1963 and 1964 and made several television appearances in addition to her stage work. She took the role of Fanny Brice to the London production of the musical and to the screen in the 1968 film version. Not only was the movie very popular, but it also earned her an Academy Award for Best Actress, making her the first to win that award for a first film. She also starred in the 1969 film version of *Hello, Dolly!*

Stage Fright. Though hugely popular, she retired from stage performances in 1968 due to extreme stage fright, focusing instead on films and recordings. She returned to live performances in 1994.

Source:
Shaun Considine, *Barbra Streisand: The Woman, the Myth, the Music* (New York: Delacorte, 1985).

KURT VONNEGUT, JR.

1922-

NOVELIST

A Writer for Youth. Kurt Vonnegut, Jr., entered the 1960s regarded as a promising but obscure science-fiction writer and left it as one of the most respected and popular figures of American literature. In particular, he was adopted by young readers on college campuses as a guru of sorts, one of the few people over thirty who could be trusted, given his cynical view of society.

From the Science-Fiction Ghetto. Since his fiction before 1960 typically used futuristic settings to critique American society, mainstream publishers shunned his work as science fiction, leading him to publish it in science-fiction magazines and paperbacks — both the kiss of death during the 1950s as far as critics were concerned. Even when he turned to World War II as a setting in his novel *Mother Night* (1962) publishers and critics refused to see him as anything but a "popular".

To Literary Stardom. Vonnegut persevered. His next novel, *Cat's Cradle* (1963), included science-fiction elements in a contemporary setting, and *God Bless You, Mr. Rosewater* (1965), though a realistic novel, introduced the eccentric science-fiction writer Kilgore Trout. Neither was a best-seller, but both were enthusiastically received by critics, who praised Vonnegut for his humor and his perceptive critiques of society. Vonnegut's next novel, *Slaughterhouse-Five* (1969), reversed the author's literary fortunes.

Of World War II and Tralfamadorians. In some respects *Slaughterhouse-Five* is a very experimental book: the narrative is fragmented rather than straightforward, the novel is metafictional since the narrator reveals himself to be the author, and it mixes science fiction with a black-humor account of Vonnegut's experiences in World War II. Like all of his fiction, though, it is written in an accessible style. These elements, however, fail to account for the immense popularity of the novel, since Vonnegut employed them to varying degrees in his earlier fiction. By the late 1960s, however, young readers comfortable with science fiction and supportive of the antiwar stance of the novel hailed it as a powerful statement against the Vietnam War and in support of their values. At the same time, professors, critics, and publishers "discovered" Vonnegut, leading to respectful articles and reviews and the rerelease of several of his earlier books in hardcover.

Sources:

William Rodney Allen, *Understanding Kurt Vonnegut* (Columbia: University of South Carolina Press, 1990);

Jerome Klinkowitz, *Kurt Vonnegut* (London & New York: Methuen, 1982);

Klinkowitz and Donald L. Lawler, eds., *Vonnegut in America* (New York: Delacorte, 1977).

ANDY WARHOL

1930-1987

ARTIST

More Than Fifteen Minutes of Fame. Andy Warhol is the pop artist known to many in the general public for saying that at some point everyone will be famous for fifteen minutes. During the 1960s Warhol himself was famous for much longer, a celebrity to both artists and the public alike. No other artist, with the possible exception of Truman Capote, was invited to as many parties and as noted for his extravagant behavior.

Pop Artist. In the early 1960s Warhol went from being a shy artist from Pennsylvania who supported himself in advertising to the flamboyant enfant terrible of pop art and the avant-garde art scene in New York. He used Campbell's Soup cans, Brillo boxes, and photographs of movie stars (notably Marilyn Monroe) as subjects. His mass-produced paintings employ silk-screening rather than conventional brush strokes, both commenting on and celebrating the commercialization of art. Similarly, he promoted himself as an artist, becoming a self-made celebrity. A failed assassination attempt in 1968 made headlines when a disgruntled actress who had appeared in one of his films critically wounded him.

Other Ventures. In 1963 he formed the Factory, a collection of artists and actors who made highly experimental films — including *Sleep* (1963), an eight-hour-long movie of a man sleeping — and other creations. He also became the manager of the rock group the Velvet Underground, which was unpopular at the time but proved highly influential in the following decades.

Still Controversial. Warhol's work has always been controversial, both in content and technique. Detractors claim he was more of a con artist than an artist, while his supporters praise his work as both a critique and an affirmation of popular culture and the connection between money and art.

Sources:

Victor Bockris, *The Life and Death of Andy Warhol* (New York: Bantam, 1989);

David Bourdon, *Warhol* (New York: Abrams, 1989);

Kynaston McShine, ed., *Andy Warhol: A Retrospective* (New York: Museum of Modern Art / Boston: Little, Brown, 1989).

PEOPLE IN THE NEWS

Contralto **Marian Anderson** gave her farewell concert at Carnegie Hall on 18 April 1965, bringing her thirty-year career to a close.

Jazz trumpeter **Louis Armstrong** began a goodwill tour of Africa, partially sponsored by the U.S. State Department, on 13 October 1960 to enthusiastic acclaim.

The New York City Ballet, under the artistic direction of **George Balanchine,** made an acclaimed tour of Russia. It was his first visit to his homeland in forty years.

On 15 March 1964 British actor **Richard Burton** married **Elizabeth Taylor** after a highly publicized romance and after the two divorced their respective spouses. It was his second marriage and her fifth.

In November 1966 writer **Truman Capote** hosted an extravagant Black and White Ball in New York — a masquerade for which attire was limited to those two colors. Its guest list of 540 included prominent figures in the arts, the sciences, politics, and high society.

Noted musician **Ray Charles** was arrested in 1965 for possession of heroin, to which he had been addicted since age sixteen. After one year in rehabilitation, he returned to performances and recording in full force.

A new dance craze shared by both teens and adults was started in 1960 by rock 'n' roll performer **Chubby Checker**'s recording of "The Twist." The popularity of the song and the dance set off a series of "no-touch" dances. In May 1962 former president **Dwight D. Eisenhower** notes that the dance represents "some kind of change" from more formal dances.

MacBird by young playwright **Barbara Garson** was a succès de scandale with its treatment of a politician who, encouraged by his wife Lady MacBird, has President John Ken O'Dunc assassinated. The book, published by Garson and her husband's Grassy Knoll Press, was published in 1966 and sold 105,000 copies before the play itself opened in New York on 22 February 1967 to a successful run.

In 1962 heiress **Rebekah Harkness** became the primary supporter of the Joffrey Ballet, headed by **Robert Joffrey.** Two years later she took over the company, renaming it the Harkness Ballet, forcing Joffrey to make a new start. His City Center Joffrey Ballet, with the help of a Ford Foundation grant, premiered in 1965.

After a twelve-year "retirement" from public performance, pianist **Vladimir Horowitz** returned to the stage at Carnegie Hall on 9 May 1965. He "retired" again from 1969 to 1974.

Gospel singer **Mahalia Jackson** sang "Precious Lord, Take My Hand" at the funeral for Martin Luther King, Jr., in April 1968.

In 1966 Beatle **John Lennon** claimed that the group was "more popular than Jesus." He later apologized for the remark. Though some disc jockeys in the South refused to play their albums, their 1966 American tour was a success.

Pulitzer Prize–winning poet **Robert Lowell** declined an invitation to the thirteen-hour 14 June White House Festival of the Arts in a 2 June 1965 letter to President Johnson, citing "dismay and distrust" of U.S. foreign policy.

In 1961 the divorce of playwright **Arthur Miller** and actress **Marilyn Monroe,** who had married in 1956, was announced.

In 1968 eighty-year-old poet **Marianne Moore,** an avid baseball fan, threw the first pitch on opening day at Yankee Stadium.

Russian-born ballet dancer **Rudolf Nureyev** and **Dame Margot Fonteyn** were the stars of an extremely successful tour of Britain's Royal Ballet in America in 1965. The young Nureyev was a particular draw, becoming one of the biggest stars in ballet in decades.

Pablo Picasso, easily the most famous living artist by the middle of the twentieth century, celebrated his eightieth birthday on 25 October 1961. Several museums staged exhibits in his honor, and in 1962 nine New York galleries showed the entire spectrum of his lengthy and prolific career in its various phases and periods. This was followed by a summer-long exhibit at the Museum of Modern Art.

In 1960 rock 'n' roll star **Elvis Presley** was released from the army after two years of service.

On 31 January 1963 sixteen-year-old pianist **André Watts** filled in at the last minute for Glenn Gould with the New York Philharmonic, conducted by Leonard Bernstein. His performance of Franz Liszt's E-flat Concerto was a major success, launching a promising career.

AWARDS

PULITZER PRIZES

1960

Fiction: *Advise and Consent*, by **Allen Drury**

Drama: *Fiorello!*, by **George Abbott, Jerome Weidman, Sheldon Harnick,** and **Jerry Bock**

Poetry: *Heart's Needle*, by **W. D. Snodgrass**

Music: *Second String Quartet*, by **Elliott Carter**

1961

Fiction: *To Kill a Mockingbird*, by **Harper Lee**

Drama: *All the Way Home*, by **Tad Mosel**

Poetry: *Times Three: Selected Verse from Three Decades*, by **Phyllis McGinley**

Music: *Symphony No. 7*, by **Walter Piston**

1962

Fiction: *The Edge of Sadness*, by **Edwin O'Connor**

Drama: *How to Succeed in Business without Really Trying*, by **Frank Loesser** and **Abe Burrows**

Poetry: *Poems*, by **Alan Dugan**

Music: *The Crucible*, by **Robert Ward**

1963

Fiction: *The Reivers*, by **William Faulkner**

Drama: no award

Poetry: *Pictures from Brueghel*, by **William Carlos Williams**

Music: *Piano Concerto No. 1*, by **Samuel Barber**

1964

Fiction: no award

Drama: no award

Poetry: *At the End of the Open Road*, by **Louis Simpson**

Music: no award

1965

Fiction: *The Keepers of the House*, by **Shirley Ann Grau**

Drama: *The Subject Was Roses*, by **Frank Gilroy**

Poetry: *77 Dream Songs*, by **John Berryman**

Music: no award

1966

Fiction: *The Collected Stories of Katherine Anne Porter*, by **Katherine Anne Porter**

Drama: no award

Poetry: *Selected Poems (1930–1965)*, by **Richard Eberhart**

Music: *Variations for Orchestra*, by **Leslie Bassett**

1967

Fiction: *The Fixer*, by **Bernard Malamud**

Drama: *A Delicate Balance*, by **Edward Albee**

Poetry: *Live or Die*, by **Anne Sexton**

Music: *Quartet No. 3*, by **Leon Kirchner**

1968

Fiction: *The Confessions of Nat Turner*, by **William Styron**

Drama: no award

Poetry: *The Hard Hours*, by **Anthony Hecht**

Music: *Echoes of Time and the River*, by **George Crumb**

1969

Fiction: *House Made of Dawn*, by **N. Scott Momaday**

Drama: *The Great White Hope*, by **Howard Sackler**

Poetry: *Of Being Numerous*, by **George Oppen**

Music: *String Quartet No. 3*, by **Karel Husa**

THE AMERICAN THEATRE WING ANTOINETTE PERRY AWARDS (TONY AWARDS)

1960

Play: *The Miracle Worker*, **William Gibson**

Actor, Dramatic Star: **Melvyn Douglas**, *The Best Man*

Actress, Dramatic Star: **Anne Bancroft**, *The Miracle Worker*

Musical: *Fiorello!* and *The Sound of Music*

Actor, Musical Star: **Jackie Gleason**, *Take Me Along*

Actress, Musical Star: **Mary Martin**, *The Sound of Music*

1961

Play: *Becket*, **Jean Anouilh**, translated by Lucienne Hill

Actor, Dramatic Star: **Zero Mostel**, *Rhinoceros*

Actress, Dramatic Star: **Joan Plowright**, *A Taste of Honey*

Musical: *Bye, Bye, Birdie*

Actor, Musical Star: **Richard Burton**, *Camelot*

Actress, Musical Star: **Elizabeth Seal**, *Irma la Douce*

1962

Play: *A Man for All Seasons*, **Robert Bolt**

Actor, Dramatic Star: **Paul Scofield**, *A Man for All Seasons*

Actress, Dramatic Star: **Margaret Leighton**, *Night of the Iguana*

Musical: *How to Succeed in Business without Really Trying*

Actor, Musical Star: **Robert Morse**, *How to Succeed in Business without Really Trying*

Actress, Musical Star: **Anna Maria Alberghetti**, *Carnival,* and **Diahann Carroll**, *No Strings*

1963

Play: *Who's Afraid of Virginia Woolf?*, **Edward Albee**

Actor, Dramatic Star: **Arthur Hill**, *Who's Afraid of Virginia Woolf?*

Actress, Dramatic Star: **Uta Hagen**, *Who's Afraid of Virginia Woolf?*

Musical: *A Funny Thing Happened on the Way to the Forum*

Actor, Musical Star: **Zero Mostel**, *A Funny Thing Happened on the Way to the Forum*

Actress, Musical Star: **Vivien Leigh**, *Tovarich*

1964

Play: *Luther*, **John Osborne**

Actor, Dramatic Star: **Alec Guinness**, *Dylan*

Actress, Dramatic Star: **Sandy Dennis**, *Any Wednesday*

Musical: *Hello, Dolly!*

Actor, Musical Star: **Bert Lahr**, *Foxy*

Actress, Musical Star: **Carol Channing**, *Hello, Dolly!*

1965

Play: *The Subject Was Roses*, **Frank Gilroy**

Actor, Dramatic Star: **Walter Matthau**, *The Odd Couple*

Actress, Dramatic Star: **Irene Worth**, *Tiny Alice*

Musical: *Fiddler on the Roof*

Actor, Musical Star: **Zero Mostel**, *Fiddler on the Roof*

Actress, Musical Star: **Liza Minnelli**, *Flora, the Red Menace*

1966

Play: *The Persecution and Assassination of Jean-Paul Marat as Performed by the Inmates of the Asylum of Charenton under the Direction of the Marquis de Sade*, **Peter Weiss**

Actor, Dramatic Star: **Hal Holbrook**, *Mark Twain Tonight!*

Actress, Dramatic Star: **Rosemary Harris**, *The Lion in Winter*

Musical: *Man of La Mancha*

Actor, Musical Star: **Richard Kiley**, *Man of La Mancha*

Actress, Musical Star: **Angela Lansbury**, *Mame*

1967

Play: *The Homecoming*, **Harold Pinter**

Actor, Dramatic Star: **Paul Rogers**, *The Homecoming*

Actress, Dramatic Star: **Beryl Reid**, *The Killing of Sister George*

Musical: *Cabaret*

Actor, Musical Star: **Robert Preston**, *I Do! I Do!*

Actress, Musical Star: **Barbara Harris**, *The Apple Tree*

1968

Play: *Rosencrantz and Guildenstern Are Dead*, **Tom Stoppard**

Actor, Dramatic Star: **Martin Balsam**, *You Know I Can't Hear You When the Water's Running*

Actress, Dramatic Star: **Zoe Caldwell**, *The Prime of Miss Jean Brodie*

Musical: *Hallelujah, Baby!*

Actor, Musical Star: **Robert Goulet**, *The Happy Time*

Actress, Musical Star: **Patricia Routledge**, *Darling of the Day*, and **Leslie Uggams**, *Hallelujah, Baby!*

1969

Play: *The Great White Hope*, **Howard Sackler**

Actor, Dramatic Star: **James Earl Jones**, *The Great White Hope*

Actress, Dramatic Star: **Julie Harris**, *Forty Carats*

Musical: *1776*

Actor, Musical Star: **Jerry Orbach**, *Promises, Promises*

Actress, Musical Star: **Angela Lansbury**, *Dear World*

ACADEMY OF MOTION PICTURE ARTS AND SCIENCES AWARDS (THE OSCARS)

1960

Actor: **Burt Lancaster**, *Elmer Gantry*

Actress: **Elizabeth Taylor**, *Butterfield 8*

Picture: *The Apartment*, **United Artists**

1961

Actor: **Maximilian Schell**, *Judgment at Nuremberg*

Actress: **Sophia Loren**, *Two Women*

Picture: *West Side Story*, **United Artists**

1962

Actor: **Gregory Peck**, *To Kill a Mockingbird*

Actress: **Anne Bancroft**, *The Miracle Worker*

Picture: *Lawrence of Arabia*, **Columbia**

1963

Actor: **Sidney Poitier**, *Lilies of the Field*

Actress: **Patricia Neal**, *Hud*

Picture: *Tom Jones*, **United Artists-Lopert**

1964

Actor: **Rex Harrison**, *My Fair Lady*

Actress: **Julie Andrews**, *Mary Poppins*

Picture: *My Fair Lady*, **Warner Bros.**

1965

Actor: **Lee Marvin**, *Cat Ballou*

Actress: **Julie Christie**, *Darling*

Picture: *The Sound of Music*, **20th Century-Fox**

1966

Actor: **Paul Scofield**, *A Man for All Seasons*

Actress: **Elizabeth Taylor**, *Who's Afraid of Virginia Woolf?*

Picture: *A Man for All Seasons*, **Columbia**

1967

Actor: **Rod Steiger**, *In the Heat of the Night*

Actress: **Katharine Hepburn**, *Guess Who's Coming to Dinner?*

Picture: *In the Heat of the Night*, **United Artists**

1968

Actor: **Cliff Robertson**, *Charly*

Actress: **Katharine Hepburn**, *The Lion in Winter*, and **Barbra Streisand**, *Funny Girl*

Picture: *Oliver!*, **Columbia**

1969

Actor: **John Wayne**, *True Grit*

Actress: **Maggie Smith**, *The Prime of Miss Jean Brodie*

Picture: *Midnight Cowboy*, **United Artists**

DEATHS

Gracie Allen, 58, comedian, wife and partner of George Burns, 27 August 1964.

Laverne Andrews, 51, oldest of the singing trio the Andrews Sisters, 8 May 1967.

Fay Bainter, 74, stage and film actress, 16 April 1968.

Tallulah Bankhead, 65, stage and screen star, 12 December 1968.

Diana Barrymore, 38, stage and film actress, 25 January 1960.

Vicki Baum, 64, novelist (*Grand Hotel*), playwright, and screenwriter, 29 August 1960.

William Baziotes, 52, abstract painter, 5 June 1963.

Sylvia Beach, 75, supporter of American writers in Paris and first publisher of James Joyce's 1922 novel *Ulysses*, 6 October 1962.

William Bendix, 58, film actor (*The Hairy Ape, The Babe Ruth Story*), 14 December 1964.

R. P. Blackmur, 61, literary critic, 2 February 1965.

Marc Blitzstein, 58, composer and translator of Bertolt Brecht and Kurt Weill's *The Threepenny Opera*, 22 January 1964.

Charles Boni, 74, cofounder of the Modern Library and of the publishing house Boni and Liveright, 14 February 1969.

Anthony Boucher (William Anthony Parker White), 56, writer, critic, and editor of mystery stories and science fiction, 29 April 1968.

Clara Bow, 60, sex symbol of the silent screen known as "the It Girl," 26 September 1965.

Charles Brackett, film writer and producer (*Sunset Boulevard*), 9 March 1969.

Van Wyck Brooks, 77, literary critic and historian, 2 May 1963.

Lenny Bruce, 40, controversial comedian, 3 August 1966.

Eugene Leonard Burdick, 46, collaborator on best-selling novels *The Ugly American* and *Fail-Safe,* 26 July 1965.

Eddie Cantor, 72, vaudeville, radio, film and television actor, 10 October 1964.

Neal Cassady, 41, Beat Generation inspiration, 4 February 1968.

Montgomery Clift, 45, film actor (*From Here to Eternity*), 23 July 1966.

Patsy Cline, 30, country singer ("Crazy," "Walkin' after Midnight"), 5 March 1963.

Nat "King" Cole, 45, popular pianist and singer ("Unforgettable," "Mona Lisa"), 15 February 1965.

John Coltrane, 40, innovative jazz saxophonist, 7 July 1967.

Gary Cooper, 60, Academy Award–winning movie star (*Sergeant York, High Noon*), 13 May 1961.

E. E. Cummings, 67, popular experimental poet, 3 September 1962.

Dorothy Dandridge, 41, singer and film actor (*Porgy and Bess, Carmen Jones*), 8 September 1965.

Sabu Dastagir, 39, film actor (*The Jungle Book, The Thief of Baghdad*), 2 December 1963.

Walt Disney, 65, animator, film producer, and theme-park impresario, 15 December 1966.

H. D. (Hilda Doolittle), 75, poet, 27 September 1961.

W. E. B. DuBois, 95, founder of the National Association for the Advancement of Colored People, author (*The Souls of Black Folk*), 27 August 1963.

Marcel Duchamp, 81, influential French-born sculptor and painter (*Nude Descending a Staircase*), 1 October 1968.

Margaret Dumont, 75, actress and frequent foil for the Marx Brothers, 23 March 1965.

Max Eastman, 86, revolutionary writer and editor, 25 March 1969.

Nelson Eddy, 65, singer and costar with Jeanette MacDonald on several romantic films, 6 March 1967.

T. S. Eliot, 76, Nobel Prize–winning poet, critic, and dramatist, 4 January 1965.

Brian Epstein, 32, British discoverer and manager of the Beatles, 27 August 1967.

William Faulkner, 64, major Nobel Prize–winning novelist and short-story writer (*The Sound and the Fury, Absalom, Absalom!*), 6 July 1962.

Edna Ferber, 82, popular playwright and novelist (*Show Boat, Giant*), 16 April 1968.

James Montgomery Flagg, 82, American illustrator, creator of World War I recruitment poster featuring Uncle Sam saying, "I Want You," 27 May 1960.

Clyde Julian "Red" Foley, 58, country musician, 19 September 1968.

Alan Freed, 42, disc jockey credited with popularizing rock 'n' roll, 20 January 1965.

Leo Friedlander, 78, sculptor, 24 October 1964.

Robert Frost, 88, acclaimed American poet ("Stopping by Woods on a Snowy Evening," "The Road Not Taken"), 29 January 1963.

Clark Gable, 59, American movie actor (*It Happened One Night, Gone with the Wind*), 16 November 1960.

Howard R. Garis, 89, author and creator of "Uncle Wiggily" stories for children, 5 November 1962.

Judy Garland, 47, film star famous for her role as Dorothy in *The Wizard of Oz*, 22 June 1969.

John Gassner, 64, playwright and critic, 2 April 1967.

Hugo Gernsback, 83, founder of *Amazing Stories,* the first science-fiction magazine, in 1926 and originator of term *science fiction,* 19 August 1967.

Edmund Richard "Hoot" Gibson, 70, film actor known for cowboy roles, 23 August 1961.

William Goetz, 66, film producer and one of the cofounders of 20th Century-Fox and Universal, 15 August 1969.

Michael Gold, 74, proletarian writer (*Jews without Money*), 14 May 1967.

Woody Guthrie, 55, influential folk musician and composer ("This Land Is Your Land"), 3 October 1967.

Moses Hadas, 66, prominent scholar and translator of classical literature, 17 August 1966.

Edith Hamilton, 95, well-known classicist (*Mythology*), 31 May 1963.

Oscar Hammerstein II, 65, Broadway lyricist and librettist, collaborator with Richard Rodgers on musicals (*Oklahoma!, The King and I, South Pacific*), 23 August 1960

Dashiell Hammett, 66, renowned writer of hard-boiled detective fiction (*The Maltese Falcon, The Thin Man*), 10 January 1961.

Lorraine Hansberry, 34, playwright (*A Raisin in the Sun*), 12 January 1965.

Otto Harbach, 89, Broadway lyricist and librettist, 24 January 1963.

Moss Hart, 57, playwright, director, and screenwriter, 21 December 1961.

Coleman Hawkins, 64, jazz saxophonist, 19 May 1969.

Gabby Hayes, 83, the archetypal Western sidekick, 9 February 1969.

Ben Hecht, 70, journalist, fiction writer, playwright, and screenwriter, 18 April 1964.

Ernest Hemingway, 61, Nobel Prize–winning writer (*The Sun Also Rises, A Farewell To Arms*), 2 July 1961.

Sonja Henie, 57, Olympic figure-skating champion who later starred in films, 12 October 1969.

Josephine Herbst, 76, writer, 28 January 1969.

Paul Hindemith, 68, German-born composer, 29 December 1963.

Hans Hofmann, 85, influential painter and teacher, 17 February 1966.

Judy Holliday, 42, Oscar-winning actress (*Born Yesterday*), 7 June 1965.

Edward Hopper, 84, painter (*Nighthawks*), 15 May 1967.

Louis Horst, 80, former husband of and collaborator with modern dance pioneer Martha Graham, 23 January 1964.

Langston Hughes, 65, major African-American poet and novelist, 22 May 1967.

Zora Neale Hurston, 59?, folklorist and novelist (*Their Eyes Were Watching God*), 28 January 1960.

Aldous Huxley, 69, British novelist (*Brave New World, Point Counter Point*) who spent his last years in America promoting experiments with religion and drugs, 22 November 1963.

Shirley Jackson, 45, noted writer of novels and short stories ("The Lottery"), 8 August 1965.

Randall Jarrell, 51, poet and critic, 14 October 1965.

Robinson Jeffers, 75, Pulitzer Prize–winning poet and playwright, 20 January 1962.

Spike Jones, 53, popular bandleader, 1 May 1965.

Helen Kane, 62, "boop-boop-a-doop" singer of the 1920s and 1930s ("I Wanna Be Loved by You"), 26 September 1966.

Boris Karloff, 81, British star of American horror films, 2 February 1969.

George S. Kaufman, 71, Pulitzer Prize–winning playwright, director, and producer, 2 June 1961.

Buster Keaton, 70, silent-film comedian, 1 February 1966.

Jack Kerouac, 47, Beat Generation novelist (*On the Road*), 21 October 1969.

Franz Kline, 51, abstract expressionist painter, 13 May 1962.

Ernie Kovacs, 42, television and movie comedian, 13 January 1962.

Fritz Kreisler, 86, Austrian-born violinist and composer, 29 January 1962.

Alan Ladd, 50, film actor (*Shane*), 29 January 1964.

Oliver La Farge, 61, supporter of American Indians and Pulitzer Prize–winning author (*Laughing Boy*), 2 August 1963.

Bert Lahr, 72, Broadway, radio, television, and film actor best known for his role as the Cowardly Lion in *The Wizard of Oz*, 4 December 1967.

Nella Larsen, 72, novelist of the Harlem Renaissance, 30 March 1964.

Charles Laughton, 63, Academy Award–winning stage and film actor, 15 December 1962.

Stan Laurel, 74, of the classic Laurel and Hardy comedy team, 23 February 1965.

Vivien Leigh, 53, Oscar-winning British stage and film actress remembered for playing Scarlett O'Hara in *Gone with the Wind*, 8 July 1967.

Frank Loesser, 59, Broadway composer and lyricist (*Guys and Dolls*), 28 July 1969.

Peter Lorre, 59, Hungarian-born film actor (*M, Casablanca*), 23 March 1964.

Mina Loy, 83, poet, 25 September 1966.

Jeanette MacDonald, 57, soprano and star of 1930s romantic films with Nelson Eddy, 14 January 1965.

Jayne Mansfield, 34, film actress, 29 June 1967.

John P. Marquand, 66, Pulitzer Prize–winning author, 15 July 1960.

Chico Marx, 70, the "Italian," piano-playing Marx Brother, 11 October 1961.

Harpo Marx, 70, the silent, harp-playing Marx Brother, 28 September 1964.

Carson McCullers, 50, southern playwright, short-story writer, and novelist (*The Member of the Wedding, The Ballad of the Sad Cafe*), 29 September 1967.

Jimmy McHugh, 74, composer for movies and Broadway ("I'm in the Mood for Love"), 23 May 1969.

Adolphe Menjou, 73, elegant movie actor (*The Front Page, A Farewell to Arms*), 29 October 1963.

Helen Menken, 64, Broadway actress and president of the American Theater Wing, 27 March 1966.

Grace Metalious, 39, author of the best-selling novel *Peyton Place*, 25 February 1964.

Dimitri Mitropoulos, 64, Greek-born conductor, 2 November 1960.

Marilyn Monroe, 36, sex symbol and film actress (*Gentlemen Prefer Blondes, The Seven-Year Itch*), 5 August 1962.

Wes Montgomery, 45, jazz guitarist, 15 June 1968.

Douglas Stuart Moore, 75, composer of folk operas, 25 July 1969.

Anna Mary Robertson ("Grandma") Moses, 101, painter who started at age seventy-six and created more than one thousand paintings, 13 December 1961.

Charles Munch, 77, conductor of the Boston Symphony Orchestra from 1949 to 1962, 6 November 1968.

Paul Muni, 71, stage and screen actor (*Inherit the Wind*), 25 August 1967.

Red Nichols, 60, jazz musician and bandleader, 28 June 1965.

Edwin O'Connor, 49, Pulitzer Prize–winning novelist, 23 March 1968.

Flannery O'Connor, 39, Southern fiction writer, 3 August 1964.

Clifford Odets, 57, writer of protest plays (*Waiting for Lefty*), 14 August 1963.

Frank O'Hara, 40, poet and critic of the New York School, 25 July 1966.

Dorothy Parker, 73, razor-tongued poet, short-story writer, and critic, one of the wits of the Algonquin Round Table, 7 June 1967.

Maxfield Parrish, 95, painter, 30 March 1966.

Sylvia Plath, 30, poet ("Daddy," "Lady Lazarus") and novelist (*The Bell Jar*), 11 February 1963.

Cole Porter, 71, Broadway composer and lyricist (*Kiss Me, Kate*), 15 October 1964.

Earl "Bud" Powell, 41, jazz pianist, innovator in bebop with Duke Ellington and Charlie "Bird" Parker in the 1940s, 1 August 1966.

Claude Rains, 77, British-born film actor (*Casablanca, The Invisible Man*), 30 May 1967.

Otis Redding, 26, popular singer ("[Sittin' on] The Dock of the Bay"), 10 December 1967.

Fritz Reiner, 74, Hungarian-born conductor, 15 November 1963.

Elmer Rice, 74, playwright (*The Adding Machine*), 8 May 1967.

Conrad Richter, 78, Pulitzer Prize–winning novelist, 30 October 1968.

Henry Morton Robinson, 62, best-selling novelist (*The Cardinal*), 13 January 1961.

Theodore Roethke, 55, Pulitzer Prize–winning poet, 1 August 1963.

Billy Rose, 66, Broadway producer and songwriter ("Me and My Shadow"), 10 February 1966.

Ruth St. Denis, 91, one of the creators of modern dance and teacher of Martha Graham, 21 July 1968.

Carl Sandburg, 89, poet and biographer of Abraham Lincoln, 22 July 1967.

Joseph M. Schenck, 82, Russian-born film pioneer, one of the founders of 20th Century-Fox, 22 October 1961.

Delmore Schwartz, 52, poet and critic, 11 July 1966.

Evelyn Scott, 70, novelist, 3 August 1963.

David O. Selznick, 63, Hollywood producer (*Gone with the Wind, The Wizard of Oz*), 22 June 1965.

Mack Sennett, 76, movie director (the Keystone Kops), 5 November 1960.

Ben Shahn, 70, Lithuanian-born artist, 14 March 1969.

Upton Sinclair, 90, socialist writer (*The Jungle*), 25 November 1968.

Cordwainer Smith (Paul Myron Anthony Linebarger), 53, science-fiction writer, 6 August 1966.

E. E. "Doc" Smith, 75, science-fiction writer, 1 September 1965.

John Steinbeck, 66, Nobel Prize–winning fiction writer (*Of Mice and Men, The Grapes of Wrath*), 20 December 1968.

Billy Strayhorn, 51, jazz pianist, arranger, and composer ("Take the A Train"), partner of Duke Ellington for twenty-six years, 10 June 1967.

Ruth Suckow, 67, novelist, 23 January 1960.

Sharon Tate, 26, actress and wife of director Roman Polanski murdered by Charles Manson's followers, 8 August 1969.

Deems Taylor, 80, pioneer in American opera, 3 July 1966.

Jack Teagarden, 58, jazz trombonist and vocalist, 15 January 1964.

James Thurber, 66, cartoonist and writer ("The Secret Life of Walter Mitty"), 2 November 1961.

Alice B. Toklas, 89, author and companion of Gertrude Stein, 7 March 1967.

Melvin B. Tolson, 68, poet, 29 August 1966.

Jean Toomer, 72, poet and fiction writer of the Harlem Renaissance (*Cane*), 30 March 1967.

Spencer Tracy, 67, Oscar-winning movie actor (*Boys' Town, Adam's Rib, Captains Courageous*), 19 June 1967.

B. Traven (Berick Traven Torsvan), 79, mysterious writer (*The Treasure of the Sierra Madre*), 27 March 1969.

Sophie Tucker, 79, singer billed as "the last of the red-hot mamas," 9 February 1966.

Carl Van Vechten, 84, critic and novelist (*Nigger Heaven*), 21 December 1964.

Edgard Varèse, 81, French-born composer, innovator in electronic music, 6 November 1965.

Bruno Walter, 85, German-born conductor, 17 February 1962.

Walter Wanger, 74, movie producer (*Stagecoach, Cleopatra*), 18 November 1968.

Dinah Washington, 39, blues singer, 14 December 1963.

William Carlos Williams, 79, poet and pediatrician, 4 March 1963.

Yvor Winters, 67, poet and critic, 25 January 1968.

Richard Wright, 52, novelist (*Native Son*) and autobiographer (*Black Boy*), 28 November 1960.

Ed Wynn, 79, radio, television, and stage performer known as "The Perfect Fool," later a successful dramatic actor (*Requiem for a Heavyweight*), 19 June 1966.

PUBLICATIONS

Movies

Carlos Clarens, *An Illustrated History of the Horror Film* (New York: Putnam, 1967);

Bosley Crowther, *The Great Films: Fifty Golden Years of Motion Pictures* (New York: Putnam, 1967);

George N. Fenin and William K. Everson, *The Western* (New York: Orion, 1963);

Pauline Kael, *Kiss Kiss Bang Bang* (Boston: Atlantic-Little, Brown, 1968);

Dwight Macdonald, *Dwight Macdonald on Movies* (New York: Prentice Hall, 1969);

Andrew Sarris, *The American Cinema: Directors and Directions, 1929–1968* (New York: Dutton, 1968);

Richard Schickel, *The Disney Version: The Life, Times, Art and Commerce of Walt Disney* (New York: Simon & Schuster, 1968);

Film Culture, periodical.

Music

Jonathan Eisen, *The Age of Rock: Sounds of the American Cultural Revolution — A Reader* (New York: Random House, 1969);

Orrin Keepnews and Bill Grauer, Jr., *A Pictorial History of Jazz*, second edition (New York: Crown, 1966);

George Martin, *The Opera Companion* (New York: Dodd, 1961);

Wilfrid Mellers, *Music in a New Found Land* (New York: Knopf, 1965);

Henry Pleasants, *Serious Music — And All That Jazz!* (New York: Simon & Schuster, 1969);

Harold C. Schoenberg, *The Great Conductors* (New York: Simon & Schuster, 1967);

Schoenberg, *The Great Pianists* (New York: Simon & Schuster, 1963);

Peter Yates, *Twentieth Century Music: Its Evolution from the End of the Harmonic Era into the Present Era of Sound* (New York: Pantheon, 1967);

Down Beat, periodical;

Opera News, periodical;

Rolling Stone, periodical.

Dance

John Martin, *John Martin's Book of the Dance* (New York: Tudor, 1963);

Olga Maynard, *The American Ballet* (New York: Macrae, 1960).

Literature and Theater

Nona Balakian and Charles Simmons, eds., *The Creative Present* (Garden City, N.Y.: Doubleday, 1963);

Eric Bentley, *The Life of the Drama* (New York: Atheneum, 1964);

Frederick C. Crews, *The Pooh Perplex* (New York: Dutton, 1963);

William Jovanovich, *Now, Barabbas* (New York: Harper & Row, 1964);

Roy Harvey Pearce, *The Continuity of American Poetry* (Princeton: Princeton University Press, 1962);

Charles Rembar, *The End of Obscenity: The Trials of Lady Chatterley, Tropic of Cancer, and Fanny Hill* (New York: Random House, 1968);

René Wellek, *Concepts of Criticism* (New Haven: Yale University Press, 1963);

Drama Review, periodical;

Publishers Weekly, periodical.

Art

Harold Rosenberg, *The Anxious Object: Art Today and Its Audience* (New York: Horizon, 1965);

Alan Solomon, *New York: The New Art Scene* (New York: Holt, Rinehart and Winston, 1967);

Susan Sontag, *Against Interpretation and Other Essays* (New York: Farrar Straus & Giroux, 1966);

Art News, periodical.

The Grateful Dead in Haight-Ashbury, 1967

BUSINESS AND THE ECONOMY

by WILLIAM FRIEDRICKS

CONTENTS

Sidebars and tables are listed in italics.

1960

- The American farm population is 15.6 million or 8.7 percent of the total U.S. population.

- Defense spending and veterans' benefits account for nearly $50 billion or 56 percent of the federal budget and 10 percent of the Gross National Product (GNP).

- Lillian Vernon publishes the first mail-order catalogue.

- The median family income (in 1971 dollars) is $7,688.

- The per-capita national debt stands at $1,582.

- The U.S. automobile industry begins to shift to compact cars to meet falling sales and increased foreign imports.

- The United States launches seventeen space satellites including *Tiros 1,* the first weather satellite, which takes 22,952 pictures of Earth's cloud cover.

4 Jan. The longest steel strike in the nation's history is settled when steel companies and the United Steel Workers agree on a wage increase. The strike had started in July 1959.

15 May Taxes reach 25 percent of earnings, according to a Tax Foundation report that lumps together federal, state, and local taxes.

16 Nov. President Dwight Eisenhower orders the ending of overseas spending whenever possible to stop the outflow of gold from the United States.

18 Nov. Chrysler discontinues production of the De Soto automobile, which had been manufactured by the firm since 1928.

1961

- General Dynamics loses $143 million.

- President John Kennedy establishes the President's Commission on the Status of Women.

Jan. Demand for steel falls below 40 percent capacity.

31 Jan. In a Project Mercury test flight NASA launches a capsule containing a chimpanzee into space and recovers the animal successfully. The capsule travels 5,000 miles per hour and reaches a height of 155 miles.

6–7 Feb. A U.S. district judge finds twenty-nine large manufacturers of electrical equipment guilty of price-fixing. Penalties include thirty jail sentences and fines totaling nearly $2 million.

23 Feb. The costliest airline strike in history ends. The six-day strike grounds Eastern, TWA, Flying Tiger, American, and National airlines.

5 May President Kennedy signs the Fair Labor Standards Act increasing the minimum wage from $1.00 to $1.15 in September 1961 and to $1.25 in September 1963. Coverage is expanded to include 3.6 million workers not previously under minimum-wage law.

29 June Three satellites are launched by single rocket in the first triple launch in history.

1962

- In the first case decided under the Celler-Kefauver Amendment, the Supreme Court blocks proposed merger between Brown Shoe Company and retail chain Kinney Shoes.

- President Kennedy issues an executive order supporting union representation among federal employees as governmental policy.

- Use of nudity in advertising becomes a national controversy when Christina Paolozzi, a twenty-two-year-old model, appears nude in a full-page color ad in *Harper's Bazaar*.

18 Jan. A twenty-five-hour workweek, with five overtime hours, is established when electrical workers finish contract negotiations with employers in New York City.

1 Mar. In the biggest antitrust case to date, E. I. Du Pont de Nemours and Company is ordered by a federal district court to divest itself of sixty-three million shares of General Motors stock.

10 Apr. United States Steel announces a 3.5 percent price hike ($6 per ton) after signing a new union contract. Five other major steel producers follow suit. President Kennedy accuses the companies of defying the public interest by raising prices.

28 May The New York Stock Exchange experiences its greatest loss since 29 October 1919; shares on the exchange lose nearly $21 billion in value. The market rebounds quickly.

10 July *Telstar,* an experimental communications satellite owned and built by American Telephone and Telegraph and Bell Telephone Laboratories, is launched. It soon relays live television pictures from Andover, Maine, to Britain and France.

27 July In settlement of a price-fixing case, General Electric agrees to pay $7.5 million in damages for excess profits.

15 Sept. President Kennedy signs into law a $900 million public-works bill for projects in economically depressed areas.

4 Oct. Congress passes the Trade Expansion Act, designed to promote overseas trade through tariff reductions.

1963

- Automobile accidents result in 40,804 deaths, an all-time high.

- Avon's return on invested capital, 34.3 percent, is highest among *Fortune 500* companies.

- Five percent of automobiles sold in the United States are foreign imports.

- The first year two companies ever register more than $1 billion in profits; GM has a profit of $1.6 billion, Standard Oil of New Jersey a profit of $1 billion.

26 Jan. The longshoremen's strike ends; it ties up shipping for nearly a month and costs more than $800 million.

31 Mar. The 114-day New York City newspaper strike ends. It is the costliest newspaper strike ever with lost revenues estimated at $100 million.

3 June The Supreme Court rules that the agency-shop labor contract (one in which an employee is not required to join a union but must pay it the equivalent in dues and fees) is constitutional where permitted by a state.

8 June The American Heart Association opens a drive against cigarette smoking.

10 June President Kennedy signs a bill requiring equal pay for equal work regardless of sex.

1 July The United Brotherhood of Carpenters, the largest U.S. building-trade union, orders all its locals to end racial discrimination on construction sites.

1964

- Encyclopaedia Britannica purchases G. and C. Merriam Company.

- Ford introduces the Mustang (brought out in late 1964, it is in the 1965 model year).

26 Feb. The Tax Reduction Act reduces personal and corporate income-tax rates.

16 Apr. Texas Gulf Sulphur Company announces a major discovery of copper, silver, and zinc in Ontario, Canada.

14 June United Steelworkers and eleven major steel companies sign an agreement to end racial discrimination in the steel industry.

24 June The Federal Trade Commission announces that starting in 1965 cigarette packages must carry health warnings.

2 July President Johnson signs the Civil Rights Act of 1964 banning racial discrimination in public places and employment.

5 Aug. Congress creates the National Commission on Technology, Automation and Economic Progress to study the effects of automation on unemployment.

7 Aug. The Gulf of Tonkin Resolution passes Congress, giving President Johnson a free hand in Vietnam.

30 Aug. The Equal Opportunity Act is signed by President Johnson, providing $950 million for youth programs, community-action antipoverty measures, small-business loans, and the creation of the Job Corps.

25 Sept. After successful contract negotiations with Ford and Chrysler, the United Auto Workers strike General Motors when they fail to reach a contract agreement. The contract is signed on 5 October, but local strikers tie up production until 7 November.

1965

- The American farm population falls to 12.4 million or 6.4 percent of the total U.S. population.

- The GNP climbs from $628 billion to $672 billion, a 7 percent increase over the previous year.

- IBM introduces its third-generation computer, the 360, after spending $5 billion on its development.

- The number of color television sets in the United States tops five million.

- Total federal appropriations reach a record high — $119 billion — for peacetime; $47 billion was spent on defense.

- Unemployment falls to 4.2 percent, an eight-year low.

- Union membership stands at 18.5 million.

17 Feb. The moon probe *Ranger 8* is launched. It sends back over seven thousand photos of the moon's surface before crashing into the Sea of Tranquillity on 20 February.

9 May	Eight hundred retired employees of the Fifth Avenue Coach Lines in New York City receive a record arbitration award of more than $9 million. The bus line was taken over by the city in 1962; in 1964 courts had ruled that the company must continue to pay its obligations to retired employees.
28 July	President Johnson announces that U.S. troop levels in Vietnam will be increased from 75,000 to 125,000.
Oct.	The Water Quality Act provides the federal government with broad powers, especially in the area of oil-spill cleanup.
10 Nov.	Alcoa, the nation's largest aluminum producer, and three other companies' plans to raise the price of aluminum by 2 percent are scrapped when the government announces it will sell a portion of its aluminum stockpile.
5 Dec.	The Federal Reserve Board raises the discount rate from 4 percent to 4.5 percent, the highest rate in thirty-five years, in an attempt to curb inflation.

1966

- Branch bank offices account for almost 65 percent of all bank offices and control 70 percent of the country's banking resources.

- In *United States* v. *Von's Grocery Company* the Supreme Court stops the merger of Von's, a Los Angeles retail grocery-store chain that held only 4.7 percent of area sales, with Shopping Bag. Together they would have held 7.5 percent of the grocery market in Los Angeles.

- Inflation begins a steady rise.

- Studebaker ceases production of cars.

- Teachers across the United States stage thirty-six walkouts (only twenty-six had occurred in the entire previous decade).

- The Vietnam War steadily escalates: total casualties since 1 January 1961 are 6,664 killed and 37,738 wounded. By the end of year, the United States has nearly 400,000 troops in Southeast Asia.

9 Feb.	The New York Stock Exchange reaches the peak of a three-and-a-half-year bull market; the Dow Jones industrial average climbs to an all-time high of 995.
16 Mar.	*Gemini 8,* with crew Neil Armstrong and David Scott, makes the first successful space docking.
22 Mar.	General Motors president James Roche apologizes to Ralph Nader before a Senate subcommittee for spying on Nader's private life. Nader's book, *Unsafe at Any Speed* (1965), identifies GM's Corvair as dangerous.
6 Apr.	Headed by Cesar Chavez, the National Farm Workers Union, which had been striking California grape growers since September 1965, declares a major victory when it is recognized as the bargaining agent for farmworkers of Schenley Industries.
13 Apr.	Pan American Airways announces a major jet aircraft order — twenty-five new Boeing 747 jets to be delivered in 1969. The huge new aircraft is designed to carry up to five hundred passengers.

2 June   *Surveyor 1* makes the first soft landing on the moon.

8 June   A merger between the National Football League and the American Football League, going into effect in 1970, is announced.

1 July   The Medicare health-insurance plan for the elderly goes into effect.

9 Sept.   President Johnson signs the Traffic Safety Act, establishing safety standards for automobiles sold to the public.

7 Oct.   Stock prices tumble; the Dow Jones industrial average falls to 744. It is the worst market decline since 1962.

15 Oct.   The Department of Transportation, the twelfth cabinet department, is created.

11 Nov.   *Gemini 12* makes a successful rendezvous with the target vehicle. This is the last of the *Gemini* missions.

31 Dec.   President Johnson announces that the supersonic transport contract (SST) will be awarded to Boeing over Lockheed. The Boeing plane will carry three hundred passengers at speeds of up to eighteen hundred miles per hour. Cost of development is estimated at $6.4 billion.

1967

- One hundred twenty-five of *Fortune 500* companies report lower sales than they did in 1966; GM's profits of $1.6 billion are down 9.3 percent from 1966.

- NASA's Project Apollo, with the goal of landing a man on the moon, begins.

- The $69.9 billion defense appropriation is the single largest appropriation ever passed by Congress.

- The Air Quality Act gives the federal government sole responsibility for establishing clean-air standards.

- There are 1.8 million retail establishments in the United States.

15 Jan.   The Commerce Department announces that the GNP rose by 5.4 percent in 1966.

10 Mar.   The New York Stock Exchange has its second largest trading day to date, exceeded only by 29 October 1929.

11 May   The one hundred millionth telephone is installed in the United States. The country has approximately half the telephones in the world.

30 June   The General Agreement on Tariffs and Trade (GATT), the result of four years of negotiations, is signed in Geneva by the United States and forty-five other nations.

5 July   American Telephone and Telegraph (AT&T) is ordered by the FCC to decrease its long-distance and overseas telephone rates by $120 million per year.

22 July   The military announces that U.S. troop strength in Vietnam will reach 525,000 by the end of 1968.

26 July   The three-month strike by the United Rubber Workers ends when the union signs a three-year contract with the nation's largest tire manufacturers; Firestone announces price increases five days later.

1968

6 Sept. The United Auto Workers strikes the Ford Motor Company — nearly 160,000 workers are involved — when their contract expires. The union is seeking a 6 percent wage increase; the strike ends in October with a new three-year contract.

- The average price of a new single-family home is $26,600.

- Corporate after-tax profits increase to $47.8 billion.

- The GNP increases to $860 billion, a record 9 percent rise.

- The decade's merger movement peaks; twenty-five hundred mergers in manufacturing and mining companies occurred.

15 Jan. The Supreme Court approves the merger of the New York Central and Pennsylvania railroads, creating the largest railroad in the country. Two years later, in 1970, the merged firm, Penn-Central, collapses under bankruptcy.

Feb. Oil discovery in Prudhoe Bay, Alaska, is announced.

19 Feb. The first statewide teachers' strike in U.S. history begins when nearly half of Florida's public-school teachers walk off the job. The strike ends on 8 March.

18 Apr. The Bell Telephone System is struck for the first time in its history by 178,000 members of the Communications Workers Union. Although the strike has little impact on telephone service, a record-breaking settlement is announced in May, with workers receiving a wage increase of 19.58 percent over three years.

13 June A new record for shares exchanged is set on the New York Stock Exchange, with 2,350,000 shares traded.

28 June President Johnson signs a bill into law combining a 10 percent income-tax surcharge with a $6 billion cut in government spending.

1 July The United Auto Workers formally separates from the AFL-CIO. The split comes after years of feuding between UAW president Walter Reuther and AFL-CIO head George Meany. Three weeks later the UAW joins the Teamsters to form the Alliance for Labor Action.

30 July Eleven major steel producers reach an agreement with the United Steel Workers of America. The new three-year contract calls for an average annual wage increase of 6 percent. The following day Bethlehem Steel raises steel prices 5 percent; the price hike is lowered, however, when U.S. Steel raises its prices a more modest 2.5 percent on 7 August.

26 Sept. Mickey Mouse celebrates his fortieth birthday.

11 Oct. The first manned *Apollo* mission, *Apollo 7,* begins its eleven-day mission.

2 Nov. Funk and Wagnalls publishing firm is acquired by Reader's Digest.

Dec. The seasonally adjusted unemployment rate of 3.3 percent is the lowest since the Korean War.

1969

- The American farm population declines to 10.3 million or 5.1 percent of the total U.S. population.

- Control Data Corporation has the highest average growth rate of any *Fortune 500* company for the decade — 48.4 percent.

- The GNP rises to $932.3 billion, a 7.7 percent increase over last year.

26 Feb.   GM recalls 4.9 million possibly defective cars and trucks, the largest automobile recall to date.

3 Apr.   U.S. combat deaths in Vietnam since 1 January 1961 total 33,641 — 12 more than were killed in the Korean War.

9 June   The prime lending rate reaches a record high at 8.5 percent.

1 July   The federal Truth-in-Lending Act is passed, requiring disclosure of all pertinent information to the borrowing customer.

8 July   The first U.S. troop reductions in Vietnam begin; 814 soldiers from the Ninth Infantry Division leave for home.

16 July   *Apollo 11*, which will ultimately land the first men on the moon, is launched.

23 July   Consumer prices rise 6.4 percent since 1 January, the largest increase since 1951.

18 Oct.   The Department of Health, Education, and Welfare bans the use of cyclamates (artificial sweeteners).

20 Nov.   The Department of Agriculture announces a step-by-step plan to phase out the use of the pesticide DDT.

17 Dec.   The Dow Jones industrial average hits its low of the year at 769.93.

OVERVIEW

American Century. In 1941 publishing magnate Henry Luce proclaimed the dawning of the American Century, and by the mid 1960s, if one looked at the business community, there was every reason to believe he was correct. At home and abroad American business was preponderant. The domestic economy was growing, unemployment was down, firms were increasingly productive, and technology was fueling constant innovation. Historians Louis Galambos and Joseph Pratt noted: "It was a good time to be in business in the United States, an era when American efficiency and entrepreneurship were the wonder of the world."

Decade of Affluence. During the 1960s the United States experienced its longest uninterrupted period of economic expansion in history. Whereas automobiles, chemicals, and electrically powered consumer durables were the leading sectors in the 1950s, they were supplanted by aerospace, housing, and the computer industry in the 1960s. By the end of the decade the average American's real income had increased 50 percent since 1950, and the country's high standard of living became the envy of the world. Median family income rose from $8,540 in 1963 to $10,770 by 1969. This newfound affluence meant that many Americans for the first time enjoyed discretionary income that could be spent for enjoyment, not necessities. This prosperity did not reach all, however; poverty remained a growing problem, and its elimination became a cause célèbre for Lyndon Johnson's presidency.

Big Business. Big business dominated the domestic economy of the 1960s. In 1962, for example, the five largest industrial corporations accounted for over 12 percent of all assets in manufacturing, the top fifty held over one-third of the country's manufacturing assets, and the largest five hundred controlled over two-thirds. Some firms grew unbelievably large — by 1965 General Motors (GM), Standard Oil of New Jersey (Exxon today), and Ford had larger gross incomes than all the farms in the United States. Viewed another way, General Motors's revenues for 1963 were nearly eight times those of New York State. In addition to controlling the U.S. market, American big business also reigned supreme globally. American overseas investment increased from $11.8 billion in 1950 to $49.2 billion in 1965. These businesses were Americanizing the world: by 1970 International Business Machines (IBM) was a major firm in every country in which it operated; Campbell's and Heinz sold their processed foods throughout the world; Procter and Gamble's products were distributed on all continents; and Coca-Cola was so widespread that some spoke of American overseas business expansion as the "Coca-Colonization of the world."

Big Government. The federal government's position in the economy continued growing during the decade. By 1970 it employed 3.9 percent of the labor force, up from 2.4 percent in 1940. This expansion of government also meant a much more active involvement in the economy. The government, in fact, played several economic roles: it was at once a consumer, an employer, a regulator, and a social-welfare agency. As a consumer it pumped billions of dollars into the economy by supporting scientific research, buying military equipment (especially at the height of the Vietnam War, when defense expenditures amounted to 10 percent of the Gross National Product [GNP] and 45 percent of the federal budget), building highways, and competing with the Soviet Union in outer space. As an employer it provided large numbers of civilian and military jobs. In 1967, for example, it employed 3 million civilians and 3.4 million military personnel. As a regulator the government stepped up its operations to control the economy and shape the business environment. And with the legislation of President Johnson's Great Society, the government greatly expanded social-security benefits and extended its obligation to care for its citizenry.

Big Labor. The 1960s were mixed for organized labor. On the one hand, union membership increased over the course of the decade — from 18 million in 1960 to 20.7 million in 1970 — largely because of the growth of public-employee unionism; but as a percentage of the workforce it decreased. While wages and benefits were up and in most cases outstripped the rising cost of living, the American Federation of Labor and Congress of Industrial Organizations (AFL-CIO) came under increasing attack by radicals who opposed the union's support of the Vietnam War and its apparent lack of support for the civil rights of African-Americans. Yet even as its critics became more vocal, the AFL-CIO piled up a series of successes through its political arms. Up until 1968 and the election of Richard Nixon the union enjoyed several political victories, placing labor-supportive liberals in the White House as well as both houses of Congress. By the end of the decade, however, unions' influence appeared to be decreasing.

Cracks in the System? Unions were not alone in their struggle by decade's end; there were clear signs that the American economy was in trouble. New competition loomed on the international horizon as Japan and a resurgent Europe challenged American corporations both at home and abroad. Meanwhile, as the costs of the Vietnam War spiraled upward, inflation put pressure on the economy, and America's long period of prosperity gave way to one dominated by stagflation in the 1970s.

Sources:

Mansel Blackford and K. Austin Kerr, *Business Enterprise in American History* (Boston: Houghton Mifflin, 1994);

Louis Galambos and Joseph Pratt, *The Rise of the Corporate Commonwealth* (New York: Basic Books, 1988);

U.S. Department of Commerce, *Historical Statistics of the United States: Colonial Times to 1970* (Washington, D.C.: Government Printing Office, 1975);

Robert Zieger, *American Workers, American Unions: 1920–1985* (Baltimore & London: Johns Hopkins University Press, 1986).

TOPICS IN THE NEWS

AGRICULTURE IN THE 1960S

Larger Farms, Fewer Farmers. During the 1960s the post–World War II agricultural trends of larger farms and fewer farmers accelerated. Over the course of the decade nine hundred thousand farms disappeared, largely because of consolidation. This meant that the average size of farms increased from 297 acres in 1960 to 374 acres by 1970. Although it was true that corporations and conglomerates were moving into agriculture, the family

Midwestern corn crop being harvested

FARM FACTS			
Year	Number of Farms (in thousands)	Farm Population (in thousands)	Percent of Total Population
1950	5,648	23,048	15.2
1955	4,514	18,712	11.1
1960	3,963	15,635	8.7
1965	3,356	12,363	6.4
1970	2,949	9,712	4.7

Source: Gilbert Fite, *American Farmers* (Bloomington: Indiana University Press, 1981).

farm remained a fixture in rural America. In 1970, 66 percent of all corporate farms were family owned, 14 percent were individually owned, and the remaining 20 percent were owned by a group larger than a family.

Increasing Production and Specialization. As farm size increased, farmers took advantage of new technology that made economies of scale possible. New machines, fertilizers, and pesticides pushed the value of farm output from $29 billion in 1946 to $54 billion in 1970. Over the same period labor productivity tripled. By 1970, for example, one farmer (making use of the latest feeding equipment) could take care of seventy-five thousand chickens or five thousand head of cattle. Assembly-line techniques, in fact, made their way into agriculture. Large-scale poultry operations are illustrative. Chickens no longer roamed the farm eating whatever they could find. Rather, they were housed in a comfortable, controlled environment stuffed with specialized foods to create a particular type of chicken for a particular market.

Continued Role of Government. Ever since the New Deal programs of the 1930s the federal government has played a major role in American agriculture, and the free

The 1964 Corvair, the car that was the target of Ralph Nader's *Unsafe at Any Speed*

market for such goods ceased to exist. In a complex scheme of government price supports, subsidies, and loans, farmers received funding depending on the situation in both the domestic and world food markets. One federal program, for example, attempted to uphold the price of agricultural goods by lessening supply; farmers were paid to take land out of production. Although this accounted for only a portion of the federal monies going to farmers, these direct government payments rose from $702 million in 1960 to $3.7 billion in 1970. But the constant problem of oversupply and chronic surpluses continued through the decade. They did not temporarily abate until the early 1970s, when the devalued dollar made American products cheaper and changing European and Japanese dietary preferences increased demand for American commodities. In addition, poor harvests in the Soviet Union opened up a huge market for American grain.

Sources:

Robert Howard, *The Vanishing Land* (New York: Villard, 1985);

John T. Schlebecker, *Whereby We Thrive: A History of American Farming, 1607–1972* (Ames: Iowa State University Press, 1975);

United States Department of Agriculture, *Contours of Change: The Yearbook of Agriculture, 1970* (Washington, D.C.: Government Printing Office, 1970).

THE BIG THREE AND THE AUTO INDUSTRY

Challenge of the Imports. By 1960 the American automobile industry had been consolidated into the Big Three (General Motors [GM], Ford, and Chrysler) and American Motors. These firms not only dominated the domestic market, they were supreme globally. In 1960 American companies built 93 percent of the autos sold in the United States and 48 percent of world sales. In the mid 1950s, however, led by Volkswagen and soon followed by Fiat, Renault, Datsun, and Hillman, imports

began to nibble their way into the rich American market. The growing presence of imports disturbed Detroit, and the Big Three responded with their own small cars — GM produced the Corvair, Ford the Falcon, and Chrysler the Valiant. They then introduced the so-called muscle cars, powerful, sleek sports models such as the Mustang. The tactic worked: Americans, dazzled by the horsepower and the style, turned away from the boxy, utilitarian imports. By 1965 American firms appeared to have beaten back the challenge, and import sales, which had risen to 668,000 in 1959, dropped to 540,000. Given the American love affair with the automobile, the country's growing affluence, and the fact that the two-car family was fast becoming the badge of the middle class, there was no reason to doubt that the Big Three's prosperity and success would continue.

Smog. Automobiles first became associated with the brown haze known as smog in the early 1950s by California Institute of Technology scientist A. J. Haagen-Smit, who estimated that 70 percent of the Los Angeles smog was created by automobile exhaust. The California state legislature finally acted in 1960, requiring all cars sold in the state to have a special part installed to limit emissions. As air pollution became a national issue, the federal government followed the pioneering steps taken in California. In 1965 Congress passed the Motor Vehicle Air Pollution Control Act, which set emission standards. Two years later the Air Quality Act gave the federal government sole responsibility over clean air standards. The auto industry complained but ultimately complied. Unfortunately, because of antitrust laws, the Big Three were not allowed to work together on an emission-control system; each was forced to develop its own. Japan, on the other hand, encouraged its auto manufacturers to pool resources and share the costs of pollution-control devices. This saved the Japanese firms a tremendous amount of research and development costs. Although expensive for the automakers, the clean air acts succeeded in decreasing dangerous vehicle emissions.

UNSAFE AT ANY SPEED

Highway Safety. Concern over automobile safety was heightened by Ralph Nader's 1965 book alleging that unsafe automobile design (particularly the Chevrolet Corvair) was the major contributor to highway accidents. This led to the passage of the National Traffic and Motor Vehicle Safety Act in 1965 and the Highway Safety Act the following year. Together they required safety features (seat belts, for example) installed in all motor vehicles and the development of comprehensive traffic safety programs. Much like the government's regulation of air quality, these new safety standards made auto travel safer and led to a decline in highway fatalities.

End of an Era. By the late 1960s foreign manufacturers — largely Volkswagen, Toyota, and Datsun — were once again putting pressure on Detroit. While the recession at decade's end hurt American auto firms because people delayed purchasing new domestic cars, it helped the foreign companies as many opted to buy less-expensive models, which often turned out to be imports. By 1970 imports had captured 11 percent of the U.S. market, and with two oil crises over the next ten years, smaller, more-fuel-efficient foreign automobiles continued to increase their share of the market. As of 1987 imports made up 31 percent of all vehicles sold in the United States.

Sources:

James J. Flink, *The Car Culture* (Cambridge, Mass.: MIT Press, 1975);

George S. May, ed. *The Automobile Industry, 1920–1980* (New York: Bruccoli Clark Layman / Facts On File, 1989);

John B. Rae, *The American Automobile Industry* (Boston: Twayne, 1984).

THE VOLKSWAGEN BEETLE

The first serious overseas challenge to the U.S. automakers came from a small, rather odd-looking, four-cylinder import from Germany called the Volkswagen (VW). It was originally designed in the 1930s as the answer to Adolf Hitler's dream of producing a car for the German masses (Volkswagen translates as people's car). World War II intervened, however, and the car was never built. At war's end American and British firms considered buying Volkswagen, but with the factory destroyed and only one model plan, they declined. The German government picked up the pieces and began production slowly. Over the next few years, the awkward "Bug," as it would affectionately be called later, became a common sight on German roads.

Volkswagen's entry into the United States went largely unnoticed until company executives realized that to break into the American market, VW had to guarantee good service and support for their auto. With a national sales

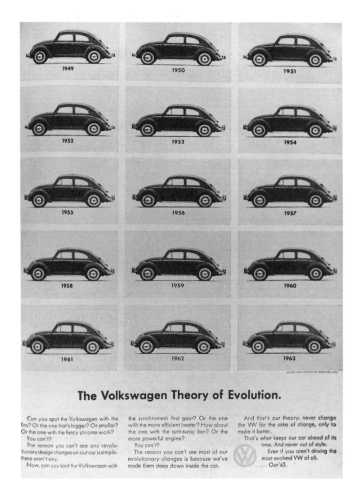

Advertisement for the Volkswagen Beetle

and service organization stretching across the country, sales began to climb. Unexpectedly, the car's lack of style caught on, and it tapped into an antisnob appeal. In 1955 VW sold 28,000 cars in the United States accounting for nearly half of all imports. This leading role among imports continued through the 1960s, peaking in 1968, when VW accounted for 68 percent of all imports sold in the United States. Like the Model T, the VW did not have annual model changes, it was inexpensive, and it was easy to fix. Such attributes made Volkswagen popular with American young people, and the Beetle became, in many ways, a symbol of the decade's youth culture.

Source:

John B. Rae, *The American Automobile Industry* (Boston: Twayne, 1984).

THE BOOM ON WALL STREET

Up, Up, and Away. Ever since mid 1949, when the Dow Jones industrial average stood at 161, the stock market had been rising. By 1959, despite the recession, the Dow Jones average was 685. In 1960, however, the market seemed to stall, and in 1962 it suffered its worst year since 1931: in June, when the market hit bottom, the Dow had lost 27 percent of its value since December. But from that point on to 1966, the market shot up, with the

Gerald Tsai, Jr., a mutual-fund innovator at Fidelity Fund

moved up the organizational ladder quickly. In 1957 Tsai requested and was given charge of a new fund — the Fidelity Capital Fund — that was to concentrate on growth stocks. He broke with the standard money-manager strategy of spreading out his risks. Instead, he invested heavily in high-technology firms such as Litton, Polaroid, Texas Instruments, and Xerox. He also bought into many of the new conglomerates. With his unorthodox leadership the Fidelity Capital Fund became one of the fastest-growing mutual funds, but in 1962, with the plummeting market, its value (and thus its appeal) declined sharply. It came back strongly, however, and over the next few years outperformed the Dow Jones. Tsai was the marvel of Wall Street. In 1966 he chose to go out on his own: he established the Manhattan Fund. But Tsai had lost his touch; the market downturn in 1966 and poor stock selections hurt the fund, which was eventually merged with CNA Financial.

Sources:

"Fresh Face in Money Management," *Business Week* (20 February 1965): 54ff;

Robert Sobel, *The Last Bull Market: Wall Street in the 1960s* (New York: Norton, 1980).

CREDIT CARDS

"I'll Just Charge It." Ubiquitous words and phrases generally associated with the 1960s — "Don't trust anyone over thirty," "the Generation Gap," "the Establishment," "peace," and "groovy" — capture only part of the decade. One important change during these years might best be depicted by the expression that revolutionized the way Americans bought things: "I'll just charge it." The burgeoning use of credit cards simplified the idea of buying now and paying later, thereby adding fuel to the economic boom already under way. Although various kinds of charge cards had been available for nearly fifty years, the credit-card industry took off in the 1960s.

Origins. Consumer credit in the form of installment-buying plans became prominent during the years following World War I. In order to encourage the purchasing of big-ticket items such as automobiles, washing machines, radios, and the like, companies in the 1920s allowed customers to spread the cost of their purchase over several months rather than making one lump-sum payment. With installment buying, more automobiles were on the road, and oil companies began issuing gasoline cards to customers permitting them to charge purchases at any of the firm's affiliated gas stations. The airline industry followed suit in the 1930s. American Airlines opened the credit door with its Universal Air Travel Plan (UATP). Beginning as a coupon book, UATP later developed into a credit card business. But these charge cards, much like the ones department stores were also giving out, could be used only at the issuers' establishments. The universal card, acceptable at many stores and shops for a variety of goods and services, awaited the creation of Diners Club.

Dow Jones gaining 460 points, inching above the 1,000 mark in January. Although it would drop from that peak, in the years 1962 through 1968 the market increase was greater than the famous bull market of the 1920s.

Mutual Funds. Although nearly thirty million Americans held stock, few knew much about the market. This limited knowledge led many to play the stock market through mutual funds. Although they had existed since the 1920s, mutual funds did not become popular until the 1950s. In essence, mutual funds were diversified stock portfolios managed by professionals. For a fee investors could put their money into one of these funds. Fund managers then bought and sold large blocks of desirable stocks in an effort to increase the fund's value. By 1965 such funds were so popular they accounted for one quarter of all transactions on the New York Stock Exchange. Three years later new ones were being started at the rate of one a week, and mutual funds were managing more than $51 billion in assets.

Gerry Tsai and Fidelity Capital Fund. Before Gerry Tsai entered the picture, people traditionally thought of mutual funds as conservative investments. In 1952 at age twenty-four Tsai joined Boston-based Fidelity Fund as a junior stock analyst. Edward Johnson, head of Fidelity Fund, was impressed with Tsai, and the young man

They'll know who you are when they see your Bankamericard

BANK OF AMERICA

1964 advertisement for what was then the only bank card in the world

Diners Club and the Others. Set up by Alfred Bloomingdale (the son of the department-store tycoon), Frank McNamara, and Ralph Synder, the Diners Club card was introduced in 1949. It was a universal, third-party card: that is, the Diners Club company acted as a middleman between the consumer and the merchant. The firm made money by charging customers for the card and charging merchants for using its services. Cardholders paid a monthly fee and were required to pay off their total balance each month. After several years operating in the field alone, Diners Club faced new competition in 1958. That year American Express, known for its traveler's checks, and Hilton Hotel's credit-card branch, Carte Blanche, each introduced universal credit cards. Later in 1958 the nation's two largest banks, Bank of America and Chase Manhattan, jumped into the growing credit-card industry.

BankAmericard and Master Charge. With BankAmericard, Bank of America created a universal revolving charge card — the cardholders were given the option of making a minimum payment, with the balance (with interest added) carried over to the next month's bill. In 1966 Bank of America decided to franchise its BankAmericard (the name was changed to VISA in 1976) across the country. In response several large banks formed another national card system known as the Interbank Card Association (Interbank purchased the rights

to Master Charge in 1969 and changed its name to MasterCard in 1980). Once established, these two rival firms battled to place their respective credit cards in consumers' hands. The method was unsolicited mass mailings of credit cards. By 1970 there were millions of bank cards in circulation, and some predicted this plastic money would one day replace paper currency altogether.

Continued Growth. During the 1970s the number of credit cards in circulation more than doubled, with the charge volume increasing 1,400 percent. Growth continued into the 1980s: by 1985 VISA had 86.4 million cardholders to MasterCard's 64.9 million. Credit cards had truly transformed the way Americans bought things. By 1984, 71 percent of American families had at least one credit card, and from 1970 to 1986 the number of families carrying a bank credit card rose from 16 to 55 percent. As finance professor Lewis Mandell suggested, consumers had apparently taken the television commercial seriously and were "not leaving home without them."

Source:
Lewis Mandell, *The Credit Card Industry: A History* (Boston: Twayne, 1990).

DOW CHEMICAL AND STUDENT ACTIVISTS

Student Protests. For many, student protests are remembered as synonymous with the 1960s. At first associated with the civil rights movement, protests spread as college students soon found other reasons for demanding change in the status quo: at Berkeley, California, for example, the 1964 free-speech movement led students around the country to attack their universities as huge impersonal places, with largely irrelevant curricula. By 1965 and 1966 the more radical students found another cause — "the illegal war in Vietnam." Starting out as teach-ins at colleges and universities across the country in 1965, the protests against the war grew to huge marches and rallies by decade's end.

Dow and the Vietnam War. Dow was one of America's largest chemical corporations and had a fine reputation. Although its major business involved selling chemicals to other companies, most consumers knew the firm as the maker of the convenient kitchen products Saran Wrap and Handi-Wrap. But in the mid 1960s Dow became widely known for a relatively small government contract that amounted to one-fourth of 1 percent of the company's total sales. The contract was for the manufacture of napalm, a gasoline gel, packed into canisters and dropped from bombers during the war in Vietnam. Napalm was designed to stick to its victims and burn them. For antiwar activists, it came to symbolize the inhumanity of the war.

The Battle against Dow. On 28 May 1966 one hundred people paraded around Dow's facility in Torrance, California, protesting its making of napalm. Meanwhile, the same day, another seventy-five demonstrators stood

The 1967 riot at the University of Wisconsin–Madison protesting production of napalm by Dow Chemical

in front of Dow's New York offices, chanting slogans such as, "Napalm burns babies, Dow makes money." Over the next couple of years the anti-Dow campaign spread to antiwar groups at universities across the country. In 1967, when a Dow employment recruiter went to the University of Wisconsin–Madison, he was harassed by student activists. A riot ensued — leaving seven police officers and sixty-five students hospitalized. In addition to these protests, Dow became the target of more aggressive opposition: on several occasions its offices were vandalized and files destroyed.

Dow Quietly Backs Down. From the beginning of the protests Dow defended its actions. Early on, it explained: "Our position on the manufacture of napalm is that we are a supplier of goods to the Defense Department and not a policymaker. We do not and should not try to decide military strategy or policy." The public opposition, however, clearly had an effect; when the government napalm contract was up for renewal, Dow intentionally did not pursue it aggressively and lost the contract to a lower bidder.

Sources:
Todd Gitlin, *The Sixties: Years of Hope, Days of Rage* (New York: Bantam, 1987);

Allen Matusow, *The Unraveling of America* (New York: Harper & Row, 1984);

Milton Moskowitz, Michael Katz, and Robert Levering, eds., *Everybody's Business* (New York: Harper & Row, 1982);

Don Whitehead, *The Dow Story: The History of the Dow Chemical Company* (New York: McGraw-Hill, 1968).

NEW ENVIRONMENTALISM

Earth Day. Perhaps most symbolic of the renewed concern for the environment was the establishment of Earth Day. Its origins dated back to a 1969 speech by Wisconsin senator Gaylord Nelson, who called for a nationwide environmental teach-in on college campuses, modeled after the antiwar protest gatherings of the same name. Held on 22 August 1970, the first annual Earth Day involved an astonishing fifteen hundred colleges and ten thousand schools; *Time* magazine estimated that overall, upward of twenty million people participated. *Audubon* magazine referred to the hugely successful event by writing: "Now, suddenly, everybody is a conservationist."

The EPA. With preservation now clearly on the national agenda, the capstone event for the environmental movement of the 1960s was the National Environmental Policy Act of 1969. The passage of this law committed

Congress to protecting the environment. Signed by President Richard Nixon on 1 January 1970, the legislation also created the Environmental Protection Agency (EPA), which soon became, in terms of both staff and budget, the country's largest governmental regulatory body.

Sources:

Samuel P. Hays, *Beauty, Health, and Permanence: Environmental Politics in the United States, 1955–1985* (New York: Cambridge University Press, 1987);

Kirkpatrick Sale, *The Green Revolution: The American Environmental Movement, 1962–1992* (New York: Hill & Wang, 1993).

FRANCHISING

Post–World War II Boom. Franchising initially became popular in the 1920s, especially with automobile manufacturers, oil companies, and restaurants setting up outlets, but the major franchise boom took place after World War II. In the mid to late 1940s thousands of veterans returned home to the United States with the notion of being their own boss. Although big business dominated major sectors of the economy, the tradition of small-business ownership remained very strong. Franchising, in effect, combined the benefits of both large and small business. Under the terms of an agreement the franchisee was a legally independent business (most often a small business) separate from the franchising company. The contract generally specified that the individual acquiring the franchise pay an initial fee, sell only specific products, conduct business in a certain manner, and often cede the franchiser a certain percentage of gross sales. For the small-business owner there were several advantages: a smaller initial investment was needed; training and advertising were provided by the parent company; and usually one was selling a product with a national, or at least regional, reputation. The strong desire to be an independent businessperson, combined with large companies' desires to distribute their products as cheaply as possible, led to a rapid expansion of franchises. By 1967 sales from franchise outlets accounted for 10 percent of the GNP.

McDonaldization of America. The franchising explosion was led by Ray Kroc and his McDonald's chain. By the late 1950s Kroc had hit upon a formula for success. His restaurants featured spotless kitchens, an assembly-line process for making standardized food — hamburgers, french fries, and soft drinks — consistent quality, speedy service, and low prices. Training for franchise owners was provided at what was called Hamburger University, and franchisees were held to strict requirements regarding food quality, store appearance, and cleanliness. By 1980 there were over sixty-five hundred McDonald's outlets with sales over $6.2 billion. So successful was McDonald's that its system became the model for other fast-food franchisers (Domino's Pizza, for example) to follow.

Beyond Fast Food. By the 1960s franchising had moved well beyond fast food. Franchise operations now

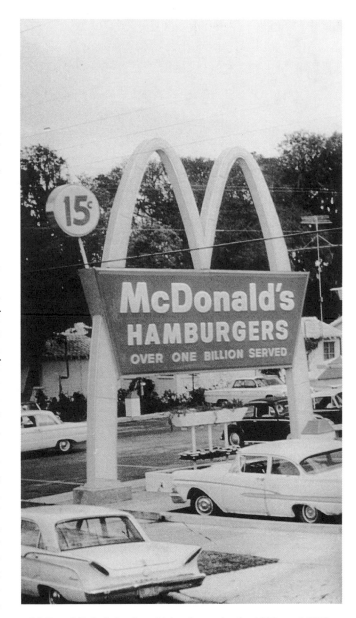

McDonald's led the franchising boom in the 1950s and 1960s

provided people with a wide variety of services ranging from renting moving equipment (U-Haul outlets), preparing taxes (H & R Block), or repairing cars (Midas Muffler shops). One franchise that took off in the 1960s rode the electronics boom to success. By middecade the electronics business had become the nation's fifth largest industry, turning out such products as televisions, radios, stereos, appliances, and high-technology equipment for the Defense Department. Charles Tandy, a Fort Worth, Texas, businessman, believed there was a huge market for electronics, and in 1963 he purchased the nine existing Radio Shack stores. He then began to sell franchises nationally. Placing the outlets in suburban malls as well as small towns and cities, Tandy provided electronic goods with a high turnover and high profit margins. Growth was rapid, and by 1980 there were seventy-five hundred Radio Shack stores, outnumbering the ubiquitous McDonald's restaurants.

An Wang on the cover of a 1969 magazine featuring one of his products

Sources:
Mansel G. Blackford, *A History of Small Business in America* (New York: Twayne, 1991);

Thomas S. Dicke, *Franchising in America* (Chapel Hill & London: University of North Carolina Press, 1992);

Ray Kroc, *Grinding It Out: The Making of McDonald's* (Chicago: Regnery, 1977).

AN WANG AND HIGH-TECH ELECTRONICS

The career of An Wang and the rise of high-technology electronics went hand in hand. A Chinese national, Wang completed his doctorate in applied physics at Harvard University in 1948 and remained there as a research assistant, where he was fortunate to work with Howard Aiken, a pioneer in the development of computers. Wang created, and then in 1949 patented, the pulse transfer controlling device, an invention that advanced computer core memory. In 1951, thinking the infant computer industry showed enormous potential, he left Harvard and set up his own firm, Wang Laboratories.

Throughout the 1950s and early 1960s Wang Laboratories became known as an aggressive firm on the cutting edge of electronics technology; it was Wang, for example, that installed the first electronic scoreboard at Shea Stadium. The firm's first major product line was in the desktop-calculator business: in 1965 it introduced LOCI,

an electronic desktop calculator. The following year Wang came out with a less expensive, more user-friendly model, and by decade's end it was the leader in this market.

Then, in a move that at first appeared puzzling, Wang suddenly stopped producing calculators in 1970 to pursue the computer business more aggressively. The strategy was successful: as Wang had correctly believed, the price of calculators tumbled, and many firms such as Bowmar Instruments went bankrupt. In 1971 Wang introduced a word processor, and the following year its small business computer was on the marketplace. By the mid 1970s Wang Laboratories had broken onto the *Fortune 500* list of largest industrials and dominated the word processing market.

Source:
An Wang and Eugene Linden, *Lessons: An Autobiography* (Reading, Mass.: Addison-Wesley Publishing, 1986).

IBM AND THE COMPUTER INDUSTRY

Dominance. By the mid 1960s IBM so dominated the computer industry that business insiders often spoke of "IBM and the Seven Dwarfs," which referred to IBM and the other major computer manufacturers. Its supremacy had been established in the early 1950s when it surpassed computer pioneer Remington Rand (later merged into Sperry Rand). IBM continued to eat up the market share, as the industry went through several generations. The first computers were giant machines using vacuum tubes. Vacuum tubes gave way to transistors in the second gen-

IBM AND THE SEVEN DWARFS – THE COMPUTER INDUSTRY BY MARKET SHARE IN 1965	
Company	Market Share
IBM	65.3
Sperry Rand	12.1
Control Data	5.4
Honeywell	3.8
Burroughs	3.5
General Electric	3.4
RCA	2.9
NCR	2.9

Source: Robert Sobel, *IBM: Colossus in Transition* (New York: Times Books, 1981).

The IBM 360, Model 30 central processing unit

eration of computers, but it was the third generation that really gave IBM the edge.

The 360 Series. IBM's 360 line of computers debuted in 1965 after a $5 billion investment. This new series used integrated circuits instead of transistors and revolutionized the industry for the next several years. The new circuits made miniaturization possible and allowed for a tremendous increase in the computational power of the machines. Accordingly, historian Robert Sobel suggested: "In the history of computers, everything is pre-360 or post-360." Improvements such as the 360 series led to greater use of computers in the business community. In 1965 nearly $3 billion worth of computer equipment was sold; five years later the figure reached $5.7 billion. Technology advanced rapidly, however, and by 1971 another development ushered in a new generation of computers that would drastically expand their use.

The Silicon Microchip. In 1971 Intel pushed the industry forward with the invention of the microprocessor — an entire central processing unit (CPU) of a computer was placed on a single silicon chip. Advertised as a "computer on a chip," these microprocessors were approximately the size of a capital letter on this printed page. By the mid 1970s a single microchip could process as much information as a giant, room-sized computer of the late 1940s. The microchip, in turn, led to the development of the personal computer in the late 1970s and the rise of a new powerhouse in the industry, Apple Computer.

Sources:
T. R. Reid, *The Chip* (New York: Simon & Schuster, 1984);

Joel Shurkin, *Engines of the Mind: A History of the Computer* (New York: Norton, 1984);

Robert Sobel, *IBM: Colossus in Transition* (New York: Times Books, 1981).

KENNEDY VERSUS BIG STEEL

During his first year in office President John F. Kennedy and his administration were involved in negotiations between the major steel firms and their workers. By the end of March 1962 a deal was cut whereby workers received no wage increase but expanded fringe benefits. With this settlement worked out, Kennedy assumed steel companies would not raise their prices. Two weeks later, however, Roger M. Blough, president of U.S. Steel, went to the White House and handed Kennedy a press release announcing a price hike of six dollars a ton. The other major steel firms immediately followed suit.

Kennedy felt betrayed: he had intervened in talks between Big Steel and labor to keep industry costs down, and now the companies raised prices. He responded by attacking the action of steel executives on television and initiated a grand jury investigation on price-fixing in the steel industry. The Pentagon threatened to shift procurement to companies that had not raised prices, and Congress was encouraged to investigate the industry as well. Three days after the price increases were announced, several firms backed down, and the following day, 14 April, Blough rescinded U.S. Steel's new price.

Although on the one hand a victory for Kennedy, the incident damaged government business relationships. During his first year in office the president had worked hard to eliminate the private sector's traditional fear of Democrats. This battle only appeared to confirm the corporate world's view that Kennedy and his party were hostile to big business.

Source:
Grant McConnell, *Steel and the Presidency — 1962* (New York: Norton, 1963).

Roger M. Blough, U.S. Steel chairman of the board, answering reporters' questions after meeting with President John F. Kennedy

LABOR IN THE 1960S

Labor at High Tide. By the mid 1960s, labor's future appeared bright. Real wages were rising, union numbers were strong, and during the presidencies of Kennedy and Johnson organized labor felt it had friends in the White House. With the advent of the Great Society the AFL-CIO leadership believed the administration was picking up where the New Deal had left off in providing benefits such as health care to the lower classes. Working hard for passage of Johnson's progressive domestic program, the AFL-CIO won plaudits from many liberals.

Changing Work Patterns. Organized labor's apparent strength, however, was fleeting. During the 1960s the percentage of blue-collar workers (those generally in the manufacturing sector) as a proportion of the total workforce declined so that by 1970 the typical American worker was a white-collar employee. Fewer relatively high-paying industrial jobs were available for unskilled workers. Although the burgeoning service sector created millions of jobs, they either were low paying — clerical or fast-food positions, for example — or, because of the expansion of science and technology, required a higher level of education. Concurrently, many companies lowered their costs by moving their manufacturing plants out of the heavily unionized Northeast and Midwest (where labor costs were higher) and relocated in southern and western states with right-to-work laws (legislation that inhibited unions and resulted in wage rates 20 percent lower than in unionized areas). From 1966 to 1976, for example, northeastern states lost a million factory jobs, while southern states picked up 860,000 manufacturing jobs. Even more damaging, however, was the movement of jobs overseas. Large multinational American firms began to take advantage of cheap foreign labor. By the mid 1970s leading U.S. firms like Ford, International Telephone and Telegraph (ITT), Kodak, and Proctor and Gamble employed over one-third of their workers overseas. The AFL-CIO estimated that between 1966 and 1971 the United States lost 1 million jobs to foreign subsidiaries of American firms. An AFL-CIO official explained that America was becoming "a country stripped of industrial capacity and meaningful work . . . a service economy . . . a nation of citizens busily buying and selling cheeseburgers and root beer floats."

Generation Gap in the Labor Movement. Rocked by a shrinking manufacturing sector, plant closings, and migration of jobs overseas, organized labor was also hurt by the general social upheaval of the 1960s. Many young production workers began to see unions' (particularly the AFL-CIO's) support of the Vietnam War and slowness to support rights of African-Americans as reactionary. Much like militant students of their generation, young

United Auto Workers participating in the 1963 march on Washington, 1963

workers often questioned the legitimacy of authority. Once viewed as allies, labor leaders were now viewed suspiciously at best and as part of the problem at worst. This tension between leadership and membership would only increase through the 1970s. By that time these internal struggles were compounded by layoffs because of a weak economy and the continued corporate policy of cutting labor costs by moving overseas or replacing workers with machinery.

Sources:

Ronald L. Filippelli, *Labor in the USA: A History* (New York: Knopf, 1984);

James R. Green, *The World of the Worker* (New York: Hill & Wang, 1980);

Robert Zieger, *American Workers, American Unions, 1920–1985* (Baltimore & London: Johns Hopkins University Press, 1986).

RISE OF CONGLOMERATES

Third Merger Wave. Beginning in the late 1950s and running through the 1960s, a third period of rapid corporate expansion enveloped the nation. Unlike the first two (in the 1890s and the 1920s), when companies either combined horizontally with firms involved in the same business or vertically with suppliers or customers, conglomerates combined companies in completely unrelated industries. This new corporate strategy was based on the the assumption that the firm would be protected by diversification during times of economic fluctuation — if the market was down for one product, it may not be for another. Such mergers accounted for 60 percent of all corporate combinations in the 1960s.

International Telephone and Telegraph. International Telephone and Telegraph (ITT) conglomerate strategy was fairly typical of the decade. Originally a telecommunications firm operating in foreign countries,

ITT's chief executive officer, Harold Geneen, became concerned about the possibilities of growth overseas. To protect the company, he instituted a policy of expanding the firm's domestic holdings through acquisition. Between 1961 and 1968 ITT purchased fifty-two companies with combined assets of $1.5 billion. Firms added to the ITT family included Avis (rental cars), Continental Baking (Wonder Bread, Twinkies), Canteen Corporation (food sales), Levitt and Sons (home construction), Sheraton Corporation (hotels), and Hartford Fire Insurance. As a result of this diversification, only 20 percent of ITT's total revenues in 1974 derived from the original telecommunications division.

Tobacco Industry. The tobacco companies had a special reason to use the conglomerate strategy. By the 1930s the industry was dominated by four major firms, R. J. Reynolds, American Tobacco, Liggett and Myers, P. Lorillard, and a smaller newcomer, Philip Morris. In the 1960s the industry was threatened by new research relating cigarettes to cancer, a ban of cigarette ads on television, and mandatory warning labels on cigarette packages and advertising. Given this environment, executives of all the tobacco companies chose to diversify by investing in nontobacco businesses. American Tobacco purchased Jim Beam, Master Lock, Franklin Life Insurance, and Sunshine Biscuits. In 1969 it even changed its name to American Brands. R. J. Reynolds bought American Independent Oil, Chun King, Del Monte, and Morton Foods. P. Lorillard became part of the Loews conglomerate, and Liggett and Myers bought Alpo dog food and Izmira Vodka. Among Philip Morris's acquisitions were Miller Brewing Company and Seven-Up.

Peak and Decline. The conglomerate wave reached its peak in 1968. Three factors account for the declining

Harold Geneen, chief executive officer of ITT

interest in this corporate form. While the Justice Department began to take a more aggressive stance against conglomerates, profits of such companies failed to live up to expectations. Finally, the recession of the early 1970s curtailed the conglomerate expansion until it was revived again in the 1980s.

Sources:
Keith Bryant, Jr., and Henry Dethloff, *A History of American Business* (Englewood Cliffs, N.J.: Prentice-Hall, 1983);

Robert Sobel, *The Rise and Fall of the Conglomerate Kings* (New York: Stein & Day, 1984).

TRADING STAMPS

Trading stamps originated in the 1890s, but it was the expansion of supermarkets and gas stations in the 1950s that led to their soaring popularity. A marketing gimmick, colored stamps were given out by many retail establishments. Patrons collected the stamps, pasted them in blank books, and redeemed the filled stamp booklets for a wide variety of prizes: the most popular redemptions were sheets and blankets, furniture, appliances, and sporting goods. Trading stamp companies such as Sperry

and Hutchinson (S&H Green Stamps) sold their stamps to retailers who used them as inducements for customer purchases. A 1966 survey reported that 49.3 million American households — 83 percent of the national total — saved stamps. By the mid 1960s there were over three hundred stamp companies nationwide employing seventeen thousand with a payroll of $68 million. The industry peaked in 1969 with sales of $825 million. For much of the decade trading stamps were part of the American landscape: parents gave them to babysitters, corporations presented them to employees as rewards, and families often gathered around the kitchen table to glue trading stamps into booklets. In the early 1970s trading stamps fell by the wayside. Gas stations had accounted for 25 percent of stamp sales. With the oil crisis gas stations were assured of customers, and they stopped offering stamps. In the midst of the recession many supermarkets, figuring that customers would prefer lower prices at the checkout rather than free gifts later, followed gas stations' example and pulled out of stamp programs. By 1975 stamp sales had fallen to $275 million, a twenty-year low.

Source:
Richard D. Smith, "Why Everyone Collected Stamps," *Audacity*, 2 (Spring 1994): 50 ff.

WOMEN AND WORK

Prior to the 1960s. An ever-increasing number of women had entered the workforce since the 1870s, but over a 120-year period, the identity of the woman worker changed. From the 1820s, with the onset of industrialization in the United States, until 1940, the average female employee was young and single, and, if married, the woman working outside the home was likely poor and African-American. From the 1940s to the 1970s, how-

WHAT THINGS COST IN 1967	
Average three-bedroom house	$17,000
New Cadillac	$6,700
New Volkswagen	$1,497
Men's gray flannel suit	$60
Portable typewriter	$39
1 pound of sirloin steak	$.89
1 gallon of regular gas	$.39
Hershey chocolate bar	$.05

Source: James K. Martin and others, *America and its People* (New York: HarperCollins, 1993).

Women working on a Chrysler assembly line in 1965

ever, married women became the largest component of the female labor force, and the number of gainfully employed, white middle-class women rose rapidly.

Domesticity of the 1950s. World War II had served as a catalyst encouraging women to take up the jobs vacated by their brothers, fathers, husbands, or sons who were off fighting the war. When the conflict ended, however, many women remained working outside the home. By 1960 over one-third of women were employed, while more and more married women went to work to obtain the many accoutrements of middle-class life. But "women's work" had certain characteristics: jobs were often part-time, they were rarely regarded as career oriented, and they were usually low paying since women's income was viewed as secondary. Such positions included clerical and secretarial jobs, teaching, and work in retail. Yet even as more women were working, the shapers of culture — educators, magazine editors, advertisers, and television executives — stressed that the proper place for women was in the home rearing children.

Betty Friedan and *The Feminine Mystique*. In 1963 Betty Friedan's best-seller, *The Feminine Mystique,* argued that women were oppressed by a culture that consistently denied them opportunities outside the domestic sphere. Friedan went on to suggest that women should have the same freedom for self-fulfillment that men possessed. This book reawakened the feminist movement: in 1964 women's groups succeeded in getting the Civil Rights Act to include a section banning discrimination based on gender; two years later Friedan and others founded the National Organization of Women (NOW). By the late 1960s the government required that all insti-

tutions receiving federal funds use nondiscriminatory hiring practices, and in the early 1970s affirmative-action laws were in place. In this atmosphere public opinion about women in the workplace began to change. In 1936 a Gallup poll reported that only 18 percent of Americans approved of married women working outside the home; forty years later the poll found that 68 percent approved of working women.

Persistent Problems. By the end of the decade women had made real strides forward. As the social stigma of working outside the home lessened, more and more women sought employment. Yet even as working became

WORKING WOMEN AND U.S. LABOR FORCE

Year	Total Labor Force (in thousands)	Working Women (in thousands)	% of Women	% Who Work Labor Force
1950	59,223	16,443	30	28
1960	69,234	22,222	36	32
1970	82,048	30,547	41	37
1980	106,066	44,741	51	42

Source: Lynn Weiner, *From Working Girl to Working Mother* (Chapel Hill & London: University of North Carolina Press, 1985).

The Growing Federal Government

Year	Federal Civilian Employees	Federal Budget Expenditures (in $1,000)	Surplus or Deficit (in $1,000)	Federal Expenditures as % of GNP
1950	1,960,708	39,544,037	2,200,000	15.9
1955	2,397,309	68,509,184	300,000	17.7
1960	2,398,704	92,223,354	300,000	18.2
1965	2,527,915	118,429,745	1,600,000	17.6

acceptable for women, three persistent problems remained. Few women were breaking into the male-dominated professions and careers: in 1969, 25 percent of all working women held traditional female jobs — secretarial, bookkeeping, domestic service, food service, or elementary-school teaching. Second, the median income for women who worked full-time was less than 60 percent of the median for men. Finally, even when both spouses worked, the woman was generally responsible for most of the housework, and coming home frequently did not mean the end of the workday.

Sources:

Lois Banner, *Women in Modern America: A Brief History* (New York: Harcourt Brace Jovanovich, 1984);

William Chafe, *The American Woman: Her Changing Social, Economic, and Political Roles, 1920–1970* (New York: Oxford University Press, 1972);

Cynthia Taeuber, *Statistical Handbook on Women in America* (Phoenix: Oryx Press, 1991).

HEADLINE MAKERS

MARY KAY ASH

1915?-

COSMETICS ENTREPRENEUR

Early Career. The founder of Mary Kay Cosmetics, Mary Kay Ash began her business career out of necessity. Divorced during World War II and raising three small children on her own, she soon moved from a secretarial position into sales with Stanley Home Products. In this new job she demonstrated Stanley's wares in people's homes. Although she enjoyed the work, she was not very successful. With the hope of improving her sales technique she attended the company's annual convention. At the meeting's awards ceremony, she saw the year's top saleswoman crowned queen of sales. Motivated by this coronation, Ash was the top seller the following year, but she was disappointed to discover her prize was an underwater flashlight. She remained among Stanley's best salespeople until she left in 1953 to take a better job at World Gift Company. She moved up rapidly in the home-accessory company to become an area manager and later the national training director. By 1963 she was making twenty-five thousand dollars per year and was happily remarried. But sexism within the company and an efficiency expert who told management that Ash had too much power led to her being transferred to a less important position. Unhappy with the new job, she retired.

Establishing the "Dream Company." Retirement did not suit her, and she decided to write a book exclusively for women on the art of selling. As she prepared the manuscript, Ash outlined her ideal company. Such a firm would feature an outstanding product line, treat males and females equally, base promotion solely on merit, and reward outstanding work with valuable prizes. These ideas seemed sensible to her, and once she hit upon a product to market, she ventured out on her own. The product was a skin cream Ash had been buying from a cosmetologist she met at a Stanley Home Product party in the 1950s. When the cosmetologist died, she pur-

chased the skin cream formula. With a cosmetics firm making her cream, she prepared to open a retail outlet, but then her husband died. Forced to rethink her situation, she turned to her twenty-year-old son to manage the financial side of the company while she oversaw its marketing. Founded in 1963 as Beauty by Mary Kay, the company's name was soon changed to Mary Kay Cosmetics.

The System. Built on the ideas she garnered from Stanley and World Gift, Mary Kay's line of cosmetics was sold by saleswomen called "beauty consultants" at house parties featuring a beauty program and makeup lessons. Unlike other sales operations, Mary Kay paid its sales force well — sometimes up to a 50 percent commission — and no sales territory was established. The latter innovation worked well, because as many of her consultants' (who often only worked nine-hour weeks and earned only two thousand dollars per year in the 1980s) husbands were transferred, they could sell their beauty products wherever they were located. To motivate her largely part-time sales force, she held huge and extravagant annual conventions where many prizes — ranging from jewelry and furs to pink Cadillacs and trips to tropical locales — were bestowed on many consultants for meeting a variety of selling levels.

Success. The new company enjoyed immediate success; sales rose from $198,000 in 1964 to $800,000 the following year. In 1967 the company went public, and sales topped $10 million in 1968. Although in many respects Mary Kay was not a pioneer — door-to-door sales had been used by Avon and Fuller Brush, and house parties had been exploited by Stanley and Tupperware — the company provided opportunities to a largely untapped labor force, women seeking a part-time or second income, and knew how to entice them to sell. In a decade that would, in its latter years, witness a rebirth of the women's movement, Mary Kay had already created a company run by and established exclusively for women.

Sources:
Mary Kay Ash, *Mary Kay Ash* (New York: Harper & Row, 1981);

Robert Sobel and David Sicilia, *The Entrepreneurs* (Boston: Houghton Mifflin, 1986).

CESAR CHAVEZ

1927-1993

LABOR LEADER; FOUNDER AND PRESIDENT OF THE
UNITED FARM WORKERS OF AMERICA

Migrant Years. The son of Mexican immigrants, Cesar Chavez saw his parents lose their small farm in Yuma, Arizona, in the late 1930s. With no other possibilities, the family headed for California and joined the ranks of migrant workers traveling throughout the state picking such crops as apricots, figs, grapes, lettuce, peas, or tomatoes. But once knowing the independence of owning a farm, the Chavez family was not as docile as many other field laborers. Chavez remembered: "We were probably one of the strikingest families in California, the first ones to leave the fields if anyone shouted *Huelga* (Spanish for strike)!" The migratory life was hard on the young Chavez; constant travel made education difficult, and many of the Anglo teachers openly disdained such children. Together, these factors forced Chavez to drop out of school after the end of the eighth grade. Wishing to get off the land, he joined the navy during World War II, but racism kept him in menial jobs. Out of the service in 1946, Chavez returned to the only life he knew — migrant farmwork in Delano, California (in the state's Central Valley).

Early Organizing. In 1952 Chavez landed a job in a San Jose lumberyard, and he and his young family took up residence in Sal Si Puedes (get out if you can), the Mexican barrio of the city. Here Chavez was introduced to the ideas of social justice by Father Donald McDonnell and the self-help social-service group, the Community Service Organization (CSO). By the end of that year he was a full-time organizer for the CSO. Just six years later Chavez was appointed its general director. Under his leadership the CSO became the most powerful Mexican-American political organization in the state. While establishing a CSO chapter in Oxnard, California, Chavez became convinced that work issues were most important to the Chicano community. When the CSO rejected his idea of forming a farmworkers union, he broke with the association in 1962.

National Farm Workers to United Farm Workers. Now thirty-five years old, Chavez created the National Farm Workers Association (NFWA). After three years of organizing, he led his small union to strike in a show of solidarity for Filipino grape pickers in September 1965. This Delano strike soon spread from its origins against table-grape growers to include many of California's leading wineries, and Chavez's use of nonviolent tactics brought the conflict national attention. Because traditional picketing could not keep scabs out of the fields, Chavez adopted another strategy — the economic boy-

cott. To keep his movement in the public eye, Chavez staged a grueling three-hundred-mile march from Delano to Sacramento, and later he fasted for three weeks to rededicate the union to nonviolence. In 1966 his NFWA merged with an AFL-CIO affiliate to establish the United Farm Workers Organizing Committee (UFWOC). After five years of struggle the economic impact of the boycott pressured the growers to settle. The UFWOC obtained contracts with twenty-six growers; this accounted for nearly two-thirds of the California grape crop.

Aftermath. Soon after his victory over the grape growers Chavez again employed the boycott against lettuce growers who were using nonunion labor. Here he attained only limited success, however, largely because the Teamsters were now competing with the UFWOC (in 1972 the AFL-CIO upgraded its status from an organizing committee to a full-fledged affiliate, the United Farm Workers of America) for members. From 1972 to 1974 membership dwindled from nearly sixty thousand to only five thousand. But Chavez continued to work long hours for *La Causa* (as the farmworkers' movement became called), and his efforts were rewarded. From 1964 to 1980 real wages of California migrant workers increased 70 percent, health-care benefits were provided, and a formal grievance procedure was established. By 1975 he also helped obtain passage of the country's first agricultural-labor-relations act in California. This legislation guaranteed farm laborers the right to organize and bargain collectively. Although membership was up again by the 1980s, the UFW's star seemed to be fading. Yet Cesar Chavez remained important; he had organized the once-thought-unorganizable migrant Mexican-American farmworkers, brought them national attention, and won for them the rights enjoyed by other American workers.

Sources:

Cletus Daniel, "Cesar Chavez and the Unionization of California Farm Workers," in *Labor Leaders in America,* edited by Melvyn Dubofsky and Warren Van Tine (Urbana & Chicago: University of Illinois Press, 1987);

Dick Meister and Anne Loftis, *A Long Time in Coming: The Struggle to Unionize America's Farm Workers* (New York: St. Martin's Press, 1977).

HOWARD HUGHES

1905-1976

TYCOON

The Eccentric Eclectic. Over his lifetime billionaire Howard Hughes pursued a variety of interests: he was a test pilot, a manufacturer of aircraft, a longtime majority owner of Trans-World Airlines (TWA), a movie producer, a hotelier, and a real-estate developer. He is best remembered, however, for his increasingly bizarre behavior beginning in the mid 1950s, when he completely dropped out of society. His desire to avoid all publicity and his proclivity for seclusion only heightened the public's interest in Hughes, his whereabouts, and his activities.

Of Tools and Movies. Howard Hughes was born in Houston in 1905. His father had pioneered drilling equipment for the oil industry and built up a successful firm, Hughes Tool Company. When his father died in 1924, Hughes, a freshman at California Institute of Technology (Cal Tech), dropped out of school to run the inherited tool firm. After soon discovering that Hughes Tool did not seem to need his leadership, the twenty-one-year-old Hughes moved to Hollywood to make movies. In the 1930s and 1940s he made such notable films as *Hell's Angels* (the most expensive movie made until 1941), *Scarface* (which featured Hughes's discovery Jean Harlow as the female lead), and *The Outlaw* (which Hughes also directed and which introduced Jane Russell). His continuing interest in the movie industry led him to purchase a controlling interest in RKO Pictures Corporation in 1948.

Of Airplanes. Meanwhile, Hughes formed an aviation company that ultimately became Hughes Aircraft. Besides owning the firm, Hughes tested many of the aircraft himself. Over the course of the 1930s he established several speed and endurance records. In September 1935 he set a speed record of 352 miles per hour in a plane of his own design. Three years later he circled the earth in record time, ninety-one hours. But his most famous airplane was the all-wooden, eight-engine *Spruce Goose*, intended to carry up to 750 passengers. Hughes flew this giant on its maiden and only flight in 1947. While the industrialist was testing planes or making movies, Hughes Aircraft grew to be a major manufacturer of aircraft. It experienced great expansion during World War II, and by 1979 it was the nation's sixth largest defense contractor. Hughes's interest in airplanes also led to his involvement in the airline business — in 1939 he purchased control of TWA; over time he increased his interest in the company to 78 percent. He sold his TWA stock in 1966 for $546.5 million.

Of Seclusion and Controversy. By the time Hughes divested himself of TWA, he had not been seen in public for years. During the 1960s he became quite active in Las Vegas real estate and the gambling industry. He purchased, for example, the Desert Inn, the Sands Hotel, and the Frontier as well as a Las Vegas radio station and Alamo Airways. These new properties, combined with Hughes Tool, Hughes Aircraft, and real-estate holdings in Arizona and California, gave Hughes an estimated net worth of $1 billion at the end of the decade. Increasing interest in the recluse led to scandal. In 1971 writer Clifford Irving claimed to have the memoirs of Hughes. Irving said he and Hughes had collaborated on the autobiography. Hughes denied the story, and in 1972 the manuscript was discovered to be a forgery. In the last years of his life the wealthy hermit grew stranger and stranger. Seen only by a few male aides, he shuttled in secrecy between quarters in luxury hotels in Las Vegas, Mexico, the Bahamas, Nicaragua, Canada, and England. Apparently becoming deranged from a poor diet and large doses of drugs, he died, oddly enough, in an airplane taking him to Houston for medical treatment in 1976. Even after his death, controversy continued. With his estate estimated as high as $2 billion, several different "wills" surfaced, one showing up in the Mormon church offices in Salt Lake City. All ultimately proved to be forgeries, and no authentic will has been located.

Sources:

Donald Bartlett and J. B. Steele, *Empire: The Life, Legend, and Madness of Howard Hughes* (New York: Norton, 1979);

Michael Drosnin, *Citizen Hughes* (New York: Holt, Rinehart & Winston, 1985);

Milton Moskowitz, Michael Katz, and Robert Levering, eds., *Everybody's Business* (New York: Harper & Row, 1982);

New York Times, 6 April 1976.

JAMES LING

1922-

CONGLOMERATE ORGANIZER; FOUNDER OF LING-TEMCO-VOUGHT

Growth Stock of the Go-Go Sixties. James Ling built one of the most exciting, widely diversified conglomerates of the 1960s — Ling-Temco-Vought (LTV). In 1965 *Fortune* magazine hailed LTV the fastest-growing company in the United States from 1955 to 1965. Three years later it was the country's fourteenth largest industrial concern with sales of $2.8 billion. Ling's assault on the business world and LTV's meteoric rise were nothing short of amazing.

Business Beginnings. A high-school dropout from a working-class background, Ling held a spate of odd jobs before becoming an electrician in Dallas, Texas. After serving in the navy, where he studied electrical engineering, Ling returned to Dallas in 1946. He then sold his house and used the proceeds to set up Ling Electric Company. The small firm originally specialized in residential wiring but soon expanded into larger commercial projects. By 1955 the company was earning $1.5 million annually, and Ling chose to incorporate. However, he soon realized that electronics had greater growth potential than the electrical business, and the following year he bought a small electronics firm that manufactured testing equipment for the aerospace industry. In 1958 he merged the two companies forming Ling Electronics and created a holding company, Ling Industries. During these transactions Ling learned a valuable lesson — the increasing value of his company's stock covered the indebtedness created by purchasing other businesses.

Creating LTV. After acquiring several more small electronics concerns, Ling obtained two other firms — Temco Electronics, an electronic-reconnaissance equipment maker, and Chance Vought, an aircraft manufacturer. The companies were combined, creating LTV. In 1964 Ling "redeployed" his holdings into three subsidiaries, and each issued its own shares of stock. The sale of securities provided capital for further acquisitions. In 1965 Ling began the great expansion with the purchase of Okonite Company, a cable manufacturer, and two years later he purchased Wilson and Company, a meatpacking, sporting goods, and chemical firm. More capital was needed for further expansion, so Ling reconfigured Wilson into three divisions, each issuing its own stock. Two giant acquisitions then followed: Greatamerica, a banking and insurance company which also held Braniff Airways and National Car Rental; and Jones and Laughlin, the sixth largest steel company in the country. By repeatedly reorganizing his companies and issuing various securities, James Ling not only built a mammoth conglomerate, he became a multimillionaire.

Collapse. After 1968, however, things began to fall apart. The Justice Department brought suit against LTV, demanding it spin off the steel firm or other holdings. Rising interest rates and the economic downturn hurt company profits and made its heavy debt load difficult to service. By 1970 LTV's stock had fallen from a high of 169 in 1967 to 7, and Ling was forced to step down as CEO. Although he continued to own a substantial amount of LTV stock and pursued other business interests, Ling's high-flying days were over. LTV struggled over the next decade, selling off subsidiaries to pay down the debt. By 1985, however, when it became clear that the company's fortunes could not be turned around, LTV filed for bankruptcy.

Sources:

Stanley Brown, *Ling* (New York: Atheneum, 1972);

Robert Sobel, *The Rise and Fall of the Conglomerate Kings* (New York: Stein & Day, 1984).

RALPH NADER

1934-

CONSUMER ADVOCATE, LAWYER

The Consumers' Watchdog. *Progressive* magazine once hailed him as "Citizen of the Republic" because of his crusading efforts to protect the public; others, less sympathetic to his causes, have referred to him as the nation's nag. But whether regarded as a hero or a villain, Ralph Nader has been the country's leading consumer advocate since the mid 1960s. Yet, in an ironic twist, this defender of consumer rights is in many ways a nonconsumer. He does not own a car, lives in an inexpensive rooming house, avoids all junk food, and dresses plainly. In fact, as of 1983, he was still wearing the same pair of shoes he purchased in 1959.

Unsafe at Any Speed. Nader graduated Phi Beta Kappa from Princeton and then attended Harvard Law School, where he became interested in automobile safety. After practicing law in Connecticut for several years, he headed to Washington, D.C., became a consultant to the Department of Labor, and returned to his research on auto safety. In 1965 he published his findings in his book *Unsafe at Any Speed.* The study attacked General Motors for selling a car, the Chevrolet Corvair, that had known safety defects. The book became an immediate bestseller, and General Motors, in a move to discredit the author, hired a detective to investigate Nader's politics, religion, and sex life. When news of the investigation leaked out, the chairman of GM was forced to apologize to Nader and ultimately paid him $425,000 to drop the invasion-of-privacy suit. With this money Nader created several consumer-interest groups, including the Center for the Study of Responsive Law. Collectively these organizations included many young, idealistic staff members who became known as "Nader's Raiders."

Protective Legislation. With the support of his raiders who were sent to investigate a wide variety of industries and products, Nader campaigned for consumer protection laws in the 1960s and 1970s. He played an essential role in obtaining the National Traffic and Motor Vehicle Safety Act of 1966 — which established a federal agency to set auto safety standards — the Consumer Products Safety Act, and the Occupational Safety and Health Act. He also successfully lobbied for job protection for whistleblowers and the creation of the Environmental Protection Agency.

Persistence. In 1972, after a flurry of legislative victories, Nader ranked seventh in a Gallup poll of most-admired people, immediately ahead of the pope and comedian Bob Hope. By the late 1970s and into the early 1980s, however, Nader's influence declined; Congress defeated, for example, his proposed Consumer Protection Agency in 1978. Yet Nader's commitment to improving people's lives never wavered, and by the end of the 1980s it was clear he remained a real political power. He was part of the California initiative effort that reduced the skyrocketing cost of auto insurance rates, and his continued pursuit of safer automobiles led major manufacturers to install air bags in most of their cars.

Sources:

Ken Auletta, "Ralph Nader, Public Eye," *Esquire* (December 1983): 480–487;

Ralph Mayer, *The Consumer Movement: Guardians of the Marketplace* (Boston: Twayne, 1989).

H. ROSS PEROT

1930-

TYCOON

The Stuff of Fiction. The life story of H. Ross Perot seems more like a good novel than reality. A U.S. Naval Academy graduate, Perot joined IBM and soon became one of its top salesmen. But Perot wanted more challenges, and choosing to go out on his own, he formed Electronic Data Systems (EDS). Six years later he took it public, and the thirty-nine-year-old Perot was a billionaire. Perot later made headlines for his failed efforts to bring American prisoners of war (POWs) home from Vietnam, and then, ten years later, he was back on the front pages for his successful covert operation that rescued EDS employees being held in an Iranian jail by the Ayatollah Khomeini. He returned to the limelight when he became the largest stockholder of General Motors. In 1992 he ran for president.

Perot and EDS. From his days with IBM, this man from Texarkana, Texas, came to believe there was a market for someone who could design, install, and operate data-processing systems for clients. In 1962, with one thousand dollars in savings, Perot founded EDS, a computer-services company, to fill this niche. By attracting major clients, mostly large insurance companies such as Blue Cross, the company was profitable, but with revenues of $7.7 million in 1968, *Fortune* magazine referred to it as an industry "pip-squeak." That same year, however, Perot recapitalized his firm with 12 million shares. Then with the brokerage house of R. W. Presspich and Company, he took his firm public. Initially offered at $16.50 per share, EDS closed its first day of trading at $23.00. Perot had offered only 650,000 shares for sale, and personally held 9 million. Overnight, his EDS shares gave him a net worth of $200 million. During the great bull market of 1969–1970 EDS shot up to $150 per share, and "the Fastest Richest Texan Ever," as *Fortune* had dubbed him, was worth $1 billion.

The Two Rescues: Win One, Lose One. From his stock-market coup on, the wiry, five-foot-six-inch Perot thrived on media attention. In the fall of 1969 Perot began his efforts to free American POWs in North Vietnam. As part of his campaign, he collected nearly thirty tons of supplies and medicine, chartered two jets, and tried to take the cargo to the POWs. When the North Vietnamese officials refused to allow the planes to land, Perot then offered $100 million for the release of the prisoners. Although rebuffed, Perot's work led to better treatment of the POWs. Much more successful, however, was Perot's daring mission to rescue EDS employees from Iranian jails. In 1979 a disguised Perot first flew to Iran to tell the employees he was going to get them out. He then organized a private group of commandos, who succeeded in extracting the EDS workers from revolutionary Iran. Best-selling author Ken Follett's *On Wings of Eagles* (1983) was based on this story.

Perot and General Motors. On his fifty-fourth birthday Perot and GM chairman Roger Smith surprised the business world by announcing GM's purchase of EDS; from the deal Perot became the largest single stockholder of GM and a member of its board of directors. As GM struggled through the mid 1980s, Perot became very critical of company management. In December 1986 Smith and GM executives purchased Perot's 11 million shares for $62.50 a share, or nearly double the market price. Historian John Ingham said in *Newsweek* that "GM had paid Perot a cool $700 million to get out and shut up."

Act Four. Although Perot once told *Newsweek* magazine that he did not see himself "as someone who can save the United States," he apparently changed his mind in 1992. Fed up with the incumbent Republican president, George Bush, and not at all satisfied with the Democratic hopefuls, Perot entered the presidential race as a third-party candidate in the spring. Addressing Americans with simple language and quotable one-liners, he portrayed himself as a political outsider who could cut through bureaucratic red tape and spur economic growth. The unpredictable Perot, however, dropped out of the race in the summer only to reenter it in October. Bill Clinton won the election, but Perot received 19 percent of the popular vote, more than any other third-party candidate since Theodore Roosevelt ran on the Bull Moose party ticket in 1912.

Sources:

Ken Follett, *On Wings of Eagles* (New York: Morrow, 1983);

"GM Boots Perot," *Newsweek*, 108 (15 December 1986): 56–60ff;

Arthur Louis, "The Fastest Texan Ever," *Fortune*, 78 (November 1968): 168ff;

Christopher Wren, "Ross Perot: Billionaire Patriot," *Look*, 34 (24 March 1970): 28–32.

JERRY WURF

1919-1981

LABOR LEADER; PRESIDENT OF THE AMERICAN FEDERATION OF STATE, COUNTY, AND MUNICIPAL EMPLOYEES (AFSCME)

Unionization of Public Employees. The spreading of public-sector unionism accounted for much of the labor movement's vitality in the 1960s. Public-employee union membership rose from less than 400,000 in 1955 to over 4 million by the early 1970s. This rapid increase can be explained in several ways. As the government assumed a larger social and economic role in post–World War II America, the number of public workers skyrocketed — by the mid 1960s one out of every eight Americans was employed by local, state, or federal government. This growth lured union leaders to mount major organizing efforts. Such unionization campaigns benefited from the steady inflation over the period that encouraged workers to worry about their salaries, but they were also aided by the federal government. In 1962 President John Kennedy signed executive order 10988, granting federal employees the right to join unions and bargain collectively. While all of these factors were important, one labor leader, Jerry Wurf, and his union, the American Federation of State, County, and Municipal Employees (AFSCME), took center stage and led the organization effort.

Early Career. Jerry Wurf's union career began in 1940, soon after he took a job as a cashier and counterman at a Brooklyn cafeteria. Unhappy with the working conditions, Wurf led the other employees to organize Local No. 448 of the Food Checkers and Cashiers Union of the Hotel and Restaurant Workers. Impressed with his efforts, the union gave Wurf a job as a staff organizer, and by the mid 1940s he had recruited workers in surrounding cafeterias, diners, and restaurants. His achievements as an organizer caught the attention of veteran labor leader Arnold Zander, head of the AFL-affiliated American Federation of State, County, and Municipal Employees, who hired Wurf in 1947 to build a union to compete with the CIO's Transport Workers Union. Unable to break the dominance of the CIO's union, Wurf was moved over to reorganize AFSCME's small New York City union. His first major success came in 1954 when Mayor Robert Wagner, Jr., issued an executive order recognizing city workers' right to organize. Four years later Wagner acknowledged the union as the exclusive bargaining agent when it had majority representation. By the end of the 1950s Wurf had rebuilt the local in New York, and his high visibility positioned him to win the presidency of the national organization in 1964.

President of AFSCME. Wurf's first years as president of AFSCME concentrated on changing Americans' attitudes toward the rights of public workers. Many still regarded such workers as public servants who did not have the right to bargain collectively. Making wide use of the strike (in 1967 alone some 250 public-workers' strikes broke out), Wurf was well on his way to accomplishing that goal. A major victory came in 1968 when members of the local in Memphis, Tennessee, largely African-American sanitation workers, went on strike protesting racial discrimination. Wurf and local union officials organized a boycott of white-owned businesses in the area, but they did not interfere with strikebreaking garbage collectors. Although the union received favorable media coverage, it was not until Martin Luther King, Jr., came to Memphis to support the strikers and was subsequently assassinated that the city finally capitulated. It agreed to recognize the union and increase wages, and base future promotions entirely on seniority. A considerable triumph for AFSCME, Wurf compared it to pivotal strikes of the past: "[It was] our Homestead, our Hart, Schaffner and Marx, our Flint sit-downs." In the early 1970s many municipal workers watched their purchasing power decline as cities faced serious financial troubles, and this led many public employees to join AFSCME. By mid-decade gaining one thousand members per week, it was the nation's fastest-growing union. By the end of the 1970s public employees' rights were recognized, their unions were well established, and AFSCME was one of the largest unions in the AFL-CIO.

Supporting Liberal Causes. Because of the growing numbers of minorities in the public sector, half of AFSCME's membership consisted of women and nonwhite minorities. This makeup, coupled with Wurf's liberal leanings, led the union to champion many progressive causes. Once called "a man with white skin but a black soul" by Rev. Ralph Abernathy, Wurf was active in supporting the cause of African-Americans. Besides civil rights, he was one of the first leaders of an AFL-CIO union to speak out against the union's support of the Vietnam War. In addition, when George Meany withheld an AFL-CIO endorsement from Democratic presidential nominee George McGovern in 1972, Wurf and AFSCME independently threw their support behind the antiwar candidate.

Sources:
Ronald Filippelli, *Labor in the USA: A History* (New York: Knopf, 1984);

Joseph Goulden, *Jerry Wurf: Labor's Last Angry Man* (New York: Atheneum, 1982).

PEOPLE IN THE NEWS

In December 1965 **Harold S. Geneen,** CEO of International Telephone and Telegraph (ITT), announced plans to acquire the American Broadcasting Company (ABC). The Justice Department did not allow the merger.

On 4 March 1964 **James ("Jimmy") Hoffa,** president of the International Brotherhood of Teamsters, was convicted of tampering with a federal jury in 1962; in July he was also convicted on fraud and conspiracy charges. Fined ten thousand dollars and sentenced to eight years in prison, he was pardoned by President Richard Nixon in 1971.

In his January 1966 budget message President **Lyndon Johnson** gave his famous "guns and butter" speech, explaining that the United States could fight a war and expand social-welfare programs simultaneously. He said, "We are a rich nation and can afford to make progress at home while meeting our obligations abroad — in fact, we can afford no other course if we are to remain strong. For this reason, I have not halted progress in the new and vital Great Society programs in order to finance the costs of our efforts in Southeast Asia."

In 1962 **Royal Little,** CEO of Textron, retired. A pioneer in the conglomerate wave of the 1950s and 1960s, he built a midsized textile company into a huge diversified firm making everything from bathroom accessories to helicopters.

In 1963 **George Meany,** president of the AFL-CIO, referred to automation as a "curse to society."

In 1968 **Robert Noyce** left Fairchild Semiconductor to found Intel Corporation. By 1971 Intel had developed the microchip.

On 3 February 1967 **Walter Reuther,** head of the United Auto Workers, resigned from the executive council of the AFL-CIO, increasing the rift between Reuther and AFL-CIO president George Meany.

On 23 September 1969 Secretary of Labor **George Shultz** ordered into effect the Philadelphia Plan, guidelines for the hiring of minorities by six skilled-craft unions working in Philadelphia on projects receiving federal funds.

In 1960 **Henry Singleton** left Litton Industries to establish his own electronics firm, Teledyne. From this Singleton created a massive conglomerate; by 1987 Teledyne had sales of $3.2 billion and was the 134th largest industrial concern in the country.

On 8 August 1968 financier **Louis Wolfson** and three associates were convicted of stock manipulation in violation of Securities and Exchange Commission regulations during the liquidation of Merrit-Chapman and Scott Corporation.

DEATHS

Benjamin Abrams, 74, founder of Emerson Radio and Phonograph Corporation, 23 June 1967.

Avery C. Adams, 65, head of Jones and Laughlin Steel Corporation (1956–1963) and Pittsburgh Steel Company (1950–1956), 11 December 1963.

Cyril Ainsworth, 71, engineer and expert on industrial and safety standards, 13 December 1964.

Frank A. D. Andrea, 77, pioneer radio manufacturer, 22 December 1965.

Elizabeth Arden, 81, founder, president, and chairman of the board of Elizabeth Arden (now owned by Eli Lilly and Company), an international organization of beauty resorts, beauty salons, and retail cosmetics, 18 October 1966.

George Arents, 85, founder of American Machine and Foundry Company and International Cigar Machinery Company, 13 December 1960.

Sewell L. Avery, 86, business executive; president (1905–1937) and chairman of the board (1937–1951) of U.S. Gypsum; in 1931 he was named chairman of Montgomery Ward and would later serve as its president, 31 October 1960.

Roger Babson, 92, stock analyst who predicted the stock-market crash of 1929, 5 March 1967.

Harold Bache, 73, president of Bache and Company, 15 March 1968.

Hugh Baillie, 75, president (1935–1955) of United Press (now United Press International), 1 March 1966.

J. Stewart Baker, 73, first president of Chase Manhattan Bank, 5 September 1966.

John W. Barnes, 62, president of his family's publishing firm, Barnes and Noble, 17 December 1964.

Arthur S. Barrows, 79, president of Sears, Roebuck and Company (1942–1946), 20 September 1963.

Bruce Barton, 80, advertising executive, who wrote the best-seller *The Man Nobody Knows* (1925), which pictured Jesus Christ as the world's most successful businessman; one of the founders of Batten, Barton, Durstine and Osborn advertising agency, 5 July 1967.

Bernard M. Baruch, 94, financier and philanthropist, 20 June 1965.

James F. Bell, 81, founder of General Mills (1928), the world's largest milling company, 7 May 1961.

Nathan J. Blumberg, 66, president (1938–1952) and chairman of the board (1952–1960) of Universal Pictures, 24 July 1960.

John Brophy, 79, one of the founders of the CIO in 1935, 19 February 1963.

Elmer Brown, 66, president of International Typographical Union, 27 February 1968.

Ralph Budd, 82, railroad executive; president of the Great Northern Railroad (1919–1932); president of the Chicago, Burlington and Quincy Railroad (1932–1949), 2 February 1962.

Charles H. Buford, 74, president of the Chicago, Milwaukee, Saint Paul, and Pacific Railroad (1947–1950), 17 August 1960.

Arthur H. Bunker, 68, chief of War Production Board (1941–1945); board chairman of American Metal Climax, 19 May 1964.

Orville S. Caesar, 73, president (1946–1955) and chairman (1955–1959) of Greyhound Corporation, 19 May 1965.

Harold Carlson, 66, head of Associated Press electronics laboratory (1946–1961); one of the developers of transmitting photos by wire, 11 September 1964.

Paul H. Carnahan, 61, president of National Steel Corporation since 1961, 26 December 1965.

Ralph Chaplin, 73, a leader of the Industrial Workers of the World (IWW) during World War I; wrote the labor anthem "Solidarity Forever," 23 March 1961.

Colby M. Chester, 88, president (1924–1935) and chairman of the board (1935–1943) of Postum Foods, now General Foods Corporation, 26 September 1965.

Martin W. Clement, 84, president (1935–1951) and chairman of the board (1949–1951) of the Pennsylvania Railroad, 3 August 1966.

Baynard S. Colgate, 65, head of Colgate-Palmolive Company (1933–1952), 8 October 1963.

Harvey N. Collison, 66, board chairman of Olin Mathieson Chemical Corporation, 1 November 1966.

Samuel Cooke, 66, an originator of the supermarket in Philadelphia in 1927, 22 May 1965.

Howard Coonley, 89, former president of National Association of Manufacturers (NAM), 25 February 1966.

Joshua Lionel Cowen, 85, founder and chairman of Lionel Corporation (maker of Lionel toy trains), 8 September 1965.

Mark W. Cresap, Jr., 53, president of Westinghouse Electric Corporation (1958–1963), 28 July 1963.

Powel Crosley, Jr., 74, car manufacturer; owner of the Cincinnati Reds baseball team, 28 March 1961.

Edward Cudahy, Jr., 80, 1900 kidnapping victim, meatpacking executive, 8 January 1966.

Harlow H. Curtice, 69, business executive; forty-four-year career with GM; president of AC Spark Plug Division (1929–1933); president of Buick Motor Division (1933–1948); and president of GM (1953–1958), 3 November 1962.

Charles B. Darrow, 78, inventor of the game Monopoly, 28 August 1967.

Roy E. Davidson, 63, head of the International Brotherhood of Locomotive Engineers, 6 July 1964.

Arthur V. Davis, 95, president of Alcoa in 1910 and board chairman from 1928 to 1957, 17 November 1962.

Walt Disney, 65, movie producer, creator of such famous characters as Mickey Mouse and Donald Duck, and the theme park Disneyland, 15 December 1966.

Edward H. Dodd, 96, president (1916–1928) and chairman (1928–1938) of book publisher Dodd, Mead and Company, 19 June 1965.

Frank C. Dodd, 92, former chairman of Dodd, Mead and Company, 4 January 1968.

Hartley M. Dodge, 82, owner and head of Remington Arms Company, 25 December 1963.

Joseph M. Dodge, 74, banker; helped rebuild Germany's monetary system (1945–1946) and reorganized Japan's economy (1949–1952), 2 December 1964.

Orvil E. Dryfoos, 50, president (1957–1961) and publisher (1961–1963) of *The New York Times,* 25 May 1963.

Irenee Du Pont, 86, president of Du Pont (1919–1926), 19 December 1963.

Roy S. Durstine, 75, a founder in 1918 of Batten, Barton, Durstine and Osborn advertising agency; had run his own advertising agency since 1939, 28 November 1962.

J. Frank Duryea, 97, codesigner (with brother Charles) of the first gasoline-engine automobile in the United States, which had its first trial run in September 1893, 15 February 1967.

Frederick H. Ecker, 96, head of Metropolitan Life Insurance Company (1929– 1951), 20 March 1964.

Charles Edison, 78, president (1926–1950) and board chairman (1950–1957) of his father's firm, Thomas A. Edison; board chairman (1957–1961) of successor firm, McGraw-Edison; Democratic governor of New Jersey (1941–1944), 31 July 1969.

Sherwood H. Egbert, 49, president of Studebaker Corporation (1961–1963) who unsuccessfully tried to return company to financial success, 30 July 1969.

Edwin Ekstrom, 78, founder of the Greyhound Bus Company, 7 May 1967.

R. A. Emerson, 54, president of the Canadian Pacific Railway, 13 March 1966.

Benjamin F. Fairless, 71, president (1938–1952) and chairman (1952–1955) of U.S. Steel, 1 January 1962.

Marshall Field, Jr., 49, president and publisher of the *Chicago Sun-Times;* chairman of the board of Field Enterprises, 18 September 1965.

Charles T. Fisher, 83, one of seven brothers who founded Fisher Body Company (a division of General Motors from 1926) in 1908, 8 August 1963.

James L. Fly, 67, businessman and lawyer, chairman of the Federal Communications Commission (1939–1944), 6 January 1966.

Bruce C. Forbes, 48, president and publisher of *Forbes* business magazine, 2 June 1964.

Roy A. Fruehauf, 57, former chairman of the board of Fruehauf Trailer Company, 30 October 1965.

Wilfred J. Funk, 82, son of the founder of the dictionary and encyclopedia publishing company Funk and Wagnalls; president of the company from 1925 to 1940, 1 June 1965.

Walter S. Gifford, 81, efficiency expert, president (1925–1948) and chairman of the board (1948–1950) of American Telephone and Telegraph Company, 7 May 1966.

Bernard F. Gimbel, 81, president (1927–1953) and chairman of the board (1931–1966) of Gimbel Brothers, a chain of retail department stores, 29 September 1966.

Tom M. Girdler, 87, president and board chairman of Republic Steel Corporation; former president of Jones and Laughlin Steel, 4 February 1965.

Eugene G. Grace, 83, president since 1913 of Bethlehem Steel Corporation, second largest steel producer in the

United States; chairman of the board (1936–1957), 25 July 1960.

Robert C. Graham, 82, one of three brothers, makers of Graham-Paige automobiles, 3 October 1967.

Chester H. Gray, 84, founder of the American Farm Bureau Federation, 1 April 1964.

Albert M. Greenfield, 79, department-store tycoon; one-time owner of Tiffany's, 5 January 1967.

Robert E. Gross, 64, owner (from 1932) and board chairman of Lockheed Aircraft Corporation, 3 September 1961.

Larry E. Gubb, 74, former board chairman, Philco Corporation, 10 November 1966.

Harold K. Guinzburg, 61, a founder (in 1925) and president of Viking Press, 18 October 1961.

Paul M. Hahn, 68, former president of American Tobacco Company, 9 August 1963.

Alfred L. Hammell, 72, president of Railway Express Agency (1949–1959), 8 February 1962.

Thomas J. Hargrave, 70, president of Eastman Kodak from 1941, 21 February 1962.

George M. Harrison, 73, labor-union leader; vice-president of American Federation of Labor (1934–1955); chairman of Railway Labor Executives Association (1935–1940); president (1928–1963) and chief executive officer (1963–1965) of National Brotherhood of Railway Clerks, 30 November 1968.

Fred A. Hartley, Jr., 66, U.S. congressman from New Jersey (1929–1949); co-author with Sen. Robert Taft of Ohio of the Taft-Hartley Labor Relations Act in 1947, 11 May 1969.

Amory L. Haskell, 72, founder and president of Monmouth Park Race Track; introduced safety glass to U.S. auto manufacturers, 12 April 1966.

John D. Hertz, 82, founder of Yellow Cab Company (in 1915) and Hertz Rent-A-Car (in 1924), 8 October 1961.

Eugene Holman, 67, head of Standard Oil of New Jersey from 1944 to 1960, 12 August 1962.

Mark C. Honeywell, 89, head of Minneapolis-Honeywell Regulators (1927–1935), makers of heating systems and thermostats, 13 September 1964.

Charles R. Hook, 83, head of American Rolling Mill Company from 1930 to 1959, 14 November 1963.

Herbert C. Hoover, Jr., 65, mining engineer; undersecretary of state (1954–1957); helped settle Anglo-Iranian dispute over the Abadan oil field; son of President Herbert Hoover, 9 July 1969.

Harry Humphreys, Jr., 66, former chairman and president of Uniroyal, 3 September 1967.

Edward F. Hutton, 86, founder of the brokerage firm E. F. Hutton and Company in 1904; chairman of Postum Cereal Company (now General Foods) from 1923 to 1935, 11 July 1962.

Edward W. Isom, 76, president of Sinclair Rubber (1942–1952) and board chairman of Sinclair Chemical (1952–1955), 19 January 1962.

Alton W. Jones, 70, head of Cities Service Company from 1939 to 1959, 1 March 1962.

Henry J. Kaiser, 85, entrepreneur and industrialist; involved in aluminum, automobiles, cement, shipbuilding, and steel; also founded one of the nation's largest health-maintenance organizations, Kaiser Permanente Medical Care Program, 24 August 1967.

Herbert T. Kalmus, 81, codeveloper of Technicolor process for motion pictures, 11 July 1963.

Natalie M. Kalmus, 87, codeveloper of Technicolor, 15 November 1965.

W. M. Keck, 84, founder of Superior Oil Company, 20 August 1964.

K. T. Keller, 80, president and chairman of the board of Chrysler Corporation, 21 January 1966.

Thomas Kennedy, 75, president of United Mine Workers (1960–1963), 19 January 1963.

Herbert A. Kent, 73, president (1942–1952) and board chairman (1952–1955) of P. Lorillard Company, a manufacturer of cigarettes, 19 July 1960.

James H. Kindelberger, 67, head of North American Aviation from 1935; the company produced 14 percent of U.S. military aircraft during World War II, 27 July 1962.

Willard M. Kiplinger, 76, founder of the *Kiplinger Letters* and *Changing Times*, 6 August 1967.

Blanche W. Knopf, 71, cofounder and president, Alfred A. Knopf, 4 June 1966.

Sebastian S. Kresge, 90, founder of S. S. Kresge Company, originally a dime-store chain, now giant Kresge Corporation, owner of discounter K-Mart, 18 October 1966.

Rush H. Kress, 85, with his brother Samuel developer of S. H. Kress and Company into a chain of variety stores, 22 March 1963.

Thomas Lamont, 68, financier and onetime partner of J. P. Morgan; convened meeting of representatives from major banking houses in an attempt to halt stock market decline in October 1929, 10 April 1967.

James M. Landis, 64, lawyer and government official; served on the Federal Trade Commission, Securities and Exchange Commission, and the Civil Aeronautics Board; drew up a report on federal regulation for President-elect John Kennedy, 31 July 1964.

Russell C. Leffingwell, 82, board chairman of J. P. Morgan and Company (1948–1955); assistant secretary of the U.S. Treasury (1917–1920), 2 October 1960.

Nathaniel Leverone, 84, founder and head of Automatic Canteen Company, which led the way in the development and production of reliable vending machines on a national scale, 30 May 1969.

Abraham Levitt, 82, building contractor; his company mass-produced over sixty thousand houses after World War II; famous for building three suburban communities, all named Levittown, in the Northeast, 20 August 1962.

John L. Lewis, 89, president of the United Mine Workers (1920–1960); in 1935 led several unions out of the AFL to found the CIO; served as its president until 1940, 11 June 1969.

Josiah K. Lilly, 72, chairman of the board, Eli Lilly and Company, a pharmaceutical firm, 4 May 1966.

Jesse T. Littleton, 78, developer of Pyrex glassware, 24 February 1966.

Henry R. Luce, 68, founder, editor, and publisher of *Time, Life,* and *Fortune,* 28 February 1967.

Alfred Lyon, 81, former president of Philip Morris, 7 May 1967.

Elliot B. Macrae, 67, publisher; president of E. P. Dutton and Company, 13 February 1968.

Walter P. Marshall, 67, former president (1948–1965) and chairman (1965–1966) of Western Union Telegraph Company, 5 May 1969.

Homer Martin, 66, first president of the United Auto Workers, 22 January 1968.

Oscar G. Mayer, 76, president of Oscar Mayer Corporation, 5 March 1965.

L. B. Maytag, 78, former president of Maytag Company, a major appliance manufacturer, 8 August 1967.

Fowler B. McConnell, 67, president (1946–1958) and board chairman (1958–1960) of Sears, Roebuck and Company, 27 December 1961.

William G. Mennen, 83, chairman of the Mennen Company, 17 February 1968.

Gustav Metzman, 73, president of the New York Central Railroad (1944–1952), 11 April 1960.

Thomas Millsop, 68, former chairman of the board, National Steel Corporation, 12 September 1967.

James P. Mitchell, 63, secretary of labor under President Dwight Eisenhower (1953–1961); opposed right-to-work laws, 19 October 1964.

Theodore Montague, 69, former president of Borden Company, 13 August 1967.

Wyndham Mortimer, 82, a founder of the United Auto Workers (UAW) and the Congress of Industrial Organizations (CIO), 23 August 1966.

Thomas E. Murray, 69, organizer in 1939 of Murray Manufacturing Company, maker of electrical switches; member of the Atomic Energy Commission (1950–1957), 26 May 1961.

Edgar A. Newberry, 75, head of J. J. Newberry Company, a variety-store chain from 1939, 25 January 1962.

Wilbur H. Norton, 59, president of Montgomery Ward (1946–1948); vice-president of General Motors (1949–1952), 2 April 1963.

Irving S. Olds, 76, board chairman of U.S. Steel (1940–1952), 4 March 1963.

William F. O'Neil, 76, founder and board chairman of General Tire and Rubber Company, 4 September 1960.

Cola G. Parker, 72, president of Kimberly-Clark Corporation (1942–1953); president of National Association of Manufacturers (1956), 27 June 1962.

Josephine B. Paul, 61, president of the brokerage firm A. M. Kidder and Company from 1956, 6 August 1962.

Frances Perkins, 83, expert on industrial relations and first woman cabinet member; served as President Franklin Roosevelt's secretary of labor from 1933 to 1945, 14 May 1965.

T. S. Petersen, 69, retired president, Standard Oil of California, 16 September 1966.

Joseph N. Pew, Jr., 76, chairman of Sun Oil Company from 1947, 9 April 1963.

Gerald L. Phillippe, 59, chairman of General Electric Company, 18 October 1968.

John Pillsbury, 90, retired head of Pillsbury Foods, 31 January 1968.

Gregory Pincus, 64, one of the developers of the birth-control pill, 22 August 1967.

Robert A. Pinkerton, 62, chairman of Pinkerton, the private detective agency, infamous for being brought in against the Homestead Steel Works strikers in 1892, 11 October 1967.

Edgar Monsanto Queeny, 70, former head of the chemical firm Monsanto, 7 July 1968.

Michael J. Quill, 60, one of the founders and president of Transport Workers Union of America, 28 January 1966.

James Henry Rand, 81, cofounder of Sperry-Rand Corporation, a business machine and computer firm, 3 June 1968.

Clarence B. Randall, 76, retired chairman of Inland Steel, 4 August 1967.

Stanley B. Resor, 83, president (1916–1955) and board chairman (1955–1961) of J. Walter Thompson Company, 29 October 1962.

Roy Reuther, 58, organizer of the United Auto Workers, brother of Walter Reuther (president of the CIO), 10 January 1968.

R. J. Reynolds, 58, heir to tobacco fortune, 14 December 1964.

Ralph O. Rhoades, 65, geologist and oil company executive; in 1935 did research that led to discovery of oil in Kuwait, 19 July 1961.

Stanley M. Rinehart, Jr., 71, founder in 1929 of Farrar and Rinehart, which in 1960 became Holt, Rinehart and Winston, a major publisher of college textbooks, 26 April 1969.

A. W. Robertson, 85, board chairman of Westinghouse Electric Corporation from 1929 to 1951, 18 December 1965.

David A. Robertson, 80, head of the Brotherhood of Locomotive Firemen and Enginemen (1922–1953), 27 September 1961.

William E. Robinson, 68, businessman; president (1948–1954) and publisher (1954) of the *New York Herald Tribune*; president (1955–1958), board chairman and chief executive officer (1958–1961) of Coca-Cola; under Robinson's leadership Coke achieved record in sales volume, 6 June 1969.

Helena Rubinstein, 94, founder and president of Helena Rubinstein, a cosmetics firm; one of the world's wealthiest women, 1 April 1965.

Margaret Rudkin, 69, founder of Pepperidge Farm, 1 June 1967.

Joseph P. Ryan, 79, president of the International Longshoremen's Association (1927–1953), 26 June 1963.

John Savage, 88, engineer who designed Hoover Dam and Grand Coulee Dam, 28 December 1967.

Joseph M. Schenk, 82, motion picture executive; president of United Artists (1927–1933) and later president and board chairman of 20th Century-Fox, 22 October 1961.

Charles F. Seabrook, 83, cofounded with Clarence Birdseye a frozen-food marketing firm (1932), 20 October 1964.

Richard L. Simon, 61, cofounded publishing firm Simon and Schuster in 1924, 29 July 1960.

Alfred P. Sloan, Jr., 90, president and later chairman of the board of General Motors in the 1920s and 1930s; famous for his reorganization of GM, 17 February 1966.

Robert L. Smith, 71, board chairman of the cough-drop manufacturers Smith Brothers from 1955, 7 January 1962.

Winthrop Smith, 67, board chairman of the huge brokerage firm Merrill, Lynch, Pierce, Fenner and Smith, 10 January 1961.

Harold Stanley, 77, head of the investment house of Morgan, Stanley and Company from 1935 to 1956, 14 May 1963.

Frank D. Stranahan, 89, cofounder of Champion Spark Plug Company in 1908, 10 November 1965.

Robert A. Stranahan, Sr., 75, cofounder of Champion Spark Plug Company, 9 February 1962.

Leon A. Swirbul, 62, founder and president of Grumman Aircraft Engineering Corporation, 28 June 1960.

Wilfred Sykes, 80, president of Inland Steel Company (1941–1949), 2 May 1964.

J. Maurice Treneer, 86, creator of Alka-Seltzer for Miles Laboratories, 2 July 1968.

Walter J. Tuohy, 65, chief executive officer of the Chesapeake and Ohio (C&O) and the Baltimore and Ohio (B&O) railroads, 12 May 1966.

J. C. van Eck, 84, Dutch industrialist; founder of Shell Oil Company in United States (1912); president of Shell Oil (1923–1936); managing director of Royal Dutch-Shell Group (1936–1947), 16 February 1965.

Guy W. Vaughn, 82, former president of Curtiss-Wright Corporation, 21 November 1966.

Jesse G. Vincent, 82, inventor of the first V–12 automobile engine, 20 April 1962.

Edward C. Werle, 56, board chairman of the New York Curb (later American) Exchange (1944–1947) and of the New York Stock Exchange (1958–1961), 7 January 1962.

Roy B. White, 77, president (1941–1953) and chairman (1953–1961) of the Baltimore and Ohio Railroad, 3 June 1961.

Arthur D. Whiteside, 77, president of the credit-rating agency Dun and Bradstreet (1933–1952), 17 June 1960.

George Whitney, 77, head of J. P. Morgan and Company from 1940 to 1955, 22 July 1963.

Albert N. Williams, 73, head of Western Union Telegraph Company from 1941 to 1946, 2 October 1961.

Charles E. Wilson, 71, president of General Motors (1946–1954) and secretary of defense (1954–1957), 26 September 1961.

Robert E. Wilson, 71, head of Standard Oil Company of Indiana from 1945 to 1958; member of the U.S. Atomic Energy Commission (1960–1964), 1 September 1964.

Edwin E. Witte, 73, economist; an expert on labor/management relations and labor law, he was executive director of President Franklin Roosevelt's Commission of Economic Security, which drafted the 1935 Social Security Act, 20 May 1960.

Robert E. Wood, 90, vice-president (1924–1928), president (1928–1939), and chairman (1939–1954) of Sears, Roebuck and Company; under his leadership, Sears became the world's largest retailer, 6 November 1969.

C. E. Woolman, 76, chairman of the board, Delta Air Lines, 11 September 1966.

Samuel Zemurray, 84, Russian-born businessman who ran United Fruit Company from 1938 to 1951, 30 November 1961.

PUBLICATIONS

Daniel Bell, *The Coming of Post-Industrial Society* (New York: Basic Books, 1973);

Alfred D. Chandler, Jr., *Strategy and Structure: Chapters in the History of the Industrial Enterprise* (Cambridge, Mass.: MIT Press, 1962);

Barry Commoner, *The Closing Circle* (New York: Knopf, 1971);

Richard Easterlin, *The American Baby Boom in Historical Perspective* (Cambridge, Mass.: National Bureau of Economic Research, 1962);

Paul Ehrich, *The Population Bomb* (San Francisco: Sierra Club, 1968);

Betty Friedan, *The Feminine Mystique* (New York: Dell, 1963);

Milton Friedman and Anna J. Schwartz, *A Monetary History of the United States, 1867–1960* (Princeton: Princeton University Press, 1963);

John K. Galbraith, *The New Industrial State* (Boston: Houghton Mifflin, 1967);

Mitchell Gordon, *Sick Cities* (Baltimore: Penguin, 1965);

Frank Graham, Jr., *Since "Silent Spring"* (Boston: Houghton Mifflin, 1970);

Michael Harrington, *The Other America* (New York: Macmillan, 1962);

Walter W. Heller, *New Dimensions in Political Economy* (Cambridge: Harvard University Press, 1966);

Scott G. Hutchinson, *The Business of Acquisitions and Mergers* (New York: Presidents Publishing, 1968);

Daniel Moynihan, *Maximum Feasible Misunderstanding* (New York: Free Press, 1969);

Ralph Nader, *Unsafe at Any Speed* (New York: Grossman, 1965);

Arthur M. Schlesinger, Jr., *A Thousand Days: John F. Kennedy in the White House* (Boston: Houghton Mifflin, 1965);

E. F. Schumacher, *Small is Beautiful* (New York: Harper & Row, 1973);

Alfred P. Sloan, Jr., *My Years at General Motors* (New York: Doubleday, 1963);

Studs Terkel, *Working* (New York: Pantheon, 1974);

Murray Weidenbaum, *The Modern Public Sector* (New York: Basic Books, 1969);

Business Week, periodical;

Forbes, periodical;

Fortune, periodical;

Newsweek, periodical;

Time, periodical.

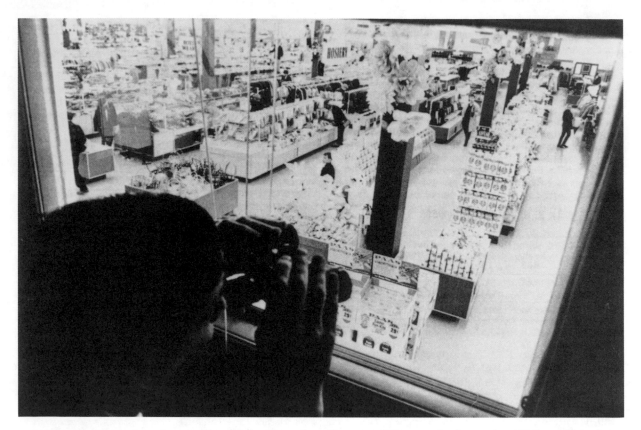

A department-store detective watching for shoplifters through a rear-window monitoring station. While retail department-store sales topped $20 billion in 1967, shoplifting losses were also in the billions of dollars.

EDUCATION

by HARRIET WILLIAMS

CONTENTS

Sidebars and tables are listed in italics.

1960

- Just before the 1960 presidential election, Congress passes a general aid-to-education bill for first time in the twentieth century.

- Myron Lieberman's *The Future Of Public Education* predicts a revolution in all aspects of education in the coming decade.

20 Feb. Black students in Greensboro, North Carolina, stage a sit-in by filling seats at a lunch counter to protest against refusals to serve seated blacks.

13 May Demonstrating San Francisco students are rebuffed with fire hoses at city hall as they protest a House Un-American Activities Committee hearing.

12 Nov. Justice Department warns Louisiana governor Jimmie Davis against blocking desegregation of public schools.

13 Nov. A special session of the Louisiana legislature approves drastic steps to avoid New Orleans school desegregation.

4 Dec. Black New Orleans minister Floyd Foreman continues to escort his five-year-old daughter to an integrated neighborhood school despite abuse.

1961

- Massive shortages in classrooms and of qualified teachers exist in all parts of the country.

- President John F. Kennedy's school legislation fails due to the controversy over proposed federal aid to private schools.

10 Jan. Two black students enroll at the University of Georgia.

13 Jan. The University of Georgia's first two black students are suspended following riots; administration officials are directed to reinstate them.

20 Mar. Louisiana's attempts to halt desegregation are held unconstitutional.

6 May Attorney General Robert Kennedy, speaking at the University of Georgia, vows strict enforcement of civil rights laws.

Nov. Students from several eastern colleges spend Thanksgiving picketing the White House to protest resumption of nuclear weapons testing.

1962

11 Jan. President Kennedy, in his State of the Union Address, announces a push to enact school legislation that failed in 1961.

6 Feb. Congress hears Kennedy's "Special Message on Education" with additional proposals: among them, scholarships to upgrade quality of teaching and aid for adult illiterates and handicapped children.

Apr. A one-day teachers' strike in New York, precipitated by years of overcrowding and low pay, occurs.

25 June The Supreme Court rules that reading of an official prayer in New York public schools violates the Constitution.

8 July The government announces plans for a study on the impact of television on schoolchildren.

14 July Anthony Celebrezze replaces Abraham Ribicoff as secretary of health, education and welfare when Ribicoff runs for Senate.

26 July	A federal judge orders Prince Edward County, Virginia, schools to open, three years after they closed to defy segregation.
31 Aug.	Roman Catholic church officials in Buras, Louisiana, close an integrated parochial school due to threats of violence.
20 Sept.	Mississippi governor Ross Barnett defies federal-court orders and refuses to allow James Meredith to become the first black student at the University of Mississippi.
24 Sept.	As the University of Mississippi board agrees to admit Meredith, Barnett issues a public threat to arrest any federal official who interferes with state officers defying desegregation orders.
26 Sept.	Lt. Gov. Paul Johnson prevents Meredith from enrolling at "Ole Miss."
28 Sept.	Barnett is found guilty of contempt of the federal court order.
29 Sept.	Lieutenant Governor Johnson is also found guilty of contempt.
30 Sept.	Meredith is escorted onto campus; federal troops are ordered there as rioting and shooting break out.
1 Oct.	After fifteen hours of rioting which leaves two dead, Meredith is enrolled.

1963

28 Jan.	Without incident Harvey Gantt registers as the first black student at Clemson College in South Carolina.
5 June	Without incident the second black student, Cleve McDowell, enters the University of Mississippi Law School.
11 June	After planning defiance of the federal desegregation order, Gov. George Wallace steps aside as two black students register at the University of Alabama.
1 July	The U.S. Court of Appeals prohibits Powhatan County, Virginia, schools from closing doors as Prince Edward County had done in 1959.
11 Aug.	One of the two black students at University of Alabama withdraws.
14 Aug.	Virginia governor Albertis Harrison details private financing organized to provide education for the seventeen hundred black children in Prince Edward County who had had no schooling since 1959.
18 Aug.	James Meredith is the first black candidate to receive a B.A. degree from the University of Mississippi.
8 Sept.	A New York teacher strike is averted as the United Federation of Teachers accepts a new contract.
24 Sept.	The University of Mississippi's only black student, McDowell, is expelled for carrying a gun on campus.
19 Nov.	Kennedy thanks National Education Association members in the Rose Garden for help in passing the aid-to-higher-education bill.

16 Dec. President Lyndon B. Johnson signs the education bill into law, saying "The enactment of this measure is a monument to President Kennedy," who had been assassinated on 22 November.

1964

- The number of classrooms under construction lags 124,000 behind need.
- More than 10,000 portable classrooms are now parked near U.S. schools to handle overflow students.

8 Jan. In his State of the Union Address President Johnson unveils his $97.9 billion budget, with increased spending for education as a hallmark.

22 Feb. The United States and the Soviet Union sign the fourth two-year agreement on educational, technological, and scientific exchanges.

12 Mar. Ten thousand New York residents march on the board of education building to protest the loss of neighborhood schools due to desegregation plans.

25 May The Supreme Court holds that Prince Edward County, Virginia, schools must reopen.

19 Nov. In his first speech after the election President Johnson calls education the "prime investment" of the future.

3 Dec. At the University of California, Berkeley, a three-month dispute between student activists and the administration reaches its most intense point as 796 students sitting in at the administration building are arrested.

1965

- Fifty new community colleges are built.

23 Jan. Air Force Secretary Eugene Zuckert announces that one hundred cadets at the Air Force Academy were involved in a cheating scandal.

25 Jan. The new federal budget is $2.2 billion over spending in 1964, with the largest expansion of welfare and education spending since the New Deal.

Feb. One thousand black schoolchildren in Selma, Alabama, are arrested while participating in Martin Luther King, Jr.'s nonviolent voter-registration campaign.

5 Mar. In Indianola, Mississippi, the Freedom School, one of first integrated schools established as an alternative to segregated public schools, is burned to the ground.

9 Apr. A $1.3 billion school-aid bill is enacted after the Senate, in a 73–18 vote, passes it without amendments.

30 May Vivian Malone becomes the first black graduate of the University of Alabama.

20–21 July The White House Conference on Education, with 709 participants and 200 observers, symbolizes President Johnson's commitment to education.

2 Sept. The Senate votes 79–3 to pass a $4.7 billion higher-education bill with major provisions for grants for needy students.

20 Nov.	The chancellor and academic dean of City University of New York as well as the presidents of Brooklyn and Hunter Colleges resign to protest a four-hundred-dollar fee to city residents for annual tuition. Previously there had been no tuition.

1966

- Ivy League schools intensify recruitment of black students.
- The number of enrolled students in graduate programs has doubled to 570,000 since 1957.

19 Feb.	Protestant Union Theological Seminary and Jesuit Fordham University agree to share professors, credits, and libraries in the first formal agreement of its kind between institutions.
3 Mar.	Veterans serving after 31 January 1955 receive new educational benefits as President Johnson signs the Veteran's Readjustment Act.
9 Mar.	President Johnson relaxes travel restrictions to Communist China, allowing scholars to travel and study there.
12 May	University of Chicago students take over the administration building to protest the university's cooperation with the selective service system.
6 June	James Meredith, on a walk from Memphis, Tennessee, to Jackson, Mississippi, to encourage voter registration, is shot by a sniper.
20 Oct.	Congress approves $6.2 billion in aid for elementary and secondary education.

1967

- Student protests — now primarily objecting to U.S. involvement in Vietnam and on-campus recruiting — intensify dramatically.
- The University of Texas chancellor suggests that because so much attention is focused on disadvantaged children, gifted students are being ignored.

14 Jan.	The Hunt Report, "A Bill of Rights for Children," is released; it cites the waste of human potential due to disastrous child-rearing patterns in poverty-stricken families.
30 June	President Johnson's task force on education recommends new and expanded federal programs to include a "moon shot" effort in curriculum and instruction to assure that all children learn the three Rs.
15 Dec.	House-Senate conferees agree to Texas senator Yarborough's bilingual education bill.

1968

- The congressional agenda for 1968 is to renew, extend, and amend the three giant higher-education acts of the past decade.

25 Jan.	Secretary of Health, Education, and Welfare John Gardner resigns after citing misgivings about the inadequacies of the Great Society.
18 Nov.	After five weeks of closed schools, the New York United Federation of Teachers votes to end its strike.
4 Dec.	The government orders the Union, New Jersey, school board to comply with the 1964 Civil Rights Act in a major move against segregation in the North.

1969

- Nine million children from low-income families receive aid for education through Title I.

- There are 716,000 children participating in Head Start programs.

- More than 4 million high-school and 845,000 technical students are enrolled in federally supported vocational education programs.

22 Apr. City College in New York is closed after 150 black and Puerto Rican students blockade one campus.

7 May Seven are injured in a battle between black and white students at City College in New York.

15 May The California National Guard, with tear gas and shotguns, breaks up a protest at the University of California, Berkeley, over the university's seizure of property being used as a "people's park."

Oct. 11 The National Education Association and the American Federation of Teachers merge in Flint, Michigan, as affiliates form the United Teachers of Flint.

Dec. Fifty thousand children enrolled in schools with individually prescribed instruction programs receive individual packets in math and reading. Each child has a study program geared to his or her learning needs and characteristics.

OVERVIEW

Educational Crisis. Americans in the 1960s became aware that the nation was suffering from a shortage of citizens whose education and training were sufficient to meet the technological challenges of modern society. The gap between the learning needs of the country and the capacity of the American educationl system to meet those needs was at a crisis point at the beginning of the decade, and the resulting demands for more and better education forced reassessment of every segment of the teaching-learning process. Education writer Myron Lieberman aptly predicted, in his 1960 book attacking the established system, *The Future of Public Education,* that sweeping transformations over the next few decades would affect "teacher organizations, professional ethics, teacher education, the theory and practice of teacher compensation, and the many interrelationships between teachers and pupils, parents, communities and governmental agencies." Lieberman's predictions were correct, but the changes were compressed into only one decade, 1960–1969.

Effects of Inertia. During this period the face of America changed. Revolutions occurred in science and technology, in economic and political affairs, and in demographic and social structures, while educational institutions struggled to catch up. Despite some attempts at upgrading math and science education at the end of the 1950s, spurred by the Soviets' launching of *Sputnik I,* tradition-bound educators clung to conventional practices merely out of habit. Changes to the system were forced — sometimes by law, sometimes by riot — resulting in tumult and, at times, chaos.

Desegregation of Education. Implementation of *Brown* v. *Board of Education of Topeka, Kansas,* the Supreme Court ruling of 1954 declaring that segregated education was inherently unequal, did not occur in any significant way until the 1960s. But the changes did not come quickly or without extensive federal intervention. The Southern Educational Reporting Service announced in 1960 that less actual desegregation of southern schools occurred in that year than in any other since the Court's original decision. Most southern school districts were practicing "ingenious procrastination," but after a federal district court order threatened schools with sacrificing state financial aid, fourteen southern school districts agreed in late 1960 to desegregate first grade that year and to desegregate a grade per year after that. In the North, where segregation of schools was de facto, the result of black/white housing patterns and illegal separation of the races, parents vigorously protested the loss of neighborhood schools. Although some school districts complied with Court-ordered desegregation without incident, many did not. This defiance in both the South and the North prompted a 1969 unanimous Supreme Court decision declaring that it is "the obligation of every school district to terminate dual school systems at once and to operate now and hereafter only unitary schools."

Higher Education Desegregation. Federal intervention was required to desegregate some southern state universities, and at times black students attempting to enroll faced rioting whites; state troopers deployed by defiant governors squared off against the National Guard sent by the president to enforce the law of the land. The most tumultuous desegregation of a southern university took place at the University of Mississippi ("Ole Miss") at Oxford in the fall of 1962. Gov. Ross Barnett had himself appointed the registrar of the school to bar James Meredith, the first black man to seek entry. Despite federal orders, despite the board of trustees' support of Meredith's candidacy, and despite the Southern Association of Colleges and Schools' consideration of suspending the college's accreditation, Barnett persisted in excluding Meredith. Only after Barnett was found guilty of contempt of a federal court order and fined five thousand dollars per day until he relented did he step aside and allow Meredith to enroll. The scene had been set for fierce rioting by students and citizens, and by 1 October, when Meredith actually began attending classes, two people had been killed. In contrast many southern colleges and schools desegregated without incident, and in the North most institutions actively sought black applicants. Ivy League schools aggressively courted bright black candidates, and by 1968 Princeton, for example, had increased its black enrollment by 200 percent from 1960.

Teacher and School Shortages. The sense of crisis caused by desegregation was intensified by the severe shortages of qualified teachers and the critical lack of classroom space to house the ever-growing numbers of students entering schools and colleges. In 1960 public-school enrollment was 1.9 million students in excess of classroom capacity, a situation that persisted throughout the decade. Portable classrooms, or mobile classroom units, arrived at thousands of schools as a temporary solution to overcrowding, but they remained parked behind schools at the end of the decade. Some secondary schools, scrambling to handle the flood of adolescent baby boomers, were forced to provide double sessions in which students attended only half days. The U. S. Office of Education estimated that in 1960, 195,000 teachers were needed to wipe out deficits, replace substandard teachers, and reduce class sizes to manageable numbers. But the average starting teacher salary of $5,160 did not compare favorably with the $10,700 average starting salary of seventeen other professions that required the same amount of college training. Even though the number of college graduates was swelling, those graduates were not choosing teaching as their professions in sufficient numbers to solve the problems in the elementary and secondary schools.

The Higher Education Boom. Colleges, too, felt the full effect of the baby boom during the late 1960s. But college enrollment boomed even faster than the college-age population. In 1960 the United States was the first society in the history of the world with more college students than farmers, and by 1969 the number of students was triple that of farmers. Todd Gitlin, author of *The Sixties: Years of Hope, Days of Rage* (1987), recalls that upon his high-school graduation from the Bronx High School of Science in New York in 1959, the principal inscribed in his yearbook, " 'About a century ago, the great editor, Horace Greeley, pointed the way of opportunity to the youth of his day in the words, "Go West, young man." Today, there are no more undeveloped western territories but there is a new and limitless "west" of opportunity. Its trails lead through the schools, colleges and universities to the peaks of higher learning. Never in history has there been so promising an opportunity for the young men and women who can make the ascent.' " Gitlin, who at age twenty became president of Students for a Democratic Society (SDS), a militant group devoted to "shaking America to its roots," was one of the thousands of high-school graduates flocking to public institutions of higher education, whose enrollments grew proportionally faster those of the private institutions.

Campus Discontent. The combination of burgeoning numbers of nontraditional college students, many of whom saw the institutions as representative of the establishment which had formerly excluded them, and the growing cynicism of many other students toward institutional leaders set the stage for a decade of student protests. The tensions of a society providing unprecedented affluence for some alongside economic and political discrimination against others helped to galvanize a new mi-

nority: a largely urban and suburban, middle-class New Left. These students who found themselves together at large universities became the New Left, an igniting force which triggered a radical student-activist movement that in some ways has defined the decade. Within a few years this minority created a culture, a style, and a set of tactics that launched effective protests against causes as diverse as the Vietnam War, racial discrimination, and dormitory regulations.

New Missions, New Constituencies. In 1966 University of California president Clark Kerr claimed that "what the railroads did for the second half of the nineteenth century and what the automobile did for the first half of the twentieth century, the universities will now do for the nation." Major research universities in the 1960s were not only the center of the knowledge process, but also the focal point for national growth. This transformation of some universities from teaching institutions to a "knowledge industry," or research factories serving the needs of government and business, left a vacuum among schools serving student needs. At the same time employment opportunities for unskilled workers were declining rapidly while positions for highly trained workers went begging. In response, the military, for example, was forced to create educational institutions providing all types of training from remedial elementary courses in reading and basic math to Ph.D. programs — all for enlisted men within the confines of the service branches. In the private sector community colleges and technical institutions were built and filled with students at a breakneck pace. During 1967, for example, 130 new community colleges were opened. New constituencies vying for more and better education emerged as well. Adults, migrant workers, the handicapped, recent immigrants struggling to learn English, and very young children from disadvantaged backgrounds all competed for attention and for the education dollar.

Expansion of the Federal Role. Public-school education has historically been under state and local controls, but during the 1960s the federal government played an ever-increasing role in the funding of American schools. This infusion of federal dollars and the accompanying spending guidelines began in a relatively small way during the Eisenhower administration with the passage of the National Defense Education Act of 1958, a response to the Soviet launching of *Sputnik I*. This effort was created to stimulate education in science, engineering, foreign languages, and mathematics. In the early 1960s, even while most school boards tenaciously rejected a national education policy, they pleaded for federal funds to help alleviate dire shortages of teachers and to supplement teacher pay. During the televised Kennedy-Nixon presidential debates in 1960, both candidates agreed that teacher salaries were a national disgrace, but whereas Nixon opposed using federal funds for improving salaries (and had cast the tie-breaking vote in opposition to a Senate bill providing just that), Kennedy reminded viewers and listeners that he had voted to provide those funds. Subsequent support of Kennedy by the National Education Association (NEA) was a significant factor in his narrow victory over Nixon. During the Kennedy-Johnson era an extraordinary transformation of federal education policy took place. At the end of the decade, massive amounts of federal aid had gone into all phases of education, from Head Start programs for deprived preschoolers to $9 billion in classrooms, libraries, and labs. One of the cruelest ironies of this era is that just as the federal government implemented programs and policies to "level up" the bottom fifth of the school population, the quality of the standard curriculum at the center of America's public-school system began to spiral downward.

"The Great Debate." During the decade a "great debate" sounded in the popular press and in the professional journals: should the essential purpose of education be intellectual training or social adjustment? If the controversy were viewed as a continuum, on one end would be critics who believed that the historic, rightful task of education is strictly intellectual training, and that in emphasizing social adjustment, the schools were meddling outside their boundaries. At the other end of the spectrum were those who believed that the true purpose of education is the task of developing students' awareness of their inner feelings generated by what they have learned or problems they have encountered. Most people's attitudes fell somewhere between these extremes, and there was some general agreement that the goals of education should emphasize critical thinking, good citizenship, social competence, and creative skills. Debate still continues about which of these goals should receive the greatest emphasis, but in the 1960s it was carried out against the backdrop of public belief that the Soviets had an educational system that was working while the American one was faulty. The public was still concerned with Soviet scientific accomplishment, imagining our ideological competitors to be ruthless, determined, fanatical, and absolutely loyal in their commitment to the values and purposes of a monolithic society. Many Americans expected a similar sense of purposefulness, loyalty, and commitment from the children. However, with general disagreement on what the essential purpose of those children's education should be, that expectation was thwarted. Despite this controversy, with millions of those children and adolescents demanding an education, and with unprecedented national financial support, teaching and learning took place — often without clear goals and in the face of chaos — and nearly always in overcrowded classrooms with underpaid teachers.

TOPICS IN THE NEWS

EXPANSION OF THE FEDERAL ROLE IN EDUCATION

Kennedy Learns from Failure. Congress renewed the National Defense Education Act of 1958 for two more years in 1961. However, President John F. Kennedy wanted new and much more sweeping programs to improve conditions for both students and teachers. The Kennedy administration pressed vigorously for federal aid from 1961 to 1963, but political opponents objecting to the form that aid might take branded the program a fiasco. Perhaps this failure was a blessing, however. Francis Keppel, then dean of Harvard School of Education, was an adviser who helped draft proposed legislation in 1960. As he later recalled, "We came up with a report that, had it been adopted, would

probably have broken the federal government's bank in no time at all." The funds were to go only to public schools since President Kennedy, a Catholic, was unwilling to risk his slender political majority by supporting federal spending for parochial schools. Catholic politicians wanted money for parochial schools, and some Republicans and southern Democrats wanted no bill at all, primarily because of attached desegregation riders. An inability to compromise spelled disaster for this first proposal, but by 1963 Kennedy had succeeded. When he was assassinated in Dallas, his major achievement in the field, the Higher Education Facilities Act of 1963, was on its way to Senate approval. When President Lyndon Johnson signed it into law in December 1963, he called it a monument to Kennedy, saying, "This session

President Lyndon B. Johnson signing the Higher Education Facilities Act in 1963

WHAT THE GREAT SOCIETY DID FOR EDUCATION

President Johnson's budget message sent to Congress on 15 January 1969 provided aggregate, six-year totals reflecting his Great Society's monumental federal efforts to transform education in America. He cited the following accomplishments:

1. We are now assisting in the education of nine million children from low-income families under Title I of the Elementary and Secondary Education Act of 1965.

2. We are providing a Head Start for 716,000 preschool children... and Follow Through for 63,500 children to preserve their gains.

3. About 182,000 children who suffer mental or physical handicaps requiring special educational methods are now enrolled in classes with Federal support. None of these programs was available in 1964.

4. Under the budget proposals for 1970, college students will receive a total of 2 million grants, loans, and interest subsidies for guaranteed loans compared with 247,000 in 1964. This assistance is reaching 1 out of every 4 students.

5. Between 1965 and 1970, the Federal Government will have assisted in the construction of more than $9 billion worth of college classrooms, libraries, and other facilities double the previous five years.

6. About 500,000 students will receive support for education and training in 1970 under Veterans Administration program — principally the GI Bill — compared with about 30,000 in 1964.

7. More than 4 million high school students and 845,000 technical students will be enrolled in federally supported vocational education programs in 1970, an increase of 200% in 5 years.

8. Creation of the Teacher Corps, which in 1970 will bring 2,400 talented and concerned young people into the most demanding classes in the Nation—those in our city slums and poor rural areas.

9. Improvement in the quality of teaching through graduate fellowships and short-term refresher training which will reach about one teacher out of 11 in 1970.

Source: Hugh Davis Graham, *The Uncertain Triumph: Federal Education Policy in the Kennedy and Johnson Years* (Chapel Hill: University of North Carolina Press, 1984), pp. 201-202.

of Congress will go down in history as the Education Congress."

Johnson Institutes Numerous Programs. President Johnson capitalized on the Kennedy momentum as well as a sense of obligation to the slain president to "move full speed ahead" with a plan to attack poverty. The plan that Johnson and R. Sargent Shriver skillfully and quickly drove through Congress in 1964 placed a premium on education — to lend a "hand up" rather than a "handout." By 1965 most Americans did not object when Keppel explained that the new federal role in education was as "a junior partner in a firm in which the major stockholders are the state, and local and private education agencies." By the end of 1968, long after Johnson's landslide victory over Barry Goldwater, the major new federal commitments were in place: the landmark Elementary and Secondary Education Act and the Higher Education Act of 1965, the National Endowment for the Arts, the National Endowment for the Humanities, Teacher Corps, Head Start, Follow Through, guaranteed student loans, college work study, scholarships for the needy, school breakfasts, public television — and aid for school construction, developing institutions, the handicapped, community colleges, and bilingual education. During Johnson's tenure, federal aid to schools and colleges surged from $1.8 billion to more than $12 billion annually, with the most novel and striking increases flowing to elementary and secondary education — from $500 million in 1960 to about $3.5 billion in 1970. These Great Society initiatives poured through Congress one after another, and by the end of the decade federal dollars and their accompanying spending guidelines were influencing virtually every aspect of American education.

Early Compensatory Education for the Great Society: Head Start and Follow Through. When President Johnson moved "full speed ahead" with his attack on poverty

WISDOM AND WIVES

The shortage of teachers and staff in higher education became so acute in 1960 that some colleges resorted to tapping a new pool of talent: faculty wives. These women, housewives with top college degrees themselves and bored by the daily grind, became perfect candidates for jobs with the stimulus of books and research. Smith College, Mount Holyoke, Amherst College, and the University of Massachusetts formed a clearinghouse for spousal talent that placed twenty-four women in academic jobs ranging from museum director to exam grader in anthropology. Charles Porter, dean of all-male Amherst, said, "There are a lot of well qualified women around here and they can do us a lot of good."

Source: "Wisdom and Wives," *Newsweek* (11 January 1960): 54.

President Johnson, with his first teacher — Kathryn Deadrich Loney — at the signing of the Elementary and Secondary Education Act of 1965

by signing the Economic Opportunity Act of 1964, Head Start — a key weapon in that attack — was created. This program, designed at first as a summer session for four- and five-year-olds, was to give poverty-stricken disadvantaged youngsters a chance to fill the cultural void that had been keeping them from beginning school on an even footing with their middle-class cohorts. The program's aims were grand: to attack poverty, raise educational levels, and narrow the chasm that separated whites and blacks. As a newsletter to workers who were in training for the first summer's work in 1965 read: "A child who has never held a crayon or scissors is likely to feel inferior, perform more slowly and establish from the beginning an expectation of failure in school." After serving over 550,000 children that first summer, the program produced such remarkable gains in many children that in late August 1965 the program became year-round, with the winter sessions serving far fewer children but taking them as early as age three. In 1967 President Johnson launched a major Follow Through program as a supplement to an expanded Head Start. In his 8 February "Special Message on Children and Youth," he reminded the American public of the ravages of poverty on children and pledged continuing support for preschool nurturance of the chil-

dren of the poor. Although there was wide political support for educational intervention to help eradicate the damages of poverty on young children, not everyone believed that expanding spending on compensatory programs was wise fiscal policy. Edwin Dale, writing in the *New Republic,* sums up the opposition's belief that the government should train its "big guns" on increasing the national rate of economic growth. He argues that increasing the growth rate by only one percentage point would solve more poverty-induced problems than all the federal programs put together. "Keep an eye on the GNP," he warned in 1965, expressing a concern that many fiscal conservatives had about the dramatically increased rate of federal spending.

Expanded Government Loan Programs for College. As a college financial officer said in 1966, "If there's a will, there's a way. Practically no high school graduate with sufficient intellectual ability will be denied support." Federal programs had produced huge increases in financial aid: the College Scholarship Service estimated that by 1966 nearly 710 million students were benefiting from one of five major programs:

1) Student Opportunity Grants — these were gifts given by colleges to needy students.

2) College work-study programs — these programs provided students with full-time summer and fifteen-hour-per-week fall and spring jobs for nonprofit organizations. The organization supported 10 percent of the funding; the federal government supported 90 percent.

3) National Defense Loans — students were able to borrow up to $1000 per year, and they would begin repayment nine months after graduation, with ten years to repay at 3 percent interest.

OPEN UNIVERSITY CONCEPT TAKES OFF

After the publication of *The Open University* in 1966 by education critic Paul Goodman, more than a dozen campuses established these friendly, examless "free universities" for do-it-yourself learning. At San Francisco State University, where Goodman himself served as a seminar leader, huts erected on campus served as classrooms for courses such as Competition and Violence and Gestalt Therapy. Established by students for students, these courses sometimes augmented the established curriculum. At Cornell, for example, Moslem students taught their peers about Islamic culture. And at least one Cornell professor enrolled — to learn jazz from one of his students.

Source: *Time* (21 October 1966): 76.

Maurice Freehill, in *Gifted Children: Their Psychology And Education* (1961), proposes the following prescription for the education of the nation's elite:

1. Programs should be organized around unit topics, projects or study themes.
2. Lessons should be organized around a problem or purpose.
3. Encouragement of side issues which develop incidental and concomitant learning should be given.
4. Special emphasis should be placed on the tools of workshop learning.
5. Informal classrooms should see reference works used more frequently than textbooks.
6. An increasing awareness of his or her own learning process should be developed in the learner.
7. Some student involvement should exist in the planning of what is studied or at least in deciding what is expected to be learned.
8. All students should participate in periodic evaluations.
9. Students should be asked to create summaries of their learning which require rearrangement and coming to conclusions as opposed to reiteration and repetition.

Harvard professor and book reviewer Robert Coles disagreed, claiming that this "prescription" to develop higher-order thinking skills should be administered to "all but the most intellectually limited." Although Freehill's suggestions are for students whose IQs exceed 120, Coles argues that this type of stimulating educational activity should not be denied to any students with average abilities. The differences, he says, should come in the speed, scope and intensity of the activities, not in the general approaches to learning.

Source: *Harvard Educational Review*, 33, 2 (Spring 1963): 356.

---

4) Guaranteed loans — students received private loans, but the government paid the lender 6 percent interest while the student was in school, then split the 6 percent with the student after graduation.

5) New GI Bill — this program provided $150 per month to any student who had put in 180 days' active service since 1955. Five hundred thousand former GIs had enrolled by 1967.

Innovations in Federal Funding: Regional Labs for Educational Research. One of the biggest pushes in federal spending was for research into ways to improve

teaching and learning. Although the major research universities were populated with scientists and social scientists who were investigating all phases of education, their new knowledge was not disseminated into the public schools. Therefore, Title IV of the Elementary and Secondary Education Act of 1965 sought to create eighteen regional research and development laboratories in order to explore orderly ways to get new ideas flowing from fertile minds and into local classrooms. The prototype for these labs was a research center initiated by Massachusetts Institute of Technology (MIT), Educational Services, Inc., that had 350 faculty members from two hundred colleges and universities doing everything from studying the best ways to teach semiconductor physics to analyzing how successful children from deprived backgrounds had overcome their handicaps. Once the regional labs were installed, up to 60 percent of the research was done by those outside the field of education. For example, Nobel laureate William Shockley explored computer-programmed instruction as anthropologist Margaret Mead studied cultural patterns of inner-city schools. At one point in 1965, twenty-eight studies were under way on the same question: How do first graders learn to read?

Sources:
Carl Bereiter, *Teaching Disadvantaged Children in the Preschool* (Englewood Cliffs, N. J.: Prentice-Hall, 1966);

Edwin Dale, "The Big Gun on Poverty," *New Republic*, 153 (7 August 1965): 13–15;

Hugh Davis Graham, *The Uncertain Triumph: Federal Education Policy in the Kennedy and Johnson Years* (Chapel Hill: University of North Carolina Press, 1984);

Time (15 October 1965): 60;

Time (14 October 1966): 112.

THE CHANGING CURRICULUM

A Different Look at Language. During the 1960s, students at all levels not only studied newly offered subjects, they also found many familiar disciplines taught in such a different way as to be almost unrecognizable. The National Defense Education Act, which had been extended from its original 1958 version, had introduced foreign-language education into hundreds of schools that had not previously offered it. By 1966 more than three thousand undergraduates were getting intensive training in thirty-six languages during summer programs at more than twenty-two institutions through provisions in that act. Many of these students were later employed in secondary schools, so that more high-school students than ever had a chance to learn a second language. For elementary and secondary students studying their native language, some dramatic changes were in store. Advances in the study of English by linguists Paul Postal and Noam Chomsky at MIT had created new vantage points from which to examine the structure of language. Working with research funds from the U.S. Army, Air Force, Navy, and the National Science Foundation, these linguists proposed a new conceptual framework of language that came to be called transformational generative grammar. In 1966 linguist Paul Roberts translated this theory into practice when he published sets of English textbooks in transformational grammar for students in grades three through nine. Children were taught to manipulate sentences instead of merely applying traditional grammar rules: they began with "kernel" sentences (subject and verb) and then learned rules intuitively as they began to transform those kernels into more complex structures.

Math and Science Students "Discover" Principles. Just as transformational grammar emphasized active participation, so did the new "discovery" approach to teaching math and science that pervaded many elementary and secondary curricula. Teachers using this method in mathematics led children through a series of problems, hoping to prompt students to discover a generalization. Then the teacher led the students toward expressing that generalization in a universal equation. Max Beberman, a University of Illinois math professor who oversaw projects in ninety-two schools, explained, "The student 'sees' the theorem or 'discovers' the principle in a form in which it can be proved. For example, junior high students, after being led through a series of math examples, expressed what they had observed in their calculations as $(N+1/2)(N+1/2)=N(N)+N+1/4=N(N+1)+1/4$." Students were enthusiastic about the new approach, some labeling the old way they had learned math, by rote, as primitive. The approach was widely used in science, too, in which a Socratic discussion led by the teacher forced students to hit upon conclusions on their own. Physics, chemistry, biology, and earth-science courses all over the country were conducted in this new way. Another innovative science/math project was tested in Saint Louis high schools before being used in classrooms around the country. Sponsored by the U.S. Office of Education, this project imported Russian eighth-grade texts for use in secondary math classes. The Russian texts, which cut out all the frills and used math to solve science problems, were well received by American students. As one boy said, "U.S. books have lots of colored pictures. This one has only small, simple figures, but it gets right to the point. You sure understand what they're getting at."

Discovering the Problems with Discovery Learning. Discovery learning was heartily endorsed by educational theorists, but it predictably ran into opposition. Some teachers were reluctant to shift from handing out textbooks and having students memorize conclusions, and they soon discovered for themselves that this new approach required much more preparation. Parents whose children, for example, were not memorizing the table of elements for chemistry classes as they had done complained that "the kids aren't learning anything" because so much of what their children were learning was basic principle, not factual bits.

"Revisionist" History Emerges. The civil rights struggle and the furor over the Vietnam conflict were mirrored in some significant changes that took place in the study

Coeds at Vassar

and teaching of history. Previously American history had been presented to students as a wholehearted success story: "the pageant of the unflagging promise of liberty," as historian Arthur Schlesinger, Jr., explained. But those who believed that the country was united by the promise of the American dream faced a "new identity crisis" during the decade. At the meeting of the American Historical Association in 1969, president C. Van Woodward of Yale reflected on this crisis, asking, "Was the U. S. record all that righteous, unique and pure, or is this a national illusion?" Many of the history texts produced during the decade were too eager to "knock down" rather than seek meaningful interpretation, claimed some historians. But most agreed with Daniel Boorstin, then at the University of Chicago, who stressed that students must be exposed to the full range of experiences of all the American people in the past, that young people should "frankly face the role of violence and oppression in our history."

New Interest in "Forgotten History." Established historians and new doctoral students "discovered" new fields of history that traditional texts had ignored: black history, urban history, and intellectual history all attracted intense interest that spread from university professors to high-school and middle-school teachers. Educators had long been critical of school texts for their continuing distortion of the influence of black Americans, both individually and as a major ethnic group, and by 1968 publishers responded. For example, Bobbs-Merrill, one of the chief publishers of social-studies texts for school children, offered *Crispus Attucks: Boy of Valor* (1965) by Dharathula H. Millender, a study of the first black to die in the American Revolution, as well as many other texts featuring black leaders and historical figures.

Expanding the Study of Sociology and Social Work. The disciplines of sociology and social work attracted a tremendous surge of interest during the decade. Student enrollment in graduate programs in sociology at the University of Southern California, for example, doubled in the years from 1963 to 1965. The study of human society was appealing: "Young people today are very concerned with catastrophic changes that are leaving people bruised and broken," explained the dean of the School of Social Welfare at the University of California at Los Angeles (UCLA). It was difficult, however, to keep professors in the field. Even though academic salaries soared (for example, compensation for sociology professors at Tulane University grew from ten thousand to twenty-one thousand dollars), scholars were defecting to higher-paying positions in government and industry. Demographers, or specialists in population trends, were in especially great demand outside of academia.

The Study of Drama. Before the 1960s aspiring actors who longed for a career in the theater had to go to New York and hope to learn on the job. But in 1959, when UCLA hired a professional troupe of actors to set up a theater on campus, opportunities to learn theater arts in academia began. During the 1960s dozens of universities established professional schools staffed by in-residence acting companies. The goal of these new drama schools was to supply trained talent for Broadway as well as for regional theaters. The schools soon became hubs for theatrical experimentation and creativity since most were subsidized by their host universities and not totally dependent on ticket sales. Universities soon began building stunning new theaters to house their productions. The $20 million Krannert Center for Performing Arts at the University of Illinois, completed in 1966, was only one example of a construction trend that would continue throughout the decade. These new theaters were crucial, claimed UCLA chancellor Franklin Murphy, who justified the expense: "What a nearby hospital means to a medical school, a theater means to a drama student."

Sources:

H. A. Gleason, Jr., "What Grammar?" *Harvard Educational Review,* 34 (February 1964): 267;

"Lessons from Moscow," *Newsweek* (25 January 1960): 82;

"Math Made Easy," *Newsweek,* 55 (8 February 1960): 91;

Newsweek (13 January 1969): 62;

Review of *Crispus Attucks: Boy of Valor, Harvard Educational Review,* 38 (March 1968): 605;

"Sociology in Bloom," *Time,* 86 (29 October 1965): 64;

"Teaching Theater as a Profession: U.S. University Programs" *Time,* 88 (25 November 1966): 66.

COLLEGE OFFICIALS AND THE MORALS REVOLUTION

Easing of In Loco Parentis. In the 1950s and early 1960s, college authorities stood in loco parentis. This fact permitted the colleges to have almost unquestioned authority over students' lives. By 1965, when college enroll-

---

THE STRAWBERRY STATEMENT: NOTES OF A COLLEGE REVOLUTIONARY

In 1968 Random House published *The Strawberry Statement,* the random thoughts of nineteen-year-old Columbia University student protester James Simon Kunen, who drafted the book on "napkins, and cigarette packs, and no-hitchhiking signs." Kunen defends his disjointed critique of his world this way: "People want to know who we are, and some think they know who we are — a bunch of snot-nosed brats. It's difficult to say really who we are. We don't have snot on our noses. What we do have is hopes and fears." He talks about himself: "My father talks about the bad associations people make when they see someone with hair. I come back with the bad associations people make when they see someone replete with a shiny new Cadillac. . . . But as for bad vibrations emanating from my follicles, I say great. I want the cops to sneer and the old ladies swear and the businessmen worry. I want everyone to see me and say, 'There goes an enemy of the state,' because that's where I'm at, as we say in the Revolution biz." And he defines the players and the issue in the Columbia University riots of 1968:

> Students for a Democratic Society — just that. Defies more specific definition. Mixed bag. Activist, but often hampered by internal dissension. Called "pukes" by the jocks. Students Opposing SDS — never could get their sh — together; majority coalition. All powerless because totally disorganized. Called "jocks" by the pukes.

> The gym — An eleven-story private building to be built on public land, Morningside Park, which separates Columbia from Harlem. The community (blacks) could use a certain section of it at certain times, through a certain door (the back). The important point was that the community was not consulted as they had not been consulted with regard to the purchase of one hundred and fifty buildings and the eviction of ten thousand people over the past seven years. The gym served as a symbol for all Columbia expansion.

---

ment had risen to 5.5 million from 2.5 million in 1955, and when new social, economic, and ethnic groups had entered this broadened world of postsecondary education, college authorities began to lose this traditional control. The sheer numbers of the new college population and demographic changes in the college population made in loco parentis a difficult position for college administrators to maintain.

Colleges Watch as the Morals Revolution Occurs. Institutions soon realized that the parental control they had previously exercised over students' sexual behavior was quickly waning. Although chastity remained an accepted virtue for many college students, attitudes were changing. As an Ohio State senior explained, "We have discarded the idea that the loss of virginity is related to degeneracy. Pre-marital sex doesn't lead to the downfall of society, at least not the kind of society we're going to build." Harvard sociologist David Riesman, who had been on campus for thirty-one years, said, "There's a change, a real change, even though you can't prove it statistically." And Gael Greene, who interviewed 614 students on 102 campuses for *Sex and the College Girl* (1964), became convinced that "there's more premarital sex now than when Kinsey published his study in the early 50s." Although many campus officials in the 1960s abandoned curfews and dropped strictures against dorm-room visitations, not all administrators were willing to give in to students' demands. As Notre Dame's president Theodore M. Hesburgh put it, "If anyone seriously believes he cannot become well educated without girls in his room, he should get free of Notre Dame."

Sources:

William A. Kaplan, *The Law of Higher Education* (San Francisco: Jossey-Bass, 1986), pp. 6, 59;

"The Morals Revolution on the U.S. Campus," *Newsweek*, 63 (6 April 1964): 52–56.

Spanish-language textbooks

How Student Unrest Changed Higher Education

Philosophical Shifts in October of 1969. Harold Taylor, author of *Students Without Teachers: The Crisis in the University* (1969), reflected on the student revolution that raged on campuses across America during the mid 1960s. "It became clear that it was no longer possible to stand slack-jawed while we made reports about civil disorders and studies of urban problems," he explains. "We could no longer stand quietly by while history rushed forward." Sometime in the mid 1960s students and society reached the end of an era, he claims, and the first protest at Berkeley in 1964 provided the "possibility of hope" for students who had never considered the possibility of revolt against their own educational systems. Risen from the civil rights movement, this revolt produced changes in curriculum, in student regulations, in policy-making decisions, and in how colleges in general did business with students. By the end of the decade,

students had affected even the most sacred of academic traditions — tenure.

Berkeley — The Beginning. Mario Savio, a brilliant philosophy student at the University of California, Berkeley, served as a voice for student dissidents who came to represent what was called "the free speech movement." What began as a petty dispute over university regulations grew into a confrontation of philosophical dimensions. Savio's speech attacking university president Clark Kerr explains the abstract nature of the earliest student complaints: "An autocracy runs this university . . . if President Kerr is the manager, then the faculty are a bunch of employees and we're the raw material. But we don't mean to be made into any product, don't mean to end up being bought by some clients of the university. . . . We're human beings." For several weeks in the fall of 1964, the disputes raged, capped by an eight-hundred-student sit-in at Sproul Hall. Gov. Pat Brown ordered six hundred police to clear the hall, and the largest mass arrest in California history was effected when the eight hundred students were taken into custody. These students, later studied by campus sociologists, bore a "remarkable resemblance" to the campus population as a whole, with every subject major except business represented. The free speech movement was subdued by the spring of 1965, but by then a sullen rage had invaded the Berkeley campus. However, the students' achievement in paralyzing a great university became legend on campuses across America, inspiring demonstrations protesting a diversity of issues at over a dozen colleges. A year later, conservative Ronald Reagan was elected governor of California, largely on a campaign against the "sit-ins, teach-ins and walk-outs" at Berkeley and on the promise to organize a "throw-out" within the university. The first target was President Kerr.

Protests Widen as Issues Evolve. The Berkeley issues may have been ill-defined, but when the American government initiated a war policy of sustained bombardment of North Vietnam, "President Johnson replaced President Kerr as an object of campus fury," recalls Milton Viorst, in *Fire in the Streets: America in the 1960's* (1979). Riding a wave of opposition to the Vietnam conflict, the student movement would soon thrive. By the end of the decade, protests were sharply targeted, demands clearly enunciated. Many of these demands involved racial issues, with blacks demanding concessions from traditionally white institutions. For example, Queens College in New York was closed when black students demanded a white administrator be removed from a program for seven hundred students from poverty areas; forty black students at Swarthmore took over the administration office until more blacks were admitted; at Brandeis, sixty-five blacks seized the building housing computer and phone switchboards to protest racism in college policies; and at San Francisco State University, a two-month protest that turned violent resulted from demands that all blacks who applied be admitted. Other demands were for greater voice in university policies in general — including decisions about which professors should be hired and granted tenure. In 1969 Columbia University boasted that it had become the first major American university with a central policy-making body that included students, alumni, and staff as well as faculty and administrators. At the same time the American Association of University Professors released a list of forty-nine institutions involved in restructuring administrative policy-making bodies. Governor Reagan recognized the power of student protests when in 1969 he agreed with Health, Education, and Welfare (HEW) director Robert Finch that federal funds should not be cut off punitively from colleges where violence had occurred.

Sources:

Todd Gitlin, *The Sixties: Years of Hope, Days of Rage* (New York: Bantam, 1987);

Max Heirich, *The Beginning: Berkeley, 1964* (New York: Columbia University Press, 1970);

Newsweek (6 January 1969): 62;

Harold Taylor, "The Student Revolution," *Phi Delta Kappan*, 51 (October 1969): 62;

Harold Taylor, *Students Without Teachers: The Crisis in the University* (New York: McGraw-Hill, 1969);

THE DEMISE OF THE ENGLISH LANGUAGE

In a 1964 *Newsweek* article entitled "The English, How She Is Spoke," educators and writers alike mourned the death of standard English. Author James Thurber condemned the "spreading malaise of 'you know' as well as du wop choruses, bop talk, slang, intellectualese, government jargon, and sloppy grammar," all of which were "continually eroding and warping the king's English." Dwight Macdonald, professor at Northwestern University agreed: "When the typical student commits his thoughts to writing, he defiles his own language." In response, in their annual meeting the National Council of Teachers of English called for massive retraining of English teachers. The College Board Commission on English suggested another remedy: a sharp increase in classroom theme writing and reading of classical literature.

Source: "The English, How She Is Spoke," *Newsweek* (13 February 1964): 87–88.

Milton Viorst, *Fire in the Streets: America in the 1960's* (New York: Simon & Schuster, 1979).

THE ORIGINS OF BILINGUAL EDUCATION

Cuban Émigrés and the Miami Educational System. In 1961 the educational system in Miami was transformed by the thousands of Cuban refugees pouring into south Florida as they escaped the Castro regime. Over seven hundred émigrés from academia, including over four hundred Havana University professors, took jobs as stevedores, gardeners, and janitors. The U.S. government investigated many proposals to get these Cubans into positions at U.S. colleges after they improved their English skills, and the University of Miami Medical School provided a three-night-per-week program to teach Cuban medical doctors so that they could qualify for U.S. practice. There was little or no grumbling on the part of the Cubans, however. As one former University of Havana law professor put it, "We're just lucky to be here." The situation in the public schools was more problematic, however. Dade County teachers struggled with over ten thousand Cuban children who were arriving at the rate of "a classroom a day." Teachers went to classes to learn Spanish at night, and the district hired 150 former Cuban teachers as Spanish-speaking assistants for classrooms.

Interest in Migrant Education. The language barrier was not limited to Florida. The children of a significant number of Spanish-speaking migrant workers were entering schools in a steady stream from Arizona through California and north to Oregon. Model programs to assist these children were established in many western school districts. One of the strongest was in Fresno, California, where the so-called cotton kids filled the schools to the bursting point. This program, started in 1960, succeeded where others failed because it relied on extensive small-group workshop methods of teaching to solve problems of immediate personal interest to the migrant children, using their native language as a starting point. By the late 1960s there was national interest in the problem of educating the migrant child. Florida State University and the University of Miami sponsored an extensive research study conducted by Harvard University professor Robert Coles, who worked directly with the children themselves. Coles concluded that migrants defy classification and are as diverse as any group in twentieth-century America. His last word on the problem: "If the schools cannot make these children feel welcome, then they cannot educate them."

Bilingual Education Act. On 17 January 1967 Ralph Yarborough, a Democrat from Texas, introduced Senate proposition S428 "to amend the Elementary and Secondary Education Act of 1965 to provide assistance to local education agencies in establishing bi-lingual American education programs and to promote such programs." Although Yarborough's efforts were primarily on behalf of Mexican-American children, the proposal had wide-ranging effects on many populations of non-English-speaking individuals, including some Native Americans. The language of the bill suggested that schools which serve an open society ought to build on the cultural strengths students bring to the classroom. Stated goals of the legislation were to:

1) Cultivate ancestral pride;

2) Reinforce, not destroy, native languages;

3) Cultivate inherent strengths; and

4) Provide children with a sense of personal identification essential to social maturation.

On 12 February 1969 Robert Finch, secretary of HEW, stated that prompt massive upgrading of bilingual education was one of the major federal policy imperatives, and a new post, Special Assistant for Bilingual Education, had been created.

Sources:

Robert Coles, "Peonage in Florida," *New Republic*, 161 (26 July 1969): 17–21;

Esther Edwards, "The Education of Migrant Workers," *Harvard Educational Review*, 30 (Winter 1960): 12–51;

Hugh Davis Graham, *The Uncertain Triumph: Federal Education Policy in the Kennedy and Johnson Years* (Chapel Hill: University of North Carolina Press, 1984), pp. 217–220;

Newsweek (27 February 1961): 58;

Newsweek (4 December 1961): 59.

PROGRESSIVE EDUCATION VERSUS BASIC EDUCATION

Defining the Camps. One point of agreement among almost all scholars of reform during the 1960s was that American education needed a fundamental restructuring. Unfortunately there was no agreement about how that new system should look. Many educators still followed the original tenets of philosopher John Dewey's progressive education. They believed that because of changes wrought by science and technology, the mind of modern man differs from that of the Victorians. They argued, therefore, that modern education should emphasize modern needs: tolerance of different beliefs and of individual liberties; an emphasis on cooperation, not competition; and the scientific approach to the solution of human problems. Problem solving is more valuable than rote learning, and traditional teaching methods create a "repressive, irrelevant, impersonal authoritarian environment," proponents believed. "The story of survival is the story of creatures who adapted to change in their environment. The dodo had no control over his lack of ability to survive. School boards do," said Commissioner of Education Harold Howe in 1969, tacitly supporting the progressive agenda. On the other hand, proponents of what came to be called "basic education" (so named after the formation of the Council for Basic Education in 1956 and the publication of *The Case for Basic Education* in 1959) believed that a commitment to traditional goals and methods had established enough continuity to accomplish a basic core of admirable successes. Moreover, they felt that progressive education had been tested and had failed. As one critic put it, "Impaired by the deliberate policy of the Deweyites, both schoolchildren and university students are 'bird brained' — not that they are stupid, but that, birdlike, they cannot bear to concentrate for more than a few moments." Both camps claimed to support creativity. However, progressives believed creativity is encouraged by liberalizing regulations and encouraging unrestrained behavior, whereas opponents believed that

---

STANFORD APPOINTS EIGHTEEN-YEAR-OLD TO FACULTY POSITION

Harvey Friedman joined the Stanford faculty two days before his nineteenth birthday in 1967. Friedman, the youngest professor ever at that time, just "thought faster" than everyone else. He spent two years at MIT earning his undergraduate degree, then one more earning his Ph.D., a regimen that normally takes seven years. Excited about his teaching assignments in both science and mathematics, Friedman commented, "It's going to be fun teaching — even if my students are older than I am."

Source: *Newsweek* (2 October 1967): 56.

New York City Board of Education recruiting teachers in Washington, D.C.

battles over this curricular issue. Max Rafferty, who would later become chancellor of the California schools, helped open the public debate in 1962 with the publication of his *Suffer, Little Children*, a critique of progressive learning. As he put it, "Our failures and low standards result from the progressive leavening which has worked its way into our schools. The further we depart from accepted norms of society, the greater our divergence from sanity." Paul Goodman, progressivist philosopher then at Berkeley, fired back: "True progressivism as defined by Dewey's best insights has never been tried. Therefore, today's failures are due to an excess of traditional approaches." The Council for Basic Education supported a study of the San Francisco schools by eight university professors who made the following recommendations:

1) Two-thirds of the day as opposed to one-half of the day should be devoted to reading and writing in the elementary schools.

2) High-school students should take four years of English instead of three.

3) High-school science lab time should double.

4) The teaching of science in elementary schools should be departmentalized and taught by specialists.

5) Teachers must be prepared in their fields, not in general education courses.

6) A certificate/diploma system should distinguish between students who merely attended and those who completed the requirements in high school.

In general, the researchers found that "a return to solid subjects is needed, and all students should be taught the same subjects."

The Basic Proponents Make Inroads. Californians appeared to support more stringent requirements such as those recommended by the Council on Basic Education researchers. The issue affected all levels of instruction. In Berkeley a nursery-school operator defied the state Department of Welfare on the issue of play periods. By insisting that children attending her nursery school, the Melody Workshop, spend time on academics, she received so much public support that the State Department backed down. Observers wrote of a "Conservative Revolution" in California educational circles. In waging his successful race for commissioner there, Rafferty ran against "John Dewey himself" (even though Dewey had died in 1952). However, the issue was not settled in California nor elsewhere in the United States, and debate continued into later decades about whether, for example, third graders learn about Alaska best by baking sourdough bread or memorizing facts. In the introduction to *The Case for Basic Education*, Clifton Fadiman argues the importance of a return to basics, but those basics sound suspiciously progressive. He writes: "Somehow the average high school graduate does not know who he is, where he is, or how he got there. He will naturally enough settle

creativity is encouraged by stricter requirements and the imposition of external discipline.

What Actually Goes on in the Classroom. Whereas progressives believed that science, for example, is best taught in the context of real-life problem solving, basic education proponents agued that skills must be taught directly. Carl Hansen, Washington, D.C., school superintendent whose Amidon experimental school in an urban-renewal area had received wide attention for academic success, came down firmly on the side of the basic proponents. He argued that instead of liberating young minds, progressive methods often imprisoned them; that if science were taught cloaked in a "home unit," students might "get stuck at the doorbell" and never get to the principles of electricity. At Amidon the curriculum emphasized Hansen's version of basic education: learning to read through phonics, formal grammar beginning in fourth grade, a geography course on specific places, and history taught in chronological order.

California as a Battleground. As one education writer put it, "When California education gets a cold, the rest of the country sneezes." It is not surprising, then, that California was the site of some of the most bitter political

for shallow and trivial meanings. . . . In accordance with his luck and his temperament, he may become happily lost, or unhappily lost. But lost he will become . . . . And if we allow these lost ones to multiply indefinitely, they will see to it that our country is lost also."

Sources:

Clifton Fadiman, Introduction to *The Case for Basic Education: A Program of Aims for Public Schools*, edited by James D. Koerner (Boston: Little, Brown, 1959), pp. 11–14;

Paul Goodman, *Compulsory Mis-education* (New York: Horizon, 1964);

Max Rafferty, *Suffer, Little Children* (New York: Devin-Adair, 1962), pp. 146–147;

Don Robinson, "The Conservative Revolution in California Education," *Phi Delta Kappan*, 42 (December 1960): 90–96;

Carmine A. Yengo, "John Dewey and the Cult of Efficiency," *Harvard Educational Review*, 34 (January 1964): 33–53.

SHORTAGES OF TEACHERS, PROFESSORS

Overcrowding, Underpaying. The shortage of teachers and classrooms was acute throughout the decade. In President Kennedy's "Special Message on Education" on 6 February 1963, he stressed the seriousness of the problem. One and one-half million students were housed in overcrowded classrooms, and approximately two million were studying amid "grossly substandard health and safety conditions." Salaries were too low to retain the ablest teachers, with some poorer districts offering starting annual wages as low as $3,000. Moreover, of the teachers in the classrooms, 7.2 percent held substandard certificates, affecting the quality of education for one pupil in thirteen, according to the U.S. Office of Education. Although the colleges were equally crowded, there were not enough students in teacher-training programs to ease the shortages in certain locales. In Nebraska, for example, fewer than 50 percent of qualified graduates remained to teach in the overcrowded Nebraska schools. In California, for each year in the decade nineteen thousand new teachers were needed to meet demands, but only thirteen thousand were being trained.

Vacancies in Administration, Higher Education. Even though the ranks of educational administration and college teaching offered better pay, many of those jobs also went unfilled. In 1962 an unprecedented number of top educational posts were open. Dozens of positions paying $20,000 and up were vacant, including U.S. commissioner of education, president of City University of New York, and the New York superintendent of schools (which paid $37,500). President Kennedy lamented the serious manpower shortage in the ranks of Ph.D.'s in engineering, science, and math. "In the last 20 years mankind has acquired more scientific information than in all of previous history," he said, but fewer than one-half of 1 percent of the school-age generation were achieving Ph.D.'s in any field. The United States was also battling to keep the professors trained in this country. Canada was "hauling in Yanks by the dozen," bragged one Canadian official. They were able to offer college professors salaries of at least $500 higher than they could earn in the States ($6,535 versus $6,021 for assistant professors; $11,071 versus $9,840 for professors).

A Remedy for the Public Schools: The Teacher Corps. The Teacher Corps, a federal program based on the success of the Peace Corps, was initiated in 1968 to help solve the shortages in the public schools. As a recruiting brochure for the corps read, "One fifth of our nation's children go to schools that — because of isolation and inaccessibility, or because of ghetto-bred violence and despair — cannot attract, cannot hold well trained teachers." This work-study program began with 54 universities and 124 school systems in twenty-eight states, its aim being to find college graduates dedicated to service, then force-feed them professional skills in summer programs, and speed them into internships in the schools that needed them most. The government paid 90 percent of the interns' salaries, but corps members were employees of the school systems in which they worked. Corps teachers' obligations were two years of mandatory service, but after that the school systems had the option of keeping them on as regular teachers. Recruiting brochures reminded interested future teachers that they would receive 2A Occupational status with the draft once they signed on.

Sources:

About the Teacher Corps (Washington, D.C.: U.S. Government Printing Office, 1968);

Clifton Fadiman, Introduction to *The Case for Basic Education: A Program of Aims for Public Schools*, edited by James D. Koerner (Boston: Little, Brown, 1959), pp. 11–14;

THE VIETNAM DRAFT AND COLLEGE DEFERMENTS

In 1965 the push for more manpower in Vietnam forced Lewis Hershey, selective service director, to admit, "We're scraping the bottom of the barrel" for available men. All draft boards were calling up nineteen-year-olds, the deferment for married men was eliminated, but few college students in good standing were being drafted. An Amherst professor jokingly explained their new grading system: A=excellent; B=good; C=fair; D=passing; V=Vietnam. "Fear is a driving force in academia these days," a UCLA professor explained. "I am damn sure students are studying more." By 1967 even graduate students were subject to the draft. Unless a student had successfully completed one year of graduate school or was enrolled in medical studies, he was draftable. Many graduate schools saw enrollments drop by one-half during the fall of 1968.

Sources: *Newsweek* (27 December 1965): 59; *Time* (24 November 1967): 56.

Television in a North Carolina classroom

"Help Wanted: Key Posts Vacant," *Newsweek,* 60 (22 October 1962): 84;

John F. Kennedy, "Special Message to Congress on Education 29 January 1963," in *Public Papers of John F. Kennedy* (Washington, D.C.: U.S. Government Printing Office, 1963), pp. 105–108, 112–116;

Newsweek (25 January 1960): 82.

THE MILITARY GOES TO SCHOOL

The "Brainpower Lag." In the fall of 1960 a U.S. captain set his compass wrong and flew over Canada, not California as planned. A major made an arithmetic error that significantly affected the fuel calculations, forcing an entire group of jets to land at the wrong airport. Observers began to question the competency of military officers. Of the air force top brass, only 43 percent of 119,000 line officers held a college degree. The military took its problem of lack of brainpower seriously, and $63 million was set aside annually for a military-education program. Among the goals were to double the number of officers with advanced degrees and to revise standards for commissions.

Classrooms in the Military. By 1964 the military's program was in full force, and two researchers, Dr. Harold Clark of Teachers College, Columbia University, and Harold Sloan, research director at Fairleigh-Dickinson College, had spent two years evaluating it. In their book, *Classrooms in the Military (1967),* they describe programs serving over three hundred thousand GIs in classrooms, with nearly a million more studying by correspondence. If these military schools were placed in one contiguous area, they would exceed the acreage of New York City, Los Angeles, and Chicago, and their subject-matter offerings ranged from the three Rs to courses required for doctoral degrees. The researchers found the schools' standards of productivity excellent and recommended that civilian schools study the impressive way these military institutions were adjusting schooling to a technological age.

Project 100,000. By 1967 the military was facing another educational problem. Due to the demand for more and more manpower to support the efforts in Vietnam, Defense Secretary Robert McNamara was forced to lower draft standards to recruits with a sixth grade education. One-third of the 1.5 million men turning twenty-one each year were failing to meet the draft's mental requirements. The army responded and began remedial reading and writing lessons "taught by the numbers." Project 100,000 (the number the army hoped to enroll by 1968) also offered Graduate Equivalency Degree classes for those who had succeeded after the basic remedial courses. Many of the recruits learned quickly with lots of positive reinforcement. As one army instructor explained, "Some of these are men who have never been commended for anything they've done well."

Sources:
"And That's an Order," *Newsweek* (15 February 1960): 67;

"The Drop Ins: Remedial Reading and Writing Classes," *Newsweek,* 70 (30 October 1967): 50–51;

Newsweek (31 October 1960): 57;

Newsweek (20 January 1964): 77.

TECHNOLOGY AND EDUCATION

Educational Television. In the fall of 1961 on the opening day of school, educational instruction literally took off on the wings of an elaborately equipped plane

sophomores received the bulk of their education via television, taking notes from a screen in a 330-seat auditorium. Professors, located in studios with projectors and tape recorders, could teach eighteen hundred students simultaneously and eighteen hundred more via tape replay. At Pennsylvania State University, researchers examined results of four hundred experiments comparing televised instruction at the college level with conventional teaching and determined that the screen conveys information at least as effectively as a live professor. Despite the fact that the practice appeared pedagogically sound, most universities resorted to televised instruction as a tool to get through tough times occasioned by soaring enrollments, not as permanent delivery systems.

Teaching Machines and Programmed Learning. As early as 1960 the American Association for the Advancement of Science held a symposium on "Data Processing Machines and Educational Research." Later that same year, the National Education Association published *Teaching Machines and Programmed Learning*, a collection of forty-seven papers, all with a messianic tone, given by

Harvey Gantt leaving the registrar's office after enrolling at the all-white Clemson College in South Carolina

which became the equivalent of an eleven thousand-foot-high broadcasting tower. This was the Midwest Program of Airborne Televised Instruction (MPATI), which served six midwestern states with carefully taped programs of the nation's finest teachers, encompassing key subjects in the curriculum from grades one to twelve. The projected cost of this state-of-the-art technology per student, per year was estimated to be about that of a single textbook. Although by 1960 the University of Michigan had already studied the effectiveness of televised instruction for fifteen years, few districts had access to such well-crafted programs as those offered by MPATI. However, when the time came to shift the financial burden from the Ford Foundation, which had developed MPATI, to the state and local systems it served, the districts were unable to agree on paying their admittedly modest shares. The entire project foundered, and by the end of the 1960s the great boom in classroom instructional television that had begun with so much promise lost momentum.

Professors on Screen. Higher education made use of televised instruction in a different way. On hundreds of campuses, professors taped their lectures so that students could receive instruction via closed-circuit television. At the University of Miami, for example, most freshmen and

psychologists, educators, and engineers. The products ranged from stimulus-presentation devices costing over one thousand dollars each to fifty-cent "sit and spit" test-scoring devices. (Digital application of saliva to a treated card revealed which multiple-choice letter — a, b, c, or d — was correct.) The field expanded rapidly, and by 1961 psychologist and scientist B. F. Skinner was writing in the *Harvard Educational Review* explaining the teaching machines he had designed "as examples of technological applications of basic science." Skinner argued that these machines must have control over the consequences of student action so that paying attention would be effectively reinforced. It was crucial to development of thinking, he claimed, that the machines provide for branching and decision making, not the mere discrimination among responses in an array. Skinner had already tested one such programmed-learning machine on thirty-four eighth graders, who completed a year of introductory algebra in one semester or less. On an achievement test, all of the students tested to the eighth-grade level or better, with 50 percent of them getting ninth-grade scores.

Computers and Education. Computers were commonplace in higher education as early as 1960, but they were not being used for instruction at that time. A typical example of computer technology at the beginning of the decade was the 1960 concordance of William Wordsworth's poetry that Cornell computer programmers punched out on an IBM system in 197 hours. The 956-page analysis of word usage in poetry had taken sixty-seven people six years to accomplish in 1911. Similar research projects were relatively common, but teaching with computers was an innovation. However, it was but a short leap to computer-assisted instruction which used the logic of Skinner's programmed learning. By 1968 computers were being used for individual drill-and-practice systems to supplement the regular curriculum taught by a teacher. By this time a computer with two hundred terminals could accommodate up to six thousand students. At Dartmouth, for example, students (most of whom were taught computer programming as freshmen) could go to one of sixteen computer stations around campus, type out a math problem, and receive the reply in a few seconds. The next type of application was more complex — a tutorial system responsible for introducing a concept and then providing examples so that students could develop skill in its use. This type of computer-assisted instruction was highly popular, especially in the study of languages. At Stanford, for example, the Russian tutorial was totally computerized, eliminating classroom instruction altogether. Computer experts wrote in 1968 about the possibility of a dialogue system, in which the students interact with the computer, but this plan was merely conceptual at the end of the decade.

Sources:

Philip Hall Coombs, *The World Crisis in Education: The View from the Eighties* (New York: Oxford University Press, 1985), pp. 127–128;

Newsweek (15 February 1960): 67;

DOGS BANNED FROM CAMPUS

When the Cornell University comptroller issued an edict banning dogs from campus, students rose as one in protest. A long-standing Cornell tradition had allowed pets not only on campus but also in classrooms with their owners. Prof. Clinton Rossiter, who found dogs no more distracting than coeds knitting during lectures, said, "Why ban dogs? Who knows, like coeds — they might learn something."

Source: "Dogs at College," *Newsweek* (4 January 1960): 39.

Newsweek (2 March 1964): 77;

Max Rafferty, "An Overview of ETV," *Phi Delta Kappan*, 51 (December 1960): 136;

Patrick Suppes, "Computer Technology and the Future of Education," *Phi Delta Kappan*, 49 (April 1968): 420–423.

PUBLIC-SCHOOL INTEGRATION

Effects of the 1964 Civil Rights Act. When the 1960s began, six years after the Supreme Court ruling that separate schools are inherently unequal schools, many districts in the South were practicing "ingenious procrastination" rather than progressing toward desegregation. In fact, there was less actual desegregation of southern schools in 1960 than in any other year since the Supreme Court decision. Until 1964 state and school officials played an elaborate game of avoidance. However, the Civil Rights Act of 1964 empowered the U.S. Office of Education to withhold federal funds from systems failing to desegregate and empowered the U.S. Attorney General to force the process. Although the 1964–1965 school year began in eleven southern states with only 604 of 2,951 school districts having even begun the process of desegregation, by fall of 1965, 2,816 systems had filed plans defining their intentions to comply with the law. This dramatic turnaround was largely the result of the financial impact of the 1964 Civil Rights Act. The efforts toward desegregation in the South proved to be only token motions in many cases, however. One typical approach was for school districts to instigate "freedom of choice" plans which granted students the opportunity to sign forms declaring the school within that district they would attend the following year. These plans did move some black students into formerly all-white schools, yet no white student in any of the southern states chose to attend schools that, by freedom of choice, remained overwhelmingly black.

Desegregation Outside the South. This system of separatism was not unique to the South, however. In Los Angeles, for example, de facto segregation was a fact of life, and the John McCone Report on the education of minorities there in 1965 concluded that the very low level of scholastic achievement in the predominantly black schools would continue to contribute to the separation of the races. Northern schools, too, remained segregated in some areas due to housing patterns. In 1964, 137 of New York City's 723 elementary and junior high schools were 90 percent or more black or Puerto Rican, and it appeared that mass busing would be the only solution to this problem. James Donovan, the newly appointed president of the board of education, insisted, however, that "This is the Board of Education, not the Board of Integration or Board of Transportation." Furthermore, 2,700 members of a Manhattan Parent-Teacher Association vowed to resist any efforts to desegregate further by busing children across neighborhood lines. As one Manhattan parent put it, "Why do our children have to be inconvenienced, just to satisfy the Negroes' whims?"

Desegregation or Integration? For a decade the Supreme Court had avoided the use of the word *integration* in writing about school cases. However, in the case *U.S. v. Jefferson County Board of Education* (1966), the terms *desegregation* and *integration* were used interchangeably, and the decision made clear that the law provided for "not white schools or Negro schools — just schools." By 1969 a unanimous Supreme Court decision stripped southern school officials of all of their favorite legal crutches to avoid compliance with the law, stating that "the obligation of every school district is to terminate dual school systems at once and to operate now and hereafter only unitary systems." Ironically, these decisions impacted southern schools more directly than schools where separation of races was de facto. By 1970 a higher percentage of blacks was attending integrated schools in the South than in the rest of the United States.

Sources:

Jack Bass, *Unlikely Heroes* (New York: Simon & Schuster, 1981);

A Statistical Summary, State by State, of School Segregation-Desegregation in the Southern and Border Area from 1954 to the Present (Nashville: Southern Education Reporting Service, 1964);

Hubert Wey, "Desegregation and Integration," *Phi Delta Kappan*, 47 (May 1966): 508–515.

MONTESSORI SCHOOLS

Education for Mentally Handicapped Children. Dr. Maria Montessori was a medical student in the 1890s serving as an intern in the psychiatric clinic of Rome, Italy, which housed the "idiot children" then relegated to insane asylums. Appalled by what she saw happening to these children, she began a lifelong study of mentally deficient children and then quickly extended her work to the study of normal young children. The approach to educating the very young which she pioneered in her "Homes of Children" over several decades resulted in successes that exceeded even her own expectations. In working with retarded children she transformed three-to-seven-year-olds into avid pupils who learned cleanliness, manners, "grace in action," and they became acquainted with animals and plants and with the manual arts. They got both sensory and motor training and learned rudiments of counting, reading, and writing. When, in 1912, Montessori published *The Montessori Method: Scientific Pedagogy as Applied to Child Education in "the Children's Houses,"* people from all over the world pressed her to communicate her methods to others. In the United States there was interest at the time, but by 1917 articles in the American press had dwindled to less than five a year.

Explosion of Interest in Montessori in the 1960s. Five decades after the publication of Montessori's book, there was an explosion of interest in the United States in her methods and theories. This renewed fascination was partially due to a 1964 publication of *The Montessori Method*, introduced by Prof. J. McV. Hunt. Hunt, a leading researcher in learning theory, reendorsed Montessori's beliefs that even very deprived children can learn if they are taught with the method: liberty for the child complemented by organization of the work by an adult (a "nonteacher" in Montessori's terms). Through movement and manipulation of the Montessori materials the child can develop order and logical thought — and a firm foundation for success in the three Rs, claimed Hunt.

How the Method Can Help Deprived Children. Various research studies in the 1930s, 1940s, and 1950s had convinced scientists that the longer children experienced cultural deprivation, the more permanent were the effects. Such considerations made it even more important to consider ways to enrich preschool experience as an antidote to cultural deprivation, and the earlier the better. Montessori's methods promised success in reversing the effects of early deprivation on those symbolic skills required for success in school and in an increasingly technological culture. Moreover, the fact that she had based her teaching methods on earlier attempts to educate the mentally retarded gave her approach a significant advantage to other, more traditional, preschool methods. In the Great Society of the mid to late 1960s, intense scrutiny was given to any approach that promised a solution to the problem of children who came to school, even to kindergarten, unprepared to learn. Montessori's program, repopularized by countless advocates of early-childhood enrichment, became a model to which many educators looked as a solution to preparing both deprived and so-called normal children for the challenges of learning.

Source:

J. McV. Hunt, Introduction to *The Montessori Method*, by Maria Montessori (New York: Schocken Books, 1964): xi–xxxviii.

HEADLINE MAKERS

JEROME BRUNER

1915–

FOUNDER AND CODIRECTOR, CENTER FOR COGNITIVE STUDIES AT HARVARD, OXFORD UNIVERSITY NEW SCHOOL FOR SOCIAL RESEARCH

Study of Thinking and Learning. During the late 1950s and early 1960s, researchers were actively investigating two different areas of learning theory — operant conditioning, generally associated with B. F. Skinner, and cognitive psychology, an area of special interest for Jerome Bruner. Bruner and colleagues at Harvard's Center for Cognitive Studies were interested in studying perception, memory, and thinking in an effort to determine what techniques constitute the most effective learning situations. In 1960 Bruner issued a significant report on the deliberations of a large group of scholars, mostly scientists, who had been researching cognitive processes. This report, entitled *The Process of Education*, offers a sweeping hypothesis: "Any subject can be taught effectively in some intellectually honest form to any child at any stage of development, providing attention is paid to the psychological development of the child." The implication of this study is that in a cognitive approach to learning, maximum advantage must be taken of the cognitive properties of both learners and subject matter. In other words, teachers must organize material into logical structures so that learners will, by use of their own logical processes, come to understand the innate framework of the subject rather than simply mastering facts or techniques.

Learning Through Active Involvement. Bruner spent decades researching the importance of students' active participation in learning events. A typical study was one from 1961, in which three groups of equally bright twelve-year-olds were given large numbers of word pairs to remember. Group 1 was told, "Remember, you'll have to repeat these later." Group 2 was told, "Remember the pairs by producing a word or idea that will tie the pair together in a way that makes sense to you." Group 3 was given the mediating words produced by group 2. Group 2 remembered an average of 95 percent of the second words when presented with the first of the pair; group 1 less than 50 percent; group 3 significantly fewer than group 2. This sample study as well as hundreds of others convinced Bruner and his colleagues that activities and attitudes that characterize "figuring out" or "discovering" things for oneself appear to make material more readily accessible to learners. For teachers conditioned to years of instruction through lecture to students who, by rote, attempted to master a subject by merely memorizing facts, the implications of the importance of student participation in a subject were significant. During the decade, many "discovery learning" projects were first instituted all over the United States to the enthusiastic support of the teachers and students who were involved.

The Experiential Curriculum. Bruner's main influence came from educators who accepted his primary contention: optimum conditions for learning take place only when material is organized in a way requiring students to involve themselves so that their own logical processes exert enough force to compel their assent to conclusions. This approach to learning requires teachers to serve more as coaches of learning rather that as givers of knowledge, and every discipline from foreign-language learning to mathematics was changed in some way by Bruner's research. As Bruner observed: "The schoolboy learning physics IS a physicist, and it is easier for him to learn physics behaving like a physicist than by mastering a textbook that talks about conclusions in a field of inquiry. His time should center upon the inquiry itself." Bruner's influence extended well after the 1960s, but it was during this decade that his theories of learning first affected a wide range of educators.

Sources:

Jerome S. Bruner, "The Act Of Discovery," *Harvard Educational Review*, 31 (Spring 1961): 21–32;

Bruner, *The Process of Education* (Cambridge, Mass.: Harvard University Press, 1960);

N. L. Gage, ed., *Handbook of Research on Teaching* (Chicago: Rand McNally, 1963), pp. 138–139, 373–374, 932–936.

JAMES B. CONANT

1893-1978

PRESIDENT OF HARVARD UNIVERSITY,
U.S. HIGH COMMISSIONER TO WEST GERMANY,
AMBASSADOR TO WEST GERMANY

A Spokesman for Education in the 1950s. After leaving the presidency of Harvard in 1953, Conant became the U.S. High Commissioner and later ambassador to West Germany. In this country, however, he remained a strong voice for educational innovation during the 1950s, and his 1959 volume, *The American High School Today,* argues for much higher standards in American education. His call for comprehensive high schools that would meet all students' needs, regardless of their abilities and goals, was particularly important in the 1960s when attempts were made to eliminate educational inequities, especially in segregated school districts.

Assessing All Segments of the American Educational System. During the 1960s Conant researched and wrote about all aspects of the American educational system. *Slums and the Suburbs,* published in 1961, closely examines northern suburbs where segregation was then de facto, or based on neighborhood patterns of housing which separated the races. In this text he advocates vocational training for young people whose low academic scores had consigned them to remedial classes. He pioneered the concept of partnering with community businesses to "target-train" students through apprenticeship programs to fill existing jobs in the area. Conant next spent two years studying U.S. systems of teacher training by visiting in sixteen of the most populous states and conducting a stratified sampling of the remaining states' teacher-preparation institutions. When the study was published in 1963, its critique of the "hodge-podge" curriculum and the paucity of coursework required in the disciplines candidates were preparing to teach influenced many institutions to revise their curricula. Next, Conant tackled educational problem solving in general in *Shaping Educational Policy,* published in 1964. He explains to the general public how policies were actually formulated in many different states and why this policy-making machinery was inadequate. Conant's analysis of New York and California as examples of excellence in policy in two different areas — New York from kindergarten through high school, California beyond high school — suggests that if the two were combined, the result would be the ideal educational organization. Again state planners took notice, and although New York did not become a model for public education, California's three-tier system of higher education was emulated in many states.

Guiding Philosophy. Conant distinguished himself in four careers: researcher in chemistry, educational administrator, ambassador to West Germany, and finally, influential advocate for reform of American public education. In a volume called *Two Modes of Thought* (1964) he attempts to define the multiple influences that affect his thinking and his attitudes as well as his own decisions and his philosophy of life. He believed that his way of thinking and analyzing problems derived from two basic modes of thought: the empirical-inductive method of inquiry, and the theoretical-deductive outlook. His particular stance, which straddled the worlds of science and social science, gave Conant a unique position during a decade that supplied copious problems to be solved.

Sources:

James Bryant Conant, *Shaping Educational Policy* (New York: McGraw-Hill, 1964);

Conant, *Two Modes of Thought: My Encounters with Science and Education* (New York: Trident, 1964).

ERIK ERIKSON

1902-1994

DEVELOPMENTAL PSYCHOLOGY

Stage Theory of Human Development and Identity. Erik Erikson, psychoanalyst with a Ph.D. in child psychology, is probably best known for his stage theory of human development. Erikson's theory suggests that each stage of life, from infancy and early childhood on, is associated with a specific psychological struggle that significantly affects personality. Erikson, who coined the term *identity crisis* in naming that particular crisis inherent in adolescence, was an innovator whose influence shaped the emerging fields of child development and life-span studies. Defining identity as a basic confidence in one's inner continuity amid change, Erikson suggested that the emergence of this identity might be precipitated by a crisis and accompanied by intense neurotic suffering, especially for creative people. This theory had particular resonance during the 1960s, during which young people heard Erikson saying, "Your life is important; your relationship to your times is important; you can make a difference in society and you can find yourself in the process," according to Dr. Robert Wallerstein, now retired as head of the psychiatry department at the University of California, San Francisco.

Research and Writing in the 1960s. As a professor of human development at Harvard in the 1960s, Erikson conducted behavioral research, lectured at MIT, and published widely discussed texts, including *Insight and Responsibility* (1964) and *Identity: Youth and Crisis* (1968). During the decade Erikson frequently sojourned in India where he became fascinated with the life of Mohandas Gandhi. Inspired by Gandhi's nonviolent civil disobedience, Erikson wrote a Pulitzer Prize–winning biography of him. Erikson, hoping to advance innovative images of youth and young adulthood, was a pioneer in considering the role that cultural and societal factors play in shaping personality.

Influence on Education. Erikson's concepts of a malleable ego in adults and the importance of the social milieu in which a person negotiates each crisis influenced educational theory in the decade and beyond. His work proposed the idea that adults, despite poor childhoods, could compensate for their deprivations; that the mold of their first five years of life was not hard and fast. This theory lent credence to the importance of special programs for the culturally deprived. In a paper entitled "Ego Development and Historical Chance" he argues that racism and joblessness could affect the mind at the deepest layers of the unconsciousness, thus providing a framework for educational spending aimed at compensating for societal conditions. Although Erikson was neither a policy adviser nor an educational theorist, his studies of children and adolescents and his belief in the richness of human potential significantly affected education theory.

Sources:

Martin Finucane, "Erikson Opened Up Child Psychology," *Columbia* (S.C.) *State*, 17 May 1994, pp. D1, D6;

Obituary, *New York Times*, 13 May 1994, p. C16;

Spencer A. Rathus, *Pyschology* (New York: Holt, Rinehart & Winston, 1987), pp. 401–402.

PAUL GOODMAN

1911-1972

EDUCATION CRITIC

Outspoken Critic of the System. Although there were numerous voices in the media during the 1960s criticizing the educational system, none was as outspoken or irreverent as Paul Goodman. Goodman, who studied classics at the University of Chicago and whose doctoral dissertation used Aristotle's *Poetics* to analyze and explain a body of contemporary literary works, attacked all parts of the U.S. educational system of the 1960s with an eye toward this question: What are the criteria for separating what appears to be from what really exists in academia? He looked at institutional relations as a direct confrontation with other humans, not impersonal establishments, and

he staged these confrontations often and loudly. Over the decade Goodman's critiques became more and more political and therefore more and more public; the subsequent arguments he made were notable for their form, their force, and their consequences.

Schooling versus Education. Goodman's strongest argument against the system claimed it was not merely failing to improve students, but it was actually harming them. As he writes in the preface to *Compulsory Mis-Education* (1964), "I do not try to be generous or fair. . . . We already have too much formal schooling, and the more we get, the less education we will get." Goodman did not spare any level of schooling. As he explained, "In the organizational plan, the schools play a non-educational role — in the tender grades the schools are a baby-sitting service during the time of the collapse of the old-type family and during a time of extreme urbanization. In the junior and senior grades, they are an arm of the police, providing cops and concentration camps paid for in the budget under the heading 'Board of Education.'" The primary educational purpose of the schools, he argued, was "to provide apprentice training for corporations, government, and the teaching profession itself, and to train the young to adjust to authority." Although he felt that the schools had served as a democratizing force, he believed that with changing conditions they had become "a universal trap," and democracy had begun to look like "regimentation." This educational practice, he argued in a debate with James B. Conant, had "saddled us with an inhumane and uncitizenly society, with slums of engineering without community planning, with unphilosophical medicine, a sheepish electorate and a debased culture. This is the education of the Organization."

Schooling as a Symptom of a Larger Problem. Goodman's criticism of the system was expressed in several major publications during the decade: *Growing Up Absurd* (1960); *Compulsory Mis-Education, and the Community of Scholars* (1962); and *People or Personnel: Decentralizing and the Mixed System* (1965). Widely quoted in the media, he was also regarded as an inspiration for emerging student radicals. As Todd Gitlin, president of SDS, remarked, "We loved him for his bad manners. He was the insider's outsider, enormously learned yet economically and socially a man of the margins." Goodman's assault on the system went beyond a critique of the schools; he extended his attack, arguing, for example, that "A major pressing problem of our society is the defective structure of the economy that advantages the upper middle-class and excludes the lower class. The school people loyally take over this problem in the war on poverty, the war against delinquency, retraining the jobless, and so forth. But by taking over the problem, they themselves gobble up the budgets and confirm the defective structure of the economy." One of Goodman's greatest influences on the decade was to shock the public into considering the real meaning of education. A liberal thinker who disdained liberal political policy, Goodman anticipated many of the problems that would arise with the Great Society's attempts to alleviate the inequities in educational opportunities.

Sources:

Paul Goodman, *Compulsory Mis-Education* (New York: Horizon, 1964);

Goodman, *Compulsory Mis-Education, and the Community of Scholars* (New York: Vintage Books, 1962);

Goodman, *Growing Up Absurd* (New York: Random House, 1960);

Todd Gitlin, *The Sixties: Years of Hope, Days of Rage* (New York: Bantam, 1987);

James Edward McClellan, *Toward an Effective Critique of American Education* (Philadelphia: Lippincott, 1968).

ARTHUR JENSEN

1923-

PROFESSOR, UNIVERSITY OF CALIFORNIA, BERKELEY

National Furor Over Black IQ Attainment. No other scientist researching learning gathered the national headlines or created such controversy as Arthur Jensen. His article setting forth his theory and research on the feasibility of boosting deprived children's intelligence quotients (IQs) appeared in the *Harvard Educational Review,* a publication that has a limited readership. However, the popular press translated his 123-page article into flat statements of only a few sentences, claiming that Jensen's conclusions were that blacks were intellectually inferior to whites according to IQ tests.

Why Jensen Was Investigating Genetic Factors. Jensen initiated his study to document whether or not the compensatory programs that the federal government was supporting with millions of dollars were capable of making significant inroads in narrowing the gap between minority and majority pupils. Essentially, Jensen argued that in his research he found that genetic factors were much more important in determining IQ than environmental factors. He attributed the majority of the genetic factors to prenatal influences primarily associated with the nourishment of the mother and the child. And these genetic factors, he believed, contributed to different, but not necessarily inferior, learning patterns in some black children.

Associative Versus Conceptual Learning. Jensen defined two different types of learning: associative (related to imaginative and intuitive thinking) and conceptual (related to logic and the ability to grasp abstract concepts). However, it is only the conceptual type of learning that is measured by IQ tests, he explained. Because our education system puts a greater emphasis on this conceptual learning rather than associative learning, those whose learning patterns are different are always going to

be at a disadvantage. According to Jensen, "Too often, if a child does not learn the school subject when taught in a way that largely depends on this conceptual framework, he often does not learn at all, so we find high school students who have failed to master basic skills that they could easily have learned many years earlier by means not totally dependent on conceptual learning." The conclusion that Jensen came to was that our educational systems should foster "diversity rather than uniformity" and spend funds attempting to "tap into other ways of learning," rather than trying to force all learners to respond in the same way.

Distortions and Responses. Immediately after Jensen's article was published, response was swift in the academic community and the general public. The next issue of *Harvard Educational Review* was, in a break from the usual format, devoted only to counterarguments. Although nearly everyone disagreed with Jensen's contention that conceptual intelligence is hereditary, there was support for his conclusions and his reasoning. Jerome Kagan, professor at Harvard, applauded the attention the article brought to problems deriving from prenatal malnutrition; J. McV. Hunt agreed that indeed children must be provided rich postnatal experiences to develop inherent intellectual structures; and James Crow supported Jensen's contentions that "the reality of individual differences need not and should not mean rewards for some, frustration for others." Although the general public never had the chance to comprehend all of Jensen's arguments, the out-of-context conclusions about so-called inferiority of blacks provided ammunition for political arguments against spending for compensatory educational programs.

Source:

Arthur Jensen, "How Much Can We Boost IQ and Scholastic Achievement?" *Harvard Educational Review,* 39 (Winter 1969): 1–123.

FRANCIS KEPPEL

1916-1990

DEAN, HARVARD GRADUATE SCHOOL OF EDUCATION, U.S. COMMISSIONER OF EDUCATION

Work to Improve Teaching. As dean of the Harvard Graduate School of Education, Keppel served for fourteen years, quadrupling the enrollment and establishing the school as a site for national leadership in education. He redesigned the master of arts in teaching (MAT) degree and expanded the program. He also created the School and University Program for Research and Development (SUPRAD), which conducted pilot projects on topics such as team teaching and the use of teaching machines.

Commissioner of Education. In his position as commissioner of education from 1962 to 1965 he worked for vastly expanded federal support of education. As the head of the 1965 Keppel Interagency Task Force, he was asked to propose programs to accomplish the following tasks:

1) Relieve the doctor, nurse, and medical technician shortage, especially in light of new Medicare demands;
2) Expand financial aid to middle-class college students;
3) Develop a year-round preschool program;
4) Refine the hastily developed ESEA Title I so as to reach more disadvantaged children;
5) Devise a grant program for quality improvement to selected institutions of higher learning;
6) Explore how best to transfer NDEA student loans, which were line items in the federal budget, to such off-budget devices as an "Educational Development Bank";
7) Improve drop-out prevention for talented students;
8) Develop a program of international education.

Keppel devised plans to make inroads on all of these problems.

Legacy of National Assessment of Educational Progress. One of Keppel's highest personal priorities during his national tenure was to establish a program for national assessment of educational progress. This testing would provide a reasonable benchmark against which to measure progress and to judge the effectiveness of all the newly established programs. To those legislators who believed firmly in local control of education, this idea sounded un-American. Keppel succeeded, however, by including such a plan in 1965 legislation couched in the rhetorical phrase "Planning and Cost Analysis." In the following decades the program came to be called the National Assessment of Educational Progress (NAEP). This national basis for comparison, as well as the sweeping federal programs he helped to form, are his legacy to education. Keppel left government in 1966 to direct private programs in educational development.

Source:
Hugh Davis Graham, *The Uncertain Triumph: Federal Education Policy in the Kennedy and Johnson Years* (Chapel Hill: University of North Carolina Press, 1984), p. 11.

B. F. SKINNER

1904-1990

PROFESSOR AT UNIVERSITY OF MINNESOTA, INDIANA UNIVERSITY, HARVARD UNIVERSITY

Operant Conditioning Theory Leads to Teaching Machines. B. F. Skinner, one of the best-known learning theorists, first attracted popular attention during the late 1950s and the 1960s. Although for decades Skinner had been actively researching how and why humans behave as they do and what role random trial and error plays in learning (for example, during World War II he had devised an operant-conditioning procedure for training pigeons to direct missile missions), it was his resounding success in teaching children with programmed learning machines that made his name easily recognizable. A pioneer in the use of automated learning, Skinner's work with colleagues in producing the first linear program for teaching introductory psychology at Harvard was widely reported, but he also devised programs for elementary-school children and for junior-high introductory algebra students. But it is Skinner's intellectual achievement in producing a philosophy of human nature appropriate to these new techniques of instruction that is his more lasting influence.

The Nature of Human Nature. His philosophy of human nature was that man is by nature an active organism that learns from interaction with the environment. He strongly believed that environmental influences shape humans into wanting some things and not wanting others, and that children's language acquistion as well as children's attitudes toward morality are shaped by conditioned responses, or positive reinforcement from adults in the community. These views were different from other theorists' beliefs, but Skinner had the public's attention more than the others did. This theory had major implications for supporting early-intervention school programs for children from deprived backgrounds, especially those from communities where there was little or no adult reinforcement for learning prosocial behavior.

Behavior Modification Goes to School. Skinner's theories had widespread effects in the schools at all levels. Nearly all teachers were exposed to his theories about reinforcement, which were incorporated into discipline policy as often as into actual teaching. For example, 1960s teachers (and those trained in following decades) were taught to attend to positive behavior of students, and, as much as possible, to ignore children who might be going out of their way to earn disapproval. Rather than reinforcing misbehaving childrens' desires for attention, even the negative kind, teachers' attention was to focus on those who were doing well. Although this approach to discipline was not startlingly new, the focus on avoiding punishment and being consistent so that undesirable behavior was not partially reinforced was an innovation. The other school-based application of Skinner's theory and research was the teaching machine. These machines, based on programmed learning, broke complex learning tasks into a number of small steps that learners would combine in sequence to form a correct behavior chain. These machines did not punish errors; instead, all learners would eventually earn perfect scores with the only variable being the time to finish the programs. Later, many computer-software manufacturers relied heavily on this Skinnerian stimulus-response theory in designing their products. Skinner's most lasting influence on education was as a champion of scientific psychology, whether that science is used to control classroom behavior or to teach children the principles of an academic discipline such as algebra or psychology.

Sources:
James Edward McClellan, *Toward an Effective Critique of American Education* (Philadelphia: Lippincott, 1968), pp. 225–250;

Spencer A. Rathus, *Psychology* (New York: Holt, Rinehart & Winston, 1987), pp. 12, 57, 197–199;

B. F. Skinner, *A Case History in Scientific Method* (New York: Appleton-Century-Crofts, 1959), pp. 76–100.

PEOPLE IN THE NEWS

Sylvia Ashton-Warner's *Teacher,* published in 1963, fascinated educators and the American public with its view of the education of the Maoris, an aboriginal people in New Zealand.

Claude Brown's 1965 autobiography of his education in Harlem before its infestation with drugs, *Manchild in the Promised Land,* was an important document about life and learning in a black urban environment in the 1940s and 1950s.

The Process of Education by **Jerome Bruner** in 1960 helped redefine learning by arguing that intellectual activity is the same whether at the frontier of knowledge or in third grade; he claimed the difference is in degree, not in kind.

The decades-long argument about phonics versus sight reading was the subject of **Jeanne Chall**'s landmark 1967 *Harvard Educational Review* essay, "Learning to Read," in which she reviews all the research and makes the case for a "code emphasis" (phonics) for beginning readers.

Robert Coles, child psychiatrist, worked with both black and white children during desegregation in the South and the North; his *Children of Crisis: A Study of Courage and Fear* (1967) told the story of how children perceived the changes they were encountering.

Nickolaus Englehardt, whose firm specialized in engineering and architecture of schools for over eight hundred school districts, eased integration pressures when he conducted a quiet campaign to locate a new school in Charlotte, North Carolina, between white and black neighborhoods in 1965.

Eli Ginzberg in 1966 published *Life Styles of Educated Women,* a study of the personalities, backgrounds, and home and career experiences of 311 women doing distinguished graduate work at Columbia Unversity.

Carl Hansen, District of Columbia school superintendent, announced in 1960 that after six years of integration the overall standing in city school achievement tests had risen.

John Holt added to the theory underlying learning with the publication of *How Children Learn* in 1967.

Jerome Kagan claimed in 1969 that perceived intellectual inadequacies of lower-class children may derive from a style of mother-child interaction.

Francis Keppel, U.S. commissioner of education and shaper of Kennedy and Johnson education policy, argued in 1967 that local autonomy is the "basic instrument in management of educational systems," but that the proper federal role is that of a "partner with vested interests."

William Heard Kilpatrick, a Teachers College, Columbia University, faculty member, turned ninety in 1961 as some blamed his progressive philosophy for everything from the missile gap to the rising divorce rate. **John Dewey,** a generation earlier, had called Kilpatrick "the best student I ever had."

James Koerner, secretary of the Council for Basic Education, attacked the preparation teachers received in 1964, claiming that "the professional curriculum is 50–75% water" and at the graduate level, the "dilution is often much higher."

Herbert Kohl popularized the open classroom concept in 1969 in *The Open Classroom;* he suggested that in this environment "the teacher is no longer required to behave like a teacher, nor are the children required to be submissive."

Jonathan Kozol spent 1964 and 1965 as a substitute-teacher in the Boston school system. Kozol, whose *Death at an Early Age* in 1967 was a polemic against the treatment of black pupils there, was fired from his teaching job after reading to his students a Langston Hughes poem not on the approved reading list.

Myron Lieberman in 1960 suggested that until teacher certification was modeled more along the lines of bar-association guidelines education would never improve and the teaching profession would never "lop off the ineffectives."

Daniel P. Moynihan, director of Joint Center for Urban Studies of MIT and Harvard and professor of education and urban politics at Harvard, published *The Assault on Poverty* in 1965.

Max Rafferty, seeking to oversee California's schools in 1960, ran against **Ralph Richardson** but saved his harshest criticism for **John Dewey** and "progressive education" which, he said, had "stripped the meat from the bones of education and replaced it with Pablum."

Sir Herbert Read in 1966 advocated nurturing creativity; he claimed the educational system taught students only what not to do — not to make a noise, not to make a mess, not to disturb busy adults.

In 1960, when Vice Adm. **Hyman G. Rickover** advocated "European academic rigor" in America's secondary schools on *Meet the Press*, his appearance resulted in the largest audience request for transcripts of the program in its history.

In 1964 **Paul Roberts** popularized the new structural linguistics with the publication of *English Syntax*, claiming that "we are all of us ungrammatical much of the time" when uttering complex sentence forms.

Theodore Sizer, the dean of the Harvard Graduate School of Education, focused attention on the private-versus-public-school debates in the journal he edited during the 1960s, *Religion and Public Education.*

Clifton Wharton, who in 1969 was the first black to be named president of a major U.S. university (Michigan State), was also the first candidate to be selected through exercise of new student and faculty rights. Both students and faculty served on the search committee, which recommended his appointment.

Sociology professor **Lewis Yablonsky** (San Fernando Valley College) was subpoenaed in 1967 to testify at the marijuana trial of one of the flower children he was studying for his book on the hippie movement. Pleading the Fifth Amendment on his own drug use, he argued that academic researchers should be free to study social problems without fear.

DEATHS

Ludwig Bemelmans, 64, best known for his illustrated children's books though he was also a writer of satire, 1 October 1962.

Edward H. Chamberlin, 68, professor of economics at Harvard University for more than forty years; his *Theory of Monopolistic Competition* attacked the theory that higher wages benefit the economy, 16 July 1967.

Sidney B. Fay, 91, historian, educator, and authority on Germany whose most important work was *The Origins of the World War,* 29 August 1967.

Wilfred John Funk, 83, publisher, poet, and lexicographer whose twenty-year feature in *Reader's Digest*, "It Pays to Increase Your Wordpower," was a vocabulary lesson for the masses, 1 June 1965.

Howard R. Garis, 89, U.S. author known for his "Uncle Wiggily" tales totaling over seventy-five books, 5 November 1962.

Virginia C. Gildersleeve, 87, U.S. educator, feminist, and internationalist, dean emeritus of Barnard College and the only woman delegate at the conference to draft the charter for the UN, 7 July 1965.

Sir Ernest Gowers, 85, British authority on English usage; revised *Fowler's Modern English Usage* and wrote *Plain Words: Their ABC,* 16 April 1966.

Sir Herbert Grierson, 94, British professor and scholar of seventeenth-century English literature; largely responsible for the renewed interest in writer John Donne, 19 February 1960.

Alfred Whitney Griswold, 56, president of Yale University since 1950; known as defender of academic freedom and critic of many aspects of American education, 19 April 1963.

Moses Hadas, 66, teacher and classical scholar who wrote more than thirty books including *A History of Greek Literature,* 17 August 1966.

George Rolfe Humphries, 74, poet, teacher, and translator, whose versions of the classics, especially Virgil and Ovid, were widely read, 22 April 1969.

Bob Jones, Sr. (Robert Reynolds Jones), 84, fundamentalist, evangelist, and educator who led national attacks on Roman Catholicism and liberalism; founded Bob Jones College, now Bob Jones University, 22 January 1968.

Carl Jung, 85, Swiss pioneer in analytic psychology who founded his own school for teaching and training psychotherapists; creator of such terms as *introvert* and *extrovert* to define the workings of the subconscious mind, 6 June 1961.

Helen Keller, 87, deaf and blind American educator; she learned to read, write, and speak; devoted her life to crusading for education for the deaf and blind; the story of her education was dramatized in *The Miracle Worker,* 1 June 1968.

William Heard Kilpatrick, 93, former professor and leading educational philosopher, known primarily for his role in the practical application of John Dewey's educational philosophy of progressive education, 13 February 1965.

Oliver La Farge, 61, author, historian, and anthropologist who fought to improve the education and welfare of the American Indian; his novel *Laughing Boy,* a portrait of Navajo life, won the Pulitzer Prize in 1929, 2 August 1963.

James M. Landis, 64, former dean of Harvard Law School and adviser to Presidents Roosevelt, Truman, and Kennedy, 30 July 1964.

C. Wright Mills, 46, U.S. sociologist and author of *White Collar; The Power Elite; Causes of World War Three;* and *Listen, Yankee: The Revolution in Cuba,* 20 March 1962.

Leander H. Perez, Sr., 76, political boss of Plaquemines Parish, Louisiana, who fought vigorously to maintain segregated schools, 19 March 1969.

Roscoe Pound, 93, dean of Harvard Law School and internationally known authority on law, 1 July 1964.

Samuel C. Prescott, 89, U.S. biologist and first dean of the School of Science at the Massachusetts Institute of Technology; pioneer in scientific methods of food canning in the 1890s, 19 March 1962.

Howard Percy Robertson, 58, professor of mathematical physics at California Institute of Technology and scientific advisor to President Kennedy, 26 August 1961.

Most Rev. Joseph Francis Rummel, 88, Roman Catholic archbishop of New Orleans, who introduced integration into southern parochial schools, 8 November 1964.

Margaret Higgins Sanger, 82, pioneer in the education of the American public on birth control; in 1916 she opened the first American birth-control clinic and was jailed for thirty days; she was a founder of the International Planned Parenthood Federation and the Case for Birth Control, 6 September 1966.

Arthur M. Schlesinger, Sr., 77, history professor at Harvard for over thirty years, editor of Pulitzer Prize winner *The American Migration,* and coeditor of the thirteen-volume *History of American Life,* 30 October 1965.

Courtney Craig Smith, 52, president of Swarthmore College and U.S. secretary of the Rhodes Scholarship Trust, 16 January 1969.

Polly (Mary Agnes) Thompson, 75, Scottish-born teacher, companion, and interpreter for deaf and blind Helen Keller, 21 March 1960.

George Macauley Trevelyan, 86, British historian whose texts *History of England* and *English Social History* were studied internationally, 21 July 1962.

John Dover Wilson, 87, Scottish Shakespearean scholar whose texts *The Essential Shakespeare* and *What Happens in "Hamlet"* were widely studied, 15 January 1969.

PUBLICATIONS

Alexander Astin, *National Norms for Entering College Freshmen — Fall 1966* (Washington, D.C.: American Council on Education, 1967);

Ray Allen Billington, *The Historians' Contribution to Anglo-American Misunderstanding: The Report of a Committee on Bias in Anglo-American History Textbooks* (New York: Hobbs, Dorman, 1966);

William Brickman, ed., *Educational Imperatives in a Changing Culture* (Philadelphia: University of Pennsylvania Press, 1966);

Philip Hall Coombs, *The World Educational Crisis: A Systems Analysis* (New York: Oxford University Press, 1968);

Robert Dentler, ed., *The Urban R's: Race Relations as the Problem in Urban Education* (New York: Center for Urban Education, 1967);

Martin Deutsch, Irwin Katz, and Arthur Robert Jensen, eds., *Social Class, Race, and Psychological Development* (New York: Holt, Rinehart & Winston, 1968);

Dan Dodson, *Power, Conflict and Community Organizations* (New York: Council for American Unity, 1961);

Education at Berkeley: Report of the Select Committee of the Berkeley Academic Senate (Berkeley: University of California Press, 1968);

Careth Ellington, *The Shadow Children: A Book about Children's Learning Disorders* (Chicago: Topaz Books, 1967);

Kalil Gezi, *Teaching in American Culture* (New York: Holt, Rinehart & Winston, 1968);

Edmund W. Gordon, *Compensatory Education for the Disadvantaged: Programs and Practices Preschool Through College* (New York: College Entrance Examination Board, 1966);

Calvin Harbin, *Teaching Power* (New York: Philosophical Library, 1967);

Leslie A. Hart, *The Classroom Disaster: How the Outworn Classroom System Cripples Our Schools and Cheats Our Children, and How to Replace it* (New York: Teachers College Press, 1969);

Philip W. Jackson, *The Teacher and the Machine* (Pittsburgh: University of Pittsburgh Press, 1968);

William Loren Katz, *Teachers' Guide to American Negro History* (Chicago: Quadrangle Books, 1968);

Bernard Klein and Daniel Icolari, eds., *Reference Encyclopedia of the American Indian* (New York: B. Klein, 1967);

James Koerner, *Who Controls American Education? A Guide for Laymen* (Boston: Beacon Press, 1968);

John Lawlor, ed., *The New University* (New York: Columbia University Press, 1968);

Elizabeth W. Miller, *The Negro in America: A Bibliography*, compiled for the American Academy of Arts and Sciences (Cambridge, Mass.: Harvard University Press, 1966);

Duncan Grant Morrison and Clinette Witherspoon, *Procedures for the Establishment of Public Two-Year Colleges* (Washington, D.C.: U.S. Office of Education, 1966);

R. Calvert Orem, ed., *Montessori for the Disadvantaged: An Application of Montessori Educational Principles to the War on Poverty* (New York: Putnam, 1967);

Emory Rarig, ed., *The Community Junior College* (New York: Teachers College Press, 1967);

Joseph Slabey Roucek, ed., *The Difficult Child* (New York: Philosophical Library, 1964);

Roucek, *Programmed Teaching: A Symposium on Automation in Education* (New York: Philosophical Library, 1965);

Roucek, *The Study of Foreign Languages* (New York: Philosophical Library, 1968);

Robert Theobald, ed., *The Guaranteed Income: Next Step in Socioeconomic Evolution?* (Garden City, N.Y.: Doubleday, 1966);

Meyer Weinberg, ed., *School Integration: A Comprehensive Classified Bibliography of 3,100 References* (Chicago: Integrated Education Associates, 1967).

Portable classrooms in Chicago, Illinois, 1962

FASHION

by DARREN HARRIS-FAIN, JOLYON HELTERMAN, and SAM BRUCE

CONTENTS

Sidebars and tables are listed in italics.

1960

- Already an important designer of women's clothing, Pierre Cardin begins to create fashions for men, pioneering a trend away from the standard of the gray flannel suit.

- Anthony Traina, of well-known clothing-design label Traina-Norrell, dies, leaving Norman Norell on his own.

- General Motors, Ford, and Chrysler introduce compact models — the Corvair, Falcon, and Valiant, respectively — in order to combat the growing foreign small-car export market.

1961

- Mary Quant opens a second Bazaar in Knightsbridge, based on the same concept that had propelled the highly successful King's Road boutique in 1955 — youth-oriented fun.

- After working for many years under haute couture figure Cristóbal Balenciaga, André Courrèges sets up his own house of fashion design.

- Minis are first introduced in couture houses by Marc Bohan at Dior and by Courrèges.

- Eero Saarinen's design for the TWA terminal at New York International Airport, built in the shape of an eagle about to take off into flight, nears completion. The architect dies on 1 September.

- In a recession-ridden production year, only compact cars show a gain in sales. Overall, the American auto industry's sales are down 25 percent, but sales of compacts are up 9 percent.

- A revival of interest in art nouveau furniture, fabrics, and wallpaper takes place, influenced partly by a Museum of Modern Art exhibition.

- Jane Jacobs publishes *The Death and Life of Great American Cities,* which lambastes large-scale, utopian urban-design plans for American cities.

1962

- Yves St. Laurent opens his own couture house after having worked as head designer at the House of Dior for five years following Dior's death.

- The Council of Fashion Designers of America is founded as a nonprofit organization designed to further American fashion design as an industry, establishing basic codes of professional decorum. Norman Norell is the first president.

- Jacqueline Kennedy redecorates the White House under supervision of the National Fine Arts Commission. She shows the results of the project in a televised tour.

- More automobiles are produced in America during the model year than in any other year except 1955. General Motors cars average about 55 percent of the industry's total sales.

1963

- Fashions from Quant and other Chelsea designers cross the Atlantic Ocean, with exports beginning to account for large percentages of total sales.

1964

- Vidal Sassoon creates short, geometrically inspired bob hairstyles to complement Quant's youthful concepts in fashion.

- Quant receives the London *Sunday Times* International Award for the revolutionary directions in which she has taken British — as well as international — fashion.

- Waistless dresses called shifts are popular, particularly for casual wear.

- Joseph Salerno's United Church in Rowington, Connecticut, represents a burgeoning new freedom of expression in architecture, with its swooping, pointed roofline.

- The Museum of Modern Art, once an example of relative freedom in architectural design, is remodeled by Philip Johnson so as to impose symmetry.

- Many American automakers enlarge their "compact" cars in both weight and length, despite the growing trend toward smaller, particularly foreign, models.

1965

- In London, Barbara Hulanicki starts Biba, a mail-order fashion business that becomes a landmark boutique for the youth market. Biba is based on the concept of cheap clothing meant to be thrown away when a particular fad changes.

- Courrèges stirs up the fashion world with innovative and youth-spirited collections that include over-the-knee skirts. His Space Age collection, in particular, causes excitement.

- Ford introduces a new car called the Mustang at the New York World's Fair, spawning the popular trend of "pony cars" — a name that applies to the Firebird, the Camaro, and a few other small, sporty models.

- The quintessentially 1950s fin finally disappears from cars — with a final run from Cadillac, the automaker that had introduced it in 1948.

- Front seat belts become standard equipment in American cars.

- Puritan Fashions, an American clothing manufacturer, imports a large amount of new fashions from London designers, including the youth-oriented fashions of Quant and of Tuffin and Foale. Clothing is presented in splashy shows rather than in the more elegant manner of traditional shows.

- The Studebaker company, started by Henry and Clement Studebaker, shows its final model, the Daytona.

- The federal government passes the Motor Vehicle Air Pollution Act, which regulates automobile design, often at considerable expense to automakers.

- Paul Young opens the first shop in the United States exclusively for mod fashions — Paraphernalia, located in New York City. His shop imports youth-spirited European clothing.

- The Houston Astrodome, an enclosed, air-conditioned stadium 642 feet in diameter, is opened on 9 April.

1966

- Robert Venturi completes a residence in Chestnut Hill, Pennsylvania, that experiments with resolving architectural-design contradictions in a manner that will later be called postmodern.

- Ford's Mustang scores bigger sales than any other American auto model. Sales of all other compacts slip.

- Op-art and Mondrianesque patterns appear on dress fabrics in youthful clothing designs.

- The British Society for the Preservation of the Mini Skirt demonstrates outside the couture house of Christian Dior in September in order to protest a forthcoming collection that includes long coats and dresses.

- Mary Quant is given the Order of the British Empire (OBE) in honor of the phenomenal success of her export market.

- Yves St. Laurent's collections include pop art–influenced fashions.

- The federal government passes the National Traffic and Motor Safety Act due to rising public concern regarding automobile safety.

- The first phase of the Salk Institute for Biological Research in La Jolla, California — designed by Louis I. Kahn — is completed.

1967

- Unisex clothes begin to show up in most of the major designers' fashion collections.

- Laura Ashley opens her first shop, in London.

- Faye Dunaway wears tailored flannel trousers in the movie *Bonnie and Clyde,* prompting a turn to men's tailoring in women's clothing.

- The House of Dior creates a resort ensemble consisting of a see-through chain-mail tunic and bikini bathing suit.

- Chevrolet introduces the two-seat Camaro SS to counter the threatening popularity of the Ford Mustang.

- Only 55.23 percent of cars that were nine years old on 1 July 1967, compared to 80.70 percent of nine-year-old cars on 1 July 1965, are still on the road — a consequence of the implementation of planned product obsolescence in order to stimulate the market artificially.

- R. Buckminster Fuller's geodesic dome is a center of attention at Expo '67 in Montreal.

1968

- Efforts are made by certain established couturiers to replace the mini, offering maxi- and midi-length clothing as alternatives. Many women reject both, though some accept the maxi as a wearable coat length.

- Cristóbal Balenciaga, perhaps the premier Paris couturier of the 1950s and teacher of Courrèges, closes his couture house. He is said to have remarked, "The life that supported the couture is finished. Real couture is a luxury which is just impossible to do anymore."

- Du Pont introduces a silklike synthetic fabric called Quiana.

- American Motors brings out the AMX in order to join the highly profitable pony-car craze. Although Craig Breedlove establishes several speed records with this car, there is not much faith in the ability of American Motors to produce a high-performance car, and the design is short-lived.

- In January the federal government begins to require expensive crash tests and emissions tests for new American auto models.

- The Volkswagen Beetle reaches record sales of 569,292 in the United States.

- The one-hundred-story John Hancock Building in Chicago by Skidmore, Owings and Merrill becomes world's tallest building. It contains 825,000 square feet of office space.

- Eero Saarinen's famous Gateway Arch in Saint Louis, Missouri, is completed posthumously.

1969

- "Hot pants" (the name was not coined until 1971) make their first appearance. They are introduced as something to wear underneath a split midi-length skirt, but women wear them alone instead.

- The "nude look" is popular on beaches, with crocheted cotton bathing suits and jeweled breastplates that are worn without a T-shirt underneath.

- Danilio Silvestri comes out with a transparent ball of acrylic that opens up into a chair — to be used by the growing pop culture as home furnishing.

- Architect Richard Foster designs a rotating residence, which makes a complete turn in forty-eight minutes.

- AMC's Hornet and Ford's Maverick are Detroit's first real challenges to the subcompact-car market, which is virtually monopolized by foreign competitors.

- The air bag is developed and implemented as a crash-safety device.

OVERVIEW

A Time of Transition. The 1960s were a time of transition in every aspect of American life, and the world of taste and fashion was no exception. To move from conservative Jacqueline Kennedy dress suits, large American-made cars with tail fins and gargantuan engines, built-to-last American modern sofas, and pure-form glass-box buildings to thigh-high miniskirts and dirty blue jeans, small foreign cars, pink disposable plastic chairs, and gaudy Las Vegas–inspired building facades in a matter of one short decade is a phenomenon that only a society charged with a sense of restlessness and turmoil could experience. Those volatile changes in taste and fashion, of course, mirrored what was happening in society as a whole.

Materialism. The result of America's victory in World War II was an unprecedented confidence in being superior to the people of every other nation in the world. The postwar years in the United States were prosperous, and many Americans enjoyed a financial security that they had never before imagined. Wartime production restrictions, which had necessarily limited what could be produced and purchased, had instilled American consumers with the desire to buy. In the years after the war, with more money than before at its disposal, the public celebrated its newfound prosperity with a rush to spend. Material possessions were symbols not only of the success of American society as a whole but of how well one was doing compared to one's neighbor. The money supply seemed to be unlimited, and people wanted to spend it on material goods such as new outfits, the latest futuristic armchair, or a high-performance car. Corporations wanted to show off their success with modernist buildings.

Built-In Obsolescence. Businesses welcomed the new consumerism. The huge demand for possessions that had immediately followed the war began to level off by the early 1950s, and manufacturers began to scramble for ways to keep up profits. Many people had money to spend, but once, for example, someone bought a new automobile, it would take years before even the most avid shopper had to buy a replacement. With clothing styles that remained basically the same as the then-revolutionary but basically conservative 1947 New Look by Chris-tian Dior, women could remain relatively fashionable from season to season with long-lasting, high-quality clothing and accessories. Manufacturers realized that if they offered items that were designed not to last a long time but to be faddish and disposable, consumers would be back in the stores sooner. For an item to be disposable meant one or both of two things: either it could be so conspicuously trendy that no one would want it once the fad had passed, or it could be designed to wear out more quickly than technology demanded. These two options worked together well. Since disposable objects were often made from cheaper materials than their built-to-last counterparts, manufacturers felt freer about taking chances with unconventional designs. The boom in the synthetic-materials industry in polyester, polyurethane, and plastics greatly contributed to the success of the disposable-goods market. Mass production worked much more effectively with plastics than with fine wood.

That's Fine with Us. But why were people willing to purchase these faddish and often-shoddier items of clothing, furniture, cars, and even homes? One reason was that more cheaply produced, disposable items meant big savings for the consumer. The desire to buy, already so deeply ingrained in Americans' minds, led to an exponential growth in the number of items that people took home. Many Americans during the late 1950s and the first half of the 1960s enjoyed the opportunity to buy on a whim. Shopping did not have to be the practical procedure it had once been. Many people enjoyed the new freedom to take a chance with off-the-wall clothing, furniture, and automobiles. It seemed like tangible proof of the high standard of living: the ability to buy one item and keep it until the whim wore off — or the item wore out — and then return to the store to purchase another style of the same item. Also, more families could afford to buy a house now that many were being offered at unprecedented low prices, largely because of the prefabricated crackerbox homes that were appearing in the newly developed suburbia.

Modern Look. Also, the modern look was impressive with a public still in awe at the enormous leaps being taken in science and technology. The space-age look, no matter how tacky in retrospect, was then exciting and daring and symbolized a celebration of the improvement of human life through new gadgets and machines. No-iron polyester clothing; cheap, glossy, stackable plastic chairs; and cars with power windows and engines that would quickly go from zero to sixty were more impressive than the durable-but-staid objects with which most people had grown up. In architecture the modernist pure-form glass skyscrapers that had been originally conceived to inspire and symbolize high human values were being adopted by large corporations, which wanted to project the cutting-edge image of these technological masterpieces.

The Youth Market. Perhaps the most important influence on taste and fashion of the 1960s was the rise of the youth market. The many babies born after World War II were in their mid teens by the 1960s, and they became a powerful commerical force. Their parents often had money to spend on them, either directly or through allowances. Also, more teenagers, girls and boys alike, worked part-time jobs, and at earlier ages. Most of their parents had learned to scrimp and save in the Depression or through the war. The younger generation had never really been forced to be thrifty. Young people developed their own tastes in clothing, cars, and, as they grew a little older, furniture. With their own money to spend, young people wanted objects that were different from those of their parents.

Fashion. Clothing was often the most visible aspect of the new trends. In general, the fashions of the 1960s were more exciting and freer than they had been for several decades. At the beginning of the decade many women were influenced by President John F. Kennedy's attractive, young wife. Jacqueline Kennedy showed American women that good taste could be achieved through simple rather than ornate clothing choices. But the Jacqueline Kennedy look was the last of the simplified styles to be popular for a long time. Around 1964 the young British designer Mary Quant became popular in America with the so-called mod look that had been successful in London's Chelsea district and Carnaby Street since the late 1950s. The mod trend was a youth movement — and a materialist movement — that resulted in a wardrobe expressly for the younger generation that included miniskirts, brightly colored shift dresses, dark eye makeup, and wild ties, blouses, and stockings. The new youthful fashions were made to be both accessible to everyone and disposable from season to season. Men began to concern themselves more with their hairstyles and clothing. Instead of the gray flannel suit and a buzz cut on the sides and back, more and more men experimented with wilder patterns and colors and went to styling salons rather than barbershops. Some men began to wear their hair much longer.

Fashion Freedom for Women. The mod look gave women more fashion choices, and in the 1960s there was a gradual relaxation in social strictures governing what women could and could not wear. Panty hose could be made using strong synthetic fabrics, eliminating awkward garter belts. In the second half of the decade some young women opted to go braless. Pants were probably the biggest fashion revolution of the decade for women. Although women had been wearing pants at home and in sports for several decades, for the first time major designers were creating high-fashion pants outfits made for going out on the town and for more formal social occasions. After a good deal of opposition from country clubs, fine restaurants, and other establishments, women were largely emancipated from the requirement that they wear skirts.

Cars. The craze for cars that had characterized the late 1950s continued into the 1960s, with some differences. Gaudy tail fins, which had been such a popular item in late-1950s cars, gradually lost popularity and finally disappeared. Planned obsolescence had been a feature of automobile design for a long time; styling naturally had been given the highest emphasis, since mechanical features were seldom selling points. Auto dealers lauded the superficial mechanical features of the cars, such as power windows, convertible hardtops, tape players, and other options. The first wave of baby boomers was at a driving age, and this youth market was targeted heavily. Sporty "pony cars" — cars smaller than Detroit had ever produced — were offered, as were high-performance, big-engine "muscle cars." High performance did not usually mean long lasting, but while they lasted the cars worked well. More cars than ever before were sold, and two- and three-car families were not uncommon.

Furniture. Furniture during the 1950s, while often colorful and modern looking, was essentially functional, rationally designed to suit human needs as efficiently as possible. Furnishings were to be "machines for human living" and were intended to reduce the number of objects needed by people as much as possible. They were also built to be durable. Furniture of the 1960s kept the exciting colors and modern look but did away with much of the rational design. Furniture was still mass-produced, but more inexpensive plastics and other materials were used to create sofas, chairs, beds, and lamps that would last for only a short time. Also, the main emphasis was on fun, unusual designs and patterns, not function. Manufacturers of course did not wish to reduce the number of items needed and desired by consumers. The more items the better was the slogan for buyers and sellers alike. The positive aspect of this trend was a huge increase in the number of furniture choices. It was cheap enough that manufacturers could have several designs of every type of furniture rather than only a few.

Architecture. In the early 1960s the modernist style was still a powerful force in architecture. Tall skyscrapers that appeared to be magically assembled with huge walls of glass supported by thin skeletons of reinforced steel were common sights in the urban centers of America. Even smaller cities had begun to take advantage of the crisp, clean, look of the pure-form modernist tower. But whereas the original modernist architects of the early twentieth century — Ludwig Mies van der Rohe, Walter Gropius, Le Corbusier, and others — had advocated a pure architectural style for buildings that would reflect high values, the style was taken up in the 1950s and the 1960s by profit-oriented corporations to celebrate instead the triumph of material values. Instead of open, graceful, floating forms, the new generation of architects created an endless succession of impersonal glass boxes with heavy-looking, ponderous supports, keeping the absence of overornamentation but often ignoring the aesthetic qualities originally intended by the modernists.

Disillusionment, Antiestablishment. The late 1960s were characterized by an overwhelming sense of disenchantment with what American society had become. Materialism and capitalist greed had brought America to the point where young men were dying in order to infringe on the rights of other cultures — at least this is how many in the younger generation viewed U.S. intervention in Indochina and the Vietnam War. The same materialism had created an automobile culture that was filling the air and the earth with harmful pollutants, using up valuable and limited resources, and killing more and more people on the highway. Environmental concerns were for the first time becoming highly charged issues. The wasteful use and unchecked disposal of plastics and other nonbiodegradable products began to cause alarm. Youth by now were much more cynical young adults and led the way of this disillusionment, which was aimed at the "establishment," most often represented by their parents' generation. The lighthearted rebelliousness that had characterized the early part of the decade — wilder clothes, cars, and furniture — had given way to a much darker sense of alienation from that generation's apparent complacency with the status quo.

Hippies and Antifashion. The hippies were an important influence, in spreading a general sentiment of "antifashion." The traditional dictums of fashion basically had been challenged in the first half of the 1960s; now fashion of any kind, traditional or not, was viewed as a suspicious alignment with establishment materialism and moral failing. Secondhand clothing, dirty T-shirts, unkempt hair, torn blue jeans, and costumes borrowed from ethnic, non-Western cultures (assumed to be less corrupt) became the alternatives.

A Challenge to the Automobile Industry. Cars in particular were seen as highly materialistic, and by the late 1960s smaller, more economical automobiles were desired. Detroit found itself sweating as foreign small-car competitors began to claim higher and higher percentages of the American market. The oil shortages of the early 1970s brought a peak to this already rising trend.

The Decline of Modernism. The late 1960s saw many divergent trends in architectural style as architects realized that modernism, despite its utopian ideals, could not solve the world's problems. When several modernist high-rise housing projects collapsed from inattention to engineering details, the result was new and more difficult problems than the ones it had set out to solve. Architects appropriated aspects of earlier styles as well as elements borrowed from the then-burgeoning pop culture to create a collage of loosely defined styles, known collectively as postmodernism.

Optimism to Pessimism. In general tastes in fashion and style of the 1960s were determined by the transition from an exuberant optimism at the beginning of the decade to a jaded pessimism at the end. The 1970s brought a frustration that affected designers and consumers alike. The next several years would be characterized by a sense of nonstyle, an indecision as to what a building should look like, where the hemline should fall, and, more generally, what stylistic forces, if any, would ever again have the power to determine American taste.

TOPICS IN THE NEWS

BIG CARS, SMALL CARS

Cars for Sale. After World War II Americans had more disposable income than ever before, and automobiles were high on their wish lists. This excitement about new cars continued into the 1960s. The showing of the new automobile models became a high-profile event, and people visited the showroom entrances to catch a glimpse and perhaps a place on the new-car waiting list.

Bigger Is Better. Although smaller models existed most cars manufactured immediately after World War II were huge by today's standards. The desires of both the consumers and the auto producers were responsible for the phenomenon. Americans had always seemed to associate largeness with power, prestige, and quality. The auto industry, naturally, was more than happy to oblige: big cars meant big profits, so the six-passenger sedan became Detroit's standard car. Besides having engines that were often much more powerful than necessary for the basic transportation needs of their owners, cars of the postwar era were quite long (up to sixteen or seventeen feet for some models), had low silhouettes, and featured excessive styling, with gaudy paint-and-chrome combinations, bulbous bodies, white-wall tires, wrap-around windows, and sculpted fins. The late 1950s were the high point in such styling excesses. The consumers seemed happy with the state of affairs: big cars were fine with them, and there were not many alternatives. American automakers had no motivation to create low-cost, smaller models: if they built big, expensive cars, those were what people would buy.

What Foreign Cars? For a long time no one offered much of a challenge to the domination of the big car producers. Some compact and subcompact automobiles being made were by foreign manufacturers, but Detroit did not at first take seriously the possible threat of competition. During the immediate postwar era foreign-made vehicles had a reputation, usually deserved, for being poorly designed, especially with regard to comfort and basic performance. Also, imported cars were practically impossible to have repaired if something went wrong. With the exception of the Volkswagen Beetle and certain expensive luxury automobiles, foreign cars were not considered a serious option for the car-buying American public in the late 1940s and the 1950s.

Change in Attitude. By the late 1950s certain changes had begun to occur. For one, the foreign auto companies made their cars more mechanically sound than before. Also, the demand for smaller, cheaper cars grew rapidly. Many people still believed the bigger-is-better notion, but foreign competitors slowly began to fill the demand left mostly unrealized by American automakers. While in 1957, for example, small imported cars accounted for only 3.5 percent of the U.S. new-car market, two years later it had climbed to 10.2 percent. Realizing that smaller profits from selling smaller cars were better than no profits at all, the Big Three (Ford, General Motors, and Chrysler) came out with compact cars during the decade. New models of 1960 included the Chevrolet Corvair from General Motors, the Falcon from Ford, and the Plymouth Valiant from Chrysler. Of the three the Falcon clearly won in terms of sales, due in part to some muckraking advertising as to the competitors' shortcomings and in part to Ralph Nader's widely publicized condemnation of the American-made car in general and the Corvair in particular.

High Performance. This remission of "big-car fever" was short-lived, and by the next model year those compact automobiles were beginning to be embellished. The American public of the 1960s no longer wanted only gimmicky styling in its automobiles — by 1962 fins had almost completely disappeared — it wanted performance. So the cars often grew bigger to match the big engines put inside them, usually powerful V-8s. The year 1964 marked an important milestone in the history of high-performance cars. Pontiac's GTO — an intermediate version of the smaller Tempest/Le Mans — became the prototype of what was quickly becoming the so-called muscle-car/pony-car craze in America. Muscle cars were automobiles with power. Pony cars were the same type of high-performance cars but with smaller bodies; they were named with the advent of the enormously popular Ford Mustang. Often there was an indistinguishably fine line between a muscle car and a pony car. Other popular muscle cars included Plymouth's 1968 Dodge Charger and highly successful 1968 Road Runner. The latter of

What was the quintessential automobile of the 1960s? Many people, car enthusiasts and non-enthusiasts alike, would be quick to choose the Ford Mustang as the car that represents that decade. It was not the fastest or most powerful car by any stretch of the imagination: until power-car builder Carroll Shelby put a giant V-8 engine into it in 1967 and called it the Cobra Mustang GT 500, the Mustang was actually at the low end of the high-performance-car lineup. It was basically a compact car, but there were smaller ones available. It was more or less in the sports-car category, but the Corvette was the most popular sports car.

But when the design was unveiled at the annual show of new models on 17 April 1964, both Ford and its competitors realized that something big was in the making. The model presented at the show was a sporty-looking convertible with a long hood and a short deck. Lee Iacocca, then the general manager of the Ford division, headed the team responsible for developing the styling of the versions of the Mustang that reached the car-buying public. Iacocca and his fellow designers had two things in mind when planning the final product: it should be sporty enough to appeal to the youth market, and it should be priced low, in the twenty-five-hundred-dollar range.

The final result was one of the most diverse collections of options ever presented to the automobile customer. It became an almost-overnight success. The Mustang was available as a convertible, a hardtop (the most popular), or a two-plus-two fastback. Besides the varied palette of colors for the body paint and upholstery, there were customer choices to be made with regard to the type of engine (6-cylinder or V-8), the transmission (three- or four-speed or automatic), tinted or untinted glass, and wheel-cover types as well as whether or not to have a tape player, a luggage rack, and so forth. The list seemed endless. Ford executives claimed that no two Mustangs were exactly the same. The performance of the Mustang could be matched by several other contemporary cars, but for a standard price of twenty-four to twenty-seven hundred dollars, its performance was hard to beat. In 1966 alone more than 541,000 units were sold, accounting for 6 percent of the market.

The Mustang was the catalyst for the so-called pony-car craze started by the Pontiac GTO. Those smaller, sportier, often high-performance cars were extremely popular during the latter half of the 1960s. The Mustang was popular because it pulled together the most desirable aspects from several different concurrent trends in the car market: the compact economy car, the performance-oriented muscle and pony cars, and the trendy little sports cars.

Sources: Leon Mandel, *American Cars* (New York: Stewart, Talbori & Chang, 1982);

Nicket Wright, *Post War American Classics* (New York: Crescent, 1983).

---

the Plymouth muscle cars was a market success because of the new concept of offering pure power in plain packaging; also, its horn made the same sound as the popular cartoon character.

Sporty Looks. As Detroit began to produce better high-performance cars that were also relatively small, a widespread taste for sportier cars began to develop. The Corvette had always maintained a high level of popularity since its introduction in 1953, and it continued to do so when it was almost completely restyled (except for the engine) in 1963 as the Stingray. At about the same time, the Falcon and Valiant were mechanically improved to offer performance that their "economy-only" introductory versions of 1960 had failed to do. In attempts to counter the formidable popularity of the Ford Mustang, Plymouth introduced a sportier version of the Valiant in the 1964 Barracuda, and, after a generally unsuccessful 1965 Rambler Marlin, American Motors offered the 1968 Javelin and two-seater AMX. The sports cars brought out by General Motors, in particular the Chevrolet Camaro and the Pontiac Firebird (both in 1966), were even more popular. All enjoyed at least moderate success, but the Mustang remained the most popular.

The Twilight of the Muscle-Car Era. In 1965 the passage of the Motor Vehicle Air Pollution Act reflected a growing concern for the effects of automobile emissions, placing restrictions on Detroit's engine-design freedom. The insurance industry's tendency to charge large premiums for muscle-car insurance as well as the growing antimaterialist sensibility of the end of the 1960s gradually pushed more and more Americans toward smaller, more economical cars. Once again the foreign competitors were there to fill the small-car market void left by Detroit in its concern with high performance. Whereas by 1962 the foreign-make share of the U.S. market had dwindled to a mere 4.9 percent, in 1967 it was at 9.5 percent, and by the beginning of the 1970s it had reached well over 10 percent of all American-bought new cars; the oil shortages of the early 1970s furthered the economy-car trend. Increasing inflation and environmental concerns helped make the economy-car design a standard American automobile permanently by the latter half of the 1970s.

Sources:

James J. Flink, *The Car Culture* (Cambridge, Mass.: MIT Press, 1975);

Leon Mandel, *American Cars* (New York: Stewart, Talbori & Chang, 1982);

Nicket Wright, *Post War American Classics* (New York: Crescent, 1983).

BIG HAIR

The Full of It. Hair for many women of the early 1960s was supposed to be full, and they spent many hours with hair lacquer, combs, and curlers to help it reach its desired height and body. The late-1950s beehive, thus called because of its final shape, was one of the most popular styles well into the middle of the 1960s. It was also, by far, the fullest.

Beehive Construction. How was a beehive made? First, the volume was created. Wet hair was rolled in curlers and then dried. Some women had their own salon-type dryers that came down over the top of their heads. After the curlers were removed, the hair was teased. After being thoroughly teased, the hair was ready to be shaped. The top or front layer was lifted, not brushed, over the entire mass and then heavily sprayed with a powerful hairspray so that the rat's-nest part was hidden from view.

Beehive Upkeep. The entire process was not repeated every day. Hair was washed only about once a week. In between full settings, the volume was maintained by wearing strategically placed curlers at night and teasing and spraying each morning. Curler caps were an important fashion necessity for most young women, and satin pillowcases were marketed as being easier on the hair.

Bouffant. Not every young woman could or wanted to achieve the formidable beehive. Hair was still worn full but in a bouffant style. The setting and teasing were still done, but the hair was not pulled back into the beehive. First Lady Jacqueline Kennedy wore a moderate bouffant hairdo, the hair tastefully lifted off the crown. Many young women finished their bouffants with curlicues called "guiche curls" over each cheek. In order to have the perfect curl in the shape of a C, girls would tape down the locks of hair onto their cheeks at night, sometimes going as far as to paint them with clear fingernail polish. Bouffants often looked immobile, but not as stiff as the beehive.

Hat's Off! With such full, fragile hairdos, women often opted to go hatless. When hats were worn, they were either large enough to accommodate the entire do, or they were small pillbox hats that crowned the top. Many women simply went without — a relatively new look in women's fashion.

Reaction. In the mid 1960s young women — influenced by folk singers such as Joan Baez — began rejecting bouffant styles in favor of long, straight "natural" styles, even ironing thier hair to achieve the right "look."

Source:

Ellen Melinkoff, *What We Wore: An Offbeat Social History of Women's Clothing, 1950 to 1980* (New York: Morrow, 1984).

LOOKS AND NEW LOOKS: THE NEW HIGH FASHION

The "New Look." French designer Christian Dior's "New Look," introduced in 1947, was simpler than previ-

Lady Bird Johnson with a bouffant hairdo

Women were supposed to wear a dress or skirt, according to what the silhouette on the typical women's-bathroom door indicated. More powerful forces than the sign maker for the local restaurant had been saying this to women for decades. During the 1960s women began to challenge that notion regularly.

This is not to say that pants had not been worn at all by women before. Pants had served for gardening, going to the beach, doing things around the house, and playing many kinds of sports. But the housedress was standard daytime attire for chores at home, and even into the early 1960s standard women's sportswear included skirts. Also, skirts and dresses remained the rule for school, the office, the street, and evening social occasions.

In the late 1950s and early 1960s women's slacks were usually tight fitting, with narrow, tapered legs that ended above the ankle. Casual "Capri" pants were zipped in the back or on the side — zippers in the front were only for men — and worn with crop tops and flats. Stretch pants, made of synthetic fibers such as Helanca nylon or a wool-nylon blend, were worn in the early 1960s. They had a stirrup strap that clung to the instep of the foot so that they would not creep up the leg. When they were worn with flats the strap was visible, but eventually they were worn with low boots. They were worn by fashionable women on the street, but most kept them for casual occasions.

By 1963 the legs of casual pants had begun to widen. Narrow, tapered trousers were still popular, but increasingly "hipster" or "hiphugger" trousers were worn. Hipsters ended on the hips, rather than on the waistline, and were often worn with wide belts. Many of these trousers had flared bell-bottom pants legs.

By the middle of the decade most top Paris designers had pantsuits in their collections. The suits were made of various fine materials, including twill, lace, silk, velvet, wool crepe, and even suede, leather, and vinyl. The last were used frequently by André Courrèges in his futuristic outfits, which often included trousers. The pants could be narrow and tapered or flared with highly decorative bell bottoms trimmed in fringe, lace, or fur. The "masculinity" of a woman wearing pants was tempered with jewelry, gloves, dressy patent-leather shoes, and ornate handbags, and thus fashionable ladies took to the street in pantsuits.

Fine restaurants and clubs took a little more convincing. Many women were turned down at the door wearing the latest, most elegantly designed pantsuit, much to the protest of well-dressed women on the cutting edge of high fashion. To make the point, Judy Carne of television's *Laugh-In* arrived at New York's 21 Club wearing an elegant pantsuit. When she was refused a table, she promptly removed the inappropriate pantsuit to reveal a technically acceptable — but much more risqué — micromini. (The restaurant's dress code was changed soon after.) The Ritz claimed that it would allow a woman to dine in its restaurant while wearing a pantsuit if the maître d' were unable to tell whether she was wearing pants, resulting in a brief stint of popularity for the culottes suit.

By the end of the 1960s even the finest establishments recognized the inevitability of accepting rather than challenging women's prerogative to wear pants. Women were going to wear them, acceptable or not, so it seemed better policy not to lose their business. Since then pants have been a standard part of every woman's wardrobe, both for casual wear and formal wear.

Source: Ellen Melinkoff, *What We Wore: An Offbeat Social History of Women's Clothing, 1950 to 1980* (New York: Morrow, 1984).

ous styles in its emphasis on the natural curve of women's shoulders — rather than the squared-off look of the early 1940s — but was still complex and unnatural. It required hip pads and highly constructed undergarments to squeeze and pull average female figures into "feminine" twenty-inch wasp waists and elegant A-lines. Fabrics were heavy and often elaborately patterned and embellished. But even the women who had discovered simple separates during the 1950s prodded their bodies into the required silhouette for evening social occasions.

Slow Improvements. Something was done to improve the situation for women, but not all at once. From around

1957 on, some designers began to be influenced by the simpler designs of casual wear. Dresses were still well tailored, but not necessarily waist squeezing; they still emphasized the hips and bust, though. They came in plainer patterns and fabrics. But many formal suits, coats, and dresses were still fancy. Women simplified their clothing styles somewhat, but there was no unified concept of how that could be done without looking sloppy.

Jacqueline Kennedy. Then there was Jacqueline Kennedy. Elegant and unassuming as she stood in public beside her husband, President John F. Kennedy, during the early 1960s, she quietly influenced American fashion with her impeccably well-thought-out, pared-down look. She seldom spoke publicly, but she became a model for many American women, who spent time and money trying to create carbon copies of her look.

The Look. Elegant clarity was key. The look included a semifitted Chanel- or Givenchy-type suit jacket that came down to the top of the hipbone or a similarly fitting overblouse with a slim A-line skirt that fell to the middle of the knee or just past. Collars were either simple and rounded or nonexistent, a novelty for formal wear, and sleeves were often above the elbow or done away with altogether. All of these clothes were in restrained solid colors with little or no embellishment, save the single, large, center button near the neck that closed an Empire-waist topcoat. The finishing touches were pumps, long white gloves, sometimes a simple strand of pearls, and her trademark pillbox hat. A classic Jacqueline Kennedy look for the evening was a dress in a single color (often black), sometimes sleeveless, and with a founded or bateau neckline.

Too French? While many women copied her style, some disapproved. A fairly common sentiment was that she spent a lot of money on foreign clothes. The emphasis was on the "foreign" part: the name Givenchy seemed a little too French to be in the wardrobe of the all-American first lady (with the maiden name Bouvier). When she replaced the French couturiers after this election-year response without altering her basic style of clothing, Americans seemed content, even if she still spent a lot of money on clothes. So American women went on wearing Jacqueline Kennedy–inspired French fashions with proper American names.

Simplicity, Not Fanciness. Naturally, this look did not come to dominate high fashion overnight. Women still sported fashions — especially casual wear — that remained popular from the 1950s well into the new decade, and the more pared-down look was saved for special occasions and outings on the town. But the message was loud, clear, and far-reaching: elegance was better achieved through simplicity, not fanciness, of dress.

Source:
Ellen Melinkoff, *What We Wore: An Offbeat Social History of Women's Clothing, 1950 to 1980* (New York: Morrow, 1984).

Jacqueline Kennedy

MEN'S FASHION: CARE MORE, DARE MORE

More Style Conscious. By the 1960s many men had generally started to think more about what they wore and to be a little more style conscious and daring than they had for several decades. Men's fashion palettes had expanded, which was not surprising, considering that clothing choices for men during the 1950s could hardly have become more conservative.

A Uniform Direction. Women's fashions of the early to mid 1960s had two different strains. While Jacqueline Kennedy was passively paring down style to a ladylike, elegant clarity, Mary Quant, the mods, and André Courrèges were turning fashion on its head, paring down little but the number of yards it took to make a shirt. The trend in men's clothing stayed in one fairly consistent direction: whether one was young, old, Chelsea mod, or New York businessman, fashion was becoming more exciting on the whole. Of course, the increasing "antifashion" sentiments of the late 1960s altered the course of all fashion trends.

Start at the Top. The days of the 1950s crew cut were also coming to an end. During the 1960s men were more concerned about having a neat, well-styled haircut. Instead of the cheap trim on the back and the sides at the local barbershop, many men began to go to hairstyling salons, which had begun to offer services to both women and men in the same large, open-design setting. Hair was neatly combed, often parted on the side, and young men hardly ever left the house without combs in their pockets. When their girlfriends fell in love with the Beatles and their look in the mid 1960s, many of the younger crowd copied the straight-across-the-front fringe of the four megastars. In the late 1960s many young men wore their hair longer, influenced by the back-to-nature sentiments of the flower children.

Suits. Suits followed a more exciting trend: men became more conscious of what they wore both to the office and on social occasions. The gray flannel suit of the 1950s had been rather boxy in appearance. By the end of that decade Italian designers had begun to influence the standard suit design with a much slimmer line. In the early 1960s the jacket was even narrower, nipped and shortened to give a more fitted look. Small dress-shirt collars were either pointed or had rounded edges; white collars were seen on checkered, striped, or colored solid shirts. Gingham checks, particularly in blue and white or black and white, were popular. Ties became narrower, as did belts. Slim-cut wool or blended pants legs without pleats were cuffed at the beginning of the decade, then cut straight. In the middle of the 1960s the Edwardian look, characterized by a single-breasted suit jacket with narrow lapels buttoned high on the chest, was popular. Vests, which had been discarded for several decades, made a fashionable reappearance.

New Dandyism. For more adventurous men, suits with brighter, more daring colors were becoming available, often made of synthetic blends. These came in many combinations: with plain oxford-cloth shirts, shirts with ruffles down the front, wide ties, bow ties, and so forth. The key was a sort of dandyism, a new freedom of dress.

Bold Experiments. As early as 1957 Pierre Cardin had introduced the collarless jacket, which was tight fitting and double-breasted. The mods adopted the collarless-jacket look, modeling themselves after the popular Beatles. To the newfound dandyism, the mods added decorative waistcoats, paisley and floral patterns, wide belts, and bell-bottom dress trousers. With the release of the Beatles' *Sgt. Pepper's Lonely Hearts Club Band* album in 1967, satin uniforms trimmed in braid, like those worn by the group on the album's cover, became popular with some. The same year experienced the short-lived popularity of the Nehru jacket, with stand-up collars and buttons to the neckline. The Nehru jacket, inspired by Jawaharlal Nehru, the former Indian prime minister, was often worn with a synthetic-fabric turtleneck shirt or sweater.

Not Everyone. Some men continued to wear gray flannel suits with oxford-cloth shirts. Not every man had the courage, or even the desire, to raise the excitement level of his wardrobe. But during the 1960s that had become a viable option.

Sources:
Maybelle S. Bigelow, *Fashion in History: Western Dress, Prehistoric to Present* (Minneapolis, Minn.: Burgess, 1979);

J. Anderson Black and Madge Garland, *A History of Fashion* (London: Black Cat, 1990).

NEW FASHIONS FOR YOUNG PEOPLE

Dress Codes. Not many high schools and colleges had school uniforms in the 1960s, but most had dress codes. For a good portion of the 1960s young women were not allowed to wear pants of any kind to class, and young men were forbidden to wear blue jeans. Students were expected to maintain a neat appearance, and until the second half of the decade they generally complied without much complaint.

Young Women. Many young women in the early 1960s wore skirt/blouse/sweater combinations, and clothes by such manufacturers as Villager, McMullen, and John Meyer of Norwich were the most sought after. Wool A-line skirts that fell about midknee, usually in muted heather colors, and flesh-colored stockings went with Bass Wee-juns. Cotton blouses, often with a button-down or Bermuda collar, had long or elbow length sleeves. They could be either in a plain solid or have a tasteful, subdued, often flowery print. The sweater was most often a cardigan, sometimes with a ribbon adorning the top button. For the really in look, the cardigan was tied loosely around the neck, and an initial pin or circle pin would be worn at the center of the collar or on the side.

New Dresses. Villager and McMullen, as well as many other large-scale manufacturers, also made one-piece dresses — also worn with a sweater around the neck — called shirtwaists. They were sometimes worn with a belt at the waist, but they departed from the twenty-inch wasp waist of the 1950s. After about 1963 completely waistless dresses known as shifts were worn to school, to the beach, or just to hang out. A reinterpretation of the not-so-popular sack or chemise dress of the late 1950s, shifts were often sleeveless and allowed more freedom to move around and to dance.

Young Men. Young men also had basic school clothes. Standard fare included a dress shirt made of cotton or a cotton blend, often in a bright solid color (especially yellow) or an interesting pattern. Plaid shirts were popular for a while, and Gant dress shirts were successful. Many young men liked to wear socks that matched their shirt. Chinos in a light khaki fabric or dress pants made of wool, cotton, or a natural-looking synthetic blend were worn with a narrow leather belt. In the warmer months short-sleeved sports shirts could be worn.

The Mod Look. The impact of the mod look was felt a few years into the decade in school wear. Young women wore as high a miniskirt as they could get away with, and brighter colors and patterns filled the school halls. But the first half of the 1960s, especially in high schools, was characterized by a general tendency to maintain a conservative manner of school dress. As the mod look became more standard, and as the tremors of the antiestablish-

The Beatles in their *Sgt. Pepper's Lonely Hearts Club Band* outfits

ment sentiments of the latter part of the decade started to be felt, many high-school and college students alike quickly adopted it.

Source:

Ellen Melinkoff, *What We Wore: An Offbeat Social History of Women's Clothing* (New York: Morrow, 1984).

THE RISE OF THE YOUTH MARKET

Adult-Targeted Market. For the first half of the twentieth century the big designers targeted adult women since they or their husbands had the money to spend. Girls dressed in basic school clothes: plain dresses or cotton blouses, cardigan sweaters, and wool skirts in conformity with school dress codes. School fashions were created by anonymous designers at clothing manufacturers. While hemline height, colors, and so forth were influenced by Paris, the fashion capital's designers seldom made direct contributions to the wardrobe of girls. For dress-up occasions, girls wore versions of their mothers' clothing.

More Money. But in the late 1950s and early 1960s teenagers had more money than previous generations. The postwar years had been prosperous, and girls often had incomes from part-time jobs or sizable allowances from their parents.

More Girls. Also, there were more girls in that generation as the early baby boomers became teenagers. Not only did this growing portion of the population have money to spend, but their generation was the first in a long time that had not grown up in an era programmed with the need to be frugal. They wanted to buy, and they especially wanted to buy clothes. However, shopping in the large department stores could be discouraging for young people. Saleswomen often were supercilious to girls who came into their sections just to browse around. Besides, the clothes sold in department stories were not all that "fun."

Mary Quant. In the late 1950s Mary Quant, a young British woman who worked in a milliner's shop, set out to do something about the lack of youth-oriented fashions. She opened a clothing shop — the first boutique — on King's Road in the Chelsea district of London. Called Bazaar, the boutique was filled with clothes designed by Quant that had a markedly new feel. Simple, figure-skimming short dresses in black or with wild geometric patterns, knee-length jumpers, balloon-style dresses, and other novel items lined the racks, and the young, trendy Chelsea crowd came en masse to browse through Quant's designs of the day. After those designs sold — usually in only a day or two — she would go home to create some new types of dresses for the next day's business.

Fun Clothes. Quant's philosophy was to make clothes fun and accessible. After opening a second Bazaar at Knightsbridge, other young London designers began to follow suit — most successfully, Barbara Hulanicki and her shop, Biba — and the youth-centered boutique era was born. The boutique shopping experience was one of relaxed browsing, often with popular music playing in the background and maybe a coffee bar on the side. The idea was to have inexpensive clothing that could be worn and then disposed of when quickly changing trends turned — a new concept in the made-to-last fashion industry.

The Mod Look. Quant and her young London compatriots dressed the trendy Chelsea set and created the mod look. The other major center for trendy mod fashions was London's Carnaby Street. Short, straight-cut dresses patterned with a combination of dots and stripes, often with wide, wildly colored ties, were a Carnaby Street–look trademark. Sally Tuffin and Marian Foale were a major fashion force for the Carnaby Street crowd, and they were demonstrative about their disenchantment with the control of high fashion by Paris. They claimed that rather than concerning themselves with being fashionably correct, they just "wanted to be ridiculous."

Coming to America. The Beatles were an important part of this new mod generation, and as they took the United States by storm in 1964 they solidified the success of the mod look, which had arrived the year before. American manufacturers, realizing the revolution in fashion that was in the making, brought Quant and her fellow young designers to America to give the country a taste of their work. Instead of the elegant collection showings of haute-couture fame, the London designers put on fashion spectaculars, impressing audiences in New York, Los Angeles, and other major U.S. cities with extravaganzas choreographed to upbeat popular music.

The Mini. One of the most influential aspects of the new mod look came from its introduction of the mini. To attain mini status, the skirt or dress had to fall somewhere above the knee. But that definition left a lot of room for interpretation. From about 1963 on, hemlines crept higher and higher up the thigh, culminating in the micromini, which just barely (but not always) hid undergarments.

The Art of the Miniskirt. Walking down almost any street in America during the mid 1960s, one would be sure to catch a glimpse of an above-the-knee hemline. Some high-school and college dress codes held out briefly, but minis were worn to class, to fine restaurants, to the office, and everywhere else. And not just by girls — many women were not immune to the advertised promises that they would look as young as they dressed. Females of all ages and sizes diligently learned the art of walking, sitting, picking up dropped pencils, and avoiding stairwells; which, if inevitable, were best negotiated as quickly as possible, while still maintaining an acceptable level of decency.

Preferred Stockings. Their efforts were helped by newly important stockings and tights. With more of the leg exposed, hosiery became fancier and had interesting patterns. Fishnet stockings and heavily textured tights spanned by strong geometric patterns became the fashion, often coordinated with an equally striking pattern in the miniskirt itself. Undulating lines and patterns borrowed from the then-fashionable op art were popular, as were Warholian pop art designs. In short, anything modern, trendy, and fun was acceptable.

Panty Hose. The introduction of panty hose was revo-

Models in mini dresses

lutionary for the way women dressed. Freeing women from the complexities (not to mention the aesthetic burdens) of the girdle, garter belt, "garter gap," and other aspects of traditional female-undergarments, panty hose allowed a more natural line.

Completing the Look. The mod look à la Mary Quant was not finished when a short checkerboard shift or a brightly colored midthigh mini and brocade-textured stockings were put on. To complete the look, hair was cut short in a geometric, often asymmetric style inspired by Vidal Sassoon. Many young American women kept their bouffants or their long straight hair for a long time, but for the real "total" look, hair was cut in this boyish crop. In order not to appear too boyish, women made up their eyes heavily. Heavy black eyeliner, with dark eye shadow filling in the space up to the eyebrows, contrasted with lips that were made as pale as possible. Twiggy, the famous model from Britain, was the quintessential embodiment of this look. Finally, on the feet was usually either a pair of Mary Janes or short boots. With mod-look enthusiasts pointed toes and thin, high heels, which had remained popular well into the 1960s, were gradually replaced by chunkier, more-squared-off footwear.

Paris Couture. Meanwhile, Paris couturiers continued to create elegant fashions for the more conservative, usually older, sector of the public. Couture fashions were not free from the influence of the new mod look's high hemlines and youthful designs, but in general the major Paris designers maintained a conservative output.

Not Everyone. A few exceptions opted to go the way of the new modern look — not necessarily mod, but with some similarities. One of the most notable of those designers was André Courrèges. From 1964 his collections featured futuristic outfits rendered in sculptured, heavy fabrics that tended to ignore the natural lines of the figure. Space-age influences were characteristic of his designs, including the stark use of white from head to toe, from a tall white helmet to white squared-off boots. The helmet was too much for most women, but the Courrèges trademark white boots fared much better. His skirts, which were usually several inches above the knee, were designed to be worn with these boots, and gradually he introduced calf-high and finally over-the-knee versions.

Sources:

Barbara Bernard, *Fashion in the '60s* (New York: St. Martins Press, 1978);

Maggie Pexton Murray, *Changing Styles in Fashions: Who, What, Why* (New York: Fairchild, 1989);

J. Anderson Black and Madge Garland, *A History of Fashion* (London: Black Cat, 1990).

SECONDHAND CLOTHES AND TIE-DYED SHIRTS: ANTIFASHION AND THE HIPPIE INFLUENCE

All in Fun. Young people of the 1960s had started the decade with an air of optimism, a confident exuberance reflecting the prosperous American society into which they were coming of age. They had an unprecedented amount of social and financial freedom to develop their own identities — identities separate from those of their parents. This sentiment manifested itself most visibly in youthful dress. The mod look was cool; the mini was daring; unusual color combinations were exciting. Mostly it was a good-natured stand against the older "establishment," with no hard feelings.

Growing Consciousness. As the 1960s moved forward, with them came a growing consciousness of social concerns, including civil rights issues and controversial U.S. intervention in Indochina. Many young people, disgusted with what they saw as rampant materialism and the moral failing of American society, found ways to separate themselves as completely as possible from the older generation — the establishment — that represented it. One of those ways was a revolution against traditional fashion values. The mods and the new youth market in general had simply rejected the older generation's clothing and its fashion choices. The youth of the late 1960s instead rejected established fashion of any kind — particularly anything worn or accepted by the establishment — in favor of their own unorthodox uniform.

Hippies. The extreme of this revolution against fashion was found in the hippies or flower children. Sometimes with a vengeance these young men and women retreated from materialistic society, adhering to their own moral views. An important aspect of this rejection of the establishment was in the way the hippies dressed themselves. Flowers, the hippie symbol of brotherly love,

FOREVER IN BLUE JEANS

Denim pants were invented by Levi Strauss in the mid nineteenth century to cater to the needs of California prospectors. The highly durable material soon was adopted by laborers of all sorts, and for the next century denim jeans remained work clothes. Starting in the late 1950s, denim pants, or blue jeans, made a remarkable transition: they became the most popular kind of pants among young people, who helped make them acceptable in sportswear in America and around the world.

Several factors were behind the popularity of blue jeans during the 1960s. The hippies took up jeans for many reasons: they were inexpensive, required little or no care, and became more comfortable with wear. In particular, jeans were an antifashion statement. As Marshall McLuhan put it, "Jeans represent a ripoff and a rage against the establishment." Hippies were not the only ones to appreciate the down-to-earth nature of jeans; the establishment also began to favor them, as sportswear became increasingly casual and as unisex fashions became popular.

During the decade jeans appeared in a wide variety of styles — patched, embroidered, rolled up, cut short, faded, and so forth — each intended as a means of personal expression. Denim jackets, skirts, and other articles also appeared. Since then blue jeans have remained an integral part of American clothing.

Source: Michael and Ariane Batterberry, *Mirror Mirror: A Social History of Fashion* (New York: Holt, Rinehart & Winston, 1977).

were often worn in the hair, but they also appeared painted, embroidered, and sewn onto buttons, shirts, and pants. Bell-bottom jeans, faded and dusty, were the basis of the hippie wardrobe. Wearing a T-shirt as outerwear was revolutionary at first, but when that seemed too tame, they were dyed in bright strident colors; later they were tie-dyed in undulating, psychedelic spirals and circles.

Secondhand. The establishment seemed much too materialistic, particularly when buying new clothes. Instead of continuing that trend, hippies often patronized secondhand shops. They claimed they bought clothes for utilitarian purposes only, rejecting the traditional associations of clothing with status and taste. Army-navy surplus stores, Salvation Army stores, and other thrift-type stores were popular sources. Along with conventional views of clothing quality, traditional notions of gender-

Day dress by Mary Quant, 1964

Provençale cotton outfits by Yves St. Laurent, 1964

Space-age design by Courrèges, 1965

Hippie-influenced evening dresses, late 1960s

distinct clothing were also discarded. Sandals were worn everywhere by both men and women.

Natural. But going barefoot was preferred. Part of the antifashion movement was a move back to naturalness. So much of fashion seemed artificially restricting as well as symbolic of the establishment's unnatural rules of stylistic conformity. The hippies moved toward an ideal of a more primitive, uncorrupted lifestyle. Hair was unkempt and usually grown long; young black men and women wore full Afro cuts. Young women wore little if any makeup. Going braless had been a radical choice for young women in the middle of the decade, but by the end of the 1960s it had become standard practice for some.

Cultural Escape. If Western capitalist societies represented materialism and an absence of morals, maybe other societies were better models to follow, the hippies believed. In fashion this meant a strong interest in the clothing of Eastern, tribal, and other ethnic cultures, including those of Native Americans and Indians. Ethnic jewelry and especially love beads abounded as did brightly colored, exotic-looking fabrics, often from India.

Hippie Influence in the Mainstream. Not every young person in the late 1960s was a hippie; in fact, most were not. But almost every person under the age of twenty-five was influenced by the hippies to one degree or another. The same antifashion trends embraced by the hippies were apparent — if to a lesser degree — in the moves toward naturalness and ethnic styles of the fashion establishment.

Stretching the Limits. School dress codes got in the way of natural expression sometimes, but they were often pushed to the limits. Whereas trying to wear a denim mini to foil the no-jeans-at-school rules of the mid 1960s had been a mischievous form of good-natured rebellion, antifashion at the end of the decade took on a new, much darker sense. More leeway was taken with grooming; long hair and no bra/no hose became, if not the standard, at least a common choice. If skirts had to be worn, they were often tattered, dirty, or secondhand, and shirts were worn untucked by both men and women.

High Fashion Attempts Hippie. Not everyone read the hippie look as the blaring antiestablishment message it was intended to be. Some of its aspects were considered charming by outsiders, if a little raw and rough edged. Put into the hands of experienced designers, some believed, it might even be worth something. So by 1968 top Seventh Avenue designers introduced new bohemian-inspired lines. Models appeared in *Vogue* and other high-fashion magazines wearing sanitized versions of patchwork skirts and flowered dresses, and pantsuits, blouses, underwear, and everything else, were elegantly tie-dyed.

Fashion Limbo. However, a three-hundred-dollar beige and plum Halston tie-dye pantsuit was not genuine hippie, and soon both designers and consumers realized it. The 1960s ended on a note of fashion uncertainty about when to trust a fashion authority. With that uncer-

Unisex outfits tailored for the youth market

tainty came a generally tolerant attitude, even in high fashion, regarding clothing choices. Minis, maxis, midis, pantsuits, hot pants, and numerous other contradictory styles appeared, then disappeared.

Source:
Ellen Melinkoff, *What We Wore: An Offbeat Social History of Women's Clothing, 1950–1980* (New York: Morrow, 1984).

A SIGNIFICANT DECLINE IN THE COUTURE SYSTEM

European Couture. Twentieth-century high fashion

had traditionally been the almost-exclusive domain of European fashion centers. Designers from European cities, especially Paris, created original clothing for particular wealthy clients or a collection of styles from which clients could choose and subsequently purchase personally tailored versions. Naturally, this method is extremely expensive, and the group who patronized personal couture was elite. Many others depended on basic manufacturer lines that, while influenced by what was going on in Paris, were usually fairly basic wear. Still others made their own clothing.

Line for Line. By the 1960s couturiers were sending their original designs abroad, particularly to the United States, where certain retail stores copied them in a system called "line for line." For a fee these American manufacturers were given permission to produce copies of designs for private customers. Manufacturers promoted this system, boasting that they could have their customers wearing an item from Parisian high fashion within several days of its introduction in the couture houses. But the affected public was still small.

Ready-to-Wear. In the mid to late 1950s certain Parisian couture houses also began to create secondary lines of fashions to be mass-manufactured. The couturiers finally realized the enormous economic potential of selling some of their designs at less expensive prices. The secondary designs were not poorly designed versions, but less expensive fabrics were often used, and sometimes the cut itself would be somewhat less intricate. Buyers from around the globe purchased rights to mass-produce the designs. These ready-to-wear clothes were sold in large numbers in retail stores, allowing more people to wear "high fashion."

The Power of Paris. While the Parisian celebrity designers at first were reluctant to allow their designs to move from the elite couture houses to the general public through ready-to-wear lines, their power over the fashion world had not yet diminished. They still had direct control over the line-for-line and ready-to-wear versions of their designs that they sold abroad, but their influence was much more diffused. Even lesser designers for American and British manufacturers who were not buying the couture designs directly were imitating the basic style coming out of Paris. Everyone wanted the Paris look. Paris dictated how far down the hemline went, whether the bust or the hips would be emphasized or deemphasized, the types of fabrics that were in fashion, and the correct colors, accessories, and hairstyles. If Paris said that rounded collars were in, the world made rounded collars.

Decentralized Power. With the rise of the youth market in the late 1950s and early 1960s, however, Paris began to lose its monopoly of control over the way people dressed. High-fashion meccas began to be established in London, New York, Rome, Milan, Madrid, and other places. In the 1960s and 1970s young people tended to reject the dictates of Paris styles, following instead their own fashion inspirations — such as young, trendy designers or popular rock superstars. The antifashion era of the hippies, as well as the general antiestablishment sentiment of many young people during the Vietnam War years, served to decentralize even more the forces governing the way people dress. Paris may still be the fashion capital of the world, but it now has some substantial rivals.

Source:
Maggie Pexton Murray, *Changing Styles in Fashion: Who, What, Why* (New York: Fairchild, 1989).

STYLE OVER SUBSTANCE: FURNITURE GOES POP

Postwar Modern. The furniture of the 1940s and 1950s, particularly after World War II, was based on the modernist aesthetic — it was rationally designed and functional. Not that it was necessarily boring: unlike many examples of modernist furniture before World War II, the furniture of the late 1940s and the 1950s was often exciting, with lively colors and patterns. Still, it was inherently functional. Furniture was designed first and foremost to be efficient, enabling people to sit, sleep, eat, or store their belongings. Modernist furniture designers took design ideas of the late-nineteenth-century and early-twentieth-century Arts and Crafts movement, as well as certain motifs of early-twentieth-century Art Nouveau and Art Deco, and incorporated them into the modernist vocabulary of rational function. Influential in furniture design of this period was the ideal of a masterfully planned living environment. From the Arts and Crafts movement also came a concern with durability. By using newly developed and perfected synthetic materials, particularly plastics, modernist designers could create objects that lasted much longer than even their Arts and Crafts counterparts. The most prolific and popular designers were from the Scandinavian countries, and Danish modern, Swedish modern, and Finnish modern furniture and other interior-design objects filled many American homes by the late 1950s.

Pop. The baby boomers coming of age at the beginning of the 1960s had a significant effect on furniture design — not surprising, since they indirectly affected the design of clothing, art, architecture, and almost all aspects of consumer society. Toward the end of the 1950s a new pop aesthetic, based on the ever-changing fads of popular culture rather than an established tradition of quality, began to emerge. Instead of durability, permanence, high-quality materials, and designs that were rational and functional, pop objects were conceived in terms of disposability, cheap materials, and whimsical, often-witty "antidesign."

More Objects. Modernists had strived to pare down the number of objects needed by humans. The theory was essentially that as more rationally designed objects that functioned efficiently were produced, many superfluous items could gradually be eliminated. As designer-architect Ludwig Mies van der Rohe succinctly put it, "Less is more." The pop ideal, on the other hand, involved providing a prosperous consumer society with many objects. Manufacturers and their designers realized that if they created more pieces of furniture with shorter life spans, consumers would shortly have to replace them. Also, if the sofa or lamp were odd and faddish enough, consumers would purchase the next fashionable item even before built-in obsolescence occurred naturally. While the use of less expensive synthetic materials had aided modernist designers in creating mass-produced but carefully designed furniture, the availability of those materials was the enabling force behind the creation of pop furniture, which depended on being cheap and quickly made.

Status No More. Mirroring certain changes in attitude regarding other areas of culture, some people expressed a new contempt for the associations of furniture ownership with status. The more youthful sector of the population advocated — and therefore spent money on — furniture that was inexpensive and accessible enough to be available to a wider range of the population, a trend similar to their response to fashion. Furniture such as Peter Murdoch's child's chair (1963) — constructed from polyethylene-coated paperboard — Roger Dean's Pumpkin Chair (1967), and Robin Day's injection-molded armchair are typical of the designs that met the demands of the new market. Each was simple and cheaply produced, and not many people could seriously associate either with

status. As furniture became less expensive and therefore more accessible, designs became more playful as well. Designers did not have to worry as much about using expensive materials for unusual creations that could easily turn out to be failures. Also, many people were tired of staid, traditional, functional designs.

Fanciful Designs. Some chairs were shaped like half globes, while others were designed as continuous ribbons folded in on themselves. There was no purpose for such designs except for sheer novelty and the knowledge that when they broke one could go to the store and buy other unusually designed chairs as replacements. Colors were often bright, and shapes and patterns were often intricate and fanciful. Pop invested a sense of the personal that had gotten lost in modernism. Some furniture, in fact, actually began to take on human and other organic shapes, a radical departure from Bauhaus-inspired starkness. French designer Olivier Morgue took this idea to the extreme with his fiberglass upholstered, chaise-longue Bouloum seats (1968) — also called "person seats" because they were shaped like a reclining human figure. One would sit in them as if one were sitting in another person's lap. The Bouloum chairs could be used singly or stacked to make the chair as high as desired. American designer Wendell Castle created furniture that suggested neosurrealist biomorphic shapes, including his Molar Sofa (1969–1970) constructed out of plastic. Italian designer Gaetano Pesce created the Up Series, which consisted of "transformation" furniture. The polyurethane-foam furniture was packed in flat boxes; when the boxes were taken home and opened, the three-dimensional forms would magically spring to life.

Modernist Footholds. Many people, however, remained basically conservative during the 1960s with regard to taste in furniture. Rationally designed, functional furniture continued to attract a substantial market, especially in corporate environments where the crisp, stark look of modernism seemed to project the right image of efficiency and success. Many examples of Scandinavian modern furniture were generally pleasing to the more conservative eye. Modernist furniture was no longer seen as the progressive wave of the future that it had been in previous decades.

Source:
Stephen Baxley, Phillipe Garner, and Deyan Sudjic, *Twentieth-Century Style & Design* (New York: Van Nostrand Reinhold, 1986).

STYLES OF MODERN ARCHITECTURE

The Modernist Influence. During the 1960s modernist architecture was still a widespread and powerful force. Buildings in the modernist style were part of the environment of virtually every urban area in America, and new ones were being erected every day. Although it was becoming increasingly evident that modernism had failed to meet its idealistic goals of raising the human spirit, it was still a basically good style and method in which to con-

Roger Dean with his pumpkin chair

New Forms of Expression. Despite many striking and original masterpieces modernism had not allowed for much overt individual expression. In fact, a modernist goal had been to subvert explicit content in favor of the beauty of pure, rational form. In the late 1950s and 1960s there was a resurgence of individual expressionism in architecture. The famous Sydney Opera House in Australia (1959) by Danish architect Jorn Utzon, with its huge, steeply arching shell forms, shows modernist engineering (but certainly not form) at its most fanciful. Finnish-born American architect Eero Saarinen designed the TWA terminal for International Airport in New York City (1962) in the shape of an eagle about to take off in flight; however, the building's "failure" in purity of form still allows for purity of rational function. Many other architects during the decade took advantage of the new freedom of form while still maintaining basic modernist concerns for function.

Historical Styles. One of the original intentions of modernist architecture had been to make a break from a tyranny to the history of architecture. At the beginning of the century many architects still used classical columns and arches as well as elements of form and ornament from various other historical styles to adorn their buildings. The modernists thought it looked ridiculous to have a skyscraper capped with a gilded dome; instead, they attempted to purge architecture of this type of outdated ornamentation and to develop a style that belonged to the twentieth century alone. With an increasing awareness of modernism's shortcomings, many architects saw no reason to exclude some of these impressive-looking older forms. By the mid 1960s a new historical trend began to emerge as a new generation of architects started to incorporate historical elements that had been deemed obsolete by the pure-form modernist architects. Roman arches, Corinthian columns, Brunelleschian loggias, flowing Baroque staircases, symmetrical facades, intricate wall ornamentation — all appeared in buildings that were still essentially modernist in both engineering and function. Louis I. Kahn's Kimbell Art Museum in Fort Worth, Texas (1966–1972), uses Renaissance cathedral ideas and forms of repeated, symmetrical nave bays and vaulted-arch ceilings but keeps the work in a modern context by using state-of-the-art engineering methods for lighting and air conditioning and other functional aspects. From afar Minoru Yamasaki's famous World Trade Center in Manhattan, conceived in the late 1960s and completed in 1974, looks like another example of the corporate modernist skyscraper. Up close, however, the Gothic ogival-arch decoration that repeats itself along the entire surfaces of the two towers becomes surprisingly apparent.

struct buildings. However, by the 1960s the modernist style began to be recognized as just one of many possible approaches. Throughout the decade architects began to branch out in various directions.

Brutalism. Some of the new stylistic options were not too far removed from the modernist style. Several architects, inspired by the late works of the French modernist Le Corbusier, created buildings that used many of the rational structural ideas of the modernist style. Instead of the sleek, buoyant steel-and-glass masterpieces of the International Style, however, these brutalist buildings were constructed using rough, blocklike materials, such as concrete and brick, fashioned into heavy and aggressive forms. An important brutalist work is Yale University's School of Art and Architecture building (constructed 1959–1963) designed by Paul Rudolph. Its rectangular forms made of large slabs of rough concrete are layered in a simplistic-looking crisscross pattern suggesting a structure made with children's building blocks. However, when one imagines the forms constructed out of lightweight steel and glass, the structure's early-modernist roots become recognizable. British architect James Stirling also created several brutalist works, notably a building for Cambridge University's history department in 1966. As Le Corbusier and other important architects suggested, the move to less perfect building materials paralleled a growing recognition of the unperfectible nature of the human condition.

Complexity and Contradiction. These divergent trends in architectural style were addressed in an important book by architect Robert Venturi, *Complexity and Contradiction in Architecture,* which was written in 1962 and published in 1966. He discusses the divergent styles of his contemporaries and argues that all of architectural

The Whitney Museum of American Art in New York, an example of brutalist architecture

history has been a continuous mixture of inconsistent styles. Venturi claims that when scholars and critics summarize a specific period or style in architecture, they pick and choose examples that fit into a neat category. These mainstream masterpieces, he explains, might include a chapel by Michelangelo, but only its altar and its sculptural forms, and then maybe a dome of one of Guarini's buildings and just the facade of the Louvre. But the elements of these same buildings that are not "stylistically correct" enough — such as an unexplained asymmetry or an unconventional ornament — to fit into the mainstream of the period are ignored. Venturi offers a revisionist way to look at the entire history of architecture, one that includes all of these so-called inconsistencies. He concludes that these inconsistent trends are actually the mainstream, while the examples that fit nicely into stylistic categories are really the exceptions. Venturi also takes modernist architects to task for ridding architecture of all content, turning Mies van der Rohe's dictum "less is more" on its head by arguing that "less is a bore." He felt that architecture should not be pure but hybrid, inconsistent, and "of messy vitality and richness of meaning."

Postmodernism. Venturi's book was influential, and it helped codify the aesthetic and stylistic trend that by the end of the 1960s was already beginning to become popular with a new generation of architects. Buildings designed by Venturi, who was admired primarily for his theoretical writings, and even more successful architects incorporated various styles and influences, including but not limited to brutalism, expressionism, historical neoclassicism, and the burgeoning pop and automobile culture. The buildings of this new breed of architecture emphasized individual expression and were often full of witty content that sometimes parodied past styles or the human situation. Charles Moore's complex of residential units for Kresge College in Santa Cruz, California (1965–1974), is modeled on the meandering nature of an Italian village and includes repeated quasi-neoclassical balconies. Parodying the modernist preoccupation with function, the whiteness of the stuccoed buildings is interrupted by primary colors that highlight such amenities as the laundromat and the public telephone. In general there began to be a much greater tolerance of individuality and stylistic freedom during this period. In the 1970s writer Charles Jencks labeled the budding movement postmodernism. Important architects who began to work in this loosely defined postmodernist style, besides Venturi and Moore, included Michael Graves, Philip Johnson, Robert Stern, and Frank Gehry.

Sources:

Stephen Baxley, Phillipe Garner, and Deyan Sudjic, *Twentieth-Century Style & Design* (New York: Van Nostrand Reinhold, 1986);

Marvin Trachtenberg and Isabelle Hyman, *Architecture from Prehistory to Post-Modernism: The Western Tradition* (New York: Harry N. Abrams, 1986).

THE TWILIGHT OF MODERNIST ARCHITECTURE

Utopian Modernism. Modernist architecture had been conceived beginning in the 1920s as a utopian stylistic force. Instead of an outdated neoclassical style (arches, columns, Doric capitals, and sculpted ornamentation), the original modernists had sought a building style that was unique to the twentieth century. That style would both celebrate human progress and technology and steer the human condition toward even higher social goals.

Technology. The first goal would be achieved by using technology to its highest advantage. Stronger, more lightweight materials were used to raise buildings to unprecedented heights. Also, with the lighter materials, entire walls did not have to bear the weight as in earlier methods of construction. This meant that much more glass could be used.

Pure Form and Rational Design. Modernist architects attempted to create buildings for people to live in and work in that were pure in form and rationally designed to suit those particular functions. Purity of form came from reducing designs to clean, simple forms — only those elements needed to make the building efficiently perform its intended function. Also, the open plans and large amounts of glass that could now be used in large buildings were intended to foster a sense of togetherness in their inhabitants, a communal environment where all would be inspired to work at the same cooperative level.

A New Approach to Housing. The new technology was used to build large urban-housing projects that were inspired by the ideals of French modernist architect Le Corbusier. Enormous housing clusters were constructed in which multiple levels of residential units were joined by enclosed walkways and covered corridors. Some even had shops, restaurants, and parks — all within the enclosed "minicity."

Respectable Results. It all sounded promising, and from the beginnings of modernist architecture up to World War II many impressive examples of pure-form buildings were created, mostly by the giants of the profession, including Ludwig Mies van der Rohe, Frank Lloyd Wright, Walter Gropius, and Le Corbusier. The style became known as the International Style, and it pervaded cities around the globe. From Mies van der Rohe in particular came the model for modernist urban skyscrapers. These buildings seem simple, particularly in their absence of surface ornamentation and their boxlike appearance. But their generous use of glass not only gives them a buoyant, floating effect but opens up to the public

Charles Moore

what could easily become closed-off, impersonal structures. Also, several huge urban-planning projects were realized, giving many low-income American families places to live that promised to be better than anything they had been able to afford previously. Observers were beginning to believe that maybe modernist methods could be used to bring about a new, brighter tomorrow.

Disenchantment with Modernism. Many of the imitators of the post–World War II era who attempted the modernist designs of the great masters ended up producing large, ugly boxes. City after city was filled with this same type of simple, unimaginative building. What the imitative architects did not understand was that simple forms and lack of decoration were not the primary considerations for designing a modernist building. Instead, those characteristics came about as a natural result of rationally planning a building to fulfill its intended function and then eliminating any parts that were unnecessary. Although the modernist masters always incorporated purity of form and function, they were also always conscious of using this purity to create strikingly beautiful structures. While Mies van der Rohe could make huge skyscrapers pleasing to the eye, many of the less observant architects covered their buildings with heavy structural bracing. The prolific architectural firm of Skidmore, Owings, and Merrill erected the ninety-five-story John Hancock Center in Chicago (1965) with heavy diagonal cross beams disrupting the rising verticals of small glass windows. Instead of the floating Miesian look, the John Hancock tower had one of brawny weight.

Social Value. Not only had the aesthetic intentions of modernist architecture been distorted, but its social goals had been subverted as well. Modernist ideals had their roots in the quasi-Socialist thought of the 1920s. While the modernist-style United Nations Secretariat building was created to house part of the nonprofit organization whose goals were international human concerns, by the 1950s and 1960s corporations had adopted the sleek, crisp look of the International Style for their own. Structures such as the Union Carbide building (1963) and the Pan Am building (1964) that symbolized the triumph of profit-oriented capitalism were far removed from original modernist intentions.

Decline. More tragic was the failure of urban-planning projects to improve the situations of low-income families. The utopian designs for high-rise, high-density housing clusters, when put into actual use, were all too often disasters. With their convenient access to restaurants, shops, and parks via enclosed hallways, assaults and other crimes happened easily without the usual defenses of a crowded outdoor street. Pollution and vandalism marred the visions of ivory-white corridors joining meticulously planned housing units. People were not disciplined and perfect enough in the real world for these modernist utopias that worked so brilliantly on paper to become realized. Many of the housing projects turned out not to have been engineered well during construction, and builders used cheap materials that necessitated frequent repairs. With so much crime, vandalism, and disrepair, often the wisest choice seemed to be to tear down the project and start over. By the late 1960s it was not uncommon for huge housing units to be dynamited com-

The Pan Am building in New York, modernist architecture subsumed by corporate interests

pletely. A writer on the period, Charles Jencks, designates the end of modernist architecture as the day in 1972 when Minoru Yamasaki's Pruitt-Igoe housing project in Saint Louis, Missouri, was dynamited to the ground.

Sources:
Stephen Baxley, Phillipe Garner, and Deyan Sudjic, *Twentieth-Century Style & Design* (New York: Van Nostrand Reinhold, 1986);

Marvin Trachtenberg and Isabelle Hyman, *Architecture from Prehistory to Post-Modernism: The Western Tradition* (New York: Harry N. Abrams, 1986).

HEADLINE MAKERS

ANDRÉ COURRÈGES

1923-

FASHION DESIGNER

Innovation and Influence. There were many important fashion designers during the 1960s — Pierre Cardin, Yves St. Laurent, Oleg Cassini, and others — but among the most influential in both Europe and the United States was the experimental French couturier André Courrèges. He is credited for being among the first to introduce hemlines above the knee and pantsuits for women, among other innovative fashions.

Apprenticeship and Early Designs. As an adolescent Courrèges was inclined toward an artistic career, but following the wishes of his practical-minded father he became a civil engineer instead. In 1948 he left a promising engineering career and moved to Paris to enter the fashion world. After a few months in a small fashion house, he joined the house of Cristóbal Balenciaga and worked his way up from the bottom, from presser to Balenciaga's main assistant and cutter. In 1961, with his mentor's blessing, Courrèges started his own line, producing fashions highly influenced by his work with Balenciaga.

Zenith. Courrèges established a name for himself during the next few years, and in 1963 he came into his own with a series of designs totally unlike anything he or anyone else had done to that point. U.S. fashion journalists praised him — he was variously called the Picasso or the Le Corbusier of Paris couture — for his short skirts, inventive pants, and snow-white designs. He followed his successes in 1964 with his trademark white boots, women's pantsuits, and the first of what were called his space-age designs.

Retreat and Return. His haute couture fashions were worn by prominent women and were often widely copied and pirated, usually poorly. At the height of his success, in July 1965, Courrèges announced that he would show no more collections until he figured out a way to exercise greater control over his designs. Later that year he sold his house to L'Oréal and worked only for private clients. He returned to the fashion world in 1967 with a highly publicized showing to which the press but not buyers were invited. His new designs featured see-through minidresses, space-age styles, and clothing with cut-out spaces exposing more of the models. In 1967 he also introduced a ready-to-wear line, Couture Future, to be licensed to particular stores as a less expensive alternative to his appointment-only designs. In 1968 stores in New York, Cleveland, Chicago, Houston, Los Angeles, San Francisco, and five other American cities opened Couture Future boutiques.

Later Success. In the later 1960s and after, Courrèges's fashions became generally more subtle and tended to be more colorful. However, his aim remained, he said, to provide women with functional modern clothing; he disliked items such as bras and high heels. While his fashions favored youthful, athletic women, his clients included Lady Bird Johnson, Jacqueline Kennedy Onassis, and the duchess of Windsor.

VIDAL SASSOON

1928 -

HAIRSTYLIST

Something Different. At his mother's suggestion, Vidal Sassoon secured his first job at the age of fourteen in a London beauty salon. After fighting for a year with the Palmach Israeli army, Sassoon returned to London, and in the early 1950s opened his own shop on Bond Street. Resolving that, if he was to be a hairstylist, he should "do something different," Sassoon introduced a new method of blunt-cutting hair and then blow-drying it rather than using rollers, resulting in geometric cuts that were unlike popular styles of the time.

International Fame. His experiments paid off, and important models and actresses began visiting Sassoon's salon. In the early 1960s the Beatles began to sport Sassoon hairstyles, and the hairdresser was soon internationally famous. Sassoon became the major influence on hairstyles in the 1960s as he introduced both very short and very long styles and initiated the natural look, as opposed to the sculpted or slick looks of earlier decades.

Beauty Business. Complaining that the financial rewards of hairstyling were not commensurate with the fame it had brought him, Sassoon founded Vidal Sassoon in the mid 1960s and began to market hair-care and beauty products. He also opened a chain of salons and hairdressing schools. His company, based in Los Angeles, California, would grow into a $100 million-a-year business by the mid 1980s.

TWIGGY (LESLIE HORNBY)

1949 -

FASHION MODEL

"Sticks." To many who knew her, a Cockney girl named Leslie Hornby would have seemed an unlikely candidate for the world's best-known model; classmates called her "Sticks," referring to her extremely slender, boyish figure. But after she adopted the name "Twiggy," dropped out of school at age fifteen, and, with the assistance of her twenty-five-year-old boyfriend Nigel Davies (who preferred to be called Justin de Villeneuve), began a modeling career in London in 1966, success quickly followed. Her androgynous appearance and the mod styles she characteristically sported captured the imagination of the younger generation.

Cover Girl. Within a few months Twiggy appeared on the cover or in feature layouts for such prestigious fashion publications as *Elle, Paris Match,* and the British edition of *Vogue.* Soon de Villeneuve founded Twiggy Enterprises to handle the young model's expanding business concerns and launched a line of dresses and sportswear bearing her name.

Twiggy in New York. On 20 March 1967 Twiggy arrived in the United States for a promotional tour and was immediately surrounded by a crowd of reporters and photographers at John F. Kennedy International Airport. She remained in New York for seven weeks, charging $120 per hour for assignments and then $240 after her picture appeared on the cover of *Newsweek.* She posed for Richard Avedon of *Vogue* for only $100 a day; de Villeneuve claimed that one of the primary reasons for Twiggy's stateside trip was the opportunity to work with the renowned photographer. Fashion photographer Bert Stern also filmed a documentary of Twiggy's visit, which

was aired in three segments (27 and 28 April and 25 May 1967) on the ABC network.

Twiggy Enterprises, U.S.A. Twiggy easily attained star status in the U.S. and was a major trendsetter in American fashion. Twiggy Enterprises lost little time in capitalizing on her success. Twiggy's dress manufacturers, Leonard Bloomberg and Sidney Ellis, arrived in the States and quickly received $500,000 worth of orders. Mattel, the toy makers responsible for the Barbie doll, brought out a Twiggy doll in September 1967, and other licensed Twiggy products included paper dolls, lunchboxes, posters, trading cards, and ballpoint pens. The androgynous, mod look that Twiggy exemplified swept America as it had Britain and much of Europe.

ROBERT VENTURI

1925 -

ARCHITECT

Early Life and Education. Robert Venturi was born in Philadelphia, Pennsylvania, on 25 June 1925. Though his father owned a wholesale fruit company, Venturi dreamed of becoming an architect from boyhood. He graduated with a B.A. in architecture from Princeton University in 1947, where he went on to earn a master of fine arts degree in 1950. He won Rome Prize Fellowships in 1954 and 1956, providing the means for Venturi to continue his studies at the American Academy in Rome.

Early Career. Venturi returned to Philadelphia and began his career with the firm of Louis I. Kahn. Kahn's firm departed from the dominant modernist architectural approaches exemplified in the work of Frank Lloyd Wright or Ludwig Mies van der Rohe, and Kahn encouraged his designers, including Venturi, to develop their own individual styles. Venturi moved on to several partnerships before forming forming Venturi and Rauch in 1964. He had joined the faculty of the University of Pennsylvania in 1957, an association that continued until 1965. In 1966 he was appointed the Charlotte Shepherd Davenport Professor of Architecture at Yale University.

Manifesto. In 1966 Venturi created controversy in the architectural community with the publication of his book *Complexity and Contradiction in Architecture.* The work was Venturi's manifesto on the making of architecture, in which he rejected the legacies of Wright, Mies van der Rohe, and Le Corbusier, who stressed carefully ordered, simple, and functional design stripped of traditional influences. His treatment of the ideas of the giants of modernist architecture was impertinent, as when he transformed Mies van der Rohe's well-known slogan "Less is more" into "Less is a bore." Invoking examples of

Renaissance, baroque, and mannerist architecture, Venturi argued for design that utilized elements of ambiguity, redundancy, and inconsistency.

Learning from Las Vegas. Venturi continued his unorthodox approach to the field with a study of commonplace urban architecture in the Las Vegas commercial strip, conducted with his wife and business associate, Denise Scott-Brown. As a result, they published a controversial and influential article in the March 1968 issue of *Architectural Forum,* titled "A Significance for A&P Parking Lots, or Learning from Las Vegas." The article led to a research project, carried out in collaboration with students of Yale, to study the phenomenon of "urban sprawl."

Ugly and Ordinary. Venturi compared the projects of Venturi and Rauch to the work of pop artists Andy Warhol and Roy Lichtenstein, in that they draw from, among other influences, the ordinary architecture of urban environments to produce the "*extra*ordinary." When the jury of the 1968 Brighton Beach housing competition rejected a design submitted by Venturi and Rauch as "ugly and ordinary," Venturi and co-authors Scott-Brown and Steven Izenour in their book *Learning from Las Vegas* (1972) ironically adopted the phrase to characterize the firm's work. Their championing of the open-ended, pluralist "U&O" architecture over the autonomous "H&O" (heroic and original) type prevailing at the time would greatly influence the development of postmodern architecture.

Source:
Christopher Mead, ed., *The Architecture of Robert Venturi* (Albuquerque: University of New Mexico Press, 1989).

PEOPLE IN THE NEWS

Pierre Cardin launched the "nude look," featuring flesh-colored panels, in 1966.

R. Buckminster Fuller was given the Gold Medal from the Royal Institute of British Architects in 1968.

In 1967 U.S. Secretary of Health, Education, and Welfare **John Gardner** publicly criticized the American automotive industry for contributing to air pollution.

In 1964 Vienna-born designer **Rudi Gernreich** unveiled his topless women's bathing suit, creating a stir of controversy.

Philip Johnson's New York State Theater in Lincoln Center opened on 23 April 1964.

Jacqueline Kennedy was inducted into the Fashion Hall of Fame in 1966.

Morris Lapidus's fifty-story, two-thousand-room Americana Hotel opened on 24 September 1962 in New York.

In 1966 pop artist **Roy Lichtenstein** designed an expensive line of china for the Durable Dish Company.

Architect **Ludwig Mies van der Rohe** was one of thirty-one recipients of the Presidential Medal of Honor in 1963.

In 1966, the year following his best-selling book *Unsafe at Any Speed,* **Ralph Nader** testified before a Senate subcommittee on automobile safety. On 9 September **President Lyndon B. Johnson** signed the resulting National Traffic and Motor Vehicle Safety Act into law to establish minimum safety standards for new domestic and foreign cars sold in the United States.

I. M. Pei received the Brunner Award for architecture from the National Institute of Arts and Letters on 17 March 1961.

The fifty-nine-story Pan Am Building, then the largest commercial office building in the world, was completed in New York in 1963. The building, designed by **Emery Roth and Sons** in collaboration with **Pietro Bulluschi** and **Walter Gropius,** was protested by some people for blocking a view of Park Avenue.

AWARDS

COTY AMERICAN FASHION CRITICS' AWARD

(The "Winnie" — to an individual selected as the leading designer of American women's fashions)

1960 — Ferdinando Sarmi

Jacques Tiffeau

1961 — Bill Blass

Gustave Tassell

1962 — Donald Brooks

1963 — Rudi Gernreich

1964 — Geoffrey Beene

1965 — No Award

1966 — Dominic

1967 — Oscar de la Renta

1968 — George Halley

Luba

1969 — Stan Herman

Victor Joris

RETURN AWARD

(Award to a designer whose work merits a top award for a second time)

1960 — No Award

1961 — No Award

1962 — No Award

1963 — Bill Blass

1964 — Jacques Tiffeau

Sylvia Pedlar

1965 — No Award

1966 — Rudi Gernreich

Geoffrey Beene

1967 — Donald Brooks

1968 — Oscar de la Renta

1969 — Anne Klein

HALL OF FAME

("Winnie" designer chosen three separate times as best of the year)

1960 — No Award

1961 — Ben Zuckerman

1962 — No Award

1963 — No Award

1964 — No Award

1965 — No Award

1966 — No Award

1967 — Rudi Gernreich

1968 — No Award

1969 — No Award

SPECIAL AWARDS

(Honoring noteworthy contributions to fashion)

1960 — Rudi Gernreich

Sol Klein

Roxane

1961 — Bonnie Cashin

Mr. Kenneth

1962 — Halston

1963 — Arthur and Theodora Edelman

Betty Yokova

1964 — David Webb

1965 — Anna Potok

Tzaims Luksus

Gertrude Seperack

Pablo

Joint Special Award: Sylvia de Gay, Bill Smith, Victor Joris, Leo Narducci, Don Simonelli, Gayle Kirkpatrick, Stanley Herman, Edie Gladstone, and Deanna Littell

1966 — Kenneth Jay Lane

1967 — Beth and Herbert Levine

1968 — Count Giorgio di Sant'Angelo

1969 — Adolfo

Halston

Julian Tomchin

THOMAS B. CLARKE PRIZE (GIVEN BY THE NATIONAL ACADEMY OF DESIGN FOR INTERIOR DESIGN)

1960 — Werner Groshans

1961 — Aaron Shikler

1962 — David Levine

1963 — Thomas Yerxa

1964 — Moses Soyer

1965 — Philip B. White

1966 — Bruce Currie

1967 — Jack Henderson

1968 — Philip B. White

1969 — Edward Melcarth

AMERICAN INSTITUTE OF ARCHITECTS (AIA)

AIA Gold Medal (Awarded annually to an individual for distinguished service to the architectural profession or to the institute. It is the institute's highest honor.)

1960 — Ludwig Mies van der Rohe, Chicago

1961 — Le Corbusier, Paris

1962 — Eero Saarinen, Bloomfield Hills, Michigan

1963 — Alvar Aalto, Helsinki

1964 — Pier Luigi Nervi, Rome

1965 — No Award

1966 — Kenzo Tange, Tokyo

1967 — Wallace K. Harrison, New York

1968 — Marcel Breuer, New York

1969 — William W. Wurster, San Francisco

AIA Craftsmanship Medal

1960 — William L. DeMatteo, Silversmith

1961 — Anni Albers, Weaving

1962 — Theodore Conrad, Model Making

1963 — Paolo Soleri, Ceramics

1964 — Jan de Swart, Stained Glass

1965 — No Award

1966 — Harold Balazs, Wood Sculpture

1967 — Sister Mary Remy Revor, Fabric Design

1968 — Jack Lenor Larsen, Fabric Design

1969 — Henry Easterwood, Fabric Design

AIA Edward C. Kemper Award (To AIA members for "significant contributions to the profession of architecture and to the Institute.")

1960 — Philip D. Creer

1961 — Earl H. Reed

1962 — Harry D. Payne

1963 — Samuel E. Lunden

1964 — Daniel Schwartzman

1965 — Joseph Watterson

1966 — William W. Eshbach

1967 — Robert H. Levison

1968 — E. James Gambaro

1969 — Philip J. Meathe

AIA Honor Awards (Initiated to encourage appreciation of excellence in architecture in the United States and by American architects working abroad.)

1960 — Sherwood, Mills & Smith

Robert L. Geddes, Melvin Brecher, Warren W. Cunningham of Geddes Brecher, Qualls

Killingsworth, Brady & Smith

Corbett & Kman Kitchen and Hunt

Eero Saarinen & Associates

1961 — Edward Durell Stone

Mario J. Ciampi and Paul Reiter

Philip Johnson

Minoru Yamasaki

Philip Johnson

Skidmore, Owings & Merrill

Birkirts & Straub

1962 — Ernest J. Kump and Masten & Hurd

Anshen & Allen

1963 — Eero Saarinen & Associates

Skidmore, Owings & Merrill

Ralph M. Parsons Company and Minoru Yamasaki

Joseph Salerno

1964 — Architects Collaborative

Skidmore, Owings & Merrill

Paul Rudolph

1965 — Reid & Tarics
Sert, Jackson & Gourley
Eero Saarinen & Associates
I. M. Pei & Associates

1966 — Eero Saarinen & Associates
Gevo Saarinen & Associates
Keyes, Lethbridge & Condon

1967 — Fred Bassetti & Company
Caudill, Rowlett, Scott
Hammel Green & Abrahamson
Vincent G. Kling
Ian MacKinley
Moore, Lyndon, Turnbull, Whitaker
I. M. Pei & Partners
Smith, Hinchman & Grylls
Neill Smith & Associates
Stickney & Hull
Edward Durell Stone
Architects Collaborative
Architects Collaborative and Campbell, Aldrich & Nulty
Toombs, Amisano & Wells

1968 — Fred Bassetti & Company
C. F. Murphy Associates, Skidmore, Owings & Merrill, and Loebl, Schlossman, Bennett & Dart
Crites and McConnell
William N. Breger
Giorgio Cavaglieri
Davis, Brody & Associates and Horowitz & Chun
Alfred De Vido

Joseph Esherick
Stevenson Flemer, Eason Cross, Harry Adreon
R. Buckminster Fuller/Fuller & Sadao Inc., Geometrics Inc., and Cambridge Seven Associates
Gruzen & Partners and Abraham W. Geller
Gwathmey & Henderson
Hirshen/Van der Ryn
Mackinley/Winnacker
MLTW/Moore Turnbull
McCue Boone Tomsick
Office of Oberwarth Associates
Reid, Rockwell, Banwell & Taries
Rogers, Taliaferro, Kostritsky, Lamb
Benjamin Thompson & Associates

1969 — Desmond-Miremont-Birks
Frank L. Hope Associates
Hugh Newell Jacobsen
Kallman, McKinnell & Knowles and Campbell, Aldrich & Nulty
Vincent M. Kling & Associates
Ernest J. Kump Associates and the Office of Masten & Hurd
Richard Meier
Neill Smith & Associates and Dreyfuss & Blackford
I. M. Pei & Partners
I. M. Pei & Partners and Pederson, Hueber, Hares & Glavin
John B. Rogers
Skidmore, Owings & Merrill
Smotrich & Platt
Walker/McGough, Foltz and Lyerla/Peden
Harry Weese & Associates, Cromlie Taylor
Wurster, Bernardi & Emmons

DEATHS

Elizabeth Arden (Florence N. Graham), 81, businesswoman who founded and ran one of the world's largest beauty-aids companies, 18 October 1969.

Bettina Ballard, 56, authority on women's fashions, fashion editor for *Vogue* (1946–1954), 4 August 1961.

William F. Bigelow, 86, magazine editor, managing editor of *Cosmopolitan* (1903–1913) and editor of *Good Housekeeping* (1913–1940), 5 March 1966.

Lord Alfred Bossom, 83, British architect, designed and renovated New York buildings, 4 September 1965.

Mead L. Bricker, 78, automobile executive, former vice-president of Ford Motor Company, 28 January 1964.

Pierre Cartier, 86, jeweler, founded Cartier's (1908) in New York City, 27 October 1964.

Le Corbusier, 77, Swiss-French architect, one of the greatest architects of the twentieth century, author of several books reflecting humanistic modernism in architecture, 27 August 1965.

Harlow Herbert Curtis, 69, business executive, served as vice-president and president of General Motors Corporation, 3 November 1962.

Taube C. Davis, 70, fashion consultant who greatly influenced women's fashions, 25 December 1962.

James Frank Duryea, 97, inventor, with brother Charles designed first successful gasoline-powered automobile in the United States (1893), 15 February 1967.

Harley Earl, 86, designer of cars, including various models of La Salles, Buicks, Cadillacs, and many others, 5 July 1969.

Hugh Ferriss, 72, architect who was a pioneer in modern architectural design, 29 January 1962.

Charles T. Fisher, 83, industrialist, founded Fisher Body Company, which became a division of the General Motors Corporation, 8 August 1963.

Assar Gabrielsson, 70, Swedish industrialist who founded Volvo Motor Company, 28 May 1962.

Irene Gibbons, 54, fashion designer, designed many clothes for film stars, 15 November 1962.

Walter Gropius, 86, German-American architect and designer, important as a founder of modernist architecture (international style), 5 July 1969.

Erwin A. Gutkind, 72, German-born U.S. city planner, wrote *Twilight of the Cities* (1962), 7 August 1968.

Jacques Heim, 67, French couturier, director of a French fashion house for nearly forty years, 7 January 1967.

Joseph Hudnut, 81, architect, wrote *Architecture and the Spirit of Man* (1949), 15 January 1968.

K. T. Keller, 80, automobile executive, president (1935–1950) and chairman of the board (1950–1965) of the Chrysler Corporation, 21 January 1966.

Paul McCobb, 51, designer who pioneered modern designs for the home, 10 March 1969.

Ludwig Mies van der Rohe, 83, German-American architect, perhaps the most important developer and proponent of the modernist architectural style, 17 August 1969.

Heinz Nordhoff, 69, German industrialist, head of Volkswagen Company (1948–1968), 11 April 1968.

Wilbur H. Norton, 59, business executive, president (1946–1948) of Montgomery Ward and Company and vice-president (1949–1952) of the General Motors Corporation, 2 April 1963.

Douglas W. Orr, 74, architect, president (1947–1948) of American Institute of Architects, 29 July 1966.

L. Andrew Reinhard, 72, architect, helped design the Rockefeller Center, the Chrysler Building, and other projects in New York City, 2 August 1964.

Helena Rubinstein, 94, cosmetics executive, owner of international chain of beauty salons, founder of successful cosmetics firm under her name, 1 April 1965.

Eero Saarinen, 51, architect and furniture designer, most famous for his designs for the Womb chair, the Saint Louis arch, and the TWA terminal in New York, 1 September 1961.

Henry R. Shepley, 75, architect who designed several college and hospital buildings, 24 November 1962.

Louis Skidmore, 65, architect, founding partner of Skidmore, Owings, and Merrill, which was responsible for the designs of some of the best-known modernist buildings in the United States, 27 September 1962.

Carmel Snow, 73, Irish-born U.S. fashion editor, edited *Harper's Bazaar* (1932–1958), 7 May 1961.

Eldridge Snyder, 66, architect who designed many buildings in the United States and the Bahamas, 24 March 1967.

Louis L. Stott, 57, industrialist, founded Polymer Corporation (1946), pioneered production of nylon in stock shapes, 4 September 1964.

Ethel Traphagen, 81, fashion designer, founded first school of fashion design (1923) in the United States, 29 April 1963.

Jesse G. Vincent, 82, inventor and automobile executive, held more than four hundred patents, including one for the first V-12 engine, 20 April 1962.

Stephen Francis Voorhees, 86, architect, chief architect of 1939 World's Fair in New York City, 25 January 1965.

Royal B. Wills, 65, prolific U.S. architect, 10 January 1962.

PUBLICATIONS

Architecture & Design

Wayne Andrews, *Architecture in America: A Photographic History from the Colonial Period to the Present* (New York: Atheneum, 1960);

Andrews, *Architecture in Chicago and Mid-America* (New York: Atheneum, 1968);

Peter Blake, *The Master Builders* (New York: Knopf, 1960);

John Burchard and Albert Bush-Brown, *The Architecture of America* (Boston: Little, Brown, 1961);

Walter Gropius, *The New Architecture and the Bauhaus* (Cambridge, Mass.: MIT Press, 1965);

Vincent Joseph Scully, *American Architecture and Urbanism* (New York: Praeger, 1969);

Robert A. M. Stern, *New Directions in American Architecture* (New York: Braziller, 1969);

Architectural Digest, periodical;

Architectural Record, periodical;

Better Homes and Gardens, periodical;

Designer, periodical;

Historic Preservation, periodical;

House and Garden, periodical;

Interior Design, periodical;

Landscape Architecture, periodical.

Fashion

Marylin Bender, *The Beautiful People* (New York: Coward-McCann, 1967);

Mila Contini, *Fashion: From Ancient Egypt to the Present Day* (New York: Crescent, 1965);

Esquire Fashions for Men (New York: Harper & Row, 1966);

James Laver, *The Concise History of Costume and Fashion* (New York: Scribners, 1969);

Phyllis Lee Levin, *The Wheels of Fashion* (Garden City, N.Y.: Doubleday, 1965);

Jane Trahey, ed., *Harper's Bazaar: 100 Years of the American Female* (New York: Random House, 1967);

Walter Vecchio, *The Fashion Makers: A Photographic Record* (New York: Crown, 1968);

The World in Vogue (New York: Viking, 1963);

Brides, periodical;

Fashion Calendar, periodical;

Gentleman's Quarterly, periodical;

Glamour, periodical;

Harper's Bazaar, periodical;

Mademoiselle, periodical;

McCall's, periodical;

Modern Bride, periodical;

Vogue, periodical.

Jacqueline Kennedy, with the president and Charles DeGaulle. Mrs. Kennedy is wearing an outfit by Oleg Cassini, with a pillbox hat.

GOVERNMENT AND POLITICS

by ROBERT M. ROOD and KAREN L. ROOD

CONTENTS

Sidebars and tables are listed in italics.

1960

1 Feb. Black college students begin a sit-in at a whites-only lunch counter in Greensboro, N.C., introducing a form of civil rights protest that spreads to other southern cities.

5 May The Soviet Union shoots down an American U-2 spy plane and captures the pilot, Francis Gary Powers.

10 May Massachusetts senator John F. Kennedy, a Roman Catholic, wins the West Virginia primary, proving that he can attract support in a predominantly Protestant state.

16 May A summit conference between President Dwight D. Eisenhower and Soviet premier Nikita Khrushchev is canceled following the U-2 incident.

13 July Kennedy wins the Democratic presidential nomination. Lyndon B. Johnson is nominated for vice-president the next day.

25 July Vice-president Richard M. Nixon wins the Republican presidential nomination.

26 Sept. Kennedy and Nixon meet in the first televised debate between presidential candidates.

8 Nov. Kennedy defeats Nixon in the presidential election.

17 Nov. The CIA briefs Kennedy on the plans to back Cuban exiles in an invasion of Cuba at the Bay of Pigs.

1961

- Kennedy begins to increase the number of U.S. military advisers in South Vietnam.

3 Jan. The United States breaks off diplomatic relations with Cuba.

17 Jan. Eisenhower gives his farewell address, warning Americans of the potential danger to democracy from the nation's large and powerful military-industrial complex.

1 Mar. Kennedy establishes the Peace Corps by executive order.

17 Apr. Cuban exiles invade Fidel Castro's Cuba at the Bay of Pigs. Cuba defeats the invaders by 20 April, and the surviving members of the force are captured and imprisoned.

4 May The Freedom Riders begin their bus travels to various southern cities, seeking to eliminate segregation in interstate transportation.

14 May A Freedom Riders' bus is attacked and burned in Anniston, Alabama.

3-4 June Kennedy and Khrushchev meet in Vienna for a summit that ends in a stalemate over the fate of East and West Germany.

13 Aug. East Germany closes its borders with West Berlin and begins construction of the Berlin Wall.

27 Oct. U.S. and Soviet tanks confront each other on the outskirts of Berlin.

1962

3 Nov.	Gen. Maxwell Taylor and State Department official Walt Rostow return from a fact-finding trip to South Vietnam and suggest that quick military action can lead to a victory.
7 Dec.	The United States begins airlifting UN troops to the Congo to assist in retaking the Katanga Province.

- Tensions mount over increasing Soviet presence in Cuba.

- U.S. troop levels in South Vietnam continue to grow.

10 Apr.	U.S. Steel, followed by several other steel companies, announces a price increase. Kennedy reacts strongly, and three days later the price increase is rescinded.
1 Oct.	James Meredith enrolls at the University of Mississippi as federal troops battle thousands of protesters.
14 Oct.	The United States discovers Soviet offensive missiles in Cuba and issues an ultimatum demanding their removal. Cuba is quarantined and placed under a U.S. naval blockade. After several days of tense confrontation, the Soviets agree to remove their missiles from Cuba on 28 October.
6 Nov.	The Democrats, as the party of the incumbent president, hold their own in House and Senate elections. They win four new Senate seats and lose only six in the House.
14 Dec.	Kennedy proposes across-the-board tax cuts to stimulate the economy and reduce unemployment.

1963

2 Apr.	The Southern Christian Leadership Conference, led by Dr. Martin Luther King, Jr., begins its campaign to desegregate Birmingham, Alabama.
11 June	The University of Alabama is integrated by court order after Gov. George C. Wallace makes a symbolic effort to block the door.
26 June	Kennedy addresses thousands in Berlin to reassure them of the continuing U. S. commitment, proclaiming "Ich bin ein Berliner."
25 July	The United States, the Soviet Union, and Great Britain sign the Partial Nuclear Test Ban Treaty.
28 Aug.	Civil rights supporters march on Washington and listen to Dr. Martin Luther King, Jr.'s now-famous "I have a dream" speech.
1 Nov.	South Vietnamese president Ngo Dinh Diem and his family are murdered in a coup backed by the United States.
22 Nov.	President Kennedy is assassinated in Dallas. Vice-president Lyndon B. Johnson becomes president.

1964

8 Jan.	Johnson declares a War on Poverty in his State of the Union message.
10 June	The Senate invokes the cloture rule, ending a southern filibuster designed to prevent a vote on the civil rights bill—the first time cloture has successfully been invoked on civil rights legislation.
21 June	Three civil rights workers are murdered in Mississippi during the "freedom summer" voting-rights drive.
15 July	Arizona senator Barry Goldwater wins the Republican presidential nomination.
18 July	Riots break out in the predominantly black sections of Brownsville and Harlem in New York City and spread to other cities.
3 Aug.	U.S. ships are attacked in the Gulf of Tonkin by North Vietnamese patrol boats, prompting a retaliation by the United States and passage of the Tonkin Gulf Resolution, giving Johnson congressional approval for all future actions he takes regarding the war.
20 Aug.	Johnson signs the War on Poverty Bill.
26 Aug.	Johnson wins the Democratic presidential nomination and selects Minnesota senator Hubert H. Humphrey as his running mate.
3 Nov.	Johnson defeats Goldwater in a landslide, carrying many Democrats into office.

1965

•	Johnson escalates the Vietnam War. By the end of the year there are more than 180,000 American troops there.
2 Mar.	U.S. aircraft begin bombing North Vietnam.
7 Mar.	As part of a drive to win voting rights for blacks, marchers set out from Selma to Montgomery, Alabama; they are attacked by Alabama state police and the local sheriff and his men. The marchers return to Selma.
8 Mar.	The first U.S. combat troops are sent to Vietnam; earlier forces had consisted primarily of military advisers and support personnel.
15 Mar.	Johnson seeks a voting bill in an address to both houses of Congress.
21 Mar.	The march from Selma to Montgomery resumes under the protection of troops and is completed on 25 March.
28 Apr.	The United States invades the Dominican Republic, ostensibly to prevent a Communist takeover.
11 Aug.	Large-scale riots break out in Watts, a black section of Los Angeles.
15 Oct.	Demonstrations against the Vietnam War occur in forty U.S. cities.

1966

•	The Vietnam War continues, with U.S. troop strength reaching 400,000 by late in the year.
7 Jan.	Martin Luther King, Jr., begins his campaign for fair housing in Chicago.
4 Feb.	Televised hearings on the war in Vietnam are begun by the Senate Foreign Relations Committee, chaired by Arkansas senator J. William Fulbright.

	5 June	James Meredith begins a solitary march across Mississippi and the next day is wounded by a shotgun blast. Civil rights leaders rush to Mississippi to continue the march, which takes twenty days.
	16 June	SNCC leader Stokely Carmichael calls for "black power" during the march to support Meredith.
	12 July	Blacks riot in Chicago. Riots occur in twenty other U.S. cities over the summer.
	8 Nov.	The Republicans, through white-voter "backlash," regain many of the congressional seats they lost in 1964.

1967

- The Vietnam War continues. U.S. troop strength reaches 475,000 by the end of the year.

15 Apr. Large antiwar demonstrations take place in New York City and San Francisco.

23 June Soviet premier Aleksey Kosygin and President Johnson meet at Glassboro State College in New Jersey and discuss the Middle East, arms control, and Vietnam.

12 July Rioting begins in Newark, starting the "long hot summer" of 1967.

23 July The Detroit riots begin, and federal troops must be brought in to control the situation.

1968

- U.S. troop strength in Vietnam rises to more than 500,000.

23 Jan. North Korean patrol boats seize the U.S. Navy ship *Pueblo* on an intelligence-gathering mission off the Korean coast. The crew is held until 22 December.

12 Mar. Minnesota senator Eugene McCarthy, an antiwar candidate, comes in a close second to Johnson in the New Hampshire Democratic primary.

31 Mar. Johnson announces to a national television audience that he is halting the bombing of North Vietnam; he invites North Vietnam to begin peace negotiations and announces he will not run for reelection.

4 Apr. Civil rights leader Martin Luther King, Jr., is murdered in Memphis, Tennessee. Riots occur in many U.S. cities.

12 May Peace talks between the United States and North Vietnam begin in Paris.

5 June New York senator Robert F. Kennedy is shot and killed hours after winning the California Democratic primary.

1 July The Nuclear Non-Proliferation Treaty is signed by the United States, the Soviet Union, and many other nations.

8 Aug. Richard M. Nixon wins the Republican presidential nomination.

21 Aug. Soviet troops invade Czechoslovakia.

28 Aug. Hubert H. Humphrey wins the Democratic presidential nomination as demonstrators battle police outside the convention hall in Chicago.

5 Nov.	Nixon wins the presidential election.

1969

- The Vietnam War continues. Nixon withdraws 75,000 troops. U.S. combat deaths reach 33,461 — more than during the Korean War. Negotiations to end the war continue.

23 June	Warren Burger becomes Chief Justice of the United States, succeeding the retiring Earl Warren.
15 Nov.	250,000 march in Washington, D.C., to protest the war.
17 Nov.	Strategic Arms Limitation Talks (SALT) are begun in Helsinki.

OVERVIEW

A Decade of Contrasts. The 1960s were years of enormous contrasts in American politics. President John F. Kennedy's challenge to "Ask not what your country can do for you — ask what you can do for your country" at his inauguration in January 1961 ushered in a new decade of activism with consequences neither he nor anyone else at that time could foresee. Young idealists flocked to join the Peace Corps and VISTA — for government service to the needy overseas and at home. Others, believing that America could indeed be a land of equal opportunity, joined the civil rights movement and Students for a Democratic Society (SDS). Yet as the decade progressed, optimism gave way to anger and pessimism.

Violence and Disillusionment. The assassinations of President Kennedy in November 1963; civil rights leader Dr. Martin Luther King, Jr., in April 1968; and Sen. Robert F. Kennedy, John F. Kennedy's brother, a few months later made Americans question the character of their nation. As the decade wore on, the "freedom now" chant of the nonviolent civil rights movement yielded to "black power" demands of black militants who saw the lives lost and the beatings borne as too great a price for rights won. President Lyndon B. Johnson, Kennedy's successor, offered a vision of a Great Society, with freedom from want and equal opportunity for all, but his programs stalled as he diverted funds to pay for an ever-growing war in Vietnam. By the end of the decade radical opponents of the war, including the Weatherman faction of SDS, and radical black nationalists were employing violent guerrilla tactics to publicize their messages. Another part of politics in the 1960s was the "backlash" triggered by civil rights advances, the antiwar movement, and the summer riots that occurred in black neighborhoods of northern cities from 1964 through 1968. Segregationist presidential hopeful George Wallace won significant support in the North as well as the South in 1964 and 1968. The wide appeal of Richard M. Nixon's call for "law and order" in his successful presidential campaign of 1968 may be seen as an index of the extent to which Americans were tired of violence and dissent.

Foreign Policy Consensus. At the start of the decade there was a broad, bipartisan consensus for the activist role of the United States in global affairs. At the end of World War II the United States had become the single most powerful nation in the world, militarily and economically. Furthermore, through a series of alliances which sought to block expansion by the Soviet Bloc and the People's Republic of China, the United States had become recognized as the leader of the "free world." In his inaugural address Kennedy summarized Americans' perceptions of their country's role when he said, "Let every nation know, whether it wishes us well or ill, that we shall pay any price, bear any burden, meet any hardship, support any friend, oppose any foe to assure the survival and success of liberty." At that time most of the American public accepted this commitment, but they were clearly cognizant of its dangers. In the early 1960s — years of confrontation between the Soviet Union and the United States — most Americans expected that there would eventually be a war between the two countries, one that might even involve nuclear weapons.

U.S./Soviet Tensions Reduced. Tensions between the United States and the Soviet Union came to a head with the Cuban missile crisis of October 1962, when the two countries came perilously close to war. In the aftermath of this crisis leaders in both countries saw a need for improved relations. Although both countries spent the 1960s building huge stockpiles of nuclear weapons, they also made several small steps toward arms control and better diplomatic relations. By the end of the decade most Americans still saw the Soviet Union as the chief adversary of the United States, but even though they believed that war was still possible they no longer saw it as inevitable. The stage was gradually being set for Nixon's 1970s policy of détente (or relaxation of tensions) with the Soviet Union.

Vietnam War Breaks the Foreign Policy Consensus. As Kennedy was inaugurated in 1961, indigenous Communist movements were threatening armed takeovers in Southeast Asia. The Kennedy administration increased levels of military aid and numbers of American military advisers, but the American public paid little attention to the situation in Vietnam until Johnson started bombing North Vietnam in February 1965 and then sent combat troops later that year. Over the next three years, as American forces took over more and more of the combat role, members of the government and the military — as well as the general public — increasingly called into question the wisdom and purpose of the war as well as the belief that Americans were fighting to "contain" communism. They called for limits to America's policy of global activism in support of its anticommunist allies. Mass public demonstrations against the war became commonplace, and the war became a principal issue in the 1968 presidential campaign. Kennedy's call for sacrifice "to assure the survival and success of liberty" was replaced by chants of "Hey, hey, LBJ, how many kids did you kill today?" and "Hell no! We won't go!" from antiwar protesters and draft resisters. By the start of the 1970s the broad, bipartisan foreign policy consensus was breaking up.

Conservatives Dominate Domestic Policy. Throughout the 1950s congressional action on social welfare proposals and civil rights legislation was effectively blocked by the conservative coalition: conservative southern Democrats acting in concert with Republicans. They effectively blocked much of Kennedy's early legislative agenda, winning 74 percent of the time in 1961 and 67 percent in 1963. Its influence was broken temporarily after the assassination of President Kennedy in November 1963. Invoking the memory of his slain predecessor, President Johnson was able to push through much of Kennedy's stalled domestic agenda in 1964, a year in which the conservative coalition won only 25 percent of the time. The massive Democratic victory of 1964 ensured liberal domination of both the House and Senate in the congressional sessions of 1965 and 1966, and Johnson used this edge to good advantage in advancing his War on Poverty, his Great Society, and civil rights legislation. Voter backlash in 1966 and 1968, however, brought the conservative coalition back to power. It was successful 67 percent of the time in 1967. Yet by this time many of the powerful southern Democrats who dominated chairmanships of major committees in both houses of Congress were beginning to retire or die and were replaced by northern Democrats. Over the next few years the conservative coalition lost its clout.

Domestic Programs Extend the New Deal. During the election of 1944 President Franklin Delano Roosevelt proposed to extend the New Deal through new initiatives on housing, education, and medical care once World War II was over. Yet preoccupation with the Cold War during the administrations of Democrat Harry S Truman and Republican Dwight D. Eisenhower — along with Republican objections to expanding the New Deal — kept these proposals from advancing. Medicare, aid to education, and housing programs proposed during the Kennedy administration and eventually passed during the

Johnson administration all had a legislative history dating back to the 1930s. Essentially they were an extension of the New Deal rather than radical new initiatives. The same can be said of many of the proposals in Johnson's War on Poverty and Great Society programs.

A Second Reconstruction. The success of the civil rights movement in challenging the legal structure of racial segregation and discrimination in the American South was one of the most striking developments of the 1960s. A series of hard-fought Supreme Court cases brought by the National Association for the Advancement of Colored People (NAACP) in the late 1940s and the 1950s had begun to crack the legal basis for segregation in the South, but the process had been slow. Modeling their tactics on the nonviolent methods used against British imperialism in India by Mahatma Gandhi, the civil rights movement sought to mobilize southern blacks and to convince northern whites of the moral rectitude of their cause. Through the lunch-counter sit-ins of 1960, the Freedom Rides of 1961, the integration of the University of Mississippi in 1962, the Birmingham campaign of 1963, the freedom summer of 1964, and the Selma campaign of 1965, civil rights groups pressed for integration of restaurants, public transportation, and institutions of higher learning and for an end to laws and intimidation that prevented southern blacks from registering to vote. Violent responses from white racists created political support for the civil rights movement as Americans reacted with moral outrage to televised coverage of beatings of civil rights demonstrators and to news about murders of voter-registration volunteers. With the passage of the Civil Rights Act of 1964 and the Voting Rights Act of 1965, the legal underpinnings of segregation and white supremacy in the South were stripped away.

From Recession to Inflation. When President Kennedy took office in January 1961, the U.S. economy was in its fourth recession since the end of World War II. Kennedy implemented a variety of measures to stimulate economic growth and reduce unemployment. By the mid 1960s the economy was the strongest it had been since 1945 — with a high gross national product (GNP), a low inflation rate, and unemployment at 4 percent (the level economists call full employment). Federal revenues were high enough to pay for President Johnson's extensive social programs. The escalation of the Vietnam War caused dramatic growth in federal deficits, as Johnson tried to fund both the war and his domestic agenda. By the end of the decade inflation became a major problem; the cost of living was rising faster than the GNP was growing.

TOPICS IN THE NEWS

ASSASSINATION AND VIOLENT PROTEST

Violence in Politics. During the civil rights struggle Americans were horrified by the televised firebombings of Freedom Riders' buses, the use of high-pressure fire-hoses and attacks by police dogs against demonstrating children, and the beatings of protesters by members of the Ku Klux Klan and the police. Little children were killed when white supremacists bombed the churches of activist black pastors. The murders of civil rights workers Medgar Evers in 1963; Andrew Goodman, Michael Schwerner, and James Chaney in 1964; and Viola Liuzzo in 1965 drew national attention.

Assassination of President Kennedy. Americans were thrown into mourning when President John F. Kennedy was struck down by an assassin's bullet on 22 November 1963 in Dallas. Kennedy was the first president to be assassinated in more than sixty years, well outside the boundaries of most living Americans' memories. Americans believed that such things happened in other countries, not in the United States. They watched in near disbelief as television covered the poignant state funeral, moved by the riderless horse following the caisson on which the casket was carried and by the salute of Kennedy's young son, John, as the caisson passed.

Assassinations in the News. While assassinations have been rare in the history of American politics, two other assassinations of major political figures occurred in the 1960s. In 1968 national attention was drawn by the murder of civil rights leader Dr. Martin Luther King, Jr., in Memphis in April 1968 and that of Senator Robert F. Kennedy, younger brother of President John F. Kennedy, two months later, as he campaigned for the Democratic presidential nomination in California. The murder in 1965 of Black Muslim leader Malcolm X did not evoke the same nationwide response as the murders of King and the two Kennedys, but it made him a martyred hero to thousands of young black nationalists. All these murders — as well as the 1967 killing of American Nazi leader George Lincoln Rockwell — were symptomatic of a growing trend throughout the 1960s toward the use of violence as a means of political expression by groups on both political extremes.

Riots in the Cities. Americans were also alarmed by riots that flared up in black sections of urban areas across the country during the summers of 1964–1968. In 1964 riots began in the Harlem and Brownsville sections of New York City and spread to other cities. In August 1965 a five-day riot in the Watts section of Los Angeles was the most destructive race riot in years and resulted in thirty deaths before the California National Guard restored order. There were more than 40 riots in black neighborhoods around the country in 1966 and more than 160 in what has been called "the long hot summer" of 1967; eight of these riots required calling out the National Guard to restore order, with those in Newark and Detroit on the same scale as Watts. There were racial disturbances across the country in response to the assassination of Martin Luther King, Jr., in April 1968 and rioting in a low-income neighborhood of Miami while the Republican National Convention was in session there that summer.

Politics of Confrontation. By 1967 radical antiwar activists were employing rhetoric and actions designed to provoke violent reactions from authorities — tactics clearly illustrated on television in October 1967, when some of the large crowd of protesters outside the Pentagon broke through lines of troops and stormed the building. More than a thousand people were injured and seven hundred were arrested as troops wielding rifle butts prevented demonstrators from entering the Pentagon. In Chicago, during the Democratic National Convention the following August, city police beat thousands of anti-war demonstrators in what an official government report at the time called a "police riot." While only a relatively small number of demonstrators at the Pentagon and in Chicago initiated violent confrontations with authorities, some radical groups went further. In October 1969 the Weatherman faction that had taken control of SDS earlier that year stormed through Chicago streets, destroying property and beating up people who got in their way — ostensibly to protest the trial of the organizers of the Chicago demonstrations in August 1968 and to "bring the war home." During these same years members of the Black Panther party engaged in several well-publicized shoot-outs with the police, and in the late 1960s and early 1970s radical antiwar and black nationalist groups

At about 12:30 P.M. on 22 November 1963 as his motorcade passed the Texas School Book Depository in downtown Dallas, President John F. Kennedy was shot and killed, and Texas governor John Connally, who was riding in the same car, was wounded. A few hours later Dallas police arrested Lee Harvey Oswald, an employee of the depository and a former Marine sharpshooter, who shot and killed a Dallas police officer while resisting arrest. Oswald had defected to the Soviet Union but later returned to the United States and spent time promoting "fair play" for Cuba. He had threatened to blow up Dallas police headquarters if FBI agents did not stop interviewing his wife and family regarding Oswald's pro-Cuban activities. A rifle identified as the murder weapon was found in the depository and was traced to Oswald. He had purchased it through a mail-order catalogue.

On 24 November while national television covered the transfer of Oswald from the Dallas city jail to the Dallas county jail, Jack Ruby, a Dallas nightclub owner, shot Oswald at point-blank range. Oswald died denying any involvement in the Kennedy assassination. Ruby died of cancer in 1967 without ever providing any information about the assassination or his motives for killing Oswald.

Kennedy's successor, President Lyndon B. Johnson, appointed a bipartisan commission headed by Chief Justice of the United States Earl Warren to investigate the events in Dallas. In September 1964, after months of inquiry, the so-called Warren Commission issued an 888-page report supported by twenty-six volumes of documents. The commission concluded that Oswald had acted alone in killing Kennedy and that Ruby had not been part of a conspiracy when he murdered Oswald.

Almost immediately the Warren Commission report was faulted by a variety of critics. Many of them questioned the sole-assassin conclusion, citing inconsistencies in witnesses' testimony and flaws in the technical testimony, including the links between a film taken by an amateur photographer and the timing of the taped sound of the gunshots. Others suggested a conspiracy directed by the Soviet Union or Fidel Castro of Cuba, or a plot by organized crime. Still others have hypothesized that the CIA, or perhaps even Texas supporters of Vice-president Lyndon Johnson, may have been involved in Kennedy's assassination.

District Attorney Jim Garrison of New Orleans, who had a reputation for making unsubstantiated charges, announced in February 1967 that Kennedy had been murdered by a conspiracy involving Oswald, who had lived in New Orleans, and several individuals from that city, and on 1 March 1967 Garrison charged New Orleans businessman Clayton L. Shaw with conspiring with Oswald and David William Ferrie (a former pilot who had died in February) to murder Kennedy. By the time Shaw was tried and acquitted a year later, Garrison had developed a new theory that Cuban exiles disgusted over the failed Bay of Pigs invasion had murdered Kennedy.

Continued efforts have been made to review and challenge the Warren Commission findings; in 1976 a U.S. Senate committee concluded that both the FBI and the CIA had inadequately followed up the available leads, and in 1979 a House committee suggested that the possibility of a second gunman had not been adequately explored. Yet the evidence against Oswald would probably have been sufficient to convict him if he had been brought to trial.

Sources: Vaughan Davis Bornet, *The Presidency of Lyndon Johnson* (Lawrence: University Press of Kansas, 1983);

Jim F. Heath, *Decade of Disillusionment: The Kennedy-Johnson Years* (Bloomington: Indiana University Press, 1975);

John Kaplan, "The Assassins," *American Scholar,* 36 (Spring 1967): 271–306.

took credit for several hundred bombings around the country.

Public Response. Antiwar activists hoped that television news pictures of soldiers and policemen beating unarmed demonstrators would mobilize public opinion against the war — just as similar media exposure had worked for the civil rights movement. To a great extent antiwar demonstrations did help to turn the American public against the war, but as these protests became more violent, the public began to view them as yet another example of how the nation was being torn apart by violence. A conservative backlash in the 1966 national elections — triggered by the summer riots of 1964–1966 — swept many Republicans into office, seriously eroding the Democrats' liberal majority. The same concerns over social and political violence contributed heavily to Richard M. Nixon's narrow victory in the presidential election of 1968. A decade that had begun on the idealistic theme of social justice ended with cries for "law and order."

Sources:

David Farber, *The Age of Great Dreams: America in the 1960s* (New York: Hill & Wang, 1994);

Hugh Davis Graham and Ted Robert Gurr, *Violence in America: Historical and Comparative Perspectives, A Report Submitted to the National Commission on the Causes and Prevention of Violence,* revised edition (New York, Toronto & London: Bantam, 1970);

Allen J. Matusow, *The Unraveling of America: A History of Liberalism in the 1960s* (New York: Harper & Row, 1984);

Robert Weisbrot, *Freedom Bound: A History of America's Civil Rights Movement* (New York: Norton, 1990).

THE COLD WAR CONTINUED: CRISIS YEARS, 1960-1965

A Summit Canceled. During the first few years of the 1960s, the Cold War continued at the same high level of antagonism as in the late 1950s. After Soviet premier Joseph Stalin's death in 1953, the United States and the Union of Soviet Socialist Republics made occasional tentative steps toward reducing tensions. President Dwight D. Eisenhower had summit meetings with Soviet leaders in 1955 and 1959, but a planned summit meeting in 1960 was canceled in the wake of the U-2 incident.

The U-2 Affair. An American U-2 spy plane, flown by CIA pilot Francis Gary Powers, was shot down over Soviet territory on 1 May 1960. Eisenhower at first denied that the United States was engaged in aerial spying over the Soviet Union, but when the Soviets put the captured pilot on display, Eisenhower was forced to admit that the incident had indeed happened. Yet he defended the U-2 spy missions and refused to apologize for the intrusion into Soviet airspace.

The Vienna Summit. Newly elected President John F. Kennedy met Soviet premier Nikita Khrushchev in Vienna on 3–4 June 1961, but the meeting ended in a stalemate over the status of Germany and the city of Berlin. At the end of World War II Germany was occupied by the United States, Great Britain, France, and the Soviet Union, and they divided the country and the city of Berlin into sectors, each of which was governed by one of the occupying powers. Berlin was geographically located within the territory controlled by the Soviets, but the four parties had guaranteed that each could have free access to the city. In 1949 the three western powers helped to create the Federal Republic of Germany (West Germany) from their three sectors of the country and their sectors of Berlin. Over the postwar years the Soviets persistently demanded a resolution of the German question and a solution to the problem of Berlin. At the summit Khrushchev demanded a settlement that year and threatened to cut off access to Berlin. Kennedy responded that the United States would go to war to keep access to Berlin open. The summit ended with nothing accomplished.

IKE'S FAREWELL ADDRESS

On 17 January 1961, three days before he left office, President Dwight D. Eisenhower issued a warning that reverberated throughout the decade. To defend its freedom in the Cold War era, he pointed out, America had created "an immense military establishment and a large arms industry" that was "new to the American experience." Then he explained the consequence of this military build-up and expressed his greatest fear:

> The total influence — economic, political, even spiritual — is felt in every city, every statehouse, every office of the federal government. . . .
>
> In the councils of government we must guard against the acquisition of unwarranted influence, whether sought or unsought, by the military-industrial complex. The potential for the disastrous rise exists and will persist.

The forces created to preserve American freedom had, ironically, the power to destroy it, and the only solution to this dilemma, Eisenhower said, was "an alert and knowledgeable citizenry" that could compel the machinery of the military-industrial complex to mesh "with our peaceful methods and goals so that security and liberty may prosper together." Already, the president added, government defense contracts threatened to control intellectual inquiry in American universities, "historically the fountainhead of free ideas and scientific discovery." Throughout the 1960s Eisenhower's warning was quoted more frequently than any other words he spoke during his presidency. As more and more of the nation's human and material resources were committed to waging war in Vietnam, antiwar protesters frequently charged that the military-industrial complex had achieved power beyond any possibility of citizen control and was in fact running the country. Eisenhower, who supported the American presence in Southeast Asia, disagreed.

Source: Stephen E. Ambrose, *Eisenhower: The President* (New York: Simon & Schuster, 1984).

The Berlin Wall. After the Vienna summit the Berlin problem continued to simmer. In an attempt to stem the tide of refugees seeking asylum in the West, East Germany sealed its borders on 13 August 1961 and began erecting a wall that divided the Soviet-controlled sector of Berlin from the other three. Throughout the fall of 1961 the East Germans and the Soviets periodically tried to hamper U.S. access to West Berlin. On 27 October there was a brief, daylong confrontation between U.S. and Soviet tanks at the border of the city. Anticipating a new confrontation over Berlin, President Kennedy obtained special limited power from Congress on 24 September 1962 to call up as many as 150,000 reservists for as long as a year and to extend active duty tours for up to a year without the declaration of a state of emergency. Despite periodic attempts at relaxing tension, the Cold War continued in a predominantly hostile tone.

Nuclear Test-Ban Negotiations. The United States, Great Britain, and the Soviet Union had teams of diplomats engaged in negotiations through 1961 and into 1962 in an attempt to ban the aboveground testing of nuclear weapons. These talks were adjourned on 29 January 1962 because of a failure to agree on terms for international control and verification. The United States had voluntarily stopped aboveground testing, but on 2 March President Kennedy announced that the United States would resume them. U.S. tests resumed in April.

Southeast Asia. Increased Communist insurgent activities in Southeast Asia — especially in Laos, Cambodia, and South Vietnam — was a continuing source of concern in the early 1960s. For a brief period after the Geneva Accords of 1954, which had created these three countries out of the former French territories in Indochina, the area had been relatively peaceful, but a resurgence of Communist activity began in 1958 and escalated as the 1960s began.

Massive Retaliation Criticized. During the 1950s the Eisenhower administration had cut back on conventional military forces and placed substantial emphasis on airpower and nuclear weapons, announcing the doctrine of massive retaliation by which any Communist attack on the free world would be met with a massive attack on the Soviet Union itself. Critics argued that this policy actually weakened the U.S. position by leaving the United States without the conventional forces needed if a crisis did not justify the use of nuclear weapons. Retired general Maxwell Taylor argued that the United States should be prepared to fight "brushfire" wars in the underdeveloped world and would also have to develop a counterinsurgency capability to combine unconventional political and military tactics to combat guerrilla warfare.

Kennedy's Flexible Response Doctrine. In its doctrine of flexible response, the new Kennedy administration sought to remedy the perceived flaws of the Eisenhower strategy. They devised a nuclear policy called the Single Integrated Operational Plan (SIOP). Instead of a single choice, a massive strike, the SIOP gave the president a series of options (all large-scale) for the type of nuclear attack to be used, the functional equivalent of an athletic team's playbook and game plan. The Kennedy administration also called for strengthening U.S. conventional forces so that the United States would be better prepared in a confrontation where the use of nuclear weapons was not appropriate, such as the anticipated conflict over Berlin. They also put more emphasis on developing a counterinsurgency capability with units such as the Special

Forces, which became known as the Green Berets. The president took the entire White House press corps to Fort Bragg, North Carolina, in October 1961 to watch the Special Forces demonstrate their skills. These troops were given training in the languages, history, and culture of the region in which they were to serve. In addition they were trained in medicine, community organization, and political skills, so that one or two individuals could live in a village and coordinate the inhabitants' military activity.

Aid to Third World Countries. The new administration also sought to shift the American response to the Third World away from an emphasis on military aid to one based on economic and humanitarian concerns. As part of the Foreign Assistance Act of 1961, the Agency for International Development (AID) was created to coordinate U.S. foreign-aid programs, and levels of economic assistance were increased. Also, in a speech on 13 March 1961 Kennedy proposed that the United States and Latin American countries form an Alliance for Progress to promote economic and social reform by attacking poverty and inequality. The alliance, which was formally created at a meeting in Punta del Este, Uruguay, on 16 August 1961, began having problems within two years when the Latin American members demanded a greater

American and Soviet tanks facing off in Berlin, 27 October 1961

role in the organization. The United States refused and provided less and less money. This process was accelerated during the Johnson administration, which preferred aid arrangements between the United States and individual countries.

Origins of the Peace Corps. One of the most successful attempts by the Kennedy administration to deal constructively with Third World problems was the creation of the Peace Corps, which sent volunteers abroad to work at low pay in capacities such as teachers, agricultural specialists, and health specialists. Several private programs operating in the 1950s served as prototypes, and several politicians had suggested similar programs, including Congressman Henry Reuss of Wisconsin, Sen. Hubert Humphrey of Minnesota, South Carolina governor Ernest (Fritz) Hollings, Lt. Gen. James Gavin, and Gov. Milton Shapp of Pennsylvania. During his presidential campaign Kennedy asked his staff to prepare a position paper on the possibility of such a volunteer organization.

Kennedy Proposes the Peace Corps. On 14 October 1960, in extemporaneous remarks to ten thousand students at the University of Michigan, Kennedy got an enthusiastic response when he laid out the basics of the Peace Corps and asked how many students would volunteer. On 2 November, six days before the election, Kennedy formally proposed the creation of a Peace Corps in a speech in San Francisco. He repeated the proposal in his election-eve broadcast. Although Republican Sen. Jacob Javits of New York had tried to persuade Richard Nixon to make a similar proposal, the Republican nominee derided the program as a haven for draft dodgers, and President Eisenhower labeled it a juvenile experiment.

Shriver Heads the Peace Corps. Subsequent to his election, John Kennedy put his brother-in-law Sargent Shriver in charge of a task force to plan the establishment of the Peace Corps. Shriver delivered the report on 28 February 1961, and the next day Kennedy established it on a temporary basis via an executive order and sent a message to Congress requesting bills authorizing and funding the Peace Corps. Within four months Congress had complied, and the first volunteers were in the field by fall 1961.

Military Responses to Third World Crises. When Americans thought the Soviets were involved in Third World problems, they tended to respond with military force, as in the Congo crisis of 1960–1961, the Bay of Pigs invasion of Cuba in 1961, and the 1965 invasion of the Dominican Republic.

The Congo Crisis. Within one week of gaining its independence from Belgium, the central African nation the Congo, now known as Zaire, erupted into civil war. One faction was led by Prime Minister Patrice Lumumba and had some minimal backing from the Soviet Union. His ties to the Soviets often led Lumumba's critics to label him a Communist. A second faction was led by President Joseph Kasavubu, considered to be a noncommunist nationalist. A third faction was the army, led by Col. Joseph Mobutu. A fourth faction, led by Moise Tshombe, controlled the mineral-rich province of Katanga. Tshombe's group had the backing of Belgian and other western mining interests. After Tshombe declared the Katanga province independent on 11 July, Lumumba and Kasavubu requested United Nations assistance to reunify the country. A U.N. force was airlifted into the country by the U.S. Air Force on 14 July 1960, but U.N. Secretary-General Dag Hammarskjold refused to let the force be used against the Katanga secessionists. Lumumba then requested assistance from the Soviet Union, but he got only token help. After Kasavubu and Lumumba openly split, paralyzing the government, Mobutu and the army took over on 14 September, placing Lumumba under house arrest. On 17 January 1961 Lumumba was assassinated with assistance from the American CIA. Mobutu relinquished power to Kasavubu in January 1961. Political conditions were chaotic. U.N. forces clashed more and more frequently with the Katanga rebels. Throughout the crisis, the United States backed the Kasavubu government and the U.N. effort. Concerned about potential Soviet inroads in Africa, the United States preferred to keep the country intact. After the United Nations backed military action to reunite Katanga with the Congo on 16 September 1961, the U.S. Air Force transported additional U.N. forces to the country in December. Eventually, in January 1963, a mixed force of Congolese and U.N. troops defeated the Katangan forces and reunited the country.

The Cuban Situation. In January 1959 a revolutionary group led by Fidel Castro overthrew the corrupt government of dictator Fulgencio Batista. After a period of uncertainty in relations with the United States, Castro began a period of slow drift toward the Soviet Union, including signing diplomatic and trade agreements in February 1960. In retaliation for Castro's seizure of American oil refineries in June 1960, the Eisenhower administration withdrew Cuba's export sugar quota. The Castro government responded by nationalizing American-owned sugar mills. In September Castro attended the U.N. session in New York, where he publicly embraced Soviet premier Nikita Khrushchev. The Eisenhower administration imposed an economic embargo against Cuba a month later and broke diplomatic relations with Cuba on 3 January 1961.

The Bay of Pigs Invasion. During the last year of Eisenhower's presidency, the CIA had begun training a secret force of Cuban exiles and devised a plan for them to invade Cuba at the Bay of Pigs. President-elect Kennedy was briefed about the plan on 17 November 1960, and in a meeting during the week prior to his inauguration was urged by Eisenhower to carry it out. After his inauguration, Kennedy, considering whether or not he should go ahead with the plan, asked the Joint Chiefs of Staff to review it. The original plan had been for the force to invade Cuba at the Bay of Pigs with the United States providing air cover and support from naval vessels. The plan was modified, removing the air cover and moving naval support farther out to sea. After intelligence reports indicated that there were no Cuban military forces in the vicinity of the Bay of Pigs and that the Cuban populace would flock to the assistance of the invaders, Kennedy ordered the invasion to go ahead. It began on 17 April 1961. The intelligence reports were wrong. Cuban military forces were in the area. In the absence of air and naval support, the invasion force was defeated within three days, and its surviving members captured. Moreover, the Cuban population did not rise in support of the invaders but stayed behind locked doors until the fighting was over. In the wake of the failed invasion Kennedy took full responsibility.

Castro Embraces Communism. After the invasion, Castro fully embraced Marxism-Leninism, made the Cuban Communist party the only legitimate political party, and moved Cuba into the Soviet camp. In response the United States ended all trade with Cuba on 3 February 1962 and in October barred any nation's ships en route to Cuba from using U.S. ports. The Kennedy administration became obsessed with Castro and tried a variety of covert schemes organized by the CIA to get rid of him. The plots against Castro included sending him a box of cigars poisoned with botulism and lacing his shoes with a chemical that would make his beard fall out, thus tarnishing his "macho" image. Through Operation Mongoose the CIA sabotaged Cuban sugar exports, damaged goods imported into Cuba, sabotaged sugar mills and oil refineries, and ran guns to opposition groups in Cuba. Further, the CIA enlisted the services of the organized-crime groups, which had operated in Cuba before the revolution, to try to assassinate Castro. Operation Mongoose continued into 1965 under the Johnson administration.

The Dominican Situation. Elsewhere in the Caribbean, Rafael Trujillo Molina, who had maintained dictatorial control in the Dominican Republic since 1930, was assassinated on 30 May 1961. Trujillo's son temporarily took power, but on 20 December 1962 Juan Bosch, a leftist leader, was elected president in the first democratic elections held in more than thirty years. His rule was short-lived. He was overthrown by the army seven months later and replaced by Donald Reid Cabral. In 1965 elements of the army seized portions of the capital, Santo Domingo, and declared their support for Bosch. Other leftist supporters of Bosch began handing out arms while another faction in the army supported Cabral. As the country verged on civil war, Ambassador W. Tapley Bennet, Jr., telephoned President Johnson and urged him to intervene, warning that if the leftists were to win, then Castro-like forces would gain control of the country. On 28 April 1965 Johnson sent a military force to reestablish order and take control of the island. After the two sides reconciled their differences, U.S. troops — which had ul-

timately numbered twenty-four thousand— were withdrawn in June of 1966. Joaquin Balaguer defeated Bosch in the Dominican election of 1966.

Public Response to the Dominican Invasion. Johnson originally said the use of American troops was necessary to protect American lives, but on 2 May he began justifying their deployment as necessary to prevent a Communist takeover. At home public reaction to the U.S. military presence in the Dominican Republic was originally positive, but support for Johnson's action diminished over the summer as people learned that the United States had failed to consult with the Organization of American States (OAS) before the invasion and that the situation in the Dominican Republic had not been as dire as originally thought. Of special importance was the reaction of Senate Foreign Relations Committee Chairman J. William Fulbright, who held secret hearings on the Dominican invasion. Then he delivered a speech on the Senate floor in September, declaring that the invasion was ruthless and that Johnson was lacking in candor. This speech began an open breach between Johnson and Fulbright that carried over to the televised Senate hearings on Viet-

RALLYING AROUND THE FLAG

When looking at the impact of foreign-policy events on presidential popularity, many observers of American foreign policy have noted a phenomenon they call the "rally-round-the-flag" effect. Regardless of the general trend in a president's popularity, specific events tend to produce a short-term upward swing in his poll ratings. This increase in popularity appears whether the president's action is wise or unwise, harmful or beneficial to the United States. President John F. Kennedy's rating went up by ten points or more following both the disastrous Bay of Pigs invasion of April 1961 and the successful conclusion of the Cuban missile crisis of October 1962. In response to his rise in popularity after the Bay of Pigs, Kennedy commented, "The worse I do, the more popular I get." President Lyndon B. Johnson's approval rating went up after the Tonkin Gulf incident, and, despite the general, steady decline of his popularity as the Vietnam War continued, he had upswings in his popularity following the invasion of the Dominican Republic in 1965, the bombing of Hanoi in 1966, and his announcement of the bombing halt and his decision not to run in 1968. This phenomenon suggests that a president's popularity will take a short-term jump upward regardless of what he does — as long as he does something.

Sources: John E. Mueller, *War, Presidents and Public Opinion* (New York: Wiley, 1973);

Bruce Russett and Harvey Starr, *World Politics: The Menu for Choice*, fourth edition (San Francisco: Freeman, 1992).

nam the following spring and to Fulbright's subsequent militant criticism of the U.S. war effort in Vietnam.

Long-Term Implications. While the Kennedy and Johnson administrations both tried to refocus U.S. efforts on the Third World toward economic and humanitarian aid, whenever it appeared that there might be Soviet involvement or that local Marxists might reach power, the United States was inclined to treat the problem as part of the Cold War confrontation with the Soviet Union and to respond with covert action by the CIA, military means, or both. This pattern continued into the 1970s with President Richard Nixon's response to the Allende government in Chile and to the Ford administration's response to the civil war in Angola. It also manifested itself in the 1980s in Ronald Reagan's invasion of Grenada and his policy of aiding the Contra movement in Nicaragua.

Sources:

Michael R. Beschloss, *The Crisis Years, Kennedy and Khrushchev, 1960–1963* (New York: Harper & Row, 1991);

Theodore Draper, *The Dominican Revolt: A Case Study in American Policy* (New York: Commentary, 1968);

Walter LaFeber, *America, Russia and the Cold War, 1945–1984*, fifth edition (New York: Knopf, 1985);

Jerome Slater, *Intervention and Negotiation: The United States and the Dominican Revolution* (New York: Harper & Row, 1968).

Attorney General Robert F. Kennedy and President John F. Kennedy during the Cuban missile crisis

THE COLD WAR CONTINUED: THE CUBAN MISSILE CRISIS

Rumors of Soviet Missiles. During the summer of 1962 there were frequent reports of unusual Soviet activities in Cuba, including rumors that the Soviets might be installing missiles there. By late August intelligence reports confirmed that several large ships had brought Soviet military equipment and personnel to the island, although neither were thought to provide any offensive military capability. For some time the United States had used aerial reconnaissance and photography to monitor all Soviet ships coming to Cuba and had been making twice-monthly reconnaissance flights over Cuba itself. On 29 August President John F. Kennedy ordered periodic flights over Cuba by high-speed, high-altitude U-2 spy planes. Although U-2 flights through 7 October showed Soviet antiaircraft missile (SAM) sites under construction and the introduction of Soviet-built patrol boats, they turned up no hard evidence of offensive missile sites or introduction of such missiles.

A Soviet/Cuban Alliance. These Soviet activities followed Fidel Castro's takeover of Cuba in 1959 and an alignment soon thereafter of the new government with the Soviet Union. They also followed the abortive Bay of Pigs invasion of 1961 and extensive naval and military maneuvers carried out by the United States in the Caribbean during spring 1962. On 2 September 1962 the Soviets announced that they would supply additional arms and personnel to meet the so-called imperialist threat to Cuba. They further warned on 11 September that attacks on Cuba or Soviet ships going to Cuba might result in war, perhaps even nuclear war.

Electoral Politics. The U.S. congressional elections of 1962 also played a role in the developing crisis over Cuba. According to political folklore, it is normal that the party of an incumbent president will lose House and Senate seats in an off-year election. Sensing that the Democrats were vulnerable, the Republicans charged that Kennedy had not responded adequately to the increasing Soviet presence in Cuba. In August Republican Sen. Homer Capehart of Indiana demanded that Kennedy order an invasion of Cuba. More Republicans joined the fray in September and early October. Former vice-president Richard Nixon, campaigning for the governorship of California, demanded that Kennedy order a quarantine of Cuba. Republican senators Karl Mundt of South Dakota, Hugh Scott of Pennsylvania, and Kenneth Keating of New York called for a naval blockade of Cuba, while Republican senator Barry Goldwater of Arizona and Democratic senator Strom Thurmond of South Carolina joined Capehart in his call for a U.S. invasion of Cuba. On 10 October Sen. Keating charged that the administration was ignoring the placement of Soviet missile sites and missiles in Cuba. In mid October the Republican national chairman declared that the Kennedy administration's policy on Cuba had become the primary issue in the fall elections.

Evidence of Missile Sites Is Found. On 14 October 1962 a U-2 mission over Cuba took photographs showing clear-cut evidence that two MRBM (Medium Range

An American U-2 spy plane photograph of a Soviet missile installation under construction at San Cristóbal, Cuba

Ballistic Missile — range about 1,100 miles) sites were under construction. Additional flights three days later found even more evidence, showing a total of nine MRBM sites and three IRBM (Intermediate Range Ballistic Missile — range about 2,200 miles) sites. Later flights found evidence that these launch sites — which had the potential of mounting nuclear strikes on Washington, D.C. — would possibly be operational by the end of October.

Kennedy Convenes Excomm. Upon receipt of the first evidence that the Soviets intended to place offensive missiles in Cuba, President Kennedy put together an ad hoc group of cabinet members and agency heads normally responsible for foreign affairs and military policy, some of whom were also statutory members of the National Security Council. Additionally, the group included trusted advisers such as his brother U.S. Attorney General Robert Kennedy, White House aide Theodore Sorensen, and a few private citizens, such as former U.S. secretary of state Dean Acheson and former U.S. secretary of defense Robert Lovett. This group functioned so well during the crisis that its existence was later formalized as the Executive Committee (Excomm) of the National Security Council. They began meeting on 16 October 1962 and met daily throughout the crisis to consider possible responses to the threat of Soviet missiles in Cuba and to assess developments as the crisis resolved itself.

Possible Responses. Among the alternatives considered were (1) secret talks with the U.S.S.R. without pub-

lic disclosure of the missile presence, (2) a public announcement that there were Soviet missiles in Cuba followed by negotiations, (3) an air strike and an invasion of Cuba, (4) a surgical air strike aimed at the missile sites, (5) a quarantine or blockade of Cuba, and (6) private negotiations with Fidel Castro. The military members of the group favored an air strike accompanied by an invasion. Attorney General Robert Kennedy led the opposition to this option on the grounds that any kind of air strike would be reminiscent of the Japanese surprise attack on Pearl Harbor and that in so doing the United States would forfeit any moral position they held in the crisis. Instead the attorney general, together with Secretary of Defense Robert McNamara and Sorensen, persuaded the group to adopt a quarantine and a naval blockade of Cuba. On 22 October President Kennedy briefed congressional leaders and then gave a dramatic, televised address announcing the presence of Soviet missiles in Cuba and demanding their removal. He explained the imposition of the quarantine and blockade, promising continued close surveillance and the reinforcement of the naval base at Guantánamo Bay in Cuba, and he called for emergency meetings of the Organization of American States (OAS) and the United Nations. He warned that a missile attack on the United States launched from Cuba would be met with a U.S. attack on the Soviet Union and that the United States would respond to Soviet countermoves elsewhere in the world, especially in Berlin, with any means necessary. On 23 October President Kennedy activated reserve units, and by Wednesday, 24 October,

In his inaugural address President John F. Kennedy stressed that leadership had been passed to a new generation. Not only was Kennedy twenty-seven years younger than his predecessor, President Dwight D. Eisenhower, but the new administration's top appointees were on average two decades younger than Eisenhower's. Moreover, Kennedy drew more from universities and think tanks than Eisenhower — appointing three times as many academics and far fewer businessmen. Educated at the best universities, Kennedy's appointees had a self-confidence derived from early service in positions of great responsibility during and immediately after World War II.

Some, like Kennedy and his brother Attorney General Robert F. Kennedy, saw military service during World War II. Secretary of State Dean Rusk served in military intelligence during the war and had then been an Asian-affairs expert in the U.S. State Department before becoming president of the Rockefeller Foundation. Secretary of Defense Robert S. McNamara, a staff officer during the war, was a member of a group in charge of logistics for bombing raids. When the war was over, the group, which had become known as the "whiz kids," reorganized the financially troubled Ford Motor Company. McGeorge Bundy, Kennedy's special assistant for military affairs, had helped to plan the invasions of Sicily and France and had worked for the agency that implemented the Marshall Plan before becoming a political analyst for the prestigious Council on Foreign Relations and then going to teach at Harvard.

Among Kennedy's top economic advisers, University of Minnesota professor Walter Heller, chairman of the Council of Economic Advisers, had an important job in the U.S. Treasury Department during the war. Harvard professor John Kenneth Galbraith, who advised Kennedy on foreign economic policy, saw wartime service as deputy administrator of the Office of Price Administration (OPA), while Charles Hitch, a member of the Council of Economic Advisers, was on the War Production Board.

Many of Kennedy's advisers worked for the CIA or its World War II predecessor, the Office of Strategic Services (OSS). Chairman of the U.S. State Department Policy Planning Council Walt W. Rostow, Secretary of Labor Arthur Goldberg, and Special Assistant to the President Arthur Schlesinger were veterans of the OSS. William Bundy, younger brother of McGeorge Bundy, resigned from the CIA to join the Kennedy administration as deputy assistant secretary of defense for international security.

Though the intelligence and self-confidence of this "Kennedy Brain Trust" were widely admired, some people worried about the group's brashness. House Speaker Sam Rayburn said to Vice-president Lyndon B. Johnson, "They may be every bit as intelligent as you say, but I'd feel a whole lot better about them if just one of them had run for sheriff once."

Sources: David Halberstam, *The Best and the Brightest* (New York: Random House, 1972);

Jim F. Heath, *Decade of Disillusionment: the Kennedy-Johnson Years* (Bloomington: Indiana University Press, 1975);

Nelson Lichtenstein, ed., *Political Profiles: The Kennedy Years* (New York: Facts on File, 1976).

the blockade of Cuba by U.S. naval forces had become operative. During a 25 October televised meeting of the U.N. Security Council, U.S. Ambassador Adlai Stevenson presented the photographic evidence of the missile sites to the world, in the face of denials from the Soviet ambassador.

The Soviet Response. The initial Soviet reaction on Tuesday, 23 October, was to condemn the decision of the United States and to accuse President Kennedy of pushing the world to the brink of nuclear war. Soviet forces and other Warsaw Pact forces were put on alert. Yet on Wednesday, 25 October, Soviet ships en route to Cuba halted at sea. On the next day a Soviet-chartered Liberian freighter was searched by U.S. vessels enforcing the

quarantine and blockade, but it was allowed to continue when no contraband was found.

Back-Channel Messages Sent. On 26 October ABC newsman John Scali was contacted by the top Soviet intelligence official in the United States. This official stated that the Soviet Union would agree to remove its missiles from Cuba under United Nations supervision and would not reintroduce them if the United States promised not to invade Cuba. Scali immediately contacted Secretary of State Dean Rusk, who sent a message expressing interest back to the Soviet official via Scali. That evening President Kennedy received a rambling letter from Premier Nikita Khrushchev, in which

Secretary of Defense Robert S. McNamara and Secretary of State Dean Rusk meeting
with President John F. Kennedy at the White House

Khrushchev suggested similar terms but was not as explicit.

The Crisis Escalates. Saturday, 27 October, was probably the darkest day of the confrontation. That morning Radio Moscow broadcast a new message from Khrushchev to Kennedy, adding the condition that the Soviets would take their missiles from Cuba only if the United States removed from Turkey its missiles aimed at the Soviet Union. A U.S. U-2 flight over Cuba was shot down that day by Soviet SAMs, which had just become operational. On the same day another U-2 flight strayed over the Soviet Union, resulting in Soviet interceptors being scrambled to shoot it down and U.S. aircraft in the area being scrambled to escort it safely back to base. U.S. intelligence reported that Soviet embassy officials at the United Nations in New York had begun destroying sensitive documents, a step normally undertaken as war is about to begin.

Kennedy's Response. At the Excomm meeting that day, Robert Kennedy suggested the unusual ploy that the United States ignore the second Khrushchev message and reply only to the first. The group agreed, and President Kennedy sent Khrushchev a message agreeing that, if the Soviets would withdraw their missiles from Cuba under U.N. supervision and promise not to reintroduce them, the United States would agree not to invade Cuba. The next day (28 October), in another broadcast from Radio Moscow, Khrushchev signaled full agreement, making no mention of U.S. missiles in Turkey. He further stated an interest in future diplomatic efforts to reduce tensions and control the burgeoning nuclear arms race. In reply President Kennedy issued a statement welcoming the Soviet decision. He stated that the naval blockade would be lifted after verification of removal of the missiles and dismantling of their launch sites, and he promised that the United States would not invade Cuba. The crisis that had brought the United States and the Soviet Union to the brink of nuclear war was effectively over. Subsequent photo reconnaissance showed the missiles gone and the launch sites dismantled. The quarantine was lifted on 21 November.

Election Results. In the aftermath of the crisis the Republicans did not do as well as they had hoped in the 1962 elections. Kennedy's handling of the Cuban situation helped the Democrats gain six seats in the Senate accompanied by a minimal two-seat net loss in the House, a far better outcome for the Democrats than had been expected. In a postelection about-face the Republicans — who had criticized Kennedy for inaction on Cuba — now accused him of manipulating the crisis to the benefit of Democratic candidates.

The Seeds of Détente. The Cuban missile crisis was also a cathartic event in U.S./Soviet relations. The realization that they had come close to nuclear war had a sobering effect on the way the two nations dealt with one another and contributed to a relaxation of tensions. In the short term the United States agreed to a hot line, a direct communications link with Moscow so that in future crises the two leaders would be able to communicate directly rather than relying on other parties to carry messages or on signaling through public broadcast messages. The initial hot line became operational in August 1963. On 25 July 1963 a treaty banning aboveground nuclear testing was signed by representatives of the United States, Great Britain, and the Soviet Union. Kennedy also announced that the United States would begin selling wheat to the Soviets. He also indicated a willingness to reduce tensions by suggesting in a speech given at American University in June 1963 that it was time to reexamine attitudes toward the Cold War. Yet the nuclear arms race between the two superpowers did not slow down. One reason the Soviets had not challenged the U.S. naval blockade of Cuba was their lack of sufficient naval power. Determined not to be in a similar situation in the future, the Soviets made a conscious decision to increase their naval capacity substantially.

Sources:

Elie Abel, *The Missile Crisis* (Philadelphia: Lippincott, 1966);

Graham T. Allison, *Essence of Decision: Explaining the Cuban Missile Crisis* (Boston: Little, Brown, 1971);

Raymond Garthoff, *Reflections on the Cuban Missile Crisis* (Washington, D.C.: Brookings Institution, 1989);

Ole R. Holsti, *Crisis, Escalation, War* (Montreal: McGill University Press, 1972);

Robert F. Kennedy, *Thirteen Days: A Memoir of the Cuban Missile Crisis* (New York: Norton, 1969);

Robert Smith Thompson, *The Missiles of October: The Declassified Story of John F. Kennedy and the Cuban Crisis* (New York: Simon & Schuster, 1992).

THE COLD WAR CONTINUED: NUCLEAR ARMS RACE, ARMS CONTROL, AND DÉTENTE

The Arms Race. After World War II the United States and the Soviet Union began a nuclear arms race that continued unabated throughout the 1960s. For most of the 1950s both countries concentrated on manufacturing atomic and hydrogen bombs and the intercontinental bomber force necessary to deliver them. Both countries also developed short-range and intermediate-range missiles that could be armed with nuclear warheads, as well as nuclear weapons to be used on the battlefield.

The Space Race. The 5 October 1957 launch by the Soviet Union of *Sputnik,* the first man-made satellite to orbit the earth, dramatically changed the arms race. Reacting with shock and embarrassment, the Americans rushed to launch their own satellites. Throughout the 1960s the United States and the Soviets competed to see which country could be the first to demonstrate a particular feat in space. On 25 May 1961 President Kennedy announced a program to put a man on the moon by the end of the decade and asked Congress to fund the project. This goal was accomplished on 20 July 1969 when American Neil Armstrong walked on the surface of the moon.

From an intelligence point of view, any nation that demonstrates the ability to launch satellites into orbit also has the capability to develop and deploy intercontinental ballistic missiles (ICBMs). Further, every successful launch of a satellite or any other space project is evidence of the reliability of all launch vehicles including ICBMs. In addition to technological advances that resulted from the space race, it also brought public relations benefits, demonstrating American technical sophistication to a marveling world.

The Missile Race. Throughout the 1960s the United States and the Soviet Union made massive efforts to develop, build, and deploy strategic forces that relied primarily on ICBMs and SLBMs (submarine-launched ballistic missiles) armed with nuclear warheads. Bombers gave way to missiles. In 1963 the United States had 630 intercontinental bombers to 190 for the Soviets; by 1972 bombers had dropped to 457 for the United States and 156 for the Union of Soviet Socialist Republics. During the same time period, however, the United States had increased its number of ICBMs from 424 to 1,054 and its SLBMs from 224 to 656, while the Soviets increased their ICBM force from 90 to 1,533 and their SLBMs from 107 to 437. The number of nuclear warheads each country possessed had grown to match the numbers of launch vehicles, with the exception of American warheads for SLBMs, which increased from 224 in 1963 to 2,096 in 1972. (A technological breakthrough allowed the United States to mount multiple warheads on their SLBMs.) By the end of the decade the United States and the Soviet Union had each stockpiled enough nuclear weapons to destroy one another — and the entire world — several times over.

Changes in Strategy. As both the United States and the Soviet Union converted from reliance on bombs delivered by intercontinental bombers to reliance on nuclear warheads delivered by ICBMs or SLBMs, strategic doctrine adjusted to the new technology. When each country's nuclear force was primarily delivered by bomber, it was possible to have time to intercept an attacking bomber with antiaircraft missiles or with interceptor aircraft, and both countries had developed elaborate air-defense systems. With the approximate thirty-minute flight time for a warhead launched from an ICBM and an even shorter flight time for warheads from SLBMs, there was too little warning time to allow interception. The Soviet Union and the United States were vulnerable to attack by one another; in effect, each held the other's population hostage. This ability led to the strategic doctrine known as Mutual Assured Destruction (MAD) — each country would be deterred from attacking the other because it could not escape the enormous damage resulting from retaliation.

Development of Spy Satellites. The space race benefited arms control. Both the Soviet Union and the United States developed and deployed spy satellites that allowed them to monitor reliably one another's nuclear tests, missile launches, and military deployments on a constant basis. Spy satellites provided a steadier flow of information than U-2 flights, and satellites were not as intrusive as spy plane overflights. By the end of the decade each side had developed and deployed sufficient technical means to simplify greatly the job of verifying compliance with arms control agreements. Problems with verification had been a major sticking point in the attempts to negotiate arms control agreements during the 1950s and the early 1960s. The spy satellites helped make possible the arms control agreements of the mid and late 1960s and the 1970s. By the end of the decade each of the two superpowers was relatively confident that it possessed the capability to destroy the other with a nuclear attack and that it had an adequate possibility of monitoring the other.

Political Climate Changes. After the Cuban missile crisis of October 1962, in which the United States and the Soviet Union came perilously close to nuclear war, both sides became less bellicose. Another factor that contributed toward reduced tension between the United States and the Soviet Union during the decade was the increased hostility between the Soviets and the People's Republic of China. On 1 January 1963 the Chinese criticized Soviet premier Nikita Khrushchev's actions during the Cuban missile crisis and his idea of "peaceful coexistence" between the Soviet bloc and the West. The Soviets responded with denunciations of the Chinese on 7 January and 30 August. The Communist Chinese added to the Soviets' concerns when they detonated a nuclear device for the first time on 16 October 1964. This event added another, potentially hostile, member to the "nuclear club," one that shared a long border with the Soviet Union. By 1969 there were armed border clashes between the Soviet Union and Communist China. In an atmosphere of reduced tensions between the United States and the Soviet Union but increased tension between the Soviets and the Chinese, several small steps were taken toward arms control.

Nuclear-Test Ban Talks. Since the late 1950s scientists and the public had become increasingly concerned that radioactive fallout from aboveground tests was a serious health hazard. During the spring of 1963 the United States, Great Britain, and the Soviet Union resumed talks on banning aboveground nuclear tests, negotiations that had been suspended in early 1962. Agreement was reached rapidly, and on 5 August 1963 the three countries signed a treaty banning nuclear testing in the atmosphere, in outer space, and underwater. Compliance was partially monitored through satellites designed to detect the radioactivity released by such tests. Since the adoption of this treaty more than one hundred additional countries have signed it. France and the People's Republic of China have refused to sign the treaty although each voluntarily refrains from violating its provisions.

U.S./Soviet Cooperation Despite Differences. The spirit of cooperation in U.S./Soviet relations in 1963 was in sharp contrast to the intense hostility of the previous fall. Kennedy's trip to Berlin — where he proclaimed, "Ich bin ein Berliner" (literally: I am a jelly doughnut; he should have said, "Ich bin Berlinisch") in a speech on 26 June 1963 — was motivated at least in part by a need to reaffirm the U.S. commitment to Berlin, whose population had become increasingly nervous in light of the improvement in U.S./Soviet relations. During the rest of the decade relations between the United States and the Soviet Union remained reasonably stable and paved the way for the policy of détente espoused by Richard Nixon when he became president in 1969. The two countries were able to compartmentalize their differences over the Six Day War involving Israel against Jordan, Syria, and Egypt, in June 1967, over the invasion of Czechoslovakia by the Soviet Union and Warsaw Pact forces in 1968, and over the escalating U.S. effort in Vietnam. They were also able to conclude two more arms control agreements during the 1960s and to begin the negotiations that resulted in another two agreements in the early 1970s. On 27 January 1967 the United States and the Soviet Union were among the sixty-two nations who signed a treaty that prohibited the military use of space.

The Glassboro Summit. After increasing tensions between Israel and Egypt during May 1967, Israel began launching attacks against several Arab countries on 5 June. By the ninth the war was over, with Israel taking control of the Sinai, the city of Jerusalem, the west bank of the Jordan River, and the Golan Heights. While the United States backed the Israelis and the Soviet Union adamantly backed Syria's demand for the return of the Golan Heights, the two countries made extensive use of the hot line to keep the relationship between them calm. In June Soviet premier Aleksey Kosygin led a special Soviet delegation to New York to take part in a U.N. effort to find a solution to the Arab/Israeli dilemma. He subsequently attended a summit meeting with President Johnson on the campus of Glassboro State College in New Jersey. They were unable to reach a consensus on the Middle East crisis, and the Arab/Israeli problem continued to be a stress point in U.S./Soviet relations into the next decade. They also discussed the Vietnam War, but they were not successful in resolving issues that prevented the United States and the North Vietnamese from starting peace talks. Three different arms control issues were on the agenda. For some time the two countries had unsuccessfully explored ways to limit the growth of their strategic nuclear arsenals. In 1964 Johnson had offered a proposal that would have frozen strategic weapons systems at their existing levels. The Soviets refused, at least in part because of security concerns rising from China's explosion of a nuclear device in 1964. Johnson and Kosygin discussed the possibility of a strategic arms limitation treaty (SALT), but the Soviets insisted they would not begin SALT talks until there was a nuclear nonprolifera-

Soviet premier Aleksey Kosygin and President Lyndon B. Johnson speaking to the press after the Glassboro Summit

Postponement of Strategic Weapons Negotiations. The talks did not start as scheduled. Throughout the spring of 1968 Czechoslovakia had enjoyed a liberalization program known as the "Prague Spring" under the government of Aleksander Dubcek. Some critics of communism called for the establishment of a democracy with free elections in a multiparty system. On 20 August 1968 the Soviet Union, fearful over the potential loss of Communist control and a Czechoslovak tilt toward the West, sent Warsaw Pact forces under Soviet command into Czechoslovakia in a move reminiscent of the Soviet invasion of Hungary in 1956. The invading force quickly took control of the country, reversed the liberalization process, and reestablished tight Communist party control. In protest the United States delayed the start of the SALT talks.

Nixon Agrees to SALT Talks. After Richard Nixon became President in January 1969 and in the absence of an agreement to limit ABM systems, his administration made a decision to go ahead with a U.S. ABM program. The delayed SALT negotiations began in Helsinki on 17 November 1969.

Sources:

Fred Kaplan, *The Wizards of Armageddon* (New York: Simon & Schuster, 1983);

Michael Mandelbaum, *The Nuclear Question: The United States and Nuclear Weapons, 1946–1976* (New York: Cambridge University Press, 1979);

Bruce Russett and Harvey Starr, *World Politics: The Menu for Choice,* fourth edition (San Francisco: Freeman, 1992).

tion treaty to prevent the spread of nuclear weapons to countries that did not have them already. They also discussed the possibility of an agreement which would place limits on antiballistic missile (ABM) systems. The Soviets had begun deploying a limited system by 1967, and the U.S. military was pressing Johnson for a commitment to build a U.S. system. Again the Soviets demurred until there was some resolution of the nuclear proliferation issue. Johnson and Kosygin did make some progress on issues that paved the way for the Nuclear Nonproliferation Treaty of 1968.

The Nuclear Nonproliferation Treaty. On 1 July 1968 the United States and the Soviet Union were among the signatories to the Nuclear Nonproliferation Treaty. This treaty, which went into effect in 1970, stipulates that none of the five (at the time) nuclear powers would transfer nuclear weapons to nonnuclear states or assist them in developing nuclear weapons. To date some 136 countries have signed the treaty although neither France nor China (two of the five original nuclear powers) has yet signed it; France has announced that it will abide by the provisions of the agreement. After the treaty was signed on 1 July the Soviet Union and the United States made simultaneous announcements that they would begin talks in September on limiting strategic weapons.

THE COLD WAR CONTINUED: THE VIETNAM WAR

Implementing the Containment Doctrine. America's involvement in Vietnam may be traced to decisions made in the late 1940s and the 1950s as the Cold War and the doctrine of containment of Communism came to be dominant considerations in U.S. foreign policy. Presidents Franklin D. Roosevelt and Harry S Truman had expected to let the Japanese-occupied French colonies in Indochina gain their independence at the end of World War II rather than allowing the French to reassert control. As the Cold War emerged in Europe during the late 1940s, prompting the formation of the North Atlantic Treaty Organization (NATO), the United States became more concerned with not alienating France, a crucial member of the new alliance, than with standing by a vague assertion of the right of self-determination for the various peoples of Indochina. The United States became increasingly concerned about Asia when civil war in China resulted in a Communist victory in 1949 and when the Communist North Koreans invaded South Korea in 1950.

The French versus the Vietminh. As they moved back into Indochina the French faced the Vietminh, an indigenous Communist independence movement led by Ho Chi Minh. During World War II the Vietminh had been the heart of armed resistance to Japanese occupation and had fully expected Indochina to be granted independence after the war. With support from the Soviet Union and later the People's Republic of China, the Vietminh seemed to the United States to be yet another example of Communist expansion at work.

The United States Backs France. In 1950 President Truman decided that supporting France in its fight against the Vietminh was important in the effort to contain communism. He began providing military aid to French forces in Indochina. Truman's decision was also guided by the domino theory, which argued that if Indochina were to fall to the Communists, then the rest of Southeast Asia would fall as well, like a row of dominoes. By 1953 U.S. military assistance to the French had reached $500 million, and the following year it rose to $1 billion. The United States was paying half the cost for the French to continue fighting the Vietminh. In 1954, after a disastrous defeat of their forces at Dien Bien Phu, the French and the Vietminh reached an agreement, the Geneva Accords. Indochina was to be divided into three countries — Laos, Cambodia, and Vietnam. Vietnam was subdivided into two supposedly temporary sectors. The Vietminh were to withdraw to the northern sector, and the French were to withdraw to the south. Elections were to be held within two years to settle the fate of Vietnam as a whole. A government was set up in the south with Ngo Dinh Diem as president. On 23 October 1954 President Eisenhower offered U.S. military assistance to the new Diem government. On 12 February 1955 U.S. military advisers took over from the French the job of training the South Vietnamese military. In addition to the dollar amounts of military aid sent to South Vietnam, the United States had an annual average of about 650 military advisers in South Vietnam from 1955 through 1960. In September 1954 the Southeast Asian Treaty Organization (SEATO), an alliance similar to NATO, was founded to counter Communist threats in Southeast Asia.

The Vietminh Reactivate. The Vietminh were relatively quiescent until 1958, when they began stepping up their activities in Laos, Cambodia, and Vietnam. In 1960 veterans of the Vietminh became the nucleus of a Communist insurgent group in South Vietnam, the National Liberation Front. The Diem government gave the group a pejorative nickname, Vietcong — meaning Vietnamese "commie" — which stuck. The Vietcong, with the assistance of the North Vietnamese, escalated the fight against the Diem government in South Vietnam.

Kennedy's Concerns About Indochina. As he took office in January 1961 President John F. Kennedy was concerned about the continued fighting in Southeast Asia and its possible spread to other Southeast Asian nations. In Laos an American-backed military government, a neutralist faction, and the procommunist Pathet Lao (also backed by the Vietminh) were fighting for control of the country. After learning that American military reserves were stretched thin because of the ongoing confrontation with the Soviets over Berlin, Kennedy expended considerable energy throughout the spring of 1961 to keep Laos neutral and independent. An agreement on a Laotian cease-fire and neutralization was reached in July 1962.

Kennedy's Vietnam Policy. On 28 January 1961, just eight days after his inauguration, Kennedy approved a counterinsurgency plan for Vietnam. The plan included additional funds, which would allow the South Vietnamese army to increase in size by 20,000 men, and authorized the use of Vietnamese agents to mount guerrilla operations in North Vietnam. He sent Vice-president Lyndon Johnson on a fact-finding tour of Vietnam in May 1961, which was followed in June by a request from South Vietnamese president Diem for additional U.S. troops to train the South Vietnamese army. In November 1961 Kennedy sent Gen. Maxwell Taylor and foreign policy adviser Walt Rostow to South Vietnam. On their return they reported that it was possible for the South Vietnamese to defeat the Communist insurgents without an American takeover of the war effort if the United States provided strong political backing for the South Vietnamese government and provided substantially increased military and economic assistance. They further recommended that President Kennedy send 8,000 combat troops to South Vietnam. Kennedy decided against sending combat troops but authorized the deployment of up to 15,000 military advisers. By the time of Kennedy's assassination in November 1963 the U.S. effort in Vietnam was costing $400 million a year, and about 12,000 military advisers were providing assistance to the South Vietnamese military effort. By the end of 1963 there had been only 70 American casualties.

Gradual Escalation. Throughout the Kennedy administration American involvement increased slowly, almost imperceptibly. On 8 February 1962 the United States announced the creation of a Military Assistance Command in Saigon. That spring it also began its involvement with the Vietnam Strategic Hamlet program, a rural pacification plan by which peasants would relocate to fortified towns where they could defend themselves. This program was intended to provide strong local opposition to the Vietcong and in turn reduce support for the Vietcong in the rural areas. Copied from a program the British had used successfully in Malaya, it did not transfer well to the Vietnamese countryside. Late in 1962 the United States introduced helicopter squadrons flown by American pilots, which helped ferry South Vietnamese troops into battle and provided close air support. Reports from the Military Assistance Command and from the embassy in Saigon repeatedly stressed how well the effort against the Vietcong was going. In early 1963 Gen. Paul Harkins, commander of the military assistance group, advised President Kennedy that he could begin troop withdrawals by the end of the year and that all U.S. forces could be withdrawn by 1965. Gen. William Westmore-

President Lyndon B. Johnson signing the Gulf of Tonkin Resolution, 10 August 1964. Standing behind the president are Rep. Carl Albert, Sen. Hubert H. Humphrey, Rep. Charles Halleck, Sen. Everett Dirksen, Sen. George Aiken, Speaker of the House of Representatives John McCormack, Sen. George Smathers, Sen. J. William Fulbright, Rep. Mendell Rivers, Sen. Bourk D. Hickenlooper, Jr., and Rep. Clement Zablocki. Secretary of Defense Robert S. McNamara and Secretary of State Dean Rusk are sitting in the first row, facing the president.

land, Harkins's successor in December 1963, maintained a similar optimism in his public pronouncements about the war throughout his tour of duty in Vietnam.

The Overthrow of Diem. Throughout 1963 the South Vietnamese political situation became increasingly unstable. On 15 February disenchanted elements of the Vietnamese air force tried unsuccessfully to kill President Diem by bombing and strafing the presidential palace. As opposition among Buddhists mounted, more and more Buddhist monks practiced self-immolation, committing suicide by dousing themselves with gasoline and setting fire to themselves, in protest of the repressive policies of the Diem regime. By late summer and throughout the fall the government was brutal in its attempts to suppress the dissidents. On 2 November the South Vietnamese military, with the acquiescence and support of the U.S. government, overthrew Diem, murdering him and his family. While Saigon celebrated, U.S. Ambassador Henry Cabot Lodge met the successful leaders of the coup in his office, where he congratulated them on their victory. He cabled President Kennedy that "The prospects now are for a shorter war." Three weeks later President Kennedy himself was dead, felled by an assassin's bullet, and replaced by Vice-president Lyndon Johnson, whose political career, especially in the U.S. Senate, had been informed by the rabid anticommunism of the McCarthy era and the political recriminations over the loss of China to the Communists.

Stepping Up the War. In 1964, a presidential election year, there was little political debate over the American military presence in Vietnam, at least in part because the two candidates, Johnson and Barry Goldwater, had agreed not to politicize the war during the campaign. In January 1964 the Joint Chiefs of Staff had sent President Johnson a memo urging him to increase the U.S. commitment and to consider a bombing campaign against North Vietnam. By following these two strategies the military hoped that the war could be won more quickly. The commitment of U.S. troops was doubled; by the end of 1964 there were 23,300 Americans serving in Vietnam. In addition Johnson ordered a study to explore the possibility of a bombing campaign.

The Gulf of Tonkin Incident. On 30 July 1964 the destroyer *Maddox* provided support for South Vietnamese commandos attacking a North Vietnamese radar installation. On 2 August, while on patrol in the Gulf of Tonkin off the North Vietnamese coast, the *Maddox* was attacked by three North Vietnamese torpedo boats. The *Maddox* crippled two of the craft and sunk the third. No further U.S. response was planned at the time. The next day the *Maddox* was joined by a second destroyer, the *C. Turner Joy*, to patrol in the Gulf of Tonkin. During a stormy night the two ships reported that they were under attack and requested air support, which was provided from the aircraft carrier *Ticonderoga*. Both destroyers fired at what they believed to be attack vessels, but the pilots from the aircraft carrier saw no signs of such vessels, and in retrospect no crew member of either destroyer was sure that he had seen an attacker. In two later reports the captain of the *Maddox* stated his doubts that either American vessel had been attacked. Washington, however, reacted to the initial report that the vessels were under attack and took action. While the captain of the *Maddox* was still quizzing his crew on 4 August, President Johnson ordered naval aircraft from the carriers *Constellation* and *Ticonderoga* to retaliate. They flew sixty-four sorties, attacking four North Vietnamese patrol boat bases and an oil depot. In addition, Johnson consulted key members of Congress on 4 August and requested a resolution of support for his actions. With the leadership of Senate Foreign Relations Committee Chairman J. William Fulbright, a resolution authorizing the president to "take all necessary measures to repel any armed attack against the forces of the United States and to prevent further aggression" passed the House of Representatives by a vote of 416–0 and the Senate by a vote of 88–2. Until its repeal in May 1970 the Tonkin Gulf Resolution provided a legal basis for the subsequent escalation and continuation of the war by both President Johnson and his successor, Richard Nixon.

Stepped-Up Bombing. In 1965 the U.S. military role in South Vietnam shifted from providing assistance to one of active combat. On 7 February 1965 the Vietcong attacked an American barracks at Pleiku, and the United States retaliated by bombing targets in North Vietnam. U.S. aircraft began bombing Vietcong targets in South Vietnam on a regular basis on 24 February. Operation Rolling Thunder, a systematic bombing campaign against targets in North Vietnam, began in earnest on 2 March. Designed to coerce the North Vietnamese into ceasing their effort in support of the Vietcong, the bombing campaign continued with occasional interruptions until Johnson halted it in fall 1968, as peace talks got under way. Originally directed primarily at military targets, the bombing campaign was expanded to include attacks on the oil depots outside Hanoi in June 1966 and on the main power plant in Hanoi itself in May 1967.

Increases in Troop Commitments. At the beginning of March 1965 General Westmoreland requested that two corps of Marines be provided to help guard U.S. facilities. Johnson agreed, and U.S. combat troops began arriving in Vietnam on 8 March. In April the Joint Chiefs of Staff recommended a commitment of 50,000 troops, a recommendation that was revised upward to 80,000 the following month. General Westmoreland upped the ante in June by requesting that troop levels be raised to 200,000. On 28 July President Johnson announced that draft calls would be increased so that the United States could raise troop strength in Vietnam from 75,000 to 125,000 men. By the end of the year there were 184,314 American troops serving there. The U.S. role was also expanded on 8 June, when Johnson authorized American troops to engage in direct combat operations.

NORTH KOREANS SEIZE THE PUEBLO

On 23 January 1968 the USS *Pueblo*, a U.S. Navy freighter equipped to gather electronic intelligence, was sailing in international waters off the coast of North Korea when it was attacked by North Korean patrol vessels. The *Pueblo*'s guns were not fired, and American naval vessels and aircraft were too far away to help, as the North Koreans seized the ship, which was commanded by Comdr. Lloyd M. Bucher, capturing its crew of eighty-three, some of whom were wounded.

The United States immediately demanded the release of the crew and the ship, but it took eleven months of negotiations, with help from the Soviet Union, before the crew was finally released on 22 December. In a news conference after the release, Bucher said that the crew had been tortured and coerced into signing confessions that they were spies.

The incident was an embarrassment to the Johnson administration in an election year. Republican candidate Richard Nixon charged that the administration had committed a tactical blunder by allowing a ship so close to North Korea without making adequate provision for assistance in the event of attack.

In March 1969 a Navy board recommended that Bucher be court-martialed for his failure to defend the ship aggressively, that the signal intelligence officer be court-martialed for not destroying sensitive documents before the capture, and that other officers and crew members be reprimanded. On 6 May, however, Secretary of the Navy John Chafee said that Bucher and his crew had suffered enough and declined to take any further action.

Source: Vaughan Davis Bornet, *The Presidency of Lyndon Johnson* (Lawrence: University Press of Kansas, 1983).

A Pattern of Escalation. U.S. forces stationed in Vietnam reached average levels of 389,000 in 1966, 485,600 in 1967, and 549,500 in 1968. At the height of this expansion the United States was employing 40 percent of its combat-ready divisions, 50 percent of its tactical airpower, and 33 percent of its naval forces in Vietnam. Throughout this expansion of the war, the administration continued to express its conviction that a victory was possible.

The Tet Offensive. This optimism seemed overstated to the American public after the Vietcong and the North Vietnamese launched an unexpected offensive on 30 January 1968 during Tet, the Vietnamese holiday celebrating the lunar new year. Although the offensive was defeated

MASSACRE AT MY LAI

On 16 March 1968 three platoons of Company C, First Battalion, 11th Brigade, American Division swept through the South Vietnamese hamlet of My Lai on a search-and-destroy mission (designed to look for enemy soldiers and kill them). Company C, which had suffered heavy losses on an earlier mission, was commanded by Capt. Ernest L. Medina, and its First Platoon was commanded by Lt. William L. Calley, Jr., an inexperienced young officer. They found no Vietcong, but during the mission hundreds of unarmed civilians, including elderly men, women, and children, were murdered and their livestock killed. The only American casualty was a soldier who shot himself in the foot to avoid participating in the massacre. After army helicopter pilots reported seeing large numbers of dead civilians in the area, the brigade and division commanders investigated but said that they had uncovered nothing unusual.

In April 1969 Ronald Ridenhour, a Vietnam veteran who had been a member of First Platoon, publicly charged that war crimes had been committed at My Lai, and reporters began uncovering details of the massacre. The U.S. Army launched an inquiry, and shortly thereafter Lieutenant Calley was charged with 102 counts of murder. At his court-martial Calley claimed that he was acting on orders from Medina — a charge Medina and others rebutted. On 29 March 1971 Calley was convicted and sentenced to life imprisonment, but in August his sentence was reduced to twenty years. Although several other officers and soldiers were court-martialed, Calley was the only one convicted.

Calley's case became a cause célèbre among conservatives and others who thought he was being made a scapegoat. In April 1974 Secretary of the Army Howard H. Calloway reduced the sentence to ten years. Calley was paroled in November 1974 and given a dishonorable discharge. In 1976 the U.S. Supreme Court upheld his conviction.

Source: William H. Chafe, *The Unfinished Journey: America Since World War II*, second edition (New York: Oxford University Press, 1991).

militarily, it created the perception that the war would not be won as easily as U.S. officials had led the public to believe. On 27 February 1968 Westmoreland requested an additional 208,000 troops, but on 22 March the administration ordered him home, signaling a shift away from a total-victory strategy. On 25–26 March the president's senior advisory group on Vietnam met and recommended against further troop increases, suggesting the need to find diplomatic means to extricate the United States from the war. The following year, newly elected President Richard M. Nixon began limited troop withdrawals, ordering home 25,000 in June and another 50,000 in December. By this time U.S. casualties had reached 33,641, a level exceeding the number killed in the Korean War.

The Antiwar Movement. Politically, there was little opposition to the U.S. involvement in Vietnam until the 1965 escalation. The number of troops in Vietnam had been small, and casualties few. For most Americans the fight was a distant one, both geographically and perceptually, and it was viewed as part of the U.S. commitment to oppose Communist expansion, a goal few Americans questioned. Moreover, individuals with expertise on Asia, inside and outside government, were reluctant to question U.S. policy on Vietnam in light of the political fallout and in recollection of careers destroyed in the wake of the Communist victory in China in 1949. There were a few who expressed their doubts. George Ball, an undersecretary of state, was very critical of the Taylor-Rostow report in 1961 and continued to question U.S. policy through much of the Johnson administration, including writing a sixty-seven-page memorandum in October 1964 that challenged the assumptions of U.S. policy in Vietnam. At a National Security Council meeting on 31 August 1963 Paul Kattenburg, a senior State Department official who had Indochina experience, argued that the United States should consider getting out of Vietnam entirely and soon found himself posted to Guyana, a small country on the Caribbean coast of South America.

Opposition in Washington. Democratic senator Mike Mansfield of Montana, Lyndon Johnson's successor as Senate majority leader, had taught Asian history at the University of Montana and had been an early supporter of the effort in Vietnam. Sent on a fact-finding tour to Saigon in late 1962, he came back pessimistic and urged that the United States reassess its policies and avoid deeper involvement. He continued to counsel against escalating troop commitments and, together with Georgia senator Richard Russell, tried hard to persuade President Johnson to find ways out of Vietnam. The chairman of the Senate Foreign Relations Committee, J. William Fulbright, led the floor fight for the passage of the Tonkin Gulf Resolution in 1964, but within two years he became very critical of the war and used televised committee hearings in the spring of 1966 as a forum to question American involvement. Attorney General Robert F. Kennedy, brother of President John Kennedy, had taken part in the decisions during the Kennedy administration that had deepened the U.S. commitment to Vietnam. In 1964 he resigned from the administration and successfully sought a U.S. Senate seat from New York. By 1968 he had become an opponent of the war and sought the Democratic nomination for president as an antiwar

Protesters at the Pentagon, 21 October 1967

candidate. Another cabinet member who served both Presidents Kennedy and Johnson, Secretary of Defense Robert McNamara, became disillusioned with the war by 1966 and resigned in November 1967. Senators Wayne Morse (D-Ore.), Ernest Gruening (D-Alaska), Frank Church (D-Idaho), Gaylord Nelson (D-Wis.), John Sherman Cooper (R-Ky.), and George McGovern (D-S.Dak.) were all early critics of the conflict. As involvement deepened and the war got more costly in terms of lives and money, more and more members of the House and Senate, as well as other political leaders — including civil rights leaders — began to question the wisdom of the U.S. effort. The Reverend Martin Luther King, Jr., gave muted criticism in 1965 and took an active leadership role against the war in 1967.

Criticism from the Military. Some retired military leaders were also critical of the U.S. policy on Vietnam. Former Marine Corps general Paul Shoup, a member of the Joint Chiefs of Staff under President Kennedy, argued that "all of Southeast Asia was not worth the life of a single American." Retired lieutenant general James Gavin, an adviser on defense issues to Kennedy's 1960 campaign, was also critical of the war, as was Gen. Matthew B. Ridgway, who had commanded U.S. forces in the Korean War and was Army Chief of Staff from 1953 to 1955. Many military critics thought the commitment of U.S. troops to a land war in Asia was folly. Others thought the United States had overcommitted its military resources to the conflict and had left itself vulnerable in the event of crises elsewhere in the world.

Public Protests. Protests from the public became more frequent after the 1965 escalation of the war. On 17 April

1965, 15,000 to 25,000 demonstrated in Washington against the bombing of North Vietnam. Teach-ins about the war were held on many college and university campuses that spring. On 15 and 16 October there were antiwar demonstrations in forty U.S. cities, and on 17 November some 15,000 antiwar protesters marched in Washington. Antiwar demonstrations continued throughout 1966 and 1967, involving larger and larger numbers. On 15 April 1967, 100,000 in New York City and another 20,000 in San Francisco attended rallies against the war. A week of draft-resistance activities culminated with a 21 October 1967 march on the Pentagon by 35,000 protesters, including such well-known liberal intellectuals as poet Robert Lowell, novelist Norman Mailer, and critic Dwight Macdonald. Mailer was arrested at the Pentagon and spent the night in jail. Radical activist Abbie Hoffman attracted media attention with a mock exorcism of the Pentagon, in which singing and chanting demonstrators engaged in a comic attempt to levitate the building. The earliest antiwar protesters had tended to be from fringe pacifist groups, anti-nuclear-weapons groups, and radical student groups. As the protests grew larger and the war escalated, the protesters became more representative of the entire political spectrum.

Public Support Steadily Declines. In August 1965, 61 percent of the American population supported the war policy. A little over a year later, in November 1966, polls showed support had dropped to 50 percent. The drop continued: in October 1967, fewer than half of those polled, 44 percent, supported the war, by spring 1968 only 40 percent did so, and by the time of the Democratic National Convention in August 1968 only 35 percent favored the war. In 1969, Richard Nixon's first year as President, support for the war had eroded to 32 percent.

The 1968 Elections. Debate over the war became fully politicized during the 1968 presidential election campaign. Sen. Eugene McCarthy (D-Minn.), running as an antiwar candidate, challenged incumbent President Johnson for the 1968 Democratic nomination and did surprisingly well in the New Hampshire primary. Newly appointed Secretary of Defense Clark Clifford became a key figure in persuading Johnson to halt the bombing and begin peace talks. On 31 March, after the meetings with his senior advisory group on Vietnam that led to the decision not to raise troop levels further, Johnson gave a televised talk to the nation, in which he announced a partial bombing halt, invited the North Vietnamese to begin negotiations, and announced — in a major surprise — that he would not run for reelection. Not long before Johnson's pullout, Sen. Robert Kennedy had entered the presidential race as an antiwar candidate. Vice-president Hubert Humphrey also sought the nomination, which he eventually won at a convention marred by violent clashes between Chicago police and demonstrators in the streets outside the convention hall. Saddled by the Johnson administration record, Humphrey lost a closely fought election to the Republican nominee, Richard Nixon, who campaigned with a secret plan to end the war.

Antiwar Demonstrations Continue. The Women's Strike for Peace on 26 March 1969 was the first large demonstration against the war since summer 1968. Late in 1969 the so-called Vietnam Moratorium Committee organized massive antiwar protests all across the country. An estimated 100,000 protesters marched in Boston. A month later, on 15 November, 250,000 marched in Washington to protest the war.

Attempts to Start Negotiations. The early strategy of the United States had been predicated on the assumption that the Vietcong could be defeated. From 24 December 1965 to 31 January 1966 Johnson tried a bombing halt as a means to persuade the North Vietnamese to start negotiations. In 1967 Soviet premier Aleksey Kosygin tried, through conversations with British prime minister Harold Wilson in February 1967 and President Johnson at the Glassboro summit in July, to bring the United States and the North Vietnamese to the bargaining table, but the efforts were not fruitful.

Peace Talks Begin. After Johnson's 31 March 1968 speech, North Vietnam agreed to preliminary talks on 3 April. A month later the two sides agreed to begin formal talks in Paris on 12 May. On 31 October Johnson announced a full bombing halt as a prelude to expanded negotiations. Throughout the preliminary talks in 1968 the Johnson administration took the stance that political and military issues could be separated. The United States and the North Vietnamese were to negotiate a military cease-fire and mutual withdrawal of troops while the

South Vietnamese and the Vietcong were to negotiate a political settlement between themselves. This strategy was hampered by the refusal of South Vietnam to be a party to the negotiations if the Vietcong were included. After months of negotiations the peace talks were expanded in January 1969 to include the Vietcong and the South Vietnamese. The new Nixon administration continued the strategy of separating the political and military dimensions of the negotiations. Despite secret meetings between National Security Adviser Henry Kissinger and North Vietnamese negotiator Xuan Thuy, the talks made little progress during 1969.

Nixon Orders Secret Bombing Campaign. President Nixon escalated the war in 1969. For years there had been North Vietnamese and Vietcong military activity along the porous border between Vietnam and Cambodia. The U.S. military had long requested that some action be taken against enemy forces using Cambodia as a sanctuary. Johnson had rejected these requests except on the most limited basis. Within a week of Nixon's inauguration the military was again pressing for permission to press the fight into Cambodia. General Westmoreland's successor, Lt. Gen. Creighton Abrams, estimated that the enemy had recently moved 40,000 troops to Cambodian bases and that they were being supplied through the Cambodian port of Sihanoukville. Abrams recommended that the United States begin a short-term bombing campaign of the enemy facilities and transportation routes in Cambodia. Nixon originally was hesitant but ordered a retaliatory bombing strike in February. A continuing bombing campaign of the bases in Cambodia began in March and went on in secret for fourteen months. Although there was some limited press exposure, the administration did not acknowledge the bombing campaign until 1973.

The Nixon Doctrine. In July 1969 Nixon announced a shift in U.S. foreign policy that has since been dubbed the Nixon Doctrine. In the future the United States would avoid military entanglements like Vietnam and limit its support to economic and military aid. Despite the shift in policy, the war continued into the 1970s, eventuating in more than 55,000 American combat fatalities. Negotiations continued, and a ceasefire went into effect on 28 January 1973.

Sources:

David Halberstam, *The Best and the Brightest* (New York: Random House, 1972);

Stanley Karnow, *Vietnam: A History* (New York: Viking/Penguin, 1983);

Paul Kattenburg, *The Vietnam Trauma in American Foreign Policy* (New Brunswick, N.J.: Transaction Books, 1980).

DOMESTIC POLICY: GOVERNMENT, CIVIL RIGHTS, AND RACE RELATIONS

Roots of the Civil Rights Movement. The civil rights movement burst onto the American political scene in the 1960s. Before then the principal tactic in the fight against discriminatory laws was the lawsuit, usually filed by lawyers for the National Association for the Advancement of Colored People (NAACP). Southern resistance to court-ordered desegregation of public schools had been strikingly demonstrated in 1957, when President Dwight D. Eisenhower had to send U.S. Army troops to Little Rock, Arkansas, to enforce a school-integration order. The successful bus boycott led by Rev. Martin Luther King, Jr., in Montgomery, Alabama, in 1956 was a preview of civil rights tactics of the 1960s. The next year King was among the founders of the Southern Christian Leadership Conference (SCLC), whose purpose was to help provide an organizational base through which activist black clergy and their churches could mount nonviolent resistance to racism.

Lunch-Counter Sit-Ins. On 1 February 1960 four black college students from North Carolina A&T University seated themselves at a whites-only lunch counter in a Greensboro, North Carolina, Woolworth's store and refused to leave until served. By the end of the year some 70,000 participants had staged lunch-counter sit-ins in 150 towns and cities, and more than 3,600 had been arrested. The movement was successful, demonstrating the power of nonviolent confrontation as a tactic to combat racism. During that same year the need to direct the energies of college students involved in these sit-ins toward future nonviolent efforts to confront racism resulted in the formation of the Student Nonviolent Coordinating Committee (SNCC, pronounced "snick"), whose membership was then primarily students at black colleges and universities in the South. While it was not an arm of the SCLC, SNCC was at first closely connected to the organization, operating out of space provided in the SCLC office in Atlanta.

A Coalition Against Discrimination. The civil rights movement that emerged from the sit-ins was a loose coalition of the SCLC, SNCC, the Congress of Racial Equality (CORE), and the NAACP. Working to mobilize the black community and prod the federal government to take action, each of the groups mounted its own projects, often with the support of the others.

Kennedy's Slow Start on Civil Rights. The newly elected Kennedy administration held out much hope to the civil rights movement. John and Robert Kennedy had helped Martin Luther King, Jr., when he was jailed during the fall 1960 election campaign, and Kennedy campaigned on a promise to push through a new civil rights program, including an executive order against discrimination in federal housing. Yet after the election President Kennedy deferred action, earning criticism from civil rights leaders. While the Congress with which Kennedy dealt in 1961 was nominally controlled by the Democrats, it was actually in the hands of the conservative coalition, a group of conservative southern Democrats and northern Republicans who over the years had been especially effective in blocking civil rights legislation. Moreover, most committees in both the House and Senate were chaired

PACKING THE HOUSE RULES COMMITTEE

By 1900 the Committee on Rules of the House of Representatives had become one of the most powerful committees in the Congress. At the start of the 1961 session all major pieces of legislation had to go through the committee before they could get to the House floor for debate. From their position as gatekeepers, members of the Rules Committee controlled the legislative agenda. Throughout the 1950s the two ranking Democrats on the committee, Rep. Howard W. Smith (Va.) and Rep. William Colmer (Miss.), had worked effectively with conservative Republican committee members to block new social programs and civil rights initiatives.

In 1961 House Speaker Sam Rayburn came up with a way to get President John F. Kennedy's legislative agenda around this roadblock. Backed by the administration, he proposed to expand committee membership from twelve to fifteen by adding two Democrats and one Republican. Assuming these two additional Democrats would be loyal to the party leadership, it would be easier to get the necessary committee votes to move Kennedy's legislative agenda to the floor of the House. Liberal lobbying groups, especially the labor unions, worked intensively for the bill, whereas conservative groups opposed it. (The American Medical Association lobbied against it because they hoped to kill Kennedy's Medicare proposal in the House Rules Committee.) Rayburn's proposal passed by a margin of only 217–212 with the assistance of twenty-two liberal Republicans. including New Yorker John Lindsay and Pennsylvanian William Scranton. The change helped Kennedy secure passage of his initial economic package in spring 1961.

Sources: Michael Barone, *Our Country: The Shaping of America from Roosevelt to Reagan* (New York: Free Press, 1990);

Jim F. Heath, *Decade of Disillusionment: The Kennedy-Johnson Years* (Bloomington: Indiana University Press, 1975).

by conservative southern Democrats who could thus dominate the legislative process. Kennedy feared that pushing the civil rights program early in his presidency would alienate these key southern Democrats and effectively kill other parts of his legislative agenda. During his first year in office Kennedy issued an executive order establishing the federal Committee on Equal Employment Opportunity to monitor and promote nondiscriminatory hiring for federal government jobs and positions with companies that contracted with the federal government. A two-year extension of the Civil Rights Commis-

A Freedom Riders' bus on fire in Anniston, Alabama, 14 May 1961

sion, established by the Civil Rights Act of 1957, was passed on 11 September 1961. Thus Kennedy's approach in his first year in office can best be described as cautious.

The Freedom Rides. In May 1961 CORE, led by James Farmer, began the first of a series of "Freedom Rides." Interracial groups traveled on two interstate buses from Washington, D.C., to New Orleans in order to test compliance with a recent Supreme Court decision forbidding racial discrimination in terminals serving interstate travelers. On 14 May one of the buses was attacked, stoned, and burned by a mob in Anniston, Alabama. Only the actions of a plainclothes Alabama state policeman, who had boarded the bus secretly in Atlanta, prevented the mob from harming the passengers. In Birmingham, Alabama, a mob attacked the passengers from the second bus, and the police did not arrive until several minutes after the melee began. It was later learned that Public Safety Commissioner Eugene (Bull) Connor had arranged to delay the arrival of the police for fifteen minutes after the Ku Klux Klan (KKK) confronted the bus riders. Because of Attorney General Robert Kennedy's conviction that public safety was the responsibility of state and local authorities, the Justice Department at first tried to work with state and local officials to ensure the safety of civil rights demonstrators. Assured by Alabama governor John Patterson that the Freedom Riders would be protected, the Kennedy administration was shocked at the events in Anniston and Birmingham. On the next freedom ride, on 19 May, a group of SNCC volunteers traveled on buses from Birmingham to Montgomery with a state-police escort, but in Montgomery the escort left the buses, and in the absence of local police

a mob again attacked the riders. Among the injured was Robert Kennedy's aide John Siegenthaler, who had been sent to Alabama to monitor developments and to persuade local authorities to protect the Freedom Riders. After threats of violence that evening, when King spoke at a church rally, the Kennedy administration sent 500 federal marshals to Montgomery. On the next evening the marshals prevented a mob from attacking 1,200 blacks attending a meeting in support of the Freedom Riders and held off the mob until the Alabama National Guard moved in to restore order. Working through Democratic senator John Stennis of Mississippi, the Kennedy administration ensured the safety of the Freedom Riders in Mississippi and in return did not contest the arrest of some three hundred of them on local charges of "inflaming public opinion." Reacting to these events in September 1961, the Justice Department convinced the Interstate Commerce Commission to tighten regulations against racial discrimination in interstate travel and facilities. Armed with these new regulations, the Justice Department had the ammunition it needed to force local compliance. The Freedom Rides continued into 1962, but by the end of that year CORE was satisfied that segregation in interstate travel had been largely eliminated.

Integrating "Ole Miss." While the state of Mississippi had ensured safe passage for the Freedom Riders, it was not nearly as accommodating when a federal court ordered that James Meredith, a black air-force veteran, be allowed to transfer to the University of Mississippi ("Ole Miss") in fall 1962. When Meredith attempted to register on 20 September, Gov. Ross Barnett personally blocked the pathway to the admissions office and later led a white-supremacy rally at the halftime of an Ole Miss football game. To enforce the court order Attorney General Robert Kennedy sent 500 federal marshals. After the marshals settled Meredith in his dormitory on the evening of 30 September, a mob — excited by an inflammatory radio speech from Governor Barnett — attacked the marshals. The mob grew to several thousand, and the battle with the marshals lasted all night. President Kennedy ordered 5,000 army and national-guard troops onto the campus to halt the rioting. Casualties included 166 injured marshals (28 by gunshot wounds), 40 injured soldiers and national guardsmen, and two dead civilians (one a French journalist). With the campus under control, Meredith attended classes under guard and graduated the following spring. On 28 September 1962 a federal appeals court upheld a lower-court conviction of Governor Barnett on contempt charges for his role in defying the order to integrate the university.

Kennedy's Response. The lessening of tensions between the Soviet Union and the United States following the Cuban missile crisis of October 1962 allowed President Kennedy to direct more attention to domestic policy, and the riots at the University of Mississippi were at least partly responsible for making him rethink his cautious approach to civil rights. On 20 November 1962 Kennedy issued his long-delayed executive order prohibiting racial discrimination in housing built or purchased with federal funds. In February 1963 he sent a message to Congress asking for additional legislation to guarantee the right to vote for all citizens regardless of race. On 27 August 1962 Congress approved a constitutional amendment barring payment of poll taxes as a prerequisite to vote in federal elections. Following its ratification by three-fourths of the states, it became the Twenty-fourth Amendment to the Constitution on 23 January 1964.

The Birmingham Demonstrations. Events in 1963 were pivotal in aligning the administration firmly with the civil rights movement. For the site of their next segregation protest King and the SCLC chose Birmingham, Alabama, which had a reputation as one of the most segregated cities in the country. Between 1957 and 1963 there had been fifty KKK cross burnings and eighteen racially motivated bombing incidents. Bull Connor's police force had a reputation for harassment in the black community. Demonstrations began on 2 April and continued peacefully until King was served with a state-court injunction against them. Defying the order, King was arrested on 12 April and remained in jail until he was released on bond on 20 April. As the demonstrations continued, many other demonstrators were jailed. On 2 May more than six hundred protesters, primarily teenage high-school students, were arrested. The next day Connor had the police turn fire hoses on a thousand demonstrators, many of them children, and he ordered police dogs to be loosed on the protesters, only twenty of whom reached the end of their march to city hall. The widely publicized newspaper pictures and evening-news television footage of young children being injured by the water from the fire hoses and being attacked by police dogs helped create support among northerners for the civil rights movement.

The Desegregation of Birmingham. After several days of meetings with Birmingham businessmen, Justice Department official Burke Marshall negotiated an agreement by which the white community would meet the desegregation demands in return for a halt to the protests. But Alabama governor George Wallace disavowed the settlement as did many white supremacist leaders, including Connor. Dynamite explosions did serious property damage at the motel where King was staying and at his brother's house. In reaction some twenty-five hundred Birmingham blacks took to the streets, overturned cars, burned stores, and fought police and firemen. President Kennedy responded by sending three thousand troops to a nearby base and federalizing the Alabama National Guard. After these actions, the violence quickly ebbed, although there were sporadic incidents throughout the year in Birmingham, including a 15 September church bombing that killed four girls.

Wallace Blocks the "Schoolroom Door." During the crisis in Birmingham, President Kennedy and his advisers developed a strategy for taking a forceful approach on civil rights issues. Governor Wallace gave the administration an opportunity to test that strategy when he sought to bar the integration of the University of Alabama by personally standing in the doorway of the admissions building on 11 June, when two black students attempted to enroll under court order. Kennedy had already federalized the Alabama National Guard, and when confronted by federal marshals, Wallace stood aside and let the students enroll. That evening Kennedy addressed a national television audience admonishing the American public that civil rights was a moral issue and that it was time for all Americans to work for racial equality. He also stated that he would send civil rights proposals to Congress. On 19 June, as he had promised, he sent a bill with provisions that would strengthen equality of opportunity in employment, public accommodations, voting, and education.

The March on Washington. In the ten weeks after the Birmingham crisis there were more than 758 civil rights demonstrations across the South. In Jackson, Mississippi, NAACP field secretary Medgar Evers was murdered on 12 June 1963, after a series of civil rights demonstrations there. With victory in Birmingham behind them, civil rights leaders — including King of the SCLC; John Lewis of SNCC; James Farmer of CORE; A. Philip Randolph, founder and leader of the Brotherhood of Sleeping Car Porters; Whitney Young of the Urban League; and Roy Wilkins of the NAACP — planned a national "March on Washington" to lobby Congress for passage of Kennedy's civil rights proposals. At first the Kennedy administration feared that the march would have an adverse effect on Congress, endangering passage

A demonstrator being attacked by a police dog in Birmingham, Alabama, 3 May 1963

of the bills. Once it was clear that King and the others were determined to go ahead with the demonstration, however, the administration worked with the civil rights leaders to make the march a success. On 28 August 1963 more than two hundred thousand demonstrators listened to King give his now-famous "I have a dream" speech declaring his vision of equality, a time when his "four little children" would "not be judged by the color of their skin but by the content of their character," and "all of God's children, black men and white men, Jews and Gentiles, Protestants and Catholics, will be able to join hands and sing in the words of the old Negro spiritual 'Free at last! Free at last! Thank God almighty, we are free at last!'"

The Civil Rights Bill of 1964. The civil rights proposals remained in committee throughout the fall. Five days after President Kennedy was assassinated in Dallas on 22 November 1963, newly sworn-in President Lyndon Baines Johnson reaffirmed the policy of the Kennedy administration by asking Congress for the earliest possible passage of Kennedy's civil rights package. The Civil Rights Bill of 1964 passed in the House in February 1964 and was sent on to the Senate, where it was fought bitterly by Southern senators who conducted a forty-seven-day filibuster — the longest in Senate history — to delay passage of the bill. On 10 June 1964 senators voted to cut off debate, and the bill passed. Senate Minority Leader Everett McKinley Dirksen (R-Ill.) provided crucial help in getting the bill through the Senate by first declar-

ing his support and then assisting in lining up key votes to invoke the cloture rule (the parliamentary rule to close debate). The bill Johnson signed on 2 July 1964 outlawed racial discrimination in public accommodations (such as hotels, theaters, and restaurants), gave the Justice Department additional powers in dealing with segregation of schools and in bringing suit against racial discrimination, strengthened the investigatory authority of the Civil Rights Commission, and allowed the federal government to cut off federal funding to any other level of government that was discriminatory. Voting rights remained to be addressed.

Voting Rights Campaigns. In 1961 SNCC, CORE, and the NAACP began a voter-registration campaign in the South. By 1964 the project added about five hundred thousand new black voters to election rolls, but many blacks remained unregistered, especially in Mississippi. They failed to register at least in part because they were intimidated by literacy tests, by fear of job loss, and by threats of violence, including loss of life. During 1963 SNCC volunteers labored hard at organizing the Mississippi Freedom Democratic Party, a new interracial political party designed to challenge the whites-only Democratic Party of Mississippi. Some eighty thousand blacks voted for Freedom party delegates, demonstrating that — contrary to the opinion of many whites in the state — blacks did want to vote. During the "freedom summer" of 1964, hundreds of volunteers, black and white, poured into Mississippi to conduct adult-literacy classes and help blacks move through the voter-registration process. It was hard and dangerous. In addition to the highly publicized disappearance and murder of Andrew Goodman, Michael Schwerner, James Chaney, and three other civil rights workers were killed that summer. There were at least 1,000 arrests, 35 shooting incidents, 30 bombings, and 80 beatings. As a result President Johnson ordered FBI Director J. Edgar Hoover to take a more aggressive role in combating violence directed against civil rights activists. The FBI, which had spent more time monitoring the civil rights movement than it had in investigating white-supremacist groups, began a long-term campaign to infiltrate racist groups such as the KKK and to gather evidence to be used against them when they broke the law.

The Freedom Democrats. In addition to the voter registration project, the volunteers helped organize Mississippi Freedom Democratic Party precinct caucuses, county conventions, and state conventions, which selected an integrated delegation to challenge the credentials of the all-white regular-party Mississippi delegation at the Democratic National Convention in July 1964. Though the Freedom Democrats failed to unseat the regular Democrats, they won some concessions, including a ban on segregated delegations at future conventions.

The Selma Campaign. Frustrated over the failure of efforts in Mississippi, the SCLC chose Selma, Alabama, the county seat of Dallas County, as the focus of a new campaign. In that county only 3 percent of the eligible blacks were registered to vote, and local black leaders requested help from the SCLC, realizing the visibility that the presence of King, who had won the Nobel Peace Prize late in 1964, could lend to their cause. Dallas County Sheriff Jim Clark was known to be easily provoked by civil rights demonstrators, and the SCLC saw the potential violence as a means to generate public sympathy for their cause. Although the first march on 18 January 1965 was uneventful, the next day Clark roughed up a protester and arrested sixty-seven blacks attempting to register to vote. Over the next several weeks thousands were arrested, including King. Clark's treatment of the demonstrators, closely covered by the national media, became more and more brutal. In one case he and his deputies arrested 165 protesters and then chased them out of town with electric cattle prods. On 17 February a state trooper shot a demonstrator, who died two days later. On 3 March King announced a protest march from Selma to the state capital at Montgomery, a distance of fifty-four miles. Although Governor Wallace banned the march, Hosea Williams, an SCLC official, and John Lewis of SNCC started out with 600 marchers on 7 May. As they crossed the Edmund Pettus Bridge on the outskirts of Selma, the marchers were attacked by Alabama state troopers with tear gas and clubs, and as they turned back to flee toward Selma they were set upon by Sheriff Clark and his men. Given full play by the networks, the beatings on the Edmund Pettus Bridge provoked moral outrage across the United States. King, who had spent the day preaching at his Atlanta church, rushed back to Selma and prepared to lead a new march on 9 May. A federal judge issued a temporary injunction to stop the marches until he could rule on the validity of Wallace's ban, creating a dilemma for King, who knew defiance of federal officials could jeopardize future federal support for the movement. Florida governor Leroy Collins, sent to Selma as President Johnson's personal emissary, worked out an agreement between King and Alabama authorities: state police would block the bridge and allow King and his marchers to stop, offer a prayer, and return to Selma unharmed. This compromise deeply wounded the civil rights movement. SNCC members were already convinced that King's absence from the first march signaled his unwillingness to risk his own safety while SNCC voter-registration volunteers were in danger every day. Now, when King ordered the marchers to return to Selma, they were angry at what they perceived as a betrayal. A third attempt to march to Montgomery was successful. President Johnson federalized the Alabama National Guard, which together with federal marshals lined the route to protect the marchers. Leaving Selma on 21 March, twenty-five thousand marchers took five days to walk to Montgomery, where King and other civil rights leaders addressed the group from the steps of the state capitol.

The Voting Rights Bill of 1965. President Johnson's landslide victory in the 1964 presidential election carried enough new liberal Democrats into both houses of Congress to break the conservative coalition blocking his domestic legislation. In January 1965, with this strong legislative majority in place, Johnson directed newly appointed Attorney General Nicholas Katzenbach to begin drafting a new civil rights bill whose focus would be on voting rights. President Johnson took advantage of the national outrage over events in Selma to push for passage of civil rights legislation. In a nationally televised address to a rare joint session of both houses of Congress on 15 March, Johnson called for a national effort to eliminate bigotry and hatred. He also outlined the basic provisions of his voting-rights proposals, which he sent to Congress four days later. Working closely with congressional leaders, including minority leader Dirksen, Katzenbach ushered the proposals through both houses of Congress, where they passed with impressive margins despite a conservative filibuster in the Senate, by 3 August 1965, and Johnson signed the bill three days later. Applying primarily to the southern states, the bill empowered federal authorities to take over the voter-registration process in jurisdictions where discrimination existed and to suspend literacy requirements. Changes in state and local election laws had to be preapproved by the Justice Department. The changes wrought by this law showed their impact by the 1968 elections. By then voter registration of blacks had gone from 31 percent of those eligible in 1965 to 57 percent of those eligible; blacks were running for office and winning. In Dallas County, Alabama, newly registered black voters defeated Sheriff Jim Clark when he ran for reelection.

Legislative Results of the Civil Rights Movement. The passage of the Voting Rights Act provided the federal government with a powerful new tool to attack voting discrimination. Under Eisenhower's 1957 Civil Rights Act the Civil Rights Commission and the Justice Department were required to investigate civil rights abuses, developing evidence and filing suit in each separate local jurisdiction on a case-by-case basis, a process by which it would have taken decades to remedy racial injustice across the South. The Voting Rights Act of 1965 established a quick test to determine probable discrimination, allowing federal officials to move quickly. A provision giving the federal government power to deny funding to segregated school districts was added to the Higher Education Act passed later in 1965, providing the federal government with a new tool to speed the process of desegregating public schools. The government no longer had to sue each individual school district to force compliance. With the exception of legislation to bar discrimination in the sale or rental of housing, the civil rights movement had achieved its purpose, the elimination of the legal structure which had allowed racial discrimination to flourish. It was an accomplishment that has been called the "second reconstruction."

The Break-Up of the Civil Rights Coalition. Just as the civil rights movement reached the zenith of its power, however, it began to fall apart. Having accomplished most of their original agenda, the various groups that made up the movement were not in agreement over future actions. Moreover, distrust among leaders had been growing since Selma. Black separatists and nationalists had begun to offer a strident alternative to the nonviolence of the civil rights movement, an alternative which had increasing resonance in the black community. With the escalation of the war in Vietnam, civil rights leaders became openly critical of Johnson's war policy, angering Johnson, whose administration became less responsive to their protests.

White Backlash. Urban violence in black sections of northern cities during 1964 and 1965 tended to decrease the enormous public sympathy aroused by civil rights violations in Mississippi and Alabama. In July 1964 riots erupted in the Harlem and Brownsville sections of New York City and were followed by racial disturbances in Rochester, Chicago, Jersey City, Elizabeth, Paterson, and Philadelphia. In August 1965 the black neighborhood of Watts in Los Angeles was the site of six days of arson, looting, sniper fire, and rock throwing over a 150-block area. Thirty-four people were killed before the California National Guard brought the area under control.

White House Civil Rights Conference. In conjunction with its War on Poverty the Johnson administration planned a 1965 conference to discuss issues of economic opportunity in the black community. A report by Department of Health, Education, and Welfare official Daniel Patrick Moynihan, which focused on the disintegration of the black family as the leading cause of poverty among blacks, was to be the centerpiece of the conference discussions, but when it was released to the public in August 1965, black leaders attacked the report as racist because it located the fundamental problem of ghetto life in the absence of adult male role models in female-headed households. The conference was postponed until June 1966. By that time SNCC had come out against the Vietnam War, and King had uttered muted criticism of it (though he did not become an outspoken critic of the war until 1967). With the White House controlling the agenda and with most of the delegates handpicked invitees, the primary accomplishment of the conference was the fact that those in attendance did not condemn the war.

Civil Rights Protests in Chicago. King turned his attention northward to Chicago, where he led demonstrations against segregation in the public schools during the summer and fall 1965. The following spring he began a campaign for fair-housing practices in Chicago. On 10 July 1966 he appeared at a rally at Soldier Field sponsored by a coalition of forty-five local civil rights groups calling for an end to racial discrimination in Chicago housing and urging blacks and Puerto Ricans in that city to boycott banks and businesses that discriminated against

them. Two days later a riot erupted in a black neighborhood of the city. King worked hard to restore peace, and once the riot was over he led a series of demonstrations in the face of escalating violence by whites against the protesters. On 26 August 1966 King reached an agreement with Chicago civic leaders, who pledged to uphold the principle of fair housing and to attempt to end de facto segregation in Chicago residential patterns.

Operation Breadbasket. At the same time he was personally directing the fair-housing campaign, King put a young minister, Jesse Jackson, in charge of Operation Breadbasket, a strategy to implement fair-employment practices that had already been successful in Philadelphia and Atlanta. The basic technique employed boycotts of businesses where employment practices discriminated against blacks, followed by negotiations for increased hiring of black workers. Jackson forged agreements with a large local dairy, soft-drink bottling plants, and the A&P grocery stores in Chicago. Yet, despite the initial success of both fair-housing and fair-employment campaigns in Chicago, the net results did little to improve the lives of the city's poor blacks.

Meredith's March. On 5 June 1966 James Meredith, who had integrated the University of Mississippi in 1962, began a 220-mile solitary march across the state to show blacks that they should not be afraid to exercise their voting rights. The very next day Meredith was wounded by a shotgun blast. As he lay in the hospital the leaders of the five major civil rights groups gathered in Memphis to complete his march. During the twenty days they were together, media coverage alerted the American public to the split in the movement that had begun a year earlier. CORE and SNCC were at variance with the SCLC, the NAACP, and the Urban League on the issue of nonviolence. Floyd McKissick, the new leader of CORE, argued that a nonviolent approach had outlived its usefulness, that white violence should be met in kind with black violence. On the night of 16 June Stokely Carmichael of SNCC, having just been released from a brief detention in jail, addressed a crowd of three thousand marchers and angrily said that the demand for freedom had to be supplanted with a demand for "black power." By the time the march ended on 26 June there had been several violent clashes between the marchers, police, and white mobs, and the chant of "black power" had drowned out "freedom now." The various groups were heading in different directions.

Backlash and the Elections. White voters — who often held the mistaken view that black urban rioters were supporters of militant revolutionary groups such as the Black Panther Party, founded in 1966 — became increasingly alarmed by urban violence in the mid and late 1960s. In addition to the riots in Chicago during 1966, there were racial disturbances in twenty other cities including Omaha, New York, Atlanta, Los Angeles, and Detroit. The riots, the shift of the civil rights focus to the North, and increasing black militancy spurred a backlash among white voters that manifested itself in the election of 1966. Law-and-order candidates were elected to Congress, and the large Democratic majority of 1965 and 1966 was whittled down. Riots in summer 1967 reinforced the popularity of law-and-order politicians. A Johnson civil rights proposal which included a strong fair-housing provision failed to get through the Congress in 1966 and 1967.

The Civil Rights Bill of 1968. A civil rights bill including a fair-housing provision finally got through the Senate, after extensive legislative maneuvering, on 11 March 1968 and went on to the House. After King was assassinated on 4 April in Memphis, Tennessee, where he was leading demonstrations in support of striking sanitation workers, black communities across the United States erupted in violence. In the wake of the assassination and the resulting riots, the House passed the bill on 10 April, and it was signed into law by President Johnson the next day. In addition to fair-housing provisions that covered 80 percent of all housing, the new law also had stringent law-and-order provisions punishing individuals who traveled interstate or used interstate means of communications to foment riots.

The Poor People's Campaign. Before his death King had begun planning a campaign designed to shift the federal government's civil rights agenda toward economic issues important to blacks. After King's death, his successor as head of the SCLC, Rev. Ralph Abernathy, decided to go ahead with King's Poor People's Campaign. On 12 May 1968 some three thousand poor people moved into "Resurrection City," a temporary shanty city in a Washington, D.C., park, to dramatize their need for jobs. A crowd of fifty thousand attended a rally at the Lincoln Memorial on 19 June, but speeches by Abernathy and others failed to stir the crowd or Congress. The mood of the country had changed, and the campaign accomplished little. The remaining residents of the shanty town were evicted by police on 24 June, after their permit expired.

Civil Rights and Nixon's Southern Strategy. Richard Nixon, campaigning on a law-and-order platform, won the presidential election in November 1968 with strong support from white southern voters. While Nixon did not turn his back on desegregation, his administration acted to solidify the support of southern whites for the Republican Party — a tactic labeled Nixon's "Southern strategy." Nixon's attorney general, John Mitchell, proposed and got an extension of the 1965 Voting Rights Act, but to mollify southerners he had its provisions extended to the entire nation. Late in 1969 the Departments of Justice and of Health, Education, and Welfare began to delay the implementation of school-desegregation orders. Nixon also used the tactic of nominating southerners to high positions. To appeal to the South he nominated South Carolina federal judge Clement F. Haynsworth to fill a vacancy on the U.S. Supreme Court. The nomination was defeated by the Senate on 21 November 1969

through the efforts of critics who charged that Haynsworth was a racist. A second southern judge nominated for the same seat, G. Harold Carswell, was also rejected by the Senate early in 1970. Later in the year Nixon succeeded in filling the vacancy when the Senate confirmed the nomination of Minnesotan Harry Blackmun.

Sources:

Jack Bass, *Taming the Storm: The Life and Times of Judge Frank M. Johnson and the South's Fight over Civil Rights* (New York: Doubleday, 1993);

Taylor Branch, *Parting the Waters: America in the King Years, 1954–63* (New York: Simon & Schuster, 1968);

Manning Marable, *Race, Reform and Rebellion: The Second Reconstruction in Black America, 1945–1990*, second edition (Jackson: University Press of Mississippi, 1991);

Robert Weisbrot, *Freedom Bound: A History of America's Civil Rights Movement* (New York: Norton, 1990);

Harris Wofford, *Of Kennedys and Kings: Making Sense of the Sixties* (Pittsburgh: University of Pittsburgh Press, 1980).

DOMESTIC POLICY: GOVERNMENT AND THE ECONOMY

Postwar Economy Sluggish. After World War II the efficiency and productivity of the U.S. economy improved markedly. From 1945 to 1975 output per hour of labor increased 120 percent while output per standard unit of energy increased 23 percent. Work hours in agriculture fell from 19.2 to 7.5 percent of the total hours spent on all types of production while output per acre increased 33 percent. At the same time though, the economy was sluggish. There were four recessions between 1945 and 1961: 1948–1949, 1953–1954, 1957–1958, and 1960–1961 — three of them during Dwight D. Eisenhower's presidency. Economic growth had hovered around the 2 percent level during the 1950s, and unemployment ran high. Beginning in 1957 the monthly unemployment rate dropped below 5 percent only three times. As the 1960 presidential election campaign got under way, the 1960–1961 recession began, with recovery from the 1957–1958 recession still incomplete.

Kennedy Promises Economic Growth. John F. Kennedy's 1960 campaign promise "to get America moving again" referred primarily to stimulating the American economy. Kennedy wanted economic growth at an annual rate of 4–6 percent and unemployment at 4 percent. A growth rate of 4–6 percent would match the growth levels being reported by the Soviet Union, and it would generate the additional revenues Kennedy needed to pay for his new defense policy and for the Medicare and federal-aid-to-education programs he intended to introduce. Lowering unemployment to 4 percent or below would also make revenues available for these programs, and it would meet the traditional Democratic Party platform promise of full employment. (Economists consider unemployment levels at or below 4 percent full employment.)

A 1962 White House meeting to discuss taxes: (seated) Budget Director Kermit Gordon, Undersecretary of Treasury Henry Fowler, Secretary of Treasury C. Douglas Dillon, President John F. Kennedy, and Assistant Secretary of Treasury for Tax Affairs Stanley Surrey; (standing) Walter Heller, chairman of the Council of Economic Advisers, and Theodore Sorensen, special counsel to the President

Differing Advice on the Economy. Among Kennedy's economic advisers there were three schools of thought on how to deal with the economy. Treasury Secretary C. Douglas Dillon and Federal Reserve Board Chairman William McChesney Martin thought it important to fight inflation, to increase business confidence, and to reduce the balance-of-payments deficit in foreign trade. They also believed that technological changes in industry caused unemployment and that the remedy was through better education, retraining, and area redevelopment. Two different groups, both proponents of the theories of British economist John Maynard Keynes, advanced this solution for a slow economy: direct use of governmental fiscal and monetary policy to stimulate growth and reduce unemployment. Moreover, both groups thought that the recession should be fought by using a planned federal budget deficit to stimulate the economy. That meant that the government would go into debt by cutting taxes or increasing spending on social programs, transferring money from federal coffers to people's pockets. People would then have more money to spend and thus buy more products, causing business to prosper. As businesses reacted to increased sales by hiring new employees, the resulting increased tax revenues would eventually eliminate the deficit. The first of these groups, led by Harvard economist John Kenneth Galbraith, favored massive increases in public spending. Galbraith had political support from

Senators Paul Douglas (D-Ill.) and Albert Gore (D-Tenn.). The second group, led by Walter Heller, chairman of the Council of Economic Advisers (CEA), considered taxes to be a fiscal drag on the economy and wanted a massive tax reduction. All three groups thought that inflation could be fought by publicizing voluntary wage and price guidelines backed by vigorous moral persuasion from the president and other governmental officials.

Initial Economic Package. The theme of Kennedy's January 1961 State of the Union address was that the economy was in trouble. Three days later he sent Congress an economic growth and recovery package consisting of twelve measures, of which seven were passed within the first six months. They were an increase in the minimum wage from $1.00 to $1.25 per hour and an extension of the minimum wage to a larger pool of workers, an increase in supplemental unemployment compensation plus increased aid to children of unemployed workers, increased Social Security benefits to a larger pool of people, emergency relief for feed-grain farmers, area redevelopment, vocational training for displaced workers, and federal funding for home building and slum eradication. Kennedy also proposed aid to elementary and secondary schools. Overall, this approach was cautious and reflected the advice of Martin and Dillon rather than the Keynesians.

The Fight with "Big Steel." Early in 1962 Kennedy got a chance to see how well his appeal for voluntary adherence to CEA wage and price guidelines would work in practice. The contract between the United Steel Workers and the steel companies was about to expire, and the administration wanted to avoid a prolonged strike, like the 116-day strike that had accompanied negotiations over the previous contract in 1959. The administration also wanted to avoid a hike in the price of steel. On 23 January 1962 Kennedy; Labor Secretary Arthur Goldberg; Roger Blough, President of U.S. Steel Corporation; and David McDonald, President of the United Steel Workers, met secretly and worked out a wage agreement that was within the CEA guidelines. On 31 March the union and U.S. Steel formalized a new contract that added marginally to fringe benefits and increased wages by ten cents per hour — the smallest increase since 1942. On 10 April Blough met with Kennedy and Goldberg and informed them that U.S. Steel would raise prices across the board by six dollars per ton — a 3.5 percent price increase. Goldberg reacted sharply and accused Blough of violating the January agreement. That same day several other major steel companies announced an identical price hike. At a press conference on 11 April Kennedy assailed the price hike as unpatriotic and against the national interest. Immediately, the Defense Department announced that it would buy steel only from those companies that held prices down. The Justice Department began an investigation of price-fixing in the steel industry, sending the FBI to Pittsburgh to begin an immediate investigation, and Congress announced that hearings would be held to investigate monopolistic practices in the steel industry. In the face of adverse publicity and government pressure, steel-industry leaders announced on 13 April that they would rescind their price increases. A year later a federal grand jury indicted executives from U.S. Steel and six other steel companies on charges of illegal price-fixing. The immediate cost to the administration was a breach with the business community that took months to heal.

Tax Relief for Business. By mid 1962 Kennedy was convinced the economy needed the additional stimulation that could be provided through a tax cut. The recession was over, but unemployment was still at 5.6 percent (down from 7 percent in April 1961), and the stock market was in a deep slump. Kennedy used his commencement address at Yale University to reach out to the business community, suggesting that business needed the tax relief that would be provided by liberalizing the depreciation allowance on new plants and equipment and by giving business a 7 percent investment tax credit. These proposals became law on 16 October 1962.

Kennedy Makes Peace with Business. Three other pieces of legislation during 1962 helped Kennedy to reconcile his differences with the business community. In

1961 Sen. Estes Kefauver (D-Tenn.), who had chaired the 1960 hearings on the drug industry, introduced a bill that would amend the patent laws and promote price competition among drug companies while giving the Food and Drug Administration (FDA) greater power to police drug quality. Failing to get his bill through in 1961, Kefauver asked the administration for help in 1962. In March 1962 Kennedy sent Congress a bill that retained Kefauver's provision for increased FDA police power, but to Kefauver's dismay it mollified the pharmaceutical industry by eliminating the portions of his bill that would have promoted price competition. In 1962 the administration also supported a bill that would establish a new Communications Satellite Corporation (COMSAT) that would have a near monopoly on satellite communications. Half the stock would be sold to the public, and half would be sold to private corporations, with AT&T guaranteed a 29 percent share. Critics in Congress held up the bill until 10 July 1962, when AT&T launched Telstar — a communications satellite — and successfully beamed live television images from Europe to the United States. The effort was a public-relations coup for AT&T and helped promote passage of the bill. A third measure that improved Kennedy's standing with big business involved the Du Pont Company, which as a result of an antitrust decision had been required to divest itself of General Motors stock. Du Pont did so by giving shares to Du Pont stockholders as dividends, and a bill was introduced in Congress to provide tax relief for those stockholders. The Treasury Department backed the bill, but the Justice Department opposed it. Kennedy broke the impasse in favor of the Du Pont Company, and the bill was passed.

Trade Bill Passes. The Trade Expansion Act, passed on 11 October 1962, was considered Kennedy's major legislative accomplishment of the year. Designed to expand U.S. trade with Europe in anticipation of Great Britain's entry into the European Common Market, the bill authorized the president to reduce tariffs up to 50 percent without seeking congressional approval, if other countries made similar concessions in return. The bill also authorized the president to negotiate the total elimination of tariffs on goods for which 80 percent of the global market was the United States and Common Market countries. With the extensive level of trade between the United States and Britain, the bill, which was highly touted by the American business community, would have placed the United States in an extremely favorable trade position if Britain had in fact entered the Common Market; but President Charles de Gaulle of France blocked Britain's entry, and the impact of the bill was muted. (Britain did not join the Common Market until 1972.)

Kennedy Proposes a Cut in Income Taxes. On 14 December 1962 Kennedy gave a major speech at the Economics Club in New York City, calling for massive across-the-board cuts in both individual and corporate income taxes to take place over a three-year period. In

In general salaries in the private sector were more generous than those in the public sector. Federal government salaries for 1964 are compared with comparable figures for the private sector for 1963.

	PUBLIC SECTOR	PRIVATE SECTOR
Cabinet member or top-level executive	$25,000	$35,000-$60,000
Undersecretary or mid-level executive	$21,000	$30,000-$45,000
Top attorney	$17,700	$23,724
Experienced engineer	$15,191	$17,526
Personnel director	$12,972	$13,440
Office manager	$ 7,979	$ 7,404
Beginning attorney	$ 6,698	$ 7,452
Beginning accountant	$ 5,606	$ 6,156
Experienced typist	$ 4,525	$ 4,125
Accounting clerk	$ 4,525	$ 4,063
Beginning typist	$ 4,025	$ 3,485

Source: "How Much It Pays to Work for the Government," *U.S. News & World Report*, 57 (20 July 1964):49-50.

early 1963 inflation was stable, corporate profits were at a record high, and the stock market had rebounded, but unemployment was still considered too high at 5.7 percent. On 24 January 1963 Kennedy sent Congress a proposal that called for $13.6 billion in tax cuts over three years. Congress was still considering the bill at the time of Kennedy's assassination in November 1963. His successor, Lyndon Baines Johnson, made passage of Kennedy's tax proposal one of his three major priorities for the 1964 legislative session — the others being the Civil Rights Bill and the War on Poverty. The tax proposal passed Congress and was signed into law on 26 February 1965.

Kennedy's Economic Legacy. President Johnson inherited a strong economy from President Kennedy. Between 1961 and 1967 the gross national product (GNP) for the United States grew from $503 billion to $807 billion. The growth rate in 1964 and 1965 gave Johnson an annual dividend of $4–5 billion in extra revenues to spend. Moreover, throughout the Kennedy years, the in-

flation rate hovered about 1 percent lower than in the Eisenhower years, and for the first two years of Johnson's presidency the inflation rate was just under 2 percent. In 1965 inflation began to pick up slightly, but the GNP grew by $9 billion and unemployment stood at 4.1 percent, or almost at the full-employment level. The economy looked even better during the winter of 1966: real growth (adjusted for inflation) was 9 percent, and with unemployment at 3.8 percent the economy was robust and showed every promise of being able to support Johnson's War on Poverty and his Great Society programs.

Impact of the Vietnam War. After Johnson escalated the Vietnam War by ordering the bombing campaign against North Vietnam in February 1965 and by sending in U.S. combat forces later in the year — and as the commitment of men and matériels continued growing over the next three years — incredible pressure was placed on the economy. Johnson tried to pay for both the war and his domestic programs with his so-called guns-

and-butter budgets. The inflation rate began rising, reaching 3 percent in 1967 and 5 percent in 1968. In the same time period the federal deficit grew rapidly, going from $8.5 billion to $25.2 billion.

The Credit Crunch of 1966. During spring 1966 Federal Reserve Chairman Martin became concerned about the increase in the rate of inflation and persuaded the Federal Reserve Board to reduce the supply of new money available to commercial banks. This tightening of the money supply restricted the availability of loans for mortgages. As a result housing starts (housing construction begun) in 1966 were one half those of 1965. The tight money supply began limiting funds for loans to businesses and to state and local governments. There was a substantial outcry in the business and financial community, and the Federal Reserve Board eased its tight-money policies on 1 September 1966.

"Jawboning" on Wage-and-Price Guidelines. As during the Kennedy administration, the CEA and Johnson continued to set voluntary wage-and-price guidelines, using moral persuasion or what they called "jawboning" to get companies and unions to adhere to them. During 1965 and 1966 the guidelines urged that increases in wages and prices be kept below 3.2 percent. The wage agreements in 1965 with the steelworkers and in 1966 with the aluminum workers both adhered to these guidelines.

CEA Recommends Action on Inflation. In 1966 the CEA became concerned about the rate of inflation. It urged Johnson to cut back on nondefense spending and to suspend temporarily the 7 percent investment tax credit, and it liberalized depreciation allowances that Kennedy had championed in 1962. On 10 October 1966 Congress, at the administration's request, suspended the investment tax credit, but on 9 March 1967 — with the economy starting to look sluggish — they restored it ten months earlier than planned. Johnson announced a budget cut of $5.3 billion from domestic programs, especially the War on Poverty.

Johnson Recommends Tax Surcharge. The Johnson administration became increasingly concerned with inflation during 1967. On 3 August Johnson asked Congress to impose a temporary 10 percent income-tax surcharge, which he hoped would dampen consumer spending and in turn curb the rise in the cost of living. Congressman Wilbur Mills (D-Ohio), chairman of the House Ways and Means Committee, held up the measure until he got a guarantee of further reductions in federal spending. The surcharge that finally became law on 28 June 1968 was tied to a $6 billion budget reduction. In December 1968, Johnson's next-to-last month in office, the growth rate was 4 percent and the unemployment rate was only 3.3 percent, but the inflation rate had reached 4.7 percent. The cost of living was growing faster than the economy.

Nixon Moves Slowly. Inaugurated in January 1969, President Richard M. Nixon moved slowly on the econ-

omy. Although some economic advisers were calling for wage-and-price controls, Nixon avoided them, relying instead on some minor trimming of federal spending during his first year. By mid 1970 the inflation rate had reached 6.5 percent.

Sources:

Congressional Quarterly Almanac, 21 (1965);

Congressional Quarterly Almanac, 22 (1966);

James Gilbert, *Another Chance* (Philadelphia: Temple University Press, 1981);

Jim F. Heath, *Decade of Disillusionment: The Kennedy-Johnson Years* (Bloomington: Indiana University Press, 1975);

Nelson Lichtenstein., ed., *Political Profiles: The Johnson Years* (New York: Facts on File, 1976);

Lichtenstein, ed., *Political Profiles: The Kennedy Years* (New York: Facts on File, 1976);

Allen J. Matusow, *The Unraveling of America: A History of Liberalism in the 1960s* (New York: Harper & Row, 1984);

Hobart Rowen, *The Free Enterprisers: Kennedy, Johnson, and the Business Community* (New Rochelle, N.Y.: Arlington House, 1969).

DOMESTIC POLICY: THE GREAT SOCIETY

The Torch Is Passed. During the 1950s, much to the disappointment of some conservative Republicans, President Dwight D. Eisenhower's administration did not dismantle the New Deal social programs of the Franklin D. Roosevelt and Harry S Truman administrations. Eisenhower's social policy was not especially innovative and tended to preserve the status quo. Sen. John F. Kennedy won the 1960 presidential election on a promise "to get America moving again," primarily by stimulating economic growth. He promised to create a cabinet-level urban affairs department, to provide federal aid to elementary and secondary education, and to establish a medical care program for the elderly.

The First One Hundred Days. In his first State of the Union address Kennedy reiterated the necessity of stimulating the economy, and within the next week he sent Congress twelve specific measures. By the end of June seven of the measures had been enacted into law. Several of these measures were precursors to President Lyndon B. Johnson's War on Poverty and Great Society programs. The Area Redevelopment Act offered grants to communities in economically depressed areas that would help them attract industry through the improvement of public facilities. It also provided low-cost loans to businesses that agreed to locate in these communities. The Omnibus Housing Act was designed to stimulate urban renewal by providing federal funds for homebuilding and clearance of slums. The Manpower Development and Training Act was designed to provide vocational training to workers whose jobs had become obsolete.

Juvenile Delinquency. Another preview of Johnson's War on Poverty was included in Kennedy's Juvenile Delinquency and Youth Offenses Act of 1961. The act provided funds to help local communities fight juvenile delinquency by building youth centers, establishing job pro-

Succeeding President John F. Kennedy, whose ability to charm even the most jaded reporter had made *charisma* a household word, President Lyndon B. Johnson faced inevitable difficulties. Kennedy was good-looking, cultured, and athletic despite back problems. Johnson was homely, "folksy," and physically clumsy. Despite his considerable political skills, Kennedy gave the impression of being statesmanlike. Johnson, noted for his off-color language and sexual jokes, was called "earthy" by his friends and "crude" by his detractors, and he had a reputation for political wheeling and dealing.

When Johnson tried to appear sober and presidential, he seemed stiff — and sometimes almost foreboding. His attempts to project a warm, family-man image also failed to endear him to the public. In May 1964, a few months into his presidency, Johnson was asked to pose for photographs with the family beagles, Him and Her. In the manner of some handlers of hunting dogs, Johnson picked them up by their ears. The dogs were unhappy, as were the American Society for the Prevention of Cruelty to Animals, the American Kennel Club, and thousands of other dog lovers, many of whom called or wrote the White House or sent impassioned letters to newspapers and national magazines. In October 1965, after removal of his gall bladder and a kidney stone, Johnson made the mistake of listening to staffers who thought showing his twelve-inch surgical scar to reporters would add a human touch to stories about the president's health. Instead, widely published photographs of the president lifting his shirt to show the incision on his belly brought storms of criticism that Johnson's behavior was unpresidential.

Johnson was obsessed with his image. On the campaign trail in 1964 journalist Theodore H. White counted at least nine different Lyndon Johnsons, from a solemn "Mr. President" and a majestic "Imperial Lyndon" to a humble and pious "Preacher Lyndon" and a country-style "Sheriff Johnson." Yet, finally, no amount of image making could overcome the fact that by 1968, despite Johnson's considerable achievements in civil rights and other areas of domestic legislation, his Vietnam War policy had made him widely unpopular with hawks and doves alike.

Sources: Paul R. Henggeler, *In His Steps: Lyndon Johnson and the Kennedy Mystique* (Chicago: Ivan R. Dee, 1991);

Theodore H. White, *The Making of the President 1964* (New York: Atheneum, 1965).

grams for teenagers, and developing organizations to get people involved in decision making that affected their children. One result of this act was New York City's Mobilization for Youth program. The community organizations founded under the program were soon addressing not only juvenile delinquency but also many other local issues, including school board elections. These new local organizations operated outside mainstream channels and thus challenged established political leaders by intruding on their turf.

Failure on Federal Aid to Education. As he had promised during his campaign, Kennedy sent Congress a proposal for federal aid to elementary and secondary education. Proposals for such aid had been introduced regularly since the 1930s but had always foundered because many in Congress — particularly in the conservative coalition — feared that federal aid to education would open the door to federal regulation in a policy area where local control was considered sacrosanct. Kennedy's mixed signals on the controversial issue of aid to parochial schools — he said first that no such aid should be provided and then suggested that special-purpose loans were permissible — gave the opponents of the bill in the House of Representatives enough ammunition to kill it on 30 August 1961. Proposals to provide aid to higher education died because Kennedy failed to push hard enough for their passage.

Other Domestic Proposals Fail. On 1 January 1962 the House voted down Kennedy's plan to create a cabinet-level department of housing and urban affairs, and on 17 July 1962 the Senate tabled his Medicare proposal. With the exception of bills passed during its first six months, the Kennedy administration record on social legislation for 1961 and 1962 was weak. This failure may be blamed in part on inept leadership, but during its first two years the Kennedy administration was forced to focus most of its attention on a wave of serious foreign policy crises. It also had to deal with a Congress that was dominated by a conservative coalition of Republicans and Southern Democrats, especially in the House. These two groups had been effective in the 1950s in combining to defeat social-welfare proposals and civil rights legislation. Moreover, most of the committees in both the House and the Senate were chaired by conservative Southern Democrats, who were thus positioned to block proposals from getting out of committee. Kennedy's ability to work with Congress was also complicated by changes in leadership. Vice-president Johnson, who had been an effective Senate majority leader, had been succeeded by Sen. Mike Mansfield (D-Mont.). Legendary Speaker of the House Sam Rayburn (D-Texas) died in November 1961 and was replaced by Rep. John McCormack (D-Mass.). Mansfield and McCormack were both capable men, but they were new to their leadership positions and had much to learn about mobilizing support for the president's programs.

Attention Turns to Poverty. In May 1962 Kennedy, influenced by Michael Harrington's March 1962 book

The Other America, which painted a stark picture of poverty in the United States, gave a commencement address at Yale, in which he called for programs to provide job training, ensure adequate nutrition, and assist education in an attempt to attack the problem of poverty. With the easing of tensions between the United States and the Soviet Union that followed the Cuban missile crisis of October 1962, Kennedy was able to turn his attention back to his domestic agenda. In 1963 he reintroduced his proposal for aid to elementary and secondary education. Late that spring he asked his Council of Economic Advisers to set up task forces to study the problem of poverty and to draft proposals for legislation to be introduced in 1964. After Kennedy's assassination in November, President Johnson requested that the task forces continue their work.

Johnson's War on Poverty. In his State of the Union address on 8 January 1964 Johnson announced that it was time for the United States to declare war on poverty and promised to introduce legislation that would establish comprehensive programs designed to eradicate it. Rather than simply providing money and jobs, Johnson hoped to equip individuals with skills which would enable them to break the poverty cycle. The Economic Opportunity Act of 1964, signed into law by Johnson on 20 August, set up a new agency, the Office of Economic Opportunity (OEO), to administer ten programs to help the poor, including Head Start for preschool children, a jobs corps for youths, job training for adults, a work-study program for needy college students, grants for farmers and rural businesses, loans to individuals and businesses willing to hire the unemployed, a domestic version of the Peace Corps — Volunteers in Service to America (VISTA) — and a community-action program modeled after the programs established in Kennedy's 1961 juvenile delinquency bill. Other social legislation that Johnson got enacted during 1964 included formal authorization for the food-stamp program begun as a pilot program by executive order in 1961, a program providing free legal counsel for indigents, a housing act that extended funding for existing programs of urban and rural renewal, and a program to build urban mass transit.

The Great Society. During his commencement address at the University of Michigan on 22 May 1964 Johnson enunciated the theme for his presidency. The United States was wealthy enough to improve the lives of all Americans, he said, not just in quantitative terms but qualitatively as well. America could become a "Great Society." Anticipating success in the 1964 presidential election, Johnson set fifteen task forces to work on proposals to be introduced in the 1965 legislative session.

Conditions Ideal for a Social Agenda. The political and economic atmosphere was ideal for pushing Johnson's domestic agenda. Tensions between the United States and the Soviet Union were substantially eased, and the Vietnam War was still a minor conflict with limited U.S. involvement. The economy was robust. Having been an effective leader in the Senate, Johnson knew the legislative process well and used his knowledge to good advantage in pushing his programs through Congress. He was also able in 1964 to invoke the memory of President Kennedy, urging passage of what originally had been Kennedy's agenda as a memorial to the fallen leader. The 1964 elections gave Johnson a landslide victory over his Republican opponent, Sen. Barry Goldwater. The power of the conservative coalition was broken by the large number of new Democrats elected on Johnson's coattails, giving him large majorities in the House and Senate with which to work in both the 1965 and 1966 sessions of Congress. Those Republicans who were elected tended to be moderates.

Unfinished Business. In his 1965 State of the Union address Johnson placed the greatest stress on his domestic agenda. He urged passage of a Medicare program and federal aid to elementary and secondary education, unfinished business from Kennedy's New Frontier. He also called for passage of an aid package for higher education and new housing programs. Three days later, on 7 January, Johnson sent the Medicare proposal to Congress, and on 12 January he sent a bill to provide federal aid to elementary and secondary education.

Medicare/Medicaid and Other Health Proposals. The resurrected Medicare proposal provided a compulsory hospital-care program for the elderly, funded by an increase in social security taxes. Republicans suggested an amendment that would set up a voluntary program to pay doctors' fees — funded by contributions from participating individuals and the government. Their motivation was twofold. They wanted to take some credit for the health-care legislation if it passed, but they also hoped that the additional Medicaid component would make the program seem too costly and thus prevent the bill's passage. Even with the addition of Medicaid, however, the bill passed, and Johnson signed it on 30 July. Six additional health-care bills were passed by Congress and became law in 1965: the program for immunization of children was continued; funding was provided for training mental-health workers and teachers of the mentally and physically handicapped, as well as for research on teaching the handicapped and disabled; health-research facilities were funded; funding was voted to construct teaching facilities for health-care professions; a loan program was enacted for students preparing for health professions; grants were made available for medical libraries; and funding was provided for vocational-rehabilitation training programs.

Aid to Elementary and Secondary Schools. Congress was still resisting federal aid to elementary and secondary schools because of its fear of federal controls, and the Johnson administration was able to get the bill passed only by dropping its most controversial provision, which allowed the federal government to deny or cut off funds from schools continuing to practice racial segregation. Once this provision was dropped, the bill passed quickly

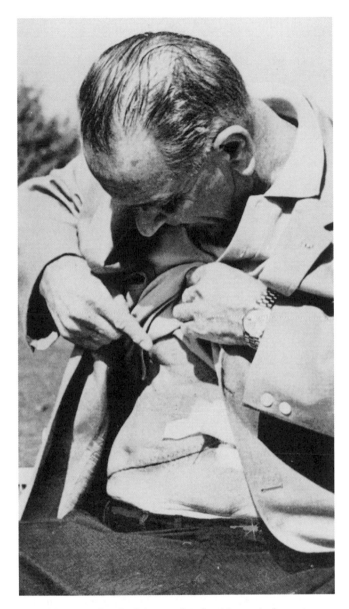

President Lyndon B. Johnson showing his surgical scar to reporters, October 1965

long history of aid to higher education dating back to the Morrill Land Grant College Act of the nineteenth century. Once a compromise satisfied banking-industry concerns regarding student loans, the Higher Education Act of 1965 (HEA) passed with minimal opposition and became law on 8 November 1965 despite the administration's addition of the controversial provision to cut off funds to segregated schools that had been dropped from the ESEA. The HEA provided federal scholarships and federally guaranteed student loans for needy students, funds for college libraries, graduate fellowships for prospective elementary- and secondary-school teachers, and provisions for a teacher corps, whose members would augment the faculties of schools in poverty-stricken areas. In 1966 Congress passed a bill providing funds to strengthen resources in undergraduate and graduate instruction in international studies and foreign languages. The Sea Grant Act of 1966 provided funds to strengthen and develop marine-science programs.

Housing and Cities. Johnson's Great Society programs also tried to deal with housing problems in both rural and urban areas. The Omnibus Housing Act of 1965 gave rent supplements for low-income housing and provided funding to build new housing for low- and middle-income families and for the elderly. It also offered grants for urban renewal. Another 1965 law finally created Kennedy's proposed cabinet-level department of housing and urban affairs, which was given the responsibility of coordinating all federal housing programs and programs for the cities. In 1966 Congress passed the demonstration-cities program, which provided cities with up to 80 percent of the costs of projects to provide housing, welfare, or transport.

Appalachia. In 1964 Johnson proposed a public-works bill that targeted 360 counties in eleven eastern states in the economically distressed Appalachian region. Passed in 1965, the bill established the Appalachian Regional Commission to develop an economic program and to coordinate projects funded under the legislation, including construction of roads, schools, and health facilities; land reclamation; and development projects.

Quality of Life. Johnson's idea of the "Great Society" implied more than his War on Poverty and programs designed to improve educational opportunity; it included dozens of proposals, designed to improve the lives of all Americans, that were enacted into law throughout the 1965 and 1966 congressional sessions. Laws were enacted to protect consumers by requiring truth in packaging and by establishing safety requirements for automobiles, children's toys, and household items. Other legislation sought to promote clean air and water. The basis of decisions made by governmental bodies was to be more open through the Freedom of Information Act. Highways were to be made less unsightly by removing billboards from interstate highways, and people's lives were to be enriched through the creation of the National Foundation for the Arts and Humanities.

and was signed into law on 11 April 1965. The Elementary and Secondary Education Act of 1965 (ESEA) was the first law to extend federal education funding to elementary and secondary schools, establishing a formula to determine the amount of aid to individual public and private schools according to the number of children in the school whose families met its poverty criteria. The bill also provided grants for the purchase of library materials and textbooks. In 1966 Congress passed a bill establishing the breakfast-in-the-schools program for poor children, extending the existing school milk and lunch programs, and providing funds for schools to acquire kitchen equipment.

Funding for Higher Education. Johnson's proposals for additional funding for higher education were far less controversial than his bill for aid to elementary and secondary schools because the federal government had a

The Great Society Falters. By the end of 1966 Johnson was forced to announce budget cutbacks in his War on Poverty and Great Society programs because of the competing need for funds to prosecute the Vietnam War, which had rapidly escalated in the last half of 1965 and through 1966. Funds for the OEO went from $4 billion in 1966 to $1.75 billion in 1967. From 1966 on, the Johnson administration became increasingly focused on the war effort. Moreover, the voter backlash resulting from the urban riots of 1964, 1965, and 1966 manifested itself in the 1966 House and Senate elections, which brought the conservative coalition back to a position of power. After 1966 Johnson introduced no major new social programs, and in 1969 his successor, Richard M. Nixon, was more interested in measures to fight crime than in finding ways to meet the demands of the poor.

Sources:

Vaughan Davis Bornet, *The Presidency of Lyndon Johnson* (Lawrence: University Press of Kansas, 1983);

Congressional Quarterly Almanac, 21 (1965);

Congressional Quarterly Almanac, 22 (1966);

Jim F. Heath, *Decade of Disillusionment: The Kennedy-Johnson Years* (Bloomington: Indiana University Press, 1975);

Allen J. Matusow, *The Unraveling of America: A History of Liberalism in the 1960's* (New York: Harper & Row, 1984).

NATIONAL POLITICS: 1960 ELECTIONS

The Democratic Nomination Race

Kennedy's Strategy. The biggest obstacle Sen. John F. Kennedy of Massachusetts faced in his bid for the presidency was his religion. He was the second Roman Catholic to run for the highest elected office in the United States on a major-party ticket. The first, Democratic governor Alfred E. Smith of New York, had won only eight states when he ran against Republican Herbert Hoover in 1928, convincing leaders in both parties that a Catholic could not win a national election. Kennedy knew that his first task in seeking the Democratic nomination was to convince party leaders that he could attract a broad range of voters. He needed not just to win primaries but to win them in ways that proved his appeal to non-Catholics.

Delegate Selection Processes. By 1972 primary elections were the principal vehicle for securing the presidential nomination of a major party, but in 1960 only sixteen states held primaries. Most national convention delegates were selected by state-party organizations and their leadership. While primaries were important vehicles for demonstrating voter strength, it was possible for the nomination to go to a candidate who had never entered a primary. With no clear front-runner at the beginning of the race to head the Democratic ticket, many believed that several rounds of voting would take place at the national convention, freeing up delegates bound by primary results on the first ballot.

Symington and Johnson Plan for a Deadlocked Convention. Sen. Stuart Symington of Missouri based his strategy on this belief. Assured of support from former president and fellow Missourian Harry S Truman but not well known in the primary states, Symington aimed his campaign at the Democratic power brokers, hoping to convince them that, with his strong record on defense and his liberal record on civil rights and labor issues, he would be the ideal compromise candidate in the event of a deadlocked convention. Sen. Lyndon B. Johnson of Texas, who had been a southern favorite-son candidate in 1956, believed that early convention balloting in 1960 would be inconclusive. As Senate majority leader since 1954, he had earned a reputation as a brilliant political strategist. With the convention deadlocked, Johnson reasoned, he could win the nomination by calling in payments on the huge pile of political debts owed him and another influential Texas Democrat, Sam Rayburn, Speaker of the House of Representatives.

Humphrey Takes the Primary Route. The fourth major candidate was Hubert H. Humphrey of Minnesota, a senator since 1948 and respected for his anti-communist stance. Nonetheless, his longtime support of civil rights and other liberal causes had convinced party regulars that he was too far left to win a national election. Like Kennedy, Humphrey had to demonstrate broad voter appeal, but unlike the independently wealthy Kennedy, he could not afford an all-out primary campaign. He decided not to enter the New Hampshire primary (8 March 1960), considering it a waste of time and money to challenge Kennedy in his own backyard.

New Hampshire and Wisconsin Primaries. Faced with no serious opposition in New Hampshire, Kennedy won 85.2 percent of the vote, with a local ballpoint-pen manufacturer coming in a distant second. Kennedy went on to face Humphrey in Wisconsin (5 April), widely viewed as Humphrey territory since he came from a neighboring state. Humphrey's campaign was no match for Kennedy's well-organized effort, and though the two candidates spent about the same amount of money, Kennedy won 56.5 percent of the vote, picking up twenty-two convention delegates to Humphrey's twelve. Yet Humphrey had won the four predominantly Protestant districts while Kennedy had done best in the four districts where the majority of the voters were Catholic.

Kennedy Overcomes the Religion Issue. The real test came when Humphrey and Kennedy faced off in West Virginia (10 May), a state that was 95 percent Protestant. During the Wisconsin campaign, the national media had picked up on religion as a means of differentiating between two candidates who shared similar views on political issues. Soon voters were hearing the same charge that had been leveled in 1928: if a Roman Catholic were elected president, the pope would be the de facto head of the executive branch. In December 1959 Louis Harris, Kennedy's personal pollster, had predicted that Kennedy would take 70 percent of the West Virginia vote to Humphrey's 30. Three weeks before the primary, after the religious issue had taken center stage, Harris discovered that Humphrey's support had risen to 60 percent while Kennedy's had dropped to 40. Going against the advice of his campaign staff, Kennedy tackled the issue head on. Two days before the voting Kennedy delivered an impassioned speech on West Virginia television. He began by asking why he should have been "denied the right to be President on the day I was baptized." Then he pointed out that in taking the oath of office, in which he swears to uphold the U.S. Constitution, the president is promising to support the separation of Church and State. "And if he breaks his oath," Kennedy added, "he is not only committing a crime against the Constitution, but he is committing a sin against God." The speech effectively redefined the religious issue as tolerance versus intolerance, and Kennedy won easily in West Virginia with 60.8 percent of the popular vote. Humphrey withdrew from the race.

Kennedy's Campaign in Nonprimary States. Kennedy won other primaries, but none was as important as West Virginia, which convinced party leaders that Kennedy was an attractive candidate. Backed by extensive research and in-depth knowledge of politics, the Kennedy campaign effectively canvassed party leaders in every state, destroying Symington's chances and earning votes even in Johnson's western strongholds.

Johnson Enters the Race. By the time Johnson declared his candidacy, less than a week before the Democratic National Convention opened in Los Angeles on 11 July, he estimated that he had 502 1/2 of the 761 votes needed to win the nomination, while Kennedy had 602 1/2 committed to him on the first ballot. If Kennedy could be stopped short of 761 on the first round of voting, the convention could go into the proverbial "smoke-filled back room," and Johnson could emerge the winner.

The Democratic Convention. Another challenge came from a powerful Draft-Stevenson movement, which continued right up to the evening of Wednesday, 13 July, when Minnesota senator Eugene McCarthy delivered an impassioned nomination speech for Adlai E. Stevenson of Illinois, who had lost to President Dwight D. Eisenhower in 1952 and 1956. Yet Stevenson declined to announce his candidacy after learning that he would not have the support of Chicago Mayor Richard Daley, head of his home-state delegation who had already committed to Kennedy. In the midst of these challenges, the Kennedy team continued campaigning. Their candidate won on the first ballot, with 806 votes, followed by Johnson with 409. Choosing Johnson as his running mate, Kennedy proclaimed in his acceptance speech that "the world is changing. The old era is ending. . . ." Americans were, he said, "standing on the edge of a New Frontier."

The Republican Nomination Race

Rockefeller Challenges Nixon. As vice-president for eight years under the popular President Eisenhower, Richard M. Nixon was heir apparent to the presidency in the eyes of most Republican Party regulars. He faced early opposition from Gov. Nelson A. Rockefeller of New York. Rockefeller had quit an appointed position in the Eisenhower administration because he considered its politics indecisive; he disliked Nixon and considered him incapable of being an effective president. Rockefeller had ranked slightly ahead of Nixon in a spring 1959 poll of Republicans, but on his trip to the Soviet Union that summer, Nixon enhanced his image as a natural leader in the so-called kitchen debate with Premier Nikita Khrushchev at a Moscow trade fair.

Party Regulars Back Nixon. By December 1959 it was apparent to Rockefeller that the party regulars who controlled most convention delegates were committed to Nixon, as were the big businessmen who would fund the Republican campaign. Though he could finance his campaign from his own large fortune, Rockefeller doubted that a nomination bought with his own money would be worth much politically. He also realized that since he could not break Nixon's lock on the party, he would have to fight Nixon in the primaries, where he would, in effect, be running against the policies of the most popular Republican president of the twentieth century.

Rockefeller Withdraws from the Race. On 24 December Rockefeller announced that he would not run for president, calling his decision "definite and final." Rockefeller's withdrawal from the race gave Nixon time to polish his image as a statesman further before entering the postconvention political frays, but Nixon and his campaign advisers had looked forward to primary battles against Rockefeller as a means of generating public excitement, diverting some of the media attention from the hotly contested Democratic race and fine-tuning their strategy for the fall campaign.

A New Challenge from Rockefeller. Nixon appeared to have the nomination locked up until the U-2 spying incident on 1 May and the resulting breakdown of the summit meeting between Eisenhower and Khrushchev sparked a Draft-Rockefeller movement. Between 1 June and 19 July, in a series of speeches and nine major documents, Rockefeller attacked the Republican leadership's handling of national affairs. Yet he treated the Democrats with disdain as well, and he was convinced that he must implement change through his own party.

The Nixon-Rockefeller Compromise. Though Rockefeller's challenge did not seriously threaten Nixon's nomination it did raise the possibility of open dissent within the party that could provide ammunition for the Democrats. A few days before the convention opened in Chicago on 25 July, Rockefeller announced that the party platform was "seriously lacking in strength and specifics." Objecting most strenuously to the defense and civil rights planks, he threatened to take his fight for changes to the convention floor. Nixon, who wanted to avoid intraparty warfare on national television, flew to New York. He and Rockefeller met in the governor's Fifth Avenue apartment and hammered out a fourteen-point statement which became known as the Compact of Fifth Avenue.

Rumblings on the Right. Nixon, who had basically accepted Rockefeller's positions, now faced two new battles, the first with the platform committee, whose views were far more conservative than those expressed in the Nixon-Rockefeller statement, and the second with an angry Eisenhower, vacationing in Newport, Rhode Island, before his appearance in Chicago. The president saw the part of the Compact of Fifth Avenue that dealt with national defense and diplomacy as a blatant attack on his competence. Despite such opposition, Nixon hammered through the civil rights plank on which he and Rockefeller agreed — calling for an end to discrimination in voting, housing, education, and jobs (one much like the Democrats') — and engineered a compromise defense plank acceptable to both Eisenhower and Rockefeller as well as the party regulars.

The Republican Convention. Rockefeller withdrew from the presidential race, and on Wednesday, 27 July, Nixon won the Republican nomination on the first ballot with 1,321 votes to 10 for Sen. Barry Goldwater, a conservative Republican from Arizona, whose name was put into nomination by the Louisiana delegation to protest a civil rights plank that they said would hand their state to the Democrats as soon as Johnson came "across the border" to "talk 'magnolia' " to Louisiana voters. For his running mate, Nixon chose Henry Cabot Lodge of Massachusetts, who had lost his Senate seat to Kennedy in 1952.

The Election Campaign

The Issues and the Rhetoric. As in most campaigns the important political issues of 1960 became lost in rhetoric and personality issues. Both candidates called for a strong defense against communism. Kennedy stressed the missile gap between the United States and the Soviet Union and pointed to incidents such as the U-2 affair and the collapse of the Eisenhower-Khrushchev summit to bolster his charge that the United States had lost international prestige. As he traveled the country he proclaimed over and over, "This is a great country. But I think it can be greater. I think we can do better. I think we can make this country move again." Defending Eisenhower's record and charging that Kennedy would be too soft on the Russians, Nixon made his campaign motto "Peace without Surrender." Kennedy scored points on the economy, warning that the United States was "slipping into its third recession in six years." As economic indicators increasingly seemed to support Kennedy's analysis, Nixon found it harder to convince voters that the downturn was temporary. In fact Nixon often appeared to be on the defensive, taking potshots at Kennedy rather than presenting his own programs. In contrast Kennedy captured voters' imaginations with his vision of a New Frontier in which public service and individual sacrifice would raise

the United States to new heights of international prestige and harmony and prosperity at home.

A Close Race from the Start. From the beginning both candidates believed the election would be close; in such cases even small tactical errors can mean the difference between winning and losing. In August a Gallup poll showed Nixon leading by 53 to 47 percent. The election seemed to be Nixon's to lose.

Nixon's Campaign Mistakes. The strong civil rights plank that Nixon pushed through at the Republican National Convention did indeed express his personal convictions on the race issue. In supporting it he seemed to commit himself to courting black voters who made the difference between winning and losing in several key Northern cities. At first he seemed to write off the South, where the Republicans were beginning to make inroads; yet a tumultuous welcome in Atlanta in August seems to have convinced Nixon that he could win over white southern voters as well as blacks. In the end he alienated both blacks and Southern whites. Another Nixon mistake that proved crucial in a close election was the promise in his acceptance speech to campaign in all fifty states. Even after he was hospitalized for nearly two weeks in late August and early September with an infected knee, Nixon refused to go back on this promise, despite the urging of his campaign staff. Late in the race he found himself in Alaska, which had only three electoral votes, while Kennedy campaigned in New York and New England, where large numbers of electoral votes were up for grabs.

Nixon Ignores His Advisers. Nixon often neglected to consult his campaign staff. He had excellent advisers and the funding for a first-rate campaign, but he was a loner by nature and tended to take too much on himself. The Nixon campaign strategy existed largely in the candidate's head; his decisions were often based on instinct, not on the advice of his political advisers. Kennedy, in contrast, was a team player. He and his advisers, headed by his brother Robert F. Kennedy, carefully mapped out their campaign strategy and followed it.

The Vice-presidential Candidates. Another factor in the election was Kennedy's running mate, the folksy, dynamic, politically astute Lyndon Johnson, who was a better campaigner than Nixon's choice, the patrician Boston Brahmin Henry Cabot Lodge, who was attractive and articulate but a leisurely campaigner.

Nixon and Kennedy Face Off on Television. Yet Nixon's biggest mistake was agreeing to four televised debates with Kennedy. As the better known of the two candidates, Nixon needed the media exposure far less than Kennedy, but he had watched Kennedy's acceptance speech and was convinced that he could outdebate his Democratic opponent.

The First Debate. At the first debate, on 26 September, Kennedy, who had spent the day practicing possible questions and answers with advisers, appeared calm and

Vice-president Richard M. Nixon and Sen. John F. Kennedy during their third televised debate, 13 October 1960

handsome; Nixon, who had spent the day alone, seemed tense and tired, even ill. Kennedy used the occasion to speak directly to the American people. Nixon rebutted or refuted portions of Kennedy's statement as if he were trying to score points from judges in a formal debate. Consequently, Nixon appeared to be picking at Kennedy's ideas rather than presenting his own.

Kennedy Scores High with Viewers. According to one poll of television viewers, Kennedy outscored Nixon on the first, second, and fourth debates, while Nixon won the third. People who listened to the debates on the radio thought the two candidates came out about even. Of the 115 million to 120 million people who watched the debates, 57 percent said they had been influenced by them. Another 6 percent, about 4 million people, said their votes were based solely on the debates; 72 percent of these people, nearly 3 million, voted for Kennedy in an election where the gap between the two candidates in the popular vote was under 120,000. As Kennedy said a few days after the election, "It was TV more than anything else that turned the tide."

Kennedy Moves Ahead. The forty-one-year-old Kennedy's performance in the debates laid to rest Republican charges that he was immature and inexperienced. His calm demeanor in these stressful situations put him on an equal footing with Nixon, whose image as a statesman was not enhanced by the debates. Kennedy moved ahead in the polls and stayed ahead, but he still faced obstacles.

Kennedy Faces the Religion Issue. Kennedy hoped he had laid to rest the religion issue in West Virginia. In September Kennedy's Roman Catholicism became an issue again, as anti-Catholic pamphlets were widely circulated and some fundamentalist preachers began charging that Kennedy was the "Pope's puppet." Then the Reverend Norman Vincent Peale, one of the most respected Protestant ministers in America, asked in a speech before a large gathering of Protestant clergyman if any Catholic could be a loyal president. Kennedy could ignore the problem no longer. Standing before the Greater Houston Ministerial Association on 12 September, he delivered what some historians have called the most important speech of his campaign: "I believe in an America where the separation of Church and State is absolute," he said, "where no Catholic prelate would tell the President (should he be a Catholic) how to act, and no Protestant minister would tell his parishioners how to vote. . . ." The speech impressed Sam Rayburn, who exclaimed, "By God . . . , he's eating 'em blood raw!" The next day, as parts of the speech were televised nationally, Nixon stated publicly that religion should not be an issue in the campaign. Kennedy's Catholicism, though not forgotten, ceased to be a major factor in the campaign. During the week before the election, when two Catholic bishops in Puerto Rico announced that it would be a sin to vote for a candidate they opposed, two prominent Catholics, Francis Cardinal Spellman of New York and Richard Cardinal Cushing of Boston, immediately provided damage control, asserting that those bishops were wrong and reaffirming, in Cushing's words, "It is totally out of step for any ecclesiastical authority here to dictate the political voting of citizens." The influence of religion on the election results is difficult to ascertain. Kennedy seems to have been most hurt by his Catholicism in the South (most of which he won anyway) and several typically Republican midwestern states (which he expected to lose and did), but close to 80 percent of all Roman Catholics voted for him. (At that time 63 percent of Catholics voted Democratic in a typical election; only 51 percent voted for Stevenson in 1956.) Kennedy's net gain in the popular vote was small, but the Catholic vote helped

Kennedy in several important, closely contested states, including New Jersey, Illinois, and Michigan.

The Black Vote Swings to Kennedy. Another important constituency was black voters, who had asserted themselves for the first time in 1948, when they won the election for Truman. Eisenhower had made some inroads into this typically Democratic group in 1956, and the Republicans' civil rights plank seemed likely to help Nixon in 1960. Yet one event late in the campaign brought the black vote back to the Democratic fold. On 25 October a Georgia judge sentenced civil rights leader Dr. Martin Luther King, Jr., to four months at hard labor as punishment for violating his parole on a minor traffic conviction by participating in a sit-in at a restaurant in an Atlanta department store. Many, including his wife, believed that he would not emerge alive from the rural Georgia penitentiary where he was imprisoned. While Nixon and Eisenhower did nothing, Kennedy, who had been warned by at least two southern governors not to intrude, called Mrs. King to express his concern. The next day Robert Kennedy called the judge who had sentenced King, and John Kennedy secretly convinced the governor of Georgia to intercede. (Neither the candidate nor the governor wanted white southerners to know of their part in the negotiations — which was not revealed until years later.)

A Major Endorsement for Kennedy. The civil rights leader was released, and his father, the Reverend Martin Luther King, Sr., announced publicly that he was switching his vote from Nixon to Kennedy. Thousands of blacks followed, probably helped in their decision by the one million or so pamphlets about the King episode that Kennedy's chief civil rights adviser, Harris Wofford, had distributed outside black churches in key locations all over the country on the Sunday before the election. The black vote not only helped Kennedy in the North, but it also kept South Carolina from going Republican and played a decisive role in winning North Carolina and Texas for Kennedy as well.

An Election Too Close to Call. Last-minute campaigning by Eisenhower caused an upswing for Nixon in the polls, but it was not enough to win the election. A record turnout, 64 percent of all registered voters, cast 49.7 percent for Kennedy and 49.5 percent for Nixon. Kennedy had a plurality of only 118,550 votes, but he took all but two of the states with large numbers of electoral votes, sometimes by the slimmest of margins. He ended up with 303 electoral votes, while Nixon took 219.

Charges of Voter Fraud. Republicans questioned the vote counts in eight states; most prominently mentioned were Illinois, New Mexico, and Texas. Yet Nixon decided not to contest the election, telling his supporters that the battle would divide the country. In all likelihood it would also have failed to change the outcome of the election. In Illinois (27 electoral votes) it might well have

been possible to find enough fraudulent votes created by Mayor Daley's political machine in Chicago to erase Kennedy's 8,858-vote lead in that state, and New Mexico (4 electoral votes), where Kennedy won by 2,294 votes, might also have been switched to the Republican column. Yet Kennedy would still have had 272 electoral votes, two more than he needed to win. Texas, with 24 electoral votes, could swing the election to Nixon, but Kennedy had won that state by 46,733 votes, a hard plurality to erase.

Kennedy Has No Coattails. A victorious presidential candidate usually carries many of his party's candidates into office behind him. Yet the 1960 presidential election was so close that Kennedy's victory did little to help the Democrats, who had gained 15 new senators and 48 new congressmen in the 1958 elections and hoped to strengthen their control over both houses of Congress in 1960. Instead the Democrats lost two seats in the Senate and twenty in the House of Representatives. (In 1961 they lost another Senate seat when Republican John Tower of Texas was elected to fill Vice-president Johnson's seat, which had temporarily been filled by an appointed Democrat.) Though the Democrats maintained majorities in both houses, these losses effectively blocked Kennedy's domestic legislation for the first two years of his presidency. The Democrats' 263–174 majority in the House included 60–70 conservative southerners who were just as likely to vote with the Republicans as with their own party on domestic matters. The Democrats had a 64–36 majority in the Senate, but faced a similar situation there. Southern Democrats headed important Senate committees by virtue of the long tenure in office and had the power to block any legislation they considered too liberal.

Senate	1958	1960	Net Gain/ Loss
Democrats	66	64	-2
Republicans	34	36	+2

House	86th Congress	87th Congress	Net Gain/ Loss
Democrats	283	263	-20
Republicans	154	174	+20

Governors	1958	1960	Net Gain/ Loss
Democrats	34	34	0
Republicans	14	16	+2

Bright Spots for the Democrats. All but one of the party's incumbent senators were reelected, including Sen. Hubert Humphrey of Minnesota, who became Senate majority whip. The Democrats had one fewer governor than they had in 1958; segregationist Orval Faubus won an unprecedented fourth term in Arkansas, while Gov. Terry Sanford of North Carolina, who had gone against old-line southern Democrats with his early support for Kennedy, was also reelected.

Significant Republican Wins. John V. Lindsay, who would be elected mayor of New York City in 1961, won a second term in the House. William W. Scranton of Pennsylvania, who would challenge Sen. Barry Goldwater for the Republican presidential nomination in 1964, defeated the Democratic incumbent in a hotly contested Congressional race.

Sources:
Congressional Quarterly Almanac, 16 (1960);

Time, 76 (16 November 1960): 3–15;

Theodore H. White, *The Making of the President 1960* (New York: Atheneum, 1961).

NATIONAL POLITICS: 1962 ELECTIONS

Democrats Hold Their Own. In off-year elections the party of the incumbent president customarily loses seats in Congress. In 1962 Republicans went after Kennedy's record — charging that he had fumbled on foreign policy and failed to win support for his domestic programs. This strategy was neutralized, however, by Kennedy's successful resolution of the Cuban missile crisis just before the election. For the first time since the 1934 off-year election, the president's party gained seats in the Senate, giving the Democrats a 68–32 majority. (They lost one seat when Democratic senator Dennis Chavez of New Mexico died less than two weeks after the election and Republican Edwin L. Mechem was appointed to serve the last two years of Chavez's term.) Reapportionment had made the House of Representatives two seats smaller than it had been in 1960, and the Democrats lost four seats, well below the average of thirty-eight losses for the president's party in off-year elections since 1900. The Republicans gained only two seats.

Senate Newcomers. Among the ten new senators elected in 1962 were Democrats George McGovern of South Dakota, Abraham Ribicoff of Connecticut, Birch Bayh of Indiana, and Gaylord A. Nelson of Wisconsin. Earlier in 1962 Edward M. Kennedy, a Democrat from Massachusetts, had been elected to complete the Senate term vacated by his elder brother, John F. Kennedy, which expired in 1964.

Republican Gains in the South. All Republican incumbents in the House were reelected, and the party won five new seats, adding to their southern strength in the House. The strong showing of the Republican Senate candidate against a four-term incumbent in Alabama also suggested growing Republican support in the South. The

Senate	1960	1962	Net Gain/ Loss
Democrats	64	68	+4
Republicans	36	32	-4

House	87th Congress	88th* Congress	Gain/ Loss
Democrats	263	258	-4
Republicans	174	176	+2

* Reapportionment after the 1960 election reduced House seats from 437 to 435; one vacant seat was filled by a Republican in 1963.

Governors	1960	1962	Net Gain/ Loss
Democrats	34	34	0
Republicans	16	16	0

"Solid South" that had voted Democratic since the end of the Civil War no longer existed.

Nixon's Valedictory. The biggest news of the 1962 elections was Richard M. Nixon's press conference after losing the California governorship to Democratic incumbent Edmund G. (Pat) Brown. In words that the staunchly Republican *Time* magazine called "too small in spirit to make for real tragedy," Nixon told the press, "You won't have Nixon to kick around any more." *Time* concluded that, "barring a miracle," Nixon's political career was over.

Presidential Hopefuls Win Governorships. Although each party ended up with the same number of governorships as it had after the 1960 elections, the impressive victories of moderate Republicans William Scranton in Pennsylvania and George Romney in Michigan inspired talk about them as potential presidential candidates. The front-runner for the Republican nomination was believed to be Gov. Nelson A. Rockefeller of New York, who easily won his second term. Democrats George C. Wallace of Alabama and John D. Connally of Texas won the governorships of their states.

Sources:
Congressional Quarterly Almanac, 18 (1962);

Time, 20 (16 November 1962): 3–28.

NATIONAL POLITICS: 1964 ELECTIONS

The Republican Nomination Race

Republicans Fear Party Split. By fall 1963 the Eastern Establishment Republicans who dominated their party at the national level began to fear that it would split in two if Gov. Nelson Rockefeller of New York and Sen. Barry

Goldwater of Arizona went head-to-head for the Republican presidential nomination. For years the Eastern Establishment — the wealthy group of (mostly) Ivy League–educated international bankers and businessmen living mainly in and around New York — were willing to let the conservative Republicans of the Midwest and West speak for the party in Congress as long as the Establishment could control the presidential nomination, placing someone with moderate views consistent with their own in the position that created the party's national image. Rockefeller, one of the wealthiest men in America, was a member of the Establishment by virtue of heredity, education, and social class, but politically he was too liberal to inspire their trust. They found Goldwater, one of the west-of-the-Alleghenies Republicans they had tended to ignore, far too conservative. Yet in the search for a candidate to represent their mainstream Republican views the Establishment found itself leaderless. Former president Dwight D. Eisenhower, who had spent most of his life as a soldier, was not experienced at party politics.

The Problem with Nixon. Richard M. Nixon, who had vowed to leave politics after losing the election for governor of California in 1962, was blamed by many in both wings of the party for creating the mess in which they found themselves. They traced the first crack in the fragile bond that held the party together to the so-called Compact of Fifth Avenue, the policy statement by Nixon and Rockefeller that had enraged conservatives at the 1960 Republican National Convention. To these conservatives Nixon had sold out the party to appease Rockefeller, and many — including Goldwater — later charged that the strong civil rights plank resulting from that Nixon-Rockefeller agreement had lost the 1960 election for the Republicans.

Rockefeller Has an Early Lead. Early in 1963 Rockefeller looked like the front-runner for the Republican nomination. President John F. Kennedy, who believed he would have lost the 1960 election if he had run against Rockefeller instead of Nixon, expected to face Rockefeller in 1964. But the equation changed in May 1963, after Rockefeller, who had been divorced from his first wife in 1961, married a divorced woman who had given up custody of her four children to her first husband. Before Rockefeller's remarriage Republicans had preferred him to Goldwater by 43 to 26 percent. In late May a Gallup poll showed that 35 percent of Republicans were for Goldwater, and only 30 percent wanted Rockefeller. With many in his party still undecided, Rockefeller reasoned that if he could make a strong showing in the primaries he could still win the nomination. He planned to battle Goldwater in three key primaries: New Hampshire (10 March 1964), Oregon (15 May), and California (2 June).

Goldwater Nearly Drops Out. The assassination of President Kennedy on 22 November 1963 almost convinced Goldwater not to seek the Republican nomina-

PRESIDENTIAL SUCCESSION

After the assassination of President John F. Kennedy and the succession of Vice-president Lyndon B. Johnson to the presidency on 22 November 1963, Americans became concerned about the issue of presidential succession. For the next fourteen months — until the inauguration of Johnson and his running mate, Hubert Humphrey, in January 1965 — the vice-presidency remained vacant. Most Americans were shocked to learn that if Johnson, who had suffered a serious heart attack in 1955, died during 1964, John McCormack of Massachusetts, the seventy-three-year-old Speaker of the House of Representatives, would become president. Next in the line of succession was Carl Hayden of Arizona, the eighty-seven-year-old president pro tempore of the Senate. They were followed by members of the cabinet, listed in rank order beginning with the secretary of state.

Americans were also concerned about who was authorized to take over the president's duties if he were temporarily incapacitated, a situation that occurred twice in the 1950s when President Dwight D. Eisenhower was hospitalized. The U.S. Constitution had no provisions that defined the conditions under which a vice-president would become acting president.

To rectify both situations Congress approved an amendment to the U.S. Constitution on 6 July 1965. After ratification by the requisite three-fourths of the states, it became the Twenty-fifth Amendment on 10 February 1967. This amendment allowed the president to nominate a new vice-president, who would take office after approval by a majority vote in each house of Congress. It also added provisions governing temporary presidential disability, specifying the circumstances and provisions by which a vice-president would become acting president.

The disability provisions have never been applied. The provisions for naming a new vice-president have been invoked twice. In 1973 President Richard M. Nixon selected Rep. Gerald Ford to replace Spiro T. Agnew, who had resigned because of his connections to a bribery scandal while he had been governor of Maryland. After Nixon resigned the presidency in 1974 in the midst of the Watergate crisis, Ford became president and tapped Nelson A. Rockefeller of New York to be the new vice-president.

Source: Vaughan Davis Bornet, *The Presidency of Lyndon Johnson* (Lawrence: University Press of Kansas, 1983).

tion. He and the president had liked each other, and Goldwater had viewed the 1964 presidential election as a perfect opportunity for them to debate the issues, giving voters a clear picture of the differences between Goldwater's conservative philosophy and Kennedy's liberal views. Though Kennedy was sure to win, Goldwater thought he could take the West and the South and claim a moral victory for the conservative cause. Against President Lyndon B. Johnson, a Texan, Goldwater could not count on the South, or even all the West. Yet he finally agreed to run because he feared the conservative cause would lose momentum if left leaderless.

Goldwater's Remarks Hurt Him. Though he had been in the Senate since 1953, Goldwater was unprepared for the sort of attention the press pays to presidential candidates. Already known for his tendency to make often outrageous off-the-cuff statements, he made several well-thought-out policy speeches in New Hampshire, but reporters found better press in remarks that social-security payments should be made voluntary, that governments could start depressions but not end them, and that the United States should have dropped an atom bomb on North Vietnam ten years earlier. All these statements unnerved even conservative New Hampshire Republicans. Rockefeller's staff carefully recorded all such pronouncements and used them against the Arizona senator. Goldwater learned to consider his words carefully, but the damage was done.

A Dark Horse Wins in New Hampshire. Rockefeller ruined Goldwater's chances in New Hampshire but failed to win the state for himself. New Hampshire Republicans found Rockefeller far too liberal and voted instead for a write-in candidate who had never set foot in the state: Henry Cabot Lodge, Jr., Nixon's running mate in 1960, whom President Kennedy had appointed U.S. ambassador to Vietnam. Lodge won New Hampshire with 33,000 votes, followed by Goldwater (20,000), Rockefeller (19,500), and Nixon, also a write-in (15,600).

Goldwater Regroups. Having hoped to win 40 percent of the New Hampshire vote and ending up with only 23 percent, Goldwater decided not to campaign in Oregon so that he could concentrate on California. Lodge's campaign was run by four political amateurs (one of whom was an expert in direct-mail advertising), and its success depended on signs of improvement in the Vietnam situation. The war got worse instead, and Rockefeller, who presented himself to Oregon Republicans as a responsible, mainstream candidate running to stop extremists from taking over the party, won the Oregon primary with 94,000 votes to 79,000 for Lodge and 50,000 for Goldwater.

Rockefeller Gains Momentum. After Oregon the Lodge campaign threw its support to Rockefeller, whose Oregon victory gave him the momentum to surge ahead of Goldwater in polls of California Republicans, but Goldwater's campaign organized an army of thousands of volunteers (9,500 in Los Angeles County alone) to go door to door and get out the vote for their candidate. Goldwater beat Rockefeller in California with 51.6 percent of the vote.

Clif White Steals the Party for Goldwater. Well before the primaries, F. Clifton White, a conservative Republican from upstate New York, had set in motion a plan that would change the face of the Republican Party for the rest of the twentieth century and beyond. Having earlier engineered a conservative takeover of the Young Republicans, he had his own national network that could work at the grassroots level in nonprimary states to seize control of the Republican Party for Goldwater. White's basic strategy was to get large numbers of conservatives to attend their local precinct meetings, thus flooding with Goldwater supporters the pool from which national convention delegates would eventually be elected. By late May Goldwater had 300 of the 655 votes he needed for the nomination. Less than two weeks after the California primary he had 588, and White was confident of delivering 200 more votes to Goldwater.

The Establishment Waits Too Long. The mainstream wing of the party controlled by the Eastern Establishment woke up to what was going on just before the California primary. Unwilling to support Rockefeller actively, they sat back and waited for him to win on his own, confident that Rockefeller would win in California, leaving Goldwater without the necessary votes to win the nomination but with enough convention votes to veto Rockefeller's candidacy. Then, they thought, the moderate, mainstream Republicans could choose their own "unity candidate."

Eisenhower Picks Scranton. Goldwater destroyed their strategy by winning the California primary, and the moderates began seeking alternatives. Eisenhower — wanting to remain publicly neutral — urged Gov. William W. Scranton of Pennsylvania to run but stopped short of publicly endorsing him. Scranton, who felt he needed Eisenhower's endorsement to have a chance, wavered for several days. Finally, Eisenhower — who was proud of having been the first modern president to get a civil rights bill through Congress — became enraged when he saw that Goldwater was about to vote against the Civil Rights Bill of 1964 and convinced the equally angry Scranton to run (still without Eisenhower's public endorsement). On 11 June Scranton began an expensive five-week campaign that was doomed from the start.

The Republican Convention. The Republican National Convention held in San Francisco on 13–16 July 1964 marked a pivotal point in Republican party history. Rallying behind Goldwater, conservatives had wrested the party away from the mainstream Republicans who had controlled the party at the national level since 1940. The repercussions of this takeover would be felt in American politics for at least the next thirty years.

Last-Ditch Efforts to Defeat Goldwater. Goldwater arrived at the convention with more than enough delegates to be nominated on the first ballot. Ambassador Henry Cabot Lodge of Massachusetts and Governors Nelson A. Rockefeller of New York and William W. Scranton of Pennsylvania, all of whom had unsuccessfully battled Goldwater in the race for delegates, now joined with other mainstream Republicans, such as Gov. George W. Romney of Michigan, Senators Jacob K. Javits and Kenneth Keating of New York, Sen. Clifford P. Case of New Jersey, and Sen. Hugh Scott of Pennsylvania, in a last-minute attempt to find some way to derail Goldwater. They decided to challenge the platform as it was presented on the convention floor by the conservative-dominated platform committee. If they could convince delegates to go along with their platform amendments, they reasoned, they could demonstrate that Goldwater's support was not as strong as it seemed, and then they might be able to shake loose enough votes to deny Goldwater his first-ballot victory. But Goldwater's people stood firm. On prime-time television, as Rockefeller stood before the convention to defend a proposed resolution condemning extremist groups — mentioning by name the Communist Party, the Ku Klux Klan, and the John Birch Society — Goldwater supporters in the galleries jeered and booed and chanted "We want Barry!" — virtually drowning out Rockefeller. Following Goldwater's instruction, his delegates on the floor were relatively quiet, and his people finally managed to squelch the uproar in the galleries. Yet millions of television viewers came away with the impression that Goldwater supporters were rabid right-wing extremists, and that image would linger in the minds of many voters.

Goldwater Has the Convention Locked Up. All minority platform proposals were handily defeated, and Goldwater won the nomination easily on the first ballot. His choice of running mate, Congressman William E. Miller, an archconservative from upstate New York, offered no possibility of conciliation with party moderates, nor did Goldwater's acceptance speech, which ended with the ringing pronouncement *"Extremism in the defense of liberty is no vice! . . . Moderation in the pursuit of justice is no virtue!"* (Goldwater's italics). On hearing these words Senator Keating and forty other members of the New York delegation walked out of the convention.

The Democratic Nomination Race

Johnson Dominates the Polls. President Johnson was content to let the Republicans' battles dominate the political news during primary season, as poll after poll showed that voters, even many Republicans, preferred him to either Governor Rockefeller or Senator Goldwater — the two most likely Republican candidates. In June, when it became clear that Goldwater had the Republican nomination sewn up, a Gallup poll showed that 81 percent of registered voters would vote for Johnson over Goldwater. Even staunch Republican businessmen,

Sen. Barry Goldwater launching his presidential campaign in his hometown of Prescott, Arizona

such as Henry Ford II, were expressing support for Johnson.

Johnson Demonstrates Leadership. Since the assassination of President Kennedy and Vice-president Johnson's assumption of the presidency on 22 November 1963, Johnson had stressed continuity with the Kennedy administration. Calling on Congress to fulfill the Kennedy legacy (and calling in the political IOUs he had amassed during his years in the Senate), Johnson used his extraordinary political skills to guide through both houses of Congress the major items on Kennedy's agenda, including a tax cut, War on Poverty legislation, and the Civil Rights Bill of 1964. This performance did much to enhance Johnson's stature as a national leader and — as he had planned — allowed him to remain above the fray of partisan politics.

A Challenge from Wallace. The president was challenged briefly from the right wing of his own party when Gov. George C. Wallace of Alabama entered a few primaries, hoping to demonstrate nationwide opposition to the Civil Rights Bill then in the Senate. Wallace won 34 percent of the votes cast in the Wisconsin Democratic primary (7 April), 29.8 percent in Indiana (5 May), and 42.7 percent in Maryland (19 May). Many of the votes in Wisconsin and Indiana came from Republican crossovers, suggesting that Wallace could hurt both candidates. Wallace announced that he would run for president as a third-party candidate. His fellow southern conservatives, however, were afraid Wallace and Goldwater would cancel out one another in the South, and they thought Goldwater had a better shot at beating Johnson. On 19 July, after a personal appeal from Goldwater, Wallace withdrew from the presidential race.

Johnson Vetoes Kennedy. There was strong public sentiment favoring the choice of Attorney General Robert F. Kennedy as Johnson's running mate, but Johnson, who was attempting to emerge from the shadow cast by one Kennedy, was not anxious to risk eclipse from another, who was perceived by many as the standard-bearer for his brother's vision of the New Frontier. Furthermore, while President Kennedy had established a good working relationship with his vice-president, Robert Kennedy and other members of the Kennedy administration had treated Johnson with barely disguised disdain and failed to seek his advice even when his superior insight on legislative matters could have been extremely useful to them. A proud man, who made a practice of always repaying friends and enemies in kind, Johnson told Kennedy privately that he would not be the vice-presidential candidate. Then, to make the decision seem like a matter of policy rather than personality, Johnson announced that no one in his cabinet would be considered for the vice-presidency.

Johnson Taps Humphrey. Johnson's choice for his running mate was Sen. Hubert H. Humphrey of Minnesota. As Senate majority whip, Humphrey, who had been a champion of civil rights since 1948, had played a crucial role in shepherding the Civil Rights Bill of 1964 through the Senate. If the election had shown signs of being close, Johnson might have thought twice about sharing the ticket with a politician as liberal as Humphrey, but Goldwater was so far behind in the polls that Johnson could afford the risk of offending conservative Democrats, especially in the South.

The Democratic Convention. The major events at the Democratic National Convention in Atlantic City, New Jersey, began to unfold just before the convention officially convened on 24 August. To dramatize the plight of southern blacks who tried to register to vote, Robert Moses, head of the Student Nonviolent Coordinating Committee (SNCC) voter-registration program in Mississippi, had organized the Freedom Democratic Party, which elected its own integrated convention delegation to challenge the credentials of the delegation sent by the regular Mississippi Democratic Party, which excluded blacks. One after another black Freedom Democrats testified to the credentials committee about the violence inflicted on them by Mississippi law officers as punishment for their legal attempts to register to vote. Johnson believed that compromise was possible, but the regular Mississippi Democrats, who stressed that their election was strictly legal, and the Freedom Democrats, who emphasized with equal fervor that morality was on their side, were totally unwilling to make concessions. The committee's decision angered both sides. It stated that no regular Mississippi delegate could be seated without first pledging to support the Democratic ticket, that two Freedom Democrats would be seated as delegates at large with full voting privileges, and that beginning in 1968 the national convention would not seat delegations from states where the party excluded citizens and deprived them of their voting rights solely on the basis of race or color. When this compromise was read aloud to the convention, Freedom Democrats swarmed onto the convention floor and took over the seats assigned to the Mississippi delegation. By the time they were ousted three hours later, the regular Mississippi and Alabama delegations had walked out. The rest of the convention was uneventful. With Johnson's nomination a foregone conclusion, not even his attempts to keep the nation guessing about his choice of a running mate could generate much drama.

The Presidential Campaign

Johnson and Goldwater's Secret Agreement. Two events of the summer of 1964 were major factors in shaping American history for the rest of the decade and beyond: on 2 July President Johnson signed into law the Civil Rights Act of 1964, and on 5 August Congress passed the Gulf of Tonkin Resolution, which later led to escalation of American involvement in the Vietnam War. Yet neither race nor the war was an issue in the 1964 election campaign. On 24 July the Republican presidential candidate, Sen. Barry Goldwater, and President Johnson met secretly and agreed not to use the war or civil rights as major campaign issues. With a relatively small number of American troops in Southeast Asia, the American public was far more focused on the Cold War with the Soviet Union than on events in Vietnam. Yet, as Goldwater pointed out, opposition to American involvement there was growing and had the potential to divide the nation.

The Race Issue. Alabama governor George Wallace's strong showing in several primaries had demonstrated the existence of a white backlash against black Americans' strides toward racial equality, and the race riots in New York and several other northern cities during July 1964 tended to reinforce the fears of some conservative whites. Goldwater might have used the white backlash to his advantage, especially in the South, but whether he did so or not Johnson might have labeled him a racist because of his vote against the Civil Rights Bill.

Johnson's Great Society. Johnson based much of his campaign on his concept of the Great Society, which he first outlined in his 22 May 1964 commencement speech at the University of Michigan. Speaking in an unprecedented period of American prosperity, he called for "an end to poverty and injustice," the enhancement of educational opportunities for all Americans, the renewal of the nation's natural beauty, and the recognition of "creation for its own sake." Yet Goldwater had provided the Johnson campaign with so much ammunition that Johnson spent little time describing specific programs.

Johnson Turns Goldwater's Words Against Him. Using Goldwater's own statements, the Democrats portrayed him as trigger happy with nuclear weapons. ("Let's lob one into the Kremlin men's room," was a frequently quoted Goldwater statement.) Johnson presented himself as the peace candidate, while his supporters amended a memorable and clever Goldwater slogan — "In your heart you know he's right" — to "In your heart you know he might." On domestic issues Goldwater needed little help from the Democrats to alienate voters. The same principled objection to the expansion of federal government that had led him to vote against the Civil Rights Bill of 1964 resulted in speeches against farm subsidies to a group of farmers, against Medicare to retirees in Florida, against poverty programs to West Virginians, against the Tennessee Valley Authority in Knoxville. At each campaign stop Goldwater seemed to alienate another group of American voters.

Johnson Wins Big. In the end Johnson won the election with 61.2 percent of the popular vote. Goldwater won his home state of Arizona and five southern states — Mississippi, Alabama, Louisiana, South Carolina, and Georgia. Helped by the black vote in Virginia, North Carolina, Tennessee, and Arkansas, Johnson took the remainder of the South and the rest of the nation, winning 486 electoral votes to Goldwater's 52. Johnson's coattails created large Democratic majorities in both the House and the Senate — as well as at the state level — causing many political commentators to ask if the Republican party could survive.

Republican Losses in Congress. The Johnson landslide helped the Democrats, who had a net gain of 38 seats in the House of Representatives. The Democrats' 153-seat majority was their largest since their party's sweep in the 1936 election. The conservative coalition of Republicans and southern Democrats was seriously damaged by the defeats of forty-two northern Republicans. GOP victories over seven southern Democrats replaced conservatives with conservatives and strengthened the influence of liberal Democrats in the Democratic Caucus. In both houses the Republicans who survived were moderates who managed to disassociate themselves from Goldwater. No congressman who voted for the Civil Rights Bill of 1964 was defeated; eleven of the twenty-one northern Republicans who voted against it lost.

Democrats Supplement Their Senate Majority. Democrats held twenty-six of the thirty-five Senate seats up for reelection in 1964 and won twenty-eight of them, giving their party its largest Senate majority since 1940. Republicans had been especially hoping to win back some of the thirteen seats taken from them by liberal Democrats in 1958, causing a major realignment of power in the Senate, but all eleven remaining members of the "Class of 1958" were reelected, including Robert C. Byrd of West Virginia, Thomas J. Dodd of Connecticut, Philip A. Hart of Michigan, R. Vance Hartke of Indiana, Eugene J. McCarthy of Minnesota, and Edmund S. Muskie of Maine. Newcomers to the Senate included Democrats Robert F. Kennedy of New York and Joseph D. Tydings of Maryland.

Governorships. Republicans won in only eight of the twenty-five states where gubernatorial elections were held in 1964, taking three governorships away from Democrats but losing two others. Republicans John H. Chafee of Rhode Island, John A. Volpe of Massachusetts, and George W. Romney of Michigan avoided backing Goldwater, whose endorsement would have most likely spelled defeat for them. All eight states that elected Republican governors gave their electoral votes to Johnson in the presidential race.

Sources:

Congressional Quarterly Almanac, 20 (1964);

Time, 84 (13 November 1964): 3–43;

Theodore H. White, *The Making of the President 1964* (New York: Atheneum, 1965).

NATIONAL POLITICS: 1966 ELECTIONS

The Republican Comeback. After its devastating losses in 1964, the Republicans came back strong in

Senate	1962*	1964	Net Gain/ Loss
Democrats	68	68	+2
Republicans	32	32	-2

* By the 1964 election there were 66 Democrats and 34 Republicans in the Senate.

House	88th* Congress	89th Congress	Net Gain/ Loss
Democrats	258	295	+38
Republicans	176	140	-38

* By the 1964 election there were 257 Democrats and 178 Republicans in the House.

Governors	1962	1964	Net Gain/ Loss
Democrats	34	33	-1
Republicans	16	17	+1

1966, erasing House and Senate deficits incurred two years earlier. Although Democrats held on to their majorities in both houses of Congress, President Johnson lost the liberal mandate that had allowed him to push through his Great Society legislation in 1965. Part of their success was attributed to former vice-president Richard M. Nixon, who campaigned actively for Republican candidates nationwide and emerged as his party's chief spokesman, filling the leadership role left vacant after Barry Goldwater's defeat in 1964.

Republican Gains in the Senate. Moderates Charles H. Percy of Illinois, Mark Hatfield of Oregon, and Howard Baker, Jr., of Tennessee took Senate seats formerly held by Democrats. Liberal Republican Edward R. Brooke of Massachusetts became the first black elected to the Senate in the twentieth century. Incumbents in both parties did well. Only one, Democrat Paul H. Douglas of Illinois, was defeated. The fifteen Democrats who won reelection included several powerful southerners. Republican southerners John G. Tower of Texas and Strom Thurmond of South Carolina, who had switched parties in 1964, were also reelected. The election of Democrat Ernest F. (Fritz) Hollings of South Carolina to fill out the term of the late Olin D. Johnston was attributed in part to the growing strength of black voters in the South.

Republicans' Strong Showing in House Races. GOP candidates took fifty-two House seats from Democrats and lost only five for a net gain of forty-seven that more than erased their net loss of thirty-eight two years earlier. Democratic liberals were hit especially hard. Twenty of the forty-seven Democrats who took House seats from Republicans in 1964 were

Senate	1964	1966	Net Gain/Loss
Democrats	67	64	-3
Republicans	33	36	+3

House	89th Congress	90th Congress	Net Gain/Loss
Democrats	295	248	-47
Republicans	140	187	+47

Governors	1964	1966	Net Gain/Loss
Democrats	33	25	-8
Republicans	17	25	+8

defeated. Four more of these Democrats, who retired, were replaced by Republicans.

Governorships Split Fifty-Fifty. Republicans made their biggest gains in gubernatorial races, picking up eight new governorships for a total of twenty-five. With the election of Ronald Reagan in California and Raymond P. Shafer in Pennsylvania and the reelection of George W. Romney of Michigan, James A. Rhodes of Ohio, and Nelson A. Rockefeller of New York, Republicans had the governorships of five of the seven most populous states. Reagan's victory over incumbent Edmund G. (Pat) Brown with a plurality of nearly one million votes enhanced the conservative Republican's standing as a possible presidential candidate. Romney's 60.1 percent victory in Michigan increased speculation about his chances for the nomination, while Rockefeller's election to a third term by a majority far greater than polls had predicted kept alive his presidential hopes. His brother Winthrop Rockefeller defeated a militant segregationist to become the first Republican governor of Arkansas since Reconstruction. Another presidential hopeful, Gov. George Wallace of Alabama, could not, by state law, succeed himself, so his wife, Lurleen Wallace, ran in his place. She easily defeated her Republican opponent.

Sources:
Congressional Quarterly Almanac, 22 (1966);
Time, 88 (18 November 1966): 3-33.

NATIONAL POLITICS: 1968 ELECTIONS

The Republican Nomination Race

Romney Leads Early. After the resounding defeat of presidential candidate Barry Goldwater in 1964 the Republican Party was left leaderless and seemed moribund. One bright spot in that year, when many Republican candidates for national and state offices had gone down in defeat with Goldwater, was the reelection of George Romney, the popular Republican governor of Michigan, where voters had favored Johnson over Goldwater by a margin of two to one. Even before he was elected to a third two-year term, Romney had emerged as the front-runner for the Republican presidential nomination in 1968, with promises of support from Gov. Nelson A. Rockefeller of New York and most other Republicans.

Romney Falters. In November 1966 polls showed Romney leading President Johnson by 54 to 46 percent, and the Michigan Republican continued to lead the president by similar margins through spring 1967. By then Romney, who was a poor public speaker, was beginning to look like a political lightweight, waffling on expressing his own "dovish" opposition to the Vietnam War for fear of offending Republican "hawks," who supported the presence of American troops in Southeast Asia. On 31 August 1967, after he had come out clearly in opposition to the war, he explained his evolution from an earlier prowar stance by saying that during a visit to Vietnam two years earlier he had been "brainwashed" by American

Richard M. Nixon opening his campaign in the 1968 New Hampshire primary

diplomats and military men. Romney never recovered from the damage this remark inflicted on his candidacy. On 28 February 1964, after polls showed Richard M. Nixon leading him five to one in the New Hampshire Republican primary, Romney withdrew from the presidential race.

The Nixon Comeback. The rehabilitation of Nixon as a viable national candidate was one of the great political surprises of 1968. After losing the California gubernatorial race to Democrat Edmund G. (Pat) Brown in 1962, Nixon had announced that he was leaving politics and joined a prestigious law firm in Manhattan. Yet he had briefly considered entering the presidential race in 1964, and in 1966 he had tirelessly and successfully campaigned for Republican candidates, establishing himself as the party's senior spokesman.

Nixon Wins Primaries. To earn his party's support for his second presidential bid, Nixon had to prove that he could win primaries. Declaring himself "better qualified to handle the problems of the Presidency than I was in 1960," Nixon accused the Johnson administration of failing "to use our military power effectively" or "our diplomatic power wisely." He promised to "End the War and Win the Peace," while curbing inflation and reestablishing law and order at home. He won the New Hampshire Republican primary on 12 March with more than 80,000 votes, more votes than the total cast for all other candidates from both parties, beating write-in candidate Nel-

son Rockefeller by a margin of seven to one. Nixon went on to win in Wisconsin (2 April), Indiana (7 May), and Nebraska (14 May) with little or no opposition before he faced and defeated California governor Ronald Reagan in Oregon (28 May).

Implementing a "Southern Strategy." On 1 June Nixon met with Sen. Strom Thurmond of South Carolina, Sen. John Tower of Texas, and other southern Republican leaders in Atlanta to clarify for them his position on civil rights. While he supported the policy of refusing federal funds to districts where schools were clearly segregated, he disapproved of withholding those funds for tardiness in complying with precise white/black student ratios mandated by federal officials, and he opposed compulsory busing to achieve school integration. Also reassuring Senator Thurmond of his belief in a strong national defense, Nixon left Atlanta with the 394 convention votes of the South and the border states virtually locked up.

Opposition from Reagan and Rockefeller. By the end of April, however, Nixon faced opposition from the right and the left of his own party. Conservative Ronald Reagan was still in the race, and in June and July he concentrated on the South, where he tried to pry loose delegates already committed to Nixon. Liberal Nelson Rockefeller, who had called a press conference on 21 March to "reiterate unequivocally" that he was not a candidate, called another on 30 April to announce that he was in the race after all. That same day he won all 34 Massachusetts delegates as a write-in candidate in that state's Republican primary. Campaigning with poll data indicating that he had a better chance than Nixon of beating any Democrat, Rockefeller had little hope of gathering the 667 votes that would give him a first-ballot convention victory, but he hoped he could win on a subsequent ballot if he and Reagan could do well enough in the first round of voting to keep Nixon below 600.

The Republican Convention. Just one week before the Republican National Convention opened in Miami on 5 August, a Gallup poll showed that suddenly Nixon was ahead of Rockefeller, Vice-president Hubert Humphrey, or Senator Eugene McCarthy, and capable of beating either Democrat. Nixon arrived at the convention believing he had just barely enough votes to win on the first ballot. He cooperated with Rockefeller, Romney, and others to revise the Vietnam War plank from a call for escalation of the war to a promise for new leadership to "offer a fair and equitable settlement to all, based on the principle of self-determination," a "pledge to develop a clear and purposeful negotiating position," and a statement of "total support" for the troops in Vietnam. On 8 August, despite a last-minute scare when Nixon's floor leader counted only 666 votes as the balloting started, Nixon won the nomination in the first round with a margin of only 25 votes: 692 to 277 for Rockefeller and 182 for Reagan.

Nixon Picks Agnew. In selecting a running mate Nixon sought to not to offend either wing of the party. Governor Spiro Agnew of Maryland was a moderate from a border state. He had nominated Nixon in a speech that had enlivened an otherwise boring convention, and no one Nixon consulted had anything bad to say about him. Armed with this compromise running mate, Nixon gave a stirring acceptance speech, promising to "bring an honorable end to the Vietnam War" and calling on the leaders of the Soviet Union and China to join him in ending "an era of confrontation" for a new "era of negotiation." Yet — as the race riots that had raged in another part of Miami throughout the convention continued — the delegates' greatest enthusiasm was for Nixon's pledge to reimpose law and order at home: "Time is running out for the merchants of crime and corruption."

The Democratic Nomination Race

Opposition to Johnson. In autumn 1967 President Lyndon B. Johnson seemed certain of winning the Democratic Party nomination to run for a second full term as president. Yet a revolt from within his own party was brewing. Since 1965 Johnson's increasing escalation of the war in Vietnam had been paralleled by an ever-growing, increasingly militant antiwar movement. Politicians in both parties had begun to question the handling of the war and to charge that the United States should never have committed troops to Vietnam in the first place. Convinced that they could not unseat a sitting president, antiwar Democrats such as Senators Robert F. Kennedy of New York, Eugene McCarthy of Minnesota, and George McGovern of South Dakota — as well as Lt. Gen. James Gavin — had all rebuffed suggestions that they oppose Johnson for the presidential nomination. Yet on 30 November, believing that someone had to take the opposition's message to the people, McCarthy announced his candidacy.

McCarthy's Moral Victory in New Hampshire. McCarthy's chances for success in the New Hampshire Democratic primary on 12 March 1968 appeared slim. Polls predicted in late January that he would get no more than 8–11 percent of the vote. Then the North Vietnamese and Vietcong launched their major Tet offensive on 30 January. Though American troops achieved total victory in the battle, the event badly eroded public confidence in Johnson's assurances that the United States was winning the war. Student volunteers who had gotten "clean for Gene" — cutting off long hair and shaving off beards and mustaches — blanketed New Hampshire in an effective door-to-door campaign to take McCarthy's message to the voters. Johnson, who had chosen to run as he had in 1964, by remaining above the political fray in Washington, was not officially entered in the primary but won 49 percent of the vote as a write-in candidate. McCarthy, however, got 42 percent and claimed a moral victory. When Republican write-ins for both candidates were added in, Johnson beat McCarthy by only 239 votes.

Kennedy Enters the Race. More of the McCarthy voters in New Hampshire were hawks disillusioned with Johnson than doves opposed to the war. Yet a nationwide Gallup poll showed a major shift to the antiwar camp during the six weeks following the Tet offensive. In February 60 percent of those polled called themselves hawks while only 24 percent said they were doves. In March the doves outnumbered the hawks by 42 to 41 percent. Kennedy realized that he had underestimated the strength of voter sentiment against the war and entered the presidential race four days after the New Hampshire primary. While he could attract students and intellectuals from McCarthy, Kennedy had a broad political base that also included minorities and working-class whites in major urban areas of the states with the most electoral votes.

Johnson Withdraws. At the end of March Johnson's aides warned him that he faced certain defeat in Wisconsin, where McCarthy was campaigning with an army of eight thousand student volunteers. On 31 March Johnson announced on television that he had ordered a partial halt to the bombing of North Vietnam and invited the Hanoi government to begin negotiations to end the war. Then Johnson made a second announcement: "I have concluded that I should not permit the Presidency to become involved in the partisan divisions that are developing in this political year. . . . Accordingly, I shall not seek and I will not accept the nomination of my party for another term as your President." Two days later McCarthy defeated Johnson in the Wisconsin primary by 56.2 to 34.6 percent.

McCarthy and Kennedy Square Off. The two antiwar candidates faced one another for the first time in the Indiana primary (7 May), where Kennedy won 42.3 percent to 27 percent for McCarthy and 30.7 percent for a stand-in for Vice-president Hubert H. Humphrey, who had announced his candidacy on 17 April, after the last filing date for the primaries. Kennedy had a bigger victory over Humphrey and McCarthy in Nebraska (14 May) — 51.7 percent of the vote — but McCarthy beat Kennedy by 44.1 to 38.1 percent in Oregon on 28 May.

Humphrey Wins Delegates. While public attention had been largely focused on McCarthy and Kennedy's primary battles, Humphrey — the choice of the party regulars — had been winning the delegate wars in nonprimary states. Of the two peace candidates, Kennedy seemed to have a better chance of stopping Humphrey, but a win in California on 4 June was crucial for Kennedy. He won with 46.3 percent of the vote over McCarthy with 41.8 and a stand-in for Humphrey with 11.9 percent. In the early hours of 5 June, just after making a victory speech to his supporters, he was shot by a lone gunman and died the next day.

McCarthy's Victory in New York. McCarthy won 62 of 123 New York delegates on 18 June; that primary also committed 30 to the late Robert Kennedy, 12 to Humphrey, and left 19 uncommitted.

McGovern Declares His Candidacy. As the convention approached, McCarthy picked up some of Kennedy's delegates, but about 300 went to Senator George McGovern, who announced his candidacy on 10 August, two weeks before the opening of the Democratic National Convention in Chicago on the twenty-sixth. Humphrey seemed to have the nomination sewn up, however, and McCarthy — never a dynamic campaigner — approached the convention with an apparent lack of direction that lent credence to McGovern's response when asked what made his candidacy different from McCarthy's: "Well — Gene doesn't want to be President, and I do."

The "Draft-Teddy" Movement. To beat Humphrey required not only rallying all the McCarthy, McGovern, and uncommitted Robert Kennedy delegates behind a single candidate, but also sparking a sizable defection from the Humphrey camp. A few days before the start of the convention, a coalition of political doves who believed Sen. Edward M. Kennedy of Massachusetts was their only hope started a "Draft-Teddy" movement. Promised support from McCarthy and Chicago mayor Richard Daley, who had secretly expressed antiwar sentiments for some time and who controlled most of the Illinois votes, the only surviving Kennedy brother unequivocally refused to run.

The Democratic Convention. The convention began and ended in acrimony. From floor fights over delegates'

credentials and rules for voting, the Democrats went on to a bitter debate on the Vietnam War platform plank.

Johnson Dictates the Vietnam Plank. Before the convention, representatives of Humphrey and Edward Kennedy had worked out a plank designed to be acceptable to both McCarthy and Johnson, but the president had expressed outright opposition to it. Rather than anger Johnson — who possessed the power to deny Humphrey the nomination — Humphrey threw his support to a majority plank that restated Johnson's policies. This plank rejected the possibility of "unilateral withdrawal" of American troops and called for an end to the bombing of North Vietnam only "when the action would not endanger the lives of our troops." The minority plank drawn up by McCarthy forces called for an immediate halt to the bombing and "an early withdrawal of a significant number of our troops." As the voting concluded, with the majority plank winning by a three-to-two margin, some peace delegates put on black armbands and chanted "Stop the War," while others sang "We Shall Overcome."

The Battle in the Streets. As the wrangling delegates moved on toward the by-then inevitable nomination of Humphrey, the real political drama was taking place in the streets of Chicago, where the police and antiwar demonstrators had been warring all week. Protesters carried out their plan to hold a major demonstration during the nominations process at the convention. The police had been clubbing and teargassing demonstrators all week. Now, as about forty-five hundred of them marched toward the convention site, police armed with clubs, mace, and tear gas charged the crowd, beating protesters, journalists, and bystanders alike. As protesters chanted "The whole world is watching," tear gas seeped into the windows of the twenty-fifth-floor hotel suite where Humphrey was working on his acceptance speech. The official report on the riot, submitted later that year to the National Commission on the Causes and Prevention of Violence, a group appointed by President Johnson, concluded that while a few protesters had deliberately provoked them, the police response was excessive, amounting to a "police riot" that injured more than one thousand mostly innocent people.

Humphrey Wins Amid Acrimony. Delegates within the convention hall were unaware of the violence in the streets until about an hour later, when television coverage of a seconding speech for Humphrey was interrupted with the first available film footage. Angry peace delegates threatened to walk out, and Connecticut senator Abraham Ribicoff used his nominating speech for McGovern to denounce "Gestapo tactics on the streets of Chicago." Finally, at 11:19 P.M., far later than the prime-time slot for which it was scheduled, the first roll call of the delegates began. Humphrey won the nomination easily with 1,760 1/4 votes to 601 for McCarthy and 146 1/2 for McGovern. The next evening Humphrey's acceptance speech failed to unite his badly divided party, and McCarthy refused to stand on the platform with

The National Mobilization to End the War in Vietnam (MOBE), headed by long-time pacifist David Dellinger, set out to attract the largest possible number of antiwar demonstrators to Chicago for Democratic National Convention week by planning a sort of multiple-choice protest like their huge October 1967 antiwar demonstrations in Washington, where the level of protest — from lawful assembly to passive resistance to civil disobedience — was left up to the individual. MOBE's plans were undermined by the refusal of Chicago authorities to grant the necessary permits and by the violent behavior of the Chicago police department during an April 1968 antiwar protest and the riots after the assassination of Martin Luther King, Jr. Many moderates who might otherwise have attended the demonstrations stayed away. About two thousand protesters had shown up in Chicago by the weekend before the convention. By Wednesday, 28 August, the day on which Hubert Humphrey won the Democratic nomination, the number had risen to about ten thousand.

Among those who did show up in Chicago were the Yippies, who had told Tom Hayden and Rennie Davis, the MOBE coordinators for the Chicago demonstrations, that they had no interest in their traditional format of speeches and a large-scale protest march. Mostly the brainchild of radical activists Jerry Rubin and Abbie Hoffman, the Yippies (short for Youth International Party) were a mock political party whose members, its founders announced, would be any hippie who came to Chicago. There the Yippies staged a "Festival of Life" to counter the "National Death Convention" (aka the National Democratic Convention) and nominated Pigasus, a real pig, as their "presidential candidate." This mock convention and other events during convention week met with violent reactions from the Chicago police, who used clubs and tear gas on demonstrators throughout the week.

The greatest mayhem occurred when — despite its inability to obtain a parade permit — MOBE attempted to carry out its planned two-mile march from Grant Park to the convention site on the night of Humphrey's nomination. Policemen waded into the crowd of about forty-five hundred, beating demonstrators, newsmen, and innocent bystanders with their billy clubs. Hundreds were injured that night, bringing the total number of injured demonstrators for the week to more than a thousand. Nearly two hundred policemen were also injured.

Though many demonstrators angered the police with verbal taunts, and a relatively small number of protesters are known to have thrown rocks and bottles or otherwise assaulted policemen, Daniel Walker's official report to President Johnson's National Commission on the Causes and Prevention of Violence concluded that "police action was not confined to the necessary force" and events in Chicago would best be described as a "police riot." Nonetheless, after the inauguration of Richard M. Nixon in 1969, Dellinger, Hayden, Davis, Hoffman, and Rubin, along with two other MOBE volunteers and Black Panther Bobby Seale (who was in Chicago just long enough to give an angry speech), were indicted under a federal anti-riot law. After a lengthy trial and appeals process, however, all convictions were overturned.

Sources: David Farber, *Chicago '68* (Chicago: University of Chicago Press, 1987);

Tom Hayden, *Reunion: A Memoir* (New York: Random House, 1988);

Norman Mailer, *Miami and the Siege of Chicago: An Informal History of the Republican and Democratic Conventions of 1968* (New York: World, 1968);

Daniel Walker, *Rights in Conflict: Convention Week in Chicago, August 25–29, 1968, A Report Submitted to the National Commission on the Causes and Prevention of Violence* (New York: Dutton, 1968).

Humphrey and his running mate, Sen. Edmund Muskie of Maine.

The 1968 Elections

The Third-Party Challenge. In the battle for the presidency Humphrey and Nixon had to fend off the advances of George C. Wallace, a segregationist former governor of Alabama, who attracted voters from the conservative wings of both parties. Wallace, who had managed to get on the ballot in sixteen states before withdrawing from the presidential race in 1964, was on the ballot in all fifty states for the 1968 elections. Between May and September 1968 Wallace's approval ratings rose steadily from 9 to 21 percent. If these numbers continued to increase at the same pace, some pollsters suggested, Wallace would get nearly 30 percent of the vote on election day. This projection suggested that Wallace's campaign strategy was working. He knew he could not win, but he hoped that he could take seventeen southern and border states (north to Delaware and Missouri) for a total

Chicago policemen clashing with demonstrators during the 1968 Democratic
National Convention

of 177 electoral votes. If he succeeded, neither major-party candidate would have a majority of votes in the Electoral College. Then Nixon or Humphrey would have to bargain with him for his electors, or the House of Representatives would be forced to choose the next president.

The Politics of Backlash. Wallace profited from the white backlash against civil rights sparked in part by the urban race riots that had been flaring up every summer since 1964 and from the conservative backlash against the antiwar movement, whose demonstrations had become larger, more disruptive, and more violent since 1964. Counting on southern support, Wallace campaigned heavily in northern states where blue-collar voters shared these sentiments, hoping not so much to win electoral votes as to demonstrate — with an eye to 1972 — that his support was not merely regional.

Wallace's Downfall. Seeking to win the same southern and border states as Wallace, Nixon based his southern campaign on the premise that most Wallace supporters were not racists, but simply voters fed up with civil unrest, the Johnson administration's expensive liberal social programs, and its conduct of the Vietnam War. Never attacking Wallace directly, Nixon found that one of the most effective weapons in his southern strategy was the suggestion that a vote for Wallace was a vote for Vice-president Humphrey. Humphrey, who saw Wallace's appeal to northern blue-collar workers cutting into the Democrats' traditional support from organized labor, got help from the AFL-CIO Committee on Political Education (COPE), whose widely distributed anti-

Wallace literature pointed out that the populist "friend of the workingman" was actually antiunion.

Wallace Frightens Voters. Wallace hurt himself as well, by often seeming to incite clashes between demonstrators and police at his campaign stops. The only candidate to call for total military victory in Vietnam, Wallace chose as his running mate Gen. Curtis E. LeMay, already well known for his remark that the United States could, and probably should, "bomb the North Vietnamese back to the Stone Age." This statement, and others advocating the use of nuclear weapons, frightened voters — just as Barry Goldwater's comments about atom bombs had scared them in 1964.

The Nonissue of the War. President Johnson asked both Nixon and Humphrey not to discuss the war lest they weaken America's position at the negotiating table. Having had no involvement in decisions about the war, Nixon could afford to stick to the law-and-order issue and to say only that he had a secret strategy to end the conflict. (Even after Nixon was elected, he never revealed this plan.) Humphrey, however, was closely associated with the Johnson administration's policies, having supported them loyally even when he disagreed privately. Since the Democratic National Convention in August, Humphrey had known that to have any hope of winning the election he had to present his own Vietnam policy, even if it angered Johnson. Finally, on 30 September he went on national television to address the issue. While Johnson tied a total bombing halt to further concessions from the North Vietnamese, Humphrey said he would stop all bombing immediately, while reserving "the right to resume bombing" if the North Vietnamese showed "bad faith." Humphrey's position was closer to Johnson's than it was to the minority peace plank voted down at the Democratic National Convention, but it was enough to silence the antiwar demonstrators who had been disrupting his campaign stops with chants of "Dump the Hump." Antiwar liberals began to consider Humphrey an acceptable candidate; campaign contributions increased; and Humphrey's numbers started going up in the polls.

An Election Too Close to Call. On 27 September a Gallup poll showed Nixon leading Humphrey by 43 to 28 percent, with 21 percent for Wallace. By 21 October — as Wallace's support faded — Nixon was still ahead, by 44 to 36 percent, but Humphrey was clearly gaining. The final Gallup poll, completed on the Saturday before the election, reported that Nixon's lead over Humphrey had dropped to only two percentage points (42–40). The last Harris poll, conducted over the weekend, showed Humphrey leading Nixon (43–40). Both pollsters considered the election too close to call.

Nixon's Narrow Victory. Nixon won 43.4 percent of the popular vote, with 42.7 percent for Humphrey and 13.5 for Wallace. Nixon took thirty-two states with a total of 301 electoral votes. If Humphrey and Wallace together had won just 34 more electoral votes, Nixon's total would have gone below the 270 votes needed to win, and the election would have gone to the House of Representatives, where the Democratic majority would most likely have made Humphrey president.

Republican Gains in Congress. Although Nixon's coattails were not long enough to carry in Republican majorities in the House and the Senate, the Republicans made gains in both houses. The liberal-dominated Congress of 1965–1966 was gone for good.

The Senate Inches to the Right. According to *Congressional Quarterly* ratings of senators without regard to party, liberal strength in the Senate remained the same — at 44 senators — before and after the election; the number of moderates dropped from 26 to 22 while conservatives increased from 30 to 34. Republicans had a net gain of five new seats, bringing the total of Republican senators to 42, the largest number since 1956. Among the 7 Republicans who won seats previously held by Democrats were Barry Goldwater, former senator (1953–1965) from Arizona, replacing retiring Democrat Carl Hayden, the ninety-one-year-old president pro tempore of the Senate; and newcomer Robert W. Packwood of Oregon, who defeated liberal Democrat Wayne Morse, one of the earliest opponents of the Vietnam War. Another Republican freshman was Robert Dole of Kansas, while Democratic newcomers included Alan Cranston of California and Harold E. Hughes of Iowa — the only Democrats who won seats previously held by Republicans — and Thomas F. Eagleton of Missouri.

Senate	1966*	1968	Net Gain/ Loss
Democrats	64	58	-5
Republicans	36	42	+5

* By the 1968 election there were 63 Democrats and 37 Republicans in the Senate.

House	90th* Congress	91th Congress	Net Gain/ Loss
Democrats	248	243	-4
Republicans	187	192	+4

Governors	1966*	1968	Net Gain/ Loss
Democrats	25	19	-5
Republicans	25	31	+5

* In 1967 the Democrats lost one more governorship to the Republicans.

Antiwar Senators Reelected. There were only two casualties among the opponents of the Vietnam War who were up for reelection in 1968. Ironically they were the only two senators to vote against the Gulf of Tonkin Resolution in 1964: Morse of Oregon and Ernest Gruening of Alaska, who lost in his state's Democratic primary. Democrats J. W. Fulbright of Arkansas, Abraham A. Ribicoff of Connecticut, Frank Church of Idaho, Birch Bayh of Indiana, George McGovern of South Dakota, and Gaylord Nelson of Wisconsin were all reelected, as was liberal Republican Jacob K. Javits of New York.

Republican Gains in the House. The GOP had hoped to win the 30 seats it needed for control of the House of Representatives. If they had come even close to that number, some Republicans thought, they could gain a majority by convincing a few southern Democrats to switch parties. But their net gain was only 4 seats, as voters tended to stick with incumbents (223 Democrats and 173 Republicans), electing only 39 newcomers (20 Democrats and 19 Republicans).

Republicans Dominate Gubernatorial Races. Having picked up the governorship of Kentucky in 1967, the Republicans added 5 more in 1968, to control the statehouses of 31 states. (This number dropped to 30 after the Maryland legislature elected a Democrat to replace Republican governor Spiro T. Agnew, who resigned after he was elected vice-president.) The victory of Richard B. Ogilvie over incumbent Democrat Samuel H. Shapiro of Illinois gave Republicans governorships in six of the seven most populous states. In fact, states with Republican governors had a total population of 132 million while Democrats governed states whose population totaled 67 million.

Sources:
Congressional Quarterly Almanac, 24 (1968);

Time, 92 (15 November 1968): 3–39;

Theodore H. White, *The Making of the President 1968* (New York: Atheneum, 1969).

RADICAL POLITICS: BLACK POWER

Cracks in the Civil Rights Movement. Chants of "black power," the slogan popularized by Stokely Carmichael and other members of the Student Nonviolent Coordinating Committee (SNCC) during the Mississippi freedom march of June 1966, were the first signs for most of the American public that some factions in the civil rights movement were beginning to question the methods of nonviolent protest advocated by the movement's popular and widely admired leader, Dr. Martin Luther King, Jr., of the Southern Christian Leadership Conference (SCLC). King argued to Carmichael and Floyd McKissick of the Congress of Racial Equality (CORE) that "black power" had connotations of violence that would (and in fact did) frighten white supporters of the civil rights movement, but Carmichael, who agreed not to use the slogan for the remainder of the march, was already convinced — as was McKissick — that passive resistance to physical force and building coalitions with sympathetic whites, the means through which the movement had already achieved most of its goals, would never make blacks fully equal with whites, who still held the reins of economic and political power and were unwilling to let go.

SNCC and Black Power. Resenting King for attracting media attention while they had done much of the hard work of running black-voter-registration drives in Georgia, Mississippi, and Alabama in 1961–1965 — and accusing him of overconcern with his own safety when they had risked death daily in those states — many members of SNCC had come to believe that self-defense was not only justified but wise. More important, the failure of the integrated Mississippi Freedom Democratic Party, organized by SNCC to unseat the regular, all-white delegation at the 1964 Democratic National Convention, brought around much of SNCC to a point of view already espoused by Carmichael: blacks should stop trying to reform the Democratic Party, he said; that would be like the Jews trying to change the Nazi party from within. Instead, he decided, blacks should form their own political party.

Carmichael's Black Panthers. In March 1965 Carmichael took the first step toward his goal in Lowndes County, Alabama, where not a single black was registered to vote, even though the population was predominantly black. As Carmichael's coworker Cleveland Sellers explained, "We intended to register as many blacks as we could, all of them if possible, and take over the county." Helped by the arrival in August of federal registrars sent under the Voting Rights Act of 1965 and undeterred by the murder of a civil rights worker, hundreds of blacks in Lowndes County registered to vote every day. In March 1966 black farmers and domestic workers formed their own political party, the Lowndes County Freedom Organization (LCFO), whose symbol — a snarling black panther — was the source of their unofficial name, the Black Panthers. By then black registered voters in the county outnumbered white voters by a large enough margin to convince members of LCFO that they could take over the county government. In the November 1966 elections they put up a full slate of black candidates for county offices and expected to win. Yet stuffed ballot boxes and other voting irregularities ensured their total defeat. While the LCFO chairman declared, "It is a victory enough to get the black panther on the ballot," many in SNCC viewed the election results as further proof that whites would never willingly give up power to blacks and moved further toward the belief that black separatism was the only solution to the subjugation of the Negro race. SNCC expelled all whites in December 1966, and CORE, which had been organizing poor blacks for community action in northern cities since 1965, followed suit in July 1968.

West Coast Black Panthers. While SNCC, led by Carmichael and H. Rap Brown, and CORE, under McKissick and Roy Innes, became increasingly militant, the American public viewed another group as the epitome of the radical black separatist movement: the Black Panther Party for Self-Defense. Founded in October 1967 in Oakland, California, by Huey Newton and Bobby Seale, the group had as its original purpose patrolling black neighborhoods to monitor police treatment of blacks. Party members' angry rhetoric — from chants such as "We want pork chops, off [kill] the pigs [police]" to Eldridge Cleaver's ultimatum "total liberty for black people or total destruction for America" — established an alarming public image that tended to obscure community programs such as health care, food giveaways, and an education center. Dressed in striking uniforms of black berets, pants, shoes, and leather jackets, and powder-blue shirts, the Panthers were also heavily armed — creating a macho image that aided greatly in recruiting new members. (Carrying a loaded, unconcealed weapon was legal in California at that time.) From a group of fewer than one hundred in Oakland, the Black Panther Party (which dropped "for Self-Defense" from its name in 1967) grew to a loosely connected organization with chapters in about thirty-five cities in nineteen states and the District of Columbia — as well as England, France, Israel, and Halifax, Nova Scotia — by late 1970. The party nearly folded in late 1967, when Newton was arrested for murder after a shoot-out with the police in which one officer was killed. Cleaver, a prison activist and writer for the West Coast radical left magazine *Ramparts*, who had signed on as Panther minister of information earlier that

Black Panthers protesting the murder trial of Huey Newton in New York City, 22 July 1968

year, emerged as a major party spokesman. The author of an influential prison autobiography, *Soul on Ice* (1968), Cleaver, who had spent nine years in prison for attempted murder, had a gift for attracting media attention and was largely responsible for the growth of the party over the next several years. (Newton was convicted of murder in 1968 but acquitted on a technicality in 1970.)

Black Liberation Ideology. Like most black power advocates, the Panthers were heavily influenced by the teachings of Malcolm X, the Black Muslim leader whose assassination in 1965 elevated him to a level of fame and prestige far greater than he had achieved in life. In the mid and late 1960s the posthumously published *Autobiography of Malcolm X* (1965) became a sort of sacred text for young black activists, with its assertion that blacks should not want "to *integrate* into this corrupt society, but to *separate* from it, to a land of our *own*, where we can reform ourselves, lift up our moral standards, and try to be godly." To these teachings the Panthers, like many of their black and white radical contemporaries, added the ideas they found in *The Wretched of the Earth* (first English translation, 1965), by Frantz Fanon, a black Caribbean psychologist who had played an important role in the struggle for Algerian independence from France. Cleaver called Fanon's book the bible of the black liberation movement, while Seale claimed he had read it six times, and Carmichael called Fanon a patron saint. They derived from Fanon an identification of the black power movement in America with the liberation efforts of the oppressed Third World peoples of Africa and Asia — a view that contributed substantially to their opposition to the Vietnam War — and a belief that "violence is a cleansing force. It frees the native from his despair and

inaction; it makes him fearless and restores his self-respect." Fanon gave the Panthers in particular — and the black liberation movement in general — the vocabulary to express their belief that black Americans' history and culture, and with it their sense of self-worth, had — like those of the Third World — been dominated, distorted, and nearly destroyed by whites, the "colonizers" who imposed their own culture and system of values on a conquered people. The solution to this state of subjugation began with reeducation of blacks to their true cultural identity — a process of empowerment best undertaken through throwing off and separating from the oppressor. Such ideas were at the heart of the Black Panther platform, especially their demand for "a United Nations–supervised plebiscite to be held throughout the black colony [that is all blacks in the United States] in which only black colonial subjects will be allowed to participate, for the purpose of determining the will of black people as to their national identity."

Cleaver Seeks White Allies. Onto the teachings of Malcolm and Fanon, the Black Panthers tacked their own version of Marxism-Leninism, what Cleaver called "a Yankee-Doodle-Dandy version of socialism." Believing that oppression of blacks was linked to oppression of the lower classes, the Black Panthers believed that they could be the revolutionary vanguard in overthrowing "all the enemies of the wretched of the earth." Although Panthers often looked on the white radicals in the antiwar movement as children playing at being revolutionaries, declining on those grounds to take part in planning for the antiwar demonstrations at the 1968 Democratic National Convention in Chicago, Cleaver and other Panthers welcomed white fellow travelers, but as foot soldiers, not generals: it was the duty of whites to participate in the black liberation struggle, the Panthers said, but blacks, not whites, would control the direction of that movement. One example of their coalition building was Cleaver's agreement to run for president in 1968 on the ticket of the Peace and Freedom Party, a mostly white group of antiwar activists, who put up as Cleaver's running mate white radical Jerry Rubin, a founder of the Yippies (Youth International Party), which planned a major role in the Chicago demonstrations.

SNCC Merges with the Panthers. At the same time Cleaver was exploring links with white radicals, he was also looking to other black groups, most notably SNCC, which was far better known than the Panthers in 1967–1968. On 17 February 1968 (Huey Newton's birthday) at one of the Panthers' many "Free Huey" rallies, they and SNCC announced that the two groups would merge, and Carmichael was named Black Panther prime minister. The union was brief and controversial. Cleaver and Carmichael were soon arguing about the place of whites in the movement, with Cleaver criticizing Carmichael's "paranoid fear" of whites and his willingness to choose allies on the basis of color rather than ideology. In August — after further infighting — SNCC officially disassociated itself from the Black Panthers and at the same time expelled Carmichael, who resigned from the Panthers in July 1969 (and was eventually denounced by them as an agent of the CIA).

Hoover Targets the Panthers. Though there were other black liberation groups that were more antiwhite and proviolence than the Panthers, the Panthers were more visible than underground guerrilla organizations such as the Black Liberation Army and the Revolutionary Action Movement and therefore a primary target of the COINTELPRO group launched by FBI director J. Edgar Hoover in August 1967 "to expose, disrupt, misdirect, discredit, or otherwise neutralize the activities of black nationalist, hate-type organizations and groupings. . . ." FBI infiltration in SNCC contributed to that organization's split from the Panthers, while other undercover agents in the Panthers and US, another West Coast black group led by Ron Karenga, instigated an August 1969 shootout between the two groups that left two Panthers dead. There was also direct action between the Panthers and law enforcement officials. In April 1968 Panther treasurer Bobby Hutton was killed, and four others, including Cleaver, were wounded during a police raid. As a result Cleaver's parole was revoked. The next December two Chicago Panther leaders, Fred Hampton and Mark Clark, were killed in a police raid of their apartment and elevated to martyrdom by fellow black nationalists. By 1970 twenty-eight Black Panthers had been killed by policemen, according to figures released by the party attorney. Cleaver had gone into exile in Algeria, taking other Panthers with him, and after Newton's release from prison that year the two disagreed on party policy. Each ended up forming his own version of the Black Panthers and expelling the other. By the mid 1970s COINTELPRO had largely succeeded in destroying or driving underground both black and white radical movements.

Defining Black Power. The black power movement as a whole was so diverse, so loosely coordinated, and in many cases so uncertain about its methods and goals that it is virtually undefinable. Although white Americans tended to interpret the "black power" slogan as a call to racial violence, blacks most often understood it as a call for racial pride and the achievement of political and economic power through peaceful, democratic means. For example, in a 1967 poll of blacks and whites in Detroit, 60 percent of the white respondents but only 9 percent of the blacks equated black power with violence and racism. Whites also tended to see black riots and looting — which erupted yearly in major American cities from 1964 through the end of the decade — as proof that huge numbers of young blacks were ready to rise up in violent revolution, but, as the Black Panthers and other groups that attempted to recruit new members in these ghettos learned quickly, the great majority of poor urban blacks wanted to be part of the middle class, not to destroy it. Because the angry rhetoric of the Panthers and SNCC made more exciting news than stories about the grassroots political activities of lower-class blacks to elect their own representatives to city and county councils, the media served to heighten whites' fears of black power groups. Not all these groups were separatist, and those that were held widely diverging, and sometimes uncertain, views on what and where the new black nation should be. While some groups called for their own black nation in Africa, others wanted to establish a new homeland in the United States. In 1968, for example, a group calling itself the Republic of New Africa (RNA) delivered a letter to the U.S. State Department in which they requested the opening of negotiations on their proposal that the United States turn over to them the states of South Carolina, Georgia, Alabama, Mississippi, and Louisiana and $400 billion start-up money for the creation of an all-black sovereign nation. (The State Department did not respond, and the RNA attempted to establish a community in Mississippi while developing urban guerrilla forces; by the mid 1970s the RNA, like other groups targeted by COINTELPRO, was defunct.) Other black power groups were simply reacting against the growing tendency of whites to move out of the inner cities while maintaining ownership of buildings and businesses as well as participation in city politics. Faced with increasingly run-down housing, price-gouging storekeepers, underfunded schools, and local governments unsympathetic to their plights, these black power groups were creating black communities in which blacks controlled their own economic and political destinies and took pride in their own history and culture. Some of these groups wanted to establish entirely new, self-sufficient black communities, such as Soul City, which Floyd McKissick established in Warren County, North Carolina. Others wanted to set up black enclaves within cities. In Newark, for example, black poet Amiri Baraka called on blacks to "take over our own space in these same shitty towns transforming them with our vision and style to be extensions of swiftshake and stomp sound." Though their rhetoric was often angry, these groups, with their emphasis on black pride and black culture and their willingness to work within the established economic and political systems, were ultimately more successful than the radical groups that dominated the media in the late 1960s.

Sources:

Hugh Pearson, *The Shadow of the Panther: Huey Newton and the Price of Black Power in America* (Reading, Mass.: Addison-Wesley, 1994);

William L. Van Deburg, *New Day in Babylon: The Black Power Movement and American Culture, 1965–1975* (Chicago & London: University of Chicago Press, 1992);

Robert Weisbrot, *Freedom Bound: A History of America's Civil Rights Movement* (New York & London: Norton, 1990).

RADICAL POLITICS: THE FAR RIGHT

Redefining the Right Wing. During the 1950s, with the emergence of the United States as a global power and as the leader of the West in the Cold War, the right wing in American politics had to reinvent itself. Though the right wing maintained its opposition to federal involvement in domestic issues that made it anti–New Deal during the 1930s and 1940s, it abandoned its isolationist position in foreign policy which was incompatible with their militant anticommunism. The far-right elements that had tended to xenophobia and nativism before World War II muted these aspects of their message after the war, when they discovered that their militant anticommunism appealed to many of the same religious and ethnic groups who had been the targets of their hate in the 1930s, notably Irish and East European Catholics. The new, militantly anticommunist right wing considered American foreign policy, including the doctrine of containment, to be too soft. It was critical of foreign aid and distrustful of American involvement in the United Nations. It was libertarian in its view of economics, opposing taxes, government regulation of business, government spending, and social programs. Finally, it was socially traditional, stressing moral order and maintenance of the "community." There were two broad strains of right-wing thinking generally agreeing on these positions but differing on how to account for the ills of American politics and policy. One group, which some have labeled the ultraconservatives or the extreme conservatives, blamed the flaws in American policy on stupidity, blindness, and bungling by American presidents and their misguided liberal advisers. William F. Buckley, Jr., has been an exponent of this point of view through the magazine *National Review,* which he cofounded in 1955, and through his television show *Firing Line.* Organizations such as Young Americans for Freedom and Americans for Constitutional Action are also considered ultraconservative. A second group on the far right has tended to see the United States as being sold out or undermined by conspiracy. This group includes Robert Welch and the John Birch Society, George Lincoln Rockwell and his American Nazi Party, and the paramilitary group the Minutemen. Representatives of the Christian Right — Gerald L. K. Smith, Rev. Carl McIntire, Dr. Fred Schwarz, Rev. Billy James Hargis — also tended to adhere to the conspiratorial explanation for folly in government policies. Despite their differences in accounting for the wrongheadedness of American domestic and foreign policies, both groups coalesced around and vigorously supported the candidacy of Sen. Barry Goldwater in 1964.

The Ultraconservatives

William F. Buckley, Jr., and the *National Review.* In 1951 Buckley, a 1950 graduate of Yale University, published *God and Man at Yale,* a scathing critique of his alma mater, in which he suggested that the faculty was overwhelmingly secular and liberal in orientation and failed to indoctrinate students properly with Christian and procapitalist values. This book, along with his 1954 defense of Sen. Joseph McCarthy, *McCarthy and His Enemies,* brought Buckley acclaim among American conservatives. In *National Review,* an outlet for conservative opinion, he repeatedly railed against the blunders of the liberal leadership of the United States and pointed out that the Communist danger to the United States comes from Moscow and Beijing rather than a conspiracy at home. Buckley provided an intellectual bridge between the prewar right and the redefined right of 1964. He was an urbane, articulate spokesman for the ultraconservative point of view, an avid supporter of Goldwater in 1964, and an editorial supporter of the states-rights position that opposed the three civil rights bills of the 1960s on the grounds that they would take away powers that legally belonged to the states and give them to the federal government.

Buckley Helps Found YAF. On 9–11 September 1960 Buckley hosted a group of conservative student activists at his Connecticut home. Early that year these activists had successfully fought a congressional proposal to drop loyalty oaths as a requirement for receiving federal aid as a college student, and in midyear they had vigorously supported an effort to win Arizona senator Barry Goldwater the Republican Party vice-presidential nomination. At their meeting with Buckley they founded the Young Americans for Freedom (YAF) — an organization designed to attract young conservatives. The early membership attracted moderate Republicans as well as ultraconservatives, and the ideology of the group emphasized libertarian views of minimal government and anti-Keynesian notions about economics. Buckley and California Congressman John Rousselot, a John Birch Society leader, served as early spokesmen for the group, providing muscle for Goldwater's bid for the 1964 Republican nomination.

Americans for Constitutional Action. Retired admiral Ben Moreell was a driving force in Americans for Constitutional Action (ACA), a group founded in 1958 and endorsed by Sen. Karl Mundt (R-S.Dak.). The ACA was modeled after and intended to be a counterforce to the liberal Americans for Democratic Action (ADA). Extremely conservative in its early rhetoric, it attacked the income tax as a policy straight out of Karl Marx and Friedrich Engels's *Communist Manifesto* and charged that the 1960 platforms of both the Republican and Democratic parties in 1960 were too liberal. Many of the early ACA leaders had close ties to the radical-right John Birch Society. The ACA promoted conservative causes, raised campaign funds, and hired campaign workers to assist in key House and Senate races during the 1960s. With the YAF the ACA provided valuable manpower and organizational resources to support conservative candidates.

The Radical Right

The John Birch Society. Given its emphasis on establishing a grassroots organization in local communities, the John Birch Society was probably the most important radical-right group during the 1960s. Founded in 1958 by Robert Welch, a wealthy former candy manufacturer and onetime vice-president of the National Association of Manufacturers, the organization grew to forty thousand members in three hundred local chapters by 1963 and to eighty thousand members in four hundred local chapters by 1967. This broad organizational base made the John Birch Society highly influential on local issues and an easily mobilized force on national issues and political campaigns. Named after an American army captain and Baptist missionary who was killed by the Chinese Communists during the Chinese revolution of the late 1940s, the organization was virulently anti-communist and idolized the late Sen. Joe McCarthy for his rabid antired crusade of the early 1950s. In a manifesto titled *The Blue Book of the John Birch Society* the society repeated McCarthy's attacks on former secretary of state George C. Marshall (also a former five-star general) and former secretary of state Dean Acheson, both of whom had been involved in the development of the Cold War policy of the containment of communism. Warning that Communist conspirators had infiltrated all aspects of American life, the John Birch Society called for the United States to withdraw from the United Nations and for the impeachment of Chief Justice of the United States Earl Warren because of his role in liberal civil rights and First Amendment decisions. Also in the 1960s it charged that civil rights leader Martin Luther King, Jr., was backed by Communists and called the civil rights movement an instrument of subversion.

Welch Embarrasses the Conservative Cause. Welch embarrassed himself and the society when he labeled former president Dwight D. Eisenhower and his secretary of state John Foster Dulles dupes of the Communist conspiracy, which by Welch's estimate controlled 50 to 70 percent of the United States by 1962. Conservative intellectuals such as William F. Buckley, Jr., and Russell Kirk denounced Welch for these attacks as did congressional conservative spokesman Rep. Walter Judd (R-Minn.). Yet they did not repudiate the society. Pressured to resign, Welch held on to his leadership position, but increasingly he lost power and influence within the organization. The society remained a force in conservative politics well into the 1970s because of its strong grassroots organization.

The American Nazi Party. Never having more than a few hundred members, the American Nazi Party gained national recognition primarily through the well-publicized activities of its leader and founder, George Lincoln Rockwell. Influenced by Christian-right leader Gerald L. K. Smith and by Sen. Joseph McCarthy, Rockwell organized the party in 1958 while he was in the U.S. Navy. Its members attended rallies wearing storm-trooper uniforms decked with swastikas. Rockwell espoused the view that America was being subverted by a Jewish-Communist conspiracy that was promoting integration and miscegenation through the civil rights movement. Paradoxically, Rockwell also attacked Robert Welch and the John Birch Society as being no better than Communist conspirators. Rockwell's energies were frequently directed to opposing the civil rights movement. In one instance of guerrilla theater he drove a "hate bus" around the South, following and mocking the Freedom Riders. In January 1965 he was arrested for disturbing the peace in Selma, Alabama, outside a church where Martin Luther King, Jr., was conducting a meeting. He also targeted the Vietnam War opposition. In November 1965 he and his followers scuffled with antiwar protesters in Washington, D.C. Rockwell and his party reached the height of their effectiveness when they participated in counterdemonstrations to King's drive for fair housing in Chicago. But Rockwell won few converts. The party began to fade from the political scene after Rockwell was shot and killed on 25 August 1967 by a disgruntled former party member.

The Minutemen. The Minutemen were a paramilitary organization founded in 1960 by Missouri businessman Robert Bolivar Depugh to protect the United States from Communist invasion from abroad and Communist subversion from within. With five thousand to six thousand members at most, the organization drew public attention because its members actively trained with rifles and other weapons. They studied guerrilla tactics and set up secret caches of arms. Minutemen were supposed to work to expose Communist influences in the U.S. national leadership. The group gradually disintegrated after their leaders were convicted in 1967 and again in 1968 of violating federal laws regulating firearms.

Gerald L. K. Smith. Rev. Gerald L. K. Smith was one of several fundamentalist preachers connected to the radical right. An aide to Louisiana governor Huey Long in the 1930s and an antiunion activist in Michigan in the

1940s, he founded the right-wing Christian Nationalist party while in Michigan and ran for president as its nominee in 1944 and 1952. Smith was not only vehemently anticommunist but also antiunion, anti-Semitic, and racist. He continued to be active in the 1960s, operating from Eureka Springs, Arkansas, where he spent much of his time promoting the construction of a seven-story statue named *The Christ of the Ozarks*. He put on an elaborate, annual passion play that depicted Jews as the killers of Christ, and he continued to promote his views through the publication of a newsletter, *The Cross and Flag*. George Lincoln Rockwell readily acknowledged Smith's influence on his own thinking.

Rev. Carl McIntire and the *Twentieth Century Reformation Hour*. Rev. Carl McIntire began his ministry in the late 1930s, and in 1941 he founded the American Council of Churches as a counter-force to the mainstream National Council of Churches, to combat what he described as the evils of religious modernism and Communist infiltration of the church. McIntire was also antiunion, anti–United Nations, and anti–Catholic. For most of his career McIntire's influence was limited to the few readers of his newspaper, *The Christian Beacon,* and listeners to a small radio station in Chester, Pennsylvania, which broadcast his views. In 1958, however, McIntire started a syndicated radio show, *The Twentieth Century Reformation Hour,* which reached six hundred radio stations by the mid 1960s. Throughout the 1960 presidential campaign, McIntire vigorously opposed the candidacy of John F. Kennedy because of Kennedy's liberalism and Roman Catholicism. McIntire helped to promote the careers of newcomers Dr. Fred Schwarz and Rev. Billy James Hargis. He also had close ties to the John Birch Society, and for a while he was on the national advisory board for Young Americans for Freedom.

Dr. Fred Schwarz. A medical doctor and a Christian evangelist from Australia, Dr. Fred Schwarz came to the United States in 1952 and founded the Christian Anti-Communist Crusade. He attacked what he perceived as the Communist orientation of American intellectuals and clergymen, and throughout the 1950s and 1960s he warned against a Communist plot to take over the United States in 1973. Primarily a fund-raiser, he and a small staff traveled, led seminars, and gave lectures promoting his views. Schwarz received public backing from Congressman Walter Judd (R-Minn.) and Sen. Thomas Dodd (D-Conn.). In 1964 he publicly endorsed Republican senator Barry Goldwater's candidacy.

Rev. Billy James Hargis. The Rev. Billy James Hargis, a radio preacher from Tulsa, Oklahoma, founded the *Christian Crusade* to promote his idea that it was every individual's Christian duty to fight Communism. He preached that the United States was being sold out to the Communists by treasonous leaders, and he attacked U.S. membership in the United Nations. He also opposed the civil rights movement because he believed that segregation was the law of God. Like McIntire he attacked the National Council of Churches as an organization treasonous to both God and country. An active supporter and member of the John Birch Society, he went so far as to charge that fellow right winger George Lincoln Rockwell and his American Nazi party were fronts for liberalism. Hargis tended to be far more overtly political than Schwarz.

Goldwater Campaign. Both the ultraconservatives and the radical right-wingers reached the height of their power in national politics when they coalesced around Goldwater's candidacy in 1964. After he lost in a landslide, taking many conservative candidates down to defeat with him, many of these organizations faded into the background, especially those that failed to build a grassroots organization. Revenues for some of the Christian-right groups started to dwindle following critical exposés of their methods and radical views. The relaxation of tensions between the United States and the Soviet Union that began after the Cuban missile crisis also tended to undermine the appeal of their militantly anticommunist messages. Groups that had set up organizational bases in local communities — including YAF, the ACA, and the John Birch Society — remained effective well after the 1960s were over.

Sources:

David H. Bennett, *The Party of Fear: From Nativist Movements to the New Right in American History* (Chapel Hill: University of North Carolina Press, 1988);

Arnold Forster and Benjamin R. Epstein, *Danger on the Right* (New York: Random House, 1964);

Jerome L. Himmelstein, *To the Right: The Transformation of American Conservatism* (Berkeley: University of California Press, 1990).

RADICAL POLITICS: THE NEW LEFT

One of the most striking and controversial political phenomena of the 1960s was the rise and decline of the New Left. It arose from the civil rights movement in 1960, played a central role in the Vietnam War protest movement, and then at the height of its influence it self-destructed. By late 1970 the New Left was essentially nonexistent.

Roots in the Civil Rights Movement. The New Left was born with Students for a Democratic Society (SDS) at the University of Michigan in 1960. Though SDS was never a single-issue organization, many of its early members saw SDS as a means of organizing northern university students to participate in the black-voter-registration drives that the Student Nonviolent Coordinating Committee (SNCC) started in the South in 1961.

C. Wright Mills, Godfather to the New Left. Much of the impetus for the direction SDS took in its early years came from the writings of sociologist C. Wright Mills (1916–1962), especially his influential 1956 book *The Power Elite*. The powerful "military-industrial complex" that President Dwight D. Eisenhower warned against in his farewell address (1960) bears a strong resemblance to Mills's "power elite." Yet Mills's interpre-

Members of SDS at a National Council meeting in Bloomington, Indiana, 1963. Tom Hayden
is standing on the far left, and Rennie Davis is on the far right.

tation goes farther than Eisenhower's in assessing the state of American democracy. Mills charged that the United States is governed by individuals from "the higher circles, the military, big business, and politics" kept in power by huge interlocking bureaucracies operating to sustain themselves rather than to serve the people. This concept underlies *The Port Huron Statement*, the first declaration of SDS policy, drafted by Tom Hayden (second president of SDS, 1962–1963) and revised by the forty-three SDS members who attended the organization's first national conference at Port Huron, Michigan, in June 1962. The statement also echoes Mills in calling for "participatory democracy": "we seek the establishment of a democracy of individual participation, governed by two central aims: that the individual share in those social decisions determining the quality and direction of his life; that society be organized to encourage independence in men. . . ."

A Noncommunist New Left. In his "Letter to the New Left" (1960) Mills predicted that young radical intellectuals all over the world would be the "real live agencies of historic change," and he rejected the Marxist idea that the working class would rise up to create a new society. While it deplored "unreasoning anticommunism," *The Port Huron Statement* declared SDS's "basic opposition to the communist system." It also criticized labor unions as too entrenched in their own bureaucracy to be agents of social change. In seeking an identity of their own — apart from the Old Left and organized labor, one of the most powerful forces in the Democratic Party — SDS limited its base of support from the start.

SDS Searches for Identity. By intention *The Port Huron Statement* was ideologically eclectic. For example, at one point it borrowed from Pope John XXIII for the statement "We regard men as infinitely precious and possessed of unfulfilled capacities for reason, freedom, and love"; at another it says the "new left must include liberals and socialists, the former for their relevance, the latter for their sense of thoroughgoing reforms in the system." In fact, SDS was willing to work with any group that shared its goals for social change. Many of the early SDS members considered themselves "radicals." Yet while Hayden spoke of the need "to disengage oneself entirely from the system being confronted," the radicalism he and his contemporaries espoused was only vaguely defined and seemed mainly to refer to the need to find and remedy the "root" causes of society's ills, an idealistic sort of radicalism that might best be described as "reformism."

Grassroots Political Action. Though SDS played a minor role in demonstrations against American involvement in Vietnam as early as September 1963, its major focus during the first half of the 1960s was on domestic issues. In 1963 the organization began its Economic Research and Action Project (ERAP) to further participatory democracy by organizing the urban poor in ten cities, including Baltimore, Boston, Chicago, Cleveland, Newark, and Philadelphia. Most ERAP projects were short-lived, though new ones sprang up as old ones died. The Newark and Chicago ERAP projects lasted into 1967, when the community organizers who had held them together, including Tom Hayden, Rennie Davis, and Todd Gitlin, turned their attention to the antiwar movement.

From Reform to Resistance: The Second Generation. In late 1964, while leaders of the first generation of SDS were still involved in grassroots domestic issues, the second generation was already starting to focus on the Vietnam War, planning an antiwar campaign that included an April 1965 protest march in Washington, D.C. U.S. bombing of North Vietnam, which began in February 1965, triggered an upsurge in opposition to the war. In December 1964 SDS had hoped to draw 2,000 to its April march; 15,000 to 25,000 showed up. SDS had been growing steadily, from 250 members in December 1960 to 2,500 in December 1964, but as the war escalated so did SDS membership, to 10,000 in October 1965 and 25,000 a year later. Though the ERAP activists had mastered the art of confrontation to achieve their political goals, they believed that the political system could be forced to reform itself. Many of the newcomers to SDS in 1965 and 1966 lacked that faith, and as the war heated up many of the old guard began to agree.

From Resistance to Revolution. Focusing on resistance to the war and the military draft, SDS had entered a new phase by late 1967, dismissing advocates of participatory democracy as "bourgeois reformists." SDS leadership began to see itself as part of a Marxist revolutionary vanguard and found its inspiration in the writings of Algerian nationalist Frantz Fanon (1916–1961), who had praised the "cleansing force" of violent revolution. "Ideological purity" became a central concern in SDS, which had previously tolerated differences of opinion within its ranks and exerted strength beyond its actual numbers by willingly working with groups that agreed with its stand on the issue at hand while disagreeing on everything else. The new SDS leadership dismissed plans for the antiwar demonstrations at the 1968 Democratic National Convention as insufficiently revolutionary, ridiculing the "old-fashioned politics" of protest coordinators Davis and Hayden — and the many other SDS veterans involved in the planning who believed they could influence electoral politics. The small number of current SDS members who went to Chicago played an inflammatory role in the demonstrations and came away believing that the young people of America were ready for a revolution on the streets.

SDS Self-Destructs. The televised pictures of the Chicago police clubbing demonstrators did, in fact, radicalize many young Americans. A poll taken soon after the convention revealed that 368,000 of them called themselves revolutionaries. Though SDS was no longer keeping careful records, its membership was estimated at 80,000–100,000. In reality many of these new "revolutionaries" were as uncertain about what the term meant to them as the SDS members of 1962 had been about their radicalism. Ironically, just as SDS should have been at the height its influence, two radical factions began to battle for its control. At the June 1969 SDS convention the Weathermen and Progressive Labor Party (PL) members (adherents of Mao Zedong's Chinese Communism) split the organization in two. Local SDS chapters declared their independence from the national organization, or organizations, and less-radical members quit in droves. By mid 1970 the PL version had faded into the background and was soon extinct. The demise of the Weathermen was explosive.

"You don't need a weatherman to know which way the wind blows" — these words from Bob Dylan's "Subterranean Homesick Blues" were the source of the Weathermen's name, but the Weathermen failed to forecast the mood of their contemporaries. In October 1969 their violent "Days of Rage" rampage through the streets of Chicago during the trial of the organizers of the demonstrations at the 1968 Democratic National Convention failed to mobilize the large numbers of young Chicagoans who had turned out for the defendants' protest marches. The Weathermen suffered more injuries and financial damage than their targets; two hundred Weatherman were arrested.

The Weather Underground. In June 1970 the Weathermen bombed the New York City Police headquarters, inflicting substantial damage, and they took credit for seven other bombings in 1970–1972. Yet on 6 March 1970 the explosion of a Weathermen bomb factory in the basement of a Greenwich Village townhouse killed three Weathermen, and the discovery of antipersonnel explosives in their arsenal further eroded their limited base of support. Under indictment for a variety of offenses, they went underground. Some took on new identities; others joined forces with Black Panthers in exile in Algeria.

Sources:
Todd Gitlin, *The Sixties: Years of Hope, Days of Rage* (Toronto, New York, London, Sydney & Auckland: Bantam, 1987; revised, 1992);

Tom Hayden, *Reunion: A Memoir* (New York: Random House, 1988);

James Miller, *"Democracy Is in the Streets": From Port Huron to the Siege of Chicago* (New York: Simon & Schuster, 1987);

Kirkpatrick Sale, *SDS* (New York: Random House, 1973).

HEADLINE MAKERS

STOKELY CARMICHAEL

1941-

CHAIRMAN, SNCC, 1966-1967; PRIME MINISTER, BLACK PANTHER PARTY, 1968-1969

Evolution of an Activist. In the course of one decade Stokely Carmichael evolved from a nonviolent civil rights activist to a black revolutionary to an ardent Pan-Africanist.

Background. Born in Port of Spain, Trinidad, Carmichael immigrated to Harlem, in New York City, when he was eleven and attended the Bronx High School of Science before enrolling at Howard University in Washington, D.C., in 1960. There he joined a group affiliated with the Student Nonviolent Coordinating Committee (SNCC) and took part every weekend in sit-ins and demonstrations to protest segregation in the Washington area. He also spent every summer of his college years as a volunteer with SNCC projects to register and organize black voters in the South, and in 1961 he spent forty-nine days in jail for taking part in one of the Freedom Rides to protest segregation of public transportation.

Work with SNCC. After graduating from Howard in 1964, Carmichael signed on with the SNCC full-time. During the Mississippi Freedom Summer Project of that year, in which ten civil rights workers were murdered and many more were beaten — frequently by officers of the law — Carmichael was project director for the second congressional district. By the time the integrated Mississippi Freedom Democratic Party, organized by SNCC, failed in its efforts to unseat the all-white Mississippi delegation to the Democratic National Convention in August, Carmichael had concluded that blacks were justified in defending themselves against white attackers and

that whites would never give up political power willingly. Blacks, he said, could take that power by forming their own political parties. He put this idea into action in 1966 as director of the SNCC voter-registration project in predominantly black Lowndes County, Alabama, where he helped black voters form their own party, the Lowndes County Freedom Organization (LCFO), with a snarling black panther as its symbol. When voting irregularities helped white candidates defeat the LCFO slate of candidates running for county offices, Carmichael became even more certain that blacks had to create their own political, educational, and economic institutions to change society — without seeking, or expecting, help from the white power structure. In May 1966 like-minded members of SNCC elected him national chairman of the organization.

Black Power. Little known to the American public when he took over as leader of SNCC, Carmichael captured media attention the very next month, during the protest march across Mississippi organized by Martin Luther King, Jr., and other civil rights leaders after James Meredith was shot at the beginning of his cross-state walk to publicize black-voter registration. On 16 June in Greenwood, Mississippi, Carmichael stood before a crowd of civil rights protesters and proclaimed: "The only way we gonna stop them white men from whippin' us is to take over. We been saying freedom for six years and we ain't got nothin'. What we gonna start saying now is Black Power!" *The New York Times* gave front-page coverage to the rally, at which Carmichael and other SNCC workers led the crowd in chanting "black power," and the slogan became part of the national vocabulary. In *Black Power: The Politics of Liberation in America* (1967) Carmichael and his co-author, Charles V. Hamilton, stressed that *black power* meant establishing political power bases through legal, democratic means, but his angry political rhetoric suggested otherwise to some observers — especially when race riots broke out in Atlanta, Nashville, and Washington after he gave speeches in those cities in

1966–1968. Though there was no proof that Carmichael directly encouraged the riots, some politicians and commentators labeled him a "professional agitator."

Black Revolutionary. Declining to seek reelection as SNCC chairman in May 1967, Carmichael, who had already denounced the Vietnam War as a white imperialist attempt to subjugate a Third World people, traveled to Europe, Africa, North Vietnam, and Cuba. Identifying with Third World freedom fighters seeking to overthrow colonial rule, Carmichael moved beyond the position stated in his book, giving a speech in Havana in August 1967 in which he called on black Americans to "take up arms and struggle for our total liberation." Back in the United States, he continued to advocate guerrilla warfare and armed struggle.

Black Panther Prime Minister. In February 1968 the SNCC merged with the Black Panther Party, which named Carmichael its prime minister. SNCC dissolved the union the following July, expelling Carmichael, who chose to stay on with the Panthers. He resigned a year later, after arguing with Black Panther minister of information Eldridge Cleaver, who believed that the party should ally itself with white radicals. By then Carmichael had become a vehement Pan-Africanist, believing that blacks should return to Africa and immerse themselves in a search for their cultural roots. In late 1968 he immigrated to the African nation of Guinea, where he changed his name to Kwame Ture and founded the All-African People's Revolutionary Party.

Sources:

Stokely Carmichael and Charles V. Hamilton, *Black Power: The Politics of Revolution in America* (New York: Random House, 1967);

William L. Van Deburg, *New Day in Babylon: The Black Power Movement and American Culture, 1965–1975* (Chicago & London: University of Chicago Press, 1992);

Robert Weisbrot, *Freedom Bound: A History of America's Civil Rights Movement* (New York & London: Norton, 1990).

ELDRIDGE CLEAVER

1935-

MINISTER OF INFORMATION, BLACK PANTHER PARTY, 1966-1971

The author of *Soul on Ice* (1968), a prison autobiography that has been called second only to the *Autobiography of Malcolm X* (1965) in its influence on young black militants, Cleaver was a leading spokesman for the Black Panther Party, notable for his willingness to recruit white radicals to the black nationalist cause.

Background. Born in Wabbaseka, Arkansas, a small town near Little Rock, Leroy Eldridge Cleaver was raised in Phoenix and the Watts section of Los Angeles. Beginning in the early 1950s he was convicted on a variety of marijuana-related charges and spent time in reformatories and prisons. In 1957 he was sentenced to two to fourteen years for attempted murder and spent the next nine years in Soledad prison.

Black Muslim. In 1958 Cleaver joined the Black Muslims and became a leader among the other Muslim prisoners. When Muslim leader Malcolm X split with Black Muslim founder Elijah Muhammad in March 1964 and moderated his views on white people, Cleaver followed Malcolm, writing later that Malcolm had drawn back "from the precipice of madness." The next year Cleaver wrote to a prominent civil-liberties attorney in San Francisco, asking her to help him get paroled. She showed some of Cleaver's prison writings to the editor of the San Francisco radical magazine *Ramparts*, which began publishing the essays later published in *Soul on Ice*. Cleaver was paroled in December 1966 and began working at *Ramparts*.

Black Panther. The following February he met Black Panther Party founders Huey P. Newton and Bobby Seale. After watching Newton call the bluff of a police officer who made a move toward his gun as the heavily armed Newton stood on the steps outside the *Ramparts* office, Cleaver decided Newton was "the baddest motherfucker ever to step foot inside of history" and signed on as the Panthers' minister of information.

New Legal Troubles. On 6 April 1968, during a ninety-minute gun battle with the police, Cleaver and three other Panthers were wounded and Panther treasurer Bobby Hutton was killed. Cleaver's parole was rescinded, and he was charged with assault and attempted murder.

Presidential Candidate. Free on bail, Cleaver ran as the presidential candidate of the predominantly white Peace and Freedom Party, using his campaign to call on black and white radicals to work together to end racial and class repression.

Exile. Having exhausted all appeals on the revocation of his parole and due to be returned to prison, Cleaver fled to Cuba on 28 November 1968. By July 1969 he was in Algeria, where he set up the international section of the Black Panthers, which became independent from Newton's party after the two disagreed and Newton expelled Cleaver in February 1971. In November 1975, having converted to Christianity, Cleaver returned to the United States, where he worked out a plea bargain under which he was sentenced to only twelve hundred hours of community service. In the late 1970s he started a clothing boutique in Hollywood and an evangelical organization in Nevada. In the 1980s he ran for national office as a conservative.

Sources:

Eldridge Cleaver, *Post-Prison Writings and Speeches,* edited by Robert Sheer (New York: Random House, 1969);

Cleaver, *Soul on Ice* (New York: McGraw-Hill, 1968);

Hugh Pearson, *The Shadow of the Panther: Huey Newton and the Price of Black Power in America* (Reading, Mass.: Addison-Wesley, 1994);

William L. Van Deburg, *New Day in Babylon: The Black Power Movement and American Culture, 1965–1975* (Chicago & London: University of Chicago Press, 1992).

TOM HAYDEN

1939-

PRESIDENT, SDS, 1962-1963; COORDINATOR OF ANTI-WAR DEMONSTRATIONS, CHICAGO, AUGUST 1968

New Left Activist. A major voice in defining the New Left, Hayden started out in the civil rights movement and worked as a community organizer in Newark, New Jersey, before he visited North Vietnam and became involved in organizing the opposition to the Vietnam War.

Background. Born and brought up in Royal Oaks, Michigan, a suburb of Detroit, Hayden attended the University of Michigan, where he edited the *Michigan Daily* and in fall 1960 helped to organize VOICE, an independent student political party that eventually became the Ann Arbor chapter of Students for a Democratic Society (SDS).

Civil Rights Activist. In fall 1961, after graduating from the university, Hayden became a field secretary for SDS, working with the Student Nonviolent Coordinating Committee (SNCC), which was beginning its efforts to help blacks register to vote in southern states. Beaten by whites in McComb, Mississippi, and arrested with members of SNCC while trying to integrate the railway station in Albany, Georgia, Hayden wrote *Revolution in Mississippi* (1961), a pamphlet about voter-registration efforts in that state.

Defining the New Left. Hayden left the South with the conviction that SDS should be the northern equivalent of SNCC, mobilizing support for SNCC's efforts in the South and organizing the urban poor of the North to influence the political decisions that affected their lives. Much of his thinking was influenced by sociologist C. Wright Mills, who had urged a new generation of young leftists to work for grassroots "participatory democracy" as a remedy to a government largely controlled by big business and high-ranking politicians and military men. This idea was at the heart of *The Port Huron Statement* (1962), the SDS manifesto, of which Hayden wrote the first draft. It was adopted at the June 1962 SDS convention in Port Huron, Michigan, where Hayden was elected SDS president for the 1962–1963 academic year.

Community Organizer. Hayden used his knowledge of SNCC community-organization methods when he helped to plan SDS's Economic Research and Action Project (ERAP) to stimulate participatory democracy in northern cities. In September 1963 he went to Newark, New Jersey, where he set up one of the longest-lasting and most successful ERAP projects, which folded after the Newark riots of July 1967. By then Hayden had become involved in the antiwar movement.

Antiwar Activist. In 1965 and twice in 1967 Hayden traveled to North Vietnam, returning from his third trip with three American POWs who had been turned over to him. In 1968, at the request of David Dellinger, head of the National Mobilization Committee to End the War in Vietnam (Mobe), Hayden and fellow SDS/ERAP veteran Rennie Davis headed the loosely coordinated efforts of the various antiwar groups that demonstrated in Chicago during the August 1968 Democratic National Convention — protests that one federal investigator described as a "police riot" because of the large number of attacks on demonstrators by Chicago police officers. For their part in planning the demonstrations Hayden, Davis, and Dellinger were among the eight men indicted in March 1969 for conspiring and crossing state lines to incite a riot. They and two others were found guilty in February 1970, but their convictions were later overturned. Hayden continued to be active in the antiwar movement, but by the mid 1970s he had moved toward involvement in electoral politics. He was unsuccessful when he ran for a U.S. Senate seat on the Democratic ticket in California, but in 1978 he was elected to the California state assembly. In 1994 he came in third when he ran for the gubernatorial nomination in the California Democratic primary.

Sources:

Tom Hayden, *Reunion: A Memoir* (New York: Random House, 1988);

Kirkpatrick Sale, *SDS* (New York: Random House, 1973).

LYNDON BAINES JOHNSON

1908-1973

VICE-PRESIDENT OF THE UNITED STATES, 1961-1963; PRESIDENT OF THE UNITED STATES, 1963-1969

Accepting the Second Slot. In 1960 Sen. Lyndon Baines Johnson of Texas, a masterful and powerful Senate majority leader since 1954, surprised Democrats and Republicans alike by agreeing to accept the Democratic nomination for vice-president, a job his fellow Texan, Sam Rayburn, Speaker of the House of Representatives, described as not "worth a pitcher of warm spit." John F. Kennedy's choice of Johnson for his running mate was also somewhat surprising. Johnson and Kennedy had made bitter remarks about one another while they had battled for the presidential nomination, and Kennedy's staff heartily disliked the Texan.

Kennedy himself, however, respected Johnson and admired his legislative skills. He also saw that Johnson could balance the ticket, helping to win votes in the South and West, where Kennedy was considered too liberal and was mistrusted because he was a Roman Catholic. There was another, strictly pragmatic reason for Kennedy's choice: "I'm not going to die in office," Kennedy told an aide; "If we win, it will be by a small margin, and I won't be able to live with Lyndon Johnson as the leader of a small majority of the Senate." The election was close, as Kennedy predicted, and Johnson's campaigning in the South and West was a major factor in assuring their victory.

Background. Johnson entered elective politics in the 1930s, having had a firsthand look at Depression-era poverty, first as a schoolteacher in West Texas, then as state director of the National Youth Administration, a New Deal program. Elected to Congress in 1937, he was an avid supporter of Franklin D. Roosevelt's social programs. His experiences during the Great Depression were important influences on the War on Poverty and Great Society programs he advanced in the 1960s. In 1948 he was elected to the U.S. Senate.

Vice-president Johnson. Entrusted by Kennedy with a more significant role than vice-presidents usually played, Johnson chaired the newly created Committee on Equal Opportunity, chartered to promote compliance with non-discrimination in hiring by the federal government and by companies contracting with the federal government. He also chaired the National Aeronautics and Space Council, playing a key role in guiding the space program.

President Johnson. After Kennedy was assassinated in November 1963, Johnson moved quickly to reassure the country that government policy would not radically change, that he would create continuity by keeping Kennedy's appointees in office, and that he would vigorously promote Kennedy's legislative package. During 1964 he pushed through Congress Kennedy's important tax cut and civil rights bills. His War on Poverty legislation, also passed in 1964, evolved from information collected by task forces created by Kennedy.

Landslide Victory in 1964. Johnson's resounding defeat of Republican candidate Barry Goldwater also gave him impressive majorities in both houses of Congress, enabling him to enact Kennedy's aid to elementary and secondary education and Medicare bills, which became part of Johnson's Great Society package that passed in 1965 and 1966, including the Higher Education Act and Voting Rights Act of 1965.

The War in Vietnam. Johnson's downfall as president was in the area of foreign policy, where he had little direct experience. His views on the subject had been formed during his early years in the Senate, as he learned from the political backlash after the 1949 Communist takeover in China and the nationwide hysteria generated when Sen. Joseph McCarthy charged in the early 1950s that Communists had infiltrated all aspects of American life. Johnson extended this lesson to the conflict in Vietnam, commenting to Henry Cabot Lodge, U. S. ambassador to Vietnam, "I am not going to be the President who saw Southeast Asia go the way of China."

Escalation. In 1965 Johnson escalated the war dramatically, first with a bombing campaign against North Vietnam in February and later by sending combat troops. By 1968 there were more than five hundred thousand U.S. troops in Vietnam, and the expanded U.S. role had begun to generate opposition that grew and became more vehement in direct proportion to ever-increasing U.S. involvement.

Johnson's Credibility Gap. Having portrayed himself as a peace candidate during the election campaign of 1964, Johnson escalated the war, leading to the perception that he had been misleading the public. The press began to point out the so-called credibility gap between Johnson's words and deeds. His explanation of why he sent troops to the Dominican Republic in 1965 reinforced this perception. First he claimed that their mission was to protect the lives of American citizens living in that Caribbean country, but subsequently he said he had sent the American military to prevent a possible Communist takeover. More and more Americans began to distrust the optimistic assurances of imminent victory in Vietnam that came from administration and military spokesmen. These predictions appeared even more unrealistic when the enemy launched its major Tet offensive early in 1968. Even before then, protests against the war had become so pervasive that Johnson limited his public appearances to safe venues, such as military bases and other federal facilities.

Johnson Drops Out. Running for the presidential nomination that should have automatically been his as incumbent, Johnson won the New Hampshire primary by a surprisingly small margin over antiwar candidate Sen. Eugene McCarthy. As one set of his advisers pressed him to make stronger efforts to get peace negotiations started, another warned him that he was about to lose to McCarthy in the Wisconsin primary. On 31 March Johnson announced on national television that he would order a bombing halt and invited the North Vietnamese to begin negotiations. Then he shocked the nation by announcing that he would not seek another term. During his last year in office, he succeeded in beginning negotiations with the North Vietnamese. After Richard Nixon's inauguration in 1969, Johnson retired to his ranch in Texas.

Sources:
Vaughan Davis Bornet, *The Presidency of Lyndon Johnson* (Lawrence: University Press of Kansas, 1983);

Robert Caro, *The Years of Lyndon Johnson: Means of Ascent* (New York: Knopf, 1990);

Caro, *The Years of Lyndon Johnson: The Path to Power* (New York: Knopf, 1982);

Doris Kerns Goodwin, *Lyndon Johnson and the American Dream* (New York: Harper & Row, 1976).

JOHN F. KENNEDY

1917-1963

PRESIDENT OF THE UNITED STATES, 1961-1963

Seeking the Nomination. John Fitzgerald Kennedy was a promising young U.S. Senator from Massachusetts when his nominating speech for Adlai Stevenson at the 1956 Democratic National Convention caught the attention of party leaders and nearly won him the vice-presidential nomination. As soon as the 1956 election was over, he put together an impressively efficient and knowledgeable campaign staff and began running for the 1960 Democratic presidential nomination. Overcoming doubts about his youth and the prevalent belief that, as a Roman Catholic, he could not be elected president of the United States, he won his party's nomination and faced Richard M. Nixon in the November 1960 election.

Campaigning for Change. Kennedy campaigned on the need for change, charging the Eisenhower administration with inaction on foreign policy matters such as growing Soviet influence in Cuba and on the economy, which was in a recession. His youthful good looks and ready wit so appealed to the American public that journalists began using the word *charisma* to describe his effect on campaign crowds, who were equally charmed by his beautiful young wife, Jacqueline Bouvier Kennedy. Turning his youth into an asset while at the same time convincing voters of his maturity, forty-three-year-old Kennedy overcame voters' qualms about his religion to win the closest presidential election in the twentieth century. He was the youngest president ever elected and the first born in the twentieth century.

The Torch Is Passed. Succeeding seventy-year-old Dwight D. Eisenhower, then the oldest man to have served as president, a hatless John F. Kennedy projected an image of youthful vigor as he stood on the steps of the U.S. Capitol on a freezing 20 January 1961 and proclaimed, "Let the word go forth from this time and place, to friend and foe alike, that the torch has been passed to a new generation of Americans — born in this century, tempered by war, disciplined by a hard and bitter peace, proud of our ancient heritage — and unwilling to witness or permit the slow undoing of human rights to which this nation has always been committed. . . ."

Foreign Policy Crises. Americans were fascinated by the new president and first lady, admiring their cultural sophistication and glamour, learning from their promotion of the arts, and enjoying the frequently photographed hijinks of their two young children. Yet the first two years of Kennedy's presidency were fraught with crises. Although he had campaigned on promises to stimulate the economy, support civil rights legislation, provide federal aid to elementary and secondary schools, and create a Medicare program for the elderly, his attention during his first two years in office was diverted by foreign policy challenges from the Soviet Union and a growing Communist threat in Southeast Asia and elsewhere in the Third World. The situation with the Soviet Union came to a head in October 1962 with the Cuban missile crisis. After he faced down Soviet premier Nikita Khrushchev, forcing him to remove Soviet missiles from Cuba, relations between the United States and the Soviet Union gradually began to improve, and Kennedy was able to turn his attention to domestic affairs.

Domestic-Policy Wars. Although the Kennedy administration worked diligently and efficiently to enforce compliance with existing civil rights laws, much of its own domestic legislation became bogged down in Congress, where the conservative coalition of southern Democrats and northern Republicans cooperated to prevent it from coming to a vote. After Kennedy's death from an assassin's bullet on 22 November 1963, his successor, Lyndon Johnson, effectively invoked the fallen leader's memory to push Kennedy's legislative package through Congress.

The Kennedy Image. Immediately after his death, Kennedy's popularity, which like most presidents' had fluctuated during his tenure in office, rose to heights surpassed only by Abraham Lincoln and Franklin D. Roosevelt in the past hundred years. Airports, schools, roads, and other public facilities were named after him. Yet his presidency was one of unfulfilled potential rather than great achievement.

Sources:

Richard N. Goodwin, *Remembering America: A Voice from the Sixties* (Boston: Little, Brown, 1988);

Arthur M. Schlesinger, Jr., *A Thousand Days: John F. Kennedy in the White House* (Boston: Houghton Mifflin, 1965);

Theodore Sorensen, *Kennedy* (New York: Harper & Row, 1965);

Harris Wofford, *Of Kennedys and Kings: Making Sense of the Sixties* (Pittsburgh: University Press of Pittsburgh, 1980).

EUGENE J. MCCARTHY

1916-

U.S. SENATOR, 1958–1971; DEMOCRATIC PRESIDENTIAL CANDIDATE, 1968

A Leader for the "Doves." As the first antiwar candidate to declare his candidacy for the 1968 Democratic presidential nomination, the scholarly and reserved Sen. Eugene J. McCarthy of Minnesota became a surprisingly strong magnet for college-age opponents of the Vietnam War. He pulled students back into mainstream politics, where they enthusiastically campaigned door-to-door for their candidate, who on at least one occasion was late for a campaign appearance because he was busy discussing literature with poet Robert Lowell.

Background. Born in Watkins, Minnesota, McCarthy, a devout Roman Catholic, spent most of the first thirteen years after his graduation from Saint John's University in that state teaching economics and sociology at Catholic high schools and colleges. He also spent nine months in 1942–1943 as a novice in a Benedictine monastery. He entered politics in the late 1940s when he helped Sen. Hubert Humphrey in a successful battle to take control of the Communist-led Minnesota Farm-Labor Party. Elected to the U.S. House of Representatives in 1948, McCarthy had a liberal, prolabor voting record and led other Democrats in forming the Democratic Study Group, which became known for advocating its own legislative alternatives to Republican policies.

Senator McCarthy. McCarthy was a member of the U.S. Senate "Class of 1958," one of the thirteen liberal Democrats who defeated Republican incumbents in the elections of that year. He continued to vote with the other liberal Democrats but quickly seemed bored with Senate politics and never took on the leadership role he had played in the House. To many of his Senate colleagues he seemed detached and sometimes condescending. Yet he attracted public attention with his passionate and memorable nominating speech for Adlai E. Stevenson at the 1960 Democratic National Convention, and became a vigorous campaigner for John F. Kennedy after the Massachusetts senator won the party's nomination. Moreover, he worked hard for aid to the unemployed and migrant farm workers. Assigned to the Senate Foreign Relations Committee in 1964, he called for an investigation of the Central Intelligence Agency (CIA), questioning its role in internal political upheavals in countries such as Vietnam and the Dominican Republic. He also criticized the sale of large quantities of American arms to Third World nations.

McCarthy and Vietnam. In August 1964 McCarthy supported the Gulf of Tonkin Resolution, giving President Lyndon B. Johnson the additional powers that eventually lend to the expansion of the Vietnam War, but McCarthy had become disillusioned with Johnson's policies by January 1966, and by early 1967 he had become a vocal opponent, calling the war "morally unjustified." In October of that year he published *The Limits of Powers*, strongly criticizing American foreign policy.

Candidate McCarthy. Agreeing to seek the 1968 Democratic presidential nomination only after popular antiwar politicians, including Senator Robert F. Kennedy, declined to run, McCarthy believed he had no hope of winning and announced that he was entering the race to be the voice of the movement for a negotiated settlement to the war. His strong showing in the New Hampshire Democratic primary demonstrated growing discontent with Johnson's policies and suggested that the president, who had seemed unbeatable a few months earlier, could be defeated after all. Faced with an almost certain loss to McCarthy in the Wisconsin primary, Johnson withdrew from the race on 31 March. McCarthy and Robert Kennedy faced off in a series of primaries, until Kennedy was assassinated just after his victory in the 4 June California primary. Meanwhile Vice-president Humphrey had been campaigning for delegates in non-primary states and won the nomination at an acrimonious Democratic Nation Convention in Chicago, where McCarthy's supporters engaged in an angry and unsuccessful floor fight for an antiwar plank in the party platform, as antiwar demonstrators and Chicago police clashed outside the convention hall. McCarthy refused to endorse Humphrey until a few days before the election and then offered only lukewarm support.

Leaving the Senate. In 1969 McCarthy surprised many observers by resigning from the Foreign Relations Committee, and he declined to seek reelection in 1970. He made halfhearted attempts to run for president in 1972 and 1976, and in 1982 he ran for his old Senate seat but lost the election.

Sources:

Jeremy Larner, *Nobody Knows: Reflections on the McCarthy Campaign of 1968* (New York: Macmillan, 1970);

Eugene J. McCarthy, *Up 'Til Now: A Memoir* (San Diego: Harcourt Brace Jovanovich, 1987);

McCarthy, *The Year of the People* (Garden City, N.Y.: Doubleday, 1969).

RICHARD M. NIXON

1913-1994

PRESIDENT OF THE UNITED STATES, 1969-1974

The Heir Apparent Falters. As vice president under Dwight D. Eisenhower, the most popular Republican president of the twentieth century, Richard Milhous Nixon seemed assured of victory at the beginning of the 1960 presidential campaign. Yet he lost to John F. Kennedy in the closest presidential election of the century. Returning to his home state, California, Nixon joined a Los Angeles law firm and began to prepare for future political involvement, keeping himself in the public eye by writing a series of syndicated newspaper columns and a political memoir, *Six Crises* (1962), which became a best-seller.

The California Governor's Race. In September 1961 — believing that he could best demonstrate his appeal to voters and establish a base for another presidential campaign by winning an important elected office — Nixon announced that he would run for governor of California, expecting full support from fellow California Republicans. Yet the right wing in the state party charged that during the 1960 election he had wandered too far toward the party's center, leaving behind the conservative, anti-Communist values with which he had started out. Some even accused him of being "soft on communism" because he had criticized the ultra-right-wing John Birch Society. Nixon defeated his conservative primary opponent by a smaller margin than he had hoped, and in the fall election he had trouble finding an issue to use against the likable incumbent governor, Democrat Edmund G. (Pat) Brown. Nixon's last-minute attempt to suggest that Brown was a Communist sympathizer was labeled "ridiculous" even in Republican *Time* magazine. After losing the election by almost 300,000 votes, Nixon lashed out at the press announcing that they would not "have Nixon to kick around anymore" because "this is my last press conference."

A Brief Hiatus Between Campaigns. Having apparently retired from politics, Nixon moved to New York City in June 1963 and became a partner in a prestigious law firm, but he continued to speak out on the issues, and he became an effective campaigner for Republican candidates. By 1964 Nixon was ready to fill the power vacuum left in the party after Barry Goldwater's overwhelming loss to Lyndon Johnson in the presidential election. Campaigning tirelessly and effectively for the party in 1966, Nixon became its chief spokesman and its leading fund raiser, placing himself in an excellent position to win the Republican presidential nomination in 1968.

President Nixon. Announcing himself better prepared to be president than he had been in 1960, Nixon managed to reclaim some of the conservative vote he had lost earlier by stressing the need for law and order — an emphasis than appealed to many Americans frightened by the inner-city riots and violent antiwar demonstrations they saw on the evening news. He won a close three-way election, as commentators wondered at his political "resurrection."

Sources:

Tom Wicker, *One of Us: Richard Nixon and the American Dream* (New York: Random House, 1991);

Jules Witcover, *The Resurrection of Richard Nixon* (New York: Putnam, 1970).

GEORGE C. WALLACE

1919-

GOVERNOR OF ALABAMA, 1963-1967

From Moderate to Segregationist. George C. Wallace, a moderate even progressive politician on most issues, attracted national notoriety in the 1960s because of his defiance of federal orders to desegregate public education in Alabama. Wallace was a political protege of populist Alabama governor "Big Jim" Folsom and established a liberal voting record in the Alabama legislature during the 1950s. In 1958 he lost a runoff in the Democratic gubernatorial primary to Alabama Attorney General John Patterson, who campaigned with a strident segregationist message. Wallace, who was considered the moderate in that race, vowed that he would never again be beaten because he appeared to be less of a racist than his opponent. In 1962 he ran for governor again and won on a militant segregationist platform; at his inauguration he vowed to uphold "segregation now — segregation tomorrow — and segregation forever."

Wallace versus King. During the drive by Dr. Martin Luther King, Jr., and the Southern Christian Leadership Conference (SCLC) to desegregate public facilities in Birmingham in 1963, Wallace tried unsuccessfully to block a settlement between the protesters and local authorities and businessmen. In March 1965 Wallace was initially successful at preventing King from organizing a march from Selma to Montgomery to protest the denial of voting rights to blacks in southern states, including Alabama. But after a federal court ordered that the marchers be allowed to proceed, Wallace did not attempt to block them.

Wallace and Alabama Schools. By 1963 Alabama was the only southern state in which no schools at any level had been desegregated. When a federal court ordered the University of Alabama to enroll two blacks, Wallace stood in the doorway of the admissions office, blocking their entrance until federal authorities ordered him to stand aside. In September 1963 Wallace sent Alabama state troopers to prevent blacks from enrolling in "whites-only" public schools in Mobile, Tuskegee, Birmingham, and Huntsville. After he replaced the state troopers with Alabama National Guardsmen, the Kennedy administration federalized those troops and ordered them back to their armories. The schools were then desegregated, but Wallace continued his quixotic efforts to block integration. In 1966 he got his state legislature to pass a bill that declared the U.S. Office of Education desegregation guidelines null and void in Alabama.

Governor Lurleen. Unable to succeed himself in 1967, Wallace tried to convince the Alabama legislature to amend the state constitution to allow a governor to serve two consecutive terms. When the legislature failed to act, Wallace had his wife, Lurleen, run for governor in the election of 1966. She won, and until she died of cancer in 1968, he served as her special assistant and essentially continued to run the state.

Presidential Aspirations. Wallace ventured into national politics in 1964, when he ran in the Democratic presidential primaries in Wisconsin, Indiana, and Maryland and did surprisingly well outside the South, appealing to blue-collar white voters. In 1968, he ran as a third party candidate in all fifty states, campaigning against the intrusive power of the federal government and stressing the law and order issue. He sought the Democratic presidential nomination again in 1972 and 1976. During the 1972 primary campaign in Maryland, Wallace was shot and partially paralyzed in an attempt on his life.

Governor Again. In 1982 Wallace won his fourth term as governor of Alabama after repudiating segregation and winning support from black voters.

Sources:

Marshall Frady, *Wallace* (New York: World, 1968);

Stephan Lesher, *George Wallace: American Populist* (Reading, Mass.: Addison-Wesley, 1994).

PEOPLE IN THE NEWS

In December 1966 the U.S. Supreme Court unanimously agreed to order the Georgia Legislature to allow civil rights worker and antiwar activist **Julian Bond** to take the seat in the State House of Representatives that he had won in 1965. The Court ruled that legislature had violated Bond's First Amendment rights when it denied him the seat because of his opposition to the Vietnam War.

In February 1965 **Robert Collier, Michelle Duclos, Walter Bowe,** and **Khaleel Sayyed** — members of the Black Liberation Front — were arrested for conspiracy to destroy government property. They had planned to dynamite the Statue of Liberty, the Washington Monument, and the Liberty Bell.

On 20 October 1969 Republican Senator **Everett M. Dirksen** of Illinois became the first senator to act in a movie when *The Monitors,* a political satire featuring Ed Begley and Kennan Wynn, was released.

In October 1963 former president **Dwight D. Eisenhower** sent House Minority Leader Charles Halleck (R-Ind.) a letter suggesting major cuts in President John F. Kennedy's budget. Kennedy responded by saying that Eisenhower's budgets had created spending deficits, gold outflows, recessions, and unemployment: "That's not a record we plan to duplicate if we can help it."

On 2 October 1968 U.S. Supreme Court Justice **Abe Fortas** withdrew as the nominee for chief justice during a controversy over his having advised President Lyndon B. Johnson on political matters while serving on the Court. Fortas resigned from the court on 15 May 1969, after it was revealed that he had accepted a twenty-thousand-dollar fee from the family foundation of industrialist Louis Wolfson, who was under investigation and later convicted for stock manipula-

tion. Fortas kept the money for a year and returned it three months after Wolfson was indicted.

On 4 December 1969 at 3 A.M. Chicago police fired more than eighty shotgun rounds into an apartment shared by several Black Panthers, killing Panther leader **Fred Hampton** and another party member.

On 7 November 1967 **Richard Hatcher** of Gary, Indiana, and **Carl Stokes** of Cleveland, Ohio, became the first two black men to be elected mayors of major U.S. cities.

On 6 August 1966 **Luci Baines Johnson,** younger daughter of President and Mrs. Johnson, married Patrick Nugent in the Roman Catholic Shrine of the Immaculate Conception in Washington, D.C.

On 9 December 1967 **Lynda Bird Johnson,** elder daughter of President and Mrs. Johnson, married U.S. Marine Corps Major Charles Robb, in the first wedding to take place in the White House since President Woodrow Wilson's daughter Eleanor was married there in 1914.

On 21 October 1964 President **Lyndon Baines Johnson** told a campaign crowd in Akron, Ohio, "We are not going to send American boys away from home to do what Asian boys ought to be doing for themselves."

For an article published in the 8 December 1963 issue of the *Saturday Evening Post,* Attorney General **Robert F. Kennedy** commented on the recently resolved Cuban missile crisis: "We all agreed in the end that if the Russians were ready to go to nuclear war over Cuba, they were ready to go to nuclear war, and that was that. So we might as well have the showdown then as six months later."

On 18 July 1969 **Mary Jo Kopechne,** a passenger in a car driven by Massachusetts Senator Edward M. Kennedy, drowned after he ran the car off a bridge on

Chappaquiddick Island, Massachusetts. Questions about Kennedy's behavior during and just after the accident essentially destroyed his hopes for winning the presidency.

In May 1964 **Howard Nathaniel Lee** was elected mayor of Chapel Hill, North Carolina, becoming the first black mayor of a predominantly white southern community.

On 3 June 1965, in a letter reprinted in the *New York Times,* poet **Robert Lowell** turned down President Johnson's invitation to a White House art festival: "We are in danger of imperceptibly becoming an explosive and suddenly chauvinistic nation. . . . I feel I am serving you and our country best by not taking part."

On 22 December 1968 **Julie Nixon,** younger daughter of President-Elect and Mrs. Richard M. Nixon, married **David Eisenhower,** grandson of former President Dwight D. Eisenhower.

On 17 April 1965 **Paul Potter,** president of Students for a Democratic Society (SDS), told the participants in the first major antiwar rally in Washington, D.C., that the Vietnam War is "the terrifying sharp cutting edge that has severed the last vestige of illusion that morality and democracy are the guiding principles of American foreign policy."

On 1 March 1967 the U.S. House of Representatives voted 307–116 to exclude black Congressman **Adam Clayton Powell** for "gross misconduct," including misuse of public funds and maintaining his wife, who lives in Puerto Rico, on the congressional pay roll. Amid charges that Powell's ouster was racially motivated, a special election to choose Powell's successor was held in April, and voters in the Central Harlem district re-elected Powell, who was disqualified from serving, by an overwhelming margin. The seat remained empty until January 1969, when Powell payed a twenty-five-thousand-dollar fine and was allowed to return to the House but was stripped of his seniority. The following June the U.S. Supreme Court rules that his expulsion from Congress was unconstitutional.

In October 1967 **Ronald Reagan,** Republican governor of California, told Republicans at a party fund-raising dinner in Milwaukee, "We have some hippies in California. For those of you who don't know what a hippie is, he's a fellow who has hair like Tarzan, who walks like Jane, and smells like Cheetah."

On 25 December 1966 **Harrison Salisbury,** associate editor of the *New York Times,* began publishing a series of articles charging — on the basis of his observations during a recent trip to Hanoi — that President Johnson was lying when he said American planes were bombing only military targets.

On 8 November 1960 in the first U.S. Senate election where one woman has run against another, incumbent Republican senator **Margaret Chase Smith** of Maine defeated her Democratic challenger Lucia Marie Cormier. The following January Smith joined Democrat Maurine Brown Neuberger of Oregon for the first Senate session that included more than one female senator.

On 1 October 1962 retired U.S. Army major general **Edwin A. Walker,** who was the commander in charge of the federal troops sent to enforce school integration in Little Rock in 1957, was arrested for insurrection after participating in the riots during the integration of the University of Mississippi.

On 18 January 1966 **Robert Clifton Weaver** was sworn in as secretary of housing and urban development, becoming the first black to serve in the U.S. cabinet.

In June 1969 **Thomas Yorty** was elected to his third term as mayor of Los Angeles after a campaign in which he associated his opponent, black former police lieutenant Thomas Bradley, with the "Black and Red Revolution."

DEATHS

Henry Fountain Ashurst, 87, senator (D) from Arizona (1912–1941), 31 May 1962.

Warren R. Austin, 85, representative to the U.N. Security Council (1947–1953) and senator (R) from Vermont (1931–1946), 25 December 1962.

Howard H. Baker, 61, representative (R) from Tennessee (1951–1964), 7 January 1964.

John F. Baldwin, Jr., 50, representative (R) from California (1955–1966), 10 March 1966.

Graham A. Barden, 70, representative (D) from North Carolina (1935–1961), 29 January 1967.

William H. Bates, 52, representative (R) from Massachusetts (1950–1969), 22 June 1969.

George H. Bender, 64, senator (R) from Ohio (1954–1967) and seven term congressman (1939–1949, 1951–1954) , 18 June 1961.

John B. Bennett, 60, representative (R) from Michigan (1947–1964), 9 August 1964.

Anthony Drexel Biddle, 64, ambassador to Spain (1961); previously served as minister to Norway (1935–1937) and ambassador to Poland (1937–1939), 13 November 1961.

Herbert C. Bonner, 74, representative (D) from North Carolina (1940–1965), 7 November 1965.

Owen Brewster, 73, Republican representative (1935–1941) and senator (1941–1953) from Maine, 25 December 1961.

Styles Bridges, 63, senator (R) from New Hampshire (1937–1961), 26 November 1961.

Overton Brooks, 63, representative (D) from Louisiana (1937–1961), 16 September 1961.

Clarence J. Brown, 72, representative (R) from Ohio (1939–1965), 23 August 1965.

Norris Brown, 96, senator (R) from Nebraska (1907–1913), 5 January 1960.

Wilbur M. Brucker, 74, general counsel of the Defense Department (1954) and secretary of the army (1955–1961), 28 October 1968.

Harry F. Byrd, 79, senator (D) from Virginia (1933–1965), 20 October 1966.

Cavendish W. Cannon, 67, ambassador to Yugoslavia (1947), Greece (1953), and Morocco (1956), 7 October 1962.

Clarence Cannon, 85, representative (D) from Missouri (1923–1964), 12 May 1964.

Francis Higbee Case, 63, Republican representative (1937–1951) and senator (1951–1962) from South Dakota, 22 June 1962.

Whittaker Chambers, 60, confessed former Communist spy whose 1950 testimony indicted Alger Hiss, 9 July 1961.

Dennis Chavez, 74, Democratic representative (1931–1935) and senator (1935–1962) of New Mexico, 18 November 1962.

Tom Connally, 86, Democratic representative (1917–1929) and senator (1929–1953) from Texas, 28 October 1963.

Eugene Dennis, 56, American Communist Party chairman and one of twelve American Communists sentenced under the Smith Act in 1948, 31 January 1961.

Everett McKinley Dirksen, 73, Republican representative (1933–1949) and senator (1951–1969) from Illinois, 7 September 1969.

Clyde Gilman Doyle, 75, representative (D) from California (1945–1947, 1949–1963), 13 March 1963.

Allen W. Dulles, 75, OSS leader in Switzerland during World War II; helped set up the CIA and was deputy director (1950–1953) and director (1953–1961), 30 January 1969.

Henry C. Dworshak, 67, senator (R) of Idaho (1946–1962), 23 July 1962.

Dwight D. Eisenhower, 78, president of the United States (1953–1961), commander of Allied forces in Europe during World War II, 28 March 1969.

Douglas H. Elliott, 39, representative (R) from Pennsylvania (1960), 19 June 1960.

Clair Engle, 52, Democratic representative (1943–1959) and senator (1959–1964) from California, 30 July 1964.

Robert A. Everett, 53, representative (D) from Tennessee (1958–1969), 26 January 1969.

John E. Fogarty, 53, representative (D) from Rhode Island (1941–1944, 1945–1967), 10 January 1967.

Felix Frankfurter, 82, associate justice of the Supreme Court (1939–1962), 22 February 1965.

Leon H. Gavin, 70, representative (R) from Pennsylvania (1943–1963), 14 September 1963.

Theodore Francis Green, 98, senator (D) from Rhode Island (1937–1961), 19 May 1966.

William J. Green, Jr., 53, representative (D) from Pennsylvania (1945–1947, 1949–1963), 21 December 1963.

Joseph Clark Grew, 84, ambassador to Japan (1931–1941); warned of plans of attack on Pearl Harbor one year prior, 25 May 1965.

David M. Hall, 41, representative (D) from North Carolina (1959–1960), 29 January 1960.

Edward J. Hart, 68, representative (D) from New Jersey (1935–1955), 20 April 1961.

Fred A. Hartley, Jr., 66, representative (R) from New Jersey (1929–1949), 11 May 1969.

Thomas C. Hennings, Jr., 57, Democratic representative (1935–1940) and senator (1951–1960) from Missouri, 13 September 1960.

Christian A. Herter, 71, representative (R) from Massachusetts (1943–1953), undersecretary (1957–1958), and secretary of state (1959–60), 30 December 1966.

Clare E. Hoffman, 92, representative (R) from Michigan (1935–1963), 3 November 1967.

Elmer J. Holland, 74, representative (D) from Pennsylvania (1956–1968), 9 August 1968.

Julius C. Holmes, 69, minister to Great Britain (1948–1953); minister to Morocco (1955–1956); special assistant to secretary of state for NATO affairs (1956–1959); consul general in Hong Kong (1959–1961); ambassador to Iran (1961–1965), 14 July 1968.

Herbert Clark Hoover, 90, president of the United States (1929–1932), 20 October 1964.

Louis A. Johnson, 75, assistant secretary of war (1937–1940), secretary of defense (1949–1950), 24 April 1966.

Olin D. Johnston, 68, senator (D) from South Carolina (1945–1965), 18 April 1965.

Estes Kefauver, 60, Democratic representative (1949) and senator (1949–1963) from Tennessee, 10 August 1963.

John F. Kennedy, 46, Democratic representative (1947–1953) and senator (1953–1960) from Massachusetts, president of the United States (1961–1963), 22 November 1963.

Robert F. Kennedy, 42, attorney general (1961–1964), senator (D) from New York (1965–1968), 6 June 1968.

Robert S. Kerr, 66, senator (D) from Oklahoma (1949–1967), 1 January 1963.

Martin Luther King, Jr., 39, civil rights leader, founder of the Southern Christian Leadership Conference, Nobel Peace Prize winner (1964), 4 April 1968.

Clarence F. Lea, 89, representative (D) from California (1917–1949), 20 June 1964.

Earl Kemp Long, 65, governor (D) of Louisiana (1939–1940, 1948–1950, 1956–1960), 5 September 1960.

Gen. Douglas MacArthur, 84, supreme Allied commander in the southwest Pacific in World War II, commander of U.S. forces in Korea, military governor of occupied Japan (1945–1951), 5 April 1964.

Russell Vernon Mack, 68, representative (R) from Washington (1947–1960), 28 March 1960.

Malcom X, 40, Black Muslim leader, 21 February 1965.

Joseph W. Martin, Jr., 83, representative (R) from Massachusetts (1925–1966), minority leader (1939–1959), speaker (1946–1948, 1952–1954), 6 March 1968.

J. Howard McGrath, 62, attorney general (1949–1952), 2 September 1966.

Pat McNamara, 71, senator (D) from Michigan (1955–1966), 30 April 1966.

Clem Miller, 45, representative (D) from California (1959–1962), 7 October 1962.

Henry Morgenthau, Jr., 75, secretary of the treasury (1934–1945), 6 February 1967.

Walter M. Mumma, 70, representative (R) from Pennsylvania (1951–1961), 25 February 1961.

Walter Norblad, 56, representative (R) from Oregon (1946–1964), 20 September 64.

W. F. Norrell, 64, representative (D) from Arkansas (1939–1961), 15 February 1961.

Hjalmar C. Nygaard, 57, representative (R) from North Dakota, 18 July 1963.

Thomas J. O'Brien, 85, representative (D) from Illinois (1933–1939, 1943–1964), 14 April 1964.

Joseph C. O'Mahoney, 78, senator (D) from Wyoming (1934–1953, 1954–1961), 1 December 1962.

J. Robert Oppenheimer, 62, nuclear physicist, 18 February 1967.

Richard C. Patterson, Jr., 80, assistant secretary and undersecretary of commerce (1938–1939); ambassador to

Yugoslavia (1944–1946), Guatemala (1947), Switzerland (1951), 30 September 1966.

Frances Perkins, 83, secretary of labor (1933–1945), 14 May 1965.

George Walbridge Perkins, 64, assistant secretary of state for European affairs (1949–1953) and ambassador to NATO (1955–1957), 10 January 1960.

Joe R. Pool, 57, representative (D) from Texas (1963–1968), 14 July 1968.

Louis C. Rabaut, 74, representative (D) from Michigan (1935–1947, 1949–1961), 12 November 1961.

Sam Rayburn, 79, representative (D) from Texas (1913–1961) had served 48 years 258 days continuously as a representative and 17 years 62 days (twice interrupted) as Speaker of the House, 16 November 1961.

B. Carroll Reece, 71, representative (R) from Tennessee (1921–1931, 1933–1947, 1951–1967), 19 March 1961.

Donald Randall Richberg, 79, coauthored the National Recovery Act while in the Roosevelt Administration, 27 November 1960.

John J. Riley, 66, representative (D) from South Carolina (1945–1949, 1951–1962), 2 January 1962.

Edith Nourse Rogers, 79, representative (R) from Massachusetts (1925–1960), 10 September 1960.

Daniel J. Ronan, 55, representative (D) from Illinois (1965–1969), 13 August 1969.

Eleanor Roosevelt, 78, first lady (1933–1945), delegate to the U. N. General Assembly (1945–1952, 1961–1962), 7 November 1962.

Andrew F. Schoeppel, 67, senator (R) from Kansas (1949–1962), 21 January 1962.

Gen. Walter Bedell Smith, 65, ambassador to the Soviet Union (1946–1949); director of the CIA (1950–1953); undersecretary of state (1953–1954), 9 August 1961.

Brent Spence, 92, representative (D) from Kentucky (1931–1963), 18 September 1967.

Charles Clarkson Stelle, 53, chief delegate to the Disarmament Conference in Geneva (1960–1963), 11 June 1964.

Adlai E. Stevenson, 65, ambassador to the United Nations (1961–1965), Democratic presidential candidate (1952, 1956), 14 July 1965.

John Taber, 85, representative (R) from New York (1923–1962), 22 November 1965.

Albert Thomas, 67, representative (D) from Texas (1937–1966), 15 February 1966.

T. Ashton Thompson, 49, representative (D) from Louisiana (1953–1965), 1 July 1965.

Keith Thomson, 42, representative (R) from Wyoming (1955–1960), 9 December 1960.

Millard D. Tydings, 70, Democratic representative (1923–1927) and senator (1927–1951) from Maryland, 9 February 1961.

John M. Vorys, 72, representative (R) from Ohio (1939–1959), 25 August 1968.

Henry Agard Wallace, 77, vice president (1941–1944), 18 November 1965.

Francis E. Walter, 69, representative (D) from Pennsylvania (1933–1963), 31 May 1963.

Joseph Nye Welch, 69, defense lawyer in the 1954 Army-McCarthy hearings, 6 October 1960.

Sumner Welles, 69, undersecretary of state (1937–1943), 24 September 1961.

Claude Raymond Wichard, 75, secretary of agriculture (1940–1945), 29 April 1967.

Alexander Wiley, 84, senator (R) from Wisconsin (1939–1963), 26 October 1968.

Charles E. Wilson, 71, secretary of defense (1953–1957), 26 September 1961.

Jesse P. Wolcott, 75, representative (R) from Michigan (1931–1957), 28 January 1969.

J. Arthur Younger, 74, representative (R) from California (1953–1967), 20 June 1967.

PUBLICATIONS

Elie Abel, *The Missile Crisis* (Philadelphia: Lippincott, 1966);

Floyd B. Barbour, *The Black Power Revolt* (Boston: Extending Horizons Books, 1968);

Daniel Bell, *The End of Ideology: On the Exhaustion of Political Ideas in the 1950s* (New York: Free Press, 1962);

Angus Campbell, Philip E. Converse, Warren E. Miller, and Donald E. Stokes, *The American Voter* (New York: Wiley, 1964);

Stokely Carmichael and Charles V. Hamilton, *Black Power: The Politics of Revolution in America* (New York: Random House, 1967);

Eldridge Cleaver, *Post-Prison Writings and Speeches,* edited by Robert Sheer (New York: Random House, 1969);

Cleaver, *Soul on Ice* (New York: McGraw-Hill, 1968);

Theodore Draper, *The Dominican Revolt: A Case Study in American Policy* (New York: Commentary, 1968);

Edward J. Epstein, *Inquest: The Warren Commission and the Establishment of Truth* (New York: Viking, 1966);

Rowland Evans and Robert Novak, *Lyndon B. Johnson: The Exercise of Power* (New York: New American Library, 1966);

Bernard Fall, *Last Reflections on a War* (Garden City, N.Y.: Doubleday, 1967);

Fall, *Viet-Nam Witness 1953–1966* (New York: Praeger, 1966);

Arnold Forster and Benjamin R. Epstein, *Danger on the Right* (New York: Random House, 1964);

Marshall Frady, *Wallace* (New York: World, 1968);

J. William Fulbright, *The Arrogance of Power* (New York: Random House, 1966);

Fulbright, *Old Myths and New Realities* (New York: Random House, 1964);

Eric Goldman, *The Tragedy of Lyndon Johnson* (New York: Knopf, 1969);

Barry M. Goldwater, *The Conscience of a Conservative* (New York: Hilman, 1960);

Richard N. Goodwin, *Triumph or Tragedy: Reflections on Vietnam* (New York: Random House, 1966);

Michael Harrington, *The Other America: Poverty in the United States* (New York: Macmillan, 1962);

Tom Hayden, *Rebellion in Newark: Official Violence and Ghetto Response* (New York: Random House, 1967);

Roger F. Hilsman, *To Move A Nation: The Politics of Foreign Policy in the Administration of John F. Kennedy* (Garden City, N.Y.: Doubleday, 1967);

Robert F. Kennedy, *Thirteen Days: A Memoir of the Cuban Missile Crisis* (New York: Norton, 1969);

Kennedy, *To Seek a Newer World* (Garden City, N.Y.: Doubleday, 1967);

Martin Luther King, Jr., *Why We Can't Wait* (New York: Harper & Row, 1964);

Mark Lane, *Rush to Judgment: A Critique of the Warren Commission's Inquiry Into the Murders of President John F. Kennedy, Officer J.D. Tippit, and Lee Harvey Oswald* (New York: Holt, Rinehart & Winston, 1966);

Seymour Martin Lipset, *Political Man: The Social Bases of Politics* (Garden City, N.Y.: Doubleday, 1960);

Samuel Lubell, *The Future of American Politics,* third edition, revised (New York: Harper & Row, 1965);

Norman Mailer, *The Armies of the Night: History as a Novel, The Novel as History* (New York: New American Library, 1968);

Mailer, *Miami and the Siege of Chicago: An Informal History of the Republican and Democratic Conventions of 1968* (New York: World, 1968);

Malcolm X, with Alex Haley, *The Autobiography of Malcolm X* (New York: Grove, 1965);

Eugene J. McCarthy, *The Limits of Power: America's Role in the World* (New York: Holt, Rinehart & Winston, 1967);

Joe McGinniss, *The Selling of the President, 1968* (New York: Trident Press, 1969);

William Manchester, *The Death of a President: November 20–November 25, 1963* (New York: Harper & Row, 1967);

Sylvia Meagher, *Accessories After the Fact: The Warren Commission, the Authorities and the Report* (Indianapolis: Bobbs-Merrill, 1967);

Daniel P. Moynihan, *Maximum Feasible Misunderstanding: Community Action in the War on Poverty* (New York: Free Press, 1969);

Benjamin Muse, *The American Negro Revolution: From Nonviolence to Black Power* (Bloomington: Indiana University Press, 1968);

Richard M. Nixon, *Six Crises* (Garden City, N.Y.: Doubleday, 1962);

Kevin P. Phillips, *The Emerging Republican Majority* (New Rochelle, N.Y.: Arlington House, 1969);

Hobart Rowen, *The Free Enterprisers: Kennedy, Johnson and the Business Community* (New York: Putnam, 1964);

Pierre Salinger, *With Kennedy* (Garden City, N.Y.: Doubleday, 1966);

Arthur Schlesinger, Jr.. *A Thousand Days* (Boston: Houghton Mifflin, 1965);

Walter Schneir, *Telling It Like It Was: The Chicago Riots* (New York: New American Library, 1969);

John Schultz, *No One Was Killed: Documentation and Meditation, Convention Week, Chicago, August 1968* (Chicago: Big Table, 1969);

Robert Sherrill, *The Accidental President* (New York: Grossman, 1967);

Jerome Slater, *Intervention and Negotiation: The United States and the Dominican Revolution* (New York: Harper & Row, 1968);

Theodore Sorensen, *Kennedy* (New York: Harper & Row, 1965);

Sorensen, *The Kennedy Legacy* (New York: Macmillan, 1969);

James L. Sundquist, *Politics and Policy: The Eisenhower, Kennedy and Johnson Years* (Washington: Brookings Institution, 1968);

Tad Szulc, *The Cuban Invasion: The Chronicle of a Disaster* (New York: Praeger, 1962);

Massimo Teodori, ed., *The New Left: A Documentary History* (Indianapolis: Bobbs-Merrill, 1969);

Daniel Walker, *Rights in Conflict: Convention Week in Chicago, August 25–29, 1968, A Report Submitted to the National Commission on the Causes and Prevention of Violence* (New York: Dutton, 1968);

Theodore H. White, *The Making of the President 1960* (New York: Atheneum, 1961);

White, *The Making of the President 1964* (New York: Atheneum, 1965);

White, *The Making of the President 1968* (New York: Atheneum, 1969);

William S. White, *The Professional: Lyndon B. Johnson* (New York: Crest Books, 1964);

Tom Wicker, *JFK and LBJ: The Influence of Personality on Politics* (New York: Morrow, 1968);

Commentary, periodical;

Congressional Quarterly Weekly Report, periodical;

Foreign Affairs, periodical;

Nation, periodical;

National Review, periodical;

New Republic, periodical;

Newsweek, periodical;

Time, periodical;

U.S. News & World Report, periodical.

Kennedy campaign workers in Los Angeles, 1960

LAW AND JUSTICE

by KEVIN M. GREEN and HALCOTT P. GREEN

CONTENTS

Sidebars and tables are listed in italics.

1960

Mar.	Trial of Richard Hickock and Perry Smith for murder of the Clutter family in Kansas. They are sentenced to hang.
6 May	The Civil Rights Act of 1960 becomes law. It seeks to protect the right of black Americans to vote by providing "voter referees," as well as empowering the Department of Justice to bring suits to force the registration of black voters.
26 June	The Supreme Court decides *Hannah* v. *Slawson*, which allows the Civil Rights Commission to keep secret the identities of persons submitting complaints. This is felt necessary in order to protect them from retaliation.
Dec.	President John F. Kennedy announces his choice for attorney general, his brother Robert Kennedy. This decision initially arouses a great deal of criticism because of nepotism concerns and because of Robert Kennedy's youth and inexperience. However, the controversy soon dies down, and Robert is easily confirmed by the Senate the next January.

1961

3 Apr.	Adoption of XXIII Amendment to Constitution giving the District of Columbia electors in voting for president and vice-president.
5 June	The Supreme Court issues the *Scales* v. *United States* opinion holding that membership in a Communist organization advocating the violent overthrow of the government is not protected by the First Amendment.
19 June	In *Mapp* v. *Ohio* the Supreme Court applies exclusionary rule to illegal searches and seizures by state police.
Nov.	The Civil Rights Commission releases its second report. Its five volumes recount disturbing episodes of police brutality against blacks in both the North and South. It calls for federal grants to upgrade police forces and for new laws allowing victims of such violence to sue local governments for damages.

1962

26 Mar.	In *Baker* v. *Carr* the Supreme Court enunciates the principal of one man, one-vote, and opens the courts to citizens seeking to challenge electoral district apportionment schemes.
1 Apr.	Justice Charles Whittaker leaves the Supreme Court.
16 Apr.	Byron White is confirmed as Supreme Court justice.
25 June	In *Engel* v. *Vitale* the Supreme Court says prayer in public schools violates the establishment clause of the Constitution.
14 Aug.	The Great Mail Robbery occurs on Cape Cod Highway in Massachusetts. The thieves get away with over $1.5 million in cash, making it the biggest cash heist in U.S. history.

1963

28 Aug.	Justice Felix Frankfurter resigns from the Supreme Court.
1 Oct.	Arthur Goldberg joins the Supreme Court.

18 Mar.	The *Gideon* v. *Wainwright* decision by the Supreme Court requires that states provide legal counsel for criminal defendants who cannot afford to hire their own attorney.
June	President John F. Kennedy submits proposal for a new civil rights bill. However, he is unable to muster enough support in Congress for its passage.
12 June	Mississippi civil rights leader Medgar Evers is gunned down by segregationist Byron De La Beckwith.
17 June	In *School Dist. of Abbington* v. *Schempp* the Supreme Court reaffirms that prayer in state supported schools violates the separation of church and state.
17 June	In *Sherbert* v. *Verner* the Supreme Court strengthens the free exercise clause of the Constitution by striking down law interfering with religious practices.
15 Sept.	Bomb explodes in largest black church in Birmingham, Alabama, killing four small girls and igniting protests and more violence.
24 Nov.	Suspected presidential assassin Lee Harvey Oswald is shot to death by nightclub owner Jack Ruby. The event is captured live by television cameras filming Oswald's transfer to the county jail.

1964

4 Feb.	The Twenty-fourth Amendment to the U.S. Constitution, prohibiting the use of a poll tax in election of federal officials, is ratified.
17 Feb.	In *Wesberry* v. *Sanders* the Supreme Court requires that congressional districts must all have approximately the same population.
Mar.	Jack Ruby is tried and convicted for the murder of Lee Harvey Oswald.
9 Mar.	In *New York Times* v. *Sullivan* the Supreme Court establishes constitutional standards for libel law which make it much more difficult for public-official plaintiffs to win libel suits.
June	The Boston Strangler begins a killing spree which soon holds the city in the grip of terror.
15 June	The *Malloy* v. *Hogan* decision by the Supreme Court applies the Fifth Amendment to the states.
15 June	In *Reynolds* v. *Sims* the Supreme Court requires that both houses of state legislatures must be apportioned on the basis of population.
21 June	Three civil rights workers are murdered in Mississippi.
22 June	*Escobedo* v. *Illinois* is decided by the Supreme Court, which requires that a suspect have access to an attorney during interrogation.

2 July   The Civil Rights Act of 1964 becomes law. The strongest such law to date, it provides for the desegregation of all public accommodations, such as restaurants and motels.

23 Nov.   In *Garrison* v. *Louisiana* the Supreme Court applies its new libel standard to criminal libel suits as well.

14 Dec.   *Heart of Atlanta Motel, Inc.* v. *United States* is decided by the Supreme Court, affirming Congress's power to order desegregation of public accommodations.

14 Dec.   *Katzenbach* v. *McClung* is decided by the Supreme Court, which establishes the broad reach of the public accommodations clause of the Civil Rights Act of 1964.

1965

5 Apr.   In *Pointer* v. *Texas* the Supreme Court applies the Sixth Amendment's confrontation clause to the states.

28 Apr.   The *Griffin* v. *California* decision by the Supreme Court holds that, when a criminal defendant exercises his constitutional right not to testify, the prosecution cannot comment on this fact to the jury.

7 June   In *Griswold* v. *Connecticut* the Supreme Court recognizes a constitutional right of privacy in striking down an anticontraceptive law.

2 July   Title VII of Civil Rights Act becomes law. This section contains the act's equal employment opportunity provision, which forbids discrimination in hiring and firing. While part of the 1964 bill, it will not take effect until 1965 in order to give the government time to study the issue.

26 July   Justice Goldberg resigns from the Supreme Court.

30 July   Medicare Act becomes law. This bill provides for governmental assistance in paying for medical needs of the elderly. It represents one component of President Lyndon Johnson's Great Society, a broad effort to employ government funding and programs to enhance the general quality of life. Other parts of the program include increased federal aid to education and anti-poverty measures.

6 Aug.   The Voting Rights Act is passed by Congress. It seeks to end racial discrimination in the voting process in the South.

4 Oct.   Abe Fortas's nomination to the Supreme Court is confirmed.

1966

Jan.   Kentucky is the first southern state to pass a civil rights law.

17 Jan.   In *Evans* v. *Newton* the Supreme Court holds that a public park cannot be segregated.

17 Mar.	In *State of South Carolina* v. *Katzenbach* the Supreme Court upholds the constitutionality of the Voting Rights Act of 1965.
24 Mar.	In *Harper* v. *Virginia State Board of Elections* the Supreme Court finds state poll taxes unconstitutional.
13 June	In *Miranda* v. *Arizona* the Supreme Court requires that individuals in police custody be informed of their rights.
1 Aug.	Charles Whitman goes on shooting spree from clock tower on the University of Texas campus, killing fifteen and wounding thirty-one.

1967

Jan.	Albert DeSalvo, who confessed to the Boston Strangler murders, is tried and convicted for sexual assault.
23 Feb.	The Twenty-fifth Amendment is ratified which provides the procedure for empowerment of the vice-president in case the president of the United States is incapacitated.
15 May	In *in re Gault* Supreme Court establishes procedural protections for juveniles in court.
June	Boxer Muhammad Ali is tried and convicted of refusing induction into the U.S. Army.
12 June	In *Loving* v. *Virginia* the Supreme Court declares that antimiscegenation laws (those which prohibit the marriage of people of different races) are unconstitutional.
12 June	Justice Clark retires from the Supreme Court.
2 Oct.	Thurgood Marshall joins the Supreme Court, becoming the first black Justice.
18 Dec.	In *Katz* v. *United States* the Supreme Court allows bugging by police if a warrant is obtained.

1968

1 Apr.	In *Avery* v. *Midland* the Supreme Court extends its one-man, one-vote requirement to local governmental elections.
11 Apr.	The Civil Rights Act of 1968 becomes law. It outlaws discrimination in the sale or rental of all housing, public and private.
May	President Johnson nominates Justice Abe Fortas to replace retiring chief justice Earl Warren.
27 May	In *United States* v. *O'Brien* the Supreme Court recognizes symbolic speech as protected by the First Amendment. However, the decision also establishes that certain limitations can be placed on this right.
17 June	In *Jones* v. *Alfred H. Mayer Co.* the Supreme Court prohibits racial discrimination in purchase, lease, sale, and conveyance of property under an 1866 civil rights law.
Aug.	Vietnam War and civil rights protestors disrupt the Democratic party National Convention in Chicago, Illinois.

1969

22 Oct.	Gun control act banning mail-order sales of guns becomes law.

24 Feb.	In *Tinker* v. *Des Moines* the Supreme Court upholds the right of high-school students to protest Vietnam War by wearing black armbands.
10 Mar.	*Alderman* v. *United States* the Supreme Court holds that the exclusionary rule only applies to the person whose rights were violated by an illegal search.
21 Apr.	In *Shapiro* v. *Thompson* the Supreme Court prohibits residency requirements for welfare benefits by states on the grounds that they violate the fundamental right to travel.
15 May	Justice Fortas is forced to resign from Supreme Court.
16 June	In *Powell* v. *McCormick* Congressman Adam Clayton Powell wins right to be seated in Congress.
23 June	Chief Justice of the Supreme Court Earl Warren retires.
23 June	Warren Burger is confirmed as the new chief justice.
23 June	In *Chimel* v. *California* the Supreme Court allows warrantless search "within reach" of a suspect.
23 June	In *Benton* v. *Maryland* the Supreme Court applies double jeopardy protection to state criminal proceedings.
9 Aug.	The Manson "Family" commits grisly murders at the home of filmmaker Roman Polanski.
Nov.	President Nixon's nomination of Clement Haynsworth to the Supreme Court is rejected by the Senate.

OVERVIEW

Change versus Consolidation. During the 1960s major changes took place in American attitudes toward and about the law. At the same time the law itself was consolidating a trend in the direction of individual rights that had begun twenty-five years before. Three notorious criminal cases — the Richard Hickock and Perry Smith "In Cold Blood" murders, the Charles Manson case, and the trial of the Chicago Seven — one at the beginning and two at the end of the decade, and a series of legislative enactments and court decisions in the area of civil rights illustrate these developments.

The Legacy of World War II. At the beginning of the decade, America was only fifteen years past the end of World War II. That conflict had been the greatest collective effort in the nation's history. By the early 1960s a large part of the men who had served in the war and the women who had maintained the home front were entering their most economically productive and socially influential years. The war effort had imbued in them a spirit of obedience to rules which carried over into their attitudes about the law. There was a strong social consensus about what was right and what was wrong. So pervasive was this agreement about the law and its supporting morality that even people who committed horrible crimes acknowledged that they had done the wrong thing.

Crime and Punishment in 1960. In early 1960 the nation's attention was focused on the trial of Richard Hickock and Perry Smith for the brutal murder of four members of a Kansas farm family. Hickock and Smith fit the popular criminal image. Both had previously spent time in prison. Smith had come from a background of rootless poverty, while Hickock matched the stereotype of the kid from a decent home who could have gone straight but turned to crime because of a flawed character. Even though the acts for which they were tried and found guilty violated the deepest moral standards of American society, neither Hickock nor Smith challenged those standards. There was no sense that either felt that what they had done was justified. They, and everyone else in America, could agree that the crimes for which they were eventually executed were morally wrong.

The Baby Boomers Come of Age. After the soldiers came home from World War II, America underwent a sharp increase in its birth rate. By the beginning of the 1960s the oldest of these children, called the baby boomers, were entering adolescence. By the decade's end they were young adults. Their attitudes toward rule obedience were very different from their parents'. Instead of spending their formative years in the greatest collectivizing experience in American history, most of them had grown up in America's greatest period of prosperity. This prosperity imbued in many of them a desire to express their individualism. They sought to stretch the rules of law and morality, to question them, and to remake them. In the course of this ferment, standards of behavior accepted as given by the World War II generation were challenged and sometimes totally rejected by their children.

Crime and Punishment in 1969. In late 1969 the nation's attention was focused on another horrific crime. Five people, including Sharon Tate, a young movie actress who was eight and one-half months pregnant, were slaughtered in a fashionable Los Angeles home. Over the subsequent months it developed that the instigator of the crime was a drifter and convict named Charles Manson. But unlike Hickock and Smith, Manson proudly proclaimed that what he and his followers had done was morally good. Even more terrifying to the average, hard-working, middle-class American of the World War II generation was the fact that Manson had been able to recruit a band of fanatical followers from the baby-boomer generation, who were intent on more acts of wanton violence.

The New Deal Fulfilled. In contrast to what was happening in the real world of American society, Congress and the courts were finishing a political and legal revolution that had begun in the 1930s. The administration of President Franklin D. Roosevelt had declared a New Deal for Americans. Two of its most revolutionary elements were the expansion of the voting franchise to black Americans and the full expression of the Bill of Rights in criminal cases. Because of their radical nature, these developments had to wait until virtually all the rest of the Roosevelt program had become law. In the 1960s the time had arrived for the New Deal to be fulfilled. As the baby boomers came of age, a half dozen men on the Supreme Court, three of whom were old enough to be their grandfathers, were expanding the individual rights of Americans to their outer limits.

Voting Rights. As the decade of the 1960s opened, the universal voting franchise which Americans had come to accept over almost two hundred years of constitutional evolution was subject to a major qualification. In many of the states of the former Confederacy, blacks were largely, though not entirely, excluded from voting by a series of legal and administrative barriers. By mid decade, federal legislation had been enacted that in fact brought those practices to an end. Universal adult suffrage had become a reality for the first time in American history. In addition the Supreme Court mandated that voting districts for members of the same representative body contain equal populations, thus ensuring that the often violated principle of "one man, one vote" enjoyed constitutional protection.

Criminal Rights. After President Roosevelt's appointees had gained control of the U.S. Supreme Court in the late 1930s, they enunciated a constitutional principle that was to have far-reaching effect. Government acts that infringed on individual rights were subject to greater scrutiny than those which affected ordinary commercial transactions. While the greater scrutiny rule was applied in subsequent years to cases involving free speech and religion, and eventually to cases involving the rights of racial minorities, criminal rights were a more difficult problem. Unlike the innocent victims of ideological and racial prejudice, most persons accused of crimes were not sympathetic figures. There was strong public pressure to short-circuit the rights of criminal defendants guaranteed in the first ten amendments to the Constitution, particularly where the accused was poor and lived outside the mainstream of white, middle-class America. But, in a series of decisions that spanned the decade of the 1960s, the U.S. Supreme Court ruled that the right to counsel, the right to remain silent, the right to be free of unreasonable searches and seizures, and other constitutional guarantees must be strictly adhered to in all criminal cases, regardless of the odiousness of the crime or the social status of the accused.

Liberty versus Order. At the end of 1969 the forces of personal liberty collided with the established legal order in the Chicago courtroom of Judge Julius J. Hoffman. At the trial of eight activists involved in demonstrations at the tumultuous 1968 Democratic Convention, the defendants and their lawyers succeeded in reducing the legal process to what was described as "guerrilla theater." In a sense the Chicago Seven case (one of the eight defendants was separated from the case in mid trial) was a parable of the growing split in American society, associated with but not entirely drawn on generational lines. Those who felt individual behavior must be constrained by strict legal limits were represented by the prosecutors and the judge. Those who felt social norms must conform to individual desires were represented by the defendants and their attorneys. The conclusion of the case, with a deeply divided jury, a mixed bag of acquittals and convictions, and contempt citations galore, left the judicial system dented but intact and the radical espousers of individual rights jailed but unrepentant. For most Americans there was a growing feeling that in cases where politics and the law were mixed, the different factions simply talked, or screamed, past one another. As always the courts were a forum for conflicts between people. But now it seemed that certain conflicts were irreconcilable.

A Portent of the Future. Like every decade, the 1960s held within itself the seeds of future change. While Congress and the courts were expanding the rights of people on the fringes of American society, behavior patterns and attitudes were spreading from the fringes toward society's heart. Many mainstream Americans found these developments to be especially threatening. To them men like Manson were not merely bad; they were positively evil in their drive to convert others to their beliefs. By 1969 a political and legal reaction to the assault of individual liberty on legal order had emerged, which set the stage for future turmoil in the field of law.

TOPICS IN THE NEWS

THE ATTORNEY GENERAL AND THE TEAMSTER

The McClellan Committee. In 1957 concerns with organized crime in labor unions led to the formation of a special congressional committee headed by Sen. John L. McClellan that was commonly referred to as the McClellan committee. McClellan brought along Robert Kennedy as the counsel for this select committee. It was in the hearings held by the McClellan committee that Kennedy first met James R. Hoffa. The committee had investigated Teamster leader David Beck who was later convicted of larceny and income tax evasion. The removal of Beck cleared the way for Hoffa to rise to command of the powerful Teamster Union, which represented truckers throughout the United States. By the mid 1950s it had become the largest union in the country both in terms of membership and funds. The Teamsters Union, and Hoffa in particular, was to become an obsession for Kennedy as the years progressed. The McClellan committee investigation of the union turned up disturbing information about its new leader. Although officials failed in several attempts to gain convictions against Hoffa, the information unearthed convinced Kennedy that Hoffa was an evil man. Kennedy came to believe that Hoffa was involved with many organized-crime figures, including the mobster Sam Giancana, reputedly the head of Chicago's Mafia. He also thought that Hoffa was siphoning money from the union funds and was engaged in other illegal acts such as extortion, assault, and even murder. However, Hoffa managed to elude law enforcement, and in 1959 a discouraged Kennedy left the committee. He felt that despite his best efforts corruption in the labor unions had grown worse and that conditions for union members had not improved. After leaving the committee Kennedy wrote a book about its work called the *The Enemy Within* (1960).

A New Attorney General. After finishing his book Kennedy turned to managing his brother's campaign for president. After John F. Kennedy's election in 1960 Robert faced the question of what to do next. He had reservations when his brother asked him to become attorney general but eventually accepted the post. The appointment raised concerns about nepotism and Kennedy's lack

James Hoffa testifying before the McClellan committee in 1961

of real courtroom experience. His legal career had so far been limited to serving as congressional counsel. Also, at age thirty-five, Kennedy would be the youngest attorney general in modern history. Yet President Kennedy wanted someone on the cabinet in whom he could confide. Also, the president felt that Robert, with his organizational skills, was a good choice for attorney general, whose primary job is not to appear in court but to administer a large department of the government.

War Against Organized Crime. Attorney General

Kennedy had not forgotten his experiences on the McClellan committee. It was not long before he turned his attention to the subject of organized crime and corruption in labor unions, two problems which he believed to be related. Under Kennedy the Justice Department began to pursue organized crime with an intensity never before applied to the problem. This led to the prosecutions of a number of organized-crime leaders and a concerted effort to break up their operations. But Kennedy wanted Hoffa, and he formed an unprecedented group of investigators and attorneys with only one purpose, to convict the Teamster leader. Kennedy seemed to believe genuinely that Hoffa, with his control over one of the country's most powerful unions, posed a threat to society. However, the attorney general was overestimating both the union and the leader's power. While it was sometimes said that the Teamsters could bring the "nation to a stop," blocking the transfer of all goods traveling by truck, the threat was overstated. The union was traditionally wary of strikes and rarely called them. Corruption was certainly a problem in the Teamsters, but other major labor unions were similarly afflicted. Kennedy's obsession with Hoffa was due in part to a belief that Hoffa was not just skimming some union funds but also that he was involved with larger organized-crime networks. But there was also a personal element to Kennedy's feelings about Hoffa, extending back to the McClellan committee hearings, when the two strong and contrary personalities had first clashed. Certainly this view was encouraged by the press which in the years ahead often depicted the suits against Hoffa as a personal battle between the attorney general and the Teamster leader.

The Get Hoffa Squad. Kennedy formed what became known as the "Get Hoffa Squad," a group of investigators and attorneys who ceaselessly pursued the union leader. The unit's function was to prosecute Hoffa using information unearthed by the McClellan committee and supplemented by its new investigations. It also sought to pursue simultaneously lower-ranking Teamster officials who were involved in the net of crimes and corruption led by Hoffa. Hoffa was kept under constant surveillance. As the head of the unit, Walter Sheridan, commented, "I knew where [Hoffa] was twenty-four hours a day." The first courtroom battle occurred in Nashville, Tennessee, where Hoffa was charged with taking illegal payments from a company employing Teamsters in violation of the Taft-Hartley Act. One of the provisions of the law prevented conflicts of interest arising from union leadership privately doing business with companies in which their unions are active. The allegation was that Hoffa had settled an employment dispute in favor of a trucking firm and then had privately done business with the firm, making hundreds of thousands of dollars personally. The trial began in October 1962. The charge was only a misdemeanor carrying at most a year in prison, but Hoffa fought it energetically, hiring a large team of capable attorneys. To the surprise of many, the Justice Depart-

ment was unable to convict Hoffa; the trial ended in a hung jury. However, the Justice Department had an informer in Hoffa's entourage. He told the government that Hoffa had conspired to bribe jurors in the case. This resulted in a second prosecution in May 1963 which was moved to Chattanooga, Tennessee, because of the publicity Hoffa had received in Nashville. With the aid of the government informant, this trial in February 1964 was successful. Hoffa was found guilty, fined ten thousand dollars and sentenced to ten years in prison. The Justice Department did not stop there. Another case was brought in Chicago in April 1964, charging fraud in the use of the Teamster pension fund. Hoffa was convicted and sentenced to another five years.

A Question of Ethics. Thus the personal campaign by Robert Kennedy against Jimmy Hoffa was largely successful. In its four years of existence, the Hoffa unit had secured two convictions against the man who had evaded all previous attempts. It also garnered 115 convictions against Teamster officials and business or personal associates of the union. However, this extensive investigation raised questions about prosecutorial prerogative and ethics. The greatest criticism went to the heart of the Justice Department's approach to Hoffa. Normally the department investigates specific charges where it has reasonable assurance that a particular wrongful act has been committed. In Hoffa's case, however, it had chosen a person as its target first and then investigated his every personal and business activity in an effort to unearth wrongdoing that could be prosecuted. To some critics Kennedy's approach more nearly resembled the inquisitions of Sen. Joseph McCarthy than conventional law enforcement. There was no doubt that Hoffa was properly convicted for illegal acts he had committed, but the questions of prosecutorial priorities and the ethical issues that accompany them were highlighted by this very personal battle.

Sources:

"Jimmy and the Jury," *Time,* 81 (17 May 1963): 30–31;

"Jimmy Wins Again," *Time,* 80 (30 November 1962): 20–21;

Victor Navasky, *Kennedy Justice* (New York: Atheneum, 1971);

Arthur Schlesinger, Jr., *Robert Kennedy and His Times* (Boston: Houghton Mifflin, 1978);

"Witness for the Prosecution," *Time,* 83 (28 February 1964): 25;

"You Bum!," *Time,* 79 (25 May 1962): 22–23.

BAKER V. CARR

Representative Government. The concept of representation is basic to local, state, and federal government. Such bodies as local councils, state legislatures, and the U.S. House of Representatives are formed by elected officials who come from a particular area or district to represent the interests of the people who elected them. If one representative comes from a district with ten people and another comes from a district with a thousand people, the people in the smaller district can be said to have a greater voice in government than the people in the

A JURY OF PEERS

In ancient days the jury for a trial was picked from people in the locale where the dispute had occurred. It was felt that people who knew the parties in the lawsuit and had witnessed or heard of the events at issue were best placed to decide the case. In the modern world a different approach is followed. It is felt that members of the ideal jury should have no preformed opinion about the case, and their knowledge should be based on the evidence presented by both sides at the trial. Given this standard, attorneys try to weed out prospective jurors who have prior knowledge or prejudices. In an effort to help attorneys in juror selection, a study was conducted in the early 1960s to determine likely objects and categories of prejudice. The study indicated that while discrimination against blacks was a topic much in the news there was little evidence of its affecting jurors. It showed that black Americans tended to be biased in favor of the young and poor. It indicated that people with low incomes are often biased against those with high incomes and vice versa but that people earning between seventy-five hundred dollars and fifteen thousand dollars were unlikely to meet bias from other groups. It found that women faced less likelihood of getting a fair trial from jurors who were men earning under five thousand dollars or who were women. The study also found that people under age thirty were less prejudiced in most categories, while retired people were the most. One unusual finding was that by occupation, salesmen had the most prejudices, being biased against low-income people, people of southern and eastern European origin, and the unemployed, but favoring women. While this study provided no hard and fast rules for attorneys picking a jury, it did give some guidance. Since the 1960s the study of jurors and their predilections and preferences has formed a growing field, though, then as now, an attorney's experience and instincts are still his best guides.

Source: *Time* (9 August 1963): 38.

est comprised only about 112,000. In the state legislature of Florida a majority of the members of both houses represented districts containing less than 15 percent of the state's population.

Districts Frozen in Time. These disparities occurred because, at the turn of the century, many state governments had frozen their legislative district boundaries. As the population flowed toward cities, there was no change in the districts from which representatives were elected. The reason was simple. The legislatures were dominated by members from rural districts, and it was not in their interest, nor in the interest of their constituents, to change the system. The best way for them to retain power was to keep things as they were. As the inequities worsened the legislatures had less and less incentive to reapportion.

Unfulfilled Promise. The only hope for reform was the courts. However, the initial attempts at judicially imposed reapportionment failed. In 1946 the U.S. Supreme Court had heard the case of *Colegrove* v. *Green*, challenging apportionment in Illinois. The Court held that the issue was a "political question." While the courts have great potential power to interfere with the legislative and executive branches of government, they are held in check by certain self-imposed limitations. Political decisions are different from legal decisions which have political effects, which courts hear all the time. The line dividing these areas can never be clearly drawn. The essence of the distinction is that courts should not make decisions on subjects that are the responsibility of another branch of government. The courts can only interfere when another branch has exceeded its constitutional powers or has breached some provision of law. For example, judges cannot appoint a cabinet officer or (except as part of an extraordinary remedy) levy a tax, but they can rule on whether a particular appointment or tax is legal.

Continuing Pressure. The reapportionment problem would not go away. With no possibility of legislative change, suits continued to be brought. Finally in 1962 the dam broke. The case that became the vehicle for this revolution was *Baker* v. *Carr*. The litigation arose in Tennessee, where the state constitution required that legislative reapportionment occur every ten years. But this responsibility had been ignored since 1901. An attempt had been made several years before to challenge the existing apportionment scheme in the state courts. The plaintiffs had relied upon the Tennessee Constitution, but the Supreme Court of Tennessee had refused to adjudicate the matter, citing the Colegrove precedent. Several other states had faced such challenges, but the Colegrove doctrine had been used repeatedly to prevent the courts from entering the fray.

Tennessee's Problem. Colegrove had been a narrow decision by a shorthanded court. The facts in the Tennessee case presented a compelling challenge to precedent. The state legislature had been intransigent in the face of

larger district. Representation is thus unequal and government may be unfair.

Unequal Representation. By the end of World War II district imbalance was especially great in the states that had the fastest growing populations. In Georgia the largest congressional district had 823,680 people in it, while the smallest had only 272,154. Illinois was another seriously malapportioned state. Its largest district, in the Chicago area, had over 914,000 people, while the small-

Albert DeSalvo, under arrest in Boston

its own constitution, and the inequalities were strong. The effects of malapportionment went beyond philosophical or theoretical arguments; they were felt in the reality of state finances. Rural sections of Tennessee commanded a majority of legislative seats and, as a consequence, took the majority of state funding, even though most of the tax dollars in the state were generated in the heavily populated urban areas. As a result, by the mid 1950s nearly ninety-eight dollars was spent per pupil in rural schools, but the schools in the state's four largest urban centers received less than sixty-four dollars per student. The effects were felt in many other aspects of state, county, and city finance.

Baker v. *Carr*. *Baker* v. *Carr* attacked the Tennessee apportionment scheme as a violation of the equal protection clause in the Fourteenth Amendment to the U.S. Constitution. That clause requires that the states treat like people the same way, and the plaintiffs argued that malapportionment violated this guarantee. There was much evidence of a violation, but before the courts could rule on the merits, they had to determine if they had jurisdiction. The case was initially heard by a three-judge panel which held that the courts had no jurisdiction. The plaintiffs then appealed to the U.S. Supreme Court. At that level the plaintiffs were joined by the U.S. government itself, represented by the solicitor general.

A Second Bite at the Apple. The Supreme Court eventually heard oral arguments twice. This unusual step indicated the divisions within the Court. Felix Frankfurter, who had authored the opinion in Colegrove, was still a justice and was active in support of its holding. In March 1962, however, the Colegrove case was reversed.

The Court held that state apportionment did not constitute a political question. It recognized the rights of voters to challenge arbitrary apportionment by a state. The Court deftly dodged the political implications of the opinion by treating the dispute as one of constitutional limitations upon state power. "One man, one vote" became the watchword.

Legal Blitzkrieg. The effect was quick and widespread. Within a year of the decision thirty-six states were involved in reapportionment lawsuits. By the end of 1963 forty-two states were dealing with lawsuits, referendums, or actual reapportionments. In 1964 the Supreme Court applied judicial reapportionment to congressional districts as well. The same year the Court also ruled that both houses of state legislatures must be apportioned according to population, even when the voters of the state had approved another system. Finally, the Court required that in elections within political subdivisions, such as for school boards, the principle of electoral equality must be applied. By the end of the decade the political landscape of the United States had been radically altered, as virtually all election districts were redrawn to meet the one man, one vote standard.

Sources:
Robert H. Birkby, *The Court and Public Policy* (Washington, D.C.: CQ Press, 1983);

Gene Graham, *One Man, One Vote* (Boston: Little, Brown, 1972).

THE BOSTON STRANGLER

A Summer of Fear. In the summer of 1962 Boston, Massachusetts, was gripped by fear. In June a fifty-five-year-old woman was found dead in her apartment. She had been sexually assaulted and strangled by a cord. The cord had been tied in a bow beneath her chin, a method which was to become the sign of the murderer known as the Boston Strangler. By the end of the month, two more elderly women were found murdered in similar circumstances. In the next two months four more women in their sixties and seventies were found strangled. The Boston police faced rising demands for action as it became clear that elderly women in Boston were being targeted by a madman. For the next several months no new bodies were found. Then in December the Strangler struck again. This time he raped and strangled two young women in their early twenties. It was now clear to the police that they had a serious problem on their hands that was not going to go away. Certain evidence suggested that the same man was responsible for all the murders. Each of the victims had been strangled with articles of clothing which had been tied with the same type of knot. Also, there was no sign of forced entry into the homes of the victims, which indicated that the killer was a smooth operator.

The Killing Continues. The Strangler struck again in March 1963. It appeared that the victim, a sixty-nine-year-old woman, had first been killed, then raped, then repeatedly stabbed with a fork, then strangled. This new technique was repeated on 6 May 1963, when the Strangler raped and killed a twenty-three-year-old college student. She had been strangled with her nylon stockings and stabbed repeatedly with a knife. The knife was found at the scene, but, as was to be expected from the experienced and cunning killer, it had been wiped clean of fingerprints.

The Killer Returns. It was four months before he struck again. On 8 September 1963 a fifty-eight-year-old woman was found who had been manually strangled. But there was no doubt as to who was responsible. On the woman's ankle was a stocking tied in the Strangler's characteristic bow. The day after President John F. Kennedy's assassination he claimed yet another victim. On 4 January 1964 the Strangler raped and murdered a nineteen-year-old woman.

An Impossible Situation. The city of Boston was in a panic. Women did not feel safe even in their own homes. The police department had established a special "Strangler Bureau" with its own detectives to try to track down all the clues and reports relating to the Strangler. The bureau focused on men with previous records of sex crimes. They kept a number of suspects under surveillance. However, the investigation was having no success. Disturbingly, the Strangler seemed to be having no difficulty entering his victim's homes, even with all the media attention on the murders and the accompanying panic. Also there was the question of why had no one ever been able to identify the murderer. He was clearly loitering around apartment buildings, yet he seemed to pass invisibly to and from the scene of his crimes.

BURIED ALIVE

In December 1968 Barbara Jane Mackle, the twenty-year-old daughter of one of Florida's wealthiest families, was abducted at gunpoint. She was staying at a motel outside Atlanta, Georgia, with her mother. She had finished exams at Emory University, and they were spending the night there before heading back to Florida for Christmas with the rest of the family. At four in the morning they were awakened by a knock at the door. The person identified himself as a policeman. When they opened the door, they faced a masked man with a shotgun and another person in a ski mask. Barbara Jane was spirited away, and her mother was left tied up. Mrs. Mackle quickly managed to get out of her bonds and call the police. The kidnappers soon contacted the family demanding five hundred thousand dollars in old twenty-dollar bills. Mr. Mackle, who with his two brothers operated a construction company worth sixty-five million dollars, decided to cooperate fully in order to get his daughter back. The money was dropped offshore in Biscayne Bay in Florida as the kidnappers had requested. However, their pickup was stopped by local police who had not been told of the ransom drop and were checking a complaint of suspicious activity. The kidnappers escaped but had to abandon the money. That evening another attempt was made, this time successfully. The kidnappers then called to tell the location of Barbara Jane. She was found buried in a coffinlike box, a foot and a half underground, about twenty miles from Atlanta. It was equipped with air tubes and a supply of food and water. Despite spending eighty hours in the box she was in good condition and was soon returned to her family.

Source: *Time* (27 December 1968): 16.

The Strangler. Despite the magnitude of the police effort, the real murderer was never regarded as a suspect. Albert Henry DeSalvo was born in Chelsea, Massachusetts, on 3 September 1931, the third of six children. When DeSalvo was eight, his father, an abusive furniture mover with a record of violent crimes, abandoned the family, returning occasionally for drunken rampages. Upon graduation from high school, DeSalvo, who already had a criminal record, joined the army. He became the army middleweight boxing champion. While in Europe, he met and married a German woman who returned to the United States with him when he was transfered to Fort Dix in New Jersey. The DeSalvos had two children.

Problems Begin. DeSalvo had an inexhaustible sex drive that took on a criminal dimension when he was stationed at Fort Dix and was accused of molesting a nine-year-old girl. The mother of the child refused to press charges, the army dropped the case, and soon thereafter DeSalvo received an honorable discharge. He worked as a handyman and later for a construction firm. But behind the carefully cultivated picture of a friendly worker and considerate family man, DeSalvo's criminal urges were mounting.

A New Approach. DeSalvo began approaching young women saying that he represented a modeling agency. He told them that they could make good money modeling but that he would have to get some information and their measurements. Apparently hundreds of women allowed him into their apartments with his clipboard and tape measure. In March 1960 he was arrested for breaking and entering and confessed to being the criminal the police had dubbed the "Measuring Man." He received a two-year sentence and was released on parole after only eleven months.

A Turn for the Worst. After his release in April 1962, DeSalvo became a rapist. He was known as the "Green Man," because he usually wore green work pants when he assaulted his victims. At times he would break in, but more often he would talk his way into women's apartments, claiming, for example, to be a building maintenance worker. He raped as many as six women a day. The police were able to confirm four attacks between nine in the morning and midday, in four separate towns. He claimed that he had assaulted over one thousand women. It was not until summer 1962 that he began killing some of his victims.

Caught. DeSalvo was never suspected by the police. Their records indicated only that he had committed crimes against property, so he was not considered to be a potential rapist. Finally, however, DeSalvo made a mistake. In October 1964 he broke into the home of a newly married young woman, tied her up, and raped her. DeSalvo left her alive, and she was able to describe him to the police. After an artist's sketch was made, he was recognized as the "Measuring Man." DeSalvo was arrested and sent to the mental hospital at Bridgewater for pretrial observation. Meanwhile other rape victims came forward. It became clear that DeSalvo was responsible for a large number of sexual assaults, not only in Massachusetts, but in neighboring states as well. However, he was not yet connected with the stranglings in Boston.

A Murderer is Revealed. The break came from DeSalvo himself. He confided his participation in the Boston stranglings to a fellow inmate at Bridgewater, who in turn passed on the word to his lawyer, the prominent criminal defense attorney F. Lee Bailey. DeSalvo subsequently hired Bailey to defend him against the assault charges he was then facing. Bailey arranged for DeSalvo to tell the story of his crimes to the attorney

general's office under an agreement that his confession could not be used against him. DeSalvo's knowledge of the crime scenes eventually convinced the police that he was in fact the Boston Strangler, but because there were no witnesses to the stranglings, the police never had enough evidence to convict him of the murders.

An Innovative Approach. Attorney Bailey's plan was to use the monstrosity of DeSalvo's acts as the Boston Strangler to convince a jury that his client was insane. The plan failed. In the January 1967 trial the jury took only four hours of deliberation to find DeSalvo sane and guilty. He was sentenced to life imprisonment but remained in Bridgewater while his conviction was appealed. Shortly thereafter DeSalvo and two fellow inmates broke out of the facility, but DeSalvo was caught within thirty-three hours and transferred to the Walpole State Prison. On 26 November 1973 he was found dead in his cell, stabbed through the heart. His murderer was never identified.

Sources:

"Bailey and the Boston Strangler," *Time*, 89 (27 January 1967): 40;

Gerold Frank, *The Boston Strangler* (New York: New American Library, 1966);

Jay Robert Nash, *Encyclopedia of World Crime: Criminal Justice, Criminology, and Law Enforcement* (Wilmette, Ill.: CrimeBooks, 1989, 1990);

John M. MacDonald, *Rape Offenders and Their Victims* (Springfield, Ill.: Thomas, 1971);

"The Phantom Strangler," *Time*, 81 (22 March 1963): 20;

"Return of the Strangler," *Time*, 89 (3 March 1967): 26–27.

THE TRIAL OF THE CHICAGO SEVEN

The Convention. In August 1968 the Democratic party held its national convention in Chicago. The Vietnam War and the civil rights movement were near their respective climaxes, charging American politics with tremendous ideological intensity. Two groups, the National Mobilization Committee to End the War in Vietnam (MOBE) and the Youth International party (Yippies) had been planning since early 1968 to conduct protest demonstrations in Chicago during the convention. Rock concerts were scheduled, parade permits were sought, and other preparations were made by the members of the two organizations. During the event there were repeated clashes among the crowds of protesters and the police and National Guard. Many were injured on both sides, and several protesters were arrested.

The Anti-Riot Act. Earlier in 1968 a group of conservative senators had added to the Civil Rights Bill of that year a provision which came to be called the Anti-Riot Act. The new statute made it a violation of federal law to travel in or use the facilities of interstate commerce with the intent to incite riot. After the convention Lyndon Johnson's Justice Department had drawn up indictments for violation of the act against five MOBE and Yippie leaders, plus three other men who also were involved in the protests. David Dellinger, Rennie Davis, and Tom

David Dellinger, at microphones, with William Kunstler, right, after his
conviction in the Chicago Seven trial

Hayden were involved in MOBE, and Jerry Rubin and Abbie Hoffman headed the Yippies. John Froines was a college professor and Lee Weiner was a graduate student. Bobby Seale was national chairman of the Black Panthers. President Johnson's attorney general, Ramsey Clark, refused to prosecute the case, but the newly elected Nixon administration decided to pursue the indictments.

Trial as Theater. From the inception the strategy of the defendants was to so disrupt the proceedings that no conviction could be obtained that would stand on appeal. In addition, the defendants correctly perceived that the trial would give them a priceless opportunity to publicize their views. To further heighten the confrontational atmosphere, the federal judge assigned to try the case, Julius Hoffman, was seventy-four years old and not known for his patience. Matters got off to a dramatic start when Judge Hoffman sought to jail four lawyers for contempt because they withdrew from the case before the trial started. In screening the jury the judge generally restricted the defendants' questions, particularly those relating to the attitudes of prospective jurors toward the Vietnam War, youth culture, and protests. Once the trial got under way the defense and the prosecution traded insults and generally offended the standards of legal decorum outrageously. At one point Dellinger charged that the defendants were being treated like Jews sent to the gas chamber. Seale was enraged that he was not able to be represented by his usual attorney, Charles Garry, who underwent surgery shortly before the trial started. After repeated attempts to prevent Seale from examining witnesses on his own, Judge Hoffman added his own touch to the proceedings by having Seale bound and

gagged. Finally, the judge separated Seale's trial from that of the remaining defendants and sentenced him to a total of forty-eight months in prison for sixteen specific acts of contempt.

The Verdict. The trial dragged on for five stormy months. Finally, after hearing almost two hundred witnesses and after having been sent from the courtroom innumerable times while the judge and attorneys wrangled, the jury retired to consider its verdict. Matters did not go much better in the jury room than they did in the courtroom. The twelve members, ten women and two men, were themselves deeply divided. In the end feelings were so aroused that the groups for and against conviction could not even occupy the same room. Determined not to let the case be mistried on account of a hung jury, they arrived at a compromise. The two academics, Froines and Weiner, were acquitted of all charges. The remaining five defendants were acquitted of conspiracy but convicted under the new Anti-Riot Act.

The Appeals. While the jury deliberated Judge Hoffman sentenced the seven remaining defendants and two of their attorneys to jail terms ranging from two months to four years for contempt of court. The appeal of the contempt sentences and the appeal from the guilty verdicts were both heard by the U.S. Court of Appeals for the Seventh Circuit in February 1972. In May the court of appeals reversed the contempt citations. It relied on a recent Supreme Court ruling that where the trial judge is the object of personal vilification and he waits, as did Judge Hoffman, until the end of the trial to cite for contempt, then a person charged with contempt is entitled to a hearing before another judge. In the main case the appeals court handed down its decision in November

1972. The Anti-Riot Act was upheld against the defendants' assertions that it was overly vague and violated the guarantee of free speech in the Constitution. However, the convictions were reversed. The court held that Judge Hoffman had not permitted the defendants' attorneys to question prospective jurors adequately about their beliefs and prejudices and about the impact of pretrial publicity. In addition, the court said the judge had demonstrated an antagonistic attitude to the defendants and had not allowed certain key witnesses to testify for the defense.

The Aftermath. The government elected not to try the defendants again on the original charges, even though the appeals court held that sufficient evidence had been presented at the trial to support the convictions of Dellinger, Davis, Hayden, Hoffman, and Rubin under the Anti-Riot Act. On the contempt citations, retrial took place in late 1973. Dellinger, Hoffman, Rubin, and one of the attorneys, William Kunstler, were convicted, but the presiding judge decided not to sentence them to any time in jail. At last, the Chicago Seven trial was over.

Sources:

David Dellinger, *From Yale to Jail, The Life Story of a Moral Dissenter* (New York: Pantheon, 1993);

USA v. Dellinger, et al., Federal Reporter, second series 472, p. 340;

John Schultz, *Motion Will Be Denied: A New Report on the Chicago Conspiracy Trial* (New York: Morrow, 1972).

Lyndon B. Johnson signing the Civil Rights Act of 1964

CIVIL RIGHTS ACT OF 1964

A Momentous Year. The most extensive and far-reaching civil rights act since Reconstruction won approval in Congress in 1964. This was not to say that the new law dealt with all the concerns of black Americans. In particular the question of effective measures to ensure that unrestricted voting would be available to blacks was left to another day. However, the Civil Rights Act of 1964 marked a major step forward for government involvement in preventing racial discrimination, particularly in the private sector.

The Act. The act was divided into eleven parts or titles. Among its provisions were: an extension of the life of the Civil Rights Commission which had been established by the Civil Rights Act of 1959; prohibition against voting registrars applying different standards to black and white applicants; prohibition of racial discrimination in public education; an authorization for the executive branch to halt the flow of federal funds to both public and private programs in which racial discrimination was allowed to continue; and authority for the attorney general to bring suits, upon written complaint of individuals, to desegregate public facilities, including those run by state or local governments.

A Question of Control. These measures basically dealt with the exercise of control over federal agencies and federal funds or with the activities of state and local governments. Control by the federal government of its own agencies and funds was relatively noncontroversial. Nor were the limitations imposed on the state and local governments novel. Since passage of the Fourteenth Amendment to the U.S. Constitution in 1868, the Supreme Court had extended constitutional protections originally applicable only to the federal government to the states as well. The Court had done this on a case-by-case basis, and not every right was necessarily protected at the state level. But the right to be free from racially based discrimination by a state government and its subdivisions was already constitutionally protected.

Titles VII and II. The other two titles dealt with a very different issue. They sought to prevent discrimination by private individuals acting independently of any governmental funding or connection. Title VII dealt with equal employment opportunity. It forbade discrimination on the basis of race, color, sex, religion, or national origin by employers or labor unions. The act initially covered those businesses which had one hundred or more employees in an industry affecting interstate commerce. It was scheduled to expand to cover any establishment employing twenty-five or more employees. The measure required that no discrimination be allowed in any phase of employment from initial hiring, to job assignments and promotions, to firings. The other section dealing with private individuals was Title II. This provision prohibited discrimination in public accommodations which might affect interstate commerce. Public accommodations included hotels, restaurants, theaters, stadiums, or gas stations.

Interstate Commerce. Both Title VII and Title II of the 1964 Civil Rights Act prohibited racial discrimination by businesses that affected interstate commerce. The definition of interstate commerce thus became crucial to the plan of desegregation in the act. The government of the United States is a government of enumerated powers. Just because the federal government seeks to act for a good cause is not enough. There must be a grant of power in the Constitution permitting it. This requirement had been a major barrier to any civil rights legislation which sought to prevent racial discrimination by private persons and businesses, rather than by governments. The Supreme Court had previously held that racial discrimination by a private business, even if licensed by the state, could not reasonably be considered state action. And if the prohibited practice was not state action, it could not be held to be a violation of the Fourteenth Amendment to the Constitution.

The Commerce Clause. The solution was the commerce clause in Article I of the Constitution, empowering the federal government to regulate the commerce between the states and with foreign nations. At first glance this may appear to be a rather limited power, allowing the federal government to control only the shipment of specific goods across state lines to the exclusion of state regulation. However, over the years the Supreme Court broadened the scope of the commerce clause to allow Congress to regulate more areas of the economy. An extreme example was the case of *Wickard* v. *Filburn,* where the Supreme Court held that a farmer who grew only twenty-three acres of wheat, which he used entirely on his own farm, was engaged in an activity which could be regulated under the commerce clause. The Court reasoned that thousands of such subsistence farmers throughout the country would affect interstate commerce if for no other reason than that they would not be buying any wheat themselves.

Supreme Court. So it was that the rather arcane issue of the commerce clause became the basis for affirming the constitutionality of the Civil Rights Act of 1964. The challenge did not take long in coming. Immediately after the act was passed, several establishments in the South announced that they would still not serve blacks. They claimed that the law was unconstitutional. Two of these cases were heard by the Supreme Court in late 1964.

Heart of Atlanta. The first case involved the Heart of Atlanta, a posh hotel located in downtown Atlanta, Georgia, which served only white patrons. This case provided a good test of the general application of the new civil rights law, because if any establishment could be found to involve interstate commerce this was it. It had 216 rooms available and was easily accessible from Interstates 75 and 85. The hotel advertised widely outside Georgia through national magazines. It also had over

THE PUNCHING PREACHER

In 1967, boxing great Cassius Clay found himself in battle outside the ring. He had captured the heavyweight championship three years before, but he now faced a jail term for claiming he was exempt from the military draft being conducted because of the Vietnam War. In March 1966 Clay had been classified 1A by his draft board in Louisville, Kentucky, but now he requested an exemption as a minister. In August of that year he had changed his name to Muhammad Ali, and claimed that he was a minister in the Black Muslims. In 1967 his case was heard in federal court. It took a jury only 21 minutes to find him guilty of draft dodging. He was sentenced to the maximum penalty, five years in jail and a ten-thousand-dollar fine. However, Ali was not beaten yet, and he appealed his case all the way to the United States Supreme Court. There his conviction was overturned in 1971. In a unanimous opinion the Court held that the boxer qualified for an exemption. On hearing the news Ali told reporters that he "thanked Allah."

Sources: Henry Abraham, *Freedom and the Court* (New York: Oxford University Press, 1988); *Time* (30 June 1967): 20.

fifty billboards and highway signs within that state. Finally, on average 75 percent of its guests were from out of state. The Court held that the difficulty blacks had in finding a place to stay when traveling clearly affected their ability to travel out of state. In a modern, mobile society such difficulties would discourage them from traveling and thus would clearly have a significant effect upon interstate commerce. The problem was so serious that special guidebooks had been published listing places where blacks could stay when traveling. Based on these findings the Court held that the use of the commerce clause to combat racial discrimination was legitimate and appropriate. Following the logic of *Wickard* v. *Filburn,* the Court noted that even if a single hotel or restaurant had a small effect on the whole scheme of peoples' movements, all the different instances taken together created a major problem. Thus the Court upheld the constitutionality of the law, both in general and as applied to any public accommodation which relied heavily on interstate customers for its existence.

Ollie's Barbeque. Another case the Court heard that same term posed a different question. Even if the use of the commerce clause was valid in some instances, how far did it go? The second case involved a restaurant called Ollie's Barbecue, run by Ollie McClung in Birmingham, Alabama. The restaurant had been in operation since 1927. It was located in a black neighborhood and two-thirds of the employees were black, but it had a policy of serving only whites on the premises, with take-out service for black patrons. It had space for about two hundred sit-down customers, most of whom were from the Birmingham area. The establishment was located some distance from the interstate highway which passed through town. It was even further from the bus and railroad stations and McClung did not seek to attract travelers. McClung did not advertise nationally, and he bought his food from a local supplier.

Widening Interstate Commerce. The Court used a different approach. Instead of looking at the clientele, as it had in the Heart of Atlanta case, it focused on the supplies used by the restaurant. While McClung bought his meat from a Birmingham wholesaler, the wholesaler bought its meat from a plant out of state. The Supreme Court noted that the restaurant purchased $150,000 worth of food per year and that of this, $70,000 worth was spent on meat. Thus about 46 percent of the restaurant's food was derived from an out-of-state source. This was enough for the Court. It held that McClung's operation did substantially affect interstate commerce, noting that the more patrons the restaurant could serve, white or black, the more food it would order. This would affect the amount of meat ordered from other states.

Greater Racial Equality. Thus the Supreme Court established that the commerce clause in its modern form was the means by which essentially any business operation in our country could be regulated by the federal government. It gave teeth to the Civil Rights Act of 1964 and opened the way to widespread integration of private institutions. But it should be noted that in doing so the Court enacted a major extension of the commerce clause. That extension was a bold but necessary step if the Civil Rights Act of 1964 was to be effective in moving the United States toward greater racial equality.

Sources:

Henry J. Abraham, *Freedom and the Court: Civil Rights and Liberties in the United States* (New York: Oxford University Press, 1972);

Richard Bardolph, ed., *The Civil Rights Record: Black Americans and the Law, 1849–1970* (New York: Crowell, 1970);

"Obliterating the Effect," *Time*, 84 (25 December 1964): 14;

"Public Accomodations on Trial," *Time*, 84 (16 October 1964): 69.

IN COLD BLOOD

The Clutters. On Saturday night, 14 November 1959, the lights did not burn late at the home of Herbert Clutter and his family near Holcomb, Kansas. The Clutters customarily rose early on Sunday to prepare for church. In many ways they represented the heartland American ideal. Herbert Clutter was a successful wheat farmer and the current chairman of the Kansas Conference of Farm Organizations. A respected man in the community, Clutter never touched alcohol or tobacco or even caffeine. His wife Bonnie was a retiring woman and something of an invalid, but she was well liked and was a caring mother of their four children, two of whom were

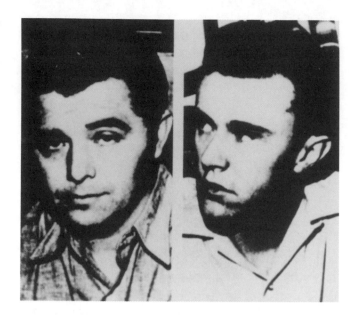

Richard Hickock, left, and Perry Smith, right, killers of the Clutter family

still at home. Their youngest daughter, Nancy, was sixteen and her brother Kenyon was a year younger. Both were straight-A students. Mr. and Mrs. Clutter had two other daughters.

The Murder Scene. The morning of 15 November, two friends of Nancy whom the Clutters took to church each Sunday were alarmed to find the house quiet. After they entered the home, they found Nancy's body in her room. By that afternoon the house was swarming with investigators. All four of the Clutters had been shot in the head with a shotgun. Nancy was lying in her bed facing the wall, her hands and feet tied. The bedcover had been drawn up to her shoulder as if she had been carefully tucked into bed. Bonnie Clutter was also tied up on her bed, and Kenyon was tied on a sofa in the basement den. His head had been placed on a pillow. Herbert Clutter lay nearby in another basement room. He also had been tied, though it appeared that he had broken some of his bindings. Apparently to ease his repose on the cold basement floor a mattress box had been moved from the other end of the room. Yet, in stark contrast to the apparent solicitude of the mysterious intruder, he had been shot in the head after his throat had been cut.

No Motive, No Clues. There seemed to be no motive for the killings. Robbery was unlikely. Nothing of value was missing. Indeed, it was well known in Holcomb that Mr. Clutter never kept cash in his home. The killer or killers had picked up the fired shotgun shells and had ripped out the telephones. The only apparent physical clues, the rope and tape used to bind the victims, were a common type obtainable anywhere. The initial belief was that the murderer or murderers were from nearby, perhaps motivated by some long-held grudge.

The Murderers. In fact, the crime was committed by

Richard Hickock and Perry Smith, who had driven over four hundred miles from Kansas City with the intention of robbing and murdering the Clutter family. Hickock was twenty-eight years old and had grown up in a stable if modest home. In high school he was an above-average student and an all-around athlete. After graduation he went to work first for the Sante Fe Railroad and then as a mechanic in Kansas City. By the end of 1957 he had been married twice, fathered three sons, and had progressed from gambling to writing bad checks to burglary, for which he was sentenced to the Kansas State Penitentiary in Lansing. In prison Hickock met Floyd Wells. As they whiled away the long hours, Wells told Hickock that one of his more pleasant experiences had been some ten years before, when he had worked for about a year on the Clutter farm. His story immediately caught Hickock's interest. He questioned Wells about the layout of the ranch and home. Wells thought Clutter kept a safe full of money in his office. Hickock was soon talking about how he would rob the place once he got out. He had worked out all the details, including choosing the man who would be his partner. Smith, thirty-one, was another inmate at Lansing. Smith's mother was a Cherokee, and his parents had been rodeo performers. After his parents left the rodeo when he was five, Smith's childhood became one of wandering poverty in the Depression. When he was sixteen Smith joined the merchant marine. He later enlisted in the army and served in Korea, receiving the Bronze Star. After his discharge in 1952, he was involved in a serious motorcycle accident which left his legs permanently weak and painful. He eventually wound up in the Kansas prison after having been convicted of burglary.

Committing the Crime. On the evening of 14 November 1959, Hickock and Smith broke into the Clutters' house, woke the family, and demanded to know where the safe was. Mr. and Mrs. Clutter told them that there was none. They locked the family in a bathroom, and Hickock kept guard while Smith searched the house. Smith then proceeded to take the members of the family out of the bathroom one by one and tie them up. He was the one responsible for the small signs of concern which had puzzled the police. All Hickock and Smith found was about forty dollars in cash and a radio. At this point Smith asked Hickock if he still wanted to go through with the killing. He stepped up to Mr. Clutter holding a hunting knife, with the intention, he later said, of calling what he believed to be Hickock's bluff. He had never favored killing them, but he wanted Hickock to back down first. While he was kneeling on the floor, his legs aching from all the activity, Smith suddenly slashed Mr. Clutter's throat. As the man began to rip apart his bonds with a last spasm of strength, Smith grabbed the shotgun from Hickock and pulled the trigger. The two men went to the next room in the basement, and Smith killed Kenyon. They then went back upstairs and either Hickock or Smith shot the two women.

On the Road. Upon returning to Kansas City, Smith and Hickock faced no questions. After about a week Hickock raised several hundred dollars by passing some bad checks, and the pair took off for Mexico. The date was 21 November 1959, and they felt that they were home free. This was far from the case. Despite Hickock's insistence of eliminating all witnesses, there was still one person who could connect him to the Clutter murders — Wells. The prisoner heard of the murders on the radio and immediately realized that his old cellmate had actually carried out his plan. Wells at first hesitated. Eventually, at the beginning of December, the inducement of a thousand-dollar reward and the encouragement of a religious friend convinced him to speak to the prison warden. The warden immediately informed the Kansas Bureau of Investigation, and a nationwide alert was issued for Hickock and his companion Smith. In the meantime, after spending several weeks in Mexico, the pair returned to Kansas City, where Hickock passed additional bad checks. Before the police could arrest them Hickock and Smith were headed for Miami to spend Christmas on the beach, oblivious to the net which was closing in around them. When they ran out of money they headed for Las Vegas, where the police brought their long journey to an end.

Trial and Execution. The authorities needed confessions. They had Wells's story but no real evidence to back it up. Hickock finally broke down and admitted his involvement. Once Smith was convinced that his partner had talked, he too confessed. The men were tried in Garden City near the scene of the Clutter murders. The trial was straightforward. The police now had some physical evidence connecting the defendants to the crime. The gun used in the murders had been found in the home of Hickock's parents, and experts were able to identify it as the murder weapon. Wells testified as to Hickock's plans in prison, and the confessions were introduced into evidence. Neither Hickock or Smith took the stand, but there was little their court-appointed attorneys could do. On 13 May 1960 they were both convicted and sentenced to hang. With the assistance of skillful lawyers who volunteered their time to help the defendants, Hickock and Smith evaded several execution dates. Eventually their appeals, and their time, ran out. On 14 April 1965 they were executed by hanging.

Epilogue. The crime attracted considerable attention, being covered extensively in the Kansas print and broadcast media, and even reported in *Time.* However, its real notoriety did not occur until Truman Capote published his book, *In Cold Blood* (1965). There seemed something about these murders that appealed to the American public: a hideous, pointless killing by two twisted individuals, a relentless and successful police investigation, a guilty verdict after a fair trial, and the eventual execution of the killers. Perhaps most satisfying was Capote's assurance that Smith's last words were "I apologize." Despite the

WARNING AS TO YOUR RIGHTS

You are under arrest. Before we ask you any questions, you must understand what your rights are.

You have the right to remain silent. You are not required to say anything to us at any time or to answer any questions. Anything you say can be used against you in court.

You have the right to talk to a lawyer for advice before we question you and to have him with you during questioning.

If you cannot afford a lawyer and want one, a lawyer will be provided for you.

If you want to answer questions now without a lawyer present you will still have the right to stop answering at any time. You also have the right to stop answering at any time until you talk to a lawyer.   P-4475

Cards with the Miranda warnings were given to Washington, D.C., policemen in 1966.

Clutters' tragic deaths, the readers could feel reassured that the legal and moral order remained intact.

Sources:

Truman Capote, *In Cold Blood* (New York: Random House, 1965);

"In Cold Blood," *Time*, 74 (30 November 1959): 18;

"The Killers," *Time*, 75 (18 January 1960): 18.

CRIMINAL LAW IN THE 1960S

A Decade of Change. During the 1960s the U.S. Supreme Court dealt with many cases involving criminal procedure. Several of these cases resulted in major changes in the way police and the courts dealt with criminal defendants. Some of the changes involved extending protections granted in the Bill of Rights to the states, others involved interpreting the Constitution's provisions in light of changing technology and circumstances that the founding fathers could not have imagined. In other cases the Court moved to enhance the protections of criminals in response to changing social values. The result of all these cases was enhancement of individual liberties and confusion for police, as the standards by which law enforcement would have to operate were in a state of flux.

Search and Seizure. The standards by which a police search for evidence was deemed valid and the admissability into evidence of anything that was found thereby became subjects of profound change. The most significant development occurred in 1961 in the case of *Mapp* v. *Ohio*. In that case state police had obtained evidence without a warrant and in violation of the Constitution. The question the Court had to answer was what to do with the evidence. It clearly linked the defendant to an illegal activity. Could the trial court consider such evidence? If federal officers had committed such an act the evidence would not have been admissible at trial under

the "exclusionary rule." The logic behind this rule was that excluding illegally obtained evidence was the best means available to deter police from making unconstitutional searches. However, up to that point the individual states had been allowed to decide for themselves how to deal with an illegal search and seizure by state or local police. But in *Mapp* the Court reversed its policy and required that henceforth the states be bound by the same requirement. This change had a great impact on criminal justice, because the large majority of criminal offenses are dealt with by the state police and courts. However, the exclusionary rule has its limits. In *Alderman* v. *United States* in 1969 the Court made it clear that the exclusionary rule would only apply in the trial of the person whose rights were violated by the illegal search. Thus, if the police improperly entered the home of one person and discovered incriminating evidence, while that evidence could not be used against the homeowner, it could be used against someone else whom it also implicated.

What Is a Search? In the years that followed *Mapp*, the Court continued to engage in defining what constituted an illegal search. In *Spinelli* v. *United States* (1969) it sought to determine what constituted probable cause to issue a search warrant. It set forth a two-prong test that had to be met before information received from a police informant could be used, which placed substantial impediments on the use of such information. That same year in *Terry* v. *Ohio* the Court also established a test for determining when a policeman could stop a person engaged in suspicious activity and search them for the limited purpose of finding any weapons. The Court said such a search was permissible if the facts available were sufficient "to warrant a man of reasonable caution in the belief that the action taken was appropriate." This "stop and frisk" rule was very subjective, which made it difficult for an officer to know if a court would later find his actions improper.

An Old Rule for New Technology. In 1967 an interesting question came before the Court in *Katz* v. *United States*: whether a search and seizure had actually occurred. The case arose from the conviction of a defendant based upon a conversation which had occurred in a phone booth. The police had attached an electronic device to the booth and were able to overhear an incriminating conversation. There was never a physical entry by the police nor any actual seizure of evidence in a tangible sense. The case involved a technology of police surveillance not available at the time of the Constitution's adoption and thus arguably fell into a gap in the document's protections. However, the Court focused on the fact that a person using a telephone booth justifiably expects privacy. The Court held that such an invasion of privacy by the police fell within the spirit of the Constitution's protection. As such, the police were required to obtain a warrant to use electronic eavesdropping equipment.

Right to an Attorney. Another issue tackled by the Court during the 1960s dealt with the right to counsel and what exactly that guarantee meant. In 1963 the Court had before it the case of *Gideon* v. *Wainwright*. Up to that time the Court had only required that counsel be appointed for criminal defendants who could not afford one if the defendant was facing the death penalty. Gideon had been charged with a lesser crime, and the state of Florida had refused to appoint an attorney when he requested it. He had defended himself at the trial and was convicted. The Court ruled that having an attorney was essential in order to have a fair trial. As a result, it held that the states must provide counsel for defendants in criminal cases who could not afford to hire their own. The next year in *Escobedo* v. *Illinois* the Court dealt with the issue of a request by a defendant to talk to his attorney while being questioned by police. The police refused and instead confronted Escobedo with a witness who had fingered him for a murder. Under subsequent questioning by the police, Escobedo implicated himself in the murder plot and was later convicted. The Court stated that once an investigation moves to the stage where a person is made a prime suspect, he has the right to an attorney, and, if he is denied this right, any confession subsequently obtained in the investigation is not admissible in court.

A New Approach. In *Escobedo* the Court had substantially moved back the time when counsel was required to be made available to the defense. The decision was criticized by some who felt that it would greatly reduce the number of confessions obtained by police. However, the Court had sought to protect the defendant's basic rights by scrutinizing the interrogation process. It continued to do so in other cases. The difference in these later cases was that the Court emphasized the Fifth Amendment right against self-incrimination rather than the Sixth Amendment right to counsel, as the basis for constitu-

tional objections to confessions. The key case was decided the same year as *Escobedo*. In *Malloy* v. *Hogan* the Court asserted that the right against self-incrimination applied to the states and that confessions in state prosecutions were to be judged by the same standards as were used in federal courts.

True Confessions. In 1966 the Court decided the case of *Miranda* v. *Arizona*. It held that a defendant must be informed of his rights before any questioning could be conducted by the police, setting out explicitly that they should inform him that he had the right to remain silent and that if he chose to speak it could be used against him in court. The reasoning was that only a person clearly informed of his right against self-incrimination was in a position later to waive it. The court also required that a

---

A KILLER'S REWARD

An interesting question faced the Supreme Court of Vermont in 1966. A woman sought to receive the estate of her dead husband, which totaled about four thousand dollars. Her husband had died without a will in 1961. The law of Vermont held that if a person was married and died without a will, then their surviving spouse was entitled to the inheritance. The problem was that the woman in this case, Mrs. Mahoney, had been tried in 1962 and convicted of voluntary manslaughter in the death of her husband. When she claimed the estate, the trial court ruled that it belonged to the dead man's parents because she had killed her husband. However, there was no state law dealing with this unusual series of events, and Mrs. Mahoney claimed that she had a legal right to her husband's property. On appeal the Supreme Court made an effort to conform to the letter of the law while reaching a just result. It said that under the law the wife had a right to the property. But the court then invoked a rule of common law, which is a form of judge-made law. It said that Mrs. Mahoney's right to the property was subject to a "constructive trust." This is a legal fiction which is invoked by courts when it would be unjust for a person with a right to property to so benefit by a wrongful act. As a result Mrs. Mahoney received the property but then had to transfer title to the parents as the next heirs under the law. After this case brought attention to the potential problems with traditional inheritance law many states, including Vermont, adopted a provision providing that a convicted murderer could not inherit property from his or her victim.

Sources: *Time* (29 July 1966): 38;
John Ritchie, Neill Alford, and Richard Effland, *Decedents' Estates and Trusts* (New York: Foundation Press, 1988).

person be informed of his right to counsel and the fact that an attorney would be appointed if he could not afford one. In *Griffin* v. *California* the Court held that the prosecution could not draw attention to the fact that a defendant had refused to take the stand. The concern was that such an agreement might lead the jury to infer his guilt from that fact instead of from the evidence, thus undermining the right against self-incrimination. *Miranda* transformed the procedures not only for arrest but also any questioning of a subject in police custody. Its profound effect has been reflected in scores of police shows and movies.

An Active Court. During the 1960s the Court dealt with many other criminal cases as well. It applied rights guaranteed in the Constitution to state prosecutions, such as the confrontation clause and protection from double jeopardy. The decade saw an activist Supreme Court striving to define and protect certain basic civil liberties while at the same time attempting to leave the police enough room to function effectively. The Court reflected the changing standards and concerns of society, though many of its decisions were criticized in some quarters for moving the balance too far in favor of criminal defendants. However, the United States is a nation of laws where the lowest and the highest, the most and the least culpable, are all guaranteed procedural protections in the criminal process. The 1960s saw an energetic effort by the Court to live up to these expectations.

Source:

Yale Kamisar, Wayne LaFave, and Jerold Israel, *Modern Criminal Procedure* (New York: West, 1990).

LAWYERS' SALARIES

In the early 1960s the majority of attorneys practiced on their own in one-man offices. The average yearly income for such practitioners was about $8,000. Yet while people often felt that the law was one of the more profitable of professions this was not necessarily the case. The average solo dentist at the time earned $12,000 a year, and the average medical doctor earned well over twice as much at $18,000. Yet those attorneys who practiced in law firms could earn a good bit more than their solitary colleagues. The average income of lawyers in two- or three-man firms was $15,000, and for those practicing in large firms with a dozen or more attorneys, it reached $28,500. As the decade progressed the earnings rose. The 1960s also saw the beginning of a movement toward more firm practice and larger law firms. This reflected the advantages of group effort as well as increasing amounts of litigation and the growing need for specialization in legal services as legislation increased in both extent and complexity. The change in lawyers' earnings over the decade was particularly striking in starting salaries for new attorneys. In 1963 new associates at the top Manhattan firms were offered a salary of about $7,000. By the end of the decade competition among such firms for the best and brightest had driven the salaries up to $15,000 a year.

Sources: *Time* (15 November 1963): 70; *Time* (23 February 1968): 54.

THE DRUG WARS

Status Is Not a Crime. In the spring of 1962 the U.S. Supreme Court heard the case of *Robinson* v. *California*, involving a Los Angeles man who had been convicted of being a narcotics addict. At trial a police officer testified that he had examined the defendant Robinson and found what appeared to be needle scars on his arm. The trial judge instructed the jury that they could find Robinson guilty if they believed he fell into the category of a drug addict. In legal terms that meant that Robinson could be convicted even if the prosecutor had failed to offer evidence of his actual use of an illegal drug. In a landmark decision handed down in June 1962, Justice Potter Stewart held that status could not be made a criminal offense. To do so, said the majority opinion, would be a cruel and unusual punishment in violation of the Eighth and Fourteenth Amendments to the U.S. Constitution. Use of banned drugs could be sanctioned by criminal penalties, and addicts could be forced by the government to enter treatment programs which involved involuntary confinement. But mere proof of addiction was no longer sufficient to send a person to prison.

The Treatment Alternative. In a series of court deci-

sions and administrative rulings in the 1920s, the punitive approach to the drug problem had become entrenched in American legal practice. Criminal sanctions reached their high point in the 1950s, when the sale of narcotics by an adult to a minor could be punished by death. At the same time, however, there was a growing body of opinion among mental health professionals that treatment was a better solution than punishment. A few months after the decision in *Robinson* v. *California*, a White House Conference on Drug Abuse was convened, leading to the establishment of the Presidential Commission on Narcotic and Drug Abuse. In its 1963 report the commission recommended that criminal sanctions for illegal drug use be relaxed and that the government increase funding of medical and psychological research into the problem of narcotic abuse. By mid decade the treatment alternative was challenging the purely punitive approach to drug control.

The Legislative Response. In response to these legal and scientific trends, Congress passed in 1966 the Narcotic Addict Rehabilitation Act. The new law empowered the U.S. Public Health Service to provide rehabilitative treatment not only for people charged with or convicted of crimes but also those who voluntarily committed themselves. Many states, such as New York and California, also launched their own treatment programs. In addition to standard psychological techniques, some of the new programs experimented with novel alternatives. One widely popular innovation involved giving heroin addicts a synthetic substance called methadone, which seemed to reduce their craving for the drug so that other treatments could become effective. In all cases the objective was to reduce self-destructive drug use and socially harmful crime while, at the same time, returning drug abusers to more productive and satisfying lives.

The Political Reaction. Unfortunately for advocates of the treatment alternative, the public perception was that drug abuse increased greatly in the latter part of the 1960s. New products like LSD appeared on the streets of America, joining traditional narcotics such as heroin and marijuana. In the 1968 presidential election the successful candidate, Richard M. Nixon, ran his campaign on a strong anticrime and antinarcotics platform. In the minds of most Americans, narcotics and crime were closely linked. It logically followed that criminal sanctions for drug use deserved a leading role in the fight against social disorder. With the inauguration of President Nixon in January 1969, the political foundation was laid for the "War Against Drugs" that was to be declared and fought in the following decades.

Sources:

James A. Inciardi, ed., *Handbook of Drug Control in the United States* (New York: Greenwood Press, 1990);

David F. Musto, M.D., *The American Disease: Origins of Narcotic Control* (New Haven: Yale University Press, 1973).

FREEDOM OF RELIGION

A Devil of a Controversy. In 1962 the U.S. Supreme Court handed down a decision which created an immense amount of controversy. The case was *Engel* v. *Vitale,* and the issue involved was the freedom of religion guaranteed by the First Amendment of the U.S. Constitution. There are few legal disputes which trigger the degree of emotional involvement among the populace as those involving the freedom of religion. Other than desegregation, there was no legal issue in the 1960s which aroused such widespread interest and criticism of the highest court in the land. In part this reaction was due to the importance of religion to many Americans. In part it was due to a dichotomy which is reflected in the Constitution itself. The freedom of religion set forth in that document really embodies two separate and often conflicting concepts. One portion of the right consists of the establishment clause which prohibits the establishment of religion by the government. The second portion of the Amendment deals with the related but distinct right of citizens to engage in the free exercise of their own religion. In this latter portion the issue is not one of government sponsor-

---

SKYJACKINGS

The 1960s saw the rise of a new criminal, the skyjacker. This new form of highjacking was the product of two developments: the birth of the commercial jet aircraft and the rise of Fidel Castro in Cuba. The jet provided long distance transport while Castro's Cuba offered a destination for various types of malcontents. Because Cuba's government was openly hostile to the United States, it offered a refuge where skyjackers could escape prosecution. Because it was a Communist destination, it had an allure for certain individuals dissatisfied with life in America. The first skyjacking to Cuba took place in May 1961, but many followed. During the 1960s nearly fifty successful attempts were made. Six more were foiled. Generally the police and airline officials tried to accommodate the skyjackers because of the great danger that an armed man poses to the airplane and passengers. A shot fired runs the risk of depressurizing the cabin or destroying essential controls on the aircraft, and in the limited space there is no place of safety to hide. Yet miraculously no injuries or fatalities were caused by these all-too-common occurrences.

Source: *Time* (11 August 1961): 12.

---

ship, but rather of government interference in people's chosen form of worship or even nonworship. The First Amendment's religious provisions reflect the concern of our nation's founders who, as former British subjects, were very conscious of the problems which arose from a state-sponsored church. England had such a church, the Church of England, which received tax revenue paid by all citizens, even those of other faiths. The British government had at various times engaged in harassment of certain religious groups and had created religious tests for certain positions in government and in the military. In an attempt to avoid these problems in our new country, the establishment clause and the free exercise clause were added to our Constitution.

A Source of Conflict. The problem is that a tension exists between these two rights. At some point governmental accommodation of religion may cross over into a violation of the establishment clause. The potential for conflict between these provisions has grown with the increasing involvement of the government into everyday affairs. In the eighteenth century there was no public-school system nor was there the myriad of other forms of government involvement taken for granted today. The scope for conflict has also increased with the extension of the rights embodied in the First Amendment to the states. Originally, the Bill of Rights, as the first ten amendments are known, only applied to the federal government. Over the years they have been gradually applied by the Supreme Court in a rather piecemeal process to the states as well. It was not until 1940 that the Court held that the states must comply with the free exercise clause, and in 1947 it held that they were also bound by the establishment clause.

School Prayer. In *Engel* v. *Vitale* the Supreme Court dealt with the question of prayer in public schools. A school in New Hyde Park, New York, began each day with a short nondenominational prayer in each class. It read: "Almighty God, we acknowledge our dependence upon Thee, and we beg Thy blessings upon us, our parents, our teachers and our Country." The prayer was recommended but not required by the state government and student participation was voluntary. Several parents of children brought suit, claiming that the prayer was contrary to their and their children's beliefs and violated their First Amendment rights. The defendants argued that because the procedure was purely voluntary and because it did not involve the expenditure of public funds that it did not constitute a violation of the separation of church and state. Instead they suggested that it merely enabled students to exercise freely their religious beliefs. While the Court had earlier held that the establishment clause required a "wall of separation" between church and state, this was the first case to deal directly with school prayer. The Court decided that prayer in public schools clearly violated this requirement of separation. However, in its opinion the Court cited no cases for its conclusion. Instead, it relied on a historical analysis of religious freedom in Britain and the United States stressing the dangers that had arisen to both the government and to religious movements when the boundary of separation was crossed. As a result, the Court found that any public involvement with religious matters through sponsoring prayers in and of itself violated the establishment clause, even if participation was wholly voluntary.

A Volatile Reaction. The opinion set off a storm of protest. Many critics of the Court felt that if the decision were taken to its logical conclusion, all reference to God in connection with any gonvernmental institution would be barred. They pointed out that such a step would apply to many basic aspects of American life such as the Declaration of Independence, the national anthem, the pledge of allegiance, the motto on coins, the words used to inaugurate the president, and even the words uttered before every session of the Supreme Court. While in fact the Court as a whole never took matters so far, the possibility was raised in the concurring opinion by Justice William O. Douglas. Justice Douglas suggested in his opinion that almost any reference to God or religion by a government official, no matter how brief or even merely ceremonial would violate the establishment clause. Following the release of the Court's opinion, newspapers were full of editorial opinions that ranged from articles which greeted the decision as a sober balancing of the

conflicting rights at issue to others predicting that it would undermine the foundations of Western civilization. Con. Mendell Rivers (D-S.C.) claimed that the Court was "legislating — they never adjudicate — with one eye on the Kremlin and the other on the NAACP." Another congressman called the decision, "the most tragic ruling in the history of the United States." Over the next several years more than 150 amendments to the Constitution were offered by 111 different members of Congress in an attempt to reverse the Court. Yet despite the strong public reaction no amendment was ever adopted.

Fuel to the Fire. However, feelings of dissatisfaction did not disappear, and they were inflamed again the very next year when the Court reiterated its position in *Abbington School District* v. *Schemp.* This case involved the reading of ten verses of the Bible, without comment, every morning at the beginning of the school day. This opinion placed less emphasis on history than before and instead pointed to the need for government neutrality with regard to religion. This neutrality would only permit government actions which had a nonreligious purpose and which neither advanced nor inhibited religion. Several years later this approach would be incorporated into the three-part Lemon test which established a standard for determining when there was a violation of the establishment clause.

The Other Side of the Coin. Also in 1963 the Court dealt directly with the meaning of the free exercise clause. In *Sherbert* v. *Verner* the Court held that the government could burden the right of religious freedom only if there was a compelling governmental interest and then only if government used the least intrusive means possible. This marked a major shift because previously the government was only required to show that it had a "rational basis" for doing so. The Court's ruling put in place a much higher degree of protection against government action which interfered with a person's religious practices.

Continuing Questions. The Supreme Court's approach to religion changed significantly during the 1960s; the court strengthened protections for both the establishment clause and free exercise clause. Yet, insofar as the two rights are sometimes at odds with one another, freedom of religion is not a matter which can be quietly laid aside by the courts. During the rest of the 1960s and up to the present day, the balancing of these two clauses has continued to provide disputes which affect the lives of many Americans every day.

Sources:

Henry J. Abraham, *Freedom and the Court: Civil Rights and Liberties in the United States,* second edition (New York: Oxford University Press, 1972);

Terry Eastland, ed., *Religious Liberty in the Supreme Court: The Cases That Define the Debate over Church and State* (Washington, D. C.: Ethics & Public Policy Center, 1993);

Kermit Hall, ed., *The Oxford Companion to the Supreme Court of the United States* (New York: Oxford University Press, 1992).

JUVENILE DELINQUENCY

A Rising Tide. By the 1960s the term *juvenile delinquency* had come to mean any sort of antisocial act committed by a young person. It included not only criminal acts but also behavior perceived as harmful to society and destructive to the people involved. While the first few years of the decade represented a continuation of trends established in the 1950s, by the late 1960s the nation faced a significant increase in youthful violence and drug use. Even more alarming was the accompanying social disaffection and overt challenges to political and social institutions.

Modern Problems. In part these developments were symptoms of an expanding society growing less personal and less integrated. In the smaller, traditional communities most people knew one another personally. Black sheep children were less likely to become a criminal statistic. Instead, their family and friends would exert pressure to conform and would provide a degree of support, assistance, and shelter. While never entirely true for the very poor, the social cohesion of the smaller communities provided a bulwark for the majority of young people. But with the development of increasingly impoverished inner-city areas and rising racial strife in the 1960s, the youth-crime statistics presented a disturbing picture. According to FBI statistics, young people under the age of twenty-five accounted for over 73 percent of arrests for murder, rape, larceny, and other major crimes, as well as over 30 percent of all traffic fatalities. Even more alarming was the fact that by the mid 1960s people under eighteen accounted for 37 percent of all serious criminal offenses. In 1964 nearly 1.4 million juveniles were arrested, with about half of these cases actually being referred to juvenile courts. It was estimated that in some urban ghetto areas over 40 percent of ten-year-old boys would be brought before such courts before they reached age eighteen. Of course, crime among the poor was not a new development, though its increasing dimensions were a cause for concern. More surprising was the rapidly rising juvenile crime rate in suburbs. There the living standards were far higher than in inner-city ghettos, yet the number of suburban juveniles arrested for serious crimes was rising at a rate well above the national crime rate.

An Uneducated Youth? Another disturbing trend was the increase of high-school dropouts. It was estimated that by the late 1960s over 7.5 million students had left school, most by age sixteen. With the increasing automation of industry there were concerns that these unskilled youths would be incapable of finding employment sufficient to support themselves, thus creating a rootless segment of society relying upon the state for support and with a greater likelihood of engaging in criminal activities. To many observers this prediction was borne out by the increased use of drugs ranging from marijuana to LSD to heroin which prevailed in the decade.

Winds of Change. Crime, drug use, and general antisocial behavior by young people were not new in and of themselves. What made juvenile delinquency in the 1960s different was the confluence of two trends, one demographic and the other social, which amplified the normal disruptiveness of youth. The demographic shift was created by the upsurge in the birth rate after World War II. This segment of the population became known as the baby boomers. They represented an increasing proportion of the populace. In 1956 the number of people

---

TRIAL BY STATISTICS

On a morning in June 1964, an elderly woman was mugged in an alley in San Pedro, California. A white woman with blond hair was seen running from the alley moments later. She got into a yellow car with a white top driven by a black man with a beard and then sped off. The police arrested Janet and Malcolm, a couple who both answered the physical description of the witnesses and owned a yellow Lincoln with a white top. The case seemed destined to become another quickly forgotten mugging case until the prosecutor sought to bolster his circumstantial evidence with mathematical probabilities. At the trial he tried to drive home the unlikelihood of another couple possessing all the same characteristics by calling a mathmetician as an expert witness. The expert stated the principle that the likelihood of a number of independent factors occurring simultaneously is equal to the product of each factor's probability of occurrence. For example, the probability of rolling a six with one die is 1/6, and the probability of rolling two sixes in succession is 1/36 (1/6 x 1/6). The prosecutor then suggested probabilities for each of the characteristics the witnesses had seen, and he calculated that the odds were 1 in 12 million that a similar couple was in San Pedro at the time of the crime. The jury was apparently convinced and found the couple guilty. However, on appeal the California Supreme Court reversed the conviction. It cited the fact that there was no evidence to support the probabilities used by the prosecutor in his calculations. The court seemed equally concerned that the use of any mathematics would usurp the traditional and more subjective standard of "beyond a reasonable doubt" in evaluating whether the evidence was sufficient to prove guilt. While this first foray into statistical analysis in a criminal trial was rejected, mathematical calculations play an increasing, if still controversial, part in the law today.

Sources: *Time* (8 January 1965): 42; *Time* (26 April 1968): 41; Eric Green and Charles Nesson, *Problems, Cases, and Materials on Evidence* (Boston: Little, Brown, 1983).

---

reaching their eighteenth year was two million. By 1965 this number had increased to four million. By 1967 there were seventy million people in the country under eighteen years of age, composing one-third of the nation's total population. The second new factor involved in juvenile delinquency during the 1960s was the product of developing social trends. After World War II the United States experienced a period of unprecedented power and affluence. This was accompanied by a feeling that there were no real limits on human action. The latter factor manifested itself in a widespread questioning of social norms relating to sexual behavior, drug use, property rights, and, most fundamentally, the right of society to limit individual behavior in any way. In combination, these factors produced the explosion of youthful rebellion which found its way into the statistics of the era as a major increase in the rate of juvenile delinquency.

Sources:

James Gilbert, *A Cycle of Outrage: America's Reaction to the Juvenile Delinquent in the 1950s* (New York: Oxford University Press, 1986);

Marshall S. Gordon III and Clifford Simonsen, *Juvenile Justice in America* (New York: Macmillan, 1982);

Ronald Steel, ed. *New Light on Juvenile Delinquency* (New York: H.W. Wilson, 1967).

JUVENILE RIGHTS

An Empty Home. At about 6:00 P.M. on 8 June 1964, the mother of fifteen-year-old Jerry Gault returned from work to her home in Gila County, Arizona, where she learned from a neighbor that her son Jerry was in the custody of the local juvenile court for having made an obscene phone call. Jerry Gault had one previous brush with the law — he allegedly stole a baseball glove two years earlier. After a brief release to his parents, Jerry Gault was summoned to an informal hearing before a judge of the superior court, who had been designated to serve as juvenile court judge. At the hearing, the judge questioned Jerry and an official at the juvenile facility where he had been held. It appeared that Jerry had been arrested by a local sheriff's deputy for making an obscene phone call to a neighbor, a Mrs. Cook, who was not at the hearing.

Declared Delinquent. On the basis of a slender collection of information, the judge declared that Jerry Gault was a delinquent child under Arizona law. He was committed to the State Industrial School until age twenty-one, unless sooner discharged by an appropriate court order. Had Jerry been an adult and found guilty of making an obscene phone call, he would have been subject to a maximum fine of fifty dollars or imprisonment for not more than two months. Because he was only fifteen, Jerry was facing six years of incarceration.

Habeas Corpus. Mrs. Gault hired a lawyer and filed a petition for habeas corpus asking the court to give her son back. The local superior court denied the petition, and on appeal so did the Arizona Supreme Court. Mrs. Gault's

counsel then filed a petition for review by the United States Supreme Court. The petition was granted by the Court, and Gerald Francis Gault stepped into history.

Some Historical Background. In a long and detailed opinion, Associate Justice Abe Fortas reviewed the background of Jerry's plight. About 1900 a movement began in the United States to reform the way the criminal-justice system handled children. At that point, any child over seven was deemed capable of criminal intent and was subject to trial and incarceration as an adult. There were horror stories of teen-age children guilty of minor offenses being corrupted by their adult fellow inmates. The idea was to put juveniles accused of criminal acts in a separate system that would treat and rehabilitate them rather than punish them. They were to be called delinquents, not criminals. To make the system work smoothly, the reformers devised a loose system of procedure which ignored many of the technicalities — and safeguards — of the criminal courts. Hence, as in Jerry's case, the complaining witness did not have to appear and testify against him, and evidence based on hearsay was freely used by the judge to arrive at his decision. By the 1960s all the states had juvenile courts similar to those of Arizona.

The body of one of the slain civil rights workers arrives in Jackson, Mississippi,
June 1964

Constitutional Theory. Since children could be detained for years under the juvenile-court system, there had to be some legal justification that would pass constitutional muster. The solution lay in the traditional law, which held that children were not entitled to liberty, only custody. If a child's natural custodians, such as the parents, failed to discharge that duty, then the state would step in as a substitute. However, as Justice Fortas pointed out, there was no support for this rationale in traditional criminal law, only in the law of guardianship. In actual practice, he noted, the broad and ill-defined powers granted to state agencies could and often did lead to results similar to that in the Gault case.

Procedural Safeguards. The best solution, according to Justice Fortas, was proper procedure. In its decision the Supreme Court held that henceforth children in state juvenile-court proceedings would enjoy four key rights, conferred by the Fourteenth Amendment to the U.S. Constitution: timely and adequate written notice of the specific charges made by the state against them; the right to be represented by a lawyer; the right to confront and cross-examine adverse witnesses in open court; and the privilege of remaining silent so as not to incriminate themselves. On all of these counts, the Arizona procedure was deficient in the Gault case. As a result the Supreme Court ordered Jerry Gault released back into his parents' custody.

A Step Backward? Criticism of Fortas's opinion began with the dissent of Justice Potter Stewart. His concern, and the concern of many, was that imposition of the new procedures would return the treatment of delinquent juveniles to the old adversarial system. While that point

was well taken, the experience of Jerry Gault lent credence to Justice Fortas's comment that "unbridled discretion, however benevolently motivated, is frequently a poor substitute for principle and procedure."

Source:
John R. Sutton, *Stubborn Children: Controlling Delinquency in the United States, 1640–1981* (Berkeley: University of California Press, 1988).

MISSISSIPPI BURNING

A Summer of Hope. In June 1964 the Council of Federated Organizations, a combination of four civil rights groups and the National Conference of Churches, organized what it called the Mississippi Summer Project. The project's purpose was to send northern college-student volunteers, mostly white, to Mississippi for the summer. There they were to work in "freedom schools" to teach blacks in the state about their constitutional rights and to take part in a campaign to assist black-voter registration. Another aim of the project was to gain greater national attention for the struggle against racial discrimination in Mississippi by involving large numbers of white civil rights workers. Unfortunately, while it succeeded in getting nationwide attention, it was at the cost of the lives of three workers based in Meridian, Mississippi. The three men were Michael Schwerner, twenty-four; James Chaney, twenty-one; and Andrew Goodman, twenty.

Michael Schwerner. Schwerner was not a summer volunteer. He had already been working in Mississippi for six months and had been an instructor at the project's training course for the volunteers. A white man from New York, Schwerner graduated from Cornell University and became a social worker in New York City. He then joined the Congress of Racial Equality (CORE), helping on various projects to combat racial discrimination in the North. However, as the summer project gained national attention, he decided that he could accomplish more in Mississippi. He and his wife were accepted by CORE as field staff workers. In January 1964 they arrived in Meridian, Mississippi, to take over a community center. They organized a ten-thousand-volume library and set up other activities for blacks. Schwerner was primarily involved in assisting voter registration, but he was also active in other areas as well. He sought to desegregate churches, stores, and other businesses. The breadth of his activities raised the concern of some of his co-workers, who thought that he was trying to do too much too fast. It also gained him the enmity of local segregationists. Schwerner and his wife had received harassing phone calls and threats. In fact he had become the focus of the local Ku Klux Klan's concern. However, Schwerner did not seem to recognize the danger inherent in this rising hostility.

Andrew Goodman. Andrew Goodman grew up in New York City where his father was a building contractor. Both his parents were involved in liberal causes, and several of their friends were affected by the anti-Communist investigations of the 1950s. The Goodman children were raised in the midst of friends and relatives of similar views, and they were educated at the progressive, private Walden School. This background encouraged an idealism and belief in individual liberties, so it was not surprising that the young man sought to join the summer project after his junior year at Queen's College. Goodman met Schwerner at the training session. Originally, Goodman had planned to spend the summer in Canton, Mississippi, but at the last minute Schwerner convinced him to join him in Meridian, where Schwerner felt Goodman's abilities and enthusiasm could be put to good use.

James Chaney. The third worker had a rather different background from the other two. Chaney was a young black man who had grown up in Meridian. When he was expelled from high school during his junior year, Chaney floated around the Deep South before returning home. He began working as a plasterer, but it did not hold his interest. Finally, he became involved through friends with CORE's activities in Meridian. When the Schwerners came to Meridian, Chaney was one of the first people they met. After he helped them get settled, he began to assist Schwerner in his registration activities. Chaney became an indispensable worker, and the Schwerners had him made an official paid member of the CORE staff.

A Routine Trip. On 21 June the three men set off from Meridian to visit a church in the all-black community of Longdale in Neshoba County. The church had been burned down five days earlier by a gang of armed white men because it had been a meeting place for civil rights groups. The three men took the usual precautions which CORE required of its civil rights workers. They planned to be back home before nightfall. They filled the car's gas tank and gave the automobile the once-over before they left. They wished to avoid having to make any unscheduled stops in rural areas. Finally, they checked in with CORE before they left town, making sure that if they were not back by 4:30 P.M., the FBI and highway patrol would be informed and local jails checked for their whereabouts. These precautions were considered necessary due to the violence and intimidation which was being practiced against civil rights workers in Mississippi.

Expected Harassment. They arrived without incident at the ruins of the church and talked with witnesses of the attack. In late afternoon they headed back to Meridian. On the outskirts of the town of Philadelphia they were pulled over by a deputy sheriff of Neshoba County. He cited them for going 65 MPH in a 35 MPH zone. He took them to the county jail located inside the town. Chaney, who had been driving, was booked for speeding, and Schwerner and Goodman were held for "investigation." They were fed dinner at the jail and were eventually released, after paying a fine, at about 10:00 P.M. The deputy, Cecil Price, later stated that he had followed their car to the county line and that they had driven on toward Meridian. However, the group never arrived. Their disappearance sparked a forty-four-day hunt to determine their fate.

The Search. At first the FBI was reluctant to get involved. There was no indication of federal violations, and the Mississippi Highway Patrol had issued a routine missing-persons bulletin. Then the burned-out car was found in a blackberry thicket beside an old logging road. As political pressure began to mount, the Johnson administration ordered the FBI to begin a full-scale search. Local officials voiced suspicion that the affair was an elaborate hoax to embarrass the state of Mississippi, but after finding the car investigators considered this unlikely. As the days passed little information was obtained. Eventually the FBI authorized a reward of up to thirty thousand dollars for anyone willing to pass on information as to the whereabouts of the three men. The offer got quick results, and the bodies were discovered at the base of a small earthen dam. They had all been shot to death.

A Matter of Murder? Once the bodies were found the investigation intensified. The fact that someone had already talked gave the agents leverage to use on various Ku Klux Klansmen within the area. Eventually two men came forward and agreed to testify to the facts surrounding the murders. Now the question was how to proceed. The FBI had acquired all the information, but murder charges could only be brought by the state. In the end an unusual course was taken. The federal government decided to prosecute the murderers under an 1870 law making it a federal crime to conspire to deprive individuals of their civil rights. The maximum penalties were a five-thousand-dollar fine and up to ten years in prison, but it offered the only likelihood of a successful prosecution, given the reluctance of local officials to pursue murder charges.

False Starts. Late in 1964 the government arrested the nineteen conspirators, including Deputy Price, who had been implicated in the murders. However, the prosecution ran into an immediate snag when a federal judge in Mississippi dismissed the charges. The government continued its efforts and had the men reindicted in January only again to have most of the indictments dismissed. The government appealed. Following a favorable ruling by the Supreme Court, further indictments were secured. The trial finally began on 7 October 1967.

The Trial. The prosecution brought forward its star witness, James Jordan, who testified that he had accompanied the party which killed the three men. He said that after releasing Schwerner, Goodman, and Chaney from jail, Deputy Price had followed them. He eventually pulled them over again and ordered them into the back of his police car. At this time the deputy was joined by a group of local Klansmen. They then drove to a deserted area where the men were shot one by one. The prosecution presented other evidence relating to Klan activities they had uncovered in their lengthy investigations. The defense presented alibis and character witnesses for the many defendants and attacked the credibility of the prosecution's informants and the characters of the deceased men. On October 18 the jury began its deliberations. It took two days to reach a decision. Finally, the jury returned a conviction against seven of the defendants, including Deputy Price. It was unable to reach a verdict for three others, so they were acquitted. None of the defendants in the federal court case has ever been tried in the state courts for the murders of Schwerner, Goodman, and Chaney.

Sources:
Seth Cagin and Philip Dray, *We Are Not Afraid: The Story of Goodman, Schwerner, and Chaney and the Civil Rights Campaign for Mississippi* (New York: Macmillan, 1988);

"Grim Discovery in Mississippi," *Time*, 84 (14 August 1964): 17;

"The Grim Roster," *Time*, 84 (3 July 1964): 19;

"Reckoning in Meridian," *Time*, 90 (27 October 1967): 32–33.

NEW YORK TIMES V. SULLIVAN

Sticks and Stones. The law of defamation deals with injury to a person's reputation and good name by false statements. One form, libel, is commonly associated with the printed word, though it can consist of statements made over other durable and widely disseminated mediums, such as television. In a libel action a person who has been defamed before a third party can sue the publisher of the statement for damages. The standard for libel claims was traditionally one of strict liability. If a person published a false statement, they were liable for damages even if they had not acted unreasonably, thus, it was easier to sue a person for libel than for most other wrongs. The justification was that great harm can result from the broadcast of false information about a person.

Up to 1964 strict liability in the law of libel had been largely ignored by the U.S. Supreme Court. It was left to the states and their courts to deal with the question of what constituted libel and what standards of proof were required. But in that year the high court, pulled along by the rush of events in the civil rights movement, made changes which would have an enormous effect on the relationship between the press and public figures.

A Controversial Advertisement. The case that brought about this shift resulted from an advertisement placed by a civil rights group in the *New York Times* on 29 March 1960 under the headline "Heed Their Rising Voices." The ad described conditions of political and racial unrest in Alabama and listed several actions which police and state authorities had taken against demonstrators at the Alabama State College campus. The ad contained a number of inaccuracies. It made reference to the police ringing the campus in response to protests when they had in fact only been deployed nearby. It stated that padlocks had been used to keep students who had protested out of the campus dining hall, when in fact no padlocks had been used. The only students excluded from the dining hall were those who had not registered for classes. The ad also said that Martin Luther King, Jr. had been arrested seven times, when he had actually only been arrested four times. It stated that police had assisted enemies of King in bombing his house, when in fact they had attempted to find the guilty parties. These and other inaccuracies formed the basis of a lawsuit by L. B. Sullivan, the Montgomery city commissioner who supervised the police department.

Sullivan Goes to Court. Sullivan claimed that he had been injured by the errors in the story. The major difficulty was that he had never been mentioned by name in the ad. But, Sullivan claimed, the references to the Montgomery police were sufficient to cause people to associate him with the abuses mentioned in the ad. The case was tried in an Alabama court in a racially charged atmosphere. The seating of spectators was segregated and the facts of the underlying civil rights controversy were on everyone's mind. The trial lasted three days. The court found that references to the police were sufficient to imply Sullivan's involvement and thus to injure his reputation. It also came to light that the *New York Times* had possessed information in its news files which contradicted some of the facts set forth in the ad. Under Alabama law, as under the libel law in most states at that time, once it was proven that the defendant had published a falsehood, it was liable for damages whether it had acted reasonably or not. The *New York Times* was found to be liable for five hundred thousand dollars in damages. This large award was an ominous sign, since the newspaper was facing a number of similar lawsuits based upon the same advertisement.

A Vulnerable Case on Appeal. The *New York Times* appealed. After the verdict was upheld by the Alabama Supreme Court, the case moved to the U.S. Supreme

Court. In the past the high court had rarely reviewed libel cases. However, this case was different because of its relationship with the civil rights movement. A string of such verdicts could be used to silence papers such as the *New York Times*, which were important allies of civil rights activists. If this decision was allowed to stand on appeal, future publication of politically controversial articles or ads would be discouraged. Moreover, Sullivan did not have a particularly strong case. Few people actually associated him with the ad. And in the political climate of Alabama at that time, any such association was likely to enhance his reputation rather than harm it.

A New Direction. *New York Times* v. *Sullivan* became the vehicle for a major change in defamation law. The Supreme Court explicitly tied the limits of libel law to the guarantee of freedom of the press in the First Amendment. In an opinion written by Justice William J. Brennan, Jr. the Court imposed a heavy burden on public officials who sue for libel. These plaintiffs now had to prove not only that a falsehood had been printed, but also that the publisher knew the information was false or recklessly disregarded whether it was in fact the truth. Proof of negligence, as in ordinary damage suits, was not enough. The Court held the Constitution permits recovery of damages for libel by a public official against a private citizen only when there is evidence that the citizen published the false statements with "actual malice." Justice Brennan felt the now higher standard was fair, since existing rules required private citizens to prove actual malice when suing state officials for libel. Thus the fact that the *New York Times* published the advertisement without checking its accuracy against information in its own files was not sufficient evidence of actual malice. The reliance of the newspaper on the reputations of those individuals who vouched for the accuracy of the advertisement satisfied the Supreme Court that the newspaper had acted, at most, merely negligently.

Conflicting Rights. The decision marked a shift in priorities. The law was now willing to allow certain types of falsehoods to go unrectified in order to provide a margin of safety for the press. The Court's rationale was that the free exchange of ideas would be unduly restricted if papers were automatically liable every time inadvertent errors occurred. The Court noted that a certain amount of mistakes inevitably occur in free debate. It felt that the cost to our society if the press were constrained by fear of suits far outweighed the cost to those individuals whose reputations were tarnished. As with many constitutional issues, the decision was ultimately based on a balancing of conflicting rights. Some scholars have felt that the Court went too far. Others have felt that it did not go far enough. Whatever one's opinion, *New York Times* v. *Sullivan* stands as an enduring legacy of a single advertisement from the civil rights era.

Sources:

Everette Dennis and Eli Noam, eds., *The Cost of Libel: Economic and Policy Implications* (New York: Columbia University Press, 1989);

Richard Labunski, *Libel and the First Amendment* (New Brunswick, N.J.: Transaction, 1987);

Rodney Smolla, *Suing the Press* (New York: Oxford University Press, 1986).

THE SHOOTIST

In the Heat of Summer. Shortly before noon on a hot summer day in Austin, Texas, a tragedy unfolded which shocked the nation. The date was 1 August 1966. A student of architectural engineering at the University of Texas began firing from the tower which soared 307 feet above the campus. The shooting spree of Charles Whitman would become one of the bloodiest rampages in recent American history.

A Typical Childhood. The sniper's background was not particularly troubled. The big, muscular, young man had grown up in Lake Worth, Florida, the oldest of three sons of a plumbing contractor. His home life appeared typical. As a child he had attended a Catholic school. He had a newspaper route and served as an altar boy at his church. He played school sports and made Eagle Scout when he was only twelve years old. His father was a gun enthusiast who insisted that his sons be able to shoot. Whitman further developed this skill during a stint in the U.S. Marines.

Unpleasant Undercurrents. Yet despite the apparent tranquility of his childhood, trouble lurked beneath the surface. His father was a rigid disciplinarian with a quick temper, who later admitted to beating his wife. Neither Whitman nor his youngest brother were on good terms with their father. Like his father Whitman had a temper and had shown a capacity for violence. Recently Whitman had been disturbed by the separation of his parents. In March his mother had called him back from Texas to help her move to Austin to be near him. She lived in a fifth floor apartment near the campus. In addition to all these problems, Whitman had been suffering from intense headaches.

Seeking Help. On 29 March 1966 Whitman visited the university's staff psychiatrist. He told the doctor of his difficulty in controlling his temper. He noted that, like his father, he had beaten his wife. He told the doctor that while he tried to control his anger he was concerned that he might explode into violence. In his notes of the session, the doctor described the young man as a person who "seemed to be oozing hostility." Whitman mentioned to the doctor that he had been "thinking about going up on the tower with a deer rifle and start shooting people." However, the doctor was not too alarmed by such comments. As he later stated, it was not uncommon for students who came to the clinic to think of the tower as the site for some "desperate action." The doctor asked Whitman to come back for another visit, but his troubled patient never returned.

A Fateful Solution. After this visit Whitman took no further action until he made his tragic decision. The

Charles Whitman

night before the shooting he sat down alone in his home and began to type out a final statement. He said that he had suffered from fears and violent impulses which were driving him to commit a final act of carnage. He wrote that he was going to kill his wife in order to spare her the embarrassment that his actions would cause. He was interrupted when a Mr. and Mrs. Fuess, friends of the Whitmans, stopped by. Whitman gave no sign of his intentions, though Mr. Fuess later commented that Whitman had seemed "particularly relieved about something . . . as if he had solved a problem." In his demented state he no doubt had. Whitman then went out to pick up his wife from work. He dropped her off at their home and then drove to his mother's apartment. He stabbed and shot her to death. Before leaving he wrote a short note saying that her suffering was at an end. He concluded by saying that he loved his mother "with all my heart."

The Hunter Returns. Whitman then drove home. It was after midnight. Entering their bedroom, he stabbed his wife to death as she lay sleeping. He then returned to his note. He set out his hatred of his father and his regret that his mother had spent the best years of her life with the man. Whitman wrote that life was not worth living. He said that he was prepared to die and requested an autopsy be performed upon his body to look for a cause of his disorders. He then gathered supplies for his final actions.

Preparing for a Tragedy. He loaded a duffel bag with a wide range of provisions: food, bottles of water, a radio,

binoculars, and other items he thought might prove useful, including a large array of firearms. He packed three pistols and two rifles, including one with a telescopic sight. The next morning Whitman visited three gun shops. He bought two more guns and some magazines. He was now equipped with an impressive arsenal and had nearly seven hundred rounds of ammunition.

A Grisly Surprise. At about eleven in the morning he drove up to the parking lot near the base of the tower, he loaded his equipment onto a dolly he had rented early that morning, and took the elevator up to the twenty-seventh floor. From there, stairs led up the three remaining floors to the observation deck, where Whitman encountered the receptionist. He hit her over the head and shot her. He then moved his equipment outside. As he spread it out a group of sightseers came onto the deck, obviously not having seen the body of the receptionist. The group consisted of a Mr. Gabour, his wife, his two teenage sons, and his sister and her husband. Gabour's sister and his youngest son were killed as they stepped out onto the deck. His wife and his older son were seriously injured. Gabour and his brother-in-law dragged the dead and wounded down to the twenty-seventh floor looking for help. They found none.

Target Practice. Whitman meanwhile had closed the door and barricaded it. He then positioned himself in the tower and began shooting the tiny figures walking to and fro beneath him. The time was 11:48 A.M. The one stroke of fortune was that the delay Whitman had encountered in dealing with the receptionist and the Gabours meant that he had missed the crowd of students who had been changing classes at 11:30. As it was, there were still plenty of targets whose fate had steered them to the wrong place at the wrong time. Whitman began to fire from various sides of the tower. Primarily relying on his rifle with the scope, Whitman picked off most of his victims in the first twenty minutes.

A Gunman in the Tower. Within four minutes after Whitman opened fire the police received a report of a gunman at the university tower. They quickly mobilized at the scene. Over one hundred city police arrived supplemented by the highway patrol, Texas Rangers, and some Secret Service agents from President Johnson's Austin office. One of the first policemen on the spot was shot dead as he tried to take cover behind some stone railings. Whitman proved his accuracy hitting pedestrians over five hundred yards away. From his perch he killed several people who were walking on streets near the campus. He injured many more, including an eighteen-year-old student who was eight months pregnant. She survived but her baby did not. Whitman continued to move around the tower firing. As the police began to return fire, Whitman continued shooting through drainage slits in the wall around the observation deck. He swept the area near the tower, which was now littered with the bodies of the dead and injured, who could not be reached because of his withering fire.

The tower at the University of Texas at Austin

door open and crept out onto the south side of the deck. One of the officers, Ramiro Martinez, started to move toward the east while Crum edged toward the west. As Martinez moved around the southeast corner Crum heard footsteps. He fired to keep Whitman at bay. Meanwhile, Martinez crept around the northeast corner. He saw Whitman crouched in the northwest corner looking toward the south where Crum had drawn his attention. Martinez opened fire and Whitman slumped to the ground dead. It was now 1:24 P.M. Fifteen people lay dead and thirty-one were injured. Whitman's reign of terror had lasted ninety-six minutes.

Source:
"The Madman in the Tower," *Time*, 88 (12 August 1966): 14–19.

THE SUPREME COURT OF THE 1960S

The Double Standard. As the decade of the 1960s opened, the U.S. Supreme Court was weighted on the side of liberal judicial activism. In virtually all matters that came before it, the entire Court adhered to the jurisprudential principle which legal scholars call the "Double Standard." Based on a series of cases from the late 1930s, this approach makes a sharp distinction between property rights and personal rights. In the former area, the Constitution is held to allow wide leeway to legislative interference in business and commercial matters. In contrast, government infringements on personal rights protected by the Constitution, such as privacy or free speech, are much more strictly scrutinized. Moreover, Chief Justice Earl Warren and three of the associate justices — Hugo Black, William O. Douglas, and William J. Brennan, Jr. — were strongly committed to judicial activism. In cases where they felt individual rights were being jeopardized by governmental acts, they did not feel constrained by legal precedent. Under those circumstances, the activist justices were willing to challenge decisions of the federal and state legislatures and of other democratically elected officials.

Excluded Evidence. The decade was barely a year old when the Supreme Court rendered its decision in *Mapp v. Ohio*. The 1961 case was the first of a series of landmark opinions on individual rights handed down by the Court in the 1960s. *Mapp* held that the exclusionary rule, which bars illegally seized evidence from being used in trials, was applicable to the states. If the illegal material which Mapp was charged with possessing was seized by the police during an unlawful search of her home, then that material was excluded from being admitted as evidence at trial. Without such evidence, the defendant could not be convicted. A majority of the Court recognized that the exclusionary sanction is drastic, and its application would sometimes result in the guilty going unpunished. However, six justices felt that the rule was justified because other methods had failed to make law-enforcement personnel fully respect the constitutionally guaranteed rights of criminal suspects.

A Tense Finale. It became apparent to the police that they were unlikely to kill or disable the gunman by shooting at him from the ground. They chartered a small plane and sent one of their best marksmen aloft, but it was difficult to shoot from a moving plane, which in any event was driven off by Whitman's return fire. Finally, three policemen and Allen Crum, a former air force tailgunner, managed to reach the tower building. They ascended to the observation level, where they forced the

The U.S. Supreme Court in 1967: front row, left to right, John M. Harlan, Hugo L.
Black, Chief Justice Earl Warren, William O. Douglas, William J. Brennan, Jr.;
back row, left to right, Abe Fortas, Potter Stewart, Byron White,
Thurgood Marshall

Justice White. Three justices dissented in the *Mapp* case — John Harlan, Charles Whittaker, and Felix Frankfurter. By the end of the following year, Whittaker and Frankfurter had resigned, and their replacements had been chosen by the new Democratic president, John F. Kennedy. Kennedy's first nominee was Byron R. White. A native of Colorado, White had been an outstanding student athlete in college. Prior to World War II he had played professional football and had attended Oxford as a Rhodes scholar. Appointed to the court from the number-two job at the Justice Department, White was usually sympathetic to law enforcement in criminal rights cases. In that sense, he did not represent a sharp break from the man he replaced, Justice Whittaker. While more liberal than Whittaker politically, White was also opposed to judicial activism.

Liberal Activism Consolidated. President Kennedy's second nominee did make a difference. After suffering a heart attack in the summer of 1962, Associate Justice Frankfurter resigned. A Roosevelt appointee, Frankfurter was a liberal but not an activist. In his later years on the bench, he had articulated a philosophy of judicial restraint that often put him at odds with Justices Black and Douglas. Frankfurter's replacement was Arthur J. Goldberg. Like Byron White, Goldberg had risen from a modest background on the basis of hard work and intellectual brilliance. In the 1950s he had been a key figure in the U.S. labor movement. Goldberg had an important role in the merger of the two main American labor organizations, the Congress of Industrial Organizations (CIO) and the American Federation of Labor (AFL), and he wrote the constitution of the resulting institution, the AFL-CIO. On the Court, Goldberg provided the fifth majority vote for the activist bloc. His most notable

opinion was in *Escobedo* v. *Illinois*. The defendant had been convicted of murder on the basis of a statement that he made to police after having unsuccessfully asked to talk to his lawyer. In a five-to-four decision reversing the conviction, the members of the activist bloc held the Constitution requires that a suspect be given access to a lawyer as soon as the purpose of the interrogation shifts to securing his or her confession.

Justice Fortas. In July 1965 President Johnson asked Justice Goldberg to resign from the Supreme Court to become the American ambassador to the United Nations. With reluctance, Goldberg left the Court, and Johnson nominated his longtime friend Abe Fortas to replace him. Johnson literally owed his political career to Fortas. In 1948 Johnson held a paper-thin lead in the race for U.S. senator from Texas. All hinged on the fate of a few contested ballots, which had gone for Johnson under questionable circumstances. With some adept legal footwork, Fortas, then a lawyer in private practice, was able to prevent Johnson's opponent from getting a hearing on his protest of the ballots' validity. Fortas had also argued some key civil liberties cases before the Supreme Court, most notably *Gideon* v. *Wainwright*, which established the right to counsel for defendants in criminal cases. Once on the Court, Fortas adopted legal positions very close to those of Goldberg on civil liberties issues, maintaining a solid fifth vote for the activist bloc. Fortas joined the majority in the landmark *Miranda* decision in 1966, and he wrote the opinion of the Court in the *Gault* case. On the other hand, Fortas dissented in certain antitrust cases, which indicated that he did not fully concur with the Double Standard.

The First Black Justice. In early 1967 President Johnson appointed Ramsey Clark attorney general of the

United States. His father, Associate Justice Tom Clark, had been a moderately liberal and activist member of the Supreme Court. While he had supported the government against private individuals in national security cases in the 1950s, he had also joined in various individual rights decisions in the 1960s. In fact, Justice Clark had written the majority opinion in *Mapp* v. *Ohio*. To avoid any appearance of conflict of interest on account of his son's appointment, Justice Clark resigned from the Court in the summer of 1967. He was replaced by Thurgood Marshall, the first African-American ever to serve on the Supreme Court. Justice Marshall was a strong judicial activist, and with his confirmation that bloc could command a clear majority in key cases.

High Tide. The last three years of the decade represented the high tide of judicial activism on the Supreme Court. In a series of cases the Court held that states cannot make marriage between people of different races a criminal offense; that the states must allow criminal defendants access to favorable witnesses and, in felony cases, must give them the right to demand a jury trial; and that desegregation of public schools must be immediate, not gradual. In these and similar cases Chief Justice Warren was consistently joined by Associate Justices Black, Douglas, Brennan, Fortas, and Marshall. However, by 1968, there were portents of change.

Replacing the Chief Justice. Early that year, Chief Justice Warren informed President Johnson that he intended to resign as soon as his successor was confirmed. The president immediately nominated his friend Fortas as chief justice and a Texas federal judge named Homer Thornberry to replace Fortas as associate justice. The Fortas nomination quickly ran into trouble. Johnson was increasingly unpopular as a result of the Vietnam War. Sensing an opportunity to delay Warren's replacement until a new president could be elected, a substantial number of anti-Johnson senators declared their opposition. With the disclosures that Fortas had continued to advise Johnson on political matters after joining the Court and had accepted a large sum of money for lecturing at a law school, the opposing senators were able to block confirmation of the nomination by use of the filibuster. In October Johnson withdrew Fortas's nomination. Fortas continued to serve as an associate justice, and Chief Justice Warren remained on the bench until a successor could be nominated and confirmed.

Scandal. Justice Fortas's problems were not over. In May 1969 it was disclosed in a *Life* magazine article that he had accepted twenty thousand dollars in 1966 from a man named Wolfson who was involved in some dubious stock-market dealings. The actual payment had been made through a charitable foundation, and Fortas had returned the money after Wolfson was indicted. However, the transaction gave the appearance that Fortas had accepted the money in return for legal advice rendered after he had become a justice. In the ensuing uproar Fortas first denied that he had done anything wrong.

Fortas and Lyndon B. Johnson

Further investigation by the Justice Department turned up letters to Fortas from Wolfson, who was now in prison, concerning his business difficulties. Facing possible impeachment, Fortas resigned on 14 May 1969. With Fortas's seat now vacant, the newly elected president, Richard M. Nixon, had two nominations to the Court.

The New Chief Justice. Nixon's choice for Chief Justice was relatively uncontroversial. Warren E. Burger was a native of Minnesota. While his parents were of modest means, Burger was able to ascend the ladder of professional success through a combination of hard work and strong intellect. In that sense he was very much like the other 1960s nominees to the Court, sharing their industrious, upwardly mobile backgrounds. After a successful career as an attorney in private practice, Burger had been an assistant attorney general in the Justice Department during the Eisenhower administration. In 1955 he had been appointed to the U.S. Court of Appeals for the District of Columbia Circuit, where he served until his elevation to the high court.

More Turmoil. The nomination to fill Fortas's vacant seat was another matter. Having just lost a close presidential election and having suffered the trauma of the

Fortas scandal, the Democrats were not about to rubber-stamp any choice that the president might make. Moreover, the Democrats commanded a clear majority in the Senate and thus had the potential to block confirmation of any nominee. Nixon's first choice was Clement F. Haynsworth, Jr. He came from a distinguished family of South Carolina lawyers and jurists, and for some years had been a judge on the Fourth Circuit Court of Appeals in Richmond. However, his nomination had opposition from the beginning. Being a conservative southerner, he was viewed with suspicion by the civil rights movement, and organized labor felt that he was too management oriented. Compounding these political problems, while on the bench Haynsworth had been involved in a case where one of the parties did business with a company in which he had a financial interest. On another occasion, prior to release of a favorable decision for a large corporation in a relatively minor lawsuit which he heard on appeal, Haynsworth had bought some stock in the corporation. While similar conflicts of interest could be attributed to many other judges, the ethical charges hit a particularly sensitive nerve in the wake of the Fortas resignation. Haynsworth's opponents successfully used all these issues to deny confirmation. The Senate, now deeply divided ideologically, refused to confirm Nixon's second choice, G. Harold Carswell, another conservative southern appellate judge. Fortas's seat was finally filled by Harry A. Blackmun, a personal friend of Chief Justice Burger, who was sworn in as associate justice in 1970.

Return to the Beginning, with a Difference. At the end of the decade, the Supreme Court in many ways resembled the 1960 Court, in terms of judicial philosophy. There remained an activist bloc of four liberal justices — Black, Douglas, Brennan, and, instead of Warren, Marshall. In the middle were Justices Stuart and White, and on the more conservative end there was the new chief justice and Justice Harlan. However, the jurisprudential trend was now moving in a less activist, more property-rights oriented, and more conservative direction. That tendency did not come to fruition for many years, but its roots lay in the wrenching events surrounding the resignations of Warren and Fortas and the nominations of their replacements.

Sources:

Clare Cushman, ed., *The Supreme Court Justices, Illustrated Biographies 1789–1993* (Washington, D.C.: Congressional Quarterly, 1993);

Kermit L. Hill, ed., *The Oxford Companion to the Supreme Court of the United States* (New York: Oxford University Press, 1992);

Arnold S. Rice, *The Warren Court, 1953–1969* (Millwood, N.Y.: Associated Faculty Press, 1987).

VOTING RIGHTS ACT OF 1965

The Federal Government Weighs In. Even though blacks were guaranteed the right to vote by the Fifteenth Amendment to the Constitution, passed in 1870, racial discrimination in voting was still widespread after World War II. Congress and the president finally began to act to redress these problems in the 1950s. The Civil Rights Act of 1957 sought to deal with continued discrimination by empowering the attorney general of the United States to bring suits on a case-by-case basis, rather than relying solely on private challenges. But even with the Civil Rights Acts of 1960 and 1964, which sought to streamline this process, case-by-case challenges were not very effective. Voting rights suits were difficult, time consuming, and slow to resolve. Preparation for a trial often required thousands of man-hours to comb voter registration records. In addition, even when the cases were carried to conclusion and the state lost, that did not necessarily solve the problem. Some states just resorted to new tests or different methods of racial discrimination not covered by the court decree, which was limited to the facts of the case before it. Broad legislative action was required to address the various and often ingenious forms that racial discrimination in voting took in the different states.

Real Solutions. The Voting Rights Act of 1965 sought to provide such a remedy by direct government action. Instead of continually challenging various state voter tests, it completely barred their use in all states which met its formula. The formula was one which essentially limited its application to the states of the South. It prohibited the use of literacy tests in states that had used them prior to 1 November 1964 and in which less than 50 percent of the population voted or were registered to vote in the 1964 presidential election. The result was that literacy tests were no longer allowed in Alabama, Georgia, Mississippi, Louisiana, South Carolina, Virginia, and in a number of counties in North Carolina. The act also banned such states from using other tests based on "educational achievement" or "good moral character" and provided for federal officials to ensure that no further racial discrimination occurred. Examiners monitored voter registration to ensure that all qualified voters were registered to vote. Poll watchers made sure that everyone who was properly registered was actually allowed to vote.

Challenges Rejected. Such a broad use of federal power brought quick legal challenge. The state of South Carolina filed an action contending that such sweeping interference in the electoral powers of the states was unconstitutional. The Court chose to treat the challenge broadly as a question of the extent of congressional powers granted by the Fifteenth Amendment. The Court's decision did not involve a great deal of detailed analysis. Resting its conclusions on the plain wording of the amendment, the Court held that it was proper for Congress to forsake the case-by-case litigation, which had failed in the past, for the more direct methods embodied in the statute. The Court said that singling out the states in the South was valid because it was the region where immediate action was most necessary.

A Necessary Decision. Thus the law was upheld. This was in some ways a predictable result. The country was

Marshall, seated left, watching as Johnson signs the Voting Rights Act of 1965

clearly calling for a drastic means of dealing with the problem of racial discrimination in voting. Also, whatever the questionable constitutionality of some aspects of the law, it clearly enacted and was based upon the text and spirit of the Fifteenth Amendment.

The Road Ahead. The effects of the law were quick and pronounced. By 1966 over three hundred thousand blacks had been registered to vote. Within two years, the percentage of eligible black voters who were actually registered had risen dramatically, particularly in the Deep South. In Mississippi the number had risen from about 7 percent of the voting-age black population to 60 percent, and in Alabama the number had risen from 19 percent to 52 percent. By the general election in 1968, the number of blacks of voting age who actually voted reached 52 percent in the South as a whole, approaching the white voting percentage of 62 percent. The breakthrough had been made, the gap was narrowing, and the ideal of truly universal suffrage was within sight.

Sources:

Henry J. Abraham, *Freedom and the Court: Civil Rights and Liberties in the United States* (New York: Oxford University Press, 1972);

Richard Bardolph, ed., *The Civil Rights Record: Black Americans and the Law, 1849–1970* (New York: Crowell, 1970).

HEADLINE MAKERS

BYRON DE LA BECKWITH

1920-

CONVICTED KILLER

A Shot in the Night. On 12 June 1963 President John F. Kennedy gave a major speech on the subject of civil rights. His administration had been criticized for not involving itself more seriously in the movement. In response Kennedy signaled a change in the direction of increased support. That evening Medgar Evers, the Mississippi field secretary for the NAACP, watched the speech on television at the organization's headquarters in Jackson, Mississippi, while his wife and three young children viewed it at home. Mrs. Evers had agreed to let the two oldest children stay up late to discuss the president's address with their father when he returned. A little after midnight Evers's family heard his car pull up in the driveway. Evers got out carrying a stack of sweatshirts from the NAACP printed with the slogan "Jim Crow Must Go." He slammed the car door and, taking out his house keys, turned to walk up the driveway. At that moment a shot rang out and a bullet tore into his back, passing through him and entering the house. The startled Mrs. Evers and her children ran out to find him sprawled on the ground. As a neighbor fired a gun to scare off the assailant, others prepared a car to carry him to the hospital. An hour later Evers was dead, and the threat of rioting and further violence hung over the city of Jackson.

A Clue Is Found. The next morning a .30-06 Enfield rifle was found two hundred feet away from the spot where Evers fell. The gun, with a telescopic sight, had been dropped by the assassin as he fled from his hiding

place in a clump of honeysuckle. A fingerprint found on the sight was soon traced to Byron De La Beckwith.

The Man Behind the Gun. Beckwith had been born in California in 1920, where his father was a prune grower. His mother was from Mississippi, with deep roots in the South. Her father had fought in the Civil War with the Confederate cavalry of Gen. Nathan Bedford Forrest. Beckwith was educated at a private school and enrolled in college at Mississippi State. However, after the bombing of Pearl Harbor, Beckwith joined the marines. He fought in the Pacific during World War II and was wounded in the bloody fighting on the island of Tarawa. Beckwith married a woman he met during the war and returned to Greenwood, where he took a job traveling throughout the state selling for a tobacco company.

Making of a Segregationist. In 1954 a few days after the U.S. Supreme Court handed down its historic *Brown v. Board of Education* decision forbidding racial segregation in public schools Beckwith attended a speech by a Mississippi judge, haranguing against the dangers of integration and the mixing of races. It was a speech which took hold upon Beckwith. He became known as a virulent segregationist. He joined the White Citizens' Council, a statewide organization advocating the continuance of segregation, passed out anti-integration literature on street corners, and began a writing campaign to promote his views. At home Beckwith's hobby was collecting and trading guns. One of the items he obtained was an Enfield rifle; another was a Japanese-made sight which he acquired in return for a revolver in May 1963.

The Trial Begins. The trial of Beckwith in January 1964 gained widespread attention both in the state and throughout the nation. Evers had been a prominent voice in the movement to end racial discrimination in Mississippi. He had been the most conspicuous civil rights leader in the state and had been a focus of the passions of people on both sides of the issue. He had received threats and had suffered intimidation and attacks before. There was wide expectation that the trial would be an empty show, with no real attempt to secure a conviction by the local prosecutor.

An Earnest Effort. Many Mississippians supported Beckwith. The White Citizens' Council provided him with an attorney and sixteen thousand dollars was raised for his defense. Yet the district attorney William Waller put forth an aggressive prosecution and Judge Leon Hendrick was considered to have presided fairly during the trial. The prosecution's witnesses identified the gun and sight as belonging to Beckwith. An FBI expert swore that the fingerprint on the sight was Beckwith's. Two cab drivers identified him as a man who had asked directions to Evers's home four days before the shooting, and another witness stated that she had seen his car parked near the Evers's home less than an hour before the attack. While the bullet which had struck Evers was too badly damaged to be proven to have been fired by the gun, the prosecution had set out a strong circumstantial case against Beckwith. However, the defense had witnesses of its own, including two policemen and another person who placed Beckwith in Greenwood both shortly before and after the murder. If this was true it would have been impossible for Beckwith to have committed the murder in Jackson which was over ninety minutes away by car. Beckwith himself took the stand and in his quiet voice denied his involvement. At the conclusion of the evidence, the jury retired to make its decision. After eleven hours it reported that it was hopelessly deadlocked in a six to six split. The judge could only declare a mistrial. Beckwith was retried in April of that year and again the jury was deadlocked. After the second trial Beckwith was released from jail, and in 1969 the indictment of murder against him was dismissed.

Laying the Ghosts to Rest. In 1990 the case was reopened. After the Mississippi Supreme Court refused to dismiss the new indictment, Beckwith, then seventy-three, was scheduled to be tried for a third time. On 5 February 1994 the new trial ended in his conviction of murder. While the reopening of the case and the guilty verdict reflect the ensuing change in the social and political climate in Mississippi, it also raises serious legal questions. The conviction followed a twenty-six-year gap between the crime and Beckwith's reindictment, which may make his the oldest prosecution in American legal history. The new trial may have violated Beckwith's right to a speedy trial and the guarantee of due process found in the Fifth and Sixth Amendments to the U.S. Constitution. The answers to those questions await the resolution of his appeals.

Sources:

Adam Nossiter, "Can Justice Delayed Become Justice Denied?" *New York Times*, 27 May 1994, B14;

Kenneth O'Reilly, *Black Americans: The FBI Files* (New York: Carroll & Graf, 1994);

Ronald Smothers, "White Supremacist Is Convicted of Slaying Rights Leader in '63," *New York Times*, 6 February 1994, A1;

Maryanne Vollers, "The Haunting of the New South," *Esquire*, 116 (July 1991): 63–66, 120.

WILLIAM J. BRENNAN, JR.

1906-1993

SUPREME COURT JUSTICE

Legal Reformer. Appointed to the U.S. Supreme Court in 1956 as a legal reformer by President Dwight D. Eisenhower, William J. Brennan, Jr. became over the next two decades the leading liberal on the court.

Background. Brennan began his judicial career in 1950, when he was appointed to the Superior Court of New Jersey. In 1952 he was promoted to the New Jersey Supreme Court. His decisions on that court show his zeal to reform court procedure in order to reduce unfair delays. They also reflect Brennan's interest in the real people whose difficulties are often overlooked by appellate judges grappling with the abstract principles presented by their cases. When Justice Sherman Minton announced his retirement from the U.S. Supreme Court in 1956, Eisenhower chose Brennan as his replacement despite the fact that Brennan was a Democrat. Brennan took his seat on 16 October 1956 during a congressional recess, and he was not confirmed until March 1957. Sen. Joseph McCarthy cast the lone negative vote on confirmation. President Eisenhower later lamented that the two great mistakes of his presidency were lifetime appointments to the Supreme Court — Earl Warren and William J. Brennan, Jr.

Leading Liberal. During his early years on the Court Brennan became the lieutenant to Chief Justice Earl Warren, joining and leading the liberal majority. Among his more than 450 majority-written opinions, many were crucial in the radical changes in American law and society in the 1960s. *Baker* v. *Carr* was the "one man, one vote" decision that was an important evolution of democratic theory in the United States. *New York Times* v. *Sullivan* made it more difficult for public officials to sue newspapers for libel. *Fay* v. *Noia* established a federal-court role in reviewing state court convictions.

A Voice of Dissent. During the 1960s Brennan very seldom dissented from court opinions — a symbol of the liberal majority of the Court. During the 1970s and 1980s he became the leader of the shrinking liberal wing against a nascent conservative majority. His persuasive personality still managed to wring court victories in that environment, though he became better known for ringing dissents that put forth his view of "the supremacy of human dignity of every individual."

Sources:

Clare Cushman, *The Supreme Court Justices: Illustrated Biographies, 1789–1993* (Washington, D.C.: Congressional Quarterly, 1993);

Stephen J. Friedman, ed., *An Affair With Freedom: Justice William J. Brennan, Jr.* (New York: Atheneum, 1970).

JOHN MARSHALL HARLAN

1899-1971

SUPREME COURT JUSTICE

Leading the Opposition. Among the justices who sat on the U.S. Supreme Court during the judicial revolutions of the 1960s, Justice John Marshall Harlan led the opposition to the activist program of the Warren court majority.

Background. Harlan was appointed by President Dwight D. Eisenhower in 1954 to the U.S. Court of Appeals for the Second Circuit, the most important appeals court in the country. When Supreme Court justice Robert H. Jackson died late that year, Eisenhower chose Harlan to fill the seat. His appointment was held up by the Senate until March 1955, because some senators were concerned that Harlan's time at Oxford University (he was a Rhodes scholar and actually received his B.A. and M.A. from Balliol College) made him too much of a believer in "world government." The Senate voted to confirm him 71 votes to 11.

Dissenting Opinions. The grandson and namesake of Supreme Court justice John Marshall Harlan (1877–1911), Harlan was a believer in judicial restraint. Throughout his tenure on the Court, Harlan held fast to federalist theory, in which each branch and level of government had distinct powers and roles. His principles of judicial nonpartisanship extended to his beliefs that judges should not vote for candidates for public office and that it violated the separation of powers principle for a Supreme Court judge to attend the president's annual State of the Union address. Harlan was a prolific author of court opinions, writing a total of 613 during his time as a justice. Of these, 296 were dissents. During 1963–1967 he averaged forty-three opinions per term. Many were dissenting opinions, though he would often write concurring opinions when he agreed with the outcome of a court case though not with the reasoning behind it. He was keenly aware that clear reasoning was as important to the law as was a particular result.

Judicial Restraint. Harlan dissented from many of the important decisions of the Court during his years there, the most famous being the *Baker* v. *Carr* "one man, one vote" ruling in 1964 and the *Miranda* v. *Arizona* police restraint ruling in 1966. Harlan was a staunch supporter of free speech, authoring the Court's 1971 opinion in *Cohen* v. *California* that upheld the right to wear clothes imprinted with vulgar language.

Great Gift. Harlan is remembered as a judge of great intellectual gifts whose principles of judicial restraint place him in the company of like-minded federal judges such as Felix Frankfurter and Learned Hand.

Sources:

Clare Cushman, *The Supreme Court Justices: Illustrated Biographies, 1789–1993* (Washington, D.C.: Congressional Quarterly, 1993);

Robert Shnayerson, *The Illustrated History of the United States Supreme Court* (New York: Harry N. Abrams, 1986);

Tinsley E. Yarborough, *John Marshall Harlan: The Great Dissenter of the Warren Court* (New York: Oxford University Press, 1992).

VIOLA LIUZZO

1926-1965

CIVIL RIGHTS WORKER

A March of Hope. In the spring of 1965 the Nobel Peace Prize winner and civil rights leader Martin Luther King, Jr. led a march from Selma, Alabama, to the state's capital of Montgomery. The avowed purpose was to present Alabama governor George Wallace with a petition protesting voting discrimination in the state. The main purpose was to draw attention to the plight of blacks in the segregated South. On 21 March thousands of participants began the fifty-mile trek to the capital. While there were some hecklers, there was little serious harassment of the marchers. The federal government had mobilized a small army to prevent any violence. Over one thousand military police were present as well as nearly two thousand federalized Alabama National Guardsmen, supplemented by federal marshals and FBI agents. Precautions even extended to having demolition experts search the bridges in the protestors' path.

Viola Liuzzo Joins the March. The marchers were composed of a wide variety of people. Many were blacks from Alabama. But the protest had drawn not only seasoned civil rights workers, but also citizens from throughout the country. One of these was Viola Liuzzo, a white, thirty-nine-year-old mother of five from Detroit, Michigan. On 16 March she took part in a civil rights march in Detroit to express support for the upcoming protest in Alabama. On the spur of the moment she decided to go to Alabama to participate in the main event. She called her husband and told him that she would be going with some friends to Selma. Her husband tried to convince her to come home and talk it over first, but she refused. She insisted that it "was everybody's fight" and that she had to go.

The Rally. The culmination of the march came on Thursday, 25 March. An immense crowd collected in front of the capital building in Montgomery, Alabama. Those who had made the march were joined by others who appeared to show support and to protest the state government's policies. A series of speakers came forward, including Martin Luther King, Jr. who called for more marches to protest other forms of racial discrimination. The governor refused the petition, claiming that the protest was a "prostitution of the legal process." However, the march and the rally had successfully attracted national attention to voting discrimination and other complaints of black Americans.

Returning Home. After the speeches were completed the crowd broke up, and the people returned to their homes. Many of the protesters lived in Selma, and Liuzzo helped out by giving rides in her car between the cities. She had walked with the marchers the first day and later had assisted by driving demonstrators back and forth along the route. On Thursday evening she carried a carload back to Selma. After dropping off her passengers she headed back toward Montgomery to pick up some more. It was 7:30 in the evening. With her in the car was a black man, Leroy Moton, nineteen, a member of the Southern Christian Leadership Conference, a civil rights group. All seemed normal until they reached a deserted stretch of highway twenty miles from Selma.

Terror on the Highway. Liuzzo and Moton were not aware that they had been targeted by a group of four Klansmen who were "looking for excitement." Eugene Thomas and William Eaton, both steelworkers, along with Collie Wilkins, a mechanic, and Gary Rowe, a bartender, had driven down from Birmingham earlier in the day. They spotted Liuzzo and Moton at a stoplight and followed them down the highway. The presence of the black man and a white woman together in the car immediately ignited their anger. Thomas insisted that they were "going to take that automobile." Outside of Selma, they speeded up, pulling alongside Liuzzo's car. Two shots were fired through the front windshield. One struck Liuzzo in the head, killing her. The car swerved off the road before coming to stop. Moton turned off the ignition and cut off the automobile's lights and waited. After about five minutes he heard a car return which shined its lights at the Liuzzo automobile. Then it drove away. Moton then managed to hitchhike back to Selma, where he informed the police of the shooting.

An Informer in the Klan. The others in the car did not know Rowe was an FBI informant. He had been used by the law-enforcement agency to obtain information on the Ku Klux Klan for over five years, for which he had been paid nine thousand dollars. His cooperation allowed the police to capture the assailants within hours of the attack. He was also the key government witness, the only one who could identify the attackers.

Justice Deferred. Wilkins was tried in May 1965 in Lowndes County where the murder had occurred. The prosecution presented the testimony of Moton regarding the events of the attack. However, from his vantage in the car he had not been able to identify the gunmen. Then came Rowe who testified that Wilkins had fired the first

two shots through the windshield, after which the other men in the car opened fire. The prosecution then presented other evidence which tended to tie the defendants to the area at the time of the shootings and which identified the gun which fired the fatal shot as a revolver found in Thomas's home. The defense attorney was a Klansman, who harangued the jury with his racist philosophy and sought to attack Rowe's credibility because he had betrayed his Klan oath of silence. After ten hours of deliberation the jury was hopelessly deadlocked, and a mistrial was declared.

A Second Chance. The difficulty of convicting Klansmen for murder of civil rights workers did not prevent the prosecution from trying to convict Wilkins again in October 1965. The attorney general of Alabama, Richmond Flowers, exercised his right to take over the prosecution from local authorities. His case was essentially a repeat of the prior trial. The main difference was that Wilkins had abandoned his Klan attorney for the less belligerent Arthur Hanes, who hammered away at inconsistencies in the prosecution's witnesses' testimonies and presented alibi witnesses. The jury found Wilkins not guilty.

Third Trial. Instead of attempting to try the remaining suspects for murder, a new course was adopted. Wilkins, Thomas, and Eaton were charged with violating an 1870 federal law which makes it a crime to conspire to deprive a citizen of his or her civil rights. Arguing that murder does just that, federal prosecutors brought the three men to trial in federal court in December 1965. The witnesses and testimony were much the same as in the earlier trials, but this time the judge refused to accept a hung jury. Although initially deadlocked, the judge sent them back to try again, and after another four hours of deliberation, they returned a verdict of guilty against the defendants. Judge Johnson then sentenced each of them to the maximum sentence allowed, ten years in prison.

Sources:
"Juries and Justice in Alabama," *Time*, 86 (29 October 1965): 49;
"The Law and De Lawd," *Time*, 86 (10 December 1965): 38;
"Protest on Route 80," *Time*, 85 (2 April 1965): 21;
"Trial," *Time*, 85 (14 May 1965): 27;
"Trial by Jury," *Newsweek*, 66 (1 November 1965): 36;
"Uncolored Justice," *Newsweek*, 66 (13 December 1965): 34.

CHARLES MANSON

1934-

MASS MURDERER

A Scene of Bloody Horror. At about 8 A.M. on Saturday morning, 9 August 1969, housekeeper Winifred Chapman arrived at 10050 Cielo Drive, the rental residence of film director Roman Polanski in a fashionable Los Angeles neighborhood near Beverly Hills. What she found that morning aroused the horrified interest of the nation. Five people lay dead in and around the blood-spattered house. The victims included Polanski's young wife, actress Sharon Tate, who was eight-and-one-half-months pregnant; Jay Sebring, a noted hairstylist; Abigail Folger, daughter of the chairman of the board of A. J. Folger Coffee Company; Folger's Polish boyfriend, Voytek Frykowski; and Steven Parent, a young man who had stopped by to sell some clock radios. The victims had been beaten and stabbed dozens of times, and the word *PIG* was written in blood on the front door. There seemed to be no motive. No money or valuables were taken, and none of the victims had been sexually assaulted. The gruesome scene baffled the police.

Deadly Reprise. Later that weekend the mystery deepened. On Sunday night the bodies of Leno LaBianca, the middle-aged president of a chain of grocery stores, and his wife Rosemary were found in their home about five miles east of Beverly Hills. They had been dead almost twenty hours. Both had been beaten and repeatedly stabbed. Again there were words written in the blood of the victims — *DEATH TO PIGS, RISE,* and *HEALTER SKELTER.*

A Break in the Case. Initially police had believed that the caretaker at the Tate residence had committed the murders there. But he had passed a lie-detector test and was in police custody when the second murders took place. After two months the police still had no suspects in either case. Breaks eventually came from two sources. One was from the members of a motorcycle gang. The other was from a prisoner in a Los Angeles jail. The prisoner told of strange conversations she had had with a fellow inmate, a young woman who was being held in connection with yet another murder involving a stabbing and a message left in the victim's blood. Both sources pointed to a man who was already being held on car-theft charges, Charles Manson.

A Career Felon. Charles Manson was born on 12 November 1934 in Cincinnati, Ohio, the illegitimate son of a sixteen-year-old girl. Manson's early years were unstable. He never knew his father. His mother was in jail for armed robbery during part of his childhood, and the boy found himself shifted among relatives, foster homes, and, finally, reformatories. His education ended in the seventh grade. In 1955, less than a year after his release from a federal reformatory in Ohio where he had been held for interstate transport of a stolen vehicle, he married a waitress, and they moved to California — in a stolen car. Manson could not give up his criminal lifestyle. While he was in prison on auto theft charges in California, his wife divorced him, and with their child, Charles Manson, Jr., moved permanently out of his life. In the following years Manson was in and out of prison on charges ranging from forging U.S. Treasury checks to pimping. In 1959 Manson was again married, according to prison records, but was divorced in 1963. The records indicate there was a child from this second marriage,

named Charles Luther Manson. One thing that set Manson apart from other career felons was his tendency to commit federal crimes, which carry longer prison terms than state offenses. He also had a temporary enthusiasm for the Church of Scientology and developed an interest in music, particularly that of the Beatles. On his release from prison in 1967, Manson was thirty-two years old, and he had spent seventeen of those years in institutions, mostly prisons.

Bizarre Motive. Manson settled in the San Francisco area after his release. He gravitated to the Haight-Ashbury district, where he accumulated an increasing number of young followers, mostly female, who came to comprise the "Manson Family." Near the end of 1967, Manson and his "family" left San Francisco, traveling through the western United States in an old schoolbus. Over a year later they arrived in the Los Angeles area, where they eventually established themselves at a former movie ranch northwest of the city. Manson wrote and recorded songs while he and his followers lived a life of leisure interrupted by occasional auto thefts and other crimes. Manson established complete control over his followers, using a combination of violence, intimidation, sex, and his powerful charisma. He preached to them his philosophy, predicting a race war in which blacks would eventually overcome whites. Manson felt that the Beatles' music, especially their *The Beatles,* known as the White Album (1969), both foretold and encouraged this apocalypse. Manson believed that the song "Helter Skelter" dealt specifically with the coming race war. While the war raged, Manson said that he and his followers would hide out in the desert. After it was over, he preached, they would be called upon to lead society by the victorious blacks. The Tate and LaBianca murders were carried out with the specific intention of horrifying the nation by creating the impression that blacks had been the perpetrators, thus starting the war Manson had predicted.

Sensational Trial. Proving this motive was the key to the prosecution's case in the trial, which began on 24 July 1970. It was the longest murder trial up to that time in American history, lasting nine and one-half months. The prosecution relied mostly on testimony from Manson family members who had agreed to talk in exchange for leniency, but there was also a small but important collection of physical evidence, including the pistol used in the Tate murders. Manson and three of his followers who had committed the murders were found guilty and sentenced to death. A fifth defendant, Charles ("Tex") Watson was subsequently tried, convicted, and sentenced to death. In 1972 the California Supreme Court found that the death penalty violated the state constitution, and all individuals on death row had their sentences converted to life in prison. In fact Manson and the other four murderers would eventually be eligible to apply for parole. Later the state of California reinstituted the death penalty, but because Manson and his followers were convicted under the prior law, their life sentences were unaffected.

THURGOOD MARSHALL

1908-1993

CIVIL RIGHTS LEADER AND SUPREME COURT JUSTICE

A Catalyst for Change. Thurgood Marshall was born on 2 July 1908 in Baltimore, Maryland. Earlier that summer there had been a riot in which two black men were lynched in Springfield, Illinois. For many blacks and white liberals the brutalities were a call to action. A series of meetings ensued which, within a year, resulted in the formation of the National Association for the Advancement of Colored People (NAACP). This was an organization upon which Marshall would have profound effects. It also was where he formed his legal reputation, which ultimately led to his appointment to the Supreme Court in 1967.

From Humble Beginnings. Marshall's great-grandfather had been a slave who was freed by his Maryland owner. Marshall's father was a proud man who worked for a time as a railroad porter and later as a steward at a country club. Marshall's mother was a schoolteacher. At that time most blacks attended one school and whites another, and as a black teacher in a black school his mother earned much less than the teachers in the white schools. However, between her income and her husband's they managed to raise their children in a relatively comfortable and stable environment.

College. With his parents' financial help and by holding down a part-time job, Marshall was able to attend the prestigious Lincoln University in Pennsylvania, known as the "Black Princeton." Despite his roguish reputation, Marshall graduated in 1930 with honors and a wife, "Buster" Burrey, who was a student at the University of Pennsylvania. His application to the University of Maryland's law school was turned down because of his race, so Marshall enrolled at Howard University Law School in Washington, D.C.

An Attorney is Born. At Howard, Marshall graduated first in his class in 1933. As he later said, in law school he "found out what my rights were." Marshall's goal was to use the law to improve the conditions of black Americans. It was at Howard that he met Professors Charles Houston and William Hastie, who helped shape the young man's interest in civil rights.

Marshall's First Case. After graduation Marshall entered private practice. It was difficult going, trying to earn a living during the middle of the Great Depression, but a new direction was offered that had great significance both for Marshall and the nation as a whole. Hastie had become chief counsel for the NAACP, and he had its Baltimore office hire Marshall. One of the first cases that Marshall handled was a suit by Donald Murray, a young black graduate of Amherst College, who had applied to the University of Maryland Law School and had been denied admission because of his race. Marshall won the case in the Maryland courts, and the school was ordered to admit Murray. The lawsuit garnered national attention and marked the beginning of what became Marshall's personal crusade to end racial discrimination in education. In 1936 Marshall joined his mentor Houston in New York as assistant special counsel to the NAACP. When Houston resigned in 1938, Marshall became the special counsel. Two years later he was appointed head of the organization's newly created Legal Defense and Educational Fund, which provided free legal assistance to blacks suffering racial discrimination. He held that position for over twenty years.

Head of the Legal Defense and Educational Fund. Marshall was involved with many important lawsuits, ranging from the ending of all-white primaries, to striking down state enforcement of agreements to keep real estate from being sold to blacks, to integrating seating on trains and other modes of interstate travel. However, his most significant project was the drive to end segregated public education. In 1952 he litigated a case in South Carolina against a school system there. Later, this case was joined with several others on appeal to the U.S. Supreme Court under the name *Brown* v. *Board of Education of Topeka*. Marshall made the oral argument, urging that the justices end segregation and an abandonment of the "separate but equal" doctrine. The resulting favorable decision crowned his long struggle against racial discrimination in education. The Supreme Court ordered the integration of public schools with "all deliberate speed," marking a new era in American education. Marshall's success was, however, followed by the death of his first wife in February 1955; later that year Marshall married Cecilia Suyat, an NAACP colleague.

Government Service. Marshall's work with the Legal Defense Fund had made him the most widely recognized and successful black attorney in the country. In 1961 he was nominated by President John F. Kennedy for a judgeship on the Federal Court of Appeals for the Second Circuit. Marshall's confirmation process lasted over eleven months. His successes in civil rights cases had created many opponents, especially among southern senators. He was finally confirmed in September 1962. While on the bench Marshall was especially concerned with safeguarding the rights of criminal defendants. He was always particularly sensitive to the claims of individuals that their rights had been violated by the government. In 1965 President Lyndon Johnson called upon Marshall to become the thirty-third solicitor general of the United States. The solicitor general handles all the government's appeals before the Supreme Court. Perhaps more important, he or she determines which few of the many possible government appeals will be made to that body. Marshall's appointment was widely viewed as a stepping stone to the Supreme Court.

The Summit Is Reached. On 13 June 1967 these predictions were proven true when Marshall was nominated by President Johnson to replace retiring Justice Tom Clark on the Supreme Court. Johnson declared that nominating Marshall as the first black justice was "the right thing to do, the right time to do it, the right man and the right place." Again Marshall faced extended questioning by senators in his confirmation hearing. This time however, the process was less drawn out. He was confirmed at the end of August of that year by a vote of sixty-nine to eleven.

Casting a Long Shadow. On the Court, Marshall made a reputation as a judicial activist. He always kept foremost in mind the defense of individual rights. He often urged his colleagues not to be so blinded by legal reasoning as to lose touch with the plight of the people behind the facts. His sympathies extended especially to the poor and members of racial minorities whose rights, he felt, could at times be protected only by the courts. Marshall was especially determined to defend the gains he and others had made in civil rights and to extend them further. On 27 June 1991 Justice Marshall announced that his health required that he step down from the bench. Marshall's retirement at the age of eighty-two marked the loss of the Court's greatest advocate for civil rights.

Sources:

Susan Low Bloch, "Thurgood Marshall" in *The Supreme Court Justices: Illustrated Biographies, 1789–1993*, edited by Clare Cushman (Washington, D.C.: Congressional Quarterly, 1993);

"Choosing a Justice," *Time*, 89 (21 April 1967): 75–76;

Leon Friedman and Fred L. Israel, eds., *The Justices of The United States Supreme Court, 1789-1978* (New York: Chelsea House, 1980);

"Negro Justice," *Time*, 89 (23 June 1967);

Carl T. Rowan, *Dream Makers, Dream Breakers: The World of Justice Thurgood Marshall* (Boston: Little, Brown, 1993);

"The Tenth Member," *Time*, 86 (22 October 1963): 94;

"Toward the Seats," *Time*, 78 (22 September 1961): 25.

JACK RUBY

1911-1967

MURDERER

A Murder Which Shocked a Nation. On the afternoon of 22 November 1963 President John F. Kennedy, riding in a motorcade in Dallas, Texas, was killed by an assassin. Within an hour and a half Lee Harvey Oswald was picked up by the police. The press coverage of the assassination and Oswald's arrest was immense. On 24 November Oswald was moved from the Dallas police headquarters, where he had been held, to the county jail. An army of reporters was on hand, and the transfer was broadcast live on national television. Suddenly, a bulky man named Jack Ruby stepped out of the crowd and fatally shot Oswald in the abdomen.

Jack Ruby. Ruby was a fifty-two-year-old nightclub owner who had lived in Dallas since receiving an honorable discharge from the army in 1946. In Dallas he changed his name from Rubenstein and eventually operated a strip joint called the Carousel Club.

An Erratic Personality. Ruby craved publicity and cultivated a rough-and-tumble persona. He had an emotional temperament tinged with violence. He acted as his own bouncer in his club, and he was always quick to take on anyone who made anti-Semitic remarks. He was a familiar sight around the police station and newsrooms, where he would often drop by to talk and do small favors for officers and media personnel.

A Day of Tragedy. On the day President Kennedy was assassinated, Ruby was at the offices of the *Morning News* drafting an advertisement for his club. When he heard of the murder he became visibly upset and changed his advertisement to a tribute to the dead president. He then returned to his club, announced that it would be closed that evening, and made a series of telephone calls to relatives and acquaintances, with whom he recounted the events of the day in an agitated manner. Later that evening he picked up some sandwiches to deliver to friends at a local radio station. On the way he stopped by the police station and arranged an interview for one of the station's personnel. He arrived in time for the midnight press conference with Oswald. It was there that he first caught sight of the accused assassin, whom he referred to as a "little weasel of a guy."

A Chance Encounter. Ruby would see Oswald one more time. On Sunday, 24 November Oswald was scheduled to be moved to the county jail. The move had been announced for 10:00 A.M., but it did not occur until about 11:20. Ruby was downtown that morning to send money to one of his showgirls. As he drove to the Western Union office, he noticed a crowd of people at the nearby police station, waiting by the ramp to the basement. He later said that after sending the money he walked over to the ramp only out of curiosity. As Ruby entered the basement, Oswald was led out. Ruby, by impulse or plan, then stepped forward, firing his gun once. He mortally wounded Oswald in front of a crowd of policemen and spectators and before a national television audience.

Belli for the Defense. Not surprisingly, the trial of Ruby for the murder of Oswald attracted immense attention and news coverage. As his attorney, Ruby chose Melvin Belli, known as "King of Torts" for his success in representing clients in personal injury suits. Belli had acquired a good knowledge of medical matters in his career, and he decided that a medical argument was the best means to defend his client. His strategy was to show that Ruby had suffered temporary insanity when he shot Oswald. However, Belli had little experience in criminal cases, and, after the verdict was in, Belli's strategy was criticized.

Questionable Decisions. The trial was conducted in Dallas in March 1964, after the judge, Joe B. Brown, refused Belli's motion for a change of venue on the grounds that the enormous media coverage and the criticism that the city had received for being hostile to the president would prevent their client from getting a fair trial. Judge Brown also allowed the prosecution to introduce testimony about statements Ruby had made to the police immediately after the shooting concerning his motivation and premeditation. Premeditation was the key to the prosecution's attempt to convict Ruby of first-degree murder, which carried the death penalty in Texas. The prosecution had to show that Ruby did not shoot Oswald on an impulse but that he had entered the basement intending to kill him. Ruby had told the police that when he had seen Oswald's sarcastic sneer at the press conference on Friday night, he had decided to kill the man if he got the chance. The fact that Ruby was carrying a pistol when he went by the police department added weight to this argument, although the defense argued that he was armed because he often carried large amounts of cash. Indeed, when he was arrested, Ruby had over two thousand dollars on his person.

A Fugue State of Mind. The defense argued that Ruby suffered from emotional instability. They suggested that he had been so upset by the assassination of President Kennedy that he had acted irrationally. He was shown to be capable of precipitous mood swings, and the defense argued that after the killing of Kennedy he had slipped into a fugue state of mind and was unable to tell right from wrong. They argued that the shooting of Oswald was the result of a quirk of fate which had placed Ruby with a gun in the same place as Oswald. However, the emphasis of the defense lawyers on Ruby's insanity may have worked against them. By spending most of their time on that argument, they neglected to build up proof to support a lesser charge if the jury found that Ruby was sane. If convicted of unpremeditated murder, Ruby would only have faced a few years in jail. But, as the case stood, once the jury was convinced Ruby was legally sane

its only real alternative based upon the evidence was a verdict of first-degree murder. After deliberating less than two-and-one-half hours, the jury returned its verdict of guilty, and he was sentenced to death in the electric chair.

Bring on the Second Team. But this was not the end of Ruby's struggle. For the appeals process Belli and the other trial attorneys were replaced by William Kunstler, Elmer Gertz, and others. These attorneys claimed that Judge Brown had made several procedural errors that had denied Ruby a fair trial. They also claimed that Judge Brown had contracted to write a book on the case, possibly influencing him to push for a conviction.

A Second Chance. Eventually, the new defense team presented their argument to the Texas Court of Criminal Appeals. The court held that the testimony of police officers concerning Ruby's confession was inadmissible. The court also found that the trial could not be fairly held in Dallas because of the widespread publicity and strong feelings in the community. The court ordered a new trial. Meanwhile, Judge Brown had excused himself; he would not be involved in the new trial. During this long legal process Ruby remained in jail, his mental and physical health deteriorating. He seemed to be losing touch with the real world, sometimes claiming that he was the object of an anti-Semitic conspiracy. Even more serious problems arose, as the preparations for the new trial began. Ruby fell physically ill, suffering from cancer. He died on 3 January 1967 without ever being retried. Like every other aspect of the Kennedy assassination, Ruby's actions before and during the murder, his trial, and his death have provided fodder for conspiracy speculations.

Sources:

"Another Day in Dallas," *Time*, 83 (13 March 1964): 24–25;

"Death for Ruby," *Time*, 83 (20 March 1964): 27–28;

Elmer Gertz, *Moment of Madness: the People vs. Jack Ruby* (Chicago: Follett, 1968);

"Like Picking a Wife," *Time*, 83 (28 February 1964): 53–54;

"The Man Who Killed Oswald," *Time*, 82 (6 December 1963): 34–35;

"A Nonentity for History," *Time*, 89 (13 January 1967): 16–17;

David Scheim, *Contract on America: The Mafia Murders of John and Robert Kennedy* (Silver Spring, Md.: Argyle, 1983).

PEOPLE IN THE NEWS

In 1961 **F. Lee Bailey** joined the defense of **Dr. Sam Sheppard**, who had already been convicted of the murder of his wife. He succeeded in having the conviction reversed by the Supreme Court and in a new trial got his client acquitted. In 1967 he represented the Boston Strangler and by legal maneuverings avoided his conviction for murder. One of the most successful criminal defense attorneys of his day, he often found himself in the center of publicity. He combined intelligent legal maneuvers with a canny ability for establishing a rapport with members of the jury.

In 1963 a scandal appeared in the United States Senate. **Bobby Baker** was the secretary for the Democratic majority in that body and had become a powerful figure in his own right. He was sometimes called the "101st senator" because of his influence on legislation and committee assignments. A close friend of **Lyndon Johnson**, he had risen along with that powerful senator and continued as his right arm in the Senate when Johnson became vice-president. However, Baker's luck finally ran out, and he resigned in 1963. There followed an investigation that was embarrassing to the many politicians with whom he had contacts. Questions were raised as to how he had managed to amass over $2 million in assets on his $19,600 a year salary. Hearings and trials dragged on through much of the decade, resulting in Baker's conviction for larceny, tax evasion, and fraud in 1967.

In 1960 **Caryl Chessman**, a convicted kidnapper, made his last attempt to avoid execution. His attorneys appealed to the California Supreme Court for clemency but were turned down. Chessman then convinced **Gov. Pat Brown** of California to grant a reprieve from his February execution date. This was to give the state legislature the opportunity to reconsider the use of capital punishment. The legislature refused to abolish such punishment, and Chessman, who had avoided eight prior execution dates, finally kept his appointment with the executioner.

In 1964 **Roy Cohn,** who made a name for himself as counsel to the Sen. Joseph McCarthy committee investigating communism, found himself under the gun.

He was tried for conspiring to prevent four accused stock swindlers from being indicted and of committing perjury. Claiming that this was a personal vendetta by Attorney General **Robert Kennedy**, Cohn was acquitted by the jury after only nine hours of deliberation.

In 1962 **Paul Crump** was sentenced to death for killing a guard in a payroll heist. His fight to avoid execution gained widespread support among prominent religious leaders and attorneys, as well as in the press and with the public at large. In jail he began reading and writing extensively, gradually gaining the respect of his fellow prisoners and prison officials alike. The campaign to prevent his execution even included testimonials of the prison's warden and of a prison guard whose life he saved. The result of this outcry was the commutation of his sentence to 199 years without parole by Illinois governor **Otto Kerner**.

In 1965 **Anthony ("Tino") De Angelis,** a soybean tycoon, pleaded guilty to fraud and conspiracy charges in federal court. He had attempted to corner the soybean market and had financed his company's rocketing growth by huge loans secured by reputed oil holdings. The problem was that there really was no oil. When the soybean futures market collapsed in 1963, so did De Angelis's scheme, bringing down several brokerage firms and causing losses running to hundreds of millions of dollars to banks and oil dealers across the country.

In 1969 **Alan Dershowitz** successfully defended the release of a sexually explicit film, the Swedish-made *I Am Curious (Yellow)*. He was involved in the defense of the Chicago Seven and has become a prominent attorney for criminal defendants.

In 1960 **Al Dewey** led the Kansas Bureau of Investigation's pursuit of those responsible for the brutal murder of the Clutter family. A former FBI special agent, he proved competent and persistent in the search, which had gained national attention.

In 1963 Supreme Court Justice **William O. Douglas** made news when he divorced his second wife. His former wife immediately married a prominent Washington attorney and Douglas, sixty-four, married twenty-three-year-old **Joan Martin** whom he had met at a speaking engagement on a college campus. Douglas's marital affairs again captured attention in 1966 when he divorced Joan. They both immediately married again, the justice to **Cathleen Heffernan**, a college senior.

In 1962 the investigations of the dealings of Texas cotton king and fertilizer magnate **Billie Sol Estes** sent shock waves from the Pecos to the Potomac. He built a massive illusory empire whose growing debts far exceeded its assets. This agricultural ponzi scheme finally collapsed, causing numerous officials in the Department of Agriculture who had had improper contacts with the Texan to be fired. By 1963, his empire in ruins, Estes had filed for bankruptcy and had been convicted on numerous fraud counts.

In 1969 the defense attorney **Percy Foreman** was hired by **James Earl Ray**, the accused killer of **Martin Luther King, Jr.** He had made a reputation as one of the foremost criminal defenders of his day. Claiming that his fee was the penance his clients were required to pay, his bills were enormous, and he was merciless about collecting them. His favorite defense tactic was to attack the character of the victim in order to gain sympathy for his client. He was a tireless worker for his clients doing most of the investigating work himself. In over seven hundred capital cases he lost only one defendant to the executioner.

In 1968 **Abe Fortas**, already an associate justice on the Supreme Court, was nominated by his close friend President **Lyndon Johnson** to fill the position of chief justice held by **Earl Warren**, who planned to retire. However, the nomination came under increasing fire; first, because of his close relation to the president, and, second, because of certain business dealings which came to light. After allegations arose in 1969 about serious ethical violations by the sitting justice, he was forced to resign from the Court to avoid impeachment by the House of Representatives.

In 1967 **Jim Garrison**, the district attorney of New Orleans, arrested businessman **Clay Shaw** on charges of conspiring with **Lee Harvey Oswald** and others to assassinate President **John F. Kennedy**. After the assassination of Kennedy, Garrison had begun an investigation, claiming that the government was involved in a conspiracy to hide the truth. His investigation gained national attention but also attracted widespread criticism and ridicule. The spectacle which had begun with such grandiose claims finally fizzled out in 1969 with Shaw's acquittal.

In 1964, late on a summer night, twenty-eight-year-old **Kitty Genovese** was attacked outside her apartment building in New York City. She was stabbed several times before her cries for help alerted neighbors. As lights flicked on in nearby apartments the attacker retreated. However, no one took any action to help her. Emboldened by the lack of response, the attacker returned and calmly raped her and stabbed her to death. The apathy of the at least thirty-eight witnesses, who did not even bother to call the police, aroused outrage throughout the country.

In 1964 **Estelle Griswold**, the director of the Connecticut Planned Parenthood League, provided contraceptives at a New Haven birth-control clinic in violation of state law. In the ensuing legal proceedings the Supreme Court found the law unconstitutional, establishing a new constitutional "right of privacy." This development in personal rights became the basis of the historic *Roe* v. *Wade* decision which legalized abortion in the next decade.

In 1969 **Clement Haynsworth** was nominated to fill the seat on the Supreme Court vacated by **Abe Fortas**. The nomination sparked a fierce partisan battle. In part it was a reaction to the Fortas fiasco and to the nomination of a southerner and a strict constructionist. It was also a reflection of the increasing politicization of the Supreme Court. Many observers point to Haynsworth's defeat as the beginning of the series of ferocious confirmation hearings that climaxed with the **Robert Bork** and **Clarence Thomas** nominations.

Late on the night of 18 July 1969, the car of Sen. **Edward Kennedy** plunged off a bridge on Chappaquiddick Island in Massachusetts. Kennedy, thirty-seven, escaped harm but his companion, twenty-eight-year-old **Mary Jo Kopechne**, was drowned. In July Kennedy pleaded guilty to leaving the scene of an accident and received a suspended sentence. Great publicity was attached to the inquest and a grand jury session which followed, but no indictment was ever brought. However, Kennedy did have his driver's license suspended for six months after a Registry of Motor Vehicles hearing found him "at serious fault" in the accident.

In 1961 **William Kunstler**, at the behest of the American Civil Liberties Union, joined the legal-defense team of the Freedom Riders in the South. Since then he has been involved in many prominent cases protecting individual's rights. He was special counsel for Martin Luther King, Jr.'s Southern Christian Leadership Conference. In 1969 he represented the seven men accused of conspiracy during the 1966 Democratic Convention in Chicago.

In 1962 **Frank Lee Morris** and two other inmates escaped from Alcatraz, the government's maximum-security prison on an island in San Francisco Bay. They sneaked out through the prison's ventilation system and set out across the bay on a handmade raft. The three men were never caught, though prison officials speculated that they had drowned. No bodies were ever recovered, and, if they were successful, it would mark the only time inmates of "the Rock" have escaped and avoided recapture.

In 1966 **Candy Mossler**, forty-six, was tried, along with her twenty-four-year-old nephew **Melvin Powers**, in the murder of her husband, millionaire **Jacques Mossler**. It was alleged that the aunt and nephew, who were supported by Mossler's money, were carrying on an affair, and they murdered the husband because he was planning a divorce. The circumstantial evidence was very strong. However, at trial the defense's strategy was to attack the prosecution's witnesses and the dead man's character. This strategy, combined with a claim that there was a conspiracy to railroad the accused, succeeded in convincing a jury of their innocence. This allowed them to inherit $28 million of Mossler's money.

In 1964 **Jack ("Murph the Surf") Murphy**, a surfer from Miami who made his living as a skin-diving instructor, was involved in an attempt to steal the giant sapphire called the Star of India. He and two friends sneaked into the American Museum of Natural History in New York City and stole the sapphire along with twenty other famous rubies and gems. Despite their initial success the amateur thieves were quickly caught by the police.

In 1966 **Ralph Nader**, a Harvard Law School graduate and author and lecturer on consumer safety, made headlines before a Senate subcommittee, testifying to harassment by the auto manufacturer General Motors (GM). He claimed that because of his book, *Unsafe at Any Speed*, which criticized the company's Corvair automobile, the company had hired detectives and used wiretapping in an attempt to embarrass him. Nader sued GM for invasion of privacy and eventually settled his claim for $425,000.

In 1967 **Adam Clayton Powell, Jr.**, a black representative from Harlem, was barred from taking his seat in Congress. This unprecedented congressional action was taken as a result of his continued refusal to pay a libel judgment and alleged misuse of committee funds. Powell brought suit to regain his seat, claiming that Congress did not have authority to refuse to seat a duly elected representative who meets the only qualifications set forth in the Constitution: age, citizenship, and residence. He was vindicated in 1969 when the Supreme Court ruled that Congress had acted unconstitutionally in denying him his seat.

In 1967 **James Earl Ray**, the accused killer of **Martin Luther King, Jr.**, fled the Missouri State Penitentiary and disappeared. His fingerprints were found on the weapon used to assassinate the black civil rights leader in Memphis on 4 April 1968. After two months of flight, traveling to Canada and then Europe, he was arrested and brought back to stand trial. He pleaded guilty in 1969 to the killing and received a ninety-nine-year sentence.

In 1964 a federal court reversed the conviction of **Dr. Sam Sheppard** for murdering his wife. The court ruled that his earlier conviction was invalid because pretrial publicity had violated his constitutional right to a fair trial. The Supreme Court affirmed this decision in 1966. He was retried for the crime and acquitted later that year.

In 1963 **Frank Sinatra, Jr.**, the nineteen-year-old son of famous singer and actor, Frank Sinatra, Sr., was kidnapped from a motel room. After a $240,000 ransom was paid, he was released unharmed.

On 5 June 1968 **Sirhan Sirhan** assassinated presidential hopeful **Robert F. Kennedy**, who had that evening won the Democratic presidential primary in California. Born in Jordan, his family moved to the United States in 1957. His apparent motive was Kennedy's avowed support of the state of Israel. He was convicted of first-degree murder in a highly publicized trial in 1969.

In 1961 psychiatrist **Robert Soblen** was convicted of spying for the Soviet Union. He was released on one-hundred-thousand-dollar bail while he appealed his conviction. Upon learning that the Supreme Court had denied his appeal in 1962 he fled to Israel. He was extradited back to the United States but died by his own hand before he arrived.

In 1969 high-school student **Mary Beth Tinker** won a major Supreme Court victory in *Tinker* v. *Des Moines Independent Community School District*. The Court declared that the school administrators could not prevent her and other students from wearing black armbands to protest against the war in Vietnam. The Court noted that, unlike issues of boys' hair length or girls' skirt length, this was an issue of free speech. To prevent students from expressing a political opinion violated their constitutional rights.

DEATHS

William J. Allen, 76, truck driver who in 1932 discovered the body of aviator Charles Lindbergh's twenty-month-old son who had been abducted by kidnappers, on 20 December 1965.

Amy E. Archer-Gilligan, 93, former nursing-home owner suspected in the deaths of over forty residents and two husbands. She was convicted of one murder for arsenic poisoning, and her death sentence was commuted to life imprisonment, on 23 April 1962.

Thurman W. Arnold, 78, prominent New Deal trust-buster as assistant attorney general from 1938 to 1943, also served on U.S. Court of Appeals for the District of Columbia before quitting to establish the Arnold and Porter law firm, on 7 November 1969.

W. Preston Battle, 60, Tennessee judge in the trial of James Earl Ray for the murder of Martin Luther King, Jr. He accepted the deal by which Ray pleaded guilty and was immediately sentenced to ninety-nine years in prison, on 31 March 1969.

Elizabeth T. Bentley, 55, former Communist whose disclosures helped convict several spies, including Julius and Ethel Rosenberg, on 3 December 1963.

Francis Biddle, 82, attorney general under President Franklin D. Roosevelt from 1941 to 1945 and a U.S. judge at war-crime trials, on 4 October 1968.

Henry Breckinridge, 73, former assistant secretary of war from 1913 to 1916, Manhattan attorney and counsel for Charles Lindbergh in the kidnapping of Lindbergh's child, on 2 May 1960.

Joe B. Brown, 59, judge in the 1964 trial of Jack Ruby for the murder of Lee Harvey Oswald, on 20 February 1968.

Harold Hitz Burton, 76, former senator appointed to the Supreme Court by President Harry S Truman where he served from 1945 to 1958, on 28 October 1964.

John T. Cahill, 62, as U.S. attorney in New York in the 1930s prosecuted gangsters, bootleggers, and the general secretary of the U.S. Communist party. He later became a prominent corporate and international lawyer, on 3 November 1966.

Whittaker Chambers, 60, former Communist spy courier who, in his celebrated and controversial testimony before the House Un-American Activities Committee in 1948, accused Alger Hiss, a high-ranking State Department official, of spying, on 9 July 1961.

Walter Chandler, 79, attorney for Memphis plaintiffs who challenged Tennessee's apportionment procedure in the *Baker* v. *Carr* case before the Supreme Court, on 1 October 1967.

Edward S. Corwin, 85, Princeton professor and distinguished scholar of the presidency and the Constitution, on 29 April 1963.

Matthew Cvetic, 53, from 1941 to 1950 he spied for the FBI against Communist organizations in the United States; he authored a book about his experiences which became the basis for the movie *I was a Communist for the FBI,* on 26 July 1962.

John F. Finerty, 82, attorney in many prominent cases involving unpopular causes, he represented the anarchists Nicola Sacco and Bartolomeo Vanzetti as well as atomic spies Julius and Ethel Rosenberg, on 5 June 1967.

Felix Frankfurter, 82, former Harvard Law School professor and adviser to President Franklin D. Roosevelt, he served as a Supreme Court justice from 1939 to 1962, on 22 February 1965.

Vito Genovese, 71, the "boss of all bosses" of the New York Mafia, sentenced to fifteen years on a narcotics conviction, he reputedly continued to run his criminal empire from a federal prison cell for the nine remaining years of his life, on 14 February 1969.

Vincent C. Giblin, 67, Florida attorney known as "Al Capone's lawyer." While he represented Capone in civil matters, he never represented the gangster in a criminal case, on 20 March 1965.

Harold Lee ("Jerry") Giesler, 77, well-known lawyer whose clients included many Hollywood celebrities. His courtroom theatrics earned him the name "The Magnificent Mouthpiece," on 1 January 1962.

Henry Clay Greenberg, 68, New York judge who banned a film spoofing Notre Dame's football team because he ruled that it would cause "irreparable harm" to the school's reputation, he was later overturned on appeal, on 9 March 1965.

Learned Hand, 89, known as "the best Supreme Court Justice this country never had," the revered Judge Hand served fifty-two years as a federal judge, thirty-seven of them on the U.S. Second Circuit Court of Appeals, on 18 August 1961.

Alexander Holtzoff, 82, judge for the Federal District Court of the District of Columbia, in 1952 he upheld President Harry S Truman's seizure of the steel industry only to be reversed later by the Supreme Court, on 6 September 1969.

Charles ("Lucky") Luciano, 64, gangster who became the narcotics and vice-ring lord of New York City but was deported back to his native Italy in 1946, on 26 January 1962.

James Patrick McGranery, 67, served as attorney general in the last year of the Truman administration. He was brought in to replace the fired J. Howard McGrath and clean up the Justice Department, on 23 December 1962.

J. Howard McGrath, 62, served as attorney general from 1949 to 1952. He was fired by President Harry S Truman in response to his own firing of a special investigator of corruption in the government, on 2 September 1966.

Delbert E. Metzger, 92, U.S. District Court judge for Hawaii who created controversy in 1944 when he ruled that martial law was no longer necessary in the islands, on 24 April 1967.

Sherman Minton, 74, former Supreme Court justice, appointed by President Harry S Truman, serving from 1949 to 1956, on 9 April 1965.

James F. Monahan, 62, also known as Boston Billy Williams, gentleman jewel thief who reportedly stole jewelry worth over $4 million but was imprisoned for thirty-one years and died in poverty, on 22 October 1960.

Edmund Morgan, 87, Harvard Law School professor from 1925 to 1950, he chaired the committee which drafted the first Uniform Code of Military Justice, on 31 January 1966.

Matthew Hobson Murphy, Jr., 51, Alabama lawyer who came to prominence representing a Ku Klux Klansman charged with the murder of a civil rights worker, on 20 August 1965.

John Francis Neylan, 74, San Francisco attorney and former chief counsel of the Hearst empire, on 19 August 1960.

Lee Harvey Oswald, 24, arrested for the assassination of President John F. Kennedy, he was himself shot to death by Jack Ruby while in police custody, on 24 November 1963.

Philip B. Perlman, 70, solicitor general from 1947 to 1952 during which time he won forty-nine cases before the Supreme Court but lost his most famous case, President Harry S Truman's seizure of the steel industry in 1952, on 31 July 1960.

Gordon Persons, 63, former governor of Alabama who placed crime-ridden Phenix City under martial law in 1954 after his candidate for attorney general was murdered there, on 29 May 1965.

Lee Pressman, 63, a prominent union attorney, he served as legal counsel for the Congress of Industrial Organizations (CIO) from 1936 to 1948 and later represented other unions in private practice, on 19 November 1969.

Melvin H. Purvis, 56, a South Carolina attorney who joined the FBI in the late 1920s, he led the units which got both John Dillinger and Pretty Boy Floyd. Died by his own hand on 29 February 1960.

Sol A. Rosenblatt, 67, prominent New York attorney who handled the marital disputes of the rich and famous, including the divorce of Alfred Vanderbilt, on 4 May 1968.

Jack Ruby, 55, nightclub owner who shot and killed Lee Harvey Oswald, on 3 January 1967.

Harry Sacher, 60, defended eleven top members of the U.S. Communist party in Smith Act trials in 1949, on 22 May 1963.

Fred W. Slater, 67, a member of the National Football League Hall of Fame, he earned a law degree and became one of the first black judges. He presided over the murder trial of Danny Escobedo and his refusal to set aside the defendant's confession was later reversed in a historic U.S. Supreme Court decision, on 14 August 1966.

David E. Snodgrass, 68, dean of Hastings College of Law who built it into a top law school by pursuing the policy of hiring eminent professors forced out of other schools by retirement rules, on 10 July 1963.

Robert Soblen, 61, Lithuanian-born psychiatrist convicted of spying for the Soviet Union in 1961. He fled the country in an effort to avoid imprisonment and died by his own hand in London, England, on 11 September 1962.

Robert F. Stroud, 73, known as the "birdman of Alcatraz," he was sent to jail for a murder in 1909 and spent the rest of his life in prison. His interest in birds began when he nursed a sick sparrow back to health. He became one of the world's foremost experts on birds and their diseases. He published many books and articles and was himself the subject of a biography and movie, on 21 November 1963.

Harry F. Ward, 93, chairman of the American Civil Liberties Union (ACLU) from 1920 to 1940, he was forced out due to his Communist sympathies, on 9 December 1966.

Joseph N. Welch, 69, an attorney who came to prominence in 1954 as the army's special counsel during the Army-McCarthy hearings. While he continued to practice law his newfound fame allowed him to become involved in television and to play the part of a judge in the movie *Anatomy of a Murder* the year before his death, on 6 October 1960.

Mabel W. Willebrandt, 73, assistant attorney general from 1921 to 1929, she was responsible for the enforcement of prohibition laws, a job which she made into a personal crusade, on 6 April 1963.

PUBLICATIONS

Patricia C. Acheson, *The Supreme Court: America's Judicial Heritage* (New York: Dodd, Mead, 1961);

Donald R. Cressey, *Theft of the Nation: The Structure and Operations of Organized Crime in America* (New York: Harper & Row, 1969);

Gerald Dickler, *Man on Trial* (Garden City, N.Y.: Doubleday, 1962);

Irving Dillard, ed., *One Man's Stand for Freedom: Mr. Justice Black and the Bill of Rights* (New York: Knopf, 1963);

Michael V. Di Salle, *The Power of Life or Death* (New York: Random House, 1965);

Harriet F. Filpel and Theodora S. Zavin, *Rights and Writers: A Handbook of Literary and Entertainment Law* (New York: Dutton, 1960);

Paul A. Freund, *The Supreme Court of the United States* (Cleveland: World, 1961);

Ronald L. Goldfarb, *Ransom* (New York: Harper & Row, 1965);

Richard Harris, *The Real Voice* (New York: Macmillan, 1964);

Ray D. Henson, *Landmarks of Law: Highlights of Legal Opinion* (New York: Harper, 1960);

Christopher Hibbert, *The Roots of Evil* (Boston: Atlantic/Little, Brown, 1963);

Otto Kirchheimer, *Political Justice* (Princeton: Princeton University Press, 1962);

Mark Lane, *Rush to Judgement* (New York: Holt, Rinehart & Winston, 1966);

Anthony Lewis, *Gideon's Trumpet* (New York: Random House, 1964);

Peter Maas, *The Valachi Papers* (New York: Putnam, 1969);

Alpheus Thomas Mason, *The Supreme Court* (Ann Arbor: University of Michigan Press, 1962);

John L. McClellan, *Crime Without Punishment* (New York: Duell, Sloan & Pearce, 1962);

James Bishop Peabody, ed., *The Holmes-Einstein Letters* (New York: St. Martin's Press, 1964);

James A. Pike, *Beyond the Law* (Garden City, N.Y.: Doubleday, 1963);

Barrett Prettyman, *Death and the Supreme Court* (New York: Harcourt, 1961);

Eugene V. Rostow, *The Sovereign Prerogative* (New Haven: Yale University Press, 1962);

Leon I. Salomon, *The Supreme Court* (New York: Wilson, 1961);

Arnold S. Trebach, *The Rationing of Justice* (New Brunswick, N. J.: Rutgers University Press, 1964);

Roul Tunley, *Kids, Crime and Chaos* (New York: Harper & Row, 1962);

Gus Tyler, ed., *Organized Crime in America* (Ann Arbor: University of Michigan Press, 1962);

ABA Journal, periodical;

Business Lawyer, periodical;

Master Detective, periodical;

Official Detective Stories, periodical;

Police Chief, periodical;

True Detective, periodical.

CHAPTER EIGHT

LIFESTYLES AND SOCIAL TRENDS

by CHARLES D. BROWER

CONTENTS

Sidebars and tables are listed in italics.

1960

- Enovid 10, the first oral contraceptive pill, is first sold at fifty-five cents a pill.

- The U.S. Census Bureau finds that Nevada, Florida, Alaska, Arizona, and California have the largest population growth of the United States.

1 Feb. Students from a nearby university stage a sit-in at a whites-only lunch counter in Greensboro, North Carolina.

17 Apr. Young civil rights activists meet at Shaw University in Raleigh, North Carolina, to establish the Student Nonviolent Coordinating Committee (SNCC).

7 Oct. A presidential debate between candidates Richard Nixon and John F. Kennedy is watched by a television audience of seventy-five million Americans.

8 Nov. Kennedy defeats Nixon by a slender margin, less than 120,000 votes.

1961

- Yo-yos become a national craze after yo-yo experts demonstrate their skills on television.

- Timothy Leary and Richard Alpert, two psychology professors, are fired from Harvard University because of their experiments with hallucinogens.

- Freedom Rides to desegregate interstate bus travel begin in May and continue throughout the summer.

- Ray Kroc buys out the McDonald brothers and opens two hundred McDonald's restaurants in southern California.

1 Mar. President Kennedy announces the formation of a national peace corps.

21–22 May A bus carrying Freedom Riders is attacked by an angry mob in Montgomery, Alabama.

24 May The Freedom Riders arrive safely in Jackson, Mississippi, and are promptly jailed.

1962

- Rachel Carson's *Silent Spring* is published.

- Fourteen-year-old Hulda Clark, a working-class African-American girl, is given a two-thousand-dollar scholarship to a Moscow boarding school by Madame Nina Khrushchev, the Soviet premier's wife.

20 Feb. Astronaut John Glenn orbits the earth three times.

29 Sept. The longest-running musical in Broadway's history, *My Fair Lady,* closes after 2,717 performances.

1 Oct. President Kennedy sends federal troops to the University of Mississippi to enforce the admission of James Meredith, Ole Miss's first black student.

1963

- The President's Council on the Status of Women issues its report.

- The Food and Drug Administration announces that supposed cancer cures krebiozen and laetrile are ineffective.

- Betty Friedan's *The Feminine Mystique* is published.

- "Piano wrecking" becomes a popular campus pastime.

4 Jan.	Pope John XXIII is named *Time* magazine's "Man of the Year."
28 Aug.	250,000 people participate in the March on Washington for Jobs and Food.
22 Nov.	President Kennedy is assassinated in Dallas.
24 Nov.	Alleged presidential assassin Lee Harvey Oswald is shot and killed by Jack Ruby outside the Dallas city jail.

1964

- The Beatles arrive in America, launching the "British Invasion" in popular music.

14 Jan.	Jack Ruby is sentenced to die for the murder of Lee Harvey Oswald.
4 Aug.	The United States begins bombing North Vietnam, citing as justification the attack on a U.S. destroyer in the Gulf of Tonkin.
28 Sept.	The Warren Commission to investigate the assassination of President Kennedy issues its report, confirming that Lee Harvey Oswald acted alone in killing the president.
30 Sept.–4 Oct.	Students at the University of California, Berkeley stage a sit-in at the campus administration building and trap a police car trying to leave with an arrested demonstrator for more than thirty hours, thus beginning the free speech movement.
14 Oct.	Dr. Martin Luther King, Jr., is awarded the Nobel Peace Prize and donates the prize money to the civil rights movement.
3 Nov.	President Lyndon Baines Johnson is elected to a full term, defeating Republican candidate Barry Goldwater.

1965

- Wham-O introduces the Superball.
- The Beatles meet Elvis Presley in Bel Air, California.

21 Feb.	Malcolm X is murdered while speaking in Harlem.
21 Mar.	Martin Luther King, Jr., leads thirty-two hundred demonstrators on a civil-rights march to Selma, Alabama.
3–7 June	The spacecraft *Gemini IV* orbits the earth sixty-two times. Astronaut Edward White walks in space for twenty minutes.
11–14 Aug.	Race riots in south central Los Angeles leave thirty-four dead, more than a thousand injured, and millions of dollars in property damage.
15–16 Oct.	Protests against the Vietnam War are held in forty cities around the nation.

1966

- Mark Lane's *Rush to Judgment*, which claims that Lee Harvey Oswald was framed as part of a conspiracy to kill President Kennedy, is published.
- Possession, manufacture, and distribution of LSD is made illegal.
- The Black Panther Party for Self-Defense is organized in San Francisco by Huey P. Newton and Bobby Seale.

- The National Organization for Women (NOW) is established.

- The first annual Conference on Black Power, organized by Adam Clayton Powell, is held.

- The television series *Batman* debuts, quickly becoming a national sensation.

13 Jan. President Johnson appoints Dr. Robert Weaver, the first African-American to hold a cabinet position, as secretary of housing and urban development.

25–27 Mar. International Days of Protest Against the War in Vietnam are held; seven American cities participate.

1967

- More than one hundred instances of racial violence around the country leave eighty-three people dead.

- The British supermodel Twiggy arrives in New York, and thinness is confirmed as the new fashion standard.

- Muhammad Ali is stripped of his heavyweight championship title by refusing to report for the military draft.

- The Gathering of Tribes for the Human Be-In is held at Golden Gate Park in San Francisco, inaugurating the Summer of Love.

12–17 July Six days of race rioting in Newark, New Jersey, leave twenty-six people dead.

23–30 July Racial violence in Detroit leaves forty-three dead.

21 Oct. Antiwar demonstrators march on the Pentagon in Washington; protestors include child-care expert Dr. Benjamin Spock, linguist Noam Chomsky, and poet Robert Lowell.

1968

- Feminists stage a rowdy protest against the Miss America pageant in Atlantic City, New Jersey.

4 Apr. Martin Luther King, Jr., is assassinated, sparking a week of rioting in forty cities around the country.

3 June Andy Warhol survives being shot by Valerie Solanis, a self-proclaimed feminist revolutionary.

5 June Robert Kennedy is assassinated.

14 Nov. Yale University admits women.

1969

- New Orleans district attorney Jim Garrison unsuccessfully tries Clay Shaw for conspiring with Lee Harvey Oswald to kill President Kennedy.

- Hell's Angels acting as security guards stab a concertgoer to death while the Rolling Stones are playing onstage at the Altamont Music Festival in San Francisco.

- A huge oil slick contaminates the coast of Santa Barbara, California.

9 Apr.   Four hundred students at Harvard University seize buildings on campus as part of a campuswide strike; police break up the demonstration after seventeen hours.

20 July   Astronaut Neil Armstrong becomes the first man to walk on the moon; the *Apollo XI*, manned by Armstrong, Buzz Aldrin, and Michael Collins, is on the moon for twenty-one hours.

9 Aug.   Five people, including actress Sharon Tate, are murdered by members of Charles Manson's family of followers.

15–17 Aug.   The Woodstock Music and Art Fair — "An Aquarian Exposition, Three Days of Peace and Music" — is held in Bethel, New York, with some four hundred thousand in attendance.

OVERVIEW

Dramatic Changes. The 1960s were a decade of change, often so dramatic that some feared for the American way of life. Minorities, women, and young people challenged the Establishment — mostly white, male, and affluent — to honor the equal rights granted to all Americans by the U.S. Constitution. The conflicts, particularly those over the civil rights of African-Americans, were frequently violent and nearly always dramatic. By the end of the decade the Establishment was still mostly white, male, and affluent, but significant steps had been taken to address the injustices in American society.

The Triumph of Nonviolence. The civil rights movement dominated the attention of white and black Americans during the decade. For African-Americans the 1960s began with the triumphs of nonviolent protestors — led by a Baptist minister from Georgia named Martin Luther King, Jr. — against segregationists in the southern states. Racist whites in the South frequently reacted with violence (and on more than one occasion, cold-blooded murder), but the protestors, mostly college students and white sympathizers from the North, stood their ground. Eventually President John F. Kennedy was obliged to send in federal troops to enforce the laws of the nation, much as his predecessor President Dwight D. Eisenhower had to force school desegregation. The partnership between whites and blacks in the quest for equal rights culminated in the 1963 March on Washington, during which hundreds of thousands of Americans, nearly a quarter of them white, sang and prayed for unity.

Terrifying Desperation. By the middle of the decade, however, frustration was leading civil rights activists to turn away from nonviolent protest of the sort advocated by King. A split formed in the movement: some thought the key to equality lay in encouraging African-Americans to register to vote and participate in the democratic process; but increasingly, radical young blacks urged nothing short of revolution. The call to arms found support among those African-Americans who lived in the inner cities of the industrial North. Fifty years earlier, 90 percent of black Americans lived in the South, but by 1960 half of them lived in the North, many in poverty and hopelessness. Rioting, touched off by episodes of police brutality or, in 1968, by the assassination of King, gave

terrifying expression to the desperation of millions of Americans. The black power movement sought to instill pride and a sense of self-reliance in the African-American community. Sympathetic whites, confused by the white-devil rhetoric of black power advocates such as Malcolm X and Huey P. Newton, wondered if there was a role for them in the struggle any longer.

La Causa. The civil rights movement inspired several similar efforts over the course of the decade. One involved the second largest racial minority in the United States, Chicanos and other Hispanic Americans. Most of them resided in the southwestern United States and California, where their original ancestors had lived before the country was colonized by the Europeans. Like African-Americans, they were frequently the victims of discriminatory laws and economic hardship. But thanks to Cesar Chavez, who organized a two-year strike among the migrant farmworkers of California's wine country; revolutionary groups such as the Alianza Federal de Los Pueblos Libres; and student protests at Los Angeles high schools, Chicanos became more politically active. No longer the "silent minority," they flocked to La Causa (the cause) by the thousands.

Woman's Day. American women asserted their right to social equality more aggressively during the decade, as well. Betty Friedan's 1963 book *The Feminine Mystique* gave voice to the dissatisfaction felt by women whose only source of fulfillment, according to society's standards, was in caring for their husbands and children. Friedan was also instrumental in forming the National Organization for Women (NOW) in 1966, which was intended to work for women's rights the way the National Association for the Advancement of Colored People (NAACP) had worked for African-Americans. As had been the case in the civil rights movement, those activists who wanted to participate in the system were mostly drowned out by strident young radicals who wanted to do away with the system entirely. Radical feminists kept their sense of fun, though, whether they were putting hexes on the Wall Street stock exchange or crowning a sheep Miss America. Feminists were never able to achieve passage of the Equal Rights Amendment to the Constitution, which would have explicitly forbidden sex discrimination, but they did successfully lobby for reforms in divorce and abortion laws and greater access to contraceptives, all of which gave women more freedom to control their own destinies.

Challenges to Marriage. The new directions in which women and young people were going added stress to the American family, which had long been considered the backbone of American life. Young people were waiting longer to marry than their parents, and more of them than ever before were questioning the necessity of marrying at all. Divorce rates climbed for married couples of all ages, and sex outside of marriage gained increased acceptance, due to effective, convenient birth control and to the efforts of young people, who had taken up free love as part of their rebellion against the Establishment.

Hippies. The generation gap grew into an abyss during the 1960s, and young people became more outspoken in their criticism of their elders than ever before. Protests against the military-industrial complex and the war in Vietnam (in which young men of draft age had a keen interest) were waged on college campuses all over the country, especially at the University of California, Berkeley, home of the Free Speech Movement. Across the bay, in San Francisco, other young people called hippies were trying to establish a whole system of their own — a counterculture — based on free love, loud music, shared property, and lots of hallucinogens and marijuana. For several years the Haight-Ashbury district of San Francisco was home to these flower children, and hippie slang, fashion, and music caught on across the country.

Time for Fun. But hippie culture was only one of the fads that entertained Americans throughout the 1960s. In the midst of considerable strife, people still knew how to have fun. One year the British Invasion (led by the Beatles) would determine what kids listened to and wore; the next it was the surfer sound. Yo-yos and Superballs were favorite toys for the kids, and for the parents, adult coloring books were a fad (they could use their children's crayons). The coloring-book fad reached its peak when the Black Panther coloring book, the fun way to learn about the coming revolution, was condemned on the floor of Congress. On the nation's dance floors a series of dances, including the pony and the swim, took their brief turns in the spotlight. And on college campuses those young scholars who were not protesting or dropping out relaxed by breaking pianos into hundreds of pieces or playing the murder game, kind of an elaborate game of tag.

A More Dangerous Fad. Drug use was a fad during the 1960s, as well. LSD ("acid") was the drug of choice for intellectuals in the early years of the decade, with Timothy Leary, a Harvard psychologist, as its leading advocate. For Leary, the drug was a way to escape the social conditioning that limited human consciousness. Other notables of the time who turned on to acid included literary celebrities Ken Kesey and Allen Ginsberg. Most of acid's leading proponents had their share of scrapes with the law once the drug was made illegal in 1966, but even after that it was consumed freely by the hippies. Likewise, the smell of burning marijuana pervaded the hippie scene. The presence of pot and acid no doubt contributed to the heady quality of the time and inspired some of its more outrageous excesses. As the joke goes, "If you can remember the '60s, you must not have been there." But there was a dark side to the drug use, as well: addiction to amphetamines and heroin caused the deaths of talented young people such as Jimi Hendrix and Janis Joplin, and the increasingly competetive (and increasingly violent) underworld drug trade soured the hippies' ideals of peace and love.

TOPICS IN THE NEWS

BLACK POWER

Frustration Sets In. As the struggle for rights for African-Americans continued during the 1960s, many activists became convinced that the nonviolent strategies used by the movement in the early years of the decade had reached the limits of their effectiveness. Many blacks expressed frustration that the civil rights movement, as represented by sit-ins and Freedom Rides, did not give them the opportunity to express their anger at racism in America any more than they had been able to in the worst days of Jim Crow. Nonviolent protest, they felt, only gave racists the opportunity to victimize them further; increasingly, black activists wanted to take the rights they had as Americans, rather than waiting to be granted them. In September 1966, for example, after a fleeing black youth accused of auto theft had been shot and wounded by Atlanta police, Stokely Carmichael, an activist and veteran of the Freedom Rides, and several other members of the Student Nonviolent Coordinating Committee (SNCC — called "snick") instigated a riot, urging demonstrating blacks to ignore the mayor's attempts to calm them. According to the Atlanta police chief, SNCC had become the "Non-student Violent Committee."

SNCC Gets Angry. By that time, under the influence of militant leaders such as Carmichael, SNCC had shifted its emphasis away from voter registration in the South. From its offices in Atlanta the organization concentrated on churning out angry propaganda, including its black power bumper stickers, which depicted a lunging black panther; SNCC's newspaper, the *Nitty Gritty;* and history pamphlets that stressed the teachings of black power advocate Malcolm X, who was assassinated in early 1965, not long after his message gained national prominence. This turn toward militancy created tension between SNCC and older civil rights leaders such as Martin Luther King, Jr., the most eloquent spokesman for nonviolence and racial harmony. But for SNCC members participation in the white-dominated system meant endangering their racial identity. As Charles V. Hamilton wrote in 1968, "To be 'integrated' it was necessary to deny one's heritage, one's own culture, to be ashamed of one's black skin, thick lips and kinky hair."

Adam Clayton Powell, left, and Stokely Carmichael, right, in Bimini

The Birth of Black Pride. The main thrust of black power, then, was to make African-Americans proud, rather than ashamed, of their appearance and their common heritage. Black Americans, they stressed, were black first and Americans second, even those who seemed to have achieved some level of success in white society. The growing class of black professionals, who frequently seemed to consider the problems of lower-class members of their race irrelevant to them, was called upon to contribute its talents to the betterment of the whole race. While the civil rights leaders of the early 1960s had welcomed the participation of whites in the effort to integrate America, black power advocates tended to view even sympathetic whites with distrust. As Malcolm X wrote in his autobiography, "Even the best white members [of black organizations] will slow down the Negroes' discovery of what they need to do, and particularly of what they can do." Toward the rest of white society the movement was openly hostile. Although Carmichael claimed that he was not antiwhite, in his speeches he took a revolutionary stance: "When you talk of 'black power,' you talk of bringing this country to its knees. When you talk of 'black power,' you talk of building a movement that will smash everything Western Civilization has created."

The Black Panthers. The most aggressive wing of the black power movement was the Black Panther Party for Self-Defense, organized in San Francisco in 1966 by Huey P. Newton and Bobby Seale. The Panthers drew the wrath of the Establishment by carrying loaded firearms to all of their public appearances. As far as they were concerned, they were at war with the white power structure. "It is not in the panther's nature to attack anyone first," they explained, "but when he is attacked and backed into a corner, he will respond viciously and wipe out the aggressor." The worst enemies of the Panthers, they proclaimed, were policemen, who serve as white America's army against blacks. "Every time you go execute a white racist Gestapo cop, you are defending yourself," Newton told black audiences. A series of riots in the nation's large cities in 1967 and King's murder in 1968 only strengthened the Panthers' case in the black community. By the end of the decade the militant party still

had considerable support, especially among young African-Americans.

Panther Hunt. The all-out race war the Panthers envisioned never occurred, however. The Panthers themselves became hunted: the Federal Bureau of Investigation (FBI) kept intelligence files on them and planted agents within the Panther ranks to try to undermine the organization. Law-enforcement officials in cities where the party was active kept close tabs on them, and on several occasions deadly gun battles broke out between the militants and the police, including one in Chicago in which Panther leader Fred Hampton was killed in his sleep. Other leaders of the party faced jail terms: Seale was imprisoned for executing a Panther informer; Newton was sentenced to fifteen years for killing a policeman; and Eldridge Cleaver, who was the presidential candidate of the Peace and Freedom party in 1968, fled to Algeria rather than return to jail for parole violations. The Panthers claimed that the white government was out to get them, and many, more mainstream black leaders tended to agree.

Black Power Survives. If the influence of the Black Panthers dwindled, however, the commitment to black power among the African-American community remained strong. Natural, nonstraightened hair and African dashiki robes became fashionable, and blackness, which for so long had made African-Americans the objects of scorn, became a source of pride. The annual Conference on Black Power, organized by Adam Clayton Powell in 1966, started small but grew in leaps each year. In workshops black leaders carved out plans for a variety of projects, including a black national bank, a black theater, and a black militia to police the country's housing projects. While the more radical proposals only met with slight support among the nation's black population, there was overwhelming support for more black-owned businesses and for a greater pride and awareness of African and African-American heritage.

Sources:
August Meier, Elliot Rudwick, and John Bracey, Jr., eds., *Black Protest in the Sixties* (New York: Markus Wiener, 1991);
"New Findings: Negro Attitudes on Racial Issues," *U.S. News & World Report*, 65 (5 August 1968): 10;
Howard Zinn, *A People's History of the United States* (New York: Harper & Row, 1980).

REACHING INSIDE

Diane Nash, one of the leaders of the Nashville Student Movement that staged the campaign to desegregate the lunch counters of the city, recalled that the movement taught young African-Americans self-respect at a time when the white society around them was trying in many ways to degrade them. "The movement had a way of reaching inside me and bringing out things that I never knew were there. Like courage, and love for people. It was a real experience to be seeing a group of people who would put their bodies between you and danger. And to love people that you work with enough that you would put your body between them and danger. I was afraid of going to jail. I said, 'I'll do telephone work, and I'll type, but I'm really afraid to go to jail.' But when the time came to go to jail, I was far too busy to be afraid. And we had to go, that's what happened."

Source: Juan Williams, *Eyes on the Prize: America's Civil Rights Years, 1954–1965* (New York: Viking, 1987).

CAMPUS PROTESTS

Cold War Laboratories. During the 1960s the baby boomers — the largest generation of young Americans in the history of the nation — reached college age; and, as a result of the general affluence of the United States in the years following World War II, more potential students were in a position to take advantage of higher education than ever before. Between 1955 and 1970 the number of college students nearly tripled, from 2.4 million to 6.4 million; nearly half a million instructors and researchers were employed by the nation's universities by the end of

Students protesting at the University of California at Berkeley during the free speech movement in 1964

the decade, up from less than 200,000 twenty years before. In large part the explosive growth of the nation's academic community was made possible by the financial support of the federal government, specifically the Department of Defense, for whom American schools were often the laboratories where the cold war battle for technological superiority over the Soviet Union was waged. In 1961 nearly half of all federal research funds came from the Department of Defense and the Atomic Energy Commission. According to Kenneth Heineman, by the end of the 1960s schools such as the Massachusetts Institute of Technology and the University of Michigan had hundreds of defense-related contracts worth millions of dollars annually; in 1969, "the Pentagon underwrote 80 percent of MIT's budget."

Education Factories. The role that the academic community played in that partnership between government and defense contractors known as the military-industrial complex tended to contribute to a conservative atmosphere on campuses. Many of the administrators of the country's state universities were corporate executives or federal bureaucrats rather than educators. By the early years of the 1960s, about the time that university enrollments began to swell with the arrival of the first baby boomers, there were indications that students and faculty were questioning the values that the administrations of their schools seemed to represent.

A United Front. The first incidence of a major student revolt against a school's administration took place in 1964 on the Berkeley campus of the University of California system, which was a major supplier of military research. At the beginning of the 1964–1965 academic year Berkeley student organizations were informed that they could no longer give political speeches or pass out literature on social issues on the grounds of the student union. Although students who had raised funds on the campus for the civil rights movement saw the new rule as primarily aimed at them, all student political groups, liberal and conservative, stood to suffer from it. A broad coalition was formed among the groups affected, and on 17 September the United Front petitioned the administration to allow continued use of the student union as long as certain rules were followed. While they waited for a response, the United Front set up tables at the union as usual and began an all-night protest vigil on 21 September. The administration stood its ground, and a series of demonstrations followed, drawing support from students who had never been politically active before.

Sit-In at Sproul. On 30 September, when eight students were issued citations from the school for continuing to man tables at the union, several hundred of their peers signed a petition saying that they were equally responsible. Demanding that they be punished as well, they occupied Sproul Hall, sitting in the building's corridors

A Washington, D.C., demonstration protesting against the exploitation of
workers by the United Fruit Company

for the rest of the day and all night. While there the demonstrators planned their next moves and argued with administrators. One demonstrator, a junior in philosophy named Mario Savio, proved to be an especially compelling speaker. When a school official claimed that the new rule was to preserve political neutrality on campus, Savio responded, "The University of California is directly involved in making new and better atom bombs. Whether this is good or bad, don't you think . . . in the spirit of political neutrality, either they should not be involved or there should be some democratic control over the way they're being involved?" For the demonstrators the issue was not one of political neutrality but of free speech.

The Captured Car. The next day, 1 October, another demonstration was held on the steps of Sproul Hall, and Jack Weinberg, who was not enrolled as a student but was manning the table of the campus chapter of the Congress of Racial Equality (CORE), was arrested for trespassing on school property. Before the police could take him away, however, the assembled demonstrators sat down in front of and behind the police car, preventing it from leaving. Jumping on top of the car, Savio led the rally from there. That evening the demonstrators grappled with policemen to keep the doors of Sproul Hall unlocked while administrators and student representatives negotiated upstairs. On Sproul Hall's steps the situation was just as chaotic, with students, faculty, and school officials arguing about the legitimacy of holding the police car. The demonstration continued until 7:30 the next evening; Weinberg remained in the car the entire time. Even when the crowd dispersed, the battered car was unable to move.

The Free Speech Movement. On 4 October the demonstrators met again to form an organization to negotiate for them, which they called the Free Speech Movement (FSM). The FSM would be led by the students who had taken the most vocal parts in the capture of the police car. Several months of demonstrations and tense negotiations followed. On 9 November members began setting up tables in the union again, starting another period of open violations of university regulations. As with the first series of demonstrations, hundreds of students volunteered to be punished for the offense. On 20 November the FSM held its largest rally yet, outside where the university's board of regents was meeting to try to resolve what seemed like an increasingly bitter stalemate. Somewhere between 2,000 and 5,000 demonstrators gathered; popular folksinger Joan Baez attended to show her support. The regents' decision was a setback: they voted to pursue new disciplinary action against the eight suspended students and enforce the rules prohibiting political activism on campus more vigorously. When the campus closed for the Thanksgiving holiday, members of the FSM were demoralized: they had been handed a defeat by the regents, and arguments over strategy were starting to jeopardize the movement's solidarity.

A Free University. On 2 December the FSM held yet another demonstration outside of Sproul Hall; after a series of tense speeches, more than 1,000 students filed into the building. Once inside, they held a free university: faculty members taught classes in languages and civil disobedience, and areas were set aside for sleep, dancing, and watching movies. The sit-in continued well into the night, until more than six hundred police from Berkeley and nearby Oakland arrived to break up the demonstration. They arrested 773 students, who, in classic civil rights style, went limp and had to be carried from the building. The process of removing all the protestors took another twelve hours. Within days, angered by the presence of state police on campus, students and then faculty called for a general strike.

Strike. The first day, a Friday, some 10,000 students participated in the strike, cutting classes or picketing the university's gates. Over the weekend the administration decided to negotiate; university president Clark Kerr announced that Monday he would propose a "new era of freedom under law" for the school. Sixteen thousand students packed into an outdoor amphitheater to hear the president's statement. When Savio tried to take the microphone at the end of the meeting, he was wrestled away by two university policemen, and pandemonium resulted. The strike continued into the week; coincidentally, a few days later student elections were held. FSM members and sympathizers received overwhelming support from the student body. On the same day they got another vote of confidence when the faculty senate passed a resolution calling for a lifting of restrictions on political activity on campus. Chancellor Edward Strong was relieved of his duties, and a new chancellor from Berkeley's academic community was chosen as his replacement. For a while it seemed as if the FSM had achieved victory. But that spring protests began again, this time over the use of obscenity in public. The FSM became the "Filthy Speech Movement," and the campus revolts continued.

Other Revolts. Campus unrest was not limited to Berkeley by any means, and particularly after U.S. military involvement in Vietnam intensified in 1965, protests developed across the country. Students and faculty members were increasingly critical of the contributions their schools were making to military research and thus to the war. The draft, understandably of great concern to eighteen-year-old students, prompted scores of hostile demonstrations. At Harvard in 1966 members of the radical group Students for a Democratic Society (SDS) jeered at Defense Secretary Robert McNamara and refused to let his car leave campus; University of Chicago students staged a sit-in to protest Selective Service examinations being held there. In 1967 University of Wisconsin students smashed university property to protest recruitment by Dow Chemical, a major defense contractor, on campus. Student radicals frequently clashed with their more conservative peers and with local authorities, most tragically perhaps at Ohio's Kent State University in May 1970, when the National Guard ended months of tense antiwar protests by shooting into a crowd of demonstrators, killing four and wounding nine others.

Sources:
Kenneth J. Heinemann, *Campus Wars: The Peace Movement at American State Universities in the Vietnam Era* (New York & London: New York University Press, 1993);

Max Heirich, *The Spiral of Conflict: Berkeley, 1964* (New York & London: Columbia University Press, 1971).

A DECADE OF BARBIE

One of the most popular toys for young American girls during the last several decades has been the Barbie doll, which debuted by the Mattel company in 1959 at the New York Toy Fair. The first Barbies were slim but shapely, eleven and a half inches tall, and sold for $3.00. Girls could not only collect the dolls but a whole range of fashions ("authentic in every detail," her makers proudly proclaimed) for the Barbie to wear. Although the earliest dolls had dead white skin and limp hair, by the early 1960s her skin tone was more natural and her designers were giving her a variety of hairstyles, especially the beehives and bubble cuts that were popular at the time. Barbie's ever-changing wardrobe also reflected the fashions of the time, from the elegance of first lady Jacqueline Kennedy to the short-skirted "Carnaby Street" look imported along with the British Invasion of 1964.

Like every popular teenager, Barbie soon had a circle of friends for girls to collect, as well. Her boyfriend Ken was introduced in 1961. (Barbie and Ken made it official in 1965, when Mattel offered a wedding ensemble for the two.) In 1963 Barbie gained a best girlfriend, Midge. In 1964 and 1966 Barbie's makers offered siblings for her: first her little sister Skipper, and then the twins Tutti and Todd. In 1966 the public was introduced to Francie, Barbie's mod cousin, and in 1968 Christie, a black friend, was added to the group. There was, of course, plenty for all of Barbie's friends to wear, too: the designers at Mattel added hundreds of new pieces to the group's wardrobe each year.

Source: Michael Forrest, "Wow! Barbie is Thirty!," *Antiques & Collecting* (September 1989): 22–25.

FADS

All Work and No Play . . . Although the 1960s were a decade of great social upheaval, Americans still knew how to have fun. A series of fads captured the public's imagination briefly. Toys, hobbies, and dances that everyone could enjoy may have helped Americans keep their sense of community at a time when the country seemed to be splintering.

Toys and Crayons. Several toys caught on with kids and grown ups alike during the decade. The yo-yo, an ancient weapon from the Philippines that had been marketed as a toy in the United States by Donald F. Duncan since 1923, suddenly surged in popularity in 1961 when Duncan's team of yo-yo experts began giving demonstrations on children's television shows. Over a period of two months New Yorkers bought 4 million yo-yos, and residents of Nashville, a city of 322,000 people, bought 350,000. Wham-O, the toy manufacturers who gave Americans slinkies and hula hoops in the 1950s, scored again in 1965 with the Superball. Made of an experimental new type of rubber, Superballs would bounce for a full minute when dropped. Another children's favorite, the coloring book, made for adult fun during the decade as well: the Executive Coloring Book hit stores in 1961 and was soon followed by the JFK Coloring Book, the Nikita Khrushchev Coloring Book, and the Psychiatric Coloring Book. By the end of 1962 sales of adult coloring books had topped the one-million mark.

It's Only Rock 'n' Roll. Rock 'n' roll music, which was not turning out to be the fad the older generation had hoped it would be, inspired teenage fads throughout the decade. In 1964 a British group called the Beatles was greeted in America by hysterical fans, and the British Invasion — during which groups such as the Beatles, the Rolling Stones, and the Dave Clark Five dominated rock music — had begun. The popularity of the Beatles was certainly more than a fad: as their music progressed from rhythm-and-blues-influenced pop to include psychedelia and Eastern mysticism, the "four lads from Liverpool" helped define the spirit of the time like no other group. They also provided the basis for a whole industry of Beatles boots, wigs, wallets, games, and movies.

Dancing. Pop music also set in motion a series of dance crazes, starting with the twist in 1961. That dance was so popular that First Lady Jacqueline Kennedy even had a twisting party at the White House. By the time the adults learned the steps of one dance, however, the teenagers had generally moved on to another one. The frug, the watusi, the mashed potato, the pony, the swim, and the jerk all had their brief spells of popularity on America's young dance fans.

Campus Fun. College campuses are traditionally breeding grounds for new fads, and the 1960s were no exception. In 1963, taking a cue from British collegians, American students took up piano wrecking as a pastime. The goal was to see how quickly a group could break a piano into small enough pieces that it could be passed through a twenty-centimeter hole. Telephone talkathons and kissathons were popular campus events during the decade, and at Atlanta's Emory University in 1962 so was going for a spin in a clothes dryer. In 1964 "t.p.-ing" became a fad: anything (or anyone) that would hold still long enough was wrapped in toilet paper. In 1966 computer dating, which matched couples scientifically, was a novel, if not especially successful, way of meeting that special someone.

Beach Party. Surfing was a fad of the 1960s, too, thanks to the music of bands such as the Beach Boys and Jan and Dean and a series of silly but popular beach movies that came out of Hollywood. Beach lingo spread across the country, leaving confused adults wondering if "boss" or "bitchin' " meant that something was good or

SEAT BELTS

Most Americans refused to wear seat belts even if they prevented deaths in car crashes.

Manufacturers also realized that they could sell cars for their safety features. They added lamination to windshields, a thin plastic layer between glass layers that keeps it from shattering as readily. They also added energy-absorbing steering columns. New safety bumpers were designed that did not crush with low-speed collisions.

Ford pursued other options. Many Americans had cars with seat belts, but few passengers wore them. Ford looked at data from the UCLA Institute of Transportation and Traffic Engineering. They conducted experiments such as putting human-form dummies in cars and crashing them. The dummies were wired to show what happens to people in a crash. Ford designed an air bag which would inflate on impact. Using data from the dummy experiments, they found the bags would give adequate crash protection. People did not choose whether to use them: the bags worked automatically. They even tested them in Air Force impact sleds using baboons and showed air bags worked. But the government, facing pressure from the automobile industry, decided air bags were something for the future.

Source: *Newsweek,* 71 (1 January 1968): 40.

bad. For those teens not fortunate enough to have an ocean nearby, skateboards let them in on some of the excitement in their own hometown streets. Skateboards enjoyed a brief popularity in 1965, until reports of injuries began to grow, and several cities cracked down on skateboarders as a public nuisance. The fad disappeared for a while, only to return in a big way in the mid 1970s.

Source:
Peter L. Skolnik, *Fads: America's Crazes, Fevers and Fancies from the 1890's to the 1970's* (New York: Crowell, 1978).

THE FREEDOM RIDES

No Free Buses. The Freedom Rides were conceived by the Congress of Racial Equality (CORE) in 1961 as the next step in protesting the segregated businesses of the southern states, encouraged by the success that the previous year's sit-in movement had in getting whites-only lunch counters to serve African-Americans. The goal of the rides was to compel the newly appointed Kennedy administration to enforce the 1960 U.S. Supreme Court ruling that made segregation of bus terminals and stations serving interstate travelers unconstitutional. Without an order of compliance from the Interstate Commerce Commission, an executive agency that was under President Kennedy's authority, southern states would simply ignore the ruling. Civil rights leaders feared, however, that federal enforcement would be slow in coming if at all, since it could cost the president the support of southern Democrats. As James Farmer, executive director of CORE, recalled, "What we had to do was to make it more dangerous politically for the federal government *not* to enforce federal law than it would be for them to enforce federal law."

A Dangerous Ride. CORE selected thirteen people, black and white, for the first ride. The white riders would sit in the back of the bus, the black riders in front. At every rest stop the blacks attempted to use all the segregated facilities in the stations. The riders they picked were trained and experienced civil rights activists, including several young veterans of the recent sit-ins. As with the sit-ins, the protest would be nonviolent. They would simply be doing what the Supreme Court had ruled was their right to do. They counted on local racists to respond violently, and thus they hoped to force the federal government's hand. Told that the segregationists intended to hold the line on the question of interstate travel, the Freedom Riders steeled themselves for the worst. Some left behind letters for their loved ones should they not survive.

Violence in Alabama. The Freedom Rides began on 4 May from Washington, D.C.; their route would take the buses through Virginia and the Carolinas, into Georgia and Alabama, and end in New Orleans, Louisiana, on the anniversary of *Brown* v. *Board of Education,* the landmark Supreme Court ruling that reversed the legal basis for school segregation. Having made it to Atlanta with only minor incidents, the riders split into two groups for the next leg of the trip, to Birmingham. That was as far as either bus got. One was met by an angry mob of some two hundred people in Anniston, Alabama, who stoned the riders and slashed the bus's tires. The bus escaped but had to stop outside of town to have a flat tire fixed. When it did, the mob caught up with it again, and someone threw a firebomb inside. The riders barely managed to escape before the bus burst into flames.

Birmingham Burning. The other bus reached Birmingham, where it, too, was met by a mob. The city's public safety commissioner claimed that he had not ordered any police on the scene because of the Mother's Day holiday. No one was on hand to protect the riders from the brutal assault which followed. One of the riders was crippled for life. John Patterson, the governor of Alabama, told the press after the attack, "When you go somewhere looking for trouble, you usually find it." Fearing for their safety, the riders managed to reach the Birmingham airport and flew to New Orleans. Over the next several days the violence against the Freedom Riders gained international press coverage; this made it especially important to the Freedom Riders that they not back

down from the segregationists' brutality. Ten students, eight black and two white, decided to return to Birmingham and finish the Freedom Ride.

Tense Days. Finding a bus line that would carry them or a driver who would consent to put his life in jeopardy proved to be difficult. The students waited in Birmingham while Attorney General Robert Kennedy, the president's brother, attempted to negotiate with the Birmingham police and the Greyhound bus company to ensure the riders' safe passage from the city. On 17 May, the day they had originally been scheduled to reach New Orleans, the riders were jailed, supposedly for their own protection. They went on a hunger strike the next day, and on 19 May they were taken to the Tennessee state line and left by the side of the highway. Securing transportation from fellow CORE members in Nashville, they immediately returned to Birmingham and attempted to buy bus tickets for Montgomery. That same day, John Siegenthaler, an aide to the attorney general, made it clear to Governor Patterson that the federal government would use whatever force was necessary to protect the riders if Alabama refused.

The Journey Continues. With assurances that Alabama state police would protect them, a group of twenty-one Freedom Riders left for Montgomery on 20 May. But at the Montgomery city limits — where city police were supposed to take over — the protection ended. The bus terminal at Montgomery seemed almost abandoned; then a mob materialized seemingly out of nowhere. The riders were beaten viciously; Siegenthaler was knocked unconscious when he tried to help a young woman rider. The state police were called in but were too late to prevent the riot. Furious that Governor Patterson had broken his promise, Robert Kennedy immediately ordered six hundred federal marshals to an air force base just outside Montgomery. Martin Luther King, Jr., came to Montgomery as well to address a rally supporting the Freedom Rides. As he spoke at Montgomery's First Baptist Church, several thousand angry whites squared off against two hundred U.S. marshals outside. The marshals used tear gas on the mob, some of which seeped inside the church. Only the intervention of the Alabama state police averted a disastrous confrontation.

Down Freedom's Main Line. The state of Alabama and the Kennedy administration hoped that the Freedom Rides would stop at least temporarily so that racial tensions might have a chance to subside. The Freedom Riders were intent on continuing; twenty-seven of them left on two buses for Jackson, Mississippi, two days after the riot at First Baptist Church. When they reached the Mississippi state line, members of the state's national guard lined both sides of the highway. The Kennedy administration had promised that no federal troops would be sent to the state if state leaders would guarantee no replays of Alabama's violence. The Freedom Riders were relieved and sang as they arrived at the Jackson bus station. There the police escorted them into the whites-only station and out the other side. They were arrested for trespassing and taken to jail. As had been the case when sit-in participants in Tennessee were arrested, the judge turned and looked at the wall rather than listening to the Freedom Riders' defense. They were sentenced to thirty days in the state penitentiary.

The Freedom Riders' Legacy. Through the rest of the summer hundreds of Freedom Riders traveled the Deep South in the effort to integrate interstate bus travel. Finally, in September the rides and the mass arrests that had followed had the desired effect. The Interstate Commerce Commission, responding to a petition by Attorney General Kennedy, drew up a set of guidelines governing the integration of all interstate bus terminals. The crisis atmosphere subsided as the focus of civil rights activism began to change to efforts to register African-Americans to vote, so that they could support the movement with their ballots. Still, workers for civil rights in the South were known by local blacks as freedom riders. As Juan Williams writes, "The courage and tenacity of those pioneers had captured the imagination and awe of blacks throughout the Southland."

Sources:

Emily Stoper, *The Student Nonviolent Coordinating Committee: The Growth of Radicalism in a Civil Rights Organization* (Brooklyn: Carlson, 1989);

Juan Williams, *Eyes on the Prize: America's Civil Rights Years, 1954–1965* (New York: Viking, 1987).

HIPPIES

New Generation of Hipsters. The hippies did not pick that name for themselves: it was given to them by Michael Fallon, a reporter for the San Francisco *Examiner,* in a 1965 story about the new bohemian lifestyle that was developing in the city's Haight-Ashbury district (named for two streets that converge there — also called the Haight). Fallon got the name by shortening Norman Mailer's term *hipster,* and he applied it to the second generation of beatniks who had moved into the Haight from nearby North Beach. This new generation of dropouts was more optimistic than the beatniks, however, more prone to talk about love, more flamboyant. They belonged to groups such as the Legalized Marijuana Movement and the Sexual Freedom League. In the summer of 1965 the hippies were few in number but were well on their way to creating a small, thriving society — a counterculture.

The Growth of a Counterculture. The hippie lifestyle, which included the use of such drugs as marijuana and LSD, drew thousands of young Americans to California in the mid 1960s. By June 1966 some fifteen thousand had moved into the Haight. That was the year that the largest generation of Americans ever — the baby boomers — reached ages eighteen through twenty. Most of these young Americans joined the workforce, married, or went to college and prepared for a career. But an increasing number of their contemporaries were chafing under

TANNING CREAM

Imagine a beautiful suntan without ever going in the sun. This was a big hit with people in the colder parts of the country in 1960, when artificial tanning cream was marketed. It was sold under such names as Man-Tan, Rapid Tan, Positan, Magic Tan, Tansation, Tanfastic, and even Tan-O-Rama.

Tan-in-a-bottle was really a bit of a technological breakthrough. The active ingredient was dihydroxyacetone. This colorless chemical was made years before, but had limited uses. In fact, it caused problems for chemists. People who came in contact with it got brown stains on their skin.

The man behind the idea was John Andre, President of the New York mail order firm Drug Research, Inc. He added alcohol and perfume to dihydroxyacetone to produce an aftershave, Man-Tan. Response by the public was tremendous, with about $15 million spent on the product in the first year. But Andre feared the big Coppertone Corporation, who came out with competing QT (for Quick Tan).

Man-Tan required three applications twenty minutes apart, or it left a splotchy mess. Hands that applied it had to be washed thoroughly or they would turn dark brown. Shirt collars tended to stain badly, and there were plenty of cases of skin irritation.

The GII Bureau *Good Housekeeping Magazine* did an investigation of the product, and results did not justify the tremendous amount spent on the product. Half the women who tried it were dissatisfied.

Without a sunscreen people could burn badly while wearing tan-in-a-bottle in the sun. The twenty-five women who volunteered to test the product applied it as directed. They noted streaks and blotches in the folds of the knees and elbows, uneven coloring, and blotches like iodine leaves. Raised warts and moles darkened more than other skin areas. While no difference was found in the eleven products tested, prices ranged from 20 to 87 cents per ounce. Weekly needs were six to eight ounces to keep the tan. Wool fabric stained (but cotton did not) if the tanning agent was applied to the cloth itself. The conclusion was you could look dirty, but not tan, by using these products.

Sources: *Good Housekeeping*, 151 (October 1960): 197;

Life, 50 (14 April 1961): 110.

Some of the most unlikely participants in the counterculture movement of the 1960s were the Hell's Angels, the large gang of outlaw motorcyclists that had roamed California's highways since the late 1940s. They were introduced to the youth scene in 1965 by author Ken Kesey and his Merry Pranksters, who thought that they could mellow the Angels out with their favorite drug, LSD. At the Pranksters' ranch in Palo Alto, California, what *Newsweek* described as a "bizarre and foolish alliance" was formed. For the next several years, the Angels provided security for the large parties and rock concerts that were part of the California hippie lifestyle. The Pranksters thought that the Angels were perfect for the job: they were dirty, mean, and an affront to mainstream sensibilities. Best of all, they worked cheap, accepting beer and drugs as payment for their services.

The relationship was destined to come to a bad end, however. The Angels were violent thugs who actually shared few of the values of the youth movement. They supported the Vietnam War: Sonny Barger, the president of the group, tried to contact President Lyndon Johnson to offer the Angels' services for "behind the lines duty" in Southeast Asia. Their weekend gatherings at different spots around the West Coast had become notorious sites of violence and rape. But the final tragic act that caused the break between the hippies and the Hell's Angels occurred at the Altamont speedway in December 1969. The Angels were working security at a free concert by the Rolling Stones, and when one of the concertgoers kicked an Angel's bike, the concert's security staff turned on the crowd. Fifty Angels beat dozens of unarmed young people with pool cues, and an eighteen-year-old African-American man, Meredith Hunter, was stabbed to death by one of the gang members. The entire incident was recorded on film by Albert and David Maysles, filmmakers who were shooting part of a documentary on the Rolling Stones' American tour, which was released as *Gimme Shelter* in 1971.

Sources: "Avenging Angels," *Newsweek* (5 January 1970): 16;
Hunter S. Thompson, *Hell's Angels: A Strange and Terrible Saga* (New York: Random House, 1966).

a community formed without greed, loneliness, or any of the other anxieties of modern society. Eastern mysticism, astrology, the novels of German writer Herman Hesse, and science-fiction utopias such as the one in Robert Heinlein's *Stranger in a Strange Land* formed the basis of the hippie philosophy.

Checking the Scene. As the population of the Haight grew, bookshops, craft stores, head shops, coffee shops, health-food stores, and other businesses catering to the young crowd opened throughout the neighborhood. The most important of these was the Psychedelic Shop, which was devoted to books on drugs and exotic religions, crafts, records, and clothes, but also served as a hangout, information center, and post office for some of the citizens of the Haight (whose addresses often changed weekly). Local bands performed at several new nightspots, including the Fillmore and Avalon Ballroom, which featured such soon-to-be famous bands such as the Grateful Dead, Big Brother and the Holding Company, and Jefferson Airplane. An atmosphere of sharing and easy living dominated the neighborhood, which was necessary, since few of the hippies had steady jobs.

The Diggers. In late 1966 a secretive group called the Diggers appointed themselves the conscience of the Haight community and began issuing fliers encouraging the hippies to take a more active stand against the society from which they dropped out. They accused the merchants of the Haight of profiting from the counterculture in the best capitalist tradition. They soon began offering free food daily: "It's free because it's yours!" their fliers proclaimed. Nearly a hundred people began attending the Digger Feeds, which offered a menu of slightly wilted vegetables, day-old bread, turkey neck stew, and whatever other food the Diggers could hustle. On Halloween 1966 the Diggers disrupted traffic at a San Francisco intersection with a street puppet show. Local merchants, meanwhile, began considering a job cooperative for the growing crowd of jobless newcomers that were showing up on Haight Street. The Diggers also started the Free Frame, where people could find free clothes and household items. In December 1966 the Diggers led hundreds of costumed marchers in a Death of Money parade.

The Death of Hippie. The climax of the hippie movement was the Summer of Love, also called the Gathering of Tribes for the Human Be-In, in 1967. Tens of thousands of mostly homeless young people came to the Haight over a period of a few months. The atmosphere actually was not very loving: the sidewalks were too crowded for anyone to get anywhere; the drug scene had become seedier and more dangerous; police were cracking down more aggressively on the neighborhood; and racial tensions, as was the case over the rest of the nation, threatened to explode into violence. Still, hippies were making a big impression on the popular imagination, thanks to hit songs such as the Jefferson Airplane's "Somebody to Love" and Scott Kendricks's "San Francisco (Be Sure to Wear Flowers in Your Hair)" and mov-

the pressure to conform that had dominated the 1950s. A growing chorus of voices was exposing the inadequacies of the Establishment and encouraging the alienated to (in the words of Timothy Leary) "Turn on, tune in, drop out." To the young people living in the Haight, they were rapidly becoming an example to the rest of the country of

ies such as *The Love-Ins.* Even car commercials had worked *groovy* into their vocabulary. Realizing that their dream had gone sour, the citizens of the Haight held a Death of Hippie service in October of that year, marching down Haight Street at sunrise with a cardboard coffin. It was time to fan out from San Francisco, they felt, taking the pure hippie message to the rest of the country.

Sources:

Charles Perry, *The Haight-Ashbury: A History* (New York: Random House, 1984);

Helen Swick Perry, *The Human Be-In* (New York: Basic Books, 1970);

Jay Stevens, *Storming Heaven: LSD and the American Dream* (New York: Atlantic Monthly Press, 1987).

TIMOTHY LEARY AND LSD

Winning the Game. Leary was a lecturer in psychology at Harvard who became one of the most recognizable figures of 1960s counterculture by espousing the value of the hallucinogenic drug lysergic acid diethylamide, known as LSD. Leary believed that LSD could be used as a tool against what he called the cultural game which regulates and prescribes the behavior of all members of society. Religion, politics, family life, and other social institutions have roles, rules, goals, and jargon all their own: to this extent, Leary claimed, they resemble baseball or basketball. The way out, the way to recognize that such social games could be played or not played as one chose, is to expand the consciousness; and the most effective way of doing that is through the use of hallucinogens.

Leary's Vision. Leary himself first experimented with hallucinogens in Mexico in 1960 by taking mushrooms purchased from an Indian spiritual healer. As he recalled, the experience made him want to tell everyone he could, "Listen! Wake up! You are God! You have the divine plan engraved in cellular script within you. Listen! Take this sacrament! You'll see! You'll get the revelations! It will change your life! You'll be reborn!" Returning to Harvard that fall, he was ready to begin experiments to determine the potential therapeutic effects of a psychedelic experience. He encouraged graduate students and fellow faculty members to participate, and he led them through weekly sessions in which they took doses of psilocybin, the chemical compound that gave the Indian mushrooms their hallucinogenic properties. He also gave psilocybin pills to 175 members of the public, mostly young men, and recorded their responses.

The Creativity Pill. Administrators at Harvard were initially enthusiastic about Leary's research; but they became nervous as word of the "creativity pill" study in Cambridge became widespread. In 1960 and 1961 Leary's experiments drew a series of notable visitors to Harvard, including jazz musician Dizzy Gillespie, British author Aldous Huxley (who had for years been an enthusiastic supporter of hallucinogens), and beatnik poet Allen Ginsberg. The meeting between Ginsberg and Leary proved to be an especially important influence on Leary's research and on the Beat literary movement. At

Timothy Leary

the poet's urging a steady stream of the East Coast's cultural elite came to enjoy a psilocybic weekend in the suburbs of Boston. Surrounded by the beautiful people, and frequently on psilocybin himself, Leary found it increasingly difficult to maintain scientific standards in his research. He came up with a new research project, one in which the conditions were undeniably more restricted: giving psilocybin to selected inmates at Massachusetts's Concord Prison. Again, the subjects reported generally favorable responses to the experience. In the fall of 1962, to the dismay of his colleagues, twenty-seven of the Harvard psychology department's thirty-two graduate students signed up to assist Leary in his research.

Enter LSD. The Harvard researchers' supply of psilocybin was impounded in 1961, but Leary had by then shifted his interest to LSD, a more powerful hallucinogen with not-always-pleasant effects. First synthesized by a Swiss chemist in 1943, LSD was used extensively by American psychiatrists and researchers in California in the early 1960s. By 1962 the psychiatric establishment was expressing concern about irresponsible overuse of the drug by therapists. That summer the U.S. Congress passed a law which gave the federal Food and Drug Administration (FDA) control over all research projects involving experimental drugs. To ensure a supply of hallucinogens from the government, Leary helped found the

DO-IT-YOURSELF FACELIFTS

In 1965 a Manhattan nurse, Clara E. Patterson, started a fad when she published the book *Facial Isometrics,* which offered a series of exercises designed to rid the user of unsightly wrinkles and sagging jowls. As *Time* magazine reported, it was not unusual for a period of several months to see commuting businessmen contorting their faces as if they were being bitten on the toes; they were really performing Ms. Patterson's daily drill.

Some of the author's suggestions, as reported in *Time:*

"Contract the muscles on either side of the nose as if sneezing, wrinkling the skin over the nose upward as hard as possible."

"Dilate the nostrils. Flare them."

"Pull the right and left corners of the mouth down and out — separately."

"Purse the lips as if for kissing or whistling, very vigorously."

"Make both sides of the neck contract at the same time to the maximum extent; hold for six seconds, with head, neck and chest rigid. The skin should rise over the upper chest."

"Open mouth as wide as possible in all directions. Hold it."

Source: "The Silent Scream," *Time* (29 January 1965): 43.

International Foundation for Internal Freedom (IFIF). The mission of the IFIF, as Leary and his comrades envisioned it, was to create a network of groups of psychedelic experimenters; each would be led by an IFIF-trained guide. Their project had a religious quality to it; Leary and his sympathizers had turned to Eastern philosophy, believing that mysticism, rather than science, contained the keys to understanding their psychedelic lifestyle. Their goal was nothing less than changing the American consciousness.

On the Run. The IFIF did not get very far along in its mission, however. The group was gaining national attention from articles in *Playboy* and *Time* and psychedelic memoirs such as Adelle Davis's *Exploring Inner Space* and Thelma Moss's *Myself and I;* but their communal style of living made them unpopular with their Cambridge neighbors, and they were viewed with suspicion by local and federal authorities and by Harvard administrators. The university declined to renew the teaching contracts of Leary and his fellow researchers when they expired in 1963. Consequently, the IFIF decided to try to seek haven abroad in Central and then South America. By the end of the year they were back in the United States, living in upstate New York on a sprawling estate owned by the family of one of the group's psychedelic supporters, again playing host to the curiosity seekers of New York's jet set.

The Merry Pranksters. Meanwhile, on the opposite side of the country, a group called the Merry Pranksters was doing its part to spread the gospel of tripping. The group was led by Ken Kesey, the author of *One Flew Over the Cuckoo's Nest,* and Neal Cassady, the original beatnik, whose exploits as a wanderer and a rogue in the 1940s inspired his friend Jack Kerouac to write *On the Road.* Also on hand was Cassady's fellow Beat, Ginsberg. As their name implies, the group approached LSD with more of a sense of fun than did Leary and his comrades. They had begun organizing huge public parties that they called Acid Tests: LSD-laced punch flowed freely, the Pranksters dressed in outlandish costumes, and everyone (sometimes thousands) danced wildly to loud, distorted guitar rock by bands such as the Warlocks (who later changed their name to the Grateful Dead).

The Government Clamps Down. LSD was becoming as vital a part of the youth rebellion against the Establishment as long hair and free love, and the Establishment decided to strike back in 1966, making possession of the hallucinogen illegal in October of that year. More rational LSD experts than Leary or Kesey, such as Sidney Cohen, author of *The Beyond Within* (1967), encouraged continued scientific experimentation with the drug, but their voices were drowned out by sensational mainstream press coverage, which was filled with lurid stories of LSD-induced madness, sex, and violence. As the government clamped down on the LSD supply, enterprising underground chemists stepped in to fill the void. Acid was increasingly plentiful around the country, prompting *Time* magazine to warn of an epidemic of acidheads in March 1966.

The Haight. Young people who were looking for ways to react against the sometimes stifling pressure to conform of the 1950s, however, were not all deterred. Many of them converged at the Haight-Ashbury district of San Francisco. Some 15,000 hippies had taken up residence in Haight-Ashbury by the summer of 1966, and tripping was one of the cornerstones of their new culture. Leary announced in September of that year the formation of an organized psychedelic religion which would have the motto "Turn on, tune in, drop out." But the hippies felt that they had gone beyond Leary: they had a social revolution already going in the Haight.

Leary and the Law. Leary spent the last years of the 1960s attempting to evade several possible jail terms he faced from a long series of drug arrests. In September 1970 he reported to a minimum-security prison in San Luis Obispo, California, but escaped less than a month

The March on Washington, 28 August 1963

later with the help of the Weathermen, a violent radical faction of the SDS. Leary spent the next several years underground, living abroad in Europe and Asia. In 1972 he was rearrested in Afghanistan and deported to the United States. He served nearly three more years in prison and was released in 1976. By then interest in LSD had subsided considerably, but Leary was pursuing new enthusiasms, about which he told audiences on his lecture circuit. He has remained a popular, if frequently obscurantist, social commentator.

Sources:

Frank W. Hoffmann and William G. Bailey, *Mind and Society Fads* (New York & London: Haworth, 1992);

Jay Stevens, *Storming Heaven: LSD and the American Dream* (New York: Atlantic Monthly Press, 1987);

Peter O. Whitmer and Bruce Vanwyngarden, *Aquarius Revisited* (New York: Macmillan, 1987).

THE MARCH ON WASHINGTON

Years of Struggle. The 1963 March on Washington, in which a quarter of a million people demonstrated for civil rights on the grounds of the Lincoln Memorial, was the largest demonstration for human rights that the country had ever seen. It was the idea of A. Philip Randolph, the aging founder of the Brotherhood of Sleeping Car Porters union, who had been a labor and civil rights activist for nearly four decades. Randolph had previously organized such a march in 1941 to demand more jobs for blacks in the wartime defense effort; when President Franklin D. Roosevelt agreed to issue an executive order calling for an end to discrimination in defense industries, Randolph called off the demonstration. But in the summer of 1963, with both job opportunities for African-Americans still lingering woefully behind those for whites and images of the Birmingham riots burned into his imagination, Randolph began organizing a new march.

Reluctant Support. Randolph and Bayard Rustin, deputy director of the march, set its date for 28 August. The goals of the march would be to call attention to the need for the passage of Kennedy's civil rights bill; job training and placement for African-Americans and an end to job segregation; and integration of the nation's schools by the end of the year. The Kennedy administration urged the march's leaders to reconsider; the civil rights bill, it was argued, would have a better chance of passing if blacks waited quietly. But when he was told that the march would go on as planned, Kennedy gave his reluctant support.

I Have a Dream. News of the planned march spread across the country, and as the day of the march drew near buses and trains arrived in Washington, pouring forth 250,000 demonstrators, nearly a quarter of them white. The attendance far exceeded what the organizers of the march had anticipated. While the crowd waited for the rally's speakers, musical personalities including Bob Dylan; Mahalia Jackson; and Peter, Paul and Mary performed. Several speakers gave stirring addresses. The featured speaker of the march, Martin Luther King, Jr., gave a speech that has become one of the most famous in American history. "I have a dream," he told the gathered crowd. He prayed for the day "when all God's children . . . will be able to join hands and sing in the words of the old Negro spiritual: 'Free at last! Free at last! Thank God Almighty, we are free at last!' "

An Image of Hope. It is difficult to determine how much of an impact the march had on civil rights policy in the government in Washington. It did, however, offer to the nation an image of blacks and whites together, giving much-needed hope to a nation that had seen too much racial strife in the past.

Source:

Juan Williams, *Eyes on the Prize: America's Civil Rights Years, 1954–1965* (New York: Viking, 1987).

MARRIAGE AND FAMILY

The Persistence of Tradition. In the early years of the 1960s family life was still dominated by the traditional roles for mother and father. Fathers were the breadwinners in the family, and mothers were responsible for household and children. According to the report of the Presidential Commission on the Status of Women (1963), the modern homemaker's challenge was to see that her family had "a place where all members . . . can find acceptance, refreshment, self-esteem and renewal of strength amidst the pressures of modern life." For many families this place was located in the suburban housing developments surrounding the nation's large cities; and "experts" on domestic life looked to the suburban family — mostly white, middle class, and able to subsist on the husband's income — as the norm. Inner-city families, on the other hand, because of a variety of social pressures, were more likely to be led by one parent, frequently the

MIXED MARRIAGE

In 1967 the daughter of Secretary of State Dean Rusk and her new husband, Guy Smith, made national headlines, because Margaret Rusk was white and Smith was an African-American. They married in California, where less than twenty years before interracial marriages had been considered illegal; until a U.S. Supreme Court ruling in 1966 struck down a Virginia law against such unions, in fact, sixteen states prohibited marriages between people of different races by law. By 1967 racial attitudes in general were somewhat more enlightened; still, Rusk's concern over the possible negative response to his daughter and Smith's marriage was serious enough to prompt the secretary to offer his resignation to President Lyndon Johnson. Johnson did not accept the resignation and gave the marriage his blessing.

One generally thinks of a marriage as being the business of the bride and groom and their families, but in the racially charged atmosphere of the 1960s almost everyone had an opinion about the Rusk-Smith wedding. In a cover story in *Time,* the magazine reported that the State Department had received hundreds of irate cards and letters from around the country. Said a businessman lunching at a Glenview, Illinois, country club, "If I were Rusk, I'd be inclined to shoot the guy." Johnson's political opponents and critics implied that the marriage was intended to gain support among liberals for Johnson and Rusk's policies. As black power advocate Lincoln Lynch said, "I wonder to what lengths Dean Rusk has to go in order to gain support for his and Johnson's war in Vietnam." Other black leaders were more generous, however: John Johnson, the editor of *Ebony* magazine, called the marriage a "measure of America's maturity," and Martin Luther King, Jr., reminded the American people that "individuals marry, not races."

Source: "A Marriage of Enlightenment," *Time,* 90 (29 September 1967): 28–31.

American history — was beginning to lose steam. By 1960 the first of the baby boomers had just reached their teenage years. A variety of factors contributed to their tendency to wait longer to marry than their parents did.

The Women's Movement. Chief among these was probably the women's movement, which achieved national prominence during the decade. Feminists appeared on television and in the national press, books such as Betty Friedan's *The Feminine Mystique* (1963) and Caroline Bird's *Born Female: The High Cost of Keeping Women Down* (1968) made the best-seller lists, and consciousness-raising groups started up in cities and on college campuses. The marriage rates for women in all age groups leveled off or fell during the decade, then fell dramatically during the early years of the 1970s, when women's liberation was in its heyday.

Free Love. Another reason the baby boomers postponed marriage was the greater social acceptance of premarital sex. Previous generations had been taught that their only proper sexual partner was a husband or wife; not everyone chose to follow that rule, of course, but those who did not risked the disapproval of their family, community, and peers. But during the 1960s the social message on sexual matters was decidedly mixed. Birth control became more convenient and effective, particularly with the introduction of the contraceptive pill in 1960. Popular movies and music became more graphic in their sexual portrayals and less likely to support the traditional morality that championed sex only in the sanctity of marriage. The traditional view had not disappeared — a Gallup poll of 1969 reported that 74 percent of women believed that premarital sex was wrong — but the trend was definitely toward greater sexual freedom: just a few years later only 53 percent of women surveyed held the same opinion. Of all the ways that youth rebelled against the Establishment during the turbulent decade, free love was the most inviting.

Divorce, American Style. Most Americans who committed themselves to becoming spouses and parents stuck with it; but the number of couples who were choosing to end their marriages climbed dramatically throughout the decade. Between 1968 and 1972 the divorce rate nearly doubled. This was in part due to the efforts of the women's movement, which lobbied for changes in divorce law that would give husbands and wives equal property rights. But for other reasons, as well, divorce was not viewed with as much distaste as Americans had had for it during the years of the baby boom, when the sanctity of marriage and family was unchallenged. For more married Americans, young and old, divorce was seen as a way to freedom they had never tasted when they were programmed into their roles of husband or wife.

Sources:
Mary Anne Guitar and the editors of *Good Housekeeping, The Young Marriage: A Handbook for Those Who Marry Young and for the Early Years of Marriage* (Garden City, N.Y.: Doubleday, 1968);

---

mother, who had to work to support her children. According to Annegret Ogden, "Between 1960 and 1970, the number of women who alone supported their families grew by 1.1 million."

The Baby Boom Goes Bust. For most of the decade marriage and children were still considered a normal part of American adulthood, particularly for women. But the baby boom — the enthusiastic burst of marrying and childbearing that began in the years following World War II and created the largest generation of children in

Annegret Ogden, *The Great American Housewife: From Helpmate to Wage Earner, 1776–1986* (Westport, Conn.: Greenwood Press, 1986);

Rosalind Rosenberg, *Divided Lives: American Women in the Twentieth Century* (New York: Hill & Wang, 1992).

THE PILL

New Control for Women. The development of a birth-control pill — which, taken daily, prevents the release of a fertilizable egg from a woman's ovaries and thus makes it impossible for her to get pregnant — raised moral issues in the 1960s on both the personal and social levels. Throughout the decade greater numbers of women took the pill (actually there were twelve different varieties), breaking the link between sex and reproduction and giving the users unprecedented control over their own sexual behavior. Health concerns were frequently expressed, and some critics argued that easy access to birth control was the same as condoning liberal sexual behavior; but, as *Time* magazine reported, by 1967 almost 20 percent of all American women who could conceive were using oral contraception.

Wonderful News for Sanger. The pill was the product of decades of human fertility research conducted in various places, but most of the credit goes to Massachusetts scientists Gregory "Goody" Pincus of the Worcester Foundation; M. C. Chang, Pincus's assistant; and John Rock of the Harvard Medical School. They had been working with the hormones progesterone and estrogen, which control the female menstrual cycle, in an effort to regulate the cycle and thus control pregnancy. By the mid 1950s an experimental version of the pill had been developed by the Worcester researchers working for the Searle Pharmaceutical Company; tested on women in Puerto Rico and Haiti, it proved to be nearly 100 percent effective. The success was wonderful news for Margaret Sanger, who had been an activist for women's reproductive rights for more than forty years and whose organization Planned Parenthood was a major financial supporter of the Worcester Foundation. Sanger was concerned, however, that the Catholic church would vigorously oppose the use of the contraceptive as it had in the past, particularly if Catholic presidential candidate John F. Kennedy were to win in 1960.

The Autonomous Girl. In May 1960 the FDA approved Searle's Enovid — as the company had named its pill — for public use. After he took office in 1961 Kennedy gave cautious support to federal research into contraceptive use, trying to balance moral concerns with the importance of slowing the nation's (and possibly the world's) population growth. American women quickly took to using Enovid: from 400,000 women by the end of 1961 to nearly 1.2 million the year after that and 2.3 million by the end of 1963. Evidence was mounting that sexual attitudes were changing just as quickly, particularly among young women. As Gloria Steinem reported for *Esquire* magazine in 1962, the pill had contributed to the

The birth-control pill

emergence of an "autonomous girl," who was less likely to accept without question the values of others. She quoted the results of a recent national study of college students, in which nearly all the respondents, male and female, offered the opinion that "sexual behavior is something you have to decide by yourself."

Sexual Anarchy. Meanwhile, Americans with a more conservative view of proper sexual behavior were expressing the fear that widespread use of the pill could lead to "sexual anarchy." In 1966 *U.S. News & World Report* offered high-school "sex clubs," wife swapping in the California suburbs, and housewives who worked as prostitutes on Long Island as examples of the declining morals the pill had helped make possible. The nation's clergymen were the most vocal critics of oral contraception: Catholic and Protestant leaders agreed that "there must be limitations and restrictions on the use of sex if we are to remain a civilized people." Reports, however, showed that 20 percent of practicing Catholic women and nearly 30 percent of Protestant women had used the pill. Not all or even most of these women fit the portrait of the unmarried autonomous girl. The pill had uses for married couples as well — to help them time the births of children or keep the family at an affordable size.

The Population Bomb. Controlling the size of families all over the world became a concern in the 1960s, as a swelling world population began to exceed the planet's limited natural resources. Unwanted pregnancies and incompetently performed abortions had become major health problems in many parts of the world, and the pill was replacing the intrauterine device (IUD) as a more effective contraceptive that women could administer themselves. The "population bomb" — as it is called by Paul Ehrlich in his popular 1968 book *The Population Bomb* — was being blamed for starvation, pollution, and the rising crime rate, among other social problems. Projecting from statistics at the time, Ehrlich warned that the populations of "overdeveloped countries" such as the United States doubled approximately every seventy years; the doubling time of underdeveloped countries, on the other hand, was much more rapid (more like twenty-five years), and they were much less able to support the growth economically. In poor rural and inner-city sections of the United States, where poverty and a high birthrate seemed to go together, the pill was frequently distributed through birth-control clinics like the mobile one operated by Planned Parenthood in Birmingham, Alabama.

An Important Advance. Most American women were not taking the pill to ease the world's overcrowding, however. They took it because it allowed them to make decisions about their sex life without having to take fear of pregnancy into account. The pill contributed more than any other factor to the appearance of the sexually liberated woman, an important advance that nonetheless was played for all the titillation it was worth in movies such as *Sex and the Single Girl* (1967) and *Prudence and the Pill* (1968).

Sources:
Time, 89 (7 April 1967): 78–84;

Paul R. Ehrlich, *The Population Bomb* (New York: Ballantine, 1968);

David Halberstam, *The Fifties* (New York: Villard, 1993);

"The Pill: How It Is Affecting U.S. Morals, Family Life," *U.S. News & World Report*, 61 (11 July 1966): 62–65;

Gloria Steinem, "The Moral Disarmament of Betty Coed," *Esquire*, 58 (September 1962): 97.

THE SIT-IN MOVEMENT

Whites Only. In February 1960 a group of black college students in Greensboro, North Carolina, refused to leave a whites-only lunch counter at which they were denied service. Their demonstration began the sit-in movement, a series of peaceful protests that brought renewed national attention to the injustices of the segregated South and eventually forced the federal government to protect the rights of African-Americans actively. Over several weeks the strategy spread to dozens of southern cities and towns; students from local colleges sat quietly for hours, studying or sometimes reading Bibles, while white employees refused to serve them. The students occupied all the seats at the counter and left only when it closed (which was often early, thanks to the

PERMANENT PRESS

Before permanent press clothes, there was wash-and-wear. Wash-and-wear had a big problem. Even after hours of ironing, it would never hold a crease. The fabric also tended to pucker if it was sewn after processing, but the problems could not be solved before processing.

Permanent press cured all these ailments of the fabric industry. The new method let manufacturers put creases, or even pleats, into the fabric. They could not be removed afterwards, and the fabric would not wrinkle with washing and drying. Needless to say, it was an instant success.

Koret of California developed the process in 1956. It was not until Levi Strauss and Co. bought the fabric for their Sta-Prest men's pants in 1964 that it caught on. Within a few weeks of the first shipment of Levi's, every major clothing manufacturer became a permanent-press fan. Koret quickly formed Koratron Co. to license users and collect royalties. Other manufacturers quickly tried to develop copycat processes, or even claim they thought of this one first.

The wash-and-wear process is simple. A fabric is treated with resins, and baked in an oven. This gives it a "set." After washing or balling up, the fabric returns to a smooth surface. The Koratron process sounds obvious but nobody else thought of it until they did.

The process was not without some problems. First, the ovens cost at least fifty thousand dollars. Dyes could not be too volatile, or coloring the fabric could produce charred remains. Some dyes were not this volatile but changed to ugly colors during processing. Overcooking ruined clothes; undercooking produced wrinkles. The Koret process also eliminated the puckering. Buttons, threads, and zippers were all added before going into the oven. Naturally, they had to be heat-resistant accessories. But without this innovation, the leisure suits of the 1970s would never have been born.

Source: *Business Week* (21 November 1964): 34.

protests). Frequently local townspeople shouted insults and threats, and in Nashville, Tennessee, the protesters were physically attacked. When the Nashville police arrived, the students, not their attackers, were arrested. As they tried to present their case in court, the judge literally turned his back to their lawyer.

Peaceful Protests. As violent as the response to the sit-ins often was, the protestors did not respond in kind. Many of them had been taught strategies of nonviolent resistance such as those used by the great nationalist leader of India, Mohandas K. Gandhi. Several clergymen, black and white, who were members of a group called the Fellowship of Reconciliation, had been touring southern college campuses since 1958, conducting workshops in which some participants would play protesters and others would play the part of segregationists. Diane Nash, who participated in the workshops while a student at Nashville's Fisk University, recalled, "We would practice things such as how to protect your head from a beating, how to protect each other. If one person was taking a severe beating, we would practice other people putting their bodies between that person and the violence, so that the violence could be more distributed and hopefully no one would get seriously injured."

The First Victory. In mid April 1960 black students from throughout the South and northern white supporters came together on the campus of Shaw University in Raleigh, North Carolina, to discuss methods for coordinating protests, raising funds, and spreading the sit-in movement to other areas. They founded the SNCC. Before dawn two days later, the home of Z. Alexander Looby, the first African-American to serve on Nashville's city council and the lawyer who had represented the sit-in protesters in court, was destroyed by dynamite thrown from a passing car. A few hours later twenty-five hundred students and townspeople marched on city hall. When asked directly by the protesters, Nashville mayor Ben West had to admit that it was wrong to sell merchandise to a customer but refuse to serve that customer at the store's lunch counter. Several weeks later, the sit-in movement achieved its first major victory when six Nashville lunch counters began to serve black patrons.

Dr. King Goes to Jail. By the end of the summer the tide of the battle over the lunch counters was turning: twenty-seven Southern cities had agreed to integrate the restaurants in their community. SNCC began to focus its attention on other areas of social injustice. They organized "stand-ins" at segregated movie theaters and "sleep-ins" at segregated hotels as well as protests at the department stores which continued to segregate their lunch counters and dressing rooms. As with the first sit-ins, the overwhelming majority of protesters were young college students. In October 1960 the Reverend Martin Luther King, Jr., was arrested in Atlanta, Georgia, for participating in a sit-in at a Rich's department store. Already serving a twelve-month suspended sentence for driving with an out-of-state license, King was sentenced to four months in the Georgia state prison system. Since 1960 was an election year, civil rights activists encouraged presidential candidates Richard Nixon and John F. Kennedy to help secure King's release. Senator Kennedy appealed to the mayor of Atlanta and also telephoned King's wife to express his sympathy. His sup-

port of the sit-in movement helped him carry several southern states in a close election. What started as a series of isolated protests in a handful of southern towns ultimately influenced the course of a presidential election.

Sources:

Martin Oppenheimer, *The Sit-In Movement of 1960* (Brooklyn: Carlson, 1989);

Juan Williams, *Eyes on the Prize: America's Civil Rights Years, 1954–1965* (New York: Viking, 1987).

WATTS

White Flight. Race riots more violent than any in the history of the United States shocked Americans during the decade; in every region of the country major cities threatened to go up in flames. Since the years immediately following World War II, middle-class white Americans had been leaving the city for nearby suburbs, and businesses that had once provided jobs and a tax base for the city soon followed. Increasingly, downtown — the inner city — was home to lower-income minorities, many of them southern blacks who came in large numbers to the North to find work. The decay of the inner cities perpetuated itself: economically disadvantaged Americans had to live in the low-rent housing such areas offered, which in turn caused more white flight to the

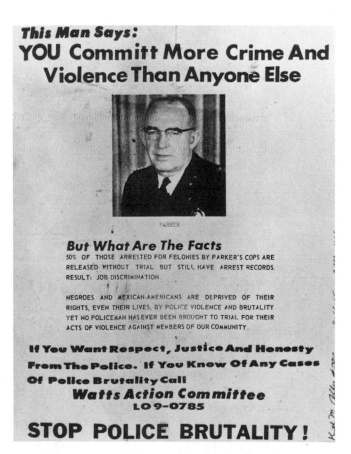

Handbill attacking Los Angeles police chief William H. Parker that was passed out during the Watts riot

suburbs for the Americans that could afford it and the businesses they patronized.

Powderkegs. As the decade progressed, African-Americans saw growing numbers of their race suffering from poverty and the health and social problems that go with it — all at a time when great gains toward the goal of racial equality had supposedly been made. Unemployment among African-Americans was well above the national average, and one-half of all black Americans lived below the poverty line (as opposed to one-fifth of whites). Not surprisingly, then, particularly during the hot months of summer, tensions ran high in black communities across the nation. On many occasions, provoked often by instances of brutality by white police against blacks, these tensions exploded into violence. In 1964 riots broke out in cities such as New York, Philadelphia, and Chicago. In 1967 alone there were eight major outbreaks, thirty-three "serious but not major" episodes, and more than a hundred minor incidents, resulting in eighty-three deaths and hundreds of injuries, mostly African-American civilians.

A Fateful Confrontation. But probably the most notorious uprising of the 1960s occurred in Los Angeles for a week in August 1965. The violence began on 11 August, a hot afternoon, in the mostly black South Central section of the city. White policemen had to use force to restrain a young black man arrested for driving under the influence. A crowd gathered at the scene, many of whom arrived too late to know what had started the confrontation. The mood was tense but nonviolent until one of the officers on the scene tried to arrest a woman he mistakenly thought had spit on him. The crowd lashed out in anger, pelting nearby cars and buses with rocks and bottles. Police reinforcements arrived, and they squared off against the angry crowd well into the night. Disturbances spread from South Central to Watts, a neighborhood several miles away. The demonstrators threw rocks; the police responded with riot sticks. Television news reporters were on the scene as well, and some of them encouraged the rioters to further violence so that they could get more exciting news footage.

Burn, Baby, Burn! At around midnight the police decided that their presence was antagonizing the crowd, and they withdrew from the scene. The mob was triumphant and had no intention of dispersing. Newsmen who stayed behind after the police left were attacked, and rioters overturned the mobile television-news vans. By this time local store owners were feeling the wrath of the crowd's anger, too: rioters smashed shop windows and made off with the merchandise they found inside. The hostility they felt for the oppressive environment in which they lived fueled their anger. "Burn, baby, burn," which was the trademark phrase for a disc jockey of one of Los Angeles's black-music stations, became the motto for the rioters over the course of the uprising. As their rage grew, they attacked blacks as well as whites: as a black automobile worker reported, he was on his way

home from work when "a man ran up to the car and struck me through the windshield with a two-by-four and ran."

The Guard Arrives. Violence continued over the next several days, encouraged by confused reports of police brutality among the black community and by leaflets distributed by the radical Black Muslims in the neighborhood. By 3:30 A.M. on Friday, 13 August, seventy-five stores in the area had been burned. African-American store owners began putting signs in their shop windows telling the rioters that they were "blood brothers"; in many cases the signs were ignored. Black leaders, including members of CORE and stand-up comedian Dick Gregory, appealed to the crowds to go home, but with little success. Gregory actually received a minor gunshot wound for his efforts. Later that day the Los Angeles Police Department decided that further support was necessary, and the California National Guard was called to help restore order. The fifteen hundred guardsmen who arrived at the scene on Friday evening clearly were too few in number, however, considering that at the height of the violence nearly ten thousand African-Americans had taken to the streets. By Saturday morning another two thousand troops had been deployed. Before the uprising was over, more than thirteen thousand guardsmen would be involved.

On the Bottom. The rioting continued for three more days. With the presence of the heavily armed guardsmen, the violence began to subside. Martial law was imposed, a curfew was established, and no one was allowed on the street without a good reason. An area of nearly fifty square miles of the city was put under military control. When the smoke finally cleared, the loss of life and property stunned Los Angeles. Thirty-four were dead, most of them participants in the riot, and more than a thousand were injured. Six hundred buildings were damaged, a third of them totally destroyed. Property damage was estimated at $40 million. When order was restored the police chief of Los Angeles, William H. Parker, was reported to say, "We're on top and they are on the bottom"; but, as Roy Wilkins, director of the NAACP, responded, "the philosophy behind the 'we're on top' expression was the tinder under the Watts explosion." The rioting in Los Angeles and throughout the country during those violent years was a dramatic demonstration that the complex relationship between black and white Americans was still far from being understood.

Sources:

Jerry Cohen and William S. Murphy, *Burn, Baby, Burn!: The Los Angeles Race Riot, August, 1965* (New York: Dutton, 1966);

Robert E. Conot, *Rivers of Blood, Years of Darkness* (New York: Bantam, 1967).

WOMEN'S LIB

Stifled Goals. American women had long struggled against the perception that they were second-class citizens, too emotional, too childish, too feminine to partic-

A women's liberation protest at the 1968 Miss America pageant

ipate in the affairs of men — which included almost everything outside of the home. Still, by the 1960s job opportunities and fair pay for women were generally lacking, and young women found that their aspirations to be anything other than a wife or mother were stifled. For many women this did not seem to matter: 96 percent of women who responded in a 1962 Gallup poll said that being a housewife made them happy. But different feelings were stirring, too. In her 1963 book *The Feminine Mystique* Betty Friedan, who was dividing her time as a housewife, a mother of three, and a freelance writer, tried to give a voice to what she called "a strange stirring, a sense of dissatisfaction, a yearning that women suffered in the middle of the twentieth century in the United States. . . . As she made the beds, shopped for groceries, matched slipcover material, ate peanut butter sandwiches with her children, chauffeured Cub Scouts and Brownies, lay beside her husband at night, she was afraid to ask even of herself the question — 'Is this all?' "

New Hope. Clearly, society was changing during the decade, however; the election of President Kennedy in 1960 gave new hope to women's rights activists when he appointed Esther Peterson as the first woman head of the Women's Bureau of the Commerce Department, a subagency that monitored women's issues in the workplace. Peterson counseled the president to consider appointing a commission with broad powers to examine the status of women in American society; included in the discussion would be the Equal Rights Amendment (ERA), a controversial (and eventually defeated) amendment to the U.S. Constitution ("Men and women will have equal rights throughout the United States and every place subject to its jurisdiction.") first proposed in 1923. The for-

mation of the commission, Peterson told President Kennedy, would likely give him a solid base of support among women voters.

A Call to Action. The Presidential Commission on the Status of Women was formed in 1961 and included experts from around the country to study the economic and legal rights of women. The commission submitted its report in 1963, and although it made several important recommendations for changes in employment policies and social services, it was criticized from within the ranks of the women's movement for not taking a strong stand on the ERA. Constitutional protection for women, the commission argued, could be found in the Fourteenth Amendment, passed shortly after the Civil War, which was intended to guarantee equal protection under the law for African-Americans but could provide the basis for women's rights as well. Despite the fact that the report may not have gone far enough, and despite the condescending treatment the work of the commission received in the national press, many women's rights activists took the report as a call to action. Thus it helped shape the direction the women's movement would take.

Jane Crow. Over the next several years American women achieved a string of successes in the form of laws against sex discrimination. One of them, the equal-pay bill of 1963, was a direct result of the recommendations made by the Commission on the Status of Women's to President Kennedy. Another came about in strange fashion. The year 1964 saw the passage of the Civil Rights Act, which granted by force of federal law many of the rights for which African-Americans had struggled. The bill had languished in Congress for several years during

National Organization for Women protest at the White House.

the Kennedy administration, but after President Kennedy's assassination it gained momentum, thanks in large part to the deal-making skills of President Lyndon Johnson, Kennedy's successor. Women's rights activists were determined to add their own demands to the bill: as they saw it, according to Rosalind Rosenberg, " 'Jane Crow' was just as repugnant to the spirit of the Constitution as 'Jim Crow.' " When the issue came up during congressional debate on the civil rights bill, it was Congressman Howard Smith, a southern Democrat and an opponent of the bill, who suggested that it be amended to include sex discrimination.

A Legislative Victory. Historians differ about Smith's motives, but it is generally thought that he introduced the sex amendment in order to ridicule the civil rights bill. Certainly, not many of his fellow House members took him seriously. According to Leila J. Rupp and Verta Taylor, "Smith's presentation and the subject itself provoked a great deal of laughter, contributing to the legend of what came to be known as 'Ladies' Day in the House.' " When the amendment passed, it was with the support of Republicans and southerners, the two groups that formed the basis of the opposition to the bill. With Title VII of the bill, which prevented discrimination in employment, now amended to include women and African-Americans, the women activists of Washington, many of whom had been involved with the Commission on the Status of Women, worked hard to see the bill pass the House and then the Senate. Signed into law in 1964, the bill was considered a major triumph for black Americans, but women rejoiced in their victory, as well.

NOW. The triumph women's rights activists felt was short-lived. Franklin Roosevelt, Jr., head of the Equal Employment Opportunity Commission (EEOC), whose job was to enforce Title VII, announced that since gender had been added to ridicule the concept of equal employment, the EEOC had no intention of enforcing the sex discrimination clause. Women's groups were outraged at the government's refusal to enforce what they had long hoped to see signed into law. At a 1966 national conference for women, Friedan and two dozen other women conceived of the National Organization for Women (NOW), whose purpose would be to represent women's issues as the NAACP did for African-Americans. At its first meeting in October, NOW elected Friedan as its first president and drew up its statement of purpose, in which the group rejected all laws and traditions that "not only deny opportunities but also foster in women self-denigration, dependence, and evasion of responsibility, undermine their confidence in their own abilities and foster contempt for women." Rather than threaten the status of men, the NOW organizers claimed that the treatment of women as inferiors damaged society as a whole.

Controversial Issues. In the months that followed NOW flexed its muscles: in 1967 members pressed President Johnson to include gender discrimination in his affirmative-action legislation (which required employers to take definite steps to rid their businesses of inequality); next, they targeted the EEOC to include more women in administrative positions. When one of the commissioners of the EEOC told NOW representatives he was interviewing "girls" for an important opening, he was told in no uncertain terms that such a demeaning title was no longer an acceptable way to refer to women. Due to its successes, NOW began to dominate the women's movement; as a result, the movement became younger, more liberal, and more vocal. Soon the group had championed two new, controversial issues: the ERA and the decriminalization of abortion.

Ain't She Sweet? In September 1968, taking a cue from the antiwar protests of the youth movement, women activists (who had adopted for themselves the name feminists) staged a rowdy public demonstration against one of the nation's most cherished institutions: the Miss America pageant. About one hundred women marched up and down Atlantic City's boardwalk, chanted, and carried signs. "Ain't she sweet?," the protestors sang about the contestants, "Makin' profit off her meat." They had a huge trash can on hand, in which they dumped girdles, bras, high-heeled shoes, copies of *Vogue* and *Ladies' Home Journal,* and other symbols of their oppressed status. Later, they led a live sheep on to the boardwalk and put a crown and a sash on it. The women were arrested when they tried to disrupt the official pageant that night. Still, as one of the protesters recalled, "It was the best fun I can imagine anyone wanting to have on any single day of her life."

The Rise of Feminism. By the end of the decade various other radical feminist groups had joined NOW in the ranks of the women's movement. There was WITCH (Women's International Terrorist Conspiracy from Hell), which was formed by Robin Morgan, the former child actress who had led the Miss America protest; the Redstockings, who led "speak-outs" on abortion in 1969; Cell 16; and the October 17 Movement. All of these groups, caught up in the heady atmosphere of the late 1960s, had become convinced that nothing short of social revolution would end the white-male domination of society. Also drawn into the radical feminist camp were African-American women, who had become alienated from the civil rights movement as it evolved from peaceful protest to black power; and lesbians, who had quickly found it difficult to cooperate with homosexual men in the developing gay liberation movement. Feminist groups formed newspapers, shelters, and health collectives to reach out to other women and inform society in general about the pervasiveness of sexism.

Consciousness-Raising. Fundamental to the movement were consciousness-raising groups, which thousands of women joined in the late 1960s. Members of these small groups could share with each other intimate details of their lives; in such an atmosphere of trust many women felt free to speak openly for the first time in their lives. In "CR" groups members realized that women everywhere shared their frustrations and hopes. The experience of consciousness-raising gave the women's movement a feeling of intimacy that made it unique among the social-protest movements of the decade. For feminists that feeling was the key to the whole movement: finally those silent yearnings about which Friedan wrote in *The Feminine Mystique* could be expressed and fulfilled. "The personal is the political" became one of the mottos of feminism.

Sources:

Betty Friedan, *The Feminine Mystique* (New York: Norton, 1963);

Edward P. Morgan, *The 60s Experience: Hard Lessons About Modern America* (Philadelphia: Temple University Press, 1991);

Rosalind Rosenberg, *Divided Lives: American Women in the Twentieth Century* (New York: Hill & Wang, 1992);

Leila J. Rupp and Verta Taylor, *Survival in the Doldrums: The American Women's Rights Movement, 1945 to the 1960s* (New York & Oxford: Oxford University Press, 1987).

HEADLINE MAKERS

RACHEL CARSON

1907-1964

AUTHOR, ENVIRONMENTALIST

Invisible Danger. Rachel Carson's 1962 book *Silent Spring* brought to the attention of the American public the dangers that pesticides pose to the plant, animal, and human life of the country. In the first chapter she tells a parable about a town that seems to be cursed: its grass is withering; its fish and wildlife are dying, as are the animals that the town's farmers raised; even the townspeople are taking ill mysteriously and suddenly, and some of them are not recovering. The balance of nature in the community had been changed forever, as if through witchcraft or enemy sabotage. But, wrote Carson, "the people had done it themselves." While no American town had suffered all these ills, she explained, many real towns had suffered one or in some cases several of them. They were caused by contamination, nuclear and chemical, the products and by-products of American industry.

DDT. Carson had worked for years for the federal Fish and Wildlife Service before becoming a writer; her first several books were popular works about the world's oceans: *Under the Sea Wind, The Sea Around Us,* and *The Edge of the Sea.* In 1958 she began serious research into the use of pesticides in the United States. A friend of Carson's had watched the birds of her bird sanctuary die because of the aerial spraying the state of Massachusetts used to kill mosquitoes. At about the same time, a group of Long Island, New York, citizens were suing to keep state officials from spraying DDT in the area to kill gypsy moths. Carson tried to interest several national magazines in covering the trial and ended up writing an article herself for *The New Yorker.*

War on Nature. Over the next several years Carson gathered information from a variety of sources, including government studies that showed that DDT accumulated in the bodies of humans and animals, passed through mother's milk to children or up the food chain from one predator to the next. The American Medical Association and the federal Public Health Service, however, had not taken a public stand on the dangers of these toxic chemicals. The Department of Agriculture continued to recommend the use of the pesticides, as well. Carson blamed the continued use of pesticides on the military mentality the government and industry brought to the "war on pests." The use of synthetic pesticides, in fact, started in World War II, when experimental chemical weapons turned out to be useful against insects. As Carson pointed out, humanity is part of nature; and when humans declared war on part of nature they declared war on themselves.

The Book's Impact. *Silent Spring* was published in 1962, despite the efforts of the pesticide industry to discredit its author. Companies threatened to withdraw advertising from magazines that reviewed the book favorably. Scientists sympathetic to the industry claimed that the impact of the book could cause famine and starvation. That summer *The New Yorker* published a condensed version of the book; that fall it became a Book-of-the-Month Club selection. Some critics predicted that the book would alert the public to the poisoning of the environment the way Upton Sinclair's novel *The Jungle* had inspired the federal Pure Food and Drug Act in 1906. President John F. Kennedy and his wife read *The New Yorker* version of the book, and about the same time that it was published in hardcover Kennedy commissioned the President's Science Advisory Committee to study the problem of pesticide use. The committee's report, issued a little less than a year later, confirmed the damaging effects of toxic pesticides. A month before the report was made public, the CBS television network broadcast a documentary called *The Silent Spring of Rachel Carson,* despite pressure from sponsors that the documentary not be shown.

An Environmental Legacy. After the publication of *Silent Spring* Carson was frequently asked to speak on the problem of pesticides in the environment. In June 1963 she testified before a Senate committee on environmental hazards, arguing that people should have the right to be free from poisons introduced by others into the environment. Two days later she appeared before the Senate

Committee on Commerce to recommend the creation of an executive government agency, free from influence by the private sector, to regulate the use and creation of pesticides. That recommendation became a reality in 1970 when the Environmental Protection Agency (EPA) was formed. In 1972 the EPA finally banned the use of DDT in response to years of lawsuits filed by the Environment Defense Fund, another organization inspired by Carson's work. Unfortunately, Carson herself was not able to see the ecological progress her work inspired: she died at her home in Maine in April 1964.

Sources:
Rachel Carson, *The Silent Spring* (Boston: Houghton Mifflin, 1962);

H. Patricia Hynes, *The Recurring Silent Spring* (New York: Pergamon Press, 1989).

BETTY FRIEDAN

1921-

AUTHOR, WOMEN'S RIGHTS ACTIVIST

Pioneer for Women. Betty Friedan was at the center of the growing women's movement in the 1960s, as the author of one of the most influential books on American women's lives (*The Feminine Mystique,* 1963) and also as one of the founders of the National Organization for Women (NOW). She was the most visible champion of women's rights at the time, even though by the end of the decade more-radical feminist groups had already begun to think of her as old-fashioned.

Stifled Aspirations. The eldest of three children, Friedan had a comfortable childhood until the Depression hit; as her parents struggled to support the family she watched her mother lash out at her father in "impotent rage." She determined that she would find the fulfillment for herself that her mother never did. In 1943, as a summa cum laude graduate from Smith College, Friedan made a decision that ran against her career aspirations: she turned down a fellowship to study psychology at the University of California, Berkeley, because her boyfriend warned her that it could end their relationship.

The Move to the Suburbs. That relationship ended anyway, and Friedan moved to New York City and began work at a labor news service. Within a few years she found herself nearly alone. Her friends had all begun to marry and move to the suburbs, as many young people did at the end of World War II. Afraid of loneliness, she met and married Carl Friedan, and in 1949 they had their first child. Friedan took a year's maternity leave. She returned to her job a little reluctantly, but when she became pregnant with a second child she was fired. Leaving New York, she and her husband found a home in the suburbs, and Friedan prepared to settle into a full-time career as a mother.

Freelance Writer. Before long Friedan began to feel frustration about her role, however: "Carl's vision of a wife was one who stayed home and cooked and played with the children. And one who didn't compete. I was not that wife." She attempted to find some fulfillment outside of the home by taking up journalism again, writing freelance articles for magazines. Her early articles were frequently about women as wives and mothers and appeared in magazines such as *Cosmopolitan* ("Millionaire's Wife," September 1956) and *Parents* ("Day Camp in the Driveway," May 1957). When she tried to sell stories about women who were living outside of traditional roles, she was told that such profiles were not really what American women wanted to read.

Women's Regret. In 1957 Friedan considered with interest the responses to a questionnaire her fellow Smith alumnae had filled out as their fifteenth class reunion approached. She had planned to use the survey results as the basis of an article for *McCall's.* Ninety-seven percent of the women who responded were married, and 89 percent of them were housewives. They claimed to be happy with their homes and family, but many of them expressed regret that they had not put their education to serious use. Depressed by her findings and by the lack of ambition she discovered among the Smith students about to graduate, Friedan wrote an article she called "The Togetherness Woman"; but because of its pessimistic tone, *McCall's* decided not to run it. Other women's magazines turned it down, as well, or agreed to run it only with substantial revisions. "Only the most neurotic housewife would identify with this," an editor for *Redbook* told her.

Writing *The Feminine Mystique*. Friedan was inspired by the success of Vance Packard, whose *The Hidden Persuaders,* a book about hidden messages in advertising, started out as an article he could not get published. Friedan began to think of "The Togetherness Woman" as a full-length book. She had little trouble selling the idea to a book publisher: while magazines might avoid controversy rather than risk offending advertisers, the books that frequently sell best are the most controversial. Over the next five years she worked on the project, accumulating overwhelming evidence of discontent among American women. The results of her research were published as *The Feminine Mystique.*

Questioning Woman's Role. The American society Friedan portrayed in the book bombards its women members with messages that they are worthy only as wifes or mothers, that they can be completely fulfilled through serving the other people in their families. She quoted *Newsweek* from 1960: "A young mother with a beautiful family, charm, talent and brains is apt to dismiss her role apologetically. . . . A good education, it seems, has given this paragon among women an understanding of the value of everything except her own worth." Even when it acknowledged the problem, the mainstream press took at face value women's insistence that their families were most important to them: as *The New York Times* observed, "All admit to being deeply frustrated at times by the lack of privacy, the physical burden, the routine of family life, the confinement of it. However, none would give up her home and family if she had the choice to make again." The effect of such statements, however, was to make the woman who might have made a different choice feel as if there was something wrong with her.

Expanding Possibilities for Women. Friedan exposed the lie of the "feminine mystique," that family and a career are not both possible for a woman. Housework should not be seen as a career, she argued, but as "something that must be done as quickly and efficiently as possible . . . to save time that can be used in more creative ways." For the women Friedan had talked to, a role in society outside the home did not distance them from their families but helped them feel more truly alive — and consequently, made life at home more bearable. "If we continue to produce millions of young mothers who stop their growth and education short of identity, without a strong core of human values to pass on to their children," she concluded, "we are committing, quite simply, genocide."

Leading the Movement. After the publication of *The Feminine Mystique* Friedan found herself in the middle of a growing movement for women's rights, dedicated to addressing seriously the very problems her book discussed. In 1966, covering the Third National Conference of Commissions on the Status of Women as a journalist, Friedan discussed with other women the idea of an organization like the NAACP to protect women's rights. Friedan wrote on a napkin the basis of the group: "to take the actions necessary to bring women into the mainstream of American society, now, full equality for women, in fully equal partnership with men, NOW. The National Organization for Women." NOW elected Friedan as its first president at its organizing meeting in October 1966.

Fighting Sex Discrimination. NOW took an aggressively political stand on matters such as divorce-law reform, child care for working women, and equal pay in the professions. One of its first major victories came in 1967, when the group persuaded President Lyndon Johnson to include sex discrimination as a basis for affirmative action. NOW also pressured the EEOC to enforce the sex-discrimination prohibition called for by the 1964 Civil Rights Act. By the end of 1967 the group had more than one thousand members. Over the next several years NOW became more liberal, taking up abortion rights as another cause and defending Valerie Solanis, the actress who shot Andy Warhol, as a feminist revolutionary. For Friedan the support of Solanis was too radical, and many younger, more militant feminists left the group to pursue their own agendas. Friedan permanently lost faith with the more liberal members of NOW when she referred to radical lesbians as a "lavender menace" which threatened to undermine the organization. Although Friedan was still a very visible member of the women's liberation movement, it had quickly grown beyond her leadership.

Sources:

Betty Friedan, *The Feminine Mystique* (New York: Norton, 1963);

David Halberstam, *The Fifties* (New York: Villard, 1993);

Rosalind Rosenberg, *Divided Lives: American Women in the Twentieth Century* (New York: Hill & Wang, 1992).

EDIE SEDGWICK

1943-1971

ACTRESS, MODEL

Chelsea Girl. Edie Sedgwick embodied several of the dominant cultural obsessions of the 1960s: glamour, celebrity, and self-destructiveness. She made a name for herself as one of the personalities that gathered around pop artist Andy Warhol and his arts Factory. As one of Warhol's "superstars" she was featured in several of his unusual films of the time, including the epic-length *Chelsea Girls*. At the same time she was a successful model, appearing in *Vogue* and *Life* magazines. A child of privilege, Sedgwick became absorbed in the often frantic social scene of the decade. She died in obscurity of a drug overdose in 1971.

A Child of Privilege. Edie Sedgwick came from a background of wealth on both sides of her family. She was born in 1943, the sixth of eight children. Her father was a gentleman rancher who added to his inherited fortune considerably when oil was discovered on his California land. Edie, a spoiled, emotional child, was sent to school in the East when she was a teenager. Unhappy at school, she did poorly; at seventeen, she was institutionalized, first at a thousand-dollar-a-month sanatorium, and then at a more restrictive facility. When she was finally released nearly three years later, she went to study sculpture in Cambridge, Massachusetts, and be near the intellectual life surrounding Harvard University.

The Factory. Beautiful and eccentric, Sedgwick became the darling of the Cambridge social circle. She was always on the lookout for new excitement, however, and soon she moved on to New York City. She met Andy Warhol there in 1965. Warhol was just starting to receive national attention for his contributions to the pop art movement, which found inspiration in the design of soup cans, pictures of celebrities, and panels of comic strips. In 1963 Warhol had moved into a loft in Greenwich Village which he called the Factory. The Factory served as his home and studio, but also as the set for his movies and as the headquarters for a growing social circle, mostly young would-be celebrities. The activity in the Factory was nonstop and had Warhol as its center; but the artist, a shy man, seemed strangely removed from it all.

Youthquaker. Warhol was immediately impressed with Sedgwick, and he began featuring her in the films he was making at the time: rambling parodies of traditional Hollywood movies that were favorites of New York's underground art scene. Sedgwick made a striking companion for Warhol, dressed in a T-shirt and black tights, her short hair bleached to look like his. Her relationship with Warhol was platonic, but Sedgwick was briefly involved with several of the more notable people to pass through the Factory scene, including singers Bob Dylan and Lou Reed. By August of that year she was receiving national attention: *Vogue* magazine proclaimed her a "youthquaker," and *Life* featured her in a fashion layout in November of that year, saying that she was "doing more for black tights than anyone since Hamlet."

Addiction. Unfortunately, at about the same time, Sedgwick became addicted to a variety of drugs, in particular the "vitamin shots" — which included heavy doses of amphetamines — that certain fashionable New York doctors administered to a large clientele. The youth scene in New York had certain ties to the hippie movement that was developing in California at the same time: both were fueled by loud rock music and widespread drug use, but the atmosphere in New York had an edgy, frantic quality that the hippies lacked (at least at first). While the hippies saw drugs as a means to a higher consciousness, the drug scene in New York City revolved around potentially lethal combinations of amphetamines, barbiturates, and heroin.

An Unhealthy "Look." As Sedgwick's drug use increased, her behavior became more erratic. In late 1965 she left Warhol and the Factory with hopes of making it as a mainstream actress. Ironically, although she was wasting away from drug use, her thinness gave her the "look" popular in fashion at the time. Consequently, she was featured in *Vogue* again in March 1966. For a time she lived in the Chelsea Hotel — a famed bohemian location — and was nearly responsible for burning it down when she fell asleep with a lighted cigarette. In December 1966 she returned to California for an unhappy Christmas reunion with her family, and she was again hospitalized. When she returned to New York she made a go at a major film project, *Ciao! Manhattan,* which featured, among other counterculture celebrities of the time, beatnik poet Allen Ginsberg; but the project was never finished, and she was unable to stop her slide into the life of a hard-core drug addict.

A Pathetic End. While the society columns in New York newspapers were wondering what had happened to her, Sedgwick was back in California, showing the effects of serious brain damage from her drug use. She finished *Ciao! Manhattan,* and the new scenes showed her in pathetic contrast to the model she had been. She married Michael Post, a fellow addict she had met in the hospital,

in 1971. Sedgwick made a brief television appearance in the landmark 1971 television documentary series *An American Family,* as a friend of Lance Loud, who, while the cameras rolled in a later episode, confessed to his family that he was gay. Sedgwick died of a drug overdose on 15 November 1971.

Source:
Jean Stein and George Plimpton, *Edie: An American Biography* (New York: Knopf, 1982).

DR. BENJAMIN SPOCK

1903-

CHILD-CARE EXPERT, PEACE ACTIVIST

Voice of Conscience. By the 1960s Dr. Benjamin Spock was known not only for his *Common Sense Book of Baby and Child Care,* which had served as a guide to the parents of baby boomers since its first edition was published in 1946 — for the next two years only the Bible was a bigger seller — he was also one of the nation's most prominent voices of conscience, participating in protests against nuclear weapons and the war in Vietnam. In 1960 Spock had campaigned for John F. Kennedy, appearing on television with Jacqueline Kennedy to help court the "mother's vote." President Kennedy's announcement of further arms testing in 1962, however, convinced Spock of the grave danger posed by the cold war arms race. "After that," he said, "I was hooked for the peace movement."

SANE. That year he became a member of SANE, an antinuclear group, despite his fears that his association with the movement would be upsetting to the parents he had spent several decades reassuring. In April 1962 he wrote the copy for a full-page advertisement in support of SANE, and the next year he became the national co-chairman of the group. In 1964 he also participated in the Doctors for Johnson Committee, believing (as did many liberal Americans) that Democratic presidential candidate Lyndon Johnson offered the best hope for ending the conflict in Vietnam. Within months after Johnson took office, however, it became clear that the president had no intention of leading the country out of the war in Southeast Asia. Frustrated that Johnson had apparently reneged on his campaign promises, Spock began to participate in peace marches.

Turning Radical. His willingness to give his support to any group that advocated an end to the war caused friction between Spock and the other leaders of SANE. In the tense days of the cold war, when any liberal ran the risk of being called a Communist, SANE had carefully weeded any Communists out of its membership. In the interest of neutrality, the organization withheld its support from any criticism of U.S. involvement in Vietnam that did not also criticize the Communist leader of North Vietnam, Ho Chi Minh. But Spock had long ago gotten over any aversion he had to demonstrating for peace and had aligned himself with the increasingly militant New Left. When SANE refused to support a series of national antiwar protests in the spring of 1967, Spock resigned from his chairmanship. In the fall of that year he accepted the cochairman's position for the National Conference for New Politics, whose radical platform was more to his liking.

Charged. Spock retired from his position as professor of child development at Western Reserve University in June 1967, a year earlier than he had planned, in order to devote his time to the peace movement and to his other love, sailing. He traveled extensively over the next several months, speaking at college campuses and rallies across the country. In December 1967 he met with two FBI agents who wanted to question him about several demonstrations in which he had participated in October. In January 1968 Spock was charged, along with five alleged "co-conspirators," for attempting to hinder the military draft and to "sponsor and support a nation-wide program of resistance" to the Selective Service. According to the accusations, Spock had helped distribute a printed statement titled "A Call to Resist Illegitimate Authority"; had helped collect draft cards at various rallies in October 1967; and on 20 October 1967 had demonstrated in front of the Department of Justice and had left the collected draft cards there.

The Trial of Dr. Spock. When the case came to trial each defendant had his own legal counsel, which made for a confusing defense. Spock's lawyer was Leonard Boudin, who was known for his defense of political activists and who had defended more than a few of the leftists who had been called before the House and Senate anti-Communist hearings in the 1940s and 1950s. The other defense counsels encouraged their clients not to take the stand, but Spock and Boudin were adamant that the doctor would testify on his own behalf. Before the trial Spock and his lawyer tried to offer a "Nuremburg defense": that is, they wanted to indict the war itself as illegal and immoral and claim that participation in it amounted to a war crime. The motion to challenge the legitimacy of the war in court was denied. During the trial Spock's counsel brought forth a crowd of character witnesses, many of whom were harrassed by the judge, who seemed hostile to the defendants. Spock's own testimony enabled him to offer his views on the war in strong, compassionate terms. "What is the use of physicians like myself trying to help parents bring up children, healthy and happy, to have them killed in such numbers for a cause that is ignoble?," he asked while on the stand.

Guilty as Charged. After three weeks of trial, the case was turned over to the jury, who found all of the Boston Five (as the defendants had come to be known) guilty as charged. Declaring that their crime had been "in the nature of treason," the judge sentenced each of them to two years in a federal penitentiary. When the convicted conspirators left the courtroom, they were greeted by a crowd of several thousand demonstrating on their behalf, including linguist Noam Chomsky and poet Robert Lowell. At a press conference that followed the sentencing, Dr. Spock gave no sign of ending his resistance to the war, calling it "totally, abominably illegal." He admonished Americans to "Wake up before it's too late! Do something now!"

Source:
Jessica Mitford, *The Trial of Dr. Spock* (New York: Knopf, 1969).

PEOPLE IN THE NEWS

Frank Caplan of Creative Playthings, introduced to the American child "Little Brother," the first anatomically correct male baby doll, in 1966.

In 1968 *Cosmopolitan* magazine chose twenty-two-year-old **Candace Bergen** to be their political correspondent with the Robert Kennedy campaign.

In 1964 **Chief John Big Tree,** 103, one of the models for the 1916 Indian-head nickel, traveled to New York City to participate in Chase Manhattan Bank's one-hundredth anniversary celebration of the nickel.

On 13 June 1960 **Jacqueline Cochran,** 54, the first woman to fly at the speed of sound, became the first woman to travel at twice the speed of sound when she rode in the backseat of a Navy 3-J Vigilante jet.

In May 1968 Stanford University elected **Vicky Drake,** 21, who worked between semesters as a topless dancer, as its student-body president.

American evangelist **Billy Graham** was attempting to hold a crusade in London's Soho district in June 1966, when he was besieged by two thousand revelers, including a stripper who jumped on to the hood of Graham's car.

James Meredith, who desegregated the University of Mississippi as its first African-American student in 1962, began a March Against Fear across Mississippi on 5 June 1966 but got less than twenty-five miles before he was shot and wounded.

Carolyn Mignini, 17, of Baltimore, Maryland, beat out fifty-one other young women to become Miss Teenage America 1964.

Actors **Kim Novak, Cliff Robertson, Burt Lancaster,** and **Zsa Zsa Gabor** and **Richard Nixon** and his wife were only a few of the hundreds driven from their homes in November 1961 in the worst brushfires in southern California's history.

Marina Oswald, wife of alleged presidential assassin Lee Harvey Oswald, sued the federal government for five hundred thousand dollars for the value of Oswald's confiscated effects, that value being the items' probable worth to collectors.

Lance Reventlow, 28, auto racer and son of Woolworth heiress Barbara Hutton, married the young star of *A Summer Place,* **Cheryl Holdridge,** on 20 November 1964.

Dr. Irving S. Wright told a meeting of the American Medical Association in December 1967 that early retirement can lead to depression, financial problems, and marital strife.

DEATHS

S. Ruth Barrett, 62, educator of the blind, director of the American Bible Society's recording department, 9 March 1961.

Bernard Baruch, 94, unpaid adviser to seven U.S. presidents, financier, and philanthropist, 20 June 1965.

Brace Beemer, 62, former radio actor who portrayed the Lone Ranger from 1941 to 1954, 1 March 1965.

Lenny Bruce (Leonard Alfred Schneider), 40, influential and controversial comedian, 3 August 1966.

Rachel Carson, 56, conservationist and author of *Silent Spring,* 14 April 1964.

Marshall Cassidy, 76, horse-racing official, inventor of stall starting gate, former director of the New York Racing Association, 23 October 1968.

Valentine Davies, president of the Academy of Motion Picture Arts and Sciences since 1960 and of the Screenwriter's Guild since 1949, 23 July 1961.

Walt Disney, 65, cartoonist, studio mogul, and designer of the Disneyland theme park, 15 December 1966.

W. E. B. DuBois (William Edward Burghardt), 95, educator and civil rights pioneer, 27 August 1963.

Ethel DuPont, 49, heiress of the multimillion-dollar E. T. du Pont de Nemours and Company fortune, former wife of Franklin D. Roosevelt, Jr., 25 May 1965.

Charles Edison, 78, industrialist, son of inventor Thomas Edison, Secretary of the Navy (1939–1940), governor of New Jersey (1941–1944), 31 July 1969.

Earl Dewey Eisenhower, 70, younger brother of the former president, electrical engineer, 18 December 1968.

Julius Fleishmann, 68, art patron and philanthropist, heir to Fleishmann Company, director of the Metropolitan Opera, 22 October 1968.

Lawrence Kelso Frank, 77, behavioral scientist, child-development authority, longtime author of the "Parent and Child" column in *The New York Times Sunday Magazine,* 23 September 1968.

Wilfred John Funk, 83, publisher, lexicographer, president of Funk and Wagnalls (1925–1940), 1 June 1965.

Dr. Carl Gottfried Hartman, 88, zoologist whose research in embryology and gynecology contributed to birth-control advances, 1 March 1968.

Spike (Lindsay Armstrong) Jones, 53, bandleader of the City Slickers musical group, 1 May 1965.

Natalie M. Kalmus, 87, codeveloper of Technicolor for motion pictures, 15 November 1965.

Helen Keller, 87, blind and deaf writer and humanitarian, 1 June 1968.

Joseph P. Kennedy, 81, financier and ambassador, father of John, Robert, and Edward Kennedy, 18 November 1969.

Jack Kerouac, 47, novelist, chronicler of the Beat Generation, 21 October 1969.

Anita King, 74, silent-film actress, the first woman to make a solo auto trip from New York to California (1916), 10 June 1963.

Lenox Riley Lohr, 76, president of Chicago's Museum of Science and Industry, former president of NBC (1936–1940), manager of the 1933–1943 Chicago World's Fair, 28 May 1968.

Daniel Longwell, 69, *Life* magazine executive, president of the American Federation of the Arts (1954–1956), 20 November 1968.

Marilyn Monroe, 36, actress and sex symbol, 6 August 1962.

Henrietta Nesbitt, 89, White House executive housekeeper (1932–1946), author of *White House Diary* (1948) and *The Presidential Cookbook: Feeding the Roosevelts and Their Guests* (1951), 16 June 1963.

J. Robert Oppenheimer, 62, nuclear physicist who directed development and testing of the first atomic bomb, 18 February 1967.

Eleanor Roosevelt, 78, former first lady, diplomat, 7 November 1962.

Helena Rubinstein, 94, Polish-born American beauty expert and cosmetics manufacturer, 1 April 1965.

Upton Sinclair, 90, writer and activist whose *The Jungle* (1906) led to the passage of the Pure Food and Drug Act, 25 November 1968.

Joan Merriam Smith, 28, woman pilot who made a 1963 around-the-world solo flight, 17 February 1965.

Doris Stevens, 70, pioneer of women's movement, organizer of the first National Convention of Women Voters in 1915, 22 March 1963.

Robert Stroud, 73, "Birdman of Alcatraz," authority on birds and bird diseases who was serving a life sentence for murder, 21 November 1963.

Princess Farid-es-Sutanah (Doris Mercer), 74, divorced wife of Iranian prince Farid-es-Sutaneh and former wife of Sebastian S. Kresge, founder of the Kresge department-store chain, 12 August 1963.

Norman Thomas, 84, American Socialist, promoter of social justice and the welfare state, 19 December 1968.

Gloria Morgan Vanderbilt, 60, Swiss-born widow of railroad heir Reginald Vanderbilt and mother of Gloria Vanderbilt, whose custody she lost in a highly publicized court case (1934), 13 February 1965.

Cornelius Westbrook Van Voorhis, 64, radio and film announcer best known for the phrase "Time marches on!" in the *March of Time* radio and movie series of the 1930s and 1940s, 13 July 1968.

Countess Elizabeth von Furstenburg, 62, U.S.-born wife of Count Franz Egon von Furstenburg and mother of actress Betsy von Furstenburg, 28 December 1961.

Aubrey Willis Williams, 74, publisher, lay preacher, and social worker who headed the National Youth Administration (1938–1943), 3 March 1965.

PUBLICATIONS

Kurt Baier, *Values and the Future: The Impact of Technological Change on American Values* (New York: Free Press, 1969);

Warren G. Bennis, *The Temporary Society* (New York: Harper & Row, 1968);

John Brooks, *The Great Leap: The Past Twenty-Five Years in America* (New York: Harper & Row, 1966);

Joe David Brown, ed., *The Hippies* (New York: Time, 1967);

Rachel Carson, *Silent Spring* (Boston: Houghton Mifflin, 1962);

Robert E. Conot, *Rivers of Blood, Years of Darkness* (New York: Bantam, 1967);

George W. Crowell, *Society Against Itself* (Philadelphia: Westminster Press, 1968);

Lincoln H. Day, *Too Many Americans* (Boston: Houghton Mifflin, 1964);

G. William Domhoff, *Who Rules America?* (Englewood Cliffs, N.J.: Prentice-Hall, 1967);

Betty Friedan, *The Feminine Mystique* (New York: Norton, 1963);

James M. Gavin, *Crisis Now* (New York: Random House, 1968);

Paul Goodman, *Drawing the Line* (New York: Random House, 1967);

Goodman, *Freedom and Order in the University* (Cleveland: Case Western Reserve University Press, 1967);

Goodman, *Growing Up Absurd: Problems of Youth in the Organized System* (New York: Random House, 1960);

Goodman, *Like a Conquered Province: The Moral Ambiguity of America* (New York: Random House, 1967);

Goodman, *People or Personnel: Decentralizing the Mixed System* (New York: Random House, 1965);

Goodman, *Utopian Essays and Practical Proposals* (New York: Random House, 1962);

Jules Henry, *Culture Against Man* (New York: Random House, 1963);

Hubert H. Humphrey, *War on Poverty* (New York: McGraw-Hill, 1964);

Jesse Kornbluth, ed., *Notes from a New Underground* (New York: Viking, 1968);

Timothy Leary, *The Politics of Ecstacy* (New York: Putnam, 1968);

Raymond Locke, *America's Race to Decadence: A Study of Political, Economic, Social and Other Decay* (New York: Exposition Press, 1966);

Raymond W. Mack, *Transforming America: Patterns of Social Change* (New York: Random House, 1967);

Edgar May, *The Wasted Americans: Cost of Our Welfare Dilemma* (New York: Harper & Row, 1964);

Robert Rienow, *Moment in the Sun: A Report on the Deteriorating Quality of the American Environment* (New York: Dial Press, 1967);

David Riesman, *Abundance for What? and Other Essays* (Garden City, N.Y.: Doubleday, 1964);

John Pearson Roche, *The Quest for the Dream: The Development of Civil Rights and Human Relations in Modern America* (New York: Macmillan, 1963);

Ronald Segal, *The Americans: A Conflict of Creed and Reality* (New York: Viking, 1969);

Anne W. Simon, *The New Years: A New Middle Age* (New York: Knopf, 1968);

Benjamin Spock, *Problems of Parents* (Boston: Houghton Mifflin, 1967).

Draft-card burning in Washington, D.C.

MEDIA

by JAMES W. HIPP

CONTENTS

Sidebars and tables are listed in italics.

1960

- Daytime radio serials and most other network radio programming end, leaving news and special events coverage.

1 June   The National Council of Churches issues a report assailing television's preoccupation with sex and violence.

26 Sept.   The largest television audience yet measured watches the first of four debates between presidential candidates Vice-president Richard Nixon and Senator John F. Kennedy.

1961

Jan.   The first presidential press conference to be broadcast live on both radio and television is held.

Jan.   Edward R. Murrow leaves CBS for a position with the United States Information Agency.

10 Jan.   Newton Minow is appointed chairman of the Federal Communications Commission (FCC).

9 Mar.   The Washington Post Company acquires *Newsweek* magazine.

May   Minow's speech to the National Association of Broadcasters labels television programming "a vast wasteland."

17 July   John Chancellor takes over from original host Dave Garroway on NBC's *The Today Show*.

24 Sept.   *Walt Disney's Wonderful World of Color* premieres on NBC.

1962

5 Jan.   The *Los Angeles Mirror* and the *Los Angeles Examiner* cease publication.

14 Feb.   First Lady Jacqueline Kennedy leads a White House tour on national television (CBS), showing recent renovations.

20 Feb.   John Glenn becomes the first American to orbit the earth; Walter Cronkite leads the news coverage.

16 Apr.   Walter Cronkite makes his first appearance as the anchorman of the *CBS Evening News*.

7 May   W. A. Swanberg is rejected as a Pulitzer Prize winner for biography by Columbia University trustees. His book *Citizen Hearst* profiles newspaper magnate William Randolph Hearst.

10 July   *Telstar 1*, a communications satellite, is launched; later that same day the first broadcast between the United States and Europe is made.

Sept.   Legislation requiring all new televisions to be manufactured with UHF band tuners is passed.

23 Sept.   ABC broadcasts its first television show in color, the animated program *The Jetsons*.

1963

14 May Newton Minow resigns as head of the FCC.

2 Sept. CBS expands its evening newscast to thirty minutes from fifteen minutes.

22 Nov. President John F. Kennedy is assassinated; television news begins an unprecedented five days of complete coverage.

1964

9 Feb. The Beatles appear on *The Ed Sullivan Show*.

2 Mar. Fred Friendly becomes president of CBS News.

25 Mar. *Relay II* satellite is launched, making transpacific broadcasting possible.

Sept. NBC becomes the first network to broadcast more than 50 percent of its programs in color.

7 Oct. NBC broadcasts the first made-for-television movie, *See How They Run*, starring John Forsythe and Jane Wyatt.

1965

1 Feb. Peter Jennings becomes anchorman for ABC's evening news for the first time.

27 Apr. Edward R. Murrow dies of lung cancer.

7 June Sony introduces the first home videotape recorder.

24 Oct. NBC becomes the first network with thirty minutes of network news every evening.

9 Dec. The first "Peanuts" television special, *A Charlie Brown Christmas*, is broadcast on CBS.

1966

1 Jan. Robert Kinter is removed as president of NBC, and David Sarnoff gives up day-to-day control of RCA.

24 Apr. The final issue of the *New York Herald Tribune* is published.

1967

Jan. National Educational Television offers the first coast-to-coast educational broadcasts.

9 Jan. ABC becomes the last network to expand its news programs to thirty minutes.

15 Jan. Super Bowl I is broadcast on both CBS and NBC; CBS wins the ratings war.

27 Aug. *I Love Lucy* is finally removed from the CBS network schedule and released to local syndication.

1968

1 Jan. Peter Jennings is replaced as ABC evening news anchorman by Bob Young.

6 Sept. Last broadcast of fifteen-minute episodes of soap operas; after a three-day break, the shows return in half-hour format.

17 Sept. *Julia* premieres on NBC; the show, starring Diahann Carroll, is the first to have a black actor in the lead role.

13 Oct. The first live broadcast from space takes place, courtesy of *Apollo VII.*

1969

17 Feb. Robert Wood becomes the president of CBS.

9 June The Supreme Court ruling in *Red Lion Broadcasting Co.* v. *FCC* establishes the fairness doctrine for broadcasters.

13 Nov. Vice-president Spiro Agnew delivers a speech critical of television news.

OVERVIEW

Not a Revolution. In the media, if not in other segments of American life, the 1960s were a decade of consolidation, not revolution. After the radical change brought about by television in the 1950s, the next decade was consumed with evolutionary change as television and radio broadcasters, newspaper and magazine publishers, and the general public attempted to come to terms with the revolution they had made in the previous decade.

Technical Problems. The television industry saw two new technological wrinkles come into widespread use, but neither was a new idea. By the end of the decade the majority of programs were broadcast in color, even if in 1967 only 15 percent of American homes were equipped with color television. UHF-band broadcasting was also given the regulatory go-ahead, though it was still looked down upon as a poor substitute for VHF broadcasting.

Content, or the Lack Thereof. Whatever the technical format of the broadcasting, the content of the programs being shown became a center of controversy during the decade. Federal Communications Commission (FCC) chairman Newton Minow came into office in 1961 with a strong condemnation of the poor quality of most television programs. Network officials responded that they only gave the audience what it wanted. And it apparently did not want the level of cultural broadcasting that Minow and other critics desired.

Public Television. One solution, if not the one Minow advocated, was the formation of the Corporation for Public Broadcasting (CPB) and the Public Broadcasting System (PBS) in 1967. Up and running by 1969, PBS and the programs funded by the CPB gave viewers alternatives to network broadcasting that were not otherwise available until the rise of cable in the 1980s. Children's television was one of the prime concerns of the CPB, one of its first programs being *Sesame Street*. The woeful level of children's programming on the networks was a topic late in the decade, but not until the 1970s was it seriously addressed.

Social Issues. With the social turmoil of the 1960s — the assassinations, the civil rights movement, the anti–Vietnam War protests, the youth culture — television was compelled to address the issues facing the American public. Black Americans gained a more prominent posi-

tion on television during the decade, as did young people. Most critics pointed out that television did a poor job in its attempts at investigating and explaining social problems but that the society at large did not do a good job either. But the goal of bringing more segments of the American public into the world of television was a new and laudable one, however imperfectly realized.

Rise of Television News. The 1960s were the decade of television news. Beginning with President John F. Kennedy, presidential press conferences began to be held according to the needs of television, a change that did not enthrall the print journalists. But even they had to recognize the superiority of television's coverage of the 1963 assassination of Kennedy. The five days of almost-continuous coverage given by the networks to the events surrounding Kennedy's death, the killing of Lee Harvey Oswald, and the Kennedy funeral had a drama and immediacy that other media could not come close to matching.

Radio. Other big news events throughout the decade — the Vietnam War, the *Apollo* moon landings — played to the strengths of television and reduced the relative stature that other media had historically enjoyed. Radio, which had for decades been the medium of immediacy, found itself becoming what Newton Minow called "publicly franchised jukeboxes." Helped by the development of the transistor and the truly portable radio set, most radio programmers adapted well to the medium's changed role of providing musical entertainment to young people and automobile drivers.

The Plight of Newspapers. Newspapers, however, were still struggling both with their mission in a world with television and the economics of their changing business. Faced with an audience which now had many more choices for news and entertainment, newspapers also were hit with rising production costs, stubborn unions, and a changing newspaper market. Newspapers found that they were outclassed by television as immediate news outlets and by radio and television as entertainment and as advertising outlets. During the decade most newspaper markets underwent severe rationalization; in New York the number of major daily newspapers shrank from seven in 1959 to three in 1967. Total newspaper circulation in the city was reduced during the same period from 5.1 million to 3.5 million. Total circulation for all newspapers in the United States rose slightly to 62.1 million by 1971 but remained stagnant thereafter. Small-town newspapers were responsible for much of this growth, so larger newspapers were left with a smaller slice of the circulation pie.

Magazines. Magazines faced many of the same troubles as newspapers. By the 1950s and 1960s general-interest magazines were no longer thought of as a major source of entertainment for the general public, despite the fact that circulations had remained steady. As a result, advertising became harder to attract in competition with television and radio. Magazines were also troubled with rising costs at a time when revenues were stagnant. One of the best-known American magazines, the *Saturday Evening Post,* disappeared in 1969, a victim not of a lack of quality but of the public's and advertisers' lack of interest. The great age of the general-interest magazine was over; successful publications were either those which ser-

viced niche markets — such as *Penthouse,* the English soft pornography magazine — or those, like the newsmagazines, which served more utilitarian purposes. The major newsmagazines — *Time* and *Newsweek* — continued to flourish, both part of media empires: *Time,* part of Henry Luce's Time-Life; and *Newsweek,* since 1961 part of Katherine and Philip Graham's Washington Post Company.

The World to Come. Change is constant, though the nature of that change is variable. Just as the revolutionary change of the 1950s had its origins in developments in the 1920s, 1930s, and 1940s, events in the 1960s would not have their full impact until the 1970s, 1980s, and 1990s. The launch of the *Telstar* and *Early Bird* satellites affected the media in the 1960s, but it would be the 1970s and 1980s before opportunities for global broadcasting would be more fully realized. The regulatory mess with UHF broadcasting would affect the development of cable television in the 1980s. The ultimate effects of media changes in the 1960s have yet to be felt fully.

TOPICS IN THE NEWS

Jim McKay, host of *ABC's Wide World of Sports,* at the World Lumberjack Championships

ABC'S WIDE WORLD OF SPORTS

No Viewers. Premiering in April 1961 as a summer replacement series, *ABC's Wide World of Sports* later became the first year-round weekly sports series on network television. Choosing to show sporting events that were uncommon for television at the time — auto racing at Le Mans, soccer in Great Britain, track in the Soviet Union — *ABC's Wide World of Sports* was an immediate critical success that attracted little or no viewer support in its first season.

Arledge. The man behind the show was executive producer Roone Arledge, who had joined ABC Sports as a field producer of *NCAA Football* in 1960. This assignment gave Arledge the idea of a "sports potpourri" to fill the network void when college football games were blacked out locally. ABC brass responded positively to the idea because, although initially the sporting events were to be taped and shown with a week's delay, commercial satellites were to be launched in the mid 1960s and the experience gained from producing *ABC's Wide World of Sports* would be invaluable in presenting live sporting events.

Regular Slot. After its short run from April to September 1961, *ABC's Wide World of Sports* returned to the air in January 1962 in its regular Saturday-afternoon time slot. Among its first shows in 1962 were water-ski championships from Acapulco, Mexico; surfing from Hawaii; and the Grand National horse race from Aintree, England. Arledge was given the opportunity to develop innovative production techniques that made ABC a leader in sports television. The ninety-minute weekly shows were in the beginning produced on a fifty-thousand-dollar budget, each sporting event edited down to eight- to ten-minute segments of highlights.

World Sports. Producer Arledge, announcer Jim McKay, and production assistant (later producer) Chuck Howard traveled around the world searching for the types of events that became a trademark of *ABC's Wide World of Sports:* cliff diving from Mexico, demolition derbies, European skiing, dog-sled racing, and such. The show became a Saturday-afternoon institution and Arledge a powerful executive at ABC.

Olympics. In 1965 he was promoted to vice-president in charge of sports programming, winning the rights for the network to broadcast both the winter and summer Olympics in 1968. In 1967 *The New York Times* television critic Jack Gould praised ABC by saying that their "expertise clearly shows that the coverage of sports on TV can be increasingly inventive, and perhaps also teach a lesson or two to the producer of entertainment programming." Arledge was named president of ABC Sports in 1968.

Sports Strategy. *ABC's Wide World of Sports* raised the level of sports programming and showed the networks that it could be an integral part of their scheduling and business strategies. Arledge was a visionary in the television business, and *ABC's Wide World of Sports* was his first great triumph.

Sources:

"Shoot Craps," *Newsweek,* 59 (1 January 1962): 52;

Christopher H. Sterling and John M. Kitross, *Stay Tuned: A Concise History of American Broadcasting,* second edition (Belmont, Cal.: Wadsworth, 1990);

Huntington Williams, *Beyond Control: ABC and the Fate of the Networks* (New York: Atheneum, 1989).

"A VAST WASTELAND"

Federal Communications Chairman Newton Minow's address to the 39th Annual Convention of the National Association of Broadcasters on 9 May 1961 started a fire of controversy over the content of broadcast television. Minow's characterization of early 1960s programming as "a vast wasteland" entered the public language.

When television is good, nothing — not the theater, not the magazines or newspapers — nothing is better.

But when television is bad, nothing is worse. I invite you to sit down in front of your television set when your station goes on the air and stay there without a book, magazine, newspaper, profit-and-loss sheet or rating book to distract you — and keep your eyes glued to that set until the station signs off. I can assure you that you will observe a vast wasteland.

You will see a procession of game shows, violence, audience-participation shows, formula comedies about totally unbelievable families, blood and thunder, mayhem, violence, sadism, murder, Western badmen, Western good men, private eyes, gangsters, more violence and cartoons. And, endlessly, commercials — many screaming, cajoling and offending. And most of all, boredom. True, you will see a few things you will enjoy. But they will be very, very few. And if you think I exaggerate, try it.

Is there one person in this room who claims that broadcasting can't do better?

Well, a glance at next season's proposed programming can give us little heart. Of seventy-three and a half hours of prime evening time, the networks have tentatively scheduled fifty-nine hours to categories of "action-adventure," situation comedy, variety, quiz and movies.

Is there one network president in this room who claims he can't do better?

Well, is there at least one network president who believes that the other networks can't do better?

Gentlemen, your trust accounting with your beneficiaries is overdue.

Source: Newton Minow, *Equal Time: The Private Broadcaster and the Public Interest*, edited by Lawrence Laurent (New York: Atheneum, 1964), pp. 52–53.

BLACKS ON TELEVISION

First Attempts. The civil rights struggles of the 1950s finally began to filter into the television industry during the 1960s. NBC had broadcast *The Nat King Cole Show* in 1956 and 1957, but southern stations refused to broadcast it, and it was canceled. The new decade saw an increase in roles for black actors, such as the guest-star roles for a couple on *The Dick Van Dyke Show*. Rob Petrie mistakenly believes that his son, Richie, has been accidentally switched at birth and tracks down the couple he believes has his son. The couple turns out to be attractive, middle class, and black.

Bill Cosby. In 1965 NBC paired Robert Culp with black actor Bill Cosby in *I Spy*, an adventure-intrigue show. The easy rapport between Culp and Cosby and the relationship of Cosby's character to Culp's (Culp played a professional tennis star, and Cosby was his trainer-masseur) defused the potential for controversy. The first network show to star a single black character was *Julia*, which premiered on NBC on 17 September 1968, starring Diahann Carroll as a widowed nurse with a young son. Though it was one of the first shows to employ black writers, the show's plots did not accomplish much more than presenting white middle-class concerns with a black character. Despite criticisms by black critics of the show's lack of realism, *Julia* was still a breakthrough.

Positive Change. *Rowan and Martin's Laugh-In* featured black comedians, the best known being Flip Wilson. Wilson had his own show on NBC beginning in 1970, and it was briefly at the top of the ratings. The first black family on a prime-time soap opera, *Peyton Place*, made its appearance in 1968. *The Mod Squad*, featuring Clarence Williams III as one of the three-member squad, premiered in September 1968. Other black characters were included in *Mission Impossible, Land of the Giants, Star Trek, Mannix, Ironside*, and *Hogan's Heroes*.

Problem Areas. Although roles for blacks on television increased during the decade, there was still little programming intended for the black community. Of the 1,135 hours of television programming broadcast monthly by the major national networks in 1969, only one hour — occupied by the monthly *Black Journal* on public television — was intended for the black audience. There were local, mainly public-affairs shows which attempted to fill the need for black programming — *Black on Black* in Syracuse, *Inside Bedford Stuyvesant* in New York, *For Blacks Only* and *Our People* in Chicago, *Jobman Caravan* in South Carolina — but there were few entertainment shows which spoke directly and solely to a black audience.

Network Myopia. The television networks saw the problem in racial terms: white audiences would not watch characters who were different from themselves, and black audiences were not large enough to support shows designed only for them. Paul Morash, executive producer of *Peyton Place*, described the network's solution: "All the

Protesters in the March on Washington decrying the lack of black television shows

Negroes I've seen on TV are colorless — absolutely devoid of character, humor or idiom. They are prideless Negroes, castrated men and desexed females. These people are really gilded Rochesters [Jack Benny's comedic manservant]." Harry Belafonte agreed that "For the shuffling, simple-minded Amos-and-Andy type of Negro, TV has substituted a new one-dimensional Negro without reality."

Problems of Society. At bottom the problem was that white, middle-class America did not know enough about black society to judge whether a representation was unrealistic or offensive. The one-dimensional Negro *was* reality for most white Americans; a realistic portrayal of black America was seemingly beyond the capabilities of network television. The more "realistic" black shows of the 1970s created their own set of problems and questions about perception. Television, as is any other form of popular entertainment, is an imperfect mirror of the society that produces it. The problems of race and television in the 1960s were manifestations of the larger struggles occurring in other segments of society.

Sources:

"Black on the Channels," *Time*, 91 (24 May 1968): 74;

Royal D. Colle, "Color on TV," *Reporter*, 37 (30 November 1967): 23–25;

B. Porter, "The Negro Stereotype," *Newsweek*, 69 (3 April 1967): 59–60;

Louie Robinson, "TV Discovers the Black Man," *Ebony*, 24 (February 1969): 27–30.

CORPORATION FOR PUBLIC BROADCASTING

A National Beginning. In 1966 there were 114 educational-television stations, up from 52 in 1961. But they remained struggling local stations with little money and almost no national, quality programming. In 1967 the tide began to turn with two events. The first was the start of the *Public Broadcasting Laboratory* (*PBL*), an experimental news and features broadcast funded by the Ford Foundation and broadcast on educational television for two hours on Sunday evenings. The second was the publication of *Public Television: A Program for Action*, a report by the Carnegie Commission on the future of educational television.

Commitment of Ford. While the programming produced by the *PBL* was widely derided as boring and without any real significance, the project underscored the commitment of the Ford Foundation to public broadcasting. From 1951 to 1977 the Ford Foundation donated more than $292 million to public radio and television, helping to support stations and to fund programming.

Public Broadcasting Act of 1967. President Lyndon B. Johnson used the Carnegie report as the basis for legislative proposals to create a national system of public broadcasting. The Public Broadcasting Act of 1967 became law in November 1967. The most important part of the legislation created the Corporation for Public Broadcasting (CPB). The purpose of the CPB was to funnel money from the federal government to educational television stations and to underwrite programming. The initial funding by Congress was $5 million.

John W. Macy. John W. Macy was named chief executive of the CPB in 1969. His first programming project was the Children's Television Workshop, which was formed to develop educational shows for children. The first product of the workshop was *Sesame Street*, which premiered on 10 November 1969 and quickly became a favorite of children and television critics.

Public Broadcasting System. The Public Broadcasting System (PBS) was created by CPB in 1969 to aid in

Sesame Street

connecting the educational-television stations. Along with the Ford Foundation, PBS helped create a network of program distribution; one of its goals was to help local stations create their own programs which could then be shared with other stations and broadcast nationally. PBS helped to raise the quality of programming seen on public television and to standardize what was shown across the country.

Slow Support. While widespread viewer support and a large audience would be slow in coming for public television, the passage of the Public Broadcasting Act was a watershed in establishing government support for quality television. While it had little direct effect on the overall quality of television, the CPB at least helped guarantee an outlet for programming not regarded as commercially viable.

Sources:
"Future of Non-Commercial TV: Exclusive Interview with John Macy, Corporation for Public Broadcasting," *U.S. News and World Report,* 67 (8 December 1969): 94–97;

"Meatier than Bonanza," *Business Week* (4 November 1967): 38;

"Whither Public TV?," *Newsweek,* 73 (21 April 1969): 104.

DEATH OF THE SATURDAY EVENING POST

Venerable Institution. When the *Saturday Evening Post* ceased publication with the 8 February 1969 issue, one of the most venerable institutions of American magazine publishing fell victim to the changing media landscape of the post–World War II era.

Middle-class America. The *Saturday Evening Post* claimed ancestry from the 1729 founding by Benjamin Franklin of the *Pennsylvania Gazette.* The *Saturday Evening Post* was, for almost sixty years, the most successful general-interest weekly magazine in the United States. The magazine had first reached its position as a magazine leader under the editorship of George Horace Lorimer, who held that post from 1899 until 1937. During Lorimer's tenure the *Saturday Evening Post* published fiction by Harold Frederic, Ring Lardner, Jack London, Joseph Conrad, William Faulkner, Stephen Crane, Thomas Wolfe, James Branch Cabell, P. G. Wodehouse, Rudyard Kipling, William Dean Howells, and F. Scott Fitzgerald. The mix of quality fiction, good reporting, and nonjingoistic Americanism made the *Saturday Evening Post* into the widely recognized voice of middle-class America. President Franklin Roosevelt was said to read the *Saturday Evening Post* when he wanted to find out what the middle class was thinking. In 1952 circulation was 4.2 million readers for the five-cent magazine.

Decline of the Mass-market Magazine. But the 1950s were the high-water mark for the mass-market magazines. As more televisions were sold and more and more television stations went on the air with broadcasts, the nature of American entertainment changed radically. Mass-market magazines fought television by trying to increase circulation, but this in turn raised the price of ads for companies who might advertise. In the mid 1950s the advertising base for the *Saturday Evening Post* was reduced when a full-page ad cost forty thousand dollars. By the end of the 1950s the Curtis Publishing Company, which owned the *Ladies' Home Journal, Holiday,* and *American Home* in addition to the *Saturday Evening Post,* had severe financial problems despite the fact that circulation and ad revenue at its magazine holdings were at all-time highs.

Last Try. From 1960 through 1963 Curtis was losing great amounts of money. The board of directors, which

Willie Morris's recollections of when he was hired to be an editor at *Harper's* magazine in 1963 give a glimpse of the New York magazine world as its old ways were dying and the new ways were yet to emerge.

Then abruptly, he [*Harper's* editor in chief John Fischer] asked:

"How would you like to come to work at *Harper's?*"

"To do what?"

"To be an editor. You've had some sturdy editorial experience, you've been around the country, your writing is adequate and sometimes better than adequate. We can't pay much, but if you're fool enough to want to live in New York, it'll get you by."

"How much?" I asked.

"$115 a week to start, and more if you work out."

$115 a week! I had been making more than that on the *Texas Observer*, and New York was rumored to be the most expensive city in Christendom. I said this, diplomatically, adding that I had a wife, and a young son who ate enough to keep three doberman-pinchers in good health.

Fischer relented, went up to $125, and said he would give me a thousand dollars to help me get settled in the city. "And if you don't like it," he said, "try it a month or so, and you can leave with no hard feelings."

"When do I start?," I asked.

"As soon as you want. Find an apartment first if you wish." He paused, waving goodbye to a publisher. "There's only one other problem, and that's space. I don't know where the hell we're going to put you. Every inch of space is taken up in the office. We'll just have to move you around until there's a permanent place." For some reason I thought he might be joking until I started to work several days later. I worked in a hallway, in an alcove, and one week in a kind of a large linen closet, carrying my manuscripts from place to place. But even the linen closet turned out to have better acreage than the reporters had at the *New York Times.*

Source: Willie Morris, *North Toward Home* (Boston: Houghton Mifflin, 1967).

---

included no members with any hands-on magazine experience, was unsure of what to do. In 1964, reacting to the demands of the staff, the board hired William A. Emerson as editor of the *Saturday Evening Post*. He would be its last. His introduction as editor made clear the plight of the magazine:

My name is William A. Emerson, Jr. I am the new editor of the *Saturday Evening Post.* I stand before you perfectly equipped to be the editor of the *Post* because the "A" in my name stands for Appomattox. My family have been losers for generations.

Old Vision. Yet economics was not the only problem at the *Saturday Evening Post*. Its optimistic picture of a self-confident America was at odds with the changing tenor of the times. The Vietnam War, the civil rights struggle, and the cold war all combined to make the Norman Rockwell view of the United States — Rockwell painted *Saturday Evening Post* covers — seem a bit naive. Technology and a changing society and world had made a great institution dispensable.

Sources:
"Death of an Institution," *Newsweek,* 73 (20 January 1969): 52–53;

Michael M. Mooney, "The Death of the Post," *Atlantic Monthly,* 224 (November 1969): 70–76;

David Schanche, "We Call on the Saturday Evening Post — For the Last Time," *Esquire,* 72 (November 1969): 40–60.

NEWSPAPERS IN THE 1960S

Struggle and Decline. The decade of the 1960s was one of continued struggle and decline for newspapers. In 1909 there were 689 cities in the United States that had competing daily newspapers; by 1963 that number had shrunk to 55. Among major cities that number was down to 20. Over 1,400 cities had only one newspaper or two papers owned by the same publisher. Chains such as Scripps-Howard, Hearst, Newhouse, Knight, and Cox bought up papers around the country, having the effect of making newspapers more alike editorially regardless of the competitive status. Also people began to move outside the cities to the suburbs, taking away circulation and targets of advertisers.

Competition. Newspapers in the 1950s and 1960s performed three functions for the public: they provided news information, they provided entertainment, and they were advertising vehicles. The decline of a competitive news environment was a product of the rise of television journalism, as network and local-affiliate news became the new competitive forces. Television obviously provided an entertainment medium more conducive to the general public. As an outlet for advertisers, the new vitality of radio along with television took away many of the advertisers the newspapers relied upon. In 1950 local radio had advertising revenues of $273 million; in 1965 this figure had increased to $889 million. Television ad receipts increased from $171 million in 1950 to $2.5 billion in 1965. Newspaper ads increased from $2.1 bil-

The televised debates between Vice-president Richard Nixon and Senator John Kennedy in 1960 changed forever the form and content of national elections in the United States. For the first time a candidate's attractiveness on television was the ammunition for a political attack. Nixon's poor makeup — an aide plastered his face to cover up his naturally heavy beard — made him appear washed out compared to the youthful, tan-faced Kennedy. Many commentators have claimed that Nixon lost the election because of his appearance. Indeed, Kennedy used the vice-president's appearance as campaign fodder throughout the rest of the election.

At a campaign stop in New Mexico, Kennedy responded to Nixon's claims that the senator was a barefaced liar:

> Two days ago, the Republican candidate, Mr. Nixon, quoted me as having said that the Republicans had always opposed Social Security, and in that wonderful choice of words which distinguishes him as a national leader, he asserted that this was a barefaced lie. Having seen him four times close up in this campaign, and made-up, I would not accuse Mr. Nixon of being barefaced — but I think the American people next Tuesday can determine who is telling the truth.

Source: Joseph P. Berry, *John F. Kennedy and the Media: The First Television President* (Lanham, Md.: University Press of America, 1987), pp. 125–126.

---

lion to $4.4 billion. But this revenue was spread among 1,751 daily papers and 562 Sunday papers as against only 604 television stations.

Paring Down. Cities were increasingly left with one newspaper because that was all that the city could support economically. Cities such as New York saw the number of daily newspapers drop because the major advertisers — such as Macy's or Bloomingdale's — could no longer afford to buy huge advertising spreads in both *The New York Times* and the *New York Herald Tribune*, for example. New York papers were also faced with union troubles, some papers having to deal with as many as ten unions when renegotiating a contract. While other cities, such as Nashville, Miami, and Tucson, had competing papers functioning under joint operating agreement — in which they shared production facilities — New York unions threatened strikes to prevent the reduction in labor that would result from such a move.

New York. The practical costs of this operating environment showed up in the stories of failed papers across the country. The most famous, and possibly best, newspaper to fold was the *New York Herald Tribune*, which finally succumbed to a long illness on 24 August 1966. The *New York Herald Tribune* was founded as the *New York Herald* in 1835 and merged with the Horace Greeley–founded *New York Tribune* in 1924. During its prime, as Jimmy Breslin writes, "It was a fatter and far better-written paper than the [New York] *Times*." Its list of contributors included John O'Hara, Walter Kerr, Richard Harding Davis, Walter Lippmann, Red Smith, Art Buchwald, and Joseph Alsop.

Strikes. The decline of the paper was due to mismanagement after the death of owner-editor Ogden Reid in 1947. In an attempt to compete with television, the new owners, Reid's widow and two sons, adulterated the editorial program of the paper, at one time placing a gossip column on page 1. The cachet of the *New York Herald Tribune* slowly evaporated, and financial losses mounted. U.S. ambassador to Great Britain John Hay ("Jock") Whitney bought the paper in 1958 and slowly began to rebuild it, both its circulation and its editorial base. By 1962 circulation was up to 411,000 and gaining 1,000 per week. Then in 1962 the head of the printers' union called a strike that lasted 114 days; when it ended, circulation was crippled and annual losses ran to $5 million.

Merger. In April 1966 the *New York Herald Tribune* was merged with two troubled afternoon dailies, the *New York World-Telegram & Sun* (itself a merged paper) and the *New York Journal-American*. On 24 April 1966 another strike started and lasted 113 days; the *New York*

In August 1962 the Soviet Union purchased advertising space in three American and four foreign newspapers to reprint Soviet premier Nikita Khrushchev's speech to the Soviet Peace Congress. For $32,500 the Soviets had the speech printed in the *New York Herald Tribune*, the *Kansas City Star*, the *San Francisco News-Call Bulletin*, the Montreal (Canada) *Star*, the Ottawa (Canada) *Journal*, the Winnipeg (Canada) *Free Press*, and the *Manchester* (England) *Guardian*.

The *Washington Post* was also approached to run the text of the speech. The *Post* instead offered to run the speech in its news columns at no cost if a Soviet newspaper would agree to run President John F. Kennedy's speech on disarmament given that month to the United Nations General Assembly. The Soviets never replied to the offer by the *Post*.

Herald Tribune was never again published. The paper that did remain, called the *New York World-Journal-Tribune*, lasted only until 1967. There were scattered successes among the failures. *New York Newsday,* founded in 1940 and actually published on Long Island to serve the suburban community, took much of the circulation and advertising revenue from the city dailies.

Lower Quality. Competition among the newspapers and with television and radio had the effect of lowering the quality of the major papers. Many executives believed that a national paper might succeed where a large city daily did not. *The New York Times* began a national edition, and the *Wall Street Journal* became a national business paper by establishing printing and distribution centers in eight locations across the country. The publisher of the *Wall Street Journal,* Dow-Jones, started the *National Observer,* a general-interest weekly paper, in 1962, but it failed to generate the huge circulation expected and was closed. It took until the 1980s and the Gannett group's *USA Today* to strike the right formula for a national general-interest paper.

Sources:

Ben H. Bagdikian, "The American Newspaper Is Neither Record, Mirror, Journal, Ledger, Bulletin, Telegram, Examiner, Register, Chronicle, Gazette, Observer, Monitor, Transcript nor Herald of the Day's Events: It's Just Bad News," *Esquire,* 67 (March 1967): 124, 138;

"Big Newspapers Hit by Move from Cities to Suburbs," *Business Week* (27 May 1961): 103–104, 109;

Jimmy Breslin, "A Struck Paper, Famous and Needed, Goes Down," *Life,* 61 (26 August 1966): 26–29;

Richard Kluger, *The Paper: The Life and Death of the New York Herald Tribune* (New York: Knopf, 1986);

"Newspapers Fight a Dollar Deadline," *Business Week* (11 September 1965): 136, 138, 140, 143;

"A Wallflower at Five," *Newsweek,* 69 (27 February 1967): 54–55;

"What's Happening to Newspapers," *U.S. News and World Report,* 54 (28 January 1963): 81–82;

"When Unions Killed a Major Newspaper," *U.S. News and World Report,* 61 (29 August 1966): 70–72;

"Winds of Change for Newspapers," *U.S. News and World Report,* 60 (25 April 1966): 67–69.

NEWSWEEK PURCHASED

Powerhouse. The purchase of *Newsweek* magazine by the Washington Post Company on 9 March 1961 created a formidable print-news company. The *Washington Post,* already powerful as the leading morning newspaper in the U.S. capital, bought the second most read newsmagazine in the country. In January 1961 *Newsweek* had a circulation of more than 1.4 million, second only to Henry Luce's *Time.*

Death of Astor. *Newsweek* had been controlled by philanthropist Vincent Astor. On his death in 1959 his controlling 59 percent stock interest was transferred to the Astor Foundation, which soon began quietly to look for a buyer. The magazine had been founded in 1933 as *News-Week.* Astor had acquired his interest in 1937 through a merger with his magazine, *Today.*

1960–1961
1. *Gunsmoke* (CBS)

2. *Wagon Train* (NBC)

3. *Have Gun Will Travel* (CBS)

4. *The Andy Griffith Show* (CBS)

5. *The Real McCoys* (ABC)

6. *Rawhide* (CBS)

7. *Candid Camera* (CBS)

8. *The Untouchables* (ABC)

9. *The Price is Right* (NBC)

10. *The Jack Benny Show* (CBS)

1964–1965
1. *Bonanza* (CBS)

2. *Bewitched* (ABC)

3. *Gomer Pyle (U.S.M.C.)* (CBS)

4. *The Andy Griffith Show* (CBS)

5. *The Fugitive* (ABC)

6. *The Red Skelton Hour* (CBS)

7. *The Dick Van Dyke Show* (CBS)

8. *The Lucy Show* (CBS)

9. *Peyton Place II* (ABC)

10. *Combat* (ABC)

1968–1969
1. *Rowan and Martin's Laugh-In* (NBC)

2. *Gomer Pyle (U.S.M.C.)* (CBS)

3. *Bonanza* (CBS)

4. *Mayberry R.F.D.* (CBS)

5. *Family Affair* (CBS)

6. *Gunsmoke* (CBS)

7. *Julia* (NBC)

8. *The Dean Martin Show* (NBC)

9. *Here's Lucy* (CBS)

10. *The Beverly Hillbillies* (CBS)

Philip Graham. The negotiating force at the *Washington Post* was Philip Graham, who had gained his position at the newspaper by marrying Katherine Meyer, the daughter of the owner of the *Washington Post,* in 1940. Graham became publisher at the *Washington Post* in 1946. Under his tenure the circulation of the newspaper doubled to four hundred thousand from 1946 to 1956. He also established a strong editorial team at the paper, knowing that a newspaper in the capital had a special burden. The Grahams were strongly partisan Democrats but worked hard to maintain the paper's editorial independence: the *Washington Post* endorsed no candidate in the 1960 presidential election.

The Sale. Graham paid $8 million to the Astor Foundation for its *Newsweek* stock but eventually paid almost $15 million for all the remaining interests. At the contract signing with the Astor group, Graham quipped that he did not know how to write the $2 million earnest check: "I didn't know how the hell to add zeroes after the two million, so I just wrote 'two million dollars' and went squiggle-squiggle with the pen." In addition to *Newsweek* the Washington Post also acquired in the deal a television station, giving the company stations in the capital, Florida, and Connecticut.

New Team. Graham quickly began putting his own editorial team in place at *Newsweek,* promoting Osborn Elliott from managing editor to editor even before the sale was closed. Most of the *Newsweek* staff members were offered new jobs at the magazine or in Washington with the paper. Walter Lippmann was hired to contribute a column, a move that enhanced the magazine's prestige.

Suicide. Graham suffered periodic bouts of manic-depressive illness that brought on erratic behavior. He once threatened to divorce his wife to deprive her and their four children of the Washington Post Company. On 3 August 1963 he shot himself after spending six weeks at a psychiatric hospital. Katherine Graham took over the job of running the Washington Post Company and quickly became an aggressive manager. In 1965 she brought Benjamin Bradlee from *Newsweek* to be the executive editor of the newspaper.

Reputation. The purchase of *Newsweek* added to the reputation of the *Washington Post* as one of the most powerful newspapers in the world and confirmed that the Grahams were a force to be reckoned with, not only in Washington but also in New York. More important, the acquisition increased the amount of editorial talent available to both publications. Over the years *Newsweek* continued to trail *Time* in circulation, but many critics considered it the stronger magazine editorially.

Sources:
"Magazine for Sale," *Time,* 77 (27 January 1961): 44;

"*Newsweek*'s News," *Time,* 77 (17 March 1961): 67;

"Restless Publisher: Philip Leslie Graham," *New York Times,* 10 March 1961, p. 17;

Harrison E. Salisbury, "Washington Post Buys Newsweek," *New York Times,* 10 March 1961, p. 17.

NEW YORK REVIEW OF BOOKS

Starting Up. First published in February 1963 during a New York newspaper strike, the *New York Review of*

CRONKITE DECLARES STALEMATE

When Walter Cronkite returned from Vietnam in March 1968, after viewing the situation on the ground following the February Tet offensive, the news anchor went on the air to express his editorial opinion about the American war effort. He first hosted a special report on the war Tuesday evening, 5 March 1968, and then read a personal statement on the *CBS Evening News* on 6 March 1968. It was the latter statement that had the greater impact.

> We have been too often disappointed by the optimism of the American leaders, both in Vietnam and in Washington, to have faith any longer in the silver linings they find in darkest clouds. . . . It seems now more certain than ever that the bloody experience in Vietnam is to end in a stalemate.

> It is increasingly clear to this reporter that the only rational way out then will be to negotiate, not as victors, but as an honorable people who lived up to their pledge to defend democracy, and did the best they could.

Cronkite's statement shocked the American public, and many scholars have traced the public's growing opposition to the war to Cronkite's disillusioned editorial. President Lyndon Johnson is said to have been influenced by the statement enough not to run for reelection. The political import was reminiscent of Edward R. Murrow's 1954 *See It Now* program on Joseph McCarthy, which was instrumental in changing the tide of McCarthyism. The direct response of the television news media in a political question had the long-term effect of reducing the credibility of the media, even if it did not injure Cronkite's reputation.

Books was intended to fill the void left by the absence of the reviews usually published by *The New York Times* and the *New York Herald Tribune.* It was also intended as a corrective to the intellectually shallow commentary contained in newspaper reviews. As critic Edmund Wilson wrote in the *New York Review of Books* in September 1963, "The disappearance of the *Times* Sunday book section at the time of the printers' strike only made us realize it had never existed." The first issue of the journal was intended to be the only one, but after nearly one hundred thousand copies were sold, the backers decided to publish a second issue in May 1963. The success of the two issues convinced the journal's backers to continue publication semimonthly.

Social Turmoil. Jason Epstein, an editor at Random House, developed the idea for the *New York Review of Books*. His wife, Barbara, and Robert Silvers, a former editor at *Harper's* magazine, have edited the *New York Review of Books* since it was founded. The social chaos in the United States over the Vietnam War led the elitist but left-leaning *New York Review of Books* to adopt surprisingly revolutionary attitudes and radical causes. The Weathermen and the Black Panther party were two of its causes célèbres in the late 1960s. The most famous, and notorious, *New York Review of Books* cover was a diagram of how to make a Molotov cocktail. As the New Left and radical movements disintegrated in the early 1970s, the magazine returned to its left-wing, literary, nonviolent politics.

Fragmentation. The success of the *New York Review of Books* in the early 1960s was a symptom of the failing power of mainstream media outlets, newspapers especially, to continue to connect with a society that, as a whole, was becoming more fragmented with fewer shared interests.

Sources:

Joseph Epstein, "Thirty Years of the 'New York Review,' " *Commentary*, 96 (December 1993): 39–43;

"Good Bet for a Baltic Baron," *Time*, 81 (31 May 1963): 51;

Philip Nobile, *Intellectual Skywriting: Literary Politics & The New York Review of Books* (New York: Charterhouse, 1974).

BROADCASTING STATISTICS, 1965

	AM	FM	TV
Number of Commercial Stations	4,019	1,270	569
Number of Noncommercial Stations	25	255	99
Total Stations	4,044	1,525	668
Network Affiliates	1,302	NA	516
Broadcast Employees	62,607 Combined		47,753
% of Households with Sets	97	40	93

RADIO IN THE 1960S

Growing. The 1960s were a decade of change for radio. Having weathered the challenge of television in the 1950s, something that most observers said was unlikely, radio was growing as an industry in the 1960s, even if individual stations faced struggles.

New Role. But radio was no longer the national entertainment medium it had been in the 1930s and 1940s, playing network programs of comedy, drama, information, and music. Starting in 1948 with the advent of network television, the networks transferred many of their popular radio shows and their stars over to television. Jack Benny, Lucille Ball, *Amos 'n' Andy*, and dozens of other stars and shows ended up on the visual medium.

Transistors. But radio survived and even prospered. In 1949 there were 80 million radios in the United States. In 1965 there were 228 million. Most of the growth was provided by a 1948 invention at Bell Laboratories, the transistor. This small electronic replacement for vacuum tubes provided the technology for the growth of a new market for radios. Radios in houses and in cars became smaller, better, and cheaper. By 1960 a typical AM/FM radio cost only thirty dollars; an AM-only radio cost fifteen dollars.

Music. These two technologies, television and the transistor, transformed radio. With expensive program development switched to television and millions of automobile commuters in need of entertainment, radio stations turned to music. The most successful format was the Top 40 station, which played only the most popular records listed by *Billboard* magazine. By 1967 the National Association of Music Merchants reported that 90 percent of all radio programming was music.

Commercialism. This 90 percent excluded commercials, which brought impressive revenues as radio audiences grew. In 1963 a radio executive testified before a government committee that twenty-five commercials per hour were not excessive. Former FCC chairman Newton Minow decried in 1965 the chaos of commercialism on the radio:

> To twist the radio dial today is to be shoved through a bazaar, a clamorous Casbah of pitchmen and commercials which plead, bleat, pressure, whistle, groan and shout. Too many stations have become publicly franchised jukeboxes.

Disc Jockey. For most stations the glue that held together the incessant mix of music and commercials was the disc jockey, a voice that moved from music to advertisement and back, reminding the listener to what station he or she was tuned. In large markets the deejay could earn up to one hundred thousand dollars annually and become a media star. Murray the K and Klavan and Finch were top deejays in New York, and Bob Crane was the top deejay in Los Angeles. In 1965 Crane left radio to star in the television series *Hogan's Heroes*.

Ethnic Radio. The demise of the national networks, which by the 1960s provided little more than an hourly news break and an occasional sports program, led to the rise of the demographically specific radio station. In addition to stations that catered solely to the young listener with rock 'n' roll music, many stations were in the market for black listeners. For example, in Chicago there were three stations for black listeners: WAAF, which featured jazz and shouts of "Uhuru" (freedom) at the end of its shows; WVON (Voice of the Negro), which played almost entirely music; and WOPA, which ran advertisements tailored to its mostly black, poor audience ("We don't care if you're on ADC [Aid to Dependent Children], just one question: do you want a wig?").

Responding to Society. Radio's success was an example of the power of new technology and the ability of entrepreneurs to adapt to it. It also responded in a telling way to the segmentation of American society.

Sources:

Alfred Bester, "The New Age of Radio," *Holiday,* 33 (June 1963): 56, 58, 61–62, 64, 87–93, 95–97;

William O'Hallaren, "Radio Is Worth Saving," *Atlantic Monthly,* 204 (October 1959): 69–72;

"Radio '65: Everyone's Tuned In," *Newsweek,* 65 (28 June 1965): 80–82;

Desmond Smith, "American Radio Today: The Listener Be Damned," *Harper's,* 229 (September 1964): 58–63.

Early Bird, the first commercial communications satellite

SATELLITE BROADCASTING

International Broadcasting. On 10 July 1962 the international broadcasting of television signals came closer to reality with the launch of *Telstar 1,* a fifty-million-dollar communications satellite owned and operated by the American Telephone and Telegraph Company (AT&T). That same day a picture of an American flag flapping in the breeze was beamed from a television station in Andover, Maine, to Europe. Eleven days later a consortium of the three major television networks broadcast a "picture album" of the United States — the Statue of Liberty, the Golden Gate Bridge, and a herd of buffalo grazing near Mount Rushmore — received by television broadcasters in Great Britain and the European Broadcast Union. The Europeans transmitted pictures of the Roman coliseum, the Louvre, and the British Museum to the United States.

Synchronous Orbit. One year later, on 10 July 1963, CBS showed the potential uses of transatlantic broadcasts when it showed a program called *Town Meeting of the World,* featuring former president Dwight D. Eisenhower, European Common Market founder Jean Monnet, West German parliamentary leader Heinrich von Brentano, and former British prime minister Anthony Eden. Two weeks later the first synchronous-orbit satellite, in step with the rotation of earth, was launched.

Early Bird. In 1965 the first commercial communications satellite, *Early Bird,* was placed in orbit. The same consortium of broadcasters that broke in *Telstar 1* collaborated in the first *Early Bird* relay. Martin Luther King, Jr., Pope Paul VI, French nuclear scientists, U.S. Marines patrolling in the Dominican Republic, and Houston heart-bypass surgeons were shown across the ocean. The following day American networks were switching so frequently from country to country that John Horn, television critic for the *New York Herald Tribune,* suggested that they were acting like a "bunch of kids with a new kite."

Dream. Fred W. Friendly, president of CBS News, issued an instruction to his company that, like so many based on principle, was forgotten in the rush for entertainment dollars:

> Now that the Bird is working for us, CBS News must now make sure it does not find itself working for the Bird. . . . There is a natural tendency to show what we can do physically with the satellite, but it is what we do with it as a news instrument that will distinguish CBS News. Let others turn it into a plaything for bland features. . . . Hard news still counts most.

Source:

Edward Bliss, Jr., *Now the News: The Story of Broadcast Journalism* (New York: Columbia University Press, 1991).

60 MINUTES

First Television Newsmagazine. The first television newsmagazine show, *60 Minutes,* premiered on CBS on

Harry Reasoner and Mike Wallace

24 September 1968 as a bimonthly program in the Tuesday night at 10 P.M. slot. Its cohosts during its first years were veteran news reporters Harry Reasoner and Mike Wallace. The *60 Minutes* format was the brainchild of *CBS Evening News* producer Don Hewitt, who saw the program as a "*Life* magazine of the air." Each hour-long show was divided into three twenty-minute segments, two handled by Wallace and one by Reasoner.

The Interview. The interview subject was the primary segment type, with Wallace and Reasoner featuring during the first year talks with Black Panther Eldridge Cleaver, French-German student radical Daniel Cohn-Bendit, Attorney General John Mitchell, rock singer Janis Joplin, Supreme Court nominee Clement Haynsworth, and My Lai massacre participants Pvt. Paul Meadlo and Capt. Ernest Medina. Some of the segments were criticized as puff pieces, but others, including the show investigating My Lai, were hailed as television journalism at its best. More important, *60 Minutes* showed the networks that news could be packaged as entertainment and sold to advertisers and the public.

The Decline of the Documentary. The newsmagazine helped spell the end of the news documentary, a genre of show that was expensive to produce and not popular with viewers or advertisers. The success of *60 Minutes* was not lost on the other networks, particularly NBC, which introduced *First Tuesday*, a two-hour monthly newsmagazine hosted by Sander Vanocur, in January 1969. *First Tuesday* was ultimately a failure, as were most competing newsmagazine shows until the premiere of *20/20* on ABC in the late 1970s.

Dominance of the Newsmagazine. The effects of the success of *60 Minutes* — the show was finally moved to 7:00 P.M. on Sundays in 1975 — were not clear until the 1990s, when newsmagazines were an increasingly dominant programming format; in 1994 there were no fewer than ten prime-time newsmagazine shows broadcast by the three traditional networks, ABC, NBC, and CBS. The blurring of news and entertainment became a more controversial subject as news budgets were slashed in the late 1980s and early 1990s, and much of the reputation for news gathering was taken by new outlets such as Cable News Network (CNN). While much of that shift was because of technology, the demands of viewers and the effects of programming shifts — some exemplified by *60 Minutes* also had an important effect.

Sources:

Richard Campbell, *60 Minutes and the News: A Mythology for Middle America* (Urbana: University of Illinois Press, 1991);

"Cloaking Pitfalls in Smiles," *Time,* 93 (10 January 1969): 39;

"The Mellowing of Mike Malice," *Time,* 95 (19 January 1970): 57;

"Merry Magazines," *Time,* 93 (11 April 1969): 86.

SMOTHERED SMOTHERSES

Censorship. Tom and Dick Smothers, two clean-cut, conservative-looking comedians, became the causes célèbres for civil libertarians in April 1969 when their television show *The Smothers Brothers Comedy Hour* was canceled by CBS, ostensibly because the Smotherses had failed to fulfill their contract obligations to provide entertainment that met the standards set by CBS. The reason put forth by the Smotherses and most independent observers was censorship.

Risqué and Political. *The Smothers Brothers Comedy Hour* premiered on CBS on 5 February 1967 as a midseason replacement. A Sunday-night show competing against the powerful Western *Bonanza*, the Smothers

The Supreme Court decision in *Red Lion Broadcasting Co.* v. *FCC* on 9 June 1969 institutionalized the modern interpretation of the Fairness Doctrine for radio and television broadcasters, which provided equal time to spokespersons representing conflicting views on political issues. The case arose in 1964 when a radio preacher, Billy James Hargis, used a prerecorded radio program to attack Fred Cook, the author of a book highly critical of Barry Goldwater, the Republican candidate for president. Cook, with Democratic party support, demanded equal time from the almost two hundred stations that broadcast the show to rebut the Hargis charges.

All of the stations except one complied with Federal Communications Commission (FCC) rules on fairness. WGCB, a station in the small Pennsylvania town of Red Lion, instead of offering free airtime to Cook, offered to sell commercial time for the rebuttal. Cook complained to the FCC, which ordered the station to provide Cook with airtime. When the station refused, the FCC took the case to court.

After years of making its way through the court system, the Supreme Court ruled in favor of the FCC. The decision spelled out the extent to which the federal government could regulate the content of broadcast media. In its ruling the Supreme Court gave greater weight to the rights of listeners over the property rights of the owners of broadcast outlets:

> It is the right of the viewers and listeners, not the right of the broadcasters, [that] is paramount. . . . It is the purpose of the First Amendment to preserve an uninhibited marketplace of ideas in which truth will ultimately prevail, rather than to countenance monopolization of that market, whether it be by the Government or a private licensee. . . . It is the right of the public to receive suitable access to social, political, esthetic, moral, and other ideas and experiences which is crucial here.

The controversial decision was unpopular with broadcasters, who believed that they had the sole right to decide what they telecast on their own stations. Most public-interest groups applauded the decision as being in the best interests of the people. The Fairness Doctrine put forth in the *Red Lion* case was abandoned by the FCC in 1987. President Ronald Reagan vetoed legislation that would have codified the doctrine, maintaining that the doctrine actually prohibited free speech by making broadcasters less likely to air controversial material.

Source: Christopher H. Sterling and John M. Kitross, *Stay Tuned: A Concise History of American Broadcasting*, second edition (Belmont, Cal.: Wadsworth, 1990).

Brothers produced a pleasant surprise by placing often among the top thirty shows in weekly ratings. But the network censors were never happy with the brothers. Their humor was sometimes risqué and always political. The favorite target was President Johnson, and there were also drug references (which the censors at CBS were too staid to recognize), sexual innuendos, and humor at the expense of those who would censor art or stifle creativity.

Defending Cuts. According to the Smotherses, CBS had tampered with 75 percent of their material during the two years of their run. During the 1968–1969 television season the Smotherses had repeatedly asked for guidance on what the network objected to and what it would accept. CBS had repeatedly ignored their request and had instead continued to cut material from the show. In defense of their cuts CBS invoked the National Association of Broadcasters Television Code, a vague list of principles, not rules, that had its origin in the proscriptions of the Catholic Legion of Decency.

False Renewal. On 14 March 1969 the show was renewed by CBS for the 1969–1970 season, yet CBS officials continued to say the future of the show was uncertain. On 27 March the Smotherses received a warning from CBS that if they could not accept network oversight it was their duty to tell the network that they wanted out. It also reminded them that their contract called for delivery of their shows on tape no later than the Wednesday before airdate, a contract that had never been met or enforced. The brothers wired back their happiness at being renewed.

Contract Violation. The tape for the 13 April show was already completed, and CBS informed the brothers that for various reasons the 13 April show would have to be shown on 6 April. The 13 April show contained several provocative pieces — a skit with black singer Nancy Wilson on interracial marriage and a "sermon" on the biblical story of Jonah that maintained that the Gentiles on the boat had behaved characteristically by throwing the nearest available Jew overboard. CBS requested and

Tom and Dick Smothers

received cuts on the material they deemed offensive. On Thursday, 3 April, the Smotherses sent a tape of the show. On 4 April CBS canceled it because the Smotherses had violated their contract by late delivery.

Press Reaction. The reaction of the press was decidedly, if not unanimously, pro-Smothers Brothers. *Life* intoned that "Such a network can no more lecture us on questions of responsibility and taste than the SDS [Students for a Democratic Society, a militant protest group] can advise us on etiquette." CBS offices and even affiliates were the objects of protests across the country. The *Wall Street Journal* and *The New York Times* were among the media outlets weighing in against CBS. Only *TV Guide* among mainstream publications was against the Smotherses.

Revealing the Limits. By August 1969 Tom Smothers had lined up a syndicated network of stations to broadcast the program, beginning with the canceled 13 April show. By the summer of 1970 ABC had picked up the show but ran it only two months before canceling it. More provocative than *Rowan and Martin's Laugh-In*, *The Smothers Brothers Comedy Hour* revealed the limits of the networks in terms of political comedy during the turmoil of the late 1960s.

Sources:

Nat Hentoff, "Smothers Brothers: Who Controls TV?," *Look*, 31 (24 June 1969): 27–29;

William Kloman, "The Transmogrification of the Smothers Brothers," *Esquire*, 72 (October 1969): 148–149, 151, 153, 160, 199–200, 201;

Betty Rollin, "The Smothers Brothers: The Naughtiest Boys on TV," *Look*, 31 (13 June 1967): 68–69, 71–73;

"The Unsinkable Tom Smothers," *Time*, 94 (29 August 1969): 52–53.

TELEVISION TECHNOLOGY: COLOR AND UHF

Quality and Growth. The 1960s finally saw the resolution of two technical issues and problems that had plagued television since its early development: color broadcasting and ultrahigh frequency (UHF) stations. Their resolution led to an improvement in broadcast quality and growth in the number of television stations.

Old Standards. Color broadcasting was a problem left over from the debate over broadcast technical standards during World War II. CBS, which had no technical patents relating to black-and-white technology, pushed during the mid 1940s for a standard that would have called for color broadcasting, which CBS had developed, and a large number of stations on the UHF band. CBS

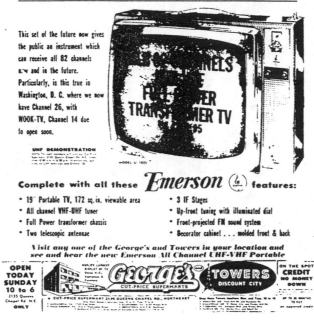

CHAIRMAN NEWTON N. MINOW
Federal Communications Commission

MR. CHAIRMAN: We applaud you for your stand requesting manufacturers to produce all 82 channel (UHF-VHF) television receivers. Emerson Radio (one of the major producers of television in the U.S.A.) now offers an all 82 channel (UHF-VHF) TV set at a price no higher, and in many cases lower, than a 12 channel VHF set.

This set of the future now gives the public an instrument which can receive all 82 channels now and in the future. Particularly, is this true in Washington, D. C. where we now have Channel 26, with WOOK-TV, Channel 14 due to open soon.

Complete with all these *Emerson* features:

- 19" Portable TV, 172 sq. in. viewable area
- All channel VHF-UHF tuner
- Full Power transformer chassis
- Two telescopic antennae
- 3 IF Stages
- Up-front tuning with illuminated dial
- Front-projected FM sound system
- Decorator cabinet ... molded front & back

Newspaper advertisement for VHF-UHF television sets

was opposed by RCA, which had an interest in black-and-white broadcasting and the status quo in regard to the broadcasting band. Joining RCA were the manufacturers of black-and-white and very high frequency (VHF) television sets, who knew that after the war consumers would buy what was available without thought to technological advance.

UHF Stifled. In 1945 the Federal Communications Commission decided that black-and-white television would be standard and that televisions would not be required to carry UHF tuners, effectively stifling that broadcasting frequency. UHF broadcasting would linger in its moribund state until the 1960s.

Government Mandate. A law was finally passed in 1962 that required television manufacturers to include a UHF tuner on every television set beginning in 1964. Still UHF remained a stagnant broadcast band, growing only because the available channels along the VHF band were beginning to become scarce by the mid 1960s. Between 1964 and 1974, 158 new stations went on the air, 111 UHF and only 47 VHF.

Color Freed. The FCC finally approved the CBS system of color broadcasting (which was not compatible with black and white and could not be received on black-and-white televisions) in 1950. In 1953 the order approving CBS color was rescinded, and RCA's system instead was approved, a ruling that recognized the state of the marketplace but also set in concrete somewhat poorer broadcasting standards. NBC, which was owned by RCA, did broadcast some programs in color, but color did not become widespread until the 1960s.

Color Becomes Common. As color television sets became more common in American households, some interesting research was undertaken on the effects on viewers. The networks found people exposed to color programming watched more television and paid more attention to commercials. The networks reacted predictably, and by fall 1965 all three had adopted complete color broadcasting as their goal. The fall 1965 schedule would be 95 percent color on NBC, 50 percent color on CBS, and 40 percent on ABC. By January 1966, 70 percent of all commercials were in color. By the end of that year there were, for the first time, more color televisions than black-and-white televisions being sold. Fifteen percent of all homes in the United States were equipped with color television in 1967; by 1976 this number had risen to 75 percent.

Evolutionary Change. These technological developments, more evolutionary than revolutionary, helped create the broadcast-television environment that lasted from the 1960s to the mid 1980s. Only with the rise of cable television did the system worked out through trial and many errors give way to a system with higher quality and more viewer choices.

Source:
Christopher H. Sterling and John M. Kitross, *Stay Tuned: A Concise History of American Broadcasting*, second edition (Belmont, Cal.: Wadsworth, 1990).

HEADLINE MAKERS

SPIRO AGNEW

1918-

VICE-PRESIDENT AND MEDIA CRITIC

Agnew's Speech. On 13 November 1969 at 7:00 P.M. Vice-president Spiro Agnew made a speech carried live by the three networks that lambasted those networks. The impetus behind Agnew's speech was the press reaction, especially the television news reaction, to a speech on the Vietnam War by President Richard M. Nixon on 3 November 1969. In the speech Nixon called on the support of "the great silent majority of my fellow Americans," asking for their help in achieving his goal of ending the war in victory.

Instant Analysis. Agnew, in his speech, concentrated on the analysis following Nixon's speech, attacking it as "instant analysis and querulous criticism":

It was obvious that their minds were made up in advance.... One commentator twice contradicted the President's statement about the exchange of correspondence with Ho Chi Minh. Another challenged the President's abilities as a politician. A third asserted that the President was now following the Pentagon line. Others, by the expressions on their faces, the tone of their questions and the sarcasm of their responses made clear their sharp disapproval.

Impugning the News Media. But Agnew had a more wide-ranging target than the response to a single speech. The speech was meant to impugn the credibility of the entire television-news medium. Agnew asserted that the network news anchormen were out of touch with Middle America:

To a man [they] live and work in the geographical confines of Washington, D.C., or New York City.... Both communities bask in their own provincialism, their own parochialism. We can deduce that these men read the same newspapers. They draw their political and social views from the same sources. Worse, they talk constantly to one another, thereby providing artificial reinforcement to their shared viewpoints.

Public Response. The public response to the speech was overwhelming. The networks reported calls running in Agnew's favor by a nine to seven margin. The White House reported calls running thirty-five to one in favor of the vice-president. A Gallup poll reported that 77 percent of the public supported the views of the vice-president. The network response was negative, though there was an air of caution given the large positive public response to the speech. CBS president Frank Stanton called the speech "an unprecedented attempt by the Vice-president ... to intimidate a news media." ABC president Leonard H. Goldenson left his response to "the ultimate judgment of the American people." Most newspeople saw correctly that, as William Safire later revealed in his White House memoir, the speech was the beginning of a concerted attack on news organizations by the Nixon White House.

Frank Reynolds. The individual focus of Agnew's ire was ABC anchor Frank Reynolds, who was thought by White House officials to have been biased and unfair during the 1968 campaign. In the case of Reynolds,

Agnew's speech was most effective. Reynolds had responded to Agnew's speech by saying that "There is something much worse than a public official attempting to frighten a broadcaster, and that is a broadcaster that allows himself to be frightened." On 4 December 1970 Reynolds was removed from the anchor desk. His reaction left little doubt whom he saw as the ultimate cause:

> I suppose I ought to say I hope I have not offended anyone in the last two and a half years, but that's not really the truth either because there are a few people I did very much want to bother, and I hope I have.

Long-term Effects. The ramifications of Agnew's speech were manifold. In the short term he garnered many political benefits, helping to restrain the television press from attacks on the Nixon program. In the long term the speech did little good for anyone involved. When the Nixon administration ran into trouble with the Watergate scandal, there was little or no political goodwill in the press. Agnew also had little support when he was forced to resign in 1973 over tax-evasion charges. Also the press suffered from the fact that many Americans agreed with Agnew that the press was out of touch and not to be trusted.

Sources:

"Agnew's Complaint: The Trouble with TV," *Newsweek,* 74 (24 November 1969): 88–90;

Edward Bliss, Jr., *Now the News: The Story of Broadcast Journalism* (New York: Columbia University Press, 1991);

"Flare-Up Over Agnew — Its Meaning," *U.S. News and World Report,* 65 (19 August 1968): 6;

William Safire, *Before the Fall: An Inside View of the Pre-Watergate White House* (Garden City, N.Y.: Doubleday, 1975).

JOHNNY CARSON

1925-

LATE-NIGHT SHOW HOST

Television Institution. Johnny Carson made the late-night NBC program *The Tonight Show* a television institution, far outpacing all competing shows in the ratings. Carson's comedic talents and ability to attract celebrity guests kept viewers tuned in to NBC.

Pat Weaver. *The Tonight Show* was the 1954 brainchild of NBC executive Pat Weaver, who had created *The Today Show* in 1952. The two programs were meant to complement each other and to lock viewers to NBC from the earliest viewing hours to the latest. On 1 October Carson officially replaced the contentious Jack Paar as host of *The Tonight Show.*

Carson versus Paar. During his five-year tenure Paar had made the show a moneymaker for NBC, but under Carson *The Tonight Show* was a blockbuster. By 1965 Carson had raised the audience to an average of 8.7 million nightly viewers, over 300,000 above Paar's peak. Sponsor revenues for the show reached $20 million in 1967, a $4 million increase over the highest billings during Paar's years.

Ballooning Salary. Carson's salary rose with the success of the show. In 1965 he made $200,000 annually, a figure that rose to more than $700,000 in 1967. After a television strike in 1967, NBC raised his salary to over $1 million. His announcer, Ed McMahon, made more than $250,000 in 1967. These salaries paled, of course, in comparison to the profits generated for NBC by *The Tonight Show.*

Beating the Competition. From the beginning the significance of *The Tonight Show* was that it justified the late-night portion of Pat Weaver's vision of programming that would attract viewers from the morning until past midnight. *The Tonight Show* under Carson quickly became a late-night institution, virtually immune to serious competition. The other networks and syndication companies were unable to compete with Carson; *The Joey Bishop Show* failed on ABC after running from 1967 to 1969; *The Las Vegas Show,* starring Bill Dana, failed in syndication in 1967 after only a few months; syndicated shows starring Mike Douglas and Merv Griffin barely made a dent in the solid ratings of *The Tonight Show.* With its ratings power *The Tonight Show* became a money machine for NBC, combining its proven ability to attract advertisers with its low production costs. Carson remained host until 1992.

Sources:

"And Here's Johnny . . . ," *Newsweek,* 59 (12 February 1962): 80;

Ernest Havemann, "24 Hours in the Life of Johnny Carson," *McCall's* (March 1965): 58, 61, 141;

"Here's Johnny," *Newsweek* (8 May 1967): 114–115;

"Insomniacs-ville," *Newsweek,* 66 (19 July 1965): 78;

"Midnight Idol," *Time* (19 May 1967): 104–106, 107, 109, 111;

"Prince of Wails," *Time* (14 April 1967): 88;

Betty Rollin, "Johnny Carson, the Prince of Chitchat, Is a Loner," *Look* (25 January 1966): 98–102;

"Wherrr's Johnny?," *Newsweek,* 69 (17 April 1967): 119.

WALTER CRONKITE

1916-

NEWS ANCHORMAN

The Newsman. During the 1960s Walter Cronkite became the most respected television newscaster in the United States. As the news figure most associated with the biggest news stories of the 1960s — the Kennedy assassination, the Vietnam War, and the *Apollo 11* moon landing — Cronkite was renowned for his honesty, character, and lack of affectation. In 1973 he was voted "the most trusted man in America."

Early Career. After a wide-ranging career as a print and radio journalist that began in 1933, Cronkite became anchorman of the *CBS Evening News* on 16 April 1962. He oversaw the expansion of the *CBS Evening News* from fifteen minutes to thirty minutes on 2 September 1963, featuring an interview with President John F. Kennedy on the first half-hour show. On 22 November 1963 the most significant event in the history of television news to that time occurred: the assassination of President Kennedy.

Covering the Assassination. The assassination was the event that marked the victory of television over newspapers as the news medium of choice for the American public. Taking place between the morning and afternoon papers, the assassination was tailor-made for the immediacy of television. Cronkite was the CBS announcer who relayed, with tears in his eyes, the news that President Kennedy was dead. For the first time CBS suspended regular programming, and it covered the death and funeral from Thursday until after the state funeral on the following Monday. Through the tragedy Cronkite and the other television figures acted as a link for all Americans in a way that other media could not. The coverage of the assassination was confirmation that television was now the leading public news outlet and that Cronkite was the leading newscaster.

Vietnam Statement. Cronkite's coverage of the Vietnam War and his on-the-air conversion from support for the war to disillusionment changed the way television news was viewed and how it went about its business. His March 1968 call for negotiations to end the war was a precedent-setting editorial for a network that had long banned editorializing by its news reporters. In a clear show of Cronkite's credibility, only seven letters were received by CBS criticizing the statement.

Moon Program. During the 1960s Cronkite was known as a staunch supporter of the space program, especially the Apollo moon project. His evident enthusiasm for the rocket launchings he covered helped galvanize public support for the costly program. When *Apollo 11* landed on the moon on 20 July 1969, Cronkite beamed:

> Boy! There they sit on the moon! Just exactly nominal wasn't it . . . on green with the flight plan, all the way down. Man finally is standing on the surface of the moon. My golly!

Following Cronkite. The strengths of Cronkite allowed him leeway in his journalistic practices that opened doors for later journalists. Many of those who followed lacked his strengths.

Sources:
"Cronkite Takes a Stand," *Newsweek*, 71 (11 March 1968): 108;
"Cronkite's Alarm," *Nation*, 204 (27 February 1967): 260–261;
"On the News Beat," *Newsweek*, 63 (1 June 1964): 74–75;
"Pad 19," *New Yorker*, 41 (3 April 1965): 38–40;
"Shake-up at CBS," *Newsweek*, 59 (26 March 1962): 82.

MARSHALL McLUHAN

1911-1980

MEDIA AND CULTURE THEORIST

Media Guru. Marshall McLuhan was the media guru of the 1960s. His controversial theories about the effect of changing media on culture and society made him into a media figure himself. Readers saw his ideas as a possible explanation of the social turmoil of the 1960s, and media executives pointed at his writings as a sign of their importance. While many of his theories have been dismissed as confused and confusing, his influence on thinking about media and culture was significant.

A New Kind of Science Fiction. A Canadian, McLuhan was born in Edmonton, Alberta, on 21 July 1911. Early in his career he was a professor of English literature. Upon taking a job teaching in the United States, McLuhan became interested in popular culture and its effect on youth. In the United States he was "confronted with young Americans I was incapable of understanding. . . . I felt an urgent need to study their popular culture in order to get through." His first book on the media and culture, *The Mechanical Bride: Folklore of Industrial Man* (1951), was a collection of short pieces on the detrimental effects of the "pressures set up around us today by the mechanical agencies of the press, radio, movies, and advertising." He described the book in a letter to his mother as "a new kind of science fiction, with ads and comics as characters."

Global Village. In *The Gutenberg Galaxy: The Making of Typographic Man* (1962) McLuhan continued to present his ideas about the effects of changes in media technology on the form of society. He points to the rise of the book and the fragmented print society as the source of the decline of the oral tribal society. The invention of electronic media changed society again, restoring some of the oral tradition and making the world into what McLuhan called a "global village." This type of sloganeering made McLuhan popular with advertisers and media figures who could reduce his complex ideas to provocative, meaningless phrases.

The Medium Is the Message. *Understanding Media: The Extensions of Man* (1964) was McLuhan's most influential book, filled with concepts that influenced how media thought about itself and how people thought about media. According to McLuhan books were obsolete, and common definitions of literacy should be expanded to include media other than print. Television was the "cool" medium, requiring more mental and sensory involvement than "hot" media, such as books. The youth of the postwar period were fundamentally different from their elders in that they did not respond as well to traditional instruction, instead becoming more tribal and less societal. The content of media is determined by its form: "The medium is the message."

Seer or Charlatan? In 1967 McLuhan published with Quentin Fiore *The Medium Is the Massage,* a book that attempted to clarify and explain his ideas. The popularity of the book — it was a best-seller — led to a television special on NBC about his theories. By the late 1960s McLuhan was regarded less seriously by academics, but he was still a good source for a provocative phrase that could be used in advertising and popular culture. His influence in the general culture, however, was longer lasting. His ideas legitimized the academic study of popular culture and justified the self-important statements by media executives. But many were convinced that McLuhan was a charlatan. Columbia University professor Jacques Barzun dismissed McLuhan with a pun on a McLuhanism: "The tedium is the massage."

Sources:

"The Hardware Store," *Time,* 92 (9 August 1968): 48;

Hugh Kenner, "Understanding McLuhan," *National Review,* 18 (29 November 1966): 1224–1225;

Richard Schickel, "Marshall McLuhan: Canada's Intellectual Comet," *Harper's,* 231 (November 1965): 62–68;

"Understanding McLuhan," *Newsweek,* 67 (28 February 1966): 56–57;

Geoffrey Wagner, "The Charlatan as Saint," *National Review,* 20 (19 November 1968): 1174–1176.

NEWTON MINOW

1926-

CHAIRMAN, FEDERAL COMMUNICATIONS COMMISSION

Appointed. A Chicago lawyer well versed in communications issues, Newton Minow was appointed chairman of the Federal Communications Commission (FCC) on 10 January 1961 by President John F. Kennedy. He was sworn in on 2 March 1961 and immediately began to do battle with bad taste and manipulative programming.

A Vast Wasteland. His speech to the National Association of Broadcasters in May 1961 set off a firestorm of controversy. His labeling of television programming as "a vast wasteland" angered network executives and pleased critics of television. In addition to the technical concerns of the FCC — license renewal, technology issues, and others — Minow made the improvement of the content of television and radio one of his main projects. While he

had no statutory authority over content, Minow used the power of the commission to hold hearings to try and change the focus of programming from shallow entertainment to culture and education.

Commission Hearings. In February 1962 the FCC held a series of hearings on network programming, devoting a week each to the programming policies of CBS, NBC, and ABC. The first week of the hearings, with CBS executives, was not marked by many confrontations. The second week of the hearings, with the executives of NBC, brought recriminations between the commission and NBC board chairman Robert Sarnoff, whose opening statement accused the FCC of seeking "regulatory power over network programs" and of trying to "impose the centralized authority of government to determine what is good for the public to see and hear." Minow, of course, denied the intention of the FCC to regulate programming, but he used the hearing to plead with the networks to provide quality shows and not to follow blindly the lead of audience ratings.

Minow's Effect. Minow's advocacy improved only slightly the offerings of the networks; it at least brought the issue before the public. But the problem remained that the networks were only providing the type of programming that viewers wanted. The television program on NBC about Minow's FCC hearings received an 8.2 rating, compared with a 12.7 for the competing *Maverick* on ABC and a 23.4 for *Mister Ed* on CBS. Still, Minow's defense of quality in television programming helped lay the foundation for the Corporation for Public Broadcasting and the Public Broadcasting System in the late 1960s. After two and a half years at the FCC, Minow returned to private life in May 1963. Although his crusade failed, Minow is remembered for his "vast wasteland" comment and his advocacy of quality.

Sources:

"Appointments: Musical Chairs," *Newsweek,* 61 (27 May 1963): 29–30;

"Minow's Farewell," *New Republic,* 149 (13 July 1963): 5;

"Pap and the Public," *Newsweek,* 59 (12 February 1962): 80–81;

" 'Plead, Bleat, Groan,' " *Newsweek,* 59 (16 April 1962): 67;

"A Pretty Long Letter — And a Pretty Long Answer," *Newsweek,* 59 (5 February 1962): 54–55;

"A Sponsor for Quality," *New Republic,* 148 (4 May 1963): 3–5.

WILLIE MORRIS

1934-

MAGAZINE EDITOR

Magazine Troubles. Willie Morris, at thirty-two years old, became the youngest editor in chief in the history of *Harper's* magazine on 1 July 1967. He replaced John Fischer, the man who hired him and brought him to New York from Texas in 1963. *Harper's* in the 1960s was suffering from competition with television. In 1966 the magazine had 277,000 readers and $1.8 million in revenues, figures which belied the problems faced by narrowly focused news and literary magazines during the 1960s. Though *Harper's* had been revered and sustained by the literary elite, the magazine's owners and editors found that the traditional readership was not able to sustain *Harper's* financially.

Early Life. The hiring of Morris was part of an editorial plan to bring the magazine more in line with the changing American society of the 1960s. Morris's background was certainly not that of the typical New York editor. He was born in 1934 in Yazoo City, Mississippi, and grew up with the discomfort associated with the racism of that society. After high school he went to the University of Texas at Austin. As editor of the college newspaper, the *Daily Texan,* Morris became a campus celebrity because of his activist stand, defending the right of the paper to comment on campus, local, state, and national issues. While at Texas he became a liberal and used his journalistic talents to expound his political beliefs in that Democratic, but conservative, state.

In Texas. Morris moved to England in 1956 after his graduation from Texas and studied history at Oxford University as a Rhodes scholar. In 1960 he received a request from Ronnie Dugger to return to Texas to edit the political weekly the *Texas Observer.* A journal with a circulation of six thousand, the *Texas Observer* had an influence far greater than its subscriber list, attempting to report honestly what went on in Texas politics, stepping on all the toes that goal entailed. During his editorship his talents as a political observer were noticed, and he was able to publish essays on southern and Texas politics in magazines such as *Harper's.*

Changes in New York. Hired first as an editor at *Harper's* in 1963, Morris worked to update the literary and journalistic content of the magazine. He signed novelist William Styron, Socialist and social scientist Michael Harrington, and psychiatrist Robert Coles to write for the magazine. After his appointment as editor in chief, a move that also brought *The New York Times* writer David Halberstam and freelancer Larry King as editors to *Harper's,* he sent Halberstam to report on the Vietnam War, printed Norman Mailer's *Armies of the Night* (in an issue-length piece), and generally upgraded the content of the magazine. He wrote the first volume of his autobiography, *North Toward Home* (1967), at age thirty-two. He did not, however, solve the problems of the magazine. He was fired as editor in chief in 1971 and returned to a more sedate lifestyle in the Northeast and, eventually, at the University of Mississippi in Oxford. In 1993 he published *New York Days* (Random House), the second volume of his autobiography.

Sources:
Susan Lardner, "Willie Morris (b. 1936 –) and Frank Conroy (b. 1936 –)," *New Yorker,* 43 (3 February 1968): 106, 109–111;

Willie Morris, *North Toward Home* (Boston: Houghton Mifflin, 1967);

"North by South," *Time,* 90 (10 November 1967): 61–62;

"A Spur for Harper's," *Newsweek,* 69 (22 May 1967): 68–69;

"Youth for Harper's," *Time,* 89 (19 May 1967): 56.

JANN WENNER

1946-

MAGAZINE OWNER, EDITOR, AND PUBLISHER

Youth Market. Jann Wenner was among the first entrepreneurs to realize the enormous commercial potential of the baby-boomer youth market of the 1960s. Born in 1946, Wenner was twenty when he started *Rolling Stone* magazine in 1967 to focus on the rock 'n' roll youth culture of the late 1960s.

Starting. Wenner's first experience as a journalist was at the University of California, Berkeley, where he wrote a music column for the campus newspaper. He also did reports on the Free Speech Movement at Berkeley for NBC. He dropped out of college after his junior year and wrote a music column for *Sunday Ramparts,* a weekend offshoot of the New Left magazine. After six months he borrowed seventy-five hundred dollars from a relative and started *Rolling Stone* with fifty-two-year-old *San Francisco Examiner* columnist Ralph Gleason.

Statement. The first biweekly issue appeared on 9 November 1967 and featured a cover portrait of John Lennon. The "Publisher's Statement" in the issue put forth the purpose of the magazine:

> *Rolling Stone* is not just about music, but also about the things and attitudes that music embraces. . . . To describe it any further would be difficult without sounding like bullshit; bullshit is like gathering moss.

Procapitalism. The magazine was solidly, if not spectacularly, successful during its first few years, reaching a circulation of more than sixty-four thousand subscribers by April 1969. Wenner has never been embarrassed by the financial success of his "counterculture" venture, rejecting the anticapitalist rhetoric of the radical Left that was linked so closely to the social upheaval of the late 1960s. "Rock and roll is now the energy core of change in American life. But capitalism is what allows us the incredible indulgence of this music."

Aging. Wenner built *Rolling Stone* into a strong media presence, building the circulation of the magazine past the one million mark by 1987. The magazine did lose its intensity as a cultural and political voice as the revolutionary trappings of the music and political rhetoric of the 1960s fell to the wayside in the 1970s. The magazine then became more of an industry voice as the baby boomers grew old enough to realize that they had little need of a voice of a generation. The median income of subscribers in 1987 was more than thirty thousand dollars.

Showing the Way. The importance of *Rolling Stone* was that it showed other companies and entrepreneurs that the youth market could be exploited on its own terms.

Sources:

Nick Ravo, "Rolling Stone Turns a Prosperous 20," *New York Times*, 23 August 1987, p. 22;

"Rocking the News," *Newsweek*, 73 (28 April 1969): 90;

"*Rolling Stone*'s Rock World," *Time*, 93 (25 April 1969): 78.

PEOPLE IN THE NEWS

In November 1969 **Walter Annenberg** sold the *Philadelphia Inquirer* and the *Philadelphia Daily News* for $55 million. Annenberg, who owned *TV Guide, Seventeen* magazine, and the *Daily Racing Form,* sold the newspapers to escape a challenge to the renewal of his FCC license for WFIL television station in Philadelphia. He had been accused of having a virtual news monopoly in the city.

Lucille Ball and **Desi Arnaz** made their final appearance together in an *I Love Lucy* special on 1 April 1960. Their divorce became final on 1 May.

John Henry Faulk, a CBS radio personality, won his libel suit in June 1962 against a sponsor who accused him of Communist leanings. He filed the suit in 1957 with the help of **Edward R. Murrow.** The court awarded him $2.8 million.

Mal Goode became the first black network correspondent on 10 September 1962, covering the United Nations for ABC.

On assignment in Colombia in May 1967 for *McCall's* magazine, **Lynda Bird Johnson,** the daughter of the president, was involved in an incident with Colombian journalists. Two Colombian newsmen sued Johnson's Secret Service agents after having been attacked and beaten while approaching her at the Barranquilla airport.

In May 1967 television star **Lassie** was named as the symbol of the Keep America Beautiful antilitter campaign. The collie had no statement on her appointment.

As a measure of his own media message, **Marshall McLuhan** recorded an album for Columbia Records in April 1967 on his theories. While in New York, McLuhan entertained reporters with his insights — one example, on the miniskirt: "It's a rediscovery of the tribalistic sculptural values. The kilt is a miniskirt."

Presidential candidate **Richard Nixon** appeared on *Rowan and Martin's Laugh-In* on 16 September 1968, delivering the show's signature line, "Sock it to *me*?"

Jack Paar walked off *The Tonight Show* set on 11 February 1960 after an NBC censor cut a joke from his performance. He returned on 7 March, but his days as host were numbered.

In December 1966 *The New York Times* reporter **Harrison Salisbury** was granted a visa to North Vietnam and began filing stories from Hanoi. Both Salisbury and *The New York Times* were severely criticized. Salisbury was voted a Pulitzer Prize for his Vietnam work, but the trustees of Columbia University refused to sanction the award.

During an AFTRA strike in April 1967, novice newsman **Arnold Zenker** replaced **Walter Cronkite** as the anchorman for the *CBS Evening News* for thirteen days. Upon his return after the strike settlement, Cronkite quipped, "Good evening. This is Walter Cronkite, sitting in for Arnold Zenker. It's good to be back."

AWARDS

EMMY AWARDS

1960

Best Dramatic Program: *Playhouse 90* (CBS)

Best Variety Program: *The Fabulous Fifties* (CBS)

Best Comedy Program: *The Art Carney Special* (NBC)

Best News Program: *The Huntley-Brinkley Report* (NBC)

Best Public Service Series: *The Twentieth Century* (CBS)

Trustees Award: Frank Stanton (CBS)

1961

Best Dramatic Program: *Macbeth, Hallmark Hall of Fame* (NBC)

Best Comedy Program: *The Jack Benny Show* (CBS)

Best Variety Show: *Astaire Time* (NBC)

Best Public Service Series: *The Twentieth Century* (CBS)

Best News Program: *The Huntley-Brinkley Report* (NBC)

Trustees Awards: National Educational Television and Joyce Hall, Hallmark Cards

1962

Best Dramatic Program: *The Defenders* (NBC)

Best Comedy Series: *The Bob Newhart Show* (CBS)

Best Variety Show: *The Garry Moore Show* (CBS)

Best Public Service Series: *David Brinkley's Journal* (NBC)

Best News Program: *The Huntley-Brinkley Report* (NBC)

Trustees Awards: CBS News and Jacqueline Kennedy for *A Tour of the White House;* heads of ABC, CBS, and NBC news departments for space coverage; David Sarnoff

1963

Best Dramatic Series: *The Defenders* (NBC)

Best Comedy Series: *The Dick Van Dyke Show* (CBS)

Best Variety Show: *The Andy Williams Show* (NBC)

Best Public Service Series: *David Brinkley's Journal* (NBC)

Best News Program: *The Huntley-Brinkley Report* (NBC)

Trustees Awards: Dick Powell; American Telephone and Telegraph for *Telstar 1* and *2*

1964

Best Dramatic Show: *The Defenders* (NBC)

Best Comedy Show: *The Dick Van Dyke Show* (CBS)

Best Variety Show: *The Danny Kaye Show* (CBS)

Best Public Service Series: *NBC White Paper: Cuba: Parts 1 and 2, The Bay of Pigs and the Missile Crisis* (NBC)

Best News Program: *The Huntley-Brinkley Report* (NBC)

1965

Outstanding Program Achievements: *The Dick Van Dyke Show* (CBS); *My Name Is Barbra* (CBS); *What Is Sonata Form?* (CBS); *The Louvre* (NBC); *Saga of Western Man* (ABC)

1966

Best Dramatic Series: *The Fugitive* (ABC)

Best Comedy Series: *The Dick Van Dyke Show* (CBS)

Best Variety Series: *The Andy Williams Show* (NBC)

Trustees Awards: Edward R. Murrow and Xerox Corporation

1967

Best Dramatic Series: *Mission Impossible* (CBS)

Best Comedy Series: *The Monkees* (NBC)

Best Variety Series: *The Andy Williams Show* (NBC)

1968

Best Dramatic Series: *Mission Impossible* (CBS)

Best Comedy Series: *Get Smart* (NBC)

Best Variety Series: *Rowan and Martin's Laugh-In* (NBC)

Trustees Award: Donald R. McGannon

1969

Best Dramatic Series: *NET Playhouse* (NET)

Best Comedy Series: *Get Smart* (NBC)

Best Variety Series: *Rowan and Martin's Laugh-In* (NBC)

Trustees Awards: William D. McAndrew and the *Apollo VII, VIII, IX*, and *X* astronauts

OVERSEAS PRESS CLUB GEORGE POLK MEMORIAL AWARDS

1965

Metropolitan Reporting: A. M. Rosenthal, *The New York Times*

Foreign Reporting: Malcolm W. Browne, Associated Press

National Reporting: Paul Hope and John Barron, *Washington Star*

Radio Reporting: Edward P. Morgan

1966

Foreign Reporting: Dan Kurzman, *Washington Post*

Editorial Writing: John B. Oakes, *The New York Times*

National Reporting: Barry Gotteher, *New York Herald Tribune*

1967

Foreign Reporting: Harrison E. Salisbury, *The New York Times*

Interpretative Reporting: Murray Kempton, *New York Post*

National Reporting: Richard Harwood, *Washington Post*

1968

Foreign Reporting: R. W. Apple, *The New York Times*

Local Reporting: J. Anthony Lukas, *The New York Times*

National Reporting: Clayton Fritchey, *Newsday Specials*

Television Documentary: *Africa*, ABC

1969

International Reporting: David Kraslow and Stuart H. Loory, *Los Angeles Times*

National Reporting: Bernard D. Nossiter, *Washington Post*

PULITZER PRIZES IN JOURNALISM

1960

Public Service: *Los Angeles Times*

National Reporting: Vance Trimble, Scripps-Howard Newspaper Alliance

International Reporting: A. M. Rosenthal, *The New York Times*

Local Reporting: Jack Nelson, *Atlanta Constitution*, and Miriam Ottenberg, *Washington Evening Star*

Editorial Writing: Lenoir Chambers, *Norfolk Virginian-Pilot*

1961

Public Service: *Amarillo* (Tex.) *Globe-Times*

Local Reporting: S. de Gramont, *New York Herald Tribune*, and Edgar May, *Buffalo* (N.Y.) *Evening News*

National Reporting: E. R. Cony, *Wall Street Journal*

International Reporting: Lynn Heinzerling, Associated Press

Editorial Writing: W. J. Dorvillier, *San Juan* (P.R.) *Star*

Cartoon: Carey Orr, *Chicago Tribune*

1962

Public Service: *Panama City* (Fla.) *News-Herald*

National Reporting: Nathan G. Caldwell and Gene S. Graham, *Nashville Tennessean*

International Reporting: Walter Lippmann, *New York Herald Tribune*

Local Reporting: Robert D. Mullins, *Deseret News* (Salt Lake City, Utah), and George Bliss, *Chicago Tribune*

Editorial Writing: Thomas M. Storke, *Santa Barbara* (Cal.) *News Press*

Cartoon: Edmund S. Valtman, *Hartford* (Conn.) *Times*

1963

Public Service: *Chicago Daily News*

National Reporting: Anthony Lewis, *The New York Times*

International Reporting: Hal Hendrix, *Miami News*

Local Reporting: Sylvan Fox, Anthony Shannon, and William Longgood, *New York World-Telegram & Sun*, and Oscar Griffin, Jr., *Houston Chronicle*

Editorial Writing: Ira B. Harkey, *Pascagoula* (Miss.) *Chronicle*

Cartoon: Frank Miller, *Des Moines* (Iowa) *Register*

1964

Public Service: *St. Petersburg* (Fla.) *Times*

National Reporting: Merriman Smith, United Press International

International Reporting: Malcolm W. Browne, Associated Press, and David Halberstam, *The New York Times*

Local Reporting: Norman C. Miller, *Wall Street Journal,* and Albert V. Gaudiosi, James V. Magee, and Frederick A. Meyer, *Philadelphia Evening Bulletin*

Editorial Writing: Hazel Brannon Smith, *Lexington* (Miss.) *Advertiser*

Cartoon: Paul F. Conrad, *Denver Post*

1965

Public Service: *Hutchinson* (Kans.) *News*

National Reporting: Louis M. Kohlmeier, *Wall Street Journal*

International Reporting: Joseph Arnold Livingston, *Philadelphia Bulletin*

Local Reporting: Gene Goltz, *Houston* (Tex.) *Post,* and Melvin H. Ruder, *Hungry Horse News* (Columbia Falls, Montana)

Editorial Writing: John R. Harrison, *Gainesville* (Fla.) *Sun*

1966

Public Service: *Boston Globe*

National Reporting: Haynes Johnson, *Washington Evening Star*

International Reporting: Peter Arnett, Associated Press

Local Reporting, Special: John A. Frasca, *Tampa Tribune*

Local Spot News Reporting: *Los Angeles Times*

Editorial Writing: Robert Lasch, *St. Louis Post-Dispatch*

Editorial Cartoons: Don Wright, *Miami News*

1967

National Reporting: Monroe W. Karmin and Stanley W. Penn, *Wall Street Journal*

International Reporting: R. John Hughes, *Christian Science Monitor*

Local General Reporting: Robert V. Cox, *Chambersburg* (Pa.) *Public Opinion*

Local Investigative Reporting: Gene Miller, *Miami Herald*

Editorial Writing: Eugene C. Patterson, *Atlanta Constitution*

News Photography: Jack R. Thornell, Associated Press

Editorial Cartoons: Patrick B. Oliphant, *Denver Post*

1968

National Reporting: Howard James, *Christian Science Monitor*

International Reporting: Alfred Friendly, *Washington Post*

Local Reporting: J. Anthony Lukas, *The New York Times*

Editorial Writing: John S. Knight, Knight Newspapers

1969

National Reporting: Robert Cahn, *Christian Science Monitor*

International Reporting: William Tuohy, *Newsweek*

Local Reporting: Albert L. Delugach and Denny Walsh, *St. Louis Globe-Democrat,* and John Fetterman, *Louisville Courier*

Editorial Writing: Paul Greenberg, *Pine Bluff* (Ark.) *Commercial*

Cartoons: John Fischetti, *Chicago Daily News*

DEATHS

Franklin P. Adams, 78, newspaper columnist, in New York City on 23 February 1960.

Gracie Allen, 58, actor and comedienne, in Hollywood, California, on 27 August 1964.

Peter Arno, 64, cartoonist, in Port Chester, New York, on 22 February 1968.

William Calhoun Baggs, 48, editor of the *Miami News*, in Miami, Florida, on 7 January 1969.

Hugh Baillie, 75, newspaperman, in La Jolla, California, on 1 March 1966.

Charles Bickford, 78, actor, in Hollywood, California, on 9 November 1967.

John Mason Brown, 68, theater critic for the *Saturday Review of Literature*, in New York City on 16 March 1969.

Whittaker Chambers, 60, journalist and spy, in Westminster, Maryland, on 9 July 1961.

Dickie Chappelle, 47, war correspondent and photographer, in South Vietnam on 4 November 1965.

Sir William Connor, 57, British newspaper columnist, in London, England, on 6 April 1967.

Thomas Costain, 80, newspaper columnist and novelist, in New York City on 8 October 1965.

Russel Crouse, 73, playwright and magazine editor, in New York City on 3 April 1966.

Jay Norwood ("Ding") Darling, 85, political cartoonist, in Des Moines, Iowa, on 12 February 1962.

Jane Darwell, 87, movie and television actress, in Hollywood, California, on 13 August 1967.

Rudolph Dirks, 91, creator of *The Katzenjammer Kids*, in New York City on 20 April 1968.

Orvil E. Dryfoos, 50, publisher of *The New York Times*, in New York City on 25 May 1963.

Allen Balcom Du Mont, 64, technical innovator of the television, in New York City on 15 November 1965.

Edward Duffy, 63, editorial cartoonist, in New York City on 13 September 1962.

Max Eastman, 86, magazine editor and author, in Bridgetown, Barbados, on 25 March 1969.

Stuart Erwin, 64, television actor, in Beverly Hills, California, on 21 December 1967.

Negley Farson, 70, newspaper correspondent, in Devon, England, on 13 December 1960.

Marshall Field, Jr., 49, newspaper magnate and editor and publisher of the *Chicago Daily News*, in Chicago on 18 September 1965.

Daniel R. Fitzpatrick, 78, editorial cartoonist for the *St. Louis Post Dispatch*, in Saint Louis on 18 May 1969.

Raoul Herbert Fleischmann, 83, cofounder and publisher of *The New Yorker*, in New York City on 11 May 1969.

Gene Fowler, 70, newspaperman and biographer, in Los Angeles on 2 July 1960.

William Goetz, 66, film producer and cofounder of 20th Century-Fox, in Holmby Hills, California, on 15 August 1969.

Harold Lincoln Gray, 74, creator of "Little Orphan Annie," in La Jolla, California, on 9 May 1968.

James A. Hagarty, 85, newspaperman, in New York City on 24 November 1961.

Jimmy Hatlo, 65, cartoonist of "They'll Do It Every Time," in Carmel, California, on 1 December 1963.

George D. Hay, 72, originator of the *Grand Ole Opry* on radio, in Virginia Beach, Virginia, on 9 May 1968.

Ben Hecht, 70, journalist, author, and screenwriter in New York City on 18 April 1964.

Marguerite Higgins, 45, newspaper reporter, in Washington, D.C., on 3 January 1966.

Hedda Hopper, 75, gossip columnist, in Hollywood, California, on 1 February 1966.

Edward Britt ("Ted") Husing, 60, radio sports announcer, in Pasadena, California, on 10 August 1962.

H. V. Kaltenborn, 86, radio and television news commentator, in New York City on 14 June 1965.

Dorothy Mae Kilgallen, 52, newspaper columnist and radio and television personality, in New York City on 8 November 1965.

Frank King, 86, cartoonist of *Gasoline Alley* strip, in Winter Park, Florida, on 24 June 1969.

William Monroe Kiplinger, 76, magazine and newsletter owner, in Bethesda, Maryland, on 6 August 1967.

Ernie Kovacs, 42, television and movie comedian, in Los Angeles on 13 January 1962.

Edwin Aloysius Lahey, 67, newspaper reporter, in Washington, D.C., on 17 July 1969.

Fulton Lewis, Jr., 63, radio commentator, in Washington, D.C., on 21 August 1966.

Henry Robinson Luce, 68, founder of Time publishing empire, in Phoenix, Arizona, on 28 February 1967.

Kingsley Martin, 71, editor of the *New Statesman* (U.K.), in Cairo, Egypt, on 16 February 1969.

Edward R. Murrow, 57, television and radio newsman, in New York City on 23 April 1965.

Kathleen Norris, 85, novelist and journalist, in San Francisco, California, on 18 January 1966.

Graham Creighton Patterson, 87, publisher of *Farm Journal*, in Evanston, Illinois, on 23 November 1969.

Drew Pearson, 71, newspaper reporter and columnist, in Washington, D.C., on 1 September 1969.

Frederick S. Pearson, 47, magazine editor and humorist, in New York City on 17 January 1960.

Westbrook Pegler, 74, newspaper columnist, in Tucson, Arizona, on 24 June 1969.

George Putnam, 88, newspaper editor, in Salem, Oregon, on 18 August 1961.

Stanley B. Resor, 83, advertising executive, in New York City on 29 October 1962.

Quentin Reynolds, 62, war correspondent, at Travis Air Force Base, California, on 17 March 1965.

Robert Ruark, 49, newspaper columnist, in London on 1 July 1965.

John Shubert, 53, part owner of the Shubert theater chain, in Florida on 17 November 1962.

Francis Striker, 58, radio scriptwriter and creator of *The Lone Ranger*, in Buffalo, New York, on 4 September 1962.

Arthur Hays Sulzberger, 77, publisher of *The New York Times* from 1935 to 1961, in New York City on 11 December 1968.

Raymond Swing, 81, radio commentator, in Washington, D.C., on 22 December 1968.

James Thurber, 66, humorist and cartoonist, in New York City on 2 November 1961.

Clarence George Wellington, former editor of the *Kansas City Star*, on 20 January 1960.

Walter Yust, 65, editor in chief of *Encyclopaedia Britannica* from 1938 to 1960, in Evanston, Illinois, on 29 February 1960.

PUBLICATIONS

Warren Kendall Agee, ed., *Mass Media in a Free Society* (Lawrence: University of Kansas Press, 1969);

Michael J. Arlen, *The Living-Room War* (New York: Viking, 1969);

Harry Bannister, *The Education of a Broadcaster* (New York: Simon & Schuster, 1965);

Erik Barnouw, *A History of Broadcasting in the United States,* 3 volumes (New York: Oxford University Press, 1966–1970);

Marvin Barrett, *Survey of Broadcast Journalism, 1968–1969* (New York: Grossett & Dunlap, 1969);

Apollinaris M. Baumgartner, *Catholic Journalism* (New York: AMS Press, 1967);

Edward Bliss, Jr., ed., *In Search of Light: The Broadcasts of Edward R. Murrow, 1938–1961* (New York: Knopf, 1967);

William A. Bluem, *A Documentary in American Television: Form, Function, Method* (New York: Hastings House, 1965);

Carnegie Commission of Educational Television, *Public Television: A Program for Action* (New York: Carnegie Corporation, 1967);

Edward W. Chester, *Radio, Television and American Politics* (New York: Sheed & Ward, 1969);

John Henry Faulk, *Fear on Trial* (New York: Simon & Schuster, 1964);

Fred W. Friendly, *Due to Circumstances Beyond Our Control* (New York: Random House, 1967);

Maury Green, *Television News: Anatomy and Process* (Belmont, Cal.: Wadsworth, 1969);

David Halberstam, *The Best and the Brightest* (New York: Random House, 1972);

Gabriel Heatter, *There's Good News Tonight* (Garden City, N.Y.: Doubleday, 1960);

John Hohenberg, *Between Two Worlds: Policy, Press, and Public Opinion in Asian-American Relations* (New York: Praeger, 1967);

Will Irwin, *The American Newspaper* (Ames: Iowa State University Press, 1969);

John Jakes, *Great Women Reporters* (New York: Putnam, 1969);

Alexander Kendrick, *Prime Time: The Life of Edward R. Murrow* (Boston: Little, Brown, 1969);

Robert E. Kitner, *Broadcasting and the News* (New York: Harper & Row, 1965);

Carl E. Lindstrom, *The Fading American Newspaper* (Garden City, N.Y.: Doubleday, 1960);

Eugene Lyons, *David Sarnoff: A Biography* (New York: Harper & Row, 1966);

Robert MacNeil, *The People Machine: The Influence of Television on American Politics* (New York: Harper & Row, 1968);

Marshall McLuhan, *Understanding Media: The Extension of Man* (New York: McGraw-Hill, 1964);

McLuhan and Quentin Fiore, *The Medium Is the Message* (New York: Bantam, 1967);

Robert St. John, *Encyclopedia of Radio and Television Broadcasting* (Milwaukee: Cathedral Square, 1967);

Alvin Silverman, *The American Newspaper* (Washington, D.C.: R. B. Luce, 1964);

Charles Side Steinberg, *Mass Media and Communication* (New York: Hastings House, 1966);

Raymond Swing, *"Good Evening!–: A Professional Memoir* (New York: Harcourt, Brace & World, 1964);

Bernard A. Weisberger, *The American Newspaperman* (Chicago: University of Chicago Press, 1961);

William Almon Wood, *Electronic Journalism* (New York: Columbia University Press, 1967);

Broadcasting, periodical;

Editor and Publisher, periodical;

Television Age, periodical;

TV Guide, periodical;

TV News Magazine, periodical.

C H A P T E R   T E N

MEDICINE AND HEALTH

by CAROLYN WILSON-BURROWS and WAYNE BURROWS

CONTENTS

Sidebars and tables are listed in italics.

1960

Feb. Frank L. Horsfall, Jr., M.D., becomes director of the prestigious Memorial Sloan-Kettering Cancer Center in New York.

Laborer Billy Smith has a severed leg reimplanted but with only temporary success.

Apr. A breast implant is made from silicone gel in a plastic bag.

Debate continues over killed- versus live-virus polio vaccines.

May Oral contraceptive pills are approved for widespread use in the United States.

July Measles vaccine developed by Dr. John Enders of Harvard shows promise in early tests.

Oct. Graft used to replace a portion of the aorta.

Percentage of babies delivered by Cesarean section doubles in twenty years to between 5 and 6 percent.

Dec. Foreign-trained doctors are required to pass special tests to practice in the United States.

1961

Mar. U.S. Supreme Court asked to overturn repressive Connecticut law preventing distribution of contraceptive advice or devices.

Apr. California recognizes equivalency between osteopaths and M.D.'s.

Teenage syphilis and gonorrhea epidemics reported.

May Drs. Jack Kevorkian and Glenn Bylsma use blood from a cadaver to give a transfusion.

Intrauterine contraceptive devices are developed as a new form of birth control.

Vaccination announced for mothers with Rh-negative blood to prevent their antibodies from affecting future pregnancies.

Nov. Application to approve thalidomide, a sedative, is retracted when it is discovered that the drug causes severe birth defects.

1962

- Dr. Irving S. Cooper pioneers cryosurgery (freezing) in the brain.

- Harrington rod operation described to cure scoliosis (excessive curvature of the spine).

- Multiple-agent therapy (radiation, chemotherapy, and steroids) used for leukemia.

- Burroughs-Wellcome Company markets the drug Allopurinol to prevent attacks of gout.

June Everett Knowles, Jr., has a severed arm successfully reimplanted.

Various government proposals are considered to give all the elderly adequate health insurance.

Sept. Rubella virus isolated.

Dec. First human kidney transplant using a nonrelative as a donor takes place.

1963

- Roche introduces the drug Valium.
- Body-function recorders are used in postoperative care to monitor patients.
- The measles vaccine is announced.

May The first human liver transplant is performed.

Several intrauterine contraceptive devices are approved for general use.

June First human lung transplant is performed.

1964

Jan. The first human heart transplant is performed using a chimpanzee donor.

The surgeon general declares cigarette smoking a health hazard.

Kidney dialysis at home introduced.

Mar. Joseph Goodman from Connecticut becomes the first American to die (on Miami Beach) of Portuguese man-of-war jellyfish stings.

Drs. Blakemore and Sengstaken begin using a two-part balloon to stop stomach bleeding in patients with liver disease.

Apr. Sterling Drug Company of New Jersey produces the hundred billionth Bayer aspirin tablet.

July Sen. Ted Kennedy fractures his spine in an air crash.

In Saint Louis women are allowed to give birth without general anesthesia.

New fertility drug Pergonal is introduced. Twins, triplets, and other multiple births are common.

A million abortions per year are done in the United States, most of them illegally.

Rubella reaches epidemic proportions in the United States.

1965

- The female hormone estrogen is found to prevent bone degeneration (osteoporosis).
- Rubella epidemic of 1963–1964 caused twenty thousand children to be born with birth defects.

Jan. One and a half million Americans have been sterilized for birth control.

Soft contact lenses are invented.

Mar. A computerized blood bank is set up in New York City (the New York Blood Center).

Artificial hearts are being developed at three sites in the United States.

May "Surfer's knees" is described as a medical consequence of kneeling on surf boards.

1966

- A live-virus rubella vaccine is first developed.

- Coronary-artery blockage is treated by surgically bypassing the blocked vessel with a vein from the patient's leg (coronary-artery bypass surgery).

Jan. Dermatoglyphics (palm prints) are used in the diagnosis of congenital defects.

Mar. An epidemic of children with thyroid disease is reported in Saint George, Utah, downwind from the Nevada nuclear test site.

Brooklyn surgeons use a gas jet to remove blockages from arteries.

A stapling device is marketed that closes incisions rapidly during surgery.

July Medicare begins to provide coverage for Americans over sixty-five years old.

1967

- The fertility drug clomiphene is marketed.

- Authorities in Evanston, Illinois, report that fluoridated water reduced cavities 58 percent over twenty years.

May Colorado becomes the first state to liberalize abortion laws.

A live-virus measles vaccine is developed.

Cook County Hospital, Chicago, hooks up a cystoscope (to look in the bladder) to a color television and videotape machine.

The drug LSD is held to produce chromosome breaks.

Leprosy is grown in the lab using an armadillo.

No American died of rabies in 1967, for the first year since records were kept.

1968

- A meningitis vaccine is developed and tested on military recruits.

Jan. Malnutrition among U.S. poor is just as severe as in developing countries, according to the Public Health Service.

Feb. Alcohol is found to be the best inhibitor of premature labor.

Tests of a new German-measles vaccine show it is safe and effective.

Nude group psychotherapy is reportedly being used in Los Angeles.

Mar. A kidney-storage unit is announced that can save donor kidneys awaiting transplant for up to three days.

Transplanting organs is reported to transplant the donor's cancer as well.

May "Supermales," with an extra male (Y) chromosome, are linked to violent crimes.

The injectable drug Depo-Provera can provide contraception for three months per dose.

June RhoGAM, for Rh-negative mothers, is marketed.

Oct. The FDA bans cyclamates (a sugar substitute), which cause cancer in lab animals.

1969

- Hysterectomies, especially in women under forty, are reported to be often unnecessary.

- MIST (Medical Information Telephone System) for consultations between doctors is started by Alabama Medical College dean, Clifton K. Meador.

- Rubella vaccine is approved for general distribution.

- Louisville pediatrician Billy Andrews develops a new incubator for premature babies.

4 Apr.   First artificial heart implant.

OVERVIEW

Changes in the Medical Profession. The medical profession transformed itself after World War II. New methods of diagnosis and treatment expanded the physician's healing powers enormously, and unprecedented social pressure was applied to assure that those new powers were exercised responsibly. Medicare and Medicaid programs initiated during the administration of President Lyndon B. Johnson routinely extended good medical care to the poor and the elderly for the first time in history, and it cost more than even the most conservative planners imagined. Between 1950 and 1970 the medical workforce tripled to 3.9 million people, and national health-care expenditures increased sixfold to $71.6 billion per year.

Evolving Practices. Innovations in obstetrics, vascular surgery, neurosurgery, transplant surgery, and other medical fields made headlines, but the ability of physicians to perform new procedures did not mean they were available, because physicans' time was limited, and complicated medical procedures took time and money. New techniques, drugs, and instruments required that physicians modify their practices. House calls, common in the years before World War II, became rare as routine diagnoses required medical tools that were not portable, and the doctor's office — or the hospital — became the place to treat illness. The influx of patients to hospitals increased the demand for interns, low-cost medical apprentices; twice as many were needed as graduated from medical schools each year, so the difference was supplied by foreign doctors wishing to gain a license to practice in the United States. Higher medical costs prompted studies into the quality of care, and some health-care consumers began to question the safety of new drugs and procedures. The government responded by instituting a federal bureaucracy to administer health programs and assure the safety of new drugs and new medical procedures.

New Methods of Treatment. Medical scientists introduced equipment during the 1960s that greatly enhanced the effectiveness and efficiency of medical care. Cryosurgical probes, used to remove or deaden diseased tissue by freezing, allowed for attractive alternatives to standard surgery, especially in removal of cancerous tumors. The home-dialysis machine, used to treat patients with kidney failure, allowed patients to undergo the lengthy and awkward process of dialysis without disrupting their lives with frequent hospitalizations. The portable electrocardiograph (EKG), which monitors electrical impulses in the heart, allowed doctors to perform a fundamental diagnostic test in their offices instead of in hospitals.

Implantation Surgery Revolutionized. The field of implant surgery was vastly expanded during the decade. Before the 1960s the only successful transplants of organs were of kidneys between identical twins. New drugs that suppressed the immune system to keep it from rejecting foreign cells and the development of a tissue-typing system that decoded genetic messages allowed physicians to begin thinking of body parts as modules that could be removed and reattached or transplanted from body to body. In 1963 the first human-liver transplant occurred when a man with liver cancer was given the healthy organ of a patient who had just died. A lung transplant was also performed that year, and the first heart transplant was performed in 1964 using a chimpanzee heart to replace a human one temporarily while a more suitable donor was located. Recipients of these early transplants did not fare well, but surgeons demonstrated the potential viability of their procedures.

Vascular Surgery. Medical researchers developed mechanical body parts for use when real donor organs were not available. Throughout the decade cardiovascular surgeons worked to design an artificial heart. The first successful models were simple pumps that supplemented the natural pumping action of the heart. The first complete artificial heart was installed in 1969 and served to keep the patient alive for several days until a donor was found. Many other advances were made in areas of cardiovascular surgery, including the coronary-artery bypass, which involves redirecting blood flow to the surface of the heart and bypassing diseased arteries. The first techniques allowed only one artery to be bypassed, but further research into grafting, or transplanting, made multiple bypasses feasible. The surgical procedure of cleaning out fat-clogged arteries was also developed and improved, and a safe and effective method for cardiac resuscitation was developed.

Vaccines. The spread of several devastating and fatal diseases triggered research and development of preventive vaccines. As researchers performed more experiments with live viruses, safety versus effectiveness became a main topic of debate. Live-virus vaccines, which involved injection of the active viral agent, were often more effective than killed-virus vaccines, but they were considered more dangerous. The oral live-virus polio vaccine developed in 1955 was extensively tested throughout the world before it was approved in 1961 for general use in the United States. Both live-virus and killed-virus vaccines were developed to combat measles; although the live-virus vaccine was more effective, it could not be administered to certain patients, and thus the killed-virus was necessary. The development of a live-virus rubella vaccine followed soon after the measles vaccines.

Cancer Research. The success of medical scientists in understanding and combating viruses stimulated research into cancer causes and armed physicians with a better understanding of cancerous diseases. Physicians and the general public became more concerned with discovering and attempting to prevent the causes of cancer. In 1964 the surgeon general warned the public of the dangers of smoking, linking it with deadly illnesses such as lung cancer, heart disease, and emphysema.

Reproduction and Sex. Numerous advances were made in the fields of gynecology and obstetrics during the 1960s. Following approval of a highly effective birth-control pill and other contraceptives, such as the intra-uterine device (IUD), women were afforded a measure of sexual freedom not previously available to them. The implications were unsettling to many people and led to a rethinking of matters related to sexuality, involving not only medical but also moral and religious philosophies. The issue of choice became a topic not only for the sexual act but also for the possible consequence involved: preg-nancy. The demand for legalization of abortion and safer procedures caused heated debate. Fertility drugs offered the opportunity for pregnancy to previously infertile women, and artificial insemination offered infertile men the possibility of fatherhood. The process of giving birth was facilitated by the use of anesthesia in the delivery room, but natural-childbirth techniques were developed and became popular after the public came to fear the use of drugs during pregnancy.

The Bad with the Good: Drugs Cause Side Effects. Although many advances were made in treating illnesses with newly developed drugs, extensive testing by the Food and Drug Administration (FDA) proved that some of the new drugs were unsafe. The most notorious episode in the 1960s involved thalidomide, a drug prescribed to treat morning sickness (nausea) in pregnant women that caused devastating birth defects in millions of cases worldwide. Because it did not pass the strict safety tests of the FDA, the drug was prohibited in the Unites States. Similarly, cyclamates (sugar substitutes) were distributed, found to have health risks, and then banned because they did not meet FDA standards.

Boom Times. Health care was the fastest-growing industry in the United States during the 1960s, and health-care professionals became more businesslike as the field grew. Helping people regain and maintain their health was still the primary motivation of medical practitioners, but they went about their jobs fully aware of market potential and profits. By 1969 the average net profit for a medical practitioner was $32,000, about four times the net income of the average worker. Some sixty-eight million Americans were covered by Blue Cross health insurance alone. It was a boom time in the field of health care, and the benefits grew proportionately with the costs.

TOPICS IN THE NEWS

Shocking Findings. Trussell deemed the care of about half the patients to be good or excellent, but he judged that one-fourth of the admissions received poor medical service. Patients fared better in nonprofit hospitals, especially those associated with medical schools, where faculty members supervised physicians in training. One out of five hospital admissions he considered unnecessary, and many hysterectomies, or surgical removals of women's uteruses, he thought were being done without good reason.

Concern over Costs. The study was sponsored by both the Teamsters members and their management, who paid the bills for medical care. They were concerned about quickly rising costs, but 80 percent of the patients themselves thought they received excellent care.

Source:
"The Patients' Perils," *Time*, 79 (18 May 1962): 47–48.

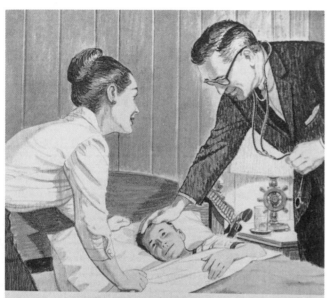

YOUR DOCTOR AND YOU

Are house calls a thing of the past?

In granddad's time, ol' Doc Brown dashed into the dark of night in his horse and buggy to reach a sick patient on the old homestead.

Those days are gone forever, and you can be glad of it! Doc Brown was a good doctor for his time, but often there was little he could do—either in the home *or* in his office—with the few pills and tonics in his little black bag.

There were no diagnostic laboratories, no x-rays, no vast array of wonder drugs, none of the innumerable testing and treatment devices that modern medicine now makes available to your family doctor.

Today he can give you much better care in his well-equipped office. And, except in the most unusual cases, there is little danger in transporting a patient. Telephones, modern highways and comfortable cars bring almost everyone within a few minutes of treatment.

Of course, if you really face an emergency at home, your doctor will hurry to you—but rely on his practiced and professional judgment whether a house call is necessary. In most instances, he can serve you sooner and better in his office.

Your doctor will be glad to explain his house call policy to you.

This is a public service message by:
THE AMERICAN MEDICAL ASSOCIATION

1964 Public Service message by the American Medical Association

CARE QUESTIONED

A Critical Study. Medical care had always been trusted as competent and adequate, but a study published in 1962 by Dr. Ray Trussell from Columbia University questioned that trust. He examined the medical charts of Teamsters Union members and their families who were admitted to New York hospitals.

THE DOCTOR'S OFFICE

In 1960 the National Broadcasting Company (NBC) introduced a service to take advantage of a captive audience—patients in doctors' waiting rooms. The Medical Radio System piped "therapeutic" music into the waiting rooms, interrupted every fifteen minutes by a spot called called *Medical News*, which actually consisted of drug-company advertisements. Drug manufacturers paid $338,000 a year for the opportunity to provide *Medical News* material.

To keep *Medical News* from putting too much pressure on patients, Dr. Chester S. Keefer of the Boston University School of Medicine acted as censor. He also evaluated the music.

Source: "Music While You Wait," *Newsweek*, 55 (22 February 1960): 92.

A CHANGING TRADITION

House Calls. Before World War II about 40 percent of doctors' visits were made by the physicians going to patients' homes. By 1960 the number of house calls had dropped to 10 percent; by 1970 they were rare occurrences. The reasons for this drop varied. Mainly, physicians considered house calls an inefficient use of their time. It was increasingly difficult for a doctor to do an adequate exam in a patient's home because all the proper equipment and drugs that had been developed and might be needed were impossible to carry. In large cities physicians were sometimes attacked for the drugs they carried.

The Public's Perspective. The public saw the change of tradition differently, and most were not pleased. They were accustomed to having the caring doctor at the bedside when someone was ill. Now doctors were charging more and making people come to them.

Source:
"The House-Call Habit," *Time*, 78 (15 September 1961): 62.

FOREIGN DOCTORS

A New Group of Interns. In 1948 Congress voted to let foreign medical-school graduates come to the United States for further training, inadvertently establishing a two-tier system of medical practice. American graduates generally took their internship and residency at prestigious university-based hospitals. The foreign graduates went mostly to fourteen hundred smaller community and veterans' hospitals, where they staffed emergency rooms and treated the poor who could not pay for care.

Tough Exam. The Educational Council for Foreign Medical Graduates (ECFMG), an agency developed by the American Medical Association (AMA) with legal backing from the government, was created to regulate the placement of these interns. This agency required special seven-hour tests in English and general medicine for the fifteen thousand foreign-trained doctors. The grueling and deliberately tricky tests were meant to fail 50 percent, causing some eight thousand foreigners to lose their visas. The exams were first given in November 1960. About twenty-five hundred foreign doctors failed and faced having their visas revoked by 31 December.

Reconsideration. There was an outcry from the hospitals where these physicians worked. Who would care for charity patients if foreign doctors were forced to leave? Public concern began to mount over the loss of medical service and the unfair way the tests were handled. The AMA strongly pressured the ECFMG to enforce its regulations strictly until State Department officials, realizing the issue could create a foreign-relations disaster, advised a reconsideration. As a result, the twenty-five hundred fired physicians received temporary reinstatements of their visas and were allowed to stay in the United States for six months to study for a repeat exam in April. They could work in their hospitals in the meantime but not see patients.

Sources:
"Chaos...," *Newsweek*, 55 (5 September 1960): 67;
"High Temperatures," *Newsweek*, 55 (5 December 1960): 69–70.

GOVERNMENT HEALTH PROGRAMS

Johnson's Health-Care Program. President Lyndon B. Johnson's Great Society program proposed far-reaching legislation on health care, the backbone of which was the Medicare program. Medicare was enacted in a bill signed in 1965 that extended social-security insurance to cover medical expenses for all citizens over 65 years of age. The program, which went into effect on 1 July 1966, was voluntary, but estimates were that 85–95 percent of those eligible would participate. Funding came from increased payroll taxes.

The Design of Medicare. Medicare has had two different parts since its inception. Part A covers hospitalization, outpatient diagnostic services, home-nursing services, and nursing-home care. Part B can be added voluntarily to cover doctor's fees and drug costs as well as other incidentals; it cost three dollars per month in 1966. The program was designed to be managed by Blue Cross or a similar organization that would pay hospitals and physicians and bill the government.

The Benefits of Medicare. Hospital stays of up to ninety days were covered, but the patient was required to pay the first forty dollars, plus ten dollars per day for each day over sixty days. Nursing-home care for patients who had been hospitalized was available for one hundred days at a cost to the patient of five dollars for each day over twenty days. Under part B doctors were paid 80 percent of "reasonable and customary fees," as determined by the government. The patient paid the 20 percent difference.

President Lyndon B. Johnson signs the bill establishing Medicare in 1965 beside former president Harry S Truman, who first proposed the program nearly twenty years earlier.

Initially, the doctor could charge more than the "reasonable and customary fee" if the physician and patient agreed on the higher amount.

Opposition to the Plan. The AMA and most physicians bitterly opposed the new law, labeling it socialized medicine. Organized medicine suggested vastly increased patient demands, with shortages of physicians, nurses, and other health professionals. Insurance companies also opposed the idea. Consumer groups, unions, and senior-citizen's groups favored the program.

Medicaid: A Plan for the Poor. Medicaid, designed to help states pay for care of the poor, was another Great Society program. It provided federal matching funds for eligible state programs. Medicaid drove health costs up significantly by extending care to many people who previously did not seek it because they were poor. By 1969 the system was already plagued with cost overruns. Administrative tangles were common and well publicized, as were scandals that resulted from news reports of health-care professionals defrauding the system. The government felt that physicians' fees were climbing too quickly, so it froze fee schedules paid under Medicaid. The costs were so high that New York dropped two hundred thousand eligible Medicaid recipients by lowering the maximum income participants could earn. Any family of four earning over five thousand dollars a year in 1969 was eliminated. As a result of the fee caps, many doctors refused to accept Medicaid patients. Only forty states had started Medicaid programs by 1969.

Sources:
"Auditing the Doctors," *Time,* 94 (11 July 1969): 38–40;

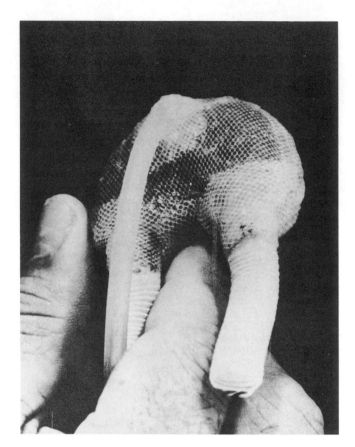

An implantable auxiliary ventricle, developed by Dr. Adrian Kantrowitz and used to assist patients with congestive heart failure, 1966

"Biggest Change Since the New Deal," *Newsweek,* 65 (12 April 1965): 88–90;

"Dr. Ward's Last Words," *Time,* 85 (21 May 1965): 28–29;

"Medicare — How It Will Work," *Business Week* (31 July 1965): 51–54;

"Medicare Is Launched into a Shambles," *Life,* 59 (3 September 1965): 52B–58.

HEART SURGERY: THE ARTIFICIAL HEART

Early Attempts. Heart donors are scarce, and recipients often do not have the luxury of time. To facilitate the process of heart transplantation, there was a concerted effort during the 1960s to develop an artificial heart for temporary use in bridging the time gap between a patient's need and the availability of a donor or as an assisting device for people whose hearts are not fully functional. Early experiments involved the use of a plastic banana-shaped device with internal valves to assist the blood in its movement from one heart chamber to another. A large pump outside the body provided the force. Dr. Michael E. DeBakey used such a device, which he called an intrathoracic pump, on a forty-two-year-old patient in 1963, but the patient died four days later, and there was some indication that the pump had caused blood clots.

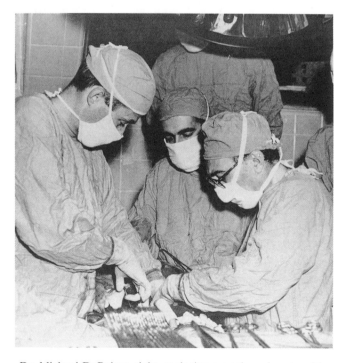

Dr. Michael DeBakey, right, replacing a weakened aorta with a synthetic Dacron substitute in 1962

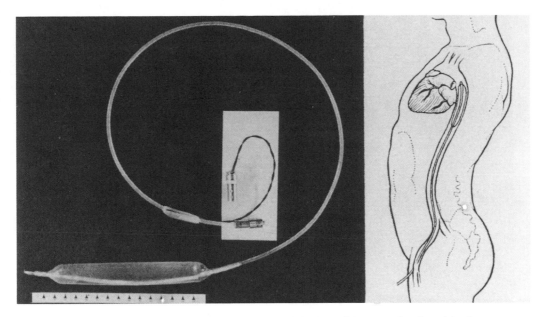

A balloon pump, with a diagram showing positioning, of the type developed by Dr. Michael DeBakey

An Improved Model. Dr. Adrian Kantrowitz of Brooklyn's Maimonides Hospital codeveloped the heart booster produced by the Avco-Everett Research Laboratory near Boston, where his physicist brother, Dr. Arthur Kantrowitz, was director. Their device, a banana-shaped booster without valves, attacked the common problem of blood clots experienced with early heart pumps. The Kantrowitz device was meant to be implanted permanently in patients with severe heart failure. It could be placed in the chest cavity and attached without open-heart surgery. The pump was intended to be turned on only when needed. The first Kantrowitz pump was implanted on 4 February in a patient who died within twenty-four hours. A second operation was more successful: the patient died of a stroke twelve days after the operation, but the pump operated properly.

Temporary Heart. In August 1966 DeBakey implanted a pump developed for a different use than the Kantrowitz device. DeBakey's pump provided temporary assistance to hearts with diseased valves and other irregularities that could be addressed surgically. It assisted the left ventricle, the chamber of the heart that pumps reoxygenated blood to the body. The DeBakey pump was first used on a rheumatic-fever victim who required valve replacements. It was successful, and the patient was released from the hospital a month after her operation.

Dispute between Colleagues. The first complete artificial heart was placed by Dr. Denton A. Cooley on 4 April 1969 in patient Haskell Karp at Baylor University Hospital. Cooley, a colleague of DeBakey, had done more heart transplants than any other surgeon in 1969, when he operated on Karp. While DeBakey and Cooley appeared to get along well in public, they were increasingly at odds with each other in private. Karp's case led to

a public break between them over an issue related to the artificial heart.

No Donor. Karp was a forty-seven-year-old dying of heart failure. His condition quickly deteriorating, Cooley tried to remove the damaged part of the heart and repair it with a Dacron graft. When Karp's heart stopped beating, Cooley removed the heart completely and put the patient on a heart-lung machine, a process that could be maintained only for a limited time.

Emergency Measures. Dr. Domingo Liotta, a colleague of Cooley's at Baylor, had been working with DeBakey on an artificial heart for ten years. His present model was ready to try, and Liotta suggested it might keep Karp alive for one or two weeks while he was waiting for a donor. The artificial heart was about the size of a real heart and made of Silastic, a silicone plastic. It had Dacron cuffs to attach to the blood vessels, and an external pump the size of a refrigerator was the power source, attached by hoses through the chest wall. Cooley installed the DeBakey-Liotta artificial heart in Karp. During the sixty-five hours he was on the pump, Karp regained consciousness and was even able to speak. On the basis of a national televised appeal, a donor was found, but Karp died of pneumonia and kidney failure thirty hours after the heart transplant.

Stolen Idea? DeBakey felt Cooley had stolen his idea and ten years of research. He thought Karp was a poor candidate for an artificial heart and that Cooley should have consulted him before using it. Cooley apparently felt he had to do something for Karp, and the artificial heart was his only choice. He felt DeBakey was primarily concerned because Cooley received credit for implanting the first artificial heart. As a result of the dispute, Cooley

Surgical sewing, or suturing, is a slow and tedious process. The technique of surgical sewing has been used in one way or another since ancient times, but it had never been automated until the autostapler was marketed in the mid 1960s.

U.S. Surgical Corporation made the original instrument, which was a monkey wrench with a gun trigger. Disposable cartridges could be placed in the instrument with different sizes of suture placed in different patterns depending on the cartridge chosen. When the autostapler was placed against a patient's skin and the trigger was pulled, it placed a series of tiny metal staples about three to four inches across at a time, closing the incision. The staples were made of stainless steel, nonreactive in human tissue.

Dr. Mark Ravitch of the University of Chicago School of Medicine was one of the first to develop an operation for the instrument itself. He used staples across the biggest vein returning blood to the heart (the vena cava) to prevent clots in the legs from getting into the lungs.

resigned from Baylor to associate with the University of Texas at Houston and form the Texas Heart Institute.

Sources:

"An Act of Desperation," *Time,* 93 (18 April 1969): 58;

"An Artificial Heart," *Time,* 93 (11 April 1969): 46;

C. P. Gilmore, "Booster Pump Gives New Life to Failing Hearts," *Popular Science,* 187 (December 1965): 48–51, 194;

"Half-Heart Replacement," *Time,* 82 (8 November 1963): 50;

"The Most Important Operation in History," *Science Digest,* 60 (July 1966): 46–49.

HEART SURGERY: CORONARY ARTERY BYPASSES

New Techniques. Two developments led to a revolution in the field of cardiovascular surgery during the middle of the decade. The first was cardiac catheterization to penetrate interior walls of the coronary arteries. This technique was pioneered by Dr. F. Mason Sones of the Cleveland Clinic in 1959. The second new method was revascularization, developed by Dr. Arthur M. Vineberg in Montreal and refined at the Cleveland Clinic by Vineberg and Dr. Donald Effer. Vineberg used a shunt to direct the flow of blood from the nonessential left internal mammary artery to the heart, bypassing diseased arteries. By the end of 1966 he had performed the surgery eighty-seven times with only three deaths due to the operation. Forty of his patients had returned to work.

A Multiple-Graft Procedure. The mammary-artery graft worked well but was useful only if one coronary artery needed repair. The heart is served by three main artery branches, and frequently more than one artery or artery branch required a shunt to provide the necessary supply of blood to the heart. The procedure that eventually allowed multiple grafts was the coronary-artery bypass graft (CABG), in which veins from patients' legs were used to repair the coronary arteries. Vineberg, Effer, Dr. C. Walton Lilledi at the University of Minnesota, and DeBakey in Houston all worked on similar procedures at about the same time, but DeBakey is usually said to have been the first to develop CABG, which became a routine procedure in subsequent decades.

Sources:
"Increasing the Blood Flow," *Time,* 87 (18 February 1966): 57–58;

J. D. Ratcliff, "New Life for Failing Hearts," *Reader's Digest,* 88 (February 1966): 181–188.

HEART SURGERY: ENDARTERECTOMY

Clogged Arteries. Cholesterol and various fats sometimes reach excessive levels in the bloodstream. One of the body's responses is to deposit some of the greasy mix on the inside walls of arteries. These deposits build up over time to form large plaques on the vessel walls, a condition known as atherosclerosis. If the buildup gets thick enough, the artery can be blocked off completely, but before this happens a very thin and irregular section of blood flow can lead to blockage by blood clots. When the flow of blood is severely restricted, the cells served by the artery die. When coronary arteries are affected, the result may be a heart attack.

Cleaning the Arteries. The technique of endarterectomy, the reaming out of arteries, was developed to remove the plaques and reopen clogged vessels. Drs. Philip Sawyer, Martin Kaplitt, and Sol Sobel of the Kings County Hospital in Brooklyn developed gas endarterectomy for use on blocked arteries in the leg, abdomen, and neck. A needle was inserted in the artery, and a jet of carbon dioxide (CO_2) was injected at a pressure of eight pounds per square inch. This tore away the lining of the artery as well as the plaques. The vessel could then be opened to remove the plaques. The technique had been successful on about seventy patients when the doctors began to try it on coronary arteries. The first patient was a forty-four-year-old woman who had experienced two heart attacks and had a life expectancy of less than two years. She was placed on a heart-lung machine, her body was cooled to eighty-two degrees Fahrenheit, and her heart was stopped for the surgery. It was successful.

A Safer Technique. In 1967 radiologist Dr. Charles T. Dotter of the University of Oregon Medical School developed a safer and more effective procedure. He inserted a long catheter in the femoral artery in the groin and fed it into the diseased coronary artery. The catheter served as a guide for a second probe that was positioned in the diseased artery at the point of the obstruction and expanded to push the spongelike plaque against the artery wall, restoring circulation. By the end of 1967, some 150 patients had been treated with this technique, which was completely successful about half of the time.

Source:
"Cleaning Out Coronaries," *Newsweek*, 69 (23 January 1967): 86–88.

HEART SURGERY: RESUSCITATION

A Cure That Kills. Imagine the following scene. In early-twentieth-century America, a middle-aged man leaving the theater clutches his chest, then he drops to the ground. The cry goes out, "Is there a doctor in the house?" Up walks a physician. He proceeds to cut open the man's chest and squeeze the heart into activity again. All cheer as the victim, momentarily revived, is rushed to the hospital. He dies a few days later. Scenes such as this were played out repeatedly as Good Samaritan physicians applied what was then state-of-the-art medicine. A few patients' lives were saved by this routine; it was better than no treatment at all, but the cure was nearly as deadly as the illness.

Hand-Pump Resuscitation. In 1960 Dr. W. B. Kouwenhoven, a Ph.D. in electrical engineering at Johns Hopkins University, started advertising a new technique for cardiac resuscitation. Calling it the hand-pump, or closed-chest, massage, he developed the technique in collaboration with a group of Johns Hopkins physicians. Kouwenhoven claimed that even nonphysicians could learn the method, and early results showed that it was very effective.

The Technique. The hand-pump method does not require cutting open the chest at all. Instead the hands are used to apply and release pressure rhythmically over the lower part of the breastbone. The pressure pushes the chest cavity down about an inch, squeezing blood out of the heart. Releasing the pressure allows blood to flow into the heart for the next cycle. This technique, now performed with mouth-to-mouth resuscitation, is known as cardiopulmonary resuscitation (CPR) and is used to revive victims of heart failure.

Encouraging Results. Before teaching the method widely, Kouwenhoven worked with Dr. Alfred Blalock to test it. They chose people who had died on the operating table. Of the twenty patients tested, 70 percent were revived. Using open-chest heart massage, only 40 percent were expected to have been resuscitated. Kouwenhoven and Blalock taught the hand-pump system to Baltimore firemen who manned the city's ambulance service. Within the first three months they revived six patients in public without opening any chests. Today the hand-pump system is the standard against which alternative methods are judged.

Sources:
Paul W. Kearney, "If a Heart Stops Beating — There's Help at Hand," *Reader's Digest*, 77 (November 1960): 96–99;

"Without the Knife...," *Newsweek*, 56 (18 July 1960): 56.

NEW METHODS: CRYOSURGERY

Cutting with Cold. Cryosurgery is surgery by freezing. Normal surgery involves cutting through tissue to reach and remove abnormal masses. In routine procedures it is usually necessary to remove some normal tissue at the edges of the surgical field. The body heals after surgery by scarring both internal and external tissues. Cryosurgery may involve an initial incision with a knife to reach an area of interest, but the main difference is the use of a precise freezing probe. A medium such as liquid nitrogen is pumped into the probe, causing it to freeze at low temperatures; the probe is then used to kill tissue it contacts but not surrounding cells. The body heals by dissolving the dead tissue. Some scarring generally occurs, but it is not as severe as that caused by surgery using a knife. Between 1960 and 1965 cryosurgery progressed in several specialty medical applications from a novelty to a commonly used surgical technique.

A Delicate Operation. Dr. Irving S. Cooper, a neurologist at New York's Saint Barnabas Hospital, was a pioneer in using cryosurgery. An example was his treatment of nine-year-old Steve Schiavo, who suffered from dystonia, a crippling condition caused by a brain tumor and characterized by tremors, muscle deformities, and loss of muscle control. Schiavo could no longer walk, and his arms had constant tremors. When Cooper performed brain surgery on him, the patient had to stay awake for the procedure because the tumor was next to the speech center of the brain, and if cells in that area were damaged, the patient could be left mute. His head was placed in a frame that kept him from moving, and Cooper injected a

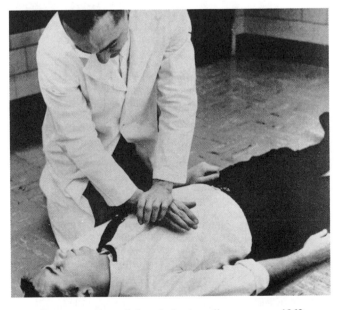

Demonstration of closed-chest cardiac massage, 1962

local anesthesia before making a small opening in the boy's skull to expose the tumor. Using X rays, Cooper accurately positioned the cryosurgical probe, freezing the tumor to minus ten degrees Celcius. As Cooper watched the tremor improve, he made Schiavo talk to ensure that only the tumorous cells were being destroyed. If too many were frozen, Cooper had thirty seconds to thaw the area before the damage became irreversible. When he was sure he had isolated the tumor, he froze it to minus eighty degrees for three minutes. The operation was a success.

Cancer Treatment. Dr. William G. Cahan of Memorial Sloan-Kettering Cancer Center also used cryosurgery. He pointed out that the main advantage of the cryoprobe to him was that it reduced bleeding in the area of surgery. Cahan used cryosurgery to treat cancer of the uterine cervix painlessly and bloodlessly; the procedure was later found to be more effective in precancerous problems of the cervix. Cahan also reduced a large tongue cancer by cryosurgery, then removed the shrunken lesion using regular surgical techniques.

Less Blood Loss. Dr. Leo Schwartz of Manhattan Eye, Ear and Throat Hospital used cryosurgery to remove small tumors of the larynx that were not cancerous. Dr. Robert W. Rand used the method on the pituitary gland at the base of the brain, approaching the surgery site through the patient's nose. University of Michigan doctors Walter Work and Mansfield F. W. Smith used cryosurgery to remove noncancerous blood-vessel tumors in the nose called angiofibromas that can cause massive nosebleeds. Traditional surgery of this type requires the transfusion of three to eight units of blood, on the average. These surgeons used cryosurgery to remove the tumors with no significant blood loss.

Sources:

"The Cold Knife," *Newsweek,* 64 (7 September 1964): 58–159;

"The Cold That Cures," *Time,* 85 (30 April 1965): 85–86;

"Freezing for Parkinson's," *Time,* 80 (6 July 1962): 29–30;

"Healing with an Icy Lance," *Life,* 58 (2 April 1965): 98–102.

New Methods: Home Dialysis

Hospital Dialysis. Kidney failure is devastating because the kidneys cease to cleanse the body of poisons that come from the digestion of food and the normal breakdown of proteins in the body. Without treatment a person with kidney failure will live for about three weeks before dying of uremia (named for a poison that builds up in the blood). Dialysis involves taking blood from the patient with kidney failure and removing the poisons by passing the blood over a membrane which has fluid on its other side. The fluid contains water, salts, sugars, and other small molecules found in normal blood. The dialysis process was designed to be used with an artificial kidney. The patient went to the hospital twice a week for four to six hours at a time. The equipment was expensive, and the medical personnel who ran it required special training. By 1964 there were one hundred patients in the United States routinely being dialyzed twice a week at a cost of about $10,000 a year each.

A Solution. Patients who required hospitalization two days a week found it difficult to keep a job so that they could pay the cost of dialysis, or at least qualify for group health insurance that paid for it. The answer was home dialysis, a refined procedure that significantly reduced the cost and the time required.

How It Works. Home-dialysis patients had two tubes placed permanently in their arms, one in a vein, the other in an artery. The tubes were normally connected so that the blood from the artery went back into the vein. During dialysis the two tubes were connected to a machine, a large stainless steel tank containing a chemical-cleansing mixture. The tubes were plugged into a membranous tube which was primed with one and a half pints of the person's blood from the last dialysis. A physician and nurse could evaluate the patient at home and connect him or her to the device.

More Comfortable and Convenient. Once the machine was started, the patient could read or sleep during the dialysis. The physician and nurse did not have to stay for the whole process as long as they could be contacted by phone in case of difficulty. The few original home-dialysis patients had spouses who monitored the process and unhooked the machine after dialysis. An alarm on the machine rang if any leaks occurred. A seven-page checklist was also provided for safety.

Cost. The initial cost for the home-dialysis machine was $2000. Supplies totaled about $170 per week. The overall cost (after purchasing the machine) was about half the price of hospital visits twice a week. Patients could often continue working during the day and sleep through the dialysis at night.

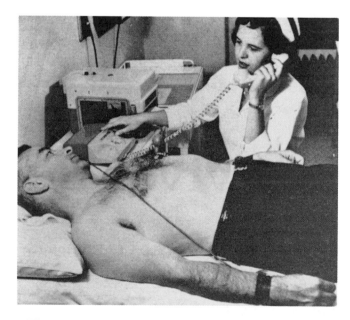

The Bell Dataphone, developed by Bell Telephone to transmit data from electrocardiograms to remote sites

Sources:
"Artificial Kidney Machine in the Home," *Life*, 57 (4 December 1964): 55–58;
"Cleaning Up the Blood," *Time*, 84 (13 November 1964): 64.

New Methods: Portable EKG

EKG. Heart activity is measured by the electrocardiogram, or EKG (the *K* is from the original German spelling), which measures cardiac electrical activity with an array of suction cups and disks placed on the patient's chest and limbs. At the beginning of the decade the EKG machine was a bulky and sensitive piece of equipment that was used strictly in hospital settings or in the offices of specialists. In 1964 the Public Health Service began local testing in the Washington, D.C., area for a more convenient method of obtaining an EKG. A nurse could go to the patient's home in Alexandria, Virginia, with a nine-pound box, place four electrodes on the patient's chest, phone George Washington University Medical School, put the phone's mouthpiece on a receptacle attached to the box, and record the results on a university computer.

Less Bulky System. Honeywell made Cardioview, the box for this function, that took advantage of all the new technology in electronics to miniaturize the system. Bell Telephone Company made the Bell Dataphone, the receptacle that allowed the EKG to be transmitted over the phone. The university computer allowed doctors to read the EKG directly with an oscilloscope, a kind of television screen, or to record the results on a paper readout of the EKG.

Source:
"Let Me Dial Your Cardiogram," *Time*, 84 (24 July 1964): 51.

Organ Transplants and Limb Reimplantation

Transplant Surgery and the Immune System. Between 1960 and 1969 numerous advances were made in the field of transplant surgery. In early 1960 the only major transplants performed were those of kidneys from one identical twin to another; surgeons had not yet learned how to suppress the body's natural tendency to reject tissue that is not its own. Each person's body has a unique chemical coding that is basic to the immune system. Body cells are protected by a complex system of protein that rejects foreign matter, including bacteria and viruses. Any matter that is not similar to the body's tissue is rejected (with the exception of some invaders, such as cold viruses). This system of protection also causes the body to reject organ implants from someone else's body.

Advances in the Field. Several developments during the 1960s revolutionized the field of transplantation. A major discovery was that certain anticancer drugs suppress the immune system and can be used to delay or prevent rejection — at a price. The immune system constantly destroys the early cancers that form in the body as

Automated blood-typing machine, 1965

well as the microscopic intruders that occasionally get inside the body. Too much suppression of this system allows foreign bacteria and viruses to kill the patient; too little fails to keep the body from rejecting a transplanted organ, or graft. Another major advance was in the field of tissue typing. It was known that a patient could receive a blood transfusion from a donor with blood of the patient's type. Solid tissue used in transplants involves more-complex differences, however, which scientists started to decode in the 1960s.

Limb Reimplantation. The easiest way to avoid rejection is to transplant the patient's tissue from one place to another on his or her own body. Burn patients are given skin grafts in this manner, for example. But until 1960 surgeons had not learned how to graft severed limbs, a frequent need for patients involved in accidents. In order for the procedure to be attempted, there are basic requirements: the severed limb must be intact; the severed tissue must be kept alive until the transplant can be performed; and connective tissue, including muscles, bones, blood vessels, and, most difficult of all, nerves must be reattached.

An Attempt and Success. In 1960 foundry laborer Billy Smith's leg, cut off in an accident at work, was reattached by surgeons at Eden Hospital in Castro Valley, California. The operation was only a temporary success. After a few months the leg became infected and had to be amputated. The first permanent transplant success was with twelve-year-old Everett Knowles, Jr., of Somerville, Massachusetts, whose arm was severed when he jumped a ride on a train. The police took the boy to the Massachusetts General Hospital, where surgeons had been preparing for a reimplantation for ten years. The severed arm was placed in ice after the blood vessels were flushed out to prevent clots. The boy was given blood, fluids, antibiotics, and other drugs to prevent blood clotting and was taken for X rays. The blood vessels of the right arm were opened under X ray. The surgery, which started only three and a half hours from the time the arm was amputated, took eight hours and six pints of blood. It was gloriously successful.

Liver Transplant. The first human liver transplant was performed in 1963 at Denver's Veteran's Hospital on William Grigsby, a forty-seven-year-old merchant marine discovered during exploratory surgery to have advanced liver cancer. The donor was a fifty-five-year-old veteran who had died of a brain tumor and had been placed on a heart-lung machine to keep his liver alive while Grigsby's surgery was started.

The Liver: A Vital Organ. The liver performs a remarkable number of functions in the body. It prepares and stores nutrients from food, makes proteins, and chemically converts poisons to less toxic forms. Without a liver a person would live less than two days. A unique feature of the liver is its dual blood supply. It has the usual circulation system, with arteries from the heart connected to veins going back to the heart. It also has another blood supply from the intestines, called the portal circulation, that delivers nutrients from food. This portal circulation makes transplanting a liver more technically difficult than transplanting other organs.

The Operation and Its Aftermath. Surgeon William R. Waddell and his team connected plastic tubes between the portal vessels below the liver and the jugular vein in Grigsby's neck. Grigsby's cancerous liver was removed, and the dead man's liver replaced it. When all the attachments were finished, Grigsby's new liver started making bile (a digestive juice) at once, proving that it was working. After the operation Grigsby was given the anticancer drug Imuran to suppress his immune system. Grigsby improved rapidly for about three weeks; then he suddenly died. An autopsy showed that his death was caused by the movement of blood clots formed in the vessels of his legs moving to his lungs. His liver was functioning well until the end.

Her children may never hear of polio

Remember, not so long ago, when parents of young children lived in dread of polio? Particularly during summer, when it sometimes struck with epidemic savagery. Take 1952. 57,879 victims that year.

Then 1963. 431 cases—the lowest number ever reported in a single year.

Then 1964—the first year when in seven of the first fifteen weeks not a single new case of paralytic polio was reported anywhere in the United States.

It was the pioneering research of Dr. John F. Enders and his associates that led to the breakthrough: the vaccine developed by Dr. Jonas Salk. This first brought down the incidence of polio. More recently an oral vaccine, developed by Dr. Albert Sabin, promises to eliminate polio entirely.

But it took the science and skills of our drug companies to make these vaccines available at low cost to millions: over one-half billion doses distributed to date in the United States.

The suffering spared, the savings over former hospital costs and special polio treatments are beyond calculation.

This is the value of modern drugs—protecting your health and reducing the cost of illness.

This advertisement is sponsored by a group of prescription drug manufacturers whose aim is to create through research continually better medicines: BURROUGHS WELLCOME & CO. · CIBA PHARMACEUTICAL COMPANY · LEDERLE LABORATORIES · MERCK SHARP & DOHME · A. H. ROBINS CO., INC. · SMITH KLINE & FRENCH LABORATORIES · THE UPJOHN COMPANY · WALLACE LABORATORIES · WARNER-CHILCOTT LABORATORIES

1964 cooperative advertisement by drug manufacturers promoting the benefits of prescription medicines

Heart Transplant. The first human heart transplant was performed in 1964 by Dr. James D. Hardy at the University of Mississippi Medical School at Jackson. The patient was a sixty-eight-year-old man dying of heart failure. Hardy explained to the patient that he was going to die and offered to attempt a risky heart transplant. The patient agreed, and a donor dying of brain damage was identified. While waiting for the donor to die, the heart patient started failing faster than expected. Convinced that he could wait no longer, Hardy tried a bold experiment. He transplanted a heart from a chimpanzee to keep his patient alive until the donor heart was available. The chimp's heart was too small to sustain the human patient, though, and he died an hour after surgery. Hardy was also the first to perform a heart-lung transplant. The patient died of kidney failure eighteen days later.

Lung Transplant. The first lung-only transplant was performed in 1963 at Pittsburgh's Presbyterian University Hospital by Dr. George Magovern and Dr. Adolph Yates, who had been doing the procedure on dogs for two years. The patient was Regis Sismour, forty-four, dying of emphysema; the donor was a thirty-three-year-old who had died of a brain hemorrhage. The donor lung (the left, because it is easier to transplant) looked like a black ball until it was completely reattached inside Sismour; then it turned pink as air expanded it. The transplant was

Dr. Albert Sabin, developer of the oral, live-virus polio vaccine, 1962

too successful though. Sismour's body was used to low oxygen levels. The new lung suddenly worked so well that Sismour got too much oxygen all of a sudden, causing him to have seizures. The doctors had to give him low oxygen air and gradually increase the oxygen to get his body used to it again. Like many other early transplant recipients, Sismour recovered well briefly, but then disaster struck. Eleven days after surgery, Sismour suddenly noticed his lung "stiffening." He could barely force air in and out, and then he died. The exact cause of death was never determined.

Sources:

"The First Heart Transplant," *Science Digest,* 55 (April 1964): 82–83;

Alix Kerr, "A Noble Failure Loses a Life But Advances Surgery," *Life,* 55 (26 July 1963): 32–34;

"A Miracle — Almost," *Newsweek,* (22 February 1960): 92;

"Setback," *Newsweek,* 61 (10 June 1963): 92;

"Sewing Back an Arm," *Time* (8 June 1962): 50–52;

Joan Steen, "The Boy Who Lost His Arm — and Got It Back," *Popular Science,* 181 (November 1962): 71–79, 186–192;

"Transplant Triumph," *Newsweek,* 61 (27 May 1963): 69, 71;

"Year of the Transplant," *Newsweek,* 63 (10 February 1964): 50–52.

THE POLIO SUGAR CUBE

Is It Safe? In 1960 a medical debate raged over the polio vaccine. In 1954 Dr. Jonas Salk had produced a killed-virus vaccine that was administered by injection and was 90 percent effective. The vaccine seemed relatively safe and cheap. Then in 1955 Dr. Albert B. Sabin of the University of Cincinnati produced a live-virus vaccine that was placed on a sugar cube and eaten, rather

than injected. Researchers, physicians, and patients were wary. Researchers suspected that the attenuated, or weakened, virus might gain the strength to cause polio once it was introduced into the human body. Physicians felt the Salk vaccine had been proven, and it was not worth the risk to switch to an oral vaccine simply for the sake of convenience. Patients were suspicious of a process of preventing polio by eating the live polio virus.

A Cautious Success. The live-virus vaccine was tested as an oral medication on children between six-months and one-year old in Houston, Texas, and on children under five in New Haven, Connecticut. In Cleveland, Ohio, newborn babies were given an eyedropper full of vaccine without the sugar cube. Large-scale testing was done outside the United States. In the Soviet Union the Sabin vaccine was given to twelve million people. By the middle of 1960 U.S. Surgeon General LeRoy Burney gave results of two years of testing on one hundred million people around the world. The Sabin vaccine was 95 percent effective and was cheaper than the Salk. It also provided "herd immunity," the ability of the vaccine to pass along its protective qualities by infection.

Sabin's Vaccine in the United States. Still, the vaccine was introduced cautiously. By August 1960, 800,000 Americans had taken the Sabin vaccine. A major study was conducted in Miami and its vicinity in Dade County, Florida. Statisticians predicted that during the term of the study twenty-seven cases of polio would occur in the county. Only eight were actually seen, however, and none of them were of the same virus type as the one used in the vaccine. The oral polio vaccine was approved for general

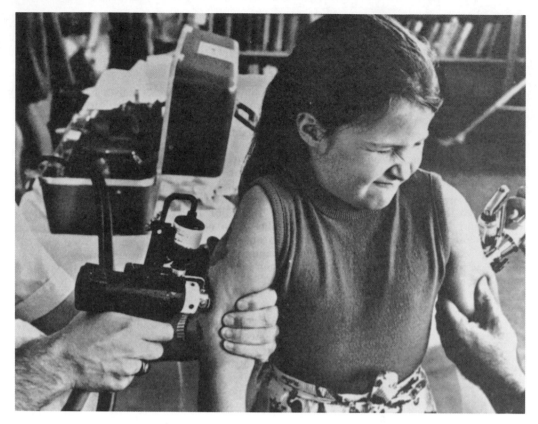

One of some ten million children innoculated in 1967 with the new measles vaccine

use in August 1961 and all but replaced the killed-virus vaccine.

Three Types. There are three types of polio virus. The Salk vaccine was effective against all three types but was weak against Type III. The oral vaccine originally approved was effective against only one type (Type I), but the Type II oral vaccine was ready for approval soon after the Type I. The Type III oral vaccine experienced a delay in U.S. distribution, though; when it was injected directly into monkeys' brains, some nerve damage resulted. Although millions of people around the world had already taken the Type III oral vaccine without experiencing problems, the Public Health Service withheld approval until the vaccine met their strict testing requirements.

Sources:

"Better than Salk?," *Newsweek*, 55 (18 January 1960): 50;

"Get Ready...Get Set...," *Newsweek*, 56 (29 August 1960): 83;

"Vaccine Free-For-All," *Time*, 78 (25 August 1961): 44.

"ROUTINE ILLNESS": MEASLES

A Serious Disease. Measles was considered a routine childhood illness in 1960. Most children contracted the disease; this was considered a good thing because an adult's infection was thought to be much more serious. Many people did not realize how dangerous measles could be for children, though. Of four million cases in America each year, four hundred — mostly children —

ended in death. One out of every four thousand children with measles recovered but was mentally retarded. This "simple" childhood illness was not at all simple.

The Enders Vaccine. In the late 1950s Dr. John Enders isolated the measles virus. In 1961 he and his colleagues at Harvard University introduced a live-virus vaccine. To reduce side effects, which included fever and rashes, the vaccine was injected in a mixture of gamma globulin. Early tests on children showed the vaccine gave nearly 100 percent immunity.

Live-Virus versus Killed-Virus Vaccine. In 1963 two vaccines were approved for general use. The Merck, Sharpe, and Dohme live-virus vaccine was grown in eggs. It was injected in a mixture of gamma globulin, like the original Enders vaccine from which it was developed. Chas Pfizer and Company was approved to distribute a killed-virus vaccine, but it required three doses injected at monthly intervals. Its effects did not last as long as those of the live-virus, however. Even though the live-virus vaccine was a superior safeguard, the killed-virus vaccine was necessary: the live-virus could not be given to pregnant women, people with leukemia, or anyone with sensitivity to eggs.

Sources:

Faye Marley, "Measles Vaccines Ready," *Science News Letter*, 83 (30 March 1963): 195;

"Measles & Hairy Ears," *Time*, 78 (22 September 1961): 92.

THE RUBELLA EPIDEMIC

Damaging Disease. Between 1963 and 1965 a rubella (German measles) epidemic swept the nation. It caused thirty thousand miscarriages; another twenty thousand pregnant women who contracted the disease gave birth to babies who suffered severe deformities, including blindness, deafness, limb defects, heart defects, and mental retardation. Infection in the first half of pregnancy meant a 50 percent chance that the baby would be affected. Later infections, in the second half of pregnancy, were less devastating (only 20 percent of babies were affected).

Identifying the Virus. Isolating the virus was the first step to developing a vaccine. Three different groups succeeded in identifying the rubella virus at about the same time: Drs. Paul Parkman and Edward L. Buescher at Walter Reed Army Institute for Research; Drs. Thomas Weller and Franklin Neva at Harvard; and Drs. John L. Sever and Gilbert M. Schiff at the National Institute of Health (NIH). Dr. Parkman moved to the NIH and worked with Dr. Harry M. Meyer on finding a way to curb the growth of the virus. Together they were first to develop a test that determined a person's immunity to rubella. Their hemagglutination-inhibition test produced results in three hours instead of the three weeks required by the old testing method.

Which Vaccine Would Work? The next step was development of the vaccine itself. The researchers started with an unsuccessful killed-virus vaccine. Next they tried a small amount of live virus in a vaccine, but this method simply gave people rubella. Then they decided on the most difficult technique — an attenuated, or weakened, virus vaccine. One way to attenuate a virus is to culture it repeatedly in nonhost cells. Because man is the host for rubella, the researchers grew the attenuated virus in kidney cells of monkeys, which are similar to those of man. By the seventy-seventh reculture in monkey kidney cells, the virus was sufficiently weakened. Parkman and Meyer used this HPV-77 strain for the vaccine.

Success. With the permission of the children's parents, physicians administered the vaccine to sixteen test patients at the Arkansas Children's Colony for retarded children. Eight were given the vaccine, and eight served as controls. These sixteen were housed together but away from anyone else. At the end of the test period, all had been exposed to rubella, but none of the children had gotten sick. Both the vaccine and its herd-immunity properties were proven. In 1969 the FDA approved a vaccine from Merck, Sharpe, and Dohme using the HPV-77 strain grown in duck embryo cells. The original Public Health Service recommendation was to vaccinate only prepubescent girls, the main concern being the possibility of a woman's being infected while in early pregnancy. Soon the policy was changed, though, and women were vaccinated immediately following delivery.

SEX ED

In the spring of 1968 Dr. Gerald Sandson, a child psychiatrist at the National Institute of Mental Health and advocate of sex education, met with a group of fifty teachers and counselors who were attending a sex education workshop. He was not pleased with what he found: "Some had their own sexual axes to grind; others almost relished their new-found sanction to pronounce four-letter words." He also observed that "few showed any knowledge of child dynamics or an appreciation that this was a subject they should approach with care."

Sandson acknowledged that a second workshop sponsored by the National Association of Independent Schools drew a more responsible and sensitive group of educators and that the first group he had observed might not have been truly representative. Nevertheless, his concerns remained, and Sandson concluded that if sex education was to be undertaken in the U.S., educators should receive proper training and counseling before being allowed to teach the subject. Based on what he had seen, Sandson believed that it was better for children to learn distorted information from their peers than from authorities in the classroom.

Source: "Teacher Problems Crop Up," *Science News*, 94 (26 October 1968): 411–412.

Sources:
"Now: A Vaccine to Conquer Another Crippler," *Reader's Digest*, 94 (April 1969): 123–127;
"Rubella Vaccine Ready," *Science News*, 95 (21 June 1969): 595;
"To Protect the Unborn," *Time*, 93 (20 June 1969): 49.

SEX IN THE 1960S: ABORTION

An Illegal Act. In 1960 abortion was illegal in every state in the union. In forty-five states an exception was made if the mother's life were in danger from the pregnancy. For the rich there was a way out: a women could go to certain doctors at certain hospitals and claim she would kill herself if forced to carry the pregnancy. Thus her life was in danger, and an abortion was permitted. Other women were having abortions illegally. Some were performed by surgeons in sterile environments for a large fee, but most were done by amateurs using dangerous methods.

Exceptions. Several states considered further exceptions. Before the end of the decade Colorado passed a law allowing legal abortion in the case of rape or incest, raising fear among conservative watchdogs that the exceptions provided a means of legal abortion for any woman willing to claim she had been raped. One married woman had to prove her husband was sterile before she was allowed an abortion for a pregnancy as a result of rape.

Changing Views. During the 1960s major changes occurred in the way the public viewed pregnancy that brought changes in abortion law during the 1970s. There was a growing concern about birth defects and advances in physicians' abilities to predict them during pregnancy. The thalidomide tragedy (see Thalidomide: Global Tragedy) disproved the prevailing theory that fetuses were protected from drugs taken by the mother. The terrible birth defects caused by thalidomide raised questions about the justness of a law that forced a woman to give birth to a seriously handicapped child. Similar concerns were raised by the rubella epidemic of the early 1960s (see The Rubella Epidemic). Rubella contracted by mothers in early pregnancy had been known to cause birth defects in about half of all cases since 1941; but there was no treatment, nor were there any means of predicting which rubella mothers would be affected until the introduction of ultrasound, a technique using sonar technology that allowed doctors to "see" inside the womb without harming the fetus. Ultrasound allowed doctors to detect some birth defects long before the baby was actually born.

Abortion Debate. These medical advances stimulated a debate that polarized Americans. Advocates of women's rights argued that the mother should have the right to choose abortion without legal restraint. Religious conservatives argued that a fetus is a human at the point of conception and that abortion is murder. In the middle were those who argued for more legal approval to provide sterile abortions for certain situations. The issue took on religious, social, and political significance in addition to its medical importance.

Source:
"The Abortion Epidemic," *Newsweek*, 68 (14 November 1966): 92.

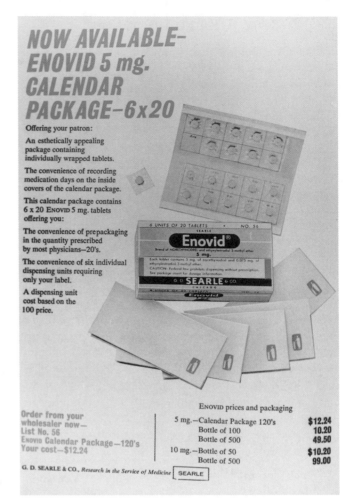

1962 advertisement for the Pill

SEX IN THE 1960S: ARTIFICIAL INSEMINATION

Proxy Parenthood. Artificial insemination involves placing sperm near a woman's cervix (the part of the uterus at the top of the vagina) by instrumental means. The physician injects the sperm of the husband into a proxy parent when he is not the cause of the couple's infertility or, in other cases, the sperm of a donor, or proxy parent. It was estimated in 1960 that one thousand to twelve hundred babies per year were artificially conceived by proxy, for a total of about fifty thousand children in the United States since the procedure was introduced.

Freezing Sperm. As reliable methods were developed to freeze sperm for storage, artificial insemination attracted more interest, and the issues related to the process posed more perplexing problems. A geneticist suggested that men freeze sperm samples before exposure to radioactivity (which can cause sterility), for example, which

seemed a valid precautionary measure. More controversial were the possibilities that long-dead men whose sperm had been frozen could still father children or that genetically attractive men — chosen for their intelligence, athletic ability, or looks — could participate in sperm markets to sell their genetic qualities to women shopping for a means of mateless conception.

Legal Questions. Legal issues arose as well. One New York physician was arrested and charged with rape for performing artificial insemination. Children artificially conceived were declared illegitimate in some states, and the children's birth certificates marked them as products of proxy parenthood. Attorneys scrambled to find answers to a host of insemination-related questions: Can a sterile husband or donor's wife sue for adultery after artificial insemination? What are the responsibilities of a sterile husband to his wife's child by a proxy parent? Could the child sue to become the donor's heir?

Procedural Questions. Physicians and scientists dealt with a different set of issues. They had to defend the integrity of the procedure after an early report described three pregnancies using frozen sperm, falsely implying that a severely deformed child resulting from one of the pregnancies was caused by the freezing process. In fact, most of these questions and issues were easily resolved, medically or through legislation, but artificial insemination was one of several fields in which modern science introduced new possibilities that previous laws and social practice had not contemplated.

Sources:

"Frozen Fatherhood," *Time*, 78 (8 September 1961): 68;

"The 'Proxy' Baby," *Newsweek*, 55 (30 May 1960): 80.

SEX IN THE 1960S: THE BIRTH-CONTROL PILL

Success in the Laboratory. The birth-control pill, developed in the 1950s, contains the female hormones estrogen and progesterone. Finding a cheap source of progesterone was an early stumbling block to development of the pill, until researchers found that the hormone could be extracted from Mexican yams. Once a pill was produced and found to be safe in lab animals, it was tested on a human volunteer population in Puerto Rico. Results were astounding. Pregnancy prevention reached a level of nearly 100 percent, and most failures were due to forgetfulness — patients had to take the pill regularly, or it did not work.

The Public Gets the Pill. In May 1960 the FDA approved distribution of the first oral contraceptive to the general population by prescription. The first pill, called Enovid, was marketed by the G. D. Searle Company of Chicago. It cost the consumer about ten dollars a month. The effects were reversible — fertility returned soon after women stopped taking the pill. The only common physical side effect was nausea.

Risks. Many conservative critics argued that the pill would promote casual sexual activity and thus undermine morality. These critics promoted unsubstantiated concerns that users of the pill risked breast and uterine can-

cer. One legitimate health risk was discovered: women over thirty-five who smoke and take the pill have increased odds for developing thromboembolic diseases, including strokes, heart attacks, and blood clots in vessels that travel to the lungs. That effect was lessened with the discovery that lower hormone doses are just as effective in contraception as the high doses in the early pills. By 1964 there were six brands of the pill available.

Source:

"Is This *the* Pill?," *Newsweek*, 55 (23 May 1960): 107.

SEX IN THE 1960S: FERTILITY DRUGS

European Precursors. Two effective drugs to combat infertility in women by stimulating the ovaries to prepare and release eggs were developed in Europe in the 1960s prior to the development of the American fertility drug clomiphene. Swedish scientists used pituitary glands obtained from autopsies to produce the fertility hormone gonadotropin. Injections were given monthly to infertile women for ten to fifteen days. A more popular drug was the Italian-made Pergonal, made from the urine of postmenopausal women. It took three gallons of urine to make one injection of Pergonal. Cutter Laboratories of Berkeley, California, was licensed to sell the drug in America. Clomiphene was more popular than the European drugs because it could be taken orally.

Results May Vary. One of the early reports of Pergonal's effects was from Columbia-Presbyterian Medical Center in New York. Of twenty-one infertile women given the drug, fifteen became pregnant. Among the first seven who delivered, three had single babies, three had twins, and one had quadruplets. Gonadotropin and clomiphene had similar effects. Prospective patients were undeterred by the risk of multiple births, however. It was several years before physicians learned how to use these drugs effectively without having to advise would-be parents to buy nursery supplies in bulk.

Source:

"Hormones for Fertility," *Time*, 84 (9 October 1964): 66.

SEX IN THE 1960S: GIVING BIRTH

Less Painful Deliveries. After World War II the process of giving birth changed. Increasingly, a woman went to the hospital for delivery instead of staying home. Through most of labor she inhaled pain-reducing anesthesia agents. Near the end of labor the woman was given general anesthesia to put her to sleep. Since she could not push the baby out, a physician used forceps, large steel spoons, around the baby's head to pull it out. This system served several purposes: pregnant women experienced less pain during labor; the hospital staff appreciated caring for less noisy patients; and physicians controlled the whole birthing process. At this time, it was thought that the baby was not greatly affected by drugs given to the mother.

Reaction against Anesthesia. Changes began after it was learned that babies seemed to be exposed to drugs the mothers took during pregnancy. Studies showed that babies exposed to high levels of anesthesia during labor had significant problems. A few hospitals introduced natural childbirth, using a technique popularized by French obstetrician Fernand Lamaze, in which mothers learned special breathing methods to control pain and were provided with practical information about the childbirth process.

Public versus Professional Perspectives. Saint Mary's Hospital in Saint Louis reported more natural deliveries than any other facility in the country in 1964 — 1,182 over a five-year period. Many women appreciated the program and the feeling that they were contributing to the well-being of their babies. Obstetricians opposed it, however. They liked neither losing control of the delivery process nor having their patients educated on the details of childbirth.

Source:
"Fewer Drugs for Happier Mothers," *Time*, 8 (25 September 1964): 81.

SEX IN THE 1960S: LIPPES LOOP

Evolution of the IUD. Ancient history relates the tale of Arabs putting stones into the uterus of a camel to prevent the camel from getting pregnant. The first recorded modern medical use of similar devices in people was during the 1920s, when Ernest Grafenberg of Germany placed rings of silk, and later silver, within the uterus of his female patients to prevent pregnancy. The procedure caused excessive bleeding and infections, and Grafenberg was forced to give up on the devices when he moved his practice to the United States. The Japanese and Israelis subsequently used such methods for birth control with greater success. The intrauterine device (IUD) gained wider acceptance in the early 1960s, when American medical researchers used new materials to develop new products. The new IUDs were made of plastic, nylon, or stainless steel. After insertion by a physician, they could be left for years. Pregnancy prevention with IUDs was almost as effective as the new birth-control pills. Most women who wanted to become pregnant could do so within a few months after having their device removed.

An Inexpensive Method. IUDs cost about two cents to manufacture, and physicians charged to insert them. Since there was only a one-time cost, IUDs were cheaper than the oral contraceptive pills, and users did not have to remember anything to get effective contraception. Over twenty thousand American women relied on the new devices in 1963.

Types of IUDs. One of the longest-lived of the IUDs was the device shaped like a double-S designed by Dr. Jack Lippes of the University of Buffalo. Various other shapes were marketed, but it became clear over time that the shape had no relation to the effectiveness of the

LIVING CULTURE TUBES

In 1968, researchers at the National Communicable Disease Center (NCDC) in Atlanta, Georgia, warned of the spread of a new strain of the venereal disease gonorrhea that was resistant to the most common treatment, penicillin.

Dr. Leslie C. Norins, director of the Venereal Disease Research Laboratory at the NCDC, traced the spread of the new strain to the war in Vietnam. The highly resistant cases were the result of women turning themselves into, Norins said, "living culture tubes." The Vietnamese women contracted gonorrhea and treated themselves with small, inadequate doses of bootleg penicillin. As a result, they became carriers of strains that were resistant to any level of penicillin. When troops returned to the United States, the new strains were introduced to the United States.

The rise of penicillin-resistant gonorrhea in the late 1960s prefigured a more serious wave of antibiotic-resistant viruses in the 1990s, led by tuberculosis.

Source: "Resistant Gonorrhea Increases," *Science News*, 94 (26 October 1968): 413.

device. Some devices had strings or other "tails" attached, so that women could examine themselves to be sure the IUD stayed in place.

Problems. After the first fifteen thousand women in America had IUDs placed, problems with the devices became apparent. In some users the devices caused heavy bleeding, and other users developed severe, life-threatening infections. The infections were later found to be related to lifestyles; the IUD is appropriate for some women, but not all.

Sources:
"Birth Control Devices and Debates Engross the U.S.," *Life*, 54 (10 May 1963): 37–40;

"Intra-Uterine Devices: A New Era in Birth Control?," *Time*, 84 (31 July 1964): 48–49;

"New Birth Control Devices," *Scientific American*, 210 (January 1964): 54–55.

SEX IN THE 1960S: THE MALE PILL

A Pill for Men? As new methods of contraception developed during the 1960s, the time-honored method of male condom use decreased. Because new contraceptives were primarily for women, birth control became a feminine imperative and responsibility. This attitude was challenged by the development of an effective male birth-control pill. One social and one medical problem led to the abandonment of the technique.

Diamines. The male pill was developed from research on diamines, protein compounds to combat amoebic intestinal infections. During animal testing it was discovered that diamines arrested maturation of the sperm in males, making them sterile. Dr. Carl Heller of the Pacific Northwest Research Foundation decided to shift the focus of his research to contraception. He tested the diamines on thirty-nine male convicts at the Oregon State Penitentiary. By taking a pill daily, they stopped producing sperm, he found. There was no effect on libido (sex drive) or the ejaculation process. When the men stopped taking the pills, their sperm counts quickly returned to normal. The female birth control pill (Enovid) cost three to four dollars a month to manufacture, but the diamine male contraceptive cost under one dollar a month. Dr. Heller's elation at the discovery of a cheap, effective method of birth control was dampened when he extended his tests to men who were not in jail: he discovered that men taking diamines could not drink alcohol. During testing, one drinker became violently ill and had to be hospitalized.

Women's Reaction. There were some early efforts to test the drug further or modify it to eliminate the adverse alcohol reaction without affecting the birth-control properties, but such research generated little enthusiasm. Drug companies considering further research conducted market studies. Many realized that an effect of the sexual revolution was that women were increasingly willing to have sex outside of marriage as long as pregnancy could be avoided. These companies conducted a poll to question sexually active single women about their reaction to the male birth-control pill. Women said they would not trust a man who claimed he had taken his pill every day.

Source:
"Male Pill," *Newsweek,* 61 (15 April 1963): 94.

SOLID PROOF: CANCER SPREADS

Cancer Virus? In 1960 a virus was proven to cause a cancer in chickens. It was the first time a virus was found definitely to cause a cancer and the first time a cancer was shown to be contagious. The proof of this finding was affirmed by using Robert Koch's postulates, a set of sensible procedures which eliminate the possibility that there is more than one cause for an effect. First the agent must be isolated from affected individuals and then grown in pure cultures. Next normal individuals exposed to the cultured agent must contract the disease the agent is assumed to cause. Finally the same agent must be isolated from the exposed individuals who contracted the illness.

Researching Sarcoma Cause. Dr. B. R. Burmester of the U.S. Department of Agriculture Regional Poultry Laboratory in East Lansing, Michigan, applied Koch's postulates to the Rous sarcoma virus, assumed to cause a certain type of cancer called sarcoma. Burmester isolated the virus in chickens with sarcoma, cultured it, and injected healthy chickens. Of the forty-five he injected, thirty-five chickens developed sarcomas. From these Burmester isolated the same virus. By Koch's postulates, then, Burmester determined that the virus caused the sarcoma.

The Cancer Connected with Contagious Virus. He continued his experiments. Healthy chickens were placed in cages with chickens injected with the virus. Even those not injected directly developed sarcomas. He concluded that the virus must be contagious. Those who were directly injected developed sarcomas much sooner than their healthy contacts. Also, healthy chickens were placed in cages with injected ones but separated by a wire screen; of these, no healthy chickens developed sarcomas. Direct contact was required for infection.

Source:
"Cancer Proved Contagious," *Science News Letter,* 78 (13 August 1960): 99.

SMOKING AND CANCER

The Government Examines Smoking. While scientists and physicians were generally convinced of the link between cancer and cigarettes by the early 1960s, the government was not. Political pressure from congressmen representing states where tobacco was grown delayed a Public Health Service report on the subject. In 1962 President John F. Kennedy asked U.S. Surgeon General Luther L. Terry to resolve the matter. Terry appointed a committee of ten, including three cigarette smokers, one cigar smoker, and one pipe smoker to review the findings of others rather than conduct their own research. Over a period of nearly two years committee members pored over eight thousand articles in the National Medical Library in Bethesda, Maryland. During the course of the inquiry Terry, who smoked cigarettes when the study started, switched to a pipe.

The Results. The report of the surgeon general was presented in the auditorium of the old State Department building on a Saturday morning, when the stock exchanges were closed, so that the findings would not have an immediate effect on tobacco company prices. The 387-page, 150,000-word report had disastrous news about the dangers of smoking. The committee found that cigarette smoking increased the rate of death and caused serious illnesses such as heart disease and emphysema. Findings were based on the number of cigarettes smoked and the number of years of smoking; there was not yet enough evidence to determine if filtered versus unfiltered cigarettes made a difference. Interestingly, former smokers seemed to face reduced risk from smoking-related illnesses. Smoking pipes and cigars seemed to raise slightly the risk of developing (rare) lip cancer but otherwise seemed less hazardous than cigarettes. The only benefit of smoking found was the psychological pleasure it gave smokers. The surgeon general's Advisory Committee on Smoking and Health advised that "appropriate remedial action is warranted."

Tobacco Industry Opposition. Tobacco industry groups quickly pointed out that a statistical association did not prove cause and effect. The committee agreed but noted they had used more than a statistical association to reach their conclusions. They had relied on animal studies, human autopsy studies, and clinical evaluations on noncancer patients, as well as epidemiological (statistical) studies. Growers and marketers of the $8-billion-per-year tobacco industry were not satisfied and decided to take the fight into the political arena.

The Report's Impact. An immediate effect was noted on cigarette sales. Sales decreased by 10 percent after release of the report, but this decline was temporary. Total 1964 sales of cigarettes were only about 3 percent less than 1963 sales. Tobacco company stocks fell initially, but prices then rose again to previous levels. Overall there was some reduction in smoking. Only 52 percent of American males smoked cigarettes in 1964 compared to 59 percent in 1955. Among senior medical students only 55 percent smoked in 1964: 44 percent had quit smoking.

Caveat Emptor. Various bills were proposed in Congress after the 1964 report, including a requirement that the tobacco industry provide a warning to consumers. This bill was opposed by southern (tobacco state) legislators, and a compromise was reached that required manufacturers to place the words "Caution: Cigarette smoking may be hazardous to your health" on cigarette packs beginning 1 January 1966. President Johnson gave a speech to Congress on health priorities in 1965 in which he proposed action on all major diseases, but he failed to mention cigarette smoking.

Advertising Ban? The National Interagency Council on Smoking and Health, composed of representatives from twelve voluntary health agencies and three government agencies, was chaired by Emerson Foote, a former advertising executive who had worked for the tobacco industry. In the wake of the surgeon general's report the council recommended a total ban on cigarette advertising. The American Medical Association (AMA) opposed that action as being taken too hastily. It later became known that the AMA had received a large grant from the tobacco industry to conduct a five-year study of smoking and health.

Sources:
"The Government Report," *Time*, 83 (17 January 1964): 42;

"One Year Later," *Time*, 85 (22 January 1965): 58;

"The Smoking Report," *Scientific American*, 210 (February 1964): 66-67.

SUGAR SUBSTITUTES

Sugar by Any Other Name? People concerned about the health effects of sugar had two alternatives in the mid 1960s, saccharin and cyclamates. Saccharin, the older of

1960 advertisement for one of the brand-name cyclamates later prohibited by the FDA

the two, is intensely sweet but may leave a bitter aftertaste. Cyclamates, the other substitute, are also intensely sweet — thirty times as sweet as sugar — and they leave no aftertaste. The positive qualities cannot outweigh the negative, however. Cyclamates can kill.

Cyclamate Controversy. Dr. Jacqueline Verrett, a researcher at the Food and Drug Administration (FDA), experimented with chicken embryos and cyclamates in 1966. She found that the chemical caused birth defects in 15 percent of the chicks exposed. She also showed that cyclamates caused chromosome breaks in rats which were fed high doses of the substance and cancer in other animals. In metabolizing the cyclamates many people's bodies formed cyclohexylamines, breakdown products known to cause bladder cancer in rats. Verrett reported her findings to FDA Commissioner Dr. Herbert Ley, Jr. Along with officials at Abbott Labs (which produced cyclamates), Ley proclaimed the product was safe. A public argument with full press coverage ensued.

A Review and a Ban. Over five million pounds of cyclamates were used each year in America in 1963, and twenty-one million pounds were expected to be used in 1969, most of it in soft drinks. Verrett accused Ley of protecting this $16-billion-a-year industry without re-

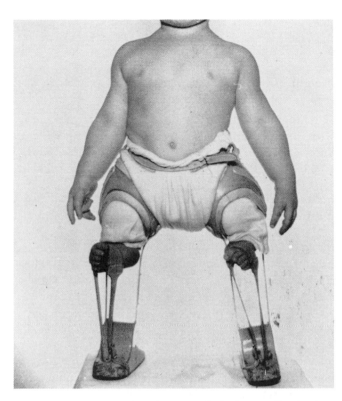

A thirty-month-old child with lower limb phocomelia, the deformity caused by Thalidomide. This patient is fitted with rocker-ended prostheses.

gard for public safety. With pressure from the press Ley was forced to ask the National Academy of Sciences Research Council to review what was known about cyclamates. Researchers there supported Verrett's conclusions. U.S. Secretary of Health, Education, and Welfare Robert Finch banned cyclamates in 1969, ordering all products containing the material off grocers' shelves by 1 February.

Sources:

"Bitterness about Sweets," *Time,* 94 (17 October 1969): 79;

"Food Additives: Blessing or Bane?," *Time,* 94 (19 December 1969): 41–42;

"HEW Bans the Cyclamates," *Time,* 94 (24 October 1969): 89.

THALIDOMIDE: GLOBAL TRAGEDY

Unexpected Benefits. Thalidomide was developed in the United States as a possible antiseizure drug, but when it was found to have no antiseizure properties, rights were sold to a West German drug company (Chemie Gruenenthal) that continued testing. Chemie Gruenenthal found that thalidomide was a reasonably effective sedative with an unusual property: there was no fatal dosage. As a sedative, the drug could be prescribed to potentially suicidal patients without risk of overdose. After testing with what seems to have been rigged results, thalidomide was approved for distribution in West Germany. Subsequently, it became apparent that it relieved nausea, or morning sickness, in many women during early pregnancy. This discovery led to a tragedy affecting thousands of lives.

Side Effects. Chemie Gruenenthal marketed thalidomide successfully, both in its pure form and in multiple-drug combinations, for a wide variety of ailments. As thalidomide use spread quickly throughout Europe, physicians began noting an increase in a rare type of birth defect called phocomelia (literally, "seal limbs"), in which a baby's limbs do not fully form; the baby might be born without an arm, for instance, its hand coming directly out of its shoulder. Heart defects, kidney problems, and deafness also increased in newborns. Some obstetricians wrote to Chemie Gruenenthal to ask if thalidomide could be associated with the explosion of birth defects. The company insisted that there was no noticeable association with thalidomide.

An American Opponent. The William S. Merrell Company of Cincinnati bought the American license for the drug, but it needed FDA approval before it could distribute. Dr. Frances Oldham Kelsey stood in the way. Kelsey taught pharmacology at the University of South Dakota School of Medicine and had her own medical practice before she transferred to the FDA. One month after starting her new job, the Merrell application reached her desk. In accordance with agency policy, Kelsey insisted on proof of safety before approving the drug. Merrell responded with political pressure. Articles were written about Kelsey's bad judgment in keeping this inexpensive, lifesaving drug off the market.

A British Report. In February 1961 a report in the *British Medical Journal* caught Kelsey's eye. It described peripheral neuritis, nerve damage resulting in tingling and numbness of the arms and legs, which was sometimes

DRUGS MUST BE EFFECTIVE

In 1962 the Drug Amendments Act, called the "thalidomide law," was passed in the wake of the thalidomide scare. Thalidomide was never proven effective for anything in animal tests. It was designed for seizure control but has no antiseizure properties. Its disastrous effects on people were discovered only after it was marketed.

A provision of the new act was a grace period for drugs approved by the FDA between 1938 (when the agency was created) and 1962. These drugs stayed on the market without having to prove they were effective, at least at first. By October 1964 drug companies had to satisfy the FDA that pre-1962 drugs were effective or pull them off the market. Many disappeared from pharmacists' shelves.

Source: "Safety & Effectiveness," *Time,* 83 (13 March 1964): 82.

permanent in long-term users of thalidomide. The report estimated this effect once in every 300,000 users. It was later learned that the incidence was 1 in 250. This report reinforced Kelsey's resolve to get adequate answers to her safety questions before approving the drug.

Disaster Averted. On 20 November 1961 West German pediatrician Dr. Widukind Lenz presented his findings that thalidomide caused phocomelia to a meeting of German pediatricians. By 29 November the drug was banned in West Germany. Chemie Gruenenthal cabled Merrell that day noting that thalidomide caused birth defects. The next day Merrell's drug application to the FDA was withdrawn. A few days before, Kelsey was about to be fired for her opposition to the thalidomide approval. Now she was a heroine.

Merrell's Persistence. The nightmare was not over in the United States. Kevadon, the name for thalidomide marketed in Canada, was distributed by Merrell for testing in the United States. FDA regulations at the time allowed physicians free distribution of a drug under consideration for approval. Twelve hundred physicians received free samples of Kevadon, and many gave it to patients, some of whom could not be traced. At least three U.S. babies were affected by the testing samples. Other deformed babies were born to mothers who were given the drug in Canada or overseas. Through Kelsey's diligence, however, the United States was spared the thousands of severe birth defects caused by thalidomide in Europe, Australia, Japan, and Canada.

Sources:
"The Doctor and the Drug," *Newsweek*, 60 (30 July 1962): 70;

John Lear, "The Reward," *Saturday Review*, 46 (2 February 1963): 47;

Lear, "The Unfinished Story of Thalidomide," *Saturday Review*, 45 (1 September 1962): 35–40;

Morton Mintz, "Dr. Kelsey Said No," *Reader's Digest*, 81 (October 1962): 86–89.

TRIPARANOL AND CHLORAMPHENICOL

Problems with Triparanol. In the same decade that thalidomide deformed thousands of babies around the world, more drugs were learned to have unexpected side effects. One was the Merrell's MER/29, or triparanol, marketed to lower blood cholesterol. The drug was found to cause baldness and blindness from an unusual form of cataracts. The FDA learned that these cataracts had been noted in animal studies required for approval of the drug, but Merrell failed to mention the finding to the FDA in the approval request. The FDA brought charges against Merrell, the parent company (Richardson-Merrell, Incorporated), and three former executives.

Antibiotic Risks of Chloramphenicol. Another drug with unexpected side effects was chloramphenicol, known by the trade name Chloromycetin (Parke, Davis and Company), an antibiotic particularly useful against some rare and tropical diseases and lifesaving against certain types of meningitis. When confined to the treatment of life-threatening infections, the risks of chloramphenicol are worth taking. Chloromycetin was introduced in 1949 with the hype given any new drug. Doctors prescribed it for minor bacterial infections, such as bronchitis and acne, and even as a placebo for viral infections such as colds — even though it was known that antibiotics have no effect on viruses. By 1952 some patients taking Chloromycetin were found to develop anemia, or low counts of red blood cells; the disorder was soon upgraded as aplastic anemia, in which the blood cells stop being made. Most people with aplastic anemia die from the disease, though male-hormone therapy, transfusions, and other hormones can save as many as 25 percent.

Accountability. A jury held that Parke, Davis acted irresponsibly in marketing the drug, in view of the fact that the link with aplastic anemia was known in 1952 and widely published in medical journals. In 1962 Carney Love, an aplastic-anemia sufferer, was awarded over $300,000 from her doctor and Parke, Davis. She had been prescribed Chloromycetin for bleeding gums after a tooth was pulled, and again for bronchitis in 1958.

Dangerous but Useful. Still, in 1968, $70 million–80 million worth of Chloromycetin was prescribed to Americans, most of it for colds or acne. Of every sixty thousand patients receiving it, one died of aplastic anemia; for newborn babies, the severe anemia rate was over 50 percent. That year an FDA panel decided the drug should continue to be approved for use, since it could be lifesaving in treating some severe infections; but Parke, Davis was required to temper its advertising and send a warning letter to doctors about the drug's side effects.

Sources:
"The Dangers of Chloromycetin," *Time*, 91 (16 February 1968): 74;

"Those Risky Side Effects," *Time*, 79 (30 March 1962): 72;

"Triparanol Side Effects," *Time*, 83 (3 April 1964): 79.

HEADLINE MAKERS

DR. DENTON A. COOLEY

1920-

HEART SURGEON

The New Specialization. After the development of the heart-lung machine in the mid 1950s, which made open-heart surgery possible, a new group of heart-surgery specialists emerged to meet the demand for new techniques. Dr. Denton A. Cooley was among the first such specialists, and he quickly rose to become one of its foremost practitioners.

Education and Early Inspiration. Cooley studied at the University of Texas at Austin and received his M.D. at Johns Hopkins University, where he then served as an intern and as a resident and worked under respected heart surgeon Dr. Alfred Blalock. In November 1944 he assisted Blalock in the first blue-baby operation, which corrected a heart defect that prevented the infant from receiving enough oxygen. This experience in particular inspired Cooley to pursue a specialization as a heart surgeon.

A Growing Reputation. In 1954 Cooley returned to his native Houston to join the faculty of the Baylor University College of Medicine, where heart surgeon Dr. Michael E. DeBakey was already well known. Cooley worked with DeBakey on techniques for removing aortic aneurysms and gained a name for himself through his work on congenital heart defects, especially in infants; through repairing damaged heart valves with artificial replacements; and through establishing the Texas Heart Institute in Houston in 1962. In the meantime his friendship with DeBakey evolved into a friendly rivalry.

Heart Transplants. After Dr. Christiaan Barnard performed the first successful heart-transplant operation in South Africa in December 1967, Cooley studied the technique and repeated the operation on 3 May 1968. His forty-seven-year-old patient received the heart of a fifteen-year-old girl who damaged her brain in a suicide attempt; the patient recovered well after the surgery but

died 204 days later. On 5 May Cooley had two patients for transplants but only one heart; he chose the younger patient. A heart for the older patient became available two days later. Its source was a man whose brain had been damaged in a barroom fight. His two opponents were charged with homicide, but since Cooley had used the man's living heart the charges were dismissed. During the late 1960s he performed as many as twenty-two heart transplants in a single year. In 1969 Cooley — who in 1968 claimed that death occurred when the brain, not the heart, ceased functioning — met in private audience with Pope Paul VI to discuss the morality of heart transplants.

The First Artificial Heart. Cooley's major claim to fame stems from his 4 April 1969 implantation of the first complete artificial heart. The device kept the patient alive, and even alert at times, for sixty-five hours, until a donor heart was received. The artificial heart was a success, but the patient died of complications little more than a day after the transplant operation. Cooley was attacked by DeBakey, who had been working on artificial heart devices — occasionally with Dr. Domingo Liotta — for ten years. DeBakey accused him of stealing his work and of not obtaining proper consent for the procedure. A committee appointed by Baylor trustees said that Cooley broke university and National Heart Institute regulations and recommended censuring him. In response Cooley resigned from Baylor and devoted his energies to his Texas Heart Institute. A $4.5 million malpractice suit from his patient's widow was dismissed in federal court in 1972, and the U.S. Supreme Court upheld the decision.

Later Career. In September 1972 Cooley received a plaque for having performed ten thousand open-heart operations, more than any other surgeon. In the early 1970s he switched from doing heart transplants, which carried a low survival rate, to coronary bypasses, which use a vein from the patient's leg to bypass a blocked artery. He also promoted a regulated diet as a way to lessen the occurrence of heart disease.

Sources:
Harry Minetree, *Cooley: The Career of a Great Heart Surgeon* (New York: Harper's Magazine Press, 1973);

Roger Rapoport, *The Super-Doctors* (Chicago: Playboy Press, 1975).

Dr. Irving S. Cooper

1922-1985

NEUROLOGIST, PIONEER OF CRYOSURGICAL
TECHNIQUES

A Remarkable Man and a Great Brain Surgeon. Praised by British writer and scientist C. P. Snow as "one of the most remarkable men alive" and "professionally one of the great brain surgeons of the world," during the 1960s Dr. Irving S. Cooper built on his already-impressive reputation from the early 1950s in treating victims of Parkinson's disease by expanding his procedures to a new field: cryosurgery. His advances led to international acclaim and to no small amount of professional jealousy and personal attacks.

Education and Early Career. Cooper earned his M.D. at George Washington University and his Ph.D. at the University of Minnesota, then worked as a fellow at the Mayo Clinic (1948–1951) before joining the faculty at New York University Medical School and the surgical staff at Saint Barnabas Hospital in the Bronx. Brilliant and compassionate, as a surgeon he devoted himself to helping people with debilitating, seemingly hopeless neurological disorders such as Parkinson's disease, which afflicts its aging victims with uncontrollable tremors. He made a name for himself as a young surgeon in the early 1950s with his discovery that by cutting off the blood supply to small portions of the brain related to Parkinson's disease — thus destroying the tissues — the symptoms could be alleviated.

Cryosurgery. During the 1960s Cooper made further advances in treating Parkinson's disease and other disorders through cryosurgery, a technique he helped to pioneer and perfect. While some surgeons used supercold probes to freeze tissues, which would then naturally dissolve, in order to reduce scarring, Cooper employed the technique as a variation on his earlier discoveries: as a way to destroy harmful tissues selectively in order to improve the patient's muscular control. He described these techniques in books such as *Parkinsonism: Its Medical and Surgical Therapy* (1961) and *Involuntary Movement Disorders* (1969). Some surgeons criticized him for not trying his techniques on animals before employing them on actual patients, but he claimed there were few appropriate animal subjects; besides, he added, his innovations worked, adding, "I'm treating desperate patients who have come to me for help, not an experiment."

Later Developments. Cooper later abandoned surgery for Parkinson's disease, instead advocating George Cotzias's drug L-dopa as a successful treatment. He continued to use cryosurgery for patients afflicted with disorders such as dystonia, a childhood neurological disease, and in 1973 he made another breakthrough with a brain implant whose electrical impulses could help patients with epileptic seizures, poststroke paralysis, and spasms caused by cerebral palsy.

Sources:

Irving S. Cooper, *The Victim Is Always the Same* (New York: Harper, 1973);

Cooper, *The Vital Probe: My Life as an Experimental Brain Surgeon* (New York: Norton, 1981);

Ronald Sullivan, "Dr. Irving S. Cooper, 63, Is Dead; Made Advances in Brain Surgery," *New York Times,* 4 November 1985.

Dr. Michael E. Debakey

1908-

HEART SURGEON

Pioneering Heart Surgeon. During the 1960s tremendous advances were made in the area of cardiovascular surgery, and Dr. Michael E. DeBakey led many of them. His work in arterial grafting and replacement and in artificial-heart devices, along with subsequent developments for which he paved the way, has saved the lives of thousands of patients. He has also been a highly visible promoter of public service for the medical profession and a prolific scholar.

Education and Early Successes. The son of a Lebanese immigrant who settled in Cajun territory to be with other French speakers, DeBakey grew up in Lake Charles, Louisiana, and studied at Tulane University in New Orleans, where he received his M.D. He spent most of the 1930s occupied with his studies, internships, and residencies, but in 1932 he developed a pump that became a stepping-stone to the heart-lung machines later used in open-heart surgery, and in 1936 he and Dr. Alton Ochsner were among the first to point out a connection between cigarette smoking and lung cancer. He taught at Tulane from the late 1930s to the late 1940s, interrupted only by military service from 1942 to 1946 in the office of the surgeon general. In 1948 he joined the faculty of the Baylor University College of Medicine in Houston, Texas, where he made his most noteworthy advances.

A Growing Reputation. Trained as a general surgeon, DeBakey came to specialize in problems related to the heart or to blood vessels. He developed a solution to usually fatal aortic aneurysms, for instance, through grafting — first with material from donors, then plastic tubing, then the highly successful Dacron graft. Soon this type of arterial reconstruction, for which DeBakey was a cowinner of Albert Lasker Award in 1963, was used for other cardiovascular problems. By this time he had an international reputation, and it was no surprise when he was selected in 1965 to head a twenty-eight-member commission, set up by President Lyndon B. Johnson, that proposed establishing regional centers for the care and study of heart disease, cancer, and strokes.

Early Heart Pumps. In May 1965 DeBakey surprised many people outside the medical community by predicting the development of a permanent artificial heart within just a few years. His claim was overly optimistic, but he and other surgeons did make great strides toward that goal in the late 1960s. In 1963 DeBakey had already developed a device that helped blood to move from one chamber of the heart to another, but the patient died less than a week later. He had better luck in 1966 with a pump that bypassed the left ventricle temporarily to ease the strain on damaged or irregular hearts until the problem could be corrected through surgery.

The First Artificial Heart. Technically speaking, though, this was not a complete artificial heart, and DeBakey's efforts to develop and employ one were upstaged by a colleague at Baylor. On 4 April 1969 Dr. Denton Cooley used an artificial heart developed by another colleague, Dr. Domingo Liotta, as a temporary measure to keep a patient alive while waiting for a replacement heart from a donor. While the heart worked, the patient died shortly after the heart transplant. Believing that Cooley had made a poor choice in using the pump, DeBakey was even more upset by his belief that his work had been stolen by Cooley and by the fact that DeBakey — at times with Liotta — had been working on an artificial heart for ten years. Cooley left Baylor as a result of the break between the two men.

Later Developments. Despite this setback DeBakey remained an influential surgeon, and his contributions to cardiovascular surgery are respectfully remembered.

Sources:
C. P. Gilmore, "Booster Pump Gives New Life to Failing Hearts," *Popular Science,* 187 (December 1965): 48–51, 194;

"Half-Heart Replacement," *Time,* 82 (8 November 1963): 50.

HARRY F. HARLOW

1905-1981

DEVELOPMENT PSYCHOLOGIST

Early Career. Harry Harlow was born in Fairfield, Iowa, on 31 October 1905. His Ph.D. was in experimental psychology, and he taught for forty-four years (1930–1974) at the University of Wisconsin. His experimental work with animals changed thinking about animal development and learning. His work had practical applications in education and in the developmental aspects of human infancy and childhood.

New Theories of Animal Behavior. Harlow was the first to show that mammals all tend to learn in similar ways, first by trial and error, then by insightful learning, in which they develop strategies, predict what will happen next, and begin to think abstractly. His work in social and developmental psychology continued with a study of motivation. It was generally thought that animal behavior was motivated by biological drives, such as the need for food or sex. Harlow showed otherwise in brilliant experiments. While much animal behavior is motivated by biological drives, it is also driven by abstract motivation. Animals' behavior can result from an urge to explore and manipulate their environment.

Experiments with Baby Monkeys. The best-known works by Harlow involved his infant monkey experiments. Monkey babies were separated from their mothers at birth. Surrogate "mothers" made of wire frames and terry-cloth covers were provided. These seemed to be enough for the babies as long as they were able to socialize with other young monkeys about their age. With only terry-cloth moms and no social contact as youngsters, the monkeys grew into creatures that could not act normally in social groups later.

Importance to Human Developmental Psychology. Harlow's work was important for monkeys, but it also had meaning for people. His research showed that as orphanages closed and children without parents were moved to foster care, the need for peer relationships at a young age intensified. Harlow died on 6 December 1981.

DR. FRANCES OLDHAM KELSEY

1914-

PHARMACOLOGIST

A Singular Contribution. Pharmacologist Dr. Frances Oldham Kelsey is credited with single-handedly preventing an outbreak of drug-related birth defects by denying approval for the distribution of thalidomide in the United States. She did so in spite of pressure and attacks claiming that she was keeping a beneficial product from potential users.

Extensive Experience. Kelsey was born on Vancouver Island, British Columbia, and studied at McGill University in Montreal before attending the University of Chicago, where she earned a Ph.D. in pharmacology in 1938. She taught there and in South Dakota, where she earned her M.D. in 1950. She became an American citizen in 1956. In 1960 she moved with her husband to Washington, D.C., where she joined the Department of Health, Education, and Welfare's Food and Drug Administration (FDA). Her new job was to screen applications from pharmaceutical companies to market new drugs.

A Useful New Drug? Kelsey's first assignment, in September 1960, involved an application from the William S. Merrell Company of Cincinnati, which had purchased the American rights to a drug called thalidomide that had been marketed under various trade names in Europe since 1957. As permitted by drug laws of the time, the company had already distributed samples to several American doctors on an experimental basis.

Cautious Response. Despite the drug's extensive use in Europe, Kelsey was suspicious after studying test reports supplied by Merrell and noticing that it behaved differently in animals from other similar drugs. She withheld approval of the drug and asked Merrell to give the FDA more information about the effects of the drug.

Suspicions and Recriminations. Kelsey still did not know exactly what she was looking for, but she was concerned that the drug might affect fetuses. Though she carefully sought more evidence as to its effects, by May 1961 the patience of Merrell had run out. Claiming that existing evidence for the side effects of thalidomide was inconclusive, it exerted extensive pressure on her to pass the drug.

Vindication. As reports of children with birth defects linked to the drug rolled in, the company withdrew it from further experiments in March 1962. In that year thousands of birth defects in Europe were blamed on the use of thalidomide during early pregnancy. The total finally reached approximately ten thousand cases worldwide, with about half of those occurring in West Germany.

Recognition. It was soon recognized that Kelsey's stand against approval of the drug prevented a similar catastrophe in the United States, and she quickly became a media figure. In July 1962 she was praised on the Senate floor for her "great courage and devotion to the public interest," and on 7 August 1962 she received the President's Award for Distinguished Service from President John F. Kennedy. With characteristic modesty she credited those at the FDA who supported her in her stance.

Effects. The thalidomide case led to stricter laws governing the testing of drugs not yet approved by the FDA, and Kelsey was invited to the White House in October 1962 to see them signed into law. A new division was created in the FDA to regulate drug testing, which Kelsey was appointed to direct.

Source:
Morton Mintz, "Dr. Kelsey Said No," *Reader's Digest,* 81 (October 1962): 86–89.

DR. LUTHER L. TERRY
1911–1985

MEDICAL RESEARCHER, TEACHER, U.S. SURGEON GENERAL

The First Surgeon General's Warning. Since the mid 1960s cigarette packs and advertisements have come with warnings from the office of the U.S. surgeon general that cigarettes may be hazardous to one's health. The surgeon general who first stated this on behalf of the federal government was Dr. Luther L. Terry, who held the position from 1961 to 1965.

Education and Early Career. Born in Red Level, Alabama, Terry studied at Birmingham-Southern College before earning his M.D. at the Tulane University School of Medicine in 1935. He taught and practiced in the South and Midwest and served four years with the United States Public Health Service, then in 1950 he joined the National Heart Institute, where he specialized in hypertension studies. He became assistant director of the National Heart Institute in 1958. President John F. Kennedy appointed Terry as surgeon general in 1961.

The Report. Researchers had long indicated a link between cigarette smoking and various health problems. Terry headed a ten-member panel that studied published reports and scholarship on the effects of smoking. The panel reached a consensus, which Terry presented on 11 January 1964. In its report the panel concluded that a strong connection existed between cigarette smoking and lung cancer, other pulmonary ailments, and heart disease. Though tobacco companies criticized the findings as inconclusive, the government proceeded to issue warnings about the possible effects of cigarette smoking. Shorter-lived effects included both a brief decline in cigarette sales and smokers (Terry among them) switching from cigarettes to pipes or cigars, which the report deemed considerably less hazardous.

Later Career. After his term as surgeon general was completed, Terry joined the faculty of the University of Pennsylvania, where he taught and served as an administrator until his retirement in 1980. During these years he promoted a ban on cigarette advertisements on radio and television, which was achieved in the early 1970s, and campaigned to control smoking in the workplace.

Source:
"The Smoking Report," *Scientific American,* 210 (February 1964): 66–67.

PEOPLE IN THE NEWS

Dr. Malcolm S. Artenstein of the Walter Reed Institute of Research developed a meningitis vaccine in 1969.

Harvard Medical School dean **Dr. George Berry** retired in 1965. He stressed the need for scientific research as a tool to understand better the patient as a person.

Fully implantable heart pacemakers with batteries were developed by **Dr. William A. Chardack** of the Buffalo, New York, Veterans' Hospital in 1961.

Dr. Thomas D. Cronin of Houston introduced the Silastic breast implant to America in 1963. It felt like normal breast tissue.

In 1961 **Dr. John Enders** and colleagues announced a live-virus measles vaccine.

In 1964 **Dr. Vincent Freda** and **Dr. John Gorman** at Columbia-Presbyterian Hospital in New York collaborated with **Dr. William Pollack** of the Ortho (Pharmaceutical Company) Research Foundation to produce Rh Immune Globulin, better known by the trade name, RhoGAM.

At the White House Conference on Children and Youth in March–April 1960 **Dr. Stanley M. Garn** of Antioch College reported on obesity in teenagers. Increased caloric intake and decreased exercise were to blame.

University of Colorado Medical Center physician **Dr. Joseph H. Holmes** reported on the painless, portable ultrasound used on pregnant women in 1964. Ultrasound provides a cheap, safe way to look inside the womb.

Dr. Frank L. Horsfall, Jr., took over the Memorial Sloan-Kettering Cancer Center in New York in February 1960. The director's position had been vacant since the death of **Dr. Cornelius ("Dusty") Rhoads** in August of 1959.

An epidemic of infectious hepatitis in New Jersey was traced to people eating raw clams in 1961 by **Dr. Roscoe P. Kandle** of the Connecticut Department of Health. He pointed out that the clams ate raw sewage dumped in public waterways, passing hepatitis to people eating the clams.

Dr. Adrian Kantrowitz of Brooklyn's Maimonides Hospital had to weld shut a new implantable heart pacemaker in 1961 while it was in the patient's open chest.

Dr. John P. Merrill at Peter Bent Brigham Hospital in Boston treated patients with kidney failure in 1962 using a "drainplug" in the abdomen. The plug could be removed to attach hoses for dialysis.

Dr. Carl Moyer at Washington University in Saint Louis reported on the healing properties of silver nitrate for burn victims in 1965; used in the proper low concentrations, it reduces pain and scarring in skin-graft procedures.

Dr. David Nachmansohn of Columbia University found out how nerves work in 1960. He used giant nerve fibers from Amazonian electric eels in his research.

In 1960 **Dr. Meyer Naide** of Philadelphia suggested excessive television watching led to heart attacks, indigestion, obesity, and even epilepsy from inactivity.

In 1961 **Dr. David Poskanzer** and **Dr. Robert S. Schwab** of Harvard found that the brain disorder parkinsonism (shaking palsy) was related to a 1915–1925 encephalitis epidemic.

The records of six thousand autopsies were reviewed by **Dr. Hans Smetana** of Walter Reed Army Medical Center in 1960 to try to find the cause of sudden, unexpected death in infants.

Ultrasound was being used by **Dr. Hans Zinsser** of Columbia-Presbyterian Hospital in New York to detect multiple fetuses before birth in 1962.

AWARDS

NOBEL PRIZE WINNERS IN MEDICINE OR PHYSIOLOGY

1960

Sir Frank McFarlane Burnet (Australia) and Peter B. Medawar (Great Britain)

1961

Georg von Bekesy (United States)

1962

James Dewey Watson (United States), *Maurice H. F. Wilkins* (Great Britain), and Francis Harry C. Crick (Great Britain)

1963

Alan Lloyd Hodgkin (Great Britain), Andrew Fielding Huxley (Great Britain), and Sir John Carew Eccles (Australia)

1964

Konrad E. Bloch (United States) and Feodor Lynen (Germany)

1965

François Jacob (France), André Lwoff (France), and Jacques Monod (France)

1966

Charles Huggins (United States) and Peyton Rous (United States)

1967

Ragnar Granit (Sweden), Haldan Keffer Hartline (United States), and George Wald (United States)

1968

Robert W. Holley (United States), H. Gobind Khorana (United States), and Marshall W. Nirenberg (United States)

1969

Max Delbruck (United States), Alfred Day Hershey (United States), and Salvador E. Luria (United States)

ALBERT LASKER AWARDS

1960

Paul W. Brand, Gudmund Harlem, and Mary E. Switzer

1961 N/A

1962

Joseph E. Smadel and C. H. Li

1963

Lyman C. Craig, Michael Ellis DeBakey, and Charles Huggins

1964

Nathan S. Kline, Renato Dulbecco, and Harry Rubin

1965

Albert Sabin and Robert W. Holley

1966

Sidney Farber and George E. Palade

1967

Robert Allan Phillips, Claude Pepper, and Bernard B. Brodie

1968

John H. Gibbon, William F. Windle, H. Gobind Khorana, and Marshall W. Nirenberg

1969

George C. Cotzias and Bruce Merrifield

DEATHS

Franz Gabriel Alexander, 73, Hungarian-born psychoanalyst, pioneered psychosomatic medicine in the United States, 8 March 1964.

W. Wayne Babcock, 90, physician, involved in the development of spinal anesthesia and introduced a variety of surgical techniques including the use of steel-wire sutures, 23 February 1963.

Louis Hopewell Bauer, 75, cardiologist, pioneered aviation medicine and served as secretary-general of the World Medical Association (1948–1961), 2 February 1964.

Alfred Blalock, 65, surgeon in chief of Johns Hopkins Hospital, codeveloped blue-baby surgery as well as the hand-pump cardiac-resuscitation method, 15 September 1964.

Paul Earle Carlson, 36, missionary doctor, killed by Congolese rebels in Stanleyville, Congo, 24 November 1964.

Frank P. Corrigan, 86, surgeon, diplomat, and first U.S. ambassador to Venezuela, helped prove the feasibility of blood transfusion, 21 January 1968.

Thomas Dooley, 34, physician, established medical missions in Laos and was a founder of the Medico organization, 18 January 1961.

Thomas Francis, Jr., 69, virologist, developed an anti-influenza vaccine and directed field testing of the Salk polio vaccine, 1 October 1969.

Casimir Funk, 83, Polish-born biochemist, discovered a substance he called a "vitamine" (the e was later dropped) while studying the disease beriberi, 19 November 1967.

Herbert Spencer Gasser, 74, physiologist, shared the 1944 Nobel Prize in medicine for research demonstrating the reaction of nerve fibers to electrical impulses, 11 May 1963.

Carl G. Harman, 88, researcher in family planning and zoologist, helped establish the basic principles of birth control through studies in embryology and gynecology, 1 March 1968.

Warren Sturgis McCulloch, 70, neurophysiologist, helped establish the science of cybernetics through his studies of the brain, 24 September 1969.

William Claire Menninger, 66, psychiatrist, cofounded and presided over the Menninger Foundation for Psychiatric Education and Research, 6 September 1966.

Hermann Joseph Muller, 76, geneticist, won the 1946 Nobel Prize for his discovery of the effects of radiation on heredity, 5 April 1967.

George Papanicolaou, 78, Greek-born medical researcher, developed the Pap-smear test for uterine cancer, 19 February 1962.

Thomas Parran, 75, surgeon general of the United States (1936–1948), helped to establish the World Health Organization, 15 February 1968.

Gregory Goodwin Pincus, 64, medical researcher and director of the Worcester Foundation for Experimental Biology, helped develop the first successful birth-control pill, 22 August 1967.

Theodor Reik, 81, theorist, researcher, and student of Freud, helped develop the theory and technique of psychoanalysis, 31 December 1969.

Alfred Newton Richards, 90, pharmacologist, was a member of the Big Six, the scientific organization overseeing the creation of war matériel and medicines during World War II, and served as president of the National Academy of Sciences (1947–1950), 24 March 1966.

Margaret Higgins Sanger, 82, pioneer in the birth–control movement, opened the first American birth-control clinic in Brooklyn, New York, and helped found the International Planned Parenthood Federation, 6 September 1966.

Bela Schick, 90, Hungarian-born pediatrician, invented the diphtheria (Schick) test and performed extensive research on allergies (a term he helped to coin), 6 December 1967.

Gordon S. Seagrave, 68, doctor known as "the Burmese Surgeon," served a long career providing medical care for the Burmese people, 28 March 1965.

Francis E. Townsend, 93, physician, founded the old-age pension plan that bore his name, 1 September 1960.

Robert J. Van de Graaff, 65, inventor of the Van de Graaff particle accelerator used in cancer therapy and nuclear physics, 16 January 1967.

PUBLICATIONS

General

Franklin Bicknell, *Chemicals in Food and in Farm Products* (New York: Emerson, 1961);

Marguerite Clark, *Medicine Today: A Report on a Decade of Progress* (New York: Funk & Wagnalls, 1960);

John H. Heller, *Of Mice, Men, and Molecules* (New York: Scribners, 1960);

Brian Inglis, *The Case for Unorthodox Medicine* (New York: Putnam, 1965);

Dr. Fritz Kahn, *The Human Body* (New York: Random House, 1965);

Henry B. Lent, *Man Alive in Outer Space* (New York: Macmillan, 1961);

Benjamin F. Miller and Ruth Goode, *Man and His Body: The Wonders of the Human Mechanism* (New York: Simon & Schuster, 1960);

Peter S. Nagan, ed., *Medical Almanac 1961-62* (New York: Saunders, 1961);

Charles Singer and E. Ashworth Underwood, *A Short History of Medicine* (New York: Oxford University Press, 1962);

Norman Burke Taylor and Allen Ellsworth Taylor, *The Putnam Medical Dictionary* (New York: Putnam, 1961).

Cancer

Orlando A. Battista, *Toward the Conquest of Cancer* (New York: Chilton, 1961).

Health Insurance and Government Programs

John Black Grant, *Healthcare for the Community* (Baltimore: Johns Hopkins University Press, 1963);

Richard Harris, *A Sacred Trust* (New York: New American Library, 1966);

Herman M. Somers and Anne R. Somers, *Doctors, Patients, and Health Insurance* (Washington, D.C.: Brookings Institution, 1961).

Heart Disease and Surgery

Nikolai M. Amosov, *The Open Heart* (New York: Simon & Schuster, 1966);

Isaac Asimov, *The Living River* (London & New York: Abelard-Schuman, 1959);

F. Kerner, *Stress and Your Heart* (New York: Hawthorn Books, 1961).

Medical Profession

Barry Commoner, *Science and Survival* (New York: Viking, 1966);

William H. Davenport, *The Good Physician* (New York: Macmillan, 1962);

Doctor X, *Intern* (New York: Harper & Row, 1965);

Iago Galdston, *Medicine in Transition* (Chicago: University of Chicago Press, 1965);

Hugo Glaser, *The Road to Modern Surgery* (New York: Dutton, 1962);

Albert Love and James Saxon Childers, eds., *Listen to Leaders in Medicine* (Atlanta: Tupper & Love, 1963);

Zhores A. Medvedev, *The Rise and Fall of T. D. Lysenko*, translated by Michael Lerner (New York: Columbia University Press, 1969).

Mental Illness and Psychology

Erik H. Erikson, *Identity: Youth and Crisis* (New York: Norton, 1968);

Martin L. Gross, *The Brain Watchers* (New York: Random House, 1962);

Carl Jung, *Memories, Dreams, Reflections,* edited by Aniela Jaffe (New York: Pantheon, 1963);

Robert Jay Lifton, *Death in Life: Survivors of Hiroshima* (New York: Simon & Schuster, 1967);

Konrad Lorenz, *On Aggression* (New York: Harcourt, Brace & World, 1966);

Norman MacKenzie, *Dreams and Dreaming* (New York: Vanguard, 1965);

John Mann, *Frontiers of Psychology* (New York: Macmillan, 1963);

R. E. Masters and Jean Houston, *The Varieties of Psychedelic Experience* (New York: Holt, Rinehart & Winston, 1966);

Charles Rolo, ed., *Psychiatry in American Life* (Boston: Atlantic-Little, Brown, 1963);

Theodore Szasz, *Analysis* (New York: Basic Books, 1965).

Physical Fitness

Better Homes and Gardens Eat and Stay Slim (New York: Meredith Press, 1968);

Marjorie Craig, *Miss Craig's 21-Day Shape-Up Program for Men and Women* (New York: Random House, 1968);

Erwin M. Stillman and Samm Sinclair Baker, *The Doctor's Quick Weight Loss Diet* (Englewood Cliffs, N. J.: Prentice-Hall, 1968);

Herman Taller, *Calories Don't Count* (New York: Simon & Schuster, 1962).

Polio

Richard Carter, *Breakthrough: The Saga of Jonas Salk* (New York: Trident, 1965);

John Rowland, *The Polio Man: The Story of Dr. Jonas Salk* (New York: Roy, 1961);

John Rowan Wilson, *Margin of Safety: The Story of the Poliomyelitis Vaccine* (Garden City, N.Y.: Doubleday, 1963).

Reproduction and Sex

Helen Gurley Brown, *Sex and the Single Girl* (New York: Bernard Geis, 1962);

William Howard Masters and Virginia E. Johnston, *Human Sexual Response* (Boston: Little, Brown, 1966);

John Rock, *The Time Has Come* (New York: Knopf, 1963).

Virology and Bacteriology

Theodor Rosebury, *Life on Man* (New York: Viking, 1969);

Wendell M. Stanley and Evans G. Valens, *Viruses and the Nature of Life* (New York: Dutton, 1961).

Periodicals

American Medical News;

Journal of the American Medical Association;

Medical History;

"Medicine," weekly report in *Newsweek;*

"Medicine," weekly report in *Time.*

Cigarette sales and health hazards

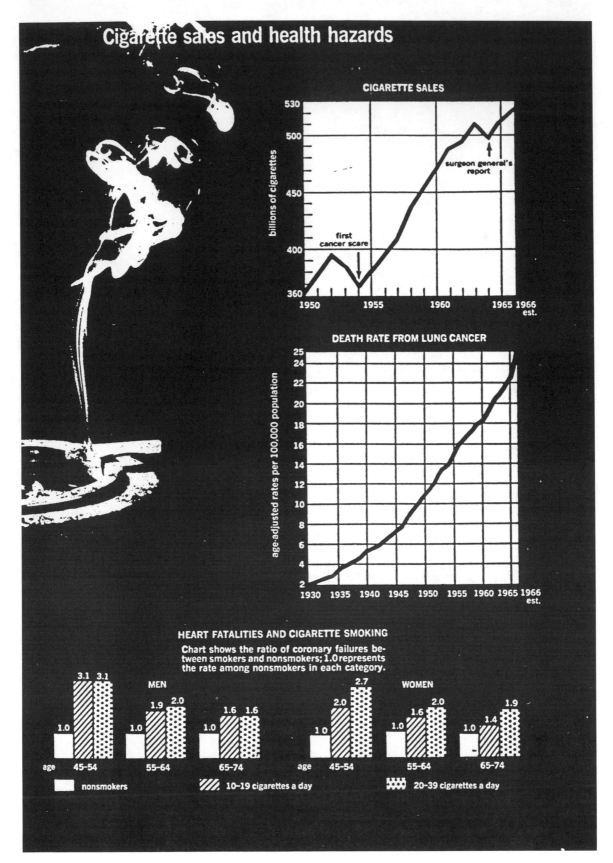

Public-service announcement, 1967

CHAPTER ELEVEN
RELIGION

by JOHN SCOTT WILSON

CONTENTS

Sidebars and tables listed in italics.

1960

- The Standing Conference of Orthodox Bishops in America is created to co-ordinate actions among the various Eastern Orthodox groups in the United States.

9 Jan. The Protestant Episcopal Church approves the use of artificial birth control.

28 Apr. The General Assembly of the Presbyterian Church, U.S. (Southern), declares that marital sexual relations without the intent of procreation are not sinful.

1961

22–23 Jan. The National Council of Churches approves the use of birth control and family planning.

29 May In *Two Guys from Harrison — Allentown, Inc.* v. *McGinley* the Supreme Court rules that a Pennsylvania law, as presently written, that requires businesses to close on Sunday does not violate the equal protection clause of the Fourteenth Amendment since the law is secular in intent and is aimed to provide workers with rest and to prevent unfair competition.

19 June The Supreme Court unanimously rules in *Toresco* v. *Watkins* that the state of Maryland cannot require candidates for office to swear they believe in a Supreme Being. This is a religious test for office and violates the First Amendment.

1962

23 Mar. Archbishop Joseph Francis Rummel of New Orleans orders the desegregation of all diocesan schools.

16 Apr. Archbishop Rummel excommunicates three people, including the powerful politician Leander Perez, for their opposition to desegregation of Roman Catholic schools.

25 June The Supreme Court in *Engel* v. *Vitale* rules that a prayer required for the public schools of New York violates the establishment of religion clause of the First Amendment.

1963

- Hebrew Union College (Reform) establishes a branch in Jerusalem.

21 May The United Presbyterian Church General Assembly passes a resolution opposing compulsory school prayer and devotions. It also opposes religious displays on public sites and tax privileges for the clergy.

23 May Elizabeth Ann Bayley Seton, founder of the American Sisters of Charity of Saint Joseph, is canonized by Pope John XXIII, making her eligible to become the first American-born saint.

9 June Black worshipers are turned away from Galloway Memorial Methodist Church in Jackson, Mississippi. The minister, Rev. W. B. Selah, and the assistant minister, Rev. Jerry Furr, resign from their positions, asking to be reassigned to other churches.

17 June The Supreme Court, in *School Board of Abington Township* v. *Schempp*, rules that states cannot require Bible reading in public schools.

4 Dec. The Second Vatican Ecumenical Council authorizes the use of vernacular languages, English and Spanish in the United States, in the Mass.

1964

- The National Catholic Reporter begins publication. This independent, lay-controlled journal becomes a major voice in Roman Catholic circles.

12 May   Rachel Henderlite is the first woman to be ordained by the Presbyterian Church, U.S. (Southern).

21 May   Elder Garrett Hawkins, pastor of Saint Augustine Church in the Bronx, is elected the first African-American moderator of the United Presbyterian Church.

May   Baptists, including members of the American Baptist Convention; the National Baptist Convention of America, the National Baptist Convention, U.S.A.; and the Southern Baptist Convention in Atlantic City, New Jersey, celebrate the 150th anniversary of the first Baptist mission organization in the United States.

14 Oct.   The Nobel Peace Prize is awarded to Martin Luther King, Jr., for his work in civil rights. He donates the $54,600 award to the civil rights movement.

1965

- The Lutheran Council in the U.S.A. is created by the three largest Lutheran bodies — the Lutheran Church in America, the Lutheran Church-Missouri Synod, and the American Lutheran Church — to coordinate their joint activities.

21 Feb.   Malcolm X is assassinated as he addresses a rally in Harlem. Members of the Nation of Islam are later arrested and convicted for the crime.

11 Mar.   Rev. James Reeb, a Unitarian minister from Boston, dies following a beating he had received in Selma, Alabama, on 9 March. He was in Selma as part of the voting rights campaign. The men tried for the crime are later found not guilty.

30 Mar.   The New York State Supreme Court rules that Black Muslims in Attica prison have the same rights to practice their religion and worship together as do Protestants, Catholics, and Jews.

May   The Most Reverend Harold Robert Perry is appointed auxiliary bishop of New Orleans. He is the first African-American bishop in the Roman Catholic church in the twentieth century and the second in the history of that church.

2 Oct.   Pope Paul VI arrives in New York on a trip to the United Nations. He is the first reigning pope to come to the United States.

1966

18 Nov.   Roman Catholic bishops announce that effective 2 December Catholics in the United States will no longer have to abstain from eating meat on Fridays, except during Lent.

1967

18 May   The governor of Tennessee signs into law a bill which repeals the "Monkey Law" of 1925. That law forbade public schools teaching "any theory that denied the story of devine creation of man as taught in the Bible" or "that man has descended from a lower order of animals." The "Monkey Law" led to the famous Scopes trial in Dayton, Tennessee, in 1925.

22 May   The General Assembly of the Presbyterian Church, U.S.A. (Northern), adopts the Confession of Faith of 1967, the first major new confession by Presbyterians since the Westminster Confession of 1647.

1968

- Troy Perry organizes the Metropolitan Community Church, a ministry directed at homosexual men and women.

Apr. The Black Catholic Clergy Caucus is organized and creates a National Office for Black Catholics.

4 Apr. Martin Luther King, Jr., is assassinated in Memphis. Riots break out in nearly 130 cities. Order is restored in some only by martial law.

16 June Rabbi Yeheda Leib Levin, chief rabbi of Moscow, arrives in the United States for a two-week visit. This is the first official representation of Russian Jewry in over fifty years. His statements that Soviet Jews have full religious freedom and that there is no anti-Semitism there fail to convince many of his audiences.

Aug. The National Black Sisters Conference of black Catholic religious orders is organized.

Oct. Richard Cardinal Cushing of Boston announces his retirement. Among his reasons is the hate mail he received for defending the recent marriage of Mrs. John F. Kennedy to the divorced Aristotle Onassis.

12 Nov. The Supreme Court strikes down an Arkansas law permitting public schools to teach the Bible version of Creation but forbidding teaching any theory that "mankind ascended or descended from lower order of animals." The Court rules this is a violation of religious freedom guaranteed under the First and Fourteenth Amendments.

24 Dec. The *Apollo 8* mission begins its orbit around the Moon, the first manned flight. The three astronauts take turns reading from the first verses of Genesis in the King James Version of the Bible.

1969

26 Apr. The National Black Economic Development Conference, led by James Foreman, issues its Black Manifesto, demanding churches and synagogues pay $500 million in reparations for their complicity in racism.

Thomas Kilgore, Jr., pastor of Second Baptist Church of Los Angles, is elected president of the American Baptist Convention; he is the first African-American to hold that office.

26 May The General Assembly of the Presbyterian Church, U.S. (Southern), passes a resolution that the theory of evolution and the traditional biblical interpretation of Creation are "not contradictory."

29 May The General Assembly of the Presbyterian Church, U.S. (Southern), passes a resolution saying that citizens have a right of conscientious objection to a particular war, in the context of the times this refers to the American involvement in the Vietnam conflict.

May Christ Memorial Church, Saint Louis, Missouri, a predominantly white Southern Baptist Convention congregation, affiliates with the National Baptist Convention, U.S.A., apparently the first Southern Baptist Convention congregation to affiliate jointly with a predominantly African-American denomination.

10 June Norman Vincent Peale, pastor of the Marble Collegiate Church, is elected president of the Reformed Church in America.

OVERVIEW

Public Issues. The "Death of God"; no compulsory prayer or Bible reading in the public schools; nuns and priest leaving their orders for secular lives, including marriage — the religious controversies of the 1960s seemed endless. While these issues aroused much emotion, other, deeper social currents concerning race, gender and sexuality, war, and the role of churches in society changed the religious landscape of the United States. The apparent religious revival of the postwar period ground to a halt in the course of the decade. While religious commitment in the United States remained the highest in the industrial world, people stopped talking of a new revival and began to discuss decline. In 1957, 14 percent of the Americans polled said religion was in decline in the United States. In 1970 that figure had increased to 75 percent.

Mainline Churches Decline. As the decade began, the mainline Protestant churches seemed to continue their dominance of society and culture. Reflecting the similarity of their views on society and faith, the leading denominations began the decade in what was called the Consultation on Church Union, which hoped to create a denomination of over twenty-five million people and preserve their leading role in the culture. In the view of many in this ecumenical movement, a united church would permit more effective coordination of their common interest in social action, such as supporting the efforts of black southerners to end legal segregation in the Jim Crow South and checking the expanded American role in the conflict in Vietnam, as well as in issues of poverty and gender. In a way those activists were successful. By the end of the decade the civil rights movement had completed its victories, and President Richard M. Nixon had promised to wind down the war. But these churches found their membership not only stopped growing in relation to the growth of population, but in some cases they even lost membership.

Conservative Churches Grow. Conservatives in those consulting denominations and members in openly conservative denominations expressed reservations, even outright opposition, to the ecumenical drive as well as to the focus on social activism by the mainline churches. Their criticism seemed justified as those ecumenical churches lost members while resurgent evangelicalism steadily brought new members to conservative Protestantism, which even begin to move back into the public arena.

The Effects of Vatican II. American Roman Catholics finally found symbolic acceptance with the election in 1960 of John Fitzgerald Kennedy, the first Roman Catholic president. And the Second Vatican Council (1962–1965) led to major changes in the conduct of the church in America. The switch of the Mass from Latin to English, the turning of the priest from the altar to the parishioners at the Mass, and the new democratic impulse released by Vatican II — the reformist council called for in 1959 by Pope John XXIII — weakened the old suspicions of American Protestants just as they reflected the weakening of the authoritarian church of the past. By the end of the decade the Roman Catholic church in the United States was an integral part of the larger community, and its members were among the most successful of American groups. But this acceptance seemed to have a price, as priests and nuns fled their orders and parishioners proved willing to act independently in religious and moral matters, particularly in regard to birth control.

Jews, America, and Israel. The Jewish community began the decade while debating the possible loss of a Jewish identity in America through assimilation, represented by a growing tendency of Jews to marry outside their religious group. But Israel's stunning success in the Six Day War against Egypt, Jordan, and Syria in 1967 triggered a rededication of Jews to their heritage and an intensified identification with the Jewish state.

New Groups Rise. Christian groups that had formerly attracted little attention from public observers began to register growth and power. Not only conservative Protestant groups, who called themselves Evangelicals, but Pentecostal Protestant churches grew in number and respectability, and Pentecostalism itself, mostly in the form of glossolalia (speaking in tongues), spread into traditional churches including Presbyterian, Episcopal, and Roman Catholic groups. The Church of Jesus Christ of Latter Day Saints (Mormon) continued to move out of its western center into the rest of the United States and the world. The increase in membership from 1,486,887 in 1960 to 1,930,811 in 1968 made it one of the fastest-growing religious groups during the decade. In 1969 the Mormons broke ground on a new temple in the Washington, D.C., area. Its six massive spires were intended to symbolize the arrival of the church at the center of American society.

New Faiths Appear. Faiths that were new to America began to appear. Islam acquired followers after the relaxation of immigration restrictions in 1965 and with the expansion of the black nationalist movement of Elijah Muhammad's Nation of Islam. Malcolm X, the Nation of Islam's most notorious spokesman, was expelled and began a more orthodox Muslim movement before his assassination in 1965. By the end of the decade plans were under way for the construction of a massive new mosque in New York City to serve the needs of both Americans and Muslim diplomats.

Asian Imports. Religions from Asia also began to pick up followers to the dismay of many traditional Christians and Jews. The Krishna consciousness movement opened in California, and by the end of the decade travelers in airports complained about the solicitations of the saffron-clad Hare Krishnas, as they were usually called. Rev. Sun Myung Moon brought his Unification church to the United States and attracted criticism ranging from that of his politics to that of his religious beliefs. For many conventional people these two groups were among the various religious cults that proliferated in the yeasty fringes of the counterculture.

A Splintering Society. As disturbing for the conventional was the organization of the Metropolitan Community Church by Troy Perry in 1968. The Metropolitan churches, later organized as the Universal Fellowship of Community Churches, served a primarily homosexual community that acquired increasing visibility in the splintering society at the end of the decade.

Change and Continuity. By earlier standards religion in the United States went through a series of wrenching changes in the decade, but at a deeper level these changes were similar to changes which had occurred in the previous centuries of the nation's history.

TOPICS IN THE NEWS

THE ARAB-ISRAELI SIX-DAY WAR, 1967

Invasion. On 5 June 1967 the developing military crisis in the Middle East exploded when the Israeli air force launched lighting raids against the Egyptian troops which had recently reoccupied the Sinai Peninsula. A United Nations emergency force had served as a buffer force in the Sinai since the clash between Israel and Egypt in the Suez Crisis of 1956 but withdrew at Egypt's request. Cairo also announced it would close Israel's access to the Red Sea through the Gulf of 'Aqaba.

Jerusalem Reunited. Anticipating an Arab war against the Jewish state, Israeli forces struck. In less than a week they first destroyed the Egyptian forces in the Sinai, then drove the military of Jordan from the west bank of the Jordan River, and finally crushed the forces of Syria and occupied the Golan Heights in southern Syria. In the process the Old City of Jerusalem was seized and annexed by Israel.

The Balance of Power. The extraordinary success of the small but highly equipped and trained Israeli forces against the combined armies of three Arab states changed the balance of power in the Middle East for the coming decades and created diplomatic problems that still echo.

Israel and American Jews. The threat of the destruction of Israel had too-obvious parallels with the Holocaust for the American Jewish community, which rallied to the Israeli cause with intense commitment. Unprecedented millions of dollars were quickly raised for Israel, and a heightened sense of religious and ethnic identity appeared. After the Six-Day War, American Jews tended to identify themselves by their commitment to the Jewish state, and many equated non-Jewish reservations about Israel with anti-Semitism.

Tensions with Christians. This led to a shift in Jewish attitude toward Christian groups. Many liberal Protestants, politically and culturally most favorable to Jews, raised questions about annexing eastern Jerusalem, noting that it was a holy city for both Muslims and Christians and that annexation would only complicate the chances for a lasting peace. Conservative Protestants, some of whom previously had been a source of anti-Semitism, now became enthusiastic supporters of Israel because the return of Jews to Jerusalem seemed to confirm biblical prophecy of the end of time. And radicals, both black and white, easily found parallels between what they considered America's unconscionable imperialism in Vietnam and Israel's relations with the Arab states and the Palestinians. This criticism of Israel, coupled with local tensions, embittered relations between Jews and African-Americans by the end of the decade. At that time a public opinion poll indicated that 33 percent of the Jews surveyed attributed a rise in anti-Semitism to militant blacks and 10 percent blamed New Left radicals.

Sources:
Arthur Hertzberg, "Israel and American Jewry," *Commentary,* 44 (August 1967): 69–73;

Martin Peretz, "The American Left and Israel," *Commentary,* 44 (November 1967): 27–34.

THE ASSIMILATION OF THE JEWS

Decline of Anti-Semitism. The postwar expansion of the American economy and the movement to the suburbs coincided with a decline in anti-Semitism. Jews, almost all now in their second or third generation in the United States, were able to move up professionally and out geographically. Their success made them the model ethnic group, offering other immigrants an example of what could be done in the United States. In spite of Zionist hopes, few Americans chose to go to the new Jewish state of Israel. By the 1960s many were Americans who happened to be Jews, and successful Americans at that.

Vanishing Judaism? While they were a successful group, what did it mean to be a Jew in America? Very little, some Jews feared. By 1964 surveys indicated that weekly religious attendance at synagogue or temple was only 17 percent, compared to the 42 percent weekly church attendance among Christians. Some Jewish observers wondered if those figures reflected the weakness of the Jewish faith and culture. They noted that Hanukkah, a minor Jewish holiday, had become the most celebrated holiday among Jews, and even the High Holidays did not attract significant numbers of worshipers.

The Problem of Assimilation. In *The Dilemma of the Modern Jew* (1962) Rabbi Joachim Prinz warned that the danger to Jews in the United States was not the anti-Semitism of the past but assimilation. His fears seemed confirmed in a study by Erich Rosenthal that appeared in the *American Jewish Yearbook* in 1963. Rosenthal discovered a growing rate of intermarriage between Jews and non-Jews, particularly among younger people. The intermarriage rate of third-generation Jews in the Washington, D.C., area was 17.9 percent. Among college students, an increasing number of whom were Jews, that rate reached 37 percent. In Iowa, where the Jewish population was small, the intermarriage rate had reached 42.2 percent. The intermarriage rate, coupled with a declining birth rate, suggested to some that the Jewish race as such might disappear in the United States.

Culture or Religion? Rosenthal's study attracted much attention in the mid 1960s among Jews and the general public. General circulation magazines such as *Time, Look,* and *Newsweek* wrote of the vanishing American Jew. Yet non-Jewish observers wondered at the issue as they saw the large new Jewish religious centers in the suburbs with their numerous classes and activities. But some Jewish observers believed that these centers demonstrated that their coreligionists saw Judaism only as a religion and not as the vital culture their parents had brought with them to the United States. Because Jewish institutions had failed to inculcate traditional values in the young, Jewish college students found themselves alienated and open to secularization and new religious cults.

Problems of Secularism. In 1968 Irving Greenberg, rabbi of an Orthodox congregation in New York and professor at Yeshiva University, published a bitter lament about the dangers to Judaism on campus, claiming that the secular rationalism of the university undermined religious faith and observance and brought young people together with a consequent increase in intermarriage. He proposed that Jewish organizations fund the Center for Jewish Survival to cope with the problem.

Dust jacket for Hannah Arendt's book that stimulated Holocaust studies

Support and Travel. Again, outsiders would be puzzled by Greenberg's concern, as the Six Day War tapped a reservoir of loyalty from American Jews. Remembering the Holocaust, in the summer of 1967 anxious Americans had raised unprecedented sums for the support of Israel. In the following years Israel became a favored travel spot for Americans, though few moved there.

Reexamining the Holocaust. Perhaps it was the Six Day War or perhaps it was only that time had begun to make it possible to confront the past, but at the end of the 1960s the Holocaust became a subject for examination and analysis. One of the triggers, obviously, was Hannah Arendt's *Eichman in Jerusalem: A Report on the Banality of Evil* (1963), which raised questions about the Jewish response to the Holocaust. As the decade wore on, the examination of the event became one of the focal points of American Jewish culture.

Sources:
Morton Adler, "What Is a Jew?" *Harper's,* 228 (January 1964): 41–45;

"Jewishness and the Young Intellectuals: A Symposium" *Commentary,* 31 (April 1961): 306–359;

Thomas B. Morgan, "The Vanishing American Jew," *Look,* 28 (5 May 1964): 42–46;

Edward Shapiro, *A Time for Healing: American Jewry since 1945* (Baltimore: Johns Hopkins University Press, 1992).

BLACK MANIFESTO

Manifesto of Revolution. In May 1969 James Foreman of the Student Nonviolent Coordinating Committee (SNCC) presented the "Manifesto to the White Christian Churches and the Jewish Synagogues in the United States of America and All Other Racist Institutions" to the New York meeting of the National Council of Churches. The manifesto, adopted earlier by the National Black Economic Development Conference, was a combination of Marxist ideology and black power rhetoric. As Foreman said in his introduction, the aim was "to bring this [American] government down . . . [and] liberate all the people in the U.S. and . . . the colored people the world around. . . . Racism in the U.S. is so pervasive . . . that only an armed, well-disciplined, black-controlled government can insure the stamping out of racism."

Reparations. The manifesto demanded that the religious bodies of the United States provide $500 million in reparations for their implication in the "capitalistic and imperialist power structure." Two days later, in what became an ongoing practice through the year, Foreman interrupted the sermon at Riverside Church in New York City to read his demands. Shortly thereafter he made the same presentation to the American Baptist Convention.

Anti-White Racism. The Black Manifesto offended most whites by its anti-white racism as well its demands for reparations for actions done by people long dead, many of whom were not even ancestors of current Americans. That anger was directed, in turn, to those church leaders who, having sensed the frustration in the black

---

CASSIUS CLAY (MUHAMMAD ALI)

After confirming rumors that he was now a Muslim, Cassius Clay, the new world champion, said that Allah had been in the ring with him in his fight with Sonny Liston. But, he clarified, "I am not a Black Muslim, because that is a word made up by the white press. I am a black man who has adopted Islam. I want peace, and I do not find peace in an integrated world. I love to be black and I love to be with my people. . . . Why do I want to get bit by dogs, washed down a sewer by fire hoses? Why does everybody attack me for being righteous? Why don't people leave me alone?"

Source: Huston Horn, "The First Days of the New Life of the Champion of the World," *Sports Illustrated,* 20 (9 March 1964): 57.

---

community that had led to the stunning race riots in the previous years, seemed willing to use church funds for programs for black improvement. Local opposition to denominational bureaucracies coupled with conservative criticism of the social and theological liberalism of national leaders to weaken the influence of the mainstream churches.

Sources:
"Black Bill Collector," *Newsweek,* 73 (19 May 1969): 74–75;

"Black Manifesto," *Time,* 93 (16 May 1969): 94;

Alan Geyer, "May Day in Manhattan," *Christian Century* (14 May 1969): 671–672;

"James Foreman's Black Manifesto," *America,* 120 (24 May 1969): 605.

BLACK MUSLIMS

Separation. In the early part of the decade the news media paid increasing attention to what they called the Black Muslims, members of the Lost-Found Nation of Islam, headed by the Honorable Elijah Muhammad. Muhammad insisted that early in the century he had come into contact with a mysterious W. D. Fard, who was later identified as Allah himself. When Fard disappeared in 1933, Muhammad took control of his organization and its Detroit mosque. Muhammad's ideas rested on a foundation of black separatism with trappings of Islam. Blacks were the original people. Whites were devils who became the oppressors of blacks. Islam was the true religion and the natural religion of blacks. They should leave the slave religion of Christianity and separate themselves from the larger white culture.

Malcolm X. Muhammad served a brief prison sentence for encouraging his followers to refuse the draft in World War II. On his release he began to rebuild his movement from his new headquarters in Chicago. One of his most astute moves was to recognize the potential of a recent convert, Malcolm Little, who had taken the name

Max von Sydow as Jesus Christ in *The Greatest Story Ever Told*

George Plimpton, "Miami Notebook: Cassius Clay and Malcolm X," *Harper's*, 238 (June 1964): 54–61.

BOOKS AND MOVIES

A Lean Decade. There were few successful movies or novels with explicitly religious themes during the 1960s. In 1961 a remake of *King of Kings*, a life of Jesus, was released. Nicholas Ray directed Jeffrey Hunter and Siobhan McKenna in this CinemaScope version, which was better received by the critics than by the audience. In 1965 George Stevens directed another version of the life of Jesus, *The Greatest Story Ever Told*, starring Max von Sydow and Charlton Heston. This version was filled with famous stars in cameo roles. John Wayne played a Roman officer supervising the Crucifixion of Jesus. The next year John Huston tackled the first twenty-two chapters of Genesis in a film called *The Bible*. The film was not a success with either the critics or the public. Huston himself made a passable Noah. Critics believed the best of the biblical films to appear in the United States during the decade was Pier Posolini's *Gospel According to St. Matthew*, which was released in the United States in 1966. This moving, simple telling of the story of Jesus was warmly received by critics and audiences in large cities, but it had limited impact on general or religious audiences because of difficulties with commercial distribution of a foreign film.

Criticism of Religion. Reflecting the declining power of religious censorship, Hollywood also ventured into stories critical of religion. In 1960 a film version of Sinclair Lewis's attack of itinerant revivalists, *Elmer Gantry*, was released. It was directed by Richard Brooks and starred Burt Lancaster, Jean Simmons, and Shirley Jones. This searing indictment of religious hypocrisy won Academy Awards for Lancaster and Jones. That same year a film version was released of the play *Inherit the Wind*. This film was loosely based on the Scopes trial in Dayton, Tennessee, in 1925. Directed by Stanley Kramer, it starred Fredric March as the William Jennings Bryan character and Spencer Tracy as a fictional version of Clarence Darrow. By middecade biblical epics had fallen from favor as the Hollywood studio system went through a series of contractions resulting from its unsuccessful struggle with television. The movie audience split, and Hollywood began to reorient itself toward more-adult, serious films or those explicitly directed toward young people. The new ratings system reflected this change.

Secular City. While little religious fiction sold well, several books with serious themes became best-sellers. In 1965 Harvey Cox found an unexpected audience for his examination of the role of religion in the current culture. While his *Secular City: Secularization and Urbanization in Theological Perspective* was not a part of the Death of God movement, his assertion that the general culture was no longer Christian and that Christianity had to adapt to make itself a meaningful part of midcentury culture

Malcolm X. (Members of the Nation of Islam replaced their "slave" names with *X*, indicating their plundered African background.) Malcolm X expanded the organization on the East Coast from his mosque in New York. A brilliant speaker, he attracted the attention of the news media and rarely left its spotlight until his assassination in 1965.

Growth and Self-Sufficiency. The Nation of Islam anticipated some of the issues of black power in its program of self-help and self-reliance. Black Muslims rejected drugs, alcohol, and pork. They dressed in sober costumes and were encouraged to patronize businesses owned by the Nation of Islam. At its height in middecade the organization had an estimated three hundred thousand members.

Scandal. The movement was rocked by scandal in mid-decade with charges that the Muhammad family profited from the organization and that Elijah Muhammad had maintained a series of sexual relationships with certain of his secretaries, having children by some. These stories, along with the expulsion of Malcolm X from the group and his subsequent assassination, caused membership to decline.

Sources:

James Baldwin, "Letter from a Region of My Mind," *New Yorker*, 38 (17 November 1962): 87–88;

Alfred Balk and Alex Haley, "Black Merchants of Hate," *Saturday Evening Post*, 236 (26 January 1963): 68–75;

Bruce Perry, *Malcolm: The Life of a Man Who Changed Black America* (Barrytown, N.Y.: Station Hill Press, 1991);

helped sell over three hundred thousand copies in only two years. In 1967 James Kavanaugh published a searing examination of the Roman Catholic church in *A Modern Priest Looks at His Outdated Church*. He left the priesthood a short time later. The denominational publishing company John Knox Press had a surprising best-seller in Robert L. Short's *The Gospel According to Peanuts* (1965), based on the popular comic strip "Peanuts." Later in the decade Short moved to a commercial press to publish *Parables of Peanuts*.

Counterculture. Not all religious best-sellers were about Christian topics. A surprise success for the Dover Press was a new translation by James Legge of the ancient Chinese classic the *I Ching*. This book taught Americans, mostly young people in the counterculture, how to answer questions by casting coins and how to read the meanings of those casts based on ancient texts. Over one hundred thousand copies were sold by the end of the decade.

CATHOLICS AND POLITICS

Religious Tolerance. In 1960 John Fitzgerald Kennedy became the second Roman Catholic to be nominated for president by the Democratic party. In contrast to the failed campaign of Al Smith in 1928, Kennedy was successful, but his success raised questions about religious tolerance in the United States.

Campaign Organization. Kennedy attracted attention as a possible presidential candidate when southern Democrats supported his nomination for vice-president in 1956. By 1960 his two years of effort had created the most-effective campaign organization of all the Democratic contenders. But his religion was an issue that worried his friends and supporters. He quieted much of that apprehension when he easily won the primary in West Virginia. If he carried this largely Protestant state, perhaps sectarian animosity was declining.

Evangelical Opposition. But opposition remained. In May the Southern Baptist Convention objected to electing Roman Catholics to office, noting "When a public official is inescapably bound by the dogma and demands of his church, he cannot consistently separate himself from these." Herbert S. Mekel, the retiring president of the conservative National Association of Evangelicals, insisted that a Roman Catholic president would lead to suffering and the persecution among those followers of the "true faith of the New Testament." Rev. W. A. Criswell, pastor of First Baptist Church in Dallas, said to be the largest church in the world, remarked that Kennedy's election would "spell the death of a free church in a free state."

Peale's Opposition. In September an ad hoc group called the National Conference of Citizens for Religious Freedom, which included Norman Vincent Peale, Daniel Poling, L. Nelson Bell, and Harold J. Ockenga, opposed Kennedy's election. The outpouring of criticism of this religious prejudice caused Peale to resign from the group three weeks later. But he continued to support Richard Nixon.

Separation of Church and State. Kennedy disarmed many of his critics when he appeared before the Houston Ministerial Association on 12 September. The candidate asserted at the beginning, "I am not the Catholic candidate for President. I am the Democratic Party's candidate for President, who also happens to be Catholic." In the course of his remarks he promised he would resign the presidency if he ever had to act in a way that would "either violate my conscience, or violate the national interest," and concluded with a pledge to "preserve, protect and defend the Constitution." He narrowly won the fall election and laid to rest the notion that a Catholic could not be elected president. Analysts of the election believe that while Kennedy lost Protestant votes from traditional Democrats he gained votes from Roman Catholics who usually voted Republican.

Sources:

Eugene Carson Blake and G. Bramley Oxnam, "The Protestant View of a Catholic for President," *Look*, 24 (10 May 1960): 31–34;

Timothy A. Byrnes, *Catholics and American Politics* (Princeton, N. J.: Princeton University Press, 1991);

John Corry, "Cardinal Spellman and New York Politics," *Harper's*, 235 (March 1968): 74–85;

Mark A. Nell, ed., *Religion and American Politics* (New York: Oxford University Press, 1990).

CHARISMATICS

The Rise of Pentecostalism. During the 1960s Pentecostalism began to move into traditional Christian denominations. Pentecostalism, the baptism by the Holy Spirit as described in the second chapter of Acts, appeared in various areas in the South in the late nineteenth century. But the revival of the black evangelist W. J. Seymour on Azusa Street in Los Angeles in 1906 began the spread of Pentecostalism throughout the United States.

Working Class Support. The phenomenon quickly spread in working-class white and black communities, particularly in the South and West, but was rejected by traditional Protestant groups who believed God had already spoken through the Bible and Catholics and others who believed that God spoke through the Church itself or through tradition. The increasing number of charismatics were dismissed by traditional groups as Holy Rollers, people who not only spoke in tongues but even indulged in more-bizarre practices, such as spiritual healing and handling serpents. But Pentecostal churches such as the Church of God, the Assemblies of God, and the Full Gospel Church were firmly established by midcentury. As these believers moved into the middle classes in the expanding economy of the postwar era, Pentecostalism became more socially respectable. The Full Gospel Business Men's Fellowship International established branches in most cities for these rising individuals.

Oral Roberts. In the postwar period the Pentecostal denominations began to attract ever-larger numbers of people. One agent of this growth was Oral Roberts, who began his Abundant Life Crusade in 1947. His tent revivals initially focused on the healing powers of the Spirit. He quickly moved to radio and then took his crusade to television and sent his program into other countries. In 1965 Roberts was invited to attend the International Conference on Evangelicalism in Berlin, where he developed a friendship with Billy Graham, the world's most famous Evangelical spokesman, and began a conciliation between Pentecostalism and conservative Evangelicals.

Effect on the Mainline Churches. The charismatic movement came into mainline Protestant and Catholic groups after Rev. Dennis Bennett, priest at Saint Mark's Church (Episcopal) in Van Nuys, California, revealed to his congregation on Whitsunday 1960 that he and some of his parishioners had been meeting privately and several of them had spoken in tongues. The announcement caused a sensation, and, while Bennett was sent to a small parish in Seattle, the charismatic movement spread. Outbreaks of speaking in tongues, or glossolalia, appeared on the campuses of Yale and Harvard Universities, and, even more startling, at Notre Dame University in 1966. The movement among Roman Catholics spread rapidly, taking the name Charismatic Renewal. By the end of the decade large convocations of people gathered to celebrate the actions of the Spirit in their lives.

Sources:

Randall Balmes, *Mine Eyes Have Seen the Glory: A Journey into the Evangelical Subculture in America* (New York: Oxford University Press, 1989);

Kilian McDonnell, *Charismatic Renewal and the Churches* (New York: Seabury Press, 1976).

CHURCH UNIONS

Ecumenicism. A series of church unions took place in the 1960s. While most of these mergers were between like-minded groups, they stimulated a belief in ecumenicism. The decade began with the creation of the American Lutheran Church by the union of the Evangelical Lutheran Church, the American Lutheran Church, and the United Evangelical Lutheran Church. In 1962 the United Lutheran Church in America, the Agustana Evangelical Church, the American Evangelical Lutheran Church, and the Finnish Evangelical Lutheran Church united to form the Lutheran Church in America.

Mergers. In 1961 the American Unitarian Association completed its merger with the Universalist Church of America, creating the Unitarian-Universalist Association. That same year the Congregational Christian Church and the Evangelical and Reform Church merged to form the United Church of Christ, with two million

EDITORIAL: "CHRISTIAN MORALITY AND RACE ISSUES"

"The faith that renews itself at Easter is the ground of Christian morals; and Christian morals this year are deeply involved in racial issues. . . . [An] issue from the past is raised by that Broadway play *The Deputy:* Was Pope Pius XII false to his trust as Christ's vicar on earth when he failed to speak out against Hitler's campaign to exterminate the Jews? . . . Even when Negroes have all the legal rights Congress can give them, only the willingness of white Americans to treat Negroes on their merits as human beings will make those rights effective. . . . The race issue will not be solved until every American conscience is involved and clarified by its personal owner."

Source: *Life,* 56 (27 March 1964): 4.

members. In 1966 the Methodist Church and Evangelical United Brethren Church united to form the United Methodist Church. Despite the merger the Southern Baptist Convention had grown to achieve the distinction of being the largest Protestant denomination in the United States.

CIVIL RIGHTS AND THE CHURCHES

Preachers and Civil Rights. The goals of the civil rights movement of the 1950s and 1960s were achieved in large part by African-American preachers who led black southerners in a successful effort to secure the rights guaranteed to them in the Thirteenth, Fourteenth, and Fifteenth Amendments. While the drive for this social revolution came from the black community, its success depended upon the support of whites at a time when the federal government had moved slowly to protect the rights of blacks in the South. A major factor in persuading whites to support these changes came from the ability of the civil rights workers to appeal to the religious and moral values of the nation.

Greensboro Demonstrations. In February 1960 white and black Americans were stunned by the sit-in demonstrations at the Woolworth's dime store's lunch counter in Greensboro, North Carolina, which students at North Carolina Agricultural and Technical College had organized spontaneously. Those demonstrations were not the first of this nature, and other groups in other cities were training themselves for the same goals. The Greensboro demonstrations triggered sit-ins by college students across the South. One such campaign was in Nashville, Tennessee, where Rev. James Lawson, a student at the School of Religion at Vanderbilt University, had been working with other black students on nonviolent protest techniques. The Nashville lunch counters were desegregated, but the president of Vanderbilt suspended Lawson, bringing charges of racism against that institution before Lawson was permitted to return and complete his degree.

SNCC. The sit-ins of 1960 had some success. Many lunch counters were desegregated, although the separation of the races in public accommodations continued. More important than securing blacks the chance to drink coffee at Woolworth's was the creation in April 1960 of a new civil rights organization, SNCC, and a new vigor for the civil rights movement.

Freedom Rides. SNCC (pronounced "snick") became the advance guard of the movement, as it demonstrated in May 1961 with the Freedom Rides. A group of white and black volunteers with the Congress of Racial Equality (CORE) rode buses across the South to test the recent order of the Interstate Commerce Commission to end segregation in interstate travel. The riots that erupted in Birmingham, Alabama, brought an end to the first rides, but volunteers from Nashville, led by Rev. James Bevel and Diane Nash, carried the ride on to Montgomery, Alabama, where another riot erupted. The federal government was forced to intervene, and, in time, nonsegregated transportation in larger southern cities was established.

SCLC. As SNCC field representatives spread out over the South to organize communities for change, the Southern Christian Leadership Conference (SCLC), headed by Rev. Martin Luther King, Jr., but strongly supported by other black Baptist ministers, continued to focus national attention on the problems blacks faced in the South. Demonstrations took place in most major southern cities and even in large towns such as Albany, Georgia.

Progressive National Baptist Convention. Not all black Baptists followed King's leadership. In 1961 he was one of the leaders of the National Baptist Convention (NBC), the largest black denomination, who opposed the reelection of Rev. Joseph H. Jackson as president of the convention. Among other things, they believed Jackson was insufficiently committed to the aims of the civil rights movement. When Jackson won reelection, King was deposed as one of the NBC's vice-presidents. Others who opposed Jackson and agreed that Baptists should be more involved in social change left the NBC to form the Progressive National Baptist Convention.

Birmingham. King unquestionably was the most famous figure in the movement, attracting such publicity that the contributions of other activists both in the SCLC and in other movement organizations were obscured. Such a situation occurred in 1963 in Birmingham, Alabama, where Rev. Fred L. Shuttlesworth, who had organized the Alabama Christian Movement for Human Rights to give direction to the campaign in that city,

failed to achieve his local goals in the momentous campaign. But the publicity that King brought to Birmingham and the inescapable evidence of violent racism there forced the Kennedy administration to commit itself to federal action to protect the rights of black southerners. Birmingham was a skirmish in the war for civil rights, which was won in Congress.

Local Involvement. As in Birmingham, the real work of the movement took place at the local level, where the churches offered places to meet and supplied committed leadership familiar with the local situation. Famously, as in the case of Sixteenth Street Baptist Church in Birmingham or Brown Chapel in Selma, Alabama, churches were the stages for demonstrations. Because the churches were so important in this function, they became targets of racial hatred and were burned and blown up, as happened to the Sixteenth Street Baptist Church in 1963, where four young girls attending Sunday school were killed. Many small, obscure rural churches throughout the region were destroyed in the course of the struggle.

Growing White Involvement. As the civil rights movement intensified in the early 1960s, more and more white clergy from the North joined the demonstrations in moral support. For the great set pieces of the movement, such as the March on Montgomery from Selma in 1965 or the Meredeth March in Mississippi in 1966, leading religious figures from around the country — Protestants, Catholics, and Jews — flew to the site for at least an expression of support. Some paid heavily. Rev. James J. Reeb, a Unitarian minister from Boston, was beaten by whites in Selma and died from his wounds. The following year Jonathan Daniel, a young student at the Episcopal Theological Seminary, was shot and killed in Lowndes County, Alabama. In both cases the killers were acquitted.

Racial Tensions in the Movement. By mid decade many young black activists were offended that the news media paid more attention to the deaths of white visitors than to the victims of the on-going brutality directed against the black community. White ministers from outside the South seemed to bring more publicity than all the efforts of black ministers on the front lines. In their rage and frustration black activists began to move toward the black consciousness that became known as black power.

Attacking the North. By the middle of the decade the movement shifted to the North, where discrimination was embedded in society's institutions, housing patterns, and shared racial attitudes rather than in laws. King and the SCLC tackled Chicago, one of the nation's most segregated communities, although separation there was based on housing patterns rather than explicit laws. As usual the news media followed King and recorded the local racial resistance to his demands. The pattern of institutionalized racism was demonstrated in other northern cities, as in Minneapolis, where Fr. James Groppi lead a series of marches demanding open housing in the late 1960s. Racism was not a Southern monopoly.

The Aim of Religion. For many others in the North as well as the South, the activism of religious leaders such as Father Groppi seemed misplaced. This was particularly true among the laity who believed the responsibility of religion was to give support in this life and a chance at a better life in the hereafter. Many objected to the violence that came with the demonstrations, and others to the aims of the movement itself. Religion, as frequently happens, was a vital force for change and a foundation of resistance. But in the privacy of their homes many Americans still harbored segregationist views.

Sources:

Taylor Branch, *Parting the Waters: America in the King Years: 1954–1963* (New York: Simon & Schuster, 1988);

David Garrow, *Bearing the Cross: Martin Luther King and the Southern Christian Leadership Conference* (New York: Morrow, 1986);

James Davison Hunter, *American Evangelicalism: Conservative Religion and the Quandary of Modernity* (Brunswick, N.J.: Rutgers University Press, 1983);

Harold E Quinley, *Prophetic Clergy: Social Activism Among Protestant Ministers* (New York: John Wiley, 1974).

COMMUNISM AND THE CHURCHES

Continued Suspicions. Although the anti-Communist hysteria of the McCarthy period had weakened by the beginning of the 1960s, charges of Communist influence and infiltration of the society in general and Protestant churches in particular continued. These charges found support from ultraright religious leaders, who in turn gained support from the military.

Military Charges. In 1960 the U.S. Air Force released a training manual that charged there was "overwhelming evidence" that Communist fellow travelers had infiltrated churches and educational institutions. Further, the manual charged, thirty of the ninety-five people who translated the Revised Standard Version of the Bible were "affiliated with pro-Communist fronts, projects, and publications."

More Controversy. In the face of sharp protests the training manual was withdrawn, but public debate continued when it was revealed that Fred C. Schwarz, president of the Christian Anti-Communist Crusade, joined E. Merrill Root, author of *Collectivism on Campus: The Battle for the Mind in American Colleges* (1955), and Herbert Philbrick, author of *I Led Three Lives: Citizen, "Communist," Counterspy* (1952), in a seminar, Education for American Security, at the U.S. Naval Air Station in Glenville, Illinois. Critics of these programs wondered that the military aligned itself against the nation's leading religious institutions.

John Birch Society. The following year public attention focused on the John Birch Society, a right-wing group named for a Baptist missionary who had been an American intelligence agent in China at the end of World War II. The society insisted that his death at the hands of the Chinese Communists made him the first casualty in the war against communism. But less paranoid people, even conservative politicians, were appalled when it was revealed that the John Birch Society's founder charged that former president Eisenhower was a "conscious agent of the Communist conspiracy." Nearly overlooked in the resulting furor were the continuing charges that the National Council of Churches was infiltrated by Communists. The founder of the John Birch Society insisted that 3 percent of the Protestant clergy were either Communists or Communist sympathizers.

Christian Echoes Ministry. Billy James Hargis of Tulsa, Oklahoma, made a career of his religious anti-communism. In 1948 he organized the Christian Echoes Ministry to fight communism and its godless allies. He attracted attention when he organized an airlift of Bibles by balloons to people in Eastern Europe. He established a headquarters in Tulsa, where he organized a National Anti-Communist Leadership School and attacked Communists and their alleged influence. He was the source of the information contained in the controversial air force training manual. In 1966 he organized the Church of the Christian Crusade and made anticommunism a tenet of faith.

Fewer Tensions. While right-wing groups and individuals in and out of the churches continued to attack the social and ecumenical actions of individuals and mainline churches, the anti-red hysteria declined, and the redbaiters drifted to the shadows of political life.

Sources:

Richard M. Fried, *Nightmare in Red: The McCarthy Era in Perspective* (New York: Oxford University Press);

Ralph A. Roy, *Communism and the Churches* (New York: Harcourt Brace & World, 1960).

CONSULTATION ON CHURCH UNION

Merger Proposal. On 4 December 1960, on the eve of the triennial convention of the National Council of Churches of Christ in America, Eugene Carson Blake, the stated clerk (chief executive officer) of the United Presbyterian Church (Northern), gave a sermon at Grace Cathedral (Episcopal) in San Francisco. The sermon, entitled "A Proposal Toward the Reunion of Christ's Church," launched a movement toward a merger of the leading mainline Protestant denominations that lasted through the decade. In his sermon Blake proposed that the United Presbyterian, Episcopal, and Methodist churches and the United Church of Christ commit themselves to official consultation toward a merger despite their varying forms of governance and crucial doctrinal divisions.

Consultation on Church Union. Other denominations joined in the program, officially called the Consultation on Church Union (COCU), in the course of the decade. They included the Christian Church (Disciples of Christ); the Evangelical United Brethren (which later merged with the Methodist Church); the African Methodist Episcopal Church; the Presbyterian Church, U.S. (Southern); the African Methodist Church Zion, and the Christian Methodist Episcopal Church. If all the members of these denominations had joined there would have been a total membership of twenty-five million.

Healing the Schism. Representatives of the various denominations met several times over the decade to address problems on governance and doctrine. As the decade drew to a close, *A Plan of Union for the Church of Christ Uniting* was readied for presentation to the mem-

ber groups. The aim of the plan was to heal the schisms among like-minded groups to make the church "a company of the people of God," relevant to Christian tradition and able to deal effectively with issues such as racism, poverty, pollution, war, and "other problems of the family of man."

Lack of Lay Support. By the time the decade ended, opponents in and out of the COCU churches were making clear their objections to the plan. Many laypeople were annoyed by the growing power of denominational bureaucrats who seemed to have little concern about denominational traditions and doctrines. A superchurch would have little relevance to the needs of people in the local community. Opponents insisted that the role of the Church was not to solve unsolvable problems such as war, racism, and poverty but to focus on bringing the individual into a proper relation with God through the gospel of Jesus.

Sources:
Eugene Carson Blake, "A Proposal for the Reunion of Christ's Church," *Christian Century*, 77 (14 December 1960): 1508–1511;

"COCU: Fervor and Candor," *Christian Century*, 86 (9 April 1969): 469–470;

"Toward a Super Church," *Time*, 93 (28 March 1969): 75–76.

THE DEATH OF GOD

God Is Dead. In October 1965 *Time* magazine stirred up a tempest among the general public with a cover story called "Christian Atheism: The 'God Is Dead' Movement." The story focused on recent developments in Christian theology in which academics discussed the need for society to recognize that it behaved as if God were no longer active in the world. They claimed that modern man functions without the need for some transcendent explanation of life, and theologians had difficulty in finding words to describe God. The argument went as follows: what could theology say about religion when God, as Friedrich Nietzsche said, is dead? The God of the Christian past no longer served a function.

Theological Stirrings. The movement got its name from the title of Gabriel Vahanian's book *The Death of God: The Culture of Our Post-Christian Era* (1961), but the controversy was stirred by the work of Thomas J. J. Altizer, *The Gospel of Christian Atheism* (1966). The movement attempted to create a theology which recognized the futility of using the traditional definitions of God, yet it accepted that the historical Jesus spoke to man in his current context, a context of a culture where mankind created a life defined in the secular. One had to discern the profane form of Jesus's presence in the world and live with the world's contradictions. As Altizer remarked, "Once we confess that Christ is fully present in the moment before us, then we can truly love the world and embrace even its pain and darkness as an epiphany of the body of Christ."

Public Disinterest. The public debate was brief. While general-circulation magazines and newsmagazines joined religious publications to carry twenty-six articles about the issue in 1966 and 1967, by the following year religious publications and journals of opinion carried only seven articles about the movement, and the issue moved back into the academic world.

Theological Liberals and Conservatives. The controversy reflected a growing split between the mainline Protestant churches, which were more open to new theological trends and focused on social issues, and conservatives in those denominations (sometimes even whole denominations), who insisted on the faith of their fathers, a faith that focused on a triune God, the inerrancy of the Bible, the need for personal salvation, and tradition. Conservatives added new theological offensives to their lists of objections to mainline leaders. One response to the controversy was a bumper sticker, an increasingly popular means of expression during the decade, reading "My God is not dead. I talked with Him this morning."

Sources:

John C. Bennett, "In Defense of God," *Look,* 30 (19 April 1966): 69–70;

Billy Graham, "God Is Not Dead," *U.S. News,* 60 (25 April 1966): 74–80;

"Toward a Hidden God: Is God Dead?" *Time,* 87 (8 April 1966): 82–87.

FREEDOM SONGS

The Importance of Music. The civil rights movement depended upon commitment from small groups of people in situations that were filled with tension and frequently with violence. Drawing on the experience of the labor struggles of the 1930s, music became a way to maintain the spirits and sense of community of the participants. Because the church was the center of the black community in the South and frequently the force behind the civil rights movement, religious songs were often adapted for the situation. With topical lyrics adapted for the changing situations, these spirituals and gospel songs encouraged the activists and brought reassurance to the singers. In time they became the way mass demonstrations expressed their moral hopes. One of the early favorites was "We Shall Not Be Moved," which spread from the Highlander Folk School in Tennessee, one of the early training centers for movement activists. The anthem of the movement was "We Shall Overcome," which became a way of ending meetings both large and small. In 1965 President Lyndon Johnson used the phrase "We shall overcome" to conclude his proposed legislation which became the Voting Rights Act. The freedom songs were a way the community held itself together in the bitter days of the civil rights struggle.

Source:

Sing for Freedom: The Story of the Civil Rights Movement Through Its Songs (Bethlehem, Pa.: Sing Out, 1990).

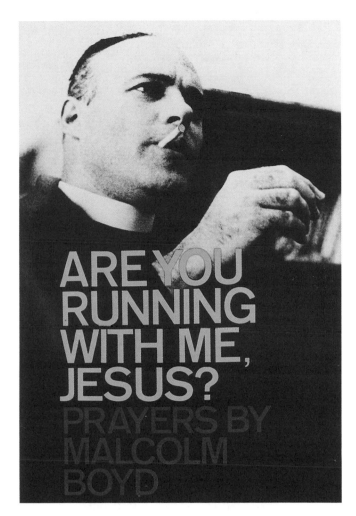

Dust jacket for Boyd's book intended to draw youth to Christianity

ON HUMAN LIFE

The Question of Contraception. By the early 1960s new contraceptive methods, particularly the birth-control pill, and growing concern about an exploding world population led some participants at the Second Vatican Council to raise the question of the church's traditional opposition to artificial birth control. The topic seemed ready for debate in the now-open climate of the church. But responding to conservatives in the Vatican, Pope John XXIII instead created a separate papal commission to review the issue. Pope John XXIII was succeeded by Paul VI in 1963, who was more responsive to conservative opposition to changes in traditional church teachings on sexual matters. In 1967 reformers were heartened when a draft report from the commission was leaked, saying that limiting the size of the family was the responsibility of the couple involved.

Humanae Vitae. But when Pope Paul VI released his encyclical *Humanae Vitae* in 1968, he reasserted the church's traditional ban on artificial birth control. American Catholics, particularly women, responded with disappointment and anger. Most ignored the ruling. By the

Pope John XXIII addressing the press during Vatican II

end of the decade 70 percent of Catholic women were privately using artificial birth control.

Catholic Disagreement. The clergy was more public in its opposition. When in 1967 Catholic University refused to renew the contract of dissident Charles E. Curran because of his views on birth control, clergy protests forced an extension of his contract. After *Humanae Vitae*, priests held news conferences and signed petitions in open opposition to the encyclical. The archbishop of Washington, D.C., disciplined fifty-one priests who said

they could not in good conscience support the ruling. Twenty-five of them later left the church.

Disastrous Impact. Fr. Andrew Greeley has concluded that *Humanae Vitae* had a disastrous impact on the church in the United States. Priests refused to enforce the ruling in confession, left their orders, and were not replaced. Attendance in Sunday schools, along with contributions and support for papal authority, dropped sharply.

Sources:

Andrew Greeley, *The American Catholic: A Social Portrait* (New York: Basic Books, 1977);

John A. O'Brien, "Humanae Vitae: Reaction and Consequences," *Christian Century*, 86 (26 February 1969): 288–289;

Xavier Rynne, "Letter from Vatican City: Consideration of Humanae Vitae," *New Yorker*, 44 (2 November 1969): 131–134.

HUMANAE VITAE

"Responsible parenthood . . . retains a . . . significance of paramount importance, which refers to the objective moral order instituted by God. . . . From this [husband and wife] are not free to act as they choose in the service of transmitting life, nor are they free to decide for themselves what is the right course to follow. On the contrary, they are bound to ensure that what they do corresponds to the will of God the Creator . . . The Church . . . teaches as absolutely required that *any use whatever of marriage* must retain its natural potential to procreate human life . . . it is a serious error to think that a whole married life of otherwise normal relations can justify sexual intercourse which is deliberately contraceptive and so intrinsically wrong."

Source: Paul VI, 25 July 1968.

THE MOD CHURCH

Counterculture Effects. As the cold war moved into its third decade, cultural currents were changing, particularly among young people. Most continued to share and operate out of the values of their parents, but a significant group, located in large cities and around college campuses, began to reflect behavior that would be called counterculture. They left traditional religion behind them. In the face of the growing attraction of aspects of this set of attitudes, there were a variety of efforts to make religion more relevant to the needs and interests of the young. Malcolm Boyd's *Are You Running with Me, Jesus?* (1967) was one of the most dramatic evidences of these efforts.

Trendiness. Conservatives complained bitterly about the trendiness of religious leaders who seemed too willing to abandon old forms simply to reach young people "where they were at." As the Roman Catholic church modified the centuries-old forms of service, it also attempted to speak to the young in their own language and joined other liturgical churches celebrating folk masses. Many older members were offended. They had lost the beauty and mystery of the traditional Latin mass; now they were losing the music and structure too.

Closing a Magazine. The United Methodist Church closed *motive*, its magazine directed at young people, in 1969, when the political costs of the redesigned, modishly illustrated publication seemed too great. The March–April 1969 issue, devoted to the issue of women's liberation, contained profanity, and when that same profanity appeared in the May issue it was labeled as clearly obscene, and the publication was ended, the excuse being that the publication was too expensive.

New Options. In spite of these efforts to meet the baby boomers halfway, many young people left traditional religious groups for conservative Evangelical groups such as the Campus Crusade for Christ. Others joined groups such as the hippie-based Jesus People or Eastern cults. Many lapsed into religious indifference.

Sources:

Shana Alexander, "Nightclub Priest," *Life,* 61 (28 October 1966): 29;

Gerald Astor, "Chaplin to the Cool World," *Look,* 31 (31 October 1967): 79–84;

John Ducha, "And Now Even the Prayers Are Pop," *New York Times Magazine* (13 November 1966): 184–185;

C. J. McNaspy, "Fold Music in the Liturgy," *America,* 114 (9 April 1966): 529–532.

NEW TRANSLATIONS

New Language. As usual the Bible remained the best-selling book during the 1960s. While Protestant traditionalists continued to rely on the King James Version, others turned to new translations. In 1961 the New Testament was published in the New English Bible translation. Nearly seven million copies were sold by the end of the decade, when it was announced that the complete New English Version of the Bible would soon be available. In 1965 a Catholic version of the Revised Standard Version of the New Testament was published, and the following year the Jerusalem Bible, the first Roman Catholic Bible translated from the original documents into English, was published. In 1965 the Anchor Bible translation began with each book coming out on a regular basis.

Torah. In 1963 a new translation of the Torah based on Masoretic (traditional Hebrew) text was published by the Jewish Publication Society of America. This translation did not depend on other Christian or Jewish translations.

RELIGION IN THE SCHOOLS

School Prayer. As late as 1962 twenty-four states permitted or required children to begin the school day with prayer. One such state was New York, whose board of

---

PRIESTS AND THE CHURCH

"I was, and always will be, a Catholic priest, but I cannot presently be the priest I was. . . . We do not need a solution to the birth-control problem. . . . We need freedom from a legalistic Church that has transformed the simplicity of a personal and Christian love into a world of fear and guilt. We do not know how to find God, we have never learned. We have only been taught to keep laws, to avoid sin, to fear hell, to carry a cross that we built ourselves. . . . No longer can I stand before my bishop and smile in shy assent when I know he is wrong. No longer will I bow before a pastor when I know his mood has formed the policy of his Church. No longer will I accept in silence the travesties that a dishonest theology has imposed on simple and unsuspecting men. Nor will I leave the Church, even if they demand it of me for it is *my* Church. I will be a Catholic, a vocal and honest one, even if my superiors forbid me to be a priest. I shall be a Catholic who follows his conscience, demands meaning and relevance from his Church, and will not permit his God to be reduced to empty ritual and all-absorbing law."

Source: James Kavanaugh, *A Modern Priest Looks at His Outdated Church* (New York: Trident Press, 1967), p. 3 passim.

---

regents devised a prayer seemingly innocuous enough to avoid offending any of the variety of religious believers in that state. The prayer read as follows:

> Almighty God, we acknowledge our dependence upon Thee, and we beg Thy blessings upon us, our parents, our teachers and our Country.

Court Rulings. On 25 June 1962 in *Engel* v. *Vitale* the Supreme Court in a six-to-one decision overturned lower-court rulings that said states could require prayer in schools if individual students were permitted to remain silent. Justice Hugo Black, speaking for the majority, ruled that any required prayer was a violation of the separation of church and state:

> There is no doubt that a daily classroom invocation of God's blessing . . . is a religious activity. . . . It is not part of the business of government to compose official prayers for any group of American people to recite as a part of a religious program carried out by government.

Widespread Protests. The ruling triggered an outburst of protest as people read the ruling as saying that children could not pray in school, rather than that they could not be required to pray. Prominent figures objected vigorously. Francis Cardinal Spellman, archbishop of New York, said,

Justice Hugo Black

> I am shocked and frightened that the Supreme Court has declared unconstitutional a simple and voluntary declaration of belief in God by public school children. The decision strikes at the very heart of the Godly tradition in which America's children have for so long been raised.

Billy Graham, probably the most famous Protestant minister in the nation, remarked,

> This is another step toward the secularization of the United States. . . .The framers of our Constitution meant we were to have freedom of religion, not freedom from religion.

Congressional Action. Numerous proposals were introduced into Congress to allow states or school districts to have children pray in school.

New Rulings. The apprehensions of traditionalists were heightened in 1963 when the same court by a margin of eight to one (Justice Potter Stewart dissenting in both cases) ruled in *School Board of Abbington Township* v. *Schempp* that schools could not require schoolchildren to read from the Bible. Madalyn Murray O'Hair, an avowed atheist whose suit contesting a Maryland law on behalf of her son was the second case connected to the Abington decision, became one of the most excoriated people in the nation.

Church and State. There were some prominent religious leaders who defended these decisions, agreeing that government-required prayer and Bible reading might infringe on minority beliefs but recognizing that the decisions did not bar students from practicing their religion as individuals even in the classroom. John C. Bennett, president of Union Theological Seminary in New York, was one of the most prominent defenders of the Court. Jewish leaders also supported the decision. But many people believed that the rules against required prayer meant there could be no prayer at all, and some protested that the Court had put God out of the schools and blacks in.

Resistance. By 1964 there were 144 proposed amendments to allow prayer and Bible reading in the schools before the House Judiciary Committee, and lawmakers in state legislatures and school boards attempted to find ways to circumvent the Supreme Court's ruling. One effective way was to ignore the ruling and continue old practices until they were challenged in the courts.

Source:
Lynda Beck Fenwick, *Should the Children Pray?: A Historical, Judicial, and Political Examination of Public School Prayer* (Waco, Tex.: Markham Press Fund, 1989).

THE SECOND VATICAN COUNCIL AND THE AMERICAN CHURCH

Vatican II. As one observer noted, by the 1960s Catholics in the United States had won their struggle to discover what it meant to be American. But after Vatican II they had to struggle with what it meant to be Catholic.

Widespread Input. In 1959 the newly elected (in October 1958) pope, John XXIII, announced an ecumenical council to bring the Catholic church up to date (*aggiornamento*). The council, the first in nearly one hundred years, opened in 1962 and was conducted in four sessions before closing in 1965, with Paul VI now the pope. Americans were active at the council, both Catholics as participants and Protestants as observers. Americans such as John Courtney Murray, Francis Cardinal Spellman, and Joseph Cardinal Ritter of Saint Louis played important roles in framing the documents of religious liberty, the absolution of the Jews for the death of Jesus, and the changes in the liturgy.

Changes. Vatican II did not create the explosion of activity that characterized the Catholic community in the last half of the decade. The tensions and desires were there waiting to develop; now they were allowed into the open. The Mass was given in English, and the priest faced the congregation, who participated fully in the service. The rigid separation from other religious groups had ended, and many interreligious contacts were initiated. The National Catholic Bishops Conference replaced the National Catholic Welfare Conference in 1966, and the American hierarchy began to guide its flock. Laypeople began to acquire a larger role in determining the affairs of the church, depending upon the local parish or diocese, and in 1967 the United States Catholic Conference was created to give laypeople a role to play along with the conference of bishops.

THE SECULAR CITY

"The forces of secularization have no serious interest in persecuting religion. Secularization simply bypasses and undercuts religion and goes on to other things. It has relativized religious worldviews and thus rendered them innocuous. Religion has been privatized. It has been accepted as the peculiar prerogative and point of view of a particular person or group. Secularization has accomplished what fire and chin could not: It has convinced the believer that he *could* be wrong, and persuaded the devotee that there are more important things than dying for the faith. . . . The age of the secular city . . . *is* an age of 'no religion at all.' It no longer looks to religious rules and rituals for its morality or its meanings. . . . For fewer and fewer [people] does it provide an inclusive and commanding system of personal and cosmic values and explanations."

Source: Harvey Cox, *The Secular City: Secularization and Urbanization in Theological Perspective* (New York: Macmillian, 1965), pp. 2-3.

Modernization versus Traditionalism. Many American Catholics were delighted with the modernizing qualities of the changes. But some of the results were disturbing. For nuns to discard their old habits and wear twentieth-century dresses was one thing; for them to challenge traditions of deference to male hierarchy was another. Worse, large numbers left their orders. More than forty-three hundred nuns returned to secular life between 1966 and 1969. Priests also challenged their constraints and acted individually in their own lives and inside the parish. Many married, often without officially leaving the priesthood. More than thirty-four hundred priests left between 1966 and 1969, it was estimated.

Change. Conservative Catholics objected to the changes. Some simply missed the old structures and habits of their lifetimes. The end of the Latin mass was particularly painful for some who went to great lengths to search out celebrations of the traditional liturgy. Others found the whole drift from authority to individual choice disturbing. But their objections were of little avail. Observers of the church later concluded that it was the hierarchy's teachings on sexuality, particularly birth control, rather than the modernization of the church that caused the weakening ties of the Catholic community.

Sources:
"Bishops Approve Liberty Draft," *Christian Century*, 82 (6 October 1965): 1214;

"Church and Religious Liberty," *America*, 113 (9 October 1965): 393–394;

"Vote Against Prejudice," *Time*, 86 (22 October 1965): 61.

VIETNAM AND THE CLERGY

Clergy Opposed to War. One of the centers of opposition to the American involvement in the war in Vietnam was the clergy. From the beginning, pacifists, such as A. J. Muste of the Committee for Non-Violent Action (CNVA), and antiwar organizations, such as the Fellowship of Reconciliation, Quakers, and the American Friends Service Committee, raised questions about the U.S. support for the regime of President Ngo Dinh Diem of the Republic of Vietnam (South Vietnam).

Minister's Vietnam Committee. In September 1963, in the wake of Buddhist protests against the Diem regime's oppression, Rienhold Niebuhr and Harry Emerson Fosdick joined ten other clergymen to form the Ministers' Vietnam Committee, which took a full-page advertisement in *The New York Times* to protest American support for the repressive South Vietnamese government.

Presidential Issue. After President Diem was toppled by the military, the situation in Vietnam deteriorated, and the question of America's role in the region became an election issue in the presidential campaign of 1964. While the crucial issues in the campaign between President Lyndon Johnson and Republican candidate Barry Goldwater were domestic, Goldwater's militaristic views on the war helped lead the traditionally nonpolitical journals *Christian Century* and *Christianity and Crisis* to support Johnson, who seemed less likely to increase American military involvement in Southeast Asia.

Increased Involvement. With the election over, the Johnson administration began a program to keep South Vietnam from being lost to communism — one which included a massive expansion of U.S. forces and direct military action in Southeast Asia. The hostilities in Vietnam became an undeclared American war. In 1965 the escalation of American involvement and growing preoccupation of the Johnson administration with foreign issues led Rev. Martin Luther King, Jr., by then a Nobel Peace Prize laureate, to speak out against the expanding conflict even though his advisers tried to prevent his public opposition.

Clergy Concerned About Vietnam. In October 1965 Rev. Richard John Neuhaus, then a Lutheran; Rabbi Abraham Heschel; and Fr. Daniel Berrigan, S.J., organized Clergy Concerned About Vietnam, which became the central organization of coordinated clergy opposition to the war. By May 1966 the organization had become permanent and took the name Clergy and Laymen Concerned About the War in Vietnam (CALCAV). Prominent clergymen such as John C. Bennett (president of Union Theological Seminary in New York), William Sloane Coffin (chaplin at Yale University), Robert McAfee Brown (Stanford University), and Martin Luther King, Jr., supported the efforts of CALCAV to organize opposition to the war among the clergy whose individual congregations or denominations were unwilling to engage in antiwar activity. CALCAV stayed independent of the direct action of the increasingly volatile antiwar movement, favoring negotiations to bring about an end to the conflict.

Religious Split. While liberal Protestant and Jewish clergy urged negotiations, conservative clergy, particularly in the Roman Catholic hierarchy and Evangelicals, openly or tacitly supported the war effort. Cardinal Spellman, vicar of the Catholics in the U.S. military, remarked in 1965, "I fully support everything it [the United States] does . . . My country, may it always be right. Right or wrong, my country," and he continued his Christmas trips to see the troops in Vietnam. It was widely believed the Cardinal Spellman was responsible for sending Father Berrigan to South America for a brief period after the creation of CALCAV in 1965 to silence his antiwar activism. Few Catholic clergy joined the antiwar movement until after 1969.

The Evangelical Perspective. Evangelicals, still believing the way to change the world was through personal conversion, ignored the questions raised by the war, although some ultraconservatives such as Rev. Carl McIntire organized demonstrations countering those organized by the clergy against the war. Billy Graham, at the request of President Johnson, made a Christmas visit to Vietnam in 1966, seemingly endorsing the American effort, and his actions later seemed to give support not just to the American troops but to the American aims themselves.

Civil Rights and the Antiwar Movement. There was a clear link between the civil rights movement and the antiwar movement among the clergy as well as the laity. The moral issues raised by the struggle against legal segregation made it easier to see the moral issues in the war and at the same time encouraged the clergy to speak out on public issues. Although the red-baiting tendency at the height of the cold war had declined, the antiwar clergy felt forced to insist they did not criticize the Johnson administration's military action because they favored communism. Rather, they wanted the nation to live up to its religious and moral values. As Martin Luther King, Jr., remarked in a speech shortly before becoming cochair of CALCAV in 1967, "I oppose the war in Vietnam because I love America." But, he insisted, the heart of the religious opposition came from the values of religion: "Our allegiance to our nation is held under a higher allegiance to the God who is the sovereign of all nations. . . ."

Draft Strategy. As the war continued and the American commitment escalated, the number of young men drafted rose. While still supporting a bombing halt and negotiations to end the conflict, the attention of some clergy shifted to the issue of conscription and the right of young men to oppose this particular war, if not war in general. In October 1967 CALCAV issued the "Statement on Conscience and Conscription," in which they

Philip and Daniel Berrigan burning draft files

endorsed the right to oppose this war alone and said they would "publicly counsel all who in conscience cannot today serve. . . to refuse such service by non-violent means. . . ." Within a matter of weeks thirteen hundred clergymen had signed the statement. More dramatically, William Sloane Coffin and Dana Mclean Greely, president of the Unitarian-Universalist Association, joined four thousand demonstrators in turning in their draft cards. Shortly after that, Coffin and Dr. Benjamin Spock delivered one thousand draft cards to the Justice Department in Washington in open defiance of federal laws. They and their three associates in turn were indicted, tried, and convicted. The convictions were later overturned.

Tet Offensive. While public opinion rallied to support the war during the fighting of the Tet offensive in early 1968, the continuing death toll as the year wore on evoked even more angry antiwar feelings and direct action. Philip Berrigan, a Josephite priest, and his brother Daniel joined in a demonstration in which blood was poured onto the records of a draft board in Baltimore. In May 1968 the Berrigan brothers and seven others broke into the draft board office in Catonsville, Maryland, to burn the draft records with napalm, used extensively in Vietnam. The demonstrators filmed the incident, and the

Berrigans and their fellow demonstrators were tried, convicted, and imprisoned for their actions.

Election Support. By 1968 the conflict in Vietnam was an overriding election issue which sharply divided the religious community. Some antiwar clergy supported Hubert Humphrey as the least offensive choice on the war and reform issues. Some Evangelicals, especially in the South and West, supported Gov. George Wallace of Alabama, running on the American Independent ticket. His running mate, Gen. Curtis LeMay, had once suggested bombing North Vietnam back to the Stone Age, and many liked Wallace's criticism of the reforms in social relations forced by the federal government during the decade. Republican Richard Nixon benefited from the votes of those who found the other candidates unacceptable on other issues, but some voted for him because they believed Nixon had a secret plan to end American involvement in the war.

Moratorium. The antiwar movement was quiet in the early months of the Nixon administration, waiting for the new president to bring an end to the conflict. When by the end of the summer of 1969 his efforts seemed ineffectual, the antiwar movement revived. On 15 October moderates, including many members of the clergy, joined in the Moratorium, a peaceful demonstration in cities around the country rather than in the traditional protest centers of New York, Washington, and San Francisco.

The organizers of the Moratorium planned to repeat the rallies in the following months, until the war was ended for the United States.

Washington March. Two days before the November Moratorium a "March Against Death" was organized for Washington, D.C. Over forty thousand marchers, each carrying a candle and representing one of the Americans killed in Vietnam, marched silently through the streets until each called out the name of the person represented. The following night five thousand heard a sermon by Eugene Carson Blake at the National Cathedral in Washington. The service closed with the congregation singing "We Shall Overcome." On 15 November hundreds of thousands of Americans demonstrated their desire for an end to the war.

Sources:
"Berrigan Brothers Say They Rob Draft Boards," *Time,* 91 (7 June 1968): 62;

Daniel Berrigan, *To Dwell in Peace: An Autobiography* (San Francisco: Harper & Row, 1987);

Robert McAfee Brown, "Because of Vietnam, in Conscience I Must Break the Law: Civil Disobedience," *Look,* 31 (31 October 1967): 48;

"Putting First Things Second: Social Activists of the Protestant Establishment," *Christianity Today,* 12 (1 March 1968): 27;

Nancy Zaroulis and Gerald Sullivan, *Who Spoke Up?: American Protest Against the War in Vietnam, 1963–1975* (Garden City, N.Y.: Doubleday, 1984).

HEADLINE MAKERS

JOHN COLEMAN BENNETT

1902-

PRESIDENT, UNION THEOLOGICAL SEMINARY, NEW YORK

Christianity and Crisis. John Coleman Bennett was born in Canada to American parents. In 1943 he became the Reinhold Niebuhr Professor of Social Ethics at Union Theological Seminary in New York; subsequently he was named dean of the seminary and then president in 1964. He was coeditor of the journal *Christianity and Crisis* and served as the vice-chairman of the Liberal party in New York City from 1955 to 1965. He spoke out extensively on issues of church/state relations, civil rights, and war. Among his publications are *Christian Social Ethics in a Changing World* (1966) and *Foreign Policy in Christian Perspective* (1966).

Source:
Robert Lee, *The Promise of Bennett: Christian Realism and Social Religion* (Philadelphia: Lippincott, 1969).

EUGENE CARSON BLAKE

1906-

GENERAL SECRETARY, WORLD COUNCIL OF CHURCHES

Protestant Pope. By the middle of the decade Eugene Carson Blake was sometimes laughingly referred to as the "Protestant Pope." He seemed to be everywhere. In 1956 he was elected stated clerk (executive officer) of the Presbyterian Church, U.S.A. (Northern), the largest Presbyterian body in the United States. He served in that position until 1966, when he became the general secretary of the World Council of Churches in its Geneva office.

National Council of Churches. He served as president of the National Council of Churches from 1954 to 1957. Not only was he one of most prominent church bureaucrats of the period, he wielded significant influence among American Protestants. His sermon proposing a consultation on church union among the mainline Protestant churches set a decade-long ecumenical dialogue in motion. He was active in the civil rights movement and was a featured speaker at the Great March on Washington for Jobs and Freedom in August 1963. He became a major voice criticizing the continued U.S. involvement in the war in Vietnam.

MALCOLM BOYD

1923-

THE ESPRESSO PRIEST

Media Background. Malcolm Boyd was ordained to the Episcopal ministry in 1951 after abandoning a promising career as a packager of shows for radio and television, during which he had served as the first president of the Television Producers Association of America. His studies included a year at Oxford and a year at Union Theological Seminary, where he studied under Reinhold Niebuhr. As the Protestant chaplain at Colorado State College, at the end of the decade he aroused controversy when he took himself and his message into the coffeehouses in Fort Collins because, he said, that was where young people who needed religion were. He resigned and moved to Wayne State University, where he again attracted notoriety with plays about social issues which he wrote and staged. His critics charged that they were obscene. In 1965 his eighth book, a collection of prayers called *Are You Running with Me,*

Jesus?, became a best-seller. Boyd then moved to a new audience, reading his prayers and meditations in nightclubs such as the Hungry in San Francisco and to Charlie Byrd's jazz guitar music at both the National Cathedral in Washington, D.C., and the Broadway United Church of Christ in New York. He was committed to the civil rights movement and from 1964 to 1968 he functioned as "chaplain-at-large" to American universities.

BILLY GRAHAM

1918-

EVANGELIST

Huge Popularity. Billy Graham entered the decade as the most famous Protestant preacher in the world. His swift movement from tent revivals to huge stadium events around the world, his effective use of radio and television, and his organization that was able to coordinate his activities as well as maintain his financial integrity made him consistently one of the most admired men in the nation. Graham continued his crusades, as he called his revivals, speaking in London, Tokyo, Yugoslavia, and Latin America, as well as in Canada and the United States. Like the Vatican, Graham had a pavilion at the New York World's Fair (1964–1965).

World Congress on Evangelism. One of his important activities was working with the World Congress on Evangelism, which met in Berlin in 1966. The congress, reminiscent of the great evangelistic conferences of the turn of the century, brought together representatives from around the world and reinvigorated the actions and growth of conservative Protestantism.

Political Influence. By the 1960s, however, Graham was such a public figure that his actions took on a political cast whether he liked it or not. He was criticized by many blacks and white liberals for his failure to speak out forcefully on the moral and religious implications of the civil rights movement in the early part of the decade. He maintained that his work with African-American evangelists and his insistence that his meetings be open to all people were a symbol of the importance of racial equality. A few months after the bombing of the Sixteenth Street Baptist Church in Birmingham, Alabama, he held a nonsegregated crusade in that city. He worked vigorously behind the scenes to lower racial tension, but his public voice was muted in this crucial area.

Vietnam. His views on the American involvement in the war in Vietnam were more complicated. He had a long history of anticommunism and a close relationship with Presidents Lyndon Johnson and Richard Nixon. Like other Americans, he strongly supported the troops actually fighting the war. In 1966, at the request of President Johnson, Graham made a Christmas trip to Vietnam. In a press conference afterward he remarked, "The stakes are much higher in Vietnam than anybody realizes. . . . Every American can be proud of the men in uniform. . . . They are paying a great price for the victory they are almost certainly winning there." An illness kept him from visiting the troops in 1967, but he returned at Christmas in 1968 even though he realized this gave an appearance of supporting the unpopular war. He remarked in early 1968, "I hope my son, who is nearing draft age, will gladly go and be willing to give his life."

Counter-Counterculture. Graham deeply disliked the challenges to authority that were characteristic of the last half of the decade. While he was able to reconcile himself to the nonviolent protests against segregation, he bitterly refused to accept the legitimacy of the antiwar protests, insisting they were threats to the nation's security and offensive to God. In regard to the ministers who were active in the antiwar movement he remarked, "Where many of these men get the 'Reverend' in the front of their names, I do not know. Certainly they don't get it from God. . . . God does not tolerate disorder."

Evasion of Race. While Graham attempted to evade political issues such as race and war, he continued to be deeply involved in politics. In 1960 he strongly supported his friend Richard Nixon's candidacy for the presidency, not because he was anti-Catholic but because he admired Nixon. His subsequent relations with President Kennedy were somewhat strained, but he had a close friendship with Lyndon Johnson. In 1968 he endorsed Nixon and quietly and effectively worked for his election. Graham fully supported the new president's regular White House church services and was the speaker at the first of these. He worked closely with the Nixon administration, supporting its efforts both publicly and privately, serving as if he were the president's chaplain.

Source:
William Martin, *A Prophet with Honor: The Billy Graham Story* (New York: Morrow, 1991).

MARTIN LUTHER KING, JR.

1929-1968

CIVIL RIGHTS LEADER

Symbol and Leader. Martin Luther King, Jr., became the symbol of the civil rights movement after leading the Montgomery bus boycott (1955–1956), which attracted the nation's attention to the growing dissatisfaction of southern blacks with the system of legal segregation. Along with a group of black Baptist preachers he helped form the Southern Christian Leadership Conference (SCLC), and in his books and sermons he laid the foundation of nonviolent direct action as a way of securing for southern blacks their rights guaranteed in the Thirteenth, Fourteenth, and Fifteenth Amendments.

Birmingham. When the SCLC joined the campaign to desegregate Birmingham, Alabama, in 1963, King's presence attracted the television and news cameras which recorded the shocking violence of the police toward the demonstrators, including children. Those displays of racism aroused the nation and forced the Kennedy administration to introduce a civil rights bill that became the Public Accommodations Act of 1964.

Nonviolence Questioned. While King was in jail in violation of an injunction to halt the demonstrations, eight of Birmingham's leading Protestant ministers published a letter asking him why violence erupted from the tension his demonstrations caused even though he insisted his was a doctrine of nonviolence. King's "Letter from a Birmingham Jail" is one of his most eloquent statements of the moral and religious basis for the civil rights movement.

Confronting Sin. He said the purpose of the campaign in Birmingham was to confront the sin of racial discrimination. The ongoing confrontations between the marchers and the police came from the failure of the white establishment to negotiate, not from the demands of the black community to modify the immoral segregated system. Only raising the tensions to an intolerable level would finally lead to a resolution of the racial injustice in the community. King denied that he advocated breaking laws, but "an individual who breaks a law that conscience tells him is unjust, and then willingly accepts the penalty of imprisonment in order to arouse the conscience of the community . . . is in reality expressing the highest respect for the law." He then expressed his great disappointment that the white church had failed to respond to the moral issue of racial discrimination and, by its silence, sanctioned the status quo, including such actions as Birmingham's efforts to maintain an unjust system.

March on Washington. King's closing speech at the March on Washington for Jobs and Freedom in August 1963, in which he said that he had a dream that America would finally live up to its values and all citizens would be able to join in the words of the spiritual "Free at last! Free at last! Thank God Almighty, we are free at last!" has become one of America's most famous speeches. The following year he was awarded the Nobel Peace Prize.

Voting Rights. In 1965 King and the SCLC joined the Student Nonviolent Coordinating Committee in the Selma, Alabama, campaign to secure the voting rights of blacks in Alabama. As in the case of Birming-

ham, the success of Selma came from the news media's attention, resulting in large part from King's presence. The publicity given the violence directed at the demonstrators secured their right to march to Montgomery and, more importantly, public support for what became the Voting Rights Act of 1965. King's greatest victories were over.

Racism and Poverty. As it became clear that Jim Crow laws were systematically being repealed, King turned his attention to the problems of racism in general and of poverty. His attempts to open jobs and housing in Chicago had limited success. His growing opposition to the American role in the Vietnam War peeled away support from the embattled Johnson administration. An upsurge of black radicalism and black nationalism among young, urban blacks shifted their sympathies from nonviolent direct action to black power. Race riots in cities reflected the growing impatience of urban blacks with their situation and weakened white support for more social reform.

Poor People's March. With his influence declining, in 1968 King began plans for another march on Washington, the Poor People's March, that would show that poverty was not solely a black issue. In April he went to Memphis to support striking sanitation workers, and he was assassinated there on 4 April. The riots that erupted in over 130 cities and towns around the country were more a cry of despair than a tribute to the man who had come to represent the civil rights struggle. The Poor People's March took place to no effect. His death was the closing of a movement and an era.

Source:
David Garrow, *Bearing the Cross: Martin Luther King, Jr and the Southern Christian Leadership Conference* (New York: Morrow, 1986).

MALCOLM X

1919-1965

BLACK MUSLIM LEADER

Childhood. Malcolm Little was born to a father who was both a preacher and a follower of the black nationalist Marcus Garvey. His father died in mysterious circumstances when Malcolm was young, and after his mother was placed in a mental institution in Michigan, Malcolm, at age fifteen, dropped out of school to live with his half sister in Boston. After a criminal career on the streets on Boston and New York, he was arrested and was sentenced to ten years in prison for robbery.

Nation of Islam. While in prison Malcolm came into contact with the writings of the Honorable Elijah Muhammad, leader of the Nation of Islam, often called the Black Muslims. Malcolm was converted and replaced his "slave name" of Little with the letter *X*. After his release from prison in 1954 he joined Muhammad and quickly proved his ability as a preacher and an organizer. He was placed in charge of the New York mosque and within a short time became the most public figure in the Black Muslim movement. He first acquired national attention when he became the focus of a CBS television documentary on the Black Muslims, *The Hate That Hate Begot* (1959). In the civil rights struggle of the early 1960s Malcolm's black-militant racial separatism seemed a stark contrast to the nonviolent tactics and integrationist demands of Martin Luther King, Jr. As Malcolm attracted more public attention, he aroused the anger and jealousy of the inner circle of the Nation of Islam. He, in turn, was dismayed by the sexual misconduct of Muhammad and by the lavish living of the leader, his family, and close associates. In 1963 Malcolm was suspended by Muhammad for remarks made after the death of President Kennedy and then expelled from the Nation of Islam.

Hajj. Malcolm then made a second trip to Saudi Arabia, this time completing his hajj, the pilgrimage to Mecca, and on his return announced his new recognition that Islam was not for blacks alone. He became more active in the civil rights movement, organizing the Muslim Mosque, Inc., and the Organization of African-American Unity. He was assassinated by followers of Elijah Muhammad while speaking to his own followers in New York in 1965.

Sources:
David Gallen, *Malcolm X as They Knew Him* (New York: Carroll & Graf, 1992);

Bruce Perry, *Malcolm: The Life of the Man Who Changed Black America* (Barrytown, N.Y.: Station Hill Press, 1991).

MADALYN MURRAY O'HAIR

1919-

ATHEIST

The Problems of Atheists. Madalyn Murray O'Hair called herself "the most hated woman in America." Although *School Board of Abbington Township* v. *Schempp* is usually cited as the case through which the Supreme Court ruled that public schools may not require Bible reading, the second decision on that issue was a case filed in 1959 by O'Hair and her son, William J. Murray (*Murray* v. *Curlett*). The decision was handed down in 1963. As atheists they protested the Baltimore school board's requirement that the public school day begin with prayer or Bible reading. Murray, as she was named then, attracted notoriety by organizing the American Atheist Center (1959), American Atheists, Inc.

(1965), and the Society of Separationists (1965). Her American Atheist Radio series was broadcast on over four thousand radio stations. She had a talent for attracting attention as, for example, when she issued statements that she planned to sue to stop governments from giving tax exemptions to places of public worship and other religious organizations. She also announced she would sue to remove the phrase "In God We Trust" from the currency. After being arrested for attacking Baltimore police, she fled to Hawaii and eventually settled in Austin, Texas, where she and her new husband established the American Atheist Association. During the 1960s the American Atheist Press published the first five of O'Hair's more than twenty-five books on the subject of atheism, including *Why I Am an Atheist* (1965).

Source:
John Howard, "The Most Hated Woman in America: Madalyn Murry," *Life*, 56 (19 June 1964): 91–92.

ORAL ROBERTS

1918-

EVANGELIST, FOUNDER OF ORAL ROBERTS UNIVERSITY

Early Career. Oral Roberts began his evangelistic career in 1947, after a brief ministry with the Pentecostal Holiness Church. At the beginning his primary emphasis was on healing services, and he attracted huge crowds in the 1950s with his tent revivals. His largest tent could seat 12,500. He soon recognized the usefulness of radio, eventually having over three hundred radio stations in the United States carrying his messages and shortwave radio beaming his program to the rest of the world. Most Americans outside Pentecostal circles grew familiar with him through the television programs he began in the mid 1950s, edited from his tent revivals. Many jeered at the healing lines he still used and scoffed at the "prayer cloths," pieces of cloth two and a half inches by five inches that he said he personally prayed over. He did not charge for these prayer cloths but maintained a list of supporters who were asked for regular contributions.

Moving to the Center. Roberts became more respectable in the 1960s, moving toward the center of the religious community without abandoning his Pentecostal roots. In his services he decreased the emphasis on healing and concentrated on simple evangelism. In 1966 he was invited to the World Evangelistic Congress on Evangelism in Berlin and there established relations with some of the leading conservative Protestants, including Billy Graham. In 1968 he startled his followers by joining the United Methodist Church. His new television programs, run in prime evening time, mixed his message with religious entertainment, and his audience grew.

Building the University. His primary work during the decade was the construction of Oral Roberts University in Tulsa, Oklahoma. This charismatic but nondenomina-tional university opened in 1965 and was dedicated by Graham in 1967.

Source:

David Edwin Harrell, Jr., *Oral Roberts: An American Life* (Bloomington, Indiana, Indiana University Press, 1983).

PEOPLE IN THE NEWS

Muhammad Ali defeated Sonny Liston on 25 February 1964 for the World Heavyweight Championship. He then confirmed rumors that he had converted to the Nation of Islam. He was stripped of his title in 1967 when he refused induction into the military for religious reasons. The Supreme Court overturned that conviction in 1971, stating that he had been improperly drafted.

In 1966 **Thomas Jonathan Jackson Altizer** of Emory University published *The Gospel of Christian Atheism.*

In 1961 **Jim Bakker** married **Tammy Faye LaValley.** They joined **Pat Robertson**'s Christian Broadcast Network in 1965 and in November 1966 began their successful religious talk show on that network.

In 1967 **David B. Berg,** operating originally out of the Light House Mission coffeehouse near the pier in Huntington Beach, California, began to convert the hippies in the area. He later turned his mission into the Children of God, one of the Jesus People groups.

In 1961 **William R. Bright,** organizer of the Campus Crusade for Christ, established the center for his national movement at Arrowhead Springs, California.

In 1967 **William Sloane Coffin, Jr.,** Yale University chaplain, offered his chapel for draft resisters. He joined in issuing "A Call to Resist Illegitimate Authority." He was later arrested and convicted for conspiring to interfere with the draft. His conviction was overturned.

In 1967 **Fr. Charles E. Curran** was removed from the faculty of the Catholic University for his opposition to the Roman Catholic teachings on contraception. Protests lead to his reinstatement, but not a change in his views. He published *Absolutes in Moral Theology* in 1968 and in 1969 edited *Contraception: Authority and Dissent,* which included his essay titled "Natural Law and Moral Theology."

In 1963 **Bill Gaither** wrote his widely recorded song "He Touched Me." In 1969–1970 he was named Songwriter of the Year by the Gospel Music Association, the first of these awards given to him.

In 1960 **Archbishop Iakovos** of the Greek Orthodox Archdiocese of North and South America, the largest Orthodox church in the United States, joined in organizing the Conference of Orthodox Bishops to bring the various Orthodox groups into contact.

Sr. Mary Corita was asked to paint the fifty-foot mural for the Vatican Pavilion at the New York World's Fair (1964–1965). A teacher of art at Immaculate Heart College in Los Angeles, her serigraphs and posters attracted wide attention. She left her order at the end of the decade, resuming her name Corita Kent.

In 1960 **Dr. Nathan Gluek,** president of the Hebrew Union College–Jewish Institute of Religion, established a branch, the Hebrew Union College Biblical and Archeological School, in Jerusalem, the first center in Israel for the teaching of Reform Judaism. He published his *Deities and Dolphins: The Story of the Nabataeans* in 1965, the result of his extensive archeological explorations in Palestine.

In 1962 **Kathryn Kuhlman** published her best-selling *I Believe in Miracles* on spiritual healing. In 1967 she began television broadcasts of her healing services from her headquarters in Pittsburgh.

Joseph Irwin Miller, a member of the Disciples of Christ and president of the Cummings Engine Company, was elected president of the National Council of Churches in 1960 for a three-year term. He was the first layman to hold that position.

In October 1961 **Pat Robertson** opened his Christian Broadcast Network in Portsmouth, Virginia. In 1963 he began his "faith partnerships," asking seven hundred of his viewers to pledge support of ten dollars a month. The response was enthusiastic, and his television network quickly moved to success.

In 1961 **Robert H. Schuller** opened a new drive-in/walk-in building for his Garden Grove Community Church in Garden Grove, California, holding on to the memory of the church's beginnings in a local drive-in movie theater. He shortly added a nine-story office building, the Tower of Power. The growth of his congregation was so spectacular that in 1969 he organized the Rob-ert H. Schuller Institute for Successful Church Leadership. In 1963 he published *God's Way to the Good Life* and in 1967 *Move Ahead with Possibility Thinking*.

In 1969 **Jimmy Swaggart** began the television broadcast of "Camptown Meeting" on stations in Atlanta, Houston, and Saint Paul. He had established his career with his annual recordings of gospel songs and his successful revivals in Pentecostal churches.

DEATHS

Bruce Barton, 80, author of best-selling religious books in the early decades of the century, 5 July 1967.

Smiley Blanton, 84, cofounded with Norman Vincent Peale the Religio-Psychiatric Clinic at Marble Collegiate Church in 1937, 30 October 1966.

Francis Cardinal Brennan, 74, the first American member of the Sacred Roman Rota, the highest Roman Catholic court; named cardinal in 1967, 2 July 1968.

Frank N. D. Buchman, 83, founder of the Oxford Group Movement (later Moral Re-Armament) in 1921, an effort to organize a "God-guided campaign to prevent war by moral and spiritual awakenings," 7 August 1961.

Father Major Jelous Devine, 88, religious-social leader who in 1942 incorporated his following as the Peace Mission Movement, 10 September 1965.

Harry Emerson Fosdick, 91, the most popular Protestant preacher in the nation and one of the country's leading liberal churchmen, 5 October 1969.

Franklin Clark Fry, 67, one of the organizers of the World Council of Churches in 1948 and the National Council of Churches in Christ in 1950, 6 June 1968.

Charles E. Fuller, 81, the most successful radio evangelist of his day, 18 May 1968.

Sweet Daddy Grace, 78, founder of the House of Prayer for All People, a Pentecostal denomination most active in the African-American community, 12 January 1960.

John Haynes Holmes, 84, one of the founders of the National Association for the Advancement of Colored People and the American Civil Liberties Union, 3 April 1964.

Robert Jones, Sr., 84, founder of the fundamentalist Bob Jones University, now in Greenville, South Carolina, 16 January 1968.

Clarence Jordan, 57, a founder of Koinonia Farms, an experimental Christian commune near Americus, Georgia, 29 October 1969.

Kenneth S. Latourette, 84, a leading historian of religion in America, 26 December 1968.

Metropolitan Leonty, 88, helped form the Russian Orthodox Greek Catholic Church, now the Orthodox Church in America, 4 May 1965.

Halford E. Luccock, 75, professor of homiletics at Yale University, 5 November 1960.

Thomas Merton, 53, author and Cistercian monk, 10 December 1968.

John Courtney Murray, S.J., 53, author, theologian, and professor at Woodstock College, Maryland, 16 August 1967.

A.(Abraham) J.(Johannes) Muste, 82, minister in the Society of Friends and a vigorous opponent of the expanding U.S. military role in Vietnam, 11 February 1967.

Helmut Richard Niebuhr, 67, author and member of the Yale University faculty from 1931 until his death, 5 July 1962.

G. Bromley Oxnam, 72, leading Protestant proponent of liberal causes and target of red-baiting even before the cold war period, 13 March 1963.

James A. Pike, 56, Episcopal bishop and religious skeptic, 2 September 1969.

Daniel Alfred Poling, 83, pastor in the Reform Church of America and owner and editor of the *Christian Herald*, 7 February 1968.

Charles Francis Potter, 79, a Baptist minister, then a Unitarian Universalist, then a humanist, 4 October 1965.

Joseph Elmer Cardinal Ritter, 74, Catholic bishop and later cardinal, a leader in integrating Catholic schools and as an American voice at the Second Vatican Council, speaking strongly for religious liberty, the absolution of the Jews for the death of Jesus, and the authority of the bishops as well as the pope in the affairs of the church, 10 June 1967.

Most. Rev. Joseph Francis Rummel, 88, Roman Catholic archbishop of New Orleans, who introduced integration into southern parochial schools, 8 November 1964.

Abba Hillel Silver, 70, Reform rabbi and leader of efforts to convince the Reform association to support the Zionist cause, 28 November 1963.

Francis Cardinal Spellman, 78, Roman Catholic archbishop and the leading Catholic figure in the United States, 2 December 1967.

Paul Tillich, 79, leading Protestant theologian and author who was forced from the University of Frankfurt by the new Nazi government in Germany in 1933, 22 October 1965.

John Ralph Voris, 87, Presbyterian minister who organized the Save the Children charity in 1932 to address the needs of children in the Appalachian Mountains during the Depression, 16 January 1968.

Harry Fredrick Ward, 93, Methodist pastor and founder of the Methodist Federation for Social Action (later the Methodist Federation for Social Service), 9 December 1966.

PUBLICATIONS

John W. Bachman, *The Church in the World of Radio-Television* (New York: Association Press, 1960);

John Coleman Bennett, *Christianity and Communism Today* (New York: Association Press, 1960);

Bennett, *Foreign Policy in Christian Perspective* (New York: Scribners, 1966);

Bennett, *Nuclear Weapons and the Conflict of Conscience* (New York: Scribners, 1962);

Daniel Berrigan, *Consequences: Truth and . . .* (New York: Macmillan, 1967);

Berrigan, *Love, Love after End: Parables, Prayers, and Meditations* (New York: Macmillan, 1968);

Berrigan, *They Call Us Dead Men: Reflections on Life and Conscience* (New York: Macmillan, 1966);

Philip Berrigan, *No More Strangers* (New York: Macmillan, 1963);

Berrigan, *A Punishment for Peace* (New York: Macmillan, 1969);

Malcolm Boyd, *Are You Running with Me, Jesus?* (New York: Avon, 1967);

George Arthur Buttrick, *Biblical Thought and the Secular University* (Baton Rouge: Louisiana State University, 1960);

Tom Driberg, *The Mystery of Moral Re-Armament: A Study of Frank Buchman and His Movement* (New York: Knopf, 1965);

A. N. Gilkes, *Faith for Modern Man* (New York: Roy, 1960);

Billy Graham, *My Answer* (Garden City, N.Y.: Doubleday, 1960);

Graham, *The World Aflame* (Garden City, N.Y.: Doubleday, 1965);

Martin Luther King, Jr., *The Measure of a Man* (Philadelphia: Pilgrim Press, 1968);

King, *Strength to Love* (New York: Harper & Row, 1963);

King, *The Trumpet of Conscience* (New York: Harper & Row, 1968);

King, *Where Do We Go To From Here: Chaos or Community?* (New York: Harper & Row, 1967);

King, *Why We Can't Wait* (New York: Harper & Row, 1964);

Robert Lee and Martin E. Marty, eds. *Religion and Social Conflict* (New York: Oxford University Press, 1964);

Charles M. Leslie, *Anthropology of Folk Religion* (New York: Vintage, 1960);

John Macquarrie, *Twentieth-Century Religious Thought: The Frontiers of Philosophy and Theology* (New York: Harper & Row, 1963);

Malcolm X and Alex Haley, *The Autobiography of Malcolm X* (New York: Grove, 1965);

Martin E. Marty, *What Do We Believe? The Stance of Religion in America* (New York: Meredith Press, 1968);

Thomas Merton, *Disputed Questions* (New York: Farrar, Straus & Cudahy, 1960);

Merton, *Faith and Violence: Christian Teaching and Christian Practice* (Notre Dame, Ind.: University of Notre Dame Press, 1968);

Merton, *Life and Holiness* (New York: Herder & Herder, 1963);

Merton, *My Argument with the Gestapo: A Macaronic Journal* (Garden City, N.Y.: Doubleday, 1969);

Reinhold Niebuhr, *Faith and Politics: A Commentary on Religious, Social, and Political Thought in a Technological Age* (New York: Braziller, 1968);

Theodore Reik, *The Creation of Woman* (New York: Braziller, 1960);

Ralph Lord Roy, *Communism and the Churches* (New York: Harcourt, Brace & World, 1960);

Christian Century, periodical;

Christianity and Crisis, periodical;

Christianity Today, periodical;

Commentary, periodical;

Commonweal, periodical;

Journal for the Scientific Study of Religion, periodical;

National Catholic Reporter, periodical, 1964– .

Anti-Catholic propaganda produced during the 1960 presidential race

SCIENCE AND TECHNOLOGY

by CAROLYN WILSON-BURROWS and WAYNE BURROWS

CONTENTS

1960

- Allan Sundage finds a starlike object in a region of the sky known as 3C48 that emits radio waves. He notices it doesn't act like either a star or a galaxy. It is later identified as a quasar, or "quasi-stellar object."

- Luis Alvarez defines extremely short-lived particles smaller than the components of atoms (protons, neutrons, and electrons) as "resonances." The resonance might be a particle or several particles associated with each other.

- The first American use of geothermal power begins near San Francisco, employing steam under high pressure to produce electricity.

- Harry H. Hess proposes his theory of seafloor spreading, paving the way for later acceptance of plate tectonics.

- Einstein's theory of relativity is confirmed under laboratory conditions at Harvard.

- Mike Todd, Jr., invents Smell-O-Vision. A spray of dust is released under theater seats to coincide with events in the movie being shown. The idea was not successful with the public.

- The USS *George Washington* is launched, carrying sixteen Polaris missiles. The first nuclear sub to carry nuclear warheads, it is able to attack anywhere at any time from an undetected location.

- A power station in Dresden, Illinois, becomes the first commercial nuclear power plant to use a boiling-water type of reactor.

- Artificial tanning cream is developed.

- The meter is redefined according to a wavelength in the spectrum of the gas krypton.

2 Jan.   After studying a meteorite that had fallen in North Dakota in 1919, Dr. John H. Reynolds of the University of California estimates the age of the solar system to be 4.95 billion years.

12 Jan.   General Electric introduces a thermoplastic tape capable of recording video and audio signals simultaneously.

23 Jan.   The bathyscaphe *Trieste* plunges to the deepest part of Pacific Ocean, almost seven miles deep. U.S. Navy Lt. Don Walsh commands the vessel. Unexpected forms of life are found at the bottom of the sea.

1 Apr.   *Tiros 1,* the first weather satellite, is launched.

10 May   The USS *Triton,* a nuclear submarine, completes an eighty-four-day journey around the world without surfacing. Knowing the starting point, speeds, and directions, a computer maps its exact location at all times. Navigation is checked by sighting the stars through the periscope. The *Triton* follows the route Magellan took centuries earlier.

July   The laser is successfully developed by Theodore H. Maimen.

12 Aug.   The *ECHO 1,* a passive communications satellite (used to reflect signals) is launched.

1961

- C. Roger Lynds at the National Radio Astronomy Observatory at Greenbank, West Virginia, detects radio waves from nebulae, regions in space that contain large amounts of gas and possibly stars.

- James V. McConnell tries to prove that smart worms (planaria, flat worms) can be fed to other worms, with memory passed along in the process. He proposes the chemical RNA is the memory-carrying molecule. Memory is later shown to be more complex.

- Marshall W. Nirenberg first cracks the alphabet of the genetic code in DNA. The code is based on the order of bases in the DNA. Every three bases in a gene codes for an amino acid in a protein.

- *Cuss I* drills 2.2 miles for core samples from the ocean bottom to study its composition and possible origin.

- Robert Hofstadter describes the structure of protons and neutrons in the atomic nucleus. Each has a positively charged core surrounded by two mesons. One meson is negatively charged in neutrons. In November Hofstadter wins the Nobel Prize in physics for his work.

- Bell Laboratories produces the first computer designed by another computer. It is used in the army's Nike-Zeus antimissile system. Bell Labs also proves that laser communication is possible.

- IBM puts its "golf ball" Selectric typewriter on the market.

- The USS *Enterprise* aircraft carrier, run by eight nuclear reactors, is launched. It can travel for three years and two hundred thousand miles between stops for refueling.

- Quartz iodide and quartz bromide lamps are used in film projectors. They are brighter than filament lamps and withstand higher temperatures.

- Texas Instruments patents the first silicon chip used for electronic circuits.

Apr.	The man-made element lawrencium, named after physicist Ernest O. Lawrence, is produced at Lawrence Berkeley Radiation Laboratory in California by Albert Ghiorso and colleagues.
12 Apr.– 5 May	The first men in space (Yuri Gagarin of the Soviet Union followed by Alan Shepard, Jr., of the United States) start the Soviet-American race for the Moon.
25 May	In his second State of the Union address, President John F. Kennedy presents his goal for the United States by the end of the decade of landing a man on the Moon and returning him safely.

1962

- The Sugar Grove radio telescope, started in 1959, is abandoned after an expenditure of $96 million. It is designed to spy on the Soviets, but satellites make Sugar Grove obsolete before it can be completed.

- Peter van de Kamp studies two thousand photos of Barnard's Star, looking at the "wobble" in its position over time. He concludes there is a planet orbiting the star. Later astronomers learn there was a telescope defect, but the way to find planets around close stars is defined.

- The U.S. scientific space probe *Mariner 2* reaches Venus 109 days after its launch from Earth.

- Rachel L. Carson publishes her book *Silent Spring*, which introduces the public to pollution and its possible effects on the environment. The book is widely read and starts an environmental movement in the United States.

- Harry H. Hess shows convection currents in the Earth's mantle cause sea-floor spreading. Plate tectonics (where the continents move on a liquid layer of the mantle underneath) will be the resulting explanation later in the decade.

- Linus Pauling and Emile Zuckerkandl show how genetic material can be used as a biological clock to determine how long ago species separated.

- Unimation markets one of the first commercially useful industrial robots. Automobile manufacturers begin ordering the machines, though they are fearful of the labor unions' reaction to such automation.

- Harvard develops an atomic clock using stable hydrogen atoms. Scientists predict that it will remain accurate for a hundred thousand years.

- RCA develops a system using metallic oxides that allows numerous electronic circuits to be put on a single silicon chip. The integrated circuit is born. The U.S. government orders three hundred thousand chips from Texas Instruments to be used in Minuteman (nuclear) missiles.

- In response to the Soviets shooting down the U-2 spy plane with Francis Gary Powers aboard in 1960, the U.S. Model 147 airplane is developed. Piloted by remote control, the plane promises safer reconnaissance.

- Kelvinator produces a dishwasher that uses neither soap nor water. High-frequency sound waves clean the dishes. The new dishwasher is never commercially produced.

- A molded car seat is made for children. The seat is locked into the car by the car's safety belt. The seat has its own safety belt for the young occupant.

- Powdered orange juice is patented.

- A braille typewriter is developed for blind people.

- Digital Equipment Corporation develops the third generation of computers. The first generation was built with vacuum tubes, the second generation with transistors. This generation uses electronic integrated circuits and is miniaturized. At fifteen thousand dollars, the price of the new machine is much lower than that of previous models.

- The noble gases have always been thought to be chemically inert — incapable of combining with other atoms to form molecules. Neil Bartlett produces the first noble gas compound, xenon platinum hexafluoride.

20 Feb.   John Glenn becomes the first American to orbit the Earth.

1 May   William Luyten of the University of Minnesota announces the discovery of the smallest known star, a white dwarf, designated LP 327-186.

July   Dr. G. Danby at Brookhaven Laboratories shows that there are two types of neutrino (a subatomic particle with no mass or electrical charge).

10 July   *Telstar*, the first privately owned and the first active communications satellite, is launched. The first live transatlantic television program is broadcast the next day.

1963

- Herbert Friedman and Riccardo Giacconi develop a satellite to be launched so that astronomers can study X-rays from space. Earth's atmosphere usually destroys X-rays from space. A strong X-ray source is found in Scorpio (Sco X-1).

- American scientists studying residual magnetism in rocks from the floor of the Indian Ocean discover periodic changes in polarity, proof of seafloor spreading.

- Mathematician Paul J. Cohen provides an alternate proof to a theorem already proven, demonstrating that two types of mathematics exist and changing views in mathematics and philosophy permanently.

- Scientists show evidence of complex molecules of life created spontaneously in artificial atmospheres resembling early Earth.

- Maarten Schmidt shows a large red shift of 3C273. The red shift proves the structure is moving away from Earth at a remarkable speed of 47,400 km/sec (29,400 mi/sec). It is almost unbelievably far away. This represents the first recognition of a quasar by astronomers.

- Kodak produces the Instamatic camera, which uses a film cartridge. Meanwhile, Polaroid produces a Polacolor camera. Film loads in flat packs, and prints are made automatically, minutes after exposure, without sending film to a lab for processing. These are immediately popular with the public.

- A Kodak subsidiary, Recordak Corporation, produces a system to store up to a million pages on microfilm. Any page can be enlarged within seconds.

- The USS *Atlantis II* clearly photographs the ocean floor.

- The Visible Man and Visible Woman models are sold. These are plastic models with transparent "skin" to show what the body's internal structures look like. The educational models create much controversy.

30 Mar. Edward J. Dwight, Jr., becomes the first black pilot chosen for astronaut training by the National Aeronautics and Space Administration (NASA).

26 July The communications satellite *Syncom 2* becomes the first to enter a geosynchronous orbit (matching the speed of the Earth's rotation).

Aug. The anti-xi-zero, a fundamental particle of antimatter, is discovered. This was predicted earlier as part of Murray Gell-Mann's resonance theory. Finding the particle makes Gell-Mann's theory much more easily accepted by physicists.

1964

- The Verrazano Narrows Bridge opens in New York City. This was the largest suspension bridge in the world at the time and a technological wonder.

- Harold Weaver describes the first natural "cosmic maser." The extreme conditions of heat and energy in some galactic regions produce maser-type emissions from certain chemical ions such as the OH⁻ radical.

- James W. Cronin and Val Fitch work with subatomic particles and prove that time reversal is possible.

- Murray Gell-Mann introduces the concept of quarks. Quarks are postulated as the most fundamental type of particle, from which all other particles are made.

- IBM uses the new chips in its innovative IBM 360 computer. IBM also produces a new product, the word processor, a hybrid of the typewriter and the computer.

- The Tokyo Olympics are broadcast live to the United States via the geosynchronous *Syncom 3* satellite.

- The U.S. Navy Research Lab produces a new "Mayday" distress radio. The radio has a nickel-magnesium battery and automatically sends a distress signal on contact with sea water. A ship cannot sink without a distress signal being sent.

- INTELSAT is formed. This is an international venture where countries pay a share of costs of developing and launching communications satellites. These payments act as stock shares, giving other nations a certain amount of time to use the U.S. satellite system.

- Dr. Stookey at Corning Glass Works in New York develops photochromic glass. Silver crystals are embedded in the glass. They absorb light and darken the glass quickly in a bright area, but lighten again in minutes in a dark area.

- *Sealab I* is the first in a series of oceanographic vessels used for research.

- Arno A. Penzias and Robert W. Wilson of Bell Labs determine that background radiation from space is left over from the "Big Bang" which started the universe.

31 July The *Ranger 7* space probe relays 4,316 close-up photographs of the Moon back to Earth and becomes the first U.S. lunar shot to be described as completely successful.

1965

- The Arecibo Observatory in Puerto Rico shows that Venus rotates in the opposite direction from the other planets. On Venus the sun rises in the west and sets in the east. They also determine that Mercury does rotate on its axis, but very slowly. One rotational day on Mercury takes 59 Earth days.

- Allan Sandage, astronomer, finds quasars that do not emit radio waves.

- Melvin Calvin determines that chlorophyll breakdown products in shale rock from the Sudan Formation are 2.5–2.9 billion years old.

- The Stanford Linear Accelerator Center becomes operational.

- John Kemeny and Thomas Kurtz develop a new computer programming language. They call it BASIC, which stands for Beginner's All-purpose Symbolic Instructional Code. BASIC will be one of the most widely used computer language for decades to come.

- The first fully electronic telephone exchange becomes operational in Succasunna, New Jersey. The new development by AT&T eventually replaces leagues of human operators with (less expensive) machines.

- The videodisc recorder is developed. Now, people can record television programs and play them back later. With a special camera they can also record home movies and play them back later.

- A magnetic highway is demonstrated in the United States. Vehicles ride above the roadway.

- Traffic control in Chicago, New York and Detroit becomes computerized. Traffic jams can be cleared more quickly. With major events like sports or big shows, traffic patterns can be controlled to avoid long tie-ups.

- A computer at the New York Stock Exchange answers questions over the telephone using an artificial voice.

- Super-8mm cassettes are developed with super-8mm movie cameras, following the lead of still picture cameras and their user-friendly technology.

- First American space walk.

- Gas chromatography is used to separate rare-earth complexes.

- Ray Dolby, an American engineer, develops a way to reduce the background noise in recordings without affecting the quality of the music.

- *Intelsat I* is launched. This satellite can handle 240 telephone circuits or one television channel between Europe and North America. It is designed to work for eighteen months and actually lasts for four years.

15 July *Mariner 4* sends the first close-up photographs of Mars.

3 Dec. *Gemini 7* sends messages to Earth by laser.

1966

- Clifford Evans and Betty J. Maggers suggest pottery from South America from 3000 B.C. was influenced by the Japanese, suggesting contact between the continents at that time.

- Robert Ardrey shows humans are territorial creatures like other animals. He tries to show that the desire to hold territory is more basic than any other instinct.

- Richard G. Doell, G. Brent Dalrymple, and Allan Cox show the Earth's magnetic field has periodic reversals.

- *Lunar Orbiter II* photographs two million square miles of the Moon from close up.

- Radar is used to measure the polar ice thickness.

- Kodak introduces a "square" flash bulb. It replaces older, more fragile bulb designs. The cube attaches to the camera and contains four separate flash bulbs, making flash photography a simpler process. Other manufacturers quickly adapt.

16 Mar. Two U.S. astronauts stage the first docking of an orbiting spacecraft.

1967

- Elwyn L. Simons determines that a skull found in Egypt is nearly thirty million years old. It is the oldest known ape skull ever found — *Aegyptopithecus.*

- R. H. MacArthur and Edward O. Wilson develop the field of biogeography.

- Charles T. Caskey, Richard E. Marshall, and Marshall W. Nirenberg find that the genetic code is essentially the same in guinea pigs, toads, and bacteria, suggesting that all life uses the same code.

- S. Manabe and R. T. Wetherald propose that human activities increase atmospheric carbon dioxide and can cause a greenhouse effect. This had been proposed before, but had been felt to be unprovable. Manabe and Wetherald use a computer model to show not only that the greenhouse effect could happen, but that it seems to be happening.

- Steven Weinberg and Sheldon Glashow independently propose electroweak unification, stating that it should be possible to unify the four basic forces of physics into one grand theory of what is.

- Computer keyboards are developed for immediate access between the operator and the computer. Punched tapes, punched cards, and magnetic tapes are no longer required.

- IBM develops a light-sensitive pen, a television screen for computers, and uses computers to assist in electronic-circuit design.

- RCA develops a compact television camera weighing 2.2 pounds.

- A cordless, battery-powered telephone is developed. It is the precursor of the cellular phone but is much more complex and expensive to use.

- Project Gassbuggy involves a 2.4-kiloton nuclear explosion used for peaceful purposes. It is intended to release natural gas in New Mexico. This is part of Project Plowshares, to use nuclear weapons for peaceful purposes.

- H. Hay and J. Yellott at the University of Arizona produce a solar-powered house using roof ponds to collect and store solar energy.

- W. J. Morgan of the United States and British scientists propose the theory of plate tectonics.

27 Jan.	A flash fire kills Gus Grissom, Ed White, and Roger Chaffee in their spacecraft at Cape Kennedy.
1 Mar.	The first overseas direct dialing begins.
9 Nov.	*Surveyor VI* makes a soft landing on the moon.
Dec.	Arthur Kornberg synthesizes active DNA in a test tube using a cell-free system.

1968

- One of the newly described pulsars in the Crab nebula is thought to have been the site of a supernova seen on Earth on 4 July 1054.

- A House of Representatives report declares Lake Erie dead from the effects of pollution. Americans become increasingly aware of and concerned about the environment.

- David Zipser breaks the last part of the genetic code — the only unknown codon (three base nucleotides in a row in the DNA known as UGA, for uracil, guanine, and adenine) codes for termination of a protein chain.

- Restriction endonucleases are described by Werner Arber, with far-reaching ramifications for the field of molecular biology.

- George Clark, Gordon Garmire, and William Kraushaar use the third orbiting solar observatory sent into space by NASA to detect gamma rays from the center of the Milky Way.

- Elso S. Barghoorn finds amino acids in three-billion-year-old rocks.

- Scientists at Cornell University map the surface of Venus using radar.

- Standard Telephones and Cables Co. lays a deep-sea cable capable of transmitting 720 simultaneous conversations between Florida and the Caribbean region.

- Bell Labs measures accurately the smallest period of time detectable at the time. The picosecond is measured by single laser pulses.

- The University of Miami uses radar to pinpoint where lightning strikes occur.

- The *Glomar Challenger* obtains seabed core samples from the deepest parts of the ocean. It uses a sonar beam to remain stationary above the drill site.

- Du Pont Corporation produces a new wallpaper from polythene. While it requires special inks to produce, it is the first truly washable wallpaper.

- Beryllium, a heat-resistant material that is lighter than steel, is used in Lockheed's C5 transport for brake disks and will later be used for heat shields in missiles and satellites.

- The Green Revolution in agriculture promises to feed a rapidly growing population by using new strains of food crops and agricultural techniques, though some of the methods require chemicals later shown to be environmentally harmful.

- Work begins on the Trans-Alaska Pipeline, designed to transport oil found in the North Slope near Prudhoe Bay on the Beaufort Sea to the ice-free port of Valdez. It will not be completed until 1977.

- J. Weber identifies gravitational waves which had been predicted by Einstein. He uses rather simple and relatively inexpensive technology to prove they exist.

16 Aug. At Cape Kennedy, Florida, the *Poseidon 3*, a new missile that can be launched from submarines, is launched for testing.

21 Dec. *Apollo 8* is launched and on 24 December becomes the first manned spacecraft to orbit the moon.

1969

- The scanning electron microscope is introduced.

- Computer bubble memory is developed. This new memory technology stores information even when the power is turned off.

- Fermilab (the National Accelerator Lab), in Batavia, Illinois, will be one of the largest in the world and will give scientists more information about subatomic particles.

- Bell Labs makes holograms (three dimensional laser pictures) practical. Lithium niobate will record holograms, will produce three-dimensional pictures, and can be used to store them. Bell Labs also produces a cable encased in petroleum jelly and plastic.

- John Cocke, Donald Taylor, and Michael Disney find a visible star associated with a (radio) pulsar in the Crab nebula.

9 Jan. A two-year study conducted by the air force reports its conclusions that UFOs are not extraterrestrial spacecraft.

22 Jan.	The Atomic Energy Commission announces the completion of the world's largest superconducting magnet.
20 July	Men land safely on the Moon, walk on its surface, and return safely to Earth four days later. An international audience watches as the Kodak Lunar Surface Camera sends back pictures of Neil Armstrong and Edwin "Buzz" Aldrin walking on the Moon's surface. The dream of the slain President Kennedy is achieved.
31 July	The unmanned craft *Mariner 6* transmits close-up photographs of the surface of Mars.
18 Nov.	Americans land on the Moon for the second time in *Apollo 12*.

OVERVIEW

The Final Frontier. The new frontier of outer space captured the imaginations of scientists and of the public in the 1960s. Astronomers discovered quasi-stellar objects, or quasars, and beamed radio messages to the stars in a search for intelligent life on other worlds. Advances in radio astronomy led to new knowledge about planets within the solar system and the stars beyond.

The Soviet-American Space Race. Perhaps even more dramatic were the advances made in the area of manned space flight as a result of the space race between the United States and the Soviet Union. In the late 1950s the Soviet Union shocked the United States by being the first nation to place a satellite in space. The launch of *Sputnik I* on 4 October 1957 had a chilling effect on most Americans, who realized that the same technology could be employed in atomic warfare. The National Aeronautics and Space Administration (NASA) was formed in 1958 to pool government resources for the formation of an American space program, and the race was on.

A Lofty Goal. In 1960 the Soviets launched two dogs and returned them safely to Earth. NASA, in the initial stages of Project Mercury, launched a chimpanzee named Ham and safely recovered him. Ham's flight was encouraging but not perfect, so NASA project director Wernher Von Braun postponed the first manned space flight from March to May 1961. The timing was unfortunate. On 12 April 1961 the Soviets launched the first man into space. America followed with a manned spaceflight launched on 5 May, and President John F. Kennedy presented Congress with a goal for the United States to reach by the end of the decade: landing a man on the Moon and returning him safely. Striving to achieve that goal, the space program made enormous advances in the 1960s, until an American became the first man to set foot on the Moon on 20 July 1969 as the world watched enthralled.

Destination: Inner Space. Scientists were also discovering a new frontier on their home planet. The mysteries of the oceans were explored in studies of dolphin communication and seafloor spreading, the latter changing the way that the scientific community viewed the Earth's crust and the behavior of continents. Oceanographers tested the viability of underwater environments for people with the Sealab projects, in which teams lived for extended periods in submerged chambers.

Learning More about Earth. The 1960s brought several important advances in the earth sciences. Americans developed means to tap into the Earth's heat to produce less expensive electricity, and climatologists discovered global warming, or the greenhouse effect. Archaeologists learned more about the history of life on Earth, discovering a skull of *Aegyptopithecus,* an early ape ancestor of humans, as well as remains of the oldest known amino acids.

Developments and New Applications. Many important breakthroughs in the science and technology of the 1960s were developed from advances of the previous two decades. A series of projects was designed to find peaceful applications for the atomic bomb. Charles H. Townes's development of the maser in the 1950s provided the basis for the creation of the laser in the 1960s. Building on advances in biology from the 1950s, scientists cracked the genetic code and succeeded in synthesizing active DNA in the laboratory.

The Information Age Begins. The development of the integrated circuit in the 1960s revolutionized electronics and, perhaps more important, the field of computer science. Computers that filled a room were replaced by machines the size of a television. In addition, the development of a new programming language made computers widely accessible, when they had previously been available only to those who could spend several years learning highly complex languages. Developments in computer technology in the 1960s would have a far-reaching impact on the United States and throughout the world in the decades to follow.

TOPICS IN THE NEWS

ARCHAEOLOGY/ANTHROPOLOGY: OBSIDIAN DATING

Stratigraphy and Seriation. Archaeologists and anthropologists have always had difficulty trying to determine how old something is. At first, they used a technique called stratigraphy, based on the assumption that older things tend to be buried under newer things. A technique called seriation is a little more sophisticated. It assumes things get more complex over time. Radiocarbon dating was developed in the 1940s, but its use is limited to material that has been alive at some time.

Thermoluminescence. Two new techniques to date old, nonliving material were developed in 1960: thermoluminescence and obsidian dating. Thermoluminescence can be used accurately to date rocks and pottery as far back as one thousand years. All rocks and pottery contain small amounts of radioactive elements. Over time the radioactive elements decay, giving off electrons in the process. These electrons get trapped within solid material. When a piece of rock or pot is heated to about 350 degrees Celsius, the trapped electrons are freed, and the material gives off a tiny bit of light. By detecting how much light is given off, the age of the material under study can be determined. This technique was developed by George C. Kennedy and Leon Knopoff at the University of California Institute of Geophysics in Los Angeles.

How Obsidian Ages. Obsidian dating was based on work by geologists and archaeologists working with the Smithsonian Institute, including Irving Friedman, Robert L. Smith, Clifford Evans, Betty J. Maggers, and Donovan L. Clark. Obsidian is volcanic glass. It is usually black and is found all over the world. People pick it up and make tools out of it by scraping its surface to form a desired shape. Once this is done, as water gets on the surface, it gradually seeps down through the material. As a result, old obsidian has an outer rind which contains water. The inner parts are dry. The thickness of this rind can be accurately measured under a microscope. The thicker the rind, the longer it has been since a person made the obsidian into a tool.

Weather and the Reliability of Obsidian Dating. Obsidian dating is not foolproof. Weather conditions can affect how quickly water seeps into the obsidian. If one obsidian tool were from the Arctic and another from the tropics, different tables would be used to determine their ages even if their rinds were equally thick. Also, different types of obsidian have different rates at which water diffuses into them. Obsidian dating is inexpensive, quick, and accurate up to about a million years old.

Sources:
"Heating Rocks Gives Age," *Science News Letter,* 77 (16 January 1960): 35;

"Volcanic Glass Moisture Helps Date Old Objects," *Science News Letter,* 77 (12 March 1960): 169.

ARCHAEOLOGY/ANTHROPOLOGY: AEGYPTOPITHECUS

Searching for the Missing Link. In the early 1960s British paleontologist Louis S. B. Leaky was searching in Kenya for the five-million-year-old missing link, an early

Skull of *Aegyptopithecus*

ancestor of man from whom evolved one line of great apes and another line leading to man himself. A much older ancestor was discovered by Dr. Grant E. Meyer and Dr. Elwyn L. Simons of Yale's Peabody Museum.

A Skull Found. The Yale expeditions started in 1961 in the Fayum desert of Egypt, about sixty miles south of Cairo. The area includes ancient lava flows. (There are no active volcanoes there now.) As wind and water eroded the lava, various remains were exposed. In the mid 1960s Meyer spotted a small bone sticking out of the lava about three hundred feet below the uppermost part of the lava flow. He carefully removed it, rock and all, and sent the entire formation back to Yale. There Simons carefully removed the rock and found an almost-intact small skull.

Aegyptopithecus. The skull belonged to an early ape ancestor, named Aegyptopithecus, the largest primate ever found in the Fayum region. *Aegyptopithecus* looked a little like modern lemurs but with different eye sockets. The most dramatic finding was the age of the skull, determined by potassium-argon dating. The skull was found to be between twenty-six and twenty-eight million years old. Aegyptopithecus was the most primitive ape ever discovered.

Sources:

"Ancient Ancestor," *Time*, 90 (24 November 1967): 62;

"Man's Earliest Known Ancestor," *Science News*, 92 (25 November 1967): 514;

Elwyn L. Simons, "The Earliest Apes," *Scientific American*, 217 (December 1967): 28–35.

ARCHAEOLOGY/ANTHROPOLOGY: ANCIENT REMAINS

Fig Tree Chert. The oldest amino acids known to exist were found in 1968 in the Fig Tree Chert, a formation of Precambrian rock located near Barberton, South Africa. The rocks were dated as being 3.1 billion years old. Older rocks containing fossils have been found since then, but this was the oldest known at the time. The rocks, studied by J. William Schopf and Elso S. Barghoorn of Harvard and Keith A. Kvenovolden of the National Aeronautics and Space Administration (NASA), were known to contain what looked like fossils of algae and bacteria, some of the earliest forms of life. Using a process called chromotography to separate chemicals, the scientists found a series of amino acids. The Fig Tree Chert contained two free and seventeen combined amino acids.

The Essential Element of Life. There are about twenty natural amino acids, and they link together to form proteins, the essential element of living organisms. Amino acids can form without any living creature making them, and the idea of spontaneously formed life molecules was a hot research topic in the 1960s. Several labs were showing that conditions on the early earth were just right for forming amino acids. The challenge facing the scientists working on the Fig Tree Chert was to prove the chemicals they found were originally in living organisms.

Proof of Organic Remains. The amino acids they found in the chert are found in life-forms today, and glycine was the most abundant, as expected, because glycine is chemically stable and some other amino acids break down to form glycine over time. To prove the hypothesis that the Fig Tree Chert contained the remains of living organisms, the scientists studied other, younger rock formations whose age was known. They knew how much organic material was present in them. They found a mathematical relationship between the age of rocks and the amount of organic material remaining in them. The mathematical formula suggested how much organic matter would remain after 3.1 billion years, which was precisely how much scientists found in the Fig Tree Chert.

Source:

"Oldest Amino Acids?," *Scientific American*, 218 (May 1968): 50.

ASTRONOMY: RADIO, X-RAY, AND INFRARED

Radio, Infrared, and X-ray Astonomy. Radio astronomers of the 1960s were as interested in sending out radio waves as they were in receiving them. In 1964 the radio dish at Arecibo in Puerto Rico was used this way. It bounced radar off planets in the solar system and detected the returning waves, allowing astronomers to make more-accurate measurements of orbits around the sun, distances from Earth, tilts of the axes of the planets, and speeds of rotation on the axes than had been possible before.

Mapping Venus. Three groups of astronomers used radar during the decade to map Venus, which is covered by clouds, so its surface is not visible to ordinary telescopes. Cornell astronomers used the Arecibo observatory. The Jet Propulsion Laboratory (JPL) in Pasadena, California, and Lincoln Laboratory at the Massachusetts Institute of Technology (MIT) bounced radar off the "veiled planet." The Cornell group found mountains on Venus. Rough spots (such as mountains) scattered the radar more than smooth spots. The MIT group used the scatter technique to look at surface features over smaller areas. The JPL group calculated the rotation of Venus on its axis. It was in the opposite direction from all the other planets.

The Development of VLBI Technology. Perhaps the most important development of the decade in radio astronomy was the development of "very long baseline interferometry," or VLBI, a technique developed in Australia that came to be used by astronomers around the world. Simply put, the limiting part of radio astronomy is the size of the antenna. The bigger the antenna, the more information obtained from it. The Australians worked on a mathematical principle to develop a new "giant" receiver. The trick was to link electronically two or more

An abandoned radio telescope site at Sugar Grove, West Virginia

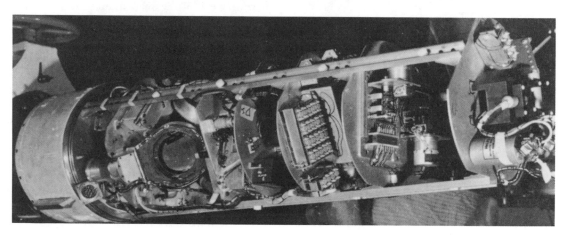

The first X-ray detector used in astronomy

radio antennas at different places. The reception was the same as it would have been for one large dish as big as the distance between the connected smaller dish antennas. The development of VLBI eventually allowed scientists to hear deep into space. The first practical VLBI system was used at Cambridge University in 1960. Linking antennas more than ten kilometers apart by cable was not practical because of the distortion in the connecting cable. American and British astronomers used microwave signals sent to a separate base station from different antennae. The Owens Valley system in the United States connected distant dishes this way in 1960. The first modern VLBI was the U.S. National Radio Astronomy Observatory, which used computers to record and transmit the data from each of the antennae, employing synchronized time at each antenna by using atomic clocks. Now the signals from each dish could be compared exactly at the base station.

The Aerobee Rocket. The first X-ray detector used in astronomy was launched on an air force Aerobee rocket in 1962. The detector was a highly sensitive X-ray telescope designed by American physicists and astronomers, including Riccardo Giacconi. The Aerobee rocket flew 150 miles up for six minutes after takeoff from New Mexico on 18–19 June. It detected a strong X-ray source in Scorpius. The X-ray source in Scorpius had no visible light source to correspond to it, suggesting that it was a neutron star, resulting from a large, dense star that had exploded. Such explosions cause massive changes in the atoms of the star: protons are crushed into electrons, destroying the atoms, and only the neutrons remain. The

Scorpius star was found to be ten miles in diameter by a Naval Research Lab rocket with an X-ray detector. Its mass was found to be one billion tons per cubic inch. The explosion left the star burning so hot it gave off X-rays but no light. Another source was later found in the Crab nebula. Still other X-ray detectors were launched in the 1960s. The Orbital Solar Observatories pointed X-ray detectors toward the Sun, which, while not a strong X-ray source, does emit some X-rays.

The Development of Infrared Astronomy. Infrared astronomy was developed in the 1960s. Infrared detectors require long periods of time without motion to be useful. Water vapor in the atmosphere is the main interfering substance, so infrared astronomy is best done using high altitude balloons rather than rockets. The first major infrared astronomical expedition was a manned mission launched by the navy in November 1959. The balloon rose to eighty thousand feet. The infrared telescope was pointed at Venus, but the motion of the balloon caused by the men and the design made the results unreliable. In 1961 the air force took over the infrared experiments and switched to unmanned balloons. In 1963 Martin Schwarzschild of Princeton launched an unmanned balloon that looked at the atmosphere of Mars. He detected water vapor around the red planet. In 1964 the air force group launched a balloon from Holloman Air Force Base in New Mexico that looked at Venus again. It did not go where it was expected to, and one of its detectors worked backward. Even so, it located Venus after nine minutes of trying. The observation lasted over two hours. Water vapor was found around Venus also. As the decade continued, the air force, Princeton, and others continued infrared astronomy. The technology of the infrared telescopes and the balloons improved. While infrared astronomy was used in learning about distant stars, it was mainly a tool for studying the solar system.

Sources:

"Ultraviolet 'Stars' Found," *Science News Letter,* 77 (6 February 1960): 85;

"Venus Observed," *Science News,* 93 (24 February 1968): 183.

ASTRONOMY: PULSARS, QUASARS, COSMIC MASERS

Quasars Discovered. One of the major discoveries of the 1960s was the quasar, short for quasi-stellar object. The first identified quasar was 3C-48. The "3C" stands for Third Cambridge Catalog of Radio Sources, a catalogue used by radio astronomers. Allan R. Sandage of Mount Wilson and Mount Palomar Observatories in California reported it at the 107th meeting of the American Astronomical Society in New York in 1960. Employing two mobile ninety-foot parabolic radio antennae, Sandage used a technique called triangulation to locate the object. Thomas A. Matthaus had noted variable radio emissions from a small area and predicted a visible star there. Sandage found the object in the predicted location. But 3C-48 did not act much like a star. It was extremely

The Crab nebula, the location of the first pulsar to be detected by astronomers

hot (over one hundred thousand degrees Celsius). Sandage looked at the spectrum of the area (spectral lines tell astronomers what elements are present in and around a star). He found no hydrogen, which is present in essentially all stars. Instead of hydrogen, Sandage found 3C-48 contained calcium ions (charged calcium), helium, helium ions, and strange ions of oxygen. He suspected it could be a star surrounded by high-energy electrons in a magnetic field moving at the speed of light. This might explain how it gave off radio and light waves. Another possibility was that it was the remnant of a supernova.

What Are They? It took some time to find that none of this was true and that 3C-48 was really a quasar. The Harvard Observatory had a collection of pictures of the region over many years. Harlan J. Smith and Dorrit Hoffleit of the Yale Observatory looked over twenty-five hundred plates in the Harvard collection taken from 1895 to 1952. In 1961 they reported they found no supernova detected by light astronomy in the region. They thought 3C-48 looked like some exploded object, though — maybe a much earlier supernova. In 1962 British astronomer Cyril Hazard located another "star" like 3C-48, named 3C-273. American Maarten Schmidt at Mount Palomar, who took photos and spectra of 3C-273, found that the normal spectrum lines were red-shifted, a condition caused by objects moving away from the observer at a high speed. Schmidt calculated 3C-273 was two billion light years away.

Quasars as Old as the Universe. Margaret Burbridge of the University of California, San Diego, studied these objects extensively. She concluded they were neither stellar objects nor galaxies, though they had some properties similar to those of stars. Thus they were quasi-stellar objects. Burbridge posited that quasars are galaxies passed through each other. Material falls to the center of a quasar where a black hole, a massive star that has collapsed on itself, is located. The black hole sucks everything around it into itself, even light. The galaxies passed through each other when the universe was young. Now the black holes are surrounded by light, and hydrogen is being sucked into them. The light can be seen by telescope, and the radio signals are energy from hydrogen racing at high speeds to the black hole, heating enough in the process to give off radio waves. Quasars, among the most distant objects visible from earth, have the energy level of one hundred or more large galaxies, resulting from gravitational collapse. They move very quickly away from earth, so the light we see today from quasars was created when the universe was young.

Masers Discovered. There was quite a bit of excitement when a maser (microwave amplification by stimulated emission of radiation) was found in outer space. Some thought it was aliens, but it was just a cosmic event. Masers explained a substance in space called mysterium. There is a region around stars where the heat causes hydrogen to ionize. Astronomers at MIT's Lincoln Laboratory figured out what caused the maser signal in one such area, the W3 area of the cosmos. In 1965 various astronomers at the University of California, Berkeley, found that W3 contained the usual elements plus a previously undetected radio-wave pattern they called mysterium. In 1966 the group from Lincoln Lab determined mysterium was an unusual form of hydroxyl ion (OH^-).

Identifying Mysterium. The chemical formula for water is H_2O. Putting a strong electrical current in water can cause it to separate. It could form hydrogen ions and hydroxyl ions: $H_2O + high\ energy = H^+ + OH^-$. The physicists and astronomers from MIT and Lincoln found mysterium was really a form of OH^- in an unusually excited state, emitting polarized radiation in a narrow band.

Solving a Mystery. The question was, How did the hydroxyl ions produce such a pattern? They could only be that narrow and polarized because they acted as a maser. But then what stimulated the hydroxyl ions to act as a maser? The Lincoln Lab group showed that the hydroxyl ions could be stimulated in this way by being close to a hot star. The heat would produce enough energy to give the hydroxyl ions maser activity.

Pulsars Discovered. Pulsars were first discovered in Britain in 1968. They were radio wave sources that had characteristic on-off cycles thought to be from neutron stars. Neutron stars rotate, and the "pulses" of the pulsar correspond to the rotation of the neutron star. The cycles resembled the pulse from the heart, so the name given them was pulsar.

American Astronomers See a Pulsar. American astronomers made a major contribution to pulsar study. Pulsars were heard but never seen until some University of Arizona astronomers, John Cocke, Michael Disney, and Donald Taylor, pointed a little thirty-six-inch Steward Observatory telescope at the Crab nebula, a supernova. The pulsar in the Crab nebula heard by radio astronomers had the fastest pulse frequency known. The

star explosion that created the Crab nebula was witnessed on Earth in A.D. 1054. Records from all over Earth indicate the explosion caused a bright spot seen for six months, even during the day, though the Crab nebula is five thousand light-years from earth. When the University of Arizona astronomers pointed their light telescope at the Crab nebula, it showed a constant light. Using computer equipment, they checked the light intensity twelve thousand times a second. They found that the light peaked thirty times a second, too fast for human eyes to see, and they also found the exact frequency of the radio pulses from the same spot. Before long, two other American observatories confirmed these findings.

Sources:

"Celestial Maser?," *Scientific American,* 214 (January 1966): 48–49;

"First Look at a Pulsar," *Time,* 93 (7 February 1969): 57–58;

"First True Radio Star?," *Sky and Telescope,* 21 (March 1961): 148;

"Quasars Are 'Crazy,'" *Science News Letter,* 86 (15 August 1964): 106;

"Radio Source 3C–48," *Sky & Telescope,* 22 (September 1961): 131.

ASTRONOMY: PROJECT OZMA — WILL THEY HEAR US?

Search for Life on Other Worlds. In the early 1960s changes in astronomy brought about Project Ozma — a search for other worlds with intelligent life — named after the princess of L. Frank Baum's Land of Oz. Dr. Frank Drake was the chief astronomer involved. The government sponsored Drake in Project Ozma, through the National Science Foundation (which owned the observatory), to make an initial search for life on other worlds. He worked at the National Radio Astronomy Observatory at Deer Creek Valley in West Virginia, where the local population referred to Drake's research as "Project Little Green Men." Drake sent and listened for radio-wave messages, hoping to make contact with extraterrestials. He was limited by the range of the radio telescope. Though he could listen to close stars, it was impossible to search the whole universe.

Narrowing the Search. Dr. Otto Struve, Russian-born director of the observatory, pointed out some ways to narrow the search. Double and triple stars could be eliminated. Planets going around such multiple-star systems would be subjected to extremes of hot and cold that would not support life. Dr. Guiseppe Cocconi and Dr. Philip Morrison of Cornell suggested that the wavelength to listen to would be twenty-one centimeters long, the wavelength of hydrogen in interstellar space. It is easy to receive this wavelength, and it also has minimal interference from Earth's atmosphere or general space noise.

Listening to the Stars. Drake's eighty-five-foot radio dish was one of the largest at the time. It was directed to outer space six hours a day, seven days a week. The radio antennae were designed to pick up two signals: one antenna was directed at the star being monitored, and the other slightly to the side. Anything picked up by both was filtered out as static from Earth, the star itself, or outer space. The difference between the two antennae was amplified using a special maser that made the signal recognizable.

No Success — So Far. The first stars to be tested were Tau Ceti and Epsilon Eridani, both only about eleven light-years away. No life from other worlds was found in Project Ozma.

Sources:
Gloria Ball, "Listen In on Other Suns," *Science News Letter,* 77 (30 April 1960): 282–283;

G. R. Price, "US Begins Search for Beings in Other Worlds," *Popular Science,* 176 (April 1960): 66–69, 209.

ASTRONOMY: THE SOUND OF THE BIG BANG

Measuring Radio Signals from Hydrogen. In 1961 German-American physicist Arno A. Penzias completed work on his Ph.D., studying the use of masers to amplify radio signals, and began work at Bell Laboratories with Robert W. Wilson measuring radio signals from hydrogen in space. They had access there to the world's most sensitive radio telescope, a six-meter horn antenna used to send and receive signals from the passive *Echo* satellite.

A Constant Noise. In 1961 the *Echo* chief engineer E. A. Ohm noted electronic noise in this antenna carefully measured at three kelvins. Penzias and Wilson tried to eliminate the noise without success. They cleaned a family of birds out of the horn and eliminated mechanical vibrations, but a constant three kelvins of noise was always there.

The Big Bang. Finally, they concluded that the noise came from space itself, from all directions in the microwave region. They were drawn to the work of P. J. Peebles and Robert H. Dicke of Princeton University, who suggested that all the elements in the universe formed in a giant explosion they called the big bang. After the big bang leftover energy was still present. Peebles said this should be detected as "background radiation" of less than ten kelvins. Peebles had suggested an oscillating universe. Penzias and Wilson found a static universe: the background radiation never varied. Penzias and Wilson's work was soon repeated by other scientists in different ways. All of them arrived at the same conclusion as the Bell Laboratories scientists. This discovery was the first solid evidence that supported the big bang theory.

BIOLOGY: MOLECULAR REVOLUTION

Cracking the Code for RNA. Marshall W. Nirenberg, working at the National Institutes of Health in Bethesda, Maryland, in 1961, performed brilliant experiments in biochemistry. These led to the molecular revolution that has continued since his work, done with his German postgraduate fellow J. H. Matthaei, was reported at the Fifth International Congress of Biochemistry in Moscow. In 1953 the physicist George Gamow worked out

Marshall W. Nirenberg

some basics of the code. A single ribonucleic acid (RNA) could only code for four possible amino acids. Pairs of nucleic acids could code for sixteen possibilities. Since there are about twenty amino acids, at least three nucleic acids in RNA must code for each amino acid in proteins. But Gamow made a mistake when he suggested that overlapping sequences of RNA provided the code for different amino acids. Nirenberg and Matthaei corrected him and broke the RNA code.

Creating Artificial Protein. They removed various chemicals required by cells to make proteins from a sample of *Escherichia coli* (*E. coli*) bacteria and put the chemicals in a test tube with no live cells left. Then the scientists added amino acids made with radioactive carbon atoms so they could measure small amounts of protein produced if they came up with the right combination of amino acids. Nirenberg made artificial RNA and successfully produced an artificial protein. By controlling the chemicals he introduced into the test tube and noting the proteins produced, he discovered the genetic code. By 1966 all sixty-four possible triplets of RNA were translated into amino acids of proteins. Some amino acids had more than one triplet code of RNA. One triplet was found to be special: it did not code for any amino acid. It told the cell (or chemicals in a cell-free system) that the code for a particular protein was ended.

Source:
"The Genetic Code," *Scientific American,* 218 (April 1968): 44.

BIOLOGY: THE FIRST GENE

Isolating Genes. In 1969 the first gene was isolated. Genes are the basis of heredity, carried by DNA. The genetic code had been broken, so science knew how DNA worked. But the process for isolating genes was

Facility used to study the behavior and communication of dolphins

elusive. Dr. Jonathan Beckwith of Harvard solved the problem using simple viruses that infected the intestinal bacterium *E. coli.* Two viruses were used, both of which tended to incorporate one of the host's genes after infecting it. Each virus could incorporate different host genes, but both these viruses took the "lac" gene, which lets the bacterium eat lactose, a milk sugar.

DNA Strands Separated, Rejoined. Beckwith removed the protein shell from both viruses, and heated their DNA separately, causing its two strands to separate. He then mixed the two types of DNA and slowly cooled them. Usually, DNA being cooled this way will seek its complementary strand to rejoin. In Beckwith's experiment DNA from the one virus attached to the complimentary DNA from the other in the only place they fit — the lac gene. Beckwith chemically removed the excess, leaving copies of the complete lac gene intact.

Source:
"An Elegant Triumph," *Time,* 94 (5 December 1969): 80.

BIOLOGY: DOLPHIN COMMUNICATION

The Complex Brain of the Dolphin. During the 1960s scientists began studying how the remarkable dolphin communicates. The dolphin is a mammal, not a fish, in the order Cetacea, which also includes whales. These mammals breathe with lungs, nurse their young, have extremely complex brains, and are otherwise similar to land mammals. In 1960 the neurophysiologist Dr. John C. Lilly reported on his four years of talking to bottle-nosed dolphins (*Tursiops truncatas*) at a U.S. Navy facility near Charlotte Amalie in the Virgin Islands. He implanted electrodes in the brains of thirty dolphins and found a "pleasure center": stimulating the electrode implanted there caused the dolphins to have wide eyes and look like they were smiling. They would also change their behavior to make Lilly stimulate the electrodes more often. Similar experiments had been performed on chimpanzees, and the dolphins learned much more quickly.

Sending a Distress Signal. Lilly also put a partly paralyzed dolphin in a pool with other dolphins. The paralyzed dolphin could not reach the surface to breathe, and so it would die without help. Other dolphins learned of their new neighbor's distress and helped him reach the surface and stay there, talking to each other in frequencies above the range of human hearing. When Lilly played back the tape of their talking, at one-quarter speed, he could hear the "mayday" call given by the paralyzed dolphin. When Lilly played the tape back to other dolphins, they reacted to the call.

A Language of Their Own. Other experiments involved Lilly's talking to the mammals. They seemed to repeat his words in high, squeaky voices. Dr. Sidney Galler, director of the Naval Researches Biological Branch, has claimed that dolphins communicate with each other in a language of their own, using sonar and special chemical-sensing organs.

Sources:
Daniel Cohen, "Dolphin: Smarty of the Sea," *Science Digest,* 48 (December 1960): 43–47;

"Dolphin Talk," *Time*, 75 (4 January 1960): 53–54;

W. S. Griswold, "The Case of the Blindfolded Dolphin," *Popular Science*, 177 (August 1960): 70–73, 184.

BIOLOGY: PRIMORDIAL SOUP

The Soup of Life. Primordial soup was the chemical mixture thought to represent the atmosphere of the early Earth, composed of ammonia, hydrogen, methane gas, and water vapor. It is a chemically rich mixture but not apparently conducive to living things. Even before 1960 scientists began to show that primordial soup could produce the types of chemicals of which life is made, but a 1960 report by Juan Oro in *Biochemical and Biophysical Research Communications* made an important advance in the subject.

Cooking the Soup. It had already been found that amino acids formed in primordial soup by performing experiments using electric sparks as simulated lightning. Stanley Miller had shown that hydrogen cyanide (HCN) was an important intermediate chemical in forming amino acids, which make up proteins. The question was, How did the all-important DNA or RNA required for life form? Oro took HCN gas and bubbled it into ammonia to form ammonium cyanide, which then reacted with itself. Oro reasoned that the atmosphere of the early Earth was much hotter than it is now, so he heated the chemical mess overnight and separated the resulting compounds using a process called paper chromatography. One product was adenine, required for DNA and RNA.

Creating a Dimer. As Oro continued his work, other scientists began similar research. Dr. Cyril Ponriamperuma, the chief of the Chemical Evolution Branch of the NASA Ames Research Center in California, took one of the bases of RNA, uridine, and formed a dimer (a combination of two similar chemicals) under primitive Earth conditions. This experiment was important, because RNA is a polymer, or a long chain of similar chemicals. Showing that a dimer forms in the test tube is a critical step in showing RNA can form without cells.

Diuridylic Acid. Ponriamperuma heated uridine and phosphate salts to 160 degrees Celsius with methane, ammonia, and a radiation source (for energy) under ultraviolet light to mimic earth conditions. The radiation acted like lightning, and he discovered that diuridylic acid would form at 50 degrees Celsius.

RNA Experiments. Dr. Sol Spiegelman of the University of Illinois was able to take RNA from a virus gene and have it reproduce itself in a test tube. There were no living cells in his system. The RNA gene was active, though, after it formed. Gary Steinman and Melvin Calvin worked on life systems at the Lawrence Radiation Laboratory in Berkeley, California. They put dicyandiamide into primitive Earth conditions in the lab. Others had shown this cyanide derivative formed in primitive-soup laboratory conditions. They found that at room temperature, with water added, peptide bonds, the unique chemical bonds between amino acids in proteins, formed. They also formed lipids (complex fats) from fatty acids and glycerol in their system. They went on to form sugar phosphates, part of the backbone of RNA and DNA.

Biological Catalysts. Sidney Fox of the University of Miami showed similar results. He formed amino acids and nucleotides (such as uridylic acid) in primordial soup. He suggested catalysts were required for complex chemicals to form. Biological catalysts are the proteins known as enzymes that speed chemical reactions. Fox concluded that there had to be enzymes before there was life in the form of cells because they would be required to allow other complex chemicals to form at a rate quick enough to form the first cell.

Sources:

"Life from Chemicals," *Science Digest*, 58 (December 1965): 40–41;

"Life May Have Begun without Preexisting Life," *Science News Letter*, 89 (8 January 1966): 25;

"New Evidence Reported on Origin of Life," *Science News Letter*, 87 (13 March 1965): 168.

CHEMISTRY: NOT SO NOBLE ANYMORE

Noble Gases. The noble gases, including helium, neon, and xenon, do not normally form compounds with other chemicals. Their atoms have enough electrons not to require sharing with or borrowing from other atoms.

Making Compounds from Noble Gases. In 1962 the American chemist Neil Bartlett was working in Canada when the idea struck him that it was possible to make compounds from noble gases. He knew that, in the complex chemical oxygen-platinum-hexaflouride, oxygen acts as if it has a positive charge (O_2^+) and the platinum and fluoride combine and act negatively charged (PtF_6^-). Bartlett knew it took a lot of energy to remove an (negatively charged) electron from oxygen and make it act positively charged, about the same amount of energy required to remove an electron from xenon. But PtF_6^- was the best oxidizer (electron remover) known.

Xenon-platinum-hexaflouride. Bartlett used the PtF_6^- with xenon and formed a new compound. Xenon-platinum-hexaflouride ($XePtF_6$) is a yellow-orange powder so stable it does not decompose at room temperature in regular room air.

CHEMISTRY: LAWRENCIUM

Plutonium. The study of man-made elements was critical in World War II. There was a need for a radioactive material to use in an atomic weapon, but not for material so radioactive it would disintegrate before the bomb could be made and dropped. The Radiation Laboratory (later the Lawrence Berkeley Lab) at the University of California, Berkeley, succeeded by producing plutonium. With a half-life (the time it takes for half of it to undergo radioactive decay) of twenty-four thousand years it allowed plenty of time to make a bomb. Plutonium, element 94 on the periodic table of the elements, was one of ten man-made elements produced by the Radiation Laboratory. The Berkeley based scientists produced all but one of the man-made elements (from 93 to 103). Swedish scientists made element 102, nobelium.

A New Element. Element 103, lawrencium, was formed in 1961. The Berkeley group took some nickel foil, coated it with a thin layer of californium (another man-made element, number 98), placed it in a helium chamber, then, with a heavy-ion linear accelerator, threw nuclei of boron 10 and boron 11 at the foil at great speeds. When the boron nuclei hit the californium, neutrons were lost, and lawrencium was formed.

A Short Life. Its chemical properties were difficult to determine, though, because it has a half-life of only eight seconds. It was produced in minute quantities and gone before it could be found. The scientists knew, though, how it would decay radioactively, so they knew what decay products to look for and thus were able to verify its brief existence. Lawrencium was named for Ernest Lawrence, founder of the laboratory.

Sources:
"Element 103 Synthesized," *Science News Letter*, 79 (29 April 1961): 259;

"Flouride Compounds of Xenon and Radon," *Science*, 138 (12 October 1962): 136–138;

"Frail Lawrencium," *Time*, 77 (28 April 1961): 46.

COMPUTER SCIENCE: BASIC KNOWLEDGE

An Awkward System. At the beginning of the 1960s, computers were expensive and difficult to operate. Because of the expense, most computers served up information to multiple clients or users from a central location. Information was input on machines capable only of punching holes in cards. The computer processed the information recorded on the cards and ran programs written by highly trained programmers. Reports were generated and returned in the form of hard copy to whomever requested them. It was an awkward system.

Making Computers Practical. In the early 1960s John Kemeny, chairman of mathematics at Dartmouth University, started working with Thomas Kurtz, director of Dartmouth's Kiewit Computer Center, on ways to make computer use practical for most of their general college students, not just the engineering, math, and physics graduate students. They got a grant from the National Science Foundation to buy equipment, and in 1964 General Electric sent them two new computers, as well as all the paraphernalia required to make them work. But without the instructions on how to hook them up Kemeny, Kurtz, and their students figured out a hookup scheme on their own. They developed a new concept of "master" and "slave" computers. The various teletype terminals fed into the master, which directed the slave to make the neces-

BUBBLE MEMORY

There was one major problem with computers. All the memory was lost when the power was turned off. But huge magnetic tapes can store vast amounts of data and do not rely on electricity to maintain them. So an electronic equivalent of magnetic tape memory had to be possible.

The breakthrough came from Bell Labs in 1969. Andrew H. Bobeck developed bubble memory. The bubble memory is based on certain iron compounds mixed with the element yttrium and a rare-earth metal. Within this structure, memory is stored in lines or stripes. If a weak magnet is placed around the material, the lines shrivel into bubbles. Moving the bubbles around in the substrate gives the controlled memory required for a computer system. As long as the magnet around the bubbles is never removed, the memory storage is permanent.

This created a major stir in the business world when it was announced. The bubble memory would revolutionize the computer industry. Computers without batteries or electricity would be the wave of the future. Bubble memory works. The problem, however, lies in mass-producing the recording material as well as in the expense of the material itself.

sary calculations. The slave fed back to the master which fed back to the teletype to print the results. This was the Dartmouth Time-Sharing System (DTSS), which solved many of the problems of time-sharing.

A Simpler Computer Language. Still, the computers accepted instructions only in highly complex languages that took programmers years to learn. So Kemeny and Kurtz developed a new language for beginners, the Beginner's All-purpose Symbolic Instruction Code, or BASIC, which had only fourteen command structures to learn and used numbered lines for individual instructions. Errors could be corrected by fixing just the particular line involved. On 1 May 1964 Kemeny and Kurtz successfully demonstrated DTSS and BASIC. Students taking the beginner's computer course learned BASIC first, and within two hours they were programming a computer. By 1968, 80 percent of Dartmouth students, most of whom were not science or math majors, were programming the computer. Then General Electric started using BASIC and DTSS. As time went on, Kemeny and Kurtz continued to improve BASIC, always keeping it simple enough for the average person to use.

One of the new generation of smaller, more powerful computers

COMPUTER SCIENCE: WHEN THE CHIPS ARE DOWN

An Electronics Revolution. During the 1960s the integrated circuit (IC) created a revolution in electronics. Previously circuit boards that ran electronic devices had to be big enough to hold components such as vacuum tubes, capacitors, and resistors. Then vacuum tubes were replaced by transistors, resulting in saving some space. But once wonder materials called semiconductors could be fabricated successfully, hundreds or thousands of complete individual components could be incorporated on a single one-inch-square silicon wafer. Computers the size of a room could now be emulated by machines the size of a television, and radios the size of a loaf of bread could be reduced to the size of a candy bar.

Mass-market ICs. The first user of these chemically etched integrated circuits was the military. It did not take long to figure out that ICs could be used in consumer products as well. Television sets still had vacuum tubes in 1960, but most black-and-white sets were transistorized by the mid 1960s. Then there was a television revolution. In the mid 1960s Congress passed a law saying all TVs had to include UHF (ultrahigh frequency) tuners in addition to the standard thirteen channels. Manufacturers turned to ICs. ICs had to be custom-made for each application. The cost of one was enormous, but a truckload did not cost much more, and so for mass-produced consumer items, such as radios and televisions, ICs were very cost-effective.

Sources:
Electronic World (November 62): 31;

Philip J. Klass, "Electron Beam Technique Makes, Inspects Semicon-
ductor Microcircuits," *Aviation Week & Space Technology*, 79 (23 September 1963): 80–93;

Barry Miller, "Integrated Circuits Cut Computer Cost," *Aviation Week*, 76 (21 May 1962): 83–84;

"Not Yet Solid in the Solid State," *Business Week* (16 May 1964): 26–27.

EARTH SCIENCES: GEOTHERMAL POWER

The Earth's Heat. Inside of the Earth is a giant source of heat called geothermal power that can be used to run electrical generators. One of the first geothermal power units was built in Larderello, Italy, in the early 1900s. Until 1960 there were not any in the United States because it cost too much to get to the heat source and carry the heat to the surface in usable form.

Superheated Steam. The Earth's crust is about twenty miles thick, but it is not the same thickness everywhere. Under the crust is magma, and cracks in the crust allow magma to come close to the surface in some places. Magma is about 10 percent water, which works its way down from the surface. When the water works its way back through cracks in the crust, it forms fumaroles — geysers with superheated steam. Normally water only reaches the temperature of its boiling point. Once it turns to steam, its temperature does not change even if heated more. But high pressure causes the steam to superheat to a temperature higher than the boiling point. This superheated steam can be used as a steady source of power to turn a generator.

Electricity from Geysers. In the valley of Big Sulphur Creek, seventy miles north of San Francisco, there are geysers. The magma reaches to about three hundred to four hundred feet below the surface. Thermal Power and Magma Power owned a lease on thirty-two hundred acres in this area, and in 1960 they used a pipeline system to ship 265,000 pounds of steam per hour to a generator built by Pacific Gas and Electric to produce electricity.

Eleven Thousand Years of Less Expensive Power. Steam pipelines had to be specially designed. They carried steam at pressures of one hundred pounds per square inch and temperatures of 348 degrees Fahrenheit. By tapping only four acres, they were able to produce forty thousand to fifty thousand kilowatts of power. It was estimated that the area could continue to supply power at this rate for eleven thousand years. Many power-generating stations boil water to make steam to produce power. Because this site did not boil the water used (it was already steam), production of electricity there was about 30 percent more economical.

Source:
Paul Corey, "Drawing Power from Nature's Steam Boiler," *Popular Science,* 176 (April 1960): 114–116.

EARTH SCIENCE: PLOWSHARES, OR GETTING THE GAS OUT

A-Bombs for Peace. Throughout the 1960s, the Atomic Energy Commission (AEC) pursued a series of projects called the Plowshares Program, an attempt to find peaceful uses for atomic bombs. In 1961 the first peaceful nuclear blast occurred. It was detonated underground twenty-five miles from New Mexico's Carlsbad caverns. The purpose of Project Gnome was to conduct various scientific experiments; the explosion was expected to supply a vast underground salt cavern and to produce steam for generating electricity. The blast occurred prematurely, and the explosion knocked the top off the underground chamber, ruining the steam "teakettle" and letting clouds of radioactive waste into the atmosphere. Gophers chewed through cables connecting some of the scientific instruments. Nonetheless, the scientists present declared Project Gnome a great success.

Project Sloop. Project Sloop, a government and industry partnership, took place near Safford, Arizona, where two billion tons of rock containing .4 percent copper lay under five hundred feet of volcanic rock. Project Sloop, designed to get the copper out, cost $13 million over thirty months. Sloop required drilling a twenty-inch shaft twelve hundred feet straight down. Then a twenty-kiloton nuclear device was exploded, leaving a two-hundred-foot-diameter cavity at the bottom. The rock inside melted with the blast and resolidified, taking 90 percent of the radioactivity from the bomb with it in a solid form. The fragmented wall of the crater below contained the copper ore. It took eight months or more for the radioactivity to cool off a bit, after which sulfuric acid (H_2SO_4) was pumped into the crater. The copper dissolved in the acid, which was pumped back out. The H_2SO_4 could be recycled as the copper was extracted.

Project Gassbuggy. Project Gassbuggy in New Mexico, a collaboration between the AEC and the El Paso Natural Gas Company, involved a twenty-six-kiloton blast 4,200 feet below the surface. Natural gas was trapped in 285 feet of sandstone unsuitable for the usual recovery methods. The nuclear device shattered the rock to let the gas escape so it could be drilled out later. Gassbuggy produced 214 million cubic feet of gas in 15 months; during the same period a conventional well would be expected to provide perhaps 80 million tons, but the Gassbuggy gas contained radioactive krypton and tritium, which was pumped into the homes of unsuspecting gas company customers.

Sources:

"A-Bomb in the Gas Field," *Science News*, 92 (23 December 1967): 610;

"Going Deep for Gas," *Science News*, 96 (20 September 1969): 236;

"Once More for the Money," *Science News*, 95 (19 April 1969): 376;

"Swords Into Plowshares," *Time*, 78 (22 December 1961): 29.

EARTH SCIENCES: THE GREENHOUSE EFFECT

The Theory of Arrhenius. The first suggestion that burning fossil fuels could warm the Earth's atmosphere was in 1896 by Svante Arrhenius, the famous chemist. Few people believed him. The atmosphere was thought to be so big and so stable that it could not possibly be affected by small fires.

Global-Warming Effect. In 1964 Syukuro Manabe and Richard Wetherald, two American climatologists, developed a computer model of the atmosphere to predict how water vapor and carbon dioxide (CO_2, which is produced by burning carbon fuel) would affect the climate. The effect they found was global warming, popularly known as the greenhouse effect.

Carbon Dioxide and Infrared Radiation. The normal carbon dioxide in the atmosphere has several specific effects, one of which is to hold the heat from the sun. Water vapor in the atmosphere blocks most infrared radiation from reaching the surface of the Earth. When visible sunlight reaches the surface, the Earth absorbs it. Part of the energy absorbed is released by the ground as infrared radiation, which is not seen, but felt as heat. The carbon dioxide in the atmosphere prevents this infrared radiation from escaping. The result is heating of the atmosphere.

The Fossil Fuel–CO_2 Connection. Manabe and Wetherald described the atmosphere as complex mathematical formulas. Using a computer to do the massive calculations, they added CO_2 to see the effects. They showed that a doubling of CO_2 would warm the atmosphere 2.3 degrees Centigrade and that the poles would warm more than the equator. The original models have been modified since they were first developed. One group pointed out that atmospheric CO_2 increased over the most recent one hundred years from burning fossil fuel but that air temperatures cooled slightly from 1940 to 1950, a phenomenon explained by aerosol particles in the air. These tiny particles come from volcanoes and from burning fossil fuel or other man-made processes. The aerosols are sometimes too small to see, but they keep sunlight from reaching Earth. So burning fossil fuels can increase CO_2 but decrease atmospheric temperature. Others pointed out that air temperature, ground temperature, and overall atmospheric temperatures are affected by various conditions, of which CO_2 accumulation is only one.

Source:

Robert A. McCormick and John H. Ludwig, "Climate Modification by Atmospheric Aerosols," *Science*, 156 (9 June 1967): 1358–1359.

OCEANOGRAPHY: SEAFLOOR SPREADING

Liquid Layer. In 1960 the theory of plate tectonics was given a huge boost by the oceanographer Harry H. Hess, who demonstrated his theory that the seafloor was

The *Glomar Challenger*

spreading. The Earth is composed of layers — the outer crust, beneath that the mantle, and below that the core. Hess suggested that the mantle, which is eighteen hundred miles thick, has two layers. The deeper layer is solid, he said, which accorded with generally accepted theories about the mantle. But the upper mantle was more like a hot liquid, according to Hess. It pushed up from below. In the deep seafloor rifts, the mantle is close to the surface. It therefore actually comes to the surface (the seabed) and pushes the Earth's crust aside on either end of the rift.

Mohorovicic Discontinuity. The easiest way to prove Hess's theory was to drill a hole in the seafloor to pierce the interface of the crust and mantle, called the Mohorovicic Discontinuity, after the Yugoslavian seismologist who discovered it. Mohorovicic was shortened by scientists to Moho; thus the idea was to drill a hole in the crust of the ocean floor until the mantle was reached — a "mohole." Moholes would have to be twenty-five to forty-five miles deep on land but are under three miles deep in some ocean regions.

Cuss I. The ocean rifts were known to contain mantle under only a few miles of crust. Thus came the *Cuss I,* a converted drilling barge named for the oil companies Continental, Union, Shell, and Superior that paid to have the former navy barge converted for Project Mohole, sponsored by the National Academy of Sciences under the direction of Dr. Gordon Lill. The vessel was 260 feet long with a 98-foot derrick. *Cuss I* would drill six miles into the ocean floor to reach the mantle, taking samples

that provided both scientific information and evidence of locations for oil beneath the sea.

Samples of Layers. The ocean floor starts with about five hundred feet of clay and soft sediment that drops from above. Then comes up to two miles of rocks and lava, then a relatively thin four miles of oceanic crust, mostly basalt rock. Finally there is the high-pressure mantle. The core samples from *Cuss I* gave indirect proof of seafloor spreading by the mantle pushing up in the ocean rifts. The closer to a rift the sample was, the younger the crust rock was found to be.

Glomar Challenger. This work continued through the decade and was facilitated by the introduction of the "floating doughnut," the $12.6 million *Glomar Challenger.* This ship could drill in water 20,000 feet deep. It had a doughnut shape, with a drill in the middle that had a 142-foot tower. It could drill up to 2,500 feet beneath the ocean floor. The problem with deep-sea drilling is keeping the ship steady on the surface while drilling miles down below. Too much ship movement can snap the drill. The *Glomar Challenger* was a technological wonder that had sonar on either side of the drill, feeding information to a computer that controlled the roll of the ship on the surface. The ship was capable of staying within 3 percent of its specified drilling depth. The drill string was made of 38,000 feet of five-inch pipe in 30-foot sections. This made it strong but flexible.

Dating Rock Samples. Rock samples from the ocean floor were dated by a radioactive-decay process. The small amount of uranium in seawater attaches to sedi-

The *Trieste*

ments, and its breakdown products, protoactinium 231 and thorium 230, also attach to sediments and sink over time. The protoactinium decays much faster than the thorium. Measuring the ratio of the two in a sample can determine the age of the sample accurately.

Proof of Spreading. The *Glomar Challenger* data showed that the seafloor was spreading evenly and gave further proof that the continents drift on a viscous layer of mantle.

Sources:

"Birth Date of Man," *Time*, 76 (11 July 1960): 53;

Wallace Cloud, "The Ship That Digs Holes in the Sea," *Popular Mechanics*, 131 (March 1969): 108–111, 236;

"Did It Break? Is It Lost?," *Life*, 50 (7 April 1961): 37–40;

Robert S. Dietz, "The Spreading Ocean Floor," *Saturday Evening Post*, 234 (21 October 1961): 34–35, 94–96;

John Steinbeck, "High Drama of Bold Thrust through Ocean Floor," *Life*, 50 (14 April 1961): 110–122;

"Time for a Theory," *Science News*, 95 (10 May 1969): 449–450.

OCEANOGRAPHY: TRIESTE

Trieste. On 23 January 1960 the bathyscaphe *Trieste*, a manned vehicle designed to dive into deep seas, dove to about 37,000 feet in the Mariana Trench of the Pacific Ocean. Inside were twenty-eight-year-old navy lieutenant Don Walsh and thirty-seven-year-old Frenchman Jacques Piccard. Piccard's father designed and built the *Trieste* in Italy for the U.S. Navy. The dive took four hours and forty-eight minutes; the *Trieste* spent half an hour at the bottom, where the hull withstood pressures of over 17,000 pounds per square inch.

Rough Descent. *Trieste* dove 4 feet per second to 27,000 feet. The first part of the dive was smooth compared to the rough seas above. Then *Trieste* hit a thermocline, where water temperatures drop sharply at a certain depth, causing the relative weight of the craft to increase. There were thermoclines at 250 feet and again about 400 feet. The second was thick and caused the craft to rock. After less than 1,000 feet the thermoclines were gone, but the passenger compartment got cold. All light from the surface was essentially gone at this depth. The passengers had a small compartment to share. They lost radio-telephone contact at 15,000 feet. After 27,000 feet the *Trieste* dumped some ballast and slowed to 2 feet per second. At 36,000 feet they slowed to .5 foot per second to avoid a crash landing.

Surprising Life. The crew was shocked to find particular forms of life at the bottom. There were a flat fish and several small shrimp where no life was thought possible. This much life in pressures of about nine tons per square inch and a temperature just above freezing (37.4 degrees Fahrenheit) was not considered likely before the *Trieste*. The divers did expect to see luminescent life, which creates its own light chemically. Luminescent creatures were only seen at 2,200 feet and again at 20,000 feet; more were expected, with greater numbers of luminescent organisms as the depth increased. Bottom dwellers had been thought to feed on dead food falling from above, but the fish were seen chasing the shrimp to eat them. No current and no radioactivity were detected at the bottom.

A Speedy Return. Plans were for the *Trieste* to stay longer on the bottom. It had mercury-vapor lights and six-inch-thick plexiglass portholes so the crew could observe. But the Plexiglas window cracked at 30,000 feet, and the crew decided to ascend early to reach the surface during daylight. To speed the trip to the surface during daytime they let two tons of ballast out. The trip to the surface took only three hours and twenty-seven minutes.

Paint-stripping Pressure. Despite the Plexiglas crack and the damages incurred getting to the dive site, the *Trieste* did well. One problem was noted: at the pressures on the deep ocean bottom the *Trieste* was compressed by about two millimeters. As a result, some of its paint came off.

Sources:
"Achieving the Ulitmate Adventure on Earth," *Life*, 48 (15 February 1960): 110–121;

"Bathyscaphe Descends to Deepest Part of Ocean," *Science News Letter*, 77 (6 February 1960): 91;

Jacques Piccard, "Man's Deepest Dive," *National Geographic*, 118 (August 1960): 224–239.

OCEANOGRAPHY: SEALAB AND FRIENDS

Living Underwater. There were Sealab projects in the 1960s numbered I, II, and III. The Sealabs were submarines of sorts equipped for scientific study. Some scientists thought that people could live and work underwater for long periods, and the Sealab project was an attempt to find out what problems such conditions would pose. The Sealabs were underwater experimental chambers where people would stay submerged for days at a time to work in and study the oceans. *Sealab I* submerged off Bermuda in 1964, and four people stayed down for nine days at 192 feet. This was a warm ocean area. The next step was *Sealab II*, taken to a cold ocean region.

Sealab II. *Sealab II* cost $850,000, a phenomenal price in its day. It was a 12-by-57-foot cylinder made of steel and containing life-support equipment and scientific research instruments. The "submarine" was attached to its support barge on the surface by an "umbilical" cable. Supplies could be lowered to the Sealab by pressurized containers. It also had an escape capsule for use in emergencies. The umbilical cable allowed closed-circuit phone and television communications with the support barge.

Problems with Pressure. Sealab worked in high pressures under water, creating some problems for the occupants. Matches will not burn at these pressures, and water had to be heated to over three hundred degrees Fahrenheit to get it to boil. Frying an egg was poisonous because of the toxic hydrogen sulfide fumes given off in the process.

Does the Air Seem Different? Oxygen was kept low — 4.3 percent instead of the normal 19 percent — because the higher amount would be toxic to people at these pressures. In fact, the whole atmosphere was regulated with unusual contents. Nitrogen was kept low at 18 percent because it could act as a narcotic at higher levels, and the rest of the air aboard was helium, causing the crew to make duck-like sounds when they talked. The crew was

Sealab I participants, (left to right) Capt. George Bond, Mate Billie Coffman, Cmdr. Scott Carpenter, and Capt. Walter Mazzone

medically monitored to see how they reacted to working at ocean depths.

Crews in Shifts. The crew could leave Sealab in wet suits, but they could not stay out long because of the cold temperatures. They were to perform certain tasks outside the lab, though, to see how well they functioned. The *Sealab II* expedition included former astronaut Scott Carpenter leading a ten-man crew off La Jolla, California. There were actually three teams that spent fifteen days each in the lab, while Carpenter stayed for thirty days. The U.S. Navy and Scripps Institute of Oceanography sponsored the *Sealab II* project. *Sealab III* continued this work at depths up to 600 feet, and the crews stayed down longer.

Sources:
Hans Fantel, "A Longer, Deeper, Daring Quest for the Secrets of Living in the Sea," *Popular Mechanics*, 130 (September 1968): 95–99, 180–182;

"Journey to Inner Space," *Time*, 86 (17 September 1965): 90, 95.

PHYSICS: PROVING EINSTEIN RIGHT

The Einstein Shift. Albert Einstein was a theoretical physicist. He used mathematics to solve problems and express new ideas, but he did not perform experiments to check his theories. Experimental work was left to others. Einstein's brillliant special theory of relativity in 1905 and general theory of relativity in 1916 proposed that space was composed of the three dimensions (length, width, and depth) plus time. The path of light moving through a gravitational field would be curved, he theorized, altering the perception of time. Stars are massive bodies, so big that space-time wraps around them.

Bending Light. As light travels from a distant star

toward Earth, it bends as it goes around a nearer star in its path. This is because the nearer star is so massive its gravitational field bends light as it travels, causing the light to lose some energy in the process and thus making it appear redder than it really is. This bending of light is called the Einstein Shift, and it is difficult to detect because the movements of stars themselves cause reddening of the light they give off.

Examining Sirius B. In 1925 the American astronomer Walter S. Adams solved the technical problem of detecting the Einstein Shift. He used a white dwarf star called Sirius B., an extremely dense body with high gravity. Adams thought the redshift of light due to gravity might be easier to detect around a white dwarf. He was right, and his experiments provided indirect proof of Einstein's general theory of relativity.

Proof in Radioactive Elements. Direct proof in the lab came at Harvard University in 1960. The general theory proposed the principle of equivalence, which holds that there is no difference between the force of gravity and the force produced by acceleration outside a gravitational field. The Harvard scientists relied on the work of the German physicist Rudolph Mössbauer in 1958. He knew that radioactive elements emit gamma rays when they decay, and they can also absorb gamma rays of exactly the same wavelength. When heated the material's atomic nuclei shake. As a result, the wavelengths of the gamma rays the nuclei give off (or receive) are redshifted.

Drilling for Confirmation. Robert V. Pound and Glen Rebka, physicists at the Jefferson Physical Laboratory at Harvard, built on Mössbauer's work. They drilled one big hole from the penthouse to the basement of their lab, a distance of seventy feet (twenty-two and a half meters), and inserted a long tube filed with helium. They put a radioactive source (cobalt 57) in the basement and a crystal absorber (iron 57) at the top. The iron should have absorbed the gamma rays produced by the cobalt if it were moved just the right distance from the source, but the gamma rays from the basement were not absorbed in the penthouse. So they calculated the amount of redshift to expect based on Einstein's general theory. By moving the emitter slightly to account for the redshift, the gamma rays were absorbed. The same was true if the source was in the penthouse and the absorber in the basement. The amount of redshift was calculated, directly proving in the lab Einstein's theory of general relativity.

Source:
"Einstein Principle True," *Science News Letter*, 77 (16 April 1960): 247.

PHYSICS: WHAT DOES IT ANTIMATTER?

Anti-xi-zero. One of the predictions of quantum theory, the branch of physics that deals with the smallest elements in the universe, was the existence of some seventeen basic particles of matter and antimatter. One fundamental bit of antimatter, the infamous anti-xi-zero,

---

NUCLEAR ACCIDENT

On 3 January 1961 an explosion occurred in the Stationary Low Power Reactor Number One at the Atomic Energy Commission's National Reactor Testing Station in Idaho Falls, Idaho. The AEC revealed that three members of the reactor's maintenance crew were killed in the explosion and that an estimated "5 per cent of the gross fission product activity contained in the core . . . were released to the building environs." They concluded that the accident was caused by the manual withdrawal of the reactor's central control rod beyond specified limits during a maintenance operation.

---

was difficult to identify for several reasons, chief among them being that it has no charge. In the usual bubble chambers where particles are studied, anti-xi-zero would leave no track, even if it were present. Physicists faced the dual challenge of finding the right combinations of particles to combine in order to produce it as a residual and of recognizing it when it was found. They also did not know what properties anti-xi-zero should have, such as how it would affect other atoms or particles during collisions.

Photographing Antimatter. Experimenters from Yale University and from Brookhaven National Laboratory started a nearly two-year search for anti-xi-zero in September 1961. They used the Brookhaven alternating gradient synchrotron to hurl antiprotons at liquid hydrogen nuclei in a twenty-inch bubble chamber. For a brief period, the particles produced phenomenal energy and new particles that were tracked in the bubble chamber and photogaphed for review later. The thirteen experimenters had to look over three hundred thousand pictures in great detail to find the evidence that anti-xi-zero hit something else and created the expected breakdown products. They found their evidence in three of the photos, even though the particle itself lasted only one ten-billionth of a second.

Sources:
"Anti-Matter Particle, Last in Nuclear Family," *Science News Letter*, 84 (24 August 1963): 115;

Wallace Cloud, "Science Newsfront," *Popular Science*, 183 (October 1963): 29;

"The Search for Anti-XI-zero," *Time*, 82 (23 August 1963): 54.

PHYSICS: IRRADIATE FOR SAFETY

Irradiated Food, Healthy or Harmful? The U.S. government in the late 1960s debated the use of radiation to kill all or most of the bacteria that cause food spoilage. The army was interested in irradiating food because during war it is hard to keep providing the troops with fresh food. Irradiation makes this task much easier. The AEC was also interested in this peaceful use of radioactivity.

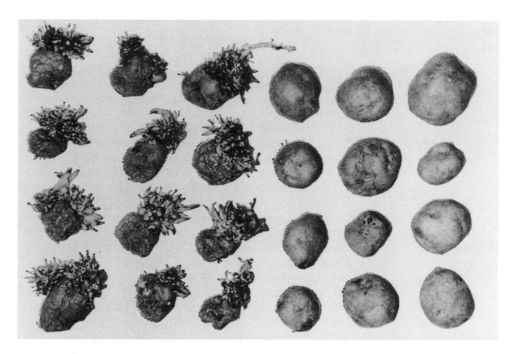

Untreated potatoes, left, and irradiated potatoes after 275 days of storage

The army and the AEC contracted with a company called Irradiated Foods, Incorporated, to provide irradiated ham that was sterilized before it was canned and could then be kept indefinitely without refrigeration. But the Food and Drug Administration (FDA) refused to approve irradiated ham for human consumption. They based their objection on studies showing that animals eating irradiated food died sooner, had fewer babies, and even weighed less than animals that ate regular food.

Studies and Results. The army and the AEC had studied irradiated food for ten years. Dr. Edward S. Josephson, associate director of the Food Irradiation Laboratory at the army's Natick, Massachusetts, center, argued that the radiation technique had been refined and improved since the animal studies the FDA was concerned about were conducted. The best tested food use for irradiation was in seed potatoes. Dr. George Pigott of the University of Washington in Seattle used cobalt 60 to irradiate twenty tons of potatoes. The potatoes were used for seed, and the crop that resulted was much larger than expected. The fishing industry also benefited from irradiation. Fish caught and irradiated at sea and again on shore could be stored in airtight containers for up to five weeks. Finally the FDA approved potatoes, wheat flour, and bacon for human consumption after irradiation but refused to approve irradiation of ham, strawberries, or oranges.

Sources:

"Irradiated Foods Go Sour," *Business Week* (25 May 1968): 160;

Andrew Jamison, "Irradiated Food: FDA Blocks AEC, Army Requests for Approval," *Science,* 161 (12 July 1968): 146–148;

Bob Nein, "Food Irradiation 'Zaps' Longer Life," *Science Digest,* 63 (February 1968): 20–23.

PHYSICS: LASER

The Search for a Laser. Once Charles H. Townes developed the maser in the 1950s, the search was on for a similar instrument that used light. Lasers and masers work on the same principle. A core of atoms are excited to a high energy state. They return to their normal energy state by releasing energy at a single, "coherent" frequency. In masers this is microwave or radio energy; in lasers it is light energy.

The First Laser. In 1960 Theodore H. Maiman at the Hughes Research Laboratory used a synthetic ruby to produce the first laser. A ruby is composed of crystals of aluminum oxide with a trace of chromium, which provides its color. The ruby allows the atoms to be excited long enough to accumulate and emit their energy packets all at once. Amplifying the light effectively is an engineering problem. While various atoms are excited and release energy coherently, some will release energy out of phase. Maiman figured out how to get rid of these out-of-phase energy packets.

Ruby Light. His ruby was about the same diameter as a pencil and four centimeters long. The ends were polished flat to form planes parallel to within about one-millionth of a centimeter of each other. Then they were coated with silver to act as mirrors that would reflect light beams back and forth between them. Any other light would escape through the curved sides of the ruby. The ruby itself made light of only one frequency (color). Maiman then made a tiny hole in the mirror at one end. This let the laser light out in a focused beam. The other engineering feat was to find a way initially to stimulate the atoms in the ruby. Maiman used a strong light shaped like a helix and wrapped it around the ruby. When he turned on the laser, it flashed a bright light for a fraction of a second. Maiman's experiment was impressive, but it took another generation of practical scientists to find a use for his discovery.

Sources:

C. P. Gilmore, "The Incredible Ruby Ray," *Popular Science*, 181 (September 1962): 89–92, 200;

Arthur L. Schowlow, "Optical Masers," *Scientific American*, 204 (June 1961): 52–61.

THE SPACE PROGRAM: PROJECT MERCURY

The Trip. The early space travelers were almost all male and were all in the military. Americans called their spacemen astronauts; the Soviets called theirs cosmonauts. The United States called its first manned space flight program Project Mercury; the first Soviet program was called Project Vostok.

The First Men in Space. Yuri A. Gagarin, twenty-seven years old, was the first human in outer space. He was launched in the *Vostok 1* space vehicle aboard a modified SS-6 Sapwood ballistic missile. He reached a maximum altitude of 203 miles above Earth and orbited Earth once in his 108-minute flight. The Soviets proved that a man could withstand the forces of lift-off and the space-capsule environment during a short space flight. On 5 May 1961 Alan Shepard, Jr., a commander in the navy, was launched into space in his Project Mercury space capsule *Freedom 7*. In military fashion he was allowed to name his space vehicle. (NASA stopped this practice in Project Gemini, which followed Project Mercury.) He was launched aboard a Redstone rocket in a fifteen-minute, twenty-eight-second flight that was less than a full Earth orbit. He reached a maximum of 116 miles above Earth, and his maximum speed was 5,180 miles per hour. For his trip into space, he received military flight pay of $14.38.

Liberty Bell 7. The next space flight, by Virgil I. ("Gus") Grissom in *Liberty Bell 7* on 21 July 1961, demonstrated the dangers of early space travel. Unlike the Soviets, who landed their craft on land, Americans landed theirs in the ocean and recovered the astronaut and space capsule by ship. After his suborbital flight Grissom's escape hatch blew open prematurely. His space ship filled with water and sank. He had to swim to his rescuers.

Vostok 2. The Soviets countered on 6 August 1961 with Gherman S. Titov, who spent a whole day in space in *Vostok 2*. While the Soviets claimed he felt marvelous, he was later found to be the first person to suffer from space sickness caused by the effects of weightlessness on the delicate balancing mechanisms of the inner ear.

An American Orbits the Earth. John H. Glenn, Jr., was the first American to orbit Earth (three times) when his *Friendship 7* was launched on 20 February 1962. Glenn, who had already been in the public spotlight as a

Alan Shepard after his fifteen-minute flight aboard *Freedom 7*

1957 contestant on the television game show *Name That Tune*, seemed likely for a few tense minutes to become the first space casualty. On reentry into the atmosphere, a space craft is moving at tremendous speed, and the resulting friction as the capsule moves through the atmosphere causes extreme heat to build up. Instruments on the ground showed that the special heat shield to protect the space capsule had dislodged. Ground-based controllers had Glenn retain retrorockets, normally fired on reentry. The idea was that they would hold the heat shield in place. In fact, the heat shield was fine, and the instruments on the ground were faulty. Components of his landing gear had failed, though, and Glenn had to direct much of the landing by hand.

Fireflies in Space. Glenn also became known for first seeing the "fireflies" of space — small, white, glowing spots seen from his spacecraft window. They were thought to be small paint chips and ice crystals from the capsule itself. Glenn left NASA soon after this flight, intending to enter politics. These plans were postponed when he slipped fixing a glass shower door in February 1964 and suffered a concussion.

A Troubled Mission. Malcolm S. Carpenter flew a troubled mission on the *Aurora 7*, with liftoff on 24 May 1962. Problems began when Carpenter enjoyed the view

PROJECT MERCURY MANNED MISSIONS

NAME OF CRAFT	LAUNCH DATE	ASTRONAUT	FLIGHT TIME	FLIGHT TYPE
Freedom 7	5 May 1961	Comdr. Alan B. Shepard, Jr., USN	15 mins., 28 secs.	Suborbital
Liberty Bell 7	21 July 1961	Capt. Virgil I. ("Gus") Grissom, USAF	15 mins., 37 secs.	Suborbital
Friendship 7	20 February 1962	Lt. Col. John H. Glenn, Jr., USMC	4 hrs., 55 mins.	3 orbits
Aurora 7	24 May 1962	Lt. Comdr. Malcolm S. Carpenter, USN	4 hrs., 56 mins.	3 orbits
Sigma 7	3 October 1962	Comdr. Walter M. Schirra, Jr., USN	9 hrs., 13 mins.	5.75 orbits
Faith 7	15 May 1963	Maj. Leroy Gordon Cooper, USAF	1 day, 10 hrs., 20 mins.	21.75 orbits

PROJECT VOSTOK MANNED MISSIONS

MISSION NO.	LAUNCH DATE	COSMONAUT	FLIGHT TIME	FLIGHT TYPE
1	12 April 1961	Lt. Yuri A. Gagarin,* AF	1 hr., 48 mins.	1 orbit
2	6 August 1961	Capt. Gherman S. Titov, AF	1day, 1 hr., 18 mins.	17 orbits
3	11 August 1962	Maj. Andrian G. Nikolaycv, AF	3 days, 22 hrs., 22 mins.	64 orbits
4	12 August 1962	Lt. Col. Pavel R. Popovich, AF	2 days, 22 hrs., 57 mins.	48 orbits
5	14 June 1962	Lt. Col. Valeri F. Bykovsky, AF	4 days, 23 hrs., 6 mins.	81 orbits
6	16 June 1962	Lt. Valentina V. Tereshkova, AF **	2 days, 22 hrs., 50 mins.	48 orbits

* First man in space   ** First woman in space

from space so much during his orbits that he got behind schedule. Meanwhile his spacesuit overheated, a problem that plagued most of the Project Mercury astronauts. On reentry he accidentally lost most of his fuel and headed back into the atmosphere at the wrong angle, causing his capsule to shake so severely that ground controllers feared it would break apart. As a result of his reentry problems, he overshot his "splashdown" target by 250 miles. Carpenter left NASA soon after as a result, some observers speculated, of NASA's intolerance of his mistakes.

Tricky Flying in Space. Some tricky flying was required to land men on the Moon. A landing vehicle had to be small and light enough to take off from the Moon's surface after the mission, but a small, light vehicle could not carry enough fuel to propel it back to Earth. So the landing vehicle had to be able to take off from the Moon and couple with a larger vehicle that carried enough fuel for the return trip, a process that required a rendezvous and docking (linking the two craft together) in space.

A Reported Rendezvous. The Soviets appeared to

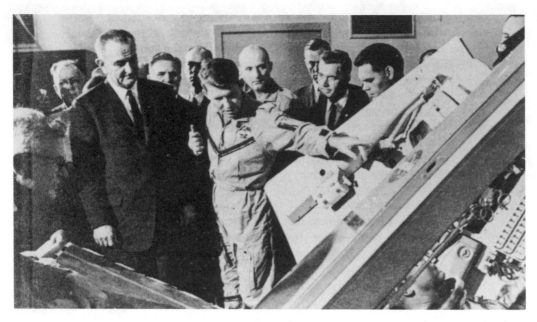

President Lyndon B. Johnson being shown a Gemini spacecraft by astronaut Walter Schirra

have accomplished a rendezvous in 1962, at least according to the American press. Andrian G. Nikolayev took off in *Vostok 3* on 11 August 1962. On 12 August Pavel R. Popovich took off in *Vostok 4*. For a short time the two were only four miles apart. In fact, neither had the maneuvering control needed for a real space rendezvous. Their takeoffs and orbits were calculated on the ground to accomplish the rendezvous. Americans, though, believed the Soviets were ahead again in the race for the Moon.

Space Flight Becomes Routine. At each stage of Project Mercury, some new technical aspect of space flight was tested. But when Walter M. Schirra, Jr., took off in the *Sigma 7* on 3 October 1962, nothing new seemed to be planned. Except for the continuing spacesuit problem, his nine-hour mission of 5.75 orbits seemed almost dull, a circumstance Schirra had anticipated by smuggling aboard a minibottle of whiskey.

New Triumphs When Machine Fails. The last Mercury flight was of Leroy Gordon Cooper in the *Faith 7* on 15 May 1963. He was a relaxed pilot who fell asleep during countdown. While the Soviets had sent men into space for days, he was the first American whose mission lasted over twenty-four hours. The automatic flight control system of his little Mercury craft had a major malfunction. This meant he had to bring the craft in manually for splashdown. He landed seven thousand yards from his rescue ship, showing the ability of men when even the most sophisticated machines fail.

First Woman in Space. The Soviets concluded Project Vostok with another dual flight. *Vostok 5* took off on 14 June 1962 with Valeri F. Bykovsky. On June 16 Valentina V. Tereshkova, the first woman in space, took off in *Vostok 6*. Tereshkova had severe space sickness, but

she was kept in orbit almost three days anyway. Bykovsky stayed in orbit almost five days and still holds the record for the longest solo space flight.

THE SPACE PROGRAM: PROJECT GEMINI

Working toward Kennedy's Goal. President John F. Kennedy had told Congress in May 1961 that the United States should have a goal of, by the end of the decade, landing a man on the Moon and returning him safely. After President Kennedy was assassinated in 1963, NASA was expected to achieve this goal in Kennedy's honor. While Project Mercury made impressive progress, the United States was still a long way from a lunar landing. The next step in the stage, Project Gemini, named after the "twin" sign in astrology, involved putting two men at a time in space.

Soviets Play a Dangerous Game. To beat the Americans again in the space race, the Soviets played a dangerous game with *Voskhod 1*, launched on 12 October 1964. They took a one-man Vostok capsule, removed the ejection seat and safety equipment, and crammed three men into the tiny capsule without protective space suits. Two of the crew had hardly any training for space flight. The flight was successful but reckless. Soviet premier Nikita Khrushchev was ousted from power while talking to the cosmonauts, and his publicity stunt may have been part of the reason for his downfall. Had anything gone wrong, *Voskhod 1* would have been disastrous publicity for the Soviets rather than being the first three-man flight.

Walk and Rendezvous. In addition to docking in space, the U.S. Moon landing was planned so that an

PROJECT GEMINI MANNED MISSIONS

MISSION NO.	LAUNCH DATE	ASTRONAUTS	FLIGHT TIME	MISSION
3	23 March 1965	Maj. Virgil I. ("Gus") Grissom, USAF Lt. Comdr. John W. Young, USN	4 hrs., 53 mins.	maneuver in space
4	3 June 1965	Maj. James A. McDivitt, USAF Maj Edward H. White, II, USAF	4 days, 1 hr., 56 mins.	space walk
5	21 August 1965	Lt. Col. Leroy Gordon Cooper, Jr. USAF Lt. Comdr. Charles ("Pete") Conrad, Jr., USN	7 days, 22 hrs., 55 mins.	rendezvous and fuel-cell power check
6	15 December 1965	Capt. Walter M. Schirra, Jr., USN Maj. Thomas P. Stafford, Jr., USAF	1 day, 1 hr., 51 mins.	rendezvous
7	4 December 1965	Lt. Col. Frank Borman, USAF Lt. Comdr. James A. Lovell, Jr., USN	13 days, 18 hrs., 35 mins.	rendezvous
8	16 March 1966	Neil A. Armstrong Maj. David R. Scott, USAF	10 hrs., 42 mins.	docking
9	3 June 1966	Lt. Col. Thomas P. Stafford, Jr., USAF Lt. Comdr. Eugene A. Cernan, USN	3 days, 21 mins.	space walk
10	18 July 1966	Comdr. John W. Young, USN Maj. Michael Collins, USAF	2 days, 22 hrs., 47 mins.	docking and re-boost
11	12 September 1966	Comdr. Charles ("Pete") Conrad, Jr., USN Lt. Comdr. Richard F. Gordon, Jr., USN	2 days, 23 hrs.	docking
12	11 November 1966	Comdr. James A. Lovell, Jr., USN Maj. Edwin E. ("Buzz") Aldrin, Jr., USAF	3 days, 22 hrs., 35 mins.	docking

astronaut could live and function outside the craft itself. The Moon has little atmosphere. Space rendezvous and docking require advanced technology allowing the spacecraft to be maneuvered. Americans began winning the space race when they showed superior skills in these matters, but the Soviets stole the show again with the first space walk.

Voskhod 2. On 18 March 1965 the Soviets launched *Voskhod 2,* manned by Pavel Belayev and Alexi Leonov. The enlarged space capsule not only included enough room for two, it had an airlock, a chamber with a hatch that could open into outer space. When the hatch was closed, the chamber could be filled with air.

Soviets Walk in Space. Leonov left the craft on 18 March 1965 while he was attached to a fifteen-foot "umbilical cord." There was some question about the effects of intense cold or heat, radiation, or even microscopic meteors flying very rapidly in space. Could a man protected only by a space suit function outside the more protective space capsule? Leonov did, but not without difficulty.

A Close Call. His pressurized space suit acted like a balloon in the vacuum of space. Trying to move and bend to return to the capsule in his suit was almost impossible. If he could not make it back, the only option would be to cut him loose and return the other cosmonaut to Earth. As soon as his life-support systems started to fail, Leonov would die alone in space. In desperation, Leonov lowered the pressure of his suit enough both to keep him alive and to allow him to bend a little. He barely made it back into the small hatch window of the capsule.

Molly Brown. The first manned Gemini flight was *Gemini 3,* piloted by Grissom and John W. Young. Unofficially named *Molly Brown* after the popular Broadway musical *The Unsinkable Molly Brown* (calling to mind Grissom's previous flight), *Gemini 3* showed that Americans could manipulate their spacecraft as was necessary to fly to the Moon and back. The only problem with the flight came after the splashdown in the Atlantic Ocean, when Grissom, whose military career was in the air force rather than the navy, became seasick waiting for the recovery ship to pick them up. It was later learned that Young had smuggled two sandwiches from a local restaurant into the spacecraft. Grissom and Young were the first to eat corned beef in space.

Americans Walk in Space. *Gemini 4* was launched 3 June 1965, manned by two air force officers, James A. McDivitt and Edward H. White. A new ground-control station in Houston had been built, and this mission was controlled from there after takeoff from Cape Kennedy, Florida. *Gemini 4* was the first launch to be shown live in Europe (via the *Early Bird* communications satellite). The astronauts attempted a rendezvous with a stage of the rocket that got them into space, but the attempt was aborted when fuel ran low. White was the first American spacewalker. He left his air hatch for twenty-one minutes

Astronaut Ed White during his *Gemini 4* spacewalk

while attached to a lifeline from the craft and used a handheld maneuvering unit. White had some difficulty returning to the craft after his space walk, and he had trouble locking the hatch. On reentry, equipment failures again caused the astronauts to land manually. McDivitt reported seeing a beer can in space; it was later determined to be part of a rocket booster.

Power Shutdown in Space. *Gemini 5* was supposed to be a big step for the American space program. Cooper and Charles ("Pete") Conrad, Jr., were to eject a radar pod from the spacecraft in orbit, back away from it, and maneuver close again for a rendezvous. The mission (the longest ever) was to last a week and was the first to test new fuel cells, which used hydrogen and oxygen to create water and electrical power. Conrad and Cooper took off on 21 August 1965 and encountered difficulty early on when the pressure in the craft dropped dangerously low. NASA decided to cut off all power that was not essential and to let the astronauts float around in space for a day while the situation was investigated. Unexplainably, the problem fixed itself the next day. The astronauts used a phantom target to test rendezvous maneuvers and stayed in space almost eight days. They were also the first to drink powered, synthetic orange juice. As they were preparing for reentry, the astronauts spotted a huge storm (Hurricane Betsy in the Atlantic) headed directly for their splashdown site. The site was changed, and the astronauts landed after traveling three million miles and 120 Earth orbits.

Successful Rendezvous. *Gemini 6* was scheduled to

take off, rendezvous, and dock in space with a separately launched Agena rocket in October 1965. The Agena took off first and broke apart before reaching orbit, so *Gemini 6* was canceled. Meanwhile, *Gemini 7* was scheduled to take off in December for various scientific experiments, so NASA took advantage of the circumstances by changing plans. *Gemini 7* was launched as scheduled on 4 December with astronauts Frank Borman and James A. Lovell, Jr., aboard. *Gemini 6* followed on 15 December with Schirra and Thomas P. Stafford, Jr., aboard and, after three orbits, made a rendezvous with *Gemini 7*. The two independently controlled spacecraft came within six inches of each other. After over five hours the two Geminis went their separate ways. *Gemini 6* splashed down after a flight lasting just over a day. *Gemini 7* continued the space endurance mission, coming down after almost fourteen days. Americans were starting to pull away from the Soviets in the space race.

Capsule Spins out of Control. *Gemini 8* was the first mission with a civilian astronaut, Neil A. Armstrong. Also aboard was David R. Scott, an astronaut from the military. On 16 March 1966 an Agena rocket was launched, followed by *Gemini 8*. Six and a half hours after rising into space, *Gemini 8* docked with the Agena rocket. Then trouble began. The paired Agena and Gemini capsule began to spin out of control. Thinking the problem was with the Agena, the astronauts moved away, but the Gemini began to spin even more wildly. The only solution was to shut down the space systems and use the reentry system to control the spin, leaving the reentry rockets very low on fuel. The mission was aborted after about ten hours, and the astronauts landed safely.

More Problems for Gemini. *Gemini 9* was plagued with problems. The mission was to be flown by astronauts Elliot See and Charles Bassett, but they were killed in a plane crash flying to the Saint Louis factory where the spaceship was being built. The backup crew included astronauts Thomas P. Stafford, Jr., and Eugene A. Cernan, who, at thirty-two, was the youngest astronaut in the American program. *Gemini 9* was another docking mission. NASA tried to launch an Agena rocket on 17 May 1966, but the rocket exploded on takeoff. This time NASA had a backup plan. A specially designed docking target (Augmented Target Docking Adapter, or ATDA) was launched 1 June for the meeting in space. Then a computer failure forced a two-day postponement of the launching of *Gemini 9* itself. Meanwhile ground-control equipment showed that two shields on the ATDA had failed to come off when expected. On rendezvous the *Gemini 9* crew described ATDA as "an angry alligator." After several rendezvous maneuvers were complete, the astronauts slept. Then Cernan was to use a backpack jet system on a space walk, a horrendous two-hour experience. He had trouble staying in one place in space and tended to float away from the mother craft. His space suit could not handle the body heat and sweat he generated, and his visor steamed up so he could not see. Then he had

Buzz Aldrin on the surface of the Moon during the *Apollo 11* mission

more trouble getting back into the craft because of his stiff space suit. Reentry and splashdown were routine for this three-day mission.

Mission Runs Smoothly. *Gemini 10* was a smooth operation. NASA launched an Agena rocket on 18 July 1966, right on schedule, followed shortly thereafter by the spaceship with Young and Michael Collins aboard. They docked with the Agena, and the locked craft were boosted into a higher orbit together. They later rendezvoused with the Agena launched from the *Gemini 8* mission.

Performing a Controlled Spin. *Gemini 11* was scheduled for a similar flight plan to that of *Gemini 10* but taking things one step forward. Astronauts Conrad and Richard F. Gordon, Jr., took off on 12 September 1966 shortly after their Agena rocket was launched. They completed a docking maneuver on the first orbit, a tactic that would be needed in an emergency takeoff from the Moon. Gordon then took a space walk that had to be cut short because of space-suit problems. The combined Gemini-Agena pair then boosted to an orbit as high as 850 miles above Earth, high enough for the astronauts to see Earth as a globe. The Agena-Gemini craft then created gravity in outer space. The two linked craft started a slow spin, and instruments on board registered some gravity by showing the astronauts were not quite weightless. The new computer systems on board controlled the entire reentry process.

Most of the Problems Solved. The final Gemini mission, number 12, had only minor glitches. Astronauts

PROJECT APOLLO MANNED MISSIONS

MISSION NO.	LAUNCH DATE	ASTRONAUTS	FLIGHT TIME	MISSION
7	11 October 1968	Capt. Walter M. Schirra, Jr., USN Maj. Donn F. Eisele, USAF Walter Cunningham	10 days, 20 hrs.	prolonged earth orbit
8	21 December 1968	Col. Frank Borman, USAF Capt. James A. Lovell, Jr., USN Maj. William A. Anders, USAF	6 days, 3 hrs.	moon orbit
9	3 March 1969	Col. James A. McDivitt, USAF Col. David R. Scott, USAF Russell ("Rusty") Louis Schweickart	10 days, 1 hr.	lunar/command module docking
10	18 May 1969	Col. Thomas P. Stafford, Jr., USAF Comdr. John W. Young, Jr., USN Comdr. Eugene A. Cernan, USN	8 days	moon orbit, module docking
11	16 July 1969	Neil A. Armstrong Lt. Col. Michael Collins, USAF Col. Edwin ("Buzz") Aldrin, USAF	8 days, 3 hrs.	lunar landing
12	14 November 1969	Comdr. Charles ("Pete") Conrad, Jr., USN Comdr. Richard F. Gordon, Jr., USN Comdr. Alan L. Bean, USN	10 days, 5 hrs.	lunar landing

Lovell and Edwin E. ("Buzz") Aldrin, Jr., took off on 11 November 1966, ninety minutes after their Agena rocket. Docking was done manually because of a radar malfunction, but all went well. NASA solved the space-walk problem at last. Using Velcro gloves and foot restraints, Aldrin could move about outside the ship without constantly fighting not to float away. The way to the Moon was paved. Men could walk in space and function, docking had been achieved, and maneuvering spacecraft had all been done. The program had gone so well that a false security pervaded NASA.

THE SPACE PROGRAM: PROJECT APOLLO

Disaster Strikes. The Soviets and Americans both started new projects in 1967 in the race to be first on the Moon. The Americans initiated Project Apollo; the Soviets, Project Soyuz. Both began with horrible disasters that set each country's space program back a year and a half. The U.S. crew of Grissom, Ed White, and Roger Chaffee were testing the new Apollo systems on the ground in January 1967. On 27 January the three were inside the spacecraft that was going to be *Apollo 1* breath-

PROJECT SOYUZ MANNED MISSIONS

MISSION NO.	LAUNCH DATE	COSMONAUTS	FLIGHT TIME	MISSION
1	23 April 1967	Col. Vladimir M. Komarov, AF	1 day, 3 hrs.	orbit
3	26 October 1968	Col. Georgi T. Beregovoi, AF	3 days, 23 hrs.	rendezvous
4	14 January 1969	Lt. Col. Vladimir A. Shatalov, AF	2 days, 23 hrs.	docking
5	15 January 1969	Lt. Col. Boris V. Volynov, AF Alexei S. Yeliseyev Lt. Col. Yevgeni V. Khrunov	3 days, 1 hr.	docking
6	11 October 1969	Lt. Col. Georgi S. Shonin, AF Valeri Kubasov	4 days, 23 hrs.	orbit
7	12 October 1969	Lt. Col. Anatoli V. Filipchenko, AF Vladislav N. Volkov Lt. Col. Viktor V. Gorbatko, AF	4 days, 23 hrs.	orbit
8	13 October 1969	Col. Vladimir A. Shatalov, AF Alexei S. Yeliseyev	4 days, 23 hrs.	orbit

ing pure oxygen. Suddenly ground control noticed they had elevated heart rates. They were heard to say, "fire in the spacecraft" and "get us out of here." Then there was a burst of flame seen from outside. It took six minutes for technicians and workers to open the hatch. By that time the three astronauts were dead. The interior of the craft was estimated to have reached 1,000 degrees Fahrenheit.

Apollo Suspended. The investigation of the accident reported that it could have been prevented. After Grissom's Mercury capsule sank, the hatches on spacecraft were bolted shut to prevent premature opening in the ocean. An electrical spark, caused by broken insulation on electrical wires run under a close-fitting door, started the fire, which burned furiously in the pure oxygen atmosphere. There were waste rags in the craft, and flammable plastics were not isolated by fire walls. NASA suspended the project to redesign the craft and review work standards. Grissom had warned NASA that the spacecraft was badly designed. After twenty thousand test failures of the engine and craft, Grissom complained loudly. He hung a lemon from the *Apollo 1* command module a week before he was killed inside it.

A Cosmonaut Is Killed. The Soviet *Soyuz 1* mission was no more successful. For once, the Soviets announced the launching in advance. There was to be a launching of two one-man Soyuz craft, docking in space, swapping of cosmonauts, and reentering. Vladimir M. Komarov, the first Soviet to fly twice in space, took off on 23 April 1967. On the thirteenth orbit, the stabilizers failed, and the Soyuz went into an uncontrolled spin. Various other equipment failed as well, including the onboard computer system. Komarov tried twice to reenter without success. On the third try he fired his reentry retrorockets to stabilize the craft, but that failed too. American listening posts monitored his conversation. Komarov realized he was doomed, with no chance of escape. He did not even have an ejection seat. He said good-bye to his wife and Soviet premier Aleksey Kosygin and began reentry. He fell to the ground like a stone. Excessive reentry heat probably killed him before he hit the ground.

Manned Apollo Missions Resume. The next space flight was *Apollo 7* (previous Apollo missions had no men aboard) using the multistage Saturn rocket. The first stage alone was capable of over 1.5 million pounds of thrust. Apollo had command, service, and lunar modules. *Apollo 7* was a test of the Apollo-Atlas system and the new designs since the *Apollo 1* tragedy. The mission started on 11 October 1968 and lasted almost eleven days, with Schirra, Donn F. Eisele, and Walter Cunningham, a civilian and former military pilot, aboard. The flight was distinguished by the bad temper of the astronauts, particularly Schirra, who seemed to be picking fights with ground control throughout the trip. All three had caught colds before blastoff.

Soyuz Tries to Keep Pace. The Soviets countered with an unmanned *Soyuz 2* on 25 October 1968 and *Soyuz 3* on 26 October, manned by Georgi T. Beregovoi. His three-day mission involved rendezvous attempts with *Soyuz 2*. There appeared to have been some difficulty with close maneuvering, and the two craft never got closer than about 650 feet.

Orbiting the Moon on Christmas Day. *Apollo 8,* launched on 21 December 1968, was a major mission. Aboard were Borman, Lovell, and William A. Anders. At about three hours into the mission, they refired the Saturn rocket's fourth stage and left Earth orbit. On 24 December they began orbiting the moon at about seventy miles above its surface. After spending Christmas Day orbiting the moon, another rocket firing directed the craft back toward Earth. Reentry was perfect.

Cosmonauts Dock Successfully. The Soviets launched *Soyuz 4* on 14 January 1969, with Vladimir A. Shatalov aboard. On 15 January *Soyuz 5* was launched with cosmonauts Boris V. Volynov, Alexei S. Yeliseyev, and Yevgeni V. Khrunov aboard. They all stayed aloft about three days. During their time in space together the two craft docked, and the cosmonauts performed a space walk.

The Lunar Module Is Tested in Space. *Apollo 9* had a special mission. The lunar module had never been tested before in space. It took off on 3 March 1969. The astronauts were James A. McDivitt, David R. Scott, and Russell Louis ("Rusty") Schweickart. Schweickart had space sickness at first, but on the fifth day he and McDivitt transferred from the command module to the lunar module. The two modules separated and later docked.

The Next to Last Step. *Apollo 10* was the final mission before landing a man on the Moon. It took off on 18 May 1969 with Young, Stafford, Jr., and Cernan. They went to orbit around the Moon, and the lunar and command modules separated. The lunar module came within nine miles of the proposed lunar landing site in the Moon's Sea of Tranquility area. On attempting to remove the descent engines from the module and fire the ascent rockets, the lunar module went into a spin, but the astronauts regained control and docked successfully with the command module.

The Big Prize. *Apollo 11* was the big one. Takeoff was on 16 July 1969. Aboard were Armstrong, Collins, and Aldrin. The command module was named *Columbia,* and the lunar module was called *Eagle.* The two separated during lunar orbit, with Collins aboard the *Columbia* and Armstrong and Aldrin aboard the *Eagle.* On 20 July 1969, at 9:18 P.M., Americans reached the Moon. Armstrong announced the arrival: "The *Eagle* has landed." Four hours later the astronauts had on space suits. Arm-

Telstar I

strong was first to come out of the lunar module. On touching the Moon's surface, he said, "That's one small step for a man, one giant leap for mankind." About a third of the population of the world watched the event on television as it happened. While Armstrong collected Moon rocks and dust, Aldrin joined him. The astronauts collected samples and set up various experiments including a laser reflector. Their Moon walk took two and a half hours. They returned to the lunar module for some needed sleep. After nearly a day on the Moon, they fired the ascent rockets and were back in lunar orbit without a problem. After docking with Columbia, the three returned to Earth. Once there, they were put into a three-week quarantine.

Goal of Soyuz Becomes Unclear. Between 11 and 13 October 1969, the Soviets launched three Soyuz missions, involving a total of seven cosmonauts (Georgi S. Shonin, Valeri Kubasov, Anatoli V. Filipchenko, Vladislav N. Volkov, Viktor V. Gorbatko, Shatalov, and Yeliseyev). Docking was not performed, but the three ships did rendezvous. There is still some question about why the Soviets embarked on this mission. Some think they had abandoned the Moon race after the *Soyuz 1* disaster and their problems with docking craft. They may have switched plans then to build a Salyut space station. The three Soyuz missions may have been a way to use up some hardware, keep their place in the space race, and perform scientific experiments.

Man Returns to the Moon. On 14 November 1969 *Apollo 12* took off for the second manned lunar landing. On board were Conrad, Gordon, and Alan L. Bean.

Conrad and Bean landed their lunar module in an area called the Ocean of Storms. The astronauts set up scientific experiments and visited the (unmanned) *Surveyor 3* which had landed nearby in April of 1967. They then took off from the Moon, docked with the command module, and returned to Earth. The most striking discovery of *Apollo 12* was life on the Moon. In a piece of insulation on the *Surveyor 3* they discovered a colony of bacteria (*Streptococcus mitis*), which had managed to live over two years on the Moon. It is generally accepted that the organisms originally came from the Earth.

THE SPACE PROGRAM: UNMANNED SPACE EXPLORATION

Echo 1. Many people have felt that sending astronauts into space has always been an expensive publicity stunt. They require costly equipment, training, and safety measures, yet unmanned satellites have proven just as useful at gathering scientific data. A major breakthrough in the use of unmanned satellites was the launching of *Echo 1* on 12 August 1960. *Echo 1* was a giant balloon designed by Bell Laboratories and NASA working in partnership. The balloon material was squeezed into a payload and launched into space. Once there, a chemical was used to inflate the balloon, made from a plastic film and covered with an aluminum skin. *Echo* also had two tiny radio transmitters so it could be tracked. (Actually, as it was large and in a low orbit, it could be seen from Earth). *Echo* was a "passive" communications satellite. When it was in the right place, radio-wave messages could be bounced off it and directed to another location.

Telstar 1 **and** *Relay 1.* More important were the 1962 launches of *Telstar I* (Bell Telephone/AT&T) and *Relay 1* (RCA), both active communications satellites. *Telstar* was a three-foot-diameter ball. It had solar cells to convert light to electricity to power it, and due to miniaturization of electronic parts it weighed only 170 pounds. *Telstar* had a receiver that picked up radio signals (such as television broadcasts and telephone messages) that were amplified in the satellite and relayed back to Earth. Special receivers on Earth used the new maser to amplify the signals from *Telstar*. The first satellite television broadcasts across the Atlantic in 1962 used this satellite.

Geosynchronous Orbit. Another concept used to make communications satellites more useful was suggested by Arthur C. Clarke in 1945. He showed how a satellite could be placed in geosynchronous orbit, an orbit 22,400 miles above the equator and circular. The satellite moves at the same speed as the Earth, so it seems to hover over one spot on Earth at all times. The first geosynchronous satellite was the communications satellite *Syncom II* launched in July 1963. Using just three geosynchronous communications satellites that can send and receive messages to each other and Earth, most of the world can stay in continuous contact. In the mid 1960s, an international group was formed to develop the INTELSAT series of communications satellites in geosynchronous orbits.

Military Missions in Space. The military was quick to see the potential of space exploration. When Cooper told ground control in 1963 that he could see individual ships, roads, and even smoking chimneys from space, they accused him of having hallucinations, but the view from space is as precise as Cooper said, and it can be enhanced by such devices as infrared detectors that can see through clouds. In August 1960 *Discoverer 13* was launched and recovered from the Pacific Ocean, having flown over the Soviet Union taking high quality pictures. A second generation of satellites was launched in 1963 that stayed in orbit much longer than the Discoverers but still had to be recovered to collect their picture information. Meanwhile, other data was transmitted back to Earth from space. By 1966 satellites were launched for orbits lasting weeks. These had high-resolution cameras and infrared detectors that sent information directly back to Earth. As each year went by, fewer satellites were launched, but they stayed in orbit longer and sent back more information. Spying from space became less expensive as the equipment improved.

Antimissile Satellites. The Midas satellites introduced in 1960 detected heat from missile launches using infrared detectors, however unreliably. They were replaced in 1968 with Ballistic Missile Early Warning System (BMEWS) satellites in geosynchronous orbit using more advanced technology. Another series of military satellites, the Velas satellite system, was used just to detect nuclear explosions. Velas satellites were launched in pairs (to see the whole Earth) starting in 1963. Still other military satellites were used for military communications and weather detection. The navy used the Transit satellites to help navigation. They provided detailed information to Polaris submarines on their underwater location. The first antimissile satellites were started in 1959 and launched in the early 1960s. The RCA SAINT (Satellite Interceptor) system was an example. SAINT was designed to inspect targets and possibly destroy them.

Weather Satellites. One of the most beneficial space programs developed was weather satellites. The United States took the lead in this in 1960. *Tiros 1*, built by RCA, looked like a giant hatbox. It was launched on 1 April 1960. *Tiros 1* used two miniaturized television cameras and a recorder. One camera had a wide-angle lens, and the other had a narrower angle for close-ups. While in orbit, the cameras took up to thirty-two images of weather patterns and recorded them on magnetic tape while *Tiros 1* was out of contact with the ground. Once over a ground station, the satellite relayed these recorded pictures back to Earth and transmitted new pictures directly. *Tiros 2*, launched in November 1960, included infrared detectors. Throughout the 1960s a series of more-sophisticated Tiros weather satellites was launched. The early detection of hurricanes and warnings

The USS *Enterprise*

to populated areas in their paths have saved innumerable lives since these satellites started working in 1960.

Studying the Sun. Satellites were also used for scientific discovery. In November 1963 the first in a series of IMP (Interplanetary Monitoring Platform) probes, satellites designed to make detailed observations of the Sun over a period of years, was launched. They supplemented the data from the Pioneer series used in interplanetary research. *Pioneer 5* was launched 11 March 1960 to study the Sun, sending back signals containing data about the Sun's activity. The first planned interplanetary probe from the United States, it continued working far beyond its expected life. *Pioneer 5* returned data to Earth from a distance of 22.7 million miles. *Pioneer 6* through *9* were launched in 1965–1968. They also orbited and studied the Sun.

Exploring Venus. In 1962 the United States launched two Mariner probes to Venus. *Mariner 1* was destroyed 22 July 1962 just after liftoff; a programmer had left out one hyphen in a multipage program for directing its course. There was only a short time period in which probes to Venus could be launched, so *Mariner 2* lifted off on 27 August 1962. It used a combination of stage 1 Atlas rocket and stage 2 Agena rocket. The Atlas boosted it to Earth orbit, then the Agena was fired to change directions and give extra thrust to send the probe to Venus. *Mariner 2* had a variety of scientific instruments aboard. Within 35,000 kilometers of Venus, it detected

no magnetic field around the planet. It noted a surface temperature of four hundred degrees Celsius on both the light and dark sides of the cloud-covered planet. Radio contact was lost 2 January 1963, 109 days after takeoff, when *Mariner 2* was 86.8 million kilometers from Earth.

Exploring Mars. Another Mariner pair was launched in 1964 for Mars. *Mariner 3* was lost when a protective covering used in liftoff failed to separate. *Mariner 4* was launched three weeks later on 28 November 1964 with a newly designed covering. On 14 July 1965 it came within 6,000 miles of Mars. It detected no radiation belts or magnetic fields around the red planet, measured the Martian atmosphere at about 1 percent of Earth's, and radioed back pictures showing a cratered surface like the Moon's. *Mariner 6* and *7* were launched for Mars in 1969.

WARFARE AND SCIENCE: NUCLEAR NAVY

More Miles to the Gallon. A nuclear-powered navy vessel can go a long way between stops for fuel. That is why Adm. Hyman Rickover pushed so hard to develop the nuclear navy and why the country was willing to pay so much to get it.

The USS *Washington*. The nuclear-powered submarine USS *Washington* was built by the General Dynamics Corporation's Electric Boat Division in Groton, Connecticut, and launched from the Charleston, South Carolina, shipyard in the fall of 1960. The *Washington* had a missile compartment containing sixteen seven-foot tubes in a 100-foot area, each holding a Polaris missile, and could stay submerged sixty days at a time. It could go three years without stopping to refuel. The sub had two crews (the "blue" and the "gold"), each consisting of ten officers and ninety enlisted men. Each crew spent sixty days on patrol. The sub's first voyage covered 1,200 miles over three months.

Run Silent, Run Deep. One of the advantages of the *Washington* was it could stay submerged and hidden just about anywhere. If war struck, the *Washington* would strike and then move silently to a new location. The trick was knowing where the sub was at all times without having to surface and give its location away. For this it had a periscope system that could see a wide swath of sky for spotting stars.

Delicate Environment. The environment inside the submarine was critical. There were lots of filters for the air, but some irritants had to be avoided. Animal fat could not be used for cooking, because it produces an irritant to people's eyes. Chlorine bleach was forbidden because it can produce breathing problems. Aerosols were avoided because they contain freon, which can build to poisonous levels.

Safeguards. At sea radio contact was limited to avoid enemy detection. The submarine communicated using a long-wave, low-frequency, constant transmission. Finally, there had to be a fail-safe system to prevent the captain from declaring war on his own volition by shooting off the missiles without authorization.

The USS *Enterprise*. The largest ship in the world in 1962 was the aircraft carrier USS *Enterprise*, with eight atomic reactors for a power supply. The flight decks were longer than four football fields, including the stands (1,123 feet). Four thirty-two-ton, twenty-one-inch propellers could move the ship at over forty miles per hour with their two hundred thousand horsepower. The *Enterprise*, built by the Newport News (Virginia) Shipbuilding and Drydock Company, cost $440 million to build and another $300 million for the planes and weapons it carried. Loaded, it weighed 85,350 tons. The forty-six-hundred-member crew had three barber shops, a complete dentist's office, a shoe-repair shop, even a closed-circuit television studio. The ship could produce 280,000 gallons of fresh water a day from the sea using evaporators. There were sprinklers capable of "soak[ing] every lawn in Des Moines" in ten seconds for fighting fires or for washing off radioactivity in the event of a near miss by a nuclear weapon in war. The *Enterprise* carried ninety airplanes at a time, including bombers that could deliver nuclear weapons deep into enemy territory. Planes could land every twenty-five seconds using the four arresting cables on the deck, which hook landing planes. There were also four launching catapults that could send a plane into the air at 160 miles per hour every fifteen seconds.

Sources:

"Deadly Teeter-Totter," *Newsweek*, 55 (11 January 1960): 55;

Frank Harvey, "85,000-Ton Hot Rod," *Popular Science*, 181 (July 1962): 58;

Andrew Jones, "Welcome Aboard the Awesome Big E," *Reader's Digest*, 81 (December 1962): 174–180;

"Polaris Goes to Work," *Time*, 76 (28 November 1960): 21.

HEADLINE MAKERS

MURRAY GELL-MANN

1929 -

PHYSICIST

Early Life and Education. Murray Gell-Mann was born in New York City on 15 September 1929. His parents were immigrants from Austria. Gell-Mann wanted to study archaeology, but his father wanted him to enter a more practical field such as engineering. They compromised, and he majored in physics. Gell-Mann received his B.S. from Yale in 1948 and his Ph.D. from MIT in 1951.

Working with Einstein. After MIT he worked for a year at the Institute for Advanced Study in Princeton with Albert Einstein, at the University of Chicago from 1952 to 1955, and then at the California Institute of Technology. He became a full professor while in his mid twenties, only four years after receiving his Ph.D.

Work with Atomic and Subatomic Particles. Some of his greatest work was done with fellow Nobel laureate Richard P. Feynman, with whom he studied the theory of weak interactions, which explains spontaneous radioactive decay in the nuclei of atoms. He also described "strangeness" (named from a quote by Francis Bacon), which explains mathematically how newfound (in 1953) subatomic particles interact.

A Theory of Subatomic Families. In 1961 Gell-Mann developed the theory of the "eightfold way" (named after a Buddhist concept of eightfold ways to reduce pain) to make sense of the "particle zoo" resulting from the discovery of more and more new subatomic particles. He showed that all subatomic particles belong to eight (or maybe ten) families, which have similar properties. His theory predicted that new particles would be found, proven with the discovery of omega minus one.

Quarks. Gell-Mann theorized that all subatomic particles are composed of three basic units, called quarks (a word Gell-Mann took from James Joyce's *Finnegan's Wake,* 1930), which have a fractional electrical charge.

His quark hypothesis was widely accepted and many additional quarks have been predicted and verified. Gell-Mann also produced some of the best science of the century. He received the prestigious Heineman Prize from the American Physical Society in 1956 and, in 1969, won the Nobel Prize.

VIRGIL I. ("GUS") GRISSOM

1926 - 1967

ASTRONAUT

Second American in Space. Virgil I. Grissom was a key figure in the United States' manned spaceflight program. He was among the seven original astronaut trainees for Project Mercury in 1959, and he became the second American to go into space when the *Liberty Bell 7* was launched on 21 July 1961 (Alan B. Shepard had been the first on 5 May). Though Grissom's flight exceeded the distance and speed of Shepard's, it experienced a glitch after splashdown when the escape hatch blew prematurely and the capsule filled with water and sank. Grissom managed to escape but was somewhat shaken by the experience.

Distinctions. Soon thereafter, NASA presented Grissom with its Distinguished Service Medal, and he, along with Shepard, received his astronaut's wings on 7 December 1961. On 15 July 1962 Grissom was promoted to the rank of major, and he received further distinction on 19 July 1962 when he was awarded the first General Thomas D. White Trophy for being "The Air Force member who has made the most outstanding contribution to the nation's progress in aerospace."

Project Gemini. Grissom helped design and construct the spacecraft of Project Gemini, a series of missions designed as an intermediate step between Project Mercury and the Apollo Moon project. On 13 April 1964 Grissom was selected to be the first Gemini pilot, and on 23 March 1965 the first two-man space flight was launched with Grissom and John W. Young copiloting

Gemini 3, nicknamed "Molly Brown" by Grissom, alluding to the title of the musical play *The Unsinkable Molly Brown* and to the fate of the *Liberty Bell 7*. During the mission Grissom achieved another first by maneuvering the craft manually from one orbit to another. Upon their return both astronauts received NASA Exceptional Service medals, presented by President Lyndon B. Johnson, and Grissom received an appurtenance to his Distinguished Service Medal.

Disaster. Grissom made headlines one last time as the focus of a tragedy. He and copilots Ed White and Roger Chaffee were engaged in a simulated mission aboard the grounded *Apollo 1* capsule. During the test a fire broke out and raged in the pure oxygen atmosphere on board. By the time technicians opened the craft's hatch, all three astronauts were dead. Ironically, Grissom had repeatedly warned NASA that the craft was poorly designed.

HARRY H. HESS

1906 - 1969

GEOLOGIST

Hess's Theory. The plate tectonics theory, basic to oceanography and geology today, was accepted because of the work of Harry H. Hess on seafloor spreading. Once seafloor spreading was shown to occur, Hess concluded that continents drift over time, the result of continental plates of the Earth's crust moving laterally around the planet. This is the theory of plate tectonics, which was developed over a period of some fifty years.

Continental Drift. German scientist and explorer Alfred L. Wegener first proposed continental displacement (or drift) in 1924 to explain how various parts of the continents seemed to fit into each other like pieces of a jigsaw puzzle. He thought they were all connected once and drifted apart, but he could not prove his theory.

Midocean Ridges. Then the midocean ridges were found. When Harry Hess was a navy captain of a Pacific attack transport, he was intrigued by flat-topped mountains under water identified by his sonar equipment. Hess named these mountains guyots, after Arnold Guyot, a Swiss-American who was Princeton's first professor of geology. In the 1950s guyots were found to be part of the Earth's mantle just below the surface. The mantle moves up in the ridges and pushes the seabed to either side. Hess said it eventually moved under the continents, pushing them apart. Hess published this theory in a 1960 report to the Office of Naval Research. His 1962 book *History of the Ocean Basins* explains his ideas in more detail.

Hess Explains the Guyots. Hess determined these guyots were volcanic islands formed along the midocean ridges. Since the peaks were submerged, water quickly (geologically speaking) eroded the cone peaks to form flat-topped mountains. The farther these were from the ridge, the deeper they were under water and the more eroded they became, so they must have moved away from their place of origination over time. This could only happen if new mantle were rising to push the guyots aside.

The First Continent. Hess proposed an early single land mass named Pangaea that broke into continental plates, which are now recognized as the continental land masses. The plates moved apart by seafloor spreading. Hess's ideas suggested the reversals of the magnetic poles should be symmetrical along the ocean ridges, a phenomenon demonstrated by British researchers in 1963.

Source:
H. W. Menard, "The Deep-Ocean Floor," *Scientific American*, 221 (September 1969): 126–142.

ARTHUR KORNBERG

1918 -

BIOCHEMIST

Reproducing DNA. Arthur Kornberg won the Nobel Prize for discovering the enzyme DNA polymerase, the substance that reproduces DNA in cells. Kornberg was able to produce DNA in the test tube in 1959, but it was not biologically active. The DNA he produced was based on a template from any natural DNA source. The DNA polymerase was from *E. coli*, a common bacterium in the human intestine that could copy a DNA template from any organism.

Phi X174. Methods to determine the sequence of bases in DNA were not exact in the 1960s, and Kornberg's test-tube DNA was not an exact copy such as living cells must produce. One of the problems of producing an active DNA was getting a good template. The *E. coli* DNA is four million base pairs long. It was almost impossible to get a good sample of DNA this long. So Kornberg used the much smaller DNA of a virus instead. The virus he chose was Phi X174, which infects bacteria (a bacteriophage). It has a single strand of DNA fifty-five hundred bases long and comes in a circle. It only contains about eleven genes. That made it easier to purify without breaking it up. It was known that even minor mutations of the DNA made the virus lose its ability to infect bacteria.

Scientists Playing God. Kornberg worked with Mehran Goulian at Stanford and Robert L. Sinsheimer of MIT. They isolated the DNA from Phi X174 without breaking it. Then they used the *E. coli* DNA polymerase to make copies in a test tube. The DNA template was copied and found to be able to infect bacteria. Kornberg and his colleagues had produced active DNA in a test tube. Then the press began to question if they were playing God by creating life.

Sources:
"Closer to Synthetic Life," *Time*, 90 (22 December 1967): 66;

"Viable Synthetic DNA," *Science News*, 92 (30 December 1967): 629–630.

JOSEPH WEBER

1919 –

PHYSICIST

Einstein's Concept of Gravity. Einstein's general theory of relativity predicted that huge bodies accelerating in space should give off gravity in waves. These gravity waves would travel at the speed of light. Physicists believed Einstein, but until University of Maryland physicist Joseph Weber published the results of a ten-year experiment in 1968, these waves had not been proven to exist.

Detecting Gravity. Weber posited that gravity waves should not be expected to be strong, so he would need a sensitive detector. But then he would need a way to eliminate the interference — Earth tremors, passing cosmic rays, electromagnetic radiation, and even atomic decay of naturally radioactive materials within the detector itself. He concluded that two detectors fairly far apart would both be influenced by all those interfering factors, but not at the same time. So if two detectors recorded activity at the same time, it was probably gravity waves, particularly if the simultaneous activity were recorded repeatedly.

The Experiment. Dr. Weber made two detectors, large aluminum cylinders one and a half tons each, designed to respond to 1660-cycle radiation, the frequency expected from gravity waves produced by pulsars. One detector was set up at the University of Maryland in College Park. The other was placed seven hundred miles away at Argonne National Laboratory near Chicago. Within ninety days there were four times when both detectors were hit by something at the same time. Statistics proved that the chance of this being a coincidence was minuscule. The only conclusion left was that gravity waves caused the effect.

Sources:
"Gravitating toward Einstein," *Time*, 93 (20 June 1969): 75;

"Gravitational Waves Detected," *Science News*, 95 (21 June 1969): 593–594;

"Gravity Wave Search," *Science News*, 94 (17 August 1968): 154–155.

PEOPLE IN THE NEWS

In 1969 **Jonathan Beckwith,** leading a team of Harvard Medical School scientists, isolated and photographed a gene for the first time.

Chemist **Kenneth Conrow** in 1967 employed a computer to assist in the complex task of naming new chemical compounds he was developing; in the process he found twenty-nine compounds that had been incorrectly named in official publications.

Astronaut **Leroy Gordon Cooper, Jr.,** made the sixth and last of the Project Mercury flights in May 1963, manually landing the craft after it developed electrical problems.

Archaeologist **Richard Daugherty** and geologist **Roald Fryxell** of Washington State University announced in 1968 the discovery in southern Washington of the oldest human remains found in the Western Hemisphere.

In 1960 **C. H. W. Hirs** and colleagues at the Rockefeller Institute and the Brooklyn National Laboratory provided the first delineation of the structure of an enzyme.

William Hayward Pickering led a team of scientists who sent the unmanned spacecraft *Ranger 7* to the Moon in 1964; it sent back approximately 4,000 close-range photographs of the Moon's surface.

Maarten Schmidt announced in 1965 the discovery of the most distant object known, the quasar 3C 9.

In January 1961 noted scientist **Glenn T. Seaborg** was designated by President Kennedy to be chairman of the Atomic Energy Commission, succeeding the former chairman, businessman John A. McCone.

In 1969 **Georges Ungar** of the Baylor University College of Medicine in Houston provided evidence of the chemical transfer of learning in animals.

Publication of **James D. Watson's** *The Double Helix* was suspended in 1968 by Harvard University Press when colleagues Francis H. Crick and Maurice H. F. Wilkins protested their portrayals in the work; the book was subsequently published by Atheneum.

In 1967 **Mary C. Weiss** and **Howard Green** produced colonies of hybrid cells combining genetic material from humans and mice.

Maj. **Robert Michael White**, U.S. Air Force, achieved in 1962 a record altitude of 310,000 feet (58.7 miles) in the rocket-powered X-15 research plane, qualifying him as an astronaut; he was the first to achieve the distinction in a winged aircraft.

In 1960 a team of chemists headed by **Robert W. Woodward** of Harvard University succeeded in synthesizing chlorophyll.

In 1963 **Chien-Shiung Wu** of Columbia University reported on her experiments confirming Richard Feynman and Murray Gell-Mann's theory of the conservation of vector current in nuclear beta decay; her results were important to scientists' understanding of weak nuclear reactions.

AWARDS

NOBEL PRIZE WINNERS

During the 1960s there were fifty-six recipients of Nobel Prizes in the sciences, and half of them were Americans. The Nobel Prize is widely considered to be the highest honor bestowed uopn scientists and signifies worldwide recognition of their work.

1960: Physics, **Donald Glaser**; Chemistry, **Willard F. Libby**

1961: Physics, **Robert Hofstadter**; Chemistry, **Melvin Calvin**; Medicine and/or Physiology, **Georg von Bekesy**

1962: Physiology and/or Medicine, **James D. Watson**

1963: Physics, **Eugene P. Wigner** and **Maria Goeppert-Mayer**

1964: Physiology and/or Medicine, **Konrad E. Bloch**; Physics, **Charles H. Townes**

1965: Physics, **Richard P. Feynman** and **Julian S. Schwinger**; Chemistry, **Robert B. Woodward**

1966: Physiology and/or Medicine, **Francis Peyton Rous** and **Charles B. Huggins**; Chemistry, **Robert S. Mulliken**

1967: Physiology and/or Medicine, **Haldan Keffer Hartline**; Physiology and/or Medicine, **George Wald**; Physics, **Hans A. Bethe**

1968: Physiology and/or Medicine, **Robert W. Holley, H. Gobind Khorana**, and **Marshall W. Nirenberg**; Physics, **Luis W. Alvarez**; Chemistry, **Lars Onsager**

1969: Physics, **Murray Gell-Mann**; Physiology and/or Medicine, **Max Delbruck, Alfred D. Hershey**, and **Salvador Luria**

DEATHS

Roy Chapman Andrews, 76, naturalist, former director of the American Museum of Natural History, 11 March 1960.

Walter Baade, 67, astronomer, first to describe supernovas, 25 June 1960.

Charles William Beebe, 84, biologist and explorer, 4 June 1962.

John Joseph Bittner, 56, geneticist whose researches in cancer were far-reaching, 14 December 1961.

Percy William Bridgman, 78, mathematician and physicist, 20 August 1961.

Dirk Brouwer, 63, Dutch-American astronomer and geophysicist, 31 January 1966.

Rachel L. Carson, 56, marine biologist and author of *The Silent Spring* (1962), which was instrumental in beginning the environmental movement in the United States, 14 April 1964.

William Weber Coblentz, 88, physicist, 15 September 1962.

Arthur Holly Compton, 69, physicist, winner of the 1927 Nobel Prize in physics for his work in quantum physics, 15 March 1962.

Peter Joseph Debye, 82, Dutch-American physical chemist, winner of the 1936 Nobel Prize in chemistry, 2 November 1966.

Lee DeForest, 87, inventor of one of the earliest processes for sound motion pictures, 30 June 1961.

James Franck, 81, physicist, worked on the Manhattan Project, though he opposed actually using the atomic bomb, 21 May 1964.

Casimir Funk, 83, biochemist who coined the word *vitamin*, 20 November 1967.

George Gamow, 64, nuclear physicist who was among the first to propose the big bang theory of the origin of the universe, 19 August 1968.

Theodore von Karman, 81, aeronautical engineer, cofounder of the Aerojet Engineering Company and the Jet Propulsion Laboratory in Pasadena, California, 6 May 1963.

Elmer Verner McCollum, 88, chemist who proved that vitamin D in dairy products and cod liver oil would prevent rickets, 15 November 1967.

Hermann Joseph Muller, 76, geneticist, 5 April 1967.

Eger V. Murphree, 63, scientist who helped establish the Manhattan Project, 29 October 1962.

Seth Barnes Nicholson, 71, astronomer who discovered the four moons of Jupiter, 2 July 1963.

J. Robert Oppenheimer, 62, physicist instrumental in developing the atomic bomb and outspoken opponent of the hydrogen bomb, 18 February 1967.

Gregory Goodwin Pincus, 64, developed oral birth control ("The Pill"), 22 August 1967.

Margaret Sanger, 82, reproductive rights activist, founder of the National Birth Control League, which later became the Planned Parenthood Federation of America, 6 September 1966.

Vesto Melvin Slipher, 93, astronomer who supervised the search that led in 1930 to the discovery of Pluto, 8 November 1969.

Otto Struve, 65, Russian-American astronomer, former president of the International Astronomical Union, 6 April 1963.

Leo Szilard, 66, physicist, helped to develop the atomic bomb, though he opposed its use, 30 May 1964.

Robert Jemison Van de Graaf, 65, physicist who developed a widely used particle generator, 16 January 1967.

Norbert Wiener, 69, mathematician and author of a famous work on cybernetics, 18 March 1964.

PUBLICATIONS

Irving Adler, *The Elementary Mathematics of the Atom* (New York: Day, 1965);

Adler, *Thinking Machines* (New York: Day, 1961);

Isaac Asimov, *Intelligent Man's Guide to Science*, 2 volumes (New York: Basic, 1960);

Asimov, *Life and Energy* (Garden City, N.Y.: Doubleday, 1962);

Charlotte Auerbach, *The Science of Genetics* (New York: Harper, 1961);

Marston Bates, *The Forest and the Sea: A Look at the Economy of Nature and the Ecology of Man* (New York: Random House, 1960);

George Beadle and Muriel Beadle, *The Language of Life* (Garden City, N.Y.: Doubleday, 1966);

Lincoln Bloomfield, ed., *Outer Space* (Englewood Cliffs, N.J.: Prentice-Hall, 1962);

Henry A. Boorse and Lloyd Motz, eds., *The World of the Atom*, 2 volumes (New York: Basic, 1966);

Hal Borland, ed., *Our Natural World* (Garden City, N.Y.: Doubleday, 1965);

R. L. F. Boyd, *Space Research by Rocket and Satellite* (New York: Harper, 1960);

J. Bronowsky, *Insight* (New York: Harper & Row, 1965);

Martin Caidin, *The Astronauts: The Story of Project Mercury, America's Man-in-Space Program* (New York: Dutton, 1960);

Nigel Calder, *Violent Universe: An Eyewitness Account of the New Astronomy* (New York: Viking, 1969);

Sally Carrighar, *Wild Heritage* (Boston: Houghton Mifflin, 1965);

Richard Carrington, *A Biography of the Sea* (New York: Basic, 1961);

Rachel L. Carson, *Silent Spring* (Boston: Houghton Mifflin, 1962);

Robert C. Comen, *Frontiers of the Sea: The Story of Oceanographic Explorations* (Garden City, N.Y.: Doubleday, 1960);

Barry Commoner, *Science and Survival* (New York: Viking, 1966);

Carleton S. Coon, *The Story of Man* (New York: Knopf, 1962);

Henry S. F. Cooper, *Apollo on the Moon* (New York: Dial, 1969);

Donald W. Cox, *The Space Race* (Philadelphia: Chilton, 1962);

John Cunningham, *The Mind of the Dolphin: A Nonhuman Intelligence* (Garden City, N.J.: Doubleday, 1967);

Nuel Pharr Davis, *Lawrence and Oppenheimer* (New York: Simon & Schuster, 1968);

Thomas K. Derry and Trevor I. Williams, *A Short History of Technology from the Earliest Times to A.D. 1900* (New York: Oxford University Press, 1961);

Theodosius Dobzhansky, *Mankind Evolving* (New Haven: Yale University Press, 1962);

Rene Dubos, *The Unseen World* (New York: Oxford University Press, 1962);

Gordon E. Dunn and I. Miller, *Atlantic Hurricanes* (University of Louisiana Press, 1960);

Wolfgang Engelhardt, ed., *Survival of the Free* (New York: Putnam, 1962);

John M. Fowler, *Fallout: A Study of Superbombs, Strontium 90 and Survival* (New York: Basic, 1960);

Edward Frankel, *DNA: Ladder of Life* (New York: McGraw-Hill, 1965);

Otto R. Frisch, *Atomic Physics Today* (New York: Basic, 1961);

George Gamow, *A Planet Called Earth* (New York: Viking, 1963);

Martin Gardner, *Relativity for the Millions* (New York: Macmillan, 1962);

T. F. Gaskell, *Under the Deep Ocean* (New York: Norton, 1960);

William Gilman, *Science: U.S.A.* (New York: Viking, 1965);

William B. Gray, *Creatures of the Sea* (New York: Funk, 1960);

James S. Hanrahan and David Bushnell, *Space Biology: The Human Factors in Space Flight* (New York: Basic, 1960);

Lucia C. Harrison, *Sun, Earth, Time and Man* (Chicago: Rand, McNally, 1960);

Frank G. Hibben, *Digging Up America* (New York: Hill & Wang, 1960);

Fred Hoyle, *Astronomy* (Garden City, N.Y.: Doubleday, 1962);

Hoyle, *Galaxies, Nuclei and Quasars* (New York: Harper & Row, 1965);

Aldous Huxley, *Literature and Science* (New York: Harper & Row, 1963);

Spencer Klaw, *The New Brahmins* (New York: Morrow, 1968);

Konrad Kraus-Kopf and Arthur Beiser, *The Physical Universe* (New York: McGraw-Hill, 1960);

Bernhard Kummel, *History of the Earth* (San Francisco: Freeman, 1961);

Ralph E. Lapp, *Man and Space* (New York: Harper, 1961);

Lapp, *Roads to Discovery* (New York: Harper, 1960);

Robert L. Lehrman, *The Long Road to Man* (New York: Basic, 1961);

George A. Lunberg, *Can Science Save Us?*, revised edition (New York: Longmans, 1961);

John W. Macvey, *Alone in the Universe?* (New York: Macmillan, 1963);

Henry Magenau, *Open Vistas* (New Haven: Yale University Press, 1961);

Martin Mann, *Peacetime Uses of Atomic Energy* (New York: Viking, 1961);

Vincent Marteka, *Bionics* (Philadelphia: Lippincott, 1965);

H. S. W. Massey and Arthur R. Quinton, *Basic Laws of Matter* (Bronxville, N.Y.: Herald Books, 1961);

Robert C. Miller, *The Sea* (New York: Random House, 1966);

Lorus J. Milne and Margery Milne, *The Senses of Animals and Men* (New York: Atheneum, 1962);

Patrick Moore, *Guide to the Planets*, revised edition (New York: Norton, 1960);

Moore, *A Survey of the Moon* (New York: Norton, 1963);

Desmond Morris, *The Naked Ape: A Zoologist's Study of the Human Animal* (New York: McGraw-Hill, 1968);

Sheldon Novick, *The Careless Atom* (Boston: Houghton Mifflin, 1969);

Hugh Odishaw, *The Challenges of Space* (Chicago: University of Chicago Press, 1962);

Stewart E. Perry, *The Human Nature of Science* (New York: Macmillan, 1966);

John Pfeiffer, *The Thinking Machine* (Philadelphia: Lippincott, 1962);

George Porter, *Chemistry for the Modern World* (New York: Barnes & Noble, 1962);

Derek J. de Solla Price, *Science Since Babylon* (New Haven: Yale University Press, 1961);

J. B. Priestley, *Man and Time* (Garden City, N.Y.: Doubleday, 1964);

Magnus Pyke, *The Boundaries of Science* (New York: Barnes & Noble, 1961);

Robert S. Richardson, *Fascinating World of Astronomy* (New York: McGraw, 1960);

Richardson, *Man and the Moon* (New York: World, 1961);

Eric M. Rogers, *Physics for the Inquiring Mind: The Methods, Nature and Philosophy of Physical Science* (Princeton: Princeton University Press, 1960);

Theodor Rosebury, *Life on Man* (New York: Viking, 1969);

Georgio de Santillana, *The Origins of Scientific Thought* (Chicago: University of Chicago Press, 1962);

Paul Shepard and Daniel McKinley, eds., *The Subversive Science: Essays Toward an Ecology of Man* (Boston: Houghton Mifflin, 1969);

Otto Struve and Velta Zebergs, *Astronomy in the Twentieth Century* (New York: Macmillan, 1962);

Ernest P. Walker and others, *Mammals of the World*, 3 volumes (Baltimore: Johns Hopkins University Press, 1965);

James D. Watson, *The Double Helix: A Personal Account of the Discovery of the Structure of DNA* (New York: Atheneum, 1968);

Heinz Woltereck, *What Science Knows about Life* (New York: Association, 1963);

R. H. Wright, *The Science of Smell* (New York: Basic, 1965);

Alfred J. Zaehringer, *Soviet Space Technology* (New York: Harper, 1961).

SPORTS

by RICHARD LAYMAN

CONTENTS

Sidebars and tables are listed in italics.

1960

- National Association for Stock Car Racing (NASCAR) Grand National tracks open at Charlotte, North Carolina, and Atlanta, Georgia.

- The New York Yankees hit a record 193 home runs during the season, winning their twenty-fifth American League pennant; they lose the series in seven games to the Pittsburgh Pirates.

- Approximately 6.5 million Americans participate in organized bowling; the top money winner among professional bowlers is Frank Clause from Old Forge, Pennsylvania, who earns over $100,000.

- Some $2 billion is wagered by an estimated 30 million people at American racetracks; Kelso is horse of the year, winning six consecutive stakes races and registering $293,310 in earnings.

- The second annual National Collegiate Athletic Association (NCAA) soccer championship is won by Saint Louis University 5–2 over the University of Connecticut.

- Professional boxing is the fifth-ranked spectator sport in the United States, attracting some 4 million people annually to live matches.

- For the first time since 1936, the United States fails to reach the challenge round of Davis Cup tennis competition.

26 Jan. Pete Rozelle is named commissioner of the National Football League (NFL).

18–28 Feb. The VIII Winter Olympics are held in Squaw Valley, California; ice-skater (and subsequent gold medal–winner) Carol Heiss is the first woman accorded the honor of reciting the Olympic oath at the opening ceremonies, which are televised live on national television.

19 Mar. Ohio State University wins the NCAA basketball championship, defeating the University of California, Berkeley, 75–55.

10 Apr. Golfer Arnold Palmer wins the Masters Tournament; he earns $71,000 for the season, also finishing first in the U.S. Open on 18 June.

29 May Jim Beatty runs the mile in 3:58, the fastest ever by an American, in the California Relays.

30 May A temporary stand collapses at the Indianapolis 500, killing two and injuring fifty; Jim Rathmann wins the race.

20 June Floyd Patterson becomes the first man to regain a heavyweight title, knocking out Ingemar Johannson in five rounds. The fight brings revenues of over $4 million; Patterson earns $636,000, Johannson $763,000.

Aug.–Sept. The XVII Summer Olympics are held in Rome. Soviets dominate the competition, but Americans Wilma Rudolph, Rafer Johnson, and Cassius Clay are star performers.

12 Aug. Ralph Boston breaks Jesse Owens's twenty-four-year-old record in the broad jump by 3 inches, leaping 26 feet, 11 1/4 inches.

20 Nov. Twenty-five-year-old A. J. Foyt, Jr., wraps up the United States Auto Club (USAC) national championship by winning at Phoenix.

29 Nov. Navy halfback Joe Bellino wins the Heisman Trophy as the outstanding college football player of the year.

Dec. There are more than 20 million paid admissions to college football games. Both Yale and New Mexico State have unbeaten seasons, but Minnesota is the consensus national champion.

26 Dec. The Philadelphia Eagles defeat the Green Bay Packers for the NFL championship; the game brings record revenues of $747,876.

1961

- Phil Hill is the first American to win the Grand Prix driver's championship.

- The American League in professional baseball expands from eight to ten teams, adding a new team in Washington while moving the Senators and renaming them the Minnesota Twins and adding the Los Angeles Angels.

- Kelso is named horse of the year for the second time in a row, posting earnings of $425,565 and winning seven of nine races.

- Saint Louis University wins the NCAA soccer championships, beating the University of Maryland 3–2.

2 Jan. Seventeen-year-old Bobby Fischer wins his fourth consecutive U.S. chess championship.

15 Feb. The entire U.S. figure-skating team is killed in a plane crash while traveling to the world championships in Prague.

Mar. Seventeen-year-old Steve Clark shatters the 100-yard freestyle swimmimg record by 1.4 seconds with a time of 46.8 seconds.

13 Mar. Floyd Patterson retains his heavyweight boxing championship, knocking out Ingemar Johannson in three rounds; this third meeting between the two makes their rivalry the longest series ever for the heavyweight championship.

25 Mar. Favored Ohio State, featuring All-American Jerry Lucas and Bobby Knight, loses the NCAA basketball championship to the University of Cincinnati 70–65; Ohio State draws 342,938 fans to its twenty-eight games of the season.

16 Apr. The Chicago Black Hawks win the Stanley Cup in ice hockey, beating the Montreal Canadiens four games to two.

6 May Carry Back wins the Kentucky Derby and two weeks later the Preakness before suffering an injury in the Belmont and thus missing the Triple Crown of horse racing.

1 Oct. Roger Maris hits a record sixty-one home runs to break Babe Ruth's record of sixty set in 1927, but he achieves the feat in a season eight games longer than Ruth's.

4–9 Oct. The New York Yankees win the World Series in five games over the Cincinnati Reds; a winning player's share is $7,979.11.

Dec. Syracuse University halfback Ernie Davis wins the Heisman Trophy; the University of Alabama is the national champion in college football.

31 Dec. The New York Giants are humiliated 37–0 by the Green Bay Packers in a freezing game in Wisconsin.

1962

- The Ford Motor Company announces that it will begin participation in auto racing.

- The National League in baseball expands to ten teams, adding the Houston Colts and the New York Mets.

- Maury Wills steals 104 bases during the major-league baseball season, breaking Ty Cobb's record of 96 set in 1916.

- The professional American Basketball League (ABL) is established.

- Don Carter, with season's earnings of $49,014, is named professional bowler of the year.

- With career earnings of over $1 million, Kelso is named horse of the year for the third year in a row.

- West Chester State Teachers College defeats Saint Louis University in the NCAA soccer championships.

10 Feb. Jim Beatty becomes the first person to run the mile indoors in under 4 minutes; his time is 3:58.9. On 8 June he sets a world record for two miles with a time of 8:29.8.

17 Mar. *Miss U.S. I* of Detroit, an unlimited hydroplane driven by Roy Duby, sets a world motorboat speed record of 200.419 MPH.

24 Mar. For the second straight year the University of Cincinnati beats Ohio State in the NCAA basketball championship.

18 Apr. The Boston Celtics win the National Basketball Association (NBA) championship, defeating the Los Angeles Lakers in a seven-game series.

30 May Rodger Ward wins the Indianapolis 500; he also wins the USAC championship for 1962.

13 July Arnold Palmer wins the second British Open in a row; he also sets a record for annual earnings in professional golf, winning $88,000 during the year.

Sept. *Weatherly*, captained by Emil Mosbacher, Jr., defends the America's Cup against Australia, winning four of five races.

25 Sept. Sonny Liston knocks out Floyd Patterson in 2:06 of the first round to win the heavyweight boxing championship. Patterson's purse is some $1.2 million.

17 Oct. The New York Yankees win their twentieth World Series in twenty-seven attempts, beating the San Francisco Giants four games to three.

27 Nov. Running back Terry Baker of Oregon State University wins the Heisman Trophy.

Dec. The University of Southern California goes undefeated in college football and is named national champion.

23 Dec. The Dallas Texans beat the Houston Oilers 20–17 in sudden death overtime to win the American Football League (AFL) title, for which a winning player's share is $2,261.80.

30 Dec. The Green Bay Packers beat the New York Giants in the NFL championship game, for which a winning player's share is $5,888.57.

1963

- General Motors tightens restrictions on support of automobile racing.

- Both Jack Nicklaus and Arnold Palmer win over $100,000; Palmer wins seven Professional Golfers' Association (PGA) tournaments; Nicklaus wins two major tournaments, including the Masters and the PGA championship.

- Kelso is named horse of the year after winning eight straight stakes races.

- Saint Louis University wins its fourth NCAA soccer championship in five years, defeating Navy 3–0 in the finals.

23 Mar. Loyola University becomes the first independent to win the NCAA basketball tournament, beating the University of Cincinnati 60–58 in overtime.

24 Apr. The Boston Celtics defeat the Los Angeles Lakers in six games to win the NBA championship.

30 May Parnelli Jones wins the Indianapolis 500 in a controversial race after stewards fail to order him off the track because his engine is throwing oil into the paths of other racers.

24 Aug. Vaulter John Pennel of Northeast Louisiana State College sets a world record of 17 feet, 3/4 inch.

25 Sept. Sonny Liston defends his heavyweight boxing championship against Floyd Patterson with a second first-round knockout.

6 Oct. Behind star pitcher Sandy Koufax, the Los Angeles Dodgers win the World Series over the New York Yankees in four games.

23 Nov. The Army-Navy football game is played on the day after the assassination of President John Kennedy at the request of the family. The president had planned to attend.

Dec. The University of Texas goes undefeated in college football to win the national championship. The Heisman Trophy is won by Navy quarterback Roger Staubach.

28 Dec. Chuck McKinley and Dennis Ralston lead the United States to a championship in Davis Cup tennis competition.

29 Dec. The Chicago Bears beat the New York Giants for the NFL championship 14–10.

1964

- Richard Petty sets a record average speed of 154.144 MPH at the Daytona 500 and wins the Grand National NASCAR championship.

- Major-league baseball games are attended by 21,280,346 fans during the year.

- Kelso breaks the all-time winnings record in horse racing as he becomes the horse of the year for an unprecedented fifth time.

5 Jan. The San Diego Chargers beat the Boston Patriots 51–10 in the AFL championship.

29 Jan. The IX Winter Olympics open in Innsbruck, Austria.

25 Feb. After being fined $2,500 by the Miami Boxing Commission for disorderly conduct at the weigh-in, Cassius Clay beats Sonny Liston for the heavyweight boxing championship when Liston fails to answer the bell for the seventh round; after his victory Clay announces that his name is Cassius X and that he has joined the Black Muslims.

21 Mar. UCLA wins thirty games in a row and the NCAA basketball championship, defeating Duke University 98–83 in the final game.

26 Apr.   The Boston Celtics defeat the San Francisco Warriers in five games to win the NBA championship.

30 May   A. J. Foyt, Jr., wins the Indianapolis 500, in which veteran driver Eddie Sachs is killed; Foyt wins ten of twelve USAC Championship Trail races during the year.

20 June   Ken Venturi wins the U.S. Open, posting a thirty on the first nine of the third round; he is treated for heat exhaustion between the third and fourth rounds.

21 June   Jim Bunning pitches a perfect baseball game against the New York Mets.

7–15 Oct.   The Saint Louis Cardinals beat the New York Yankees four games to three in the World Series.

10 Oct.   The XVII Olympics open in Tokyo; American swimmer Don Schollander wins four of the U.S. team total of thirty gold medals.

27 Oct.   Driving the $60,000 Green Monster, driver Art Arfons breaks the land speed record, traveling 536.71 MPH.

24 Nov.   John Huarte, Notre Dame quarterback, is the Heisman Trophy winner.

Dec.   The Universities of Alabama and Arkansas are undefeated in collegiate football, and Alabama wins the national championship.

26 Dec.   The Buffalo Bills beat the Boston Patriots 24–14 for the AFL title.

27 Dec.   The Cleveland Browns beat the Baltimore Colts 27–0 for the NFL championship.

1965

- Ned Jarrett is the NASCAR points champion.

- The Daytona Beach Continental sports car race is lengthened to twenty-four hours to rival the twenty-four-hour endurance race at Le Mans.

20 Mar.   UCLA beats the University of Michigan 91–80 to win their second consecutive NCAA basketball championship.

10 Apr.   Jack Nicklaus wins the Masters by a record nine strokes.

25 Apr.   The Boston Celtics win their seventh NBA title in a row, defeating the Los Angeles Lakers four games to one.

8 May   Randy Matson sets a world record in the shot put with a throw of 70 feet, 7 inches.

25 May   Muhammad Ali retains his title in a first-round knockout of Sonny Liston and on 22 November a twelfth-round knockout of Floyd Patterson.

30 May   Jim Clark, the world driving champion, wins the Indianapolis 500.

6–14 Oct.   The Los Angeles Dodgers beat the Minnesota Twins four games to three in the World Series.

15 Nov.   Craig Breedlove sets a world land speed record of 600.601 MPH in the Spirit of America.

23 Nov.   Mike Garrett, University of Southern California running back, wins the Heisman Trophy.

Dec.	Michigan State is the consensus national collegiate football champion.
11 Dec.	Saint Louis University wins the NCAA soccer championship over Michigan State 1–0.
26 Dec	The Green Bay Packers beat the Cleveland Browns 23–12 to win the NFL championship.

1966

- Chrysler announces that it will no longer support a factory racing team after the current NASCAR season; David Pearson is Grand National driving champion.

- William D. Eckert is named commissioner of baseball.

- Frank Robinson wins the Triple Crown, leading major-league baseball players in runs batted in (RBIs), home runs, and batting average; he hits the longest home run ever at Baltimore Memorial Stadium—540 feet.

- Buckpasser, the first three-year-old thoroughbred ever to win $1 million, is named horse of the year.

- The University of San Francisco beats Long Island University 5–2 to win the NCAA soccer championship.

- Chicago Black Hawks wing Bobby Hull scores a record fifty-four goals in his twentieth season as a professional hockey player.

- The National Hockey League (NHL) expands to twelve teams, awarding franchises to Los Angeles, San Francisco–Oakland, Pittsburgh, Saint Louis, Minneapolis–Saint Paul, and Philadelphia for the 1967–1968 season.

2 Jan.	The Buffalo Bills beat the San Diego Chargers 23–0 to win the AFL championship.
27 Feb.	Seventeen-year-old, three-time U.S. champion Peggy Fleming wins the world figure-skating championship in Switzerland.
19 Mar.	Highly favored, all-white University of Kentucky is upset in the finals of the NCAA tournament by Texas Western College, 72–65.
8 Apr.	The first athletic event ever is played on astro turf at the Houston Astrodome.
11 Apr.	Jack Nicklaus is the first golfer ever to win two Masters titles in succession.
28 Apr.	The Boston Celtics beat the Los Angeles Lakers in seven games to win the NBA championship. Bill Russell is named coach of the Celtics; he is the first black ever to coach a major-league team.
30 May	After eleven of the thirty-three cars are so damaged they cannot continue on the first lap of the Indianapolis 500, British driver Graham Hill wins the race, and Scotsman Jim Clark is second; only four cars complete the five hundred miles.
8 June	The AFL and NFL announce plans to merge.
20 June	Billy Casper beats Arnold Palmer in a play-off to win the U.S. Open golf championship.

1967

17 July   Nineteen-year-old Jim Ryun sets a world record of 3:51.3 in the mile, lowering the previous record by 2.3 seconds.

5–9 Oct.   The Baltimore Orioles sweep the World Series in four games over the Los Angeles Dodgers; after the series Dodger pitcher Sandy Koufax retires at the peak of his career.

19 Nov.   Before the largest television audience ever for a regularly scheduled game (30 million), the University of Michigan and Notre Dame University battle to a 10–10 tie as Notre Dame is criticized for playing a safe game at the end rather than going for a win; the two teams split the accolade of national champion.

22 Nov.   Quarterback Steve Spurrier of the University of Florida wins the Heisman Trophy.

- Richard Petty is NASCAR points champion, winning ten straight races.

- Damascus is named horse of the year, although he finished third in the Kentucky Derby won by Darby Dan.

- Larry Mahan wins the all-around rodeo championship with earnings of $51,966 for the year.

- The NCAA championship soccer game between Michigan State and Saint Louis ends in a 0–0 tie.

- The NFL expands to sixteen teams, adding the New Orleans Saints; the AFL adds the Cincinnati Bengals.

15 Jan.   The Green Bay Packers beat the Kansas City Chiefs 35–10 in the first professional football Super Bowl.

25 Mar.   Star center Lew Alcindor is named player of the year, and John Wooden is named coach of the year as they lead UCLA to an undefeated season and NCAA basketball championship over the University of Dayton, 79–64.

24 Apr.   The Philadelphia 76ers, led by league Most Valuable Player (MVP) Wilt Chamberlain, win the NBA championship over the San Francisco Warriors in six games.

30 May   Andy Granatelli's STP Special turbine-powered car driven by Parnelli Jones dominates the Indianapolis 500 but drops out three laps before the finish as A. J. Foyt, Jr., wins.

20 June   Muhammad Ali is found guilty in federal court of draft evasion. His boxing titles are stripped from him.

23 June   Jim Ryun lowers his world record in the mile to 3:51.1 and on 8 July sets a new world mark in the 1,500 meters of 3:33.1.

23 July–6 Aug.   The United States wins 225 of the 537 medals awarded to twenty-seven nations in the Pan-American games.

Sept.   The *Intrepid* defends the America's Cup with four straight wins against the Australian yacht *Dame Pattie*.

4–12 Oct.	The Saint Louis Cardinals beat the Boston Red Sox in seven games to win the World Series.
28 Nov.	Quarterback Gary Beban of UCLA wins the Heisman Trophy.
Dec.	The University of Southern California is the consensus national collegiate football champion.

1968

- David Pearson wins the NASCAR points championship, but fellow South Carolinian Cale Yarborough wins the most money (over $130,000) during the season.

- The NBA expands to fourteen teams, adding franchises in Phoenix, Milwaukee, Seattle, and San Diego.

- The new American Basketball Association (ABA) establishes a legitimate bid for a professional league to rival the NBA.

- Larry Mahan wins the Rodeo Cowboys Association all-around championship for third time in a row.

- For the second straight year, the NCAA soccer championship game ends in a tie as Michigan State and the University of Maryland end their game with the score 2–2.

14 Jan.	The Green Bay Packers beat the Oakland Raiders 33–14 in the second Super Bowl.
10 Feb.	Peggy Fleming wins an Olympic gold medal in figure skating.
23 Mar.	UCLA beats the University of North Carolina 78–55 to win the NCAA basketball championship.
Mar.–Apr.	ABC television jointly sponsors an eight-man tournament to determine the heavyweight boxing championship; Jimmy Ellis wins on 27 April, but Joe Frazier, who had refused to compete because of the promotions contract required by tournament organizers, is generally acknowledged as the best of the heavyweights.
14 Apr.	Bob Goalby wins the Masters golf tournament when Roberto de Vicenzo signs a scorecard that records one more stroke than he actually played; de Vicenzo would have tied had the score been kept accurately, but tournament rules stipulate that once a player signs his card, it cannot be changed for any reason.
2 May	The Boston Celtics, led by player-coach Bill Russell, win the NBA championship in six games.
4 May	Dancer's Image is disqualified as winner of the Kentucky Derby after a urine test shows signs of a painkiller. Two weeks later the horse is disqualified for obstruction after finishing third in the Preakness.
30 May	Bobby Unser wins the Indianapolis 500, his fourth victory in a row.
30 July	Ron Hansen of the Washington Senators makes an unassisted triple play, the first in forty-one years.
8 Sept.	Billy Schumacher in *Miss Bardahl* wins the Gold Cup for hydroplane racers with speeds of up to 130 MPH in straightaways.

8 Sept. Tennis player Billie Jean King turns pro; she loses in the finals of the U.S. Open to Virginia Wade.

2–10 Oct. In a pitching duel the Detroit Tigers beat the Saint Louis Cardinals in seven games to win the World Series.

14–28 Oct. The XIX Olympics open. In the thin air of Mexico world-record performances are commonplace. In track and field events fourteen world records are set, nine by Americans. Al Oerter wins his fourth Olympic gold medal in the discus throw. American medal winners Tommie Smith (who set a world record in the 200-meter race) and John Carlos are stripped of their honors and suspended from the team for raising their fists in a black power salute during the playing of the national anthem at the awards ceremony.

26 Nov. University of Southern California running back O. J. Simpson wins the Heisman Trophy.

1969

- David Pearson wins his third NASCAR points championship in four years.

- The NFL and AFL receive $34.7 million from CBS and NBC for the rights to televise professional football games.

- Arnold Palmer is forced to qualify for the U.S. Open, won by Orville Moody.

- Saint Louis University beats San Francisco 4–0 to win the NCAA soccer championship.

- Despite winning nine of ten races and beating Arts and Letters two races to one in head-to-head competition, Majestic Prince loses out to Arts and Letters in voting for the best three-year-old of the thoroughbred racing season and horse of the year.

1 Jan. Ohio State is named national collegiate football champion after beating the University of Southern California 27–16 in the Rose Bowl.

12 Jan. The New York Jets beat the Baltimore Colts 16–7 in the third Super Bowl, becoming the first AFL team to win the championship and establishing the competitiveness of the AFL.

1 Feb. Vince Lombardi retires as coach of the Green Bay Packers.

4 Feb. Bowie Kuhn replaces William Eckert as commissioner of baseball.

22 Mar. Lew Alcindor wraps up his collegiate basketball career by leading UCLA to its third straight NCAA championship over Purdue, 92–72.

5 May The Boston Celtics win the NBA championship for the eleventh time in thirteen years, defeating the Los Angeles Lakers in seven games.

30 May Mario Andretti wins a record purse of $809,627 in the Indianapolis 500.

14 June Don Aronow wins the Bahamas 500 powerboat race in the *Cigarette*, breaking the previous course record by 2:35:45.

16 June   Weight lifter Bob Bednarski, competing in the 242-pound class at the American Athletic Union senior championships, sets U.S. and world records in the snatch (347 1/2 pounds), clean and jerk (462 1/2 pounds), and total lifts (1,215 pounds).

11–16 Oct.   The New York Mets, who had finished ninth in the National League in 1968, win the World Series over the Baltimore Orioles in five games.

1970

1 Jan.   The University of Texas is named the national collegiate football champion after beating Notre Dame 21–17 in the Cotton Bowl.

11 Jan.   The Kansas City Chiefs beat the Minnesota Vikings 23–7 in the Super Bowl.

OVERVIEW

Winning. Vince Lombardi's motto "Winning is not everything; it is the only thing" defines fans' and players' attitudes toward sports during the 1960s. It was the decade when American cynicism infected athletic competition. The ideal of amateurism, in which physical achievement was viewed as a complement to intellectual development, was considered increasingly naive as sports became big business.

The Decline of Amateurism. The showcase of amateur athletic competition is the Olympics, which were held three times during the 1960s, each meeting demonstrating with sharper clarity the evolution of the new-age athlete as an entertainer who performed for money and for a paying audience. The first televised Olympic Games were in 1960, and by 1964 the sports businesspeople were poised to take advantage. At first a star performance in the United States brought its rewards after the games were over, when the athlete could capitalize on his or her fame, endorsing products or performing professionally, especially in ice skating and boxing. By 1964 commercialism had invaded the games themselves, as shoe manufacturers paid contestants to sport their logos in front of television cameras, and the world's greatest athletes hawked products with nearly as much energy as they pursued their games. Winning was the only thing because that was how a performer attracted sponsors, ensured endorsement contracts, and prepared for a professional career.

Drugs and Gambling. As the urgency to win increased, so did the lengths athletes would go to achieve victory. Steroids were popularized in the United States during the 1960s to provide good performers the edge they needed to achieve greatness. The long-term health cost was not yet fully known, but it was clear that the performance-enhancing drugs of the day had unpleasant side effects. Drugs, long a staple in horse racing, were the subject of sports headlines in 1968 when Dancer's Image was disqualified as winner of the Kentucky Derby after it was found he had been injected with a painkiller. Sports gamblers wanted surer bets than athletic superiority could provide. It came as no surprise to savvy fans when a Senate committee exposed mob influence of televised boxing and proved that some professional boxing matches were fixed. It was more shocking, however, when the New York district attorney uncovered widespread cheating in college basketball early in the decade, the second such scandal since World War II. In 1962 two of the most respected professional football players in the nation, Paul Hornung of the Green Bay Packers and Alex Karras of the Detroit Lions, were suspended for betting on football games and associating with undesirables. Karras had been All-Pro three years in a row, and Hornung had set the single-season scoring record in 1960, but they were suspended even though there was no evidence of game fixing. Team owners were eager to cover up any appearance of corruption.

The Fans. But fans were undeterred. Television brought a new dimension to sports as it developed the technology to present games so that viewers could watch them at home with full appreciation of every nuance. Sports broadcasts were enhanced by the explanations of commentators and the opportunity to see instant replays of key action, in slow motion if necessary. The major sports vied with one another for recognition as the nation's game. Americans did not abandon their beloved baseball, but they found that on television it lacked the drama of a good football game and fell far short of the action offered by even routine basketball. College sports were attractive to television producers because they were cheaper to broadcast. Professional team owners had learned by the end of the decade how to negotiate a television contract, but collegiate athletic directors lagged behind. Coaches at individual schools knew the basic element of fan appeal, however, whether the audience was in the stands or in the living rooms: fans like winners, and so winning was, in the view of many college coaches, the only thing. It assured their jobs and attracted the support they needed to recruit the best athletes possible, regardless of the cost.

Players Band Together. The players, both professional and amateur, were not so busy at their games that they failed to see the business opportunities the new sports-entertainment industry offered. They organized to ensure that their interests were served as revenues they generated increased. The Major League Baseball Players Association negotiated its first contract halfway through the decade, National Football League (NFL) players agitated for better benefits and higher pay, sports agents began representing individual athletes, and even the predominantly southern National Association of Race Car Drivers banded together in 1969 to form a union in the region of the country where unions were least favored. Money was not the only issue pursued by athletes' organizations. In 1968 the Olympic Project for Human Rights represented radical black athletes who demanded an end to racism in sports and demonstrated at the Olympic Games to make their point.

Race. As in all of America during the 1960s race was an overriding issue in sports. Black players were openly admitted to be superior to whites in basketball, and black players clearly changed the character of the game during the decade, bringing speed, jumping ability, and showmanship to a sport that had been dominated by shooters and methodical defenders. Heavyweight boxing champion Muhammad Ali used his position as the most recognizable sports figure in the world to express his controversial views on race. Black baseball players achieved something like parity with white players during the decade, but the attitude did not extend to the front office. Managers and owners were white. Similarly, in football there were as many black players as white by the end of the decade, but the thinking positions — quarterback and middle linebacker — were reserved for white players, who also tended to make more money.

Money. During the 1960s athletes were paid well. In baseball Sandy Koufax and Don Drysdale made well over $100,000 a year in 1966, though the average player made one-fifth of that amount. Professional golfers Jack Nicklaus and Arnold Palmer routinely made over $100,000 a season during the decade, but they were outstanding performers who set earnings records year after year. A winner at Indianapolis won a purse of nearly $200,000 by the end of the decade (of which the driver made about 10 percent), and National Association of Stock Car Auto Racing (NASCAR) driver Lee Roy Yarbrough earned over $188,000 in 1969, but he won seven Grand National races, a rare achievement. Football star Joe Namath signed with the New York Jets for over $400,000 in 1965, but starting professional football players made about $20,000 on average by the end of the decade.

Memories. Sports may have suffered the indignities of commercialization, the embarrassment of scandals, and the trauma of racial strife during the 1960s, but fans were rewarded nonetheless with memorable performances by remarkable athletes: the masterful pitching of Koufax and the meteoric rise from cellar to championship by the amazing Mets in baseball; the gritty domination of the Green Bay Packers in professional football, and the All-American performances of Navy stars Joe Bellino and Roger Staubach, for whom professional fame was less important than satisfying their obligations to their country in the armed services; the record-setting championship streak of the Boston Celtics, and Bill Russell's demonstration that a black man could not only play center for a National Basketball Association (NBA) championship team — he could coach it as well; the dramatic career of Muhammad Ali, one of the finest boxers in history, whose career is just as notable for his activities outside the ring as for his remarkable boxing skills; the racing genius of A. J. Foyt and Richard Petty, who took their sport to a new level of speed and daring. These were among the most famous of a generation of athletes who achieved unprecedented status as cultural heroes.

TOPICS IN THE NEWS

AUTO RACING: NASCAR

Bill France and NASCAR. The National Association of Stock Car Auto Racing (NASCAR) was founded by racing promoter Bill France in 1947 to showcase the talents of southern whiskey runners in their modified street cars, souped up so they could outrun country sheriffs. By 1960 NASCAR had developed a well-organized professional racing circuit confined, largely, to the South. NASCAR was southern: most of its driving stars and its core of fan support came from the South. The sport had national appeal, though, as the American automobile manufacturers recognized. Early in the decade they sponsored the NASCAR racing season by providing high-performance versions of current showroom models. It was an effective sales tool in a time when speed sold cars, and by the time manufacturers abandoned racing because it was too expensive and because of social pressures to refrain from endorsement of a dangerous sport, NASCAR was self-sufficient.

Whiskey-Running Tradition. At the beginning of the 1960s NASCAR racing was dominated by former whis-key runners turned legitimate. They drank hard up to the night before a race and knew no limits on the track. Fans delighted in the frequency of pileups and in the uninhibited style of the drivers, who would hit and bump their competitors at high speeds and go all out to win regardless of the conditions. Midwesterner Fred Lorenzen was the only major NASCAR driver in the early 1960s who did not serve his apprenticeship on dirt tracks.

Factory Sponsorship. The Automobile Manufacturers Association agreed in 1957 not to provide factory sponsorship of organized racing. In 1962 Ford announced that it would no longer abide by the agreement, and the other major manufacturers soon followed suit. NASCAR racing was the beneficiary. A key NASCAR statistic was the manufacturers' rating, which listed the number of wins by the make of car; race lineups always named the manufacturer just after the driver.

Fireball Roberts. By 1964 the sport had become too dangerous for the manufacturers to support. Richard Petty won the Daytona 500 that year with an average speed of 154.33 MPH, 7 MPH faster than A. J. Foyt,

The crash during the 1964 World 600 at the Charlotte Motor Speedway in which Glenn ("Fireball") Roberts was killed. His car is engulfed in flames at right.

Lee Roy Yarbrough after winning the 1969 Southern 500 at Darlington, South Carolina.

Jr.'s winning average at the Indianapolis 500. At the World 600 one of the finest drivers of the day, Fireball Roberts, died after a fiery crash. Roberts was burned over 40 percent of his body, and in his thirty-nine days in the hospital he received 123 pints of blood. When he died on 2 July 1964 the *Charlotte* (North Carolina) *News* wrote, "Fireball Roberts, perhaps the most nearly perfect of all stock car drivers, is dead and it is like awakening to find a mountain is suddenly gone." Veteran driver Jim Pardue died at the same track later in the year. Chrysler announced that it was withdrawing from sponsorship of NASCAR racing. Ford followed suit the next year, temporarily, though less in response to the danger of the sport than to the NASCAR ruling that the company's new 427-cubic-inch engine would have to carry 427 pounds of additional weight during races as an equalizer.

Richard Petty. Factory sponsorship was limited by 1967, when thirty-year-old Richard Petty stood out as the preeminent stock-car driver of the time. With his father, former driver Lee Petty, serving as mechanic, Richard Petty won twenty-seven of forty-eight races and finished in the top five in all except ten. He won ten straight races and set a season earnings record of $130,275. In 1969 the season's earning record was eclipsed by Lee Roy Yarbrough of Columbia, South Carolina, who won seven major races, including the Daytona 500, the Rebel 400, the Firecracker 400, the Dixie 500, and the Southern 500, for total earnings of $188,605.

Petty for President. By 1969 NASCAR had a membership of twenty thousand race supporters and sponsored a full complement of fifty-one sanctioned races. The drivers had organized the Professional Drivers' Association, with Richard Petty as president, and had begun acting like a labor union, boycotting the new Grand National (the designation for NASCAR-sponsored feature events) track at Talladega and lobbying for better health insurance, pension plans, and more accessible bathrooms. The factory sponsors were gone, but NASCAR racing was thriving.

Sources:
Kim Chapin, *Fast as White Lightning: The Story of Stock Car Racing* (New York: Dial, 1981);

Collier's Encyclopedia Yearbooks.

JUST GOOD OLD BOYS

Fireball Roberts and Fred Lorenzen were rivals, even when they raced Fords together on the Moody team beginning with the 1963 season. Before that, they were dangerous when they got close to one another on the racetrack, as they often did, Roberts in his gold Pontiac and Lorenzen in a black Ford. In 1962 at Martinsville, Virginia, the two drivers crashed. Here are two versions of what happened.

Lorenzen: "I was running good, but I wasn't thinking. Sometimes I'd lose my head and Moody couldn't get to me that day. I was still a little cocky, I suppose, and I felt that I was running so much faster than Fireball that, Move, boy. I'm coming through. Because I couldn't go around. It was too hard at Martinsville. But He wouldn't move, so I rapped him in the bumper a little bit."

Ford Factory representative Jacque Passino: "Lorenzen kept tapping him, tapping him, trying to get around, and Fireball was glib enough that he wouldn't let him. But he finally got tired of it. So they're going into the goddamned third turn, and Fireball spiked the brakes. Now Christ, Lorenzen hit him a ton. He broke the gas tank in Roberts's car, but he broke his own radiator, too. So the both of them were out of the race. They thought that was the funniest thing that ever happened to them."

Source: Kim Chapin, *Fast as White Lightning: The Story of Stock Car Racing* (New York: Dial, 1981).

Auto Racing: USAC

The founding of USAC. In the major leagues of auto racing there are two types of cars: Indianapolis, or Indy-type racers, made expressly for the race course and undrivable on public roads are the sleekest; stock cars, radically modified versions of automobiles available in dealer showrooms, run at about the same speed as the Indy racers and seem closer to life to many race fans, especially in the South. The United States Auto Club (USAC), the governing body for Indy-type racers, was formed in September 1955 by the owner of the Indianapolis Speedway, Tony Hulman. The Indianapolis 500 has since 1911 been the most respected automobile race in America, and Hulman wanted to be sure it stayed that way. USAC ran a full season of racing and named a champion each year, but the crowning event of the season was the Indianapolis 500.

New Cars for a New Age. During the 1960s Indianapolis was under assault from new kinds of cars with new kinds of engines. Colin Chapman, the respected British carmaker whose Lotus chassis had carried its drivers to Grand Prix championships in Europe, developed a revolutionary Indianapolis car; Ford brought its engineering expertise to the track and by the end of the decade had replaced the venerable Offenhauser engine; car owner Andy Granatelli introduced the turbine engine that protesting drivers said should be outlawed because it was better suited to power airplanes than race cars.

A. J. Foyt. The most successful USAC driver of the decade was a brash, cocky, temperamental young man named A. J. Foyt, Jr., who proclaimed, "All I want to do is win. It just makes me madder than hell to lose." Foyt was twenty-six in 1960, the year he won his first USAC championship. He won that title again in 1961, 1963, 1964, and 1967. In addition, he won the Indianapolis 500 in 1961 and 1964; in 1967, twelve days after winning the twenty-four-hour race at Le Mans in a Ford Mark IV prototype, a much different car from the Indy-type racer,

he won his third Indianapolis 500 in record-breaking time (averaging 151.207 MPH) in a rear-engine Coyote-Ford that he designed himself. His 1967 Indianapolis win brought him a purse of $171,227.

European "Funny Cars." The first signs that Indy racers were about to be transformed appeared in 1961, when Australian driver Jack Brabham qualified for the race with a modified grand prix car that Foyt said looked like "a bunch of pipes lashed up with chicken wire." The car was called a European "funny car," in derision of the Formula One racers that were run on the European grand prix circuit. Before the European invasion Indy cars were more or less uniform: 96-inch wheelbase, tubular frame, solid axles front and back, with 18-inch tires on the back and 16-inch tires on the front. The engine was a four-cylinder, 256-cubic-inch Offenhauser mounted in front of the driver. The car weighed about 1,700 pounds.

Colin Chapman. Prompted by Brabham's respectable showing, grand prix driver Dan Gurney invited British designer Colin Chapman to the 1962 Indianapolis 500 as a spectator. Chapman went home and designed three cars for Indianapolis. They were rear-engine, independent-suspension cars with modified Ford Fairlane engines that developed 370 horsepower, about 80 horsepower less than the Offenhausers. But Chapman's Lotus cars weighed only 1,150 pounds; in 1963 at Indianapolis they were driven by Gurney and the greatest race-car driver of the day, Scots sheep farmer Jimmy Clark. That year, in a car with a suspension not yet tuned for the two-and-a-half-mile oval at Indianapolis and on a track slippery at the end of the race with oil thrown from the engine of race leader Parnelli Jones, Clark spun out three times in the turns and showed his driving skill each time by clutching, revving his engine to prevent it from stalling while he gained control of the car, and continuing on his way to a second-place finish. In 1965, with a new Ford engine, Clark and Colin Chapman won the race. By the end of the decade Ford had replaced Offenhauser as the engine of choice, and Chapman's Lotus chassis was the most respected design at Indianapolis.

Turbine Power. In 1967 owner Andy Granatelli, who had tried for eighteen years to field an Indy winner, entered a turbine-powered car in the race. It was a revolutionary design that swooshed rather than roared down the sraightaways. Driven by Parnelli Jones, who seemed ruthless in pursuit of victory, Granatelli's car, called the STP Special, seemed clearly superior. Jones led for most of the race; then with three laps remaining a six-dollar ball bearing in the gearbox failed, and Jones was unable to continue. A month after the race, USAC changed the rules to limit the power the turbine could generate.

Source:
Charles Fox, *The Great Racing Cars & Drivers* (New York: Grosset & Dunlap, 1972).

A. J. Foyt, Jr., in his winning car at the 1967 Indianapolis 500

Maury Wills (30) stealing his 104th base of the 1962 season, breaking Ty Cobb's record

BASEBALL: THE GAME FACE

A Two-Faced Game. Baseball had two faces during the 1960s, one shown on the field, the other in the board room. On the field baseball was a glorious game played by enthusiastic athletes who seemed truly to enjoy their participation in the nation's game. Their performances were spectacular as they demonstrated skills that reshaped the game.

1960: Stengel Retires. The 1960s began with a changing of the guard. Casey Stengel, arguably the greatest manager of modern times, was forced to retire at the age of seventy. He was down but not out. A year later he returned to baseball as the bemused manager of the expansion team New York Mets. Ted Williams, the great Boston Red Sox hitter, retired in his nineteenth season at the age of forty-two; he hit .316 his last season. The New York Yankees hit 193 home runs in 1960, the most ever in an American League season, but their hitting power was inadequate to secure a World Series victory against the Pittsburgh Pirates, who played in their first championship series since 1927, when Babe Ruth and Lou Gehrig led the Yankees to a four-game sweep. In 1960 it took seven games and a bad bounce on a grounder to Yankee shortstop Tony Kubek in the eighth inning for the Pirates to win the Series.

A New Home-Run Record. Roger Maris hit a record-breaking 61 home runs in 1961, breaking the single-season record set by Babe Ruth in 1927; even though Maris's record carries an asterisk, indicating that his season was eight games longer than Ruth's, the 1961 season was enlivened by Maris's play. Maris's teammate Mickey Mantle, often playing hurt, had a much better batting average than Maris and hit 54 home runs while batting .314. Willie Mays, meanwhile, proved himself perhaps the best all-around player in the game. In 1961 he hit 4 of his season-total 40 home runs in a single game, and he hit 49 homers in 1962; his grace and speed in the outfield delighted San Francisco Giants fans. The best hitters in the game that season had batting averages nearly .100 better than Maris; they were Norman Cash of the Detroit

Tigers, with .361, and Roberto Clemente of the Pittsburgh Pirates, with .351. After 1961 batting performances declined markedly, due in part to rules changes that altered the strike zone. In the World Series the Yankees beat the Cincinnati Reds handily in five games.

Maury Wills, Stealer. In 1962 the fleet Los Angeles Dodger Maury Wills stole 104 bases (including 2 steals of home base), breaking the record of 96 set by Ty Cobb in 1915. American League pitchers threw four no-hitters in 1962, and another was registered in the National League. The National League pennant race was won the last day of the season when the San Francisco Giants caught the Los Angeles Dodgers after trailing all season and won the playoff. Despite excellent hitting the Giants lost the World Series to the Yankees in seven games.

The Great Koufax. Sandy Koufax, the Brooklyn-born pitching star of the Los Angeles Dodgers, struck out 306 men in 1963, a record. A twenty-five-game winner, Koufax lead the major leagues with an earned run average (ERA) of 1.88 and threw two no-hitters. In the Dodgers' World Series sweep against the Yankees, Koufax pitched two full games. He threw no-hitters in four successive seasons, 1962 through 1965, including a perfect game in 1965.

Bunning Is Perfect. New York Yankee domination had come to be expected in the American League by 1964, when they had won fourteen of the last sixteen pennants, but the team showed signs of weakening when they did not clinch a World Series berth until the next-to-last day of the season. The Saint Louis Cardinals won the National League pennant in a tight race and went on to defeat the Yankees in seven games behind excellent pitching by Bob Gibson, who won two Series games and struck out thirty-one Yankees in twenty-seven innings. In 1964 Jim Bunning of the Philadelphia Phillies pitched a perfect game against the far-from-perfect New York Mets, in their third bungling season. Bunning threw only eighty-six pitches to beat the Mets single-handedly.

Berra and Stengel Out. The World Series seemed diminished, somehow, in 1965 when the Minnesota

Bowie Kuhn, named commissioner of baseball in 1968

home runs (44), and leading in RBIs (112) and hits (189). But he could not overcome the solid pitching in the Series of the Saint Louis Cardinals, led by Bob Gibson. Roberto Clemente of the Pittsburgh Pirates continued a truly remarkable hitting career, with a .357 average, to lead the National League.

A Pitchers' Year. Pitchers, Gibson chief among them, so dominated the 1968 season that the pitcher's mound was lowered to take away some of the throwing advantage and to make hitting easier. There were 340 shutouts during the year and an all-time low composite batting average of .236. Gibson, who pitched five straight shutouts, had the lowest ERA ever of 1.12, breaking the fifty-three-year-old record of Grover Cleveland Alexander. He won two World Series games but lost the decisive seventh game to the flamboyant Mickey Lolich of the Detroit Tigers. In a year marked by five no-hitters, Jim ("Catfish") Hunter pitched a perfect game for the Oakland Athletics.

The Amazing Mets. The 1969 season, more than any other in the 1960s, generated excitement and pure delight when the New York Mets, who had finished in the cellar every year since they had begun playing major-league baseball except for 1966 and 1968, when they finished next to last, won the World Series. The Mets began the season as 30–1 shots to win the Series, odds that seemed generous to some, and they struggled through the season, finding themselves 9 1/2 games back in the pennant race on 15 August. They had no hitting stars, but the pitchers were stunning: Cy Young Award–

Twins represented the American League after the Yankees finished eleven games back, due, some said, to injuries but clearly attributable, it seemed, to the firing of Yankee manager and former star Yogi Berra. He was replaced by Johnny Keane, manager of the Saint Louis Cardinals, after his team beat the Yankees in the 1964 World Series. It was a year dominated by Yankee-tinged disappointments. Casey Stengel, who had achieved an enduring reputation as the manager who built the Yankee powerhouse of the 1950s and early 1960s, retired in something like disgrace after fifty-six years in baseball when his fledgling New York Mets won only fifty games and finished the season forty-seven games out of first place.

Robinson and Koufax. Two stars overshadowed all others in 1966. One was Baltimore Oriole Frank Robinson, the first player since Mickey Mantle in 1956 to win the triple crown. He batted .316, hit 49 home runs, and had 122 runs batted in (RBI). More attention was attracted by Sandy Koufax, who won twenty-seven games despite an arthritic elbow, led the National League for the ERA title (with a 1.73) for the fifth straight year, and became the first pitcher ever to strike out three hundred hitters in three different seasons. After the season Koufax retired, explaining that he feared permanent damage to his arm if he continued to pitch. He was thirty years old. In the World Series the underdog Baltimore Orioles swept the Dodgers in four straight games in a series marked by record-setting bad Dodger hitting.

Hitting Is Not Enough. Nineteen sixty-seven was the year of Carl Yastremski. He led the Boston Red Sox to the World Series, winning the league batting title (.326), leading, along with Harmon Killebrew of the Twins, in

Ed Charles, Jerry Koosman, and Jerry Grote celebrating their 1969 World Series victory

winner Tom Seaver, Jerry Koosman, Gary Gentry, and star reliever Nolan Ryan. The Series lasted only five games. The Mets had the lowest team batting average for the Series of any winning team in history, a meager .220, but the Baltimore Orioles did even worse and the Mets won, providing an unforgettable thrill for all those fans who habitually rooted for the underdog.

BASEBALL: THE BUSINESS FACE

The Day of the $2 Ticket. If the game of baseball flourished on the field, it seemed that the occupants of the front offices, where baseball was big business, had to scramble to save the game's vitality. Attendance declined steadily during the first half of the decade as television transformed spectators from bleacher bums into couch potatoes. At the beginning of the decade 25 percent of team revenues was from broadcast licenses; by the end of the decade the total was 30 percent. Although ticket prices averaged from two dollars to three dollars in the 1960s, fans increasingly found it more convenient to watch games on television than to go to the park. Still, the twenty teams in major-league baseball attracted 22.4 million paying fans to the ballpark in 1965, setting a per-club attendance record. The 150 or so minor-league teams drew less than half that number.

The Cost of Baseball. As a result, team revenues declined while the owners figured out how to negotiate broadcast contracts to their best advantage. In 1960 each club in baseball averaged $200,000 in national broadcast revenues; in 1970 revenue had increased to $700,000; in 1993 it was $14 million. About three times as much was earned from local broadcast rights. Many teams during the 1960s reported losses, but in fact they were profitable to the owners because of available tax advantages. By the end of the decade seven of the twelve teams in each league claimed to have lost money. The average cost to purchase a non-expansion major-league franchise during the 1960s was $7.6 million. Expansion teams were cheaper, costing about $2 million in 1961 and 1962. In 1969 investors paid $5.6 million for American League teams and $12.5 million for National League teams.

Players' Salaries. Players were well paid during the 1960s, but they earned what they made, in the view of most fans. In 1967 the average major-league player made $19,000, and the owners raised the minimum salary that year to $10,000 per year. A player receiving a full share on a World Series winning team got under $10,000 during the decade and a member of the losing team about half that amount. In 1966 the great Los Angeles Dodgers pitchers Sandy Koufax and Don Drysdale made headlines when their contracts came up for renewal at the same time and they jointly agreed to hold out for a $1 million three-year contract between them. They gave in two weeks before the season opened and agreed to separate one-year contracts; Koufax signed for $130,000 and Drysdale for $115,000 per year. They were at the top of the salary scale.

Players' Union. Marvin Miller emerged in 1966 as a spokesman for players' rights. He represented the Major League Baseball Players Association (MLBPA) and in December 1966 negotiated the first labor agreement between the owners and the players. He began to establish a set of player rights that gave players some freedom to change teams in contract disputes and to protect themselves from the hated reserve clause that gave owners the right to demote a player to the minors rather than release him for play on other teams. Among the provisions of Miller's 1966 contract was a meal allowance for players of $15 per day.

STENGLE'S LAST EXHORTATION

On 2 September 1965 Casey Stengel stepped down as manager of the New York Mets, and his number, 37, was permanently retired. He had recently broken his hip, and he claimed the injury affected his ability to work: "I've got this limp and if I can't walk out there to take the pitcher out, I can't manage."

He spoke to his team for the last time that day before their game with Houston. In part he said, "I've been fortunate in being able to watch some of you men on television, where you can see some things you can't see from the bench. And if you could see yourselves, you might be surprised at some of the improvement you're making in which was possibly some of your weakness. You've got a month to go, and I think you can still do something. Your manager and coaches have been doing splendid work, and you can see now that a baseball season is a long time, and that some of those good clubs can't win in August and September, especially when they play each other. The season is too long for some of them. But you've made progress, and I mean the green men as well as the others, and if you keep on you can be here four or ten years. Now, that's it."

In a pregame interview, with the glass case in which his retired jersey was to be placed in the background, Stengle remarked, "I'd like to see them give that No. 37 to some young player so it can go on and do good for the Mets. I hope they don't put a mummy in that glass case."

Sources: Leonard Koppett, *The New York Mets: The Whole Story* (New York: Macmillan, 1970);

Jack Lang and Peter Simon, *The New York METS: Twenty-five Years of Baseball Magic* (New York: Holt, 1987).

Expansion. In an effort to broaden the appeal of baseball the owners voted three times during the 1960s to expand. There were eight teams in both the American and National Leagues in 1960. In 1961 the Washington team moved to Minneapolis–Saint Paul to become the Minnesota Twins, and two new American League teams, the Washington Senators and the Los Angeles Angels, were created. In 1962 the National League expanded to ten teams, adding the Houston Colts and the New York Mets. In 1969 four more teams were added: the Kansas City Royals and Seattle Pilots in the American League, and the Montreal Expos and San Diego Padres in the National League. Now major-league baseball teams were spread throughout the country, and owners were able to stimulate fan loyalty on a geographical basis.

New Commissioner. It became clear during the 1960s that baseball had entered a new era and that the owners needed a strong commissioner with business savvy to lead them into the 1970s. They found the man they needed on Wall Street. He was Bowie Kuhn, a 6 foot 5 inch lawyer whose stature projected his power. In August 1969 he agreed to a seven-year, $1 million contract that named him the commissioner of baseball, succeeding William D. Eckert, who had been fired.

Sources:

Kenneth M. Jennings, *Balls and Strikes: The Money Game in Professional Baseball* (New York, Westport, Conn. & London: Praeger, 1990);

Gerald W. Scully, *The Business of Major League Baseball* (Chicago & London: University of Chicago Press, 1989);

Andrew Zimbalist, *Baseball and Billions: A Probing Look Inside the Big Business of Our National Pastime* (New York: Basic Books, 1992).

BASEBALL: THE AMAZIN' METS

The Beginning. In 1957 and 1958 New York lost two National League baseball teams to the West Coast. The Giants left for San Francisco in 1957 and the Dodgers for Los Angeles in 1958. That left the Yankees, who were on one of the grandest winning streaks in baseball history, but National League fans wanted a team of their own. In the National League expansion of 1962 they got their wish, the New York Mets. The majority owner was former Giants fan Joan Whitney Payson, one of the wealthiest women in the nation. Her pockets were deep, and a five-year, $6 million broadcast-rights deal with Rheingold brewery assured that the Mets were solvent.

Cost. The team cost a total of $2.3 million — $500,000 induction fee to the league and $1.8 million in draft fees from a league-created draft pool of shockingly bad players. The Mets managers got to pick twenty players, of which sixteen were chosen from a group of players released from their contracts by other teams and for which the Mets paid $75,000 each; two were picked from a group of lesser players at a cost of $50,000 each; and four picks were allowed from a premium pool at $125,000 each. But there was some hope. Payson convinced Casey Stengel, the seventy-one-year-old, recently fired manager of the Yankees, to manage the Mets. Stengel began trad-

ing, and by the time he won his first game, only three of the original draft picks were starting.

The First Season. The Mets lost their first game to the Cardinals 11–4, and the season went downhill from there. Third baseman Don Zimmer went 0 for 34 at bat and got only 4 hits in 52 trips to the plate during the season. He was traded for Cliff Cook, who informed Stengel after joining the team that he had a bad back and had trouble bending over for ground balls. Marv Throneberry was not a bad player, but he was error prone and thus became a common butt of Mets jokes. The best pitcher was Roger Craig, who won 10 and lost 24 games. The Mets ended their first season with a record: they lost 120 games in a 156-game season. No other team in major-league history had ever matched that performance.

A Losing Tradition. At the beginning of the 1963 season Stengel pronounced, "We're still frauds. We're cheating the public." They lost 111 games that year, 109 the next, and 112 in 1965. The joke was wearing thin. Stengel was retired permanently and replaced with Wes Westrum, who managed to lose only 95 games in 1966 and finish in ninth place in the league standings. The following year Westrum was replaced in midseason by Salty Parker; together they lost 109 games and returned to the cellar. Then came Gil Hodges, a former Mets player and a favorite of New York National League fans from his days as star of the Brooklyn Dodgers. He was paid $60,000 per year to manage the Mets, and in his second year he delivered a world champion.

Hodges's Team. In 1968 Hodges's Mets showed real promise. The pitching team of Tom Seaver and Jerry Koosman combined to win 35 games, and relief pitcher Nolan Ryan contributed 133 strikeouts. But the hitting was subpar, and the team finished in ninth place, losing 89 games. Hopeful Mets fans were shocked at the end of the season when Hodges suffered a heart attack during a game. The team seemed ready for success but they needed Hodges's leadership.

You Gotta Believe. Hodges returned in 1969 and predicted that the Mets could win 85 games that year. In fact they won their 85th with 20 games remaining, on the day they took over first place in the National League pennant race. Of the last 40 games of the regular season they won 38, earning the right to play against the Baltimore Orioles in the World Series. The Mets were unstoppable. They won the Series in five games with solid, error-free defense. Stengel delivered the summary commentary: "This club doesn't make many mistakes now, you can see they believe in each other, and the coaches all live in New York and you can get them on the phone. So I'm very proud of these fellas, which did such a splendid job, and if they keep improving like this, they can keep going to Christmas. The Mets are amazing."

Source:

Jack Lang and Peter Simon, *The New York METS: Twenty-five Years of Baseball Magic* (New York: Holt, 1987).

The 1962 Boston Celtics: in front, Bill Russell, K. C. Jones, and Gene Guarilia; in back, Carl Braun, Bob Cousy, Tom Sanders, Red Auerbach, Frank Ramsey, and Tommy Heinsohn.

BASKETBALL: THE PROS

Professional Basketball Expansion. The National Basketball Association (NBA) began the decade with eight teams. By the end of the decade the league had expanded to seventeen teams, had a fat television contract, and had seen attendance jump from under two million in 1965 to over five million. Throughout much of the 1950s professional basketball was being played in the shadow of the college game and was searching for an identity; toward the end of that decade the sport saw its future in Bill Russell — the big man with grace and speed. But professional basketball did not catch up with Russell until the 1960s, when men emerged who along with Russell defined the modern game. Most notable among the new breed of athletes was Wilt Chamberlain. Wilt the Stilt, as he was called, combined imposing size, intelligence, and legendary strength in challenging Russell for basketball supremacy. The rivalry between the two superstars gave professional basketball much-needed drama. Despite the influx of great basketball talent from the college ranks into the pros during the 1960s, there remained only one true super team, the Boston Celtics.

The Celtics. No professional sports team — neither the 1950s Yankees nor the 1960s Green Bay Packers — dominated its sport in the same way the Celtics ruled basketball during the decade. Led by their cigar-smoking coach Red Auerbach, the Celtics won ten of eleven NBA championships between 1959 and 1969, only four of them requiring the maximum seven games. The combination of the masterful guard Bob Cousy and the best center to that time, Bill Russell, with such supporting players as Bill Sharman, John Havlicek, Tommy Heinsohn, K. C. Jones, and Sam Jones was all but unbeatable. Only the Philadelphia 76ers, led by Chamberlain, were able to challenge the Celtics' supremacy by winning the title in 1967, the year Auerbach turned over coaching duties to Bill Russell, who continued to play for another year. The thirty-two-year-old Russell was the first black ever to coach a professional major league sports team.

The ABA. In 1962 the American Basketball League (ABL) was created to take the professional game into cities without hope of an NBA franchise. The ABL instituted the three-point shot, giving an extra point for shots made beyond twenty-five feet from the goal, but the incentive to shooters was insufficient to attract the audience the league needed to survive, and the ABL died in December 1963. In 1967 another attempt was made to organize an alternative league. The American Basketball Association (ABA) was better funded and better organized than the ABL. By the end of the decade the ABA was able to attract some star prospects from the college draft, providing it the credibility among fans it needed to survive. Even so, the ABA was considered second-rank basketball. Commissioner George Mikan instituted a red, white, and blue ball for league play. Critics suggested that the ABA ball looked as if it had bounced off the nose of a seal.

Black Man's Game. Outside of Boston basketball was by the middle of the decade considered a black man's game, and in an era of racial strife, that perception inhibited the marketability of the game. Nonetheless, the play

Boston Celtics general manager Red Auerbach toasting player-coach Bill Russell in 1967

was so good, the rivalries so intense, and the promotion so expert that the NBA managed to overcome spectators' racism.

BASKETBALL: THE COLLEGE TEAMS

A Live-Action Game. Neil D. Isaac, author of *All the Moves* (1975), a history of college basketball, argues that basketball is the most popular sport in the United States, but that it is more successful as a live-action spectator sport and as a participation sport than on television. While baseball fans might question that claim, there is an undeniable attraction to basketball, particularly at the college level. The continuous action and high scoring of the game make it exciting to watch, even if it does not televise well. The roughly one thousand college basketball teams in the United States attracted fifteen million fans in 1960.

A National Audience. College basketball became a national game at the major-college level in the 1960s. Before that time college coaches recruited locally and promoted what might be called regional game styles. But television and the rise in fan interest affected basketball as it did other major sports. The game became faster and the players bigger as a system of high-school feeder teams was developed. Coaches traveled throughout the country searching for fast, big boys they could mold into team

players. The game attracted the attention of gamblers too. In 1951 there was a cheating scandal, involving players from seven schools, that had shocked naive fans. In 1961 there was another, bigger scandal that uncovered undeniable evidence of point shaving at twenty-two colleges affecting forty-four games. In fact, New York district attorney Frank Hogan, who announced the scandal, claimed the cheating involved more schools. Some of the best college teams in the East and the South were implicated: NYU, Columbia, Saint Johns, North Carolina State, Mississippi State, and Tennessee, and it was suggested that gambling interests had infected teams throughout the nation. But the 1961 cheating scandal caused little more than a brief show of righteous outrage among fans and sports administrators. By 1962 it was business as usual.

Integration. The most dramatic change to basketball at the college level resulted from the integration of the game. Black players with remarkable skills took the game to a new level of athleticism. Sportswriters began making a distinction between white basketball and black basketball: black basketball was fast and flashy, and players who could not jump had better stay home. When Adolph Rupp, the masterful but unquestionably racist coach of the segregated University of Kentucky team, was asked why black players were so fast, he replied that the lions and tigers caught all the slow ones. Celtic great Bob Cousy said, "when coaches get together, one is sure to say, 'I've got the one black kid in the country who *can't* jump.' When coaches see a white boy who can jump or who moves with extraordinary quickness, they say, 'He should have been born black, he's that good.'" Oscar Robertson of the University of Cincinnati epitomized black basketball in the early 1960s. He had superior dribbling skills; his elusive drives to the basket frustrated bigger and slower defenders; as a sophomore in 1958 he won the national scoring title, an accomplishment no other sophomore had achieved. He won the scoring title again as a junior and as a senior, scoring more points in his career than any player ever had.

The Stubborn SEC. Some southern coaches insisted on what they referred to as the purity of the game — that meant segregation. In 1959 Mississippi State won the Southeastern Conference (SEC) and had a 24–1 record on the season, but the team refused to participate in the National Collegiate Athletic Association (NCAA) tournament because they would be required to play teams that included blacks. Auburn, 12–2 in the SEC in 1960, deferred their NCAA invitation to runner-up Georgia Tech. In 1961 and 1962 Mississippi State players and students decided they should compete against teams with black players, but the board of regents forbade it. Finally, in 1963 the team was allowed to compete in the national championships but feared reprisal from hometown racists.

White Vincibility. The 1966 NCAA championship was a basketball-court battle to decide the viability of

Sophomore Lew Alcindor in 1967

if they lost," he said. In the championship game Kentucky met Texas Western University, a small independent school that had never been in contention for a national title in any sport; they were black, they were young (starting three sophomores), and they played what was called black basketball. In the championship they humiliated Kentucky. The smallest man on the court, Bobby Joe Hill, stole the ball twice from Kentucky and drove the length of the floor to score. Texas Western led in scoring most of the game and was up by eleven points with three minutes to play. The final score was 72–65, and it marked the death of all-white basketball. In 1969 Rupp recruited a black, and then he retired.

UCLA. In the last years of the decade college basketball was dominated by UCLA. Coach John Wooden's name seemed to describe his character. He was humorless on the court and seemed to live by aphorisms. He was

CONNIE HAWKINS

In 1961 Connie Hawkins was a freshman at the University of Iowa when the cheating scandal broke. Hawkins had never played in a professional game, but he was accused of having served as an intermediary between gamblers and players and so was stripped of his scholarship by Iowa and blacklisted by the NBA for eight years. In high school Hawkins already had a national reputation as one of the nation's best basketball players. He was 6 feet 7 inches tall and reputedly could beat NBA starters in one-on-one games by the time he was a high-school senior. He was recruited by over 250 colleges despite having an IQ of 65 on standardized tests. He went to Iowa because they offered him the best deal: a full scholarship and $150 a month.

When the cheating scandal broke, Hawkins testified freely before relentless questioning. One investigator remarked that he believed Hawkins because he was too stupid to lie. Hawkins confessed, under duress he later claimed, and his career was threatened. After being blackballed by the NBA, he was a star player for the Pittsburgh Pipers of the American Basketball League, the predecessor of the American Basketball Association. In 1968, the first year of the ABA, he led the Pipers to the league championship, led the team in scoring, and was named most valuable player. In 1969 Hawkins won a lawsuit against the NBA for the right to play. He won and was signed by Phoenix.

Source: Randy Roberts and James S. Olson, *Winning is the Only Thing: Sports in America Since 1945* (Baltimore & London: Johns Hopkins University Press, 1989).

all-white teams. Adolph Rupp, age sixty-four, had won four national championships as coach of Kentucky, and he had never allowed a black player on his team. In 1966 the Kentucky Wildcats were undefeated going into the NCAA final, and Rupp had nothing but praise for his boys: "They are regular to the last man. It would be *mean*

able to enforce military-style discipline, and he studied the game of basketball with a scholar's dedication. He also recruited, from three thousand miles away in Manhattan, the most dominating college basketball player ever to play the game to that time: Lew Alcindor. Alcindor (who later changed his name to Kareem Abdul-Jabbar) was seven feet tall when he came to UCLA, and Wooden showed him how to capitalize on his height without depending on it.

Ten Championships in Twelve Years. UCLA was good before Alcindor. They had won the national championship in 1964 and 1965 with superbly coached, well-balanced teams that emphasized defense. Led by the shooting of left-hander Gail Goodrich and the quickness of Walt Hazzard that year, UCLA seemed to win because they worked harder than other teams. In 1965 Goodrich continued the tradition by leading a team that seemed to approach the game as if it were an academic subject, beating opponents because they seemed to know more. In 1967 Wooden had Alcindor. Now he had the advantage of superior coaching and the most imposing player in the game. UCLA won the national championship with a team on which five of the first six players were sophomores. They went on to win the next six national titles, for a record ten championships between 1964 and 1975.

Sources:

Neil D. Isaacs, *All the Moves: A History of College Basketball* (Philadelphia & New York: Lippincott, 1975);

Joe Jares, *Basketball: The American Game* (Chicago: Follett, 1971);

John D. McCallum, *College Basketball, U.S.A. Since 1892* (New York: Stein & Day, 1978).

BOXING

Boxing Decline. The sport of professional boxing seemed to be in decline at the beginning of the 1960s. Boxing had been the most frequently televised sporting event during the 1950s because it was easy to produce: the action between two men in a small ring could be captured easily and cheaply by a single camera. By the end of the 1950s fights appeared routinely on television; Pabst Blue Ribbon Beer sponsored the Wednesday night fights on ABC, and Gillette sponsored the Friday night fights on NBC. Televised fights used up fighters and distorted an already-corrupt sport.

Television and Boxing. Television imposed a level of commercialism on fighting that the sport had never confronted before. Television audiences, and thus television sponsors, demanded more glamour and more drama than the sport could deliver. There were not enough white hopes or inspiring role models in boxing to supply televised fights at least two nights every week and more nights most weeks. Moreover, there was increasing evidence that television boxing was corrupt. The International Boxing Club, controlled by mobster Frankie Carbo, monopolized the promotion of fights for television, and Carbo was under investigation at the beginning

Cassius Clay at the weigh-in before his 1963 fight for the heavyweight boxing championship against Sonny Liston

of the decade. By December 1960 he had been sentenced to a prison term for what amounted to the rest of his life for violation of the Hobbes Act, which prohibited interstate extortion. Television no longer needed boxing by 1960 — the networks had developed the technical proficiency to televise other sports action — and NBC was the first network to announce cancellation of its weekly fight programming in September 1960. Audience share had fallen to about 10 percent from a high of 30 percent in the mid 1950s. The other networks followed suit, and the big-money boxing matches were given over to producers of closed-circuit, pay-per-view broadcasts.

Scandals. The image of boxing during the early 1960s was tarnished by testimony before the Senate Anti-trust and Monopoly Subcommittee in December 1960, chaired by Sen. Estes Kefauver, in which mob interests in boxing were thoroughly examined. Two deaths in the ring caused escalated expressions of outrage at what critics called the barbarity of the sport. On 24 March 1962 Emile Griffith met Benny ("Kid") Paret for the world welterweight championship at Madison Square Garden in New York City. Before a live television audience Griffith beat Paret to death, pounding the defenseless champion against the ropes in the twelfth round. Paret was taken from the ring unconscious, and he died a week later in the hospital. In 1963 featherweight champion Davy Moore fought Sugar Ramos for the world title. Moore fought gamely through nine and a half rounds; then Ramos unleashed a two-fisted attack that ended with Moore falling into a corner and striking the back of his head against a ring post. Moore died two days later, and the call to ban boxing resumed.

Heavyweights. The heavyweight division dominated boxing interest during the 1960s, and with good cause. It was the decade of Muhammad Ali, a talented boxer and a remarkable sports personality capable of taking full advantage of the expanded arena provided by the media. Cassius Clay won the gold medal in boxing at the 1960 Olympics in Rome, and he promptly turned pro. He was handsome, skilled, fast, and flashy. He seemed to enjoy

It was commonly held during the 1950s that boxing attracted a bad element. At the beginning of the decade about one-third of all active fighters had criminal records. Boxing is not for choirboys, defenders argued.

Oscar Bonavena was not a choirboy. He was a brawling heavyweight from Argentina who was good enough to give Muhammad Ali a tough fifteen-round fight in December 1968 and to knock Joe Frazier down twice, but he fell short of championship caliber. Like many professional boxers, he had a giant sexual appetite that was not tempered by good sense. Bonavena liked the girls at the Mustang Ranch, the legal brothel near Reno, Nevada, especially the owner's wife, Sally Conforte. Her husband Joe, described as a "proud Sicilian" by his friends and as a mobster by the police, was not prudish when it came to his wife's liaisons with other men, but Joe Conforte did not like Bonavena.

On 16 May 1969 someone broke into Bonavena's trailer and stole some of his personal papers. Apparently believing that Joe Conforte had arranged the break-in, the hot-tempered Bonavena showed up at the Mustang Ranch six days later and demanded to see the owner, or else. One of Conforte's men, a former con, chose the latter option: he shot Bonavena in the chest with a .30–.06 rifle and killed him. The gunman, Willard Rose Brymer, pleaded guilty to voluntary manslaughter and served two years in prison.

Bob Foster was light heavyweight champion from 1968 to 1974. He won the title and proved his worthiness of it by being the first man to knock out Dick Tiger. Foster went on to defend the title a record fourteen times. His first defense against Frankie DePaula, a five-to-one underdog, was meant to be routine. DePaula came out swinging in the first round and with his first flurry knocked the new champion down. Foster got up and started to work. He knocked DePaula down three times before the round was over. The referee stopped the fight, awarding Foster a TKO.

DePaula had been a respectable fighter before his match with Foster, but afterward training, which had never been his strong point, seemed to be too much trouble, especially when there was better money to be made outside the ring. In May 1969 DePaula was tried for hijacking $75,000 worth of copper ingots from the Port Newark docks. He was acquitted on charges of theft and possession of stolen property, but the jury was unable to reach a verdict on the charge of conspiracy. While awaiting retrial in June 1970, DePaula was shot and killed in his girlfriend's apartment. He had apparently bought some drugs from a local hood and refused to pay. "He was the kind of kid you knew from the beginning was gonna end up like Swiss cheese," mused his trainer, Al Braverman. "By that I mean, he had to get shot. He was that kind of crazy, crazy human being."

Source: Nigel Collins, *Boxing Babylon* (New York: Citadel, 1990).

himself both in and out of the ring, and he had a brash yet engaging personality, in stark contrast to the sullen and silent Sonny Liston, who had been a gangland enforcer and looked the part, or the shy, self-effacing champion Floyd Patterson, who brought disguises to his second and third fights against Ingemar Johannson so he could slip out of the boxing arena without embarrassment should he lose.

The Bear. After Patterson hung on to the championship by beating Johannsen in their second (a fifty-round knockout on 20 June 1960) and third fights (a sixth-round knockout on 13 March 1961), it was Liston's turn. He was 25 pounds heavier than Patterson, who weighed only 189 pounds for the fight, and he had a ferocious attitude enforced with a devastating left jab and left hook. In their first fight in Chicago on 4 December 1961, Liston knocked Patterson out in two minutes, six seconds of the first round before a live audience of 18,894 and a closed-circuit audience of more than 700,000. It was the third fastest knockout in heavyweight championship history. In their rematch on 23 July 1963 Liston took two minutes, ten seconds to knock out Patterson before a live audience of 8,000 fans and closed-circuit audiences in some 160 locations throughout the nation who paid over $2 million to view the action.

Liston and Carbo. Liston was an unpopular champion. He had a criminal record and was known to have connections with organized crime. Indeed, Frankie Carbo owned a 50 percent interest in Liston's boxing career and promoted his fights indirectly from jail. As a result of his criminal connections, Liston was denied a license to fight in many states. Liston was also functionally illiterate and felt uncomfortable among reporters, unlike his first challenger after Patterson, Cassius Clay.

The "Louisville Lip." Clay, called the "Louisville Lip" after his hometown and his loquacious manner, was given no chance against Liston by outsiders. He was young, innocent by contrast with his opponent, and seemed hysterical before the fight. Liston was supremely confident and apparently prepared himself to go no more than four rounds. Clay had calmed by fight time, and when the bell rang he delivered on his prefight promise to "float like a butterfly and sting like a bee." He proved himself a superior boxer, dancing rings around Liston and frustrating the champion's attempts to land a haymaker left. By the end of the third round Liston was exhausted, and in the corner he asked his manager for the secret weapon, eye-stinging liniment that was rubbed on his gloves. At the end of the fourth round Clay was blinded by the liniment, and he continued the fight only at the urging of his manager. He danced through the fifth round, and Liston was unable to capitalize. In the sixth Clay was back in full form, punishing the champion. Liston sat on the stool in his corner for the seventh, a mouse under his left eye but otherwise unmarked. He was too tired to go on. Liston's handlers sought to counter charges that the fight was fixed or that their fighter was a quitter by claiming Liston had torn a muscle in his left arm early in the fight, but it was a story believed only by those who wanted an excuse.

Down and Out. In a rematch in Las Vegas on 25 February 1964 Liston went down in the first minute of the first round the first time he was hit. Clay stood over him, gesturing and daring him to get up, but Liston stayed down for a long count. Because Clay would not retreat to a neutral corner, the referee did not begin marking Liston's time on the canvas for nine seconds. But Liston wanted no more. In subsequent years he continued to fight and had more brushes with the law. He died under mysterious circumstances in 1970, perhaps of a drug overdose.

Muhammad Ali. After his first fight with Liston, Cassius Clay announced that he had joined the Nation of Islam, known as the Black Muslims, and that he had abandoned his slave name Clay. He called himself Cassius X briefly until Muslim leader Elijah Muhammad changed his name to Muhammad Ali. Boxing fans were outraged, but Ali had only begun his assault on white culture. After the second Liston fight he was classified 1-A by his draft board. Claiming exemption because of his religion and because he was a conscientious objector, Ali refused to accept the authority of the government to draft him. "Keep asking me, no matter how long. / On the war in Viet Nam, / I sing this song / I ain't got no quarrel with the Viet Cong" was Ali's statement on the matter. He fought what he called his bum-of-the-month schedule (inviting comparison with Joe Louis, who first used the phrase), dispatching Eddie Machen, George Chuvalo (twice), Floyd Patterson, Henry Cooper, Doug Jones, Brian London, Karl Mildenberger, Cleveland Williams, Ernie Terrel, and Zora Foley in a two-year period

before the federal courts challenged him. On April Fools' Day 1967 Ali was formally ordered to report for induction into the armed services. He refused, and on 20 June he was found guilty of draft evasion.

Frazer's Rise. The appeals process took nearly three years, and during that time Ali was banned from the ring. He was still champion in the view of most fight fans though. While many considered his behavior obnoxious, clearly Ali had a magnetic charm uncommon among boxers. Joe Frazier was the dominant heavyweight during the last years of the decade, but he had to wait for Ali's return before he was accepted as a great boxer, and he had to beat Ali before he was considered a champion.

Sources:
Sam Andre and Nat Fleischer, *A Pictorial History of Boxing* (Secaucus, N. J.: Citadel, 1987);

Jeffrey T. Sammons, *Beyond the Ring: The Role of Boxing in American Society* (Urbana & Chicago: University of Illinois Press, 1988).

FOOTBALL: THE PROS

Popularity. By the beginning of the decade professional football was surpassing baseball in popularity. The Baltimore Colts' stunning overtime victory over the New York Giants to win the National Football League (NFL) championship in 1958 had thrilled a nationwide television audience and helped attract a new generation of fans to professional football. The NFL championship game had as large a television viewing audience as the World Series. By the end of the decade professional football was the national pastime. NFL attendance had climbed above 90 percent of stadium capacity — figures that were the envy of the baseball owners. Sunday afternoons — traditionally reserved as time spent with family — were taken over by the sport, as fathers sat in their living rooms glued to their television sets. Even the football widows — the wives of armchair fans — came to recognize the names and the language of football. A new breed of superstar emerged from the media hype that surrounded the sport; slick, brash, and attractive players like Joe Namath had charisma, sex appeal, and, as endorsers of products, great selling power.

Television. During the 1960s television money poured into professional football at an increasing rate, as Pete Rozelle, who became NFL commissioner in 1960, successfully marketed the sport. Having convinced team owners that it would be best to negotiate a television contract as a group, Rozelle in 1961 pressed for and won legislation that exempted the NFL from federal antitrust regulations. The league continued to grow as well; cities such as Dallas and Minneapolis–Saint Paul became homes to successful NFL franchises. Beginning in 1960, however, the NFL faced competition. The American Football League (AFL) emerged as a legitimate contender for the hearts and wallets of football fans. The new league also managed to sign major college talent from under the NFL's nose. In 1966 the NFL — having once believed that the upstart AFL would meet a quick end in financial ruin — entered into a merger with their competitors. The merger guaranteed further financial stability for both leagues, as the CBS and NBC television networks paid out nearly $10 million for the right to televise the AFL-NFL championship game, later referred to as the Super Bowl.

The AFL. The American Football League was the brainchild of two wealthy Texans. Oil millionaires Bud Adams and Lamar Hunt had become tired of having their applications for an NFL franchise regularly rejected, so they decided to start their own professional football league. Other would-be owners similarly rebuffed by the NFL, such as Ralph Wilson of Buffalo, soon joined the Texans in their drive to enlist backers and land major venues for a new league. Within a few months AFL franchises sprang up in Houston, Dallas, Oakland, Los Angeles, New York, Boston, Denver, and Buffalo.

The Challenge. NFL officials publicly expressed little worry about their new competition. Their league had beaten back newcomers in the past; in the late 1940s the All-American Conference had been formed in an attempt to cash in on a postwar resurgence of interest in professional football, but the enterprise was short-lived, and its few successful teams were absorbed by the National Football League. The NFL moved quickly to steal some of the markets for which the AFL was vying. NFL franchises were awarded to Dallas and Minneapolis, causing the AFL to withdraw its proposed team from Minnesota and offer the franchise to Oakland. It soon became clear that the AFL challenge to the NFL's monopoly was a serious one. Guaranteeing the immediate future of the new league, AFL officials, under the leadership of league president Hunt, successfully negotiated a five-year television contract with ABC.

The Chiefs Bring Credibility. Many of the players on AFL rosters had come to the new league from the NFL. Called "NFL rejects" by many sportswriters critical of the new league, they were often men who were past their prime and no longer able to survive the rigors of an NFL training camp. Many others who were signed by AFL teams during the early days of the league had been sandlot journeymen, former Canadian Football League players, or young and raw talent unable to play their way onto an NFL team roster. Nevertheless, talented players and coaches did find their way to the new league. Fired by the NFL's Los Angeles Rams, Sid Gilliam moved across town to take over the Los Angeles (later San Diego) Chargers. Gilliam was a brilliant coach and talented administrator who soon turned the Chargers into the class organization of the AFL. Hunt hired the head coach of his team, the Dallas Texans (later the Kansas City Chiefs), from the college ranks. University of Miami coach Hank Stram was reputed to be one of football's most innovative coaches, and in imparting his imaginative brand of offense and defense to his Texans, Stram created the AFL's all-time winningest team.

Blanda and Cannon. Perhaps the two most dramatic signings during the early days of the AFL involved Bud Adams's Houston Oilers. The Texas millionaire coaxed veteran pro George Blanda to quarterback the new team. Adams had also written a large check to land Heisman Trophy–winner Billy Cannon of Louisiana State University. Both players became major stars in the new league, as the Oilers under their leadership went on to win the first two AFL championships. The signings proved more significant, however, in what they demonstrated to the owners in the old league and to football fans. Proven stars such as Blanda helped legitimize the new league. The signing of Cannon proved that the AFL was willing to spend money on the top college stars and battle the NFL to sign them. The Oilers fought and won a bitter court battle with the Rams over rights to Cannon. A nasty recruiting war between the two leagues had begun.

Homeless and Hungry. Largely because of Cannon and Blanda, Houstonites crowded Jeppesen Stadium (the Oilers later played at Rice University and in the Astrodome) to watch the team play. Most of the other teams in the new league, however, were not as fortunate. Typical of the experience of many teams, the Boston Patriots had difficulty finding a permanent home field. It seemed a bad omen when, for the opening game of the league's inaugural season, the Patriots settled on old and decrepit Braves Field, former home of perennial losers the Boston Braves and the Boston Yanks, a pro football team that had failed for lack of fan support.

"People Showed Up Disguised As Empty Seats." The league's two major-market teams, the Los Angeles Chargers and the New York Titans, had miserably low attendance. The Chargers — an otherwise fine ball club that lost the crosstown public-relations battle with the NFL's Rams — soon moved to San Diego and larger, more appreciative fan support. The Titans, on the other hand, were a team whose football abilities ranged from mediocre to embarrassingly poor. It soon became clear that the organization, owned by New York radio personality Harry Wisemer, could not hope to control an equal share of the market with the New York Giants, one of the NFL's most successful teams. In their first season, played at the Polo Grounds, the Titans drew only 114,000 fans to their home games, and Wisemer took to inflating the attendance figures given to the press. As one reporter wryly commented upon hearing Wisemer's figures for a particular game, "People showed up disguised as empty seats."

Scoring for Fans. The AFL tried to attract television contracts and lure fans into the stadiums by offering a spicy alternative to the NFL's running-dominated offensive schemes that resulted in "three yards and a cloud of dust." Many of the AFL teams featured passing-oriented offenses, often making for thrilling plays and high-scoring games. The new league offered other innovations. A team could attempt to pass or run for two points after a touchdown — instead of just kicking for the extra point.

THE VIOLENT WORLD OF SAM HUFF

The value of defense in football was demonstrated by two television events in the early 1960s. On 30 October 1960 one in four televisions in America was tuned in to the "Violent World of Sam Huff," an episode of *The Twentieth Century*, a CBS news series hosted by Walter Cronkite. Huff was the best of the vicious pro-football middle linebackers, and Cronkite's hour-long documentary showed just how rough that job was. Huff wore a microphone in his helmet during practice and a game as the television cameras recorded his actions with narration by Cronkite. "Anytime that you play football on the field there is no place for nice guys. I mean you have to be tough," Huff explained. "When we're out on the field, we have to shake them up. It's either . . . an expression . . . kill or be killed." Huff made as dramatic an impact on viewers as the one he routinely made on opposing halfbacks.

Source: Dan Daly and Bob O'Donnell, *The Pro Football Chronicle* (New York: Collier-Macmillan, 1990).

the end of the 1960s he took the field with a noticeable limp, having endured knee surgery in 1965, 1966, and 1968, so he made an easy target for head-hunting linebackers. In 1968 in a game against the Oakland Raiders Namath endured two crunching hits by Ben Davidson and then Ike Lassiter, who brought both his fists into Namath's chin as he tackled him. Namath's cheek was broken, but he was back on the field the next week with an altered face mask to provide him extra protection.

Super Bowl. The first championship game between the AFL and the NFL took place on 15 January 1967. It was, as most analysts predicted, a rout, in which the Green Bay Packers humiliated the Kansas City Chiefs 35–10. On 14 January 1968 the Packers repeated the performance in the game dubbed Super Bowl II, this time bullying the Raiders 33–14. When the New York Jets and the brash Namath won the right to face the NFL champion Baltimore Colts in 1968, Namath's fans feared for his safety in the face of the ferocious Colts defense, and Namath did not soothe them with his reckless bragging. When the Colts were named seventeen-point favorites to beat the Jets, Namath promised not only to beat the spread but he guaranteed a victory, and then he took to

Also, a player's name was stenciled on the back of his jersey so he could be easily recognized by fans and broadcasters.

Star Search. To stave off the disaster and ultimate ruin the Titans would cause the entire league if they were to fail in the nation's media center, the AFL stepped in and assumed the operation of the team. (Wisemer, who had been running the organization from his penthouse, was unable to make the payroll.) In 1962 a five-man syndicate led by David A. ("Sonny") Werblin purchased the Titans. Werblin immediately went to work sprucing up the organization. In search of a new image, Werblin changed the team name from the Titans to the Jets and hired Weeb Ewbank as head coach. Werblin had a visionary's understanding of the new direction professional football was taking and of the increasing commercialization of the sport during the 1960s. "Football is show business," he asserted. "The game needs stars. Stars sell tickets." In 1965 Werblin backed up his assertions with his checkbook and signed University of Alabama sensation Joe Namath for the astronomical sum of $427,000.

Namath. No football player was more successful at managing his celebrity than Joe Namath, a former college star on Coach Paul ("Bear") Bryant's University of Alabama team. Namath was a playboy and did not seem to take his fame too seriously. He was part owner of a successful New York City bar called Bachelors Three; he partied without apology and played flamboyantly on the field. He proved his toughness on the field, however, as the target of linemen resentful of his frivolous image. By

BIG DADDY

Eugene ("Big Daddy") Lipscomb, defensive tackle for the Baltimore Colts, was the most feared lineman in professional football. He was 6 feet 6 inches tall and played at 303 pounds. When asked how he went about his job, he replied that he just reached out and grabbed a handful of the opposing players and discarded them one-by-one until he found the man with the ball. Lipscomb was a legend off the field too. He consumed straight V.O. blended whiskey by the water glass full, and he had a drug habit to match his size. "I'm a B and B man — booze and broads," Lipscomb bragged.

Lipscomb was a material man: "I didn't mind losing the second wife as much as the '56 Mercury to her. I loved that car. It was the first decent car I ever owned." He replaced the Mercury with a yellow Cadillac convertible, and on the night of 9 May 1963 he picked up two women in it, bought a six-pack of malt liquor, and drove to the apartment of his drug dealer, where he paid twelve dollars for four grams of heroin. That night he died of an overdose. He had four needle marks on his arm, ten milligrams of morphine in his bile, and a blood-alcohol level of .09. "New York, New York. So big they had to say it twice," Lipscomb liked to say.

Source: Dan Daly and Bob O'Donnell, *The Pro Football Chronicle* (New York: Collier-Macmillan, 1990).

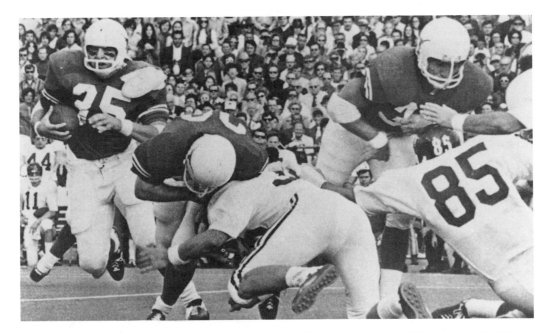

University of Texas halfback Jim Bertelsen (35) in 1969, the year he scored 78 points and led his team to a perfect season

the field to deliver. By the end of the day on 12 January 1969 the Jets had beaten the respected Baltimore Colts, led by quarterback Johnny Unitas; the AFL had proven its ability to compete among the best teams in professional football; and Joe Namath had sealed his reputation as one of the outstanding players of all time.

FOOTBALL: THE COLLEGE TEAMS

Instant Replay. An anecdote related by sports historians Randy Roberts and James S. Olson demonstrates the evolution of college football (and all televised sports, for that matter) during the 1960s, as television began to redefine the game for fans. In 1960 Roone Arledge asked ABC engineer Bob Trachinger if it would be possible to replay a piece of sports videotape in slow motion to show how a play developed and to verify a close call by a referee. Trachinger went to work on what became instant replay, which was tested during the Boston College–Syracuse University football game that year. Arledge recalled, "That was a terrific game, and at one point Jack Concannon, a sophomore quarterback, was trapped in the pocket but ended up running seventy yards for a touchdown. Six or eight people had a shot of him and we replayed the whole thing in slow motion with Paul Christman analyzing the entire play as it unfolded. Nobody had ever seen anything like that before and the impact was unbelievable. That moment changed television sports forever."

The Star System. The change in college football may not be traceable to that moment, but technology nonetheless had its impact on the game, which took on a new character during the decade. Television had two effects on college football fans. First, it created followings throughout the country for national teams. Notre Dame, Navy, Michigan State, Ohio State, Southern California (USC), and Alabama were among the glamour teams of the 1960s. They played excellent football, and they had sports stars of the first magnitude: Navy had Joe Bellino

A GUIDE FOR FOOTBALL WIDOWS

In 1969 Elaine Tarkenton, wife of New York Giants quarterback Fran Tarkenton wrote *A Wife's Guide to Pro Football,* dedicated "To the long-suffering wives of pro football fans—with the hope that in some small way this book can explain and communicate the fascination of The Game for husbands everywhere." Mrs. Tarkenton's book was the first recorded attempt to counsel what were commonly called "football widows" in methods of regaining their husbands' attentions on fall Sunday afternoons.

In her introduction Mrs. Tarkenton describes game day from a woman's point of view: "A few, a very few, share the excitement of the game with their husbands. But for most, Sunday afternoon means hours of pro-football widowhood—a slam-the-door retreat to kitchen or bedroom in an often unsuccessful attempt to get beyond range of a sportscaster whose excitement is reflected in a rising crescendo of incomprehensibility, from a tense "Third and inches, triple flankers right" to a shrieking "He breaks out into the clear.""

Source: Elaine Tarkenton, *A Wife's Guide to Pro Football* (New York: Viking, 1969).

and Roger Staubach; Alabama had Joe Namath, Ken Stabler, and Ray Perkins; USC had O. J. Simpson. And there were the star coaches: Bear Bryant at Alabama, John McKay at USC, Ara Parseghian at Notre Dame, Woody Hayes at Ohio State, and Darrell Royal at the University of Texas, among others. When their teams played on national television, fans watched. Thirty-three million viewers tuned in to the 1966 game between Notre Dame and Michigan State, which ended in a 10–10 tie. That meant revenue, which the colleges and universities used to build stronger, better teams.

The Thrill of Attending. A second effect of technology on the fans was that it increased their interest in teams within driving distance. Seeing a team on television, with the benefits of slow motion and instant replay, provided a far more coherent view of the game than live action, but it lacked the excitement, and fans hooked by television coverage wanted the pleasure of rooting for their favorite teams in person. During the 1962 season 22,337,094 fans attended college football games. That same season University of Michigan football home games attracted 585,369 spectators, including a record-breaking 101,450 at the game with conference rival Michigan State.

Evolution of the Game. Technology, and the infusion of revenue it brought, had its effect on the game as well. The 1960s were a golden age of college football. When *The Sporting News* chose its list of the twenty-five greatest college football teams in 1988, six of them were teams from the 1960s. The game changed during the decade from a conservative T-formation offense to spread wings and I-formation sets copied from the pros. Defense became more sophisticated as well, with the development of linebackers as the most potent of the defensive weapons and more emphasis on pass coverage. Positions became specialized, and different squads were commonly used for offense, defense, and various special-teams situations.

Competition. As the stakes grew in the college game, so did the fierceness of the competition both on and off the field. Recruiting became a national endeavor for the best teams, and college football's governing bodies were challenged to protect the amateur status of the players. Players in the major divisions were students only as football allowed them the time, and often not at all. During the 1960s college football became a flourishing entertainment business, producing magnificent athletes devoted to developing their skills at any cost.

Source:
Randy Roberts and James S. Olson, *Winning Is the Only Thing: Sport in America Since 1945* (Baltimore & London: Johns Hopkins University Press, 1989).

THE GREATEST COLLEGE FOOTBALL TEAMS OF THE DECADE

1. University of Texas Longhorns, 1969. Darrell Royal, in his fifteenth year as coach of the Texas Long-

1969 Heisman Trophy winner O. J. Simpson

horns, led his team to an undisputed national championship and a perfect season in 1969. The Longhorns scored 45 or more points in six different games en route to the Cotton Bowl in the postseason, where they overcame a strong Notre Dame team 21–17. Quarterback James Street passed for 699 yards, often to Cotton Speyer, his favorite receiver. Halfback Jim Bertelsen averaged 7.1 yards per rush, and Steve Worster, a talented blocking back, averaged 4.8 yards to lead the Longhorns to the nation's best offensive performance on the ground with an average of 363 yards per game. Placekicker Happy Feller scored 61 points during the season, second on the team only to Bertelsen, who had 78. At home the Longhorns were invincible, with an average winning point spread of 43 points.

2. Ohio State University Buckeyes, 1968. Woody Hayes was coach of the year in 1968 as he led the Buckeyes to an undefeated season and an undisputed national championship. During nine of the next ten seasons Ohio State won or shared the Big Ten conference title. Hayes coached a ground-based offense. His star fullback, Jim Otis, rushed 189 times during the season for an average of 4.7 yards, and Rex Kern rushed 119 times for 4.2 yards per carry. The rushers were supported with a solid passing game directed by quarterback Rex Kern, whose completion percentage was 56.9. The Buckeyes beat the University of Southern California team that featured Heisman Trophy winner O. J. Simpson 27–16 in the Rose Bowl, but the most satisfying victory of the year was against archrival Michigan, 50–14.

3. University of Southern California Trojans, 1967. In 1967 O. J. Simpson transferred from City College of San Francisco, and under the skillful coaching of John McKay he led the Trojans to a national championship and a 10–1 record in 1967. In 266 attempts Simpson rushed for 1,415 yards that year, averaging 5.3 yards per carry, scoring 23 touchdowns and some 80 percent of the team's points on the ground; in 1969 he gained 1,709 yards. His efforts were supported by an excellent defensive team that featured Tim Rossovich at defensive end and Adrian Young at linebacker. The Trojans lost 0–3 to Oregon State in the ninth game of the season but recovered to beat crosstown rival UCLA 21–20 and Indiana University in the Rose Bowl 14–3.

4. Notre Dame Fighting Irish, 1966. Ara Parseghian earned a record of 95–17–4 during his eleven years at Notre Dame beginning in 1964, and he was credited with returning the team to its past glory. With quarterback Terry Hanratty and defensive stars Jim Lynch and Alan Page, he put together one of his finest teams in 1964 and achieved the particularly difficult task for an independent of winning the national championship in a close race with Michigan State, posting a season record of 9–0–1. Defense was the key to the success of the 1966 Notre Dame team. They shut out six of their last eight opponents of the season. The Irish also led the nation in scoring offense under the leadership of the fiery Hanratty, who passed for 1,247 yards on the season. Only Michigan State avoided defeat by the Irish; they played to a 10–10 tie in the next-to-last game of the season.

5. Michigan State Spartans, 1965 and 1966. Duffy Daugherty was coach of the year in 1965, and in the two years 1965 and 1966 he dominated college football. The Spartans were 10–1 in 1965, losing only in the Rose Bowl to UCLA. The team was ranked number one in the nation by the United Press International (UPI) and number two by the Associated Press (AP). In 1966 Michigan State finished second in both polls to Notre Dame, compiling a 9–0–1 record marred only by the tie with the Irish. Running backs Clint Jones and Bob Apisa led a potent offense, but the team's success was attributed to one of the best defenses ever, with All-Americans Charles ("Bubba") Smith at defensive end and George Webster at rover. In 1965 they gave up only 6.2 points per game.

6. Penn State Nittany Lions, 1968 and 1969. Despite his team's back-to-back undefeated seasons in 1968 and 1969, Joe Paterno was unable to secure a national championship. He finished second in the AP poll to Ohio State and third in the UPI poll in 1968; in 1969 his team was overshadowed by Texas in both polls. A solid defense was the core of the Nittany Lions teams. Defensive tackle and Outland Trophy–winner Mike Reid was considered

Notre Dame quarterback Terry Hanratty and coach Ara Parseghian in 1964

among the most talented ever at his position, and linebacker Dennis Onkotz was All-American both years. The offense was dependable if not flashy. Charlie Pittman, Bob Campbell, Franco Harris, and Lydell Mitchell combined to provide a dependable rushing attack, the hallmark of an offense that averaged a 21-point margin of victory over the two seasons. Penn State beat Kansas 15–14 in the Orange Bowl in 1968; they beat Missouri 10–3 in the Orange Bowl in 1969.

Source:

John Hoppel, Mike Nahrstedt, and Steve Zesch, *College Football's Twenty-Five Greatest Teams* (Saint Louis: Sporting News, 1988).

GOLF

Palmer and Nicklaus. The two most talented golfers of the 1960s made their marks as the decade opened. In 1960 Arnold Palmer won the Masters and the U.S. Open and earned $77,000 to lead all professional golfers. Second place in the U.S. Open went to a twenty-year-old amateur, an undergraduate at Ohio State named Jack Nicklaus. He shot a 269 over the seventy-two holes of the tournament. Nicklaus's last year as an amateur was 1961. He won the U.S. amateur title that year by eight and six strokes respectively in the final two rounds. He was prepared in 1962 to enter a head-to-head competition with

Jack Nicklaus

cade, and he demonstrated his prowess at the 1965 Masters tournament, where he beat Palmer, who came in second, by nine strokes. In 1965 Nicklaus won $140,752 in PGA prize money, breaking Palmer's record set in 1963. He won the Whitemarsh, Memphis, Thunderbird, and Portland tournaments.

Nicklaus on a Roll. In 1966 Nicklaus became the first golfer ever to win back-to-back Masters tournaments. With his victory in the British Open, Nicklaus had by his fifth year as a pro won the four major golf titles in the world: the Masters (three times; he would later win twice more, establishing an intimidating record), the U.S. Open (he won again in 1967, 1972, and 1980), the PGA championship (he also won in 1971, 1973, and 1980), and the British Open (which he also won in 1970 and 1978). Nicklaus lost the World Series of Golf in a playoff to Gene Littler. Palmer did not qualify.

A Record Year. Arnold Palmer may not have been Nicklaus's equal on the golf course by the late 1960s, but he was still among the leading money winners on the tour. In 1967 his PGA earnings of $184,065 were just behind Nicklaus's $188,998. Palmer won the Los Angeles Open, the Tucson American Classic, and Thunderbird tournaments. Nicklaus, though, won money and set records. In the U.S. Open he shot a 275 for the seventy-two holes, breaking a twenty-year-old record and finish-

Palmer to determine who was the greatest golfer of the decade and, arguably, of all time.

Palmer in 1962. Palmer won his third Masters title and the British Open for the second year in a row in 1962, but Nicklaus beat him in a playoff at the U.S. Open. Promoters seized the opportunity to exploit their rivalry by arranging the World Series of Golf at the Firestone Country Club in Akron, Ohio. Devised for a television audience, this event pitted the three best golfers of the year against one another in a thirty-six-hole competition. Nicklaus won with a 135; Palmer and South African Gary Player tied for second, with 139s.

$100,000 Winners. In 1963 Palmer and Nicklaus became the first professional golfers ever to win over $100,000 in a single year: Palmer won $128,230; Nicklaus trailed with $100,040. Palmer did not win a national title in 1963. Nicklaus won the Masters and the Professional Golf Association (PGA) championship, and he won the World Series of Golf against Palmer and U.S. Open champion Julius Boros.

Palmer and Nicklaus by Ten for the United States. In 1964 Palmer beat Nicklaus in a close match at the Masters, and the two tied for second behind Bobby Nichols in the PGA championship. They paired up to win the Canada Cup international competition by ten strokes. Nicklaus had eclipsed Palmer by the middle of the de-

Arnold Palmer and "Arnie's Army"

Mickey Wright, four-time winner of the U.S. Women's Open golf championship

ing four strokes ahead of the second-place finisher, Palmer. Nicklaus also won the Bing Crosby, Western Open, Westchester Classic, and the World Series of Golf. He was at his peak.

Arnie's Army. Palmer's age had caught up with him by the end of the decade. He had suffered bursitis in his hip since 1966, and in 1969 he had to play in the qualifying round to earn the right to compete in the U.S. Open. Chief among the critics of the decision not to award Palmer an automatic bid to the Open that year was Jack Nicklaus, who had a gentleman's respect for his friendly rival. Less gentlemanly were members of Arnie's Army, the collection of fans who followed the popular Palmer from hole to hole in his tournament appearances. Palmer qualified for the Open, but he finished well back. He did muster the strength to win the last two tournaments on the PGA tour, though, vindicating the loyalty of his army. Palmer was the only golfer in 1969 to win back-to-back tournaments. He never won another of the four major titles, but he continued to attract the respect and attention of fans for the next two decades.

Women's Golf. Women's golf did not attract the sponsorship or the audience that men's golf did. The outstanding lady golfer of the decade was Mickey Wright. She won the Ladies Professional Golf Associa-

tion championship a record four times — in 1958, 1960, 1961, and 1963 — and she took the women's U.S. Open four times as well. In 1964 at the Tall City Open, she shot a 62, the lowest score for eighteen holes in the history of women's golf. Three other women have since matched that feat, but none has ever shot a better game. Then she retired in 1965 to attend college. No other woman controlled the women's game during the decade as Wright did.

Source:
Collier's Encyclopedia Yearbooks.

OLYMPICS: THE CONTEMPORARY VERSION

The Contemporary Olympic Era. What were called the modern Olympic Games, the phrase that referred to the revival of the Olympics in 1896, gave way to the contemporary games in 1960. The ideal, championed by International Olympic Committee (IOC) president Avery Brundage, of international amateur competition held in an arena unaffected by worldly influences was in its death throes. The forces that undermined the ideal — politics, commercialization, and drugs — were introduced in the 1950s, and by the 1960 games their influence was inevitable.

President Brundage. In 1952 Avery Brundage was elected president of the IOC. He was a controversial choice because members of the international committee feared the power that a president from a superpower nation would wield. The cold war affected most aspects of international relations, and observers feared that an American president would use the games to promote nationalism. Brundage managed to avoid serious charges that he used his position to promote American diplomatic goals, but during the Brundage years, due to the intrusion of forces he could not control, nationalism became the underlying theme of the Olympics, and politics was played as calculatingly in the IOC boardroom as in diplomatic gathering places.

Politics of Participation. Olympic politics boiled down to the question of participation. The Soviet Union had first participated in the Olympics in 1952 with an impressive showing. By 1960 the Soviet Olympic Committee, along with the Chinese, presented challenges to the IOC based on political and social dogma. Who would be recognized as the Olympic team from China, the Nationalist Chinese, who had been driven to the island of Formosa, or the Communist Chinese People's Republic, which occupied the mainland? (The Nationalists competed under the flag of Formosa in 1960 and 1964; the People's Republic withdrew in protest of the Nationalists' participation in 1964; the Nationalists competed as the Republic of China in 1968.) Would the East Germans be allowed to participate under their own national banner or would they be required to compete alongside their bitter enemies, the West Germans? (The two Germanies competed on the same national team in 1960 and 1964; in 1968 they were on separate teams.) Did the national policy of apartheid in South Africa, in direct conflict with IOC rules, preclude that country's participation in the games? (South Africa was banned from Olympic competition beginning in 1964.) These and many other basically political disputes came before the IOC for resolution under the guise of administrative questions. Brundage directed the IOC skillfully but made enemies all along. As a result he was criticized and called a racist, an apologist for black equality, a sexist, a hypocrite, a Fascist, and a Communist toady, among other names, by members of factions who opposed his decisions.

Soldiers of Sport. As sports historians Randy Roberts and James S. Olson observed, Olympic participants from the United States, Europe, and the Soviet Union acted as "national soldiers of sport" fighting for their country's honor and were encouraged by media commentators. Two statistics were followed with particular interest — the national tally of gold medals, and the national performance measured by a new system developed by the press that assigned points to the first six finishers in each event. The key rivalry was between the Soviet Union and the United States, and the Soviets established their superiority during the decade, raising a fundamental question about participation that, again, had its basis in opposing social and political systems.

Blurred Amateurism. The Soviets had a different view of the role of sports in society than the Americans did. They believed that sports was a vocation, like engineering or law or coal mining, and that athletes should train and work at their vocation with the support of the state. In the West professional athletics was becoming an important source of entertainment, and the best athletes made respectable livings (but not yet huge fortunes) by playing their sports professionally. Because it still clung to the ideal of amateur competition, the IOC banned participation by professional athletes. The best Soviet athletes, who were supported by the state, were not considered professionals, largely because the president of the Soviet Olympic Committee assured the IOC that the Soviet athletes were not paid to compete; yet the best Americans and Western Europeans, who played their games for money, were unquestionably pros. When the United States began losing in the medals competition with the Soviets, the system was challenged and began gradually to erode. Throughout the 1960s Western European Olympic soccer players and bicyclists were clearly professionals in non-Olympic years; the French Olympic skier Jean-Claude Killy received Fr 300,000 from the French Olympic Committee to buy his way out of an endorsement contract with an Italian manufacturer, and when he was forbidden by the IOC from displaying the logo of his new French sponsor, Killy arranged for television cameras to show him embracing a friend who brandished the logo for the world to see. American Olympians began receiving national financial support, which reached $2

million for the 1968 team, and the Western system of paying amateur athletes for appearances at meets began to blur the meaning of amateurism.

Commercial Competition. The 1960 Olympics, held in Rome for the summer competition and in Squaw Valley, California, for the winter games, was the first Olympics telecast live to American audiences. CBS paid $660,000 for the American rights to prime-time coverage of the summer games. When the games began earning significant sums of money, the amateur standard was further challenged, as the IOC found itself in the position of making money from contests staged on the principle of pure competition untainted by outside influence. By 1968 American rights to coverage brought $4.5 million, and the IOC had agreed to accept some of the profits to underwrite its operating expenses. By that time merchandisers and media analysts had been attracted to the potential for exploitation the Olympics offered. In 1968 Brundage complained, "We had Olympic butter, Olympic sugar, Olympic petrol." Sports-equipment manufacturers paid large sums for endorsements, and marketers of consumer products offered successful athletes fortunes for the use of their names in advertising. Meanwhile, press analysts and sportscasters scrambled to tell the public what the games meant, introducing and promoting layers of significance and controversy that had not occurred to many Olympics spectators.

The Drug Wars. In 1954 Dr. John Ziegler, the U.S. team physician, noted the spectacular gains Soviet weight lifters were making and wondered if there was some connection between their strength and the frequency with which young lifters had to be catheterized because they could not urinate naturally. A friendly Soviet trainer explained that the Soviets were taking raw testosterone, which gave them strength but caused enlarged prostates. Ziegler began research into an artificial testosterone that led to the development of steroids for use by athletes. Drug use was forbidden by the IOC, but prevention required a method of detection. By 1960 the race between developers of performance-enhancing drugs and developers of methods of identifying users had begun. By the end of the decade drug use had clouded even the question of gender. Soviet and Eastern European women showed up for competitions looking suspiciously masculine, and when they were subjected to chromosome tests, they had one too many to be properly called women. A Hungarian doctor called these athletes "genetic mosaics," but there was no such category for competition.

Sources:

Allen Guttmann, *The Olympics: A History of the Modern Games* (Urbana & Chicago: University of Illinois Press, 1992);

Randy Roberts and James S. Olson, *Winning is the Only Thing: Sports in America Since 1945* (Baltimore & London: Johns Hopkins University Press, 1989).

OLYMPICS: THE 1960 GAMES

The Soviet Standard. The XVII Olympiad was held in Rome in August and September and the Winter Olympics in Squaw Valley, California, in February. Over 7,000 athletes from 85 nations participated in the summer games, which were promoted as the most spectacular ever, staged at a cost of some $30 million. The Soviets won forty-three medals to thirty-four for the Americans, and in the point system, introduced by the media to measure performance, the Soviets won the games with 807.5 points to 564.5 for the United States, 319.25 points for the Germans, 270 points for the Italians, with Hungary, Australia, Japan, and Great Britain following, in that order.

Men's Performance. The Americans were strongest in track and field, despite some disappointments. The men won eight of the twenty-four track and field events, but sprinters David Sime and Ray Norton, expected to win, lost in the 100- and 200-meter races, and world-record holder John Thomas finished third in the high jump. Rafer Johnson lost seven events in the decathlon but won the gold medal with a victory in the 10,000-meter race six seconds faster than his previous best time. Male swimmers won half the swimming events, and American male divers won gold and silver medals in both springboard and platform competition. The U.S. men won three gold medals in boxing, including a dominating performance by Cassius Clay in the light heavyweight division. The American basketball team, led by Jerry Lucas, beat Brazil 90 to 63 for the gold medal.

Wilma Rudolph (117), winner of three gold medals in the 1960 Olympics

Women's Performance. The success of the women's track and field team was mostly due to the spectacular performance of Wilma Rudolph, who won gold medals in the 100-meter and 200-meter events and as anchor for the 400-meter relay. Aside from Rudolph's relay teammates, no other woman won a medal in track and field. American women swimmers won five of seven events, with two Olympic records.

Soviet Gymnasts. Gymnastic events were dominated by the Soviet men and women, who won twenty of thirty-nine possible medals.

Winter Olympics. The Winter Games drew 850 athletes from 31 nations and 240,900 spectators to Squaw Valley, where Walt Disney assisted in the preparations, providing elaborate ice sculptures among the decorations. Americans won three gold medals: Carol Heiss and David Jenkins won their respective competitions in figure skating, and the U.S. hockey team beat Canada to win the competition. The winter games were dominated by the Soviet Union, competing in only their second winter Olympics and winning seven gold medals. Their total performance-point score was 165.5; they were followed by Sweden with 71.5, the United States with 71, and Germany with 70.5.

Bobsledding? The bobsledding competition was canceled due to lack of interest.

OLYMPICS: THE 1964 GAMES

The First Asian Olympics. The XVIII Olympiad was held in Tokyo in October 1964; the winter games were in Innsbruck, Austria, in January and February 1964. It was the first Olympics held in Asia and marked the recovery of Japan from defeat in World War II. The Japanese were eager to stage a showcase for their culture, and toward that end they spent $2.7 billion to prepare. The preparations were largely lost on American audiences, though, due to the indifference of NBC, which had the broadcast rights. There was anticipation of live satellite coverage and cooperative efforts between Americans and Europeans to share video, but NBC balked at the expense and the practical difficulties of coping with a fourteen-hour time difference. They attempted one live transmission, of the opening ceremonies, and delayed telecast until after *The Tonight Show* in deference to Johnny Carson and his audience. The Japanese were infuriated, as was the State Department, which hoped to claim a show of American technological superiority if the United States was the first nation to broadcast these Olympics live.

The American Men. The Tokyo Olympics attracted 5,500 athletes from 94 nations, who competed in 163 events in 20 sports. From a national perspective the games were more competitive than the 1960 games. The Soviets won 96 medals to the 90 of the United States, but Americans won 36 gold medals to 30 for the Soviets. American men won half the gold medals awarded in track

Eighteen-year-old swimmer Don Schollander with the four gold medals he won at the 1964 Olympics

cord in the 400-meter freestyle, and swam anchor on the U.S. teams that set world records in the 400-meter and 800-meter freestyle relays.

Other Events. The United States basketball team won, as usual, beating the Soviet team 73–59. The boxing team was disappointing; the only gold medal was won by heavyweight Joe Frazier, and the team members tied for bronze medals in the featherweight and lightweight divisions. The U.S. team was not a factor in the gymnastics competition.

The American Women. Wilma Rudolph was retired, but her memory was recalled by the gold-medal performances of Wyomia Tyus and Edith McGuire, both from Rudolph's alma mater, Tennessee State; they won the 100- and 200-meter sprints, the only women's gold medals in women's track and field. Women swimmers, the oldest of whom was nineteen, were very strong, winning seven of ten swimming and diving events, setting four world records and two Olympic records in the process. Sharon Stouder set the world record in the 100-meter butterfly and swam on the world-record-setting 400-meter freestyle and 400-meter medley relay teams. Cathy Ferguson won the 100-meter backstroke in world-record time and swam on the 400-meter medley relay team.

A Disappointing Winter. The Winter Olympics in Innsbruck attracted about 1,000 athletes who competed in 34 events. The ten-day competition was disappointing for the United States. A Michigan barber named Terry McDermott was the surprise winner of the 500-meter speed-skating race in Olympic-record time. The only other bright spots were in skiing events, when Billy Kidd and Jimmy Huega finished second and third in the slalom and Jean Saubert won the bronze in the women's giant slalom. The Soviets were the overwhelming winners, taking one-third of all the gold medals and 25 medals overall. Norway won 15 medals, and Austria won 12.

and field and set Olympic records in 5 of their 12 victories. Bob Hayes earned the title "world's fastest human" with a ten-second flat time in the 100 meter, equaling the world record, and as anchor in the 400-meter relay he took the baton in fifth place and won the race by three yards in world-record time. Henry Carr was equally impressive with an Olympic record in the 200 meter and as anchor for the 1,600-meter relay team that set a world record. Mike Larabee, at the age of thirty, was the oldest man ever to win the 400 meter, and Billy Mills, who had never won a major race, won the 10,000 meter. Al Oerter won the discus in his third successive Olympics, overcoming the excruciating pain of torn muscles in his back in a come-from-behind victory over the world-record holder.

Male Swimmers. In swimming and diving the United States won 8 of 12 gold medals, bolstered by the performance of eighteen-year-old Don Schollander, who set an Olympic record in the 100-meter freestyle, a world re-

OLYMPICS: THE 1968 GAMES

The Political Games. The XIX Olympiad in Mexico City was as dedicated to political activism as to athletic excellence. The participation of South Africa was a controversy that grew in significance as the date of the games approached. At first the South Africans were invited. Then when threatened boycotts by black African nations and black athletes in the United States seemed likely to disrupt the games, the IOC voted to recommend that South Africa decline the invitation, effectively barring their participation. In the United States athlete-sociologist Harry Edwards organized the Olympic Project for Human Rights to coordinate protest movements by black American athletes, and when some members of his group agreed to participate in the games after the South African invitation was rescinded, Edwards promised a protest.

Street-Fighting Men. Meanwhile in the host city there was open fighting in the streets. Mexican students

Heavyweight boxer George Foreman after winning his gold medal at the 1968 Olympics

protesting the betrayal of revolutionary ideals by the present government rioted, and some estimated that as many as 267 people were killed in street riots. As the time for the opening ceremonies approached, army guards in battle dress were mobilized to protect the visiting athletes and spectators. Even so, 7,226 athletes from 119 countries and some 150,000 spectators traveled to Mexico City for what *Sports Illustrated* called "the most intriguing modern Olympic Games."

American Record Setters. American men won 12 of 22 gold medals in track and field with an array of spectacular performances that included 8 world records and 4 Olympic records. Bob Beamon set a world record in the long jump of 8.9 meters that broke the old record by 63 centimeters, and the record stood for twenty-three years; Dick Schaap called Beamon's the greatest athletic achievement ever. Dick Fosbury introduced a new style of high jumping, his Fosbury flop, that changed the sport; Al Oerter won a gold medal in the discus throw for the fourth consecutive Olympics. But for American audiences the track and field competition was dominated by a nonathletic event — the awards ceremony for the 200-meter sprint, which Tommie Smith won in world-record time and in which teammate John Carlos finished third. During the playing of "The Star Spangled Banner" at the ceremony, Smith and Carlos, both members of the Olympic Project for Human Rights, raised their black-gloved fists in the air, a symbol of black power. Avery Brundage suspended them immediately and sent them home, stripped of their medals. When Lee Evans set a world record in the 400 meter, he and teammates Larry James and Ron Freeman, who finished second and third, mounted the awards podium wearing black berets as a

symbol of black pride, but they removed them before the national anthem was played and avoided reprimand.

High jumper Dick Fosbury performing the "Fosbury flop" at the 1968 Olympics

Long jumper Bob Beamon during his world-record leap of 29 feet 2 1/2 inches at the 1968 Olympics

Tommie Smith and John Carlos at the 1968 Olympics awards ceremony for the 200-meter dash

All Work. American men won 10 of 17 swimming and diving medals, setting 5 Olympic and 2 world records in the process. The basketball team won easily again, even without the help of Lew Alcindor (who later changed his name to Kareem Abdul-Jabbar); he said he had too much studying to do and had no time left for the Olympics. American boxers won two gold medals, the most publicized being the victory of heavyweight George Foreman, who circled the ring with a small American flag in his hand to demonstrate his displeasure with the protesters.

Women's Track and Swimming. American women had an uneven showing in track and field, though Tyus and Manning set world records in the 100- and 800-meter races and the 400-meter relay team set a world record. Sonja Henne, Debbie Meyer, and Kolb were the stars of a magnificent women's swimming team that won 12 of 16 swimming and diving events, two in world-record time, 8 setting Olympic records.

Goldless. In the winter games the Americans were not contenders. Figure skater Peggy Fleming won the only gold; her women team members won 3 silvers, all in the 500-meter speed racing final, which ended in the first triple tie in Olympic history, and a bronze medal. The men won 2 silvers, in figure skating and 500-meter speed racing. There were a total of 105 medals awarded.

Sources:
Collier's Encyclopedia Yearbooks;

John Underwood, "Mexico 68: Games in Trouble," *Sports Illustrated* (30 September 1968): 44–51.

HEADLINE MAKERS

BOBBY FISCHER

1943-

CHESS CHAMPION

Prodigy. Bobby Fischer was thirteen in 1956 when he became the youngest national junior chess champion in history, fourteen when he won the U.S. Open Chess tournament and the right to challenge Arthur B. Bisguier for the U.S. Championship, fifteen when he became the youngest International Grandmaster in the history of chess and won the U.S. Championship, and sixteen when he ended his formal education: "The stuff they teach in school, I can't use," he explained. Erasmus Hall High School, his alma mater, presented him with a gold medal for his accomplishments in chess the year he quit school.

Charges against FIDE. Before he was twenty Fischer was the most outspoken critic of the world chess establishment. He boycotted the U. S. Championships in 1961 because he said the prize money of one thousand dollars to the winner was insulting. Three months later he won the world interzonal tournament in Stockholm, earning the right to play for the world championship. In June 1962, nine months before his twentieth birthday, Fischer finished fifth among eight players in the world championship tournament in Curaçao. Russians finished in the first four places, and Fischer charged that the tournament was rigged. He announced that he would not play in any other tournament sponsored by the governing body of world chess, the Fèdèration Internationale de Échecs (FIDE), and he thus voluntarily eliminated himself from competition that might have brought him the title of world chess champion during the 1960s.

Eccentric Genius. Fischer's eccentricities and his genius attracted media attention. As a result he was able to play in exhibitions and in events not sponsored by FIDE and command large fees for doing so. He revamped his image during the 1960s as well. To replace the casual clothing that had caused reporters to dub him "the Sweatshirt Kid" and "The Corduroy Killer," Fischer bought himself seventeen similar suits after the 1962 world championships. "If you have seventeen suits you can rotate them. They wear a long time. That's where the poor man gets it coming and going. His suits wear out fast."

Withdrawal. Sometime in the mid 1960s Fischer was converted by radio preacher Garner Ted Armstrong to the Worldwide Church of Christ, a fundamentalist, evangelistic group. He gave the church some ninety-three thousand dollars in donations before his bitter break in the early 1970s and moved to Pasadena to be near the headquarters, where, reportedly, he studied chess. In 1966 his *Bobby Fischer Teaches Chess* was published by Basic Systems books, and in 1969 Simon & Schuster published *My Sixty Memorable Games: Selected and Fully Annotated*, regarded by chess experts as the best chess book ever written.

World Champion. In 1970 Fischer went into total seclusion for a year, then emerged to announce that he was tired of being the unofficial chess champion of the world. He was ready to play for the title. He did so in brilliant — analysts say unparalleled — style, beating all contenders handily. In 1972 he met Soviet world champion Boris Spassky and did not so much defeat as humiliate him to earn the official title of world champion. Then he reverted to his seclusion, eventually forfeiting the title because he refused to belittle himself by defending it.

Source:
Ivan Solotoroff, "Bobby Fischer's Endgame," *Esquire*, 118 (December 1992), pp. 106+.

EMILE GRIFFITH

1938-

WELTERWEIGHT AND MIDDLEWEIGHT BOXING CHAMPION

Two Championships. Emile Griffith was the third man in history to hold both the welterweight and middleweight championships. The first two were Sugar Ray Robinson and Carmen Basilio. Griffith was born in Saint Thomas, Virgin Islands, and came to New York City when he was thirteen to join his mother, who worked in a hat factory. He eventually took a job working with his mother and came to the attention of the factory owner, who introduced Griffith to trainer Gil Clancy, one of the best in the business. Two years later Griffith was one of the top amateur fighters in the East.

Battle for the Welterweight Crown. He turned professional in 1958 and won twenty-two of twenty-four fights before he earned the right to fight Benny ("Kid") Paret for the world welterweight championship. He won the fight with a knockout in the thirteenth round, but his championship was short-lived. After one title defense he met Paret again and lost. Six months later, on 24 March 1962, the two fighters met for the third time in a decisive battle fought in the Virgin Islands and televised nationally. In the twelfth round Griffith, angry because Paret had called him a homosexual, pounded his opponent relentlessly as the referee watched without stopping the action. When Griffith was finally called off and awarded the fight, after twenty-one blows in the final sequence, Paret was in a coma. He died a week later never regaining consciousness.

The Middleweight Campaign. Griffith continued his career, though some critics accused him of concentrating too much on finesse and too little on hard punching afterward. He began his attempt to win the middleweight championship in 1963 and found that at 5 feet 7 inches he lacked the bulk to be as dominating as he had been as a welterweight. He was knocked out for the first time in his career in the first round by Rubin ("Hurricane") Carter in December 1963, and he lost to the brawling Don Fullmer before beating Nigerian titleholder Dick Tiger in a fifteen-round decision on 25 April 1966 to win the middleweight championship. Griffith held the championship belt for one year before beginning a three-fight series with the strong Italian Nino Benvenuti, who was 3 1/2 inches taller and over five pounds heavier. Griffith

lost the first fight on 29 September 1967, won the second six months later, and lost the third on 4 March 1968. All three fights were fifteen-round decisions.

Retirement. Griffith went on to fight impressively, but his championship days were over. He met Carlos Monzon for the middleweight title twice in the early 1970s, but he lacked the size and strength to prevail. He retired in 1977 after twenty years in the ring and 112 professional fights. After his retirement he worked as a juvenile officer and a fight trainer.

Source:
Nat Fleischer and Sam Andre, *A Pictorial History of Boxing* (Secaucus, N.J.: Citadel, 1987).

PAUL HORNUNG

1935-

FOOTBALL PLAYER

The Golden Boy. Paul Hornung was called "The Golden Boy," partly because of his blond good looks, but more so because he seemed to shine when the occasion warranted. He played on championship football teams from the time he was a senior at Flaget High School in Louisville, Kentucky. He went to Notre Dame, though Coach Frank Leahy did not offer encouragement that he would make the team. He practiced with the scrubs as a freshman, played third-string quarterback as a sophomore, made the All-American team and was named outstanding back in the nation by United Press International as a junior, and won the Heisman Trophy as a senior, despite playing on a team that lost eight of ten games. He graduated from Notre Dame with excellent grades, adding further luster to his athletic achievement.

Professional Career. Hornung signed a three-year contract with the Green Bay Packers for sixteen thousand dollars a year when that was a lot of money for a professional football player. He soon earned a reputation as a playboy who lacked a professional's seriousness about the game. Vince Lombardi changed that perception. Under his tutelage Hornung became known as one of the best backs in the league. Sharing ball-carrying duties with fullback Jim Taylor and accepting full responsibility for kicking field goals and points after touchdowns, Hornung was the star of a talent-laden team. In 1960, though suffering from a pinched nerve in his neck, he set the all-time NFL record for scoring in a season: 176 points, including 15 touchdowns, 41 extra points, and 15 field goals.

Military Service. In 1961 Hornung joined the National Guard to fulfill his military obligation. He missed only two games that season and once again led the league in scoring, an achievement capped by his nineteen points in the championship game that Green Bay won. He received most of the accolades given to professional football offensive stars that year and started the 1962 season optimistically, his military duty having ended before the season's open. Early on, though, he was injured and had to miss six games. The Packers won both with and without him.

Suspension for Gambling. His career was rudely interrupted in 1963 when he and Alex Karras of the Detroit Lions were indefinitely suspended from professional football for betting on league games, even though Hornung bet on the Packers to win. Since 1959 he had placed bets of up to $500 on college and pro games. Hornung was repentant but not financially strapped. He modeled Jantzen sportswear and lectured widely for generous fees.

Reinstatement. In March 1964 Commissioner Pete Rozelle reinstated Hornung and Karras, but Hornung was through as a football player. In the 1964 and 1965 seasons he gained only 499 total yards, and he kicked only 12 of 38 field goals in 1964. He retired in 1966 and was named to the Football Hall of Fame in 1981.

Source:
Dan Daly and Bob O'Donnell, *The Pro Football Chronicle* (New York: Collier-Macmillan, 1990).

SANDY KOUFAX

1935-

BASEBALL PITCHER

College Dropout. Sandy Koufax was a hard-throwing pitcher who lacked control during his high-school years in Brooklyn. He was an outstanding baseball and basketball player and was recruited by the University of Cincinnati. In 1955, after his freshman year, he dropped out of college to play professional baseball for the Brooklyn Dodgers. It was not until the Dodgers moved to Los Angeles that Koufax began to show promise as a major leaguer. He won eleven of twenty-two games in 1958 and tied a major league strikeout record of eighteen against the Giants in 1959.

Cy Young Awards. By 1961 Koufax was a star, and he continued to improve throughout the decade. Between 1963 and his retirement in 1965, his highest season's earned run average (ERA) was 2.04, and he won a total of seventy-seven games, including twenty-five in 1963, twenty-six in 1965, and twenty-seven in 1966, all years in which he won the Cy Young Award as the best pitcher in baseball.

Last Contract. In 1966 Koufax, a lefthander, and Dodger star righthander Don Drysdale decided to ask jointly for a three-year $1 million contract, the most lucrative demand to that time. When the Dodgers refused to meet those terms, the two stars held out. Just before the season's opener, they capitulated and signed to one year, six-figure contracts. Koufax got the fatter deal and made over $130,000 during his last year in major-league baseball.

Chronic Arm Problems. Because he threw the ball so hard, Koufax had chronic arm problems. He pitched in only twenty-eight games in 1962 and only twenty-nine in 1964 due to an arthritic elbow. Partly because he did not wish to injure his arm further and partly because of bitterness from the salary dispute with the Dodgers, he retired after the close of the 1966 season after the Baltimore Orioles swept the Dodgers in the World Series. Despite a World Series loss, it had been his best year in professional baseball: he won more games than he had ever won before and had the lowest ERA of his career. He was the youngest man to be elected to the Baseball Hall of Fame and one of the few elected in his first year of eligibility.

VINCE LOMBARDI

1913-1970

PROFESSIONAL FOOTBALL COACH

Winning Is the Only Thing. Vince Lombardi is regarded as professional football's greatest head coach. Lombardi guided the Green Bay Packers to league titles in 1961, 1962, 1965, 1966, and 1967 and to Super Bowl victories in 1967 and 1968; the Packers never finished lower than second during the Lombardi era. In his nine seasons in the National Football League he compiled a record of 141 wins and 39 losses, with 4 ties. Sportswriters, fans, and students of the game consider Lombardi's winning numbers all the more impressive given the poor-quality football teams he inherited at Green Bay and later at Washington as coach of the Redskins. The success of these teams under Lombardi is due largely to his demand that his players share his drive and determination to win at all cost. He once insisted, "Winning isn't everything. It is the only thing."

Lombardi the Ram. Reared in Brooklyn, New York, the son of Italian immigrants, Lombardi attended local Catholic schools and graduated with honors from Fordham University in 1937. In that year, Lombardi also had led the Fordham Rams to a 7-0-1 record, the tie coming in a scoreless game with heavily favored Pitt. The Rams enjoyed an immense following among fans in the New York area, and the team's front line, popularly known as the Seven Blocks of Granite, was one of the Rams' main attractions. Standing only five feet eight inches and weighing 175 pounds, Lombardi was a standout guard, winning the respect of his larger opponents for his ferocious style of play.

The Altar or the Bar? Lombardi considered entering the priesthood after graduation from college. He attended church daily, and the depth of his religious devotion away from the football field — where he was mostly known for his fury and profanity — would later be a source of wonder and amusement to his players. (Green Bay quarterback Bart Starr concluded that his coach "*needs* to go to church every day.") Lombardi, however, decided to study law instead, and attended law school for one year while supporting himself playing football for the Brooklyn Eagles, a minor league team, and working as an insurance investigator.

Fordham. In 1939 Lombardi left law school for a $1,700-a-year job as an assistant football coach and a teacher of science, math, and Latin at St. Cecilia High School in Englewood, New Jersey. He soon became head coach of the football, basketball, and baseball teams. During his seven-year stay at St. Cecilia, the football team won six state championships and had a remarkable stretch of thirty-six consecutive victories. Lombardi returned to Fordham in 1947 to coach the freshman squad, and in 1948 became an assistant under Ed Danowski. Lombardi left Fordham in 1949 to become a member of the football coaching staff at West Point. While there he was influenced by head coach Col. Earl Blaik, whose military style of discipline Lombardi much admired.

The Giants. Lombardi entered professional football in 1954 as an offensive coach under Jim Lee Howell, who was rebuilding one of the National Football League's prize franchises, the New York Giants. At the age of forty, Lombardi was considered too old by NFL standards to be entering into his first job as a professional coach; assistant coaching positions throughout the league were filled by much younger men who by forty years of age either became head coaches or moved out of the game entirely. Lombardi nevertheless soon gained a reputation at New York as a brilliant tactician whose offenses displayed a stylish and imaginative brand of football. In commenting on Lombardi's evolution as an offensive coach in the NFL, Giants star Frank Gifford once said, "Vince didn't understand our game; at first we players were showing him. But by the end of the season he was showing us."

Complete Control. Despite quick success at New York, Lombardi did not receive an offer to become a professional head coach until 1959. When the offer finally came, however, it met Lombardi's demands; the directors of the Green Bay Packers made him the team's head coach *and* general manager, giving him complete control in running the organization. His agreement with the directors stipulated that Lombardi had five years to revive Packer football. At the time many NFL insiders and sportswriters believed that a turnaround of Packer

fortunes within five years would be impossible. The community-owned franchise representing the small Wisconsin city of seventy thousand had recorded its worst record the year before, finishing the season at 1-10-1; the team's last winning season had come in 1947.

Developing a Winning Attitude. Lombardi wasted no time establishing a domineering presence at Green Bay. He made it clear to the Green Bay directors that all decisions regarding the team would be made solely by him and that the organization would no longer be run by committee. He immediately sought to land players with talent and experience — which had been especially lacking at Green Bay — through trades. In choosing players to cut or trade, Lombardi weeded out those who would "not make the sacrifices," later explaining that he had to make an immediate "example of them" to other players. From the beginning the message he sent to his players was clear: anything less than a winning attitude would not be tolerated.

Lombardi Time. Lombardi ordered many of the local bars off limits to his players and demanded that they show up on time for meals, meetings, and workouts. (Players soon realized that "on time" to Lombardi meant arriving fifteen minutes early, soon known as "Lombardi time.") Those who were overweight were ordered to get into shape by spring training, and everyone was expected to play with "small hurts." Players soon learned that Lombardi played fairly in handing out fines for rule violations; star veterans and rookies were treated alike. Lombardi purchased green sport jackets with a gold Packer emblem and required his players to wear them with a dress shirt and a tie when the team appeared in public or traveled on the road. He wanted his players to take pride in their organization and community — once regarded by the athletes as the Siberia of the NFL.

Practice, Practice, Practice. In the preseason of his first year at Green Bay, the full brunt of Lombardi's obsession with excellence was felt by the Packers assembled at training camp. Players found Lombardi's drills to be sadistic in their intensity. Most of the players came to respect Lombardi and his system, when they found themselves in the best shape of their football careers and well prepared mentally as well as physically for game day. They appreciated their coach's ability to make quick decisions and command the team authoritatively. Some players even considered him a moral leader, crediting his Jesuit training. Lombardi believed that in imparting football wisdom he simultaneously was offering important lessons about life to his players, and many of his ex-players credited Lombardi for their success outside of football.

The Payoff. Success on the football field for the Green Bay Packers came quickly under Lombardi's leadership. In his first season, the Pack played to a 7-5 record and finished third in the western division. The next year they won their division with an 8-4 record and lost to the Philadelphia Eagles in a close title game. In 1961 the Packers won the league championship, and in the following season they successfully defended the title. Green Bay, Wisconsin, became known as Title Town, U.S.A.; the Pack continued to championships three years in a row, beginning in 1965. In the first two Super Bowls (1967 and 1968) Lombardi's Packers routed the AFL champion, taking the trophy that would later be named after Lombardi.

Coaching Respite. Early in 1968 Lombardi retired as Packers head coach, remaining in the organization as general manager. By 1967 it had become clear to him and to his wife Marie that the immense pressures of running a football team coupled with his maniacal desire to win was taking a physical and mental toll. Retirement, however, proved to be even more of a strain than coaching. Lombardi had to watch from the general manager's box as the Packers limped to a losing record of 6-7-1 in their first season under another head coach, and he began looking for a way to return to coaching. He found it early in 1969 with the Washington Redskins, a once-proud organization that had fallen on hard times. The Redskins recorded their first winning season in fourteen years, going 7-5-2 under Lombardi. Considering that he started with much less talent and experience in Washington than he had found at Green Bay, Lombardi's 1969 campaign is considered by some to be his greatest as a head coach.

Coach Goes to Washington. Lombardi did not get another season with the Redskins. He died on 3 September 1970 of cancer. He had finished his coaching career at Washington without ever having suffered a losing season. The *way* in which he won — his often harsh and unrelenting style — however, increasingly made him the object of criticism, especially among the younger generation. To many Lombardi came to symbolize much of what was wrong with sports and with the social beliefs of the older generation. Social critics and sportswriters alike castigated Lombardi for his hold over his teams and what was perceived to be his win-at-all-costs attitude. By the end of the decade Lombardi became identified with the government's hawkish policies in Vietnam. He had come to Washington at a time of social unrest, and he viewed with outrage the contemptuousness of anti-war demonstrators as they squared off against authority. Although he was often unsympathetic to the masses of demonstrators whose hair, he believed, was too long and whose actions he deemed unpatriotic, Lombardi's social and political beliefs were simple. To him life was football and vice versa, and when asked to comment on the ills of American society he summed up his views as he might upon hearing a rookie had violated curfew: "What's the matter with the world? There has been a complete breakdown of mental discipline."

Sources:

Michael O'Brian, *Vince: A Personal Biography of Vince Lombardi* (New York: Morrow, 1987);

Joseph J. Vecchione, ed., The New York Times *Book of Sports Legends* (New York: Times Books, 1991).

AL OERTER

1936-

FOUR-TIME OLYMPIC GOLD MEDAL DISCUS THROWER

Four World Records. Al Oerter was the first man ever to throw the discus over 200 feet, the first of his four world records in a sport he excelled at throughout the 1960s. At the age of twenty, the 6 feet 4 inches, 290 pound sophomore at the University of Kansas was rated second in the world in the discus throw. He had set a national high-school record and had won two NCAA championships. At the 1956 Olympic games Oerter won the gold medal with a personal best throw of 184 feet 11 inches.

A Career-Threatening Accident. He returned to college and to a career-threatening challenge. In 1957 Oerter was involved in a serious automobile accident that nearly took his life. He trained furiously to regain his strength, and he never again competed without pain. After graduating from the University of Kansas in 1958, he continued to compete as a discus thrower as a member of the New York Athletic Club.

The 1960 Olympics. In 1960 Oerter lost in the Olympic trials to the world-record holder Richard Babka, but he made the Olympic team. He threw poorly in the early rounds, and then Babka suggested he adjust his throwing position. On his last throw in the competition, Oerter tossed the discus 194 feet 2 inches to win his second gold medal.

The 1964 Olympics. In 1964 Oerter was twenty-eight and hurting. He had a chronic cervical-disc problem and tore cartilage in his ribcage during practice for the Olympics. At the games Oerter faced a Czechoslovakian who had won in forty-five consecutive meets. On his fifth throw, again, Oerter won the gold and set a world record of 800 feet 1 inch.

The 1968 Olympics. His fourth Olympic gold medal came in 1968 at the politically charged games in the thin air of Mexico City. He had a pulled muscle in his right thigh in addition to his chronic neck problems that by now required him to wear a neck brace, even in competition. After two throws he was in fourth place. Then, in frustration, he removed the neck brace and won the gold medal with a throw of 212 feet 6 inches, 5 feet further than the next best throw of the games.

Return to Competition. Oerter persevered for one more season before he retired — for a time. In 1977 he reentered world competition stronger than ever. He made a throw of 227 feet 11 inches to qualify for the 1980 Olympic Games in Moscow, but he did not compete because of the American boycott of that competition. When he is not training or competing, Oerter is a systems analyst for a New York electronics company.

BILL RUSSELL

1934-

BASKETBALL PLAYER AND COACH

College and Olympics. The University of San Francisco won NCAA championships in 1955 and 1956 during Bill Russell's junior and senior years; they were 29–0 during his last year, and Russell won most valuable player (MVP) awards in five of the last six college tournaments he played in. The outstanding college player of the time, he was chosen for the 1956 Olympic basketball team, which won an Olympic gold medal after an eight-game series in which the narrowest margin of victory was thirty points. Russell also qualified for the Olympic team as a high jumper, but he withdrew so that another athlete could have the honor of representing his country.

Contract with the Celtics. When he turned professional Russell was the most-sought-after player of the year. The Harlem Globetrotters, who played at clowning basketball exhibitions for pure entertainment, offered him a one-year contract for $32,000. The Harlem Clowns, another exhibition team, offered Russell part ownership of their organization. He signed with the Boston Celtics for $24,000, joining the most formidable sports dynasty of modern times. The Celtics, under Coach Red Auerbach, won their first NBA championship during Russell's rookie year. In the next twelve years they won ten times more; then Russell retired. He was named league MVP five times during those years. In 1967 Auerbach retired as coach and named Bill Russell to succeed him. He was the first black man in history to coach a major league professional team, and during his coaching years he played as well. He retired before the start of the 1970 season.

After Retirement. After his retirement Russell wrote two books, *Go Up in Glory* (1966) and *Second Wind: The Memoirs of an Opinionated Man* (1979). He was active in the civil rights movement and worked frequently as a sports announcer. In 1987 he agreed to coach the NBA Sacramento Kings, but he did not do well and was replaced after one year. He was named vice-president of the Kings in 1988.

Greatest Player. In 1980 Bill Russell was named the "Greatest Player in the History of the NBA" by the Professional Basketball Writers Association.

Source:
Joe Jares, *Basketball: The American Game* (Chicago: Follett, 1971).

PEOPLE IN THE NEWS

Alphonse Bielevich catches a world record 98-pound 12-ounce Atlantic cod off the Isle of Shoals in New Hampshire on 8 June 1969.

Three professional football quarterbacks throw for seven touchdowns in a game during the 1960s. **George Blanda** of the Houston Oilers against the New York Titans (19 November 1961), **Y. A. Tittle** of the New York Giants against the Washington Redskins (28 October 1962), and **Joe Kapp** of the Minnesota Vikings against the Baltimore Colts (28 September 1969).

Philadelphia Warrior basketball player **Wilt Chamberlain** scores a record 4,029 season points in 1961–1962, including seven games played between 16 and 19 December 1961, in each of which he scores over 50 points.

Washington Senators pitcher **Tom Cheney** strikes out a record twenty-one batters in a sixteen-inning game on 12 September 1962.

Atlanta Braves pitcher **Tony Cloninger** hits two grand slams on 3 July 1966.

Michael Eufemia reportedly pockets a run of 625 balls at Logan's Billiard Academy in Brooklyn on 2 February 1960.

New York Yankee pitcher **Whitey Ford** pitches thirty-two consecutive scoreless innings in 1961, breaking Babe Ruth's forty-three-year-old record.

In 1965 **A. J. Foyt, Jr.**, wins a total of ten starting pole positions, awarded to the race-car driver who qualifies fastest for a race.

Darryl Greenmeyer wins the National Championship Air Race Unlimited Class championship every year from 1965 to 1969; he also wins in 1971 and 1977.

Professional bowler **Billy Hardwick** is the first ever to win the three legs of the triple crown in bowling: the national championship, in 1963; the Firestone Tournament of Champions, in 1965; and the U.S. Open, in 1969.

Jockey **Bill Hartack** wins the Kentucky Derby four of his record five times during the 1960s — in 1960, 1962, 1964, and 1969.

Judy Hashman wins a total of sixteen United States National Badminton Championships in the 1960s, including seven singles titles, six women's doubles titles, and three mixed doubles titles.

Phil Hill becomes the first American ever to win a Formula One title in 1961.

Elmer Hohl, a Canadian, throws fifty-six consecutive ringers at the 1968 world horseshoe-pitching championship.

University of Southern California baseball player **Bud Hollowell** is the first ever to hit four home runs in the college World Series in 1963.

In 1960 **Junior Johnson** posts the slowest winning time ever in the Daytona 500, averaging 124.470 MPH.

Between 1964 and 1970 **Homer Jones** of the New York Giants and the Cleveland Browns gains an average of 22.26 yards per play, catching 224 passes for 4986 yards.

Gerry Lindgren is the first cross-country runner to win the men's individual title three times — in 1966, 1967, and 1969.

Collegiate basketball player **Pistol Pete Maharavich**, playing for Louisiana State University, scores over fifty points three times between 10 and 15 February 1969.

American **Chuck McKinley** wins the national tennis doubles title with Dennis Ralston and advances to the finals of the singles competition at Wimbledon, where he is beaten in three sets by Rod Laver.

Carroll Resweber is the first man to win three NASCAR grand national championships in a row.

Frank Robinson is the only man to have won the Baseball Writer's Award as the most valuable player in both leagues: in 1961 with the Cincinnati Reds in the National League and in 1966 with the Baltimore Orioles in the American League.

Janice Romary wins the United States National Foils Championship in the women's division in 1960, 1961, 1964, 1965, 1966, and 1968.

Boston Celtic center **Bill Russell** pulls down forty rebounds twice, against the Saint Louis Hawks on 29 March 1960 and against the Los Angeles Lakers on 18 April 1962.

Norbert Schemansky wins a record number of Olympic weightlifting medals in the 1960 and 1964 Olympics: one gold, one silver, and two bronze.

Dick Weber wins the bowling U.S. Open four times, in 1962, 1963, 1965, and 1966.

Los Angeles Laker basketball player **Jerry West** hits a season record 840 free throws in 1965–1966.

AWARDS

1960

Major League Baseball World Series — Pittsburgh Pirates (National League), 4 vs. New York Yankees (American League), 3

National Football League Championship — Philadelphia Eagles, 17 vs. Green Bay Packers, 13

Collegiate Football National Champions — University of Minnesota

Heisman Trophy, Collegiate Football — Joe Bellino (Navy)

National Basketball Association Championship — Boston Celtics, 4 vs. Saint Louis Hawks, 3

National Collegiate Athletic Association Basketball — Ohio State University, 75 vs. University of California, Berkeley, 55

National Hockey League Stanley Cup — Montreal Canadiens, 4 vs. Toronto Maple Leafs, 0

Kentucky Derby, Horse Racing — Venetian Way (jockey, Bill Hartack)

Preakness, Horse Racing — Bally Ache (jockey, Bob Ussery)

Belmont Stakes, Horse Racing — Celtic Ash (jockey, Bill Hartack)

Masters Golf Tournament — Arnold Palmer

United States Open Golf Championship — Arnold Palmer

Professional Golfers of America Championship — Jay Herbert

United States Women's Open Golf Championships — Betsy Rawls

Professional Golfers of America Ladies Championship — Mickey Wright

U.S. National Tennis Tournament — Neal Fraser, Darlene Hard

United States Auto Club Racing Championship — A. J. Foyt

National Association of Stock Car Auto Racing Championship — Rex White

Indianapolis 500 Auto Race Champion — Jim Rathmann

1961

Major League Baseball World Series — New York Yankees (American League), 4 vs. Cincinnati Reds (National League), 3

National Football League Championship — Green Bay Packers, 37 vs. New York Giants, 0

American Football League Championship — Houston Oilers, 10 vs. San Diego Chargers, 3

Collegiate Football National Champions — University of Alabama

Heisman Trophy, Collegiate Football — Ernie Davis (University of Alabama)

National Basketball Association Championship — Boston Celtics, 4 vs. Saint Louis Hawks, 1

National Collegiate Athletic Association Basketball — University of Cincinnati, 70 vs. Ohio State University, 65

National Hockey League Stanley Cup — Chicago Black Hawks, 4 vs. Montreal Canadiens, 2

Kentucky Derby, Horse Racing — Carry Back (jockey, Johnny Sellers)

Preakness, Horse Racing — Carry Back (jockey, Johnny Sellers)

Belmont Stakes, Horse Racing — Sherluck (jockey, B. Baeza)

Masters Golf Tournament — Gary Player

United States Open Golf Championships — Gene Littler

Professional Golfers of America Championship — Jerry Barber

United States Women's Open Golf Championships — Mickey Wright

U.S. National Tennis Tournament — Roy Emerson, Darlene Hard

United States Auto Club Racing Championship — A. J. Foyt

National Association of Stock Car Auto Racing Championship — Ned Jarrett

Indianapolis 500 Auto Race Champion — A. J. Foyt

1962

Major League Baseball World Series — New York Yankees (American League), 4 vs. San Francisco Giants (National League), 3

National Football League Championship — Green Bay Packers, 16 vs. New York Giants, 7

American Football League Championship — Dallas Texans, 20 vs. Houston Oilers, 17

Collegiate Football National Champions — University of Southern California

Heisman Trophy, Collegiate Football — Terry Baker (Oregon State University)

National Basketball Association Championship — Boston Celtics, 4 vs. Los Angeles Lakers, 3

American Basketball League Championship — Cleveland Pipers, 3 vs. Kansas City Steers, 2

National Collegiate Athletic Association Basketball — University of Cincinnati, 71 vs. Ohio State University, 59

National Hockey League Stanley Cup — Toronto Maple Leafs, 4 vs. Chicago Black Hawks, 2

Kentucky Derby, Horse Racing — Decidely (jockey, Bill Hartack)

Preakness, Horse Racing — Greek Money (jockey, John Rotz)

Belmont Stakes, Horse Racing — Jaipur (jockey, Willie Shoemaker)

Masters Golf Tournament — Arnold Palmer

United States Open Golf Championships — Jack Nicklaus

Professional Golfers of America Championship — Gary Player

United States Women's Open Golf Championships — Murle MacKenzie Lindstrom

U.S. National Tennis Tournament — Rod Laver, Margaret Smith

United States Auto Club Racing Championship — Paul Goldsmith

National Association of Stock Car Auto Racing Championship — Joe Weatherly

Indianapolis 500 Auto Race Champion — Rodger Ward

1963

Major League Baseball World Series — Los Angeles Dodgers (National League), 4 vs. New York Yankees (American League), 0

National Football League Championship — Chicago Bears, 14 vs. New York Giants, 10

American Football League Championship — San Diego Chargers, 51 vs. Boston Patriots, 10

Collegiate Football National Champions — University of Texas

Heisman Trophy, Collegiate Football — Roger Staubach (Navy)

National Basketball Association Championship — Boston Celtics, 4 vs. Los Angeles Lakers, 3

National Collegiate Athletic Association Basketball — Loyola of Chicago, 60 vs. University of Cincinnati, 58

National Hockey League Stanley Cup — Toronto Maple Leafs, 4 vs. Detroit Red Wings, 1

Kentucky Derby, Horse Racing — Chateaugay (jockey, B. Baeza)

Preakness, Horse Racing — Candy Spots (jockey, Willie Shoemaker)

Belmont Stakes, Horse Racing — Chateaugay (jockey, B. Baeza)

Masters Golf Tournament — Jack Nicklaus

United States Open Golf Championships — Julius Boros

Professional Golfers of America Championship — Jack Nicklaus

United States Women's Open Golf Championships — Mary Wills

U.S. National Tennis Tournament — Rafael Osuna, Maria Bueno

United States Auto Club Racing Championship — A. J. Foyt

National Association of Stock Car Auto Racing Championship — Joe Weatherly

Indianapolis 500 Auto Race Champion — Parnelli Jones

1964

Major League Baseball World Series — Saint Louis Cardinals (National League), 4 vs. New York Yankees (American League), 3

National Football League Championship — Cleveland Browns, 27 vs. Baltimore Colts, 0

American Football League Championship — Buffalo Bills, 20 vs. San Diego Chargers, 7

Collegiate Football National Champions — University of Alabama

Heisman Trophy, Collegiate Football — John Huarte (Notre Dame)

National Basketball Association Championship — Boston Celtics, 4 vs. San Francisco Warriors, 1

National Collegiate Athletic Association Basketball — University of California, Los Angeles, 98 vs. Duke University, 83

National Hockey League Stanley Cup — Toronto Maple Leafs, 4 vs. Detroit Red Wings, 1

Kentucky Derby, Horse Racing — Northern Dancer (jockey, Bill Hartack)

Preakness, Horse Racing — Northern Dancer (jockey, Bill Hartack)

Belmont Stakes, Horse Racing — Quadrangle (jockey, M. Ycaza)

Masters Golf Tournament — Arnold Palmer

United States Open Golf Championships — Ken Venturi

Professional Golfers of America Championship — Bobby Nichols

United States Women's Open Golf Championships — Mickey Wright

U.S. National Tennis Tournament — Roy Emerson, Maria Bueno

United States Auto Club Racing Championship — A. J. Foyt

National Association of Stock Car Auto Racing Championship — Richard Petty

Indianapolis 500 Auto Race Champion — A. J. Foyt

1965

Major League Baseball World Series — Los Angeles Dodgers (National League), 4 vs. Minnesota Twins (American League), 3

National Football League Championship — Green Bay Packers, 23 vs. Cleveland Browns, 12

American Football League Championship — Buffalo Bills, 23 vs. San Diego Chargers, 0

Collegiate Football National Champions — Michigan State University

Heisman Trophy, Collegiate Football — Mike Garrett (University of Southern California)

National Basketball Association Championship — Boston Celtics, 4 vs. Los Angeles Lakers, 1

National Collegiate Athletic Association Basketball — University of California, Los Angeles, 91 vs. University of Michigan, 80

National Hockey League Stanley Cup — Montreal Canadiens, 4 vs. Chicago Black Hawks, 3

Kentucky Derby, Horse Racing — Lucky Debonair (jockey, Willie Shoemaker)

Preakness, Horse Racing — Tom Rolfe (jockey, Ron Turcotte)

Belmont Stakes, Horse Racing — Hail To All (jockey, Johnny Sellers)

Masters Golf Tournament — Jack Nicklaus

United States Open Golf Championships — Gary Player

Professional Golfers of America Championship — Dave Marr

United States Women's Open Golf Championships — Carol Mann

U.S. National Tennis Tournament — Manuel Santana, Margaret Smith

United States Auto Club Racing Championship — Mario Andretti

National Association of Stock Car Auto Racing Championship — Ned Jarrett

Indianapolis 500 Auto Race Champion — Jim Clark

1966

Major League Baseball World Series — Baltimore Orioles (American League), 4 vs. Los Angeles Dodgers (National League), 0

National Football League Championship — Green Bay Packers, 34 vs. Dallas Cowboys, 27

American Football League Championship — Kansas City Chiefs, 31 vs. Buffalo Bills, 7

Super Bowl — Green Bay Packers (NFL), 35 vs. Kansas City Chiefs (AFL), 10

Collegiate Football National Champions — Notre Dame

Heisman Trophy, Collegiate Football — Steve Spurrier (University of Florida)

National Basketball Association Championship — Boston Celtics, 4 vs. Los Angeles Lakers, 3

National Collegiate Athletic Association Basketball — Texas Western College, 72 vs. University of Kentucky, 65

National Hockey League Stanley Cup — Montreal Canadiens, 4 vs. Detroit Red Wings, 2

Kentucky Derby, Horse Racing — Kauai King (jockey, D. Brumfield)

Preakness, Horse Racing — Kauai King (jockey, D. Brumfield)

Belmont Stakes, Horse Racing — Amberoid (jockey, W. Boland)

Masters Golf Tournament — Jack Nicklaus

United States Open Golf Championships — Billy Casper

Professional Golfers of America Championship — Al Geiberger

United States Women's Open Golf Championships — Sandra Spuzich

U.S. National Tennis Tournament — Fred Stolle, Maria Bueno

United States Auto Club Racing Championship — Mario Andretti

National Association of Stock Car Auto Racing Championship — David Pearson

Indianapolis 500 Auto Race Champion — Graham Hill

1967

Major League Baseball World Series — Saint Louis Cardinals (National League), 4 vs. Boston Red Sox (American League), 3

National Football League Championship — Green Bay Packers, 21 vs. Dallas Cowboys, 17

American Football League Championship — Oakland Raiders, 40 vs. Houston Oilers, 7

Super Bowl — Green Bay Packers (NFL), 33 vs. Oakland Raiders (AFL), 14

Collegiate Football National Champions — University of Southern California

Heisman Trophy, Collegiate Football — Gary Beban (University of California, Los Angeles)

National Basketball Association Championship — Philadelphia 76ers, 4 vs. San Francisco Warriors, 2

National Collegiate Athletic Association Basketball — University of California, Los Angeles, 79 vs. University of Dayton, 64

National Hockey League Stanley Cup — Toronto Maple Leafs, 4 vs. Montreal Canadiens, 2

Kentucky Derby, Horse Racing — Proud Clarion (jockey, R. Ussery)

Preakness, Horse Racing — Damascus (jockey, Willie Shoemaker)

Belmont Stakes, Horse Racing — Damascus (jockey, Willie Shoemaker)

Masters Golf Tournament — Gay Brewer

United States Open Golf Championships — Jack Nicklaus

Professional Golfers of America Championship — Don January

United States Women's Open Golf Championships — Catherine Lacoste

U.S. National Tennis Tournament — John Newcombe, Billie Jean King

United States Auto Club Racing Championship — A. J. Foyt

National Association of Stock Car Auto Racing Championship — Richard Petty

Indianapolis 500 Auto Race Champion — A. J. Foyt

1968

Major League Baseball World Series — Detroit Tigers (American League), 4 vs. Saint Louis Cardinals (National League), 3

National Football League Championship — Baltimore Colts, 34 vs. Cleveland Browns, 0

American Football League Championship — New York Jets, 27 vs. Oakland Raiders, 23

Super Bowl — New York Jets (AFL), 16 vs. Baltimore Colts (NFL), 7

Collegiate Football National Champions — Ohio State University

Heisman Trophy, Collegiate Football — O. J. Simpson (University of Southern California)

National Basketball Association Championship — Boston Celtics, 4 vs. Los Angeles Lakers, 2

National Collegiate Athletic Association Basketball — University of California, Los Angeles, 78 vs. University of North Carolina, 55

National Hockey League Stanley Cup — Montreal Canadiens, 4 vs. Saint Louis Blues, 0

Kentucky Derby, Horse Racing — Forward Pass (jockey, I. Valenzuela)

Preakness, Horse Racing — Forward Pass (jockey, I. Valenzuela)

Belmont Stakes, Horse Racing — Stage Door Johnny (jockey, H. Gustines)

Masters Golf Tournament — Bob Goalby

United States Open Golf Championships — Lee Trevino

Professional Golfers of America Championship — Julius Boros

United States Women's Open Golf Championships — Susie Maxwell Berning

U.S. Open Tennis Tournament — Arthur Ashe, Virginia Wade

United States Auto Club Racing Championship — Bobby Unser

National Association of Stock Car Auto Racing Championship — David Pearson

Indianapolis 500 Auto Race Champion — Bobby Unser

1969

Major League Baseball World Series — New York Mets (National League), 4 vs. Baltimore Orioles (American League), 2

National Football League Championship — Minnesota Vikings, 27 vs. Cleveland Browns, 7

American Football League Championship — Kansas City Chiefs, 17 vs. Oakland Raiders, 7

Super Bowl — Kansas City Chiefs (AFL), 23 vs. Minnesota Vikings (NFL), 7

Collegiate Football National Champions — Pennsylvania State University (Associated Press), University of Texas (United Press International)

Heisman Trophy, Collegiate Football — Steve Owens (University of Oklahoma)

National Basketball Association Championship — Boston Celtics, 4 vs. Los Angeles Lakers, 3

National Collegiate Athletic Association Basketball — University of California, Los Angeles, 92 vs. Purdue University, 72

National Hockey League Stanley Cup — Montreal Canadiens, 4 vs. Saint Louis Blues, 0

Kentucky Derby, Horse Racing — Majestic Prince (jockey, Bill Hartack)

Preakness, Horse Racing — Majestic Prince (jockey, Bill Hartack)

Belmont Stakes, Horse Racing — Arts and Letters (jockey, B. Baeza)

Masters Golf Tournament — George Archer

United States Open Golf Championships — Orville Moody

Professional Golfers of America Championship — Ray Floyd

United States Women's Open Golf Championships — Donna Caponi

U.S. Open Tennis Tournament — Rod Laver; Margaret Court

United States Auto Club Racing Championship — Mario Andretti

National Association of Stock Car Auto Racing Championship — David Pearson

Indianapolis 500 Auto Race Champion — Mario Andretti

DEATHS

John Franklin ("Home Run") Baker, 77, from 1911 to 1914 led the American League in home runs, 28 June 1963.

Jack Barry, 73, former shortstop for the Philadelphia Athletics, 23 April 1961.

Tony Bettenhausen, 44, racing driver, killed while testing a car at the Indianapolis Speedway, 12 May 1961.

Maureen Connolly Brinker, 34, the first woman to win a tennis "grand slam" (the national championships of the U.S., Great Britain, France, and Australia), 21 June 1969.

Jimmy Bryan, 33, race car driver and former winner of the Indianapolis 500, of injuries suffered in racing accident, 19 June 1960.

Primo Carnera, 60, Italian-born boxer who won the heavyweight title in 1933 from Jack Sharkey and then lost it in 1934 to Max Baer, 29 June 1967.

Tyrus Raymond ("Ty") Cobb, 74, played with the Detroit Tigers for 22 years; the first member of the Baseball Hall of Fame, 17 July 1961.

Gordon Stanley ("Mickey") Cochrane, 59, former catcher for the Philadelphia Athletics and manager from 1934 to 1939 of the Detroit Tigers, 28 June 1962.

Samuel Earl ("Wahoo Sam") Crawford, 88, at the time of his death the only baseball player to have led both leagues in home runs, 15 June 1968.

Ernest R. ("Ernie") Davis, 23, former halfback at Syracuse University and the first black player to win the Heisman Trophy, died of leukemia, 18 May 1963.

Charles ("Chuck") Walter Dressen, 67, major-league baseball manager, 10 August 1966.

James E. ("Sunny Jim") Fitzsimmons, 91, the "grand old man of horse racing," trained Gallant Fox and Omaha, winners of the 1930 and 1935 Triple Crown, 11 March 1966.

James ("Jimmy") Emory Foxx, 59, played for the Philadelphia Athletics and Phillies, the Boston Red Sox, and the Chicago Cubs and was ranked third in career home runs (534), 21 July 1967.

Walter Hagen, 76, the leading professional golfer of the 1920s, 5 October 1969.

Ray Harroun, 89, winner of the first Indianapolis 500 in 1911 and inventor of the "hot spot" carburetor and pressed-steel auto wheels, 19 January 1968.

Sonja Henie, 57, Olympic figure-skating champion who went on to star in motion pictures and Hollywood Ice Revues, 12 October 1969.

Maximilian Justice ("Max") Hirsch, 88, leading horse trainer, 3 April 1969.

Rogers Hornsby, 66, won the National League batting title seven times in 23 years and was considered by many to be baseball's greatest right-handed batter, 5 January 1963.

Edward Britt ("Ted") Husing, 60, noted radio sports announcer, 10 August 1962.

Fred Hutchinson, 45, major-league manager and former pitcher for the Detroit Tigers, 12 November 1964.

Duke Paoa Kahanamoku, 77, Olympic swimmer who introduced the flutter kick, the one-time holder of every freestyle record up to one-half mile, 22 January 1968.

John Joseph Keane, 55, baseball coach and manager who was responsible for the 1964 rise of the Saint Louis Cardinals, 7 January 1967.

Ernie Knox, 26, boxer, died in the ring in Baltimore, Maryland, 16 October 1963.

Curley ("Earl") Lambeau, 67, one of the founders of the National Football League and coach for 31 years of the Green Bay Packers, 1 June 1965.

Anthony ("Champagne Tony") Lema, 32, professional golfer who won most of the major U.S. tournaments and was ranked tenth in official money earnings, died in a plane crash, 24 July 1966.

Eugene Allen ("Big Daddy") Lipscomb, 31, well-known football player, died of an overdose of heroin, 10 May 1963.

Dave MacDonald, 26, race-car driver, 30 May 1964.

Jack Mara, 57, president for 29 years of the New York Giants, helped to develop football into a leading spectator sport, 29 June 1965.

Rocky Marciano (Rocco Marchegiano), 45, former undefeated world heavyweight boxing champion, died in a plane crash, 31 August 1969.

George Preston Marshall, 72, owner and retired president of the Washington Redskins, 9 August 1969.

Bobby Marshman, 28, race-car driver, 3 December 1964.

John Leonard ("Pepper") Martin, 61, former outfielder and third baseman for the Saint Louis Cardinals, 5 March 1965.

Charles Mohr, 22, college boxer, died from injuries sustained in the ring at Madison, Wisconsin, 17 April 1960.

Davy Moore, 29, boxer, of injuries sustained in a featherweight championship boxing match, 23 March 1963.

Francis D. Ouimet, 74, the first amateur golfer to win the U.S. Open (1913), 2 September 1967.

Branch Wesley Rickey, 83, important major-league manager and executive who was instrumental in developing the Saint Louis Cardinals and Brooklyn Dodgers, 9 December 1965.

Glenn "Fireball" Roberts, 37, stock car driver, of injuries suffered during a race, 2 July 1964.

Robert A. ("Red") Rolfe, 60, named the all-time best third baseman of the New York Yankees, 8 July 1969.

Barney Ross, 57, former lightweight and welterweight boxing champion, 18 January 1967.

Jimmy Ryan, 33, former Indianapolis 500 winner, died in a car crash in Langhorn, Pennsylvania, 19 June 1960.

Eddie Sachs, 37, race car driver, 30 May 1964.

Earl Sande, 69, leading jockey in the 1920s and 1930s who won 967 races, including the 1923, 1925, and 1930 Kentucky Derby, 20 August 1968.

Burton Edwin Shotton, 77, major-league manager who in 1947 and 1949 took the Brooklyn Dodgers to pennant victories, 24 July 1962.

Helen Sobel Smith, 59, considered by many to be the best female bridge player in the world, 11 September 1969.

Amos Alonzo Stagg, 102, known as "the grand old man of football," spent seventy years coaching college teams and pioneered the forward pass and T-formation, 17 March 1965.

Lou Stillman, 82, owner of the renowned Stillman's Gym in New York City, where Jack Dempsey and Primo Carnera had worked out, 19 August 1969.

Harry A. Stuhldreher, 63, former football coach and the quarterback of the Four Horsemen of Notre Dame, 26 January 1965.

Reese ("Goose") Tatum, 45, former member of the Harlem Globetrotters, known as "the clown prince of basketball," 18 January 1967.

Dazzy Vance, 69, National League strikeout leader from 1922 to 1928 and member of the Hall of Fame, 16 February 1961.

Billy Wade, 34, race-car driver, 5 January 1965.

Paul Glee ("Big Poison") Waner, 62, a former outfielder for the Pittsburgh Pirates, was the third highest hitter in the National League and was elected in 1952 to the Hall of Fame, 29 August 1965.

Joe Weatherly, 44, race-car driver, 1 January 1964.

Armand ("Al") Weill, 75, manager of four world-championship boxers, including Rocky Marciano, 20 October 1969.

Wallace Werner, 28, Olympic skier, died in an avalanche at Saint Moritz, 12 April 1964.

Jess Willard, 86, world heavyweight boxing champion (1915–1919), 15 December 1968.

Craig Wood, 66, professional golfer, winner in 1941 of the U.S. Open and the Masters, 7 May 1968.

PUBLICATIONS

Hank Aaron, *Aaron, r.f.* (Cleveland: World, 1968);

Furman Bisher, *Miracle in Atlanta: The Atlanta Braves Story* (Cleveland: World 1966);

Al Bloemker, *500 Miles To Go: The Story of the Indianapolis Speedway* (New York: Coward-McCann, 1966);

Ty Cobb, *My Life in Baseball, The True Record* (Garden City, N.Y.: Doubleday, 1961);

Bob Cousy, *The Last Loud Roar* (Englewood Cliffs, N.J.: Prentice-Hall, 1964);

Robert Curran, *Pro Football's Rag Days* (Englewood Cliffs, N.J.: Prentice-Hall, 1969);

Robert Daley, *Cars at Speed: The Grand Prix Circuit* (Philadelphia: Lippincott, 1961);

Daley, *The Cruel Sport* (New York: Bonanza Press, 1963);

Joseph Durso, *The Days of Mr. McGraw* (Englewood Cliffs, N.J.: Prentice-Hall, 1969);

Harry Edwards, *The Revolt of the Black Athlete* (New York: Free Press, 1969);

Albert Hirshberg, *Basketball's Greatest Stars* (New York: Putnam, 1963);

Jack Johnson, *Jack Johnson is a Dandy: An Autobiography* (New York: Chelsea House, 1969);

Sanford Koufax, *Koufax* (New York: Viking, 1966);

Elmer Layden, *It Was a Different Game Then: The Elmer Layden Story* (Englewood Cliffs, N.J.: Prentice-Hall, 1969);

Mickey Mantle, *The Education of a Baseball Player* (New York: Simon & Schuster, 1967);

Peter McIntosh, *Sport in Society* (London: C.A. Watts, 1963);

Stirling Moss, *All But My Life* (New York: Dutton, 1963);

Joe Namath, *I Can't Wait Unitl Tomorrow . . . 'Cause I Get Better-Looking Every Day* (New York: Random House, 1969);

Jack Orr, *The Black Athlete: His Story in American History* (New York: Lion Press, 1969);

John George Pearson, *The Last Hero: The Gallant Story of Donald Campbell and the Landspeed Record, 1964* (New York: McKay, 1964);

George Plimpton, *Out of My League* (New York: Harper, 1961);

Plimpton, *Paper Lion* (New York: Harper & Row, 1966);

Edwin Pope, *Baseball's Greatest Managers* (Garden City, N.Y.: Doubleday, 1960);

Branch Rickey, *The American Diamond: A Documentary of the Game of Baseball* (New York: Simon & Schuster, 1965);

Fred Russell and George K. Leonard, *Big Bowl Football: The Great Football Classics* (New York: Ronald Press, 1963);

Marvin B. Scott, *The Racing Game* (Chicago: Aldine, 1968);

Louis Shecter, *The Jocks* (Indianapolis: Bobbs-Merrill, 1969);

Sam Snead, *The Education of a Golfer* (New York: Simon & Schuster, 1962);

Elaine Tarkenton, *A Wife's Guide to Pro Football* (New York: Viking, 1969);

Richard Thompson, *Race and Sport* (London: Oxford University Press, 1964);

Johnny Unitas, *Playing Pro Football to Win* (Garden City, N.Y.: Doubleday, 1968);

Baseball Digest, periodical;

Bowling Magazine, periodical;

Football News, periodical;

Golf, periodical;

Golf Digest, periodical;

Ring, periodical;

Sport, periodical;

Sporting News, periodical;

Sports Illustrated, periodical.

GENERAL REFERENCES

GENERAL

John Brooks, *The Great Leap: The Past Twenty-five Years in America* (New York: Harper & Row, 1966);

Chronicle of the 20th Century (Mount Kisco, N.Y.: Chronicle Publications, 1987);

Collier's Encyclopedia Yearbook (New York: Crowell-Collier, 1960–1969);

Current Biography Yearbook (New York: Wilson, [various years]);

John Patrick Diggins, *The Proud Decades* (New York: Norton, 1988);

John W. Dodds, *Everyday Life in Twentieth Century America* (New York: Putnam, 1965);

Andrew Jamison, *Seeds of the Sixties* (Berkeley, Cal.: University of California Press, 1994);

Paul Johnson, *Modern Times: From the Twenties to the Nineties*, revised edition (New York: HarperCollins, 1991);

Gerald McConnell, *Thirty Years of Award Winners* (New York: Hastings House, 1981);

Thomas Parker and Douglas Nelson, *Day by Day: The Sixties*, 2 volumes (New York: Facts on File, 1983);

Michael Downey Rice, *Prentice-Hall Dictionary of Business, Finance, and Law* (Englewood Cliffs, N.J.: Prentice-Hall, 1983);

This Fabulous Century, 1960–1970 (Alexandria, Va.: Time-Life Books, 1970);

Time Lines on File (New York: Facts on File, 1988);

James Trager, *The People's Chronology* (New York: Holt, Rinehart & Winston, 1979);

Claire Walter, *Winners: The Blue Ribbon Encyclopedia of Awards* (New York: Facts on File, 1982);

Leigh Carol Yuster and others, eds., *Ulrich's International Periodicals Directory: A Classified Guide to Current Periodicals, Foreign and Domestic, 1986–1987*, twenty-fifth edition, volume 2 (New York & London: R. R. Bowker, 1986).

ARTS

Liz-Anne Bawden, *The Oxford Companion to Film* (New York: Oxford University Press, 1976);

Carl Belz, *The Story of Rock,* second edition (New York: Oxford University Press, 1972);

Joachim Ernst Berendt, *The Jazz Book: From Ragtime to Fusion and Beyond* (Westport, Conn.: Hill, 1982);

Gerald Bordman, *The Oxford Companion to the American Theatre* (New York: Oxford University Press, 1984);

Malcolm Bradbury, *The Modern American Novel*, new edition (New York: Viking, 1992);

Reginald Smith Brindle, *The New Music: The Avant-Garde Since 1945,* second edition (Oxford & New York: Oxford University Press, 1987);

Elston Brooks, *I've Heard Those Songs Before, Volume II: The Weekly Top Ten Hits of the Last Six Decades* (Fort Worth, Tex.: Summit Group, 1991);

Steve Chapie, *Rock 'n' Roll Is Here to Pay* (Chicago: Nelson-Hall, 1977);

Ann Charters, ed., *Dictionary of Literary Biography 16: The Beats: Literary Bohemians in Postwar America* (Detroit: Bruccoli Clark/Gale Research, 1983);

Samuel B. Charters, *The Bluesmen* (New York: Oak, 1967);

Jim Curtis, *Rock Eras: Interpretations of Music and Society, 1954–1984* (Bowling Green, Ohio: Bowling Green University Popular Press, 1987);

Thadious M. Davis and Trudier Harris, ed., *Dictionary of Literary Biography 33: Afro-American Fiction Writers After 1955* (Detroit: Bruccoli Clark/Gale Research, 1984);

Davis and Harris, ed., *Dictionary of Literary Biography 38: Afro-American Writers After 1955: Dramatists and Prose Writers* (Detroit: Bruccoli Clark/Gale Research, 1985);

J. W. Ehrlich, ed., *Howl of the Censor* (San Carlos, Cal.: Nourse Publishing, 1961);

Jonathan Eisen, *The Age of Rock: Sounds of the American Cultural Revolution — A Reader* (New York: Random House, 1969);

Marc Eliot, *Rockonomics: The Money Behind the Music* (New York: Franklin Watts, 1989);

Philip H. Ennis, *The Seventh Stream: The Emergence of Rock'n'roll in American Popular Music* (Hanover, U.K.: Wesleyan University Press, 1992);

A. G. S. Enser, *Filmed Books and Plays, 1928–1983* (Aldershot, U.K.: Gower, 1985);

David Ernst, *The Evolution of Electronic Music* (New York: Schirmer-Macmillan, 1977);

David Ewen, *History of Popular Music* (New York: Barnes & Noble, 1961);

Leonard Feather, *The Book of Jazz: A Guide to the Entire Field* (New York: Horizon, 1965);

Feather, *The Pleasures of Jazz* (New York: Horizon, 1976);

Joseph J. Fucini and Susan Fucini, *Entrepreneurs: The Men and Women Behind Famous Brand Names and How They Made It* (Boston: G. K. Hall, 1985);

Harry F. Gaugh, *Willem de Kooning* (New York: Abbeville Press, 1983);

Louis D. Gianetti, *Understanding Movies* (Englewood Cliffs, N.J.: Prentice-Hall, 1987);

Barry K. Grant, ed., *Film Genre: Theory and Criticism* (Metuchen, N.J.: Scarecrow Press, 1977);

Donald J. Greiner, ed., *Dictionary of Literary Biography 5: American Poets Since World War II*, 2 volumes (Detroit: Bruccoli Clark/Gale Research, 1980);

Serge Guilbaut, *How New York Stole the Idea of Modern Art: Abstract Expressionism, Freedom, and the Cold War*, translated by Arthur Goldhammer (Chicago: University of Chicago Press, 1983);

Allen Guttman, *From Ritual to Record* (New York: Columbia University Press, 1978);

Michael Haralambos, *Right On: From Blues to Soul in Black America* (New York: Da Capo, 1979);

Jeffrey Helterman and Richard Layman, eds., *Dictionary of Literary Biography 2: American Novelists Since World War II* (Detroit: Bruccoli Clark/Gale Research, 1978);

Robert Carleton Hobbs and Gail Levin, *Abstract Expressionism: The Formative Years* (Ithaca, N.Y. & New York: Herbert F. Johnson Museum of Art and Whitney Museum of American Art, 1978);

Phil Hood, ed., *Artists of American Folk Music: The Legends of Traditional Folk, the Stars of the Sixties, the Virtuosi of New Acoustic Music* (New York: Morrow, 1986);

Penelope Houston, *The Emergence of Film Art: The Evolution and Development of the Motion Picture as an Art, from 1900 to the Present* (New York: Norton, 1979);

Pauline Kael, *5001 Nights at the Movies: A Guide from A to Z* (New York: Holt, Rinehart & Winston, 1982);

Frederick R. Karl, *American Fictions, 1940–1980: A Comprehensive History and Critical Evaluation* (New York: Harper & Row, 1983);

Alfred Kazin, *Bright Book of Life* (Boston: Little, Brown, 1973);

Orrin Keepnews and Bill Grauer, Jr., *A Pictorial History of Jazz*, second edition (New York: Crown, 1966);

James E. Kibler, Jr., ed., *Dictionary of Literary Biography 6: American Novelists Since World War II, Second Series.* (Detroit: Bruccoli Clark/Gale Research, 1980);

Lawrence O. Koch, *Yardbird Suite: A Compendium of the Music and Life of Charlie Parker* (Bowling Green, Ohio: Bowling Green University Popular Press, 1988);

Mike Leadbitter and Neil Slaven, *Blues Records 1943–1966* (New York: Oak, 1968);

Ernest Lindgren, *The Art of the Film* (New York: Macmillan, 1963);

Herbert I. London, *Closing the Circle: A Cultural History of the Rock Revolution* (Chicago: Nelson-Hall, 1984);

John MacNicholas, ed., *Dictionary of Literary Biography 7: Twentieth-Century American Dramatists* (Detroit: Bruccoli Clark/Gale Research, 1981);

Joseph H. Mazo, *Prime Movers: The Makers of Modern Dance in America* (New York: Morrow, 1977);

Don McDonagh, *The Rise and Fall and Rise of Modern Dance*, revised edition (Pennington, N.J.: A Cappella, 1990);

Jim Miller, ed., *The Rolling Stone History of Rock and Roll* (New York: Rolling Stone Press/Random House, 1976);

Robert Myron and Abner Sundell, *Modern Art in America* (New York: Crowell-Collier, 1971);

Frank O'Hara, *Art Chronicles, 1954–1966* (New York: George Braziller, 1975);

Charles Payne, *American Ballet Theatre* (New York: Knopf, 1978);

Norman Podhoretz, *Doings and Undoings: the Fifties and After in American Writing* (New York: Farrar, Straus, 1964);

G. Howard Poteet, *Published Radio, Television, and Film Scripts* (Troy, N.Y.: Whitston, 1975);

Robert George Reisner, *Bird: The Legend of Charlie Parker* (New York: Da Capo Press, 1962);

Charles Rembar, *The End of Obscenity: The Trials of Lady Chatterley, Tropic of Cancer, and Fanny Hill* (New York: Random House, 1968);

Nancy Reynolds, *Repertory in Review* (New York: Dial, 1977);

Neil V. Rosenberg, *Bluegrass: A History* (Urbana & Chicago: University of Illinois Press, 1985);

Barney Rosset, ed., *Evergreen Review Reader, 1957–1967: A Ten-Year Anthology* (New York: Grove, 1968);

Paul Rotha and Richard Griffith, *The Film Till Now* (London: Spring Books, 1967);

Irving Sablosky, *American Music* (Chicago: University of Chicago Press, 1969);

Irving Sandler, *American Art of the 1960s* (New York: Harper & Row, 1988);

Russell Sanjet, *From Print to Plastic: Publishing and Promoting America's Popular Music 1900–1980* (Brooklyn, N.Y.: Institute for Studies in American Music, 1983);

Andrew Sarris, *The American Cinema: Directors and Directions, 1949–1968* (New York: Dutton, 1968);

Eileen Southern, *The Music of Black Americans: A History*, second edition (New York: Norton, 1983);

Irwin Stambler and Grelun Landon, *Encyclopedia of Folk, Country, and Western Music*, second edition (New York: St. Martin's Press, 1984);

Tony Tanner, *City of Words: American Fiction, 1950–1970* (New York: Harper & Row, 1971);

C. Robertson Trowbridge, *Yankee Publishing, Inc.: Fifty Years of Preserving New England's Culture While Extending Its Influence* (New York: Newcomen Society, 1986);

Daniel Wheeler, *Art Since Mid-Century: 1945 to the Present* (Englewood Cliffs, N.J.: Prentice Hall / New York: Vendome, 1991);

Joel Whitburn, *The Billboard Book of Top 40 Hits*, fifth edition (New York: Billboard Books, 1992).

Mason Wiley and Damien Bona, *Inside Oscar: The Unofficial History of the Academy Awards* (New York: Ballantine, 1986).

BUSINESS AND THE ECONOMY

Daniel Bell, *The Coming of Post-Industrial Society* (New York: Basic Books, 1973);

John Brooks, *The Autobiography of American Business* (Garden City, N.Y.: Doubleday, 1974);

Keith L. Bryant, Jr., and Henry C. Dethloff, *A History of American Business* (Englewood Cliffs, N.J.: Prentice Hall, 1983);

Bryant, ed., *Encyclopedia of American Business History and Biography Railroads in the Age of Regulation, 1900–1980* (Columbia, S.C.: Bruccoli Clark Layman / New York: Facts On File, 1988);

Rachel L. Carson, *Silent Spring* (Boston: Houghton Mifflin, 1962);

Alfred D. Chandler, Jr., *Strategy and Structure: Chapters in the History of the Industrial Enterprise* (Cambridge, Mass.: MIT Press, 1962);

Barry Commoner, *The Closing Circle* (New York: Knopf, 1971);

Edward F. Denison, *The Sources of Economic Growth in the United States and the Alternatives Before Us* (New York: Committee for Economic Development, 1962);

John M. Dobson, *A History of American Enterprise* (Englewood Cliffs, N.J.: Prentice Hall, 1988);

Richard Easterlin, *The American Baby Boom in Historical Perspective* (Cambridge, Mass.: National Bureau of Economic Research, 1962);

John K. Galbraith, *Economic Development* (Cambridge, Mass.: Harvard University Press, 1964);

Galbraith, *The New Industrial State* (Boston: Houghton Mifflin, 1967);

George Gilder, *The Spirit of Enterprise* (New York: Simon & Schuster, 1984);

Charles E. Gilland, Jr., ed., *Readings in Business Responsibility* (Braintree, Mass.: D. H. Mark Publishing, 1969);

Mitchell Gordon, *Sick Cities* (Baltimore: Penguin, 1965);

Frank Graham, Jr., *Since "Silent Spring"* (Boston: Houghton Mifflin, 1970);

James R. Green, *The World of the Worker: Labor in Twentieth-Century America* (New York: Hill & Wang, 1980);

Michael Harrington, *The Other America* (New York: Macmillan, 1962);

Walter W. Heller, *New Dimensions in Political Economy* (Cambridge, Mass.: Harvard University Press, 1966);

G. Scott Hutchinson, *The Business of Acquisitions and Mergers* (New York: Presidents Publishing, 1968);

Bruce B. Kurtz, *Contemporary Art 1965–1990* (Englewood Cliffs, N.J.: Prentice Hall, 1992);

William M. Leary, ed., *Encyclopedia of American Business History and Biography: The Airline Industry* (Columbia, S.C.: Bruccoli Clark Layman / New York: Facts On File, 1992)

Ann R. Markusen, *The Rise of the Gunbelt: The Military Remapping of Industrial America* (New York: Oxford University Press, 1991);

George S. May, ed., *Encyclopedia of American Business History and Biography: Banking and Finance, 1913–1989* (Columbia, S.C.: Bruccoli Clark Layman / New York: Facts On File, 1990);

Daniel Patrick Moynihan, *Maximum Feasible Misunderstanding* (New York: Free Press, 1969);

Ralph Nader, *Unsafe at Any Speed* (New York: Grossman, 1965);

Glenn Porter, ed., *Encyclopedia of American Economic History: Studies of the Principal Movements and Ideas,* 3 volumes (New York: Scribners, 1980);

Joseph C. Pusateri, *A History of American Business* (Arlington Heights, Ill.: Harlan Davidson, 1984);

John B. Rae, *The American Automobile: A Brief History* (Chicago & London: University of Chicago Press, 1965);

Sidney Ratner, James H. Soltow, and Richard Sylla, *The Evolution of the American Economy* (New York: Basic Books, 1979);

Archie Robinson, *George Meany and His Times: A Biography* (New York: Simon & Schuster, 1981);

Graham Robinson, *Pictorial History of the Automobile* (New York: W. H. Smith, 1987);

E. F. Schumacher, *Small Is Beautiful* (New York: Harper & Row, 1973);

Larry Schweikart, ed., *Encyclopedia of American Business History and Biography: Banking and Finance, 1913–1989* (Columbia, S.C.: Bruccoli Clark Layman / New York: Facts On File, 1990);

Bruce Seely, ed., *Encyclopedia of American Business History and Biography: Iron and Steel in the Twentieth Century* (Columbia, S.C.: Bruccoli Clark Layman / New York: Facts On File, 1993);

Herbert Alexander Simon, *The New Science of Management Decision* (New York: Harper, 1960);

Alfred P. Sloan, Jr., *My Years at General Motors* (Garden City, N.Y.: Doubleday, 1963);

Studs Terkel, *Working* (New York: Pantheon, 1974);

Athan G. Theoharis, *The Boss* (Philadelphia: Temple University Press, 1988);

Murray Weidenbaum, *The Modern Public Sector* (New York: Basic Books, 1969).

EDUCATION

Philippe Aries, *Centuries of Childhood* (New York: Knopf, 1962);

Mary Knapp and Herbert Knapp, *One Potato, Two Potato . . . The Secret Education of American Children* (New York: Norton, 1976);

Fritz Machlup, *The Production and Distribution of Knowledge in the United States* (Princeton, N.J.: Princeton University Press, 1962);

Jean Piaget, *Play, Dreams and Imitation in Childhood* (New York: Norton, 1962);

Wilbur Schramm, J. Lyle, and I. de Sola Pool, *The People Look at Educational Television* (Stanford: Stanford University Press, 1963);

Schramm, ed., *The Eighth Art* (New York: Holt, Rinehart & Winston, 1962);

Joseph Turow, *Entertainment, Education, and the Hard Sell: Three Decades of Network Children's Television* (New York: Praeger, 1981).

FASHION

Bettina Ballard, *In My Fashion* (New York: McKay, 1960);

Michael Batterberry, *Mirror, Mirror: A Social History of Fashion* (New York: Holt, Rinehart & Winston, 1977);

Curtis F. Brown, *Star-Spangled Kitsch* (New York: Universe Books, 1975);

Jane Dorner, *Fashion in the Forties and Fifties* (London: Ian Allen, 1975);

The Encyclopedia of Fashion (New York: Abrams, 1986);

Madge Garland, *The Changing Form of Fashion* (New York: Praeger, 1970);

Georgina Howell, *In Vogue: Six Decades of Fashion* (London: Allen Lane, 1975);

Udo Kultermann, *Architecture in the 20th Century* (New York: Reinhold, 1993);

Jane Mulvagh, *"Vogue" History of 20th Century Fashion* (New York: Viking, 1988);

John Peacock, *20th Century Fashion: The Complete Sourcebook* (New York: Thames & Hudson, 1993);

Mary Shaw Ryan, *Clothing: A Study in Human Behavior* (New York: Holt, Rinehart & Winston, 1966);

Anne Stegemeyer, *Who's Who in Fashion* (New York: Fairchild, 1988);

Jane Trahey, *Harper's Bazaar: One Hundred Years of the American Female* (New York: Random House, 1967);

Elizabeth Wilson, *Adorned in Dreams: Fashion and Modernity* (Berkeley: University of California Press, 1987);

Tom Wolfe, *From Bauhaus to Our House* (New York: Farrar, Straus & Giroux, 1981);

Doreen Yarwood, *Fashion in the Western World, 1500–1990* (New York: Drama Book Publishing, 1992).

GOVERNMENT AND POLITICS

Graham T. Allison, *Essence of Decision: Explaining the Cuban Missile Crisis* (Boston: Little, Brown, 1971);

Stephen E. Ambrose, *Eisenhower: The President* (New York: Simon & Schuster, 1984);

Michael Barone, *Our Country: The Shaping of America from Roosevelt to Reagan* (New York: Free Press, 1990);

Jack Bass, *Taming the Storm: The Life and Times of Judge Frank Johnson and the South's Fight over Civil Rights* (Garden City, N.Y.: Doubleday, 1993);

David Bennett, *The Party of Fear: From Nativist Movements to the New Right in American History* (Chapel Hill, N.C.: University of North Carolina Press, 1988);

Michael R. Beschloss, *The Crisis Years: Kennedy and Khruschev, 1960–1963* (New York: Harper & Row, 1991);

Alexander M. Bickel, *Politics and the Warren Court* (New York: Harper & Row, 1965);

Vaughan Davis Bornet, *The Presidency of Lyndon Johnson* (Lawrence: University Press of Kansas, 1983);

Taylor Branch, *Parting the Waters: America in the King Years, 1954–1963* (New York: Simon & Schuster, 1988);

Franklin L. Burdette, *Readings for Republicans* (New York: Oceana, 1960);

Robert A. Caro, *The Years of Lyndon Johnson: Means of Ascent* (New York: Knopf, 1990);

Caro, *The Years of Lyndon Johnson: The Path to Power* (New York: Knopf, 1982);

William H. Chafe, *The Unfinished Journey: America Since World War II*, second edition (New York: Oxford University Press, 1991);

Rowland Evans and Robert Novak, *Nixon in the White House* (New York: Random House, 1971);

David Farber, *The Age of Great Dreams: America in the 1960s* (New York: Hill & Wang, 1994);

Benjamin Frankel, ed., *The Cold War, 1945–1991: Leaders and Other Important Figures in the United States and Western Europe* (Detroit: Gale Research, 1992);

Milton Friedman and Rose Friedman, *Capitalism and Freedom* (Chicago: University of Chicago Press, 1962);

Raymond Garthoff, *Reflections on the Cuban Missile Crisis* (Washington, D.C.: Brookings Institution, 1989);

James Gilbert, *Another Chance: Postwar America, 1945–1968* (Philadelphia: Temple University Press, 1981);

Todd Gitlin, *The Sixties: Years of Hope, Days of Rage* (New York: Bantam, 1987; revised, 1993);

Doris Kearns Goodwin, *Lyndon Johnson and the American Dream* (New York: Harper & Row, 1976);

Richard N. Goodwin, *Remembering America: A Voice from the Sixties* (Boston: Little, Brown, 1988);

David Halberstam, *The Best and the Brightest* (New York: Random House, 1972);

Nigel Hamilton, *J.F.K.: Reckless Youth* (New York: Random House, 1992);

Tom Hayden, *Reunion: A Memoir* (New York: Random House, 1988);

Jim F. Heath, *Decade of Disillusionment: The Kennedy-Johnson Years* (Bloomington: Indiana University Press, 1975);

Jerome Himmelstein, *To The Right: The Transformation of American Conservatism* (Berkeley: University of California Press, 1990);

Godfrey Hodgson, *America in Our Time* (Garden City, N.Y.: Doubleday, 1976);

Ole R. Holsti, *Crisis, Escalation, War* (Montreal: McGill University Press, 1972);

Fred Kaplan, *The Wizards of Armageddon* (New York: Simon & Schuster, 1983);

Stanley Karnow, *Vietnam: A History* (New York: Penguin, 1983);

Paul Kattenburg, *The Vietnam Trauma in American Foreign Policy* (New Brunswick, N.J.: Transaction Books, 1980);

Robert F. Kennedy, *Thirteen Days: A Memoir of the Cuban Missile Crisis* (New York: Norton, 1969);

Henry Kissinger, *White House Years* (Boston: Little, Brown, 1979);

Walter LaFeber, *America, Russia and the Cold War, 1945–1984*, fifth edition (New York: Knopf, 1985);

Nelson Lichtenstein, ed., *Political Profiles: The Johnson Years* (New York: Facts on File, 1976);

Lichtenstein, ed., *Political Profiles: The Kennedy Years* (New York: Facts on File, 1976);

John Lukacs, *Outgrowing Democracy: A History of the United States in the Twentieth Century* (Garden City, N.Y.: Doubleday, 1984);

Lukacs, *Passing of the Modern Age* (New York: Harper & Row, 1970);

Robert MacNeil, *The People Machine: The Influence of Television on American Politics* (New York: Harper & Row, 1968);

Myron Magnet, *The Dream and the Nightmare: The Sixties' Legacy to the Underclass* (New York: Bantam, 1993);

Michael Mandelbaum, *The Nuclear Question* (New York: Cambridge University Press, 1979);

Manning Marable, *Race, Reform and Rebellion* (Jackson, Miss.: University Press of Mississippi, 1991);

Allen J. Matusow, *The Unraveling of America: A History of Liberalism in the 1960's* (New York: Harper & Row, 1984);

James Miller, *"Democracy Is in the Streets": From Port Huron to the Siege of Chicago* (New York: Simon & Schuster, 1987);

Charles R. Morris, *A Time of Passion: America 1960–1980* (New York: Harper & Row, 1984);

Steve Neal, *The Eisenhowers: Reluctant Dynasty* (Garden City, N.Y.: Doubleday, 1978);

Hugh Pearson, *Huey Newton and the Price of Black Power in America* (Reading, Mass.: Addison-Wesley, 1994);

Edward Reed, ed., *Readings for Democrats* (New York: Oceana, 1960);

Kirkpatrick Sale, *SDS* (New York: Random House, 1973);

Arthur Schlesinger, Jr., *A Thousand Days* (Boston: Houghton Mifflin, 1965);

Eleanora W. Schoenbaum, ed., *Political Profiles: The Nixon/Ford Years* (New York: Facts on File, 1979);

John E. Schwaarz, *America's Hidden Success: A Reassessment of Twenty Years of Public Policy* (New York: Norton, 1983);

Theodore Sorenson, *Kennedy* (New York: Harper & Row, 1965);

Mark Stern, *Calculating Visions: Kennedy, Johnson, and Civil Rights* (Brunswick, N.J.: Rutgers University Press, 1992);

William L. Van Deburg, *New Day in Babylon: The Black Power Movement and American Culture, 1965–1975* (Chicago: University of Chicago Press, 1992);

Robert Weisbrot, *Freedom Bound: A History of America's Civil Rights Movement* (New York: Norton, 1990);

Theodore H. White, *The Making of the President 1960* (New York: Atheneum, 1961);

White, *The Making of the President 1964* (New York: Atheneum, 1965);

White, *The Making of the President 1968* (New York: Atheneum, 1969);

Gary Wills, *Nixon Agonistes* (New York: New American Library, 1970);

Harris Wofford, *Of Kennedy and Kings: Making Sense of the Sixties* (Pittsburgh: University of Pittsburgh Press, 1980).

LAW

Howard Ball, *The Warren Court's Conceptions of Democracy* (Cranbury: Associated University Presses, 1971);

R. Stephen Browning, ed., *From Brown to Bradley* (Cincinnati: Jefferson Law Book, 1975);

John Denton Carter, *The Warren Court and the Constitution* (Gretna, U.K.: Pelican, 1973);

Mildred Houghton Comfort, *J. Edgar Hoover, Modern Knight Errant* (Minneapolis: Denison, 1959);

David P. Currie, *The Constitution in the Supreme Court: The Second Century* (Chicago: University of Chicago Press, 1990);

Warren Freedman, *Society on Trial: Current Court Decisions and Social Change* (Springfield, Ill.: Thomas, 1965);

Alvin H. Goldstein, *The Unquiet Death of Julius and Ethel Rosenberg* (New York: Hill, 1975);

William W. Keller, *The Liberals and J. Edgar Hoover* (Princeton, N.J.: Princeton University Press, 1989);

Robert G. McCloskey, *The Modern Supreme Court* (Cambridge, Mass.: Harvard University Press, 1972);

Kenneth O'Reilly, *Hoover and the Un-Americans* (Philadelphia: Temple University Press, 1983);

Richard Gid Powers, *G-Men: Hoover's FBI in American Popular Culture* (Carbondale: Southern Illinois University Press, 1983);

Arnold S. Rice, *The Warren Court, 1953–1969* (Millwood, N.Y.: Associated Faculty Press, 1987);

Richard H. Sayler, Barry B. Boyer, and Robert E. Gooding, Jr., eds., *The Warren Court* (New York: Chelsea House, 1969);

Bernard Schwartz, *The Law in America* (New York: American Heritage, 1974);

Schwartz, *Super Chief: Earl Warren and His Supreme Court* (New York: New York University Press, 1983);

Robert Shnayerson, *The Illustrated History of the Supreme Court of the United States* (New York: Abrams, 1986);

Burton B. Turkus, *Murder, Inc.* (New York: Da Capo Press, 1992);

G. Edward White, *Earl Warren* (New York: Oxford University Press, 1982);

Stephen J. Whitfield, *A Death in the Delta* (Baltimore: Johns Hopkins University Press, 1991).

LIFESTYLES AND SOCIAL TRENDS

Beth L. Bailey, *From Front Porch to Back Seat: Courtship in Twentieth-Century America* (Baltimore: Johns Hopkins University Press, 1988);

Robert H. Bremner, and others, eds., *Children and Youth in America: A Documentary History*, 3 volumes (Cambridge, Mass.: Harvard University Press, 1970);

The Culture of Consumption: Critical Essays in American History, 1880–1980 (New York: Pantheon, 1983);

Jacques Ellul, *The Technological Society*, translated by John Wilkinson (New York: Knopf, 1964);

Betty Friedan, *The Feminine Mystique* (New York: Norton, 1963);

John K. Galbraith, *A Life in Our Times* (Boston: Houghton Mifflin, 1981);

Galbraith, *The New Industrial State* (Boston: Houghton Mifflin, 1967);

Park Dixon Goist, *From Main Street to State Street: Town, City, and Community in America* (Port Washington, N.Y.: Kennikat, 1977);

Kenneth T. Jackson, *Crabgrass Frontier: The Suburbanization of America* (New York: Oxford University Press, 1985);

Carl Kaufmann, *Man Incorporate: The Individual and His Work in an Organized Society* (Garden City, N.Y.: Doubleday, 1967);

William Kowinski, *The Malling of America: An Inside Look at the Great Consumer Paradise* (New York: Morrow, 1985);

Bart Landry, *The New Black Middle Class* (Berkeley: University of California Press, 1987);

Herbert Marcuse, *Critique of Pure Tolerance* (Boston: Beacon Press, 1965);

Marcuse, *An Essay on Liberation* (Boston: Beacon Press, 1966);

Marcuse, *Negations: Essays in Critical Theory* (Boston: Beacon Press, 1968);

Marcuse, *One Dimensional Man: Studies in the Ideology of Advanced Industrial Society* (Boston: Beacon Press, 1968);

John K. M. McCaffery, ed., *The American Dream: A Half-Century View from "American Magazine"* (Garden City, N.Y.: Doubleday, 1964);

Daniel O. Price, *Changing Characteristics of the Negro Population* (Washington, D.C.: GPO, 1969);

Charles A. Reich, *The Greening of America: How the Youth Revolution Is Trying to Make America Livable* (New York: Random House, 1970);

Milton Rokeach, *The Nature of Human Values* (New York: Free Press, 1973);

Ellen K. Rothman, *Hands and Hearts: A History of Courtship in America* (New York: Basic Books, 1984);

Mary P. Ryan, *Womanhood in America: From Colonial Times to the Present* (Danbury, Conn.: Franklin Watts, 1977);

Peter L. Skolnik, *Fads: America's Crazes, Fevers, and Fancies from the 1890s to the 1970s* (New York: Crowell, 1978);

Roger H. Smith, ed., *The American Reading Public: What It Reads, Why It Reads* (New York: R. R. Bowker, 1963);

Rick Tilman, *C. Wright Mills: A Native Radical and His American Intellectual Roots* (University Park: Pennsylvania State University Press, 1984);

100 Years of the Automobile (Los Angeles: Petersen, 1985).

MEDIA

Bart Andrews, *Lucy & Ricky & Fred & Ethel: The Story of "I Love Lucy"* (New York: Dutton, 1976);

Irwyn Applebaum, *The World According to Beaver* (New York: Bantam, 1984);

Association of National Advertisers, *Magazine Circulation and Rate Trends: 1940–1967* (New York: ANA, 1969);

Erik Barnouw, *Tube of Plenty*, second edition (New York: Oxford University Press, 1990);

Charles O. Bennett, *Facts Without Opinion: First Fifty Years of the Audit Bureau of Circulation* (Chicago: ABC, 1965);

A. William Bluem, *Documentary in American Television* (New York: Hastings House, 1965);

Tim Brooks, *The Complete Directory to Prime Time TV Stars: 1946–Present* (New York: Ballantine, 1987);

Robert Campbell, *The Golden Years of Broadcasting: A Celebration of the First 50 Years of Radio and TV on NBC* (New York: Scribners, 1972);

Harry Castleman and Walter J. Podrazik, *Watching TV: Four Decades of American Television* (New York: McGraw-Hill, 1982);

John Dunning, *Tune in Yesterday: The Ultimate Encyclopedia of Old-Time Radio 1925–1976* (Englewood Cliffs, N.J.: Prentice-Hall, 1976);

Walter B. Emery, *National and International Systems of Broadcasting: Their History, Operation, and Control* (East Lansing: Michigan State University Press, 1969);

Jay S. Harris, ed., *TV Guide: The First 25 Years* (New York: Simon & Schuster, 1978);

Laurence W. Lichty and Malachi Topping, *American Broadcasting: A Source Book on the History of Radio and Television* (New York: Hastings House, 1975);

J. Fred MacDonald, *Television and the Red Menace* (New York: Praeger, 1985);

Marshall McLuhan, *The Medium Is the Massage* (New York: Random House, 1967);

McLuhan, *Understanding Media: The Extensions of Man* (New York: McGraw-Hill, 1964);

Alexander McNeil, *Total Television: A Comprehensive Guide to Programming from 1948–1980* (New York: Penguin, 1980);

James Robert Parish, *Actors' Television Credits: 1950–1972* (Metuchen, N.J.: Scarecrow Press, 1973);

Jeb Perry, *Universal Television: The Studio and Its Programs, 1950–1980* (Metuchen, N.J.: Scarecrow Press, 1983);

Harry J. Skornia, *Television and Society: An Inquest and Agenda for Improvement* (New York: McGraw-Hill, 1965);

Gary A. Steiner, *The People Look at Television* (New York: Knopf, 1963);

Christopher Sterling, ed., *Broadcasting and Mass Media: A Survey Bibliography* (Philadelphia: Temple University Press, 1974);

Sterling, ed., *The History of Broadcasting: Radio to Televi-*

sion, 32 volumes (New York: New York Times/Arno, 1972);

Sterling, ed., *Telecommunications,* 34 volumes (New York: New York Times/Arno, 1974);

Vincent Terrace, *The Complete Encyclopedia of Television Programs: 1947–1979,* second edition (New York: Barnes, 1980);

Antoon J. van Zuilen, *The Life Cycle of Magazines: A Historical Study of the Decline and Fall of the General Interest Mass Audience Magazine in the United States During the Period 1946–1972* (Ulthoorn, the Netherlands: Graduate Press, 1977).

MEDICINE AND HEALTH

Leonard Berkowitz, *Aggression: A Psychological Analysis* (New York: McGraw-Hill, 1962);

The Cambridge World History of Human Disease (New York: Cambridge University Press, 1993);

Rick J. Carlson, *The End of Medicine* (New York: Wiley, 1975);

Frederic Fox Cartwright, *Disease and History* (New York: Crowell, 1972);

James H. Cassedy, *Medicine in America: A Short History* (Baltimore: Johns Hopkins University Press, 1991);

Faith Clark, ed., *Symposium III: The Changing Patterns of Consumption of Food,* International Congress of Food Science and Technology, Proceedings of the Congress Symposia, 1962, volume 5 (New York: Gordon & Breach Science, 1967);

Companion Encyclopedia of the History of Medicine (London: Routledge, 1993);

Marjorie Curson, *Jonas Salk,* (Englewood Cliffs, N.J.: Silver Burdett, 1990);

Bernard Dixon, *Beyond the Magic Bullet* (New York: Harper & Row, 1978);

John Patrick Dolan, *Health and Society: A Documentary History of Medicine* (New York: Seabury, 1978);

Martin Duke, *The Development of Medical Techniques and Treatments: From Leeches to Heart Surgery* (Madison, Conn.: International Universities Press, 1991);

Esmond R. Long, *A History of Pathology* (New York: Dover, 1965);

Albert S. Lyons, *Medicine: An Illustrated History* (New York: Abrams, 1978);

William A. Nolen, *A Surgeon's World* (New York: Random House, 1972);

Sherwin B. Nuland, *Doctors: The Biography of Medicine* (New York: Knopf, 1988);

John R. Paul, M.D., *A History of Poliomyelitis* (New Haven & London: Yale University Press, 1971);

Stanley Joel Reiser, *Medicine and the Reign of Technology* (New York: Cambridge University Press, 1978);

Rosemary Stevens, *American Medicine and the Public Interest* (New Haven: Yale University Press, 1971);

Elliot S. Valenstein, *Great and Desperate Cures* (New York: Basic Books, 1986).

RELIGION

Nancy T. Ammerman *Bible Believers: Fundamentalists in the Modern World* (New Brunswick, N.J.: Rutgers University Press, 1987);

Michael Baignet and Richard Leigh, *The Dead Sea Scrolls Deception* (New York: Summit, 1991);

Bernham P. Beckwith, *The Decline of U.S. Religious Faith, 1912–1984* (Palo Alto, Cal.: B. P. Beckwith, 1985);

Robert N. Bellah and Frederick E. Greenspahn, eds., *Uncivil Religion: Irreligious Hostility in America* (New York: Crossroads, 1987);

Charles C. Brown, *Niebuhr and His Age: Reinhold Niebuhr's Prophetic Role in the Twentieth Century* (Philadelphia: Trinity Press International, 1992);

Jackson W. Carroll, *Beyond Establishment: Protestant Identity in a Post-Protestant Age* (Louisville, Ky.: Westminster/John Knox, 1993);

Samuel McCrea Cavert, *The American Churches in the Ecumenical Movement, 1900–1968* (New York: Association Press, 1968);

John Cooney, *The American Pope: The Life and Times of Francis Cardinal Spellman* (New York: Times Books, 1984);

Harvey Cox, *Turning East: The Promise and Peril of the New Orientalism* (New York: Simon & Schuster, 1977);

Jay P. Dolan, *The American Catholic Experience* (Garden City, N.Y.: Doubleday, 1985);

John L. Eighmy, *Churches in Cultural Captivity: A History of the Social Attitudes of Southern Baptists* (Knoxville: University of Tennessee Press, 1987);

Robert S. Ellwood, *The Sixties Spiritual Awakening: American Religion Moving from Modern to Post Modern* (New Brunswick, N.J.: Rutgers University Press, 1994);

David Garrow, *Bearing the Cross: Martin Luther King, Jr., and the Southern Christian Leadership Conference* (New York: Morrow, 1986);

Andrew M. Greeley, *The American Catholic: A Social Portrait* (New York: Basic Books, 1977);

Carol V. George, *God's Salesman: Norman Vincent Peale and the Power of Positive Thinking* (New York: Oxford University Press, 1992);

Langdon B. Gilkey, *Catholicism Confronts Modernism: A Protestant View* (New York: Seabury, 1975);

Gilkey, *Gilkey on Tillich* (New York: Crossroad, 1990);

James Davison Hunter, *American Evangelicalism: Conservative Religion and the Quandary of Modernity* (New Brunswick, N.J.: Rutgers University Press, 1983);

Donald G. Jones and Russell E. Richey, eds., *American Civil Religion* (San Francisco: Mellen Research University Press, 1990);

Wayne W. Mahan, *Tillich's System* (San Antonio: Trinity University Press, 1974);

Bernard Martin, *The Existentialist Theology of Paul Tillich* (New York: Bookman Associates, 1963);

William C. Martin, *A Prophet with Honor: The Billy Graham Story* (New York: Morrow, 1991);

Martin Marty, *Pilgrims in Their Own Land: 500 Years of Religion in America* (Boston: Houghton Mifflin, 1984);

Robert Moats Miller, *Bishop G. Bromley Oxnam: Paladin of Liberal Protestantism* (Nashville: Abingdon Press, 1990);

Wilhelm and Marion Pauck, *Paul Tillich: His Life and Thought* (New York: Harper & Row, 1976);

Richard Quebedeaux, *The Worldly Evangelicals* (New York: Harper & Row, 1978);

Peter Rowley, *New Gods in America* (New York: McKay, 1971);

Edward S. Shapiro, *A Time for Healing: American Jewry since 1945* (Baltimore: Johns Hopkins University Press, 1992);

Ronald H. Stone, *Reinhold Niebuhr: Prophet to Politicians* (Nashville: Abingdon Press, 1972);

Ruth Wagerin, *The Children of God: A Make-Believe Revolution?* (Westport, Conn: Bergin & Garvey, 1993);

Brooks R. Walker, *Christian Fright Peddlers* (Garden City, N.Y.: Doubleday, 1964);

Edmund Wilson, *The Dead Sea Scrolls, 1947–1969* (New York: Oxford University Press, 1969).

Irving I. Zaretsky and Mark P. Leone, eds., *Religious Movements in Contemporary America*, (Princeton: Princeton University Press, 1974);

SCIENCE AND TECHNOLOGY

Gary M. Abshire, ed., *The Impact of Computers on Society and Ethics: A Bibliography* (Morristown, N.J.: Creative Computing, 1980);

Jack Belzer, Albert G. Holzman, and Allen Kent, eds., *Encyclopedia of Computer Science and Technology,* 16 volumes (New York: Marcel Dekker, 1975–1981);

Herman H. Goldstein, *The Computer from Pascal to von Neumann* (Princeton, N.J.: Princeton University Press, 1972);

J. Haugelan, *Artificial Intelligence: The Very Idea* (Cambridge, Mass.: MIT Press, 1985);

Leslie Katz, ed., *Fairy Tales for Computers* (Boston: Nonpareil Books, 1969);

Anthony O. Lewis, ed., *Of Men and Machines* (London: Dutton, 1963);

McGraw-Hill Encyclopedia of Science and Technology, fourth edition, 14 volumes (New York: McGraw-Hill, 1977);

Sam Mescowitz, ed., *The Coming of Robots* (New York: Collier, 1963);

N. Metropolis, ed., *A History of Computing in the Twentieth Century* (New York: Academic Press, 1980);

Lewis Mumford, *The Myth of the Machine: The Pentagon of Power* (New York: Harcourt, Bracc & World, 1964);

Cass Schichtle, *The National Space Program from the Fifties to the Eighties* (Washington, D.C.: GPO, 1983);

Science & Technology Desk Reference, edited by Carnegie Library of Pittsburgh, Science and Technology Department (Detroit: Gale Research, 1993);

Robert Silverberg, ed., *Men and Machines* (New York: Meredith Press, 1968);

Herbert Alexander Simon, *Sciences of the Artificial* (Cambridge, Mass.: MIT Press, 1969);

C. P. Snow, *The Two Cultures and the Scientific Revolution* (New York: Cambridge University Press, 1961).

SPORTS

Charles C. Alexander, *Our Game: An American Baseball History* (New York: Holt, 1991);

Arthur R. Ashe, Jr., *A Hard Road to Glory: A History of the African-American Athlete Since 1946* (New York: Warner, 1988);

William J. Baker and John M. Carrol, eds., *Sports in Modern America* (Saint Louis: River City Publishers, 1981);

Jim Benagh, *Incredible Olympic Feats* (New York: McGraw-Hill, 1976);

Edwin H. Cady, *The Big Game: College Sports and American Life* (Knoxville: University of Tennessee Press, 1978);

Roger Caillois, *Man, Play, and Games* (London: Thames & Hudson, 1962);

Erich Camper, *Encyclopedia of the Olympic Games* (New York: McGraw-Hill, 1972);

John Durant, *Highlights of the Olympics* (New York: Hastings House, 1965);

James B. Dworkin, *Owners Versus Players: Baseball and Collective Bargaining* (Boston: Auburn House, 1981);

Ellen W. Gerber, Jan Feshlin, Pearl Berlin, and Waneen Wyrick, *The American Woman in Sport* (Reading, Mass.: Addison-Wesley, 1974);

Elliott J. Gorn, *The Manly Art* (Ithaca, N.Y.: Cornell University Press, 1986);

Peter J. Graham and Horst Ueberhorst, editors, *The Modern Olympic Games* (Cornwall, N.Y.: Leisure Press, 1976);

Will Grimsley, *Golf: Its History, People and Events* (Englewood Cliffs, N.J.: Prentice-Hall, 1966);

Grimsley, *Tennis: Its History, People and Events* (Englewood Cliffs, N.J.: Prentice-Hall, 1971);

Allen Guttman, *A Whole New Ball Game: An Interpretation of American Sports* (Chapel Hill: University of North Carolina Press, 1988);

Dorothy V. Harris, ed., *Women and Sport* (College Park: Pennsylvania State University Press, 1972);

Robert J. Higgs, *Sports: A Reference Guide* (Westport, Conn.: Greenwood, 1982);

Neil D. Isaacs, *All the Moves: A History of College Basketball* (Philadelphia: Lippincott, 1975);

Bill James, *The Bill James Historical Baseball Abstract* (New York: Villard Books, 1986);

William O. Johnson, *All That Glitters Is Not Gold* (New York: Putnam, 1972);

Roger Kahn, *The Boys of Summer* (New York: Harper & Row, 1972);

Kahn, *The Era: 1947–1956, When the Yankees, the Giants, and the Dodgers Ruled the World* (New York: Ticknor & Fields, 1993);

Ivan N. Kaye, *Good Clean Violence: A History of College Football* (Philadelphia: Lippincott, 1973);

Lee Lowenfish, *The Imperfect Diamond: A History of Baseball's Labor Wars* (New York: Da Capo, 1991);

Richard D. Mandel, *Sport: A Cultural History* (New York: Columbia University Press, 1984);

Robert Mechicoff and Steven Estes, *A History and Philosophy of Sport and Physical Education* (Dubuque, Iowa: William C. Brown, 1993);

James A. Michener, *Sports in America* (New York: Random House, 1976);

Jack Olsen, *The Black Athlete: A Shameful Story* (New York: Time-Life Books, 1968);

Robert W. Peterson, *Only the Ball Was White* (Englewood Cliffs, N.J.: Prentice-Hall, 1970);

Benjamin G. Rader, *American Sports: From the Age of Folk Games to the Age of Spectators* (Englewood Cliffs, N.J.: Prentice-Hall, 1983);

Martin Ralbovsky, *Destiny's Darlings* (New York: Hawthorn Books, 1974);

Steven A. Riess, ed., *The American Sporting Experience* (West Point, N.Y.: Leisure Press, 1984);

Charles Rosen, *Scandals of '51* (New York: Holt, Rinehart & Winston, 1978);

William F. Russell, *Go Up for Glory* (New York: Coward-McCann, 1966);

Leverett T. Smith, Jr., *The American Dream and the National Game* (Bowling Green: Bowling Green University Popular Press, 1975);

Betty Spears and Richard A. Swanson, *History of Sport and Physical Education*, third edition (Dubuque, Iowa: William C. Brown, 1983);

Jules Tygel, *Baseball's Great Experiment* (New York: Oxford University Press, 1983);

David Q. Voigt, *America Through Baseball* (Chicago: Nelson-Hall, 1976);

Herbert Warren Wind, *The Gilded Age of Sport* (New York: Simon & Schuster, 1961);

Wind, *The Realm of Sport* (New York: Simon & Schuster, 1966);

Earle F. Zeigler, ed., *A History of Physical Education and Sport in the United States and Canada* (Champaign, Ill.: Stipes Publishing Company, 1975).

CONTRIBUTORS

ARTS
DARREN HARRIS-FAIN
Bruccoli Clark Layman, Inc.

BUSINESS AND THE ECONOMY
WILLIAM FRIEDRICKS
Simpson College

EDUCATION
HARRIET WILLIAMS
University of South Carolina

FASHION
DARREN HARRIS-FAIN
Bruccoli Clark Layman, Inc.

JOLYON HELTERMAN
Columbia University

SAM BRUCE
Bruccoli Clark Layman, Inc.

GOVERNMENT AND POLITICS
ROBERT M. ROOD
University of South Carolina

KAREN L. ROOD
Bruccoli Clark Layman, Inc.

LAW AND JUSTICE
KEVIN M. GREEN
Nashville, Tenn.

HALCOTT P. GREEN
University of South Carolina

LIFESTYLES AND TRENDS
CHARLES D. BROWER
University of South Carolina

MEDIA
JAMES W. HIPP
Bruccoli Clark Layman, Inc.

MEDICINE AND HEALTH
CAROLYN WILSON-BURROWS, M.P.H.
South Carolina Department of Health and Environmental Control

WAYNE BURROWS, M.D.
University of South Carolina Medical School

RELIGION
JOHN SCOTT WILSON
University of South Carolina

SCIENCE AND TECHNOLOGY
CAROLYN WILSON-BURROWS, M.P.H.
South Carolina Department of Health and Environmental Control

WAYNE BURROWS, M.D.
University of South Carolina

SPORTS
RICHARD LAYMAN
Manly, Inc.

INDEX TO PHOTOGRAPHS

GENERAL INDEX

Aronow, Don, 496

Arrangement in Grey and Black (Whistler), 35

Arrhenius, Svante, 462

The Art Carney Special (television), 369

Art Deco, 160

Artenstein, Malcolm S., 405

Artificial insemination, 394–395

Art News, 36

Art Nouveau, 142, 160

Arts and Letters, 496, 536

Art thefts, 25

Ash, Mary Kay, 93

Ashbery, John, 49

Ashe, Arthur, 535

Ashley, Laura, 144

Ashton-Warner, Sylvia, 136

Ashurst, Henry Fountain, 251

"A Significance for A&P Parking Lots, or Learning from Las Vegas" (Venturi), 168

The Assault on Poverty (Moynihan), 137

Assemblies of God, 420–421

Assembly (O'Hara), 25

Associative learning, 134

Astaire Time (television), 369

Astor, Vincent, 355

Astor Foundation, 356

Astounding Science Fiction magazine, 24

Astrodome, Houston, 143

A Taste of Honey (Delaney), 45, 61

Atheism, 435

Atlanta, Ga., 273

Atomic Energy Commission, 316, 450, 462

A Tour of the White House (television), 369

At the End of the Open Road (Simpson), 60

Audubon magazine, 84

Auerbach, Red, 507, 530

Aurora 7, 468–469

Austin, Warren, R., 251

Autobiography of Malcolm X, 235

Automobile Manufacturers Association, 500

Automobiles and automobile industry, 70, 80–81

    compact cars, 142

    compact cars get bigger, 143

    compact models, 149

    decline of the muscle car, 150–151

    declining sales, 142

    desire for high performance, 149

    foreign competition, 150–151

    growing foreign competition, 149

    imports, 80, 81

    increased production, 142

    large and gaudy, 149

    planned obsolescence, 144

    pollution, 168

    pollution control, 80–81

    safety, 81, 96, 144, 145, 145

    seat belts, 143

    smaller cars, 148

    taste for sport cars, 150

Avco-Everett Research Laboatory, 385

Avedon, Richard, 167

Avery, Sewell, L., 100

Avery v. *Midland*, 261

Avis rental cars, 89

Avon, 71, 93

Awards (lists), 62

    in the arts, 60–62

    in the fashion world, 169–171

"A Whiter Shade of Pale" (song), 29

A Wife's Guide to Pro Football (Tarkenton), 515

Baade, Walter, 484

Babaka, Richard, 529

Babbitt, Milton, 33

Babcock, W. Wayne, 407

Babson, Roger, 100

Baby Boom, 326

Baby Boomers, 263

"Baby Love" (song), 41

Bach, Johann Sebastian, 30

Bache, Harold, 100

Back, Carry, 489

Baez, Joan, 33, 37, 40, 151

Baeza, B., 532, 536

Baggs, William Calhoun, 372

Bailey, F. Lee, 270, 301

Baillie, Hugh, 100, 372

Bainter, Fay, 63

Baker, Bobby, 301

Baker, Howard, Jr., 227

Baker, Howard H., 251

Baker, John Franklin ("Home Run"), 536

Baker, J. Stewart, 100

Baker, Terry, 490, 533

Baker v. *Carr*, 258, 266–268, 294

Bakker, Jim, 436

Bakker, Tammy Faye, 436

Balaguer, Joaquin, 188

Balanchine, George, 32, 59

Balazs, Harold, 170

Baldwin, James, 25, 46

Baldwin, John F., Jr., 251

Balenciaga, Cristóbal, 142, 145, 166

Ball, Culiee, 357

Ball, Lucille, 368

"The Ballad of the Green Berets" (song), 28

The Ballad of the Sad Cafe (McCullers), 52

Ballard, Bettina, 172

Ballet, 32, 34

    regional companies, 44

Ballistic Missile Early Warning System, 476

Balsam, Martin, 61

Baltimore Colts, 492, 496, 512, 514–515, 533, 535

Baltimore Orioles, 494, 497, 504, 505, 534, 536

Bancroft, Anne, 29, 61, 62

Band of Gypsies, 54

"Bang-Shang-a-Lang" (song), 38

BankAmericard (VISA), 83

Bankhead, Tallulah, 63

Bank of America, 83

Baraka, Amiri, 46

Barbarella (movie), 30

Barber, Jerry, 532

Barber, Samuel, 60

Barbie Doll, 318

Barden, Graham A., 251

Barefoot in the Park (Simon), 45

Barger, Sonny, 322

Barghoorn, Elso S., 448, 453

Barnard, Christian, 401

Barnes, John W., 100

Barnett, Ross, 109, 113, 203–204

Barracuda, Plymouth, 150

Barrett, S. Ruth, 339

Barron, John, 370

Barry, Jack, 536

Barry, Jeff, 38

Barrymore, Diana, 63

Barth, John, 24, 28, 30, 47, 48

Barthelme, Donald, 29, 48

Bartlett, Neil, 444, 459

Barton, Bruce, 100, 437

Baruch, Bernard, M., 100, 339

Barzun, Jacques, 366

Baseball Hall of Fame, 527

BASIC, 446, 460

Basic education, 124–126

Basilio, Carmen, 526

Bass, Fontella, 28

Bassett, Charles, 473

Bassett, Leslie, 60

Bassetti & Company, 171

Bates, William H., 251
Batista, Fulgencio, 187
Batman (movie), 28, 310
Battle, W. Preston, 304
Bauer, Louis Hopewell, 407
Baum, Vicki, 63
Bayer aspirin, 377
Bayh, Birch, 221, 233
Bay of Pigs invasion, 176, 187–188
Bazaar, 155
Baziotes, William, 63
Beaamon, Bob, 523
Beach, Sylvia, 63
Beach Blanket Bingo (movie), 44
The Beach Boys, 26, 27, 28, 33, 38, 39, 319
Bean, Alan L., 476
The Beatles, 27, 28, 30, 31, 33, 38, 39, 154, 156, 167, 297, 309, 313, 319, 345
Beat movement, 49
Beatty, Jim, 488, 490
Beatty, Warren, 24, 29
Beauty by Mary Kay, 93
Beban, Gary, 495, 535
Beberman, Max, 120
Bebop, 33
Beck, David, 265
Becket (movie), 27, 61
Beckett, Samuel, 45
Beckwith, Byron De La, 259, 293–294
Beckwith, Jonathan, 458, 482
Bednarski, Bob, 497
Beebe, Charles William, 484
Beemer, Brace, 339
Beene, Geoffrey, 169
Beetle, Volkswagen (VW), 81, 145
Begley, Ed, 249
Behan, Brendan, 44
Bekesy, Georg von, 406, 483
Belafonte, Harry, 351
Belayev, Pavel, 472
Bell, James F., 100
Bell, L. Nelson, 420
Bell Dataphone, 389
Belli, Melvin, 299
Bellino, Joe, 488, 499, 532
The Bell Jar (Plath), 26
Bell Laboratories, 71, 357, 443, 449, 476
Bellow, Saul, 27, 50
Bell Telephone Company, 389
Bell Telephone System, 75
Belmont Stakes, 532–536
Bemelmans, Ludwig, 137
Bender, George H., 251

Bendix, William, 63
Ben-Hur (movie), 41
Bennet, W. Tapley, Jr., 188
Bennett, Dannis, Rev., 421
Bennett, John B., 251
Bennett, John C., 428, 429, 432
Bennett, Tony, 25, 33
Benny, Jack, 351, 357
Bentley, Elizabeth T., 304
Benton v. Maryland, 262
Benvenuti, Nino, 526
Beregovoi, Georgi T., 476
Berg, David B., 436
Bergen, Candice, 28, 338
Berger, Thomas, 27
Berlin Wall, 176, 185–186
Berning, Susie Maxwell, 535
Bernstein, Leonard, 26, 33, 43, 60
Berrigan, Daniel, 429, 430
Berrigan, Philip, 430
Berry, Chuck, 40
Berry, George, 405
Berryman, John, 49, 60
Bertelsen, Jim, 516
The Best Man (play), 61
Best-seller lists, 25
Best-sellers, 50
Bethe, Hans A., 483
Bethel, N.Y., 311
Bethlehem Steel, 75
Bettenhausen, Tony, 536
Betti, Ugo, 52
Bevel, James, Rev., 422
The Beverly Hillbillies (television), 355
Bewitched (television), 355
Beymer, Richard, 24, 43
Beyond the Fringe (revue), 45
The Beyond Within (Cohen), 324
The Bible (movie), 419
Bible translations, 427
Bickford, Charles, 372
Biddle, Anthony Drexel, 251
Biddle, Francis, 304
Bielevich, Alphonse, 530
"Big Bad John" (song), 25
Big Brother, 40, 54, 322
Bigelow, William F., 172
"Big Girls Don't Cry" (song), 25
Big Tree, John, 338
Bilingual Education Act, 124
Billboard magazine, 357
Bill of Rights, 279–280
Birch, John, 238
Birch Society, 237, 238, 423
Bird, Caroline, 326
The Birdman of Alcatraz (movie), 25

The Birds (movie), 26
Birkirts & Straub, 170
Birmingham, Ala., 203, 204, 320, 422, 434
Birth control pill, 395
Birthing problems, 395–396
Bisquier, Arthur B., 525
Bittner, John Joseph, 484
Black, Hugo, 288, 427
Black Aesthetic, 32, 46, 46–47, 47
Black Arts Movement, 32, 46–47, 49
The Blackboard Jungle (movie), 56
Black Catholic Clergy Caucus, 414
Black Fire (Baraka and Neal), 46
Black humor, 47–48
Black Journal (television), 350
Black Liberation Army, 236
Black Liberation Fromt, 249
Black Manifesto, 418
Black Mountain College, 35
Blackmun, Harry, 208, 291
Blackmur, R. P., 63
Black Muslims, 243, 330, 413, 418–419, 434–435
Black on Black (television), 350
Black Panther Party, 234–235, 236, 242–243, 243, 357
Black Panther Party for Self-Defense, 309, 315
Black Panthers, 183, 234, 249
Black Power, 234, 236
Black Power: The Politics of Liberation in America (Carmichael), 242
Blacks, 329, 350–351, 368, 418
    become militant, 234–235
    civil rights riots, 178
    colleges protests, 123
    conference on economic opportunities, 207
    education of, 137
    influence of vote, 220
    issue of IQ, 134
    on the Supreme Court, 261
    police brutality against, 258
    riot in Chicago, 179
    sit-ins, 108, 176
    study of their history, 120–121
    university integration, 108
    voter registration campaigns, 283–285
    and voter rights campaigns, 205, 205–206
    and voting registration, 234
    voting rights, 263, 264, 272
Blaik, Earl, 528

Blake, Eugene Carson, 424, 431, 432
Blakemore, Dr., 377
Blalock, Alfred, 387, 407
Blanda, George, 513, 530
Blass, Bill, 169
Bliss, George, 370
Blitzstein, Marc, 63
Bloch, Konrad E., 406, 483
Blonde on Blonde (Dylan), 54
Blood, Sweat and Tears, 33, 40
Blood banks, 377
Bloomberg, Leonard, 167
Bloomingdale, Alfred, 83
Blough, Roger, 87, 210
"Blowin' in the Wind" (song), 26, 38, 54
Blow-Up (movie), 42
The Blue Book of the John Birch Society, 238
Bluegrass, 33, 38
Blue jeans, 157
"Blue Velvet" (song), 26
Blumberg, Nathan J., 100
Bobbs-Merrill, 121
Bobby Fischer Teaches Chess (Fischer), 525
Bob Dylan (Dylan), 54
Bock, Jerry, 60
Bohan, Marc, 142
Boland, W., 535
Bolt, Robert, 45, 61
Bonanza (television), 355
Bonavena, Oscar, 511
Bond, Julian, 249
Boni, Charles, 63
Boni and Liveright, 63
Bonner, Herbert C., 251
Bonnie and Clyde (movie), 29, 30, 42, 144
Boorstin, Daniel, 120
Borgnine, Ernest, 30
Bork, Robert, 302
Borman, Frank, 473, 476
Born Female: The High Cost of Keeping Women Down (Bird), 326
"Born to be Wild" (song), 30
Boros, Julius, 533, 535
Bosch, Juan, 188
Bossa Nova, 33
Bossom, Alfred, 172
Boston, Celtics, 534
Boston, Mass., 268–270
Boston, Ralph, 488
Boston Celtics, 490, 491, 492, 493, 495, 496, 507, 530, 532, 533, 535, 536

Boston Five, 338
Boston Globe, 371
Boston Patriots, 491, 492, 513, 533
Boston Red Sox, 495, 504, 535
Boston Strangler, 259, 261, 268–270, 301
Boucher, Anthony, 63
Boudin, Leonard, 338
Boutique shopping, 155
Bow, Clara, 63
Bowe, Walter, 249
Bowling, 488
Bowmar Instruments, 86
Box (Albee), 52
Boxing, 488, 489
Boyd, Malcolm, 426, 432–433
"A Boy Named Sue" (Cash), 31, 53
Brabham, Jack, 502
Brackett, Charles, 63
Bradlee, Benjamin, 356
Bradley, Thomas, 250
Brand, Paul W., 406
Brandeis College, 123
Brando, Marlon, 25, 28, 42
Braniff Airways, 96
Brautigan, Richard, 27, 29, 30
Braverman, Al, 511
Breakfast at Tiffany's (movie), 24, 43
"Breaking Up Is Hard to Do" (song), 25
Brecher, Melvin, 170
Breckinridge, Henry, 304
Breedlove, Craig, 145, 492
Breger, William N., 171
Brennan, Francis Cardinal, 437
Brennan, William J., Jr., 286, 288, 290, 294–295
Brentano, Heinrich von, 358
Breuer, Marcel, 170
Brewer, Gay, 535
Brewster, Owen, 251
Bricker, Mead L., 172
Bridges, Styles, 251
Bridgman, Percy William, 484
Bright, William R., 436
Brinker, Maureen Connolly, 536
British Medical Journal, 399
British Open, 490, 518
British Society for the Preservation of the Mini Skirt, 144
Brodie, Bernard B., 406
Brooke, Edward R., 227
Brookhaven National Laboratory, 466
Brooklyn College, 111
Brooklyn Dodgers, 506
Brooks, Donald, 169, 169

Brooks, Gwendolyn, 46
Brooks, Mel, 30
Brooks, Overton, 251
Brooks, Richard, 419
Brooks, Van Wyck, 63
Brophy, John, 100
Brouwer, Dirk, 484
Brown, Clarence, 251
Brown, Claude, 136
Brown, Edmund G. (Pat), 227
Brown, Elmer, 100
Brown, Helen Gurley, 50
Brown, H. Rap, 234
Brown, James, 28, 30
Brown, Joe B., 300, 304
Brown, John Mason, 372
Brown, Norris, 251
Brown, Pat, 122, 301
Brown, Robert McAfee, 429
Browne, Malcolm W., 371
Brown Shoe Company, 70
Brownsville, NYC, 178, 183, 207
Brown v. *Board of Education*, 113, 298
Browone, Malcolm W., 370
Brubeck, Dave, 33, 52–53
Bruce, Lenny, 63, 339
Brucker, Wilbur M., 251
Brumfield, D., 534, 535
Brundage, Avery, 519, 523
Bruner, Jerome, 131–132, 136
Brunner Award, National Institute of Arts and Letters, 168
Bryan, Jimmy, 536
Bryant, Bear, 516
Brymer, Willard Rose, 511
Bucher, Lloyd M., 198
Buchman, Frank N. D., 437
Buchwald, Art, 354
Buckley, William F., Jr., 237, 238
Buckpasser, 493
Budd, Ralph, 100
Bueno, Maria, 533, 534, 535
Buescher, Edward L., 393
Buffalo Bills, 492, 493, 534
Buford, Charles H., 100
Bulluschi, Pietro, 168
Bundy, McGeorge, 191
Bundy, William, 191
Bunker, Arthur H., 100
Bunning, Jim, 492, 503
Buras, La., 109
Burbridge, Margaret, 455
Burdick, Eugene Leonard, 63
Burger, Warren, 180, 262, 290
Burmester, B. R., 397
Burnet, Frank McFarlane, 406

Burns, George, 63
Burroughs, William S., 25, 25, 27
Burroughs-Wellcome Company, 376
Burrows, Abe, 60
Burton, Harold Hitz, 304
Burton, Richard, 26, 27, 28, 41, 59, 61
Buskie, Edmund S., 226
Butch Cassidy and the Sundance Kid (movie), 30
Butterfield 8 (movie), 62
Bye, Bye Birdie (musical), 61
Bykovsky, Valeri, F., 470
Bylsma, Glenn, 376
Byrd, Harry F., 251
Byrd, Robert C., 226
The Byrds, 28
Cabell, James Branch, 352
Cable News Network (CNN), 359
Cabral, Donal Reid, 188
Cadillac, 143
Caesar, Orville S., 100
Cage, John, 33, 35, 57
Cahan, William G., 388
Cahill, John T., 304
Cahn, Robert, 371
Calder, Alexander, 36
Caldwell, Nathan G., 370
Caldwell, Zoe, 61
California, 308
"California Girls" (song), 28
California Supreme Court, 281
Calley, William L, Jr., 199
Calloway, Howare H., 199
Calvin, Melvin, 446, 459, 483
Camaro SS, 144
Cambridge Seven Associates, 171
Camelot (musical), 61
Campbell, Aldrich & Nulty, 171
Campbell, Bob, 517
Campbell's Soup, 77
"Camptown Meeting" (television), 437
Campus Crusade for Christ, 427, 436
Camus, Albert, 45
Cancer and smoking, 397–398, 402, 404
Cancer research, 380, 397
Candid Camera (television), 355
Candy Spits, 533
Cannon, Billy, 513
Cannon, Cavendish, W., 251
Cannon, Clarence, 251
"Can't Buy Me Love" (song), 27
Canteen Corporation, 89
Cantor, Eddie, 63

"Can't Take My Eyes Off of You" (song), 29
Capehart, Homer, 189
Caplan, Frank, 338
Caponi, Donna, 536
Capote, Truman, 28, 48, 50, 59, 275
Cararet (musical), 61
Carbo, Frankie, 510, 511
Cardin, Pierre, 142, 154, 166, 168
Cardinal Football League, 513
Cardiopulmonary resuscitation (CPR), 387
Carlos, John, 496, 523
Carlos, Walter (Wendy), 30
Carlson, Harold, 100
Carmichael, Stokely, 179, 207, 234, 236, 242–243, 314, 315
Carnaby Street, London, 156
Carnahan, Paul H., 100
Carne, Judy, 152
Carnegie Commission, 351
Carnegie Hall, NYC, 24, 37
Carnera, Primo, 536
Carnival (musical), 61
Carpenter, Malcolm S., 468–469
Carpenter, Scott, 465
The Carpetbaggers (movie), 43
Carr, Henry, 522
Carroll, Diahann, 61, 346, 350
Carry Back, 532
Carson, Johnny, 364, 521
Carson, Paul Earle, 407
Carson, Rachel, 308, 334–335, 339, 444, 484
Carswell, G. Harold, 208, 291
Carte Blanche, 83
Carter, Don, 490
Carter, Elliott, 60
Carter, Jimmy, 49
Carter, June, 53
Carter, Rubin ("Hurricane"), 526
Cartier, Pierre, 172
Cartier-Bresson, Henri, 32
Casals, Pablo, 25
Case, Clifford P., 224
Case, Francis Higbee, 251
The Case for Basic Education, 124
The Case for The South (Workman), 128
Cash, Johnny, 26, 31, 53
Cash, Norman, 503
Cashin, Bonnie, 169
Caskey, Charles t., 447
Casper, Billy, 493, 535
Cassady, Neal, 55, 63, 324
Cassidy, Marshall, 339
Cassini, Oleg, 166

Castle, Wendell, 161
Castro, Fidel, 187–188
Cat Ballou (movie), 27, 62
Catch-22 (Heller), 25, 47
Catcher in the Rye (Salinger), 51
The Catholic Legion of Decency, 42, 43, 44, 360
Catholics, 27, 413
Catholic University, 426
Cat's Cradle (Vonnegut), 26, 57
Caudill, rowlett, Scot, 171
Cavaglieri, Giorgio, 171
CBS *Evening News* (television), 344, 356, 365, 368
Celebrezze, Anthony, 108
Cell 16, 333
Celler-Kefauver Amendment, 70
Celtic Ash, 532
Censorship, 27
Center for Cognitive Studies, Harvard, 131
Center for Jewish Survival, 417
Center for the Study of Responsive Law, 96
Central Intelligence Agency (CIA), 176
Central Park, NYC, concerts, 28
Cernan, Eugene A., 473
Cesarean sections, 376
Chafee, John, 198, 226
Chaffee, Roger, 448, 474, 481
Chall, Jeanne, 136
Chamberlain, Wilt, 494, 507, 530
Chamberlin, Edward H., 137
Chambers, Lenoir, 370
Chambers, Whittaker, 251, 304, 372
Chancellor, John, 344
Chance Vought, 96
Chandler, Gene, 25
Chandler, Walter, 304
Chaney, James, 183, 205, 284
Chang, M. C., 327
Channing, Carol, 61
Chaplin, Ralph, 100
Chapman, Colin, 502
Chappaquiddick Island, Mass., 250
Chappelle, Dickie, 372
Chardack, William A., 405
Charger, Dodge, 149
Charismatic Renewal, 421
Charles, Ray, 24, 25, 25, 59
A Charlie Brown Christmas (television), 345
Charlotte, N.C., 136
Charly (movie), 62
The Chase (movie), 28

Corbett & Kman Kitchen and Hunt, 170
Corita, Mary, Sr., 436
Corman, Roger, 24
Cormier, Lucia Marie, 250
Cornell University, 118, 129
Corporation for Public Broadcasting, 347, 351, 351–352, 366
Corrigan, Frank P., 407
Corruption in the Palace of Justice (Betti), 52
Corvair, Chevrolet, 80, 81, 91, 142, 149, 150
Cosby, Bill, 350
Cosmopolitan magazine, 338
Costain, Thomas, 372
Cotton Bowl, 497
Coty American Fashion Critics' Award, 169
Cotzias, George C., 406
Council for Basic Education, 124, 125, 136
Council of Economic Advisers (CEA), 212
Council of Fashion Designers of America, 142
Council of Federated Organizations, 283
Country music, 39, 53
Couples (Updike), 30
Courrèges, André, 142, 143, 152, 157, 161, 166
Court, Margaret, 536
Cousy, Bob, 507, 508
Couture Future, 166
Coutures, 156
Couturiers, 159–160
Cowen, Joshua Lionel, 101
Cox, Allan, 447
Cox, Harvey, 419
Cox, Robert V., 371
Cox papers, 353
Cozzens, James Gould, 27, 30
Crab nebula, 448, 449, 456
Craig, Lyman C., 406
Craig, Roger, 506
Crane, Bob, 357
Crane, Stephen, 352
Cranston, Alan, 233
Crawford, Joan, 25
Crawford, Samuel Earl ("Wahoo Sam"), 536
Creationism, 414
Credit cards, 82–83
Creedence Clearwater Revival, 31, 40
Creeley, Robert, 49

Creer, Philip D., 170
Cresap, Mark W., Jr., 101
Crick, Francis H., 483
Crick, Harry C., 406
"Crimson and Clover" (song), 31
Crispus Attucks: Boy of Valor (Millender), 121
Criswell, W. A., Rev., 420
Crites and Mcconnell, 171
Cronin, James W., 445
Cronin, Thomas D., 405
Cronkite, Walter, 344, 356, 364–365, 368, 514
Crooners, 39
Crosby, Stills, Nash and Young, 40
Crosley, Powel, Jr., 101
Cross, Eason, 171
The Cross and the Flag (Smith), 239
Crouse, Russel, 372
Crow, James, 134
Crowther, Bosley, 30
The Crucible (Ward), 60
Crum, Allen, 288
Crumb, George, 60
Crump, Paul, 301
"Cryin" (song), 25
The Crying of Lot 49 (Pynchon), 28, 47, 56
Cryosurgery, 387–388, 402
The Crystals, 26
Cuba, 176, 177, 187–188, 279
Cuban migrants, 123
Cuban Missile Crisis, 189–193, 221
Cuban missiles, 177
Cudahy, Edward, Jr., 101
Culp, Robert, 350
Cummings, E. E., 34, 63
Cunningham, Merce, 32, 35, 46, 57
Cunningham, Walter, 475
Cunningham, Warren W., 170
Curran, Charles E., 426, 436
Currie, Bruce, 170
Curtice, Harlow H., 101, 172
Curtis, Tony, 24
Curtis Publishing Company, 352
Cushing, Richard Cardinal, 219, 414
Cuss I drilling barge, 463
Cutter Laboratories, 395
Cvetic, Matthew, 304
Cyclamates, 378, 398
Cy Young Award, 527
Czechoslovakia, 179, 194, 195
Daily Racing Form, 368
Dale, Edwin, 118
Daley, Richard, 217, 230
Dallas Cowboys, 534, 535

Dallas Museum, 36
Dallas Texans, 490, 533
Dalrymple, G. Brent, 447
Damascus, 494, 535
Dana, Bill, 364
Danby, G., 444
Dancer's Image, 495, 498
"Dancing in the Street" (song), 27
Dandridge, Dorothy, 63
Dangerous Visions (Ellison), 51
Daniels, Jonathan Myrick, 422
The Danny Kaye Show (television), 369
Danowski, Ed, 528
Dante, Ron, 38
Darby Dan, 494
Darling (movie), 62
Darling, Jay Norwood ("Ding"), 372
Darling of the Day (musical), 62
Darrow, Charles B., 101
Dartmouth College, 129
Dartmouth Time-Sharing System, 460
Darwell, Jane, 372
Dastagir, Sabu, 63
Datsun, 80, 81
Daugherty, Duffy, 517
Daugherty, Richard, 482
Dave Clark Five, 319
David, Brody & Associates, 171
David, Ernie, 489, 532
David Brinkley's Journal (television), 369
Davidson, Ben, 514
Davidson, Roy E., 101
Davies, Valentine, 339
Da Vinci, Leonardo, 26, 27, 29, 36
Davis, Adelle, 324
Davis, Arthur V., 101
Davis, Bette, 25
Davis, Ernest R., 536
Davis, Jimmie, 108
Davis, Miles, 33, 47, 53
Davis, Rennie, 231, 240, 244, 270–271
Davis, Richard Harding, 354
Davis, Taube C., 172
Davis Cup, 489, 491
Day, Robin, 161
"Day Camp in the Driveway" (Friedan), 335
Days of Wine and Roses (movie), 25
Daytona, Studebaker, 143
Daytona 500, 491, 501
Daytona Beach Continental, sports car race, 492
DDT, 76, 334

Dean, Jimmy, 25
Dean, Roger, 161
De Angelis, Anthony ("Tino"), 301
The Dean Martin Show (television), 355
Dear World (musical), 62
The Death and Life of Great American Cities (Jacobs), 142
Death at an Early Age (Kozol), 136
The Death of Bessie Smith (Albee), 52
The Death of God: The Culture of Our Post-Christian Era (Vahanian), 424
The Death of the Novel and Other Stories (Sukenick), 31
DeBakey, Michael E., 384, 385, 402–403, 406
Debye, Peter Joseph, 484
Decidely, 533
The Defenders (television), 369
DeForest, Lee, 484
De Gaulle, Charles, 210
Deities and Dolphins: The Story of the Nabataeans (Gluek), 436
De Kooning, Willem, 34
Delaney, Shelagh, 45
De la Renta, Oscar, 169
Delbruck, Max, 406, 483
A Delicate Balance (Albee), 52, 60
Dellinger, David, 231, 244, 270–271
Del Monte, 89
Delugach, Albert L., 371
DeMatteo, William L., 170
Democratic campaign, 1960, 420
Democratic National Convention, 1960, 217
Democratic National Convention, 1964, 205, 225
Democratic National Convention, 1968, 183, 230–231, 235, 261, 264, 270
Democratic nomination campaign, 1960, 216–217
Democratic nomination campaign, 1964, 224–225
Democratic nomination campaign, 1968, 229–230
Democratic Party, 177
Denim, 157
Dennis, Eugene, 251
Dennis, Sandy, 28, 61
Department of Agriculture, 76, 334
Department of Defense, 316
Department of Health, Education, and Welfare, 76
Department of Transportation, 74

DePaula, Frankie, 511
Depo-Provera, 378
Depugh, Robert Bolivar, 238
The Deputy (Hochhuth), 27, 421
Dershowitz, Alan, 301
DeSalvo, Albert, 261
Desegregation, 108, 260, 272, 283–285, 412
Desert Inn hotel, 95
DeSlavo, Albert Henry, 268–270
Desmond, Paul, 52
Desmond-Miremont-Birks, 171
De Soto automobile, 70
Detroit, Mich., 179, 310
Detroit Red Wings, 533, 534
Detroit Tigers, 496, 504, 535
Developmental psychology, 132–133, 403
De Vicenzo, Roberto, 495
De Vido, Alfred, 171
Devine, Major Jelous, Fr., 437
De Voto, Bernard, 26
Dewey, Al, 301
Dewey, John, 124, 136, 137
Diamond, Neil, 38
Diana Ross and the Supremes, 29
Dicke, Robert H., 457
Dickey, James, 49
The Dick Van Dyke Show (television), 350, 355, 369
Didion, Joan, 49
"Did You Ever Have to Make Up Your Mind?" (song), 28
Diem, Ngo Dinh, 177, 196, 197
The Diggers, 322
Digital Equipment Corporation, 444
The Dilemma of the Modern Jew (Prinz), 417
Dillon, C. Douglas, 209
Diners Club, 83
Dion, 25
Dior, 142
Dior, Christian, 142, 144, 146, 151
Dirks, Rudolph, 372
Dirksen, Everett McKinley, 205, 249, 251
Disc jockeys, 357
Discoverer 13, 476
Disney, Michael, 449, 456
Disney, Walt, 63, 101, 339, 521
Divorce, 326
Dixie 500, 501
Dixieland jazz, 33, 38
DNA, 443, 448, 451, 458, 459, 481
Doctorow, E. L., 24

Doctors for Johnson Committee, 337
Doctor Zhivago (movie), 27
Dodd, Edward H., 101
Dodd, Frank C., 101
Dodd, Thomas J., 226, 239
Dodge, Hartley M., 101
Dodge, Joseph M., 101
Doell, Richard G., 447
Dolby, Ray, 447
Dole, Robert, 233
Dolenz, Mickey, 38
Dominican Republic, 245
Dominic, 169
Dominican Republic, 178, 188, 245
"Dominique" (song), 26
Domino's Pizza, 85
Donne, John, 137
Donovan, James, 130
"Don't Come Home a-Drinkin' (with Lovin' on Your Mind)" (song), 28
Dooley, Thomas, 407
The Doors, 29, 30
Door-to-door sales, 93
Dorvillier, W. J., 370
Dotter, Charles T., 386
Douglas, Kirk, 24, 55
Douglas, Melvyn, 61
Douglas, Mike, 364
Douglas, Paul, 209, 227
Douglas, William O., 280, 288, 290, 301
Dover Press, 420
"Do Wah Diddy Diddy" (song), 27
Dow Chemical Company, 83–84, 318
Dow Jones average, 74, 76, 81
Downbeat, 53
"Downtown" (song), 28
Doyle, Clyde Gilman, 251
"Do You Know the Way to San Jose?" (song), 30
Dozier, Lamont, 41
Drake, Frank, 456–457
Drake, Vicky, 338
Drama schools, 121
Dress codes, 154, 159
Dressen, Charles Walater, 537
Dreyfull & Blackford, 171
Dr. No (movie), 25, 44
Dr. Strangelove or: How I Learned to Stop Worrying and Love the Bomb (movie), 55
Drug Amendments Act, 399
Drug Research, Inc., 321
Drug side effects, 381, 399–400

Drury, Allen, 60
Dryfoos, Orvil E., 101, 372
Drysdale, Don, 499, 505, 527
Dubcek, Aleksander, 195
DuBois, W. E. B., 63, 339
Duby, Roy, 490
Duchamp, Marcel, 63
Duclos, Michelle, 249
Duffy, Edward, 372
Dugan, Alan, 60
"Duke of Earl" (song), 25
Duke University, 491, 534
Dulbecco, Renato, 406
Dullea, Keir, 30
Dulles, Allen W., 251
Dulles, John Foster, 238
Du Mont, Allen Balcom, 372
Dumont, Margaret, 63
Dunaway, Faye, 29, 144
Dune (Herbert), 27
DuPont, Ethel, 339
Du Pont, Irenee, 101
Du Pont Corporation, 71, 145, 210, 449
Durable Dish Company, 168
Durstine, Roy S., 101
Duryea, James Frank, 101, 172
Dutchman (Jones)
Dwight, Edward J., 445
Dworshak, Henry C., 251
Dylan (play), 61
Dylan, Bob, 28, 31, 33, 37, 38, 53–54, 241, 325, 337
"The *Eagle* has landed," 476
Eagleton, Thomas F., 233
Earl, Harley, 172
Early Bird, 348, 358
Earth Day, 84
Eastern Establishment Republicans, 221, 222, 223
Easterwood, Henry, 170
East Germany, 519
Eastman, Max, 63, 372
Easy Rider (movie), 30
Eaton, William, 296
Eberhart, Richard, 60
Ebony magazine, 326
Eccles, John Carew, 406
Echo satellite, 442, 457, 476
ECHO 1, 442, 476
Echoes of Time and the River (Crumb), 60
Ecker, Frederick H., 101
Eckert, William D., 493, 506
Economic Opportunity Act (Head Start), 118, 214

Economic Research and Action Project (ERAP), 240, 244
Ecumenicism, 421
Eddy, Nelson, 63
Edelman, Arthur and Theodora, 169
Eden, Anthony, 358
The Edge of Sadness (O'Connor), 60
The Edge of the Sea (Carson), 334
Edison, Charles, 101, 339
The Ed Sullivan Show (television), 39, 345
Education
  antidiscrimination laws, 272
  basic vs. progressive, 124–126
  bilingual, 111, 123–124
  busing, 130
  campus discontent, 114
  criticism of the system, 133
  de facto segregation, 113
  desegregation of colleges, 113
  desegregation of secondary schools, 113
  discovery learning, 120
  expansion of community colleges, 114
  federal aid to, 213, 214
  foreign language training, 119
  government funding, 116
  increased college enrollment, 114
  intellectual training vs. social adjustment, 115
  the leadership of California, 125
  learning theory, 131, 134, 135
  loan programs, 118–119
  local vs. federal role, 136
  national assessment of, 135
  of migrant workers, 123–122
  of military personnel, 127
  of the mentally handicapped, 130
  the open university, 118
  policy making, 132
  private vs. public, 137
  programs for gifted children, 119
  revision of history, 120
  teaching machines and programmed learning, 128–129
  use of television, 127–128
Educational Council for Foreign Medical Graduates, 383
Educational Services, Inc., MIT, 119
Edwards, Harry, 522
Effer, Donald, 386
Egbert, Sherwood H., 101
"Ego Development and Historical Chance" (Erikson), 133

Ehrlich, Paul, 328
Eichman in Jerusalem: A Report on the Banality of Evil (Arendt), 418
"Eight Days a Week" (song), 28
18 Happenings in 6 Parts (Kaprow), 35
Einstein, Albert, 465
Einstein Shift, 466
Eisele, Donn F., 475
Eisenhower, David, 250
Eisenhower, Dwight D., 59, 70, 176, 222, 223, 238, 251, 294, 312, 358
  farewell address, 176, 185
  social policy, 212
Eisenhower, Earl Dewey, 339
Ekstrom, Edwin, 101
El Cid (movie), 24
"Eleanor Rigby" (song), 28
Elections
  1960, 218–221
  1962, 189, 192, 221
  1964, 221–226, 226
  1966, 207–208, 226–227
  1968, 201, 231–234
  poll tax, 259
The Electric Kool-Aid Acid Test (Wolfe), 49
Electrocardiogram (EKG), 389
Elementary and Secondary Education Act, 117, 119, 215
Eliot, T. S., 49, 63
Elizabeth, N.J., 207
Elle, 167
Ellington, Duke, 26, 28, 33
Elliott, Douglas, H., 251
Elliott, Osborn, 356
Ellis, Jimmy, 495
Ellis, Sidney, 167
Ellison, Harlan, 51
Ellison, Ralph, 46
Elmer Gantry (movie), 24, 62, 419
El Paso Natural Gas Company, 462
Emerson, R. A., 101
Emerson, Roy, 533, 534
Emerson, William A., 353
Emmy Awards, 369
Emory University, 319
Encyclopaedia Britannica, 72
Enders, John, 376, 392, 405
The Enemy Within (Kennedy), 265
Engel v. *Vitale*, 258, 279, 280, 412, 426, 427
Engle, Clair, 252
Englehardt, Nickolaus, 136
English Syntax (Roberts), 137
Environmentalism, 84–85

Environmental Protection Agency (EPA), 84–85, 96, 335
Envoid, 308, 327, 395, 397
Epstein, Barbara, 357
Epstein, Brian, 64
Epstein, Jason, 357
Equal employment opportunity, 260, 272
Equal Employment Opportunity Commission (EEOC), 332
Equal Opportunity Act, 72
Equal Rights Amendment, 312, 331
Erikson, Erik, 132–133
Erwin, Stuart, 372
Escobedo v. *Illinois*, 159, 277, 289
Eshbach, William W., 170
Esherick, Joseph, 171
Esquire, 49
Esslin, Martin, 45
Estes, Billie Sol, 302
Eufemia, Michael, 531
Evangelicals, 415
Evangelical United Brethren, 424
Evans, Clifford, 447, 452
Evans, Lee, 523
Evans v. *Newton*, 260
Everett, Robert A., 252
Evers, Medgar, 183, 204, 259, 293
"Everybody Loves Somebody" (song), 27
Everything That Rises Must Converge (O'Connor), 27
Evolution, 414
Evolution teaching, 413
Executive Committee of the National Security Council (Excomm), 190
Executive Coloring book, 319
Exploring Inner Space (Davis), 324
Expo '67, Montreal, 144
Exxon, 77
The Fab Four, 38
The Fabulous Fifties (television), 369
Faction literature, 48
The Factory, 58, 336–337
Fadiman, Clifton, 125–126
Fair Labor Standards Act, 70
Fairless, Benjamin F., 101
Fairness Doctrine, 360
Faith 7, 470
Falcon, Ford, 80, 142, 149, 150
Fallon, Michael, 321
Family Affair (television), 355
Fanny Hill (Cleland)
Fanon, Frantz, 235, 241
Farber, Sidney, 406
Farid-es-Sutanah, 340

Farmer, James, 203, 204, 320
Farm population, 72
Farm price supports, 79–80
Farm size and productivity, 79
Farrow, Mia, 30
Farson, Negley, 372
Fashion Hall of Fame, 168
Faubus, Orval, 221
Faulk, John Henry, 368
Faulkner, William, 33, 50, 60, 64, 352
Fay, Sidney B., 137
Fay v. *Noia*, 294
Federal Aid to the Arts Bill, 35
Federal Bureau of Investigation, 236, 284, 315
Federal Communications Commission, 344, 360, 362, 366
Federal Republic of Germany, 185
Federal Reserve Board, 73, 212
Federal Trade Commission, 72
Federation Internationale de checs (FIDE), 525
Feller, Happy, 516
Fellowship of Reconciliation, 329, 429
The Feminine Mystique (Friedan), 91, 308, 312, 326, 331, 335–336
Feminists, 312
Ferber, Edna, 64
Ferguson, Cathy, 522
Ferlinghetti, Lawrence, 49
Fermilab (National Accelerator Lab), 449
Ferrie, David William, 184
Ferriss, Hugh, 172
Fertility drugs, 377, 378, 381, 395
Fetterman, John, 371
Feynman, Richard P., 483
Fiat, 80
Fiddler on the Roof (musical), 33, 61
Fidelity Capital Fund, 82
Fidelity Fund, 82
Fiedler, Leslie, 24
Field, Marshall, Jr., 101, 372
Fifth Avenue Coach Lines, 73
The Fifth Dimension, 31
Fig Tree Chert, South Africa, 453
Figure skating, 489
Filipchenko, Anatoli V., 476
Finch, Robert, 123, 124, 399
Finerty, John F., 304
Finney, Albert, 26
Fiore, Quentin, 366
Fiorello! (Abbott, Weidman, Harnick, and Bock), 60, 61
Firecracker 400, 501

Fire in the Streets: America in the 1960's (Viorst), 123
Firing Line (television), 237
First Amendment, 258
First Baptist Church, Montgomery, Ala., 320
First Tuesday (television), 359
Fischer, Bobby, 489, 525
Fischer, John, 366
Fischetti, John, 371
Fisher, Charles T., 101, 172
Fisk University, 329
Fitch, Val, 445
Fitzgerald, F. Scott, 352
Fitzpatrick, Daniel R., 372
Fitzsimmons, James E. ("Sunny Jim"), 537
The Fixer (Malamud), 28, 50, 60
Flagg, James Montgomery, 64
Fleischmann, Raoul Herbert, 372
Flemer, Stevenson, 171
Fleming, Peggy, 493, 495, 524
Flemings, Ian, 50
Flora, the Red Menace (musical), 61
Florida, 308
Florida State University, 124
Flower children, 157
Flowers, Richmond, 296
Floyd, Ray, 536
Fluoridated water, 378
Fleishmann, Julius, 339
Fly, James L., 101
Foale, Marian, 156
Foale fashions, 143
Fogarty, John E., 252
Foley, Clyde Julian ("Red"), 64
Foley, Zora, 512
Folger, Abigail, 297
Folk music, 33, 37–39, 39, 53–54
Folk rock, 38
Follow Through program, 118
Follow Through program, education, 117
Fonda, Jane, 27, 28, 30
Fonda, Peter, 30
Fonteyn, Margot, 32, 59
Food and Drug Administration (FDA), 467
Food and Drug Adminstration, 210, 308, 323
Food Checkers and Cashiers Union, 98
Football Hall of Fame, 527
Foote, Emerson, 398
Foote, Horton, 50
Forbes, Bruce C., 101
For Blacks Only (television), 350

The Great White Hope (Sackler), 60, 62
Greek Money, 533
Greeley, Andrew, Fr., 426
Greeley, Horace, 354
Greely, Dana Mclean, 430
Green, Howard, 483
Green, Theodore Francis, 252
Green, William J., Jr., 252
Green & Abrahamson, 171
Green Bay Packers, 489, 490, 493, 494, 495, 507, 514–515, 526, 527, 528–529, 532, 533, 534, 534, 535
The Green Berets (movie), 30, 186
Greenberg, Henry Clay, 304
Greenberg, Irving, Rabbi, 417
Greenberg, Paul, 371
Greene, Gael, 122
Green Eggs and Ham (Seuss), 51
Greenfield, Albert M., 102
Greenhouse effect, 462
Greenmeyer, Darryl, 531
The Green Revolution, 449
Greensboro, N.C., 108, 176, 202, 308, 328, 421
Gregory, Dick, 330
Grenada, 189
Grew, Joseph Clark, 252
Greyhound Bus Company, 320
Grierson, Herbert, 137
Griffin, Merv, 364
Griffin, Oscar, Jr., 370
Griffin v. California, 260, 278
Griffith, Emile, 510, 526
Grigsby, William, 390
Grissom, Gus, 448
Grissom, Virgil I. ("Gus"), 448, 468, 472, 474, 480–481
Griswold, Alfred Whitney, 138
Griswold, Estelle, 302
Griswold v. Connecticut, 260
Gropius, Walter, 148, 164, 168, 172
Groppi, James, Fr., 423
Groshand, Werner, 170
Gross, Robert E., 102
Gross National Product, 70, 72, 74, 75, 76, 211
The Group (McCarthy), 26, 28, 50
Growing Up Absurd (Goodman), 133
Gruening, Ernest, 200, 233
Gruzen & Partners, 171
GTO, Pontiac, 149
Guarnteed loans for students, 119
Gubb, Larry E., 102

Guess Who's Coming to Dinner (movie), 29, 56, 62
Guggenheim Museum, 31
Guinness, Alec, 61
Guinzburg, Harold K., 102
Gulf of Tonkin incident, 197–198, 309
Gulf of Tonkin Resolution, 72, 178
Gun control, 262
Gunsmoke (television), 355
Gurney, Dan, 502
Gustines, H., 535
The Gutenberg Galaxy: The Making of Typographic Man (McLuhan), 365
Guthrie, Arlo, 29, 40
Guthrie, Woody, 33, 37, 54, 64
Guthrie Theatre, Minneapolis, 27
Gutkind, Erwin A., 172
Guyot, Arnold, 481
Gwathmey & Henderson, 171
Haacke, Hans, 36
Haagen-Smit, A. J., 80
Hackett, Buddy, 30
Hadas, Moses, 64, 138
Hagarty, James A., 372
Hagen, Uta, 52, 61
Hagen, Walter, 537
Haggard, Merle, 31
Hahn, Paul M., 102
Haight-Ashbury, San Francisco, 39, 313, 321, 324
Hailey, Arthur, 51
Hail To All, 534
Hair (musical), 33
Hair styles, 153–154, 156, 166–167
Halanicki, Barbara, 155
Halberstam, David, 367, 371
Hall, David M., 252
Hall, Joyce, 369
Hallelujah, Baby! (musical), 61, 62
Halley, George, 169
Hall of Fame award, fashion, 169
Halston, 169, 170
Hamilton, Charles V., 242, 314
Hamilton, Edith, 64
Hammarskjold, Dag, 187
Hammell, Alfred L., 102
Hammerstein, Oscar, II, 64
Hammett, Dashiell, 64
Hampton, Fred, 236, 249, 315
Hancock Building, Chicago, 145
Hancock Center, Chicago, 164
Hand, Learned, 305
H&R Block, 85
"Hang On, Sloopy" (song), 28
Hannah v. Slawson, 258

Hanratty, Terry, 517
Hansberry, Lorraine, 64
Hansen, Carl, 125, 136
Hansen, Ron, 495
Happenings, 35
The Happy Time (musical), 62
"Happy Together" (song), 29
Harbach, Otto, 64
Hard, Darlene, 532, 533
The Hard Hours (Hecht), 60
Hard Rock, 39–40
Hardwick, Billy, 531
Hare Krishnas, 416
Hartford Fire Insurance, 89
Hargis, Billy James, Rev., 237, 239, 360, 423
Hargrave, Thomas J., 102
Harkey, Ira B., 370
Harkness, Rebekah, 59
Harkness Ballet, 59
Harlan, John, 289, 295
Harlem, Gudmund, 406
Harlem, NYC, 178, 207
Harlem Globetrotters, 530
Harlem riot, NYC, 183
Harlow, Harry F., 403
Harlow, Jean, 95
Harman, Carl G., 407
Harnick, Sheldon, 60
Harper's magazine, 366–367
Harper's Bazaar, 71
"Harper Valley P.T.A." (song), 30
Harper v. Virginia State Board of Elections, 261
Harrington, Michael, 213–214, 367
Harris, Barbara, 61
Harris, Franco, 517
Harris, Julie, 62
Harris, Rosemary, 61
Harrison, Albertis, 109
Harrison, George, 39
Harrison, George M., 102
Harrison, John R., 371
Harrison, Rex, 27, 62
Harrison, Wallace K., 170
Harris polls, 216–217
Harroun, Ray, 537
Hart, Edward J., 252
Hart, Moss, 64
Hart, Philip A., 226
Hartack, Bill, 531, 532, 533, 534, 536
Hartke, R. Vance, 226
Hartley, Fred A., Jr., 102, 252
Hartline, Haldan Keffer, 406, 483
Hartman, Carl Gottfried, Dr., 339

International Business Machines (IBM), 72, 77, 86–87, 443, 446, 448
International Conference on Evangelicalism, 421
International Days of Protest Against the War in Vietnam, 310
International Foundation for Internal Freedom, 324
International Pop Festival, 1967, 39
International Telephone and Telegraph (ITT), 88, 89, 99
Interplanetary Monitoring Platform probes, 478
Interstate Commerce Commission, 320
In the Heat of the Night (movie), 29, 56, 62
Intrauterine device (IUD), 328, 396
Intrepid, 494
Involuntary Movement Disorders (Cooper), 402
In Watermelon Sugar (Brautigan), 30
Ionesco, Eugéne, 45
Irma la Douce (musical), 61
Ironside (television), 350
Irradiation of food, 466–467
Irving, Clifford, 95
Isbrandtsen Lines, 34
"I Second that Emotion" (song), 29
Isom, Edward W., 102
I Spy (television), 350
Israel/Arab conflicts, 194
Isaac, Neil, 507
"I Think We're Alone Now" (song), 29
"It Pays to Increase Your Wordpower" (Funk), 137
It's a Mad, Mad, Mad, Mad World (movie), 26
It's Like This, Cat (Neville), 51
"It's My Party" (song), 26
"It's Now or Never" (song), 24
Ives, Burl, 37
Ives, Charles, 28
"I Walk the Line" (Cash), 53
"I Want to Hold Your Hand" (song), 27
I was a Communist for the FBI (film), 304
Izenhour, Steven, 168
Izmira Vodka, 89
Jabbar, Kareem Abdul. *See Alcindor, Lew*
The Jack Benny Show (television), 355, 369
Jackson, Jesse, 207

Jackson, Joseph H., Rev., 422
Jackson, Mahalia, 59, 325
Jackson, Michael, 41
Jackson, Miss., 308, 320-321
Jackson, Shirley, 64
Jackson, Thomas Jonathan, 436
Jackson Five, 41
Jacob, François, 406
Jacobs, Jane, 142
Jacobsen, Hugh Newell, 171
Jaipur, 533
James, Howard, 371
James, Larry, 523
James, Tommy, and the Shondells, 29, 31
Jan and Dean, 319
January, Don, 535
Japanese automobile industry, 80–81
Jarrell, Randall, 64
Jarrett, Ned, 492, 533, 534
Javelin, AMC, 150
Javits, Jacob K., 187, 224, 233
Jazz, 33
Jeffers, Robinson, 64
Jefferson Airplane, 29, 33, 40, 322
Jefferson Physical Laboratory, Harvard, 466
Jencks, Charles, 163, 165
Jenkins, David, 521
Jennings, Peter, 345, 346
Jensen, Arthur, 134
Jerk all, 319
Jersey City, N.J., 207
Jerusalem, 416
Jet Propulsion Laboratory, 453
The Jetsons (television), 344
Jewish Museum, NYC, 36, 57
Jews, 415, 416
JFK Coloring Book, 319
Jim Beam whiskey, 89
The Jimi Hendrix Experience, 54
Jobman Caravan (television), 350
The Joey Bishop Show (television), 364
Joffrey, Robert, 59
Joffrey Ballet, 59
Johannson, Ingemar, 488, 511
John Birch Society. *See Birch Society*
Johns, Jasper, 28, 57
Johnson, Edward, 82
Johnson, Haynes, 371
Johnson, Junior, 531
Johnson, Louis A., 252
Johnson, Luci Baines, 249
Johnson, Lynda Bird, 249, 368

Johnson, Lyndon B., 74, 88, 99, 168, 218, 249, 302, 309, 326, 332, 336, 351, 356, 383, 398, 425, 429, 433
aid to education, 214–215
appoints Warren commission, 184
as president, 245
as vice-president, 245
attack on poverty, 117–118
becomes president, 177
Civil Rights Bill, 1964, 205
and civil rights movement, 206
does not run for reelection, 201
Dominican Republic policy, 188
education acts, 111
education policies, 116–117
elected president, 178
election campaign, 1964, 225–226
election campaign, 1968, 232–233
Glassboro Summit, 194
Great Society programs, 181, 214–216, 225–226
Gulf of Tonkin incident, 197
Gulf of Tonkin resolution, 178
health care policy, 214
housing policies, 215
image problems, 213
meets with Kosygin, 179
nominated for vice-president, 244–245
nominated vice-president, 176, 217
nomination campaign, 1964, 224–225
nomination campaign, 1968, 229
opposition to Vietnam policies, 123
State of the Union address, 214
support for education, 110
Supreme Court appointments, 289, 290, 298
tax policies, 211, 212
and Vietnam War, 178
voting rights, 178
Voting Rights Bill, 1965, 206
wage and price policy, 212
War on Poverty, 178, 178, 182, 214
Johnson, Paul, 109
Johnson, Philip, 143, 163, 168, 170
Johnson, Rafer, 488, 521
Johnson, S. C., and Son, 34
Johnston, Olin S., 252
John Wesley Harding (Dylan), 54

John XXIII, Pope, 309, 415, 425, 428
Jones, Alton W., 102
Jones, Bob, Sr., 138
Jones, Clint, 517
Jones, Dave, 38
Jones, Dean, 30
Jones, Doug, 512
Jones, Elvin, 53
Jones, James Earl, 62
James, K. C., 507
Jones, LeRoi, 45
    See also Baraka, Amiri
Jones, Parnelli, 491, 494, 502, 533
Jones, Robert, Sr., 437
Jones, Sam, 507
Joncs, Shirley, 25, 419
Jones, Spike, 339
Jones, Spile, 64
Jones and Laughlin, 96
Jones v. *Alfred H. Mayer Co.*, 261
Joplin, Janice, 313
Joplin, Janis, 40, 40, 54–55, 359
Jordan, Clarence, 437
Jordan, James, 285
Joris, Victor, 169
Josephson, Edward S., 467
Judaism, 417
Judd, Donald, 37
Judd, Walter, 238, 239
Judgment at Nuremberg (movie), 24, 62
Julia (television), 346, 350, 355
Julvenile Delinquency and Youth Offenses Act, 212
"Jumpin' Jack Flash" (song), 30
Jung, Carl, 138
The Jungle (Sinclair), 334
The Jungle Book (movie), 29
Juries, character of, 267
Juvenile delinquency, 281–283
Kagan, Jerome, 134, 136
Kahanamoku, Duke Paoa, 537
Kahn, Louis I., 144, 161–162, 167
Kaiser, Henry J., 102
Kallman, McKinnell & Knowles, 171
Kalmus, Herbert T., 102
Kalmus, Natalie M., 102, 339
Kaltenborn, H.V., 372
Kandel, Roscoe P., 405
The Kandy-Kolored Tangerine-Flake Streamline Baby (Wolfe), 49
Kane, Helen, 64
Kansas Chiefs, 534
Kansas City Chiefs, 494, 497, 514–515, 536

Kansas City Royals, 506
Kansas City Steers, 533
Kantrowitz, Adrian, 385, 405
Kantrowitz, Arthur, 385
Kaplitt, Martin, 386
Kapp, Joe, 530
Kaprow, Allan, 35
Karenga, Ron, 47, 236
Karloff, Boris, 64
Karman, Theodore von, 484
Karmin, Monroe W., 371
Karp, Haskell, 385
Karras, Alex, 498, 527
Kasavubu, Joseph, 187
Katanga Province, Congo, 177, 187
Kattenburg, Paul, 199
Katzenbach, Nicholas, 206
Katzenbach v. *McClung*, 260
Katz v. *United States*, 261, 277
Kauai King, 534, 535
Kaufman, George S., 64
Kavanaugh, James, 420
Kazan, Elia, 24
Keane, John Joseph, 507, 537
Keating, Kenneth, 189, 224
Keaton, Buster, 64
Keats, Ezra Jack, 51
Keck, W.M., 102
Keefer, Chester S., 382
The Keepers of the House (Grau), 60
Kefauver, Estes, 210, 252, 510
Keller, Helen, 138, 340
Keller, K.T., 102, 172
Kelly, Ellsworth, 36, 37
Kelsey, Frances Oldham, 399, 403–404
Kelso, 488, 489, 490, 491
Kelvinator, 444
Kemeny, John, 446, 460
Kempton, Murray, 370
Kendricks, Scott, 322
Kenetic sculpture, 36
Kenndey, John F., 109
Kenndey, Joseph P., 340
Kennedy, Edward, 302, 377
Kennedy, Edward M., 221, 230, 249
Kennedy, George c., 452
Kennedy, Jacqueline, 26, 49, 142, 147, 151, 153, 153, 168, 319, 344, 369, 414
Kennedy, John F., 49, 50, 71, 246, 252, 302, 308, 309, 312, 325, 327, 329, 334, 344, 345, 354, 365, 420, 433, 443, 451, 470
    advisers to, 191
    aid to education efforts, 213

    assassination, 177, 181, 183, 299
    assassination of, 184
    attacks poverty, 214
    and Bay of Pigs, 176, 187–188
    chooses RFK as attorney general, 258
    and civil rights movement, 202
    civil rights policy, 203–204
    economic policies, 208–211
    education policies, 114–115, 116, 126
    elected president, 176
    election campaign, 1960, 218–221
    establishes Peace Corps, 176
    flexible response doctrine, 186
    inaugural address, 191
    inaurguration, 181
    in Berlin, 177
    issue of Catholicism, 219
    nomination and campaign, 216–217
    on civil rights, 293
    opposition to legislation, 182
    primaries, 176
    proposed Alliance for Progress, 186
    proposes civil rights bill, 259
    proposes tax cuts, 177
    relations with business community, 210
    relations with Congress, 213
    school legislation, 108
    State of the Union address, 209, 212
    Supreme Court appointments, 289
    tax policies, 210–211
    and the Berlin Wall, 185–186
    and the black vote, 220
    and the Cuban Missile Crisis, 189–193
    and the steel industry, 87, 210
    trade policy, 210
    unionizing of public employees, 98
    and U.S. Steel, 177
    Vietnam policy, 196
    Vietnam War, 176
    visit to Berlin, 194
Kennedy, Robert F., 108, 183, 190, 191, 201, 203, 220, 225, 226, 229, 230, 249, 252, 301, 303, 310, 320
    appointed attorney general, 258
    as attorney general, 265–266
    assassination, 179, 181

Los Angeles Lakers, 490, 491, 493, 533, 534, 535, 536
Los Angeles Mirror, 344
Los Angeles Times, 370, 371
Lost-Found Nation of Islam, 418
Lost in the Funhouse: Fiction for Print, Tape, Live Voice (Barth), 30
"Louie, Louie" (song), 26
The Louvre (television), 369
Love, Carney, 400
Love and Death in the American Novel (Fiedler), 24
The Love Bug (movie), 30
The Love-Ins (movie), 323
Lovell, James A., Jr., 473
Lovett, Robert, 190
Loving v. *Virginia*, 261
The Lovin' Spoonful, 28, 38
Lowell, Robert, 49, 59, 200, 250, 310
Lowndes County Freedom Organization, 234, 242–243
Loy, Mina, 65
Loyola University, 491, 533
LSD (lysergic acid diethylamide), 279, 309, 313, 322, 323–324, 378
Luba, 169
Lucas, Jerry, 489, 521
Luccock, Halford E., 437
Luce, Henry Robinson, 77, 103, 373
Luciano, Charles ("Lucky"), 305
Lucky Debonair, 534
The Lucy Show (television), 355
Lukas, J. Anthony, 370
Luksus, Tzaims, 169
Lumumba, Patrice, 187
Lunar Orbiter II, 447
Lunden, Samuel E., 170
Lunds, C. Roger, 443
Lung transplant, 390
Luria, Salvador, 483
Luther (Osborne), 61
Lutheran Church in America, 413, 421
Lutheran Church-Missouri Synod, 413
Lutheran Council, U.S.A., 413
Luyten, William, 444
Lwoff, Andr, 406
Lyerla/Peden, 171
Lynch, Jim, 517
Lynen, Feodor, 406
Lynn, Loretta, 28
Lyon, Alfred, 103
Lysergic acid diethylamide (LSD), 55

MacArthur, Douglas, 252
MacArthur, R. J. H., 447
Macbeth, Hallmark Hall of Fame (television), 369
MacBird (Garson), 59
MacDonald, Dave, 537
Macdonald, Dwight, 123, 200
MacDonald, Jeanette, 63, 65
Machen, Eddie, 512
Mack, Russell Vernon, 252
MacKinley, Ian, 171
Mackinley/Winnacker, 171
Mackle, Barbara Jane, 269
MacLaine, Shirley, 24
MacMurray, Fred, 24
Macrae, Elliot B., 103
Macy, John W., 351
Maddox, U.S. destroyer, 197–198
Magazines, 348
Magee, James V., 371
Maggers, Betty J., 447, 452
Magovern, George, 390
Mahan, Larry, 494, 495
Maharavich, Pistol Pete, 531
Mailer, Norman, 27, 29, 34, 48, 200
Mail-order clothing, 143
Maiman, Theodore H., 442, 467
Majestic Prince, 496, 536
Major League Baseball Players Association (MLBPA), 498, 505
Malamud, Bernard, 28, 50, 60
Malcolm (Purdy), 52
Malcolm X, 183, 235, 243, 252, 309, 312, 314, 315, 413, 416, 418–419, 434–435
The male pill, 396–397
Malloy v. *Hogan*, 259, 277
Malnutrition, 378
Malone, Vivian, 110
Malraux, André, 26
The Mamas and Papas, 28
Mame (musical), 61
The Man (Wallace), 51
Manabe, Syukuro, 448, 462
Manchild in the Promised Land (Brown), 136
The Manchurian Candidate (movie), 25
Mandell, Lewis, 83
Manhattan Fund, 82
Mann, Carol, 534
Mann, David, 36
Mann, Manfred, 27
Mannix (television), 350
The Man Nobody Knows (Barton), 100
Man of La Mancha (musical), 61

Manpower Development and Training Act, 212
Mansfield, Mike, 199, 213
Manson, Charles, 66, 262, 263, 296–297, 311
Man-Tan, 321
Mantle, Mickey, 503, 504
Mapp v. *Ohio*, 258, 276, 288–289, 290
Mara, Jack, 537
March, Fredric, 419
March on Washington, 204, 309, 312, 325, 434
Marciano, Rocky, 537
Mariana Trench, 464
Marin, Luis Muoz, 25
Mariner 1, 478
Mariner 2, 443, 478
Mariner 3, 478
Mariner 4, 447, 478
Mariner 6, 450
Maris, Roger, 489, 503
Mark Twain Tonight! (play), 61
Marquand, John P., 65
Marr, Dave, 534
Mars, 447, 450, 478
Marshall, Burke, 204
Marshall, George C., 238
Marshall, George Preston, 537
Marshall, Richard E., 447
Marshall, Thurgood, 261, 290, 298–299
Marshall, Walter P., 103
Marshman, Bobby, 537
Martha and the Vandellas, 27, 41
Martin, Dean, 27
Martin, Homer, 103
Martin, Joan, 302
Martin, John Leonard ("Pepper"), 537
Martin, Joseph W., Jr., 252
Martin, Kingsley, 373
Martin, Mary, 61
Martin, William McChesney, 209, 212
Martinez, Ramiro, 288
The Marvelettes, 25, 41
Marvin, Lee, 27, 62
Marx, Chico, 65
Marx, Harpo, 65
Mary Kay Cosmetics, 93
Mary Poppins (movie), 27, 62
Masers, 456, 467
The mashed potato, 319
Mason, James, 25
Massachusetts Institute of Technology, 316, 453

Massive retaliation policy, 186
Masten & Hurd, 170, 171
Master Charge (MasterCard), 83
Master Lock, 89
Master of arts in teaching (MAT), 134
Masters Golf Tournament, 488, 492, 493, 495, 518, 532–536
"Masters of War" (Dylan), 54
Matson, Randy, 492
Mattaei, J. H., 457
Mattel Company, 318
Mattel toys, 167
Matthau, Walter, 30, 61
Matthaus, Thomas A., 455
Maverick (television), 366
Maverick, Ford, 145
May, Edgar, 370
Mayberry R.F.D. (television), 355
Mayer, Oscar G., 103
Mays, Willie, 503
Maysles, Albert, 322
Maysles, David, 322
Maytag, L.B., 103
McAndrew, William D., 370
McCarthy, Eugene J., 179, 201, 217, 226, 229, 230, 246–247
McCarthy, Joseph, 238, 294, 356
McCarthy, Mary, 26, 50
McCarthy and His Enemies (Buckley), 237
McCartney, Paul, 39
McClellan Committee, 265
McClung, Ollie, 273–274
McCobb, Paul, 172
McCollum, Elmer Verner, 484
McCone Report, 129
McConnell, Fowler B., 103
McConnell, James V., 443
McCormack, John, 213, 222
The McCoys, 28
McCullers, Carson, 52, 65
McCulloch, Warren Sturgis, 407
McDermott, Terry, 522
McDivitt, James A., 472, 476
McDonald, David, 210
McDonald's, 85, 308
McDonnell, Donald, Fr., 94
McDowall, Roddy, 30
McDowell, Cleve, 109
McGannon, Donald R., 370
McGinley, Phyllis, 60
McGovern, George, 98, 200, 221, 229, 230, 233
McGranery, James Patrick, 305
McGrath, J. Howard, 252, 305
McGuire, Edith, 522

McHugh, Jimmy, 65
McIntire, Carl, Rev, 237, 239, 430
McKay, Jim, 349
McKay, John, 516, 517
McKenna, Siobhan, 419
McKinley, Chuck, 491, 531
McKissick, Floyd, 207, 234, 236–237
McKuen, Rod, 50
McLuhan, Marshall, 157, 365–366, 368
McMahon, Ed, 364
McNally, Terence
McNamara, Frank, 83
McNamara, Pat, 252
McNamara, Robert, 127, 190, 191, 200, 318
Mead, Margaret, 119
Meadlo, Paul, 359
Meador, Clifton K., 379
Meany, George, 75, 99
Measles vaccine, 376, 377, 378, 392, 405
Meathe, Philip J., 170
The Mechanical Bride: Folklore of Industrial Man (McLuhhan), 365
Medawar, Peter B., 406
Medicaid, 214, 380, 384
Medical care costs, 382
Medical Information Telephone System (MIST), 379
Medical News (television), 382
Medical Radio System, 382
Medical service, 382, 383
Medicare, 74, 202, 213, 214, 378, 380, 383
Medicare Act, 260
Medina, Ernest L., 199, 359
The Medium is the Massage (McLuhan), 366
Meet the Press (television), 137
Meier, Richard, 171
Mekel, Herbert S., 420
Melcarth, Edward, 170
Mellon, Paul, 29
Memphis, Tenn., 98
Meningitis, 378
Menjou, Adolphe, 65
Menken, Helen, 65
Mennen, William G., 103
Menninger, William Claire, 407
Men's Fellowship International, 421
Men's suits, 154
Mercer, Doris, 340
Merck, Sharpe & Dohme, 393
Mercury, 446
Meredith, Burgess, 28

Meredith, James, 109, 111, 113, 177, 179, 203–204, 207, 242–243, 308, 339
Mergers, 89–90
Meridian, Miss., 283–285
Meriwether, Lee, 28
Merrell Company, 399, 404
Merriam, G. and C., Company, 72
Merrifield, Bruce, 406
Merrill, John P., 405
Merrit-Chapman and Scott Corporation, 99
The Merry Pranksters, 55, 324,
Merton, Thomas, 437
Metafiction, 48, 58
Metalious, Grace, 65
Metropolitan Community Church, 414, 416
Metropolitan Museum of Art, NYC, 28, 36
Metropolitan Opera, NYC, 25
Metzger, Delbert E., 305
Metzman, Gustav, 103
Meyer, Debbie, 524
Meyer, Frederick A., 371
Meyer, Grant E., 453
Meyer, Harry M., 393
M-G-M Studios, 29
Miami Boxing Commission, 491
Miami educational system, 123
Michigan State Spartans, 493, 495, 517, 534
Michigan State University, 137
Mickey Mouse, 75
Midas Muffler shops, 85
Midnight Cowboy (movie), 30, 42, 62
Midwest Program of Airborne Televised Instruction, 128
Mies van der Rohe, Ludwig, 148, 161, 164, 167, 168, 170, 172
Mignini, Carolyn, 339
Migrant workers, 94
Mikan, George, 507
Milky Way, 448
Mildenberger, Karl, 512
Milhaud, Darius, 52
Military-industrial complex, 185
Millender, Dharathula H., 121
Miller, Arthur, 45, 59
Miller, Clem, 252
Miller, Frank, 371
Miller, Gene, 371
Miller, Henry, 27
Miller, Joseph Irwin, 436
Miller, Marvin, 505
Miller, Norman C., 371

Miller, Roger, 28
Miller, Stanley, 459
Miller, William E., 224
Miller Brewing Company, 89
"Millionaire's Wife" (Friedan), 335
Mills, Billy, 522
Mills, C. Wright, 138, 239–240, 244
Mills, Wilbur, 212
Millsop, Thomas, 103
Milwaukee Art Center, 34
Minimalism, 32, 37
Miniskirts, 142, 144, 147, 156
Ministers' Vietnam Commitee, 429
Minnelli, Liza, 61
Minnesota Twins, 489, 492, 504, 506, 534
Minnesota Vikings, 497, 536
Minow, Newton, 344, 345, 347, 350, 357, 366
Minton, Sherman, 305
Minuteman missiles, 444
Minutemen, 237, 238
The Miracles, 41
The Miracle Worker (Gibson), 61, 62
Miranda v. *Arizona*, 261, 277–278, 295
Miscengenation, 261
The Misfits (movie), 24
Miss America pageant, 310, 333
Missile race, 193
Mission Impossible (television), 350, 369
Mississippi Freedom Democratic Party, 205
Mississippi Freedom Summer Project, 242–243, 283
Miss U.S. I, 490
Mister Ed (television), 366
Mitchell, James P., 103
Mitchell, John, 208, 359
Mitchell, Joni, 38
Mitchell, Lydell, 517
Mitropoulos, Dimitri, 24, 65
MLTW/Moore Turnbull, 171
Mobilization for Youth program, NYC, 213
Mobutu, Joseph, 187
Modern dance, 32
Modern Library, 63
Mod fashions, 143
Mod look, 147, 154–155, 156
Mods, 154
The Mod Squad (television), 350
Mohorovicic Discontinuity (Moho), 463
Mohr, Charles, 537

Molly Brown (Gemini flight), 472
Momaday, N. Scott, 31, 60
Monahan, James F., 305
Mona Lisa (da Vinci), 26, 27, 35
"Monday, Monday" (song), 28
Mondrian, Piet, 161
The Monitors (movie), 249
Monk, Thelonious, 27, 33, 53
The Monkees, 28, 38, 39, 369
The "Monkey Law," 413
Monnet, Jean, 358
Monod, Jacques, 406
Monroe, Marilyn, 24, 59, 65, 340
"The Monster Mash" (song), 25
Montague, Theodore, 103
Monterey Pop Festival (1968), 54
Montessori, Maria, 130
The Montessori Method... (Montessori), 130
Montessori schools, 130
Montgomery, Ala., 285, 308, 320
Montgomery, Wes, 65
Montreal Canadiens, 489, 532, 534, 535, 536
Montreal Expos, 506
Monzon, Carlos, 526
Moody, Orville, 496, 536
Moog synthesizer, 30
Moon, 450
Moon, Sun Myung, Rev., 416
Moon landing, 74, 470, 472, 476
Moon walk, 193
Moore, Charles, 163
Moore, Davy, 510, 537
Moore, Douglas Stuart, 65
Moore, Lyndon, Turnbull, Whitaker, 171
Moore, Marianne, 59
Morash, Paul, 350–351
Moreell, Ben, 238
Morello, Joe, 52
Morgan, Edmund, 305
Morgan, Edward P., 370
Morgan, Robin, 333
Morgan, W. J., 448
Morgenthau, Henry, Jr., 252
Morgue, Olivier, 161
Mormons, 415
Morning Noon and Night (Cozzens), 30
Morrill Land Grant College Act, 215
Morris, Frank Lee, 302
Morris, Richard
Morris, Robert, 37
Morris, Willie, 353, 366–367
Morrison, Philip, 456–457

Morse, Robert, 61
Morse, Wayne, 200, 233
Mortimer, Wyndham, 103
Morton Foods, 89
Mosbacher, Emil, Jr., 490
Moscow State Symphony, 24
Mosel, Tad, 60
Moses, Anna Mary Robertson ("Grandma"), 65
Moses, Robert, 225
Moss, Thelma, 324
Mössbauer, Rudolph, 466
Mossler, Candy, 303
Mossler, Jacques, 303
Mostel, Zero, 30, 61
Mother and Child (Picasso), 29, 36
Mother Night (Vonnegut), 25, 57
Mothers of Invention, 33
Motion Picture Association of America (MPAA), 34, 42
Motive, 427
Moton, Leroy, 296
Motor Vehicle Air Pollution Control Act, 80, 150
Motown, 33, 40–41
Mount Holyoke, 117
A Moveable Feast (Hemingway), 27
Move Ahead with Possibility Thinking (Schuller), 437
The Moviegoer (Percy), 25
Movie ratings, 42–43
Moyer, Carl, 405
Moynihan, Daniel Patrick, 137, 207
MPAA ratings of movies, 31
"Mrs. Robinson" (song), 30
Muhammad, Elijah, 416, 418, 419
Muller, Hermann Joseph, 407, 484
Mulliken, Robert S., 483
Mullins, Robert D., 370
Mumma, Walter M., 252
Munch, Charles, 65
Mundt, Karl, 189, 238
Muni, Paul, 65
Munson-Williams-Proctor Institute, Utica, NY, 35
Murdoch, Peter, 161
Murphree, Eger V., 484
Murphy, Franklin, 121
Murphy, Jack ("Murph the Surf"), 303
Murphy, Matthew Hobson, Jr., 305
Murphy Associates, 171
Murray, John Courtney, S.J., 428, 437
Murray, Thomas E., 103
Murray the K, 357
Murray v. Curlett, 435

Murrow, Edward R., 344, 345, 356, 368, 369, 373
Museum of Modern Art, 25, 27, 31, 32, 36, 59, 142, 143
The Music Man (movie), 25
Muskie, Edmund, 231
Muslim Mosque, Inc., 435
Mustang, Ford, 72, 80, 143, 144, 150
Mustang Ranch Reno, Nev., 511
Muste, A. J., 429, 437
Mutiny on the Bounty (movie), 25
Mutual funds, 82
"My Boyfriend's Back" (song), 26
"My Cherie Amour" (song), 31
My Darling, My Hamburger (Zindel), 51
My Fair Lady (movie), 27, 62, 308
"My Favorite Things" (Coltrane), 53
"My Girl" (song), 28
"My Guy" (song), 27, 41
My Lai massacre, 199
My Name Is Barbra (television), 369
Myra Breckenridge (Vidal), 30, 51
Myself and I (Moss), 324
My Sixty Memorable Games: Selected and Fully Annotated (Fischer), 525
"My Way" (song), 31
Nabokov, Vladimir, 25, 31
Nachmansohn, David, 405
Nader, Ralph, 73, 81, 96, 149, 168, 303
Naide, Meyer, 405
Naked Came the Stranger ("Penelope Ashe"), 31
Naked Lunch (Burroughs), 25
Namath, Joe, 499, 512, 514, 516
Napalm, 83
Napoleon XIV, 28
Narcotic Addict Rehabilitation Act, 278–279
Narducci, Leo, 169
Nash, Diane, 315, 329, 422
Nashville, Tenn., 319, 328
Nashville Skyline (Dylan), 54
Nashville Student Movement, 315
National Academy of Sciences Research Council, 399
National Aeronautics and Space Administration (NASA), 448, 451
National Anti-Communist Leadership School, 423
National Assessment of Educational Progress, 135

National Association for the Advancement of Colored People (NAACP), 182, 202, 207, 298
National Association of Broadcasters, 344
National Association of Broadcasters Television Code, 360
National Association of Evangelicals, 420
National Association of Music Merchants, 357
National Association of Stock Car Auto Racing (NASCAR), 488, 500–501
National Association of Stock Car Auto Racing championship, 532–536
National Baptist Convention, 422
National Baptist Convention, U.S.A., 413
National Baptist Convention of America, 413
National Basketball Association (NBA), 488, 489, 490, 508
National Basketball Association championship, 532–536
National Black Economic Development Conference, 414, 418
National Black Sisters Conference, 414
National Book Awards Symposium (1968), 49
National Broadcasting Company (NBC), 345, 345, 366, 382, 510
National Car Rental, 96
National Catholic Bishops Conference, 428
National Catholic Office of Motion Pictures, 42, 44
National Catholic Reporter, 413
National Collection of Fine Arts, 35
National Collegiate Athletic Association basketball, 532–536
National Collegiate Athletic Association basketball tournament, 508
National Commission on Technology, Automation and Economic Progress, 72
National Commission on the Causes and Prevention of Violence, 230, 231
National Conference of Churches, 283
National Conference of Citizens for Religious Freedom, 420

National Conference of Commission on the Status of Women, 336
National Council of Churches, 239, 344, 412
National Council of Teachers of English, 123
National Council on the Arts, 35
National Defense Education Act, 114, 116, 119
National Defense Loans, 118
National Educational Television, 345, 369
National Education Association, 112, 115, 128
National Endowment for the Arts, 35, 44, 117
National Endowment for the Humanities, 35, 117
National Environmental Policy Act, 84
National Farm Workers Association, 73, 94
National Fine Arts Commission, 142
National Football League, 74, 488, 499, 512–513
National Football League (NFL) championship, 532–536
National Foundation for the Arts and Humanities, 215
National Gallery of Art, 27, 29, 36
National Guard, Cal., 112
National Hockey League, 493
National Hockey League Stanley Cup, 532–536
National Interagency Council on Smoking and Health, 398
Nationalist Chinese, 519
National League, 489
National Liberation Front (Vietcong), 196
National Mobilization Committee to End the War in Vietnam, 231, 270
National Observer, 355
National Office for Black Catholics, 414
National Organization for Women (NOW), 91, 310, 312, 332, 335, 336
National Radio Astronomy Observatory, 443
National Review (magazine), 237
National Traffic and Motor Vehicle Safety Act, 81, 96, 144, 168
Nation of Islam, 413, 416, 419

Reed, Lou, 337
Regional Labs for Education Research, 119
Reid, Beryl, 61
Reid, Mike, 517
Reid, Ogden, 354
Reid, Rockwell, Banwell & Taries, 171
Reid & Tarics, 171
Reik, Theodor, 407
Reiner, Fritz, 65
Reinhard, L. Andrew, 172
Reiter, Paul, 170
The Reivers (Faulkner), 50, 60
Relay 1, 476
Relay II, 345
"Release Me" (song), 29
Religion and Public Education (journal), 137
Religious freedom, 279–280
Rembrandt, 36
Remick, Lee, 25
Remington Rand, 86
Renault, 80
Republican National Convention (1960), 217
Republican National Convention (1964), 223–224
Republican National Convention (1968), 229
Republican nomination campaign (1960), 217–218
Republican nomination campaign (1964), 221–224
Republican nomination campaign (1968), 227–229
Republicans, 179
Republic of New Africa, 236
"Rescue Me" (song), 28
Resor, Stanley B., 104, 373
"Respect" (song), 29
"The Responsive Eye" (exhibition), 36
Resweber, Carroll, 531
"Return to Sender" (song), 25
Reuss, Henry, 187
Reuther, Roy, 104
Reuther, Walter, 75, 99
Reventlow, Lance, 339
Revisionist history, 120
Revolutionary Action Movement, 236
Revolution in Mississippi (Hayden), 244
Revor, Mary Remy, 170
Reynman, Richard P., 480
Reynolds, Frank, 363–364

Reynolds, John H., 442
Reynolds, Quentin, 373
Reynolds, R. J., 104
Reynolds Tobacco, 89
Reynolds v. Sims, 159
Rheingold Brewery, 506
Rhinoceros (play), 61
Rhoades, Ralph O., 104
Rhoads, Cornelius, 405
Rhodes, James A., 227
RhoGAM, 378
Rhythm and blues, 39
Ribicoff, Abraham A., 108, 221, 230, 233
Rice, Elmer, 65
Richards, Alfred Newton, 407
Richardson, Ralph, 137
Richberg, Donald Randall, 253
Richtenstein, Roy, 168
Richter, Conrad, 65
Rickey, Branch Wesley, 537
Rickover, Hyman G., 137, 478
Ridenhour, Ronald, 199
Ridgway, Matthew B., 200
Riech, Steve, 37
Riesman, David, 122
The Righteous Brothers, 28
Right to privacy, 260
Right-to-work laws, 88
Right-wing politics, 237
Riley, Jennie C., 30
Riley, John J., 253
Riley, Terry, 37
Rinehart, Stanley M., Jr., 104
"Ring of Fire" (Cash and Carter), 53
"Ring of Fire" (song), 26
The Rise and Fall of the Third Reich (Shirer), 50
Ritter, Joseph Elmer Cardinal, 428, 438
Rivers, Mendell, 280
Riverside Church, NYC, 418
RKO Pictures Corporation, 95
RNA, 457, 459
Road Runner, Dodge, 149
Robb, Charles, 249
Robbins, Harold, 50
Robbins, Jerome, 32, 43, 45
Roberts, Glenn ("Fireball"), 501, 537
Roberts, Oral, 421, 435–436
Roberts, Paul, 120, 137
Roberts, Randy, 515, 520
Robertson, A.W., 104
Robertson, Cliff, 62, 339
Robertson, David A., 104
Robertson, Howard Percy, 138

Robertson, Oscar, 508
Robertson, Pat, 436
Robinson, Frank, 493, 504, 531
Robinson, Henry Morton, 65
Robinson, Smokey, 41
Robinson, Smokey and the Miracles, 29
Robinson, Sugar Ray, 526
Robinson, William E., 104
Robinson v. California, 278
Roche, James, 73
Rochester, N.Y., 207
Rock, John, 327
Rockefeller, Nelson A., 217–218, 221–224, 227, 228–229
Rockefeller, Winthrop, 227
Rockefeller Foundation, 44
Rock 'n' Roll, 38, 39, 319
Rockwell, George Lincoln, 183, 237, 238
Rockwell, Norman, 353
Rodeo Cowboys Association, 495
Rodger, Richard
Roethke, Theodore, 49, 65
Roe v. Wade, 302
Rogers, Edith Nourse, 253
Rogers, John B., 171
Rogers, Taliaferro, Listritsky, Lamb, 171
Rolfe, Robert A. ("Red"), 537
Rolling Stone magazine, 49, 367
The Rolling Stones, 28, 29, 30, 39, 319
Romary, Janice, 531
Romeo and Juliet (movie), 30
Romero, Cesar, 28
Romero, George, 30
Romney, George W., 221, 224, 226, 227
Ronan, Daniel J., 253
Roosevelt, Eleanor, 253, 340
Roosevelt, Franklin, Jr., 332
Roosevelt, Franklin D., 352
Root, E. Merrill, 423
Rose, Barbara, 37
Rose, Billy, 65
Rose Bowl, 496
Rosemary's Baby (movie), 30, 51
Rosenberg, Rosalind, 332
Rosenblatt, Sol A., 305
Rosencrantz and Guildenstern Are Dead (Stoppard), 61
Rosenthal, A. M., 370
Rosenthal, Erich, 417
Ross, Barney, 537
Rossiter, Clinton, 129
Rossovich, Tim, 517

Schweickart, Russell Louis ("Rusty"), 476
Schwerner, Michael, 183, 205, 283–284
Schwinger, Julian S., 483
Science fiction and fantasy, 51
Scofield, Paul, 61, 62
Scott-Brown, Denise, 168
Scott, David, 73, 473, 476
Scott, Evelyn, 66
Scott, George C., 27
Scott, Hugh, 189, 224
Scranton, William, 202, 221, 223, 224
Screen Gems, 38
Scripps-Howard papers, 353
The Sea Around Us (Carson), 334
Seaborg, Glenn T., 482
Seabrook, Charles F., 104
Sea Grant Act, 215
Seagrave, Gordon S., 407
Seal, Elizabeth, 61
Sealab I, 446
Sealab I, II, and III, 465
Seale, Bobby, 231, 234, 243, 271, 309, 315
Searle Pharmaceutical Company, 327, 395
Seat belts, 319
Seattle Pilots, 506
Seaver, Tom, 505, 506
Sebring, Jay, 297
Second Baptist Church, Los Angeles, 414
Second Skin (Hawles), 27, 47
Second String Quartet (Carter), 60
Second Vatican Council, 412, 415, 425, 428
Second Wind: The Memoirs of an Opinionated Man (Russell), 530
Secular City (Cox), 419, 429
Sedaka, Neil, 25
Sedgwick, Edie, 336–337
See, Elliot, 473
Seeger, Pete, 37, 38
See How They Run (television), 345
Segal, George, 28, 36
Segregation, 128, 182
Selah, W.G., Rev., 412
Selective Service, 338
Sellers, Cleveland, 234
Sellers, Johnny, 532, 534
Sellers, Peter, 27, 55
Selma, Ala., 110, 178, 205–206, 309
Selma march, 295–296
Selznick, David O., 66

Senate Foreign Relation Committee, 178
Sendak, Maurice, 51
Sengstaken, Dr., 377
Sennett, Mack, 66
"The Sense of Abstraction" (exhibition), 32
Seperack, Gerturde, 169
Sermons and Soda-Water (O'Hara), 24
Sert, Jackson & Gourley, 171
Sesame Street (television), 347, 351
Seton, Elizabeth Ann Bayley, 412
Seuss, Dr., 51
Seventeen magazine, 368
1776 (musical), 62
77 Dream Songs (Berryman), 60
Seven-Up, 89
Sever, John L., 393
Sex and the College Girl (Greene), 122
Sex and the Single Girl (Brown), 50
Sex and the Single Girl (movie), 328
Sexton, Anne, 49, 60
Sexual Freedom League, 321
Seymour, W. J., 420–421
Sgt. Pepper's Lonely Hearts Club Band (record), 39, 154
Shafer, Raymond P., 227
Shahn, Ben, 66
Shankar, Ravi, 40
Shannon, Anthony, 370
Shaping Educational Policy (Conant), 132
Shapiro, Karl, 49
Shapiro, Samuel H., 233
Shapiro v. *Thompson*, 262
Shapp, Milton, 187
Sharif, Omar, 27
Sharman, Bill, 507
Shatalov, Vladimir A., 476
Shaw, Clayton L., 184, 302, 310
Shaw University, 308, 329
Shea Stadium, 86
Shelby, Carroll, 150
"She Loves You" (song), 27
Shepard, Alan, Jr., 443, 468
Shepley, Henry R., 172
Sheppard, Sam, 301, 303
Sheraton Corporation, 89
Sherbert v. *Verner*, 259, 280
Sheridan, Walter, 266
Sherluck, 532
"Sherry" (song), 25
Sherwood, Mills & Smith, 170
Shevelove, Burt
Shift dresses, 143, 147

Shikler, Aaron, 170
Ship of Fools (Porter), 50
The Shirelles, 25
Shirer, Wiliam L., 50
Shockley, William, 119
Shoemaker, Willie, 533, 534, 535
The Shoes of the Fisherman (West), 50
Shonin, Georgi S., 476
Shopping Bag, 73
Short, Robert L., 420
Shotton, Burton Edwin, 537
Shoup, Paul, 200
Shriver, R. Sargent, 117, 187
Shubert, John, 373
Shultz, George, 99
Shuttlesworth, Fred L., Rev., 422
Siegenthaler, John, 203, 320
Sigma 7, 470
Silent Spring (Carson), 308, 334, 444
The Silent Spring of Rachel Carson (television), 334
Silicon microchips, 87
Silver, Abba Hillel, 438
Silvers, Robert, 357
Silvestri, Danilio, 145
Sime, David, 521
Simmons, Jean, 24, 419
Simon and Garfunkel, 28, 30, 33, 39
Simonelli, Don, 169
Simon, Neil, 45
Simon, Richard L., 104
Simons, Elwyn L., 447, 453
Simpson, Louis, 60
Simpson, O. J., 496, 516, 517, 535
Sinatra, Frank, 25, 28, 31, 33, 39, 40
Sinatra, Frank, Jr., 303
Sinatra, Nancy, 28
Sinclair, Upton, 66, 334, 340
Singer, Isaac Bashevis, 25, 25
The Singing Nun, 26
Single Integrated Operational Plan, 186
Singleton, Henry, 99
Sinsheimer, Robert L., 481
Sirhan, Sirhan, 303
Sismour, Regis, 390
Sit-ins, 176, 202, 328–329, 422
Six Crises (Nixon), 247
Six Day War, 194, 415, 416–417
Sixteenth Street Baptist Church, Birmingham, Ala., 422
The Sixties: Years of Hope, Days of Rage (Gitlin), 114
60 Minutes (television), 358–359

Waddell, William R., 390
Wade, Billy, 538
Wade, Virginia, 496, 535
Wages, 88
Wagner, Robert, Jr., 98
Wagon Train (television), 355
Wald, George, 406, 483
Walden School, NYC, 284
Walker, Daniel, 231
Walker, Edwin A., 250
Walker/McGough, Foltz, 171
"Walk Like a Man" (song), 26
Wallace, George C., 109, 177, 204, 206, 221, 224–225, 227, 231–234, 248–249, 295, 431
Wallace, Henry Agard, 253
Wallace, Irving, 51
Wallace, Lurleen, 248
Wallace, Mike, 359
Wallerstein, Robert, 132
Waller, William, 294
Wall Street Journal, 355, 361
Walsh, Denny, 371
Walsh, Don, 442, 464
Walt Disney's Wonderful World of Color (television), 344
Walter, Bruno, 66
Walter, Francis E., 253
Waner, Paul Glee ("Big Poison"), 538
Wanger, Walter, 66
Wang Laboratories, 86
Ward, Burt, 28
Ward, Harry Fredrick, 305, 438
Ward, Robert, 60
Ward, Rodger, 490, 533
Warhol, Andy, 36, 58, 168, 310, 336
War on Poverty, 178, 212, 214, 216
War on Poverty Bill, 178
Warren Commission, 184, 309
Warren, Earl, 261, 262, 288, 290
Warren, Leonard, 24
Warwick, Dionne, 28, 30
Washington, D.C. (Vidal), 29, 258
Washington, Dinah, 66
Washington Post, 354, 355, 356
Washington Post Company, 344, 355
Washington Redskins, 529
Washington Senators, 506
Water Quality Act, 73
Watson, Charles "Tex", 297
Watson, James Dewey, 406, 483
Watterson, Joseph, 170
Watts, André, 60
Watts, Los Angeles, 207

Watts, Los Angeles riot, 178, 183, 329–330
The watusi, 319
Wayne, John, 30, 62, 419
The Way to Rainy Mountain (Momaday), 31
"The Way You Do the Things You Do" (song), 27, 41
Weatherly, 490
Weatherly, Joe, 533, 538
Weathermen, 183, 241, 325, 357
Weather satellites, 70, 476
Weaver, Harold, 445
Weaver, Pat, 364
Weaver, Robert, 250, 310
The Weavers, 33
Webb, David, 169
Weber, Dick, 531
Weber, Joseph, 449, 482
Webster, George, 517
"We Can Work It Out" (song), 28
Weese & Associates, 171
Wegener, Alfred L., 481
Weidman, Jerome, 60
Weill, Armand ("Al"), 538
Weinberg, Jack, 317
Weinberg, Steven, 448
Weiner, Lee, 271
Weiss, Mary C., 483
Weiss, Peter, 61
Welch, Joseph Nye, 253, 306
Welch, Raquel, 28
Welch, Robert, 237, 238
Welcome to Hard Times (Doctorow), 24
Welfare residency requirements, 262
Weller, Thomas, 393
Welles, Sumner, 253
Wellington, Clarence George, 373
Wells, Floyd, 275
Wells, Mary, 27, 41
The Well-Tempered Synthesizer (recording), 30
Wenner, Jann, 367–368
Werblin, David A. "Sonny", 514
Werle, Edward C., 104
Werner, Wallace, 538
Wesberry v. *Sanders*, 259
"We Shall Not Be Moved" (song), 425
"We Shall Overcome" (song), 425
West, Adam, 28
West, Ben, 329
West Chester State Teachers College, 490
West Germany, 519
West, Jerry, 531

Westmoreland, William, 196–197, 198
West, Morris, 50
Westrum, Wes, 506
West Side Story (movie), 24, 43, 43, 62
Wetherald, Richard, 448, 462
WFIL, 368
Wham-O, 319
Wharton, Clifton, 137
What Ever Happened to Baby Jane? (movie), 25
What Is Sonata Form? (television), 369
"What the World Needs Now" (song), 28
"When a Man Loves a Woman" (song), 28
"Where Did Our Love Go?" (song), 41
"Where Have All the Flowers Gone?" (song), 25
Where the Wild Things Are (Sendak), 51
Whistler, James, 35
Whistler's Mother (Whistler), 35
White, Byron, 258, 289
White, Ed, 309, 448, 472, 474, 481
White, F. Clifton, 223
White, Philip B., 170
White, Rex, 532
White, Robert Michael, 483
White, Roy B., 104
White, Theodore H., 213
Whitechapel Gallery, London, 57
White Citizens' Council, 293, 294
White flight, 329–330
White House, 142, 344
White House Conference on Drug Abuse, 278
White House Conference on Education, 110
White House Festival of the Arts, 59
"White Rabbit" (song), 29
Whiteside, Arthur D., 104
Whiting, Leonard, 30
Whitman, Charles, 261, 286–288
Whitman, Walt, 49
Whitney, George, 104
Whitney, John Hay ("Jock"), 354
Whitney Museum of Art, 34
Whittaker, Charles, 258, 289
The Who, 40
Who's Afraid of Virginia Woolf? (movie), 28, 42, 45, 52, 61, 62
"Who's Your Baby?" (song), 38